The Shell
International
Encyclopedia
of Golf

Edited by Donald Steel and Peter Ryde
Advisory Editor: Herbert Warren Wind

The Shell International Encyclopedia of
Golf

Ebury Press and Pelham Books Limited
London

First published in Great Britain by
Ebury Press
Chestergate House, Vauxhall Bridge Road,
London sw1 and
Pelham Books Ltd
52 Bedford Square, London wc1
1975

ISBN 0 7207 0697 1

This book was designed and produced by
Rainbird Reference Books Limited
Marble Arch House, 44 Edgware Road, London w2
House Editor: Peter Coxhead
Assistant Editor: Raymond Kaye
Designer: Alan Bartram

The text was set by
Oliver Burridge Filmsetting Limited,
Crawley, Sussex, and
Jolly & Barber Limited, Rugby, England
The book was printed and bound by
Dai Nippon Printing Company Limited,
Tokyo, Japan

Foreword by Arnold Palmer

The year 1960 was highly significant in my career. I won the US Open at Cherry Hills, my second Masters – and made my first tournament trip overseas. While my quest for the British Open title failed, that week at St Andrews instilled in me the feeling that golf was, or should be, a game for the world, both as a spectator and participant sport.

This is perhaps the main reason why I have continued to play in Britain and in other parts of the world, and have encouraged other American professionals to do the same – as part of the obligation we have to promote the game that has meant so much to us. In the years when British golfers ruled the game, they apparently felt the same way. That is why Vardon and Ray happened to be at Brookline in 1913.

In like manner golf writing has come to reflect more and more the international aspect of the game. The trend has been away from provincialism and towards wider horizons. This book, edited by Donald Steel and Peter Ryde, is certainly a reflection of that trend. Their encyclopedia might so easily have been no more than the views of two experienced observers of the golfing scene, casting a limited look at the game beyond British shores. Instead, in making their judgments and selections of great players and courses to be described, they enlisted the help of many knowledgeable writers in the increasing number of countries where golf is played.

The result of this arduous procedure is a book which I have found informative, entertaining and far more comprehensive than any other golf encyclopedia I know. The statistics of the game are there, but not in such abundance that they reduce readability. It accomplishes this primarily because these two men with the help of Herb Wind, all three of whom I have come to know well over the years, established from the start what seems to me to be the proper aim of such a work.

After sifting through the mass of material from their own experience and from that supplied by the contributors, they decided to include only what they wanted to include. The last thing they wanted was that it should read like a telephone book.

This book is anything but that. In what other golfing encyclopedia, for example, will you find a description of a course where giraffes poke their long necks over the boundary fences to see what those fellows are up to with their sticks; an account of a course with canvas bunkers which are folded up and taken in at night? You may discover which national championship was restricted to players over 40, the winner being awarded a certificate from the Minister of Sport, and which club, in the opinion of the editors, serves the best chocolate cake in the world. No, there is nothing routine about this extensive literary survey and, what is most important, it carries the real spirit of golf.

I am happy to wish it the success it undoubtedly deserves.

Acknowledgments

The editors would like to thank the contributors, listed on pages 11 and 12, for the large part they played in this compilation. Additionally, the people mentioned below provided much information without which the book would have been the poorer:

Jimmy Alexander, British Transport Hotels Ltd
Konrad R. Bjarnason, The Golf Union of Iceland
T. B. Clark, Rhodesia Golf Union
P. B. L. Coghlan, Mount Irvine, Tobago
Henry Cotton MBE
Tom Crow, Australia
M. D. de Haaff, Uganda Golf Union
Peter Doswell, One Boat Golf Club, Ascension Island
Donald Grant MA, FRGS
Leonard 'Skip' Guinto, Secretary-General Asia Golf Confederation
Einar Horn, Norwegian Golf Union
H. B. Keartland, South Africa
André-Jean Lafaurie, Editor of *Golf Européen*, Paris
Jorge C. Ledesma, Asociación Argentina de Golf
Peter Lim, China Oceanic Development Corporation
R. F. Mackie, Waipukurau, New Zealand
Piero Mancinelli, Editor of *Golf Selezione*, Rome
Seymour G. Marvin, Director, Associação Brasileira de Golf
E. Nohrlind, Danish Golf Union
Larry Null, Professional Golfers' Association of America
Otto Rezac, Czechoslovakia
W. H. Richardson, Australian Golf Union
R. A. S. Sturgess, Golf Union of Malawi
D. G. Sutton, New Zealand Golf Association
S. J. H. Van Hengel, Nederlands Golf Comité

It is impossible to compile a book of this nature without the help of other books – the editors are particularly indebted to the following:

Golf Between Two Wars by Bernard Darwin
The Golfer's Handbook
Golf in New Zealand (A Centennial History) by G. M. Kelly
A History of Golf by Robert Browning
Oporto Golf Club by John Delaforce
Royal Liverpool G.C. by Guy Farrar
Royal Lytham and St Annes G.C. by John Grime
The World of Golf by Charles Price

Contents

List of Colour Plates

List of Contributors

The Editors

DONALD STEEL

By winning international honours as a golfer after starting a career as a golf writer, Donald Steel has achieved a unique distinction. Since his appointment as the *Sunday Telegraph*'s first golf correspondent in 1961 at the age of 23, he has competed regularly in the major amateur events in Britain.

He has twice won the President's Putter at Rye, beating Michael Attenborough and David Marsh, two Walker Cup players, in the finals of 1964 and 1970. In 1972 he won the deciding match for Berks, Bucks and Oxon in the County Championship final against Yorkshire at Woodhall Spa; and in 1970 he qualified for the British Open championship at St Andrews – the year in which he was selected to represent England in the Home Internationals.

Educated at Fettes and Christ's College, Cambridge, he has always been a notable player of games. He was a member of an unbeaten school rugby XV which included three subsequent Scottish Internationals and was the first cricketer from a Scottish school to play for the Public Schools against the Combined Services at Lord's.

He played minor county cricket for Buckinghamshire and was selected to play against Lancashire in his first year at Cambridge. It was about that time that he began to turn his attentions to golf, winning a Blue in each of his three years and in one foursomes match against Oxford playing against his brother. In his last year, he received the great honour among Cambridge sportsmen of being elected President of the Hawks Club.

After graduating with a BA degree in Agriculture, he was fortunate enough to go straight into Fleet Street and for the last 13 years has been one of the best-qualified writers on the game. He has watched and played golf in many countries and has edited two editions of the 'Golfer's Bedside Book' as well as three editions of the popular 'The Golf Course Guide' produced by the *Daily Telegraph*. In addition, he is a past captain of Denham Golf Club, where he learned his golf under John Sheridan, and when he was elected a partner in the firm of Cotton (C.K.), Pennink, Lawrie and Partners, was one of the youngest golf-course architects in the world. He is a member of the British Association of Golf Course Architects as well as its Honorary Secretary and Treasurer.

PETER RYDE

Golf correspondent of *The Times* for 22 years, Peter Ryde had a dream of getting down to single figures which vanished when he fractured his spine in a fall, but in any case he always regarded himself as having a lower handicap in Fleet Street than on the fairways. Educated at Charterhouse and Trinity College, Oxford, he began a career in journalism that was interrupted by six years' war service with the Royal Gloucestershire Hussars and the Fife and Forfar Yeomanry. After the war he joined the staff of *The Times* from the *Daily Express* in Manchester, working successively as correspondence and obituary editor. It was in his contributions to that paper's light Fourth Leaders that his path first crossed that of Bernard

Darwin, whom he succeeded when Darwin had completed 47 years in the post. Until the publication of this work Peter Ryde took the view that any writing he did outside his job should be a contrast. As a result he undertook translations from the French, including among his published works ' Metternich and His Times' and the 'Life of Pope John XXIII'.

HERBERT WARREN WIND

Born in Brockton, Massachusetts, in 1916, Herbert Warren Wind graduated from Yale University in 1937 (AB) and then attended Cambridge University (Jesus College) in 1937–9, where he read Literature and received an MA degree. He started to play golf at ten, his family being golf-minded and Brockton being unusually golf-orientated for a city of 63,000, having four golf courses. As a young boy Wind saw Francis Ouimet, Walter Hagen, Gene Sarazen, and other top players in action and this whetted his enthusiasm for the game considerably. So did his years in Britain, where he was fortunate enough to get to know the singular charm and merit of Mildenhall, to meet Bernard Darwin at the 1939 Oxford–Cambridge match and to attend the 1938 Walker Cup match at St Andrews. During the war he served as an administrative officer in the US Army Air Corps in China and later was stationed at SCAP headquarters in Tokyo during the Occupation of Japan. On his return to New York, he wrote his first book, 'The Story of American Golf' (1948). He worked as a Profile writer for *The New Yorker* magazine, left to become one of the original editors and writers for *Sports Illustrated*, and returned to *The New Yorker*, where he has been, and is presently, a contributor to the Sporting Scene department. He has been the author, co-author, editor, or co-editor of over a dozen books, nine of which have been devoted to golf and which include 'Thirty Years of Championship Golf' in collaboration with Gene Sarazen, 'The Modern Fundamentals of Golf' in collaboration with Ben Hogan, and 'The Greatest Game of All', in collaboration with Jack Nicklaus.

The Contributors

BENGT E. ANDERSON. Contributor to *Golf i Sverige* ; Hon Secretary and Treasurer of the Swedish Golfing Society, London

JAMES P. ANGLIN QC. Past President and now a Governor of the Royal Canadian Golf Association

HEINZ BIEMER. Secretary of the German Golf Association

FRED BYROD. Sports Editor of *The Philadelphia Inquirer* and its leading golf writer for many years ; contributor to golf magazines

KEN COTTON. Late President of the British Association of Golf Course Architects and Vice-President of the Association of Golf Club Secretaries

GEOFFREY COUSINS. Deputy President of the Association of Golf Writers; author of books on golf

JOSEPH C. DEY JR. Sometime Executive Director of the USPGA and former Commissioner of the USPGA's Tournament Players Division

CHARLES DISNEY. Nairobi

PIERRE DUCREY. Editor of *Swiss Golf Review*; contributor to *Golf Européen*, Paris

MURAD FYZEE. Leading Indian golf writer; contributor to *The Times of India* and *Indian Sportsweek*

ROSS GOODNER. Golf historian and Executive Editor of *Golf Magazine*

FRANK HANNIGAN. Assistant Director of the United States Golf Association

RAYMOND JACOBS. Golf correspondent of the *Glasgow Herald* and contributor to golfing publications on both sides of the Atlantic

AL LANEY. International golf correspondent (1920–1966) to the late New York *Herald Tribune*

J. STEWART LAWSON. Former Chairman and Member of the Rules of Golf Committee, St Andrews

HENRY LONGHURST, CBE. Golf correspondent of the *Sunday Times* and television commentator

DONALD LAMOND MACNIE. Golf historian and writer on many subjects

PAUL MACWEENEY. Sports Editor and golf correspondent of the *Irish Times*

JESÚS PORRAS MARTÍNEZ. Executive Secretary of the Colombian Golf Association

G. S. MIZOTA. Sometime Hon Secretary of the Japan Committee of the World Golf Association and of the Kasumigaseki Country Club

DICK SEVERINO. International golf consultant; Publisher/Editor, Golf Promotion Services, Beirut

ROBERT SOMMERS. Director of Public Information, USGA

PAT WARD-THOMAS. Golf correspondent of the *Guardian* and *Country Life*; author of books on golf

ENID WILSON. Formerly women's golf correspondent of the *Daily Telegraph*; golfer and writer of books on the subject

Preface

Why, the reader may ask himself, do the editors give 51 lines to Tom Craddock and only 42 lines to Julius Boros? Who was this guy Craddock anyway? Well, part of the object of this work is to answer that kind of question.

To answer the first question, we can only offer two reasons: firstly, that it is impossible to compare the relative importance of, for example, George Fazio and Ken Bousfield or of Eric Cremin and 'Jumbo' Ozaki. The *Encyclopaedia Britannica* gave 38 columns to baseball and 13 to Johann Sebastian Bach – they too had their problems. Secondly, the truth is that length is no criterion of importance. The length of the entry may depend on the amount of space needed to explain something; in our case, it has been largely, though not entirely, determined by such considerations as what there is to say about the golfer, how much we know or could find out, the suitability of the person to be written about. We are, after all, no more than journalists finding our living in what is writable – and providing, we hope, what is readable.

We have written about those people and things about which we have wanted to write. We believe that the same motive has moved the contributors. We have always felt the warm certainty that golf in the United States of America would be done full justice. The golf courses that have been included may be open to dispute – we should like to think that they are – but we have the certainty that the hundred courses included have been recommended by the expert opinions of Herbert Warren Wind and other American experts.

The same confidence has sustained us in respect of the other contributors. Neither of us can be sure that we have included the best courses in every country, but the authority of those who have recommended them is such that we have slept easily at night.

Since we undertook this work more than three years ago, we, the editors, have never ceased to be surprised at the number of points on which we have found ourselves in agreement, the more so since there is a considerable disparity between our two handicaps. At first sight it looked a formidable undertaking but, once we had agreed that we were not setting out to find the standard scratch score or the price of lunch at every obscure nine-hole course in the world, we began to feel a little better.

We have been frankly subjective and selective in our choice, aware, too, that the game does not consist solely of professional players; and, if encyclopedia is not considered the right word for such a work, then we can only plead that nothing else seemed adequately to express a book that attempts to encircle the globe and embrace the history of golf.

What finally emerged was the conception of a book that would settle arguments, which is why, so far as possible, we have recorded dates and records, and added an appendix of major results. But even more we have tried to remain faithful to the purpose of arousing not only the reader's curiosity but also, here and there, his nostalgia and perhaps leaving him with the same feeling that has struck us most forcibly throughout, that there is always something new to learn about the game.

DONALD STEEL

PETER RYDE

Notes and abbreviations

The book is arranged in a single alphabetical sequence. Cross references have been used where necessary; married women golfers, for example, will be found under the name by which they are known on the golf course and a cross reference to that name. The major achievements of the golfers are summarized at the beginning of their entries, the various championships, etc, being referred to in their commonly known shortened form. 'Royal' golf clubs will be found under the initial letter of the next key word in their names, with the exception of the Royal and Ancient GC.

The following abbreviations occur:

CC	Country Club
GC	Golf Club
GCC	Golf and Country Club
GTC	Golf and Tennis Club
LGU	Ladies' Golf Union
LPGA	Ladies' Professional Golf Association
R. and A.	Royal and Ancient Golf Club of St Andrews
USGA	United States Golf Association
USPGA	The Professional Golfers' Association of America; also its Championship

A

Aaron, Tommy AMERICAN
b. Gainesville, Ga., 1937. Canadian Open 1969; Lancôme Trophy (Paris) 1972; Ryder Cup 1969, 1973; US Masters 1973; Walker Cup 1959.

After a distinguished amateur career in which he was runner-up to Charlie Coe in the US Amateur Championship in 1958, and a member of Coe's American Walker Cup team at Muirfield in 1959, Aaron, a graduate of the University of Florida, joined the American Professional tour in 1961.

In the mid-1960s he was often a fast starter and in 1965 opened 12 tournaments with scores under 70, including the US Masters and the USPGA Championship at Ligonier, Pa. He was unable then, however, to master the art of keeping his game going through the later stages. He finished 2nd or tied for 2nd place nine times before he conquered this habit by winning the 1969 Canadian Open. A final round of 64 took him into a tie with Sam Snead on 275 and he won the play-off.

His name will always be linked with the unfortunate scorecard incident at the 1968

Tommy Aaron

Masters when, as Vicenzo's partner, he wrote down the wrong score at the 17th, which both he and Vicenzo failed to notice. In 1969 and 1970 he won over $90,000 on the tour, maintaining his reputation for wonderfully consistent scoring. In August 1972, Aaron finished equal 2nd with Jim Jamieson to Gary Player in the USPGA Championship at Oakland Hills. Then in 1973 he won the Masters, finishing strongly with 68: the old bogey – being able to do everything but win – was finally laid, although as with other victors this was followed by a lean period on the tour.

Abercromby, J. F. BRITISH
Abercromby, or Aber, as he was always known, was one of the best of the early British golf-course architects; but he also guided Addington as a club for many years. He was the sole dictator of its fortunes; the designer of the Old Course and the lovely New Course which, sadly, did not survive long after World War II. He was a familiar figure in a velour hat, a wooden putter tucked under his arm.

He could be immensely formidable and the story is told of a member who, in Aber's hearing, asked 'Where is the Suggestion Book?' Aber looked him up and down, prodded him with a bony finger, and replied, 'I am the Suggestion Book.' Addington is the course by which he is perhaps best remembered as an architect, but he was also responsible for the original course at the Manor House Hotel, Moretonhampstead, and for the first Haagsche course near The Hague in the Netherlands.

Aberdeen GC, Royal SCOTLAND
Balgownie, Aberdeen. 18 holes; 6,451 yd (5,899 m); par 70
An entry in the Aberdeen Town Council register of 1598 concerning a statute against 'playirs on the links during the time of the sermones' may well be the first recorded instance of official displeasure at Sunday golf, but the enthusiasm of the locals for the game led in 1780 to the founding of the Society of Golfers at Aberdeen. The Aberdeen GC emerged in 1815, becoming Royal in 1903, and is ranked as the sixth oldest club in the world.

The club was primarily responsible for creating and expanding an interest in the game locally and other clubs were duly formed. Aberdeen had to share the public links not only with the newcomers but with other sports as well. After negotiations that began in 1885, its own course was opened in 1888 at its present site, Balgownie. A clubhouse followed two years later; members

previously used a room at the Bridge of Don Hotel.

The course, on the northern outskirts of the city, follows the traditional lay-out of a links. It runs almost straight out for nine holes, largely under the lee of tall sand dunes and over natural terrain of valleys and hillocks. On the run home the fairways are rather less irregularly contoured, but the whole course makes a fine test, especially in a wind.

The qualities of Balgownie, as the course is more shortly known, have been recognized by various golfing authorities, who over the years have taken a number of important events to it. John Langley won the British Boys' Amateur Championship there in 1935 and the club has been host to the Scottish Amateur Championship six times, the Northern Open four times, and the Scottish Professional Championship once.

Aberdovey GC WALES
Aberdovey (Aberdyfi), Merioneth
Bernard Darwin once wrote, 'About this one course in the world I am a hopeless and shameful sentimentalist and I glory in my shame.' His opinion was based on a lifelong acquaintance with, and love of, the place and his own memory of the beginnings of golf there in 1886. Legend has it that Colonel Ruck, one of Darwin's uncles, borrowed nine flower pots from a woman in the village and cut nine holes on the marsh in which to put them.

The land in those days was little more than a wilderness and the game was of a rather primitive kind, but gradually more ground became playable. The green of the famous 'Cader' hole was built, and in 1892 the club was formed. The first meeting was held in April of that year, when some dozen players took part and the scratch medal was won by the young Darwin with a score of 100.

Aberdovey is rightly proud of its origins but though the course has happily retained something of an old-fashioned character, it has progressed rapidly as one of the finest in Wales. Situated at the mouth of the Dovey estuary, and looking out over Cardigan Bay, it is open to the winds. The famous architects Colt, Fowler and Braid each had a hand in the changes to the course, which lies between the railway and the big sandhills skirting the shore, but the main characteristics of the golf have remained wonderfully constant. The greens are small and in some cases have been protected from straying animals by the erection of wire fences. The player is confronted by a variety of irregular stances and lies among the hummocks and undulations. It is a course of character for which many golfers have a great fondness, and over the years it has been a regular venue for the Welsh Amateur and Welsh Ladies' championships.

Abu Dhabai SEE DESERT COURSES

Ace
American slang for a hole-in-one.

Acquasanta GC ITALY
Rome. 18 holes; par 71

This senior Italian course opened in 1903; a natural course in full view of the majestic arches of the Claudian aqueduct, and of the Appian Way.

Although frequently altered, the course has retained the individual character of the *compagna Romana*. From the back tees it is a very testing course, particularly in a wind. The greens are tilted and usually fast, and the streams provide obstacles as formidable as Scottish burns. The 8th and 9th are two of the better par-4 holes, but the outstanding hole is the 17th, a long par 4 with streams ready to catch the overbold long hitter, and a second shot to a green also well guarded by water and a steep bank. The first Italian championship, won by an Englishman, Denys Scott, was held there in 1906.

Adair, Rhona (Mrs A. H. Cuthell) IRISH
d. 1961. British Ladies' 1900, 1903; Irish Ladies' 1900-3

Rhona Adair first appeared in the British Ladies' Championship at Portrush in 1895, and immediately made her mark by winning the handicap award in the medal competition open to competitors in the championship. Four years later she was runner-up to May Hezlet in the Irish Championship, at Newcastle, County Down.

Rhona Adair played for Ireland many times and in 1900 she achieved the double of winning the British and the Irish Championships. She won the British title for the second time in 1903 at Portrush, this being her third final in the British over a period of four years. In 1901 she was runner-up to Miss M. Graham.

At Lytham and St Annes in March 1900 she won a long-driving competition with a drive of 173 yd 2 ft (158.8 m).

She was for some years president of the Irish Ladies' Golf Union, and showed particular interest in young players. Her life was spent in the vicinity of her beloved Portrush, scene of three of her championship victories.

Adams, James BRITISH
b. Troon, Ayrshire, 1910. Runner-up British Open 1936, 1938; Penfold Tournament 1936; runner-up British Professional Matchplay 1937, 1946, 1951; Dunlop Masters 1946; Ryder Cup 1947, 1949, 1951, 1953; Belgian Open 1949; Dutch Open 1949; Italian Open 1951

One of the finest British professionals of the pre- and early-postwar period, Adams twice came near to winning the Open Championship. He was an interesting player because his unusually long swing displayed remarkable lissomness for a person of substantial build but, although the club went far beyond the horizontal at the top of the backswing, it was a lovely easy swing; this could have been influenced by the fact that, as a boy at Troon, he carried the clubs of the great Willie Fernie. Being double-jointed also helped him achieve this.

His first challenge for victory in the Open came in 1936 at Hoylake, when he finished one stroke behind Alf Padgham. When Adams started the last round, he needed a 72 to tie and took 38 to the turn; two long

putts put him back in the picture and he came to the 17th needing two 4s to tie. He was bunkered at the 17th and took five although he was in and out of the hole for a three at the 18th; but his total of 288 (71, 73, 71, 73) was a great achievement.

His successes also owed much to his beautifully smooth putting stroke. In 1938 he was contending in the Open again, in what reports of the time described as 'a gorgeous duel' with Reg Whitcombe, who eventually prevailed.

Adams never came as near to victory again although he led after a first-round 68 at Portrush in 1951, only to finish equal 4th. He finished with two 69s in 1954 to tie for 5th. He was a leading tournament player for many years and played in four postwar Ryder Cup matches, in 1949 winning both his foursomes and singles matches.

Addington GC ENGLAND
Addington, Surrey. 18 holes; 6,216 yd (5,706 m)

Addington has long been acknowledged as one of the best courses within half an hour of London. To the generation that remembers its founding in 1914, Addington and J. F. Abercromby were synonymous. He laid out the course himself (he later became a leading golf-course architect) and, until a few years before World War II, he held sway there, autocratically but benevolently. The modern generation, however, can remember him only by his work, which included building Addington's New Course in the early 1930s: this divided the members who forever argued about the respective merits of the two courses, both of which were first rate.

It was said that Abercromby only built the New Course to disprove those who believed that it could not be drained. It was laid out among the bracken, heather and

Ace: Tony Jacklin gets a hole-in-one at Royal St George's during the final round of the 1969 Dunlop Masters

Acquasanta GC: a view of the 7th fairway with the Claudian aqueduct in the background

James Adams

silver birch that are such a feature of
Surrey's best golf, but had a distressingly
short life. After World War II the local
council took over the land and the club was
left with the Old Course which, thanks to
the skill of 'Aber's' design, has changed little,
remains a fine test of golf, and has been used
for many Surrey Championships.

Address

The position which a player adopts in order
to hit the ball. A player is said to have
'addressed' the ball when he has taken his
stance and grounded his club; except that,
in a hazard, a player has addressed the ball
when he has taken his stance.

Adelaide GC, Royal AUSTRALIA

Seaton, S. Australia. 18 holes; 7,010 yd
(6,410 m); sss 73

The Adelaide GC was founded in 1870
with a membership of 25 on a 9-hole course
on a site which is now the Victoria Park
racecourse, but in 1876 the club was dissolved until 1892 when it was re-formed on a
9-hole course laid out in the North Adelaide
parklands at Peterhead.

It was transferred to Glenelg in 1896 but,
because of difficulties with the lease, the club
decided to purchase land at Seaton in 1904.
An 18-hole course was designed, a clubhouse erected on a site still in use today. In
March 1923 King George V conferred the
title 'Royal'.

Royal Adelaide is one of two South

Australian clubs given championship status
by the Australian Golf Union and many
Australian Open, Amateur and Ladies'
championships have been housed at Seaton,
the first being the Australian Open of 1910.

The course is adequately bunkered and,
being only a mile from the sea, is much
influenced by the wind. Most of the course is
undulating with a good depth of natural
sand, water being provided by three bores,
each drilled to a depth of 600 ft.

Ado, Jean-Baptiste FRENCH

b. St Jean-de-Luz, Basses-Pyrénées, 1913.
French Native Professional 1951

A massive figure with a rather rough
style, Ado survived the firing squad at the
hands of the Germans during World War II,
falling and feigning death before the shots
were fired. Famous for his very long hitting.

Afghanistan

This remote kingdom, tucked high in rugged
mountainous country between Iran,
Pakistan and Russia, provides a good
example of golf inevitably finding its way to
the far corners of the globe. This example is
found in the course at the Kabul GC. From
a purist point of view, the course is not up to
much, but it is there, the only one in
Afghanistan, and thus important to resident
foreigners, the few local residents who play,
and to the occasional keen visitor.

The club is located several miles outside
Kabul, the capital, beneath a dammed lake

that supplies water to the city. The course
spreads over meadowland strewn with shale,
partly overgrown with weeds and rough
grass; the greens are sand. It is hardly the
place to go for a golfing holiday but, for the
curious tourist, it is an experience of something different.

Air Shot

A total miss. A shot in which nothing is hit
but the air, sometimes called a fresh-air shot.
Although the ball is not moved or touched,
such a shot counts in the score for the hole.

Albatross

A term used for a hole completed in three
under par. In America it is known as a double
eagle. The most celebrated double eagle was
that performed at Augusta, Ga., in the 1935
Masters. Gene Sarazen holed a no. 4 wood
shot at the par-5 15th, tied with Craig Wood,
and then beat him in a play-off.

Aldeburgh GC ENGLAND

Aldeburgh, Suffolk. 18 holes

This course undulates gently among the
heather and gorse of pleasant heathland.
Close to the sea, it has some of the qualities
of a links, such as sandy free-draining soil; it
forms part of the East Anglian golfing riches,
which are not as widely known as they
deserve, and is one of the oldest clubs in the
area, dating from 1884.

It is not recorded who designed the lay-
out but many years ago J. H. Taylor made

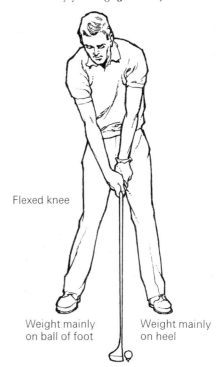

Flexed knee

Weight mainly
on ball of foot

Weight mainly
on heel

Address: *above*, Charlie Green and, *centre*,
Al Balding addressing the ball: *right*, the
address from the front

one or two alterations, which have stood up well to the advance of modern equipment. Not surprisingly, therefore, Aldeburgh has been in regular demand for Suffolk championships, but an even truer reflection of its testing quality is the fact that it has been host to three English Ladies' championships. In 1930, Enid Wilson beat Mrs R. O. Porter in the final by 12 and 11; in 1938 Elsie Corlett beat Miss J. Winn by 2 and 1; and in 1959, Ruth Porter defeated Mrs Frances Smith by 5 and 4.

Alexander, Stewart AMERICAN
b. Philadelphia 1918. Ryder Cup 1949, 1951
'Skip' Alexander turned professional in 1940. He was an established tournament player, winner of two tournaments, when he broke both ankles and was badly burned in a plane crash. Within a year, however, he was back in the Ryder Cup team and beat John Panton by 8 and 7 in the singles; but, though he won the Skyway Open in 1954, he turned his attention to becoming a club professional. In 1959 he was awarded the Ben Hogan Trophy as a golfer 'who overcame injury and physical handicap and continued to play the game'.

Alexandria Sporting Club EGYPT
Alexandria. 18 holes; 6,150 yd (5,624 m); par 69
An all-grass course, including the greens, situated near the Mediterranean, within the racecourse. It is essentially flat with some slightly elevated greens, and is generally better maintained than the course at the nearby Social Sporting Club.

Alison, Charles Hugh BRITISH
b. Preston, Lancashire, 1882; d. South Africa 1952
Educated at Malvern and New College Oxford, where he won his blue, C. H. Alison

was a member of the Oxford and Cambridge Golfing Society's team that toured America in 1903. He earned the distinction of halving the 18th hole of his University match by playing his ball from the clubhouse roof at Woking in 1904, but he is principally remembered as a golf-course architect in partnership with H. S. Colt and John Morrison. Much of his work was done outside Britain.

He played a little cricket for Somerset, was a journalist for a period, and secretary of Stoke Poges GC, Buckinghamshire.

Allan, A. J. Travers BRITISH
b. 1875; d. 1898. British Amateur 1897
Jack Allan had a very short career, but was something of an unusual champion. A medical student at Edinburgh, he never saw a golf club until 1891. He began playing on the Braids course in 1892 and two years later made the course record of 69. He was blessed with great coolness, self-possession, and had a wonderfully easy, if somewhat loose, style. In the last three rounds of the 1897 championship at Muirfield he accounted for Laurie Auchterlonie, Leslie Balfour-Melville and, finally, the redoubtable James Robb.

It was a great victory. He was the youngest champion at the time and seemed destined for a notable career but, within a year, he contracted a lung disease and died in March 1898, after taking up an appointment on the staff of the Mavisbank Asylum, Lasswade, Scotland.

Allen, Donald C. AMERICAN
b. 1938. New York State Amateur 1959, 1961, 1963-4; Walker Cup 1965, 1967
Allen, an insurance salesman, had his best year in 1965 when he tied 3rd in the US Amateur Championship, and was 2nd amateur in the Masters tournament and

runner-up in the North and South Amateur Championship. He played in the Americas Cup match with Mexico and Canada in 1965.

Alliss, Percy BRITISH
b. Sheffield, Yorkshire, 1897. German Open 1926-9, 1933; Italian Open 1927, 1935; 3rd British Open 1931; British Pro. Matchplay 1933; Ryder Cup 1933, 1935, 1937
Percy Alliss was one of the foremost British professionals between the wars, although he spent a long time out of the country as professional at Wannsee, Berlin. He was a consistent performer, being particularly noted for the quality of his long iron play.

After holding appointments in Wales, Essex and his native Yorkshire, he moved to Ferndown in Dorset, where he stayed until his retirement. Percy Alliss was in the first six of the British Open Championship seven times, coming nearest to winning in 1931, when he finished two strokes behind the winner, Tommy Armour. His two sons, Percy and Peter, followed their father into professional golf, Peter becoming, in his turn, a Ryder Cup player.

Aldeburgh GC: the 7th green   'Skip' Alexander   *Top*, Donald C. Allen: *above*, Percy Alliss

Alliss, Peter BRITISH

b. Berlin 1931. British PGA 1957, 1962, 1966; Spanish Open 1956, 1958; Portuguese Open 1958; Italian Open 1958; Vardon Trophy 1964; Ryder Cup 1953, 1957, 1959, 1961, 1963, 1965, 1967, 1969

As the son of Percy Alliss, Peter Alliss was born into golf and throughout a professional

career, which began in 1946, was one of the leading British professionals. He had superb natural talents and a swing of classical grace and power but he never succeeded in winning any of the major championships.

He won a host of professional tournaments in Britain and a number of open championships in continental Europe but, though he

Top and above, Peter Alliss

only once reached the semi-final of the Matchplay Championship, he had a fine record in Ryder Cup matches.

His introduction to the Ryder Cup in 1953 had unfortunate repercussions that left their mark on him for some time. He took 4 from the edge of the 36th green at Wentworth to lose by one hole to Jim Turnesa, while Bernard Hunt took 3 putts from the back of the same green. Britain only lost by one match. However, in 1959 Alliss and O'Connor won their foursome and Alliss halved his single with Jay Hebert.

In 1961, he won another foursome with O'Connor, halved with the mighty Arnold Palmer in one single and beat Bill Collins by 3 and 2 in the afternoon. Two years later in Atlanta, he beat Palmer by one hole and halved with Tony Lema; in 1965 at Birkdale he beat Casper and Venturi, winning a total of 5 points out of 6 for the match; in 1967 he beat Gay Brewer by 2 and 1 on the last afternoon.

At the end of 1970, Alliss moved from Parkstone in Dorset to become professional at the Moor Allerton Club in Leeds. He is a regular commentator on golf on BBC Television, an engaging storyteller, a fine after-dinner speaker and a golf-course architect.

Alternate

Replacements ready to make up the numbers in a strokeplay event when others withdraw. They would have been next to qualify and are placed in order according to their qualifying score. The term is also used in America for reserves in a team event.

Aluminium (Aluminum) Shafts

Shafts made out of aluminium that were fitted by many manufacturers to their new clubs during the 1960s. Generally speaking they never really 'caught on' because they did not become popular with the professionals.

Alwoodley GC ENGLAND

Alwoodley, Leeds, Yorkshire. 18 holes; 6,755 yd (16,177 m)

Alwoodley, within easy reach of the centre of Leeds, forms part of a famous stretch of golfing country; and though close to the city, it provides the perfect escape. The course stretches over the part of Lord Harewood's estate known as Wigton Moor and, with its natural moorland character, is one of quality and beauty.

The club was founded in 1907 with several people having a share in the layout of the course. H. S. Colt was perhaps the most notable, although another eminent golf-course architect Dr Alister Mackenzie, the

club's first secretary, also made his influence felt. The result is one of the finest tests of inland golf in Britain, calling for great control on the exposed fairways, which are set among sand and heather, whins and other shrubs. It is a course for which those who know it have great affection.

For many years it was an entirely private club and it was not until 1965 that the Yorkshire Union was allowed to hold its county championship there. This quickly led to the staging of the 1967 English Ladies' Championship, won by Ann Irvin, and in 1971 to the British Ladies' Championship, which ended in victory for Michelle Walker, at 18, the second youngest winner in the history of the event and the youngest this century.

Amateur

Broadly speaking, a player who plays for the love of the game rather than for any financial gain; but his status is carefully and rigidly defined by the Rules of Amateur Status laid down by the Royal and Ancient, and the USGA. Contravention of these rules

may lead to a player's suspension from competition.

American Amateur Championship see USGA MEN'S NATIONAL CHAMPIONSHIP (p. 460)

American Open see USGA MEN'S OPEN CHAMPIONSHIP (p. 393, tables p. 452)

American PGA Championship see USPGA CHAMPIONSHIP (p. 311, tables p. 466)

Americas Cup

A cup presented by Jerome P. Bowes of Chicago for a match played every two years by teams of men amateur golfers from clubs affiliated to the United States Golf Associ-

Amateur: The British Amateur Trophy being presented to Richard Siderowf

ation, the Royal Canadian Golf Association and the Asociación Mexicana de Golf.

The first match was played in 1952 but the series was discontinued after the 1967 event because of congestion of fixtures. Teams comprised three foursomes pairs and six singles, each foursome playing a pair from the other two countries and each single playing two matches at the same time.

The United States scored eight victories out of nine, their supremacy being broken by Canada in 1965 in Winnipeg.

Amory, Lady Heathcoat see WETHERED, JOYCE

Anderson, James BRITISH
b. St Andrews, Fife, 1842; d. 1912. British Open 1877-9

Jamie Anderson, son of David Anderson or 'Old Daw', and a caddie at St Andrews, was the first person to emulate Young Tom Morris by winning the Open Championship three years in a row, although neither he nor anyone else has ever matched Young Tom's record, four in a row.

Like most young St Andreans, he began to play at an early age, and developed into a fine player, who was often compared to Willie Park. He lacked Park's length but was deadly accurate with his approach shots, which he played so quickly that he scarcely seemed to give himself time to take aim.

He achieved his first championship victory, at Musselburgh, with a score of 160, an average of 40 per round, and followed it with another fine win in 1878 after a dramatic finish. Knowing that he had to play the last four holes in 17 strokes to beat J. O. F. Morris, he remarked 'I can dae't', and promptly did, by four strokes, including a one at the 17th which was the first in championship golf.

His third victory came at St Andrews

when he beat Andrew Kirkaldy and Jamie Allan into 2nd place with a total of 170. Though this marked the end of his championship successes, Anderson was a regular participant in foursome matches and, at various times, had four big matches with Bob Ferguson who won three Opens in a row after him.

Anderson was what is known today as a percentage player, although he was a thorough judge of the game. He was also a fine clubmaker, working for many years on his own before going to Ardeer and thence to Perth. His brother, David, was a good professional.

Anderson, Jessie see VALENTINE, MRS GEORGE

Anderson, Mrs J. see DONALD, JEAN

Anderson, Peter C. BRITISH
b. 1873

Anderson won the 1893 British Amateur Championship, beating J. E. Laidlay at Prestwick, while still a student at St Andrews University. Before that he was little known outside St Andrews but showed himself to be a fine putter; a tall man, he was extremely powerful in the wrists and shoulders. He later became a clergyman and schoolmaster, and settled in Australia.

Anderson, Willie SCOTTISH-BORN
b. 1878; d. 1910. US Open 1901, 1903-5; runner-up 1897; Western Open 1902, 1904, 1908-9

The first man to win four US Open championships, a feat since equalled only by Bobby Jones and Ben Hogan, although the biggest field against which Anderson competed was 89, and one of his winning totals, 331, was the highest in the history of the championships.

He won on a play-off in 1901, defeating Alex Smith 85 to 86, and again in 1903 when he beat David Brown by 82 to 84. His 73 in the opening round of that championship set a new record for a single round. He had a notable record in the Western Open, second only in importance to the US Open in those days.

A slim, dour figure, who attended strictly to business, he was the first of the early champions whose game was formed in America rather than in Scotland. He had a smooth, deliberate swing with a full pivot, which extended to his whole body; the mashie was his favourite club. Much more might have been heard of him, for he was an outstanding player, had he not died of arteriosclerosis at the age of 32. His death came as a shock for outwardly he appeared in perfect health right to the end. He played three 36-hole matches the week before his death. He held professional posts at 10 clubs in 14 years, notably Pittsfield CC, Apawamis, New York, and Onwentsia, Ill.

Andrews, Gene AMERICAN
b. 1913. US Public Links 1954, semi-finalist 1955; semi-finalist United States Amateur 1959; Walker Cup 1961

In 1954 Andrews emerged from relative obscurity at the age of 40 to win the US Public Links title. The championship was held in temperatures of more than 100 °F. After reaching the semi-finals in defence of his title, he moved on to bigger things, making his mark in the amateur championships of both America and Britain. In 1959 he was twice defeated one up over 36 holes by Nicklaus – in the final of the North and South and in the semi-finals of the US Amateur.

In the latter event at Broadmoor, where the greens are notoriously tricky, against the background of the Rocky Mountains,

The Americas Cup

Willie Anderson – the first golfer to win four US Open championships

Gene Andrews

Andrews plotted every one in practice rounds so that he would know the amount of borrow from every angle. In 1961 he earned his place in the Walker Cup match. With Bob Cochran, also well past 40, he defeated what was considered the strongest British pairing of Michael Bonallack and Ronnie Shade.

Andrews continued to play well through the early 1960s and, as he reached 50, his game showed little deterioration.

Angelini, Alfonso ITALIAN
b. Rome 1918. Italian Native Professional 1947, 1951-3, 1958-9, 1961-2, 1964-5, 1969; Dutch Open 1955; Swiss Open 1957, 1966; Portuguese Open 1962, 1966; runner-up British Seniors' 1972

After World War II, when he lost some of his toes from frostbite in Russia, Angelini became one of the most famous of Italian professionals. He played regularly in continental Europe with a good deal of success. He was professional at the Varesa Club for many years before accepting a post in Switzerland.

Throughout his career he had a strong swing for such a small man, but his real strength was great competitive spirit.

Anstey, Veronica (Mrs J. Beharrell) BRITISH
b. 1937. Australian Ladies' 1955; New Zealand Ladies' Open Matchplay 1955; Victoria State Open 1955; Curtis Cup 1956; semi-finalist British Ladies' 1957

Within 15 months of her introduction to the game, Veronica Anstey was picked to play for the English Girls' team in their annual match against Scotland. The game came naturally and easily to her, and she also had the advantage of a wonderful temperament.

During the tour the British Junior Team made to Australia and New Zealand in 1955 she won three championships. She was the youngest player to have captured the Australian title, and the first to win both it and the Victoria State event in the same season. She was five under par in the Australian final in which she beat Joan Fletcher by 10 and 9. In the New Zealand final she was two down to Gillian Atkinson, another British junior, after 33 holes, but won the next three.

She played for England in 1955-7 and was captain in 1961.

Antwerp GC, Royal BELGIUM
Kapellenbos, Antwerp. 27 holes; Championship Course 6,700 yd (6,126 m)

Royal Antwerp (Kon. Antwerpsche GC – Royal GC d'Anvers) was founded in 1888. It began modestly, as the Antwerp GC, with a few enthusiasts playing golf on the sands of a military training area.

In 1910, 133 acres (54 ha) of land among conifer woods was bought at Kapellenbos and Tom Simpson, the English architect,

successfully undertook the difficult task of building a new course. In 1924 the course was extended to include an 18-hole and a 9-hole lay-out. The club has subsequently housed a number of Belgian championships. The spacious clubhouse was entirely reconstructed in 1964 to offer modern comfort to the 850 members.

Apawamis Club USA
Rye, N.Y.

The Apawamis Club is in the area stretching from Long Island Sound to the Hudson River just north of New York City and called by its residents 'Westchester, the golfingest county in the world'. There may be some doubt about this statement, but none about

Apawamis, one of the oldest, pleasantest and quietest of American golf clubs.

Apawamis is a close neighbour of some quite famous golfing places, but the club itself is not particularly well known in other parts of the golfing world. This is surprising, and yet quite in keeping with Apawamis' character as a gracious and dignified gathering place for a quietly distinguished membership in an affluent neighbourhood.

It is surprising because things have happened there that might have been expected to spread the fame of a club. From this place the US Amateur title went overseas for the only time (although Ross Somerville took it over the Canadian border in 1932, as did Gary Cowan in 1966 and 1971); in 1911 Harold Hilton, of England, defeated Fred Herreshoff with one of golf's more celebrated shots on the first extra hole of their 36-hole final. For his second stroke on this par-4 hole Hilton hit a tremendous shot far off the line to the right, but the ball struck a boulder and bounced back onto the green to give him victory. At least that is the story they tell, and those who tell it will show their

hearers different rocks, and still others will relate that the ricocheting ball did not reach the green at all. There is a picture of the historic occasion in the clubhouse, showing the players, markers, and caddies on the green.

Some caddies who later became famous men worked at Apawamis at about that time. Ed Sullivan, the TV man, and Gene Sarazen used to compete in the caddie yard for bags at 50 cents a round. Also at this club senior golf was born in 1905, and every summer since that time members of the US Seniors' Golf Association, often as many as 500, descend on Apawamis for their annual meeting and competitions.

The course itself is a very good and re-

Alfonso Angelini   Apawamis Club – the 5th hole

warding one to play, nearly always in excellent shape, and can be reached by train, since the clubhouse is just up the road from Rye station.

Approach

A shot played to the green from the fairway or rough. Most commonly applied to the shorter distances.

Apron

The area in front of the green that is cut a little closer than the fairway, but not as short as the putting surface.

Arana e Ybarra, Javier SPANISH

b. Bilbao, Vizcaya, 1904

One of the leading Spanish golfers of his day, winner of the Spanish Amateur and Spanish Open Amateur Championships more than once. He is better known as one of the world's leading golf-course architects although he has worked only in Spain. He began this work after the Civil War (1936) and was responsible for a number of Spain's best courses: La Galea (Bilbao), Club de Campo (Madrid), El Prat (Barcelona), Los Monteros (Marbella), Real Autómovil de España (Madrid), Ulzama (Navarra), Guadalmina (Marbella), El Saler (Valencia) and the former Reina Cristina (Algeciras).

It is a pity that Arana did not do more work in this field, particularly in other countries, but he has contributed greatly to the Spanish scene and is generally recognized as a master of a specialized art. One of his trademarks is the single tree isolated in the fairway.

Arc

The path through the air taken by the clubhead as it is swung.

Archer, George AMERICAN

b. San Francisco, Cal., 1939. US Masters 1969; 3rd money winners' list 1968, 4th in 1971

Before turning professional in 1964, Archer worked on the ranch of a Californian cattle baron, who wished to sponsor him on the American Professional tour and give him the chance to hit hundreds of practice shots every day while still in his employment. He claims he never learned to milk a cow, let alone ride a pony. At 6 ft 6 in, Archer became the tallest major champion in history. After winning his first victory in the 1965 Lucky International, he became one of the leading players on the US circuit.

He won the Greensboro Open in 1967 and the Pensacola and New Orleans Open in

1968, the year in which his official earnings amounted to $150,972, putting him third in the money rankings. Although this figure dropped to just over $102,000 the following year, 1969 was memorable because he won the first prize of $25,000 in the Bing Crosby in January, despite finishing his third round of 72 with a double and a triple bogey; he

Approach: *top*, Henry Longhurst plays an approach to the 18th hole at Sunningdale's Old Course

Centre, George Archer driving at the 6th hole, St Andrews and, *above*, at the top of the backswing

then won the Masters at Augusta in April.

Archer won this event because he was the man who came through the pressure of the final round after Casper, the overnight leader, spoiled his chances by taking 40 for the first 9. With 9 holes to play, Archer was 3 strokes in front, but an anxious back 9 followed before he edged home. It was typified by his skirmish with the water at the 15th but he showed his reputation of being just about the best putter in America by holing downhill from 13 ft to save his par. His total of 281 (67, 73, 69, 72) was one shot better then Tom Weiskopf, George Knudson and Billy Casper.

For Archer 1970 was not a good year, but he finished 4th in the money list in 1971 behind Nicklaus, Trevino and Palmer with two victories to his credit. He made a wonderful start to the 1972 season, including victories in the Los Angeles Open after a play-off with Dave Hill and Tommy Aaron, and the Greater Greensboro Open, also in a play-off.

Archerfield GC SCOTLAND

In the days before and after the Honourable Company of Edinburgh Golfers adopted their new home at Muirfield, Archerfield, the private course of Archerfield House, formed part of the rich golfing neighbourhood of East Lothian. It occupied the land on the other side of the stone wall from Muirfield's present 6th and 8th greens, and once received the ultimate in tributes from Bernard Darwin, 'there is no more enchanting short course in the world'.

It was opened as a purely private course in April 1869 with an entry fee of five shillings and an annual subscription of four shillings, and had the reputation of providing some wonderfully enjoyable golf in a setting of perfect peace. It was not designed to test long drivers although it might easily have been made much more severe. With rabbits acting as the chief greenkeepers, it had splendid turf despite the fact that the rabbits occasionally made it possible to lose a ball on the fairway.

It existed happily for many years, for much of the time under the ownership of the Russell family, but in World War II it was ploughed to meet the demands of the agricultural war effort and was never revived. Archerfield Wood is the Graden Sea Wood in Robert Louis Stevenson's *Pavilion on the Links*.

Arda, Ben FILIPINO

b. Cebu City 1929. Philippines Open 1960, 1963; Singapore Open 1967, 1973; Indian Open 1969; Malaysia Open 1970

Ben Arda started playing golf at the age of twelve at the Cebu CC, where his father worked, turned professional in 1952 and rapidly became one of the leading tournament players in the Far East, and certainly the best that the Philippines have produced. Not surprisingly, he has played many times for his country in the World Cup, and throughout the 1960s, as the Asian Golf Circuit developed, he became a steady money winner. His career was punctuated with several victories and he earned an invitation to the US Masters at Augusta. In 1972 he won exemption from qualifying for the British Open, and made his first appearance in the championship at Muirfield.

Argentina

As with many other sports, it was the British who were mainly responsible for golf's development throughout the world; and, towards the end of the 19th century, they brought it to Argentina. At first, the new game caused a few eyebrows to be raised and the chronicles of those days remarked, with a shade of irony, on the wanderings of a few Britons devoted to such a strange sort of amusement in the uninhabited locality of San Martín and the surroundings of Buenos Aires.

The wide expanses of land served as their courses and the pioneers played with clubs, balls, bags and special dress, which had formed part of their luggage when they arrived; but, when the Lomas GC was founded in 1892, many Argentinians had already taken up the new sport; and after the Lomas, there came other golf clubs, that of San Martín and the Flores, and in 1900, the Mar del Plata. This was founded on the Atlantic coast and was followed five years later by the Golf Club Argentino, laid out among the woods and gardens of the district of Palermo in Buenos Aires, and which

today has become the municipal course. As a result of the increasing number of golfers, a great many more clubs sprang up and, by 1926, they agreed to form the Asociación Argentina de Golf.

The progress and development of golf in Argentina is due, very largely, to the work of this association, which organizes and supervises important championships and annual tournaments. These competitions have acquired universal fame and attract international golfers, who have a high regard for many of the courses and the standard of local players.

Argentine national championships are as old as the game there, and by 1972 there were some 20,000 golfers in the country. The Amateur Championship was played for the first time in 1895, and the Argentine Open in 1905 (it was then called the Open Championship of the River Plate). Argentine golf plays an important role in South America, its women's and men's teams having won the Los Andes Cup, contested by South American sides, the majority of times.

In the professional field, the prestige of Argentine golf has been greatly enhanced by several players all over the world. In 1931, José Jurado nearly won the British Open at Carnoustie and for years Tony Cerda was a regular competitor in Britain. But nobody has done as much as Roberto de Vicenzo, who has won championships in 15 countries, not to mention the British Open Championship in 1967 and his performance in the Masters tournament at Augusta in 1968. In the last 25 years, he has been undoubtedly one of the world's leading professionals as well as one of the most popular.

Argentina has also been host to several international occasions including the World Cup of 1962 and 1970, and the 1972 World Amateur Team Championship (Eisenhower Trophy). Argentina won the first World

(formerly Canada) Cup in 1953 through Cerda and de Vicenzo, and the latter won the individual title in 1962 and 1970.

Throughout the country, there are over 100 courses, of which 70 are affiliated to the association, and in the outskirts of Buenos Aires alone, there are 20 courses in addition to Golf Club Argentino, which is today almost completely surrounded by skyscrapers.

The best known are the Jockey Club, Olivos and Hindu, all of them around Buenos Aires; and the Mar del Plata.

Armour, Thomas Dickson AMERICAN

b. Edinburgh 1896; d. USA 1968. (British) Walker Cup 1922; (US) Ryder Cup 1926; Canadian Open 1927, 1930, 1934; US Open 1927; USPGA 1930; British Open 1931

One of the great expatriate company who, at the beginning of this century, learned their golf in Britain and made their fortune out of it in the United States. In addition to winning three of the Big Four events, Armour achieved the unique distinction of playing for Britain against the United States as an amateur and later for the country of his adoption against Britain as a professional.

When the Masters was first held, Armour was already 39; had he been a younger man he might have joined the very few who have won all four big events, for he had picked up the other three within seven years of turning professional. With his lively mind and strong personality, Armour became one of the most renowned teachers the game has known. His two best-known works, *How to Play Your Best Golf All the Time* and *A Round of Golf with Tommy Armour*, quickly became bestsellers. He was born in Edinburgh and fought in World War I, losing an eye. After the war he played in the first two British Amateurs and took part in the first unofficial meeting between the amateurs of Britain and the United States defeating the American, J. W. Platt, by 2 and 1. The following year, when he accompanied the British team to their first official Walker Cup match, he stayed in America and turned professional in 1924.

His first success was in the National Open at Oakmont in 1927, one of the toughest courses in the United States. He played the last 6 holes in 2 under par to tie with the leader, Harry Cooper. At the last hole he struck a no. 3 iron to 10 ft and holed the putt for a birdie, and then went on to win the play-off by 3 strokes. Three years later he defeated Gene Sarazen by one hole in the final of the USPGA Championship, and in 1931 won the first British Open to be held at Carnoustie, 50 miles from his birthplace.

Ben Arda of the Philippines during the 1970 John Player Classic

Argentina: Fidel De Luca during the World Cup in 1973

He showed in winning that his style was as graceful as it had ever been but American training had made it more workmanlike. He had a reputation for being a supremely good iron player, but some thought him an even better driver. His putting had improved by this time, and he had become extremely deliberate on the greens and close to them, taking a great many sidelong glances at the hole and as many waggles with his club. But as Bernard Darwin said of him, 'If he had not mastery over his waggles he had it over himself, and that is what counts'. The habit could, in part at least, be attributed to his having only one eye.

Armour was blessed with an immensely strong pair of hands, and one of the stories that gathered round this sparkling personality was that he could pick up a horizontal billiard cue between finger and thumb holding it at the thin end. His was the kind of personality that generated stories and, like Walter Hagen, he did nothing to discourage them. His respect for the rules is well illustrated by the story that he once saw a player tee-up his ball in the rough. He went across and, as he ground the ball into the earth with his spiked shoe, he muttered, 'Play it from there.' Another story concerns the finish of a professional challenge match in which the loser missed from 6 ft. A bystander expressed his disgust, whereupon Armour hauled him out from the crowd and bet him $500 that he could not hole out from there for that sum. He added shrewdly that the

man could have as long as he liked to practise, and went off to the clubhouse for a drink. When he returned, the man was in no mental state to hole anything. Armour refused to take his money, saying he had only done it to teach him a lesson.

After his playing days were over, he gained a great reputation as teacher both at Boca Raton in Florida, and at the Winged Foot Club near New York. Golfers as diverse as Bobby Jones and President Nixon are said to have sought his advice.

Artisan

The word, which originated in England, defines a special class of club member who usually have their own simple quarters and enjoy restricted conditions of play laid down by the parent club, in return for which they pay a reduced subscription.

The Artisan Golfers' Association was founded in 1921 by Lord Riddell, J. H. Taylor and F. G. Hawtree with the object of uniting artisan clubs in the British Isles and encouraging the formation of others.

Ascona GC SWITZERLAND

Patriziale, Ticino canton. 18 holes; 6,400 yd (5,850 m); par 71

No golfing tour of Switzerland is complete without playing south of the Alps, in the 'riviera' of Italian Switzerland. Patriziale is the best course in the area, running alongside Lake Maggiore. The sun shines there for much of the year, and the mild climate encourages the growth of palm trees, magnolias and other exotic plants. The course is flat, but long enough and difficult. Amply provided with bunkers and trees, it can be numbered among the best in Switzerland. It welcomes in the season a large influx of people, who come to a region that is Italian in language but Swiss in ambience.

Ashburnham GC WALES

Pembrey (Pen-bre), Carmarthenshire. 18 holes; 6,450 yd (5,982 m); par 71

Formed in 1894, this is one of the oldest clubs in Wales, lying along the southern coast near Llanelli with an occasional view at the far end towards the Burry estuary and Worms Head. The course, extended from 9 to 18 holes in 1902, was altered in some respects by J. H. Taylor in 1914, and by F. H. Hawtree in 1923. Like many links courses, there is a contrast between the opening holes which are inland and adventurous, and the rest of the course which runs out and back in traditional seaside manner. Two notable par-5 holes distinguish the inward nine, the 14th in particular being a model of its art. The last two holes run along each side of an old railway embankment, thence back to the last green up the hill beside the clubhouse.

The Welsh Amateur Championship has been held there several times, and in 1959 the professionals found the course at its toughest in wind and rain when the PGA Close Championship was played there.

Ashdown Forest GC, Royal ENGLAND

Forest Row, nr East Grinstead, Sussex. 18 holes; 6,098 yd (5,576 m); par 72

A hilly course on the edge of Ashdown Forest containing no artificial bunkers but a wealth of natural hazards in the form of heather lining most fairways, gorse, streams, pits and other undulations. Formed in 1888 by a group of enthusiasts headed by a parson and operating from a nearby hotel, it acquired the present clubhouse in 1894, and its royal title after the Duke of Cambridge had reviewed troops in the nearby forest. He arrived in the full panoply of war and drove a ball off the first tee. The first professional, Jack Rowe, stayed for 55 years. The artisan club, the Cantelupe, has produced famous

Tommy Armour

The announcement in the *News of the World* of the first annual Artisan Golfers' Tournament

golfers such as Abe Mitchell, Jack Smith and Alf Padgham, the Open Champion whose cousin, H. A. Padgham, is the present professional. Streams form hazards at the 2nd and 5th holes, and again at the 6th 'island' hole. A visitor was so taken by the charm of the latter hole endowed it with £5, the accumulated interest to go to anyone

who holed in one during important club medals. It was won for the first time in 1947, at which time quite a sum was handed over, but when it was done again three months later there was nothing in the kitty. The hole measures only 124 yd (113 m), but a stream guards the front and left side and the long narrow green is double terraced. The three holes just after the turn are newer than the rest, dating from just after World War I.

Ashley, Jean see CRAWFORD, MRS JEAN

Asia Golf Confederation

The governing body of Asian golf had its origins in 1963 in Manila with an invitation team tournament contested by Japan, China and the Philippines. While the representatives of these countries were in Manila, the idea of enlarging the event was put to them in the hope of inviting other Asian countries to participate in an Asian team championship.

The idea came from Leonardo 'Skip' Guinto, then Secretary-General of the Philippines Golf Association and now

Secretary-General of the Asia Golf Confederation; it received enthusiastic approval and invitations were sent to all the countries of Asia with the result that membership rose to seven the following year. In 1965 the second Asia Amateur Team Championship was held with six countries participating.

At the golf congress held during this championship, Guinto presented a constitution and by-laws that were officially adopted and the Asia Golf Confederation became the governing body of Asian golf.

By 1972, the member countries had risen to 13: Burma, the Republic of China, Hong Kong, India, Indonesia, Japan, Korea, Malaysia, Pakistan, the Philippines, Singapore, Sri Lanka (Ceylon), and Vietnam.

Among other things the Confederation supervises the Asia Men's and Women's Amateur Team Championship, the Seniors' Team Championship and the now popular Asian Golf Circuit (sometimes known as the Far East Circuit). There are only three officials of the Confederation, the president, vice-president and a permanent secretary-general. The first two positions are for a two-year term and are rotated among the member countries.

Asian Golf Circuit

Nowhere in the world has golf developed faster commercially in the 1960s and early 1970s than in parts of the Far East. In the 1950s the tournaments and championships

that existed produced little more than local interest but today, with ever-rising prize money, they can probably boast a more international entry than any others in the world.

It all dates back to 1959 when Eric Cremin, the Australian professional, was asked by Kim Hall, then a Welsh inter-

national serving in the Royal Air Force, to arrange an exhibition match. After that, their ideas grew; they persuaded the *South China Morning Post* to put up £1,000 to sponsor the Hong Kong Open which the Royal Hong Kong Club ran in conjunction with Hall, who had his tour of duty extended. Twenty-eight professionals, including Crampton, Charles, Nagle, Angel Miguel and several Chinese and Koreans, took part. Soon after the Philippines and Singapore Opens were added, together with a tournament in Tokyo.

Hall later became co-ordinator of the whole circuit, but the organizing committee now comprises Leonardo 'Skip' Guinto as chairman, Hall, vice-chairman, and Peter Thomson, the professional representative. Thomson's influence and reputation were important in the early days in raising the status of the events. By 1972 the circuit comprised nine tournaments with an average of US $25,000 prize money, starting in the last week of February and lasting until the second week in April. The tournaments consist of the Open Championships of the Philippines, Singapore, Malaysia, India, Thailand, Hong Kong, Taiwan (or China Open), Korea, and the Sobu International tournament in Tokyo.

Top foreign professionals as well as many good amateurs from all over the world take part each year. As a mark of recognition of its growing importance, the Royal and Ancient GC now offers four exempted places

Royal Ashdown Forest GC: a general view

Asian Golf Circuit: *left to right,* Murad Fyzee, Peter Thomson and 'Skip' Guinto

to the British Open Championship, based on the final order of merit of the Asian circuit.

As It Lies

Unless a player is allowed special relief as governed by the Rules or Local Rules, or his ball is lost or unplayable, he is obliged to play it 'as it lies' once it has been struck from the tee of any hole.

Atlantic City CC USA

Northfield, N.J.

Atlantic City is famous for its wide sandy beaches and autumnal beauty. A few miles away at the Atlantic City CC in the town of Northfield, two incidents occurred that have had some direct effect on American, and indeed worldwide, golf. The word 'bird' to signify a hole played one stroke below par is said to have been first used there. George Crump, who later designed Pine Valley, was playing with A. H. (Ab) and his brother William Smith when he hit a bird in flight with a tee shot. Then, when he put his second shot only inches from the hole, so legend says, one of the Smith brothers cried,

'Now there's a bird of a shot'. Bird eventually became birdie. When the 1901 United States Amateur Championship was held at Northfield, Walter Travis became the first player to win an American national championship using a rubber-core ball.

The golf course has been relatively little changed since World War II. The lower 9 holes overlook Lakes Bay and Atlantic City itself, and much of the generally flat course is only a few feet above sea level. High winds blowing off the sea are a major consideration, sometimes making a difference of three or four clubs in the play of most holes. Atlantic City is also a horror for slicers for out-of-bounds stakes line the right side of 10 holes.

The club, which was the scene of the 1965 US Women's Open, has long been owned and operated by Leo Fraser, who recently served with distinction as the president of USPGA and is a staunch supporter of the

As it Lies: a reproduction of a coloured cartoon by Charles Crombie

Ryder Cup matches.

Attenborough, Michael Francis BRITISH

b. Wiltshire 1939

A fine competitor who, after captaining Oxford in his third year, played for England for four years and gained a place in the 1967 Walker Cup team. He was twice winner of the President's Putter.

Auchterlonie, Laurence BRITISH

b. St Andrews, Fife, 1904

Laurie succeeded his father, William Auchterlonie, as professional at the Royal and Ancient in September 1964, but is better known for his skill as a wooden club-maker and as a collector of antique clubs; on both counts a pilgrimage to Auchterlonie's shop, some 200 yards from the first tee of the Old Course, is part of the ritual for regular visitors to St Andrews.

A set of Auchterlonie woods is almost as much of a rarity as one of the old clubs he has in his museum; his own output is necessarily small and highly selective. The visitor will, however, be enthusiastically

shown his private collection of around 200 clubs, restored by him and bearing the names of such illustrious 19th-century makers as McEwan and Philps, for which he was once offered £20,000. He gives frequent lectures at home and overseas on this aspect of golf, in which he is recognized as a leading authority.

Michael Attenborough

Auchterlonie, William BRITISH

b. St Andrews, Fife, 1872; d. 1963. British Open 1893

A professional of the old school, Willie Auchterlonie first played in the Open Championship when he was 16 years old. He won the title in 1893 and remains the last Scottish-born player resident in Scotland to do so. Like many of his generation Willie was first and foremost a clubmaker. In September 1935 he was appointed honorary professional to the Royal and Ancient, in succession to Old Tom Morris and Andrew Kirkaldy.

Auckland GC NEW ZEALAND

Middlemore, Auckland, N. Island.
18 holes: 6,564 yd (6,002 m)

To the Auckland GC fell the honour in 1971 of staging the Commonwealth Tournament in the year in which New Zealand golf celebrated its centenary. The weather was appallingly wet and the New Zealand side, having performed so well in the Eisenhower Trophy in 1970, fared disappointingly but the Middlemore course, rated by Arnold Palmer as the finest he played in New Zealand, was the venue of a memorable occasion.

The characteristically parkland type of course and the excellent facilities of the club presented the modern face of the Auckland Club at its best but its traditions are deep rooted, stemming from a meeting at the Northern Club in February 1894. The first course was at Green Lane with a transfer in 1901 to land administered partly by the One Tree Hill Domain Board and partly by the Cornwall Park Trustees.

Although the course had a profound influence on the development of golf in Auckland, it had its disadvantages and in July 1907 the club bought 144 acres (58 ha) of land near Otahuhu Borough which had once been held by the Fairburn family. It was W. T. Middlemore Fairburn who had given the estate its name. The property was mainly on heavy clay-silt soil with gentle undulation and a number of gullies and creeks. Middlemore was officially opened on 2 April 1910, with 18 holes ready for permanent play in 1912, two years before Middlemore staged its first National Championship. The course was laid out by the professional, F. G. Hood.

The course developed rapidly after World War I and about 1928 a number of alterations were carried out. Though there were inevitable setbacks during the Depression and World War II years, the club survived, and by 1950 membership was 300. As the game spread in popularity, other clubs began to blossom, but Middlemore's age gives it a special position and though it chooses not to stage the sponsored tournaments, the championships, international and local events which it is asked to house are an undoubted reflection of its quality. Altogether it had been host to five Open Championships by 1972 and has been the scene of exhibition matches by Arnold Palmer and Jack Nicklaus.

Augusta National GC USA
Augusta, Ga. 18 holes; par 72

The Augusta National GC, the home of the annual Masters Tournament, was founded as recently as 1931. The previous year, Robert T. Jones Jr – the immortal Bobby – had retired from competitive golf following his amazing Grand Slam, and now he had the time to do something about a project he had long thought about: building his dream golf course. Various groups approached Jones with suggestions and ideas, but he did not seriously consider any proposals until a number of well-to-do men, who wintered in Augusta and played their golf there, arranged for him to look at a tract of land at the west of the city. Called Fruitlands, it was a plantation that Baron Berckmans, a distinguished Belgian horticulturalist, had developed into the South's first great nursery. On his inspection trip to Fruitlands, Jones walked onto the terrace behind the stately antebellum manor house and, as he gazed at the upland pines and the rolling terrain that sloped down to Rae's Creek in the distance, he knew instantly that this was the ideal site for the course he had in mind. In fact, Jones, an Atlantan, had always had a warm spot for Augusta; it was his wife's home town and he had enjoyed the golf visit he made early in 1930 when he won the Southeastern Open by 13 shots from the full professional pack. That victory, Jones's friends have always felt, did much to put him in the frame of mind that made a Grand Slam possible.

To assist him in designing the course at Augusta, Jones selected Dr Alister Mackenzie, the Scottish architect whose work he admired – Cypress Point in particular. The 18 holes, however, largely embody Jones's tenets, many of which were radical and a few revolutionary. For example, he thought that a first-rate course should, at one and the same time, provide a stern test for a tournament golfer and a reasonable test for an average golfer. To this end, the fairways at Augusta are extremely broad, there is no rough to speak of, and there are fewer than 45 bunkers. For the Masters the course is extended close to its maximum – 6,980 yd

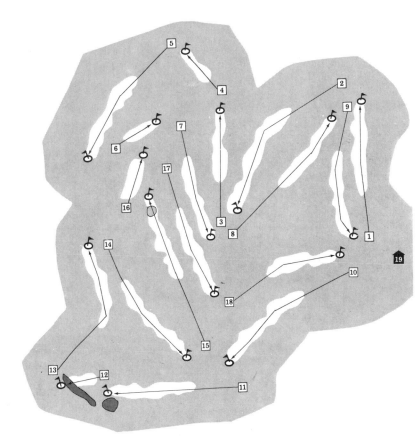

(6,383 m) – by moving the markers to the backs of the long tees, and the shots to the greens are made far more demanding and dangerous by tucking the pins in difficult positions on the large and severely contoured greens that recall those at St Andrews and other British links, which Jones had played in the British Open and Amateur and had

come to admire. The essential quality of the course that Jones built was that it was strategic in design as opposed to penal – that is, instead of being primarily set up to punish a golfer whenever he strayed from the straight and narrow, the holes encouraged him to play attacking shots, rewarded him when he brought them off, and made him

Top, Augusta National GC: the 2nd hole to the green and, *above,* the plan of the course

pay for his failures in a just proportion to his degree of error. The Augusta National came to exert an immense influence on American golf architecture. Almost single-handedly it brought to a halt the national infatuation with penal architecture (which reached its apogee at Oakmont with its two hundred-plus bunkers) and inaugurated a more sensible era of design.

When the club was formed in 1931, the founding fathers decided to call it the Augusta *National*, for it was their intention that the membership should be drawn from the length and breadth of the United States (which it has been). In 1931 no one had any idea that the club would become the venue of an important annual tournament. This, the Augusta National Invitation Tournament, which came to be known as the Masters, began in 1934 as a small, informal get-together which Bob Jones thought his old friends in golf might enjoy. A nice representative field of pros and amateurs assembled, and Horton Smith won the 72-hole event with some typical clutch putting on the final round. Jones, making his first competitive appearance since his retirement, finished in a tie for 13th, an excellent showing, but it was clear that during his years of inactivity he had lost not so much his superb swing as his ability to concentrate under pressure. That reunion was so entirely successful that Clifford Roberts, one of the founders of the club and the perennial chairman of the Masters since its inception, worked with Jones on formulating plans for holding a similar tournament the next spring. That was the year, of course, that Gene Sarazen won the Masters in a play-off after tying with Craig Wood by holing his historic 235-yd (215-m), 4-wood second shot on the par-5 15th, the 69th hole of the tournament – the famed double eagle 2. That shot put the Masters on the front page of the newspapers, and from that time on the tournament continued to grow in stature and esteem until, shortly after World War II, it came to be universally accepted as one of the game's four major championships.

What makes the Augusta National such an exceptional course is that its golf beauty is matched by its natural beauty. It may well be the most beautiful course in the world, for it has made the most of its Berckmans inheritance. Each hole is named after the flower, shrub, or tree that predominates along its borders. For example, the magnificent 10th, a 470-yd (430-m) par-4, is called Camellia; the 475-yd (433-m) par-5 13th, a typical Jones 'par 4½', is called Azalea; and the 190-yd (174-m) 16th, with its famous all-liquid fairway, is called

Red Bud. The course, which is seeded with Bermuda and rye grass, has other distinctions. It is probably the best spectator course in the world, for through the years mounds and ridges have been built alongside the holes to provide better vantage points. These changes were often accomplished at the same time that Jones made periodic functional changes to strengthen certain aspects of particular holes. As for the club itself, Clifford Roberts is reputed still to have something to say about its internal proceedings. Its membership includes Charlie Yates and Charlie Coe, but its most celebrated member was General Dwight D. Eisenhower who, during his years in the presidency, made his 'vacation White House' in the

bungalow, called Mamie's Cabin, behind the practice green.

Augusta National Invitational Tournament
The original name of the US Masters Tournament.

Australia
Doubt exists about the early beginning of golf in Australia except that the Scots had a profound influence upon it. It is generally agreed that the honour of hitting the first ball on this continent fell to the Hon. James Graham, who brought his own supply of golf clubs and featheries from the Kingdom of Fife to Melbourne around 1847, and that he even conducted a club for a few years.

His hopes of establishing the game in that period were defeated by the gold rush, although about 1851 another Scot, John Dunsmore, was reported to be hitting a ball about a paddock in Sydney. Geelong, another Scottish stronghold, may have formed a club, and possibly there were other enthusiastic pioneers as well. If so, they

appeared in an unsympathetic environment. Even Royal Adelaide and the Australian GC in Sydney made false starts. Royal Adelaide, which claims a start in 1870, dissolved for 16 years in 1876. The Australian GC, founded in 1882, was disrupted by road building and ceased to function in 1888 for five years.

The Brisbane Club came next, in 1890, with 9 holes at Chelmer; it subsequently changed names and, much later, amalgamated. This leaves Royal Melbourne, established in 1891, with the claim of being the oldest club in Australia with complete continuity. But then, despite the primitive communications between remote centres, golf came with a rush: Royal Sydney and the revived Royal Adelaide followed in 1893, Royal Perth in 1895, and in 1896 the Newlands GC in Tasmania.

With so many clubs in existence it soon became obvious that some form of co-ordinating body was needed and on 16 October 1908, a meeting at the Royal Melbourne resolved to form the Australian Golf Union and, subject to the agreement

Australia: *above,* a view of the 18-hole course at Coff's Harbour, N.S.W.

Australia: *top,* Albert Park, three miles from the heart of Melbourne

of Royal Sydney, to hold the Australian Amateur Championship there.

The union's objects, as defined in its original rules, were the general advancement of golf, control of Australian championships and the 'settlement of disputes and advice to any Clubs desiring it'.

In the last half century, Australia's golfing

development has been spectacular and rapid; 1,200 clubs were registered with the Australian Golf Union by 1972. Waiting lists exist at most city clubs and, since about 1960, golf is probably played by a higher percentage of the population than anywhere else in the world. The game has never been allowed to become as expensive as it is in many countries; to this extent its Scottish origins have been preserved.

The Australians are perhaps the most sports-minded people in the world and it is no surprise that they should be attracted by a game that lasts a lifetime. Another reason for the great expansion of interest in modern times has been the emergence of players of world standing, like Peter Thomson, Kel Nagle, Bruce Crampton and Bruce Devlin; and by the fact that up to 1972 Australia had won the World (Canada) Cup three times, and the Eisenhower Trophy twice.

In the years following World War II, when the youthful Thomson began to challenge the supremacy of such established Australian professionals as Norman von Nida and Ossie Pickworth, there were no sponsored

tournaments. Today, in keeping with the general trend, there are many chances of competition and since 1970 the Australian Open has been sponsored by Qantas, the Australian airline.

The manufacture of golfing equipment has grown and one firm, Precision Golf Forgings Pty Ltd, has established markets in many countries. There has been an increased demand for public golf courses and these have been constructed in many places.

The women, or associates as the Australians prefer to call them, have not taken a back seat. In fact, before the men had played their first open championship, the ladies had already decided their first, played on 29 and 30 August 1894 at Geelong, Victoria, with 17 entries. The Australian Ladies' Golf Union was formed on 22 September 1920, and there are now well over 1,100 affiliated clubs, yet another indication of the thriving state of golf in Australia. If the Hon. James Graham were alive today, he would find that it would take more than another gold rush to distract the Australian golfer.

As Peter Thomson once said, 'Australian golf has developed a maturity in the postwar years that has lifted the sport from monopolistic pleasure to the few to the enthusiastic pastime of hundreds of thousands.'

Australian GC, The AUSTRALIA
Kensington, Sydney, N.S.W. 27 holes;

Championship Course 7,148 yd (6,536 m); 9-hole Course 2,302 yd (2,105 m)

Royal Adelaide may dispute the fact, but some claim that the Australian GC, founded in 1882, is the oldest existing club in Australia – although continuity was broken by a dormant period of a few years starting in 1888. Together with Royal Sydney, this club was responsible for founding what is now the New South Wales Golf Association: in fact the State Amateur Championship was limited to these two clubs until 1903, the year in which the Australian GC finally came to rest at its present location. This site, near Sydney Airport, now adjoins a government highway constructed in 1968. The intrusion of this road necessitated the reconstruction of many holes. Although the club, which has always been a regular home for Australian championships and professional events, was inconvenienced by the alterations, they resulted in a course now measuring 7,148 yd.

It occupies undulating sand country and is subject to winds from the sea, so trees are scarce; the winds have scored and deepened the many bunkers, which form a considerable hazard.

The club's early history is reflected in the fact that the cup presented by C. N. Cadogan is still played for twice a year, and further emphasized by the fact that gross scores of under a hundred were rare in the early days – the handicaps of the 53 members in 1895 ranged from a lower limit of 10 to an upper of 55.

The clubhouse with its high-pitched roof has been a Kensington landmark for many years. A further wing with residential suites for members was added in 1969. One of the club's most unusual facilities is a ski lodge, high in the Australian Alps, for members to use in the snowy season.

Australian Open Championship
First played in 1904 when it was won by the Hon. Michael Scott, this is one of the few commercially sponsored major Australian championships. In 1970 Qantas, Australia's international airline, took on financial responsibility and shared with the Australian GU the administration of it. Before World War II the championship seldom had a strong international field and five times the title was won by an amateur, Ivo Whitton. Its most distinguished winner was the American, Gene Sarazen, in 1936, but after the war victories by some leading Australians – Pickworth, Thomson, Cremin, Nagle, and Crampton – added lustre to it, and with the spread of professional tournaments, it began to assume a new importance. Arnold Palmer,

Australia: a picture taken in 1953 showing some of the 15,000 spectators who watched the McWilliam's Wines Golf Tournament at the Australian GC, Sydney

Gary Player (six times) and Jack Nicklaus (twice) added their names to the roll of champions; in 1971 Nicklaus said after his 8-stroke victory at Royal Hobart that he felt it ranked next in importance to the world's four major championships (the British and American Opens, the US Masters, and the USPGA Championship).

Austria

By the end of 1972 there still seemed to be more castles than golfers in Austria. Only about 1,800 people belonged to four 18-hole and a dozen 9-hole courses. None the less, the game in Austria dates back to 1901 when the Emperor Franz Josef I became acquainted with it. He gave land at an annual rent of one Krone for the course at Wien-Krieau, constructed by the French architect M. C. Noskowski. This first course became the home of Golf Club Wien (Vienna).

In 1931, when the Austrian Golf Federation was founded, the number of players had increased to 1,200, and the number of clubs to six: the Vienna; the Golf and Country Club, Lainz; Igls, near Innsbruck; Dellach; Semmering; and Achensee. At the start of World War II, however, the number of golfers was down to 250, and it was some time after the war before real progress was made.

King Edward VIII was patron of the Lainz club (it was thought to be the only non-British club to claim this patronage). After

his abdication the king used to stay with Baron Rothschild at Enzesfeld near Baden, Vienna, where the baron built a 9-hole course between 1931 and 1935.

The first Austrian Amateur Open Championship was held at the Wien-Krieau course in 1909, and the first Ladies' Championship took place in 1925. The latter event was won in 1937 by Mrs Maria Moss, now the wife of Henry Cotton. Austria joined the European Golf Association in 1937, in a troubled period. After World War II Dr Hugo Eckelt, president of the Austrian Federation for 13 years, was largely responsible for Austria's return to the association. In 1963, Professor Heinrich Harrer, the well-known explorer and author,

Austria: *top,* the Golf Hotel at Dellach am Wörthersee; *above,* the Austrian golfer Oswald Gartenmaier during the 1972 Dunlop Masters

who was a member of Austria's first Eisenhower Trophy team at St Andrews in 1958, started on a long term as president.

Golf is growing in popularity in Austria, if slowly, and in the last few years two young golfers, Klaus Nierlich and Alexander Maculan, have dominated the championships. From 1961 to 1971, Nierlich won seven national and two international championships of Austria; his friend and rival Maculan won three national and four international titles.

Away

It is a natural rule of golf that a player takes his turn when his ball lies further from the hole. He is then said to be 'away'. In certain circumstances on the putting green, however, particularly in a medal competition, a player who has already putted once may hole out before his partner, who may be further from the hole, takes his shot.

Aylmer, Colin C. BRITISH

b. Cheltenham, Gloucestershire, 1884. Runner-up British Amateur 1910; semi-finalist 1913; Walker Cup 1922; *Golf Illustrated* Gold Vase 1924

In the 1910 British Amateur Aylmer lost the final to John Ball at Hoylake by 10 and 9. In the match against America in 1921 he partnered Tommy Armour and won his single. In the 1922 Walker Cup match he partnered Roger Wethered to victory but lost his single to Francis Ouimet.

Ayton, Laurie B. BRITISH

b. St Andrews, Fife, 1914. Runner-up British Professional Matchplay 1948; Ryder Cup 1949

Born into a well-known St Andrews golfing family, Laurie Ayton followed in his father's footsteps as a professional. He held a number of club posts and also had some success as a tournament player. His best performance was as runner-up to Fred Daly in the 1948 Professional Matchplay Championship. The following year he was chosen for the Ryder Cup team without getting a game.

Bachli, Douglas W. AUSTRALIAN

b. Victoria 1922. Australian Amateur 1948, 1962; British Amateur 1954; Commonwealth Tournament 1954, 1959; Eisenhower Trophy 1958

Bachli was a prominent State golfer from 1948 onwards, winning the Victoria and Queensland championships a number of times. But it was in 1954 that his chance came to make a wider impression when he played at St Andrews in the inaugural Commonwealth Tournament which marked the bicentenary of the Royal and Ancient Golf Club. He not only won all his matches in that event, but went on to win the British Amateur Championship at Muirfield, defeating Bill Campbell of the United States in

the final. He remains the only Australian to have won the title. During his visit to Britain that year he was undefeated in 22 consecutive matches. There was no outstanding feature to his game, apart from a great steadiness on the greens, but he thrived on keeping the ball in play. Bachli was also a member of the Australian team that won the first World Amateur Championship for the Eisenhower Trophy after a play-off with the United States in 1958. He now works for an airline company in Melbourne.

Backdoor see TRADESMAN'S ENTRANCE

Backspin

The spin imparted to a ball so that the front

of the ball is spinning upwards and the back spinning down. The dimples on golf balls, the marking on the faces of clubs, particularly irons, and the loft of the club all influence backspin, which is an essential part of the game.

As a result of the aerodynamic effects of spin, a ball driven to a good height will stay airborne about twice as long as a stone thrown to the same height.

The straighter-faced clubs, such as the driver, required for distance, are usually hit with a flat trajectory but maximum backspin is achieved with a firm strike from a barish lie with a wedge to a softish green. The amount of stop achieved is often dramatic and is a source of delight to crowds at tournaments.

Apart from the force and the manner in which the ball is struck, the lie also determines the amount of backspin.

Backswing

The part of the swing in which the club is moved away from the ball at address before beginning the downward movement, with the intention of striking the ball.

Bad Ems GC WEST GERMANY

Bad Ems. 18 holes; 6,650 yd (6,081 m); par 72

An outstanding course from the point of view of character and scenery, Bad Ems was the principal German championship course before 1939. It was here in the last event before World War II that Henry Cotton won the German Open for the third year running, and Percy Alliss won in 1933 for the fifth and last time.

The course suffered from the rigours of war but was revived by Mr Hoffman, a golf-course architect of the older school. Situated on the Denzerheide hills above the city, the course undulates in and out of valleys from the old-fashioned clubhouse, giving far-ranging views and a tendency for hanging lies. The back 9 is a less exacting test but contains a most attractive last hole. There is accommodation at the clubhouse.

Bad Ragaz GC SWITZERLAND

18 holes; 6,300 yd (5,760 m)

Not far from the principality of Liechtenstein, Bad Ragaz is situated close to the Rhine and to the eastern frontier of Switzerland. Designed primarily for the amusement of those taking the waters, it is host each year to its own golfers in the Oberrhein Championship, and is included among the country's best championship venues. The fundamental challenge lies in the narrowness of the fairways, in several

cases closely bordered by trees. The course is crossed by a number of streams which punish the more wayward golfers.

The playing season lasts from April until the end of October.

Baffy

A hickory-shafted wooden club manu-

factured in the days of the feathery and gutty ball. It roughly corresponds to the modern 4 or 5 wood.

Bahamas

A century before golf was ever played in North America a Scottish officer, Captain Alexander Campbell, who commanded the British military establishment in Nassau, introduced golf to the Bahamas and so sowed the first seed in an area which is now brimming with good courses.

Like so many of his countrymen, Campbell, once a caddie boy in Glasgow, was an obvious golfing enthusiast. He made a crude set of clubs from some old blades and bamboo shoots, moulded golf balls from knots of the local lignum vitae trees and really brought about the birth of the game in the New World by laying out a course round the parade grounds that now form the playing fields below Fort Charlotte in Nassau.

Although these were romantic beginnings, it was well over a hundred years before the first permanent club was formed, in the late 1920s. This was the Nassau, which has recently undergone extensive modernization and a change of name. Other clubs followed slowly, but the really significant part in the golfing history of the Bahamas has come comparatively recently through the successful attempt to popularize the many islands with tourists.

Elaborate private and semi-private development schemes have sprung up all over the Bahamas. Treasure Cay, Great Harbour Cay, Lyford Cay, Cotton Bay, Cat Cay, Bahama Reef CC and Blue Hill all have delightful courses in keeping with their colourful names, but perhaps the most remarkable development area has been Grand Bahama Island.

Since its first club, the Grand Bahama Hotel and CC, was opened in 1960, the King's Inn, Lucayan, Shannon and Fortune Hills courses have enriched the scene. There is no doubt that golf has brought wealth to the Bahamas, a fact that the Bahamian Government acknowledged by undertaking to sponsor the Bahama Islands Open (1970, 1971) which for two years formed the last stop on the USPGA's tournament circuit in December.

Bahrain SEE DESERT COURSES

Balding, Al CANADIAN
b. Toronto, Ont., 1924. Canadian Professional 1955-6, 1963, 1970; Mexican Open 1963

Balding caddied in his home town as a boy and then spent six years in World War II with the Royal Canadian Artillery. On discharge, he held a number of jobs, including one in a brickworks and another as a truck driver. He came to golf by working as an assistant professional at a Toronto club.

One of a small group of Canadian professionals who have competed successfully on the American circuit, Balding was the first Canadian to win a major American tournament, the Mayfair Inn Open in Florida in 1955.

Two years later he won three tournaments in the same area; he then went into a slump but recovered in 1963. In the United States he finished four times in the first four without winning. However, in addition to victories in his own country, he won the Mexican Open. In 1968, the year, ironically, when the Canada Cup was renamed the World Cup, Balding and Stan Leonard won the team championship in Rome, Balding having the lowest individual score of the event. It was a high note on which the elegant swinger apparently passed from the scene.

Balfour, Arthur James BRITISH
b. Whittingehame, East Lothian, 1848

Although he was not a great golfer, Balfour's enthusiasm for the game as a cabinet minister at the turn of the century gave the game a boost. After he had been appointed Chief Secretary for Ireland in 1866 he used to play at North Berwick accompanied by two detectives skirmishing among the sandhills. He wrote of the game: 'I am quite certain that there has never been a greater addition to the lighter side of civilization than that supplied by the game of golf.'

Balfour-Melville, L. M. BRITISH
b. Edinburgh 1854; d. North Berwick, East Lothian, 1937. British Amateur 1895

Leslie Balfour-Melville's championship victory came in the same year as his brother's success in the second Australian Amateur Championship. A lawyer by profession, Balfour-Melville was an example of the all-round sportsman typical of the period. He represented Scotland at rugby football and cricket as well as golf, and also won the Scottish Lawn Tennis Championship.

Balfour-Melville took time out in the summer from cricket to play golf and only entered for competitions if they were held at convenient courses. Beside his championship victory, he was four times a semi-finalist, and was runner-up in the event in 1889. He captained the Honourable Company of Edinburgh Golfers in 1902-3 and in 1906 was elected captain of the Royal and Ancient.

Ball, John BRITISH
b. Hoylake, Cheshire, 1861; d. North Wales 1940. British Amateur 1888, 1890, 1892, 1894, 1899, 1907, 1910, 1912, runner-up 1887, 1895; British Open 1890

John Ball was one of the most famous of the early names in British championship golf and one of the finest amateur golfers of all time.

His father owned the Royal Hotel at Hoylake which stood near the site of the old Liverpool Hunt Club racecourse and served as the Royal Liverpool GC's first headquarters. At the time of the club's formation John Ball was a boy of eight or nine and it was not surprising that golf quickly captured his interest.

When he was only 15, he competed in the Open Championship, finishing 6th, and between 1888 and 1912 won the British Amateur a record eight times. During three of those years, when he was serving with the Cheshire Yeomanry in the Boer War, he played no golf at all.

Al Balding

A. J. Balfour features in this painting of the members of the R. and A. Old Tom Morris is teeing the Captain's ball

In 1890 he became the first Englishman and the first amateur to win the Open Championship, a feat followed in 1892, and again in 1897, by Harold Hilton, a member of the same club. Ball captained England against Scotland continuously from 1902 until 1911 and competed in his last championship at the age of 60 in 1921, reaching the sixth round at Hoylake. It was Ball who was largely responsible for the winner of the 1902 Open, Sandy Herd, playing the event with the newly invented Haskell rubber-cored balls.

It is often hard in modern times to comprehend the record of John Ball. Competition was not so intense or universal in those days but Ball's dominance was truly remarkable. He was also the possessor of a particularly beautiful style which once drew a supreme compliment from no less a judge than Bernard Darwin: 'I have derived greater aesthetic and emotional pleasure from watching John Ball than from any other spectacle in any other game.' His swing was a reliable asset in many of those close finishes for which he was famous and was a mark of his calibre as a competitor. However, it is curious that it took him some time to do himself full justice on the big occasions.

No man ever came to be more of a legend in his own lifetime, the more surprising since he was a man of few words, shy and reserved. After his championship days were over he retired to a farm in North Wales.

Ball, Tom BRITISH
b. Hoylake, Cheshire, 1882; d. 1919.
Runner-up British Open 1908-9; British Professional Matchplay 1909; Belgian Open 1913

Only 5 ft 6 in tall and weighing less than 140 lb, Tom Ball managed to hit the ball a long way and was, above all, a beautiful iron player. But his style was unorthodox; at one time he used to move his left foot in the middle of his swing, and he always had a loop in his swing which ended with a pirouette on his left foot. He died from the effects of a chill contracted in World War I.

Balls see EQUIPMENT, GOLF BALLS, HISTORY OF

Ballybunion GC IRISH REPUBLIC
Ballybunion (Baile an Bhuinneánaigh), Co. Kerry. 18 holes; 6,417 yd (5,868 m); par 71

The recently built clubhouse and large hotel could turn Ballybunion into a magnet for tourists, for the buildings command wonderful views of countryside and sea, and the linksland course is of the highest quality.

The small resort town of Ballybunion stands on the southern shore of the Shannon estuary facing the Atlantic and, because of its relative remoteness, is not as well known as a golfing area as it deserves.

The resiting of the clubhouse has led to the renumbering of the holes, thus improving the start. Previously the 17th and 18th, two somewhat featureless long holes, were criticized. Now coming at the 4th and 5th they fit better into the picture. The present 18th, some 376 yd (344 m), is played from a plateau tee into a valley, with the approach up to a plateau green tucked in between high sand ridges. Many of the other holes, especially those close to the sea – the 7th, 10th, 11th, 12th, 15th, 16th and 17th, provide an unforgettable experience. So towering are the sandhills that they give the effect of a vast amphitheatre with the fairways threading through them below.

Ballybunion has been the scene of several national championships. The first time the Close Championship was staged there, in 1937, the precocious James Bruen, aged 17, beat John Burke, king of the Irish amateur game, in the 36-hole final.

Although the club records go back to 1896 the first championship was not held there until 1932 when a local member, Betty Latchford of Tralee, won the Irish Ladies' title.

Two expert opinions serve to show the bright future lying ahead for the club. After a visit there in the 1960s Herbert Warren Wind said: '... very simply Ballybunion revealed itself to be nothing less than the finest seaside course I have ever seen.' And Christy O'Connor's words emphasize its undoubted quality: 'Anyone who breaks 70 here is playing better than he is really able to.'

Bally Haly Golf and Curling Club
CANADA
St John's, Newfoundland. 18 holes; 5,664 yd (5,179 m); par 70

The remorseless winds from the nearby Atlantic Ocean blow perpetually across the course, whose undulating terrain seldom affords a level stance. Thus this short and compact course, one of only two 18-hole courses found in Canada's newest province, is a challenging one. Its par figures are seldom equalled, even by accomplished golfers. Started as a 9-hole course at Buckmasters Fields in 1900, the course was moved in 1908 to its present location, where it offers fine views of the ocean from many of the holes. It has grown without the benefit of a professional architect into the finest course in Newfoundland.

Baltimore CC USA
Five Farms, Md. 6.659 yd (6,089 m)

The Baltimore CC has had three golf courses since its foundation in the 1890s. The first of these was the Roland Park Course, where Willie Smith won the Open Championship in 1899 by a margin of 11 strokes, a record that still stands.

Now all the golfing activity is centred at Five Farms, about 15 miles from the centre of Baltimore in the rolling, green Maryland landscape, in fox-hunting country.

The East Course has been the site of three competitions of national or international importance, and each time something momentous has occurred. In 1928, 18 months after the course was completed, it was host to the USPGA Championship which, surprisingly, Walter Hagen lost. He had won five straight PGA Championships, but at Five Farms he was defeated in the semi-final round by Al Espinosa. The 1932 Amateur was played at Five Farms, and Ross Sommerville became the first Canadian to win. Then in 1965, Great Britain and Ireland tied with the United States in a marvellously tense Walker Cup match, with Clive Clark holing a 35-foot birdie putt on the last hole to halve his match with Mark Hopkins and force a tie.

The original Five Farms were owned by Stuart Oliver, a prominent Baltimore citizen, who sold the land to the Baltimore CC in 1924. The Oliver farmhouse was used as the Five Farms clubhouse until the modern redbrick building was put up in the 1960s.

Five Farms East was designed by A. W. Tillinghast, who was responsible for Winged Foot, Baltusrol, and other championship courses. It is short by modern standards but it calls for a variety of shots, and it is not always prudent for a golfer to hit his longest shot from the tee. For instance, too long a drive on holes 2 or 15 would leave the player with a hanging lie, and too long a drive on the 7th will run through the fairway into rough. On the other hand, too timid a drive on the 12th will leave the player with another hanging lie and a difficult medium iron across a nest of deep, white bunkers to an elevated green. Probably the most challenging shot on the course is the drive on the 6th, the 575-yd (526-m) Barn Hole.

Great rewards await the man who can clear the roofs of the red wooden maintenance barns at the bend of the right-to-left dogleg, and tragedy the man who attempts the carry and fails to bring it off. The successful corner-cutting tee shot that pulls up short of the cross bunkers around the bend leaves only a medium iron to the green

and sets up a likely birdie. However, the sound of underpowered drives clattering about the maintenance buildings is quite common. On the 18th, a fine finishing hole, the right side is lined with apple trees.

The club has 3,000 members, most of them non-golfers. Jess Sweetser, the first native American to win the British Amateur, was a member for many years. Although the original golf course at Roland Park, not far from the city centre, has been gone for a number of years, three holes remain, weaving down a steep hill from the old stone clubhouse, a popular lunch-time retreat, and back up again.

Baltusrol GC USA
Springfield, N.J.

Baltusrol is unique in that its two courses have both served as sites for the US Open Championship. The Lower Course has been employed for most of the 11 national championships held at the club, but the Upper Course was good enough for the 1936 Open, won by Tony Manero with 282, a record score then. The Upper is the shorter of the two, and its slick greens – their grain runs away from Baltusrol Mountain, which rises over the course – require some enormous borrows that simply cannot be read by novitiates.

As interesting and as much fun as the Upper Course at Baltusrol, the Lower is the course that adapts the better to the demands of the big game associated with today's

championships. It was the course on which Ed Furgol won the Open in 1954 and Jack Nicklaus in 1967 with a record score of 275, thanks to an awesome 65 on his final round.

The earlier Opens at Baltusrol, in 1903 and 1915, were played on a course that no longer exists. When A. W. Tillinghast constructed the two present courses in 1920, the original course was ploughed up and a fresh start made. The great strength of the Lower Course lies in its multiformity. There is no repetition – each hole is a different test. Consider the par 4s on the second 9: the 10th is a very big hole with a slight right-to-left swing to it; the 11th is somewhat shorter, with a sharp dogleg to the left; the 13th is a dogleg to the right across a creek that must

be carried on the drive; the 14th is an uncomplicated hole to a rather open green; the 15th parallels the 14th but is totally different, rising to an elevated green with tricky contouring. The course plays to a par of 72 for members, but when the USGA moves in, it advances the tees on the two shortest par 5s (the 1st and the 7th) and converts these into two prodigious 2-shot holes. The course then concludes with its only par-5 holes, the 17th and 18th, providing a probably unique arrangement at the finish.

Tillinghast had wonderful land to work with at Baltusrol and he did some wonderful things with it, especially on the 4th hole of the Lower Course, which is now regarded as an American classic. The furniture for this, one of the most attractive holes to be found in the game, includes a lake; the green itself, a huge two-levelled affair; three large bunkers behind the green; and a backdrop of oak and dogwood.

The USGA learned a good deal about the psychology of the contemporary touring professionals when it used alternative tees on the 4th hole in 1967. When the hole was played from the back, at about 194 yd (177 m), requiring a long iron or even a wooden club, the players would have nothing to do with the water and simply banged the ball onto the upper level at the back of the green without respect to where the hole was cut. However, when the tee was pushed forward to 162 yd (148 m), perhaps a 6-iron shot, the temptation to have a go at the flag – was irresistible, and so the shorter distance proved the more exciting and made the hole play as it was always intended to.

Baltusrol is big in many ways. The clubhouse is a vast, castle-like edifice. The membership is very large and includes a great many important figures from the worlds of business, finance, and law. It was Richard Nixon's golf club during the mid-

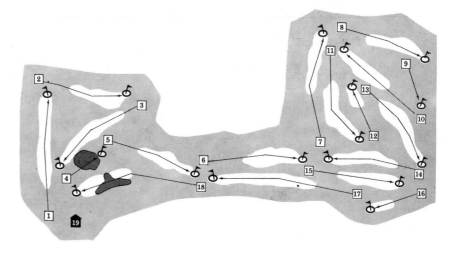

The 10th hole at the Five Farms Course of the Baltimore CC

Layout of the Baltusrol Lower Course

1960s, and the Duke of Windsor, although not a member, used to call every summer for lessons from Johnny Farrell, the US Open Champion of 1928 and Baltusrol's professional since 1934.

Barbados
Until about 1972, Barbados, better known for its cricketers than its golfers, had two courses, Rockley and Sandy Lane. The Rockley, founded after World War II, was the senior; Sandy Lane, designed by 'Happy' Ward and started about 1961, was increased from 9 to 18 holes at the end of 1972. However, by that time, the fine new Barbados Golf and Country Club had been completed and later Rockley amalgamated with it.

Barber, Jerry AMERICAN
b. Woodson, Ill., 1916. Ryder Cup 1955, 1961; USPGA 1961
At 5 ft 5 in, bespectacled Barber was one of the smallest professionals on the tour,

which he joined in 1948. He became one of the hardest practisers in the game and altogether won seven tournaments, but his most notable success was in the 1961 USPGA Championship at Olympia Fields, where he finished by holing from about 6, 12, and 20 yd on the last three greens to tie with Don January. Barber won the play-off with 67 to 68. In 1959, Barber and Doug Sanders finished runners-up in the same championship to Bob Rosburg.

Largely as a result of his PGA victory, he was voted 1961 Player of the Year and he also captained the 1961 American Ryder Cup team at Royal Lytham and St Annes.

Barber, Miller AMERICAN
b. Shreveport, La., 1931. Ryder Cup 1969
A former US Air Force officer who, after a spell working on several phases of his game in New York City, became a highly successful tournament professional. Barber was 29 before he left the amateur ranks.

A quiet, retiring man, Barber has a most distinctive, looping swing with a high-flying right elbow at the top, but it has been the source of much wealth to him. He won the Cajun Classic in 1964, but it was from about 1966 that he began to be a force on the tour. He won the Oklahoma City Open in 1967, the Byron Nelson Classic in 1968, when his official winnings topped the $100,000 mark, the Kaiser International in 1969, and followed with victories in the 1971 Phoenix Open and the Tucson Open.

Top, the clubhouse of the Baltusrol GC

Above, a watercolour, by Richard Elm, of the 4th hole at Baltusrol, designed by the architect, Trent Jones

Jerry Barber and the Ryder Cup in 1961

b. 1939. Vagliano Trophy 1961, 1969; Curtis Cup 1962; English Ladies' Championship 1968; European Team Championship 1969, 1971

Handicapped in these long-hitting days by lack of length, Mrs Barber has nevertheless shown the sterling competitive spirit that is associated with her famous brother, Michael Bonallack. Considering her size and the fact that she is unable to devote herself full time to the game, her record of three English finals in four years is a remarkable feat. On each occasion her opponent was Dinah Oxley, one of the game's longest hitters, and the contrast in length could not have been more marked. Her deliberate method makes her one of the slower players, but she uses her talent to good effect.

Barnes, Brian BRITISH
b. Addington, Surrey, 1945. British Youths' Championship 1964; Agfa-Gevaert Tournament 1969; Ryder Cup 1969, 1971, 1973; Under-25 Professional 1969; Australian Masters 1970

A strong, long-hitting golfer who turned

professional shortly after winning the British Youths' Championship, Brian Barnes played well in finishing 4th in the first Alcan Golfer of the Year tournament at St Andrews in 1967, and has appeared in many countries of the world. He qualified for his player's card in America but his success was limited there. He later became one of the leading British tournament professionals. He played well in one or two Open's and was always liable to play best on the big occasions. He is immensely strong and hits the ball a long way. He married the daughter of Max Faulkner.

Barnes, James M. AMERICAN
b. Lelant, Cornwall, 1887. USPGA 1916,

1919; US Open 1921; British Open 1925

Jim Barnes, as he is generally known, was a quiet, methodical golfer who had neither the inclination nor the ability to project himself as a personality. Nevertheless, this tall, spare-framed man, taciturn but always courteous, was greatly admired and respected. Although a naturalized American, he was always proud of his English birth. He started his golf career in his native Cornwall, becoming assistant to the Lelant GC professional at the age of 15. Nearly four years later he emigrated to the United States and in 1913 finished 4th in the US Open. He was three times in the first six before he won the title in 1921, but afterwards was never prominent in that event. A few weeks before visiting Britain in 1925 he had finished only 24th in the US Championship and was a surprise winner in the British Open at Prestwick following the sad collapse of Macdonald Smith. Barnes was 5 strokes behind Smith with one round to go and, as an early starter, escaped the chaotic crowd conditions that defeated his rival. Barnes was a fine player, his long straight driving in windy conditions

giving evidence of his early training on the Cornish coast. His *Picture Analysis of Golf Strokes* (1919) was a pioneer work in the field.

Barron, Herman AMERICAN
b. New York 1909. Western Open 1942; runner-up Canadian Open 1945; Ryder Cup 1947

In 1969 he won over $90,000 and also had the distinction of finishing in the first 10 in all the world's major championships, and had a good chance of winning the Masters and the American Open. In the Open at Houston he led going into the last round but took 78 to finish three shots back. In the Masters, paired with the three-round leader, Billy Casper, he made the mistake of playing Casper rather than the course and ended in 7th place. He won the first World Open, at Pinehurst in 1973, and thus the world record prize of $100,000.

Barber lives in Sherman, Texas, where he owns and runs his own golf course.

Barber, Mrs Sally (née Bonallack) BRITISH

Top, Miller Barber

Above, Mrs Sally Barber

Brian Barnes playing an iron shot during the 1970 Qantas Australian Open

Herman Barron

Barron was closely identified with golf in the New York Metropolitan area from the age of 10, when he began to caddie and work in the shop. He played consistently well in the US Open through the 1930s, but it was not until the 1940s that he gained national recognition. He was 5th in the 1941 US Open and missed tying for the 1946 Open by one stroke, dropping strokes at each of the last two holes when he had two pars to win outright. On the strength of this and two other tournament victories in 1946, he was picked for the 1946 Ryder Cup team. He has been professional at Fenway since 1935.

Barry, A. Gordon BRITISH
b. Cornwall, 1885; d. 1942. British Amateur 1905; British Army Champion 1922, 1925

Barry won the British Amateur Championship while still a student at St Andrews University. He remained the youngest winner of the championship until John Beharrell in 1956. A big swinger and an admirable putter, Bernard Darwin wrote of him: 'If victory was a flash in the pan, it was a bright flash.'

Barry, Beth AMERICAN
b. Mobile, Ala., 1948. Curtis Cup 1971; runner-up US Women's Amateur 1971

A relentless chipper and putter, Beth Barry adapted herself rapidly to strange conditions in Britain. Her victory in the final series of the Curtis Cup match over Kathy Phillips was convincing and crucial. An accident in childhood affected the muscles in her left hand, and this led to her adopting an ungainly swing with a quick break of the right wrist, but her long game is among the most accurate.

Barton, Pamela BRITISH
b. London 1917; d. 1943. Curtis Cup 1934,

Beth Barry

1936; French Ladies' Open 1934; US Women's 1936; British Ladies' 1936

Bright, cheerful and attractive, Pam Barton was a shining star of women's golf between the world wars. Her smiling, freckled face, youthful confidence with no trace of arrogance, and equable disposition made her popular with everyone; and from an early age, she displayed remarkable skill. She was only 19 when, in 1936, she won the British and American titles within the space of a few weeks, being the first British player to hold both since 1909, when Dorothy Campbell (Mrs D. C. Hurd) had that distinction. Miss Barton was of medium stature, strongly built, and one of the most powerful women drivers of her time. As a youngster, she achieved the unusual privilege of being allowed to play on the men's course of the Royal Mid-Surrey Club, women members being normally restricted to their own course. True to her adventurous spirit, she joined the Forces soon after war broke out in 1939 and served in the Women's Auxiliary Air Force until November 1943, when she was tragically killed in a plane crash in Kent. She was only 26.

Baseball grip
A grip in which the hands are separated as in baseball, though not as far. Also known as the two-handed grip. There is no overlap.

Basel GC SWITZERLAND
Geisberg, nr Hagenthal, France. 18 holes; 6,700 yd (6,126 m) par 72

Opened in 1965, Basel is one of Switzerland's newest courses with a season running from April to October. The site of the course is not, in fact, on Swiss soil, but over the frontier in Alsace. This has come about because the town of Basel, with its industries, has spread over all available territory on the Swiss side of the frontier.

In true Swiss fashion a good deal of trouble has been taken over it: a modern clubhouse, a difficult championship course, well wooded, plenty of bunkers and gentle slopes. It has one drawback, namely that even on the chosen site land is not unlimited, and at the early holes a long series of out-of-bounds chastens the loose hitter. Par is difficult to achieve because, apart from artificial hazards such as these out-of-bounds, there are a number of natural ones as well.

Båstad GC SWEDEN
18 holes; 6,300 yd (5,760 m)

Båstad Golfklubb was founded in 1928 on the initiative of Ludvig Nobel, a nephew of Alfred Nobel, instigator of the Nobel Prizes.

He engaged Messrs Hawtree and Taylor for the design and the great J. H. Taylor himself laid out the holes. The course is situated on hills with beautiful views towards the Kattegat. Lush and windy, the course is a good test, and it takes numerous holiday visitors each year, particularly from Britain, despite its rainy weather. According to legend, the grass on the greens always grows towards the sea.

The forming of the Båstad club and an open invitation competition in 1931, with Henry Cotton and Percy Alliss among the participants, did much to further interest in golf in Sweden. Several Swedish championships have been played there.

Bastanchury, Jane see BOOTH, MRS JANE

Baugh, Laura Zonetta AMERICAN
b. Gainesville, Fla., 1955. Los Angeles Women's Amateur 1969-70; US Women's Amateur 1971; Curtis Cup 1972

Laura Baugh (pronounced 'baw') is the youngest player to have won the US Women's Amateur this century. There is

some doubt whether she is the youngest ever for the date of birth of Beatrix Hoyt who won in 1896, also aged 16, is not known, but for the record Miss Baugh won the championship when she was 16 years, 2 months, and 21 days. She played in her first National Pee Wee tournament at the age of six, won her age-group championship at seven and on four subsequent occasions, winning once by 36 strokes and another time by 41 strokes. In the final of the US Amateur she defeated Beth Barry on the last green of a 36-hole match. She played in the Curtis Cup match the following year, halving her match with the British champion, Michelle Walker.

Laura Baugh qualified for the American Women's professional tour in June 1973;

Laura Baugh

she led for most of the first tournament in which she played and finished one shot behind the winner. Blonde and chic, she brought glamour to the professional circuit, and before joining the tour at 18 had already visited Japan and taken part in exhibition matches under the management of Mark McCormack. Her father, an Olympic pentathlon competitor in 1948, has been her only coach.

Baxter, Rex, Jr AMERICAN

b. Amarillo, Tex., 1936. USPGA Junior 1953; Trans-Mississippi 1957; Walker Cup 1957

A handsome young Texan who never quite fulfilled in the professional ranks the promise he showed as an amateur. Baxter's successes as a young man were glittering. These included the USGA Junior Championship in 1953, the Trans-Mississippi Championship in 1957 and the National Collegiate title in the same year, when he was also picked for the Walker Cup.

After two years' military service, during which he won the US Army Championship,

he turned professional in 1959. His first victory on the tour came in the last tournament of 1963, the Cajun Classic.

Bayer, George AMERICAN

b. Washington, D.C., 1925. Canadian Open 1957; tied 3rd USPGA 1962

Generally regarded as the longest hitter in the history of golf. He weighs 240 lb and is 6 ft 5 in tall. Bayer was an all-rounder at Washington University and made his reputation first in football, being drafted by the Washington Redskins. He turned professional at golf in 1954 and his first success came in the Canadian Open, 1957. He won two more tournaments in 1958 and became a consistent money winner once he decided to sacrifice length for accuracy. But this was not easy, for when he first joined the tour he became a sensation. Crowds came just to see him drive, and his temper sometimes wore thin for he was constantly expected to produce the kind of golf which he knew must jeopardize his chances of making a living. He scored four holes in one on the tour.

Once, his request to withdraw from a tournament having been refused, he took the matter into his own hands, slapping the ball around the 17th green until he had taken 17 strokes and finished in 90. For this he was fined $200 and put on 90 days' probation. In spite of his height and strength, he was past the horizontal at the top of the backswing, which gave him great clubhead speed.

Beard, Frank AMERICAN

b. Dallas, Tex., 1939. Texas Open 1965; Tournament of Champions 1967; Ryder Cup 1969; American Golf Classic 1970

Frank Beard has been one of the most consistent golfers on the US circuit and one of its best putters. A bespectacled player with an orthodox swing, he almost cultivates a quiet personality. He comes from a sporting background: his father was a professional golfer and his brother a basketball star.

In 1964 Beard was forced to leave the tour with encephalitis and lay in a coma for three days, but he recovered in five weeks and was back on the tour in another five. When nominated for the Ben Hogan trophy awarded to the golfer who has overcome the greatest adversity, it was typical of him to decline with the comment: 'I didn't do anything; I just got well'. He once summed himself up as 'a colourless guy who just plays'. In spite of this, in 1969, he finished first in the Order of Merit, earning $175,000. Two examples of his putting came in 1970. His decisive round in winning the Tournament of Champions was a 64 over the Lacosta club course, during which he took only 24 putts. Later that year in winning the American Golf Classic he returned a 67, taking only 10 putts for the last 9 holes. Beard was a member of the USPGA Tournament Committee in 1968 and has written a book about the tour.

Beardies

The row of four bunkers, invisible from the tee, that form part of the menace to the drive at the 14th hole on the Old Course at St Andrews. The bunkers are small, deep and devilish.

Beck, John Beaumont BRITISH

b. Luton, Bedfordshire, 1899. *Golf Illustrated*

Rex Baxter Jr

George Bayer

Frank Beard during the 1969 Ryder Cup

Gold Vase 1925; Walker Cup 1928 (captain 1938-1947); Royal St George's Grand Challenge Cup 1933; President's Putter 1937; captain Royal and Ancient 1957-8

John Beck played for England in 1926, 1930 and 1933, and for Britain in the foursomes of the 1928 Walker Cup match in America, but his special distinction was to be non-playing captain of the first victorious British team in the Walker Cup, at St Andrews in 1938.

Beck, Mrs John B. (née Dorothy Pim) IRISH

b. Cabinteely, Co. Dublin, 1901. Irish Ladies' 1938, runner-up 1949; Veteran Ladies' 1952, 1955-6, 1959; Curtis Cup 1954; semi-finalist British Ladies' 1961

Universally known as Baba, Mrs Beck has the distinction of having won the Irish Championship at Portmarnock while her husband, John, was captaining the victorious British Walker Cup team at St Andrews. She completed a unique family double by herself captaining a team against the United States, and she also captained a touring team to South Africa in 1951. In winning a bronze medal in the British Ladies' at the age of 59 she defeated a succession of younger players thanks to her outstanding skill with the putter. In addition to playing for Ireland in the Home Internationals for more than 20 years, she also represented that country at hockey. In 1955-6 Mrs Beck was chairman of the LGU executive council.

Beharrell, John Charles BRITISH

b. Solihull, Warwickshire, 1938. British Amateur 1956

His performance in winning the British Amateur Championship in 1956 at the age of 18 at Troon earned John Beharrell a special place in the records of the game.

It was a triumph beyond the realms of probability: in a week when Troon's famous links played very easily, he appeared like a man in a trance chipping and putting effortlessly. He defeated a succession of distinguished adversaries, who included C. D. Lawrie, I. Caldwell, Gene Andrews, as well as Frank Deighton and Reid Jack, both highly experienced Scottish Walker Cup players, and in the final he accounted for Leslie Taylor by 5 and 4 to become the youngest winner of the championship, a distinction equalled later by the 1966 winner, Bobby Cole.

Not surprisingly he was picked for England that autumn and for the British side that played the Professionals and the Rest of Europe, but his name faded from the national scene almost as quickly as it had arisen.

Beharrell, Mrs J. see ANSTEY, VERONICA

Bel-Air GC USA

Los Angeles, Cal.

The community of Bel Air, from which this club gets its name, is a part of Los Angeles. It is a region of estate-type homes most of which occupy the hilltops surrounding the course, leaving the slopes and the valleys and canyons for the golf holes to run along, over and through. The club is only a few minutes from the Los Angeles CC and overlooks the campus of the University of California at Los Angeles.

Bel-Air's membership no doubt includes any number of just ordinary wealthy men, but it is a club that has attracted a large contingent of celebrities from the movie colony and some very big businessmen. The setting is beautiful, and the course, which was built in the 1920s by Jack Neville, was later remodelled by Dick Wilson. Its members feel it is now the equal of the Los Angeles CC.

The clubhouse is handsome, and Bel-Air has one feature that may well be unique. On the 9th, a par 3, you play across a deep canyon and then walk across a suspension bridge to the green which sits quite a way below the clubhouse, sited atop a high hill. After you hole out on the 9th, you walk through the hill via a tunnel, to an elevator that takes you up into the clubhouse. Then you walk through the clubhouse and out onto the 10th tee.

Belgique, Royal GC de BELGIUM

Château de Ravenstein, Tervuren. 27 holes; Championship Course 6,627 yd (6,060 m)

Situated about 6 miles from Brussels, this course was built by royal command in 1904 to enable British businessmen to play golf when visiting Belgium: this was King Leopold II's idea when he invited Tom Simpson to design a course at Tervuren. In 1908 the club engaged a professional, George Pannall, who acted as greenkeeper and clubmaker, and gave lessons. He remained with the club for the rest of his life.

The present clubhouse, listed as a national monument, is the château built by the Infanta Isabella of Spain in the 17th century to replace Philip of Cleves' beautiful late-15th-century hunting lodge which was burned down.

King Baudouin of the Belgians and his father, ex-King Leopold III, are honorary presidents of the club; the office of the president is usually held by a member of the Royal Household. The château is also the headquarters of the Fédération Royale Belge de Golf.

Belgium

Though not a pastime for the man in the street, golf in Belgium has always attracted attention because of the keen interest Belgian royalty has taken in it. In 1903 Leopold II said: 'When British businessmen come to Belgium, they must have the opportunity of playing one of their favourite sports, golf'; and he later made land available for courses at Tervuren (Royal GC de Belgique), Ostend and in the Ardennes near Dinant (GC du Château Royal d'Ardenne).

Belgium's first course was Royal Antwerp, founded in 1888. Others followed steadily

John Beck

John Beharrell playing in the British Amateur Championship in 1956

the fairways of a number of holes and cutting across a few others. For instance, on the 4th hole, a mild little 301-yd (275-m) par 4, the drive is played across the creek to the right, and then the hole turns so that the approach must be played back across the creek again.

Belle Meade traces its history back to 1901 when it was chartered as the Nashville CC. The name was changed when it moved to the stud farm in 1921. The present course is another of those wonderful Donald Ross designs, altered in the late 1950s by Robert Trent Jones and more recently by Pete Dye. It has been the site of a number of state and sectional tournaments such as the Southern and Western Amateurs, and also of the first Senior Amateur Championship conducted by the USGA.

Belleview-Biltmore GC USA
Clearwater, Fla.

A certain old-fashioned atmosphere lingers around the Belleview-Biltmore Hotel, said to be the largest wooden structure of its kind in the world, yet possessing dignity and elegance despite its vast proportions; it recalls the life of an earlier day. The golf is first class and up to date.

The area was a favourite winter playground – or rather gathering place – at the turn of the century for wealthy Americans. Whole families, accompanied by squads of servants, were housed in its hundreds of suites and in the cottages on the grounds. They would arrive soon after Christmas each winter, and many a private railroad car was parked in its sidings. In those days, the hotel was called simply the Belleview. Much more golf is played there today. There are two courses of almost equal quality, but the regulars seem to prefer the older and somewhat more difficult West Course.

The terrain has been left with small depressions and miniature ravines that make simple-looking fairway shots difficult at times. Some of the holes run along a modest bluff above Clearwater Bay and the Gulf of Mexico, and there are often westerly winds to disturb both the golfers and the tall pines, live oaks and palms that line many of the fairways. Everybody seems to love this old place, especially the Senior Golfers, who hold several of their better tournaments there each winter.

Belvedere Golf and Winter Club CANADA
Prince Edward Island. 18 holes; 6,372 yd (5,827 m); par 72

The course is set in a scene of typical Prince Edward Island beauty. Tall spruce trees bound the rolling fairways which have such thick grass and soft turf that they allow

and the first Belgian Open Championship was played in 1910 and won by the Frenchman Arnaud Massy.

Royal interest in the game was maintained by King Leopold III, both before and after his exile, and by his son, King Baudouin. King Leopold occasionally played in championships besides being a keen follower, and his son had a handicap which, at one time, was as low as three.

Belgium's golfing affairs are run by the Fédération Royale Belge de Golf, to which the country's 13 clubs are affiliated. Belgium's most notable player is undoubtedly Flory van Donck, the great professional who more than once came close to winning the British Open. Several of the

good links suffered during World War II, but the ravages have gradually been repaired and the Belgian coast is rich in good courses.

Belham River Valley GC SEE MONTSERRAT

Belle Meade CC USA
Iroquois, Tenn. 6,668 yd (6,097 m); par 72

The great American horse, Iroquois, who won the Epsom Derby in 1881 was bred at the Belle Meade Stud Plantation in a pleasant valley near Nashville, Tenn. Today the stud farm is gone and in its place is the Belle Meade CC, whose golf course wanders through that former pastureland. The club is surrounded by hills, and Richland Creek flows quietly through the property, bordering

Top, the clubhouse at Knokke, Belgium

Above, a view of the course of the Belleview-Biltmore GC

little run to the ball. Many of the greens are unusually small by modern standards, and the value of accurate iron play is accordingly enhanced. The greens are also considered to be remarkably fast. Established in 1906 as Charlottetown GC with a 9-hole course, the layout was expanded to 18 holes in 1928. With the addition in 1963 of curling facilities for winter activity, the club adopted its present name. Most of the major golf tournaments of the Maritime Provinces have been played over the course at one time or another, and it was also the scene of the 1964 Canadian Junior Championship.

Beman, Deane R. AMERICAN
b. Bethesda, Md., 1938. British Amateur 1959; Walker Cup 1959, 1961, 1963, 1965; US Amateur 1960, 1963; Eisenhower Trophy 1960, 1962, 1964; Texas Open 1969; Greater Milwaukee Open 1970; Commissioner USPGA

It took Beman much longer than most to decide to turn professional, seven years after winning his first Amateur championship. He made a good living from a group-

insurance partnership and the prospect of making a fortune quickly among the professionals did not attract him very strongly. He used to say he stayed amateur because he preferred to have control over his own life and not have someone fill his engagement book for him.

An additional reason may have been that being only 5 ft 5 in tall, he had no great length off the tee and might have been at a disadvantage among longer-hitting professionals, whereas among amateurs he reigned supreme. Yet, when he did turn professional he was by no means outclassed, thanks to his consistently high-class putting and also to his mastery of fairway woods. Unknown when he came to Muirfield in

1959 with the Walker Cup team along with another unknown, Jack Nicklaus, Beman beat Bonallack on the 36th green, and in his last appearance at Baltimore six years later holed from 12 ft on the last green to beat Saddler in a match that ended in a tie between the two countries.

His putting stance is locked and compact but with a long backswing on the putting stroke. He pays particular attention to the line rather than to the length and concentrates on not making the stroke until he is absolutely ready to do so. In the 1969 US Open won by Orville Moody, Beman led the field at the halfway stage but faded to 4th place in the final. In 1974 he succeeded Joe Dey as the Commissioner of the USPGA.

Bembridge, Maurice BRITISH
b. Worksop, Nottinghamshire, 1945. Assistant's Champion 1967; Kenya Open 1968-9; British Professional Matchplay 1969; Ryder Cup 1969, 1971, 1973; Dunlop Masters 1971

Having entered the game from school at the age of 15, Bembridge became a much-

travelled tournament professional whose consistent play in Britain won him a place in the Ryder Cup team of 1969. In 1968, he was leading British player in the Open (5th) but his most notable achievements were in winning the last matchplay championship sponsored by the *News of the World* in 1969 and the Dunlop Masters in 1971 at St Pierre. In the 1973 Ryder Cup match he played Nicklaus twice in one day, halving one match and losing the other one on the last green. The following year he scored a record-equalling 64 in the US Masters and won the British PGA Championship with a final 65.

Benka, Peter BRITISH
b. London 1946. Leading amateur British

Open 1967; British Youths' Champion 1967; County Champions' Champion 1967; Sunningdale Foursomes (with P. Oosterhuis) 1969; Walker Cup 1969

Bent
A finely textured grass commonly used in the sowing of putting greens and fairways.

Bentley, Arnold Lewis BRITISH
b. Southport, Lancashire, 1911. English Amateur 1939

Although he did not equal his brother's achievement of Walker Cup honours, Arnold Bentley was just as good a golfer and had one of those indestructible swings which kept him in the low handicap class for longer than many of his contemporaries. He played several times for England but his finest performance was in winning the English Amateur Championship of 1939 when he beat W. Sutton by 5 and 4 in the final at Birkdale.

Bentley, Harry Geoffrey BRITISH
b. Manchester 1907. French Open 1931;

German Open Amateur 1933; English Amateur 1936; Walker Cup 1936, 1938; Italian Open Amateur 1954

Harry Bentley was one of Britain's outstanding amateurs between the wars. Associated with his brother Arnold in a paper-making firm, he made many trips to the Continent in the course of which he won

Deane Beman

Maurice Bembridge

Peter Benka

game. Since turning professional in 1940, she has been the first president of the LPGA of America, has travelled extensively and given clinics all over the world. In 1954–5 and 1957 she was the leading money winner in the LPGA.

Patty Berg came to the fore on her home course, Interlachen, in reaching the final of the US Amateur in 1935, the title she won in 1938. In 1952, at Richmond, Cal., she scored a 64 which stood for 12 years as the LPGA competition record for 18 holes.

Berkshire GC ENGLAND
Ascot, Berkshire. 36 holes

This club, 30 miles southwest of London, combines two courses of almost equal merit;

72-hole medal tournament which is an established guide to international team selection, and the Avia International Women's Foursomes. In 1965 the merits of the club were recognized when the English Championship, won by Michael Bonallack, was held there, a combination of holes from both courses being used to produce a championship test of the highest quality. The match between Great Britain and Ireland and the Continent of Europe has twice been played there.

Bermuda
A coarsely textured species of grass used for both fairways and greens, especially in hot climates.

various titles. He took part in the 1938 Walker Cup at St Andrews that produced Britain's first victory. Harry Bentley also made several appearances for England in home internationals and against France.

Berg, Patricia Jane AMERICAN
b. Minneapolis, Minn., 1918. Curtis Cup 1936, 1938; US Women's Amateur 1938; US Women's Open 1946; Vare Trophy 1953, 1955, 1956; World Champion 1953-5, 1957

A redhead with blue eyes, Patty Berg has a personality that has made her one of the outstanding figures in women's golf. She achieved success as a teenage prodigy, then as a professional promoter achieved fame and recognition from sources outside the

so at least they appeared to the members who in consequence named them Red and Blue rather than give either of them an implied superiority. Both have been fashioned from pinewoods and heath, and both measure about 6,500 yd (5,944 m).

During World War I the vast expanse of forest outside Ascot was partly cut down and the idea grew that a golf course could be constructed there. With the support of the Crown Commissioners, who owned the land, the courses were laid out by Herbert Fowler. The variety of natural hazards and the springiness of the turf as the courses wind their secluded way up and down hill give them their charm. Two major events have found a home there: the Berkshire Trophy, a

Bermuda
Bermuda, discovered in the 16th century by a Spanish sailing captain, Juan Bermudez, has been a British possession since 1684 and, in keeping with the best British tradition where sport is concerned, has become one of the world's most remarkable areas for recreation.

Golf was not the first of the island's sports to be introduced but since the first course was opened on the shores of Riddell's Bay the game has flourished and today there is a bigger area of golf courses per square mile than anywhere else in the world. On an island only 21 miles long, there are five 18-hole courses, two 9-hole courses and a par 3.

Top, Harry Bentley, English Amateur Championship, 1954

Above, Patty Berg at Wentworth

The 10th hole on the Red Course at the Berkshire GC

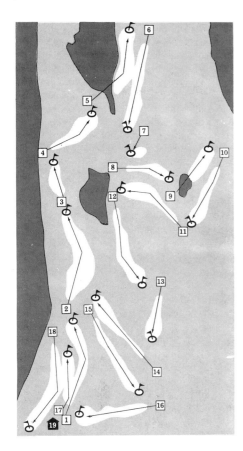

the Bermuda government in the hills of Southampton, is the most recent, opened in 1970. Golfers arrive in their hundreds each year for the Goodwill Tournament, which is the annual highlight.

Bernardini, Robert ITALIAN

b. Rome, 1944. Italian Professional 1967-8; BP Open 1968-9; Garlenda Open 1969; Swiss Open 1968-9; Walworth Aloyco Tournament 1969

Probably the best of the current Italian professionals and one of the leading players in Europe, Bernardini, whose two brothers are both professionals, turned professional when almost 16 and played most of his early

golf at the Acquasanta club in Rome. He has a fine style and quickly broadened his competitive horizons by playing in Britain and America, although his main successes have all been on the Continent.

Besselink, Albert Cornelius AMERICAN

b. Merchantville, N.J., 1924. Tournament of Champions 1953

A big, brash, free-spending player, Besselink added colour to the American circuit during the 1950s. The son of an immigrant Dutch artist, he started golf at the age of eight and won two inter-collegiate tournaments while at the University of Miami.

To the world at large golf in Bermuda means Mid-Ocean, a club with a famous, romantic-sounding name conceived by the great American golfing pioneer, Charles Blair Macdonald, in 1924. The course was full of natural features from the outset, and as Robert Trent Jones revised the layout of the course in 1953 its basic character has survived.

Mid-Ocean's name is a little misleading because, except at the start and the finish, the ocean plays little part in the design. The majority of the holes filter through colourful valleys or undulate gently, providing a great test of driving, but nobody forgets the opening hole, fittingly named Atlantic, where it is simple enough to pull the second shot onto the beach; or the 18th where the whole exciting setting unfurls itself. No wonder Archie Compston, who left Britain to be professional there for many years, found it such a compelling place.

Castle Harbour, with its spectacularly beautiful 1st tee, Riddell's Bay, Belmont Manor and Port Royal are the other 18-hole courses which complete a variety that is remarkable on such a small island. Port Royal, a Trent Jones creation belonging to

The Mid-Ocean Club, Bermuda

Top, an aerial view of the Mid-Ocean Club and its private beach

Above left, Roberto Bernardini during the 1970 John Player Classic at Hollinwell

Above right, Al Besselink

He turned professional in 1949, won his first tournament in 1952, and then won five more events in the next six years. He made a name for himself by backing himself for $500 at 25 to one to win the Tournament of Champions, which he did.

Best ball

A match in which one player competes against the better score of two or more other players. It is not a fourball.

Better ball

A match, usually a fourball, in which the better score of the two or more players determines the result of the hole.

Beverly CC USA

Beverly, a little way outside Chicago, is an interesting golf course and a rather old one by American standards, dating from the first decade of the century. It is of moderately good length – around 6,900 yd (6,310 m) but when the professional tourists move onto it from time to time, they play the course just as it stands for the members, using the figures from the regular scorecard. Beverly, nevertheless, resists the sort of wholesale birdie assault usually found on the tour, even though Jack Nicklaus won the Western Open there with 274 in 1967. (What Nicklaus does on the occasions when he is in peak form is not the yardstick by which a course should be graded.) The fact that the Western Open has been played at Beverly

several times speaks well for the quality of the course, for the Western is one of the most important tournaments on the American scene. The US Amateur has also been played there – in 1931, when Francis Ouimet won the title for a second time after a gap of 17 years.

Beverly's unusual layout provides for five drive-and-pitch par 4s, five par 3s ranging from 125 to 235 yd, (114-218 m), and four par 5s, including two which cannot be reached with two woods. It is a pretty course with tree-lined fairways that roll enough to give the player a variety of lies. The greens are small, fast and well protected.

Bevione, Franco ITALIAN

b. 1922. Italian Close Amateur 1940, 1946-7, 1949-50, 1953-5, 1959-61, 1967-8, 1971; Italian Open Amateur 1952, 1956-7; Swiss Open Amateur 1956; Scandinavian Open Amateur 1959

Franco Bevione and his sister, Isa Goldschmid, dominated Italian amateur golf for many years. He was almost unbeatable in the Italian Close Championship for some years, but he had his successes in other countries too and twice played for the Continent of Europe against Great Britain and Ireland.

Bielke, Count Gustav Adolf SWEDISH

b. 1930. Swedish Junior 1948; Swedish Open Amateur 1951; Swedish Close Amateur 1956; Scandinavian Open Amateur 1956; Swedish Amateur Strokeplay 1958, 1961

One of the stalwarts of Swedish teams during the 1950s and 1960s, Count Bielke was a member of the Swedish sides that won the European team championships of 1959 and 1961.

He played a total of 28 times for his country between 1950 and 1965, played for Sweden in the World Cup (Eisenhower Trophy) in 1960 and 1962, and was a member of the Continent of Europe teams which played Great Britain and Ireland in 1958 and 1962. Earlier he had several times been junior champion of Sweden, Germany, Belgium, Norway, Italy and France.

Biella GC ITALY

Piedmont. 18 holes; 7,080 yd (6,474 m); par 72

Situated some 15 miles outside Biella, a town famous for its flourishing weaving industry, the course, known as La Betulle, is the longest in Italy. The architect was John Morrison and the par 72 is a tough one. It is a typical inland park course, literally sunk in the middle of a silver-birch

wood. In addition to its length, it possesses many of the difficulties to be expected of a well-thought-out modern course: water hazards, bunkers, hollows, hillocks and fast deceptive greens are generously distributed along the undulating course, requiring every shot to be carefully studied.

Billows, Ray AMERICAN

b. Wisconsin 1914. Runner-up US Amateur 1937, 1939, 1948; Walker Cup 1938, 1949

Although he won many tournaments, including the New York Amateur seven times, Billows is perhaps best remembered for having failed to win the National Amateur. In addition to being three times runner-up, he was a semi-finalist once, and

twice in the last eight. Between 1936 and 1948 he accounted for such established players as Jimmy McHale, Chuck Kocsis, Reynolds Smith, Johnny Fischer, Ross Somerville, Bud Ward, Frank Stranahan and Charlie Coe. In his two Walker Cup matches he scored 2 points out of 4.

Birdie

A term of American origin and uncertain derivation for a score of one under par for a hole. It became current between the two world wars.

Birkdale GC, Royal ENGLAND

Southport, Lancashire. 18 holes; 7,080 yd (6,474 m)

Royal Birkdale, one of a succession of fine courses seen on either side of the railway line between Liverpool and Southport, is the most junior course on the British Open Championship list. It was not added until the year of Peter Thomson's first victory, 1954, but since then it has seen more important events than almost all the other clubs put together.

The 11th hole of the Beverly CC

Ray Billows

Nowadays, so much is asked of championship surroundings, quite apart from playing requirements, that a number of courses can no longer be considered suitable. Birkdale, however, with enough surrounding land for car parks, tented villages, and grandstands, is better equipped than any in this respect. Only one other British Open championship course, Muirfield, has the advantage of the first nine ending near the clubhouse. Birkdale, too, has had members with the necessary enthusiasm to plan and supervise and upon whom the Royal and Ancient still rely to some extent. With all the changes the character of the golf has remained the same in dune country typifying the best of British seaside golf. With a length of more than 7,000 yd from the championship tees and with four par 5s in the last six holes, it is immensely demanding, particularly as many of the fairways are flanked by willow scrub of the most unyielding kind; but Birkdale's scrupulous fairness has earned it the respect of the world's golfers.

Birkdale's first national championship was the British Ladies' of 1909 won by Miss Dorothy Campbell, but it was many years after before they began to come in any numbers. One significant pre-World War II championship was that in which 16-year-old James Bruen won the British Boys' Amateur in 1936 over the same course on which 10 years later he defeated Bob Sweeny in the final of the British Amateur. Within the space of 25 years Birkdale has been the setting for the Curtis, Walker and two Ryder Cup matches, two English and two strokeplay championships, two international professional events, the Carling and the Alcan, and four Open Championships.

Because of its fairly recent connections with the Open, it is sometimes assumed that Birkdale's origins are relatively modern but the distinguished history of Britain's newest Royal club (1951) began in 1889 and it is, in fact, one of the oldest clubs in the North of England, an area very conscious of its traditions.

It owed its formation to a group of eight enthusiasts who met at the home of J. C. Barrett on 30 July 1889 and decided to lease a piece of land which they later converted into 9 holes. The rent was £5 and there they stayed, using part of the nearby Portland Hotel as a clubhouse, until 1897 when they were forced to look elsewhere for land on which to build a new course.

They chose wisely in the great expanse of sandhills on the Liverpool side of Southport. In those days they started from a point which is now the 5th, and it was not until 1931, when the course was also redesigned by Messrs Hawtree and Taylor, that the present clubhouse was built and the existing sequence of holes introduced.

In more recent years, as the course was prepared to meet the demands of modern championships, many of the holes have been lengthened and a new short 12th has been designed by Fred Hawtree to replace the old 17th which caused too much of a bottleneck with the huge crowds attracted by Birkdale's great occasions.

The name of Peter Thomson will always be associated with Birkdale because it was there in 1954 that he won his first championship, and in 1965 equalled the feats of J. H. Taylor and James Braid in winning for the fifth time. Only Harry Vardon has won more often.

In 1954 the course was playing fairly short and with the emphasis on straightness and control, Thomson drove mostly with a spoon. It was the first sign of the poise, nerve and golfing intelligence which soon became familiar in Britain and though Sid Scott, Dai Rees and Bobby Locke had their chances, Thomson holed the winning putt with the back of his putter.

Eleven years later, the weather was fairly calm again and Thomson reaffirmed his mastery of British seaside conditions, but this time he beat a formidable American invasion. The field included Arnold Palmer who won in 1961 when he was established as the most formidable competitor of his time.

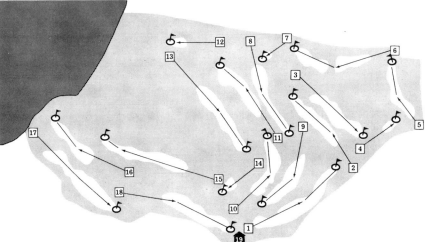

Top, the 13th green at Royal Birkdale GC

Above, course layout of Royal Birkdale

But he needed all his courage, strength and resilience before winning a protracted championship with a total of 284.

As an example of the virtue of holding on to an opponent throughout a long 36-hole match, few can equal the way in which Birkdale's own Ronnie White pursued and finally caught Charlie Coe in their Walker Cup single, in 1951.

The tall, elegant Coe played the first 7 holes in 24 strokes and if he had not missed a shortish putt for a 2 at the 7th and if White, laid a stymie, had not chipped over his ball into the hole, Coe might have got away. White, however, was unshakable. Only 1 down leaving the 7th, he rallied when Coe became 3 up and though Coe was still 2 up after 28 holes, White won the next 3 holes and the match by 2 and 1.

At the time White was peerless as a striker among amateurs throughout the world and when he reached the final of the 1953 English Amateur Championship on his own course, few gave Gerald Micklem a chance against him. It was a daunting task but White, worn down by the strain of never being able to get away from Micklem who time and again saved himself on the greens, lost on the short 17th, now no more, when Micklem found the green with a superb shot with a spoon.

Another event won by excellent work on the greens was the 1959 Matchplay Championship in which David Snell beat Harry Weetman in the final. In 1963, however, putting was a nightmare on greens which were badly scarred after the severe winter. Peter Butler won the PGA Close Championship with a score of 306 and Ronnie Shade the Brabazon Trophy with the same score after a play-off with Peter Green.

In 1958 Arthur Perowne gave the finest performance of his career in winning the Brabazon Trophy with a wonderful exhibi-tion of wooden-club play and a score of 289. Birkdale, however, is more often associated with the deeds of the professionals. Bruce Devlin won the Carling finals in 1966 and Gay Brewer another huge 1st prize in the second Alcan Golfer of the Year Championship in 1968; but neither event matched the excitement of the Ryder Cup matches of 1965 which America clinched by fine play in the singles, or the unforgettable halved match in 1969.

Britain had a slight edge for the first five rounds and went into the last round of singles with a lead of 11 matches to 9. Hopes of a home victory, though high, were tempered by the knowledge of what had happened in the past, and the Americans made their inevitable rally; but, in a desperate finish, Brian Huggett holed two heroic putts on the last two greens to halve with Billy Casper and Tony Jacklin, the Open Champion, halved the last hole with Jack Nicklaus, having holed a long putt for a three on the 17th. In its comparatively short history of housing great events, Birkdale has known nothing better, not even Trevino's victory in the 1971 Open.

Birmingham CC USA

The Country Club of Birmingham, Ala., was founded in 1897 and is one of the older golf clubs in the southern United States. It has occupied its present location, its third, since 1927 when it engaged Donald Ross to design two 18-hole courses; but little of Ross's work remains: Robert Trent Jones was engaged to modernize the West Course in 1960, and George Cobb to remodel the East Course some four years later.

The club has been the site of the Southern Amateur six times, including the 1916 championship won by Bob Jones, and the Women's Southern three times. It is also among the larger clubs in the deep South;

it has 1,700 members. The club owns some 300 acres (120 ha) of land and its maintenance budget in 1970 was $90,000. Obviously it is well tended. And should Alabama ever come under attack, one of the safer refuges might be its clubhouse, whose native sandstone walls are 3 ft thick.

Bisgood, Jeanne BRITISH

Curtis Cup 1950, 1952, 1954 (non-playing captain 1970); English Ladies' 1951, 1953, 1957; Swedish Ladies' 1952; German Ladies' 1953; Italian Ladies' 1953; Portuguese Ladies' 1954; Norwegian Ladies' 1955

Jeanne Bisgood, daughter of a former president of the English Golf Union, was a trained administrator and became a Justice of the Peace as well as being concerned from time to time with the running of women's golf. Her playing career was, nevertheless, very full and highly successful. She was one of the leading women golfers in the 1950s when she won the English Ladies' Championship three times in seven years, and played three times in the Curtis Cup.

Royal Birkdale, teeing off at the 7th

Top, Jeanne Bisgood

Above, Stanley E. Bishop

Bishop, Stanley E. AMERICAN
b. 1923. US Amateur 1946; Walker Cup
1947, 1949

In the 1946 US Amateur, Bishop beat
Smiley Quick at the 37th hole of the final at
Baltusrol, after having been 3 down.

Bisque

A handicap stroke taken at the discretion of
the player provided that he announces his
intention of using it before playing the next
hole. It is not uncommon for players to
hoard their bisques until it is too late to use
them.

Blackheath GC, Royal ENGLAND
Eltham, London. 18 holes; 6,024 yd
(5,508 m); par 69

The claim that this club is the oldest in the
world is based on the circumstances that
King James VI and his Scottish Court took
the game south when he became James I of
England, in 1603, and they are known to
have played golf on a portion of Blackheath
near the Royal Palace at Greenwich. But
James had learned golf at Perth (where he
had his appointed clubmaker), and on the
definition of a club or society as a group of
people with like interests meeting together
for their pursuit, there must have been
many unrecorded 'clubs' in Scotland a century or two earlier (golf was already popular
at St Andrews when its university was
founded in 1411). Blackheath, however, is
certainly the 'mother' of golf in England and
has proved a benign parent of many off-
spring clubs at home and overseas. Evidence
of a society exists in the silver club presented
in 1766 by Dr Henry Foot to the Captain,
Alexander Duncan, and a letter written in
1831 by the Registrar of the Blackheath
Winter GC remarking that 'the Society has
kept together notwithstanding all intervening convulsions for nearly a century to
perpetuate the national game as well as the
social customs of its ancestors'.

In the mid-18th century golf was played at
Blackheath in summer only, originally over
five holes, later extended to seven. In 1789
some hardier members took to playing in
winter and formed themselves into the
'Knuckle Club', their name deriving from
their liking for this as food. In 1825 the
Knuckle became the Winter Club and
finally winter and summer came together in
1844 and Royal Blackheath was born, with
the Knuckle Club gold medal of 1789 as its
senior trophy and one of the oldest in golf.

The club remained at Blackheath until
1923 when building encroachment forced a
move to the Eltham Club (founded in 1891).
The course was redesigned by James Braid

who produced a real test in lavishly wooded
parkland, making full use of water and other
natural hazards.

Blackheath has had many notable members but produced no greater player than
George Glennie, whose memory is perpetuated in a gold medal for strokeplay struck in
1881. Glennie, a civil engineer, had been a

Top, 'The Blackheath Golfer'

Above, David Blair

member of the Burgess Society of Edinburgh
from 1845, winning its gold medal twice,
and setting a St Andrews record of 88 which
stood for many years. He then went south
and became captain of Blackheath and
honorary secretary and treasurer from 1868
to his death in 1886. He was celebrated for
his part in the first inter-club foursome held
at St Andrews over three days in 1857. This
contest was suggested by the Prestwick Club,
organized by the Bruntsfield Society, and 11
clubs sent two players. Blackheath, the only
English club entered, triumphed. But onlookers did not fail to notice that both
members, Glennie and Lieutenant J. C.
Stewart, were Scots.

There is strong evidence in favour of
Blackheath's claim as the home of the gutta-
percha ball. Mention of it in the memoirs of
James Balfour as being used at Blackheath in
1848 is reinforced by the historian of Prestwick St Nicholas, William Galbraith, who
states that such balls were on sale at Blackheath two years before that.

Blackwell, Edward B. H. BRITISH
b. St Andrews, Fife, 1866. Runner-up
British Amateur 1904

Ted Blackwell was consistently the longest
driver among the leading amateurs of his
day, although he declared his favourite shot
to be a half-shot with an iron. In Bernard
Darwin's phrase, Blackwell hit the ball
malignantly hard and at St Andrews in 1892
he drove a gutty ball a distance of 366 yd
(335 m), claimed to be the world record.

Blackwell represented Scotland against
England 11 times between 1902 and 1925,
was runner-up in the 1922 Scottish Championship, and won many medals at meetings
of the Royal and Ancient club, where he was
captain 1925-6. He is also remembered for
his play in the final of the 1904 British
Amateur Championship at Royal St
George's when he lost to the Australian-born
American, Walter J. Travis, the first overseas competitor to win the title.

Blair, David A. BRITISH
b. Nairn 1917. Scottish Boys' 1935; British
Army Champion 1947; low amateur British
Open 1950, Scottish Amateur 1953, runner-
up 1950; St George's Gold Vase 1953, 1964,
1967; Commonwealth Tournament 1954;
Golf Illustrated Gold Vase 1955-6; Walker
Cup 1955, 1961; Scandinavian Open 1961

David Blair emerged after World War II
as one of the country's outstanding players
of the 1950s and early 1960s. Apart from
winning the Scottish Amateur in 1953, he
regularly represented Scotland between
1948 and 1957. In the 1955 Walker Cup

match he was one of only two British players to win a singles point. In 1960 he tied 9th in the British Open.

Blair's swing, a model of style and elegance, was built to last. An accurate striker through the range of clubs, surprisingly he was never the complete master of the bunker shot; for several years he had a very fair measure of success putting with a no. 3 iron.

Blairgowrie GC SCOTLAND

Rosemount, Perthshire. 27 holes; 18-hole course 6,646 yd (6,077 m), 9-hole course 2,323 yd (2,124 m)

Heather, pine and silver birch usually go to make the best type of inland golf and so

Blairgowrie rates high among the inland courses of Britain. It is more wooded than most Scottish courses and recalls the golfing country of Surrey and Berkshire. Its appeal derives from its wooded Perthshire setting as well as from its golfing merits.

The club was constituted in February 1889 after 9 holes had been hewn out of the Marquis of Lansdowne's densely wooded Meikleour estate. It was known as the Lansdowne course for many years and as early as 1901 was the scene of a notable exhibition match between James Braid and Harry Vardon which clearly aroused local interest. Dr J. G. McPherson, writing in the local paper, confessed, 'I never saw so many bicycles at an inland course, and the ladies were triumphant in their enthusiasm. They were perfectly astonished at the driving of James Braid – his rocket drives being perfectly terrible. Yet Vardon showed his marvellous skill in emergencies, though the course does not afford many test holes.'

Blairgowrie, popularly known as Rosemount, was extended to 18 holes on the advice of Dr Alister McKenzie, in June

1927. In 1934 eight new holes designed by James Braid completed the present layout. It has always been a regular choice for tournaments and society meetings including the inter-zone matches. Then in 1972 it housed a major British professional tournament, in 1973 staged the British Boys' Championship and in 1974 was scheduled to hold the Scottish Strokeplay Championship.

Blaster

A forerunner to the sand wedge. A broad-soled, lofted club used for blasting the ball out of bunkers and other unwelcome places.

Blind

A hole is said to be blind when the player cannot see the target at which he is aiming. It may apply to a fairway or a green. Modern architects strive to eliminate such shots from their design but, before the days of earth-moving equipment, they were particularly common on British courses and not unknown in America.

Bloemfontein GC SOUTH AFRICA

Orange Free State. 18 holes; 7,014 yd (6,496 m)

The Bloemfontein GC was in existence in 1895 but the course had to be moved more than once, early records were lost in a fire, and it was not until 1953 that the club took up its present position on the Mazelspoort Road. The spruit running through the course is crossed four times in the 18 holes; greens and fairways are of a generous size and width, and thousands of trees were planted to cover the bareness of the course. In 1958 the club staged its first South African Open and Amateur Championships, the first time the city had seen them since 1904.

Blum, Arnold AMERICAN

b. Georgia 1922. Southern Amateur 1951, 1956; Walker Cup 1957

Prominent in Southern golf from 1946 and at a national level from 1951, when he reached the quarter-finals of the US Amateur for the first time, Blum was one of the relatively few players ever to win more than 20 matches in the Amateur, his total being 23 matches out of 13 tournaments. In the 10 years from 1946 he won the Georgia State Amateur five times.

Blumisberg GC SWITZERLAND

nr Wünnewil. 18 holes; 6,660 yd (6,090 m); par 72

The course, opened in 1959, lies at the heart of the Swiss plain which separates the Alps from the Juras. The 4th and 6th holes run between the woods of pine and other

trees, while some run alongside a belt of great oaks. In contrast, the second 9 open out into the typical Freiburg (Fribourg) countryside of farmland with only a scattering of trees.

The course is the creation of the German designer, Bernhard von Limburger. Some holes require length and accuracy and are full of interest, others call for intelligence and shrewdness. The general effect is of hilly countryside with plenty of out-of-bounds and blind second shots. The Blumisberg course is certainly worth a visit, not only for its quality but also because its surroundings are a little-known part of Switzerland.

Boatwright, Purvis James AMERICAN

b. Augusta, Ga., 1927. Carolina Amateur 1951; Carolina Open 1957

'P.J.' Boatwright, after serving 10 years as Assistant Executive Director of the US Golf Association, became Executive Director in 1969, upon the departure of Joseph C. Dey Jr. He became involved in golf administration in 1955 when he was appointed

Blairgowrie GC, Jacklin drives at the 16th hole

Top, Arnold Blum

Above, P. J. Boatwright

Executive Secretary of the Carolina GA, in which post he remained until he joined the USGA in 1959.

A tall, calm, and methodical man, Boatwright has had an impressive career in competitive golf. Besides his victories in the Carolina Amateur and Open, he qualified for the US Open and handled Merion so well that he made the half-way cut and played the full 72 holes. He has qualified for four US Amateurs. Veteran administrators rate Boatwright an excellent rules man and point out that he has few peers when it comes to setting up courses for championships. Boatwright has his home in Peapack, N.J., which is near the headquarters of the USGA.

Bob Jones Award
This award is made annually by the United States Golf Association in recognition of 'distinguished sportsmanship'. The citation says that 'sportsmanship' can be difficult to define but the USGA has in mind 'the demonstration of personal qualities esteemed in sport: fair play, self control and perhaps self denial; generosity of spirit towards the game as a whole, and the manner of playing or behaving so as to show respect for the game and the people in it'.

The recipients of the Bob Jones award have been:

1955	Francis D. Ouimet
1956	William C. Campbell
1957	Mrs Mildred Zaharias
1958	Miss Margaret Curtis
1959	Findlay S. Douglas
1960	Charles Evans Jr
1961	Joseph B. Carr
1962	Horton Smith
1963	Miss Patty Berg
1964	Charles R. Coe
1965	Mrs Glenna Collet Vare
1966	Gary Player
1967	Richard S. Tufts
1968	Robert B. Dickson
1969	Gerald H. Micklem
1970	Roberto de Vicenzo
1971	Arnold Palmer
1972	Michael F. Bonallack
1973	Gene Littler
1974	Byron Nelson

Bob O'Link GC USA
Highland Park, Ill.

Bob O'Link, which lies in Highland Park, a rather elegant neighbourhood a little way north of Chicago, is an unusual golf club in at least two respects. It is composed of men only, and it has a large number of elevated greens. Some of these greens are merely set at the top of slopes or gentle rises, but the player at any rate finds himself hitting up to them a great number of times. Bob O'Link members do not consider either of these features as handicaps but the visitor must beware of sand, water and vegetation protecting greens whose surfaces he may not see entirely.

This is a well-tended course and the straighter driver receives favourable lies, unlike the wanderer who is almost certain to find trouble severe enough to test his powers of recovery.

Bob O'Link has been in existence for more than half a century but few changes have been needed.

Bogey
In Great Britain, the number of strokes in which a good player was expected to complete a hole – bogey has been largely replaced by par. In America it means a hole played in one stroke more than par.

Bolivia
One of the smallest golfing nations, Bolivia has only a handful of clubs, with good courses at the capital, the La Paz and Los Pinos, and others at Mallasilla and Oruro. The country's golfing affairs are run by the Bolivian Golf Federation.

The Bolivian courses are among the highest in the world; that at Oruro, the mining town, is about 12,000 ft (3,660 m) above sea level.

Bolt
To bolt a putt is to hit the ball so hard that it enters the hole still travelling fast. The expression is not generally used in America.

Bolt, Tommy AMERICAN
b. Haworth, Okla., 1919. US Open 1958; World Seniors' 1969

Although a somewhat fiery temperament

Tommy Bolt

and an inclination to throw clubs earned him the reputation of 'Thunder Bolt', he was a fine shotmaker who won the 1958 US Open Championship at Southern Hills, by four shots from Gary Player. On the last day in burning heat when two rounds were played and Bolt started one stroke ahead of Player, he played two fine rounds of 69 and 72, and a year or so later, after Player had won the 1959 British Open, he beat Player in a 'challenge' series in South Africa by four games to one.

At the time Bolt, though over 40, was one of the best players in the world. Altogether, he won 14 tour victories and preserved his game so well that in 1969 he won the World Seniors' Title, beating the British Champion, John Panton, at the 39th hole at Portsmouth, Va.

In 1971 he finished 3rd in the USPGA Championship at the PGA's course in Florida, a further tribute to a fine lasting method.

Bombay Presidency GC, The INDIA
Chembur, Bombay. 18 holes; 6,230 yd (5,697 m); par 70

This club has a history interwoven with others in and around this teeming Indian city. Among them was the Royal Bombay GC (no longer in existence), founded in 1842 and outside of Scotland and England the second oldest in the world. As early as 1846 the 'Golfing Society of Bombay' presented to the Royal and Ancient GC of St Andrews a silver medal which was competed for in that year at the R. and A.'s spring meeting, thus predating the Calcutta Cup by 39 years.

Before 1927 Bombay had three courses: a 9-hole course on the Oval and Maidan (recreation grounds), where only morning play was permitted and canvas bunkers, erected early every morning, were brought in at noon; another 9-hole course in the northern suburb of Pali Hill, Bandra, then thickly wooded, which had browns instead of greens; and the exclusive Willingdon Sports Club, founded in the heart of the city by the Viceroy, who gave it his name. Of these only Willingdon – 4,387 yd (4,011 m), par 59 – remains.

Bombay badly needed another course so in 1927 Patrick Carron, executive engineer with the Bombay Port Trust, and a band of golf enthusiasts formed the New Golf Club. The course was near the Haji Bunder docks at Sewri. The club's name was changed to the Bombay Presidency GC in 1931; it had 100 founder members. But Bombay was growing fast and it was inevitable that this valuable land close to the docks would have to be given up. The suburb of Chembur, on the western side of Trombay Hill, was still uncrowded and here a survey was made. In 1939 C. R. Clayton, greenkeeper at Royal Calcutta GC, was appointed to lay out the new course, which was opened in January 1940. Eventually it became the venue for the Western India Championship. For many years this had been held at the Royal Western India GC, a picturesque course on the main road to Delhi, 2,000 ft (610 m) up on the Deccan Plateau, but this club was obliged to close down and Chembur became the home of the Western India, and also the Bombay Championship.

With the support of an enthusiastic golf community in Bombay, and encouraged by Col. Leslie Sawhny of the Indian Golf Union, and Rajkumar Pitamber, captain of golf at Oxford, the IGU agreed to allow the All-India Amateur Championship to rotate between Delhi, Calcutta and Bombay. In December 1964 the first All-India was staged at Chembur and was won by the Bombay Amateur Russi Panday.

Thanks to Peter Thomson's planning, Chembur has become a fine test of golf. The greens are the slickest and best in India. The fairways do not provide the lush lies of Delhi and Calcutta and are much finer and tighter, requiring a more exacting wood shot. In addition Chembur, being not far from the sea, experiences variable breezes and humidity is much greater than at Delhi or Calcutta. Bombay amateur Surendar Lall holds the course record of 66.

The beauty of this 110-acre (44-ha) course lies 'across the road'. Here the 441-yd (403-m) 14th played from the championship tees, with its lightning-fast green and the dogleg 430-yd (393-m) 15th, are as challenging holes as can be found anywhere. And as the prevailing southwesterly breeze freshens towards evening, the 218-yd (199-m) 17th provides a test of not only technique but also of courage.

Bonallack, Michael Francis BRITISH
b. Chigwell, Essex, 1934. British Boys' Amateur 1952; British Army 1955; Walker Cup 1957, 1959, 1961, 1963, 1965, 1967, 1969, 1971, 1973 (captain 1969, 1971); Commonwealth Tournament 1959, 1963, 1967, 1971; Eisenhower Trophy 1960, 1962, 1964, 1966, 1968, 1970, 1972 (captain 1968, 1970, 1972); British Amateur 1961, 1965, 1969-70; tied *Golf Illustrated* Gold Vase 1961, 1967, 1969, winner 1968, 1971; English Amateur 1962-3, 1965, 1967-8; English Amateur Strokeplay 1964, 1968, 1971, joint winner 1969

Besides these successes, Michael Bonallack

has had victories on various occasions in the Berkshire Trophy, the Lytham Trophy, the St George's Champion Grand Challenge Cup, the Prince of Wales Challenge Cup, the Hampshire Hog, the Sunningdale Foursome with Douglas Sewell, and the Worplesdon Foursomes with his wife Angela. His formidable record is proof of enormous competitive powers and, in terms of championship victories, he is unquestionably the leading British Amateur of modern times. Among the many new standards of play he has set have been five victories in the British Amateur; his five victories in the English Amateur, which have never been approached; and his appearance for England in more matches than anyone else.

Ever since he won the Boys' Amateur while still more interested in cricket, Bonallack's powers developed steadily, although his swing has never been classical. It has, in fact, been the subject of much comment but has always shown the control and the capability to manoeuvre the ball, the ultimate factor in judging success. It is highly consistent and reliable, and backed in

Top, Michael Bonallack and, *above*, receiving the English Amateur Cup from Gerald Micklem in 1965

devastating fashion by a short game second to none. No amateur has ever holed more crucial putts and this has been the key to his remarkable record at home.

Bonallack won the 1961 Amateur Championship final at Turnberry against Jimmy Walker and the English Championship finals of 1962 and 1963 against Michael Lunt at Moortown, and Alan Thirlwell at Burnham and Berrow. In the latter final he was down in two from off the green no fewer than 22 times in the course of a 36-hole match. In winning the British and English titles at Royal Porthcawl and the Berkshire, he beat Clive Clark twice, having been down at lunch on each occasion. In 1968 he beat Joe Carr, his great friend, at Troon; and in the English final, he defeated David Kelley by 12 and 11 at Ganton, going round in the morning in an incredible 61. In 1969 he beat the American, Bill Hyndman, by 3 and 2 in the final of the British Amateur Championship at Hoylake, and in the first repeat final, he won in 1970 at Royal County Down. The margin then was 8 and 7 although at lunchtime Bonallack had stood one down, and the victory gave him a hat trick in the event.

Behind all these successes was a simple though unsuspected will to win; but no man accepted victory or defeat with a finer grace or dignity. Fortunate in having time to devote to the game, he has always been a true amateur, a man of kindness respected throughout the golfing world. Bonallack's wife Angela was herself a champion and Curtis Cup player, and to add to a distinguished list of family achievements, his sister, Sally Barber, played Curtis Cup golf, and his brother Tony county golf for Essex.

To mark his services to golf, Michael Bonallack was awarded the OBE in 1971, a great year for him. In addition to winning the Brabazon Trophy, the *Golf Illustrated* Gold Vase, the Amateur medal at the Open Championship and tying for the Berkshire Trophy, he captained the Walker Cup team to victory in May.

Having been a member of every Walker Cup side since 1957, victory over the Americans was one of his last remaining unfulfilled ambitions and it was largely his leadership that inspired his team to rally bravely on the final afternoon. In a desperate last hour, Britain achieved a series of narrow singles victories so that eventually the Cup was won back from the Americans after 33 years.

Bonallack, Mrs M. (née Angela Ward) BRITISH
b. Kent 1938. British Girls' 1955; German Ladies' Open 1955; semi-finalist British

Ladies' 1956, 1958, runner-up 1962, 1974; Curtis Cup 1956, 1958, 1960, 1962, 1964, 1966; Portuguese Ladies' Open 1957; English Ladies' 1958, 1963, runner-up 1960, 1962, 1972, semi-finalist 1964; Vagliano Cup 1959, 1961, 1963; Astor Salver 1966, 1968

The tall, athletic figure of Angela Bonallack was a familiar sight on the fairways in the 1950s and 1960s, and the determination in her stride was reflected in her competitive spirit. A fine upright swing gave her outstanding length and accuracy, but she will be remembered mainly for her fighting qualities in a series of six consecutive Curtis Cup matches. At her first appearance in the team in 1956 she won her single against Mary Ann Downey and contributed to the second British victory of that decade.

She had a fine foursomes record, losing only one out of five matches, but her singles record was hardly given a chance for she came up against the leading player of the United States, JoAnne Gunderson, on three occasions and never beat her. There was friendship and a great rivalry between them, but the English girl seemed to draw the best

out of her opponent. After 1964, with 4 children, Angela Bonallack was not able to continue to the top. She still hankered after winning the British Championship, the one major event that escaped her, but it was in vain, although in 1974 she again reached the final, and in 1972 she was runner-up once more in the English Championship.

Bonallack, Sally see BARBER, MRS SALLY

Boomer, Aubrey Basil BRITISH
b. Grouville, Jersey, 1897. French Open 1921-2, 1926, 1929, 1931; Belgian Open 1922, 1926; Dutch Open 1924-6; Ryder Cup 1927, 1929; joint runner-up British Open 1927; Italian Open 1932

Angela Bonallack

Aubrey Boomer spent most of his career on the Continent, being at one time professional at St Cloud, Paris, and later at the Royal Golf Club de Belgique. A handsome, charming man, he was a very consistent scorer, and also a resourceful matchplayer (he helped considerably towards Britain's Ryder Cup win in 1929); but his Continental commitments restricted his appearances in Britain. On the only occasion that he was really prominent in the British Open he had the misfortune to run up against Bobby Jones in sparkling form. Jones beat Boomer and Fred Robson into 2nd place by 6 strokes at St Andrews in 1927, with a record low aggregate.

Booth, Mrs Jane (née Bastanchury)
AMERICAN
b. Whittier, Cal., 1948. Women's Trans-Mississippi Amateur 1967, 1969; Women's National Collegiate 1969; World Women's Amateur Team Championship 1970; Curtis Cup 1970, 1972

A mainstay of American international teams from 1970 on. Like other small figures before her, such as Marlene Streit and Ann Irvin, Jane Booth commands above-average length by getting up on her toes at the shot, and on the greens she is a tigress. She was in the US team for the World Women's Amateur Team Championship at Madrid in 1970 after successfully competing in the Curtis Cup at Brae Burn, and helped her team to a narrow victory over France. Two years later in 1972 she formed part of another victorious Curtis Cup Team; her single against the British Amateur Champion, Michelle Walker, in the final series was one of the great head-to-head contests in women's golf. Although she played well she lost on the last green, and subsequently in the course of the British Women's Championship and the Trans-Mississippi she lost a second and third time to the English girl.

Boros, Julius AMERICAN
b. Connecticut 1920. US Open 1952, 1963; tied 2nd 1956, tied 3rd 1960; leading money winner 1952, 1955; Ryder Cup 1959, 1963, 1965, 1967; USPGA 1968

Without taking any effort to project his personality, Boros, of Hungarian extraction, has been one of the most captivating figures in postwar golf. His victories in the US Open lie 11 years apart, the second after a three-way play-off with Jack Cupit and Arnold Palmer at the age of 43, making him the second oldest winner of the title. At the age of 48, he was the oldest USPGA champion. His longevity in the game is in large measure due to the trueness of his swing, surprisingly

easy and long for so heavy a man, and also to his relaxed approach to the game.

He turned professional late but he did not have to wait long for success. In 1952, in the full heat of a Texan summer, he won the Open by four shots from Porky Oliver, breaking the supremacy which Ben Hogan had had in the event for two years. Through the years his form fluctuated sharply, so that it came as a surprise when he won his second Open in 1963 after finishing out of the first 20 in the prize money for the previous three years. But he always played well in the big events. He finished nine times in the first 10 in the Open, being runner-up twice and 3rd once. His best finish in the Masters was tied 3rd in 1963.

Top. Mrs Jane Booth during the 1970 Espirito Santo (World Women's Amateur Team Championship) at Madrid

Above, Julius Boros

Boros reckons that in recent years he has developed a twitch, not with his putting stroke but in trying to keep the clubhead still at address, but even in his late forties he retained the nerve to win big tournaments when the chance came (as might be expected from a man of his temperament, he is one of the keenest fishermen on the tour). In his four Ryder Cup contests he lost only three matches out of 16.

Borrow
The aim-off in putting required to compensate for the natural rolls or slopes of the green.

Bourn, Thomas Arundale BRITISH
French Amateur 1928; President's Putter 1930; English Amateur 1930, runner-up 1933; runner-up British Amateur 1933

A difficult golfer to assess, for although not always reliable, he could play astonishingly eccentric, match saving shots. 'Dale' Bourn's graceful swing sometimes let him down, and he had a short jabbing putting style, but it was in matchplay that he was seen to his best advantage, invariably rising to the occasion, and never giving up hope. This made him the best of foursomes partners and he was a member of the often victorious Carthusian team in the Halford Hewitt Challenge Cup before the war. He took neither life nor his golf very seriously, but Bernard Darwin wrote an enviable epitaph for him: 'He had pluck, a quality that everyone must long for in his heart, and for which there is no substitute.' He was killed in World War II.

Bousfield, Kenneth BRITISH
b. Marston Moor, Yorkshire, 1919. Ryder Cup 1949, 1951, 1955, 1957, 1959, 1961; British Professional Matchplay 1955; PGA Close 1955; German Open 1955, 1959; Belgian Open 1958; Swiss Open 1958; Portuguese Open 1960-1; British Seniors' 1972

One of the leading British tournament players of the 1950s he is a kindly, charming man but one with a deceptive toughness of spirit which has been responsible for his competitive success. Not a powerful striker but a master of control and accuracy, particularly on fast courses where finesse was required, his swing had a beautiful, unfalteringly slow rhythm and he was an outstanding short pitcher.

Bousfield won the 90-hole Dunlop Tournament at Southport and Ainsdale in 1957 with rounds of 70, 70, 70, 71, 72, never taking more than 5 for any hole. His best year was 1955 when he won the first PGA

Championship at Pannal, Yorkshire, the German Open, and the Matchplay Championship at Walton Heath, in which he beat Eric Brown in the final.

He also had a good record in the Ryder Cup, notably as a foursome partner with Dai Rees.

Boyer, Auguste FRENCH
b. Cagnes-sur-Mer, Alpes-Maritimes, 1908. Italian Open 1926, 1928, 1930-1; German Open 1930, 1932, 1935-6; Swiss Open 1930, 1934-5; French Open 1931, 1933-4, 1936; Dutch Open 1932; Belgian Open 1933, 1936

Perhaps the most formidable Continental player between the two wars, with a fine temperament and capable of intense concentration. Boyer's rhythmic, fluent swing was of no great length but he was diabolically accurate round the greens.

Boyle, Hugh IRISH
b. Omeath, Co. Louth, 1936. Daks Tournament 1966; Yomiuri (Japan) Open 1966; Irish Professional 1967; Ryder Cup 1967; World Cup 1967

Boyle left the Irish Republic for Birmingham at the age of two. He came to golf through the caddie ranks, but he was nearly 30 before a score of 61 on the rain-soaked East Course at Dalmahoy, Midlothian, gave him a lead in the Senior Service Festival, 1965; he tied 2nd with Jackie Cupit, one of a dozen invited Americans. He finished 2nd again in 1966 and in the

interval became the first golfer from the British Isles to win a Japanese tournament. The following year he was in the Irish team for the World Cup. In 1971 he finished 10th in the order of merit but did not find a place in the Ryder Cup team.

Bradshaw, Harry IRISH
b. Delgany, Co. Wicklow, 1913. Irish Native Professional 1941-4, 1947, 1950-1, 1953-4, 1957; Irish Open 1947, 1949; runner-up British Open 1949; Dunlop Masters 1953, 1955; Ryder Cup 1953, 1955, 1957; World (Canada) Cup 1958

A natural Irish golfer, his golf was instinctive, uninhibited and free of affectation. Bradshaw never analysed his style but, with

Ken Bousfield

Top, Hugh Boyle

Above, Harry Bradshaw

three fingers of the right hand overlapping the left, he swung the club with a superbly constant rhythm. For many years he was one of the best professionals on the British circuit, and his simple philosophy allied to a cheerful disposition made him an attractive figure.

He came very close to winning the British Open Championship of 1949, and the way in which he lost is quoted as a test case which led to the Royal and Ancient Golf Club revising the rules of golf. The famous incident occurred at the 5th hole at Royal St George's when his drive finished inside a broken bottle. Rather than risk disqualification and without waiting to see if he could get relief – which he could not then, but could now – he smashed the bottle with his second shot, sending the ball about 30 yd and losing a stroke or more.

It was a disturbing incident but it is impossible to say whether Bradshaw would have won without it. A glance at his other rounds of 68, 68 and 70 shows that in his second round of 77, he was clearly unsettled. Locke eventually won the play-off by 12 strokes. After more successes in Ireland and winning both his matches in the 1953 Ryder Cup at Wentworth, Bradshaw won his first victory outside Ireland in the Dunlop Masters which was played on the old course at Sunningdale; he played the last 6 holes in 20 strokes, 3 under par.

Bradshaw was a safe player but he had powers of chipping and putting that were the envy of most men. One of his most remarkable performances was in winning the Canada Cup for Ireland in 1958 with Christy O'Connor in Mexico City at an altitude at which Olympic athletes have felt the strain. After giving up tournament golf, he carried on his duties at the Portmarnock Club outside Dublin.

Brady, Michael Joseph AMERICAN
b. Massachusetts 1887. Runner-up US Open 1911, 1919; North and South 1917; runner-up Canadian Open 1921, 1925

One of the first of the American-bred professionals to become a championship contender, Brady was outstanding as a golfer; yet he is better remembered for the events he did not win than for those he did. Until 1926, when he had been playing in the Open for twenty years, he never scored better than 74 in a final round of the event. In 1911, carrying only six clubs, he tied with Johnny McDermott and George Simpson, losing the play-off with an 82. The following year he held a 4-stroke lead after three rounds but finished in 80 for a tied 3rd place. His most famous failure was in 1919 when he led by 5

strokes after three rounds and again finished with 80. Walter Hagen tied him with a 75 and won the play-off by one stroke. It was against Brady that Hagen practised a famous piece of gamesmanship, summoning him from the clubhouse to make him watch the holing of an 8-ft putt on the last green that would give Hagen victory. The ball lipped the hole and stayed out, but Hagen unabashed won the play-off.

As evidence of Brady's talent, he broke 100 for 27 holes in 1917 and the same year holed twice in one in a single round at Siasconset, Mass. After service at Commonwealth, Wollaston, Oakley and Oakland Hills, Brady was for many years professional at Winged Foot.

Brae Burn CC USA
West Newton, Mass. 36 holes; No. 1 Course 6,516 yd (5,958 m), par 66; No. 2 Course 5,120 yd (4,682 m), par 66

The origins of golf at Brae Burn reach back to the early 1890s, but the picturesque course bears the unmistakable signature of Donald Ross. He worked on the course three different times, changing it to fit the club's property and to make better use of the land at hand. Ross tinkered with Brae Burn for 45 years in all, and his last changes were made in 1947. The best hole on the big course is probably the 11th, a 445-yd (407-m) par 4 with bunkers squeezing the fairway in the drive zone and with out-of-bounds running parallel to the left side. The

drive should favour the left in order to open up the green for the player and help him to avoid the trees overhanging the right edge of the green. As is the case with most early American courses, the trees at Brae Burn influence the play of the holes dramatically.

One of the most difficult holes is the par-3 17th, downhill for 255 yd (233 m) to a particularly fast undulating green. This is the hole where Walter Hagen lifted his ball from a muddy lie to identify it and then made a 4 en route to defeating Mike Brady in the play-off for 1919 Open.

Brae Burn also was the site of the 1928 United States Amateur won by Bob Jones, and the Women's Amateur of 1906, won by Harriot Curtis. It is the only course to have been host to the Curtis Cup twice. (Jones's victory was historic because it was the only time the British and American Amateur Champions have met in the final.) Among Brae Burn's more illustrious members in the past were Francis Ouimet and John Anderson, twice runner-up in the Amateur. It is also the home club of Mrs Henri Prunaret, one of the organizers of the Women's World Amateur Team Championship. It has 500 members today and in addition to golf offers swimming, skating, tennis and curling.

Braid, James BRITISH
b. Earlsferry, Fife, 1870; d. London 1950. British Open 1901, 1905, 1906, 1908, 1910; British Professional Matchplay 1903, 1905,

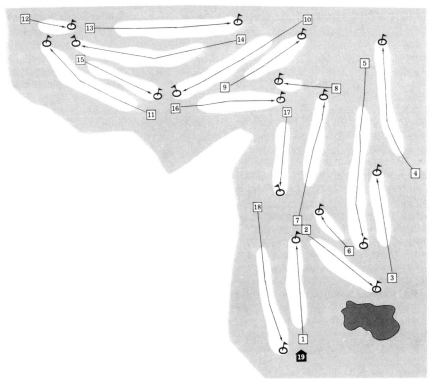

Plan of the course at the Brae Burn CC

1907, 1911, runner-up 1913, 1927; French Open 1910

James Braid, a member of the old school of Scottish professionals, belonged to a rich era. Within a year of Braid's birth, Harry Vardon was born at Grouville in Jersey and John Henry Taylor at Northam in Devon, the two who, with Braid, were later to become famous the world over as the Triumvirate.

Braid came from a humble background, the son of an Elie ploughman. His father never played golf, a fact which helps to explain his lack of sympathy with his son's taking up the game professionally. Elie then had a busy golfing world of its own, independent of Earlsferry, to which the young Braid was soon attracted. Although there were many good local models for Braid to watch and copy, he did not consciously do so. After leaving school at 13 to become an apprentice joiner in a nearby village, he began a brief amateur career which was highlighted by winning the Braid Hills tournament where he played when sent to work in Edinburgh. He turned professional in 1893 when his friend, Ralph Smith, persuaded him to go to London as apprentice clubmaker at the Army and Navy Stores. Here he earned eightpence an hour and later a shilling. He could play on Sundays around London (this was not possible in his native Scotland) and with plenty of evening golf after work, he developed the individual swing which Bernard Darwin once described as 'always essentially a full swing and, in his earlier days, a most dashing one, with a very free loose knee at the finish of the shot, when he really went out for it'. Horace Hutchinson once wrote that he hit with 'a divine fury'.

He played his first professional match at Limpsfield in December 1893, and the following summer played in his first British Open Championship when it was held for the first time outside Scotland at Sandwich.

An opening round of 91 kept him out of the money, although the rounds of 84, 82

and 84 that followed were some indication of what was to come.

At the end of 1895, he sprang to much wider fame, through a match which he played against J. H. Taylor, then champion for the second time, at West Drayton. Braid halved the match and his performance had an important bearing on his future. By the following spring, he had a post of his own at Romford, Essex, but it was not until 1901 that he achieved his greatest ambition, victory in the British Open Championship.

By then, Taylor and Vardon had each won three times; Braid had a sudden golden era. He became the first man to win the Open Championship five times although Taylor equalled this record (as later did Peter Thomson) and Vardon beat it. His victories came in 1901 at Muirfield, 1905 at St Andrews, 1906 at Muirfield again, 1908 at Prestwick and 1910 at St Andrews. In those days professional tournaments, as known today, were few and far between. Braid won his money more in challenge and exhibition matches, but he was the first winner of the *News of the World* (later the British Professional) Matchplay Championship and not surprisingly followed with more victories in 1905, 1907 and 1911. There was, too, a famous 72-hole foursome match between England and Scotland or Vardon and Taylor against Braid and Sandy Herd, but after leading by 2 holes at the end of the first round, Braid and Herd lost by 13 and 12.

A detail of a painting by Clement Flower showing, *left to right* John Henry Taylor, James Braid and Harry Vardon

Two testimonials, now hanging at the Walton Heath GC, presented to James Braid

In 1904, Herbert Fowler completed his design of Walton Heath and Braid began his long and happy association with the club which lasted for the rest of his life. As a training ground Walton Heath was of great benefit to Braid. When World War I broke out he carried on playing. He was then 44, and well over military age but he, Vardon and Taylor gave their services freely for various war charities.

Although Braid, like his two rivals, played on in the Open Championship until well into his fifties, he settled down to life as a club professional and almost to the year of his death was regularly seen on the course.

He was much in demand as a golf-course architect and throughout his life a highly respected figure who did much, by his influence and conduct, to raise the status of the golf professional. Like many Scotsmen, he was reserved in his actions in contrast to his game. He was an immensely painstaking man of few words, a warm and true friend.

In 1950 Braid, J. H. Taylor and Willie Auchterlonie were elected honorary members of the Royal and Ancient GC of St Andrews, the first professionals to receive such distinction.

Brantford GCC CANADA
Brantford, Ont., 18 holes; 6,601 yd (6,036 m); par 72

The fourth of Canada's golf clubs to be formed during the 1870s was established at Brantford in 1879. It occupied four different homes before it settled at its present location in the city's western outskirts in 1906. Its site on a bluff overlooking a fertile valley and the Grand River is one of great natural beauty. The initial 9-hole course was extended to 18 holes in 1920. In 1937 it became one of the first courses in Canada to install a full course-watering system covering the fairways as well as greens. As now constituted, the course has five par-3 holes and five par 5s, presenting most interesting golf. An unusual feature is a hoist, constructed to relieve players of an otherwise strenuous uphill climb from the 18th green to the 1st tee near the clubhouse. The course has played host to three Canadian Championships, the Seniors, Junior and Professional, as well as the Open and Amateur Championships of Ontario. *The Canadian Golfer* was started at Brantford, where it continued to be published for some 18 years.

Brassie
The no 2 wood: the golfer had two drivers in his set in the early days, the play club (driver) and the grassed driver (brassie). The

name derives from the brass plate attached to the base of the slightly more lofted type of wooden club.

Brazil
One of the leading golf nations of South America. Brazil's first club dates back to around the turn of the century when a group of British engineers working with the São Paulo Railway Company founded the São Paulo GC. This was followed in 1923 by the Gavea GCC in Rio de Janeiro. Since then the number of clubs has risen to around 30, the main centres being Rio and São Paulo. The Brazilian Golf Association, Brazil's governing body of golf, operates from São Paulo.

Mario Gonzales is the best of all Brazilian golfers. The Brazilian Amateur Championship, started in 1934, and the Brazilian Open, which dates from 1945, attract a good entry. Brazilian teams have been regular entrants in the World (formerly Canada) Cup and World Amateur Team Championship for the Eisenhower Trophy.

Brewer, Gay AMERICAN
b. Middletown, Ohio, 1932. Hawaii Open 1965; National Four-Ball (with Beard) 1965; Seattle Open 1965; Pensacola Open 1966–7; Alcan Golfer of the Year 1967–8; Ryder Cup 1967, 1973; US Masters 1967, tied 1966; Pacific Masters 1972

A golfer with a distinctive loop in his swing, Gay Brewer joined the tour in 1956 and from about 1960 onwards was one of the best of American professionals. He tied in the 1966 US Masters Championship: he took three putts from the top of the 72nd green and then lost a play-off to Nicklaus and Tommy Jacobs. He achieved his greatest performance in the Masters in 1967 when he won with a total of 280 (73, 68, 72, 67). He played the front nine beautifully

all four days, but it was not until he sank a 10-footer on the 11th that he got his first taste of the lead, or at least a tie for it.

From then on Brewer's inspired putting gave Nichols little hope and Brewer was the new champion. Afterwards he contended 'A golfer doesn't know how well he can play until he wins one of the big tournaments under pressure', and proved his point later the same year by winning the Alcan Golfer of the Year Championship at St Andrews. This carried a first prize of just over £23,000, though this was not captured without a play-off with Casper. In 1968 Brewer successfully defended this title, winning with the same score of 283 at Royal Birkdale. Brewer spent the summer of 1972 recovering

from a stomach complaint contracted at the Masters, but he finished 3rd in the John Player Classic at Turnberry and the next week won the Pacific Masters Championship in Tokyo after a sudden-death play-off with David Graham.

Brews, Sidney F. BRITISH
b. Blackheath, London, 1899; d. South Africa 1972. South African Open 1925, 1927, 1930–1, 1933–4, 1949, 1952; Belgian Open 1929; runner-up British Open 1934; Dutch Open 1934–5; French Open 1934–5; Philadelphia Open 1934; US Metropolitan Open 1935

Before the arrival of Bobby Locke, Brews was the outstanding South African profes-

Two old brassies

Gay Brewer

sional golfer and dominated the scene in that country for 20 years. Altogether he won 42 major tournaments. Yet he was of an age when professionals took pride in working for their clubs and the members in them; Brews was well loved in the Houghton GC in South Africa which he served for more than 30 years. He had been taught by his father who was employed as a clubmaker at the Minchinhampton course in Gloucestershire.

Brews was persuaded by his brother Jack to follow him to South Africa, where he immediately won a tournament. It was reckoned in those days that if Sid did not win, his brother Jack would. Besides winning the Transvaal Open eight and the Natal Open four times, he had a remarkable record in the South African Open, for his victories in it covered four decades from the 1920s to the 1950s. His last victory came in 1952 when he was 53, and after playing the last 9 holes in a strong wind in 1 under par. It was said of Sid Brews that he addressed the ball in a flash, but that it took him longer to play a drive or hit a brassie shot than it took him to putt.

Brickman, Eric BRITISH
b. Lasswade, Midlothian, 1900

From 1953 to 1967 Brigadier Eric Brickman DSO was secretary to the Royal and Ancient GC. These were years when the club's administrative tasks were expanding faster than the means to cope with them, but 'Brick' took it all in his stride and carried on the work with quiet, unassuming charm. By the time he retired the British Open had grown considerably in importance and he had a host of friends at home and overseas.

Briggs, Clare AMERICAN
b. Wisconsin, 1875; d. 1930

The outstanding delineator of the American golf scene since A. B. Frost, Briggs began as a newspaper artist with the St Louis *Globe Democrat* when he was 21. After several stints with New York and Chicago papers, he became associated in 1914 with the New York *Tribune* syndicate which distributed his work nationwide throughout the remainder of his career. A man who had the gift of seeing the funny side of life and depicting it with a bright, clean line, Briggs drew a daily comic strip called 'Mr and Mrs' that ran for decades. An enthusiastic golfer – he played mainly at the Wykagyl CC in Westchester – he produced for magazines and newspapers endless sketches, drawings, and cartoons that caught the flavour of the post-World War I golf boom with marvellous vividness and humour. An excellent selection of his work is presented in *The Duffer's*

Handbook of Golf which he and Grantland Rice published in the late 1920s.

Brightwood GCC CANADA
Dartmouth, N.S., 18 holes; 5,704 yd (5,216 m); par 68

The Brightwood course is situated in the centre of Dartmouth, facing the port of Halifax across Bedford basin. Being on the top and side of a mountain has both advantages and disadvantages. Several of the holes afford panoramic views of unusual beauty. On the other hand, the course is exposed to the winds which blow in from Halifax harbour and the Atlantic. Often it is with the weather rather than particular difficulties of the course itself that the golfer has to contend. Like so many Nova Scotian courses, Brightwood is rather short. A compensating factor is the narrowness of the holes which demand uncommon accuracy. On most of them the penalty for straying from the fairway is severe, such is the nature of the rough which abounds with trees, shrubs and rocks. A most delightful course to play, Brightwood is as much a test of a golfer's ability to think his way around the course as it is of his shotmaking skill.

British Amateur Championship see
p. 463

British Open Championship
The once quiet fishing town of Prestwick on the Ayrshire coast now has a busy international airport; diesel trains clatter on their way to Glasgow; but alongside the grey stone wall at the end of the station platform there is a link with the past: one of golf's historic courses. Critics may say the course is no longer severe enough for the professional or that some of its holes leave too much to chance, but it is where championship golf began, and even the earliest champions would still recognize it. The Open Championship is the oldest in the world and owes its origins to the Prestwick GC. In 1857, when private matches formed the main competition, Prestwick succeeded in getting eight clubs to take part in a foursomes knock-out. In the following year the club held an individual tournament for amateurs and in 1860, at the suggestion of Major J. O. Fairlie, staged a similar event for professionals. This was well timed: the death of the invincible Allan Robertson in 1859 had left the world with no obvious successor as leading player. The meeting that took place on Wednesday 17 October 1860 over three rounds of the Prestwick 12-hole course is therefore generally regarded as the first Open Championship. It was won from a

field of eight players by Willie Park of Musselburgh. There was a difference of 58 strokes between first and last, and the scores were:

174 Willie Park (Musselburgh)
176 Tom Morris (Prestwick)
180 Andrew Strath (St Andrews)
191 Bob Andrew (Perth)
192 Daniel Brown (Blackheath)
195 Charlie Hunter (Prestwick St Nicholas)
196 Alex Smith (Bruntsfield)
232 William Steel (Bruntsfield)

Strictly speaking this was not the first true Open since the meeting was for professionals only, but in 1861 the second contest was 'open to all the world'. So it has remained, although only three amateurs, John Ball, Harold Hilton (twice) and Bobby Jones (three times) have ever become champions.

Of the first eight championships Old Tom Morris won four and Willie Park three, but the most famous period of dominance by one player began in 1868 when Old Tom was dethroned by his son Young Tom, who by completing three victories in a row made the championship belt his own. This caused the club to think again and look for a new trophy. In 1871 there was no championship – the only gap apart from the war years – but then came a significant move. Prestwick, which had run all previous championships, persuaded the Royal and Ancient GC and the Honourable Company of Edinburgh Golfers to subscribe to the purchase of a trophy and to help run the championship. For the next 22 years the event was played in rotation at Prestwick, St Andrews and Musselburgh, the Honourable Company's home at this time.

The beginning of this era was marked by Young Tom's fourth successive victory, although his score was 17 more than the exceptional and never-beaten 149 which he

British Open Golf Championship: Bob Charles with the Trophy, 1963

returned in 1870; his death on Christmas Day 1875, at the age of 24, was one of the game's great tragedies. Playing the championship on different courses led to a marked increase in the size of the entry, and in 1885 it exceeded 50 for the first time. The period 1877-82 was dominated by Jamie Anderson and Bob Ferguson with three successive victories each, and the next decade brought the victories of John Ball and the first of Harold Hilton, the two famous Hoylake amateurs. Hilton's first victory was in 1892, the first year that the championship was held over 72 holes. The next important landmark was the emergence of J. H. Taylor in 1894. Not only was he the first English professional to win the Open, but he did so at Sandwich, the first time the championship was taken out of Scotland. It marked the first of 16 victories recorded by himself, Vardon and Braid: the Triumvirate. Vardon's contributions to that total were six, a number unsurpassed before or since. One of the few to break the Triumvirate monopoly between 1894 and 1914 was Sandy Herd who in 1902 became the first player to win using the new rubber-cored ball. Another was the Frenchman, Arnaud Massy, who in 1907 became the first overseas winner of the title. By 1909 Muirfield, Hoylake and Deal had been added to the list of championship venues, although it was fitting that Vardon's last victory should have been at Prestwick. That was in 1914, the year in which for the first time two

qualifying rounds were introduced, limiting the field to 80 and ties.

When play resumed after World War I it soon became obvious that the championship had become so big that some form of centralized control was necessary. At a meeting in Edinburgh in 1919, Robert Maxwell of the Honourable Company moved: 'Believing that the time had now arrived when there should be a supreme ruling authority for the management and control of the game, that the Royal and Ancient golf club be asked to accept the management for the championship and the custody of the cup.' The motion was carried unanimously and the R. and A. began what in modern times most people regard as their most important function. It was a significant hand-over for it coincided with the championship's becoming an international rather than a national gathering, thus confirming in the eyes of the world the status of that club as the governing body of the game.

Although it led to the eventual eclipse of the British players, this was an exciting period because it introduced the British public to the great Americans of that time – Walter Hagen, Bobby Jones and Gene Sarazen. Hagen was the first to win, in 1922 at Sandwich (the year after Jock Hutchison had beaten Roger Wethered in a play-off, Wethered thus nearly joining the distinguished band of amateur winners). Hagen's victory was followed by that of Arthur Havers at Troon, a new course on

the list, but that was the end of the British successes for a decade. During that time, Hagen won another three times, Jones three times, Barnes, Armour, Sarazen and Shute once each. Although this was, in many ways, the making of the championship for the future in that other Americans later strove to emulate their predecessors, it made the British impatient for a home player to win again, and when the tide began to turn with Henry Cotton's victory in 1934, their relief can easily be appreciated.

Even more heartening was Cotton's second success in 1937 against the might of the American Ryder Cup team at Carnoustie. This crowned him as the outstanding figure in British golf of his time, but the clouds of war were forming and it was another 11 years before he added his third title, a number which no other British golfer has achieved since the Triumvirate.

Snead's victory in 1946 and the historic journey of Ben Hogan to Carnoustie apart – the latter one of the great compliments paid to the championship – the Open after World War II suffered from the growing richness of the American circuit which made the average American professional, who was more interested in dollars than titles, reluctant to journey to Britain. Peter Thomson and Bobby Locke thus dominated the championship for 10 years with eight victories between them, including a hat trick from Thomson, but in 1960, one hundred years after the first Open, Arnold Palmer, America's new

The British Open Golf Championship: teeing off at St Andrews in 1895 – a painting by Michael Brown

sporting idol, appropriately set in motion a revival which has brought the event to a new level of importance. On this his first appearance Palmer was runner-up to Kel Nagle, but he won in 1961 and 1962, the latter year with a total of 276. Thereafter the challenge was maintained and strengthened by players from all over the world, including in recent years the best players from the Far East. The Open became a great spectacle, watched on television by millions in Europe and the United States, its organization reflecting much credit upon the R. and A. Not only did the ancillary benefits accruing to the winner become worth a fortune, but the prize money itself went up sharply. From a total of £1,000 in 1946 and £5,000 in 1959 it soared to £50,000 in 1972, with the winner's share up to £5,500. Other changes included the introduction in 1962 of exemptions from qualifying and in 1966 the extension of play to four days with one round each day, a far cry from the time when it was all over in a day.

Only once, in 1926, was a regional qualifying round tried, but the size of the modern entries made three qualifying courses necessary in 1970 and four in 1972 when entries were close to 500. In 1964 the play-off for the championship was reduced from 36 holes to 18, but there have been few of them in the Open history, the last being in 1970 when Jack Nicklaus beat Doug Sanders in a titanic struggle after Sanders had missed from a yard for the championship, generally

reckoned to be one of the most expensive putts ever missed. Sanders was a loyal and popular supporter of the Open during the 1960s which saw a series of eventful championships, including a first-time victory for Tony Lema in 1964 for which he hardly allowed himself time to get to know the Old Course at St Andrews, a fifth victory for Thomson in 1965 – a number exceeded only by Vardon – and an emotional and highly popular win by Roberto de Vicenzo after years of coming close. Finally in 1969 victory by Tony Jacklin broke the overseas spell and evoked scenes of wild delight. The period between 1951, when Max Faulkner won at Royal Portrush, and 1969 was the longest in the Open's history without a British winner, but it only underlined how competitive it had become and how well established in the eyes of the players who make it, together with the United States Open, the most important and highly regarded championship in the world. 1971 and 1972 belonged to Lee Trevino and 1973 to another American, Tom Weiskopf, on the championship's return to Troon; but in 1974 Gary Player won again in the first British Open to be played with the large ball.

Courses used

PRESTWICK 1860-72 (except for 1871), 1875, 1878, 1881, 1884, 1887, 1890, 1893, 1898, 1903, 1908, 1914, 1925

ST ANDREWS 1873, 1876, 1879, 1882, 1885, 1888, 1891, 1895, 1900, 1905, 1910, 1921, 1927, 1933, 1934, 1946, 1955, 1957, 1960, 1964, 1970

MUSSELBURGH 1874, 1877, 1880, 1883, 1886, 1889

MUIRFIELD 1892, 1896, 1901, 1906, 1912, 1929, 1935, 1948, 1959, 1966, 1972

HOYLAKE 1897, 1902, 1907, 1913, 1924, 1930, 1936, 1947, 1956, 1967

SANDWICH 1894, 1899, 1904, 1911, 1922, 1928, 1934, 1938, 1949

ROYAL LYTHAM 1926, 1952, 1958, 1963, 1969, 1974

DEAL 1909, 1920

PRINCES 1932

CARNOUSTIE 1931, 1937, 1953, 1968

TROON 1923, 1950, 1962, 1973

ROYAL BIRKDALE 1954, 1961, 1965, 1971

ROYAL PORTRUSH 1951

Broadmoor GC USA
Colorado Springs, Colo. 36 holes

High in the Rocky Mountains at Colorado Springs, Broadmoor is a wonderful place for golf. The vistas are majestic and the accommodation beyond criticism. Moreover, the golf is stimulating, and the two 18-hole courses, the older East in particular, are of a standard well above the common level of what are called resort courses.

It was on the East Course that Jack Nicklaus won his first national title, defeating Charlie Coe 1 up in a momentous 36-hole final in the 1959 US Amateur. The East is rated somewhat higher than the West, over which Bob Dickson won the Amateur in 1967. The holes on both courses are designed to reduce the climbing that might be expected in the Rockies. The fair-

ways are rugged, and the roll of the greens extremely hard to read, which is invariably true of mountain courses – certainly those which are a full mile above sea level.

Brook Hollow GC USA
Dallas, Tex. 6,686 yd (6,114 m); par 71

Brook Hollow in Dallas is one of those clubs that manages to maintain a quiet dignity even though it has a membership of 930. The course is meticulously groomed, and although it has not been tested by the touring professionals since the Dallas Open in 1946, it has been the site of occasional sectional amateur tournaments, including three Trans-Mississippi Amateur Championships.

The British Open Golf Championship: Norman Von Nida and Bruce Devlin weigh up a shot

Broadmoor GC

Brook Hollow was designed in 1920 by A. W. Tillinghast. It measures 6,686 yd from the back tees, which is in keeping with some of Tillinghast's other courses.

For member's play, Brook Hollow can be shortened to a more manageable 6,176 yd (5,647 m) and can be set as short as 5,456 yd (4,989 m) for ladies. The club was a pioneer in its time, and it is said to have had the first complete fairway watering system in the United States. In 1939 it became the second course in the Southwest to install bent-grass greens, which require a great deal of care in a climate like Texas. It is laid out on sandy soil near the point where Elm Fork empties into the Trinity River north of the centre of Dallas. Water for the irrigation system is pumped from the Elm Fork.

Brook Hollow came into being in a curious way. Cameron Buxton, an enthusiastic golfer, was playing at the Dallas CC in March 1920. One of his drives hit a worm cast and veered sharply left into thick rough. Buxton was, of course, upset, and the next Monday he and some friends were searching for worm-free land on which to build a new golf

course. The result of that search is Brook Hollow.

Brooks, Andrew BRITISH
b. Lanark 1946

A Scottish international at boys', youths' and senior level as an amateur, Andrew Brooks played in the 1969 Walker Cup match in Milwaukee and was unbeaten in three matches. He turned professional in October that year.

Brown, David BRITISH
b. Musselburgh, Midlothian, 1860. British Open 1886; tied US Open 1903

A slater by trade who in the early days only competed in golf events when they

Andrew Brooks

came to Musselburgh or when trade was poor. He first came to light by winning the British Open at Musselburgh in 1886 with a total of 157. Horace Hutchinson described this Scotsman as 'a very painstaking player, brimful of confidence, a long, powerful driver, and an extremely dexterous wielder of Park's patent lofter' – recommendation enough for a player who later went to America and tied for the US Open in 1903. His score was the same as Willie Anderson (307) but Anderson won the play-off at Baltusrol with 82 to 84.

Brown, Eric Chalmers BRITISH
b. Edinburgh 1925. Scottish Amateur 1946; Swiss Open 1951; Italian Open 1952; Irish Open 1953; Portuguese Open 1953; Ryder Cup 1953, 1955, 1957, 1959, (captain 1969, 1971); Scottish Professional 1956-8, 1960, 1962; Dunlop Masters 1957; Vardon Trophy 1957; British Professional Matchplay 1960, 1962

Eric Brown, in his younger days a railway fireman, came out of nowhere to win the Scottish Amateur Championship at Car-

Top, Eric Brown in play during a Canada Cup tournament and, *above*, practising for the 1968 Dunlop Masters

noustie in 1946. Later that year he turned professional and began a career in which he combined a particular liking for the man-to-man combat offered by matchplay with a volatile temperament.

Unquestionably the centrepiece of Brown's reputation has been his Ryder Cup record. He played four matches against the United States and won all his singles, then over 36 holes, in turn beating Lloyd Mangrum, Jerry Barber, Tommy Bolt and Cary Middlecoff. When Brown came to captain the side first, in 1969, Britain gained a halved match, the first, and so far only such result in the series. Two years later, again under Brown's leadership, Britain achieved the best result of a visiting side to America.

When Brown began his career, the PGA rules prevented him from competing in major domestic events until he had been a professional for five years. During this period he began his joint domination of the game in Scotland with John Panton which lasted for some 20 years. In addition to making a start on a multiple series of victories in the Scottish and Northern Open championships, as well as in many other Scottish events, Brown also competed with notable success on the Continent and in Ireland.

At his peak Brown was a great inspirational player, capable of marvellous bursts of scoring, but dogged by lapses which were more attributable to flaws in technique, particularly in his grip, than of temperament. Thus although Brown was unable to do himself complete justice in strokeplay tournaments, he shares on 65 the record low score for the Open Championship, in which he twice finished in 3rd place, and was the first player to score 30 twice for 9 holes.

Brown, John Arthur AMERICAN
b. 1895

Pine Valley, cut through thick pine forests and sandy wastelands near Clementon, N.J., is one of America's most awe-inspiring golf courses, and John Arthur Brown, its president since 1929, is equally impressive. A six-footer of commanding presence, Brown still played regularly in his 87th year. He has bettered the Pine Valley par of 70 at least 10 times, a good many years ago, and has scored lower than his age on countless occasions. Since 1953, Brown has lived in a home he built on the course, the last of 14 constructed on the club grounds. He has always run the club with a tight rein – a self-admitted and cheerfully accepted autocrat – keeping an eye on every facet of its operation and never hesitating to speak out forthrightly

and without fear for what he considers its best interests. To put this in proper perspective, it should be noted that Pine Valley's wide-ranging membership of over 800 includes at least 30 millionaires, and touches the mainstreams of American industry, banking and government. In recent years, while many other American clubs were struggling against sky-rocketing operating costs, Pine Valley installed a complete new irrigation system and greatly expanded its clubhouse facilities.

Brown served four times as president of the US Seniors' Golf Association, and up to the late 1960s was a frequent prize winner in its competitions.

Brownlow, William George Edward
BRITISH
b. London 1902

William Brownlow (later Lord Lurgan) reached the semi-final of the British Amateur Championship in 1926, losing to the eventual winner, Jess Sweetser, at the 21st. He was in the 1926 Walker Cup team.

Bruen, James IRISH
b. Belfast, 1920; d. 1972. British Boys' Amateur 1936; Irish Close Amateur 1937-8, semi-finalist 1963; Irish Open Amateur 1938; Walker Cup 1938, 1949, 1951; British Amateur 1946

Jimmy Bruen with his famous loop had the strangest swing that first-class golf has ever known. It was neither very graceful nor

John Arthur Brown

very orthodox for at the top of the swing the clubhead would be pointed in the direction of the tee box. It was then whipped down into the hitting area with almost frightening force; his power was phenomenal and his feats of long hitting a constant source of stories. It defied all the theorists but although it lent a dramatic appeal to his golf and gave him a great advantage on heavy courses and in his remarkable recoveries from rough and sand, his pitching had a rare delicacy and he was the best approach putter of his day.

Bruen, a citizen of Cork, developed his method largely on his own and at 16 won a rather one-sided British Boys' Amateur Championship at Royal Birkdale in 1936. At 17, to continue his explosive introduction, he played in the British Amateur Championship at Sandwich and the following spring went round St Andrews with obvious maturity, and apparently almost at will, in 69 or 70, sending his Walker Cup trial opponents flying like ninepins. His play in the build-up to the match was, in fact, a considerable factor in undermining the Americans though, after halving his foursome in partnership with Harry Bentley, he lost his singles to Charlie Yates who had just won the 1938 British Amateur Championship at Troon.

The following year, Bruen lost to the eventual winner of the British Amateur, Alex Kyle, in the last eight of the championship, but he led the qualifiers for the Open Championship at St Andrews, finishing leading amateur, eight shots behind the winner, Dick Burton. He was then still only just 19.

The World War II years were a great blow to Bruen's progress and there is no telling how good he would have otherwise become; and Ireland rightly felt it had found something of a phenomenon. In 1946 Bruen won a memorable victory in the British Amateur, beating the American, Robert Sweeny, champion of 1937, in the final.

It would be unfair to describe him as erratic because a swing of that nature was bound to have variations, and he had the recovery powers to redeem almost anything; but a tiresome, recurring wrist injury began to affect his strength and his confidence. He played in the Walker Cup matches of 1949 and 1951 but he was never the same player again and, except for the British Amateur at Portrush in 1960, when his wrist forced him to retire early on, as it had done against America in 1951, competitive golf saw him no more. He died in May 1972 of a heart attack.

Bruntsfield Links Golfing Society
SCOTLAND
Davidson's Mains, Edinburgh. 18 holes; 6,775 yd (6,195 m); par 70

There is a romantic theory that the Bruntsfield Association (the original name) was formed in 1761 by members of the Burgess Society who, being supporters of the cause of Prince Charles Edward Stuart, did not relish having to drink a toast to the Hanoverian George III, and broke away. Any split between the two factions did not last long, however, for by 1818 these political differences had been buried. The two clubs not only shared Bruntsfield Links for more than 100 years, until both were forced by encroachment and overcrowding to move to Musselburgh in the 1870s, but joined forces to protect their ancient golfing rights: notably in 1843 when there was a threat to hold the annual Hallow Fair on the links, attended by 40,000 head of cattle and lasting several days. The Burgess and Bruntsfield enlisted counsel who advised application for interdict against the magistrates and council; a public meeting was held, a petition with more than 400 signatures presented – and the Hallow Fair was not held on the links. In 1856 the two clubs successfully threatened interdict against a proposed carriage drive through the course. This was only a delaying action, for soon Bruntsfield Links, part of a 12th-century grant of forest made to Edinburgh by David I, was surrounded by houses. (Golf is still played there, on a short municipal course: a fitting memorial perhaps to the stout resistance of the Bruntsfield and Burgess clubs.)

The Bruntsfield society may also take credit for what is believed to be the first inter-club tournament, held at St Andrews in July 1857. The idea originated with Colonel J. O. Fairlie, captain of the Royal and Ancient in 1850 and of the Prestwick Club in 1853; Bruntsfield took the initiative; and an invitation went out from St Andrews to recognized clubs to send two of their best players to take part in a competition, with a contribution of £4 towards expenses. Blackheath, represented by George Glennie and Lieutenant Stewart, both top Scottish club players, beat the Royal and Ancient in the final.

A house on the links near the Golf Tavern served Bruntsfield as a clubhouse until the society's move to Musselburgh in 1874, where it had bought a property which it occupied until 1898 when overcrowding again forced a move, this time to the fine course at Davidson's Mains laid out by Willie Park.

Park's course was reconstructed in 1923-4.

In further recent alterations several holes
have been improved and a new circuit has
been created, with four par 3s, two par 5s
and the rest par 4.

Bulawayo GC RHODESIA
Bulawayo. 18 holes

Rhodesian golf was born in Bulawayo just
over a year after the British occupation of
Matabeleland, and the Bulawayo club was
the first to be formed in January 1895. The
first recorded president was Dr Leander
Starr Jameson, followed closely by Earl
Grey.

The first club championship in 1900 was
won by F. C. Dugmore, his prize being the
Rhodes Challenge Shield. Later Cecil
Rhodes, an enthusiastic follower of the
game, presented the Rhodes Cup, still played
for today.

In 1910 the course was extended to 18
holes, the original clubhouse was sold for
£35 and a new one built which stood for 20
years. Two years later the first Rhodesian
Amateur Championship was played at
Bulawayo. The winner, F. C. Dugmore once
more, was awarded the Gladstone Cup given
by Lord Gladstone, then High Commissioner for South Africa.

Today membership has reached 800, there
is a fine new clubhouse which was opened in
January 1970, to commemorate the club's
75th anniversary, and the course frequently
has professional tournaments.

Bulgaria

There is one course in Bulgaria, a few miles
from the capital city of Sofia. Paul Tomita,
the Rumanian professional, assisted the
architect with its design.

Bulger

An obsolete wooden club with a convex face.
The theory was that the ball could not be hit
out of the heel or toe. The invention of
Henry Lamb, it was fashionable for a time
although Willie Park, who made himself a
'Bulger', never actually used it.

Bulla, Johnny AMERICAN
b. West Virginia, 1914. Runner-up British
Open 1939, tied 2nd 1946; last 8 USPGA
1948, 1951; tied 2nd US Masters 1949

Bulla won only one tournament of any
significance, the Los Angeles Open in 1941,
but he came close to winning every major
championship, sometimes more than once.
When just starting on his career in 1939 he
came within measurable distance of achieving both the US and British Opens. At
Spring Hill in the US Open he led the field
after 54 holes but finished 6th with a 76. In

the British Open he finished 2nd, 2 strokes
behind Dick Burton, rallying strongly after
an opening 77. Again in the British Open
after World War II he finished in a tie for
2nd after leading the field for three rounds.
In the US Open he tied 3rd in 1941, 4th in
1952 and was in the top 10 of both the British
and American Opens in 1948. Two finishing
rounds of 69 took him to 2nd place in the
1949 Masters. A natural left-hander who
played right-handed, he once said that his
trouble had been that he had been playing
right-handed and thinking left.

He gained notoriety before the war by
playing the circuit with a low-priced ball
sold only in drugstores.

Bunker

A crater or hole in the ground filled with
sand; derived from a Scottish word for a
storeplace or receptacle. The American
term is trap. A bunker, as laid down by the
rules of golf, is a hazard in which a player
must not ground his club before striking the
ball.

Burke, Billy AMERICAN
b. Connecticut 1902. North and South
Open 1928; Ryder Cup 1931, 1933; US
Open 1931; semi-finalist USPGA 1931

Although a good player with several
tournament victories to his credit, Burke is
chiefly remembered as the man who 'had to
play two Opens to win one'. In 1931 he tied
on 292 at Inverness, Toledo, after 72 holes

Top, Johnny Bulla

Bunker: *centre,* Sheila Vaughan playing out of
the sand and, *above,* Nicklaus and Player at
practice

Billy Burke

with George von Elm; both returned 149 in a 36-hole play-off the next day, and in a second 36-hole play-off Burke emerged the winner of the US Open Championship by 1 stroke with 148.

Burke (his real name was Burkauskus and he was of Lithuanian descent) lost part of the fourth finger of his left hand and damaged the fifth when working in an iron mill and this led him to insert a piece of sponge into the finger of his glove to increase his grip. He had no great length off the tee but had a most accurate short game. He won his single and a foursome in the 1931 Ryder Cup and also won his foursome in 1933. His other best performances in the US Open were tied 7th in 1932 and tied 6th in 1934, a

first American defeat since the war. However, he was captain again in 1973, when he led his side to a fine victory.

Burke, an exceptionally fine putter, was at his best in rough weather. In 1952 his 69, which brought him into 2nd place behind Snead, was played in the strongest winds of any duration experienced at the Masters. It was the only score under 70 on the last two days. The year of his victory, 1956, was another occasion of bad weather. His winning total of 289 is the highest ever recorded in the event, but his final round of 71, which caught up 8 strokes on the amateur Ken Venturi, was again an exceptional round. In winning the 1960 Texas Open he scored 260 – 67, 65, 64, 64 – one of the lowest totals on

eight successes in the native championships. He also played for Ireland from 1929 to 1949.

He was the first Irish-based player to appear in a Walker Cup contest and in 1932 at Brookline, Mass., he halved his singles with Jack Westland. After World War II he had to face the rising challenge of the young Joe Carr, but defeated him in the 36-hole final of the Irish Open Amateur at Royal Dublin – his only success in that event – and added two more native titles to his list. Since he became tragically afflicted with a spinal disease he had been confined to a wheelchair, but he still followed the play in a car driven around Lahinch course when important tournaments were held there, keeping in

round of 77 in each case destroying his chances of winning.

Burke, Jack, Jr AMERICAN
b. Texas 1923. Ryder Cup 1951, 1953, 1955, 1957 (captain 1957, 1973); Texas Open 1952, 1963; US Masters 1956, runner-up 1952; USPGA 1956; Japanese Open 1958

One of the most popular of the American professionals and a star attraction during the 1950s, Burke enjoyed great success over a comparatively brief period. His peak year was 1956, and though he played the tour for a number of years afterwards, a painful hand injury and the interest of the Champions Club, Texas, which he runs with Jimmy Demaret, reduced his appearances. In his 10-year career, he won nearly $240,000, a figure which at the time had been exceeded by only 10 other professionals, although the boom in prize money has caused it to be passed by several since. He had a very fine Ryder Cup record, being undefeated in seven matches, but losing his single to Peter Mills in 1957 at Lindrick when the team he captained suffered the

record. The 1963 Lucky Championship was the 15th tournament win of his career, four of which had come consecutively in 1952. Burke turned professional in 1940, but it was 10 years later, after he had held several club jobs and served in the wartime US Marines, that he joined the circuit.

Burke, John IRISH
b. Lahinch, Co. Clare, 1900; d. 1972. South of Ireland 1928-31, 1939, 1941-6; Irish Close Amateur 1930-3, 1936, 1940, 1946-7, runner-up 1935, 1937; Walker Cup 1932; West of Ireland 1933-4, 1936, 1938, 1940-1; Irish Open Amateur 1947

Over a period of 21 years, John Burke was the most consistent amateur in Ireland. A big, strong man, bred among the Lahinch sandhills, he had a wide and handsome arc to his swing, and although he had complete command of every shot it was his length with wood out of thick clinging rough that was phenomenal. He was a tigerish match player whose pleasant character both on and off the course concealed his strong competitive spirit, proved by his record total of

touch with old friends and judging the form of the rising generation.

Burkemo, Walter AMERICAN
b. Detroit, Mich., 1918. Ryder Cup 1953; USPGA 1953, runner-up 1951, 1954, semi-finalist 1957

Distinguished by his notable record in matchplay, Burkemo was a capable golfer before World War II, good enough to be a medallist in the 1938 Public Links Championship. At that time he had not decided on golf as a career, and had seriously thought of becoming a professional boxer. After war service as an infantry sergeant, he turned professional in 1944, but it was not until 1950 that he tried his luck on the tour. Although he scored only one victory, the Mayfair Inn Open in 1957, he was a consistent money winner, showed an ability to be 'up' for major tournaments, and played regularly on the circuit for several years. His best performance in the US Open was to finish tied 4th in 1957 after a record-tying round of 65; the following year he finished 5th.

Jackie Burke with his victorious 1973 Ryder Cup team

Walter Burkemo

Burma

As in the Indian subcontinent and Sri Lanka (Ceylon), golf in Burma can be traced to the efforts of British administrators to lighten the burden of their colonial tasks. The early clubs were founded by, and for the exclusive use of, the British community. There are 50 courses in Burma but only one or two of international standard. In Rangoon, the capital, there are the Rangoon GC and three other courses: the Burma GC, 5,900 yd (5,395 m), par 71; the Defence Service GC, 6,000 yd (5,486 m); and the Syriam GC. The New Moulmein course, founded in 1935, is a 12-hole affair. The Namtu 9-hole course, revived after World War II by the Burmah Oil Corporation, was reported as almost derelict in the early 1970s.

Generally the best conditions for play are in the 'cool' weather season, November to February. In the hot season – March, April and May – the ground is hard and dry, providing a roll on the ball as long as 100 yd; in the monsoon month of August the ground is wet and boggy. The Burma Amateur and Open championships are held in December or January.

Burnham and Berrow GC ENGLAND
Burnham-on-Sea, Somerset. 27 holes

At a meeting attended by Thomas Holt and 11 others at the Royal Clarence Hotel, Bridgwater, in September 1890, a list of 51 people willing to become members of a proposed new club at Burnham was produced; in June 1891 the club was opened with J. H. Taylor as the first professional. The site chosen was a rabbit-infested stretch of sand-dune country next to the sea and the first course was therefore a modest one, although J. H. Taylor considered that it afforded splendid opportunity to develop his mashie play. In those days there were quite a number of blind holes but, as the course was

lengthened and increased to 18 holes on ground out beyond Berrow church, these were eliminated by degrees and the club quickly established a justifiable reputation as a fine test.

Its setting beside the Bristol Channel with distant views of Wales and the green hills of Somerset is ideal; Burnham is a good example of British seaside golf. The little town has been the home of two famous English golfing families: the Whitcombes (Reg won the 1938 Open Championship) were better known for their playing achievements, but eight Bradbeers became golf professionals and built up wonderful records of long service to their various clubs. The eight were all sons of the local baker and Bob, Fred, and Bob's son Richard, have served the club consecutively for more than half a century.

Burnham has more than once housed the British Ladies' Championship, the English Ladies', the English Amateur and the University match. Michael Bonallack won his second English title there in 1963 and Warren Humphreys became the youngest winner of the championship in 1971.

There has always been a strong link with women's golf largely through the influence of Dolly Fowler, a Burnham member who was English Champion in 1925; but it is equally well known for its annual staging of the West of England Open Amateur Championship whose large and varied entry is a tribute to the qualities, friendliness and hospitality of the club. A new 9-hole course was recently added by Fred Hawtree.

Burning Tree GC USA
Bethesda, Md. 18 holes; 6,662 yd (6,092 m); par 71

A rumour occasionally makes the rounds in Washington to the effect that Babe Zaharias once played golf at Burning Tree.

It has never really been confirmed, but everyone agrees that if she did, she was disguised as a man, because women simply are not allowed there. Women were once allowed in for the New Year's celebration, but the party was discontinued some years ago.

This is an ultra-exclusive men's club in Bethesda, Md., in the suburbs of Washington, D.C. Completely enclosed inside a chain-link fence, Burning Tree has been a retreat for Presidents, Cabinet officers, Congressmen and lobbyists. Presidents as far back as William Howard Taft have played golf there, Harry Truman played cards, and, of course Dwight Eisenhower was a frequent visitor, along with his cordon of secret servicemen carrying firearms in empty golf bags so as to be inconspicuous. They looked just what they were – secret servicemen with rifles in golf bags.

As might be expected, the condition of the course is immaculate. It is laid out on somewhat hilly woodland in the Potomac River valley, and from its back tees it measures 6,662 yd with a par of 71. It is 6,175 yd (5,646 m) from the front tees. The holes are routed through forests of pine and spruce, oak and maple, set close along the fairway, so that on most holes an accurate tee shot is essential. The course has just three par-5 holes, all under 500 yd (457 m) in length. The longest is the 16th, 496 yd (453 m). On the other hand, eight of its 11 par-4 holes are over 400 yd (366 m).

Burning Tree has a very 'clubby' atmosphere, and the big event of any week is the Sunday breakfast fourball. The breakfast gong rings at 8 a.m. sharp, and play begins at 8.45. The club was organized in 1923 and among its presidents have been Walter Tuckerman, the founder; Joseph E. Davies, a former ambassador to the Soviet Union; and John L. Sullivan, a former Secretary of the Navy.

Burnham and Berrow GC: the church in the middle of the course

The clubhouse at Burning Tree

Burton, Richard BRITISH
b. Darwin, Lancashire, 1907; d. 1974.
Ryder Cup 1935, 1937, 1949; British Open
1939

Dick Burton, the better known of two
Lancashire brothers who both distinguished
themselves in tournament golf, owes his
eminence to victory in the Open at St
Andrews, the last to be played before World
War II. During the war Burton served in the
RAF and lost valuable years during which he
might have exploited his position as champion. But afterwards he continued to be
prominent in golf and in 1949, aged 42, he
won a tournament at Brighton with rounds
of 68, 66, 64 and 68, his aggregate of 266
being then a record low total for a major
British 72-hole event. After holding
professional appointments in Lancashire and
Cheshire, Burton moved to London and for
many years was professional at Coombe Hill.

Bussell, Alan Francis BRITISH
b. Glasgow 1937. British Boys' 1954; British
Youths' 1956; Walker Cup 1957; *Golf
Illustrated* Gold Vase 1959

Top, Dick Burton

Above, Alan Bussell during the 1959 Brabazon
Trophy

After a highly successful beginning in
junior golf, Alan Bussell became one of the
best amateurs in Britain and in his Walker
Cup single at Minikahda in 1957 he beat
J. Campbell by 2 and 1. This, however, was
his only appearance in the match instead of
the first of many. After moving from Scotland
to the Nottingham area, business allowed
little time for golf outside local events and a
fine player who had represented Scotland was
thus lost to the international scene in Britain.

Busson, John Joseph BRITISH
b. Hinckley, Leicestershire, 1910. British
Professional Matchplay 1934; Ryder Cup
1935

John Busson, one of two golfing brothers
(Jack Busson was professional at Formby,
Lancashire, before moving to Walton Heath,
Surrey), was 23 and attached to Pannal GC
near Harrogate, Yorkshire, when he made
his name by winning the *News of the World*
Tournament which was later recognized as
the British PGA Matchplay Championship.
His reward a year later was a trip to New
Jersey with the British Ryder Cup team,
where he played top in both foursomes and
singles and gave Gene Sarazen a close match.
John Busson's best British Open Championship year was 1938, when he shared the lead
after 36 holes and struggled manfully
through the last day's gale to tie 4th.

Butler, Peter J. BRITISH
b. Birmingham 1932. British PGA Close
1963, runner-up 1965; runner-up British
Professional Matchplay 1964; Ryder Cup
1965, 1969, 1971, 1973; French Open 1968;
World (Canada) Cup 1969, 1973

A high-class British professional, who
throughout the 1960s built up a solid record
of success without ever quite carrying off a
big championship. He was not the most consistent of players, but he won a big tournament almost every year. He has a full loose
swing, but is double-jointed which enables
him to keep a good grip on the club throughout. His strongest point is his short game.

As a boy Butler was a good all-rounder; he
took readily to golf as an escape from a
clerical career when he joined the Harborne
club in Birmingham as a young man. It was
some time before he began to make an impact but, after increasing successes in the
Midlands he won the Swallow-Penfold
tournament in 1959 with a first prize of
£1,000, which was rare in those days. In
1964 he started to play in the US Masters
where he showed a fine capacity for keeping
going in years when British professionals
made no mark at all in the event. His best
performances were tied 13th in 1964 and

1966. He was in the English team in the 1969
World Cup and captain of PGA, 1971-2.

Bye
Informal match played over the holes remaining when the main match has been
completed. Thus if a match finishes with a
score of 6 and 5, a bye can be played over the
remaining five holes. If one side wins this
match 3 and 2, the players can then engage
on the bye-bye. Byes are never played in
serious golf but are often used in friendly
matches to renew interest in a round.

In a matchplay competition the advancement of a player from the first to second
round without meeting an opponent, in
order to achieve a proper balance in the
draw for which an exact multiple of four is
ultimately needed.

Byers, Eben M. AMERICAN
b. Allegheny, Pa., 1880. US Amateur 1906
Byers, only 5 ft 4½ in tall, lost to Louis
James and Walter Travis in successive US
Amateur finals and then in 1906 defeated the
Canadian champion, G. S. Lynn.

Top. Peter Butler recovers from a bunker during
the Agfa-Gevaert Golf Tournament, 1967

Above, Eben M. Byers

Opposite. Canada, Banff GC *above* and
Kelowna GC *below*

Caddie

Originally, and in some cases still, a man skilled in the game who for a fee carries a player's clubs and offers advice. The traditional golfer's companion, he is recognized by the Rules of Golf as part of the 'side'. His errors and omissions incur the same penalties as if committed by the player himself. The

word caddie is the Scots form of the French *cadet*, a term applied, for example, to the younger sons of French noble families who went to Edinburgh in the train of Mary Queen of Scots.

Caernarvonshire GC WALES

Conway (Aberconwy), Caernarvonshire. 18 holes

Within a mile of the heart of the historic town of Conway with its ancient castle and its suspension bridge, the Caernarvonshire GC enjoys a romantic setting between the

mountains and the sea. It is one of the oldest and best courses in Wales and there is evidence of golf having been played on The Morfa as long ago as 1869. A visitors' book provides definite proof that the present club was in existence in 1890. It had some notable early contacts with distinguished players when Alex Herd, British Open Champion in 1902, set up a course record of 71 in 1909, but a year later it was reduced to 65 by George Duncan during his appointment with the club. His engagement, however, was terminated in a dispute with the committee over Duncan's inclination to disappear on Saturday afternoons to play football for Conway Town (he had turned down an offer to play professional football

for Aberdeen before he moved south).

The course, an ideal site for army training, was requisitioned during both World Wars but made a fine recovery each time and became known as a characteristic test of seaside golf with a difficult finish among the gorse. It was some time before it was recognized as a championship course by the Welsh golfing bodies, but in recent years it has become a regular choice for national championships and in 1970 was the scene of the Martini professional tournament which ended in a tie between Peter Thomson and Doug Sewell.

Cairns, Lady Katherine Olive BRITISH
b. Bath, Somerset, 1912; d. 1955

Youngest daughter of the 4th Earl Cairns, she was an all-round sportswoman, playing tennis, squash, lacrosse and hockey with success, and also fencing. Her outstanding achievements in golf were the captaincy of the Curtis Cup team in 1952 – the first time Britain scored a victory in that event; chairing the Ladies' Golf Union Executive Council in 1953-4, during its reconstitution;

and the formation of the English Ladies' Golf Association. She reached the final of the English Ladies' Championship at Burnham and Berrow in 1949 when she was runner-up to Mrs A. C. Critchley, captained the British Isles in matches against France and Belgium, in 1953, and played in those matches, besides representing the British Isles against France in 1947 and 1951. She played for England in the Home International matches on seven occasions. During World War II she served with the ATS.

She died a few days after vacating the chair of the LGU Executive Council. Her intimate friends knew she was suffering from cancer, but she had kept the gravity of her condition from them.

Her golf was not pretty to watch, but she provided an object lesson in determination, and was a tremendous competitor.

Calamity Jane

The name of the famous, hickory-shafted blade putter used by Bobby Jones throughout his career. A model of it was later mass produced and marketed and is still available today. Its trademark consists of three bands of twine round the shaft.

Calcutta GC, Royal INDIA

Toliganj (Tollygunge), Calcutta. Old Course 18 holes; 6,968 yd (6,372 m); par 73

India was the first country outside Britain where golf was played and clubs were established. Royal Calcutta was founded in 1829, at Dum Dum, a northeast suburb of Calcutta and now the site of the city's international airport. In December 1830 *The Oriental Sporting Magazine* published names of 30 'subscribers to the Dum Dum Golfing Club', congratulating them 'on the prospect of seeing that noble and gentleman-like game established in Bengal'.

At some later date the club moved to the Maidan, the vast recreational expanse in the heart of the city, but soon returned to Dum Dum. But with more and more Europeans, particularly those living around Dum Dum and Barrackpore, setting up residence in the more salubrious south Calcutta area, a golf course was once again laid out in the Maidan.

The Royal's records are not traceable before 1874, but from that date they have been meticulously kept – and preserved. In 1874 a minute records that Royal Blackheath, England, presented Royal Calcutta with a medal to be competed for and this was reciprocated the next year by the presentation of a 'magnificent cup'. In 1876 there were 70 members and with golf spreading in

Top, Caddie: 'Caddie Willie', a lithograph by C. H. Robertson: *above,* a cartoon by Charles Crombie

Today's caddie

Opposite, Brian Barnes in the 1969 British Open

India, cups and trophies were presented to, and enthusiastically exchanged with, the Bangalore and the Madras clubs. In 1882 Royal Calcutta wrote to the Royal and Ancient, St Andrews, and asked them to accept a silver 'Cashmere Cup'. On 15 May 1883, the cup was dispatched by overland parcel post and received a month later, and the first Calcutta Cup event was played at the R. and A. in 1885. The first Amateur Golf Championship of India, a 54-hole strokeplay event, was played in 1892.

In 1895 Calcutta's second golf club, the Tollygunge, in the southern suburb of the same name, was established and the Royal became its neighbour towards the end of the century. The 'Royal' was conferred on the club in 1911 by King George V at the time of the Delhi Durbar. In 1938 Walter Hagen played an exhibition match at Royal Calcutta, and so did Pamela Barton. Both she and her sister Mervyn were given honorary membership of the Royal (the club does not admit lady members).

The first Indian to win the All-Indian in 1949 was Mohinder Bal, a Kashmiri (major tournaments in the subcontinent had previously been exclusively European affairs). In 1958, for the first time in 56 years, the venue for the All-India was changed; since that year it has been shared between Royal Calcutta and Delhi.

In the 1965 Indian Open at Royal Calcutta, history was made when Major P. G. ('Billoo') Sethi, India's outstanding amateur, beat the five-times British Open Champion, Peter Thomson, and twice equalled his own previous course record of 1959 by scoring 68 each in the first two rounds. Ben Arda, the Filipino Champion, broke the course record, with 67, when he won the 1969 Indian Open. It was again equalled by Richard McClean, of the United States in the 1972 Indian Open, which was won by

21-year-old Brian Jones of Sydney, Australia, playing in his first major golf tournament.

The land over which the Royal Calcutta course was laid out had originally been paddyfields and is flat. Successive committees have built mounds and planted thousands of trees, but the Royal's conspicuous features are its numerous lotus-filled tanks (large ponds). Of these hazards, the most notable are the two large tanks across the 10th fairway, a hole of 457 yd (418 m), as tough as could be found anywhere. From the tee the tiger line is over the first tank and must carry a full 230 yd (210 m). The safer route to the right leaves a very long second shot over the second tank, a good 100 yd (91 m) wide, to a small undulating green wickedly trapped all round. The out-of-bounds wall hugs the entire left flank of this excellent 10th hole.

Greens are small by modern standards but undulations make them tricky, and there is some nap. From the tee the course looks deceptively easy, but its strength lies in its par 4s, and to score requires good long and medium irons.

Caldwell, Ian BRITISH
b. Streatham, London, 1930. Walker Cup 1951, 1955; English Amateur 1961

A leading British amateur with a fine swing but one whose only championship victory came almost at the end of his international career. That was in the 1961 English Championship at Wentworth when he beat Gordon Clark at the 37th hole in the final, having led practically all day. He drove out of bounds, however, at the 35th and then had to hole from 12 ft to save himself on the 36th but he found the 37th green with a drive and a brassie, strokes of a true champion.

He had a distinguished Walker Cup singles record, halving with H. D. Paddock at Birkdale in 1951 and beating Dale Morey by one hole at St Andrews in 1955. He had a fine record, too, as a boy golfer and won well over half of the 64 matches he played for England.

Calgary GCC CANADA
Calgary, Alta. 18 holes; 6,260 yd (5,724 m); par 70

At the foothills of the Rocky Mountains, which are some 80 miles to the west and can be seen from the higher parts of the course, lies this lovely course designed in 1911 by the famous Scottish professional Willie Park, Jr. The club had its beginnings about 14 years earlier and had occupied two different sites before coming to the present one beside the Elbow River. At the second of these there were square, sand greens which had to be surrounded by wire to keep off the range cattle which abounded. The existing course represents a great transformation of the bare hardpan which the rolling foothills country originally presented. All the trees and shrubs resulted from an intelligent planting programme carried out over many years. And new topsoil had to be provided or formed by years of top dressing to achieve the fine, soft fairways that are now encountered. The course is always immaculately groomed. Its greens are small, but seldom is a level lie encountered on the fairways. It occupies two different levels, with a steep uphill climb at the start of each of the two 9s. One must be negotiated on the par-5 1st hole, but the physical effort of the 2nd has been eliminated by the provision of an escalator 330 ft (100 m) long between the 10th green and the 11th tee. Of national championships, the club has been the scene of the Canadian Amateur Championship in 1955, the Canadian PGA Championship in 1958, and the Canadian Ladies' Open Championship in 1964. It is the home club of three of Canada's long-established inter-

The clubhouse at the Royal Calcutta GC

Ian Caldwell during the 1961 English Amateur Championship

national players, Keith Alexander, Douglas Silverberg and Robert Wylie. Alexander was also Canadian Amateur Champion in 1960. The club's museum contains one of the best collections of ancient golf clubs and balls in Canada.

Campbell, Dorothy Bona BRITISH

(Mrs J. V. Hurd)
b. 1883; d. 1946. Scottish Ladies' 1905-6, 1908, runner-up 1907, 1909, semi-finalist 1903; British Ladies' 1909, 1911, runner-up 1908, semi-finalist 1904-6; US Women's Amateur 1909-10, 1924, runner-up 1920, semi-finalist 1928; Canadian Ladies' Open 1910-12

Dorothy Campbell won 11 major cham-

pionships, 10 of them between 1905 and 1912, and six of them in the United States and Canada. She was the first British-born player to win the US Women's Amateur Championship, and also the first to achieve the coveted double of the British and American titles in the same year – 1909, when the venues were Birkdale and Merion.

She had already become the outstanding woman player in Scotland, winning the Scottish Championship three times. She represented Scotland in home international matches; in 1928 she was placed 2nd on the Scottish side, and beat Cecil Leitch at the 20th. Dorothy Campbell was also one of the members of the 'English' team that played the Americans at Cromer in 1905.

At Birkdale in 1909, after defeating her third-round opponent on the 11th green, she forgot to report the result of the match to the LGU officials, who later met to discuss whether she had rendered herself subject to disqualification. While awaiting their decision she went out and practised lofting stymies. She was not disqualified and won her fourth-round match from Mrs Willock Pollen on the last green by brilliantly lofting a stymie. After winning the championship she was invited to America and subsequently only returned to Britain as a visitor.

In 1910 Dorothy Campbell was living in Canada and carried off the American and Canadian Open double. Her opponents in the finals of the British Championship were sisters, Florence and Violet Hezlet, in 1909 and 1911 respectively.

Dorothy Campbell's last championship was the US Women's Amateur in 1924 which she entered from Merion Cricket Club, and her opponent in that final was Mary K. Browne, a former American singles tennis champion.

Campbell, Sir Guy BRITISH

b. 1885; d. 1960

Campbell had a profound knowledge and love of golf, which was not surprising for his great-grandfather was Robert Chambers, an early chronicler of the game, and Campbell's distinctive style as a writer no doubt owed something to the poetic manner of his ancestor. Campbell was responsible for much of the earlier part of the official *History of Golf in Britain* which appeared in 1952. He became best known as a course designer. Killarney, West Sussex, North Berwick, Deal, Rye, Seacroft, and Trevose are examples of courses in the lay-out or redesign of which he had a hand. He was responsible with John Morrison for restoring Prince's after the war, and undertook work also in Switzerland, France and Holland. In 1920, after service in World War I, he joined the staff of *The Times* as a special correspondent. He helped Bernard Darwin when that writer was also competing in the championships he was covering, and he frequently contributed to magazines. His book, *Golf for Beginners*, 1922, had several novel aspects to it, specially in respect of the importance of practice. He also started his instruction with mastery of the putt on the grounds of 'learn to hit your short putt truly and on that foundation the rest of the edifice can be raised'. He also pressed the view that the stance had a great deal to do with the hitting or missing of iron shots. At Eton, Campbell had been captain of cricket and he was also a good oarsman, but golf was his real love and in 1907 he was semi-finalist in the British Amateur Championship. If he was steeped in the lore of St Andrews, he was a man of original ideas who never allowed himself to be restricted by convention. When World War II broke out he was nearly 55, but he was passed fit and managed to rejoin, as a 2nd lieutenant, the King's Royal Rifle Corps (the 60th).

Campbell, Joe AMERICAN

b. Anderson, Ind., 1935

Member of 1957 Walker Cup team who turned professional in 1958 and became fairly successful, winning three tournaments before injuring his back in 1966. He won $50,000 by holing in one during the 1960 Palm Springs Classic.

Campbell, William BRITISH

b. Glasgow 1900. Glasgow Amateur 1926, 1928, 1932, runner-up 1923; Walker Cup 1930; runner-up Scottish Amateur 1934

Campbell played for Scotland on many occasions and captained the side in 1935.

Campbell, William C. AMERICAN

b. West Virginia 1923. North and South Amateur 1950, 1953, 1957, 1961; W. Virginia Open 1950, 1953, 1955; Walker Cup 1951, 1953, 1955, 1957, 1965, 1967, 1971 (captain 1955); runner-up British Amateur 1954; Bob Jones Award 1956; Mexican Amateur 1956; US Amateur 1964, semi-finalist 1949, 1973

Top, Calgary GCC – the 18th hole and clubhouse

Above, Joe Campbell

ships in his own country, being beaten several times in the fifth round, until it began to look as though he would never win the title his game merited. Then, after a break of six years from the Walker Cup team, he won the 1964 title and began a new golfing lease of life.

In the British Amateur, too, Campbell frequently sailed through the earlier rounds easily only to come to grief before the semi-finals were reached. He maintained the highest traditions of amateur golf and was a much respected ambassador whether in the Eisenhower Trophy, Walker Cup, or Americas Cup events. He captained the victorious US Walker Cup side in 1955. He went to great lengths to ensure that his men adapted themselves to the strange con-ditions at St Andrews. He was a member of that team again when 16 years later it failed to learn that lesson in time. He served on the USGA executive committee, 1962-5, and the uniform ball committee 1970-1.

His first success in the game came at the age of 15 when he won a pro-am event with Sam Snead whose game he has much ad-

mired. His career at Princeton was inter-rupted by World War II in which he served as an infantry captain. He had an outstand-ing record as a collegiate, having a streak of 22 consecutive matchplay victories, and won the West Virginia Amateur 11 times. Campbell has been a member of the West Virginia legislature, is a qualified pilot, and is engaged in insurance brokerage.

Canada

Canadian golf is older than American; the game was introduced at Montreal in 1873, 15 years before the founding of America's first club at Yonkers, New York. There is little doubt that the game had been started unofficially in Canada many years before – possibly by the fur traders of Hudson's Bay Company– but the honour of being the first organized club on the North American con-tinent belongs to the Royal Montreal (Royal since 1884), which celebrated its centenary in due style in 1973.

As might be expected, the founders of golf in Canada (as nearly everywhere else in the world) were Scots. Montreal already had

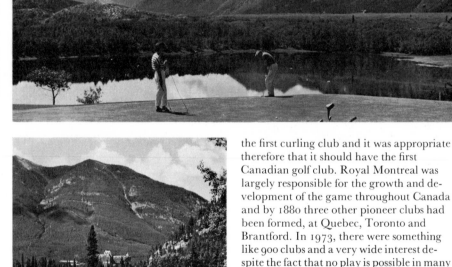

Campbell has been prominent in amateur golf on both sides of the Atlantic for the past 20 years. A tall, elegant swinger of the club, he has been one of those classical stylists – like his fellow countryman, Bill Hyndman – who have endured in the game long after others have begun to decline. He came close to joining the select band of those who have won the championships of both coun-tries, but his grip on the final of the 1954 British Amateur weakened, and Douglas Bachli took his chance to turn the tables on him. A player of fine intelligence with many outside interests, Campbell possessed per-haps too sensitive and aware a mind to be a ruthless competitor in his own cause. He has played in 28 Amateur champion-

the first curling club and it was appropriate therefore that it should have the first Canadian golf club. Royal Montreal was largely responsible for the growth and de-velopment of the game throughout Canada and by 1880 three other pioneer clubs had been formed, at Quebec, Toronto and Brantford. In 1973, there were something like 900 clubs and a very wide interest de-spite the fact that no play is possible in many areas during the long winter. The Canadian Open Championship, started in 1904, ranks high behind those of Britain and the United States, and Canada has had her share of great players.

If Royal Montreal did good work in guiding Canadian golf in the early days, that

Top, William C. Campbell at practice and, *above*, playing in the US Masters in 1972

Two of Canada's beautiful golf courses: *top*, Waterton Lake National Park, Alberta; *above*, Banff Springs Hotel, the 15th tee

role has long been assumed by the Royal Canadian Golf Association which was formed in 1896 with less than ten founder member clubs. The objects of the association were to promote interest in the game of golf; to establish and enforce uniformity in the rules of the game; and to control the Amateur, Ladies' and Open championships, the Inter-Provincial and other matches and competitions. Today the Canadian Ladies' Golf Union and the Canadian Professional Golfers' Association are also concerned with golf affairs in Canada. The first Amateur Championship was played at Royal Ottawa in 1895.

Canada Cup see WORLD CUP

Canberra GC, Royal AUSTRALIA
Yarralumla, Canberra. 18 holes; 7,116 yd (6,507 m)

Royal Canberra was founded in 1926 but was forced to move from its site on the banks of the Molonglo River when the Federal Government decided in 1959 that it would implement the lake scheme originally proposed by Burley Griffin, the designer of the national capital. In 1960, despite bitter opposition from some Canberra residents who claimed that the area should be preserved as a park and for public recreation, the club was granted a 50-year lease to build a new course at Yarralumla.

This was done to the design of John Harris at Westbourne Woods, near Government House, on 228 acres (92 ha) of what was formerly sheep country and clay pan. The area, however, had gradually been developed by Forestry School students. A strong argument in favour of giving the area to golf was that there would be less danger from fire. Although Harris had to design the course around rare trees, whose removal was prohibited under the terms of the lease, the trees generally give the golf a strong character together with huge, two-level greens on most holes.

The club became 'Royal' in 1955. Apart from New South Wales GA and LGU events, the Dunlop International was held at the new course in 1967 and 1970, and the Australian Professional Championship in 1969.

Canterbury GC USA
Warrenville, Ohio

Although it has held the US Open and the Amateur twice, Canterbury, 10 miles from Cleveland, is not quite as well known as its virtues warrant. Inverness, its Ohio neighbour, is more renowned, but those who are well acquainted with both courses

usually rate Canterbury a little higher. It is an undulating course with some spectacular holes (that do not seem so at first glimpse) and one of the most formidable finishes in American golf. There used to be a saying that if you parred the last 5 holes at Canterbury on every round, you were sure to win whatever championship you were playing.

Both Opens at Canterbury required play-offs. In 1940, Lawson Little won in an 18-hole play-off with Gene Sarazen, who had finished in a tie in the championship 18 years after first winning it at Skokie, Ill. In 1946, Lloyd Mangrum won from Byron Nelson and Vic Ghezzi after the three of them still were tied at the end of the first 18-hole play-off. In that second play-off, Lloyd was trailing Ghezzi by 3 strokes and Nelson by 2 with four holes to play. Just as he teed up, a storm broke with deafening thunder, frightening flashes of lightning, and drenching rain. Lloyd finished birdie, par, birdie, birdie, sinking a good putt to win on the water-logged home green after the other two had holed out in 73. In 1964, William C. Campbell had the distinction of becoming the last matchplay US Amateur Champion for a few years by defeating Ed Tutwiler 1 up in the final and in August 1973, Jack Nicklaus, by winning the USPGA Championship there, secured his 14th major championship victory, thereby breaking the record of Bobby Jones.

Cape GC, Royal SOUTH AFRICA
Wynberg, Cape Province

The pioneer golf club in South Africa and the oldest on the continent. Founded in 1885 thanks to General Torrens, commanding the British troops in South Africa, it was situated at first at Waterloo Green in front of the military camp at Wynberg. The course was somewhat rough by modern

A scene at the Canterbury GC

standards as the first monthly medal competition was won by General Torrens with a score of 94, and handicaps as high as 65 are on record at that time. The course is flat but provides a good test. Lack of natural undulations is made up for by clever design and by the prevalence of winds. The stress is on accuracy and the ability to place long shots, both from the tee and through the green. A good example of this is the 5th, chosen by Bobby Locke for inclusion in his ideal course. In 1891 the course moved to Rondebosch Common, and this lay-out also seems to have had its hazards for the best score in that year was 93 by a player whose handicap was plus 15, and bogey for the course was over 100. In 1905 the land at Wynberg was purchased and the club moved back. The Commonwealth Team Championship was held there in 1959.

Capilano GCC CANADA
West Vancouver, B.C. 18 holes; 6,538 yd (5,978 m); par 72

Internationally known for its scenic grandeur, the course overlooks the city and harbour of Vancouver five miles away from its vantage point on the north shore of Burrard Inlet. The attractive clubhouse is gracefully poised on a 700-ft (213-m) elevation. It is surrounded on all sides below by the course, which was hewn from a forest of giant Douglas fir and other conifers. By their very size they create the impression that the fairways are narrow when, in fact, they are of generous width. Their awesomeness has been relieved by plantings of willows and flowering dogwood. Throughout the course are many openings in the woods offering breathtaking views of the snow-capped mountains of the Coastal Range towering close to the north, and of the waters of the inlet below to the south.

The course was built in 1936 by Stanley Thompson. His main problem was one of levels and contours, for the whole of the course lies below the clubhouse. His solution is a tribute to his skill. The long opening hole descends sharply, as it must. Then after three holes which maintain approximately the level of the first green come two more which plunge down to the lowest part of the course. The 7th and 8th holes play out and back before the inevitable ascent starts at the 9th. From there through the 12th hole the climb continues, but so gradually as scarcely to be noticed, pausing only for the architect's favourite hole. This is the beautiful 155-yd (142-m) 11th, which requires a full carry across a pond in front of a green in a cathedral-like setting and slightly below the level of the tee. The remainder of the

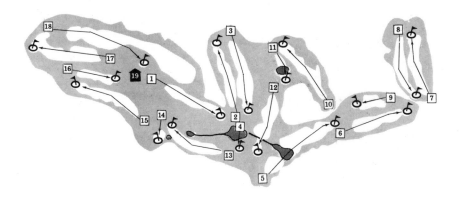

climb is reserved for the final hole, which provides a test of stamina as it rises for the whole of its length of 575 yd (526 m) to a plateau green immediately below the clubhouse. Throughout the course advantage has been taken of many fine mountain streams and three natural lakes to enhance golfing interest. First impressions notwithstanding, the course is a friendly one on which good scoring is within the reach of even the ordinary golfer. The fact that it is not often achieved is largely due to the subtle contouring of the large and rolling greens. They yield their secrets reluctantly, and then only to those who know them well.

The record for the course was established at 64 by Bob Fleming of Victoria in the British Columbia Amateur Championship of 1966. Because it does not lend itself to crowds, the course has not often been used for national championships, but it was the scene of the 1952 Canadian Amateur Championship and of the 1971 Canadian Ladies' Championship.

Jock McKinnon, who came from Angus, Scotland, at the age of 21, has been the club's only professional since it opened in 1937. By 1959 he had established a remarkable eclectic record for the course which he never bettered afterwards. Possibly it is a world record for a course of comparable length. He has played four of the holes in one, thirteen in two, and only the long, uphill 18th hole in three, for a total of 33 for the course.

Carey, John BRITISH

John Carey was one of the best known of the early caddies who carried for Willie Park Jr during his heyday. 'Fiery' was the calmest of men and his nickname did not refer to his disposition but to his ruddy complexion which contrasted strongly with the light Balmoral bonnet he always wore.

He was the most efficient of caddies and it was said that his services were worth several shots a round on the courses near North Berwick which he knew so well. He never seemed to offer advice but, when asked, merely handed over the club which was nearly always right.

Carlander, Stig Gunnar SWEDISH

b. 1937. Swedish Amateur 1954; runner-up Norwegian Open Amateur 1955; runner-up Scandinavian Open Amateur 1956; Swedish Open Amateur Strokeplay 1956, 1960, runner-up 1959; Eisenhower Trophy 1958, 1964; European Amateur Team Championship 1959, 1961

Carlander is regarded as one of Sweden's greatest golfing talents. At 16 he was the youngest-ever Swedish Amateur Champion, in 1954. He represented his country 30 times between 1953 and 1964, being in the winning Swedish side in the European Amateur Team Championship in 1959 and 1961. Carlander played for Scandinavia against Scotland in 1956, 1958, 1960 and 1962, and for the rest of Europe against the British Isles in 1960 and 1962.

Carlsbad see KARLOVY VARY GC

Carner, Mrs D. R. (née JoAnne Gunderson) AMERICAN

b. Massachusetts 1939. US Junior Girls' 1956; US Women's Amateur 1957, 1960, 1962, 1966, 1968, runner-up 1956, 1964; Curtis Cup 1958, 1960, 1962, 1964; Women's Western Amateur 1959; Women's Trans-Mississippi Amateur 1961; quarter-finalist British Women's Amateur 1963; US Women's Open 1971, low amateur 1962

The outstanding woman amateur in the United States with the exception of Babe Zaharias before she turned professional, Mrs Carner won a record number of five national amateur titles before herself turning professional. While still at high school near Washington in 1956 she won the junior title and a few weeks later found herself 4 up with 11 to play against the Canadian, Marlene Stewart, who had already won the Canadian and British championships that year. The occasion caught up with her and she lost by 2 and 1. In winning her first title the following year, she became the second youngest after Beatrice Hoyt in 1896 ever to win the championship. JoAnne Gunderson, as she then was, had great physique and was an expert in physical training; this enabled her to hit the ball vast distances with little more than a half-swing that left the clubhead pointing to the sky at the top. She relied on her footwork and strong wrists to get her length. An extrovert personality, she was strong in matchplay. Her decision to leave the amateur ranks came comparatively late, in 1969, when she was 30, prompted as much as anything by the need for a fresh challenge to her outstanding talent.

She joined the tour, travelling with her husband in a luxurious trailer; her first victory was the Wendell-West Open at

Ocean Shores, Wash., in 1970, and she finished 11th that year in the official prize winner's list. Great though her talent is, she is not a willing practiser, adopting the view that everything will click into place on the first tee. But when she did get down to it she was irresistible, as she showed in winning the 1971 US Women's Open.

Carnoustie GC SCOTLAND

Links Parade, Carnoustie, Angus. 18 holes; 6,701 yd (6,127 m); par 70 (medal); Championship Course 7,200 yd (6,584 m); Burnside Course 18 holes; 6,398 yd (5,850 m); par 72

The Championship Course is one of the sternest tests to be found anywhere, where

Course plan of the Capilano GCC, West Vancouver

Mrs D. R. Carner plays out of a bunker at Lindrick during the 1960 Curtis Cup

length, difficulty and exposure to wind are concerned. Its turf is of the finest and no two holes resemble each other. The most violent contrast is provided by the 10th hole, whose island green, which originally formed part of a garden, more resembles an inland hole. But in other ways there is great variety; holes are played to all points of the compass, and there is every kind of hazard: dunes at the 2nd and 15th, for example, the Barry burn at the 10th and the last three holes, out-of-bounds from the 6th to the 9th, trees at the 3rd and 14th, heather everywhere except the start and finish. The 6th is a notorious and invulnerable par 5 with out-of-bounds and stream threatening. Connoisseurs of shorter holes may appreciate the subtleties of the 5th with its dogleg and steep, two-banked green, which baffled Hogan in the 1953 Open until he chipped in for a birdie in the final round and shook off the last doubt about his victory.

It is the last three holes that have given Carnoustie its notoriety with the Barry burn threatening on six occasions and providing a 25-ft (7.6-m) wide barrier to the last green. The motto on the Carnoustie banner – 'Stay the Course' – was well chosen. With a military firing range flanking one side and railway sheds the other, and with the severity of its finish, it is not surprising that the course's reputation inspires respect rather than affection, yet it remains a pleasant course for the higher handicap player who is not afraid of length. The foundation of the course's fame was built by generations of holidaymakers who continue to flock to the course. Many of the bunkers are designed for the better golfer, and the annual summer competition for the Craw's Nest Tassie draws a huge entry.

Golf is indeed the birthright of the town. First mention of the game there was four centuries ago when a certain Sir Robert Maule, described as 'a gentleman of comlie behaviour, of hie stature, sanguine in colour both of hyd and haire, and colarique of nature, exercisit the gowf'. It was early in the last century that holiday golf began to develop, the first club, an artisan one, opening in 1842. In its original form the course consisted of 10 holes laid out by Allan Robertson; it was extended to 18 by Old Tom Morris some 25 years later, but it was not until James Braid undertook the tightening up of the course in 1926 that it became ready to receive the Open Championship.

Those were the days of the money matches between such giants of the game as Archie Simpson, Willie Park and Willie Campbell; it was here also that Young Tom Morris at the age of 16 beat all the leading profes-

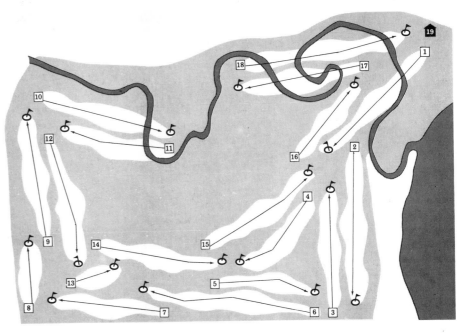

sionals. The number of Carnoustie's sons – around 300 – who emigrated towards the end of the century is evidence that golf had long been established there. Most went to the United States, among them three brothers, Alex, Willie, and Macdonald Smith who did much to spread the gospel. The first two won US championships, but Mac was cheated of more than one.

Carnoustie in its four Opens has not once failed to produce high drama. The tragic finish of José Jurado and Macdonald Smith in 1931, the year of Tommy Armour's victory, the splendour of Henry Cotton's final 71 in torrential rain six years later, and Gary Player's dramatic eagle at the 14th in 1968 which drew him clear of

Nicklaus – all these, and the quality of the champions, reflect in a way the challenge of a great course. But Carnoustie will remember longest the calculated triumph of Ben Hogan. In 1953 he completed his Grand Slam reducing his score in every round under new and alien conditions to him, so that he finished 4 strokes ahead of the field. The reception from the townsfolk, and from thousands further afield, that greeted him as he walked in a daze from the 18th green was emotional. It completed his triumph; it also raised the stature of the course to a new level and attracted golfers from all over the world.

Three Amateur championships have been held there, in 1947 (W. P. Turnesa), 1966

Top, Carnoustie GC, a view of the 18th hole

Above, a plan of Carnoustie's Championship Course

(R. E. Cole over 18 holes) and 1971 (S. Melnyk). The gap of 20 years between the first and second may be accounted for primarily by the course's inaccessibility, a state of affairs that has been put right by the opening of the Forth and Tay road bridges. The two courses, the Championship and the Burnside, are held in trust by the town council and managed by a joint committee in which are represented the three clubs – Carnoustie, Caledonian, and Dalhousie – which together with Carnoustie Ladies' Club enjoy the use of the course.

Carr, Joseph Benedict IRISH

b. Dublin 1922. Irish Open Amateur 1946, 1950, 1954, 1956; Walker Cup 1947, 1949, 1951, 1953, 1955, 1957, 1959, 1961, 1963, 1967 (captain 1965, non-playing captain 1967); *Golf Illustrated* Gold Vase 1951; British Amateur 1953, 1958, 1960, runner-up 1968, semi-finalist 1951-2, 1954; Irish Amateur Close 1954, 1957, 1963-5, 1967; leading amateur British Open 1956, 1958; Walter Hagen Award 1957; runner-up Dunlop Masters Tournament 1958; semi-finalist US Amateur 1961; Eisenhower Trophy 1966, 1968; Bob Jones Award 1967

The biggest name in British and Irish amateur golf between the end of World War II and the rise of Michael Bonallack in the mid-1960s. Joe Carr's three victories in the British Amateur Championship were unparalleled at the time. He took part in every Walker Cup match after the war until 1967, a record unequalled by any player on either side, and was captain in 1965 and 1967. During the same period he represented Ireland in the home internationals and his supremacy in his native Ireland is shown by some 30 national and regional titles. In 1966 and 1968 he captained the British and Irish team in the World Amateur Team Championship. He had great flair for

matchplay, his ability to recover from the desperate situations into which his driving sometimes landed him making him a master of the counter-thrust. His record in individual championships was better than in team events.

Although matchplay was his forte, he also had a redoubtable record as a stroke player. In his prime he held his own with professionals, leading the field in the Dunlop Masters Tournament at Portmarnock in 1959 and being beaten only in a great finish by Christy O'Connor. Similarly in 1963 at Royal Birkdale in freakish conditions he was within sight of winning the PGA championship. Three times he has been leading amateur in the British Open, remaining among the leaders in 1960 until a rainstorm led to the cancellation of a final round in which he had started 3, 4, 4. He won the Berkshire Trophy in 1959, and was a frequent competitor in the Lytham and Brabazon trophies.

Even so, he was, above all, a great matchplayer – bold, ruthless in victory, never accepting defeat until it was inevitable.

Although he seldom looked convincing on the greens and at one time took to putting with a 3 iron, his short pitching and chipping were very fine, and there have been few professionals who were his equal in bunker play. In the best Irish tradition his style was unorthodox with a tendency to flail at the ball and to 'lean into' the shot. He was slender

and wiry, but his height and an immensely strong pair of hands endowed him with great power.

In matches all over the world – whether against the United States, the Commonwealth, or Europe – his open and vital personality attracted crowds as much as the pure excitement of watching him play. His tall, lanky figure topped by a white cap with green pom-pom on it became familiar to a worldwide audience, and his engaging Irish manner combined with his love of battle specially endeared him to Americans, who in 1967 awarded him the Bob Jones trophy for sportsmanship in golf.

The first of his British Amateur victories came at Hoylake in 1953 at the end of a week during which he had consistently failed to find his form and frequently came close to defeat. But in the final against Harvie Ward he established a 3-up lead in the first six holes and was never brought back to all square. It was perhaps his finest victory. His second victory in 1959 over Alan Thirlwell ended a comparatively lean spell in which it looked as though he had already reached his peak. This would not have been surprising for although he was only 36 at the time, he had been in first-class golf 17 years, having won his first championship, the East of Ireland, in 1941. He had made special preparation for the Amateur in 1958, concentrating on driving, short pitching and putting, the latter being the weakest department of his game. The policy was triumphantly successful.

He found it harder to compete for a team than he did in individual championships, although he was very much a team man whose infectious high spirits were an asset to any international side. His early years in the Walker Cup team were successful, specially in partnership with Ronnie White, but his singles record was not as impressive as his own personal record would suggest. One notable victory was in 1959 at Muirfield when he defeated Charlie Coe after a schoolboy had stepped on his putter and broken it. He completed the match putting with a no. 3 iron. When his second son, Roddy, was chosen for the 1971 Walker Cup, it meant that between 1947 and 1971, only in 1969 was there no Carr in the British team.

Carr, Roderick J. IRISH

b. Sutton, Dublin, 1950. East of Ireland 1970; runner-up North of Ireland 1970; Turnberry Foursomes (with J. Martin) 1970; Walker Cup 1971; West of Ireland 1971

The second son of Joe and 'Dor' Carr, Roddy was brought up in a family that lives and breathes golf. His choice for a place in

Carnoustie Championship Course: the 6th hole. one of the longest and toughest of the course

Joe Carr

the Walker Cup team was something of an inspiration, for he had not made much impact outside Ireland, yet he played a crucial part in the match; still only 20, he won 3½ points out of 4, his three victories all coming on the last green. Carr played for Ireland in the home internationals and was also a member of the British and Irish youth team. He hits an outstandingly long ball and is a first-class putter, but since turning professional in the autumn of 1971, he has had to wait some time before showing the ability he displayed as an amateur.

Carry

The distance from the point at which the ball is struck to the point at which it first touches the ground. The word is also used in the sense of succeeding in 'making the carry', which is one of the commonest and most challenging hazards in golf. The distance necessary to hit across a lake or clear a ravine may also be called the 'carry'.

Carter, Edwin J. AMERICAN

b. Marietta, Ohio, 1907

A dynamic man who served as tournament manager of the USPGA during the late 1950s and contributed greatly towards making the tournament circuit a multi-million-dollar business. Carter, whose sports background included football at Northwestern, had sold insurance and cars, had been a department-store buyer and merchandiser and had run a string of weekly newspapers before moving into golf. After leaving the PGA to do full-time promotion work on his own, Carter continued to serve as manager or business manager of the PGA championship each year. He suffered a mild heart attack in 1964 but was soon back in action. He was once described as the only man who could stand still and look as if he was moving.

Casera, Aldo ITALIAN

b. San Remo 1920. Italian Open 1948; Italian Professional 1948-9, 1956; Swiss Open 1950

With Grappasonni and Angelini, Casera was one of the leading Italian professionals of the post-World War II era. He was not as successful as the other two but won both the Italian Open and Professional championships, played throughout Europe and was in the Italian World (Canada) Cup team. He was club professional at Barlassina for many years.

Casper, William Earl, Jr AMERICAN

b. San Diego, Cal., 1931. US Open 1959, 1966; Vardon Trohpy 1960, 1963, 1965-6, 1968; Ryder Cup 1961, 1963, 1965, 1967, 1969, 1971, 1973; Canadian Open 1967; US Masters 1970

From the time that he won the US Open at Winged Foot in 1959, Casper was the most consistent player on the American tour over a period of 10 to 12 years. During that time, he inevitably suffered by comparison with the Big Three (Palmer, Player and Nicklaus) when it came to championship victories and often he did not receive the recognition he deserved.

He turned professional in 1954 while still in the US Navy and in the next 12 years won 33 titles or tournaments. This was the time when professional golf was reaping the full benefit of a rapidly expanding commercial market and Casper was one of those to profit most. When he won the Open in 1959, it was something of a surprise since he was not quite fully established in the front rank and there were those who felt his golf was based on a magical short game, though he had finished 2nd in the USPGA Championship the previous year. In the four rounds he needed only 112 putts. In 1968, one of his greatest years, the IBM

computer showed him to be the leading putter, but he had long since become a master in the control of his long game as well. This, together with the shedding of about 40 lb in weight on a much publicized anti-allergy diet, was responsible for the supreme consistency of a swing which had a superb, rounded and rhythmic flow. He also became one of the fastest players in America.

With an admirable equanimity of mind, a reputation as a sober dresser, and a lack of exhibitionism, he was never quite seen by the Americans as their hero. In a country where the extrovert is king, these were factors which at times seemed to work against him but his second victory in the US Open at the Olympic Club, San Francisco, in 1966 had an almost fictional climax. It will be remembered as much for being one of Palmer's most bewildering failures on the course where, 11 years before, the unknown Jack Fleck beat the seemingly invincible Ben Hogan.

It was some time before the 1966 Open boiled down to Palmer v. Casper and some time before anyone gave Casper more than the ghost of a chance. With 9 holes to play in the final round, Palmer was 7 strokes ahead of Casper and 9 ahead of Nicklaus. Palmer had turned in 32 and going to the short 13th was still six in front. He lost another stroke by missing the green there but five shots still seemed as good as 50. If he had been content to cruise home, Casper would have had no chance but Palmer being Palmer was

Joe Carr and his son Roddy

Ed Carter

Billy Casper in action at Wentworth in 1970

anxious to beat Ben Hogan's 1948 Open record of 276 and it was this which led him to disaster.

The play-off followed somewhat the same pattern as the last round. Palmer, out in 33, took a 2-stroke lead but Casper gained 2 strokes on the 11th, Palmer dropped 4 strokes to par at the next 5 holes and Casper had completed one of the most remarkable recoveries in the history of the game. Casper's total was 278 (69, 68, 73, 68).

The year 1966 was notable for Casper in other ways. He was elected player of the year, finished leading money winner and topped $100,000 in a year for the first time. His official winnings were $121,000, $129,000 in 1967 and then $205,000 in 1968 when he was again player of the year in America and leading money winner.

His official earnings dropped in 1969, which was the year when he missed a great chance of winning the US Masters, but there was some consolation in winning the Alcan Championship at Portland, Ore., in September with another extraordinary finish. He made up 7 shots on Lee Trevino over the

last three holes to win by 1 stroke with a total of 274.

He was second in the money list in 1970 but the highlight of his year was his victory in the US Masters at Augusta. He had several times previously been accused of playing the course conservatively – particularly the par 5s – and the previous year it had proved his undoing, but a change of attitude allied to some fine golf enabled him to beat Gene Littler in a play-off.

Casper has played in Britain many times, and is a member of the British PGA, but oddly enough without winning a tournament. He is married with five children and is a member of the Church of Jesus Christ of Latter Day Saints (Mormon) and preaches

Billy Casper recovering from a bunker at Wentworth during the semi-finals of the World Matchplay Championship, 1967

regularly at their meetings. He has had many interests outside the United States; for years he visited the troops in Vietnam, and he also paid many visits to Morocco to give lessons to the King.

Casual Water

Any temporary accumulation of water

which is visible before or after a player takes his stance and which is not a hazard of itself or is not a water hazard. Snow and ice are either casual water or loose impediments, at the option of the player. The most common cause is flooding after heavy rain.

Cater, J. Robin BRITISH
b. Edinburgh 1919. Semi-finalist British Amateur 1952: Walker Cup 1955

The peak of Robin Cater's career lasted the comparatively short time of five years. But Cater, a good all-round golfer, achieved much within that period, reaching the semi-final of the 1952 British Amateur and the 1954 Scottish Amateur championships, playing for Scotland without interruption

Top. Casual Water: P. Toussaint finds some in a bunker

Above, Alec Caygill

from 1952 to 1956, and taking part in the 1955 Walker Cup match.

Caven, John BRITISH
b. Castle Kennedy, Wigtownshire, 1891. Runner-up British Amateur 1922; Walker Cup 1922; semi-finalist Scottish Amateur 1925

Besides being runner-up to Ernest Holderness in the 1922 British Amateur, this Scottish player reached the sixth round in 1924.

Caygill, Gordon Alexander BRITISH
b. Appleby, Westmorland, 1940. British Youths' Open 1960, 1962; Assistant Professional 1963; Rediffusion Tournament 1963; joint winner Martini International Tournament 1969; Penfold Tournament 1969; Ryder Cup 1969

Not constitutionally robust and plagued for a time by ulcers, Alec Caygill faded from the scene just when he appeared to be breaking through. Showed much courage in returning to the circuit and playing well enough in 1969 to be picked for the Ryder Cup.

Centre Shaft

A club with the shaft inserted in the middle of the head instead of the heel. The idea came from America at the turn of the century in the shape of the 'Schenectady' putter used by Walter Travis in winning the 1904 British Amateur Championship. This was named after its place of origin, consisted of a rectangular piece of wood, with straight sides and had the shaft set vertically into the centre of it. Its legality was disputed between the US Golf Association and the Royal and Ancient GC; it was banned in Britain though not in America. The British ban lasted until 1949, after which centre-shafted putters quickly became popular.

From left to right: a Schenectady putter of 1904; a centre shafted putter; and an adjustable centre-shafted putter of 1904

Cerda, Antonio ARGENTINIAN
b. 1921. Runner-up British Open 1951;
World (Canada) Cup 1953

Tony Cerda, one of several great golfers
from the Argentine, was a great favourite
with spectators during several years when he
competed on the British circuit. In the 1951
Open at Portrush he made a brilliant effort
in the last round to overhaul Max Faulkner
and looked like doing so until a 6 at the
short 14th killed his chances. Cerda and de
Vicenzo won the World Cup for Argentina
in 1953 and were runners-up in 1954.

Cerrudo, Ron AMERICAN
b. Palo Alto, Cal., 1945. Runner-up British
Amateur 1967

After a distinguished amateur career, at
the peak of which he was chosen for the 1967
US Walker Cup team, and lost to Bob
Dickson in one of the fastest-played finals of
the British Amateur Championship, Ron
Cerrudo turned professional the same year
and soon made his mark.

Cerrudo won the final tournament of the
1968 season, his first full one on the Ameri-

can circuit, and had another victory in 1970,
bringing his total prize money in less than
three years to $100,000. But later that year
Cerrudo had an operation on an interverte-
bral disc and did not return for tournament
play until the 1971 season.

Ceylon see SRI LANKA

Chadwick, Elizabeth (Mrs A. D. Pook)
BRITISH
b. Inverness 1943. Runner-up English
Ladies' 1963; Vagliano Cup 1963, 1967;
British Ladies' 1966-7; Curtis Cup 1966;
Commonwealth Tournament 1967

Elizabeth Chadwick came to the fore
when she reached the final of the English

Ladies' Championship at Liphook in 1963.
Her subsequent victories in the British
Ladies' in 1966 and 1967 were rewards for
dedication and determination. Above average height and, in her teens, hampered by a
tendency to overweight, she worked at her
golf assiduously. At Ganton in 1966, after
taking 48 for the first 9 holes of the first

qualifying round, including a 10 at the 7th,
where she incurred a 2-stroke penalty and
was twice bunkered, she was one under an
average of 4s in the final for 16 holes when
she defeated Vivien Saunders.

Next year at Royal St David's, Harlech,
her defence of the British title was helped by
the excellence of her putting. In her quarter-
final with Ann Irvin, Miss Chadwick had
single putts on 10 greens.

Having achieved her ambition of winning
the championship, and having proved that
the feat was no fluke by retaining the title
the following year, Elizabeth Chadwick
retired from serious golf.

Chambers, Doris Elaine BRITISH
b. Liverpool. British Ladies' 1923, semi-
finalist 1909; Curtis Cup (captain) 1934,
1936, 1948

Britain's greatest golfing ambassadress.
Her services to the game were recognized
when she received the OBE in 1960. She
began playing in championships when the
founders of the Ladies' Golf Union were still
active organizers, and has continued to
uphold the principles that inspired them.
She was made vice-president of the LGU in
1952, and was president in 1961-3.

When the LGU sent their first touring
team abroad, to South Africa in 1933, she
was an automatic choice as captain. She
also captained Britain's Curtis Cup teams in
1934, 1936 and 1948. Besides leading the
British side in its away match with Canada

in 1934, she played for Britain on that
occasion. She represented England in many
home international matches.

Her outstanding achievement was winning the British Ladies' Championship at
Burnham and Berrow in 1923, when she
defeated one of her closest friends, Mrs Allan
Macbeth, by two holes in the final over 36
holes. She had previously won a bronze
medal by reaching the semi-final of the
British Ladies' at Birkdale in 1909. Her feat
at Burnham was hailed both as the 'triumph
of a promising young golfer' and as a
'Cheshire veteran's success'. No one enjoyed
the joke more than the champion.

Besides acting as the official LGU relations officer with overseas unions and clubs,
and entertaining overseas visitors, she has
given much time and support to the encouragement of young players.

Champions GC USA
Houston, Tex. 36 holes

It was by no means an accident that the
1969 US Open Championship was played
over the Cypress Creek course of the Champions GC, for this lush golf course set on
gently rolling woodland north of Houston
was built with this aim in mind. Into it went
the accumulated knowledge and instincts of
two superior tournament professionals –
Jimmy Demaret and Jackie Burke – who
had dreamed and planned such a course for
15 years before the bulldozers moved in.
They had played around the world and felt
that they knew the qualities that made some
courses good and others not so good; and
with the help of Ralph Plummer, the architect, they tried to blend these features into
their creation. They did not attempt to
re-create other holes contour for contour,
because they realized that a hole that may
be playable on the Pacific Coast might not
be workable in a Texas forest. Rather, they
attempted to work toward their concept of
what made for sound and interesting golf.

When the course was opened for play in
1960 it was called by many the finest course
in the Southwest, which is probably an
exaggeration. Still, it is a strong test which
was the site of the Houston Champions
International for a number of years, the
1967 Ryder Cup match, and the 1969 US
Open, won by Orville Moody. All these
have been played over the Cypress Creek
course, which was stretched out to 7,166 yd
(6,552 m) for the Ryder Cup match but
played at 6,986 yd (6,388 m) for the Open.
(A second course, the Jackrabbit – named
after a road that borders many of its holes –
was designed by George Fazio, and has a
good deal of charm and style.)

Ron Cerrudo during the British Amateur
Championship of 1967

Elizabeth Chadwick during the Avia Ladies
Foursomes at Berkshire GC in 1967

The first impression of Champions is of the trees. Demaret claims there are 70,000, mostly pine. Best known of them all is a little pink-flowering mimosa planted squarely in a greenside bunker at the 17th hole. The impish Demaret, called by Burke the resident nurseryman, planted it there for reasons best known to himself. Other trees are used to route certain holes into doglegs.

Two of the strongest holes on the course are the 4th and 12th, which are fairly long par 3s. The 12th cost Miller Barber 2 strokes in the last round of the 1969 Open, when he made 5 on it after Moody made 3. A pond crowds against the left side and curls partially in front of the green, and pines are close to the right. The 4th is very flexible and can play from 190 to 220 yd (174-200 m). It calls for a shot across a wild, snake-infested dry gulch which has defeated two of the finest players of any age. Lee Trevino hit his tee shot into that gulch in the first round of the 1969 Open, slipped as he tried to play out, injured himself, and missed the 36-hole cut. In 1971 in the Champions International, Ben Hogan hit four successive shots into the gulch, made 11 on the hole, apologized to his playing partners, said, 'Never grow old' to a friend, and withdrew after completing the first nine.

Championship Belt

The original prize awarded to the winner of the British Open Championship when it started in 1860. Presented by the Earl of Eglinton, it was an ornate piece of work made out of red morocco leather and silver plates. Under the regulations of the Championship, the winner held it for a year but, in the event of the same player winning it for three successive years, it automatically became his property. Young Tom Morris achieved this in 1868, 1869 and 1870. The belt remained in the possession of the Morris family until Old Tom Morris presented it to the Royal and Ancient at St Andrews where it remains to this day.

Chantilly GC FRANCE
Chantilly, Oise. 27 holes

Golf de Chantilly, at the famous racing town 20 miles north of Paris, is on land once owned by the Duc d'Aumale and now by the nation. It is an area of splendid woodland inhabited by deer and wild boar. Horse racing may seem to dominate the district, but the golf club has had a distinguished connection with the game in France. It was founded in 1906 at about the same time as Morfontaine, Hosségor, Chantilly le Lys and Chiberta, and, like these four, owed much to the skill and influence of the British golf-course architect, Tom Simpson, who did much of his best work in France. At Chantilly, however, only about 10 holes remain from the pre-World War II lay-out, which was largely on different ground.

The club's first president was Prince Murat and the first course officially opened in October 1909 with an exhibition match between the two great French professionals, Arnaud Massy and Jean Gassiat. Its association with French championship golf began shortly afterwards. Down the years Chantilly has produced more than its share of fine players but, above all, it is a happy, friendly club with a course whose quality is beyond doubt.

Curiously, perhaps, it has a parkland rather than a wooded character, although oak, beech and maple form a continuous background to the golf and there are plans to build a further 9 holes in the woods. The trees that provide a feature of the golf were planted for the purpose, with the possible exception of those guarding the second shot to the 5th. There is plenty of contrast and holes such as the 5th, 9th, 10th and 11th are quite outstanding. When groomed to a championship pitch with the rough fully grown, the course is a long and severe test.

Chapman, Brian H. G. BRITISH
Walker Cup 1961; *Golf Illustrated* Gold Vase 1962

Brian Chapman gained his place in the

An aerial view of the 4th green at the Champions GC

The short 14th hole and the ladies' tee at the Chantilly GC

1961 Walker Cup team after he had been at Cambridge. He played for England in 1961-2. His grandfather founded the Chapman GC in Salisbury, Rhodesia.

Chapman GC RHODESIA

Eastlea, Salisbury. 18 holes; 7,124 yd (6,514 m); par 72

The Chapman GC, formerly the Henry Chapman GC, is situated in a suburb virtually within walking distance of the city, and is one of the best in Southern Africa; its undulating fairways, water hazards, difficult though well-manicured greens, and clusters of conifers and willows provide a stern test.

Its history dates back to 1928 when it was founded by Henry Chapman who, at the time of his retirement, was general manager of Rhodesian Railways and director of the British South Africa Company. He was also grandfather of Brian Chapman, the British Walker Cup golfer.

A working committee began the considerable task of clearing the 121 acres (49 ha) of very rough ground, heavily covered with indigenous trees and scrub bush; and they had to bridge and ford a fast-running tributary of the Makabusi River 15 times. This work was completed in about two years together with the planting of some 2,000 trees; today there are nearer 9,000. Within 10 years, the club could boast greens and fairways sown with grass and, over the years, successive committees have maintained the quality of the golf at the same high level Henry Chapman and his founder members planned for it.

Chapman, Richard Davol AMERICAN

b. Greenwich, Conn., 1911. French Open 1939, 1952; US Amateur 1940, semi-finalist 1938; Walker Cup 1947, 1951, 1953, 1955; *Golf Illustrated* Gold Vase 1948; Canadian Amateur 1949; British Amateur 1951,

runner-up 1947, 1950; North and South Amateur 1958; Italian Amateur 1960

Chapman has devoted much of his life to the game and won every major championship for amateurs, making frequent visits to Europe. A great theorist, he has tried many swings – the one which he used to win the US Amateur was anything but classical; but he developed a style that was polished and neat in the manner of the professional swing in the era between the wars. His strokes were crisp and decisive and in the dominance held by Americans over British golf after World War II, he played a notable part. He had already had a taste of the British Amateur before the war, in which he served as a major in the US Air Corps, and in 1947

he lost in the final at Carnoustie to another American, Willie Turnesa, in a match which was distinguished for its quality and the spirit in which it was played. Chapman gained an early lead with birdies and was 4 up at the turn; at the 10th, the South America hole, he appeared certain to become 5 up when Turnesa from the rough hit a low second towards the wide burn guarding the green, but the ball played ducks and drakes and scrambled up the far bank. Chapman, his composure disturbed, took 6 and lost the hole, from which point Turnesa's short game slowly began to undermine him.

Notwithstanding his successes in match-play Chapman also acquired a reputation in strokeplay. In the year he won the US Amateur he was also medallist in the qualifying round. In the 1954 US Open he had a record low round of 67, and his 65 at Sunningdale held the record there for years. He also scored 63 at Pinehurst and, competing in the British Amateur at Sandwich, he once took only 29 strokes in reaching the turn.

Charles, Robert James NEW ZEALAND

b. 1936. NZ Open 1954, 1966, 1970; NZ Professional 1961; Swiss Open 1962; British Open 1963, joint 2nd 1968, runner-up 1969; Canadian Open 1968; runner-up US Professional 1968; Piccadilly World Matchplay Tournament 1969, runner-up 1968; Dunlop Masters, John Player Classic 1972; South African Open 1973

The finest left-hander and the finest New Zealander in golfing history. After a good amateur career in which he became NZ Open Champion in 1954 and played with distinction for his country in the first two Eisenhower Trophy tournaments, he gave up life as a bank teller in Christchurch and turned professional in 1960. Bob Charles is a holder of the OBE.

It seemed then that, though he had the qualities of an outstanding competitor, his game lacked the power to challenge the Americans on their own courses but he won a tournament there in 1962 and, apart from one lean spell, continued to do well. He also possesses a first-class short game, an expressionless calm and, above all, a beautifully constant rhythm; it was these virtues that enabled him to win the 1963 British Open at Royal Lytham, easily his best achievement and one which really brought him to the fore.

At the outset, his name was not too seriously mentioned as a possible winner but the weather was not rough and Charles, hitting the ball firmly enough and excelling with

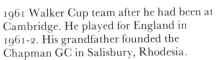
Brian Chapman

Top, a portrait of Richard D. Chapman and, *above*, in action during the British Amateur Championship, 1951

the putting stroke that has made him a fortune, eventually holed a putt of about 5 ft to tie with the American, Phil Rodgers. Charles' total was 277 (68, 72, 66, 71), one shot outside Palmer's record set the year before. With some more great putting, Charles beat Rodgers in what proved to be the last 36-hole play-off by 8 strokes.

In 1963 he won the Houston Classic; his other victories on the American tour were the Tucson Open in 1965, the Atlantic Classic in 1967, and the Canadian Open in 1968, which was also his best official money-winning year with $70,000.

In 1969 Charles won the Piccadilly Matchplay Tournament at Wentworth, beating Gene Littler with devastating

putting in the final at the 37th hole. He had finished as runner-up to Tony Jacklin in the British Open at Lytham three months before. He was also joint 2nd to Gary Player at Carnoustie in 1968 and joint 2nd with Arnold Palmer the same year in the USPGA Championship.

In 1972 he won the John Player Classic at Turnberry and a week later won the Dunlop Masters at Northumberland GC. His ability to master tigerish courses was shown again, as it had been at Turnberry, by his victory at Durban in the South African Open Championship. It was becoming ever more obvious that his prospects of victory were much higher outside than inside the United States where he had made his home. In 1973 he left America but returned the next year and won a major tournament.

Chaume, Simone Thion de la

(Mrs René Lacoste) FRENCH
b. Paris 1908. British Girls' 1924; French Ladies' Close 1925-30, 1936-8; French Ladies' Open 1926-7, 1930, 1935, 1938-9, runner-up 1925; British Ladies' 1927, semi-finalist 1926

The first French player to win the British Ladies' Championship, in 1927, three years after she had been the first French girl to take the British Girls' title; in both of these events her opponent in the final was Dorothy Pearson. Simone de la Chaume was from 1926 to 1939 the dominating figure in French golf and provided her country-women with a superb example of style, her method being simple and orthodox, her easy rhythm never disturbed by overhitting.

She arrived in top-class golf by running-up to Glenna Collett in the French Open at Versailles in 1925, and the following year defeated Charlotte (Cecil) Leitch in the French Open at that stage. But honours were shared between the English and French players that season, for Cecil Leitch defeated her in the semi-final of the British Championship at Royal St David's. After her success in the 1927 British Championship at Royal County Down, she went to America to compete in the Amateur National Championship at Garden City, New York, and reached the third round, where she lost to Alexa Stirling (Mrs Fraser). Altogether Simone de la Chaume played in 11 Vagliano Cup matches.

She married René Lacoste, the tennis champion. Their daughter Catherine, inheriting their skill and aptitude for games, has surpassed her mother's records at golf. They have the unique distinction of being the only mother and daughter each to have won the British Ladies' title.

Chaume, Mrs R. Thion de la see
LE BLAN, NANETTE

Chen Chien-chung TAIWANESE
b. Taipei 1936. Korean Open 1968; Indian Open 1970; Philippines Open 1971

Son of Chen King-shih, the famous professional who has done so much for the game in Taiwan, Chen Chien-chung turned professional in 1957 and has become one of the best players in the Far East. He is based at the Shizuoka Prefecture in Japan.

Chen Ching-po TAIWANESE
b. Taipei 1931. Japanese Open 1959, runner-up 1961-2, 1964; Kanto Open 1962, runner-up 1965, 1968; First Champions Tournament 1964; Golf Nippon Series 1964; Third Champions Tournament 1966; Grand Monarch Tournament 1966; Million Golf Tournament 1967

Chen Ching-po turned professional in 1952 and was the first of Taiwan's tournament players to make a name for himself in world golf, becoming known, in fact, as the Ben Hogan of Asia. He played at Wentworth when Nationalist China made its first appearance in the World (Canada) Cup and was the mainstay of the team for the next 10 or 11 years. He won a number of tournaments in the Far East but was unlucky that he was at his prime just before the circuit achieved its present wealth.

Chen King-shih TAIWANESE
b. 1910

A caddie at 14, Chen King-shih turned professional in 1930 and later, known as 'Old Man Chen', played a big part in the development of golf in Taiwan. He was responsible for the coaching of a number of good professionals; in fact, nearly all the leading professionals there have come under his guidance in one way or the other.

More recently, because of his advancing years, his teaching has been on a more selective basis. His son, Chen Chien-chung, is a professional in Japan.

Cherif el Sayed Cherif EGYPTIAN
b. Cairo 1923. Egyptian Professional 1955; Egyptian Open 1959, 1968

In the 1955 Egyptian Professional Championship he beat the great Hassan Hassanein by one stroke at the Alexandria Sporting Club. Sayed Cherif played 13 times for Egypt in the World (Canada) Cup, beginning in 1954 at Montreal and including 1956, when he teamed with Hassanein at Wentworth, and 1971 at Palm Beach Gardens. He had an innate talent for building and maintaining courses. He is head professional

Top, Bob Charles – a close-up, and, *above,* Charles driving at the final hole during the 1968 Piccadilly World Matchplay Tournament

and course superintendent simultaneously at the Gezira Sporting Club, Cairo, and the Lebanon GC, Beirut; a popular figure on the international tournament circuit, though he plays much less now than in past years.

Cherry, Don AMERICAN
b. Wichita Falls, Tex., 1924. Semi-finalist US Amateur 1952; Anderson Memorial 1953; Canadian Amateur 1953; Walker Cup 1953, 1955; Sunnehanna Amateur 1954

After more than a decade as a successful amateur, Cherry turned professional in 1962, although he was in his late thirties at the time. During the 1950s he made two very good showings in the US Amateur (semi-finalist in 1952 and quarter-finalist in

1954), and was a member of two Walker Cup teams. Although he won dozens of tournaments in Texas alone and was well-known throughout golf, he had an even bigger reputation with the general public as a popular singer.

Cherry Hills CC USA
Denver, Colo. 18 holes; 7,000 yd (6,401 m)

Cherry Hills was host to one of the most exciting and chaotic of all US Opens – the 1960 Open in which Arnold Palmer, 7 strokes off the pace, began his final round with 6 birdies on the first 7 holes, finished with a 65, and won the championship by 2 shots. The details of that incredible Saturday afternoon – in those days they still played two rounds in one day – will no doubt fascinate future golf historians. At one stage in the afternoon, Jack Nicklaus, then a 20-year-old amateur, jumped into the lead – with only 7 holes to go. Nicklaus was paired that day with Ben Hogan who that afternoon made his last serious bid to win a fifth Open. Ben was thwarted on the long 71st where, gambling on a birdie 4, he found the water hazard

before the small green and missed his par.

Cherry Hills is situated in Denver, a mile above sea level, with the snow-capped Rockies in the distance. The way drives travel in the thin atmosphere should make any golfer feel like Nicklaus. Although the course measures over 7,000 yd from the back tees, it is a bit too short now to present a true championship test. This is particularly true for the modern tournament stars. The second 9 is appreciably stronger. It includes the 14th, a long dogleg par 4 with a creek on the left, which Hogan rates as one of the best of its kind in the country. The 18th is a splendid finishing hole, another long par 4. A lake guards the left side of the fairway, and the the fairway begins a gradual climb

up a rugged slope to a subtly contoured green.

The 1960 Open was not the first held at Cherry Hills. The championship had been staged there in 1938, and Ralph Guldahl, the defender, won it decisively. His total of 284 was four strokes higher than Palmer's 22 years later.

Chicago GC USA
Chicago, Ill.

The city of Chicago is a golfing centre the equal of any, and there has been a great deal of play in and around the city since the game arrived there in the early 1890s. There are many old clubs and noteworthy courses in the district, and they have put on a large number of major events – nine US Opens, ten US Amateurs, and three PGA Championships. Several golf associations have their headquarters in Chicago, and the plants of some of the biggest golf-equipment manufacturers are located there.

Above all this stands the Chicago GC, a Midwestern golfing monolith and about as impressive a survivor of the old days as can be found in America. The club was founded in 1892 when Charles Blair Macdonald, that pillar of American golf, assembled a few adventurous souls and set up business in Belmont, a western suburb. The course became so popular that two years later the club decided to move to Wheaton and build a better course. Macdonald was in charge of this project, and the course he built stands today without radical alteration, a monument to his genius as an architect. The visitor will find it in perfect order, and he probably will not have to wait to tee off, for this is probably the least-used course in the district. Pete Thomas, who was the club professional for many years, used to say that if a foursome walked out on the clubhouse porch and saw another foursome moving down a fairway, they would call off their game because the course was crowded.

Three US Opens and four US Amateurs have been held at the Chicago GC. In 1911 it was the scene of the first victory in the US Open by an American-born player, Johnny McDermott, a product of the Philadelphia caddie yards. The last important event played there was the 1928 Walker Cup match.

Don Cherry

Cherry Hills GC

An early photograph of the clubhouse of Chicago GC

The Chicago GC was one of the five clubs that formed the US Golf Association in 1894. The others were Newport, Shinnecock Hills, St Andrews, and The Country Club.

Chile

Los Leones in Santiago is, in the opinion of Roberto de Vicenzo, the best of the courses in Chile where golf began in the last century at the Granadilla CC, Vino del Mar. Altogether there are more than 30 clubs in the country but many have only 9 holes and the game is not as popular as in some of the other South American countries.

The Chilean Golf Federation controls the country's golfing affairs. The Chilean team first entered for the World Cup (Eisenhower Trophy) in 1964 and finished in 23rd place level with Japan. Chile has been playing in the World (Canada) Cup since 1954 in Montreal; the best finish was in 1963 when Oralana and Salas tied 15th with New Zealand.

China

In an age when golf is developing rapidly in many countries it is perhaps a pity that the game has ceased to exist in China since the founding of the People's Republic in 1949. Golf was established there by Westerners before the end of the 19th century. It remained largely a British, and particularly a Scottish, affair. In 1947 the Shanghai GC was closed down. One of its two courses became a public park; the other six or seven throughout China were presumably put to more strictly utilitarian purposes. Of the two Shanghai GC courses, Kiangwan and Seekingjao, the latter was perhaps the best in China on account of its natural greens and wealth of natural hazards. During the Japanese invasion it was the scene of an engagement in which the clubhouse was blown up, but this was later rebuilt. There was a course at Hungjao where Chinese equipped with nets were employed to retrieve balls from the frequent water hazards, and another in the Hankow racecourse.

Other clubs were at Peking, Foochow (Minhow), Tsingtao, and Tsientsing, but the most romantic was a 9-hole course on Weihaiwei island. It had silver sand greens, an adjoining rifle range, an old fort inhabited by scorpions, and a short 9th where one recommended way to play the ball was to bounce off the clubhouse roof. All in all, a treacherous round for a caddie whose master was lacking in control.

The China Open Amateur Championship was started in 1924 and played every year until 1940, and once only after that, in 1948.

Chip

A short approach consisting almost entirely of run. It is usually played from just off the green with a variety of clubs. Most players would choose a fairly straight-faced club but Bobby Locke, for one, could get the same effect with a wedge.

Christchurch GC NEW ZEALAND

Shirley, Christchurch. 18 holes; 7,005 yd (6,405 m)

Founded in 1873, Christchurch was the second club to be formed in New Zealand, but interference from cattle and the variety of other sports engaged in at the Hagley Park site made this a false start. A new start was made in 1891 and a move further out of town came in 1898. Two years later the club moved to undulating land with sand dunes in the Shirley district: true links country where Denis O'Rorke and L. B. Wood laid out a course. Nine holes were opened in 1900 and the other 9 were ready the following year. The course is still an undulating one with dunes, and a creek is a feature of several holes.

In 1910 the New Zealand Open was held there for the first time but the course was on the short side until redesigned by D. Soutar of Sydney. A watering system was installed to prevent the greens from becoming burned up in summer, a complaint common elsewhere in New Zealand.

Membership built up after the Depression

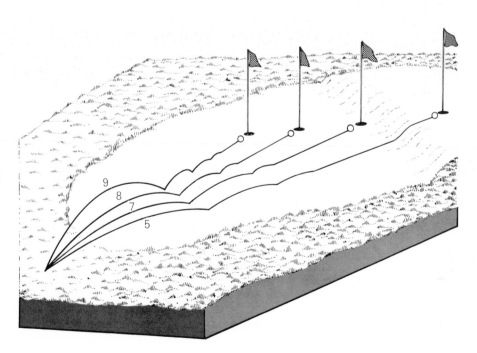

Chip: F. Rodesch *(top)* of Belgium playing a chip shot to a green, and, *above,* a diagram to illustrate the choice of club, which depends upon the distance the hole is from the edge of the green

Opposite, Billy Casper

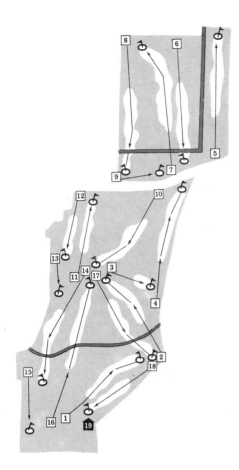

the 1961 Walker Cup match at Seattle, being the only member of his team to win his singles match. He was a severe loss to British amateur golf when business commitments compelled him to give up tournament play.

Cinque Ports GC, Royal ENGLAND
Deal, Kent. 18 holes; 6,659 yd (6,089 m); par 72

The Royal Cinque Ports GC, or Deal as it is more familiarly known, is the type of seaside links found only in the British Isles. Its traditional golfing terrain – running out alongside a ridge of pebbles by the sea and returning on a parallel strip – is one of Nature's masterpieces. Although Deal can

be described as typical of links golf, it retains a personality of its own. It lies a mile or so south of Royal St George's beside the pebble beach, but its dunes are flatter and the fairways, though full of undulations, have become almost inland in texture, except on the top of the numerous hillocks. The 1st hole is unusual in that the clubhouse stands almost halfway along it, so that the second shot over a stream guarding the first green can be gloated over by those not playing. The last 5 holes can be very arduous. The 14th is a short hole reached with wood when playing against the prevailing wind, and the length and undulation of the last 4 makes judgment of distance difficult. They are more often won or lost than halved, which makes them specially suitable for the foursomes matches played in one of the most famous of all British amateur tournaments, the Halford Hewitt Challenge Cup. The balcony of the clubhouse makes an ideal grandstand for spectators, and the Chequers Inn, near the 15th tee, a suitable port of call for victors and vanquished at an earlier stage.

Deal has seen sterner stuff. Two British Opens have been held there; the first in 1909 provided J. H. Taylor, whose total was 295, with his fourth victory. In 1920 George Duncan won after a remarkable final day, at the beginning of which he trailed Abe Mitchell by 13 strokes. With rounds of 71 and 72 he overtook him and won the championship with 303. Difficulties of access and accommodation have since made Deal unsuitable for the championship.

In the only British Amateur championship held there Roger Wethered beat Robert Harris by 7 and 6, having survived a far more uncomfortable time in the semi-final after he had been 4 up on the 14th tee against Francis Ouimet. It was on that tee that on another occasion Lionel Munn, runner-up in the 1937 Amateur, was once asked to

and again after World War II and although other clubs have sprung up near Christchurch, Shirley maintains a respected position, proud of its past which it celebrated at its centenary in 1973. The Christchurch Club has been the home course of Bob Charles for a number of years. It enjoys one unusual distinction: M. H. Godley and W. T. D. Harman halved the 9th hole in one during a fourball match in 1936.

Christmas, Martin J. BRITISH
b. 1939. Runner-up English Amateur 1960; joint winner English Strokeplay 1960; semi-finalist British Amateur 1961, 1964; Walker Cup 1961, 1963; Wentworth Foursomes (with E. R. Whitehead) 1962; Eisenhower Trophy 1962

A classic swinger of the club whose attacking strokes played right up to the pin brought him quick recognition in amateur golf. His defeat in the final of the 1960 English championship by Doug Sewell was only decided at the 41st hole, the longest match in the championship's history. Christmas gave one of the best British performances in

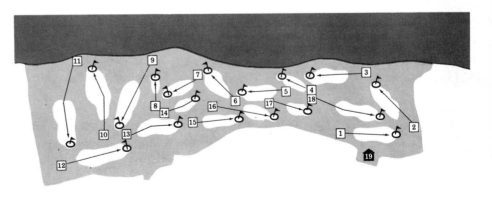

The course plan of the Christchurch GC

Opposite, Royal County Down GC

Top, Martin Christmas driving during a semi-final, British Amateur Championship

Above, The Royal Cinque Ports GC's course plan

oblige a photographer by making a stroke. He did so and struck the ball into the hole some 200 yd away. In the two English championships played at Deal John Langley featured in both finals, losing in 1936 while still at school to Harry Bentley, and beating Ian Patey in 1950. In 1949 the Open had been allotted to Royal Cinque Ports but it was decided against because the course had not recovered from wartime requisitioning. The course has also suffered much flooding from time to time from the sea but this is now a thing of the past. Leading the way in championships, as they did at Troon, were the ladies; May Hezlet won there in 1902.

Clark, Clive Anthony BRITISH

b. Winchester, Hampshire, 1945. Runner-up British Boys' Amateur 1961; runner-up Carris Trophy 1962-3; runner-up British Amateur 1965; runner-up English Amateur 1965; joint winner English Amateur Open Strokeplay 1965; *Golf Illustrated* Gold Vase 1965; joint winner Lytham Trophy 1965; Walker Cup 1965; Danish Open 1966; Agfa-Gevaert Tournament 1968; John Player Tournament 1970; Ryder Cup 1973

Clark studied architecture for a time at London University, but in 1965 his golf reached such a sustained level of excellence that he decided to make it his career, and he turned professional at the end of the year. He was unlucky in reaching the final of the British and English Championships to find in each case that he was up against Michael Bonallack at his peak, although Clark led in both matches after 18 holes. Clark was joint winner or runner-up in the three main British strokeplay events which made him winner of the Scrutton Jug, the trophy based on the aggregate of two of those events. With Mrs Anderson (Jean Donald) he was runner-up in the Worplesdon Foursomes. The climax to his career as an amateur came in the 1965 Walker Cup match against the United States at Baltimore. In the key match he was 1 down with 2 to play against John Hopkins, who had struck his tee shot deep into the trees at the short 17th. A miraculous recovery gave Hopkins a half there, and at the 18th Clark was left with a 33-ft putt which he bravely holed to give the British side their best result in the United States.

He made a slow start as a professional but his game gradually began to blossom as it did when he was an amateur. In 1967, when he ended the season 3rd in the Order of Merit, he tied for 3rd place in the British Open Championship at Hoylake, being beaten only by de Vicenzo and Nicklaus. He was also runner-up in the Sunningdale Four-

somes with Brigitte Varangot.

He tried his hand briefly on the American tour but thereafter decided to stick mainly to Europe. He won two tournaments in Britain in 1969, another in 1970, and in 1972 finished 10th in the Order of Merit. Such consistency won him a place in the 1973 Ryder Cup team.

Clark, Gordon James BRITISH

b. 1933. Runner-up British Amateur 1961; British Amateur 1964, semi-finalist 1967; Walker Cup 1965

A leading Northumberland golfer for many years, Gordon Clark's most notable distinction was in winning the 1964 British Amateur Championship at Ganton, the first

Top. Clive Clark

Above, Gordon Clark

time the Championship had been held inland. Although Clark had been runner-up in the 1961 English Championship, losing a thrilling final to Ian Caldwell at the 37th, his victory at Ganton surprised many who thought that Michael Lunt would repeat his 1963 triumph. However, after beating Martin Christmas in the semi-final with a stern recovery over the last few holes, Clark did the same again against Lunt in the longest final in the Championship's history.

He was a semi-finalist again at Formby, losing to Bob Dickson by 4 and 3, and played in the 1965 Walker Cup match, winning over half his matches for England. In British golf his merit as a player who could keep the ball in play, and was not afraid of winning, has perhaps been underrated. Certainly for a time his fellow Northumbrians were of that opinion.

Cleek

A shallow-faced, hickory-shafted iron with loft roughly corresponding to the modern no. 2 iron. Used in the days of the feathery and gutty ball to control long shots.

Clubs see BAFFY, BLASTER, BRASSIE, CALAMITY JANE, CENTRE SHAFT, CLEEK, DREADNOUGHT, DRIVER, EQUIPMENT, IRONS, JIGGER, LOFT, LIE, MASHIE, NIBLICK, PLAY CLUB, RUT IRON, SAND IRON, SHAFT, SHANK, SPADE MASHIE, TEXAS WEDGE, TORSIONS, TRACK IRON

Cochran, Robert AMERICAN

b. St Louis, Mo., 1912. Runner-up British Amateur 1960; runner-up US Western Amateur; Walker Cup 1961

Bob Cochran had been a good golfer for 30 years before gaining attention by reaching the final of the British Amateur when nearly 48, and making it his best year with other successes in the United States. He lost

A cleek

in the final of the British at Royal Portrush to Joe Carr by 8 and 7. His record that year caused him to be picked for the 1961 Walker Cup match at Seattle; here, in his 50th year, and partnered by G. Andrews, he won the foursome against Britain's strongest pair, the champion, Michael Bonallack, and Ronnie Shade. He was still winning local tournaments after he had passed 50.

Cock

The cocking of the wrists is the sideways bending or breaking movement necessary in the backswing or downswing in order to hit the ball. The degree of 'cock' varies from player to player as does the stage in the swing at which it is done.

Top, Bob Cochran

Above, Charles Coe playing in the final of the British Amateur Championship of 1951 at Porthcawl

Coe, Charles R. AMERICAN

b. 1923. US Amateur 1949, 1958, runner-up 1959; Walker Cup 1949, 1951, 1959, 1961, 1963 (captain 1959); runner-up British Amateur 1951; Eisenhower Trophy 1958; Trans-Mississippi 1947, 1949, 1952, 1956

One of the greatest postwar American amateurs. Coe's long career owes much to a beautiful, elegant swing, which in 1970 enabled him to finish well up in the US Masters at Augusta. This was an outstanding performance by an amateur of 46 but Coe, who in recent years has been a member of the committee responsible for organizing the Masters, often played with distinction among the great professionals there. Five times between 1949 and 1958 Coe finished in the first 24: in 1959 he was 6th and in 1962 equal 9th with Venturi. One of the finest performances by any amateur in recent years came when he finished 2nd in 1961 with Arnold Palmer, one stroke behind Gary Player.

It is probable that Coe was a finer stroke-player than matchplayer and, if the US National Amateur Championship had deserted matchplay sooner than 1965, it is likely that he would have won it more than twice. He was exceptionally slim in his early days and his physical resources could be severely strained at the end of a long week. This was the case when he lost the final of the British Amateur to Dick Chapman at Royal Porthcawl in 1951 by 5 and 4. Nevertheless in 1949 he crushed Rufus King by 11 and 10 in the final of the US Amateur at Rochester and in 1958 beat Tommy Aaron, now a professional, by 5 and 4 in San Francisco.

In the summer of 1959 after Coe had captained the victorious American Walker Cup team at Muirfield, he lost a memorable US Amateur final at Broadmoor to Jack Nicklaus. Coming to the last hole all square, Coe slightly overhit his second and though he almost holed his chip, Nicklaus pitched to 5 ft and holed for a 3.

Coe played many notable matches in the Walker Cup, especially that with Ronnie White at Birkdale in 1951, but none was more important to his side than the one with Charlie Green at Turnberry in 1963. Given the responsibility of playing last by his captain, Dick Tufts, he won by 4 and 3 thus completing a remarkable recovery and victory for America.

Cog Hill's Men's Club USA

Lemont, Ill. No. 4 Course 6,656 yd (6,086 m); par 72

Cog Hill comprises four daily-fee courses in industrial Lemont, in the southwestern suburbs of Chicago, and its No. 4 Course is rather special. It ranks among the very best courses open to the public in the United States, and it is worthy of a national championship. The course is impeccably groomed, with bent-grass fairways and greens, and it has a complete watering system. Dick Wilson laid it out in the early 1960s, over relatively flat terrain with heavy clay soil. It is easy to reach by car over good roads, and the green fee in 1972 was under $10.

Like most Wilson courses, Cog Hill No. 4 is of moderate length. The greens are of only average size, extremely well contoured and protected by bunkers. The 14th hole, for example, is a par 3 of a modest 124 yd (113 m), and yet the green is extremely hard to hit. To begin with, it sits well below the tee; it is quite small and is ringed by six quite large bunkers. The 16th is a 393-yd (359-m) par 4 with a narrow fairway and a deep basin, perhaps an old gravel pit, to the left of the green.

Cog Hill is owned by Joe Jemsek, a self-made man, son of immigrant parents, and former Cog Hill caddie. He bought the

property from the Coghill family, after whom it is named, at the end of a successful career as a golf professional and owner of another Chicago golf course. At the time Jemsek acquired Cog Hill, the No. 4 Course had not been built. It is Joe Jemsek's creation, and his pride.

Coldham Common GC ENGLAND
Cambridge

Bernard Darwin wrote eloquently and with obvious feeling about many courses in Britain but of Coldham Common he said, 'I am quite sure it was the worst course I have ever seen, and many others would probably award it a like distinction.' It deserves, none the less, a special place because

Cog Hill's Men's Club

in fact, he established a great liking for Wentworth where in 1964 he was unlucky not to beat Arnold Palmer in the first final of the Piccadilly Matchplay Championship.

Coles' record in the British Open has been disappointing, although he tied for 3rd place in 1961, and for 2nd in 1973 with a last round of 66. Ever since he spent long hours as an assistant developing his swing, he has had a remarkably repetitive method with a fine, flowing rhythm and a lovely high, statuesque finish. At the top of his swing the clubface, hooded slightly at address, is peculiarly shut but there has been no more likely winner of tournaments in Britain for more than a decade.

it was the course where the Cambridge University GC began in 1875. The course has long since been swallowed up by housing.

Cole, Robert SOUTH AFRICAN
b. 1948. British Amateur 1966; Natal Open 1969, 1970; South African Open 1974

Bobby Cole burst upon the golf world in the 1966 British Amateur at Carnoustie. Almost unknown in Britain, except to those who had heeded Gary Player's words about a rising young star, and those who had seen him tie for the *Golf Illustrated* Gold Vase a few weeks before, he beat Shade in the final by 3 and 2. Cole was still just 18 – an almost exact tie with John Beharrell for the youngest player ever to win the title.

Backed by a rich South African, he turned professional soon after and joined the group managed by Mark McCormack, and at the USPGA school to qualify recruits for the tour he finished top in 1967 ahead of Beman, Murphy, Jacklin, and Townsend.

Great things may be expected of him once he achieves the breakthrough, for he is a classic swinger of a golf club, and although he is slim, weighing little over 140 lb, he is one of the very longest drivers in the game.

A sign of his progress came in the 1969 South African circuit, where he finished with the best stroke average over the seven tournaments. The year 1974 was his best yet. He started by winning the South American Open finishing with an eagle on the last green and a record-breaking 64. He also finished well in American tournaments and was in contention for most of the British Open. His youthful good looks and smart turn-out, combined with a handsome swing, make him attractive to watch.

Coles, Neil C. BRITISH
b. London 1934. Assistant Professionals' 1956; Ryder Cup 1961, 1963, 1965, 1967,

1969, 1971, 1973; British Professional Matchplay 1964-5, 1973, runner-up 1966; Dunlop Masters 1966; German Open 1971; Scottish Open 1972; joint 2nd British Open 1973; Spanish Open 1973

Although not exactly cast in the colourful mould of such modern professionals as Doug Sanders, Neil Coles was for 10 years or more one of the best and most consistent of the British professionals. With a little more devil in him and a little wider ambition, he might well have enjoyed conspicuous success overseas, but having an acute dislike of flying and therefore travelling as little as possible has not helped him. It is no coincidence that he has played his best golf when able to stay at his own home during a tournament and,

He won the Harry Vardon Trophy in 1963 and again in 1970. Then 1971 was another fine year which included victories in the Penfold and the Carrolls International tournaments, and in the German Open, his first championship title. In the 1967 Ryder Cup in Houston he won both his singles matches against Doug Sanders and in overall matches up to 1971 he scored 6½ out of 12.

Collett, Glenna (Mrs E. H. Vare)
AMERICAN
b. New Haven, Conn., 1903. US Women's Amateur 1922, 1925, 1928-30, 1935, runner-up 1931-2; Canadian Ladies' Open 1923-4; French Ladies' Open 1925; runner-up

Bobby Cole

Neil Coles – a portrait and in action

Glenna Collett

British Ladies' 1929-30; Curtis Cup 1932, 1936, 1938, 1948 (captain 1934, 1936, 1948, non-playing captain 1950)

Glenna Collett's record of six US Women's Amateur Championships is likely to remain unsurpassed, and while achieving this string of victories she set fresh standards for her countrywomen. A natural all-rounder at games, she was fascinated by golf at the age of 15, but her successes were only achieved after intensive study and practice. Her attack on the ball with woods and irons made her outstanding.

Her endeavours to obtain the British title were twice thwarted in what have since become historic encounters, with Joyce Wethered. The first of their meetings was at Troon in 1925, when Miss Wethered won by 4 and 3, after playing the 15 holes in level 4s. Their next meeting was more memorable, for it was in the final of the British, in 1929, on the Old Course at St Andrews. Playing inspired golf, Glenna Collett with a 2, a 3, and nine 4s, was 5 up after 11 holes, and missed from 4 ft to increase her lead on the 12th. At the end of the first round her lead had been reduced to 2, and after 27 holes she was 4 down. A counter attack of two 3s enabled her to obtain two holes back, but Joyce Wethered held on to the lead.

The following year Glenna Collett reached the final of the British Ladies' Championship at Formby, and was unexpectedly beaten by a 19-year-old English girl, hitherto comparatively unknown, Diana Fishwick (Mrs Critchley). Her subsequent visits to Britain were with the American Curtis Cup team, during which she was more concerned with the success of her side than with her own endeavours in the British championships that came afterwards. As a sportswoman she specially endeared herself to the players she met and to the galleries who watched her play in Britain.

Bill Collins

Collins, Bill AMERICAN

b. Meyersdale, Pa., 1928. Greater New Orleans Open 1959; Houston Classic 1960; Hot Springs Open 1960; Ryder Cup 1961; Buick Open 1962

A hefty ex-Marine whose successes, though covering a brief period, were enough to gain him a place in the 1961 Ryder Cup match at Royal Lytham. He turned professional in 1951 but did not join the tour full time until 1958. Collins had a reputation for being one of the best-dressed players.

Cologne GCC see KÖLN-REFRATH GCC

Colombia

Golf in Colombia began in 1917 in Bogotá,

the capital, with the founding of the Country Club of Bogotá on a site which has long since been engulfed by warehouses and a football stadium. The ground on which the first course was built belonged to the Bank of Colombia. One of the pioneers of the club was Enrique Samper whose enthusiasm was aroused during a visit to London. While shopping he saw a man swinging his umbrella and thought that he had gone mad. He was told that the man was a golf fanatic and, on the strength of this, Samper got himself invited to a club. He became fascinated and, upon his return to Colombia, took with him golf clubs and other equipment.

When the first course came into existence, there were no lawn mowers, and sheep were used to keep the grass short. With the rapid commercial growth of the city, the club had to move to an area known as the 'Old Country'; then in 1947 it moved a second time to one of the most beautiful parts of Bogotá, where it has remained to this day. The club now has two fine 18-hole courses, a polo field, tennis courts and swimming pool.

The Colombian golfer, A. Rivedeneira, in the 1973 German Open

Following the lead given by the Country Club, enthusiastic nationals and resident foreigners became interested in golf; a number of other clubs were set up in various parts of the country and in 1972 they numbered 23 with a total membership of about 5,500. A total of 60 professional golfers of various nationalities serve these clubs, all of which are affiliated to the Colombian Golf Federation which was established in 1945 as the governing body of the game in Colombia.

Colombo GC, Royal SRI LANKA (CEYLON)
Colombo. 18 holes; 6,286 yd (5,748 m); par 71

The Colombo GC was founded in 1882, exclusively for the European community. The club moved to its present home on the south side of the capital in the 1890s; the course is also known as Ridgeway Links, after a former British governor who allocated the land.

The Amateur Championship of Ceylon was instituted in 1891, one year earlier than the Indian and two years before the US Amateur. It was held every two years, alternating between Colombo and the hill station of Nuwara Eliya until 1905; since then the championship has been competed for annually at alternate courses.

With the coming of independence Ceylonese nationals were allowed membership of Royal Colombo. The first Ceylonese champion had been Timothy de Silva, in 1923; in that same year W. P. Fernando, Ceylon's outstanding amateur golfer, was born. He has won the Championship 10 times and been runner-up six times. Pin Fernando also holds the amateur record of 68 at the Royal Colombo, beaten only by Max Faulkner's professional record for the course of 66.

Royal Colombo is characterized by deceptive simplicity, demanding accurate driving. It is possible to go out of bounds or into clear water or swamp off almost every tee. In addition there are many trees to contend with, and a railway line, not to mention the changing winds of the southwest and northeast monsoons. The first hole, a 430-yd (393-m) par 4, is a severe opening which the player might wish had been left for somewhere later in the round. It makes a formidable 19th when doing overtime in a match that will not finish. The 10th, 11th, and 12th, all par 4s, are Royal Colombo's counterpart of the St Andrews 'loop'. Though all are on the short side they give the chance of laying the foundations of a good score. The 186-yd (170-m) par-3 13th is the best short hole on the course. The tee

shot is played over a large expanse of water and marsh on to an elevated plateau green well trapped and guarded by yawning bunkers.

When playing Royal Colombo, the vital stage is the 'Ridgeway finish', comprising the 484-yd (443-m) 14th, the 533-yd (487-m) 15th, both par 5s, and the 459-yd (420-m) par-4 17th. The good player with some length is generally able to reach the 14th in two shots, against the southwesterly wind. But even in the balmiest weather the 15th defies the best, for apart from the flanking tract of rough country there is a formidable expanse of water and marsh stretching all the way from the 12th tee to the 15th green. Finally the 17th is the best hole on the

course, requiring an accurate drive and a good stiff iron.

Many rulers, statesmen and politicians of world fame have played over Royal Colombo, and a host of admirals, generals, and air marshals during World War II when SEAC headquarters were at Kandy.

Like Royal Calcutta, Colombo has kept its designation despite the constitutional changes that have taken place since independence.

Colonial CC USA
Fort Worth, Tex.

Colonial has become well known everywhere because it conducts an annual tournament that stands head and shoulders above

the average tour event, because it has been the golfing home of Ben Hogan, and because its golf course is one of the most stringent tests in the country. One US Open has been held there, in 1941, and it will be long remembered since Craig Wood, a most amiable and well-liked man who encountered much tough luck during his career, won it while wearing a corset arrangement to keep vertebra in place and relieve pain. This was the same Craig Wood who lost in a play-off to Denny Shute in the 1931 British Open, who lost on the second extra hole to Paul Runyan in the final of the 1934 PGA Championship, and who was also the victim of Gene Sarazen's double eagle in the 1935 Masters.

Colonial was a comparatively new course when the Open was held there, having been inaugurated in 1936. It was well designed and few changes were necessary to prepare it for the national championship. As a matter of fact, no substantial changes were made until 1969 when flooding from the Trinity River damaged several holes. The results of the rehabilitation programme have been most successful, and Colonial is again the superlative challenge it was before. It is approximately 7,000 yd (6,400 m) long, measuring just over or under that figure depending on which tees the golfer plays. It demands tremendous skill in controlling the ball, for the fairways are narrow and bend through woods of pecan and oak, and, on top of this, the ubiquitous Trinity River moves menacingly through or alongside many of the fairways. To cope with Colonial, it helps if a golfer can move the ball both ways off the tee and on his approach shots as well. The greens are on the small side and they are not easy to putt. The finishing hole, a modest-looking but deceitful par 4 of 434 yd (397 m), features a right-to-left sloping fairway and a water hazard that guards the left side of the green, and it has produced some spectacular wind-ups to several editions of the Colonial Open, or Colonial National Invitation, as the club calls it.

The main force behind the building of Colonial was Marvin Leonard, the owner of one of Fort Worth's largest department stores. Leonard wanted to build a course fit for the US Open, and towards that end he insisted that the greens at Colonial be seeded with bent grass and not with Bermuda. Leonard was the man who gave Hogan the helping hand he needed when he was trying to establish himself in golf. As it turned out, Hogan, who developed his game on Colonial, could handle the course better than any other golfer, for he could meet the high demands it placed on pinpoint

Top, The clubhouse of the Royal Colombo GC

Above, A crowd watching play, several years ago, at the Colonial CC

accuracy better than any other. He was always the man to beat in the Colonial Open, and he carried it off five times. When Marvin Leonard built a new course, Shady Oaks, on the man to beat in the Colonial Open, and he friend there. Today Colonial is a very crowded club, and at Shady Oaks Hogan is able to have the privacy he values.

Colt, H. S. BRITISH
b. 1869; d. 1951

Harry Colt is remembered as one of the leading golf-course architects of his time and a man whose work in Britain and elsewhere has brought players a great deal of pleasure. Royal Portrush, Moor Park, Denham, Wentworth (with his partners Alison and Morrison), Rye, Northamptonshire County, Sunningdale (New Course), Trevose, St Andrews (Eden Course), Stoke Poges and, in Holland, Kennemer GCC are just some of his creations. In addition he made major alterations at Royal Porthcawl, Southerndown, Sunningdale (Old Course), Alwoodley, Aberdovey and Royal Dublin.

Colt played much of his own early golf at St Andrews and his admiration for the Old Course undoubtedly influenced his concepts of design. These became known after he had left Cambridge and spent some time as a solicitor in Hastings. It was during this period that he designed the course at Rye, but he did not become fully engaged in this new career until 1900 when he was made the first secretary of the Sunningdale Club, where he remained for 12 years.

He later became so famous in the golfing world as an architect that the younger generation may tend to think of him solely in this role, but Colt was also a fine golfer who played for England in 1908, besides reaching the semi-final of the 1906 Amateur Championship at Hoylake and the sixth round in two other years.

In his book *Sheridan of Sunningdale*, Jimmy Sheridan, the much-loved caddiemaster, referred to Colt as 'a great and wonderful man', although in the early days there were several clashes between these two strong personalities. Later in his career Colt formed a company with C. H. Alison and J. S. F. Morrison as partners and together they did a great deal of work in Britain and Europe.

In his earlier days as an architect Colt made one special journey to America in the summer of 1913 to work with George Crump during a brief but critical period in the lengthy construction of Pine Valley.

Columbia CC USA
Chevy Chase, Md. 6,400 yd (5,852 m)

A casual look at Columbia's scorecard could lull the golfer of medium skill into a euphoric trance, induced by the certain knowledge that here at last is a golf course where he can reach most of the greens in the allotted shots without straining his back muscles. And then comes the revelation. The scorecard shows that Columbia measures barely 6,400 yd from the back tees, but this does not take into consideration the many intimidating hills. They have little effect on the reasonably long hitter, for he can fly his tee shots over the crests, but the moderate hitter constantly drills his shots into the side of those hills, and so a 350-yd hole plays as long as the average 400-yd hole, and the 400-yd holes become almost out of reach.

Columbia is an old-style course with rather small greens, and its bunkers are more like sandpits than the modern, flared type of hazard. It is located in Chevy Chase, barely 15 minutes' drive from the centre of Washington, D.C., at the intersection of two busy roads, and within reach of the White House. Clubhouse and course are used by political figures. Bud Wilkinson, once a famous football coach at the University of Oklahoma and more recently the Chairman of the President's Commission on Physical Fitness, has also played there.

Columbia was the site of the 1921 National Open, won by Jim Barnes (by 9 strokes), as well as the 1955 Canada (now the World) Cup Match in which Flory Van Donck of Belgium, set the course record of 66 and tied with Peter Thomson of Australia and Ed Furgol of the United States for low individual total. Furgol won the sudden-death play-off on the 3rd hole, a tantalizing 352-yd (322-m) par 4 on which the only problem is a tulip tree on the right side of the fairway in the drive zone. The tree's age is indeterminable, but it is kept up by wire cables that bind every branch to the trunk. Cut the wires and the hole would be nothing. Thomson made a 5 there, and Furgol won with a 4.

Columbia finishes with a 412-yd (377-m) par 4 through a saddle-like dip to a mammoth green, 10,000 square feet (930 m²) on four levels, with a vast bunker partly blocking the approach.

Since 1912, the club has had only two head professionals. Fred McLeod, the wonderful old Scot who captured the US Open in 1908, served for over 50 years, and he was held in such esteem by the members that his portrait hangs in the panelled grill room.

Committee
Any group of men or women elected or appointed to take responsibility for and advise on any particular function in a club. Besides a general committee golf clubs normally have greens, house, and handicap committees to govern affairs.

Another type is the championship or tournament committee for major events. Such committees are responsible for organization, the welfare of the players and for any decisions which may have to be taken during play.

Company of Gentlemen Golfers see HONOURABLE COMPANY OF EDINBURGH GOLFERS

Compston, Archibald Edward Wones BRITISH
b. Wolverhampton, Staffordshire, 1893; d. 1963. Runner-up British Open 1925; British Professional Matchplay 1925, 1927; Gleneagles Tournament 1925; Ryder Cup 1927, 1929, 1931; Eastern Open 1928

Archie Compston was one of the greatest personalities in British golf between the wars. Big, with a confident stride and a rugged appearance, he had a will to win, a fierce attacking style, and an uncompromising attitude to the outside world. He learned the game on Penn Common near his birthplace and was noted in his youth for exhibitions of temper which included club throwing. He mellowed with the years but he remained to the end a 'character'. He became an assistant at the age of 16 and held professional posts at Coventry and North Manchester before going to Coombe Hill, where he coached the Prince of Wales and a number of prominent amateurs, including Pam Barton. His greatest achievement was the 18 and 17 victory over Walter Hagen at Moor Park, and his most spectacular failure the fourth round of 82 in the 1930 Open at Hoylake, after he had taken the lead with a record-breaking third round of 68. During the latter years of his life, partly for health reasons, Compston was resident professional at the Mid-Ocean CC, Bermuda, where his ruggedness, tempered by maturity, fitted into the frame of opulent sophistication just as easily as it had done in Britain.

Concede
A hole To allow that an opponent has won the hole before he has completed the playing of it.
A putt When in matchplay a player puts a shot so close to the hole that his opponent considers it impossible for him to miss the next, the latter can 'concede' the putt without another stroke being played.

Congressional CC USA
Bethesda, Md.

In the years immediately after World War I, Washington, D.C., found itself with much more government and many more citizens but with no more golf courses than it had in the pre-war years when it was simply a small Southern town. With the end of that war came a period of expansion in American golf courses, and it was in this atmosphere

Sinclair. In the end, life memberships, no matter to whom they were sold, did not insure financial stability, and the club suffered through the Depression. It never really became financially sound until after World War II when improvements in roads brought the club much closer, seemingly, to the city. During World War II, the club was taken

controversial holes that has ever been played in the US Open: the 9th is a 600-yd (549-m) par 5 with a ravine just in front of a smallish green. The fairway narrows considerably at the point above the ravine, and it is just about impossible to reach the green in two shots. Jack Nicklaus tried several times in practice rounds before the Open and failed.

Long as the course played for the 1964 Open was, the winning score was 278, until that time the second lowest in Open history and the first time 280 was broken in 16 years.

CONGU (COUNCIL OF NATIONAL GOLF UNIONS)
The body set up in 1924 following a meeting between the Royal and Ancient and the Golf Unions of England, Scotland, Ireland and Wales. It is comprised of members of each and is responsible for:

1. running the handicapping system in Great Britain and Ireland;

2. managing the annual international matches between the four countries;

3. arranging dates.

Conley, Peggy AMERICAN
b. Spokane, Wash., 1947. Pacific Northwest 1963; runner-up US Women's Amateur 1963; semi-finalist 1967; US/Girls' Junior 1964; runner-up 1963; Curtis Cup 1964, 1968; Western Women's 1966

At 17, Peggy Conley was one of the youngest ever to have played in the Curtis Cup. In 1963 she had burst upon the scene, showing up well in several events, and losing only to Anne Welts in the final of the US Women's Amateur which she reached by beating three Curtis Cup players. Still a student at High School that year, her precocity as a golfer heralded a gradual lowering of the age in international contests.

that two Indiana Congressmen conceived the idea of a club where members of Congress could play golf and entertain friends. From dream to fulfilment took about three years, and in 1924 an 18-hole golf course was ready for play, located in the Potomac River valley about 15 miles from central Washington. This is the Congressional CC.

Its clubhouse is immense. A white stucco structure with a red tiled roof, it sits on the highest hill of the grounds. It has an utterly commanding presence, along with an outdoor swimming pool, grill rooms, banquet rooms, bedrooms, and at one time a system of secret passages in its upper floors that led from bedrooms to conference rooms. It must have been rather unsettling to be seated at a conference table and see a wall part to reveal Herbert Hoover in his starched collar coming through the woodwork.

Hoover was then Secretary of Commerce, and he was made Founders Club president. Life memberships were sold to John D. Rockefeller, Vincent Astor, Charlie Chaplin, William Randolph Hearst, and Harry

over by the Office of Strategic Services, and cloak-and-dagger operations were planned on what is now the second 9.

The original course, although pleasant enough, has been revised considerably, a third 9 has been added, and now the main course is composed of the first 9 of the original course and a new second 9, created in the mid-1950s by the golf architect, Robert Trent Jones.

Before the 1964 United States Open, the one that produced such a dramatic victory for Ken Venturi was played there, Jones returned and remodelled the first 9. Congressional measured well over 7,000 yd (6,400 m) for the Open, and although the members do not play it to that length, it is understood throughout Washington that a 2-handicapper at Congressional must be a somewhat better player than a 2-handicapper at any other club in the city.

Typical of Jones's courses, Congressional is festooned with doglegs which twist through forests of pine and oak, up or down an occasional steep hill, but mostly through pleasant woodland. It has one of the more

The pleasant woodland course at the Congressional CC

Peggy Conley

Conrad, Joseph W. AMERICAN
b. San Antonio, Tex., 1930. Southern
Amateur 1953-4; Trans-Mississippi Amateur 1953; British Amateur 1955; low
amateur British Open 1955; Walker Cup
1955

Joe Conrad was a member of the 1955
American Walker Cup team in Britain while

serving as a USAF lieutenant. He experienced
a remarkable variation in fortune. In the
match against Britain at St Andrews he
partnered Dale Morey to win a foursome
point, yet these two were the only Americans
to lose their singles. Then Conrad went on to
win the British Amateur Championship at
Royal Lytham and, on returning to St
Andrews for the Open Championship later
that year, finished leading amateur.

Conrad also won many matchplay tournaments in the 1950s and played twice on
Americas Cup sides. He turned professional
in December 1956, but, a comparatively
short hitter, was not able to make the same
impact on the tournament circuit as he had
done during his amateur career.

Coody, Charles AMERICAN
b. Texas 1937. Semi-finalist US Amateur
1962; Dallas Open 1964; Cleveland Open
1969; US Masters 1971

Coody's reputation is largely based on his
victory in the Masters, for although he had
four or five years of solid financial success
before that, few outright victories came his

way. After leaving high school in 1954 and
attending Texas Christian University he won
some 30 amateur tournaments in Texas,
some of them while serving as an Air Force
lieutenant. He qualified for the US Open in
1960 and 1961, and the following year
reached the semi-finals of the US Amateur,
turning professional a year later. In 1969 he

had a chance to win the Masters, a tournament on which he has concentrated, but
dropped strokes at the last 3 holes through
adopting a defensive policy, and was beaten
into 5th place. Early the next year his entire
set of clubs was stolen, and he tried some 20
drivers before finding one that suited him.
The resultant loss of confidence affected his

game. But he came back in 1971 and showed
that he had learned his lesson from the 1969
Masters. This time he established an early
lead, lost it, but was never out of touch with
the leaders, and finished strongly as Nicklaus
failed to take his chance. Coody is a well-
built 6 ft 2 in with a flowing, compact swing.

In 1973 he made two profitable visits to
Britain, winning the Wills tournament and
the John Player Classic in appalling conditions at Turnberry.

Cooper, Harry AMERICAN
b. Leatherhead, Surrey, 1904. Texas Professional 1923-4; Del Monte Tournament 1926;
Los Angeles Tournament 1926; Canadian
Open 1932, 1937; runner-up US Open 1936

'Lighthorse' Harry Cooper was ineligible
for American Ryder Cup honours as he was
born in England. Otherwise he would surely
have played more than once in those
matches, for he was certainly in the first 10
of American professionals of his day. In 1927
he took three putts on the last green on
which Tommy Armour holed a 10-ft birdie
putt to force a play-off in the US Open
Championship, which Armour won. In the
1936 Championship Cooper again had his
aggregate on the board with every chance of
winning, but lost by 2 strokes to Tony
Manero, who beat the course record with a
last round of 67.

Copenhagen GC DENMARK
Eremitagen. 18 holes; 6,315 yd (5,763 m)

København Golf Klub, Denmark's oldest
golf club, was founded on 6 December 1898
at a meeting held in the *Kongen af Danmark*
(King of Denmark) hotel. The founders
were G. Hage, E. Schmidt and L. Friis. The
beginnings were a little primitive: golfers
simply went out to a stretch of parkland
called Fælled, made some holes and started
to play. There was no proper course, although eight holes lay close together, and no
official permission to play golf had been
obtained; as golfers had to share Fælled with
children playing and adults sunning themselves on the grass, activity did not continue
long in these dangerous conditions.

In 1899 the club moved to the Klampenborg deer park, a few miles north of the city,
in which stands the 18th-century Ermitage.
Nine holes were laid out in this beautiful
setting with many fine old trees and excellent
turf. There was a shed where members could
store their clubs and a restaurant at the
castle where they could dine. Today the
course has 18 holes. Grazing deer – the
Danish kings used to hunt here – add to the
charm of the golf.

A new clubhouse was built to replace one

Joseph W. Conrad

Top, Charles Coody

Above, Harry Cooper

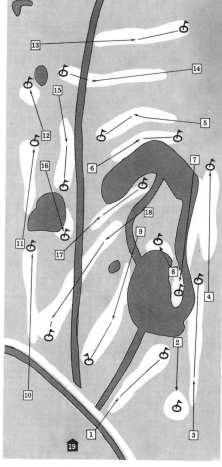

destroyed during the German occupation in World War II; dining out on its terrace in the long evenings of the northern summer is one of the pleasant features of this club, which has been the venue for several Danish championships.

Corcoran, Fred J. AMERICAN
b. Cambridge, Mass., 1905.

A professional promoter and adviser, Fred Corcoran is one of the best-known personalities in the American golf world. He was also executive director of the Professional Golfers' Association of America in the sometimes stormy years between 1936 and 1947. He began as a caddie at Belmont, Mass., in 1916 and soon rose to be caddiemaster, and eventually a club secretary. He was Massachusetts state golf handicapper from 1927 to 1936; that year he moved to Pinehurst to join Bob Harlow, whom he succeeded as tournament director of the PGA. His first winter tour in that capacity was also Sam Snead's first and the two soon began what was to be a long and profitable association. In addition to Snead, Corcoran also served as adviser to baseball players, such as Ted Williams and Stan Musial, footballers like the Gogolak brothers, and other golfers including Tony Lema, Ken Venturi, Roberto de Vicenzo, Babe Zaharias, George Knudson, Bobby Nichols, and Tom Weiskopf. During his years as tournament manager the American tour grew from a few scattered tournaments into a regular rotation of events that brought organization and players to the threshold of big money and gave golf a major-league stature. Additionally he organized the tour for the Women's PGA and served as director from 1949 to 1961. He also had a hand in forming the Golf Writers' Association, and was, with John Jay Hopkins, a principal promoter of the International Golf Association which stages the

World (formerly Canada) Cup. A genial companion, with a quixotic humour and a fund of stories, he acted as manager for four Ryder Cup teams, in 1937, 1939, 1941 and 1953. He has received a number of awards, including the 1968 Walter Hagen Award.

Corfu GC CORFU
18 holes; 6,800 yd (6,218 m); par 72

This course is 10 miles (16 km) inland from Corfu town and international airport. Five artificial lakes are fed by a river running through the property, and 20,000 trees have been planted for aesthetic and tactical reasons.

Corlett, Elsie BRITISH
b. Lytham, Lancashire, 1902. Vagliano Cup 1931, 1936-9; Curtis Cup 1932, 1938 (captain 1964); runner-up British Ladies' 1938, semi-finalist 1934, 1937; English Ladies' 1938, runner-up 1926, 1935; Veteran Ladies' 1954

One of the most consistent performers during the 1920s and 1930s. Elsie Corlett had limited opportunities for golf, which left

her at a disadvantage against those with more time for competition. Self-taught, essentially a swinger, she concentrated on playing within her potential. During her first championship the bottom fell out of a caddie bag she had borrowed – an embarrassing moment she likes to recount.

Cosh, Gordon B. BRITISH
b. Glasgow 1939. Walker Cup 1965; Eisenhower Trophy 1966, 1968; Scottish Amateur 1968, runner-up 1965

Gordon Cosh was in the British Isles team v. Europe in 1966 and 1968, and represented Scotland in internationals from 1964 to 1969. He was frequently a hostage to the unpredictable whim of his driving, but he had an abundance of competitive spirit and regularly retrieved an apparently lost cause with his flair in the short game and the reliability of his holing out.

Cotton, Charles Kenneth BRITISH
b. Sonning-on-Thames, Berkshire, 1887

Ken Cotton, a graduate of Cambridge (where, ironically, he played virtually no

Top, Copenhagen GC, Denmark

Above, Fred Corcoran

The course plan of Corfu GC

golf), became a scratch player and from 1927 was secretary at the former Hendon GCC, London; Parkstone; Stoke Poges, Buckinghamshire; and Oxhey. After World War II, Cotton decided on a new career as a golf-course architect since the pre-war generation of practitioners had diminished in numbers. Most of the work in Britain in those days consisted of reclaiming courses disrupted by the war. Cotton, however, soon showed a great deal of talent in his original work. He was also active abroad and when the boom in golf-course building came about 1960 he was soon busy enough to take on a number of partners.

A tall kindly man, he is perhaps best known for his design of Olgiata, Rome; St Knuds in Denmark; St Pierre, Monmouthshire; Ross-on-Wye; Brickendon Grange, Hertfordshire; the new Frilford Heath, Berkshire; the major redesign of West Lancashire, Liverpool, and Downfield, Dundee; and the 9-hole course at Wentworth.

Cotton, Thomas Henry BRITISH

b. London 1907. Ryder Cup 1929, 1937, 1947 (captain 1947, non-playing captain 1953); Belgian Open 1930, 1934, 1938; British Professional Matchplay 1932, 1940, 1946, runner-up 1928, 1930, 1949, semifinalist 1947, 1951; British Open 1934, 1937, 1948; Italian Open 1936; Czechoslovak Open 1937-8; German Open 1937-9, runner-up 1933-6; Harry Vardon Trophy 1938; French Open 1946-7

In an age when no Briton won the Open Championship more than once, Henry Cotton, three times holder of the title, stood out like a colossus. The circumstances of each of those victories added lustre to his reputation. In 1934 at Sandwich he put an end to 10 years of American domination of the event. His brilliant opening rounds of 67

and 65 meant that, after a third round of 72, he stood ten strokes ahead of the field. Before the final round he had an attack of stomach cramp and, starting badly, went out in 40, but he recovered and won by 5 strokes.

Three years later at Carnoustie he won again from a field containing the entire US Ryder Cup team. His last round of 71, in torrential rain on a waterlogged course, was in the conditions one of the finest ever played; it was surpassed in his own career only by the 66 which set a new course record for Muirfield and gave him his third victory in 1948. He was not naturally gifted but reached the top by intensely hard practice which, as a young man, sometimes left his hands sore and blistered. Once he had left Alleyn's School, Dulwich, and decided that golf was to be his life, sheer character brought him success and, when he had achieved it, he was shrewd enough to make the most of it.

His position as the greatest British golfer of his age rests on more than his record of achievement. As teacher, writer of several books, inventor, and even in putting on an act at the London Palladium, he exploited his talents to the full. His belief that the public would pay well for what professionals had to offer opened up new fields for his colleagues and carried on the work of emancipation begun by Walter Hagen. He has an original and inquiring mind – at his golf school in Monte Carlo his pupils drove golf balls into the sea – and probably no Briton

has studied the game more thoroughly. By his fastidious way of living and the ease with which he mixed with all kinds of people, he brought style and dignity to his profession. In all these things he was staunchly supported by his Argentinian-born wife, 'Toots'.

His first full professional job was at Langley Park, Kent, whence in 1933 he went to the Royal Waterloo club in Belgium. Apart from a short spell in Cannes, which was the beginning of a long association with the south of France where he has always felt very much at home, he remained there until returning to Britain and taking up a post at Ashridge, Hertfordshire, before his second victory in the Open.

From Fulwell, Middlesex, his first post, he went as assistant to Rye where his ambition drove him to practise even by moonlight. World War II interrupted his career at its peak; his services to the Red Cross in raising funds were recognized by the award of the MBE, and he was for a time in the Royal Air Force, but although physically very strong – he was a great believer in muscle-building exercises – he was not so constitutionally and was invalided out.

When golf resumed after the war he soon showed that his game had endured. Although not a natural golfer, he had very strong hands and his swing was full of grace and power; by comparison, his putting, good though it was, appeared laboured. His third victory in the Open came when he was 41, but in the postwar years he continued to win many lesser tournaments, as he had done before. Notable among these were three matchplay championships, an event in which he was also three times runner-up, and four Continental championships. He also won some important challenge matches against individual players.

He played in three Ryder Cup matches and was captain twice. At 46 he won a five-round tournament at Wentworth, and final proof of his enduring style came in 1956 when in his 50th year he tied 6th in the Open, ahead of every other Briton except John Panton. When competing ceased to be a pleasure, he spent more and more time on the Continent, settling eventually in Penina in the Algarve district of Portugal, where he had designed a course from an old ricefield. He also was responsible for a number of other golf courses in Europe and Britain.

Country Club, The USA

Brookline, Mass.

Brookline is a residential suburb of Boston. Settled in 1634, 14 years after the *Mayflower* landed, Brookline should not be confused with Brooklyn, one of the five

Gordon Cosh

Henry Cotton

boroughs of New York City, which has more people but less grass.

Brookline is the home of The Country Club, a tradition-drenched institution which, among its other distinctions, was the very first country club. The founders did not think it necessary to add a qualifying place-name to their invention, and so it remains to this day The Country Club, the first of its type, on the site of what is generally thought of as the most significant golf tournament ever: the 1913 US Open in which Francis Ouimet made golf an important game in the United States by defeating Harry Vardon and Ted Ray in the most storied of all play-offs.

Golf was not mentioned by the club's founders in 1882. A 6-hole course was laid out in 1893. Today there are 27 holes divided into nines named the Clyde, Squirrel, and Primrose. Customarily, the Clyde and the Squirrel nines are played as an 18-hole test, leaving the Primrose nine, according to one member, 'for ladies, children, and beginners'.

The course used today for great events at The Country Club – e.g. the 1963 US Open – is drawn from each of the three nines. Holes 10, 11, and 12 of the normal 18-hole test are discarded and replaced by three selected from the Primrose. One of these, the 11th on the revised course, is actually two holes for the members – a short par 4 followed by a short par 3 over water. When combined to form a brute of a par 4 over water, it works surprisingly well. The overall length of about 6,800 yd (6,218 m) presents no problem to the modern long hitter, but the greens are rather small and the rough is always allowed to grow very close to the putting surfaces.

The scores for the 1963 Open, held at The Country Club specifically to celebrate the 50th anniversary of Ouimet's triumph, were the highest in modern times. Julius Boros (who won the play-off), Jacky Cupit, and Arnold Palmer tied with 293, 9 over par. In calmer weather the scoring would no doubt have been lower, for extraordinary winds blew during three of the four rounds.

The Country Club, with four other clubs, founded the USGA in 1894. Since then, six of its members have been presidents of the association. Golf is not, by any means, the only game which has been under the considerable influence of The Country Club. Six members have won a total of 41 United States figure-skating titles, including Olympic gold medallist Tenley Albright (now Dr Tenley A. Gardiner). Tennis has been brightened by both the skills and generosity of Hazel Hotchkiss Wightman, another member, who donated the Wightman Cup. She has won a total of 53 national tennis championships. Curling was first played indoors in the United States at the club's covered rink. The club also entertained an annual race meeting until such private events were replaced by state-sanctioned tracks with their automatic betting machines.

The 1973 Walker Cup match marked the 11th national or international event for The Country Club and made it the first American club to host the Walker Cup twice. The first occasion was in 1932, a memorable match which featured the denting of the cup, on display behind the 18th

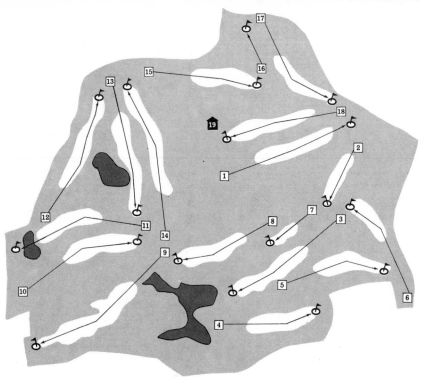

Top, The Country Club, Brookline, Mass., and *above*, the plan of the course

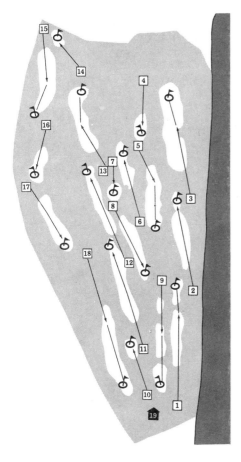

a part of Newcastle's appeal. Although there have been various alterations to his original design, notably those completed in 1908, his efforts were an immediate success. In 1898 in the *World of Golf* the links were described as 'undoubtedly the finest in Ireland' and in 1908 Harry Vardon added, 'The course now holds its own with all others.' In that year

at Newcastle. She remains the youngest winner of the British Ladies' title to this day. She went on to win four titles at Newcastle, the Irish of 1906 and the British again the following year. Her opponent in both those finals was her sister, Florence Hezlet (Mrs Cramsie). The entry on the latter occasion included the Curtis sisters who years later

green, by an errant shot of Leonard Crawley's. Crawley, undaunted as always, went on to win his match and the only British point that year.

County Down GC, Royal NORTHERN
IRELAND
Newcastle, Co. Down. 36 holes

Few championship courses in the world offer a more majestic setting than the Royal County Down GC. It lies between the Mourne Mountains and the sandy shores of Dundrum Bay about 30 miles south of Belfast. It is widely regarded as one of the best examples of the type of seaside golf peculiar to the British Isles.

The County Down club was formed in 1889 and at a meeting held in June of that year 'the Secretaries were empowered to employ Tom Morris to lay out the course at a cost not to exceed £4'. Compared with construction costs today such a meagre budget seems incredible, yet Tom Morris managed to build a course out of rough ground and sandhills. There is no doubt that nature was on his side – a fact that is so much

the club became 'Royal' and in the Coronation year of 1953 the Duke of Edinburgh became its patron. By this time the club was renowned and esteemed throughout the golfing world.

The first national championship played at Newcastle was the 1893 Irish Amateur Open, won by John Ball, and the first professional tournament was that in 1898 when Harry Vardon beat J. H. Taylor by 12 and 11. Fifty-six years later Harry Bradshaw won the Irish Professional Championship after a play-off with Christy O'Connor. In 1957 the home internationals were held at Newcastle for the first time. The club also has a proud connection with British championships and other international occasions to couple with the many other Irish championships to which it has been host.

These began when the British Ladies, who have always been faithful to Royal County Down, held their championship there in 1899: an historic landmark because the title went to May Hezlet who had celebrated her 17th birthday the week before, and won the Irish Ladies' title the week before that, also

gave their name to the Curtis Cup. Charlotte (Celia) Leitch won the first British Ladies' after World War I, in 1920, and in 1927 there began a trio of French victories interrupted by that of Wanda Morgan in 1935.

The first French winner was Thion de la Chaume, followed by the Vicomtesse de Saint-Sauveur who beat Mrs Valentine (Jessie Anderson) in 1950, and Brigitte Varangot who defeated Philomena Garvey in 1963. Largely because of their happy association with the club, the LGU took the Curtis Cup to Newcastle in 1968 and had a week of glorious weather and a close match.

Like all overseas visitors the Americans were enchanted by the beauty of the place in summer with a gentle breeze off the sea and the sun on the mountains. At such times golf has little better to offer: it has always seemed a pity that the Royal County Down's relative inaccessibility, shortage of accommodation and qualifying courses should have denied it an Open championship. The course certainly warrants it and the members have all the energy and enthusiasm to ensure

The course plan of Royal County Down GC

Royal County Down GC nestles at the foot of the Mourne Mountains

success. However, in 1970 there was the consolation of the British Amateur Championship which provided Michael Bonallack with his third successive victory. It is a nice coincidence that only John Ball, who won Newcastle's first championship in 1893, has achieved the British Amateur more times than Bonallack's five.

Besides the Championship course there is a No. 2 or ladies' course – much shorter but none the less sporting and demanding, and, in some parts, extremely narrow.

County Louth GC IRISH REPUBLIC

Baltray (Baile an Tragha), Co. Louth. 18 holes; 6,712 yd (6,137 m); par 73

One of the best linksland courses, established in 1892. Spread out over an unusually large area, four miles from Drogheda, it has plenty of room between holes and work on the greens has raised them to top quality. In the Irish Close Amateur Championship played there in 1962, history was made when Michael Edwards of Shandon Park beat Jack Harrington of Adare Manor at the 42nd hole, the longest championship final in any country. The following year the final was reduced from 36 to 18 holes.

In 1947 Harry Bradshaw, at the peak of his game, won the Irish Professional Championship there with 291, a score indicative of the quality of Baltray (as the course is commonly called, after the nearby fishing village of that name). Although the start is unimpressive with a hole of 320 yd (293 m) and somewhat featureless, there are some very testing holes. The finish is tough with the 17th and 18th both par 5s, and when the wind blows, as it generally does beside the sea, Baltray demands careful shot control as well as long hitting.

Baltray is unique among Irish clubs in that its most famous players have been women, Philomena Garvey and Mrs Val Reddan who, as Clarrie Tiernan won the Irish Ladies' title in 1936, and in 1938 became the first Irishwoman to be selected for a Curtis Cup team. After the war she faced her new local rival, Miss Garvey, in the final of the Irish. After one of the finest matches ever played between women Miss Garvey won at the 39th and went on to dominate the home scene for the next 17 years.

It was a woman, too, Mrs Josephine Connolly, who inaugurated the East of Ireland Championship in 1941, and 30 years later was still running it with striking success. In all but name this is the national amateur strokeplay championship and attracts a top-class field every year. The first winner was Joe Carr who went on to take first place

eleven more times and then see his son, Roddy, presented with the trophy in 1970.

County Sligo GC IRISH REPUBLIC

Rosses Point (Na Rossa), Co. Sligo. 18 holes; 6,457 yd (5,904 m); par 71

A linksland course situated in some of the most beautiful scenery in Ireland with breath-taking views on all sides. This is the countryside made famous by Ireland's poet W. B. Yeats. To the north is Lissadell and to the south Knockarea, both intimately associated with him as well as with Lady Gregory, one of the founders of Ireland's national theatre, the Abbey. To the south are the mountains of Sligo-Antrim, and dominating everything the strangely shaped Ben Bulben, with its long, flat top.

No hole is exceptionally long but the ever-present winds add the essential variety.

The first 4 holes and the 18th form what could be termed a separate section of the course from the other 13, for the 5th tee looks down on a vast panorama which embraces that hole and the remainder up to the 17th green. There follows a steep climb to the 18th tee, a short par 4 with its green close to the clubhouse. There is a sense of intimacy about the scene which greets the visitor who has turned the corner at the end of the little village of Rosses Point. Nearby a superb beach faces the Atlantic.

With space no object each hole is a separate entity and there are many fine testing ones, notably the 3rd, a long downhill switchback, and the 5th, another long one, its tee perched on what seems a cliff edge. The 14th has a stream snaking across the fairway two-thirds of the way to the green, making it a problematical two-shotter if the wind is adverse, and at the 17th, which doglegs to the left, the best placement for the drive is an alarmingly small area; anywhere else means much trouble.

Founded in 1894 Rosses Point, as it is universally known, has provided two famous Irish players, Cecil Ewing and James Mahon. The Ewing family association has been most important for they originally owned the hotel that in the early years served also as the clubhouse. Cecil Ewing was brought up on the course and showed exceptional talent from an early age. The West of Ireland Championship, going back to 1923, is traditionally the opening tournament of the Irish golfing season at Easter, and the Irish Close and Inter-Provincials are frequently staged at the club.

Course

The area upon and within which the game is played. In many cases, this area has to be

defined by the committee of the club and the boundaries can take many forms, but on some courses there are no limits or out-of-bounds, a ball being 'in play', unplayable or lost.

Course Architecture SEE GOLF COURSE ARCHITECTURE

Course Rating

The evaluation of the playing difficulty of a course compared with other rated courses, for the purpose of providing a uniform, sound basis on which to compute handicaps. *See also* Standard Scratch Score and Par.

Cowan, Gary CANADIAN

b. Kitchener, Ont., 1938. Canadian Junior 1956; Canadian Amateur 1961, runner-up 1959-60, 1964, 1968; Ontario Amateur 1964, 1968, 1971. US Amateur 1966, 1971; Ontario Open 1968; North and South Amateur 1970; winner New Zealand Centennial Invitation Tournament 1971.

Gary Cowan's aggressive play and his powerful, if occasionally erratic, game have gained him brilliant victories which have brought him international renown. Perhaps his supreme achievement was in 1971 when he became the first foreigner to win the US Amateur more than once, and the first person ever to win it at strokeplay. His first victory in that event was gained after a play-off with Deane Beman; but his second was won in explosive fashion. Playing in the last pairing on the final day, he needed a par 4 on the 396-yd (362-m) last hole to win by a stroke. From a difficult lie in the rough, he holed his second shot of 135 yd (123 m) with a no. 9 iron for an eagle to win by three shots.

Although Cowan has only once won his own national championship, he has been runner-up on four other occasions. He has also won a great many lesser titles in Canada and the United States, has been 14 times a member of the Ontario team in the Willingdon Cup Interprovincial Matches, and has played in 16 Canadian international teams – in six World Amateur Team Matches, six Americas Cup Team Matches and four Commonwealth Team Matches. In addition, he has been low amateur in both the Canadian Open Championship and the Masters Tournament in Augusta.

An insurance agent and a family man with two sons, Cowan has steadfastly resisted the lure of professional golf. In 1972 he chose to devote himself to his business and his family and to forego tournament golf, for a year at least, even at the cost of allowing his US Amateur Championship to go undefended.

Cox, Wilfred H. AMERICAN

b. Brooklyn, N.Y.C., 1897; d. 1969. North and South Open 1931; Ryder Cup 1931; tied 4th US Open 1931, tied 5th 1932, tied 3rd 1934

A well-known touring pro in the 1930s who became professional at Congressional in Washington, D.C., in 1937. Wiffy Cox helped form the Long Island PGA and was its first president. He was later president of the Middle Atlantic PGA and served on the national PGA tournament committee. Cox's wide stance and three-quarter backswing carried him to many tournament victories, five of them (including the San Francisco Matchplay, the Massachusetts Open and the North and South Open) in 1931, when he also tied for 4th in the US Open and was selected for the Ryder Cup team. The matches were played at Scioto that year and Cox won both his foursome and singles.

Cox, William James BRITISH

b. Chalfont St Giles, Buckinghamshire, 1910. Ryder Cup 1935, 1937

Bill Cox did not win a major tournament or championship during his playing career, but he was a consistent performer. Besides playing in Ryder Cup matches he toured South Africa in 1936-7 with the British PGA team. At the height of his career in 1938 he shared the halfway lead in the Open Championship at Sandwich but, like most of the field, he was beaten by the gale that raged on the final day.

After RAF service in World War II Cox settled down to the rewarding life of a club professional and coach, quickly obtaining a great reputation in the latter category. His services to sport brought him an OBE in 1967. Cox's early experience was wide, varied and valuable; he was assistant at Beaconsfield, Buckinghamshire; under Henry Cotton at Langley Park, Kent, and Royal Waterloo, Belgium; and at Addington. He took his first full professional appointment at Wimbledon Park, Surrey, and after the war went to his present club, Fulwell, Middlesex.

Craddock, Tom IRISH

b. Malahide, Co. Dublin, 1931. Irish Open Amateur 1958; East of Ireland 1959, 1965-6; Irish Close Amateur 1959; European Amateur Team Championship 1965, 1967, 1969, 1971; Walker Cup 1967, 1969; Lytham Trophy 1969

Sporting talent in families tends to run more strongly in Ireland than in other countries and four Craddock brothers, Tom, Joe, Mick and Paddy, all became first-class players. Malahide, on the coast north of Dublin, is a lively golfing area and the Craddock boys were swinging clubs almost as soon as they could walk. Tom was marked for international honours from an early age and his début for his country could hardly have been more auspicious. It occurred at Royal Birkdale in 1955 when he not only won all his three singles but by margins of 6 and 5 twice and 4 and 2.

That standard was fully maintained during the next six years. Selection for Ireland was automatic for he won the Irish Open Amateur over 72 holes on the last occasion that event was held; in 1959 he was crowned native champion after a memorable final against Joe Carr at Portmarnock which was decided at the 38th hole. He added the East of Ireland title to his list, also in 1959.

Then came a long break, for through pressure of work and ill-health he was absent from the Irish team from 1961-4 and not until winning the East of Ireland for the second time in 1965 was he in the news again. That year he resumed his place on the Irish team and was the hero of the European Amateur Team victory at Sandwich. The long-awaited and, in the opinion of many, overdue Walker Cup honour came to him in 1967; he retained his place in 1969, in which year he also beat a top-class field for the Lytham Trophy.

No amateur has a more classical style. Craddock's swing is round and full with the fractional pause at the top and the ball dispatched long distances. His iron play is of similar quality and his touch close to the greens is excellent. Had his putting been up to the same level few of his rivals could have lived with him.

Crail Golfing Society SCOTLAND

Crail, Fife. 5,499 yd (5,028 m); par 68

Founded in 1786 and ranking eighth among the oldest clubs, Crail has experienced, and survived, more ups and downs than most of its fellows, and it is distinguished by having kept its original name through all vicissitudes. James Gordon Dow, in his history of the club, states that Crail was the port of entry for golf balls imported from Holland for James VI and his fellow players – in 1618, however, the king granted patent to James Melville 'to furnish the Kingdom of Scotland with better golf balls and at an easier rate than has been for many years past' the price not to exceed 4 Scots shillings each.

The question of allegiance to the Stuart or the Hanoverian cause arose here as at the Bruntsfield Links Golfing Society, for in 1794 members were required to subscribe to a resolution of 'loyalty and affection' to George III, or be 'looked upon as having withdrawn from the Society'. Forty-five members signed; no abstentions are recorded. But such sentiments were not enough to sustain the society: membership shrank to 20 by 1810 and in 1812 the society suffered its first dissolution. An 1815 revival failed and another of 1824 was short-lived, but in 1832 there were 25 regular and 25 honorary

Wilfred H. Cox

Tom Craddock

members. At that time the society played on the former Sauchope Links and three rounds made 24 holes. In 1849 the February Medal meeting was cancelled because a 'Hare Hunt' had been arranged for the same day and this apparently led to another collapse until 1856 when the society moved to Balcomie Links.

It may be that the Crail Society pioneered one aspect of greenkeeping for in 1874 it was decided that 'iron cases be got for the holes on the links to prevent the holes from being destroyed' and subsequently officials inspected a course of eight rings, agreeing that they be left in the holes 'during that part of the year when there is most play on the links'. The 'eight' is significant as it is noted that in 1878 when the grass was very long on Sauchope 'play was very bad, with 104 a good score for 16 holes'. By 1892, Sauchope was overcrowded, and Tom Morris laid out a proper course at Balcomie that is still in use. It is pleasantly off the beaten track to St Andrews and with its wide, open vista of the Firth of Forth it is still a beautiful and historic place for holiday golf.

Crampton, Bruce AUSTRALIAN
b. Sydney, N.S.W., 1935. Australian Open 1956; World (Canada) Cup 1957; Milwaukee Open 1961; Texas Open 1964; Bing Crosby National Pro-Am 1965; Colonial National Invitation 1965; '500' Festival 1965; Hawaiian Open 1969; Westchester Classic 1970; American Golf Classic

1973; Houston Open 1973; Phoenix Open 1973; Tucson Open 1973.

Crampton has survived more than a decade on the gruelling US circuit, in which time he has risen to be one of the leading money winners. He took some time to make his mark in the United States because he was not a sound driver, but he made up for it on

the greens with a putting stroke which Gary Player has described as one of the best he has seen. More important to his success has been his stamina and strength of will: these enabled him, after he began playing regularly in the United States in 1959, to compete in 38 tournaments without a break in some years. In 1964 the only tournament he missed the whole year was in the week when his golfing equipment was stolen. Crampton is strong and keeps himself fit, neither drinking nor smoking.

He first travelled to Britain in 1956 with Norman von Nida from whom he learned much of his early golf. Like von Nida he gained a reputation for outspokenness which was not well received in some quarters in Britain. In the States, where he first competed in 1957 when he was invited to the Masters, he at once felt at home. He took easily to the tough life of pre-qualifying, and though it was some time before he began winning big prizes, he reckoned the competition more rewarding than elsewhere.

Crampton has made well over $100,000 every year since 1968. The years 1972 and 1973, when he had passed 35, were his best and showed his remarkable durability on the tour. In 1972 he finished 2nd behind Nicklaus in both the US Masters and the US Open. In spite of finishing high among the leading money winners he won no tournament that year, but as though in compensation he had three victories on the tour in 1973 and raised his total winnings to more than $1,000,000, which placed him 5th on the all-time money list.

Crans GC SWITZERLAND
Crans-sur-Sierre, Valais. 27 holes; Championship Course 6,870 yd (6,282 m); par 73

Sir Arnold Lunn, one of the pioneers of international skiing, who had already built the Palace Hotel at nearby Montana, laid out the first Crans course in 1905. In the absence of the tourists for whom it was designed, the course closed down during World War I. It was 1923 before a new course was contemplated and carried through by Elysée Bonvin. The growth of tourism in the area and the fact that the Swiss Open Championship has been held there every year except in wartime have given the club a position second to none in Switzerland.

The present two courses of 9 and 18 holes cover about 124 acres (50 ha) of land which the club leases from some 300 owners. Crans extends over an undulating plateau 5,000 ft above the Rhône valley with views across it to the Matterhorn and Monte Rosa. In one or two places steep grass-covered ravines cut

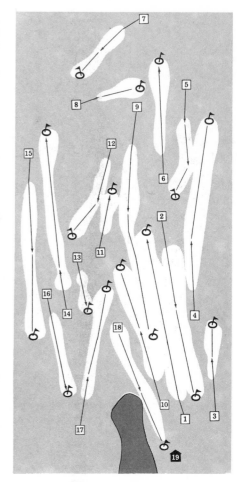

across the slopes (in winter the latter serve as nursery ski slopes), but on the whole the features are gentle and contrast with the majestic surrounding scenery. Crans is generally open from the end of May to the middle of October. The course can be stretched to nearly 6,900 yd for championships, but in the rarified air the ball travels about 10 per cent further than under normal conditions and yardage gives little indication of the club that may be required.

Crawford, Harry BRITISH
Harry Crawford, commonly known as 'Big Harry', was one of the famous figures around North Berwick at the end of the last century. Formerly a professional, he later got permission from the club to set up a ginger-beer stall on the course to act as a halfway house. He was a huge man, had a fog-horn voice, a ready wit and was well known for his friendship with Arthur Balfour, who later became Prime Minister.

He often caddied for Ben Sayers, one of his favourites, and also struck up a great association with Old Tom Morris. They had

Bruce Crampton

The course plan of Crans GC

an understanding that whoever died first should be accompanied by the survivor on his last journey. Harry outlived Tom and set off from North Berwick for St Andrews, a journey which meant a long leave of absence from his ginger-beer stall.

It was said that funerals were Crawford's great weakness and, whenever his stall was

Essex and Worcestershire, and for the MCC on their tour of the West Indies in 1926. He was a classical stylist at both sports, possessing one of the finest swings in golf.

He won the English championship at Hunstanton in 1931, beating W. Sutton in the final by 1 hole. In the 1932 Walker Cup at Brookline, Mass., he won Britain's only

point with a 1-hole victory over George Voigt.

Crawley won his foursome match with Frank Pennink in the victorious Walker Cup team in 1938 and won again with Laddie Lucas in 1947. He lost his singles to Francis Ouimet in 1934, to Johnny Fischer who had six threes in a row in 1938, and to M. H.

unmanned, the question was invariably, 'Whose funeral today?'. But he was a kind man who would always help those in need and, when he died at well over 75 in about 1910, his passing was much mourned.

Crawford, Mrs Jean (née Ashley)
AMERICAN
b. Kansas 1939. Curtis Cup 1962, 1966, 1968 (captain 1972); US Women's Amateur 1965, runner-up 1960, 1967

A graduate of Kansas University, Jean Crawford beat Mrs J. D. Welts (Anne Quast) for the US Women's title in 1965. In 1960 she lost to JoAnne Gunderson (Mrs D. R. Carner) and in 1967 to Mary Lou Dill.

Crawley, Leonard George BRITISH
b. Nacton, Suffolk, 1903. English Amateur 1931, runner-up 1934, 1937; President's Putter 1932, 1947, 1951-2; Walker Cup 1932, 1934, 1938, 1947; Gleneagles Silver Tassie 1934; runner-up French Open 1937

A double blue at Cambridge, Leonard Crawley was one of the great games players of this century, playing county cricket for

Ward in 1947; but on the last two occasions he found his opponents playing 'career' rounds against him.

It was easy to capture his lovely, strong, slow rhythm, his faultless footwork and balance. He fitted the description of the old cricketer, 'Elegance, all elegance, fit to play before the king in his parlour'.

Top, Crans: a view of the 16th green during the final round of the Swiss Open Championship. 1972

Above, Mrs Jean Crawford

Top, Leonard Crawley in action, *and above,* demonstrating croquet putting

He had a profound knowledge of the game and for more than 25 years wrote with authority as golf correspondent of the London *Daily Telegraph*. He also wrote golf and other articles for *The Field*.

Creavy, Tom AMERICAN
b. Tuckahoe, N.Y., 1911. USPGA 1931, semi-finalist 1932

Creavy's victory in the USPGA Championship in 1931 equalled Gene Sarazen's feat of winning at the age of 20. As a youngster he caddied for such players as Sarazen and Johnny Farrell and it was Farrell who sponsored him for PGA membership in 1928. Two weeks later, Creavy beat Farrell in the quarter-finals of the Metropolitan

PGA tournament. On his way to the national title, Creavy defeated Jock Collins, Peter O'Hara, Cyril Walker, Sarazen and Denny Shute. In the 1934 Open at Merion, he finished with a remarkable 66 to tie for 8th place. It was the only round under 70 in the tournament. Illness disrupted Creavy's tournament career and he confined himself primarily to his duties as club professional in upstate New York and to work within the PGA organization.

Cremin, Eric AUSTRALIAN
b. Mascot, N.S.W., 1914. Australian PGA 1937-8; Australian Open 1949

One of the leading professionals of his generation, although his career suffered

from the war years and the fact that Australia had few tournaments in the immediate postwar period. He did, however, win a total of 32 tournaments; his best years were 1949 when he won the Australian Open at Kensington with a fine finish, and four other tournaments, and 1950 when he won seven events. Cremin did not travel a great deal, but he was in Britain in 1951 with Kel Nagle. (This was Nagle's first season in Britain and also Peter Thomson's.)

When Cremin, who was an outstanding putter, gave up tournament play, he gained a great reputation as a teacher. For years he visited the Far East as golf instructor on the P and O liner *Canberra* and later became the senior professional at the Singapore Island CC. He also played a very significant part around 1959 in the development of the Far Eastern circuit. It was largely his influence which persuaded many leading players to take part in the Hong Kong Open and other events.

Crenshaw, Ben AMERICAN
b. 1952

No amateur since Jack Nicklaus came to the professional circuit with more advance publicity than Crenshaw, and none has so quickly justified his reputation. He did not stay amateur long enough to win the US Amateur Championship but achieved something that is even more difficult: victory three times running in the National Collegiate, sharing it in the second year, 1972, with Tom Kite, a fellow member of the University of Texas team. In addition to this he won numerous regional titles and in 1973, the year that he turned professional, he compiled as an amateur an aggregate of 69·9 over 42 competitive rounds. In the course of this he finished tied 3rd in a professional tournament at the Heritage club.

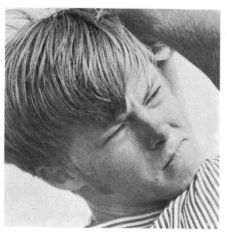

With such a record, some reaction might have been expected when he began competing for money, but in the San Antonio – Texas Open, he opened with a 65 and won the event by 2 strokes, becoming the first player to win his inaugural event as a professional since Marty Fleckman in 1967. He followed that with 2nd place and $44,000 prize money in the World Open Championship, a new event held at Pinehurst. After that he quietened down a little, but left no doubt that his magnetism and his intelligent approach to the game would help him to go a long way.

Critchley, Mrs A. C. SEE FISHWICK, DIANA

Critchley, Bruce BRITISH
A player with a beautiful style who never quite fulfilled his early promise. He won the Worplesdon foursomes with Frances Smith in 1961 but business kept him out of serious competition for several years. When he returned, he won a place in the 1969 Walker Cup team and in 1970 reached the semi-final of the British Amateur Championship. His mother won the British Ladies' Championship in 1930 as Diana Fishwick. He gave up competitive golf in the early 1970s.

Crocker, Helen Fay URUGUAYAN
b. Montevideo 1914. US Women's Open 1955, 3rd 1958; runner-up Tam O'Shanter World 1957; runner-up LPGA Championship 1958

Tom Creavy

Ben Crenshaw

Bruce Critchley

Fay Crocker's great-grandfather was captain of a New England whaler; her grandfather settled in Montevideo, built a 9-hole course, and introduced golf to that country. He worked hard to make his family play the game. Her father won the championship of Uruguay 37 times and she followed him by winning the women's title 20 times; she also won the Argentine Championship 14 times before moving to the United States and turning professional. Before she did that in 1954 she played two or three times in the US Women's Amateur; in 1950 she lost in the third round to Mae Murray at the 27th hole, the longest match in the history of the event. Her performance in that match at East Lake, Atlanta, drew favourable comment from Bobby Jones who watched her play.

Croome, Arthur C. M. BRITISH
b. Uplands, nr Stroud, Gloucestershire, 1866; d. *c.* 1929

A fine golfer who also hurdled and played cricket for Oxford and was a member of the Gloucestershire cricket side with Dr W. G. Grace. He was cricket correspondent of *The Times* and wrote for the *Morning Post* on golf, a game he took up when his cricketing days were done. He was co-founder of the Oxford and Cambridge Golfing Society and was honorary secretary until 1919, when he succeeded John Low as captain. He was a man of many talents who, in his one excursion into golf-course architecture, designed the lovely course at Liphook.

Croquet Putting
A method of putting similar to that of striking a croquet ball, with hands separated on the shaft, legs astride the line of putt. It was declared illegal in 1967 on the grounds that it did not constitute a golf stroke, to the dismay of those who found in it a cure to the shakes. The new Rules demanded that 'a player shall not make a stroke on the putting green from a stance astride, or with either foot touching, the line of the putt or an extension of that line behind the ball'. They also introduced a regulation governing the angle of the shaft to the head of the putter, requiring a divergence of at least 10 degrees from the vertical. The croquet method called for a shaft set at right angles to the head.

Cros, Claudine (Mrs Rubin) FRENCH
b. Paris 1943. French Ladies' Open 1960, 1968; German Ladies' Open 1961; French Ladies' Close 1964-5; World Women's Amateur Team Championship 1964, 1966, 1968, 1970; runner-up British Ladies' 1968, 1972

With the Vicomtesse de Saint-Sauveur, Brigitte Varangot and Catherine Lacoste she dominated Continental women's golf throughout the 1960s. She had a simple classical style, devoid of all frills, and was one of the purest strikers of a golf ball of her age. From a motionless, statuesque address she swung the club with perfect rhythm, stroking rather than punching her iron shots with great accuracy. Yet she lacked some 'devil' in matchplay which prevented her, in spite of her successes, from doing herself full justice; or it may have been that her style inspired others to play their best.

She reached the semi-finals of the British championship three times in addition to 1968 and 1972 when she was beaten in the final at Walton Heath by Miss Varangot. That was the nearest she came to a victory she seemed to have deserved. Miss Varangot, a close friend with whom she had shared lodgings throughout the week, squared at the 18th with a 13-ft putt for a birdie and won at the 19th.

Born into an athletic family, Claudine Cros's game was from the start matched against two low-handicap brothers (Patrick played for France before turning professional). If she had a weakness it was in her chipping, but this much improved after she went to live in America and Venezuela, where she married a Frenchman. In the world team championship she played every time from its beginning in 1964 until 1972. Her final 74 in the first year when France won

was made with superb iron play but without holing a putt of any length. At Madrid in 1970 her 70 was the lowest score in the championship. In 1972 she made intense preparations for the British championship at Hunstanton and reached the final, having defeated an American Curtis Cup player on the way, Barbara McIntire. Mrs Rubin's swing was as pure and graceful as ever, although she was by now a mother of two, but she began to tire in the final and Michelle Walker, after a shaky start, was not to be denied. In 1973 she went to live in Tokyo and found that only by turning professional could she enjoy the standard of golf she was used to. She played well enough to make it financially worthwhile.

Croquet Putting: Peter Butler with croquet putter watched by Leonard Crawley

Top, the Sam Snead method of croquet putting

Above, Claudine Cros

Crosby, Bing AMERICAN
b. Tacoma, Wash., 1904

Harry L. Crosby's love of golf was born when he took part in Paul Whiteman's great musical *The King of Jazz* in 1930. With other musicians, he played at Lakeside in Los Angeles, a club of which he was often champion and is now a life member. Macdonald Smith was his great hero and his own easy rhythm as a golfer stemmed from the days when he used to watch him with admiring eyes. Golf game fairly easily to Crosby, just as his singing had done, and he eventually acquired a handicap of 2 and took part in championships. In 1950 he played in the British Amateur at St Andrews and, with as large a gallery as Ben Hogan might have

had, began with two 3s against one of the local players. He shares the distinction with one other golfer of having holed in one at the 16th at Cypress Point. In all the world there is no finer hole at which to achieve it.

In 1971 he went back to St Andrews for a return friendly match – although the word soon got around and another huge gathering turned out to watch, and in 1972 he was over again to organize a seniors' tournament at St Andrews. Crosby's great contribution to the game has been in staging and sponsoring the Bing Crosby Pro-Am Tournament which is now part of the American professional circuit. It started in 1936 at Rancho Santa Fe, Cal., and has developed into a unique occasion. After World War II,

Bing Crosby

having joined Cypress Point, Crosby suggested that the tournament should be played there. Later, as it grew in size and importance, Pebble Beach, also in California, became the headquarters with everyone playing two rounds there and one round at Cypress Point and Spy Glass Hill.

For some years, Crosby himself guaranteed the tournament but always the profits went to charity. A dozen or more youth centres have been built; others, together with universities in 26 states, have received endowments from him.

Cruickshank, Robert Allan AMERICAN
b. Grantown-on-Spey, Moray, 1894.
Runner-up US Open 1923, tied 2nd 1932,

3rd 1934, 1937; North and South Open 1926-7, 1943, runner-up 1944

In 1920, two young Scottish amateurs, Bobby Cruickshank, who had been a prisoner in World War I, and Tommy Armour, played in the British Amateur Championship. Cruickshank gave Cyril Tolley, the eventual winner, his hardest match; but, like Armour, Cruickshank turned professional and moved to the United States. He never succeeded in winning the British or American Open championships but he tied with Bobby Jones in the American Open of 1923 at Inwood, finishing with a birdie on the 36th for a total of 296 (73, 72, 78, 73). In the play-off, he and Jones were level going up the last fairway

Robert A. Cruickshank

but Cruickshank, by pulling his drive and having to play his second over a lagoon, failed to make four and Jones thus won his first major championship.

Without Jones on the scene, Cruickshank might well have become better known than he was but he was one of the best American professionals during the 1920s and 1930s, and twice more came close to capturing the US Open, tying 2nd in 1932 3 strokes behind Sarazen, who played the last 28 holes in 100 strokes, and finishing 3rd equal in 1934 and 3rd in 1937.

Small of stature, Cruickshank maintained his game splendidly and in 1950 tied for 25th place in the US Open at Merion at the age of 56.

Crystal Downs CC USA
Frankfort, Mich. 18 holes; 6,670 yd
(6,099 m)

From a bluff above Crystal Lake, a small stretch of water on the western rim of Michigan about 180 miles north of Chicago, the view commands rolling meadowland, dunes, wooded ridges, and the blue-green waters of Lake Michigan blending with the distant horizon. This expanse strongly resembled a British moor in its natural state, and it is fortunate that it did. Were it not for its appearance, it is unlikely that Crystal Downs would have its present place in the world of golf: only this persuaded Alister Mackenzie to undertake its design in 1928.

Crystal Downs was actually in operation then, the members playing a 9-hole course laid out by Eugene Goebel, who was primarily a park planner and landscape architect, although he had designed some golf courses around Grand Rapids, 100 miles or so to the south. By mid-1927, Walkley Ewing, one of the original members, began to realize the full potential of the terrain and he was afraid the club might have missed a chance to construct a truly outstanding course. Mackenzie had just finished Cypress Point and was eager to return home to Britain, but through Robert Hunter, the author of a book on golf-course architecture, Ewing lured Mackenzie to the shores of Crystal Lake. The ground appealed to Mackenzie; then and there he and Perry Maxwell set about designing an 18-hole course. Even though they had no assurance they would be paid for it, the two men went ahead and completed a basic plan for a new course. Eventually they received $5,000 for their work.

The course was completed in 1933, and it has remained basically the same ever since. It is a typical Mackenzie layout, if there is such a thing. It is not exceptionally long at

6,670 yd from the back tees, but the holes present an intriguing variety of golf problems, and it is a delight just to be out on the fairways trying to solve them.

Cudd, Bruce H. AMERICAN
b. 1934. Oregon Amateur 1952-3; runner-up Pacific Northwest Amateur 1952-3; Pacific Northwest Open 1953; semi-finalist US Amateur 1953; Western Amateur 1954; Walker Cup 1955

One of the country's leading amateurs in the early 1950s. After reaching the semi-finals of the 1953 US Amateur and winning the Western in 1954, he was selected for the 1955 Walker Cup.

Cumming, George CANADIAN
b. Bridge of Weir, Renfrewshire, 1879; d. 1949. Canadian Open 1905, runner-up 1906-7, 1909, 1914

A transplanted Scot who became the dean of golf professionals in Canada. Cumming emigrated to Canada as a youth, served for over 50 years as professional at Toronto GC, and may fairly be claimed as a Canadian.

having the lowest 18-hole score in the 1908 Open Championship.

Cup
Another name for the hole cut on the putting green. It particularly refers to the lining or tin which must be 'sunk at least one inch below the surface of the putting green, unless the nature of the soil makes it impractical to do so'.

Cupit, Jack AMERICAN
b. Longview, Tex., 1938. Canadian Open 1961; runner-up US Open 1963

One of the leading young players on the PGA tour despite an unorthodox looping swing, Jacky Cupit won many amateur tournaments in Texas and was a member of the University of Houston team that won three straight National Collegiate titles. His first victory as a professional came in the Canadian Open of 1961 and he won the Western Open the next year, but it was not until 1963 that he attracted wide attention. That year he tied with Julius Boros and Arnold Palmer in the Open at Brookline,

Before leaving Scotland he had caddied and been assistant professional at Ranfurly Castle GC, learned clubmaking at Forgan's, and spent three years as professional at the Dumfries and Galloway GC. Renowned for his play, but equally for his teaching of many fine Canadian golfers, both professional and amateur, and in the early years for clubmaking, he also has to his credit the design of dozens of fine courses in Canada. He was largely responsible for raising greatly the standard of his profession in his adopted country. He was a pioneer in the formation of the Canadian Professional Golfers' Association, of which he was captain on five occasions.

One of his golfing distinctions was that of

Mass., and finished 2nd in the play-off. He has four brothers who are golf professionals.

Cuppy
A lie in which the ball rests in a tiny depression in the ground.

Curtis Cup see INTERNATIONAL MATCH FOR THE CURTIS CUP

Curtis, Harriot S. (b. 1878) and **Margaret** (b. 1880) AMERICAN
On 25 May 1905, at Royal Cromer, before the British Ladies' Championship on that course, a party of visiting American players had a match with the leading British women players. The pleasure of that contest so im-

pressed two of the visitors, the Curtis sisters, that they were inspired with the idea of having regular international fixtures involving 'women golfers of many lands', but it was not until 1932 that their dreams were realized. In that year were established the biennial matches for the Curtis Cup, between representatives of the United States and the British Isles.

Both the Curtis sisters were winners of the American Women's National Amateur Championship. Appropriately, Miss Harriot won it first, in 1906. The following year they both reached the final; this was the only occasion on which two sisters have met at that stage of the event. Margaret won in 1907, and again in 1911 and 1912.

Bruce Cudd

Jack Cupit chipping to the 6th at Dalmahoy GC

Top, Margaret Curtis – a portrait by Charles Hopkinson

Above, Harriot and Margaret Curtis

Altogether, Margaret played in 25 championships, her first in 1897. She was runner-up in 1900, and again in 1905. Fifty years after her first appearance in the National Amateur, Margaret competed in 1947, and entered for the last time in 1949 at the age of 65. In 1958 she was nominated fourth winner of the Bob Jones Award. She died in September 1965 aged 81. Besides being a champion golfer, Margaret was also an outstanding lawn-tennis player, and won the Women's National Doubles title with Evelyn Sears.

The Curtis sisters' family home is at Manchester, Mass., nearby the Essex CC, which was their course, and on which the 1938 Curtis Cup match was held.

in'. In executing the cut-up shot, the clubface is intentionally laid back and open to increase loft and thus produce more backspin effect on landing. It is mainly used in recovery or pitch shots.

Cyprus

Cyprus is an attractive holiday island; but though the climate favours all-year golf, the game is not one of the attractions of this Greco-Turkish state in the eastern Mediterranean. Nor, despite some talk of developing golf there as a tourist amenity, is the game likely to become a factor in international holiday planning in the near future.

Interest in golf in Cyprus is centred

Cut

The type of spin imparted to the ball by coming across it from 'outside to in'. It is usually unintentional, not to be confused with the 'fade' which is often a sign of control, the ball flying from left to right in a prescribed curve. A more severely cut shot or faded shot played without apparent control is a slice.

Cuthell, Mrs A. H. see ADAIR, RHONA

Cut-up

A shot more familiar in the days of hickory-shafted clubs, though the term is still applicable today when the face of the club is laid open and drawn across the ball from 'out to

largely on the British Joint Services GC at Episkopi. That club has a 13-hole seaside, all-sand course. The Cyprus Mines Corporation operates a 9-hole, part-grass, part-sand course at Pendayia for company staff and invited guests; and there remains a sketchy sort of course at the Nicosia GC which, once active, has fallen into relative disuse, particularly since the troubles between the Greek and Turkish communities that began in the early 1960s.

Cypress Point GC USA

Pebble Beach, Cal. 18 holes; 6,464 yd (5,911 m); par 72

Possibly the most exciting diversified plot of golf land in the world is that occupied by

Cypress Point on the Monterey Peninsula. One local golf expert has analysed the 18 holes as follows: typical seaside holes: the 1st, 13th, 14th, and 18th; typical inland holes: the 8th, 9th and 12th; holes of seaside escarpment type: the 15th, 16th and 17th; holes of wooded, hillside character: the 5th, 6th, 7th and 10th. Not everyone may agree exactly with this analysis, but the point is well taken: the variety of golf holes at Cypress Point is probably unique.

Cypress Point was laid out in the 1920s by Alister Mackenzie who had been engaged by Marion Hollins, a top woman golfer who had gone into real-estate promotion. Most people think that Mackenzie, a Scot whose first profession was medicine, utilized the marvellous land at his disposal with imagination and taste. (Bobby Jones, for one, was enormously impressed by Cypress Point, and it was a main reason why he asked Mackenzie to assist him in laying out the Augusta National.) On the other hand, there has always been a faction that believes that Mackenzie failed to exploit the full potential of the terrain and, for the most part, created routine holes that succeed only because of their magnificent setting.

Be that as it may, nearly everyone is agreed that the 15th, 16th and 17th holes form one of the most thrilling passages in golf. On the 15th, 139 yd (127 m) from the back tees, a deep inlet, booming with the sound of waves crashing into rocks, separates the tee from the green. The 16th, a 233-yd (213-m) 3, requires a carry of about 210 yd (192 m) across the Pacific to reach a green sited on a virtual island that is lined with cliffs of yellowish-brown rock. It is the great picture-postcard hole of the golf world. The satisfaction of hitting the green is enormous, and the visiting golfer should always give it a go unless he is working on an especially good scoring round. Then he should play a safe iron onto the fairway that arcs around to the left of the direct line. The 17th, 375 yd (343 m), sweeps to the right in a long curve that hugs the cliffed coast. It is fatal to get into the ice plant in the rough by the cliffs but, on the other hand, the cautious tee shot out to the left will often end up either directly or partly stymied by the huge trees that command the middle of the fairway.

Cypress Point is not a long course – from the back markers, it is still under 6,500 yd – but from start to finish it is one of those insidious courses on which an error can cost the golfer not just one stroke but two or three or four, or more. It is a joy to play because of the diversity of holes it offers, its splendid natural backdrop, and its lack of traffic. With luck a glimpse can be had of the wild

Curtis Cup 1972 – Hollis Stacy of the US team holes a long putt

deer that roam this section of the peninsula. In the 1960s when Tommy Bolt was playing a round on the course in the Bing Crosby Pro-Am and playing so badly that he was looking for an excuse to lose his temper, he was just about to hit his tee shot on one of the homeward holes when a deer darted out of the woods and bounded across the fairway. Bolt hurled his club to the ground and growled with anger, 'Did you ever see such rotten marshalling?'

Czechoslovakia

In 1899, when Bohemia was still part of the Austro-Hungarian empire, casual observers at the old Imperial Common in Prague, where horseraces were usually held, were

times during a round. Another well-known spa in western Bohemia, Mariánské Lázně (Marienbad), followed with its own 9-hole course, opened by King Edward VII. In 1913 Baron Ringhofer built his own private course at Volesovice and, in the same year, the first Slovak course was opened at another watering place, Piešťany.

By this time many players from Prague were competing in tournaments abroad, although it was not until 1924 that a club was formed in the capital. It owed its existence to the initiative of Sir George Clark, British Ambassador to the new republic of Czechoslovakia, and its course was built on the site of the military training grounds in Motol. Three years later the Piešťany course was

Czech Open Men's and Women's Championships were held from 1932 to 1938, and the Czech Open from 1935 to 1938, Henry Cotton winning twice. Czechoslovakia was one of the 12 founder members of the European Golf Association in 1937.

A beautiful new 9-hole course was ready in 1938 at Klánovice, 30 miles southeast of Prague, making a total of two 18-hole and six 9-hole courses in the country, but after World War II only Mariánské Lázně, Klánovice and Lisnice were playable. Karlovy Vary was gradually reconstructed and by 1949 was considered the most attractive course in the country.

The Czechoslovak Golfers' Union is now responsible for about 1,000 golfers and once more holds annual national and international championships with regular weekend competitions at all the clubs. The Union is again a member of the European Golf Association and its players take part in the World Cup.

A third 18-hole course is now in use at Moravská Ostrava in northern Moravia. In 1972 two more were under construction in Prague and Poděbrady and several others were planned. The number of courses had risen to 14 by 1972.

Generally speaking, golf is not expensive, nor is accommodation, particularly in the western spas. Visitors are welcome to compete in tournaments and championships.

surprised by the behaviour of a group of men. They were hitting small white balls with club-shaped sticks into holes marked with red flags. By so doing, they introduced golf to what is now Czechoslovak territory. A little later they had to forsake the common for a remoter region on the outskirts of the city. But the first course, as it happened, was not built in Prague.

That distinction fell to Karlovy Vary (Carlsbad), the famous spa, where, on 6 September 1904, the Gentlemen's Fencing Club changed its name to the International Sporting Club. Its main facilities were for tennis and golf. Nine holes were laid out in the Imperial Park in the valley of the Teplá; the golfer had to play over the river five

reopened and another one, which still exists, was laid out at Lisnice, 15 miles south of Prague.

Up to this time all the clubs had 9-hole courses. Karlovy Vary became the first 18-hole course in 1932. Mariánské Lázně also completed a second 9 holes that year. In 1935 the first Moravian club was formed in Brno, also at a military training ground.

The Czech Golfing Association was founded in 1932 with the staging of the first championship for a cup presented by the President. It was won by S. Samek of Berlin. Other winners of various early championships included J. W. Bailey, Count John de Bendern, Henry Cotton, and Eva von Szlavy who won the women's title in 1937. The

The 16th hole of the Cypress Point GC

Dailey, Allan Marshall BRITISH

b. Leuchars, Fife, 1908. Ryder Cup 1933;
Dunlop-Southport Tournament 1935; tied
4th British Open 1936; captain PGA 1956

Although born within a few miles of St
Andrews, Allan Dailey has spent practically
all his golf career in England and for many
years has been attached to the Berkshire GC
near Ascot. He first became prominent by
beating three international golfers in succession to win the Roehampton matchplay
tournament in 1933, and later the same year
he was chosen for the Ryder Cup team. In
1936 he toured South Africa with the British
team. His brother Russell is professional at
Royal Wimbledon.

Dallemagne, Marcel FRENCH

b. Paris, 1898. Belgian Open 1927, 1937;
French Close Professional 1930, 1932, 1935,
1937, 1939, 1950; Swiss Open 1931, 1937,
1949; Dutch Open 1933; equal 3rd British
Open 1936; French Open 1936-8; Italian
Open 1937

Dallemagne was the first of several French
professionals who, following long after
Arnaud Massy and Jean Gassiat, established
themselves as serious rivals to the British
and American elite between the wars. Tall
and easy of movement, he had a fine swing
with plenty of power and, as his record
shows, was good enough to win many Continental titles at a time when they were considered almost the prerogative of British and
American challengers.

Daly, Fred IRISH

b. Portrush, Co. Antrim, 1911. Irish Open
1946; British Open 1947, runner-up 1948,
tied 3rd 1950, 3rd 1952; British Professional
Matchplay 1947-8, 1952; Ryder Cup 1947,
1949, 1951, 1953

One of the best golfers on the British
circuit after World War II, Daly was also an
outstanding personality. He was not a stylish
golfer, for his wide arc and consequent
movement away from the ball gave his swing
the appearance of a lurch, but for a small
man he commanded great length and his
golf was full of character. He walked jauntily
along with a rolling gait, whistling to himself
for relaxation and taking anything up to a
dozen waggles and sideways glances at the

hole before putting. But for a time he reigned
supreme, not only by the consistency of his
play, but thanks to his strong competitive
spirit. He played with great tenacity, defeating 'Tiger' Poulton in a match of the British
PGA Championship at the 30th hole;
shortly after returning to the clubhouse he
was out again in the next round covering the
first 5 holes at Walton Heath in 16 strokes.

It was at Portrush where he was born and
grew up as a caddie that he learned to drive
long and straight and to withstand the strong
winds. He moved to Mahee GC, Co Antrim,
first as assistant and then as professional.
Most of his successes before the war were
confined to Northern Ireland, whose championship he won seven times, starting in
1936. After the war he came quickly to
prominence adding the Irish Dunlop
Masters and another North of Ireland
championship to victory in the Irish Open.
His success in the 1947 British Open owed
something to his finishing his final round
before a strong wind got up, but he showed it
to be no fluke by winning the British Matchplay Championship the same year, which
had not been achieved as a double since
James Braid in 1905. The next year he won
it again, a feat only previously achieved by
Abe Mitchell (Rees, Coles and Thomson
later defended their titles successfully). In
winning the British Open he had holed two
significant long putts – one of 20 yd at the
13th which steadied him after two bad shots,
and one of 12 yd at the 18th, which drew him
clear of Reg Horne who eventually finished
2nd. This ability to hole putts under pressure
was a feature of his play; he showed it again
notably during the 1953 Ryder Cup match
at Wentworth when he holed a long putt on
the 36th green to win his foursome with
Bradshaw, and the following day continued
to hole long putts in inflicting a heavy defeat
on Ted Kroll. His policy with the putts was
to let the ball die at the hole rather than to
give the hole a chance, and none can say
that he was not most successful. In winning a
professional tournament at Mere, Cheshire,
in 1949, he completed the first nine holes in
29 and went on to finish with 63, which
established a winning lead.

Darwin, Bernard BRITISH

b. Kent 1876; d. 1961. Golf writer for *The
Times* and *Country Life* 1907-53. *Golf
Illustrated* Gold Vase 1919; semi-finalist
British Amateur 1921; Walker Cup 1922;
President's Putter 1924; Worplesdon Four-
somes (with Joyce Wethered) 1933; captain
Royal and Ancient 1934-5

Darwin's fame as a golf writer was based
not only on his deep knowledge of the game

and a charming style but on his achievement
in developing golf reporting from a collection
of figures at the foot of the column into a
branch of literary journalism. What he
was seen to do for golf was soon attempted in
other sports. His philosophy of writing was
to describe what he saw regardless of whether
it was the most sensational event of the day,
never to strain for an effect, to underwrite
the drama but paint the lesser events larger
than life, to spread the golf details thin to
attract a wider audience. Like Lamb and
Hazlitt – as an essayist he somewhat resembled both – he was far from gentle. A
bagful of prejudices and partisan foibles
added savour to his writing, whether it was
on golf, books, children, prizefighters or
well-known criminals. His observations
were sometimes waspish, but on the rare
occasions that he criticized a player in print
the tone was almost invariably kind and
generous. He never lost his sense of humour
or proportion, he restrained his affection
almost austerely, and underwrote rather
than overwrote. The human friendliness
born of the game delighted him even more
than its thrills.

After Cambridge, whose golf team he
captained in his third year of playing for the
university, he practised law for a time,
which gave him his lifetime's interest in
famous criminals; but he turned gladly from
it to writing in 1907. He first played for
England against Scotland in 1902 and did so
eight times up to 1924. He served for two
years in Macedonia in World War I and
joined the staff of *The Times* in 1919. In 1922
he went with the first Walker Cup team to
visit the United States, and took the place of
the British captain when he fell ill. Beaten
with Tolley in the top foursome, he won his
single against the US captain, Bill Fownes.

Darwin's passion to win made him a
difficult foursomes partner and highly
critical of his own performance, but his
feelings never lasted beyond the last green.
His weekly column was avidly read and his
anonymous leading articles for *The Times*
were often betrayed by his weakness for
quotations from Dickens, an author he knew
almost by heart. In 1934 he drove himself in
as captain of the Royal and Ancient – a
good drive although he said he found the
ball assuming the shape of an egg as he
reached the top of the backswing. He
received the CBE in 1937 for his services to
sport and literature. His works on golf
include *Present Day Golf*, with George Duncan; *Tee Shots and Others*; *Golf Between Two
Wars*; *Green Memories*; *Rubs of the Green*;
Playing the Like; *Out of the Rough*. Other
works are *The Game's Afoot*, a sports an-

thology; *A Dickens Pilgrimage*; *W. G. Grace*; *Dickens*; *John Gulley and his Times*; *Life is Sweet Brother*; and his autobiography, *The World that Fred Made*.

Davies, Richard D. AMERICAN
b. California 1930. Runner-up Mexican Amateur 1957-8; British Amateur 1962; low

amateur US Open 1963; Walker Cup 1963
One of the more surprising winners of the British Amateur, beating John Povall of Wales at Hoylake by one hole in the 1962 final, thereby securing a place in the 1963 Walker Cup team.

Davis, Zara Grace Bonner (Mrs S. M. Bolton) BRITISH
b. London 1914. Curtis Cup 1948 (non-playing captain 1956, 1966); runner-up English Ladies' 1948
Zara Davis's outstanding capabilities of leadership were recognized by the Ladies' Golf Union when she was appointed captain of the British Curtis Cup team in 1956 and again in 1966. In 1957 she captained the British team in the Commonwealth Tournament at Hamilton, Ont. Before these assignments she had led England in home nationals in 1955. She was a first-class player as well as leader and represented Britain in the 1948 Curtis Cup and Vagliano Cup matches. She was also a member of the British team that toured South Africa in 1951 and played for England in seven home

Richard Davies

international matches between 1939 and 1956. In 1939 she married S. M. Bolton, then captain of Royal Portrush GC, and has since lived in this Northern Irish town.

Dawson, John W. AMERICAN
Semi-finalist British Amateur 1929; runner-up US Amateur 1947; US Seniors' 1958-60; runner-up French Amateur 1960
One of the country's top amateurs for many years with several victories to his credit. His record, illustrious enough as it is, would no doubt have been better but for his absence from national competition for almost 20 years. He reached the quarter-finals of the US Amateur in 1928 after upsetting Chick Evans in the first round, but was asked to withdraw from the 1929 event because of his affiliation with Spalding, the sports equipment firm. He did not enter the Amateur again until after World War II when he was runner-up in 1947. During those years as a promotion man for Spalding, Dawson won many sectional titles and proved his ability by winning the 1942 Crosby Invitational by three shots from the nation's leading professionals. He went into real estate that year and is generally given credit for developing Palm Springs into the famous resort that it is. He came close to winning a major championship as early as 1929 when he reached the semi-finals of the British Amateur. But, after being three up on the 16th tee in the semi-final match, he lost the next four holes, against J. N. Smith of Earlsferry Thistle.

Dead
A shot that leaves the ball so close to the hole that the holing of the putt is as near as can be a certainty is said to be 'dead'.

De Bendern, Count John (John de Forest) BRITISH
b. 1907. British Amateur 1932, runner-up 1931; Walker Cup 1932; Austrian Open Amateur 1937
John de Forest, a popular player with a compact, unorthodox swing, was well known in London golf circles as a member of Addington and Sunningdale, as well as of the Royal and Ancient. His elder brother, Count Alaric de Bendern, was also a fine golfer who won the Swedish and Dutch Open Amateur titles. John de Forest, having finished runner-up in the British Amateur Championship to Eric Martin Smith in 1931, went one better the following year, beating Eric Fiddian by 3 and 1 at Muirfield.

Decker, Mrs J. D. SEE SANDER, MRS ANNE

de Forest, John SEE DE BENDERN, COUNT JOHN

Deighton, Dr Frank William Gordon BRITISH
b. Glasgow 1927. Walker Cup 1951, 1957; Commonwealth Tournament 1954, 1959; Scottish Amateur 1956, 1959
A graduate of Glasgow University, Frank Deighton became one of the leading amateurs in Britain in the 1950s. A fine swinger, he won the Scottish championship twice and in 1957 played in the Walker Cup match in Minikhada. He was picked in 1951 but did not play. He has remained a fine player and has won many medals at Royal and Ancient meetings at St Andrews.

Delhamyeh CC LEBANON
9 holes; 6,530 yd (5,971 m); par 72 (for 18 holes)
The course has slanting Bermuda-grass fairways and Japanese-grass greens which break sharply toward the sea below.

Delhi GC INDIA
New Delhi, 18 holes; 6,972 yd (6,375 m); par 73
In 1928, a golfing Scot, chief of Delhi's horticulture department, headed a Governmental committee to select and make an 18-hole golf course worthy of the Indian capital. The Scot, with a secret passion for excavation, hoped that laying out a course in an archaeologically promising area might lead to sensational discoveries.
Borrowing two elephants, he set off through the dense undergrowth between the Moghul Emperor Humayun's tomb and the historic Babarpur *tehsil* (estate), southeast of Delhi, a vast burial ground for Moghul nobles, and a storehouse of archaeological relics.
The Scot nominated himself first captain of the Lodhi GC, but, despite much flattening of burial mounds, nothing came to light except angry snakes and scorpions. Three years later the amateur archaeologist died.
From 1931 the club languished and almost closed, until in 1950, with a special lease drawn up at Prime Minister Jawaharlal Nehru's bidding, the Delhi GC was founded. Jungle was partly cleared, the area extended, tube wells sunk, new greens and tees were laid, and thanks to the efforts of the Commonwealth War Graves Commission, over two hundred trees were planted – a single coconut palm sways a thousand miles from its native ocean strand – together with thousands of flowering shrubs and bushes, providing sanctuary for more than 300

species of birds, monkey, jackal, mongoose, cobra and squirrel.

On the par-4, 442-yd (404-m) 6th, the player can ponder the placing of a drive from the peaceful shade of an arched lantana-covered family tomb. Near the 6th green, monkeys sit scratching on a weathered tombstone, and along Lodhi Road passing turbaned peasants stop bullock and camel carts to watch.

The sandy loam has produced a rich turf, good for the most exacting fairway wood shot, and the greens are true. On a hillock behind the 7th green is the Barah Khamba (Twelve Pillars), a splendid ruined mausoleum of the Afghan-Lodhi dynasty with a solitary nameless tomb. Another mausoleum, the Lal Bangla, stands next to the clubhouse.

Indian golf is forever indebted to Australia's international star, Peter Thomson, for getting it on the world golfing map with the establishment of the annual Indian Open and also for making India a part of the Asia golf circuit which alternates annually between Delhi and Calcutta. In 1964 the first Indian Open was played in Delhi and appropriately won by Thomson, who lowered the course record to 67. In the 1971 Indian Open, the winner, fellow Australian Graham Marsh, further lowered the course record with two consecutive 66s in the first two rounds. National Amateur championships are also played here.

Delhi's outstanding feature is its four strong finishing holes: the par-4 15th, par-3 16th, the long par-5 17th and tricky par-4 18th, the latter two both doglegs, placing premiums on accurate driving, the crux of golf at Delhi.

Demaret, James Newton AMERICAN
b. Houston, Tex., 1910. US Masters 1940, 1947, 1950; Argentine Open 1941; Ryder Cup 1947, 1949, 1951

A highly respected figure in American golf who, with Jack Burke, owns and operates the Champions GC in Houston, Tex., scene of the Ryder Cup match in 1967 and the US Open Championship in 1969. In 1940 when competition was extremely fierce, Demaret, then a nightclub singer, won six tournaments in succession, finishing with the Masters at Augusta which he won by four strokes from Lloyd Mangrum. In his first round of 67 he played the back 9 in 30, a record which still stands, though equalled by Gene Littler in 1966 and Ben Hogan in 1967.

He won the Masters again in 1947 by 2 strokes from Byron Nelson. Then in 1950 he became the first to win the Masters three times, although it needed a swing of seven

strokes on the last six holes for him to catch and overhaul Jim Ferrier. Ferrier was 5 over par for this stretch and Demaret two under. Demaret's winning totals were 28 in 1940, 281 in 1947 and 283 in 1950.

In 1948, Demaret was runner-up to Ben Hogan in the US Open Championship at the Riviera Club, Los Angeles, and he and Hogan made a formidable foursomes pair in the Ryder Cup matches of 1947 and 1951, winning both games together. Demaret, in fact, won all his matches, a third foursome in 1949 with Clayton Heafner, two singles against Dai Rees and one against Arthur Lees: a unique record.

Denmark
Golf found its way to Denmark some time before the Copenhagen GC was founded at the end of the 19th century. A few members of the aristocracy had golf holes on their estates and the game was also played on public open ground near the famous Tuborg breweries, now a built-up area. It was F. Hansen and Mrs Ingeborg Aagesen, son and daughter of J. G. Hansen, who took back clubs and balls from a stay in England, cycled out to the Fælled, as the area was called, and surprised Copenhageners with their unknown game.

This particularly Anglophile family has pioneered several sports in Denmark. J. G. Hansen, a councillor of state, had introduced tennis to his country, playing it in a prison exercise yard. He and his family

were also the first to play bandy, a form of ice hockey.

At this time there was no thought of founding a golf club. However, on his return from America, Charles R. Jensen, who had been an employee of the Spalding sports equipment company and was later a professional, invited friends to a demonstration of the game in the park at the Eremitage. After other Danes had been invited to try their hand it was agreed that a club should be formed.

Progress away from the capital was slow and by 1954 there were only 12 clubs throughout Denmark. One more had been added by 1965, but then the dramatic growth in the game's popularity in most countries of the world was also reflected in a surge of activity in Denmark. Fifteen new courses were built between 1965 and 1970, and others have been constructed since. At the same time there has been a marked improvement in the standard of play, with Danish teams doing well in European competitions, notably in winning the 1966 European Junior Team Championship in the Netherlands.

Desert Courses of the Middle East
The desert courses of the Persian Gulf area are a world of golf unto themselves: balls are red not white; the greens are not green but brown or black or a shade between; the fairways are more like runways on a deserted unpaved country airport; and the rough is a

Jimmy Demaret

Denmark: the golf course on the island of Fanø

Petroleum Company (Bapco), the Kuwait Oil Company (KOC), and others have done very well indeed. Beginning some 35 years ago at Bahrain, they have fashioned courses which, although neither green nor great, even as sand courses, are a formidable challenge to the golfer's determination to score well. Having devised the courses, they employ local rules, varying from course to course, to provide relief from playing conditions considered impossible or unfair. Though these at times tend to stretch the basic Rules of Golf, generally they seem not unreasonable, considering the course conditions.

The kingdom of Saudi Arabia, with the biggest number of sand courses, has a special place in Arab world golf. Of its nine courses, eight are sand. Of these, three are 18-hole, one is 6-hole. Except for the 6-hole course, which lies within the US Embassy compound in Jiddah, all the courses in the country were built by Aramco, Tapline and the Arabian Oil Company (Japanese) for use by employees.

The ninth course is the 9-hole Bedouin Hills at Rahfa, the only green course on the vast and desolate Arabian peninsula. Designed by an American oil engineer, John Arnold, Tapline resident manager at this pumping station along the pipeline which carries oil some 1,500 miles to the Mediterranean terminus in Lebanon, the course measures 2,650 yd (2,423 m), par 33. With alternate tees, it is set up to play to 5,700 yd. (5,212 m), par 65, for 18 holes. Though relatively short, with the longest hole 395 yd, (361 m), the existence of a grass course in this remote desert location is a tribute to Arnold and his colleagues who planned and built it. Arnold, incidentally, assisted in developing the Zahrani CC course when he was stationed in Lebanon.

Bahrain, with Bapco's 18-hole course at the Awali GC and a 9-hole course at the Rifa's GC, and Kuwait, with KOC's 18-hole course at the Ahmadi GC, and others, add to the list of unusual desert courses in that part of the world. So, too, do the tiny oil-rich gulf sheikhdoms of Abu Dhabi, Dubai and Qatar; each of these states has one 9-hole course.

The Awali course in Bahrain, 6,286 yd, (5,748 m), par 71, site of the annual Bahrain Open Championship, is generally considered the best of the five 18-hole courses in the gulf area. The greens are better than the others'; it has trees which help to define the course, and the ball is played as it lies in the rough (on some of the others, a free move is permitted, to avoid rocks and buried lies in soft sand).

distressing mixture of sand and rock which plays havoc with scores and chews cruelly into new clubs imported all the way from the United States and Britain.

This description generally fits the sand courses of Saudi Arabia, Bahrain, Kuwait, Abu Dhabi, Dubai and Qatar. As Lee Trevino would say more succinctly, 'Man, they're something else!' and he is from Texas, and no stranger to sand courses.

The balls are red because in the glare of the desert sun a white ball cannot be seen against the sand and greyish rocks; the greens, called 'browns', are formed from oil-treated sand, with the colour depending upon the type of sand and the amount of oil used; the fairways resemble makeshift run-

ways because they are made of sand or a type of local marl, sprayed with oil and compacted to preserve them from the desert wind.

The peculiarities of these courses arise from climatic and geographical conditions, and practical economic considerations. In the desert, with extreme heat and little, if any, water, grass does not grow unless induced artificially by irrigation and soil preparation requiring imported grass seed, fertilizers and special equipment. Lacking these the only thing to do is to make the best of what there is.

The employees of Arabian American Oil Company (Aramco), Trans Arabian Pipeline Company (Tapline), the Bahrain

Top, the 2nd hole of the Awali GC, Bahrain – a photograph taken during the 1972 Bahrain Open – camels often wander across the line of play creating an unusual 'hazard'

Above, a scene on the course of Detroit CC

The other four, Aramco's three courses in Saudi Arabia and KOC's Ahmadi course in Kuwait, vary in character. Of the Aramco courses, which host the annual Aramco Invitation Tournament, Surf Side at Ras Tanura, 6,175 yd, (5,646 m), par 71, part of which borders the gulf, is the most picturesque; Rolling Hills at Dhahran, formerly 27 holes, now 6,018 yd (5,503 m), par 72, has the most rugged terrain; and the Ain Nakhl (Palm Springs) at Abqaiq, 6,145 yd (5,619 m), par 71, has the best fairways. Ahmadi, 6,100 yd (5,748 m), par 69, where the annual Kuwait Open Championship is played, has a number of open greens which invite run-up shots.

In general, these courses are more primitive than the old sand courses of Egypt, such as the Maadi Sporting Club course near Cairo, where the Desert Open was played until 1956, after which the course was abandoned. There, with Nile water readily available, the sand fairways and greens were watered and rolled, with no oil used. Though hard, the fairways were smoother, more playable; the rough was not nearly so rocky; and the ball was always played where it lay.

Climate and course conditions affect time and technique of play. During those months when temperatures rise to 110°F (43°C) by nine o'clock in the morning and reach 130°F (54°C) by noon, accompanied by high humidity along the gulf, tee-off time is as early as 4.30 am. Sun-shaded motorized golf carts make it possible to play later and still withstand the weather; but these are not always available.

Once off the tees, which are usually rubber mats on elevated platforms, getting the ball to the greens in anything like par figures requires a different striking technique from that used in hitting from grass. Whereas on grass the proper way to strike the ball, at least with the irons, is to hit down onto it and take a divot from the turf, this is impossible on these courses because there is no divot to take. The local rules permit placing the ball in the fairway; and it is necessary to sweep the ball off the ground, picking it cleanly from the surface. Otherwise, the clubhead either buries in the sand or bounces off rocks or compacted fairway material which, compared to turf, has little if any give; in either case, the shot is killed.

Playing from portable artificial-turf mats has been introduced at some of the courses, with the ball placed on the mat for every shot. Mats are controversial, and prohibited on some courses. Apart from making the game more enjoyable under conditions which, even with them, are still far removed from normal golf, the argument in their

favour is protection of the player and his clubs from injury and damage sustained in striking rocks. But, it is an axiom for the man who wants to play well on these courses that he sacrifice his clubs on the altar of success. If he worries about damaging them, his score will suffer badly, and the damage will still occur.

Where local rules do not permit moving the ball in the rough, fairway limits are indicated by wires, cables, lines or stakes, without which it is difficult to determine where the rough begins.

The greens, or browns, are usually bounded by white lines, to make it easier to apply the rules governing play on the putting surface. Local rules permit the greens to be swept or dragged to eliminate footprints on the sand surface. Spiked shoes are not permitted.

The courses have bunkers (despite the abundance of sand), a limited number of artificial water hazards, and other local features. They also have moving diversions in the form of camels, donkeys, goats, sheep and their keepers, wandering at will across the line of play. One of the better Aramco woman golfers, in search of a birdie, struck a shot soundly down the middle and felled a sheep. It was a good shot, but expensive. According to the local tribal law of compensation, she was obliged to buy her 'sheepie'; the negotiated price was something like $40 in Saudi rials. Such is the way of golf in Arabia.

Not far away, across the gulf in southern Iran, there are several sand courses which are generally similar to those on the Arabian side. These were also built by western oil companies for use by their staff and visitors. On either side of the Gulf it is all a far cry from golf on the lushly turfed desert courses of California and Arizona or the parkland courses in Britain.

Design of Golf Courses SEE GOLF-COURSE ARCHITECTURE

Detroit, CC of USA
Grosse Point Farms, Mich. 18 holes; 6,875 yd (6,286 m)

The Country Club of Detroit in its fashionable setting is noted in golfing circles as the place where Arnold Palmer emerged on to the national golf scene. There, at the age of 24, Arnie, only a few months out of the Coast Guard and virtually unknown, won the US National Amateur in 1954. Naturally, he did it in a succession of dramatic matches culminating in a 1-hole victory in the final over Bobby Sweeny, the former British Amateur Champion.

That match was played on a course that is flat but unusually appealing. H. L. Colt designed the original course in 1911 and Robert Trent Jones remodelled it and brought it up to date in the early 1950s, extending it to 6,875 yd. Many prominent figures from the automobile industry live in palatial houses bordering the course.

Detroit GC USA
Detroit, Mich. 36 holes; North Course 6,864 yd (6,218 m); par 72; South Course 5,920 yd (5,395 m); par 68

The Detroit GC is a complex of 36 holes entirely within the city limits, about 15 minutes from central Detroit by expressway. This makes it highly convenient for lunch, dinner, conferences – and surreptitious afternoon rounds of golf. It was established in 1899 by some captains of industry, among them pioneers of the automobile industry: one of them was Clarence A. Black, who had the distinction of dismissing Henry Ford from the Detroit Automobile Company and of helping to organize the Cadillac Motor Company.

Black was the first president of the Detroit club and found its first home, a 45-acre (18-ha) tract on which a temporary course of six holes was laid out. Within a few years enough land was acquired to build two fully fledged courses. Donald Ross was engaged as the architect. When the project fell behind schedule in 1916, Ernie Way, who was in charge of construction, put up lights and work was carried on at night. At first glance, the North appears to be the more testing of the two courses – the South has 6 par-3 holes – but both have par-4 holes of more than 400 yd.

The club has had great success with its professionals. Alex Ross became the professional in 1916 and stayed until 1946. His will specified that when he died, he was to be cremated and his ashes strewn over the fairways. He was succeeded by Horton Smith, who lasted 18 years, from 1946 until his death in 1963.

As in its early days, Detroit GC is not for the downtrodden. The cost of membership was $2,000 in 1971 which was necessary as the maintenance budget rose to $177,885 in 1970. The membership totals over 1,000.

Devlin, Bruce AUSTRALIAN
b. Armidale, N.S.W., 1937. Australian Amateur 1959; Australian Open 1960; French Open 1963; World (formerly Canada) Cup 1970

Devlin, whose trade was plumbing, turned professional in 1961 after a fine amateur career in which he won the Australian

Amateur and Open championships and finished as joint leader in the individual section of the first World Amateur Team Championship at St Andrews in 1958.

With such success behind him, he decided to go in search of wealth in the United States but he won so little in 1962 and 1963 that he was faced with the prospect of being unable to afford to stay. In 1964, however, he won the St Petersburg Open, and has since turned out to be one of the most successful non-Americans in the history of the USPGA tour.

Victories followed in the 1966 Colonial Invitational, and the 1969 Byron Nelson Classic; but two of his most profitable and distinguished successes came in international events outside America. In 1966 he won the Carling World tournament at Royal Birkdale (first prize £12,500) and in 1970 he became Alcan Golfer of the Year at Portmarnock, Dublin (first prize about £23,000). His nearest challenger, Bob Rosburg, was 7 strokes behind his total of 278 (69, 71, 70, 68). Devlin's victory was largely attributable to a quite outstanding round in a gale of wind with the big ball which those present claim to be one of the best rounds they ever saw. It is not perhaps surprising that a feeling prevails that this craggy Australian with a smooth swing has never quite realized his full potential.

Devlin's best year in America was 1970 when he finished 11th in the official money list, winning the Cleveland Open and finishing in the top ten of tournaments eight times.

Since then he has limited his playing programme in order to carry out commitments as a highly successful golf-course architect in partnership with Robert von Hagge, but he showed his form by winning the USI tournament in America in 1972 and so manages to combine the best of both worlds.

Dey, Joseph C., Jr AMERICAN
b. Virginia 1907

Executive Director of the United States Golf Association until 1968, when he switched to become Commissioner of the Tournament Players Division of the USPGA, Dey has been one of the game's outstanding administrators. He was educated at the University of Pennsylvania and started work as a sports writer on the *Philadelphia Public Ledger* and subsequently on the *Philadelphia Evening Bulletin*. He had intended to study for the ministry, and it is not surprising that he brought to his task in golf administration a strong sense of justice and fair play. He became a steadying influence in the game's rapid rise in popularity. During more than 35 years of distinguished office with the USGA, five new championships were launched and two international contests. He also helped to codify the rules of the USGA; this last work gave him special pleasure. He was also one of the prime movers in the establishment of Golf House, at that time in New York. When he transferred to the professional ranks, the Professional Golfers' Association was split by dissension and it took all his powers of diplomacy to set matters right. When he retired at the end of his term of office in 1974, the USPGA had healed its breach and moved forward into smoother waters with an $8,000,000 programme in 1973.

Dickinson, Gardner AMERICAN
b. Dothan, Ala., 1927. Ryder Cup 1967, 1971; Cleveland Open 1968; Doral Open 1969; Atlantic Classic 1970

Gardner Dickinson turned professional in 1952, but gained the majority of his victories on the American circuit in the late 1960s and early 1970s. At 5 ft 10 in and weighing only about 140 lb, Dickinson's custom of wearing a flat white cap earned

him the description of 'mini-Ben' after Ben Hogan, whose protégé he was and on whom he modelled his swing. Dickinson was also a central figure in the dispute between the tournament players and the USPGA that came to a head in 1969 and led to the formation of the Tournament Players Division.

Dickson, Robert B. AMERICAN
b. McAlester, Okla., 1944. British Amateur 1967; US Amateur 1967; Walker Cup 1967; Haig Open 1968

Bob Dickson's promise as a student of Oklahoma State University was soon manifested by two amateur victories in 1967. His victory in the British Amateur at Formby after the Walker Cup match was one of the fastest pieces of play by two Americans ever seen; he defeated Ron Cerrudo at the 35th. He was low qualifier in the 1969 spring school, but found the professional circuit a difficult one in which to make his name. His first major tour win was the Andy Williams in 1973. In 1968 he received the Bob Jones Award.

Didrickson, Mildred SEE ZAHARIAS, MRS G.

Bruce Devlin

Joseph C. Dey Jr

Top, Gardner Dickinson

Above, Bob Dickson

Diegel, Leo AMERICAN

Tied 2nd US Open 1920; USPGA 1928-9; 3rd British Open 1929, joint runner-up 1930

Leo Diegel had the depressing reputation of being as it were 'always the bridesmaid and never the bride'. During a career of some 15 years in the top flight of American professional golf he failed in several close finishes in open championships in Britain and America, and because of the regularity of his lapses when in good positions became known as 'third-round Diegel'. Although twice USPGA Champion, his temperament was not always proof against the stress of critical situations, but he was a likeable man with a good sense of humour and known for a leaning towards the unorthodox. His most striking departure from the normal in style was when he adopted a putting posture, with the elbows bent so much that the forearms were almost horizontally opposed.

Dietschiberg GC SWITZERLAND

Lucerne (Luzern). 18 holes; 5,625 yd (5,143 m); par 71

The Lucerne course, perched on a hill some 2,200 ft (670 m) above sea level, and open from April to October, looks out over the Lake of the Four Cantons. From a strictly golfing point of view, the course is outdated; the holes are generally short and tricky. In its early days – it was founded in 1903 – it enjoyed considerable popularity thanks to the number of British visitors to the city. The view from the course remains incomparable, yielding a glimpse of what is called 'primitive' Switzerland, also of historic Switzerland, with in the background the peaks of Mounts Rigi and Pilatus.

Dill, Mary Lou AMERICAN

b. Texas, 1948. US Women's Amateur 1967; Curtis Cup 1968

A comparatively inexperienced winner of the national championship at the age of 20 while she was still attending college in Nacogdoches in Texas. She defeated Peggy Conley and Jean Ashley in the final stages.

Direction Post

A post specially erected to show the player the line to the hole. Most frequently direction posts reveal the line to a concealed fairway but are also used to show the location of a 'hidden' green. If a ball strikes a direction post, it must be played 'as it lies'. Similarly, if a ball ricochets off a direction post and finishes out of bounds, no relief is allowed. In America direction flags are used.

Divot

The piece of turf uprooted in making a shot. It is common etiquette that all divots must be replaced. No relief is allowed for a ball coming to rest in a divot mark.

Dod, Charlotte BRITISH

b. 1872; d. June 1960. British Ladies' 1904, semi-finalist 1898-9

Lottie Dod was an all-round athlete: she won the women's singles at Wimbledon five times and was also an international hockey player, a champion skater, a skilful archer, fine billiards player, and noteworthy member of the Alpine Club.

Having had her fill of tennis, she turned her attention to golf, and was a member of the Moreton Ladies GC, Birkenhead, Cheshire.

Apart from her championship successes, she played top for Britain in the match against America at Cromer, Norfolk, 1905, and lost at the 20th to Georgina Bishop, the American champion. She also played for England in the match against Ireland at Portrush in 1895, and at Newcastle, Co. Down, in 1899 when the two countries met again. She led the English team in the first official international matches between the home countries, at Cromer in 1905, and was a member of the committee formed to establish county golf in England.

She was noted for her excellent wooden club play, and for her powers of recovery. She was also a good putter. Her capabilities as a golfer were crowned in the championship she won at Troon in 1904, when she defeated Dorothy Campbell in the semi-final, and May Hezlet in the final. The final was unusual, being attended by a large, unruly, crowd, through which the players had to fight their way. Lottie Dod, accustomed to playing tennis before a gallery, was the less affected.

Dodd, Muriel (Mrs Allan Macbeth) BRITISH

b. 1891. British Ladies' 1913, runner-up 1923, semi-finalist 1914; Canadian Ladies' Open 1913

Her best year was 1913 when she won the British Ladies' Championship and the Canadian Open title. In 1923 she was runner-up in the British Ladies' at Burnham and Berrow to Doris Chambers, and in the semi-finals of that championship achieved the distinction of inflicting defeat on Joyce Wethered by 2 up and 1 to play, thereby joining Cecil Leitch, the only other player to stop Miss Wethered in a national championship.

Dogfight

A tight match of moderate quality in which the fortunes fluctuate although little is given away by either side.

Dogleg

A hole whose fairway is marked by a gentle or acute bend, usually about 200 yd (183 m) from the tee, with a hazardous area within the bend; this poses the player the problem

Leo Diegel

Mary Lou Dill

Divot – demonstration by Valentin Barrios

of attempting the carry or of playing more safely. Doglegs are most common on tree-lined courses and may curve left or right. A double dogleg curves twice.

Dog Licence

Slang in Britain for a defeat in a match by 7 and 6, the price in old shillings and pence of a British dog licence.

Doleman, William BRITISH

b. Musselburgh, Midlothian, 1838; d. Glasgow 1918

One of four Scots brothers, all natives of Musselburgh, who had a strong influence on golf for a long time. William was the best player. After a spell at sea as a young man, during which he sailed out of Sebastopol under Russian gunfire in 1854, he became first amateur in competition for the Championship Belt five times, in 1866-70. Thereafter in the Open Championship he was 3rd amateur in 1872, 1st in 1874, 2nd in 1875, and 1877-8, and 1st in 1879 (and 3rd overall), 1881 and 1884. He played in nearly every Amateur championship until 1911, and in 1910 won his first round match when 73 years of age.

A. H. Doleman was one of the pioneers of golf in England, founder of golf at Royal Lytham and St Annes, and one of the principal founders at Cambridge University. John, the eldest, introduced golf to Nottingham, and the fourth brother, Frank, carried on a clubmaking business in Edinburgh.

Dominican Republic

There used to be several courses in the Dominican Republic, but there are now only two, the Santa Domingo Country Club and the Campo de Golf Cajuiles or La Romana GC. The senior of these, Santa Domingo, a private members club, is a pleasant course, the first nine holes being rather flat, and the second more undulating. There are a number of elevated greens and young trees to provide features. At La Romana the character of the golf and the club is different. This club, planned to attract tourists, caters for a number of sports including deep-sea fishing, and in an area where it seldom rains and the winter temperature is in the 80s Fahrenheit, is a popular spot. The course, designed by the American, Pete Dye, and officially opened towards the end of 1971, has four or five holes by the ocean, small tricky greens and big sand traps.

The Dominican Republic entered its first team in the World Amateur Team Championship at Mexico City in 1966, and, at the last moment, undertook to stage the 1974 series.

Donald, Jean (Mrs J. Anderson) BRITISH

b. North Berwick, East Lothian, 1921. French Ladies' Open 1947; Scottish Ladies' 1947, 1949, 1952, runner-up 1953, semi-finalist 1951; runner-up British Ladies' 1948, semi-finalist 1946-7, 1951, 1953; Curtis Cup 1948, 1950, 1952; Sunningdale Foursomes 1951, 1953, 1958, 1961

Jean Donald's arrival in big golf was delayed by World War II, part of which she spent in the Middle East as a WAAF cypher officer. When the major events were resumed, she immediately made her mark, reaching the last four of the British championship in 1946. Victories in the first of her three Scottish championships in 1947, and also that year, in the French Open Cham-

pionship, established her in the front rank of British women's golf. Her subsequent successes in the Scottish were in 1949 and 1952, but the British title eluded her. The nearest she came to it was a memorable final at Royal Lytham and St Annes in 1948, with the American champion, Louise Suggs. Wet, weary, and level with 4 holes to play, they exchanged the next two, and halved the 35th. After both had been in trouble getting there, and each played three strokes to reach the 36th green, Miss Donald was 6 yd from the hole and Miss Suggs 6 ft away from it. The American had been deadly from that range all day, and Miss Donald endeavouring to bolt her putt went 5 ft past the hole. After Louise Suggs had left herself on the brink, Jean Donald missed coming back. She was a semi-finalist four times in the British championship, each time being put out by the eventual winner, Jean Hetherington (Mrs Holmes), 1946, Mildred Zaharias, 1947, Frances Stephens (Mrs Smith) 1951, and Marlene Stewart 1953.

The outstanding feature of Jean Donald's game has been the power of her woods and long irons, and her ability to redeem the stray shots when she found trouble.

At the end of 1953 she joined the sales

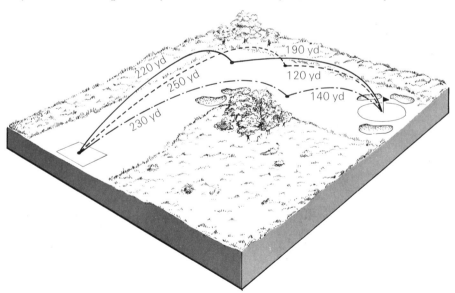

Dogleg

Jean Donald playing a no. 4 iron

staff of Slazengers and became a much respected representative in the golf trade. She travelled extensively, and visited Australia, Scandinavia and the Continent.

Donck, Flory Van BELGIAN
b. Brussels 1912. Belgian Professional 1935, 1938, 1949, 1952-7, 1959-60, 1963-4; Dutch Open 1936-7, 1946, 1951, 1953, runner-up 1957; Belgian Open 1939, 1946-7, 1953, 1956, runner-up 1935, 1951; runner-up British Professional Matchplay 1947, 1952; German Open 1953, 1956; Italian Open 1953, 1955; Swiss Open 1953, 1955, runner-up 1947, 1952, 1956-7; Vardon Trophy 1953; French Open 1954, 1957-8, runner-up 1946, 1956; Uruguyan Open 1954; World (Canada) Cup 1954-64; Portuguese Open 1955; 2nd British Open 1956, 1959; Venezuelan Open 1957

An elegant figure with a stylish swing, Van Donck is best summed up perhaps as a fastidious golfer. His tall figure and good looks, together with an artist's pair of hands and courteous manner (though he was capable of flashes of temper) made him a prince among golfers. His record is fine and covers many years, but he never quite reached the top rung. In 11 consecutive years from 1949 he finished only twice out of the first ten in the British Open and twice was beaten only by the winner. He was most at home on the Continent where he reigned supreme and set several course records. His 65 round Troon in the third round of the Open in 1950 set a new low record for any round in that championship. He won numerous tournaments in Britain and in 1953 finished with the best average. His style was fluent and orthodox but he had a most individual putting method, using what was almost a two-handed grip, holding the hands low and slightly cocking the toe of the putter. He was a regular visitor to the British circuit from Belgium, where he was successively attached to the Royal GC, Brussels and the Ravenstein club.

He represented Belgium for a decade in the Canada Cup and twice came near to winning that individual event. In the 1955 he lost a play-off at Washington to Ed Furgol and Peter Thomson and he was 3rd at Wentworth in 1956 to Ben Hogan. He captained the Continental team against the British Isles four times, 1954-6, 1958.

Dorado Beach GTC PUERTO RICO
36 holes
Dorado Beach is a creation of Laurence Rockefeller, one of the sons of John D. Rockefeller Jr, who conceived the resort area as an aid to the economy of Puerto

Rico. It is situated on the northern shore of the island some 10 miles west of San Juan. It began with 18 holes in the late 1950s, but now is a 36-hole complex. Both courses were designed by Robert Trent Jones.

The first of the two courses was an unbelievable operation: over 1,000,000,000 cubic yards of material was brought in to reclaim a swampy area. A planeload of hybrid Bermuda grass was imported from the United States and planted on one fairway, and then sprigs from this were used to establish the grass over the rest of the course. Rather than cut down the graceful coconut palms that might be in the line of a planned fairway, the trees were dug up and transplanted. The result is certainly among the best of Jones's courses, and the routing of the holes is especially pleasant, particularly on the second nine of the West course. A difficult hole is followed by an easier hole; if one

green is strongly protected by bunkers, the next is relatively open; this fairway may be tight, the next much less so.

Ironically, and regrettably for a resort that was developed in Puerto Rico partly to provide jobs for local people, all the caddies have been dismissed from Dorado Beach. A few years ago six of them, with legal counsel, decided that since they wore uniforms they were regular employees of the hotel and were entitled to all benefits, including the pension plan. If all Dorado's caddies for 10 years had been included, the hotel would have had to pay out more than $1,000,000. The case was settled out of court and all the caddies have now been replaced.

Doral CC USA
Miami, Fla. 4 × 18 holes; Blue Course 7,028 yd (6,426 m); par 72

If it is ever completed, the Doral CC may

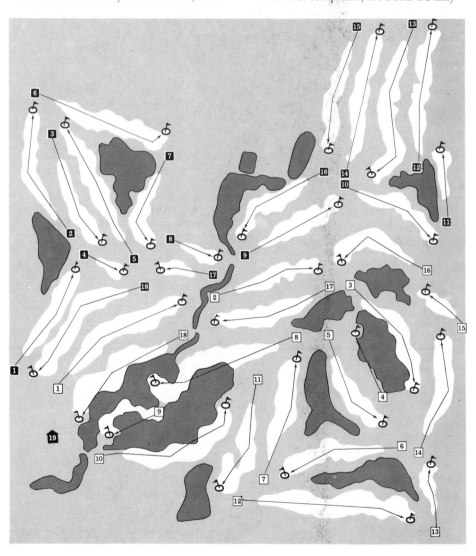

Two of Doral CC's courses; the tees of the Blue are shown as white squares, those of the Red as black

have more holes of golf than any complex in the United States. At the beginning of the 1970s, the club, located in former marshland near Miami Airport, had 81 holes made up of four regular 18-hole courses and another 9-hole par-3 course. Plans call for a fifth 18-hole course, and when it is completed Doral will have 99 holes. Pinehurst CC has five regulation 18-hole courses, or 90 holes.

Each of Doral's 18-hole courses is known by a colour – Red, White, Blue, and Gold; but people talking of Doral usually mean the Blue Course, where each season the touring pros play the Doral Open.

Because of the nature of most land in Florida (the entire state is hardly more than a sand pit, flat as an ironing board with the same general shape), only an architect with great imagination can design an interesting course. Fortunately, in Dick Wilson the proprietors of the hotel that owns the golf complex found one of the keenest minds in the business. The land is swampy, and so Wilson built eight lakes within the boundaries of the Blue Course, and then routed the holes round and over the water. Naturally, since this is a subtropical region, Doral has its quota of palm trees, but it is the lakes that give the course its character. Two holes are notable for their strategic design. The 8th is a 528-yd (483-m) par 5 that calls for two shots across a lake and allows absolutely no room for error with the approach, for the green is set on a peninsula; to approach it from the most advantageous angle, the second shot must take a big bite from the lake so that the third shot is coming straight down a chute. The 9th hole, a 180-yd (165-m) par 3, is all carry across part of that same lake, and again the green is on a peninsula; hit the shot right or left, or leave it short, and a player is in the water. A skin diver makes three sweeps a week through the waters around the 9th and he does very well. It is estimated that the lake swallows 50 balls a day.

Robert von Hagge, a talented product of Wilson's office, has been in charge of the recent course construction at Doral.

Dormie

A player is dormie when he is as many holes up as there are holes left to play. It follows that a player can be dormie only when the match is to finish at the 18th or at another fixed point. He is never dormie, i.e. able to 'sleep' in the knowledge that he cannot be beaten, when the match is to be played to a finish.

Dornoch GC, Royal SCOTLAND

Dornoch, Sutherland. Old Course 18 holes; 6,515 yd (5,957 m); No. 2 Course 9 holes

Royal Dornoch, on the southeast coast of Sutherland, is the most northerly first-class course in the world. It is in the same latitude as Hudson's Bay or southern Alaska; and yet, because of the Gulf Stream, golf is played there the year round with surprisingly little interruption from snow and frost.

Given a less remote setting, Royal Dornoch might easily have housed an Open championship. It possesses all the qualities of seaside golf and presents the kind of challenge that has won the hearts of many respected judges who journey to the far north of Scotland on the recommendation of those who have been enchanted by the golf and by the surrounding beauty. They are seldom disappointed.

Dornoch, with a cathedral dating back over 700 years, seems to centre around the game of golf. The course lies only a few hundred yards beyond the main square and has probably not changed much since the glorious stretch of linksland first aroused the interest of golfers as long ago as 1616. Only St Andrews and Leith preceded it as a golfing nursery yet the Royal Dornoch GC was not founded until 1877. In the 1880s Old Tom Morris was commissioned to lay out a proper nine holes.

A second nine was added shortly afterwards and in 1904 Dornoch was transformed from being just another course into one with championship rating by changes carried out under the direction of John Sutherland, a remarkable man who was secretary of the club for over 50 years.

The leading golf professionals began to include Dornoch in their exhibition tours. In the first decade of the century, Vardon, Braid, Massy and Herd all played there, Vardon describing the old 14th as 'the finest natural hole I have ever played'.

In 1909 six Dornoch golfers distinguished themselves in the Amateur championship at Muirfield. Tom Grant, a baker, beat John Ball; W. Henderson beat the American, Jerome D. Travers; and the veteran Dornoch secretary, John Sutherland defeated Harold Hilton to reach the last 16. Both Ball and Hilton, taking notice, visited Dornoch for a week that summer. Its fame had begun to spread. Before 1900, discerning Londoners had already discovered its peace and beauty, as well as its fine golf. Before World War I, Dornoch had become a popular holiday retreat for families from the south; prominent among them were such famous golfers as Sir Ernest Holderness and the Wethereds.

A further remodelling of the course after World War II kept pace with the modern advances of equipment and it has continued to be admired by connoisseurs. Dornoch's character is true British seaside links: beautiful turf and a feeling that everything has been untouched by the centuries. Yet, unlike many old links, nothing is hidden; the greens are not large but they are well guarded and nothing but the best will do. The first eight holes curve out at two levels to the point towards Embo where the 9th turns for home along the shore, but, because of the careful placing of the tees, the wind's attack is nicely varied.

The 14th, 'Foxy', is a gem with the sort of raised green that Donald Ross introduced when he revised the Pinehurst No 2 course and which became the hallmark of his work. But one thing nobody could ever reproduce is the splendour of the surroundings at Dornoch. The broad sweep of the Dornoch Firth, the lighthouse on its remote headland, and the great hills of Sutherland are as much a source of joy and inspiration to Dornoch men as its historic links and noble traditions, which include the staging of several Scottish championships, though not the British Amateur.

Double Eagle see ALBATROSS

Douglas, Dave AMERICAN

b. Philadelphia 1918. Canadian Open 1953; Ryder Cup 1953

Dave Douglas's grandfather ran a golf course near Edinburgh. His father emigrated to the United States at the age of 20. Dave was a consistent performer for several years after 1945. Tall, slim, and quiet, his best year was 1953 when he won the Canadian Open and finished well enough up on the tour to gain a place in the Ryder Cup match. He won his foursome with Ed Oliver, and halved a dramatic single with Bernard Hunt.

Douglas, Findlay S. AMERICAN

b. St Andrews, Fife, 1874; d. 1959. US Amateur 1898, runner-up 1899, 1900, semi-finalist 1897, 1901; US Seniors' 1932

Douglas emigrated to the United States in 1896 and became a leading figure during the early years of amateur golf in that country. He was a long hitter and this was never more apparent than in his final in 1900 with Walter Travis who was on the short side. However, the better putter won on that occasion. From 1932 to 1934 Douglas was president of the Metropolitan Golf Association. He was president of the USGA in 1929-30.

Douglass, Dale AMERICAN

b. Wewoka, Colo., 1936. Azalea Open 1969;

Kemper Open 1969; Ryder Cup 1969

Douglass turned professional in 1960 after graduating from Colorado University. He knew some lean years before winning his first tournament in 1969. This was his best year, with winnings just below $100,000, and a place in the Ryder Cup team. Known as one of the iron men of the American circuit for the number of tournaments in which he plays, he has averaged more than 35 tournaments a year recently. This matches his golf philosophy: if a player goes on hitting fairways and greens the putts must eventually drop.

Draw

A stroke, usually deliberate, played across the ball from 'in to out' causing it to travel at first to the right and then curve back towards the line required. A half brother to the hook. The most notable player who used the controlled draw on nearly all his shots was Bobby Locke.

It is also the method of deciding who plays against whom in a competition by drawing the names out of a hat. The published result is known as the 'draw' for the event.

Dreadnought

A special type of driver with a big head popular for a time around the turn of the century. Its name was derived from the Royal Navy's big battleships which were being built at the time with a fine array of heavy guns.

Drew, Norman Vico IRISH

b. Belfast 1932. East of Ireland 1952; Irish Open Amateur 1952-3; North of Ireland (Amateur) Open 1952; Walker Cup 1953; Irish Dunlop Tournament 1959; Irish Native Professional 1959; Ryder Cup 1959; *Yorkshire Evening News* Tournament 1959; World (Canada) Cup 1960-1

Although Drew's major successes as an amateur were confined to Ireland, they were so concentrated in the early 1950s that he won a place in the 1953 Walker Cup team. When six years later he had another strong run of success as a professional he became one of the few golfers to play for his country as an amateur and as a professional. He did specially well to hold Doug Ford to a half over 36 holes at the top of the Ryder Cup singles that year.

Driver

The no. 1 wood used from a tee at a hole where a player needs maximum distance with his shot. This shot is known as the 'drive' although it is not necessarily played with the driver.

Driving Ranges

Driving ranges were first introduced in America and have since become common throughout the golfing world. They are built on a limited area of land and provide a line of bays or stalls from which golfers can practise shots. Golfers hire the balls but do not have to pick them up.

Some driving ranges form part of a more elaborate golfing centre which may provide catering facilities, a golf shop, par 3, and pitch and putt courses. They are usually floodlit for evening activity. In some cases, notably in Japan, they consist simply of a multi-storey hitting deck and a large net to trap the balls shortly after they have been hit. For a great number of Japanese, golf begins and ends there but for most golfers, a driving range only complements golf on a full-length course.

Drottningholm GC SWEDEN

Drottningholm. 18 holes; 6,584 yd (6,020 m)

Of the 10 courses in the Greater Stockholm area that belonging to Drottning-holms Golfklubb is the best. It is situated near Drottningholm royal palace in beautiful parkland where golfers may encounter herds of deer. A number of championships have been played there, including the Volvo Open.

Dub SEE DUFF

Dubai SEE DESERT COURSES

Dublin GC, Royal IRISH REPUBLIC

Dollymount (Baile na gCorr), Dublin 3.
18 holes

Royal Dublin, the second oldest club in Ireland, and the oldest in the Republic, was founded in 1885 by John Lumsden, a Scotsman from Banffshire, and some of his friends. For a year or two its home was in Phoenix Park, then after a move to Sutton, a new links was established in 1889 on the North Bull at Dollymount.

On 22 May 1891, Dublin GC became the Royal Dublin and ever since has been one of the best courses in a country noted for its golf.

Three old drivers

Top, Findlay S. Douglas

Above, Dale Douglass

In its early days, the landlord of the links disapproved of Sunday golf but those who did play effected their entry to the clubhouse through the back door while the front door, in deference to his lordship's wishes, remained closed. Bombardier Fletcher and his wife invariably had a pot of Irish stew on the stove and the members sat on forms in the locker room with plates on their knees and a bottle of Guinness on the floor.

During World War I, the military used the links. After the war the course, almost unrecognizable, was redesigned by H. S. Colt. In August 1943 the renovated clubhouse was burned to the ground but was rebuilt in 1954 and modernized in 1962. Royal Dublin has always been a home for Irish championships and professional events and since 1959 Christy O'Connor has been its professional.

Dudley, Edward Bishop AMERICAN b. Brunswick, Ga., 1901; d. 1963. Oklahoma Open 1925-6; California Open 1929; Pennsylvania Open 1929-30; Philadelphia Open 1929, 1933, 1936, 1940; Ryder Cup 1929, 1933, 1937; Los Angeles Open 1931; Western Open 1931; semi-finalist USPGA 1932; Walter Hagen Tournament 1939; Utah Open 1942

A big man with a relaxed and exceptionally smooth swing. Henry Cotton once called it the most beautiful he had ever seen; Chick Evans said Dudley was the only man with a swing comparable to Harry Vardon's. Dudley was a consistent winner on the American tour for more than 10 years, but did not capture a major title. After three rounds he led the 1937 US Open, finished with a 76 and dropped to 5th. In 1928 he had moved into a challenging position with a third-round 68, only to score a closing 75 that tied him for 6th place. Six times he

reached the quarter-finals of the USPGA Championship; once he reached the semi-finals, but never a final. Dudley led the 1933 British Open at St Andrews for 36 holes and finished tied for 7th.

Dudley was active in the USPGA for many years, serving as national president from 1942 to 1948. It was largely through his efforts that Bing Crosby, Bob Hope and other entertainers volunteered to play exhibition matches for war relief and to support the sale of war bonds. He served for more than 20 years as professional at the Augusta National club in the winter and at the Broadmoor in Colorado Springs in the summer. He was several times the playing partner of President Eisenhower at Augusta.

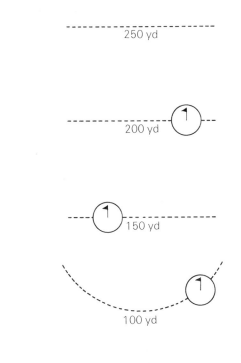

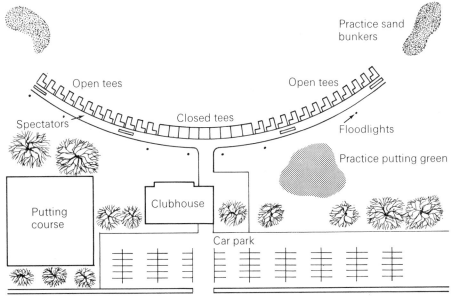

A layout for a typical driving range

Ed Dudley

Duff

To foozle a shot; commonly associated with indifferent players who hit the ground instead of the ball, although it may apply to any player who makes a poor stroke. A duffer is a really incompetent player. In America, no one duffs a shot – he dubs it.

Duncan, Colonel Anthony Arthur

BRITISH

b. Cardiff 1914. British Army 1937-8, 1948, 1952, 1954, 1956; Welsh Amateur 1938, 1948, 1952; runner-up British Amateur 1939; President's Putter 1948, 1958; Walker Cup 1953 (non-playing captain)

One of the most famous of all Welsh golfers, his greatest playing achievement was in reaching the final of the last pre-war British Amateur. Captain of Oxford University a year or two before, Duncan lost to Alex Kyle by 2 and 1 at the Royal Liverpool, Hoylake in what Bernard Darwin described as a 'capital match'. Darwin also said that he should have felt very much inclined to have played him in the Walker Cup foursomes of 1938 because, he added, it would be hard to imagine a better foursome partner or a much better putter. Although he never actually played in a Walker Cup match, these virtues were largely responsible for his great success in foursomes. In 1953 he was non-playing captain of the team at Kittansett.

The match gave rise to the famous incident when the American foursomes pair Jackson and Littler were disqualified when Jackson discovered a 15th club in his bag; but Duncan, applying Rule 36(5) eventually got the decision changed.

The Americans were penalized 2 holes instead of being disqualified, a decision that gave rise to one ingenious newspaper headline, 'Britannia waives the rules'.

Duncan continued a remarkable playing record for Wales but his career developed more in the role of administrator. He was chairman of the Walker Cup selection committee and inaugurated the Duncan Putter, an annual 72-hole medal at Easter, which has done much to provide more competition for Welsh golfers.

Duncan, George BRITISH

b. Oldmeldrum, Aberdeenshire, 1893; d. 1964. British Professional Matchplay 1913; British Open 1920, runner-up 1922; Ryder Cup 1927, 1929 (captain), 1931

James Braid, who knew Duncan well, once wrote, 'I cannot make him out; he plays so fast that he looks as if he doesn't care, but I suppose it must be his way. He's the most extraordinary golfer I have ever seen.' A reminder of this was given in the title of

his autobiography, *Golf at the Gallop*. Duncan was son of the village policeman, one of a family of 10. His first experience of golf came at the age of eight on the Old Links at Aberdeen where he later used to caddie and, though his father insisted on his becoming a carpenter, his love for the game won through.

At 17, he became professional at Stonehaven but, within a year, after rejecting an offer to play football for Aberdeen, he secured the professional's job at Rhos-on-Sea, North Wales, before moving to Caernarvonshire GC, Conway. As a playing professional he was somewhat overshadowed by the Triumvirate of Taylor, Vardon and Braid but he was a great player, a 'pros' pro' with something of an artist's temperament.

If ever there was a natural golfer, Duncan was one. Though he was a great 'experimenter', Vardon's influence on him as a swinger was considerable and, like Vardon, he became a believer in the 'all-air route' in the flight of his shots. He was a player of brilliance and inspiration rather than consistency. In 1913 he beat James Braid in the final of the matchplay championship on Braid's own course at Walton Heath and in 1920 won one of the most remarkable victories in the history of the Open Championship.

After two rounds at Deal, he trailed Abe Mitchell by 13 strokes but a third round of 71, with a new driver acquired in the exhibition tent, worked wonders. Mitchell, in one of the famous 'disaster' rounds, took 84; his huge lead had been wiped out and by the time he finished, Duncan was on his way round again. Duncan finished in 72 which, in view of the morning, was too much for Mitchell who took 76 and surrendered 2nd place to Sandy Herd, then 52 years old. It is ironic that Duncan had persuaded Mitchell not to get to the course too early that day

because of his late starting time around noon, but Mitchell arrived as Duncan drove off at 8.45, a factor that was generally regarded as contributory to his collapse.

In 1924, Duncan left the old Hanger Hill club for Wentworth where, in 1926, he played for Britain against America. Two years earlier he won his single against Jock Hutchison in a similar match at Gleneagles and at Wentworth he and Mitchell beat Jim Barnes and Walter Hagen in the foursome by 9 and 8, while in the singles he beat Hagen 6 and 5.

When the Ryder Cup was instituted in 1927, he beat J. Turnesa at Worcester, Mass. One of his finest performances came when, as captain of the British side, he beat Hagen again, this time by the embarrassing margin of 10 and 8 at Moortown in 1929. It was said that Duncan's game at its best was the 'champagne of golf and the fizziest champagne at that'.

In 1934 he moved to Mere GC at Knutsford, Cheshire, where, despite many offers to settle in America, he remained for the rest of his working life.

Dunch

British term for an unintentional shot, similar to a duff, in which the ball is not hit cleanly.

Dunes Golf and Beach Club USA

Myrtle Beach, S. Car. 18 holes; 7,027 yd (6,425 m); par 72

One of the most frightening shots in American golf is the second to the 575-yd (526-m) par-5 13th hole at the Dunes. The 13th is crescent-shaped, curving around Singleton Lake, a brackish appendage to the Atlantic Ocean that roars ashore behind the red-brick clubhouse. The second shot must be played with a wood, and it must be a good one to carry across the lake and leave a reasonable shot to the double-tiered green. It is on record that in the more than 20 years of the club's life, only Mike Souchak has been able to reach that green in two.

The Dunes is a creation of Robert Trent Jones, built on a former private wild turkey and deer-hunting preserve which was used as an Air Force target range during World War II. The land was acquired in 1947, and construction was somewhat hazardous, with an occasional unexploded bomb turning up in the path of a bulldozer.

The course plays mostly away from the Atlantic and weaves among pines, holly, and scrub oak, all of them bent slightly by the constant wind from the sea. Bass and mullet abound in the waters of Singleton Lake, and somewhere out there is an alligator. Once he

George Duncan, left, British Open champion in 1920 with J. H. Taylor, champion in 1894-5, 1900, 1909 and 1913

ginning to suspect that 69s round a golf course were not the end-all and be-all of life'.

Dunn, 'Old' Willie BRITISH
b. Musselburgh, Midlothian, 1821; d. North Berwick, East Lothian, 1880

An early Scots professional who achieved fame as the first club professional at Royal Blackheath, and in a number of challenge matches. The most famous of these was the foursome over three greens – St Andrews, Musselburgh, and North Berwick – in which he was partnered by his twin brother, Jamie, against Old Tom Morris and Allan Robertson from St Andrews. They lost the match by two greens to one, but had the satisfaction of beating the

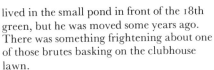

lived in the small pond in front of the 18th green, but he was moved some years ago. There was something frightening about one of those brutes basking on the clubhouse lawn.

Dunk, Bill AUSTRALIAN
b. Gosford, N.S.W. 1938. Australian Professional 1962, 1966, 1971; Malaysian Open 1963

A golfer with a remarkable record in Australian events, although he has been much less successful in other countries. Altogether Dunk had won 86 professional tournaments up to January 1972 and had set or equalled some 50 course records in Australia, New Zealand, Malaysia, the United States, and Japan.

On 15 November 1970 he had a round of 60 at Merewether in a $A10,000 tournament, which is the lowest score ever recorded in a major golf tournament in Australia, and he has won the Australian Professional Championship three times. However, despite a spell in America and regular appearances on the Asian circuit, he has never quite repeated the devastating form he has shown in Australia. Dunk has represented Australia several times in the World Cup.

Dunlap, George T., Jr. AMERICAN
US National Collegiate 1930-1; North and South Amateur 1931, 1933-6, 1940, 1942, runner-up 1938; Walker Cup 1932, 1934, 1936; US Amateur 1933; Metropolitan Amateur 1936

Dunlap, a member of the publishing family of Grossett and Dunlap, was a fixture at Pinehurst and was the favourite and often the winner in almost every tournament played there for more than 15 years. He almost made the North and South Amateur his personal property, winning it seven times in the dozen years before World War II. He

won the US National Collegiate while at Princeton in 1930, again in 1931 and that season won his first North and South title. This earned him a place in the 1932 Walker Cup team and in the matches at the Country Club he shot a 66 in the course of winning his singles, 10 and 9. He had to win a play-off to gain a place in the 1933 Amateur, then went on to take the championship. Max Marston, his opponent in the final, also qualified for the tournament in a play-off. Dunlap, an amiable man, continued to play championship golf for a number of years, but he did not work as hard at his game after the mid-1930s. Henry Longhurst, in reporting the 1936 Walker Cup matches, wrote that 'the New York "socialite" was already be-

'foreigners' from St Andrews by 12 and 11 over their home course. The following year, 1844, Dunn went to Royal Blackheath to act as custodian of the links and club master. While Dunn was there, during the 1850s, Lord Starmont is said to have been sent to the club by his doctor, to lose weight. By the end of the first 7 holes (one round) his lordship had broken the entire set of clubs and his caddie came in for another set; these suffered almost the same fate, and at the end of the day the noble lord professed himself pleased with the day's exercise and asked Dunn to have another set ready by Thursday when he would be down again.

Dunn played a number of matches in those years, all of the challenge variety for

Dunes Golf and Beach Club

Top, George T. Dunlap Jr

Above, 'Old' Willie Dunn, second from right, in the first known golfing photograph, taken at St Andrews, c.1845

there was no championship. On another occasion he was paired with Sir Robery Hay in a match for £200 at St Andrews. Some idea of what that meant to him can be gauged from the fact that when Willie was first employed at Royal Blackheath he earned about 10 shillings a week. They lost, but Sir Robert had been up till the early hours at the Fife Hunt Ball. Willie Dunn returned to Scotland after 20 years at Royal Blackheath. He went to Leith and eventually to North Berwick.

Dunn, 'Young' Willie BRITISH
b. Musselburgh, Midlothian, 1870; d. 1952.
US Open 1894 (unofficial), runner-up 1895 (official)

Son of Old Willie Dunn, he emigrated to the United States in 1891 when, after designing a course in France at Biarritz, he was commissioned by W. K. Vanderbilt to build one at Shinnecock Hills, near Southampton, N.Y. The site was two miles from Shinnecock Indian reservation and 150 Indians helped Dunn lay out 12 holes. At the time his one desire was to return to France, which he believed had a great golfing future, but he stayed on in America where his designs included the popular Ardsley, N.Y.

In 1894 Young Willie Dunn won an unofficial Open Championship, contended by four competitors and decided by matchplay; he was runner-up the following year in the first Open run by the newly formed USGA. He was soon followed by two nephews, Seymour and John D. Dunn, who became prominent course architects and teachers.

Durban CC SOUTH AFRICA
Durban, Natal. 18 holes; 6,965 yd (6,369 m); par 72

Fashioned from the sandhills that run parallel to the seashore south of the Umgeni River. The architect, who started work in 1920, was Laurie Waters, a famous South African professional and four times winner of the South African Open, and he was assisted by G. Waterman. The course has changed little and every national championship allocated to Natal has been held there. Many distinguished visitors have tried their skill at Durban, including the Duke of Windsor, after whom the short 12th is named in honour of the extraordinary number of strokes he required to complete the hole. Durban has one of the largest memberships in the world.

Dutra, Olin AMERICAN
b. Monterey, Cal., 1901. Southern Californian Professional 1928-30, 1932-3; Southwest Open 1931; USPGA 1932;

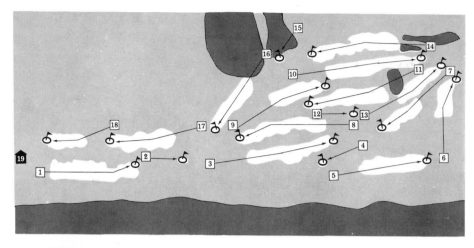

Ryder Cup 1933, 1935; US Open 1934; 3rd US Masters 1935

As a teenager Dutra worked in a hardware store and for three days a week he got up before dawn to practise his golf. This was his routine for several years; he continued it after turning professional so as to hold two jobs. Dutra earned a reputation as a tireless teacher, but still found time to improve his game. The quality of that game, one of the best in the early 1930s, is shown by Dutra's performance in winning the 1934 US Open at Merion. Although ill, he had closing rounds of 71 and 72, overhauling Gene Sarazen who had a final round of 76. Twenty-seven years later, in 1961, Dutra was still able to shoot a 61 over the Jurupa Hills course in Riverside, Cal., the club where he was professional.

Dutra's achievements in the 1930s included touring with Walter Hagen in 1933 and being chairman of the USPGA tournament committee in 1935.

Dye, Pete AMERICAN
Paul Dye, who is always referred to as Pete,

began his career in golf architecture after a spell in the insurance business in his home town of Indianapolis, Ind. He wanted a more meaningful life, and he has apparently found it, judging by the zest and high creativity he brings to his work. Many informed critics consider that he is the most successfully experimental of the postwar American architects. In this period when many architects have made it a practice to build a dozen or more courses simultaneously, Dye has made a point of limiting himself to three or four overlapping jobs. A great admirer of the old Scottish courses, such as Dornoch, he tries to infuse those 'natural' qualities into his American courses. These include The Golf Club (Columbus, Ohio), Crooked Stick (Indianapolis), Harbour Town (Hilton Head Island, S. Car.), and Campo de Golf Cajuiles (Dominican Republic). Dye, a fine golfer, has played in many US Amateur Championships. His wife is Alice Dye, who was a member of the 1970 American Curtis Cup team.

Dykes, John Morton, Jr. BRITISH
b. Bearsden, Dunbartonshire, 1905. Walker Cup 1936; Scottish Amateur 1951

Possessed of a buoyant enthusiasm and great strength and stamina, Morty Dykes's competitive golfing life spanned almost 20 years. He played in the 1936 Walker Cup match, having reached the last eight of the British Amateur Championship in that and the preceding year, and in 1951 won the Scottish Amateur Championship. Dykes also represented Scotland in six years, playing first in 1934 and for the last time 17 years later.

Top, course plan of the Durban CC

Above, Olin Dutra

East, J. Victor AMERICAN b. Scotland

One of golf's all-rounders, East was first apprenticed as a professional at Elie. In 1901 he went out to Australia where he became professional to the Royal Sydney GC, and was instrumental in forming the Professional Golfers' Association of Australasia in 1906, of which body he was elected secretary and treasurer. In 1921 he made a world tour with the trick artist Joe Kirkwood, and a year later settled in the United States, becoming professional to the Biltmore Forest CC. In the course of a long career East was also journalist, author of *Better Golf in Five Minutes* and a designer of clubs, associated first with Spalding in America and later with Wilsons.

Easterbrook, Sydney BRITISH

Ryder Cup 1931, 1933; tied 3rd British Open 1933

Syd Easterbrook was one of the very few golfers who gained Ryder Cup honours without winning a major tournament. He went to the United States with the 1931 team but his finest performance was at Southport and Ainsdale two years later, when he beat Densmore Shute in the deciding match on the home green, to give Britain the Cup. A few weeks later Easterbrook came very near to being Open Champion. He took a seven at the 14th hole in a final round of 77 and lost by one stroke, Shute winning after a play-off.

East London GC SOUTH AFRICA

East London, Cape Province

The present course, lying between the Eastern Beach and Nahoon, was carved out of virgin bush and sandhills overlooking the Indian Ocean. The work was carried out almost by hand, members devoting weekends to it and taking their African gardeners to help them. The result was a course of natural beauty, but considerable replanning was needed before it could stage its first national championship in 1927. Three more championships have been held there, including Bobby Locke's last victory in a South African Amateur championship before turning professional. Other improvements have been made regularly to keep abreast of modern developments. The club has pro-

duced two national champions, C. E. Olander (1932, 1934, 1936) and B. R. Ryan (1948).

Eagle

A hole performed in 2 strokes below par.

Edgar, John Douglas BRITISH

b. Newcastle upon Tyne 1884; d. 1921. French Open 1914; Canadian Open 1919-20; runner-up USPGA 1920

Professional for a time at Gosforth GC, Edgar won the French Open in 1914 and later emigrated to the United States where he worked in Atlanta. In 1919 he won the Canadian Open, finishing several shots ahead of Walter Hagen, then at the height

of his powers, and repeated the victory in 1920. In 1921 he was found dead in a city street, the victim, it was said, of a gang fight. Edgar wrote an instructional book *Through the Gate* in which he set out his own method of teaching the swing. He made his pupils swing at the ball passing the clubhead through a gate set up behind the ball, a gate which could be gradually closed as the pupil improved. In this way he was able to develop his theory of the in-to-out method of striking, of which he was one of the first exponents.

Edmunston GC CANADA

Edmunston, N.B. 18 holes; 6,610 yd (6,044 m); par 73

Tucked in the northwest corner of New Brunswick, just across the St John River from the most northerly town of Maine in the United States, lies one of the finest and most difficult courses in eastern Canada. Begun in 1922 with only seven holes, it was expanded and rebuilt in 1947 under the direction of Albert H. Murray, winner of the Canadian Open Championship in 1908 and 1913 and of the Canadian PGA in 1924. With his golfing knowledge and experience, Murray made splendid use of the more than 250 acres (101 ha) of varied terrain at his disposal. Built on two levels, the course is long and has fairways of ample width. But its well-bunkered greens are of only medium size, ranging in area from 3,500 to 5,000 square feet (325-465 m²). They reward long and well-placed tee shots. In winning his second straight Canadian Amateur Championship there in 1956, Moe Norman of Kitchener, Ont., played one of the most perfect rounds of golf ever seen in Canada. His opponent in the morning round of a 36-hole semi-final match, with the course rain-soaked and playing unusually long, scored a fine 72, one under par. But he found himself 8 down to Norman's 64, made up of 9 birdies and 9 pars.

Egan, Henry Chandler AMERICAN

b. Chicago, Ill., 1884; d. 1936. Western Amateur 1902, 1904, 1907, runner-up 1903; US Amateur 1904-5, runner-up 1909, semi-finalist 1929; Pacific-Northwest Amateur 1915, 1920, 1923, 1925, 1932, runner-up 1914, 1921; Californian Amateur 1926, runner-up 1928; Walker Cup 1934

The outstanding American amateur golfer in the years between the heydays of Travis and Travers. He built up an impressive record in the first decade of the century, then abruptly disappeared from competition after moving to Oregon in 1911, where for a few years his home was 300 miles from a golf

Top, J. Victor East

Above, Henry C. Egan

course. During those years he gave his occupation as fruit grower. He began competing in Pacific-Northwest tournaments in 1914 but did not enter for the US Amateur again until 1929 when the event was held in the West for the first time, at Pebble Beach. In his first appearance in the event since he had been runner-up in 1909 he reached the semi-finals – some indication of what he might have accomplished had he competed regularly in the Amateur during the intervening 20 years.

Chandler Egan first played golf in 1896 at Lake Geneva, Wis., while on a visit to his cousin, Walter Egan. His father joined Exmoor, Ill., in 1899 and Chandler soon developed into a first-class player possessing a style that few equalled. He moved to California in the late 1920s and took up golf-course architecture: it was Egan who re-modelled the Pebble Beach course and influenced the decision to hold the 1929 US Amateur there.

Egan won his fifth Pacific-Northwest Amateur in 1932 at 48, and was chosen for the 1934 Walker Cup at 50. He was stricken with pneumonia in 1936 while working on a course at Everett, Wash., and died six days later.

Egypt

Golf in Egypt dates back over 50 years to the 1914-18 period when the British introduced the game. For some 40 years, until 1956, this nation, because of the British influence, led the Middle East in having the best golf clubs and courses and the strongest international identification in golf. After the Suez conflict of 1956, however, Egyptian interest in the game waned, there was a general British exodus and from these reverses golf in Egypt has not yet recovered. But it is not beyond restoration. There is a growing appreciation of its value as a tourist attraction. In this

Egypt: teeing off at Maadi Sporting Club's sand course. The tee is merely an elevated platform of sand with mats laid on top

there is hope for its eventual revival. Egypt still has the climate that makes golf there specially attractive in the autumn, winter and spring months. Perhaps one day Egypt will resume its place in the golfing sun.

Egyptian golf flowered originally in two famous British clubs: the Gezira Sporting Club, founded in 1882 as the Khedivial Sporting Club (the name was changed to Gezira in 1914); and the Alexandria Sporting Club, founded in 1880. Both were horse-racing and social clubs; golf was introduced at Gezira about the time of World War I and at Alexandria about 1920, when courses were laid out within and around the race-tracks. These eventually became respectable 18-hole grass courses.

In the early 1930s a second 18-hole course was built in Alexandria at the Smouha City suburb. Built inside the racetrack on re-claimed swamp which had been used for many years as a garbage dump, the course was known and still is for rich carpet-like turf.

Several other courses contributed to the development of golf in Egypt: the 18-hole course at the former Heliopolis GC near Cairo; the picturesque 9-hole grass course at the Mena House hotel in the shadow of the Pyramids of Giza; and several sand courses, now abandoned, including the Maadi Sporting Club course outside Cairo, where the famous Desert Open was played annually until 1956.

From the early 1950s the annual Egyptian Open Championship, inaugurated in 1921, the Egyptian matchplay Championship, and other special events, attracted international tournament stars who lent glamour and class to the Egyptian golf scene and brought it into the limelight. The fields included Bobby Locke, and Gary Player, from South Africa, and England's Ryder Cup player Bernard Hunt, who won the 1956 Open at Gezira. Then came Suez, followed by the decline of golf in the country. Today Egypt has five courses in play, two in Alexandria and three in Cairo. They are open to tourists, but range from mediocre to poor, suffering from lack of proper maintenance and much less used than in the days when the country was foremost in Middle Eastern golf, led by its native professional Hassan Hassanein and, later, World Cup players Cherif El Sayed and Mohammed Said Moussa.

Eichelberger, Martin Davis AMERICAN
b. Waco, Tex., 1943. Semi-finalist US Amateur 1964; Walker Cup 1965; Greater Milwaukee 1971

Dave Eichelberger attended Oklahoma State University, nursery of several good

young professionals; but before turning professional in 1967 took part in the Americas Cup matches in 1965 and in the tied Walker Cup match at Baltimore. He lost both foursomes on that occasion but contributed a crucial point on the final afternoon, defeating Michael Bonallack, reigning British champion, by 5 and 3. For four years after turning professional he had a lean time, becoming a regular figure trying to qualify on Mondays, but in 1971 he suddenly made the grade, his winnings rising above the $100,000 mark for the first time. In addition to recording his first tour victory at Milwaukee, he finished in the top ten on eight other occasions.

Eindhoven GC NETHERLANDS
Valkenswaard. 18 holes; 6,669 yd (6,098 m)

The Eindhovensche Golf Club, about five miles from the centre of Eindhoven, was started by Dr A. F. Philips, brother of the founder of the electrical and radio company, and his wife, and opened in 1930. Designed by H. S. Colt, it is reminiscent of the sand-and-heather courses round London. With sandy fairways twisting a path through attractive pinewoods, it is one of the best in Holland. The club is well equipped to cater for championships and its clubhouse has recently been extended and modernized. During the Dutch Open championship of 1964 Harold Henning established the course record of 64. It has also been the scene of several other national and international events, including the 1972 European Junior Team Championship.

Martin Roesink, generally regarded as Holland's best professional player, was once assistant to Piet Witte at Eindhoven.

Eisenhower, General Dwight David
AMERICAN
b. Denison, Tex., 1890; d. 1969

Martin D. Eichelberger

Dwight Eisenhower undoubtedly did more to popularize the game of golf with the average American than any other single individual during the last quarter of a century. From its first appearance in the United States, golf had been viewed by the large majority of Americans as a rather sissified pastime of the snobbish rich, but after Eisenhower had revealed his infatuation with the game so publicly and regularly, Americans changed their minds, perhaps feeling that there must be something good in a game he liked so much.

An all-round athlete at West Point, Eisenhower did not take up golf until many years later during one of his tours of duty in Washington, D.C., where he played the

game at the Chevy Chase club. When he became President, he joined the Burning Tree club because it was felt that it offered him more privacy. Knowing how he liked to relax during his Presidency by hitting a few shots, friends arranged for a practice green and bunker to be built on a side lawn of the White House, and he used these often. At Camp David, the Presidential retreat, Eisenhower practised iron shots on a compact little layout – a green and three differently angled tees – designed by Robert Trent Jones. But, he is most closely associated with the Augusta National GC. During his term as President, he made his 'vacation White House' the Colonial cottage (called 'Mamie's Cabin') that stands close by the

large practice putting green. It is said of him that he competed hard to win in all his matches. He was not a particularly impressive swinger – an old football injury had left him with a game knee – but he kept the ball nicely in play and was often in the mid-80s. His pitch shots were the best part of his game. He enjoyed the company of golfers and knew many of the champions well, being a particularly close friend of Arnold Palmer, and of Bob Jones. The Eisenhower Trophy awarded for the World Amateur Team Championship was named after him in 1958.

Eisenhower Trophy see WORLD AMATEUR TEAM CHAMPIONSHIP FOR THE EISENHOWER TROPHY TABLE (p. 470)

Ekwanok CC USA
Manchester, Vt.

Henry Leach, perhaps the best of the pre-Darwin British golf journalists, rated Ekwanok the best golf course he had come across on his several visits to America. A favourite among the American gentlemen-

golfers of that period, Ekwanok came to international attention in 1914 when the US Amateur Championship was held there: Francis Ouimet was making his first start in the Amateur since his landmark victory over Vardon and Ray in the 1913 US Open, and everyone was naturally interested to see what account the young man would give of himself. He won the championship, defeating Max Marston, W. I. Howland, Bob Gardner, Bill Fownes, and Jerry Travers, in that order. This performance went far to show the world that Ouimet was a substantial golfer and not just a one-week wonder. In the 36-hole final against Travers, the great match player, Ouimet, 4 down after 16 holes, swept the next seven in a row to take firm command. He was off-line only once during the 31 holes of the match.

Since 1914, Ekwanok has not been used for an important championship, but it continues to be a much-admired course. It is not a long layout, but its small greens are poised in engaging positions on the tumbling ground, and it takes first-class golf to hit them and to score. The charming village of Manchester – Robert Todd Lincoln, the president's son, was a summer regular – has changed little over the years, and there are few pleasanter spots in the world to play golf, especially when autumn is colouring the Green Mountains. Manchester has a second 18-hole course, Equinox, which ranks close to the top among the country's public courses.

Eldorado CC USA
Palm Desert, Cal. 6,840 yd (6,254 m); par 72

Eldorado was opened for play on 22 November 1957, during an era when the desert country of south-central California was being developed as a vacation area. Grass is not a common crop in this parched land, but this Palm Springs and Palm Desert area had other attractions – bright blue skies, a mild, inviting climate, and of course little rain. Because of the arid climate, a generous water supply was essential, and seven lakes were built into the design of the course. All of them are in play.

Eldorado is set in a canyon among craggy mountains rising thousands of feet. The fairways wind among orange groves and date palms. Two years after opening it was the site of the Ryder Cup match. The British had won in 1957, and they were in position to win two of the four foursomes matches on the first day. Harry Weetman and Dave Thomas were 1 up on Sam Snead and Cary Middlecoff playing the last hole, but the British lost that hole when Weetman hit his approach into a water hazard, and Snead

Top, General Dwight D. Eisenhower

Above, the Eisenhower Trophy

Ekwanok CC

and Middlecoff saved a half. The United States ultimately won the match, 8½-3½.

Each year now, at least one round of the Bob Hope Desert Classic is played over Eldorado. Part of the proceeds from this tournament help finance the Eisenhower Medical Center nearby. This desert region is strong in Eisenhower tradition; the former President lived in a home alongside the 11th fairway at Eldorado.

Elie Golf House Club SCOTLAND
Elie, Fife. 18 holes; 6,294 yd (5,755 m); par 70

James VI in a charter of 1589 reaffirmed the golfing rights of the people of Earlsferry on certain common land first established in a much older charter. Over the centuries the royal burgh of Earlsferry and the neighbouring burgh of Elie grew together, not least in their golfing affairs on contiguous links. Eventually the Earlsferry and Elie Club was formed in 1858, followed in 1875 by Earlsferry Thistle and Elie Golf House Club, these two sharing the original club's trophies when it was disbanded, and continuing to flourish on the common course. The ancient course of 9 holes was extended to 11, then to 14 in 1886. In 1895 Tom Morris stretched it to 18 and some alterations were made in 1921 by James Braid, a local man. Elie, 10 miles south of St Andrews, is perhaps best known for the golfers it has produced, the giant of them all being James Braid himself, who represented Earlsferry Thistle when he was only 15. He is commemorated by a plaque at the town hall and a club trophy. Another was A. H. Scott, a great player, teacher and craftsman, appointed clubmaker to the Prince of Wales (later Edward VII), and inventor of the original short-socket club known as 'Scott's unbreakable neck' and his 'straight-line putter'. His son David, who died in 1967, carried on the business for many years and is to be commemorated in a golfer's stained-glass window in Elie parish church, depicting his famous dog Paddy, an Irish setter, and marking their combined feat, after David Scott's retirement, of raising £1,000 for the kirk restoration fund by retrieving and selling lost golf balls. Other notable golfers produced by Earlsferry/Elie were J. N. Smith, Bob Simpson and Douglas Rolland, a stonemason of magnificent physique, famous for his prodigious driving. To Elie Golf House Club must also go the credit for creating one of the earliest Ladies' Clubs, in 1881.

Ellison, T. Froes BRITISH
English Amateur 1925-6

No great stylist but a fine temperament

for matchplay, Ellison had the knack of getting down in two from greenside bunkers to the discomfiture of his opponents. He won the first English championship in 1925, which was held over his home course, Hoylake, and successfully defended his title at Walton Heath the following year, a feat achieved since only by Frank Pennink, Alan Thirlwell, twice by Michael Bonallack, and Harry Ashby. He hit the ball a powerful blow with a short backswing, but lacked the timing essential for long driving, a flaw that may have excluded him from the highest honours.

El Prat GC SEE REAL CLUB DE GOLF 'EL PRAT'

El Saler GC SPAIN
Cullera. 18 holes; 7,108 yd (6,500 m)

Club de Golf El Saler, situated very close to the sea several miles south of Valencia, was authorized by the Spanish Ministry of Information and Tourism which realized from the success of private ventures along the eastern seaboard what a tourist attraction golf had become. The ministry enlisted the skill of Spain's leading course architect, Javier Arana. At 7,108 yd it was the second longest course in Spain at the time. El Saler includes a 9-hole par-3 course. An unusual feature of El Saler is that it is open to the public and forms part of the government-run 'Luis Vives', a *parador* on motel lines. It is one of two state-managed golf courses in Spain.

El Shams GC EGYPT
An 18-hole, all-grass course. This new club, located on a stretch of bare desert near Heliopolis and the Cairo international airport, replaces the now defunct Heliopolis GC. El Shams is an elaborately planned all-sports club, with a racetrack surrounding the flat course. The course is partly open and generally featureless.

Elysian Fields
On the 14th hole of the Old Course at St Andrews, the area of safety golfers strive to find with their drive: from the back tee this is possibly the most dangerous drive on the course. It lies between the stone out-of-bounds wall on the right and the row of bunkers called the Beardies.

Emery, Walter AMERICAN
b. Okla. 1912. US Intercollegiate 1933 Runner-up to Lawson Little in the US Amateur Championship 1935, Emery was in the 1936 Walker Cup team, winning his single and halving his foursome in partnership with Charlie Yates.

Engadine GC SWITZERLAND
Samedan. 18 holes; 6,250 yd (5,715 m); par 70

Samedan, not far from St Moritz, is the oldest course in Switzerland, having been founded in 1898. It is close to the celebrated Palace Hotel and Suvretta House. Perched above the Engadine valley, it is, at about 5,700 ft, the highest course in Europe. Even in July and August snow may be found there. The course is flat but there are many obstacles: pine trees, the only trees to grow at this altitude, a stream, and above all wind which blows down almost all the time from the Maloja pass and at its worst adds greatly to the difficulties. In the rarefied atmosphere the ball travels easily 300 yd and more.

Equipment
The modern golfer drives in his car to the clubhouse, puts on his spiked shoes, gets his trolley from the shed, loads it with a big bag containing 14 clubs, a waterproof suit, a shooting stick and an umbrella, with a pocketful of balls, left-hand glove and other paraphernalia. Before setting out on the round he puts a scorecard in his pocket and calls in at the professional's shop to replenish his stock of balls and tee pegs. As he saunters out to the first tee dressed in pullover, wind-cheater and nylon cap, and as he removes the paper wrapper from a ball and drops it into the teebox, he is not conscious of how far he differs from the players of previous generations. This is golf as he knows it, yet all the equipment of his round is of the 20th century, the culmination of many years' development from primitive beginnings.

For most of the four or five hundred years of golf history the player's equipment consisted only of clubs and balls, often just one of each. He wore what might be called his everyday clothes, including smooth-soled shoes. His clubs, if he had more than one,

Walter Emery

were carried loose under his arm or that of his caddie. He had no protection against the weather. He or his caddie teed the ball on a pinch of sand, and the score was kept by comparing the number of shots he had taken with those expended by his opponent. In the very early days the club was an all-purpose implement of no set design, being often nothing more than a rudely-fashioned stick cut from the hedgerow and having at one end sufficient curve and bulk to give it balance.

As in the case of the ball there is no documentary evidence earlier than the latter part of the 15th century to give any clue as to the nature and appearance of golf clubs, but the fact that clubs were bought by the nobility and gentry implied the existence of craftsmen who sold them. The first of these makers to be named was William Mayne, a bowmaker by trade who in 1603 was appointed, among other things, clubmaker to James VI of Scotland shortly after his accession to the throne of England, as James I. There is no direct means of identifying the kind of clubs Mayne and his immediate successors made, but from what is known of the products of the 18th and 19th centuries it is certain that the basic components were a shaft of ash or hazel, and a head of blackthorn, beech, apple or pear. The usual method of joining them was to plane longitudinal bevels in the end of the shaft and the neck of the head, glue the planed surfaces together and bind with twine. The heads were fashioned to lie at a much flatter angle than those of today; they were also narrow and long, rarely more than 1 in. thick from face to back and usually 4 or 5 in from heel to toe. These dimensions were consistent with the sweeping swings used in the feather-ball era.

Although the earliest golfers were content with one club for all the shots, by the end of the 15th century there were clubs for special purposes. Shots from the tee, and many of those through the green, where the lies were good, were made with the 'play club', the forerunner of the driver, and there were other wooden clubs with greater angles of loft which were used for shots played from doubtful lies or in approach play where the ball had to be given more air. The early iron clubs were few in number and used specifically for playing out of bunkers and rough places, being given names like bunker iron, rut iron and track iron. All approach play from reasonable lies was with the lofted wooden clubs – the long spoon, the short spoon, baffy or baffing spoon, and so on. The putter also had a wooden head and was often used also for short approaches.

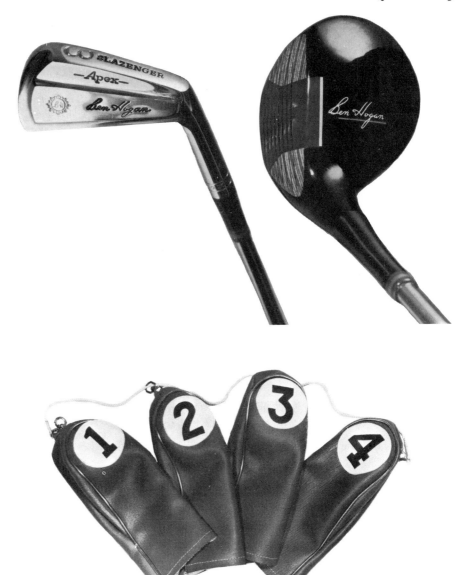

With the advent of the gutta-percha ball there were changes in the design of clubs, dictated by the fact that a solid ball yielded less than the hardest-packed feathery on impact with the clubhead. Consequently it became necessary to strengthen clubs at the weakest part – the joint between head and shaft – and to use soft woods like apple and pear instead of thorn and other hard wood. The heads were shortened to lessen the strain on the spliced neck, and it became the fashion to put leather insets in the clubfaces which otherwise were liable to become dented and worn by constant collision with the ball. A more yielding substance than ash was required for the shaft, and this problem was solved by the discovery that North

American hickory, at first imported for pick handles and similar tools, was ideal for the purpose. Hickory was supple and springy and supplied the resilience that the gutty did not possess. These shafts also had more torsion than those of ash and other woods used up to that time, and this brought about a change in method. Swings became more upright than the flat ones formerly used to sweep the feathery on its way.

One important change in club design resulting from the introduction of the gutty was that splicing head and shaft together was abandoned in favour of inserting the end of the shaft into a hole bored in the head. The other main change was in the role of iron clubs. Formerly employed only

Two modern clubs and a set of club covers

for getting out of trouble, they were now being used more and more in approach play, and the skill of the makers of forged iron heads was allied to the new skills of the professionals in establishing a standard of iron play that transformed the game. Before then iron heads were clumsy and oddly shaped, but the late-19th-century golfers found uses for the mid-iron, the cleek, the niblick and finally, towards the close of the century, for the mashie, made famous by John Henry Taylor.

But another time of change was at hand. The introduction of the rubber-core ball demanded the use of harder wood for clubheads than apple and pear. The need was met by persimmon, again from North America, and this has remained the standard material, although in recent years laminated heads and even composition ones have been increasingly employed, mainly because of dwindling supplies of good persimmon.

The present use of lead for giving necessary weight to the heads of wooden clubs dates from feather-ball days, but bone insets to preserve the sole of the club in contact with the ground eventually gave place to brass sole plates. For a long time persimmon heads had no insets on the striking faces, but nowadays most clubheads have faceplates of hard material, sometimes bone or ivory but more usually plastic, to preserve the wood from damage on contact with the ball.

With the big expansion of golf in the 1890s the output of individual clubmakers in professionals' shops was insufficient to supply the growing demand, and this led to the establishment of factories ranging from workshops run by resident professionals to big commercial concerns using machine tools for shaping heads and gradually developing into mass-production units. Yet even in the most advanced establishments most of the work was still done by hand, and expert craftsmen remained in great demand.

Soon after World War I all this was changed. The growing shortage of suitable hickory led to experiments with steel shafts, and these were legalized in the United States in 1926. Britain did not follow suit till 1930, but the effect in both countries was the same. Clubmaking, from being a craft, depending on the skilled eye and hand of the individual workman, became a mechanical process. Shafts were acquired from the tube makers, heads were fashioned half a dozen at a time by jig tools, and clubmaking was reduced to little more than an assembly job.

The results of this development were far reaching. For the first time it was possible to turn out implements made to a set design and identical in dimensions, appearance and

characteristics, and so the age of the 'matched set' dawned. In the days of hickory much depended upon the selection of good shafts and the fitting of those shafts to suitable heads. Skilled work with saw, plane, spokeshave, rasp, glasspaper, lead ladle and polish bottle was required to produce a perfectly balanced club that would please the eye and the hand. It was possible for craftsmen to copy clubs within certain limits, and a golfer with the necessary experience could build up a 'set' of clubs, each feeling in his hands similar to the rest. But the factories, using steel shafts and the latest equipment including 'swing-weight' balances, could match up a set of clubs differing from each other only in loft and shaft length.

However damaging this was to the clubmaking craft, there was an even more serious outcome which for a time threatened to bring the game into disrepute. Manufacturers, having established a constant relationship between loft and distance obtainable, sought to bring even greater precision into golf by making clubs in intermediate sizes. Already the long-established names like mid-iron, mashie-niblick and mashie had given place to numbers, and the last refinement, at least from the trade's point of view, was to produce a $1\frac{1}{2}$ iron in between the no. 1 and no. 2, and so on down the scale. The craze reached such ridiculous proportions that in the 1930s caddies were staggering under big loads, as many as 25 clubs being stowed into vast bags.

The Royal and Ancient and the USGA agreed on a rule limiting to 14 the number of clubs that one player might carry in a competition. This number, with a difference of approximately 10 yd between lofts, seemed to give golf as much precision as any one could desire. Any more would ruin the game, and there were many conservative golfers, scornfully referring to 'shots bought in the shops', who believed that a limit of 10 or even fewer would be to the general benefit. But in these commercial days any big change of that kind would cause undesirable upheaval. Golfers generally seem satisfied, but the plain and inescapable fact is that prices have risen to a point that makes initiation into golf on a grand scale very expensive.

It is not only that clubs now cost as many pounds as they did shillings 60 years ago, but that accessories have grown in number and variety. This growth mainly belongs to the last half century, for the only important addition to the golfer's equipment between the arrival of the gutty and the introduction of the rubber-core ball was a bag for the clubs, previously carried loose in the crook of an arm. The first caddie bags were loose canvas cylinders with shoulder straps but without hoods, and they were liable to concertina to the ground, scattering the clubs, if the golfer lost control. Stiffeners made from split cane were introduced and eventually the bag was made quite rigid by being constructed round an iron frame, with rings top

An umbrella is sometimes a very necessary piece of equipment – Eric Brown in earnest, and damp, conversation with his caddie

and bottom to keep the shape. For many years golfers had difficulty in protecting their clubs in wet weather. Rain could fall into the bottom of the bag, soaking the grips, and at first the only way of keeping them dry was to reverse the clubs and wrap a mackintosh round the protruding grips. Hoods began to come in after World War I and at first were detachable, being fastened to the rim of the bag with press studs or wing nuts.

The introduction of steel shafts and the subsequent development of matched sets and large armouries brought a revolution in the design of bags. They became larger and heavier and acquired various embellishments. Some of the most expensive had internal compartments to hold shoes, waterproof suits, towels and other accessories. The ball pockets increased in size to accommodate scorecards, cigarettes or pipes, and zip fasteners proliferated.

Waterproof clothing specially designed for golfers is also a product of the inter-war period. Before then golfers in wet weather just got wet and changed into dry clothing at the end of the round. The waterproof fashion began with rubberized mackintosh trousers introduced in the 1920s, and much later came the windcheater jacket. After World War II full mackintosh suits were regular items of the golfer's wardrobe and bags were big enough to accommodate them, although when nylon became popular many suits could be carried in the golfer's pockets. With an umbrella in its socket and perhaps a seat-stick thrust in among the clubs, and an extra pullover stowed away somewhere else, the modern golfer is prepared for any weather and the longest round. He is also fortunate in being able to relieve his shoulder of the burden. The trolley or caddie cart was developed after World War II as a natural result of the fact that the numbers of caddies had decreased in inverse ratio to the sums required for their services. The days when even small clubs had caddie masters and groups of caddies waiting for Sunday morning employment have passed. Nowadays caddies in any number can be found only at exclusive or affluent clubs, or on duty at championships and tournaments. The trolley was first viewed with scepticism mixed with ridicule. Some clubs even went so far as to ban it – a few still do – but it was a heaven-sent solution to a difficulty and is now in general use. Mechanical trolleys powered by battery-electric motors were developed in the United States for carrying two golfers and their clubs. Very few are even now seen in Britain for the average British golfer, apart from questions of cost, still prefers to walk in pursuit of the small white ball. More recently smaller mechanical trolleys that the owner can control by hand while walking have appeared and these seem more likely to appeal to the British golfer.

Greenkeepers and green committees look askance at trolleys in winter and when conditions are really bad they are banned. But golfers are not easily put off from playing and soft and slippery going holds no difficulty if spiked shoes are worn. Yet spikes are also products of the last fifty years. They first appeared about 1920 and were then rather stubby spikes of the kind fitted to cricketers' boots. They were also integral parts of the shoe and could only be replaced *in toto* when the shoe itself was repaired. Uneven wearing of the spikes inevitably occurred. After World War II this difficulty was overcome by the introduction of spikes that could be screwed into and out of sockets permanently fixed in the soles and heels.

Very early golfers wore smooth-soled shoes, which in some of the old prints look as slight as court shoes or dancing pumps. Probably the lower-class golfers and the professionals, wearing heavy boots with thick soles, were rather better equipped for the job than more affluent players. When golf became popular in the gutty-ball era it was customary to play in clothes used for other outdoor pursuits like fishing and shooting, and stout boots with ribs of leather or metal plates went with Norfolk jackets and breeches and gave fairly good foothold without causing the pockmarks and scratches on the putting greens which today annoy not only the greenkeeper but also the late starters in a tournament round.

Although many golfers do not use trolleys or spikes there can scarcely be one who does not carry tee pegs. These handy articles made from wood or plastic were introduced shortly before World War II, and before long sand disappeared after hundreds of years as the standard material for making tees. A tee was made deftly by the caddie with an expert pinch of sand on which to perch the ball, or clumsily by the inexperienced amateur who built an ungainly pyramid. A player with a caddie was accustomed to tap the required spot with his driver head and leave the caddie to do the rest. But tee pegs are so easy to use that even champions do their own teeing up. The tee box, once a receptacle for sand, now does duty as a waste-paper basket and a tee marker.

No golfer thought of using an umbrella until bigger caddie bags made them easier to carry. The seat-stick is also popular with golfers, and perhaps a necessary piece of equipment in these days of interminable fourball matches and general slow play. Left-hand gloves (for right-handed players) are also fashionable, popularized by Henry Cotton and scarcely seen before the 1930s. Probably no scorecards existed until about the middle of the 19th century. Certainly they were not used even in the Open Championship until 1865, five years after that event started, and for long afterwards they were simple in layout, giving only the numbers of the holes with columns for scoring, but no yardage or par figures. Towards the end of the gutty-ball era, with more and more people taking up the game and clubs multiplying, the scorecard became more complicated, giving lengths of holes, par figures, columns for gross and net scores, and other information, with spaces for signatures and, on the back, the local rules for the course. They were often folded in two, and cut so that they measured 6 in, either in length or diagonally, and could be used to determine stymies in case of dispute.

Equity
The rules of Golf, Rule II, Subsection 4, state 'If any point in dispute be not covered by the Rules or Local Rules, the decision shall be made in accordance with equity.'

Espinosa, Al R. AMERICAN
b. Monterey, Cal., 1892, d. 1957. Illinois Open 1925-6, 1930; runner-up USPGA 1928, semi-finalist 1927; Ryder Cup 1929, 1931; runner-up US Open 1929; Ohio Open

1932-3, 1936; Indianapolis Open 1935; Mexican Open 1944-7

A consistent winner on the limited tournament circuit of the 1920s and early 1930s. He was runner-up in the 1928 USPGA and tied with Bobby Jones for 1st place in the 1929 US Open, only to be crushed by 23 strokes in the 36-hole play-off the

Al Espinosa

next day. He had made up 4 strokes to catch Jones on the last round at Winged Foot. Al, a brother of Abe Espinosa, was a member of two Ryder Cup teams. He moved to Mexico late in his career and was still winning the Mexican Open when over 50.

Espirito Santo Trophy see WOMEN'S WORLD AMATEUR TEAM CHAMPIONSHIP FOR THE ESPIRITO SANTO TROPHY (p. 470)

Estoril GC PORTUGAL

Portugal's early golfing history is centred around the Oporto GC which was founded in 1890 but since its founding Estoril GC has come to be regarded as the 'headquarters' of Portuguese golf. It started in 1929 as 9 holes laid out by Jean Gassiat and in 1938 was extended to 18 holes by Mackenzie Ross. Control has always been

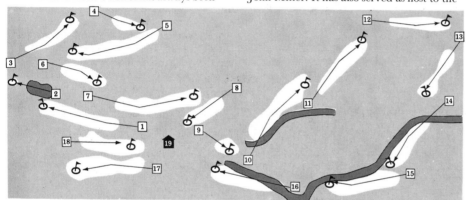

more necessary than length at Estoril.

Located in a fashionable seaside town close to Lisbon, it has been a popular golfing retreat and between 1930 and 1961 every Portuguese championship was held there. In 1961, the Portuguese National Amateur went to Espinho, which became the country's first 18-hole course in 1934, and in 1967 the Portuguese Open Amateur was taken to Penina, the first of several fine courses in the Algarve. In time, these may take over from Estoril as the championship centre but nothing can detract from the influence that Estoril has had upon Portuguese golf.

Etiquette

The general conduct or code of behaviour that all players are expected to observe on the course. It includes such things as consideration for other players, replacing divots and pitch marks, smoothing out footprints in bunkers and playing without delay.

Eugene CC USA

Eugene, Ore. 18 holes; 6,908 yd (6,317 m); par 72

One look at Eugene CC should be enough to convince the golfer that he must keep the ball on the fairway. Eugene is in Oregon, a state known for its timber, particularly the giant Douglas fir that reaches 250 ft and whose trunk at its base can be 6 ft or more in diameter. Clumps of these trees stand along every fairway, and it soon becomes clear that they cannot be played over.

Eugene can play very long, at 6,908 yd from the back tees. It was originally designed in 1924 by H. Chandler Egan, the US Amateur Champion of 1904 and 1905, and was remodelled by Robert Trent Jones in 1967. Eight of its holes play either across or alongside water, and it has two par-5 holes over 500 yd (460 m).

Eugene was the site of the 1964 National Junior Championship which was won by John Miller. It has also served as host to the National Collegiate Championship and the Trans-Mississippi Amateur.

European Golf Association

The European Golf Association was founded in 1937 at a meeting held in Luxembourg and has grown in importance and stature over the years. The Association concerns itself solely with matters of an international character. It has no jurisdiction in the domestic affairs of its affiliated organizations, whose independence it recognizes.

The Association declares that it will observe the Rules of Golf and Amateur Status as laid down by the Royal and Ancient Golf Club of St Andrews and its prime objects may be stated as follows:
(a) to encourage the international development of golf and to strengthen the bonds of friendship existing between the national organizations and to encourage the formation of new organizations;
(b) to co-ordinate the dates of the Open and Amateur championships of its members;
(c) to arrange, when such have been decided upon, European team championships and matches of international character;
(d) to decide and publish the calendar dates of the Open and Amateur championships of Europe, and matches.

The EGA is responsible for selecting teams for the following matches: St Andrews Trophy (men), Vagliano Trophy (women), EGA Trophy (youths).

The EGA has a president elected for a period of two years, and is represented on the Rules of Golf and Amateur Status committee of the Royal and Ancient. The member countries are Austria, Belgium, Czechoslovakia, Denmark, England, Finland, France, German Federal Republic, Iceland, Ireland, Italy, Luxembourg, Netherlands, Norway, Portugal, Scotland, Spain, Sweden, Switzerland and Wales.

Evans, Albert David BRITISH

b. 1911. Welsh Amateur 1949, 1961; semifinalist British Amateur 1951

Albert Evans, now retired as a farmer, is one of the three most capped players for Wales over a period of 30 years. He was twice Welsh Champion, the second time at the age of 50, and was semi-finalist in the 1951 British Amateur Championship, losing to Charlie Coe by 3 and 2 over the Porthcawl links which he loves so well.

A kindly man, he has done much to encourage young Welsh golfers and has performed devoted service as a British selector for many years. He was also responsible with a small band of dedicated helpers for the construction of the new Ross-on-Wye GC in

Top, the course plan of Estoril GC

Etiquette, *above:* the British comedian, Eric Sykes, distracting Pat Tallack at the start of his backswing

Herefordshire and was captain in the first year in its new home.

Evans, Charles, Jr AMERICA

b. Indianapolis, Ind., 1890. Western Amateur 1909, 1912, 1914-15, 1920-3; Western Open 1910; French Amateur Open 1911; North and South Amateur 1911; US Amateur 1916, 1920, runner-up 1912, 1922, 1927; US Open 1916, runner-up 1914, tied 6th 1920

Chick Evans's influence on American golf was second only to that of Francis Ouimet in broadening the social base of the game. Like Jones and Ouimet, he showed great promise at an early age, winning the first of his six Chicago City Amateur championships at the age of 17, and following it three years later with victory over a strong professional field in the Western Open, second only to the US Open in importance at that time. It is a tribute to the soundness of his technique that 43 years later he was still good enough to play in and qualify for the US Open Championship. But although his outstanding talent was obvious, it took him time to win his first National Amateur. By 1916 he had played in seven of them; he had reached the final in 1912, and had been three times in the semi-final, beaten each time by players he should not have lost to. Part of the reason for this was that although on the course he had an extrovert manner, his putting was quite insecure by comparison with the rest of his game. In 1916 everything seemed to click into place. Playing with seven clubs – but he had three reserve putters – he won the Open at Minneapolis with a record score of 286 which was to remain unbeaten for the next 20 years. He led all the way. His putting held up throughout the Amateur Championship that followed, and like Ouimet he won the Amateur after victory in the Open. Evans achieved it in the same year, a feat that has since been equalled only by Jones in the year of his Grand Slam. It is said that Evans's mother encouraged him to do what he wanted to do from childhood, and she was again influential in his decision not to turn professional, but to treat the game as a sport. He continued to compete for many years and played in 50 consecutive national championships; in 1927 only Bobby Jones, with seven 3s in 11 holes, stopped him from winning a third Amateur. Before he retired, Evans, who had been a caddie, set up a scholarship fund at Northwestern University that has given scores of caddies a chance in life they would not otherwise have had.

Everard, Mary BRITISH

b. Leeds, Yorkshire, 1944. English Ladies'

1972, runner-up 1964; runner-up British Ladies' 1967; European Team Championship 1967, 1971, 1973; World Women's Amateur Team Championship 1968, 1972; British Women's Strokeplay 1970; Curtis Cup 1970, 1972, 1974

An inconspicuous but highly effective player who hides a strong determination behind a nonchalant manner. The fact that she played in a world event before she played against the United States owed something to her having a bigger reputation in strokeplay than in matchplay, which was confirmed by her victory in the second British strokeplay championship to be held; but, in fact, she developed into a most dependable match player, showing both mental and physical toughness. From the time she made her first Curtis Cup appearance in 1970 this became apparent; in the match she won 2½ points out of 3, and the following year she won all but one of her matches in the European team championship and the Vagliano Trophy contest against the Continent of Europe. Possessed of no great length – her admirers always complained that she did not hit the ball hard enough – she compensated for this by missing fewer fairways than most, and showing fine judgment in the short pitch. When her game reached its peak she had added considerably to her length.

Ewing, Reginald Cecil IRISH

b. Rosses Point, Co. Sligo, 1910; d. 1973. West of Ireland 1930, 1932, 1935, 1939, 1941-3, 1945, 1949-50; Walker Cup 1936, 1938, 1947, 1949, 1951, 1955; runner-up British Amateur 1938; Irish Close Amateur 1948, 1958, runner-up 1946; Irish Open Amateur 1948, 1951

Born and bred within a few yards of the Co. Sligo links at Rosses Point, Cecil Ewing was in the ideal situation to make use of his natural golfing talent and no amateur perhaps in any country has been more closely connected with the game over a long period of years: that his first and most recent championship successes covered a span of 40 years is evidence of this. After his early achievements in his native western province international recognition was not long in following, but curiously he was more prominent in major events in Britain than in his own country in the years just before World War II.

By being selected for the 1938 Walker Cup team he shared in the sole triumph over the Americans until the feat was repeated at St Andrews in 1971. He did not play in the foursomes but contributed a point in the singles by beating Ray Billows. Immediately afterwards he confirmed his status by reach-

ing the British Amateur Championship final in which he lost narrowly to America's number one, Charlie Yates.

When competitive golf was resumed after the war he and his close friend and rival Joe Carr stood out above all the other Irish players and Ewing won his four national open and native titles, bringing off the rarely accomplished double in 1948. With his remarkably economical style, feet close together at the address, compact three-quarter swing with a limited pivot, the power coming mainly from massive forearms and wrists with more than 224 lb behind the shot, he was able to defy the passage of time and capture the native trophy for the second time at the age of 48.

After his retirement from the championship scene he took on the non-playing captaincy of the Irish teams, a position he held for 10 years, 1960-9, and led his teams to two European championship triumphs, at Sandwich in 1965 and Turin in 1967.

His experience and shrewd judgment were invaluable as Ireland's representative over a number of years on the Walker Cup selection committee. He played continuously for Ireland in the Home Internationals from 1934 to 1958, the great feature of his play being an inborn ability to hit long-iron shots low whatever the weather.

Mary Everard in a deep bunker during the English Ladies' at Woodhall Spa in 1972

Face

The surface of the club designed and prepared for hitting the ball; the only part *intended* to make contact with the ball. Bunkers also have faces: that part of the sand that rises steeply at the front.

Fade

The opposite of draw; a shot moving slightly from left to right towards the target (*see* draw). Usually deliberate and controlled, unlike a slice.

Fagnes, Royal GC des BELGIUM

Balmoral, Spa. 18 holes; 6,273 yd (5,736 m)

Royal GC des Fagnes was founded in 1927 and officially opened with an exhibition match in which Cotton and Compston played against Massy and A. Boyer. Later Cotton described the course as a 'Continental Sunningdale'.

It has been the scene of many big amateur tournaments. As might be expected at a resort, it is busiest during the holiday season.

Fairway

The specially prepared and cut part of the course between tee and green, surrounded by rough, bunkers and other hazards. Sometimes the fairways can be interrupted by strips of rough, cross bunkers, lakes and roads etc., but it usually extends as far as the apron of the putting green.

Falkenstein GC WEST GERMANY

Blankenese, Hamburg. 18 holes; approx. 6,600 yd (6,035 m); par 73

One of the best known, if not one of the oldest, of Hamburg's eight courses, Falkenstein is situated on the outskirts of a suburb 10 miles out of the city. The course, which has seen some memorable championships, consists of five par 5s, nine par 4s and four par 3s. It winds its way through heather and wooded areas, which are hilly in parts. During a normal season the fairways are lush and the greens – most of them fairly large – form a challenge to the best of putters. At one point, from a small summit, a view can be had over the nearby River Elbe, and every hole can be said to have a character of its own. There are several narrow drives and accuracy and length off the tee is of the first importance. The club

was founded in 1906; the course at Falkenstein, designed by the British architects Colt, Alison, and Morrison, was completed in 1930. Dr von Limburger later made a number of changes.

Falsterbo GC SWEDEN

Founded in 1909, Falsterbo Golfklubb has Sweden's only true links course, on a peninsula some 21 miles south of Malmö. Many Swedish Close and Open championships have been played there and also several Scandinavian Open Amateur championships. In 1964 the winner was Major D. A. Blair, who later wrote: 'Falsterbo incorporates all the best characteristics of the great seaside links. The turf, the natural hazards and swift changes in wind and weather make it as fine a golfing test as the championship links of Great Britain. In fact, within a day I had discovered a gem which is now one of my favourites.' In 1963, the European Amateur Team Championship was played at Falsterbo with England taking part in it for the second time. Captained by Michael Bonallack, England won and received the trophy from King Gustaf VI. The first nine holes were originally laid out at a total cost of £70 on the Baltic side of the Falsterbo peninsula. Eighteen holes were completed in 1930 and although vastly improved since then, very little has, in fact, been altered from the original design. Falsterbo is internationally known for the great flocks of birds passing the peninsula in the autumn on their southward migration.

Far East Circuit SEE ASIAN CIRCUIT

Farrell, Johnny AMERICAN

b. New York, 1901. Philadelphia Open 1925, 1927; Florida Open 1926; Ryder Cup 1927, 1929, 1931; US Open 1928, tied 3rd 1925-6; runner-up British Open 1929;

runner-up USPGA 1929, semi-finalist 1926, 1933

During the 1920s and early 1930s Farrell was one of the most colourful and competent players. In winning the 1928 US Open, Farrell tied with Bobby Jones and had the distinction of defeating him by one stroke in a 36-hole play-off. In addition to that Open, Farrell was in the first five on three other occasions. He had a consistent record in the USPGA championship, but was beaten five times in the quarter-finals. Starting as a caddie in the Westchester area, his first success came with victory in the Shawnee Open in 1922. It was not until 1926 that he began to win regularly; that year he took five events and then eight the next year, thereby establishing himself as a front-rank player. In 1929 he finished 2nd in the British Open and also in the USPGA, but without coming close to winning either. Farrell was a short hitter, even in his prime, but compensated with a fine short game and outstanding putting. Late in his competitive career he became professional at Baltusrol. His brother, James, and two sons are professionals.

Faulk, Mary Lena AMERICAN

b. Thomasville, Ga., 1930. US Women's Amateur 1953; Curtis Cup 1954

A tall graceful swinger, whose outstanding year as an amateur was 1953, when she won the US Women's Amateur. Earlier that season she had reached the semi-finals of the British Ladies' Championship, at Royal Porthcawl, after which she toured Europe. Not wishing to be encumbered with any golfing gear on that trip, she shipped her clubs home. They had not arrived when she checked in for the US Amateur at Rhode Island, and the clubs she used in winning that event were a miscellaneous lot borrowed from friends. She played in the Curtis Cup

Royal GC des Fagnes

Mary Lena Faulk

in 1954 and in defence of her Amateur title went to the semi-finals. She turned professional soon afterwards, and quickly made her mark by tying with Louise Suggs for 2nd place in the US Women's Open, 1955.

Faulkner, Max BRITISH

b. Bexhill, Sussex, 1916. Ryder Cup 1947, 1949, 1951, 1953, 1957; British Open 1951; Spanish Open 1952-3, 1957; British Professional Matchplay 1953; British Senior 1968, 1970; Portuguese Open 1968

Since the war, Max Faulkner has been one of the best and certainly the most colourful of all British professionals. His greatest distinction was in winning the Open championship in 1951, a performance enhanced by the failure of any other British player to emulate his feat for 18 years. No other golfer has won the Open, the matchplay championship and the Dunlop Masters; no other British golfer has abandoned the serious approach so readily and no British golfer has shown such a liking for bright clothes. He has an engaging, uninhibited manner and is an amusing storyteller but he is also a superb striker of the ball and with his strong physique has preserved his fine swing remarkably well.

At Portrush in 1951 he had the good fortune to be safely in the clubhouse on the second afternoon while his close challengers were contending with an afternoon of wind and rain, and that evening was said to be signing autographs putting 'Open Cham-

pion 1951' after his name. That was typical of a likeable, uncomplicated man and the following day's events proved him correct in his prediction. Although he had his anxious moments, only Cerda threatened to catch him and he eventually won by two shots with a total of 285 (71, 70, 70, 74). Cerda was 2nd.

Faulkner was for long the centre of attraction for British crowds and though he did not win as often as he might have done, he maintained his enthusiasm for the game and combined it with his other love, fishing. He won the British Senior Championship in 1968, losing the world final narrowly to the American, Chandler Harper. In recent years he has helped several young players, notably his son-in-law, Brian Barnes, and Tommy Horton, with their games.

Fazio, George AMERICAN

Tied 1st US Open 1950

Over the last 10 years, George Fazio has moved into the front line of American golf-course architects. He had earlier enjoyed a most successful career as a professional golfer. He served as the club professional at Pine Valley for many seasons and compiled an excellent record during his excursions on the tour. In the 1950 US Open, he tied 1st with Hogan and Mangrum (Hogan won the play-off). Fazio also figured prominently in the national championship in 1952 and 1953, finishing 5th and 4th respectively. A man of affability and taste, Fazio takes his time when he builds his courses, and his insistence on not rushing and getting things right has resulted in such sound and freshly conceived layouts as Moselem Springs, in Fleetwood, Pa., and Jupiter Hills, north of Palm Beach, Fla., one of the country's outstanding new courses.

Feel

The sensation of a ball on the club or of a club in the hands with regard to its weight and balance. In a more abstract sense, a player is said to have 'feel' for the game if he takes naturally to it and shows instinct and artistry in his shotmaking.

Feldafing GC WEST GERMANY

Feldafing. 18 holes; 6,340 yd (5,797 m); par 71

Situated some 20 miles south of Munich along the shore of the Starnberger See, one of the largest Bavarian lakes. From the clubhouse terrace and from some of the holes the ranges of the Bavarian Alps come sharply into focus on clear days. On the whole it is not a difficult course; here and there a tight spot, but more often there is room enough to stray and a fairly low score

is within reach of the good golfer. Fairways and greens recover quickly from the harsh winters which in this part of Germany last longer than elsewhere, and at the peak of the summer season the golfer could hope for no better playing conditions. Starting from the elevated clubhouse close by a road, the holes descend to lake level, then continue almost

touching the shore before climbing steeply to the 18th green. The greens are not large but bunkers guard many of them. A large hotel lies across the road from the clubhouse.

Ferguson, Bob BRITISH

b. Musselburgh, Midlothian, 1848; d. 1915. British Open 1880-2, runner-up 1883

One of the famous early Scottish professionals whose performance in winning the Open championship three times in succession, though equalled by Peter Thomson, 1954-6, and Jamie Anderson, 1877-9, has only been bettered by Young Tom Morris. His first Open victory was on his own links at Musselburgh, within sight of the house where he was born. His score then was 162; at Prestwick and St Andrews it was 170 and 171.

Anderson and Ferguson were the outstanding players after the era of the Morrises. Ferguson started to caddie at the age of eight on the Musselburgh links. The first real sign of his fulfilment as a player came at the age of 18 when he beat all the great professionals of the day in the Leith tournament with a bag of borrowed clubs. His prize was £10. As a result, he was backed in many matches; one of his sponsors was Sir Charles Tennant, who put up money in 1868 and 1869 when Ferguson beat Tom Morris six times. He and Morris also represented Scotland in a foursome at Hoylake in 1875, their opponents and victims being Bob Kirk of Blackheath, and John Allan of Westward Ho!

Max Faulkner

George Fazio

A man of powerful physique, he was particularly strong with cleek and iron and, because of this, showed up well when the wind was high or the ground soft. An attack of typhoid after the 1883 championship drew the sting from his game which was never the same again.

Fergusson, S. Mure BRITISH

b. Perthshire 1855. Runner-up British Amateur 1894, 1898; 4th (leading amateur) British Open 1891; St George's Challenge Cup 1906; captain Royal and Ancient 1910

Fergusson had a great reputation for holing critical putts, looking supremely confident from six feet. He was a lover of St Andrews who collected at least 12 medals at R. and A. spring and autumn meetings, nearly 40 years separating the first and last. A master of the stiff-armed push shot in a wind, he was generally reckoned unlucky not to have won at least one championship, notably the Amateur of 1894.

Fernie, Willie BRITISH

b. St Andrews, Fife, 1851; d. Troon, Ayrshire, 1924. British Open 1883, runner-up 1882, 1884, 1890-1

Willie Fernie, one of the great St Andrews professionals, went to Dumfries as greenkeeper in 1880. In 1874, while a plasterer by trade, he went by donkey cart to Wemyss with several other golfers, including the 14-year-old Andrew Kirkaldy, to take part in a tournament where a first prize of £6. In 1882 he was runner-up in the Open to Bob Ferguson and the following year at Musselburgh foiled Ferguson's attempt to win the Open for a fourth successive year.

Fernie's victory cannot have been very popular at the time for Ferguson was playing at Musselburgh, his own course, and local feeling was high. Ferguson, in fact, had to finish with three 3s to tie on 159, but in the play-off Fernie, one behind on the last tee, drove the green and holed a long 'steal' for a 2 to win by 1 stroke.

He remained a good player, was runner-up in the Open four times and took part in several challenge matches. He was professional at Felixstowe, Suffolk and Ardeer, Ayrshire, before moving to Troon where he remained until he retired shortly before his death. He was a good teacher and also played a considerable part advising on golf-course design, notably the original courses at Turnberry.

Ferrier, James AMERICAN

b. Manly, N.S.W., 1915. Australian Amateur 1935-6, 1938-9; runner-up British Amateur 1936; Australian Open 1938-9;

USPGA 1947, runner-up 1960; Canadian Open 1950-1; runner-up US Masters 1950

Although he won only one of the big four events, the Australian-born Ferrier has a fine all-round record throughout the world. A big, burly figure more than six feet tall, he started out in life as a sports, and in particular, a golf writer. While writing he won four Australian Amateurs and several State championships, and in 1936 had a successful trip to Britain, losing a fine match in the final of the British Amateur to a birdie on the last green from Hector Thomson. In Britain he won the Gleneagles Silver Tassie and the *Golf Illustrated* Gold Vase. He was still an amateur when he won the last two Australian Opens before World War II. He then emigrated to the United States, where he arrived with the reputation of having won 25 major championships in his own country. An injury to his leg when he was young gave him a curious action in golf with a drop and swivel of the body, but he was a very fine short-iron player, and it was not long before he was making his mark in the United States. He had intended to play in the 1940 US Open as an amateur, but there were doubts about his status, as interpreted in that country, because of his instructional book *How I Play Golf*. His entry was accepted as an amateur but the doubt may have influenced him in turning professional later the same year. It was in 1944, while serving as a sergeant in the US Army, that he won his first professional tournament in Oakland, Cal. In 1945 he scored two holes in one in the course of the San Francisco Open, and he had soon earned a reputation as a consistent money player. His victory in the USPGA championship came as the result of such a dazzling display with his pitching clubs that he was not asked to putt a second time on any of the 34 greens against Chick Harbert. Strongly placed at the halfway stage in both the 1947 and 1950 US Opens, he could not

James Ferrier

sustain his game and finished 6th each time. He played consistently well in the US Masters after the war; his best finishes were 2nd to Jimmy Demaret in 1950 and tied 3rd in 1952. In 1950 he needed a 38 to beat the winner but took 41 home.

Fescue

A finely bladed grass which forms the basis of many putting greens. The fineness of the grass gives a good surface and prevents nap.

Fiddian, Eric Westwood BRITISH

b. Stourbridge, Worcestershire, 1910. Runner-up British Amateur 1932; English Amateur 1932; Walker Cup 1932, 1934

Eric Fiddian, better-known of two Midland brothers, had a short but distinguished career, the cares of the family business taking him more or less out of big golf when he was still in his 20s. He had the curious distinction of doing a hole in one in each round of a 36-hole match and losing – that was in the Irish Open Amateur Championship final in 1933 against Jack McLean.

Field

All the contestants in a tournament or championship.

Fields GC IRAN

Masjed Soleyman. 18 holes; approx. 6,300 yd (5,760 m); par 72

Fields GC, about 125 miles northeast of Abadan, was founded in 1924 as a private course for staff and guests of the National Oil Company and the Iranian Oil Exploration and Producing Company. It is generally considered the best of several sand courses in southwest Iran.

Finland

Golf came to Finland in 1930 through the initiative of a Dane, Charles P. Jensen, who had travelled extensively in America. Helsingfors GCC (Helsingfors is the Swedish name for Helsinki) was founded in June 1932 at the Tali estate a few miles outside the capital. The first tournament on its 9-hole course took place in 1933. The club later adopted the Finnish form of its name, Helsingin Golfklubi. It extended its course to 13 holes in 1936, to 15 in 1938. In 1952 it became Finland's only 18-hole course. The designer of this senior Finnish course, Mr Arkkola, was not an architect, but had worked as a greenkeeper in Ontario from 1922 to 1930. He planned the first nine holes and constructed them with a couple of men and primitive equipment. Tali is rather flat but clumps of trees add interest. All the

Finnish men's championships and most of the women's have been played there; Aulanko has accommodated some of the latter in recent years.

In 1939 clubs were started at Pori and Viipuri (Vyborg – now in Soviet Russian territory). The number of Finnish clubs rose to 13 in 1957 with the formation of those at Kokkola, Lahti and Aulanko. The last-named course and the one at Turku (Åbo) are beautifully set in old parks. The rest of the country's courses are fairly modest. The airfield site of 6-hole Mikkeli makes it unique.

The season in the south of Finland lasts only from mid-May to mid-October; in the north it is even shorter. By way of compensation the long hours of daylight in summer enable the popular Midnight Sun tournament to be held.

Finsterwald, Dow AMERICAN

b. Athens, Ohio, 1929. Harry Vardon Trophy 1957; Ryder Cup 1957, 1959, 1961, 1963; USPGA 1958; tied US Masters 1962

By means of a steady control in which he concentrated on keeping the ball in play Dow Finsterwald was for a time a phenomenally consistent money winner. After returning a 61 in the St Louis Open in 1950 as an amateur he turned professional and moved steadily to the top. In the late 1950s he was as successful as anyone on the tour (11 victories in 1957 and in 1958 he won the USPGA championship at Havertown, Pa. It was the first year that the championship was decided by strokeplay rather than matchplay and his winning score was 276. Billy Casper finished 2nd.

From 1956 to 1965 Finsterwald had a fairly good record in the US Masters, finishing 3rd in 1960 and tying with Palmer and Player in 1962. He lost the play-off with 77

against Palmer's 68 and Player's 71. He also had good results in four Ryder Cup matches, winning nine games and losing only three.

Firestone CC USA

Akron, Ohio. 36 holes; South Course 7,180 yd (6,565 m), par 70; North Course 7,100 yd (6,492 m), par 70

Harvey Firestone, Sr, founder of the Firestone Tire and Rubber Company, was an industrial baron who early recognized that contented employees were good for business; his should have good jobs, certainly, and also good homes; and in the mid-1920s he decided they should also have their own golf course.

Company saw an alliance with professional golf as an effective form of publicity, and therefore it associated itself with the Rubber City Open, which continued over that aging course until 1959, when Firestone was invited to entertain the 1960 USPGA Championship. The club then engaged Robert Trent Jones to redesign the old course. He lengthened it to 7,180 yd, slashed par to 70, added bunkers, put a water hazard in front of the 3rd green and yet another in front of the 16th, a par-5 hole of 625 yd (569 m), and either moved or enlarged all 18 greens.

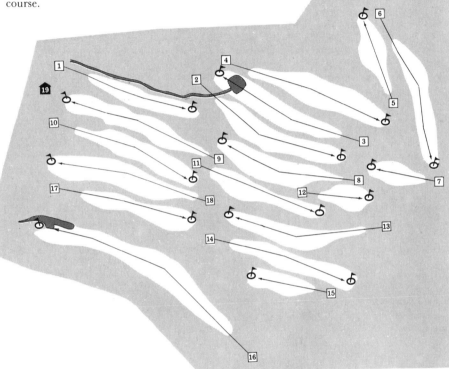

Some years earlier he had acquired 800 acres (324 ha) of rich Ohio farmland south of Akron that could be used either as an extension of the Firestone Park residential area or for additional production sites. Eventually he turned it into a golf course for all company employees. The Firestone CC currently has 1,440 members, 800 family or golf memberships. The remainder are social members awaiting an opening in the family membership rolls.

Bertie Way designed the original course of 6,585 yd (6,021 m) and a par of 72. Construction began in 1927, and it opened for play in 1928. The club existed quietly until the early 1950s when professional golf suddenly increased in popularity. The Firestone

This is Firestone's South Course, very compact for its length, with many parallel fairways, but they are so well screened from their neighbours that the result is not unpleasant. The course is always in impeccable condition. (Its tees, for example, would serve very nicely as greens on many golf courses with 'fancier' reputations.)

The new 7,100-yd North Course was added in 1968 across the road from the main course, set amid the waters of the Tuscarawass Reservoir. The reservoir comes into play on 10 holes. Since 1961, the South Course has been the site of the American Golf Classic, now one of the major events. A smaller version, the Little American Golf Classic, has been played on the North Course.

Dow Finsterwald

The plan of the Firestone CC. the South Course

In 1966 the USPGA Championship was played over the South Course a second time.

Perhaps most fame has come from the World Series, which has been played on the South Course since its inception in 1962.

Fischer, John W. AMERICAN

b. Cincinnati, Ohio, 1912. US National Collegiate 1932; Walker Cup 1934, 1936, 1938 (non-playing captain 1965); US Amateur 1936, semi-finalist 1937

One of the leading American amateurs during the 1930s and one of the best competitors. He was a 'never-say-die' man who was frequently down but seldom beaten throughout his career. This specialist in comebacks once admitted that he could not play well when he was in front because he then lost the nervousness that kept him on his toes. It started in his second year at Michigan University when he won the US Collegiate title, scoring three birdies on the last 4 holes to win by two and one. In the 1936 US Amateur, with both Walker Cup teams taking part, he reached the final against Jack M'Lean and found himself 1

down with 3 to play. He saved the 34th only by virtue of a stymie, halved the 35th with a birdie, and on the 36th holed from 12 ft to save the match with a birdie 2. On the first extra hole Fischer holed from 20 ft for yet another birdie against the unfortunate Scot. In the 1938 Walker Cup match Fischer was four down to Leonard Crawley at lunch, but completely turned the tables by scoring seven consecutive 3s from the 8th and winning by 3 and 2.

He even carried this knack of fighting finishes into the professional world, for he was once 4 down with 5 to play against Walter Hagen in an exhibition match, but finished with an eagle, three birdies and a par to halve the match. Appropriately

Johnny W. Fischer

enough, when he captained the American team in the 1965 Walker Cup match at Baltimore, his team fought back on the final afternoon from an apparently hopeless position to halve the contest. Fischer, who is an attorney in Cincinnati, was for a time on the USGA executive committee.

Fishwick, Diana Lesley (Mrs A. C. Critchley) BRITISH

b. London 1911. British Girls' Open 1927-8; British Ladies' 1930; Curtis Cup 1932, 1934 (non-playing captain 1950); English Ladies' 1932, 1949; French Ladies' Open 1932, runner-up 1946; Florida West Coast 1933; German Ladies' Open 1936, 1938; Belgian Ladies' Open 1938; Dutch International Ladies' 1946

Diana Fishwick established herself as a golfer of the highest class at the age of 19 by winning the British Ladies' Championship at Formby. Her opponent in the final was the famous American Glenna Collett. The occasion might well have daunted a less resolute character, but she is reputed to have said 'What a lark', when told whom she had

to meet in that final, and went out and won it by 4 and 3. In the autumn of 1949 she was nominated as captain of the British Curtis Cup team for 1950 and in order to obtain first-hand knowledge of the players she entered for the English Championship at Burnham and Berrow, and without any prior preparation regained the English

Diana Fishwick, captain of the British Curtis Cup team in 1950

title she had previously won in 1932.

Her admirable temperament and skill with her putter have always made her a difficult opponent to beat. She reduced putting to simplicity by knocking the ball at, and very frequently into, the hole without any fussing over the line, or preliminary practice swings. She married Brigadier-General Critchley. Their son Bruce won Walker Cup honours in 1969.

Flagstick

Marker used to show the position of holes on a golf course. The flagstick fits into the metal cylinder that secures the sides of the hole. Flags should be of different colours for the first and second nine holes.

Flat

A flat swing is one in which the club moves through a plane nearer the horizontal than the vertical. *See also* Upright.

Fleck, Jack AMERICAN

b. Bettendorf, Iowa, 1921. US Open 1955

All else in Jack Fleck's career was surpassed by his victory in the 1955 US Open, one of the most surprising in the history of the championship. Although he had turned professional in 1939, Fleck was little known nationally when he came in late on a Saturday afternoon in June 1955 at the Olympic Club at San Francisco with a final round of 67 to tie with Ben Hogan.

He had got down in 2 from an unlikely place at the 18th, holing from 8 ft for a birdie 3 to finish with a total of 287 after playing the stroke of a lifetime from the rough. Few people gave him a chance with a round to play; virtually nobody gave him a chance in a play-off with Hogan, at the time the greatest player in America. However, the next day Fleck was round in 69. Hogan, one shot behind, took six at the 18th for 72 and Fleck achieved the seemingly impossible.

Fleck had a lean period for the next three or four years but in 1959 he had seven finishes in the top 10 – his first year playing the tour full time. He won the Phoenix Open in 1960 and made a great attempt to win the US Open at Cherry Hills the same year, eventually finishing equal 3rd.

Fleckman, Marty AMERICAN

b. Port Arthur, Tex., 1944
Walker Cup 1967; Cajun Classic 1967

Fleckman turned professional in 1967 after winning a place in the American Walker Cup team at Sandwich earlier that year. He reached the semi-final of the British Amateur Championship at Formby, losing to Cerrudo at the 19th hole. Though his

golfers in America ever since. He is a strong, long-hitting player and the key to his game is confidence.

In 1965 Floyd won the St Paul Open. His best year so far came in 1969 when he won the Jacksonville Open; the American Golf Classic at Firestone, where he became the first person to shoot four consecutive below-par rounds over the course and had a record total of 268; and the USPGA Championship over the National Cash Register course at Dayton, Ohio, achieving an 8-under-par 276. These victories gained him a place in the Ryder Cup team that year.

Fluff

A stroke that hardly moves the ball at all. Common with short wedge shots.

Follow Through

The part of the swing after the ball has been hit; the follow through cannot alter the way the ball has been hit but it reflects the way the club has been swung.

Ford, Doug AMERICAN
b. New Haven, Conn., 1922. Ryder Cup 1955, 1957, 1959, 1961; USPGA 1955; US Masters 1957, joint runner-up 1958

A thoroughly professional pro who was never out of the top 20, and usually in the first 10 of the money winners list during his first 12 years on tour. He was also one of the fastest of players who made up his mind quickly and played the shot without fuss.

amateur career was relatively undistinguished, he surprised everyone by leading the 1967 US Open at Baltusrol after three rounds. A last round of 80 left him in a tie for 18th.

Fleisher, Bruce AMERICAN
b. Union City, Tenn., 1948. US Amateur 1968; Eisenhower Trophy 1968; Walker Cup 1969

At 19 one of the youngest-ever winners of the US National Amateur. His victory qualified him for the Walker Cup and Eisenhower Trophy teams. In 1968 he also finished low amateur in the US Masters, opening with a 69 – 4 strokes lower than Arnold Palmer with whom he was paired. Fleisher turned professional in 1970 and won his player's card in 1971.

Flight

The line the ball takes through the air. It is governed by the loft of the club and also the control of the player who, if he is good enough, can make it fly high or low, or hit it with draw or fade.

Floyd, Raymond AMERICAN
b. Fort Bragg, N. Car., 1942. Ryder Cup 1969; USPGA 1969

Ray Floyd joined the American tour in 1963, played in 10 events without making the 36-hole cut, but won the 11th, the St Petersburg Open; he was voted 'Rookie of the Year' and has been one of the leading

His putting was seen at its best in the final of the USPGA championship when he defeated Cary Middlecoff by 4 and 3. In the 1957 Masters his final 66 was the lowest last-round score ever made until Bert Yancey's 65 in 1968; after three rounds he was 3 strokes behind Sam Snead but overtook him and won the tournament by 3 strokes. The fol-

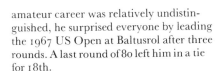

Flat swing: one of the flattest – John Schlee. *top*, during the 1973 British Open

Above, Jack Fleck

Top, Marty Fleckman

Centre, Bruce Fleisher

Above, Ray Floyd

Follow Through: a good example from Johnny Miller

lowing year he was 2nd to Arnold Palmer. He was an outstanding amateur in the New York district before turning professional in 1949. Ford attributed his skill on the greens to the many hours he had spent in billiard saloons.

Fore!

The golfer's traditional warning call when other players or bystanders are in peril of being struck by a ball. It also warns, or requests, others to get out of the line of play, or, less politely, encourages those in front to hurry. The usage probably derives from 'Beware before!', a military command, mentioned by John Knox in the 16th century, warning troops to drop to the ground so that the guns might fire over them.

Forecaddie

Formerly an extra caddie employed by a player to go forward to show him the position of the ball, or to indicate when blind shots could safely be played. Forecaddies have been banned since the 1950s: some of their actions were open to suspicion, and the minority of players who could afford them were thought to have an unfair advantage. It is now left to organizing committees to appoint 'spotters' to act on behalf of all competitors, if deemed necessary.

Formby GC ENGLAND

Formby, Lancashire. 18 holes; 6,875 yd (6,286 m); par 73

Doug Ford

A links course in sandhills and pinewoods 14 miles north of Liverpool and five miles south of Southport. Formby is a championship course of character distinguished by the quality of its turf and the variety and seclusion of its holes. Formed in 1884, it then covered nine holes; in 1901 the present imposing clubhouse was opened by Lord Derby, whose family has since shown a continuing interest in the club. The flatness of the opening holes beside the railway contrasts with the rest of the course among sandhills to which the outstanding 5th hole forms an introduction. The remoteness of the distant holes beside a bird sanctuary in unspoiled woodland makes it difficult to believe that industrial Lancashire is not far away. The short 9th and long 10th with their elevated tees are close to Formby Point with views on a clear day south to the Welsh mountains and north to the Lake District. The 12th with its undulating fairway and well-guarded green is a hole of special quality; the 18th green is one of the longest in the country, comparable to the first at Royal County Down. In still dry weather several holes are within reach of a wedge second shot but as on all links its character changes completely when the wind blows and it becomes a severe challenge. Several championships there attest to its value: the English in 1934, 1949, 1959, when Guy Wolstenholme won a classic encounter with Michael Bonallack on the 36th green, and 1973; the English Ladies' in 1958; and the

Formby GC – venue of the British Amateur Golf Championship in 1967

British Amateur Championship for the first time in 1957, and again 10 years later when Bob Dickson won an all-American final at exceptional speed. The Home Internationals have also been played there, and each year a scratch Open medal tournament, the Formby Hare, is held; several distinguished names appear on this trophy. Jack Barlow has been a loyal and respected servant and steward of the club for more than 60 years.

Alongside the men's club is Formby Ladies' Club, proudly independent and separate since its formation in 1896. The 18-hole course, measuring 5,300 yd (4,846 m), runs within the senior course and has many of the same beguiling characteristics. The ladies' club has continued to administer its own affairs and resists any suggestion that it should be absorbed by the men's club.

Formosa see TAIWAN

Forsell, Liv (MRS L. WOLLIN) SWEDISH

b. 1945. Scandinavian Ladies' Open Amateur 1963-5, 1967, 1970-1; Swedish Ladies' Close Amateur 1963-4, 1966-9; Portuguese Ladies' Open Amateur 1967; semi-finalist British Ladies' 1968; Moroccan Ladies' Open 1972

Liv Forsell has been Sweden's dominant woman golfer since 1963. She has represented her country 28 times between 1962 and 1971. She was voted 'Woman Sports Personality of Sweden' in 1966, and 'Sweden's Golfer of the Year' in 1966 and 1968.

Forward Press

A slight forward movement originating in the right knee that pushes the weight from the inside of the right foot on to the left and breaks the inertia before starting the backswing. Although the hands move forward slightly, they are in fact virtually passive and merely respond to the pressure of the right leg. There are varieties of forward presses but every first-class player has some movement of this nature at the start of his swing.

Foster, Rodney BRITISH

b. Shipley, Yorkshire, 1941. Semi-finalist British Amateur 1962, 1965; Berkshire Trophy 1964; runner-up English Amateur 1964; Eisenhower Trophy 1964; Walker Cup 1965, 1967, 1969, 1971, 1973; Lytham Trophy 1967-8

One of the finest of all Yorkshire-born amateur golfers. Foster was a leading figure in English amateur golf during the 1960s. He first caught the notice of the selectors by reaching the semi-final of the Amateur Championship at Hoylake in 1962 when only 20, and was a member of the four-man team that won the Eisenhower Trophy in Rome two years later. He represented England and Britain many times after this, but his particular strength lay in medal play, in which he had as consistent a record as any of his contemporaries except Bonallack. His most notable achievement was in winning the English Open Amateur Strokeplay Championship for the Brabazon Trophy at Little Aston in 1970.

Foulis, James AMERICAN

b. Scotland 1868. US Open 1896, tied 3rd 1897

In the 1890s James Foulis emigrated to the United States with his brother, Dave, and became professional at Chicago GC.

He won the second US Open at Shinnecock Hills in 1896 with a score of 78, 74 (152): the 74 stood as a record for seven years, although it should be noted that it was achieved over a course measuring only 4,423 yd (4,044 m). The next year, when the Open was held at the Chicago GC course, Foulis tied for 3rd, 6 strokes behind Joe Lloyd.

Fourball

A match in which four players take part, usually two against two, the better ball or aggregate of each pair deciding the winning of each hole or the total points. It has outstripped the foursome in popularity, giving the weekend player the chance of hitting his own ball. But it increases the time needed to play a round and is not considered good practice for players wishing to stand on their own feet competitively.

Foursomes

Matches in which two play against two, each pair hitting alternate shots with the same ball, driving at alternate holes irrespective of who played the last stroke on the previous hole. Foursomes medal and Stableford competitions are also played on the principle of alternate shots, although in these each pair plays against all other pairs.

Foursomes are a traditional form of golf still popular where British influence is strong, but much less so elsewhere. In America, where they are known as 'Scotch foursomes',

they now occur mainly as one part of international matches such as the Ryder, Walker and Curtis Cups. Representative matches elsewhere also usually include foursomes and singles.

Fowler, W. Herbert BRITISH

b. London 1856

A fine golfer who won several medals at St Andrews and Muirfield, and played for England on a number of occasions, Fowler is principally remembered as a golf-course architect. A contemporary of Colt, Simpson and Abercromby, he did much fine work, his most notable creations being Walton Heath, Saunton and the Berkshire.

Fownes, William Clark, Jr AMERICAN

b. 1878; d. 1950. Runner-up North and South Amateur 1910, 1917, 1929; US Amateur 1910, semi-finalist 1905, 1907, 1914, 1919; Walker Cup 1922, 1924

A prominent figure in American golf for 50 years as a championship player, an administrator and a man dedicated to keeping the formidable Oakmont course one step ahead of the golfers who played on it. Fownes won the US Amateur in 1910 and was in the semi-finals four times in 16 years. He was captain of the first American Walker Cup team in 1922 and was in the team again in 1924. Apart from the national championship, most of Fownes's tournament activity was in Pennsylvania (where he won over 15 titles from 1904 to 1921), although

he also played regularly in the North and South Amateur and was runner-up four times, the last in 1929 when he had turned 50. After completing a two-year term as president of the US Golf Association in 1927, Fownes was chiefly known to American golfers as the man who made Oakmont so awesome. In 1903, the architecture of the

Liv Forsell

Rodney Foster

Foursomes: Arthur Lees and Ted Dexter studying a putt on the 13th green of the Old course at Sunningdale

course had been entrusted to his father, Henry C. Fownes, but after a few years William stepped in and took charge. Even though Oakmont was a good course, Fownes was not satisfied; he trapped the greens, shaved the grass short and furrowed the bunkers. As scores got lower generally, he made the course even tougher so that it was not until Sam Parks's 299 in 1935 that 300 was broken there. It was said at the time that trying to stop a putt at Oakmont was like putting down a flight of stairs and attempting to stop the ball on the third step.

Frame, David William BRITISH
b. Woking, Surrey, 1924. Walker Cup 1961; semi-finalist English Amateur 1963

Frame won the Worplesdon Foursomes, with the Vicomtesse de Saint-Sauveur (Lally Segard), and the Hampshire Hog in 1971.

France
In spite of isolated attempts to popularize the game, golf has remained an exclusive and expensive sport confined for the most part to the Paris region and resorts along

the Channel coast. To the present day it has a small but exclusive following and such development as there has been was largely concerned with the growth of the tourist industry. Starting about 1970 a French international player, Gaetan Mourgue d'Algue, has made repeated efforts to popularise the game by organizing competitions with world-class golfers taking part. Two examples have been the Trophée Lancôme and the Marlboro Nations Cup. A certain amount of success has been achieved by getting time on television. It is perhaps too early to judge the results, but by comparison with Spain, for example, the number of promising young professionals remains very small.

Yet France has an honoured history in the game. The Pau club, founded in 1854, was one of the first outside Britain and the French Open Championship deserves to rank among the distinguished championships of the world for its seniority – it started in 1906 two years after the first French Amateur Championship – and for the famous names that have adorned it. The Triumvirate of Vardon, Braid and Taylor competed in it in various years, the first two winning the title; Hagen and Nelson, in the evening of his career, were also winners; Cotton, Locke and Thomson added their names. The growth of international golf, and in particular of the prize money attaching to it, has tended to cause the champion-

ship to be overshadowed by other more recent events, and in spite of its proximity to the British Open, few Americans have stayed long enough to take part. But among British and other overseas golfers it has maintained its popularity, especially since it is now played earlier in the season.

The venue for the Open has been mostly in the Paris region where for years the most polished inland courses were to be found. Occasional visits to the Channel coast were made, but damage done in World War I to such courses as Dieppe and Fourqueux caused them to be ruled out for the championship. The last Channel coast resort to be visited was Deauville in 1956. Le Touquet has two of the best courses in the north, but the club has not been affiliated to the Fédération Française de Golf and so the championship has stayed away. In recent years, in order to fulfil its commitments to the British PGA, which in return offers its cooperation in the event, it undertook to find a minimum of £10,000 prize money, and the championship has been taken to a strong golfing area, the Côte Basque. There are several delightful courses in that area – such as La Nivelle, Hosségor, and the newly rejuvenated Chiberta – but only Chantaco has any pretensions to championship quality. Nevertheless, the championship in returning there has recognized the debt it owes to that region, for from it have sprung nearly all the Frenchmen players of note. Starting with Arnaud Massy, through Marcel Dallemagne, to the modern generation of Jean Garaialde and Bernard Pascassio, all have come from that crowded and pleasant country north of the Spanish frontier, several of them even from the same village of Ciboure. Nor must one forget the remarkable contribution of the French ladies, Catherine Lacoste, Brigitte Varangot, Claudine Cros (Rubin), the Vicomtesse de Saint Sauveur and Mme Lacoste who, in terms of championship achievement, have far surpassed the men. Another area of delightful courses, but lacking championship qualities, is the Riviera.

Frankfurt GC WEST GERMANY
Frankfurt am Main. 18 holes; 6,445 yd (5,893 m)

The Frankfurter Golfklub, situated on the city boundary within easy reach of the centre, is one of Germany's finest courses. It has been the venue of numerous national and international championships. Although the course is of average length, it provides as stern a test as could be asked for. It is generally flat with fairways carved out of attractive forest land. Good-sized greens,

William C. Fownes, Jr

Top, David W. Frame

Above, France, represented here by Mme J. Garaialde hitting her tee shot at the 16th during the European Team Championship in 1971, watched by Miss M. Petersen

many of them well guarded by bunkers, demand accurate placing of the shots if the player is to score well. A background of trees around most of them makes judgment of distance comparatively easy, but the individual character of the holes ensures that a player has to use every shot in the bag. There are four par-3 holes, four par 5s and 11 par 4s, the last-named averaging 430 yd (393 m) each. Except for some modernization in 1968 the course has been altered little since it was first laid down in 1928 by Harry Colt. The three opening holes; which might look easy at first glance, have proved the downfall of many golfers who failed to be on the alert from the start. An international atmosphere prevails in the clubhouse, due in part to the importance of Frankfurt as a trade centre.

Fraser, Mrs W. G. SEE STIRLING, ALEXA

Frearson, Mrs Diane (née Robb) BRITISH b. 1943. British Girls' 1961; runner-up British Ladies' 1961; Curtis Cup 1962, 1972

A fine stylist who showed early promise by reaching the final of the 1961 Ladies' Championship at the age of 18. In the Curtis Cup match in 1962 she was the only Briton to win her single. Shortly after this she married and retired from national competition, but after the death of her husband she returned to the game, playing well enough in the championship in 1968 to take Ann Irvin's place on the World Cup team after the latter had been obliged to withdraw. In the year or two before the Curtis Cup match of 1972 she worked up her game, and after winning one tournament and playing through the Home Internationals of 1971 undefeated she was picked – 10 years

Top, France, Chantaco course, near St Jean-de-Luz, with the Basque Pyrenees in the background. *Above,* the course at the northern coastal resort of Hardelot

after her first appearance in the match. She remarried in 1973.

Freeze
A condition in which players seem to seize up over a shot, usually a putt. A 'freeze', nervous in origin, may afflict a player half-way through a swing, preventing him from completing his stroke.

Furgol, Ed J. AMERICAN
b. New York Mills, N.Y., 1919. Semi-finalist Amateur Public Links 1940; North and South Amateur 1945; US Open 1954; Ryder Cup 1957

One of the most remarkable players in the history of the game, certainly in the history of the US Open. He remained in the front rank of professionals for nearly 20 years until taking a club job in 1962. Injured in a childhood playground accident, his left arm was badly set and permanently impaired. It became too short, the muscles atrophied, and it bent rigid at an angle of 70 degrees. It became virtually useless except to help guide the club, but the fact that it was rigid may have helped him to groove his swing, ungainly though it was. Furgol compensated for his left arm by bending over at the address and employing a rather lunging swing. The backswing was of necessity short but his position at the top was compact and sound, and his power came from a powerful uncoiling of his body. Nothing but intense determination could have overcome such a handicap. His record in public links tournaments was good and by 1945, when he won the North and South, he was one of the country's leading amateurs. At that point he turned professional: after some years all the hard work paid off and he won the 1954 Open at Baltusrol. There his towering drives gave him enough length and when he came to the final hole he was leading.

There after a 20-minute wait for the couples ahead he hit a smothered hook, but played out onto an adjoining fairway and made his par. The same year he won two tournaments at Phoenix and Havana. Another highly successful year was 1956; he played in only 21 events, but won two of them and lost another only on a play-off; he

also finished 4th in the Open and reached the semi-finals of the USPGA championship. His fifth and most recent tournament victory came in 1957 after which he appeared infrequently on the tour, taking a full-time club position in 1962. But the following year this remarkable golfer turned up in the US Masters and lay only one stroke behind Nicklaus entering the final round.

Furgol, Marty AMERICAN
b. New York Mills, N.Y., 1918. Western Open 1951; Houston Open 1951; Ryder Cup 1955; runner-up Canadian Open 1956; El Paso Open 1959; San Diego Open 1959

A familiar figure on the American circuit from the late 1940s into the 1960s. Furgol turned professional in 1941, but had to spend five years as an artillery sergeant before he could get down to the serious business of tournament golf. He established himself as a player of ability when he won the Western and Houston Opens in 1951. He was 3rd leading money winner in 1954 and was chosen for the 1955 Ryder Cup team. Marty Furgol is no relation to Ed Furgol, but they were born in the same town and once caddied at the same course.

Mrs Diane Frearson playing from the rough during the LGU Team Golf in 1961

Top, Ed J. Furgol chipping

Above, Marty Furgol

Gallacher, Bernard BRITISH

b. Bathgate, West Lothian, 1949. Scottish Open Amateur Strokeplay 1967; Ryder Cup 1969, 1971, 1973; Schweppes Championship 1969; Wills Open 1969; Dunlop Masters 1974

Bernard Gallacher had a brief but distinguished career as an amateur, playing for Scotland at both junior and senior level and winning the first Scottish Open Amateur Strokeplay Championship at Muirfield in 1967. Later that same year he turned professional and made a slow start in 1968, but his progress and success throughout 1969 were remarkable. He won the Schweppes Championship, the Wills, finished 2nd three times and earned a place in the Alcan Golfer of the Year event in Portland, Ore. In addition he played in the Ryder Cup scoring a notable victory over Lee Trevino and winning a point with Bembridge in the foursomes.

He inevitably suffered some reaction in 1970 but re-established himself well in 1971, retained his place in the Ryder Cup team, winning $3\frac{1}{2}$ points out of 5 in St Louis, a tribute to the strong competitive will that drives a slender frame. In 1973 he and Brian Barnes gave Britain a good start by twice winning the top foursome, but an illness on the second day was an unfortunate setback to British hopes.

Gallardo, Angel SPANISH

b. Sitges, 1943, Portuguese Open 1967; Spanish Open 1970; Mexican Open 1971; Calle Open (Colombia) 1972

Angel Gallardo, the eldest of six brothers, three of whom are golf professionals, has been the pioneer of world travel among Spanish players. The Miguels and Ramón Sota were well known in Europe, but Gallardo has played throughout the world and enjoyed a good deal of success. Like nearly all Spanish professionals, he began golfing life as a caddie and came up the hard way. He has always remained independent of people prepared to sponsor him. After turning professional at 17, he won several local tournaments around Barcelona but it was not until he won £900 in a tournament

in Biarritz when he was 20 that his potential became apparent.

By widening his tournament horizons, he quickly became a challenger to the Miguels' and Sota's crown. Of a cheerful spirit, he has proved a popular figure wherever he has played. Besides Europe he has played in Australia, America, the Far East and the

Caribbean, and has represented Spain in the World (formerly Canada) Cup from 1969 to 1972. He has won the Spanish Open only once in 1970, at Nueva Andalucía, but he played a prominent part in the formation of the Spanish PGA and was its first captain in 1972.

Gamesmanship

The art, as defined by Stephen Potter, of winning 'without actually cheating'. It takes many forms in golf, where there is so much scope for its practice, but championship golf is mercifully free of it. It is an art of subtle ploys and inferences, a form of psychological warfare.

Gancedo, José F. SPANISH

b. Málaga, 1938. Spanish Close Amateur 1966-9, runner-up 1959, 1965, 1970; Eisenhower Trophy 1966, 1968, 1970, 1972; Worplesdon Mixed Foursomes (with Catherine Lacoste) 1967; Continent of Europe v Great Britain and Ireland 1968, 1970, 1972; Spanish Open Amateur 1968-9, runner-up 1963, 1971

A dashing, long-hitting player who is perhaps the best amateur that Spain has produced. He took up the game in 1954 in Málaga where he had lessons from Julio Casana. He made several visits to Britain, showing up well in a number of strokeplay events and gradually earning the reputation of one of the best of Continental players. In 1971, he took seriously to golf-course archi-

Bernard Gallacher

Top, Angel Gallardo holes a birdie putt

Gamesmanship: *Above,* Eric Sykes demonstrates, at the expense of Pat Tallack, the gentle art of coughing during the backswing

José Gancedo during the English Strokeplay Championship at Hillside in 1971

tecture and was responsible for two new courses on the Costa del Sol at Torrequebrada and Costalita.

Ganton GC ENGLAND

Ganton, Yorkshire. 18 holes; 6,823 yd (6,239 m); par 72

Although Ganton is not on the Open Championship roster it holds a special place in the history of British golf because of its early association with Harry Vardon, and its quality as an inland links course on which nearly every major event apart from the Open has been held. Situated about nine miles inland from Scarborough, the course has many seaside features, notably the deep sandy bunkers. It lies at the foot of the Yorkshire Wolds, a setting of distinctive charm, and the quality of golf is enhanced by the excellence of the dry, springy turf. For a time it was decided to try to recapture the aspect of the old links by reducing watering to a minimum on the course, but the experiment was not a success, and the fairways and greens have for years been of the highest inland quality.

The course was founded in 1891, five years before Harry Vardon took up his post there. While at Ganton he was to win three Open Championships and bring back from the United States the coveted US Open trophy in 1900. It was also the scene of a famous contest between Harry Vardon and Willie Park, the first 36 holes of which had been played at North Berwick leaving Vardon with a small lead. Vardon was irresistible on his home course and gave a wonderful exhibition of driving in defeating Park over the 72 holes. Vardon was followed by another professional who was to win the US Open, Ted Ray, and the succession of famous designers who have had a hand in shaping the course makes impressive reading: Vardon, Colt, Fowler, Hutchison, Hilton, Braid, and C. K. Cotton. The last-named was brought in to prepare the course for the 1949 Ryder Cup. Other international events that have found their way there are the European Women's Team Championship, the British Ladies' Championship in 1954 and 1966, the Brabazon Trophy in 1952 and 1960, the British Amateur Championship in 1964, and the English Championship in 1947, 1955, and 1968. It is also the only inland course ever to house the British Amateur Championship, the final in 1964 between Gordon Clark and Michael Lunt producing the longest match on record.

In an area of England where championship courses are scarce, it is probable that the course would have been in even greater

demand for the big events but for the fact that it can play on the short side, and that hotel accommodation on the spot is scarce, although there is no lack of that in Scarborough.

It is sometimes said that it would just be possible to start with five 3s as Dutch Harrison did when the Americans came out for the singles breathing fire and brimstone in 1949 after losing the foursomes in the Ryder Cup match, but thereafter the course toughens up. The 7th, a long dogleg with a beautifully placed nest of bunkers at the angle, is as good a hole as could be found anywhere. The 12th has changed its character at least three times over the years but has now settled down into a respectable par 4 of sharp dogleg quality. Most fascinating is the finish; the last four holes have swung many a match, and after a series of well-placed but artificial bunkers, the road is crossed to the 17th where a giant, sprawling dune bunker serves its purpose for the last two holes. The most recent champion to pay tribute to the greens was Michael Bonallack who in the first 18 holes of the final against David Kelley in the 1968 English Amateur, went round in 61 and stood 10 up at lunch. He said he saw the line of every putt he had to make and knew that if he struck it properly it would run true into the hole.

Garden City GC USA

Garden City, N.Y.

Garden City was the golfing seat of Walter Travis, who also designed the course. Travis set out to conquer the golf world in the early years of the century and in 1904 became the first overseas player to carry off the British Amateur. The controversy over the Schenectady putter with which he won the British title has long since ceased to reverberate, but his combative personality is still remembered. Travis was an excellent architect, and the course at Garden City, which calls for a high quality of control on all shots, is still one of the very best in the New York area. Five national championships and one Walker Cup match have been played there, but it has not had a big event since 1936, when Johnny Fischer won the US Amateur in a dramatic extra-hole final with Jack M'Lean of Scotland. Because of Garden City's long absence from the tournament list, it has largely been forgotten how splendid a test of golf it is. It is an inland course on flat ground near the middle of Long Island, about halfway between Long Island Sound and the Atlantic Ocean. It is, nevertheless, a course with a strong seaside feeling, and it is full of subtleties.

Gardner, Robert Abbe AMERICAN

b. Hinsdale, Ill., 1890; d. 1956; US Amateur 1909, 1915, runner-up 1916, 1921, semi-finalist 1923; Chicago Open 1914; Chicago District Amateur 1916, 1924-5; runner-up British Amateur 1920; Walker Cup 1922 (captain 1923-4, 1926)

Ganton GC – a view from the 12th tee

A fine all-round athlete who was a major figure in amateur golf for almost two decades. He burst into prominence in 1909 by winning the US Amateur while a freshman at Yale. He beat Chandler Egan in the final. Seven of the eight quarter-finalists were from Chicago.

University, other sports, and finally

business, kept him from playing enough golf for the next few years and it was not until 1914 that he began to recover his game. In 1915 he again won the Amateur but only after a series of narrow escapes. He defeated John G. Anderson in the final. Gardner sailed to the final in 1916, only to be put out by Chick Evans, who was winning at last after being heir apparent for several years.

After World War I, in which he served as a lieutenant of field artillery, Gardner continued to play championship golf. In the British Amateur final of 1920 he birdied the 36th hole to square with Cyril Tolley, but lost to a birdie on the 37th. In 1921 he reached the US Amateur final for the fourth

time and was beaten by Jesse Guilford in a duel of long hitters. His last serious challenge was in 1923 when he lost in the semi-finals to Jess Sweetser, the defending champion.

Gardner hit all shots with an ease and lack of effort that was the envy of his contemporaries, and when he reached the 1916 US Amateur at Merion he silenced critics who said he could not play well on a tight course.

Gardner, Robert W. AMERICAN
b. 1921. California State Amateur 1947, 1950; Metropolitan (New York) 1958, 1960-2; runner-up US Amateur 1960; Eisenhower Trophy 1960; Walker Cup 1961, 1963

He lost to Deane Beman in the final of the 1960 US Amateur and was a member of the American team that won at Merion the same year by the biggest margin in the history of the Eisenhower Trophy. In his two Walker Cup appearances, Gardner was unbeaten. Gardner dominated golf in the New York area by winning the Metropolitan Amateur six of the seven years from 1958 to 1964.

Garstedt GC WEST GERMANY
nr Bremen. 18 holes; 7,250 yd (6,629 m); par 74

One of the most difficult lay-outs on the entire Continent, and certainly in Germany. Its length, combined with narrowing fairways at strategic points, makes for an outstanding challenge. Undulating fairways, interrupted by patches of heather – a natural feature of this area – demand well-placed shots if a good score is to be achieved. The wayward shot meets with immediate disaster, either in high, dense rough or bushes bordering the forest. Considering the size of the course, the greens are comparatively small. One consolation is that there are only 18 bunkers in all, and the outward holes allow for some free hitting. But there is no room for a mistake coming in. On the whole the course is rather flat. Forward tees compensate the average golfer for the rigours of the course. Until a few years ago the members of the Zur Vahr GC had to be content with a 9-hole course at Bremen, but the rapid growth of the port finally obliged them to look further afield. The village of Garstedt lies on the road to Bremerhaven.

Garvey, Philomena IRISH
b. Drogheda, Co. Louth, 1927. Irish Ladies' 1946-8, 1950-1, 1953-5, 1957-60, 1962-3, 1970; Curtis Cup 1948, 1950, 1952, 1954, 1956, 1960; British Ladies' 1957, runner-up 1946, 1953, 1960, 1963

Philomena Garvey was runner-up to Jean

Hetherington (Mrs Holmes) in the final of the 1946 British Ladies' Championship at Hunstanton. This was the first major tournament after World War II, and the 36-hole final was decided on the last green. That year she also began her domination of Irish golf by taking the Irish title which she was to win 5 times. Finalist again in the

British, at Royal Porthcawl in 1953, she lost to brilliant golf by the Canadian Marlene Stewart. Reaching that stage of the British Championship for the third time she prevailed at Gleneagles in 1957, when her opponent was Mrs Valentine (Jessie Anderson). Her fourth British final was at Royal St David's, Harlech, in 1960 when she was defeated by the American Champion Barbara McIntire, and her fifth at Royal County Down in 1963, when she lost to Brigitte Varangot of France.

Her work as a saleswoman in a Dublin store left her limited opportunities for golf, but did not prevent her from being the best woman player in the country, and despite lack of practice she was able to amass 14 championships out of a possible 18 in the years 1946-63 Philomena Garvey relaxed her hold of the championship by turning professional, but was reinstated as an amateur in 1968, and won the Irish title again in 1970. A fine, powerful striker of the ball with woods and irons, she is one of the few class women golfers who have used the interlocking grip.

Gassiat, Jean FRENCH
b. Biarritz, Basses-Pyrénées, 1883. French Open 1912; French Professional 1912, 1919, 1927, 1929

With Arnaud Massy, Gassiat was a pioneer of Continental golf. A regular competitor in Britain, his best performance in the Open Championship was tied 7th in

Top, Robert Abbe Gardner

Above, Robert W. Gardner

Philomena Garvey in the 1968 British Ladies'

1912. He continued to be a force on the circuit for many years but he is specially remembered for the curiously shaped putter of his own design. It consisted of a large block of wood with a shallow face, but a very wide, large head, and was once described by an eminent player as 'the grand piano'.

Gavea GCC BRAZIL

Rio de Janeiro. 18 holes; 6,032 yd (5,516 m)

Gavea GCC, the second oldest golf club in Brazil, is most beautiful and picturesque, situated in a valley between mountains and the sea. It was founded in 1923 when a group of Scots and Englishmen, aided by a few Americans, and Brazilians who had been educated abroad, bought the present piece of land. They appointed Arthur Davidson, a young assistant professional from Peterhead

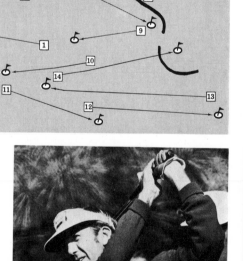

in Scotland, to lay out the course which was officially opened for play in 1926. Davidson then stayed on for some 20 years as professional.

More than ten Brazilian Opens have been staged at Gavea, which has seen a number of great players from all parts of the world. The course itself, bisected by a busy highway, requires great accuracy and knowledge, combining a number of hilly holes, with several along the beach reminiscent of a Scottish links. It is the home course of Mario Gonzales.

Geiberger, Allen L. AMERICAN

b. Red Bluff, Cal., 1937. National Junior Jaycee 1954; Caracas Open 1962; Ontario

Open 1962; American Golf Classic 1965; USPGA 1966; runner-up Carling World Tournament 1967

Al Geiberger joined the professional ranks in 1959 after a dazzling record in junior and amateur golf. The year he won the junior title in 1954, he travelled to Europe with the short-lived junior Walker Cup team, played in Britain and won the French junior championship. As a member of the powerful University of Southern California team he won 34 out of 36 collegiate matches and helped his side to an unbeaten streak of 51 victories. At that time he used to carry a card bearing the word 'attack' given him by his coach, because he was considered a conservative player. This has been the key-note of his game, which relies principally on consistently accurate driving and putting. In the year that he turned professional he

had won 10 consecutive amateur titles in the Californian region and tied 5th in a strong field for the Los Angeles Open. In 1967, although he won no major event, his earnings were higher than the year before when he won the USPGA. But in 1967, reducing his number of tournaments to 24, he completed every one and drew money in all of them except one, finishing nine times in the top 10.

Geneva GC SWITZERLAND

nr Geneva. 18 holes; 6,900 yd (6,309 m); par 72

Opened in 1973, the Golf Club de Genève course is situated about three miles south-west of the town and is open from March to December. Designed by the American architect, Robert Trent Jones, high on the residential slopes of Cologny, it commands an exceptional view over the lake and the town of Geneva. To the south, beyond a belt of venerable oaks, the foothills of the Mont Blanc massif can be seen. The course itself exemplifies the best and most modern ideas of a distinguished architect. Gentle slopes, water hazards and majestic trees have all been put to use with consummate skill. Bunkers and greens have been planned down to the minutest detail – nothing has been left to chance.

A new clubhouse has grown up beside an 18th-century farmhouse now used for maintenance equipment. The 9th and 18th greens, below the clubhouse, form one surface.

Germain, Dorothy (Mrs Mark Porter)
AMERICAN

US Women's Amateur 1949, semi-finalist 1959; Curtis Cup 1950 (non-playing captain 1966)

Dorothy Germain defeated Dorothy Kielty by 3 and 1 in the final to win the 1949 American Women's Amateur National

Top, the course plan of Gavea GCC   *Above*, Al Geiberger in the US Masters, 1970   Dorothy Germain and her daughter

Championship at Merion's East Course. That year the field had been limited to 128 for the matchplay stages by 16 sectional qualifying competitions. In the 1950 Curtis Cup match, at Buffalo, she halved her single with Frances Stephens (Mrs F. Smith). Previously she had combined with Beverly Hanson to defeat Jean Donald and Mrs G. Valentine (Jessie Anderson).

Germany

Several elements contributed to the foundation of German golf. In 1891 those members of London Society who frequented the German spas were in the habit of taking their golf clubs with them, which filled the natives with astonishment, especially when the visitors began digging up nearby parks. The first display of golf was at the spa of Bad Homburg, where 9 holes were laid out by a General Duff of the Brigade of Guards. Other resorts followed suit, and at Baden-Baden an Anglican minister, the Rev. T. White, was responsible for starting a course. It was not until 1895 that the first two German courses were opened. In this connection American dentists, businessmen trading abroad, diplomats and members of the Royal Prussian Navy were all instrumental in forming German golf. The German Freudenberg family brought the game back from Ceylon (Sri Lanka) and started the Bremen club on the city's racecourse. Foreign diplomats in particular were responsible for the formation of the Berlin Club. In 1899 the third oldest German course, Bad Homburg, came into existence; at first its 18 holes covered only 1,300 yd (1,188 m). Within ten years it had some 2,500 members.

At the beginning of this century Reinbek, Kiel, Leipzig-Gaschwitz, and Hamburg appeared. There was at that time no uniformity of rules; at Bad Homburg the starting list was determined by the players' social standing; at Baden-Baden the lowest handicaps had preference; and in some northern clubs older members preceded the younger. It was not until 1907 that uniformity was achieved by the foundation of the German Golf Union with seven clubs represented. That number soon increased to 19, but the first chairman, Johan Wentzel, encountered difficulties. At some courses he found that a rock had to be struck instead of holing out, or that greens were not mown. The first German Open Championship was held in 1912 at Baden-Baden where William Roosevelt, a nephew of Theodore Roosevelt, was president. The prize money was 5,000 Reichsmarks, a vast sum for those days, which attracted such players as Vardon and Herd, and also the winner, J. H. Taylor.

Fourteen courses survived World War I, and by 1928 as many as 30 – among them three championship courses at Bad Salzbrunn, Frankfurt, and Berlin-Wannsee – were in existence. The game continued to develop throughout the 1930s, thanks to the efforts of Karl Henkell in fostering international interest. After World War II, with the courses in East Germany lost and the remainder no longer operating, German golf started once more from scratch. Equipment was almost unobtainable, courses were requisitioned by the forces of occupation and signs such as 'Germans allowed only on Mondays' appeared in many clubhouses. In 1950 the European Golf Association readmitted the German Association to membership. There were 32 member clubs by 1950; 55 by 1962 and by 1970 almost one hundred. Although all these clubs are private and golf is still a privileged sport, a drastic change of attitude in favour of broadening the sport may soon take place. First signs of this appeared in the 1971 Open championship when there was a strong international entry and more than 3,000 spectators.

Gezira Sporting Club EGYPT

Cairo. 9 holes; 5,809 yd (5,312 m); par 69 (for twice round)

Formerly an 18-hole course but reduced to 9 since 1956-7. It is situated on Gezira, an island in the Nile, five minutes by taxi from central Cairo, and lies partly within and partly outside Gezira racecourse. Gezira is the most beautiful of the Egyptian courses, with many large trees and flowers, reminiscent of the best parkland golf. It is the best-maintained club and course in Egypt, although it has fallen below pre-1956 standards.

Ghezzi, Victor AMERICAN

b. Rumson, N.J., 1911. Los Angeles Open 1935; Maryland Open 1935; runner-up Canadian Open 1935, tied 2nd 1948; Hollywood (Fla.) Open 1936; New Jersey Open 1937, 1943-4; North and South Open 1938; USPGA 1941, semi-finalist 1947; tied 2nd US Open 1946; Greensboro Open 1947

Vic Ghezzi first came to national prominence when he won the Los Angeles Open in 1935. In 1936, in his second try at the US Open, he shared the lead after 36 holes only to finish tied for 18th after a dismal final round of 81. A decade later he tied with Lloyd Mangrum and Byron Nelson for 1st place in the 1946 Open at Canterbury; in the play-off over 36 holes on the following day, Ghezzi and Nelson finished one stroke behind Mangrum. In 1947 he finished with

a 69 and tied for 6th place at St Louis. In winning the 1941 USPGA he defeated Mangrum, 1 up, in the semi-finals and beat Nelson at the 38th hole of the final. Ghezzi, an accurate player with a good short game, was selected for the Ryder Cup team in 1939 and 1941, but neither match was held because of World War II.

Giles III, Marvin M. AMERICAN

b. Charlottesville, Va., 1943. Eisenhower Trophy 1968, 1970; Walker Cup 1969, 1971, 1973; US Amateur 1972, runner-up 1967-9

In an age when so many promising young players in America turn professional, Giles has remained an amateur, working as an investment banker in Richmond. His record in the US Amateur is wonderfully consistent and for long he was unfortunate not to have won. Besides being runner-up three years running, he was 6th in 1970. In 1968 he scored a 65 at Scioto, the lowest single round since the Amateur Championship became strokeplay in 1965. He won at last in 1972, a victory that gave a great deal of pleasure.

In the 1968 Eisenhower Trophy event in Melbourne his total of 286 tied with Michael Bonallack for the lowest individual score and he more than once showed up well in the US Masters at Augusta. He was low amateur in 1968 and 2nd low amateur in 1970, a period when he was the best amateur in America without having won the championship. When he chipped in off the road at

Vic Ghezzi

the 17th at St Andrews in his 1971 Walker Cup single with Michael Bonallack, it seemed as though the whole contest had taken a vital turn, but the British made an even better recovery on the second day and went on to victory.

Gimmie
Term, shortened from 'give me [this]', for a conceded putt. One short enough for a player to be certain that his opponent cannot miss the next.

Givan, Harry AMERICAN
Seattle Amateur 1931; Washington Amateur 1933; Pacific Northwest Amateur 1936-7, 1945-6, runner-up 1950; Walker Cup 1936; Washington Open 1936

One of the best players in the Pacific Northwest for three decades.

Gleneagles Hotel Golf Courses SCOTLAND
Auchterarder, Perthshire. 45 holes (King's Course 18, Queen's Course 18, 'Wee' Course 9)

Any group of well-travelled golfing

Americans asked to name their favourite British courses would undoubtedly put Gleneagles high on their list. It may lack the age-old traditions of St Andrews, Prestwick or Dornoch, and it has accommodated only one modern, major international event – the 1957 British Ladies' – but its appeal is well grounded. It occupies a stretch of wild, heathery moorland in the heart of Perthshire, possesses a hotel of great splendour and boasts two courses that, besides showing British inland golf at its best, epitomize the glories of Scotland.

The courses belong to the British Transport Hotels Ltd and owe their existence to the vision of a Scotsman, Donald A. Matheson, who became general manager of the Caledonian Railway Company. Work started on the hotel in 1913, and James Braid was commissioned to design two courses, an 18-hole course to be known as the King's, and a 9-hole course, the Queen's. All work was stopped by the outbreak of World War I but by 1919 the golf courses were completed and ready for play, although the hotel was not opened until June 1924. Both hotel and golf courses were an immediate success, the golf providing a test on the grandest scale yet conceived in Britain. The holes were long, there was no run on the ground and such mighty hitters of the ball as J. H. Taylor and Sandy Herd were often beaten by the length of it all.

Today the ceaseless tramp of golfers has hardened the beautiful turf, the ball now runs freely and the shots do not seem quite so formidable with modern equipment, but the handiwork of the architects, Braid and his henchman, Major C. K. Hutchison, remains a monument to them. Golf was so popular there that, shortly after the hotel was opened, it was decided to extend the Queen's to 18 and to construct the 9-hole 'Wee' Course.

Gleneagles is a course of hills and valleys, heather and bracken, and superb views of the Ochils and Grampians. The King's used to be regarded as the sterner test, and there are many who still stick to this judgment, but fairly recent alterations to the Queen's by James Alexander, former superintendent of all British Transport Hotel courses, have evened the balance.

The charm of Gleneagles is endless: tackling inviting drives from elevated tees to heather-lined fairways, relaxing on the 'Wee' after tea, or strolling within sound of grouse, geese or woodcock in a blaze of autumn colour. Gleneagles also established a milestone in the history of the BBC with weekly pre-war broadcasts from the ballroom. During World War II it became a hospital. Nowadays, the courses rarely see major tournaments; they are busy with hotel guests, visitors and society bookings.

In 1924 George Duncan beat Abe Mitchell in the final of a professional tournament and later the same summer lost a challenge match over 72 holes to Macdonald Smith. Enid Wilson completed her hat trick of British Ladies' Championship victories there in 1933 and Mrs George Valentine, who was born in nearby Perth, won her title there in 1957. It was her second triumph at Gleneagles. As Jessie Anderson she had in 1936 achieved the status of heroine by holing a putt across the 18th green to win a point and halve the Curtis Cup match against the United States.

Glennie, George BRITISH
d. 1886

In what was a forerunner to the Open Championship in 1860, the Prestwick Club devised an inter-club foursomes competition which was played at St Andrews in 1857. The winners were Royal Blackheath in the

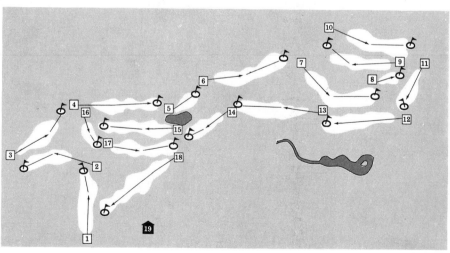

Top, Marvin Giles holes a chip shot during the 1971 Walker Cup at St Andrews

The plan of the King's Course at Gleneagles Hotel

Above, Harry Givan

persons of George Glennie and Lieut. J. C. Stewart, both Scots, who were made life members of Royal Blackheath in recognition of their success. The pair were also well known at St Andrews, Glennie becoming Captain of the Royal and Ancient in 1884, two years after the George Glennie Medal was presented to the R. and A. by the Royal Blackheath Club, for competition among members.

Glennie was a fine player and a deadly putter whose score of 88 in the autumn meeting of the R. and A. in 1855 was unbeaten for almost 30 years. He was also well known as Blackheath's honorary secretary for many years, and was a much-loved figure in the club.

Glen View GC USA

Golf, Ill. 18 holes; 6,574 yd (6,011 m); par 72

Glen View, situated in a village about 20 miles north of Chicago, has such an abundance of trees that when Dutch elm disease practically eliminated the elms in the United States, they were hardly missed here, even though they had made up a large portion of the timberland over which the course was laid out. Tall spreading oaks and maples still line the fairway for most of the course's length.

This is one of the older clubs in the Chicago area, and in 1899 it was the site of the first Western Open and Western Amateur. Jock Hutchison was the club

professional for many years, and he is today an honorary member. Laurie Auchterlonie and Tom McNamara also served as Glen View professionals. Chick Evans has played at Glen View since his own Edgewater passed out of existence. The club's membership has included Warren G. Harding, Fred W. Upham, S. L. Avery, General Charles C. Dawes, and Merrill C. Meigs. Its membership today is just over 300, and it includes many figures prominent in the railroad industry. The village of Golf was so named because many years ago Harry E. Byram, president of the Milwaukee Railroad, was a member of what was then the Glen View Golf and Polo Club. His office was in central Chicago, and when he wanted to play golf he would arrange to have his private car

dropped off at a siding about a quarter of a mile from Glen View. This became known first as the 'golf siding' and later simply as Golf.

Glyfada GC GREECE

Glyfada, nr Athens. 18 holes; 6,715 yd (6,140 m); par 72

Glyfada, on the edge of Athens airport and two miles from Glyfada's marina, was the first 18-hole course in Greece and has thus played a significant part in the development of the game in the country. It was originally planned by the National Tourist Organization of Greece and the first 9 holes were ready for play by the end of 1962. Then in 1967, four years after the second 9 were opened, a club was formed to run its own

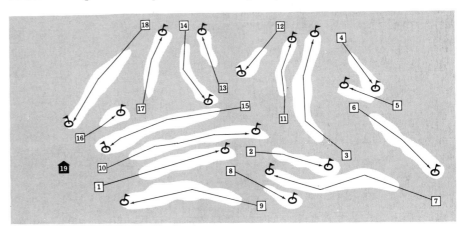

Top, a view of the 13th green on the King's Course at Gleneagles

The course plan of Glyfada GC

affairs as well as house the annual International Amateur and the International Ladies' Amateur championships of Greece which generally attract a good field.

Situated at sea level on terrain that rolls gently between the foothills of Mount Imitos and the Saronic Gulf, the course, designed by the British architect Donald Harradine, was carved out of a forest of small pine trees. The fairways are for the most part narrow. This calls for great control. Many holes have groups of pine or individual trees actually on the fairway.

The club has excellent facilities. Hector Thomson, one of the most famous names in British amateur golf before World War II, is the professional.

Goalby, Robert AMERICAN
b. Belleville, Ill., 1931. Joint runner-up US Open 1961; US Masters 1968

Although three major league baseball teams were interested in him, it was football that Bob Goalby played for the University of Illinois before becoming a car salesman, and later a professional golfer in 1957 at the age of 26. His progress was punctuated with periodic victories on the tour: he was joint 2nd, one stroke behind the winner in the 1961 US Open. He was a member of the PGA tournament committee from 1962 to 1964. In 1963 he played in the Ryder Cup match at Atlanta, where he won both his singles matches and was unbeaten in the foursomes. For the next few years his name was almost forgotten. Then in April 1968 came his victory in the Masters, the tournament in which his previous highest finish was 25th in 1962. It was a victory clouded for him by the scorecard mistake that befell Roberto de Vicenzo. Nobody regretted Vicenzo's misfortune more than Bob Goalby. He was deprived of the chance of proving himself the outright winner in the

Bob Goalby on the 10th tee during the US Masters at Augusta in 1970

play-off that should have followed; this was hard on Goalby who deserves to be remembered for surviving the extreme pressures of the last round and finishing the tournament with a 66, one of the best in Augusta's history. It was a spell of two birdies and an eagle in 3 holes from the 13th which proved decisive. His total was 277 (70, 70, 61, 66). After the Masters, he won a tournament in each of the next three seasons.

Godfrey, Walter John Ihaka
NEW ZEALANDER
b. Auckland, N. Island, 1941. New Zealand Open Amateur 1958; Eisenhower Trophy 1960, 1962; Hong Kong Open 1972; Victoria Open 1972

Godfrey's third name reflects his Maori heritage, his mother being of that race. He was a leading New Zealand amateur until 1963, when he turned professional and played the whole tour in Britain that summer. Thereafter he confined his tournament appearances largely to the Far East, New Zealand and Australia. Though he has won few major tournaments, he has victories in about 40 events to his name. He played in the British Opens of 1970-2, on the exemptions earned by his performances in the Far East, and in the year beginning July 1971 had a most rewarding spell, highlighted by his victories in the Victoria Open, Australia, and the 1972 Hong Kong Open.

Golf, History of
Trying to find the origin of golf is as pointless as trying to discover who invented bread. Moreover, there is a danger that in making such research we might overlook the delights of both of them. There is another danger: if the work is done by an historian he may bore the golfer with his erudite findings; if by a golfer, he may be too ignorant of history to make a proper job of it. A number

of writers in the past twenty years have avoided both pitfalls, notably Sir Guy Campbell, who produced a most scholarly survey in Cassell's *History of Golf in Britain*, and Robert Browning whose *A History of Golf* gives a most readable and informative account; in that work at least scholarship stopped short of pedantry, and love of the game did not lure him into romanticism. There is room for many variations of opinion between the blunt assertion of the *Encyclopaedia Britannica* that golf originated in Scotland and the shrewd evasion of Sir Walter Simpson who said it was probably invented by a shepherd, any shepherd, knocking a pebble with upturned crook, and left the rest to the now somewhat discredited version of a bold pioneer in the subject, Robert Lang. From the other side of the Atlantic W. K. Montague presents a sympathetic and stylish account in *The Golf of Our Fathers*. What follows can be no more than a broad picture based on these works, with the bare bones of the matter given separately as a list of dates.

Encyclopaedia Britannica is on safe ground; if golf had not originated in Scotland, the legend that it did has grown such deep roots that no amount of erudite evidence to the contrary would change things now. Besides, the Scots got golf on to the Parliamentary statute books at an early date, and no historian can ignore that. It is a matter of great delight among golfers that the practice of the game in those early years was constantly upsetting Government and Church. In the second half of the 15th century three edicts called for the cessation of golf in favour of the practice of archery. The threat from south of the border was real at that time, but, from the tone the authorities adopted, golf might be thought to be some form of sabotage. The extracts from the decrees issued by the parliaments of the Scottish

The news of the Irish Rebellion was brought to Charles I while he was playing golf at Leith. A painting by Sir John Gilbert (1817-97)

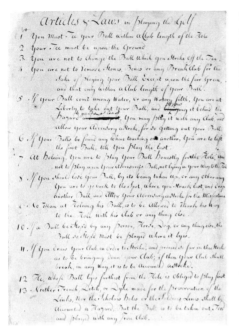

With the accession of Dutch William to the throne, followed by the House of Hanover, golf ceased to make news in the court circular, and it was left to the increasing flow of Dutch pictures on the game to remind historians that it had not gone out altogether. It was not until the early Scottish clubs began to take definite shape between 1740 and the end of the century that concrete evidence became abundant again. Robert Browning, editor of the magazine *Golfing* for nearly half a century, bridges the gap with clarity:

It is necessary to clear our mind of any assumption that the existence of links and of a community of golfers playing over it implied the existence of any authority to look after the course or to regulate play. Courses in those days were wholly natural; the only greenkeepers were rabbits. Clubs and competitions – apart from private matches – were quite unknown. Nobody had thought of the idea of keeping a score by counting the number of strokes taken for a round.

Golf knew nothing then of the social snobberies that afflict parts of it today. According to the Statistical Account of Scotland:

... the greatest and wisest of the land were to be seen on the links of Leith mingling freely with the humblest mechanics in pursuit of their common and beloved amusements. All distinctions of rank were levelled by the joyous spirit of the game. Lords of session and cobblers, knights, baronets and tailors might be seen earnestly contesting for the palm of superior dexterity.

The British have acquired a reputation for forming themselves into clubs, but in the 18th century these bodies were rare, and it was only gradually that they came to resemble clubs as we know them today with office bearers, articles of association, and a headquarters. Browning settles on dates for the formation of golf clubs by taking the years in which they first agreed to play for a trophy. They might still be only a company loosely formed and meeting in the premises of others, but they are definable as a group. In this context he gives the earliest date to the Honourable Company of Edinburgh Golfers in 1744. Slowly other clubs took shape, and a century later some 30 of them could be counted in Scotland.

From the minute books of those early clubs can be gained some idea of how the game survived. Players who could afford it – and there must have been a majority who could not – took as many as six or eight clubs on the round, carried under the arm by

---

kings have become famous, but their language is too rich not to give one sample of it. The third of these proscriptions in 1491 is beginning to get a little scornful:

It is statute and ordinit that in na place of the Realm be usit fut-bawis, gouff or uthir sik unprofitable sports bot for the commone goode and defence of the relm be an it bowis schutting and yfore markis ordinit.

The warning three times repeated in seventy years does not suggest any great enthusiasm for observing it, but makes it perfectly clear that the game had a good hold on the public, not least among the peasants. A similar edict in 1427 mentioned 'fut-bawis' but not 'gouff', and most people would be content to conclude from that that somewhere between 1425 and 1450 gouff took such a hold on Scotland as to be deemed one of its national sports. The partiality for the game of Scottish royalty was unflagging, and when the Treaty of Glasgow brought together in marriage the Scottish king's son and the English king's daughter, removing for the time being any threat from the Sassenachs, the king himself celebrated with a round or two of golf; and a year later, in 1603, according to the Lord High Treasurer's accounts, the king lost a £2 wager playing against the Earl of Bothwell and was also ordered to pay nine shillings for clubs and balls.

On this sparse but firm evidence the argument of golf originating in Scotland was formed. Much of the rest is well-informed conjecture, the shading in of probabilities.

Let *paganica*, a rustic pastime of the Romans, be called the grandfather of golf; let us regard as cousins *cambuca* as played in England, *chole* in Belgium, *kolfspel* (some references prefer the verbal noun *kolven*) in Holland, and *jeu de mail* in parts of France; and a fig for their relative dates. All of them differed in one respect or another from golf, *chole* perhaps the least. Each represents man's overpowering desire to swing any stick that he holds and thence to direct it at something whether that object be a pebble, a puffball or a golf ball. Something of the kind would have had to be invented anyway. Let us study instead the backswing of the player in the stained-glass window in Gloucester cathedral, dating back to 1450 – he has broken his wrists a little early and his footwork looks a little leaden, but his weight transference is correct and he had already learned not to move his head; and while we are studying art take a look at the neat grip of the two-year-old boy in 'Child with a Club', the painting by an unknown artist believed to be of the infant son of King James VI.

It is largely through royal archives and minutes from parish meetings that track is kept of the sport through the Middle Ages. The Church did not attempt a full-scale assault on the game. Its quarrel was with those renegades who preferred the links to listening to its two-hour broadsides from the pulpit. When James VI became James I of England and Scotland, golf moved over the border in a royal way and its standard was raised at Blackheath outside London.

Two items from a Royal and Ancient scrapbook: *left*, 'Articles and Laws in playing the Golf', from the club minute book, 1754 and, *right*, 'Regulations for the Game of Golf', 1842

caddies who early formed an integral part of the game. The duties of the latter were numerous. They had to warn other members of the public using the common land to keep out of the way; they would shoo away the rabbits that were everywhere; and they acted as forecaddies, marking the vague line to the next hole. Perhaps they were also left to extricate the ball from the hole into which it had finally been conjured. and which sometimes became elbow deep from the sand that had been scraped from the bottom to provide a tee on ground only a few club lengths from the hole itself.

In the early days golf had been frowned on by the recruiting officers and by the elders of the Kirk. Golfers always had to fight for what they considered their rights. They fought against Mr Dempster who bred too many rabbits on St Andrews common land until golf became nearly impossible; at Bruntsfield in 1798 they fought against the Quartermaster of the Royal Edinburgh Light Dragoons who wished to use the ground to drill his cavalry. Though on the other side it must be recorded that in 1800 when a party left London in a landau to visit David Garrick at his Thames-side house, men of the Coldstream regiment changing guard outside Kensington Palace cheered when they saw the party's clubs.

The history of Westward Ho!, the first links course in England, has been bedevilled down to modern times by the question of grazing rights. We may believe that in the

18th century such worries were the common lot of the golfer. Golf might have become lost as it did elsewhere; instead, thanks to the Scots, hard-headed and stubborn in their allegiance to the game, it grew and flourished in the decades after it had ceased to amuse a royalty whose roots were in Hanover. Indisputably Scotland can claim to have fought for the game's survival and cherished it before its roots had fully taken.

Foursomes were the general rule, and it is strange to reflect that a form of the game that is almost unknown among the several millions of golfers in the United States today should be the form that sustained golf for centuries in Scotland. The picture is not one of gloom. The nobility – among them the two and twenty noblemen of Fife who formed the St Andrews club in 1754 – must have lent powerful support to the cause; the turf over which they played had that special tough quality that made it thrive on wear and tear; and the company was good. In days when households had to make their own entertainment in the evenings it is easy to picture how much the groups of habitual opponents looked forward to their regular dinners, when matches were made and bets taken, and when in the fine phrase of Smollett 'they never went to bed without having each the best part of a gallon of claret in his belly'. He was referring to the old cronies past 80 seen at the Musselburgh club, but we may be sure they were in no way exceptional.

Slowly a sense of rivalry developed between the local groups. Each area developed its own heroes, treating them as gladiators and pouring unbridled scorn on their opponents when the match was on. Golf, as other sports, has always demanded its super-stars; they may have gone by horse and trap instead of transcontinental jet, but the support they were accorded was every bit as keen. Nor were the personalities lacking.

One of the earliest was Sir Robert Maule, born in 1497, who is described as being

. . . ane man of comlie behaviour, of hie stature, sanguine in collure both of head and haire, colarique of nature and subject to sudden anger. . . . He had gryt delight in haukine and hountine . . . likewakes he exercisit the gowf and oft times past to Barry Links, when the wadsie [wager] was for drinks.

An even more formidable opponent appears to have been William St Clair of Roslyn, captain of the Honourable Company of Edinburgh Golfers in 1766. Sir Walter Scott draws this picture of him at the height of his powers:

. . . a man considerably above six feet, with dark grey locks, a form upright but gracefully so, thin-flanked and broad shouldered, built it would seem for the business of war or the chase, a noble eye of chastened pride and undoubted authority.

Anyone might be excused for starting two down on the first tee to such a figure.

The Golfers', a coloured engraving by Charles E. Wagstaffe from a painting by Charles Lees

No vexed rules separated amateur from professional; the matches that drew the biggest crowds were usually foursomes between the leading players among the gentry, sons and grandsons of those two and twenty nobles and gentlemen of Fife; but gradually a race of giants was being bred among the club and ball makers who earned a precarious trade by supplying those who played. Before the time when the coming of the railways and better roads made inevitable the desire for a nationwide championship, these players, forerunners of the full-time professionals, fought battles that thrilled the natives of St Andrews, Prestwick, Musselburgh or North Berwick. First among them in time and skill, though not in stature, was Allan Robertson, who enjoyed the enviable reputation of never having lost a match in singles playing level. We cannot call him the champion for there were no championships, only challenge matches which threw the locals into a fever of excitement, where the sums at stake represented a whole year's wages to the players. The most famous match, because the best chronicled,

was that in 1849 between old Allan and his promising assistant Tom Morris against the Dunn brothers over the water at Musselburgh.

'Yon wee divil canna play gouf at a', the Dunn supporters shouted at Allan Robertson, but he and Old Tom came from 4 down with 8 holes to play in the deciding encounter and won by 2 holes, their opponents losing their heads badly at the 17th when their ball got behind a rock.

Allan is credited with having developed the most famous of the early iron clubs, the cleek. If so the fashion in iron clubs was slow to catch on. Bernard Darwin wrote of young Tom Morris, in his prime just before 1870, making 'great daring' use of the tiny-headed iron niblick for pitching over bunkers. Until late in the 19th century three or four iron clubs was as much as anyone carried. With the death of Allan Robertson, the Prestwick club turned its thoughts to an open event to establish who was the leading professional. Like so much else that has become traditional – the British Open is the oldest of the national championships – its origin was

chancy and disjointed. The entry for what is recognized as the first Open at Prestwick was eight, a laughable figure by modern standards – but they would laugh just as much at the number of times we handle the ball between tee and hole.

Although it was some years before the entry increased appreciably – it first reached three figures in 1901 – a new era had begun; golf for the first time was to have a show window as its best players began to be better known. In the years before the turn of the century golf went through a period of stability in preparation for the great explosion that heralded the 20th century. English golf began to make up for the slow start which had left it far behind Scotland, and a great number of the clubs that are household names today derive from that period. Hoylake, with its brilliant band of amateurs, and Royal (as it later became) Wimbledon, were the missionary posts that helped to propagate the game in England. In 1894 the Open crossed the border of Scotland for the first time, going as far south as the cliffs of Dover – and was won by a

The participants of the Perth Tournament of 1864

Devonian. It was the first sign on the horizon of the age of the great Triumvirate – Taylor, Vardon and Braid – which was to dominate golf for the next 20 years. Each has his individual place in history but their combined impact on the publicizing and spread of the game was as great as any group before or since until we reach the present age of the Big Three in the United States. They travelled about the country playing golf of such quality as had never been seen before and giving impetus to the growth of the game. Vardon at his peak was a sublime player and gave his name to a now orthodox grip which Laidlay and Taylor had used before him. As equipment became more refined, scores were reduced; but some who saw both eras swore that nothing ever exceeded in greatness Taylor's round in a storm on his way to an 8-stroke victory over the field in the 1913 Open at Hoylake. In the wind that flattened every tent and brought the rain across the course in great flurries, in a wind that made Taylor use his driver three times at the 3rd and still need a short pitch to reach the green, he holed the course in 77 'his cap pulled well down, his chin stuck out, his feet flat upon the ground'.

Already the seeds sown in the United States were beginning to bear fruit. Traces of golf being played there in the 18th century can be found, and historians will dispute among themselves whether the notice of a Golf Club Ball at Savannah in 1811 was merely a social affair or based on the real thing, but the late 1880s were the significant time, when the eccentric Charles Blair Macdonald was trying to transplant the Scottish golf he knew to a new climate, and when Dr Lockhart of Dunfermline was arrested in Central Park, New York, for hitting golf balls in a sheep pasture.

From the beginnings of the game in the Yonkers apple orchard, at Shinnecock Hills, and at Belmont outside Chicago, Charles Price in *The World of Golf* estimates that in the decade up to 1900 a thousand courses came into existence in the United States. Enthusiasm was fanned by the emigration to that country from Scotland of clubmakers and professionals from Carnoustie and other centres of the game until the list of early winners of the US Open begins to read like a parish register from Midlothian. Golf had taken root abroad in isolated spots many years before the United States, or even England, had properly woken to its charms. Where this happened – in Bombay, Delhi, Hong Kong and the Cape – it is no coincidence that there was also evidence of Scottish regiments or Scottish engineers. The start of the first course on the European continent, at Pau in 1856, is sometimes ascribed ultimately to Scots officers sent to recuperate there after the Peninsular War and liking the place well enough to settle down.

Vardon won the first American Open of this century, Walter Travis and his accursed Schenectady affronted the Sandwich members by winning the British Amateur in 1903, and the same year the newly formed Oxford and Cambridge Golfing Society sent over the first transatlantic team to start the rivalry that has grown steadily. From then on the history of golf is interwoven with American influence. The victory of that slip of a lad from Boston, Francis Ouimet, crystallized a trend that was inevitable once sheer weight of numbers and American inventiveness took a hand in golf. Once that country had become fired with enthusiasm for the old game, with its customary vigour and strong financial backing, it soon became dominant, through the skill of such players as Jones, Hagen, Sarazen, Nelson and Hogan.

Britain stood out for a time against such innovations as the centre-shafted putter and dragged its feet in tolerating the steel-shafted club, an invention that revolutionized the technical side of the game as much as the change from feather-filled to gutta-percha balls had done nearly a century before. Under American influence, golf has become increasingly a science rather than an art, an impression that is emphasized by the modern professional tendency to rely on mathematical precision rather than visual judgment to gauge the strength of an approach. Other directions in which American influence has made itself felt are in the slower rate of play that is natural to a warmer climate; the watering of greens and fairways which encourages the pitch to the target rather than the run-up type of shot; and in the predominance of strokeplay over matchplay. In the face of American victories, isolated British champions like Henry Cotton, Max Faulkner and Tony Jacklin stand out almost in defiance of a mainstream. After World War II, American interest in British championships declined and the cream was skimmed off the tournament prize money in Britain by Commonwealth players like Thomson and Locke. In the 1960s there looms across the scene the figure of Arnold Palmer, the first of the modern Big Three and one of the most dynamic personalities golf has ever seen. Not only has he revived American interest in the British Open, but his personality was well suited to television which was then beginning to enter golf in a big way – although BBC television

cameras fixed to open lorries were present at a tournament outside London as early as 1939.

The growth of golf throughout the world, given impetus by the American predilection for starting tournaments on a world scale, led other countries to develop tournaments of their own. South African, Australasian, and Far East circuits offer increasingly worthwhile prizes, and there are signs that all these parts may be co-ordinated into a year-round programme. On the other side of the picture, the heavy cost of playing the game and the shrinking of the leisured class has narrowed the gap between amateurs and professionals. Sport has come to the fore as one of the best mediums for advertising, and the elimination of the frontiers between the two, of the firmer defining of that boundary, is one of the most baffling but urgent problems confronting the game in the 1970s.

Golf History – A Chronology

1340-50	To commemorate his comrades who fell fighting the French at Crécy, Sir Thomas Broadstone erects in Gloucester Cathedral a stained-glass east window in which there is a medallion showing a man swinging a club at a ball on the ground
1424	Football forbidden by Act of Parliament in the reign of James I of Scotland
1457	First of three references to the 'gouf' in Acts of Parliament under the Scottish Kings James II, III, and IV, discouraging the playing of it because of the need for archery practice. The other two dates are 1470 and 1491
1502	King James IV buys clubs and balls from a bowmaker in Perth
1504	Golf match between James IV and the Earl of Bothwell
1527	Sir Robert Maule described as playing regularly on Barry Links at Carnoustie
1567	Mary Queen of Scots reproached for playing golf in the grounds of Seton House so soon after the death of Darnley, her husband
1592	Proclamation at Leith against the playing of golf 'in time of sermonis' on Sundays
c. 1620	First mention of the feathery ball
1641	King Charles I playing golf at Leith when news is brought to him of the outbreak of the Irish rebellion
1646	Charles I plays golf at Newcastle while a prisoner of the Scots
1682	First international golf match between the Duke of York (afterwards James II) and a shoemaker named John Patterson on the one hand and two English noblemen

1721	Evidence of golf on Glasgow Green	1865	London Scottish Golf Club at Wimbledon
1744	First club meeting of the Honourable Company of Edinburgh Golfers, competing for a silver club presented by the City of Edinburgh	1867	First Ladies' Golf Club at St Andrews
		1870	Royal Adelaide Golf Club
		1873	Royal Montreal Golf Club
1754	Twenty-two noblemen and others of Fife hold open competition for which the prize is a silver club. Taken as the formation of the St Andrews Club which subsequently became the Royal and Ancient Golf Club	1878	First Oxford v. Cambridge match at Wimbledon
		1881	Royal Belfast Golf Club
		1884	Oakhurst Golf Club, White Sulphur Springs, Va.
		1885	First British Amateur Championship
1764	St Andrews course reduced to 18 holes	1885	Royal Cape Golf Club, South Africa
1773	Burgess Golfing Society of Edinburgh in existence	1888	St Andrews Golf Club, Yonkers, N.Y.
		1893	Ladies' Golf Union formed
1780	(Royal) Aberdeen Golf Club	1894	First British Open Championship held in England, at Sandwich
1786	Crail Golfing Society		
1786	South Carolina Golf Association formed at Charleston, USA	1894	United States Golf Association
		1895	First US Open Championship
1810	First mention of a ladies' golfing society – the 'Fish Wives' of Musselburgh	1901	Rubber-cored ball introduced by Coburn Haskell
1829	Royal Calcutta Golf Club	1902	First international match between Scotland and England
1818	Golf at Kersal Moor, Manchester		
1833	First Royal golf club named by William IV at Perth	1903	Walter Travis of the United States the first foreigner to win the British Amateur
1834	Royal and Ancient Club granted its name	1905	First full international match between Britain and the United States: women's teams at Cromer, Norfolk
1848	Introduction of the gutta-percha ball		
1856	Continent of Europe's first course at Pau, France	1907	Arnaud Massy of France the first foreigner to win the British Open
1857	First championship meeting played as a foursomes by club pairs at Prestwick	1911	US Open won for first time by homebred American, J. J. McDermott
1860	First Open Championship by strokeplay over Prestwick Links	1913	Francis Ouimet becomes first amateur to win US Open
1884	Royal North Devon. First links course in England	1919	British Open and Amateur championships taken over by Royal and Ancient
		1921	Jock Hutchison the first American to win the British Open
		1926	First (unofficial) professional match between Britain and the United States
		1930	Bobby Jones wins the Amateur and Open championships of Britain and the United States in one year
		1932	First Curtis Cup match
		1951	Francis Ouimet elected first American captain of the Royal and Ancient

Allan Robertson (1815-59), maker and supplier of feathery balls

Golf Ball, History of the

The Rules lay down maximum weight and minimum diameter for the golf ball and any player using one of illegal dimensions risks disqualification. Such stringent control is of recent origin, in comparison with the great age of the game, for it was not until the early 1920s that any form of standardization was introduced officially. By that time the ball had acquired basic characteristics, but dimensions could still vary. The evolution of the ball took place over many centuries and involved a number of changes none of which, until modern times, made strict regulations either desirable or feasible.

Three types of ball figure in the history of golf from the earliest recorded times in the 15th century: first the feather-stuffed ball, or feathery; then the gutta-percha ball, or gutty; and finally the rubber-core ball, which no one so far has ventured to call the rubbery. Considering the relative qualities of the three types, it is extraordinary that the feathery reigned supreme for at least 400 years, and possibly for much longer. There was in fact no adequate substitute until someone discovered the suitability of gutta-percha in the mid-19th century. No doubt in the course of its long career the feathery was improved from time to time, but it was never an easy ball to play and was produced only by dint of much hard labour. Given the nature of its materials and the method of construction it could never have been standardized. Examination of any collection of old featheries would show quite wide differences in size and manufacturing techniques. This is not surprising because each ball was hand made throughout, although the process itself was similar in every workshop. A spherical bag was made by stitching together segments of cowhide and this was filled with feathers, rammed in through the gap left for that purpose. The feathers, as many as would fill a top hat, were first boiled to facilitate handling and to soften the pinions, and when the hard work of packing them in was finished the gap was sewn up. The ball was hammered all over to make it as globular as possible, and then painted. The various ballmakers had their individual tricks of the trade, and the size and therefore the weight of each ball was determined by the amount and thickness of the leather used.

The feathery was never a reliable ball. It was usually ovoid or oblate rather than spherical, and this affected its passage through the air and particularly its behaviour on the ground. Wet weather not only made it heavier and less manageable, but, combined with wear and tear, rotted and broke the stitches with predictable results. An unkind cut with an iron club or collision with a sharp stone could also cause irreparable damage. For these reasons, and also because the slow and tedious process of manufacture made it expensive, only well-to-do golfers could afford to buy the feathery and the less fortunate players had to be content with old balls or improvised substitutes. But this ball, with all its faults lasted until about 1848 when the peculiar properties of a Malayan elastic gum called gutta-percha came to the notice of golfers. This, it was discovered, could be softened in hot water, made into a ball by rolling with the hand on a flat board, and allowed to get hard, when it would stand up to almost anything a club could do to it. Being completely spherical it rolled true. The only snag it encountered in the experimental stages was that it flew badly. Those early gutties, smooth and round, left the clubhead satisfactorily but ducked to earth like shot partridges after travelling a short distance through the air, much to the amusement and satisfaction of the feather-ball makers who had viewed the innovation with suspicion mixed with fear. Their fears were not groundless, for those who persevered with gutties soon found that after a few shots they behaved better and at the end of the round were outdoing the feathery in every way. But as they were then much battered and nicked by the blows of the clubs and contact with stony ground, they were restored to smoothness by being soaked in hot water. This got rid of the wrinkles – and made them virtually unplayable again at the start of the next round. It was not long before the pioneers realized that the trouble was caused by the smoothness. So the gutties were artificially nicked and bruised all over with the point end of a hammer head, and all was well. Eventually the gutty was made in an iron mould which turned out perfect spheres. The final refinement was a mould with patterns on the inside which did away with the laborious and haphazard business of hand-hammering.

The gutty had many advantages over the feathery, including consistency of flight and roll, but the most important were cheapness and durability. The ballmakers who had laboured all day to produce three or four featheries could turn out gutties by the dozen in the same time, and the rate of production was speeded up by the introduction of moulds. Although gutties occasionally broke into pieces and were prone to lesser ailments like 'flats' and 'scars', the hot-water cure was equal to most problems, and remoulding was a simple job. It was not such a pleasant ball to hit as the feathery, but it was superior in all other respects and was responsible for the great increase in the golfing population that took place during the second half of the 19th century.

The next catalyst of change came at the end of the century when Coburn Haskell successfully experimented in the United States with a theory that elastic wound round a soft core and enclosed in a gutta-percha cover would provide a livelier and more resilient substitute for the comparatively unresponsive gutty. The appearance of this invention in Britain caused as much consternation as the gutty had done half a century earlier. There were even discussions

among the golf leaders of the day as to whether it should be banned by rule. The professionals, doing good business with gutties, were sceptical to a man, but one of their number, Alexander Herd, happened to play with the great Hoylake amateur John Ball in a practice round before the 1902 British Open Championship. John Ball was using the Haskell and Herd not only found himself outdriven consistently but also saw the ball was behaving better in approaching and putting. He was invited to try one with the inevitable sequel that he obtained a supply – and won the championship. That was virtually the end of the gutty.

It is unnecessary to dwell on the advantages of the rubber-core ball over its immediate predecessor, for they must be obvious, even to present-day golfers who have never hit a gutty. Because of its qualities the rubber-core ball had two effects on the development of the game. It made golf much more pleasant for everyone, and considerably easier for the beginner and long-handicap player, since their mis-hits had less disastrous results, and this accelerated the already steady advance of the game towards its present position. The other effect was to create the need for controlling the power of the ball. There had been no necessity for either standardization or control with its predecessors. The feathery came from the bench in all manner of sizes, weights and shapes. The gutty was made in various sizes, too, but these were definitive and did not have any noticeable effect on performances. Gutties were made in a range of weights from 26 to 30 pennyweight (1.4-1.7 oz; 40-47 g), the golfers used those they thought suited them best in different weather conditions and on different courses. The makers of the rubber-core ball, on the other hand, were able to give their products different characteristics based on the tension of the windings, the nature of the core and the thickness of the cover. They were not slow to realize the value of being able to build in more resilience and greater length. Soon a rat-race began with firms claiming more and more distance for their particular products. Competition became so keen that sober golfers feared the sport would be ruined and golf courses made out of date.

In 1912 St Andrews obtained the co-operation of the ball manufacturers in a voluntary restriction on efforts to get greater distance, but there was still variety in sizes and even up to the end of World War I golfers had the choice of at least four recognized weights: 27 pennyweight (approx. 1.5 oz; 42 g), which floated, and non-floaters at 29, 30, and 31 dwt (approx. 1.6,

1.7, 1.8 oz; 45, 47, 48 g). Two obvious advantages of this range were that a heavier ball could be used in windy conditions and a floater put down at a 'water' hole. As soon as golf started again after the war it was generally realized that the only way to make control effective was to introduce precise dimensions. The Royal and Ancient and the USPGA conferred and agreed that 'on and after May 1st, 1921, the weight of the ball shall be not greater than 1.62 ounces [45.88 g] and the size not less than 1.62 inches [41.15 mm]'.

This agreement lasted 10 years. On 1 January 1931 the USGA made legal 'an easier and pleasanter ball for the player'. Its dimensions were 'not less than 1.68 inches [42.67 mm] in diameter and not heavier than 1.55 ounces [43.89 g]'. One year later, after experience had shown that the new ball was too light, the US specifications became 1.68 in and 1.62 oz, and so it has remained. Britain stayed wedded to the 1.62-1.62 ball but in 1948 Canada adopted the American size, and efforts were made during the next few years to agree on universal measurements. At a conference in 1951 Britain and America agreed on a new code of rules with one exception – the size of the ball. But the USGA, while sticking to the 1.68-in diameter, conceded that international teams visiting the United States could play the smaller ball if they wished.

From that time, there developed in Britain a campaign for the adoption by the R. and A. of the larger diameter ball based on the theory that American superiority in international matches with Britain was due to the fact that the US ball demanded more accurate striking and therefore produced a higher standard of shot production. The controversy between the 'small-ballians' and the 'big-ballians' raged for years and the advocates of change were fortified by the

A modern golf ball

Opposite, A painting of John Whyte Melville by Sir Francis Grant in the Royal and Ancient GC

Overleaf, The original sketch for 'The Golfers' by Charles Lees

BBC's colour system is manifestly the best in the world. It has added much to the general enthusiasm to be able to show to people in their own homes such scenes as Turnberry with its white lighthouse, Arran, the Mull of Kintyre and the great granite rock of Ailsa Craig; or Muirfield, looking over the Firth of Forth and away up to the distant tracery of the great Forth Bridges; or Gleneagles, where the view extends for 40 miles in almost every direction; or Killarney, or the Bay of St Andrews – the list is almost endless.

These courses and many others, among them Puerto Rico, scene of a play-off after a three-course match, 'The Big Three in Britain', between Palmer, Nicklaus and Player, had ended in a three-way tie, were included in a series of no fewer than 46 matches played specially for BBC television. Each took a minimum of eight hours to play and film, but there is little doubt that their popularity made a substantial contribution to the so-called explosion of golf as a popular game.

In the United States development of television followed much the same pattern. The first outside broadcasts on television began round the beginning of the 1950s. The way was shown by coverage of political conventions. Sport followed, but for a time such coverage was only regional and confined to the easier sports of boxing and football. Golf presented special difficulties, in particular the number of cameras needed to ensure getting a view of the winner. Coverage was for years restricted to the last few holes, and the need for this contributed greatly to the decline of matchplay in America. Not only were sponsors discouraged from adopting it, but the hundreds of thousands of viewers who learned of golf through television were led to believe that medal play, in which the action must finish on the last green, was the only form of the game. In spite of the difficulties, golf offered such compensations in the form of change of view and the lovely places where it is played, it needed only the impact of a magnetic personality to establish it firmly as a television sport. As often happens, the need provides the man. Arnold Palmer had all the qualities required to bring the game to life on the screen: a pleasing personality, a bold adventurous game, and an ability to impart to his audience the full range of emotions he himself was feeling. When he missed a putt, everyone watching felt they too had missed the putt. With the help of Mark McCormack, his business manager, Palmer's name became a household word from coast to coast. Although towards the end of the 1960s Jack Nicklaus overshadowed him in the record books, it was Palmer who was acclaimed as sportsman of the decade by sports writers. In making golf popular on television the US Masters played its part. At first its coverage was regional but in recent years it has through the Columbia Broadcasting Corporation appeared before a wider public. The beautiful setting of holes ringed by water against a background of azaleas and other flowering shrubs made golf something pleasing to watch, even for those who had a small understanding of it. In the last few years appreciation of that fact has led to a greater cooperation between the United States and Great Britain in the exchange of golfing films.

Goodman, John G. AMERICAN

b. Omaha, Nebr., c. 1908. Trans-Mississippi Amateur 1927, 1931, 1935; US Open 1933; Walker Cup 1934, 1936, 1938; Mexican Amateur 1936; US Amateur 1937, runner-up 1932; semi-finalist 1935-6

Johnny Goodman was the fifth of 10 children and was left an orphan while still at school. He left school to earn money for his younger brothers, then completed his education at night school and, immediately after graduating, set off to win his first Trans-Mississippi. His financial difficulties persisted and in 1929 we find him travelling to Pebble Beach on a cattle car with a cattleman's pass, supplied him by a friend, and putting out Bobby Jones in the first round of the National Amateur. Although his golf was cradled in the caddie ranks at Omaha Field Club, his game was a contrast to the usual free-flowing caddie swing: his was short and compact. Also in 1929 he finished 2nd low amateur to the winner, Bobby Jones, in the US Open. He tied for 11th, in spite of a second round of 80. With Jones no longer competing, he finished low amateur in the 1932 Open (tied 13th) and looked ready to win an Amateur Championship, but like Jones, Ouimet and Evans before him, he was to win the Open before the Amateur. In the 1933 Open, a second round 66 put him into the lead and he was never overtaken, although a 6-shot advantage over Ralph Guldahl going into the last round was reduced to a 1-shot lead by the end.

In the 1935 Amateur, Goodman was beaten in the semi-finals by Lawson Little who shot four birdies at him in the last 6 holes, and the following year he was defeated by Johnny Fischer at the same stage. In 1937 he was low amateur again in the US Open (tied 8th) and won the Amateur at last. Some said he should have been picked for the 1932 Walker Cup team. His chance

Johnny Goodman

Henry Longhurst, left, one of Britain's best-known television commentators, receives the Simpson Trophy from Dr Simpson in 1973, Fred Corcoran supporting the proceedings

results of a tournament at Wentworth in 1960 in which every competitor had to play the 1.68-in ball. Christie O'Connor won with the low aggregate of 277 for 72 holes, and the big-ball brigade received further encouragement in 1964 when the PGA adopted for one experimental year a rule making the big ball compulsory in all tournaments under PGA auspices. The experiment was not repeated in 1965, but the rule was reintroduced for a three-year period in April 1968 and has remained in force ever since, an attempt in 1970 to repeal it meeting with overwhelming defeat.

The PGA regulation did not apply to amateur golf, nor to the Open Championship, and in that event practically everyone played the small ball until 1974, when the R. and A. made the bigger ball compulsory for the Open. Before that the R. and A. had appointed a ball subcommittee to investigate the whole question and submit suggestions. This led to a joint Anglo-American proposal in 1971 that there should be a universal compromise ball of the standard weight, 1.62 oz (45.88 g), but a minimum diameter of 1.66 in (42.16 mm). A ball of these dimensions had been under test for some time before the announcement, and the proposal required only ratification by the R. and A. and USGA before being implemented, but it ran into difficulties and was later dropped.

However, bearing in mind the fundamental changes that brought the gutty and the rubber-core ball into existence, and the fact that manufacturers have recently introduced types of solid ball which are claimed to be more durable and not noticeably less effective than the rubber-core, it would be unwise to assert too confidently that further development is not likely. A new material, a 20th-century Dr Haskell, or some scientific and technical advance could all bring about another golfing revolution.

Golf Club, The USA

Columbus, Ohio. 6,300 yd (5,761 m); par 72

It is conceivable that in some future time the early creations of Pete Dye will be looked on as the heralds of a new concept of golf-course design. But like most new concepts, Dye's courses have borrowed heavily from the past, and close examination reveals that his ideas are skilful and imaginative blends of the classic and the *avant garde*.

The first of Dye's new-style designs was Crooked Stick in Indianapolis. His second was The Golf Club, a course of quality developed in the mid-1960s near Columbus, Ohio, not far from Donald Ross's Scioto.

Looking at The Golf Club, the viewer is struck by the imagination that went into the design, for the ground is flat, uninteresting, and only partly wooded in second-growth oak, beech and ash. From the water level of a small creek that meanders through the property, to the top of the highest hill, the 18th tee, the difference is only 20 ft (6 m) and the 18th tee was raised to that height by bulldozers.

From the back tees, The Golf Club can be stretched to 6,700 yd (6,126 m), but it plays more comfortably at 6,300. The creek comes into play on three holes; it runs parallel to the 5th, a 390-yd (357-m) par 4; cuts diagonally across the 6th twice; and runs in front of the 16th, a short par 3. The green of the 16th is less than 3,000 square feet (280 m²) in area. The 6th hole, 440 yd (402 m) long, could well be the most interesting on the course. First, the drive must clear the creek in order to put the golfer in position to reach the green. Then the creek turns, and cuts back across the fairway just in front of the green. In his studies of the famous old courses, in books and on the spot, Dye had seen railroad ties (sleepers) used to shore up the face of bunkers, and he used this device on the 3rd, another par 3. The green is a little higher than fairway level, and Dye constructed three tiers of bunkers, each of them faced with the railroad ties. At times, it is wise to play backwards from the bunker towards the tee rather than try for the green. Countless players have progressed from trap to trap, rather like salmon swimming upstream.

Two holes are outright copies of famous holes on famous courses. The 5th is patterned after the 15th at Dornoch, a short par 4 over a sandy hill, and the 18th after the home hole at Prestwick, an even shorter par 4 on which the drive is the key shot.

Golf-Course Architecture

The beginnings of golf-course architecture are generally put at about the year 1880. Before that time little serious thought was given either to design or construction of golf courses. Such as there was went no further than advice from Scots, not only amateurs but also professionals such as Tom Morris and the Dunn brothers, Willie and Tom. Their ideas were mostly confined to the construction of flat greens of formal and unnatural shape, also of fairway bunkers made in the form of rectangular ramparts stretching at regular intervals across the course, without architectural value.

Later Willie Park Jr began to design courses showing more imagination. He was responsible for the first lay-out of Sunning-

date which was later improved by Harry Colt, secretary of the club. Park also designed Huntercombe, still little altered from its original lay-out and with several good, really imaginative holes.

Between 1900 and 1905 course design was rescued from what might have been fatal deterioration by such well-known amateur golfers as Colt, among whose best creations was Swinley Forest, Berkshire; Herbert Fowler (Walton Heath Old); Tom Simpson (Sunningdale New); and J. F. Abercromby (Addington). And from then until 1914, and afterwards between the wars, they were joined by A. C. M. Croome (Liphook), Sir Guy Campbell (Killarney), Mackenzie Ross, C. K. Hutchison (West Sussex) and Major Hotchkin (Woodhall Spa). Colt had two partners, Hugh Alison, who designed two or three of the first courses in Japan, and John Morrison, who was responsible for Wentworth. Tom Simpson and Colt both designed several Continental courses and the latter also worked in the United States.

The Triumvirate of Vardon, Taylor and Braid also designed courses. Sandy Lodge, and Oxhey (now defunct) were both designed by Vardon. Braid's best is to be seen at Carnoustie, which he redesigned for the 1939 British Open Championship, Blairgowrie and Gleneagles; Taylor, in partnership with Hawtree senior, was responsible for Royal Birkdale.

Golf-course architects owe a special debt of gratitude to Tom Simpson who made a deep study of the principles of design and construction, and wrote on the subject with humour and authority. His works include the *Architectural Side of Golf*, written in collaboration with Roger Wethered; his chapters on course architecture in *The Game of Golf* set a pattern that has withstood the passage of time. Another useful book to which, with several other designers, he contributed, was *Golf Course Design, Construction and Upkeep*.

The main principles of golf-course design, evident in the work of architects mentioned above, are:

(a) Holes should be of good length; par-4 holes of less than about 340 yd (310 m) should be avoided because of the advantage they offer the good player over the long-handicap man.

(b) Fairway bunkers and hazards should be sited strategically rather than from an intent to penalize, as was evident in the early days.

(c) Holes should be designed to encourage the placing of shots, with the natural corollary that the drive should not necessarily be directed to the centre of the fairway. Most skilled players and committee members do

Opposite, Glyfada GC *above* and Huntingdale GC *below*

not accept the presence of a central bunker on a fairway at 250 yd (230 m), but the architect's view is that if a player really is skilled he should be able to place his drive and that, if he does so, he will have an easier shot to the green with his next. On the Old Course at St Andrews the line between tee and green at most of the longer holes is interrupted by bunkers. It follows that when a fairway bunker is centrally placed, the green should be orientated to that side of the fairway on which the tee shot should finish.

(d) A frontal attack on a hill should be avoided wherever possible.

(e) The triangular system should be adopted in the skeleton plan so that the playing of a number of consecutive holes with or against the wind is avoided. This also implies avoiding placing consecutive holes parallel with each other.

(f) A judicious use of natural hazards, such as trees, streams, ponds, and the use of as few artificial hazards as possible.

(g) At one-shot holes the longer axis of the green is generally on a straight line from tee to green, but by orientating the green at an angle to the tee shot the hole is made more interesting and testing.

The architect may sometimes use the principle of *suppressio veri*, though not that of *suppressio falsi*. For example, the ground in front of a green may appear flat from a distance, whereas in fact there is a grass hollow short of the objective which is invisible. This is fair, for no one should criticize a hole until he knows it well. In recent years big prize money and the increase in medal tournaments has led to a revival of an old theory that as far as possible the element of luck should be eliminated.

Over the years there has been a steady increase in the length of shot, due partly to improvements in clubs and balls, but also to the increased skill and power of the first-class players. The stage has now been reached where two rounds a day on a course of 6,800 yd (6,220 m) leaves a middle-aged player exhausted; yet golf is for fun, or meant to be, for most people. Only in the case of the minority should it mean business. In Britain land is expensive and the cost of constructing an 18-hole course increases almost from month to month. More often than not the architect is given about 100 acres (40 ha) on which to work, barely enough for a course of 6,200 yd (5,670 m) at the best. If he is given 120 acres (48 ha) the architect is thankful; with 140 acres (57 ha) he is not only surprised but delighted. The huge distances that top-class players now cover from the tee threaten to destroy the design and testing quality of many of our

finest courses, and it is surely desirable to set a limit. One way of achieving this would be to set a minimum limit to the degree of loft of any club except the putter somewhere between that of a no. 2 and a no. 3 wood. In this way the length that could be driven off the tee would be reduced and brought under control.

Design in the United States followed similar principles to those used in Britain; particularly good work was done there by the British architect Donald Ross who achieved an international reputation. Colt visited the United States and helped in the lay-out of the famous Pine Valley Course. Dr Alister Mackenzie was another who worked in America. As the number of courses increased the name of Robert Trent Jones, the great American designer, became known throughout the world. On the whole American architects have gone in for much larger greens, bunkers that are simply flat areas of sand, and a profusion of water hazards. They have also greatly increased the lengths of their courses, a yardage of 7,000 (6,400 m) being regarded as quite acceptable. At least one course measures 8,000 yd (7,315 m). There are signs that vast greens and excessive yardage are not as popular as they once were.

Before 1900 inland courses were largely prepared by hand by large labour forces. One contractor working on a new course in the south of England is reported to have employed 300 men. Earth moving was by horse-drawn scoops. Steam traction engines and ploughs were used, and for pulling out the roots of large trees a winding engine was the normal method. Machinery slowly began to take the place of men with wheelbarrows, spades and shovels, but in many countries the horse was still in use for moving earth and cutting grass until shortly before World War II. Motorized machinery is now universally used and for course construction today a work force of 10 to 12 is sufficient. A 'mole' is commonly employed for installing water pipes, and this method is increasingly used for laying plastic drainage pipes. But the final shaping of greens and bunkers and the preparation of proper seed beds for tees and greens can still be done only by hand. Although a machine can shape up greens, tees and bunkers roughly, the man with the spade and rake is, and probably always will be, essential.

An architect's responsibilities seem to be at least as onerous as those of the designer of any skyscraper, suspension bridge or factory in the sense that his product must be able to withstand the ravages of time. He must plan for perpetuity and get things right first time:

inaccurate assessment of future needs can cause his client much future expense. He will rightly be tempted to recommend the spending of rather more money than his client contemplates if he can thereby produce more pleasant and exciting courses.

Informed criticism of new courses is generally rare and an important aspect of the game – possibly the most important – is being left largely to chance. The architect receives no guidance from any ruling body. The client invariably asks for a championship course even though he stands no chance of getting one on the ground provided. On the other hand, it is good for the man responsible to feel free of pressures and conventions. In addition to gazing into a crystal ball, every designer has one objective in mind – to make the fullest use of the ground at his disposal and to produce a course that looks as though nature and not he had designed it.

Golf on Television

The first golf on the air in Britain was almost certainly broadcast on 27 March 1927 by Eleanor Helme from the original BBC studio, 2LO London: 'An eye-witness account of the London Ladies' Foursomes Golf Tournament at Addington'. It was only just before World War II that the first attempt was made to broadcast the game live. This was at the English Amateur at Birkdale; the commentator, Bernard Darwin, was accompanied by a team of two technicians, one carrying the apparatus slung on his back and the other the transmitting aerial. From Darwin's comments on his return it was gathered that he saw little or no future in this form of activity. It was tried again for the semi-final rounds of the 1939 Amateur Championship at Hoylake, the commentator this time being Henry Longhurst. The result was not a happy one, since it became at once obvious that if the team accompanied the players the commentary could be overheard, and if they did not, they could not see the play. On this occasion the signal to go was given by an engineer on the clubhouse roof lowering a white handkerchief. By this time both semi-finals had passed out of view and out of the one-mile range of the transmitter, and a 10-minute account of non-existent play was nobly rendered by the commentator, only to find that the last eight of what had seemed a very long 10 minutes had been cut off through a technical hitch.

Although regular accounts of the main events continued to be broadcast on sound, with Tom Scott as the main commentator, it soon became clear after the war that radio would eventually give pride of place to TV.

Here again the first attempt had been made by Bernard Darwin.

In 1947 a further attempt was made with a little mock-up competition on high ground, the 15th fairway at Moor Park, perhaps more to test the reception of the picture back at Alexandra Palace in North London than to entertain the public, practically none of whom yet had TV sets. A monitor set was housed in a wooden box on the fairway while the commentator, again Longhurst, had a microphone on a long length of cable enabling him to alternate between seeing the play from a neighbouring mound and running to see the picture in the monitor, which was by this time inaccessible because of the crowds seeing TV for the first time.

The first attempts seriously to televise a real tournament took place under an enthusiastic golfer-producer, Antony Craxton, who had for many years produced the Royal broadcasts on Christmas Day. The scene was Wentworth, where a huge, and to those who had to climb it, intimidating 70-ft tower was erected, overlooking four holes at the furthest end of the course. All concerned were beginners in an unknown art and it was naturally assumed that the main object of televising golf was to show as many people as possible playing golf shots. The result of constantly flashing from one player to another turned out, however, to be somewhat 'bitty' but a surprisingly large audience, including housewives who knew

nothing of the game, was found to watch – many of them, as they said, 'because it seemed to be such a lovely place'.

Another natural object was to show the winner winning but, transmissions in those days being at fixed times, there was no guarantee of being able to do so. The first improvement came when it was decided to send the players out on the final two days, as had been done in the United States for some time, in reverse order of merit, i.e. the leaders going out last. From this period improvement in presentation was constant. From America was copied the idea of concentrating on the last five holes, plus any 'bonus' holes the cameras might also be able to see, as on the Old Course at St Andrews where they can also see the first five, since the first and last five share the same fairways.

Another vast improvement was the scoring system by which players were quoted as being so many under (or, very rarely, over) par. In earlier days it had been so many under or over 4s, i.e. an average of 4 per hole. For scorers, commentators and public alike this was a headache. If the par of all the holes to be shown was 4 apiece, all would have been easy, but the difficulty may well be imagined when one player was 4 under 4s but with a par 5 to come, whereas another was 5 over but with a par 3 to come. Now all is simple. If a player is 4 under par with 5 to play, it does not matter what the remaining par is. If he continues with par figures he remains 4 under; if he makes a birdie, he goes to 5 under, and every single person can understand.

Yet another great improvement was the creation of the miraculous instant-playback video tape by which it is possible not only to see a player's stroke again within a second or two, if necessary in slow motion, but also to tape long periods for transmitting when there is nothing of equal interest live at the time of transmission. To commentators brought up on fixed times, 'as advertised in the *Radio Times*', the video tape came as a mixed blessing. Instead of 'Nothing more till 4.20', it would be 'Don't go yet. We will stay and record the last five holes of Nicklaus', to be transmitted later. On one occasion, the cricket with which the day's transmissions were to be shared having been washed out, the BBC actually put out 6½ hours of golf from the British Open, a tremendous mental and physical strain on director and producer, who have to remain confined in a dark operations-room type of trailer known as the Scanner, with perhaps 10 different pictures showing simultaneously on their screens.

Of all outdoor games, golf perhaps gained more than any from colour, especially as the

The John Player Classic of 1973 being televised and, *above*, TV preparations for the Wills Open at Dalmahoy

BBC's colour system is manifestly the best in the world. It has added much to the general enthusiasm to be able to show to people in their own homes such scenes as Turnberry with its white lighthouse, Arran, the Mull of Kintyre and the great granite rock of Ailsa Craig; or Muirfield, looking over the Firth of Forth and away up to the distant tracery of the great Forth Bridges; or Gleneagles, where the view extends for 40 miles in almost every direction; or Killarney, or the Bay of St Andrews – the list is almost endless.

These courses and many others, among them Puerto Rico, scene of a play-off after a three-course match, 'The Big Three in Britain', between Palmer, Nicklaus and Player, had ended in a three-way tie, were included in a series of no fewer than 46 matches played specially for BBC television. Each took a minimum of eight hours to play and film, but there is little doubt that their popularity made a substantial contribution to the so-called explosion of golf as a popular game.

In the United States development of television followed much the same pattern. The first outside broadcasts on television began round the beginning of the 1950s. The way was shown by coverage of political conventions. Sport followed, but for a time such coverage was only regional and confined to the easier sports of boxing and football. Golf presented special difficulties, in particular the number of cameras needed to ensure getting a view of the winner. Coverage was for years restricted to the last few holes, and the need for this contributed greatly to the decline of matchplay in America. Not only were sponsors discouraged from adopting it, but the hundreds of thousands of viewers who learned of golf through television were led to believe that medal play, in which the action must finish on the last green, was the only form of the game. In spite of the difficulties, golf offered such compensations in the form of change of view and the lovely places where it is played, it needed only the impact of a magnetic personality to establish it firmly as a television sport. As often happens, the need provides the man. Arnold Palmer had all the qualities required to bring the game to life on the screen: a pleasing personality, a bold adventurous game, and an ability to impart to his audience the full range of emotions he himself was feeling. When he missed a putt, everyone watching felt they too had missed the putt. With the help of Mark McCormack, his business manager, Palmer's name became a household word from coast to coast. Although towards the end of the 1960s Jack Nicklaus overshadowed him in the record books, it was Palmer who was acclaimed as sportsman of the decade by sports writers. In making golf popular on television the US Masters played its part. At first its coverage was regional but in recent years it has through the Columbia Broadcasting Corporation appeared before a wider public. The beautiful setting of holes ringed by water against a background of azaleas and other flowering shrubs made golf something pleasing to watch, even for those who had a small understanding of it. In the last few years appreciation of that fact has led to a greater cooperation between the United States and Great Britain in the exchange of golfing films.

Goodman, John G. AMERICAN

b. Omaha, Nebr., c. 1908. Trans-Mississippi Amateur 1927, 1931, 1935; US Open 1933; Walker Cup 1934, 1936, 1938; Mexican Amateur 1936; US Amateur 1937, runner-up 1932; semi-finalist 1935-6

Johnny Goodman was the fifth of 10 children and was left an orphan while still at school. He left school to earn money for his younger brothers, then completed his education at night school and, immediately after graduating, set off to win his first Trans-Mississippi. His financial difficulties persisted and in 1929 we find him travelling to Pebble Beach on a cattle car with a cattleman's pass, supplied him by a friend, and putting out Bobby Jones in the first round of the National Amateur. Although his golf was cradled in the caddie ranks at Omaha Field Club, his game was a contrast to the usual free-flowing caddie swing: his was short and compact. Also in 1929 he finished 2nd low amateur to the winner, Bobby Jones, in the US Open. He tied for 11th, in spite of a second round of 80. With Jones no longer competing, he finished low amateur in the 1932 Open (tied 13th) and looked ready to win an Amateur Championship, but like Jones, Ouimet and Evans before him, he was to win the Open before the Amateur. In the 1933 Open, a second round 66 put him into the lead and he was never overtaken, although a 6-shot advantage over Ralph Guldahl going into the last round was reduced to a 1-shot lead by the end.

In the 1935 Amateur, Goodman was beaten in the semi-finals by Lawson Little who shot four birdies at him in the last 6 holes, and the following year he was defeated by Johnny Fischer at the same stage. In 1937 he was low amateur again in the US Open (tied 8th) and won the Amateur at last. Some said he should have been picked for the 1932 Walker Cup team. His chance

Johnny Goodman

Henry Longhurst, left, one of Britain's best-known television commentators, receives the Simpson Trophy from Dr Simpson in 1973, Fred Corcoran supporting the proceedings

came in 1934 and again in 1936; both times he played top, and won in foursomes and singles. In the years between Jones and the full power of Little, Goodman was regarded as supreme among amateurs. But in the fateful British victory of 1938 he lost twice: by this time a slight falling off of his best form was discernible. Little more was heard of him; when he turned professional shortly before World War II he ceased to be active in championships.

Goose Neck

A curved neck on a putter so arranged as to bring the line of the shaft, as the player looks down it, slightly in advance of the putter head.

Gordon, Jacqueline BRITISH

b. Stanmore, Middlesex; d. 1970. Runner-up British Ladies' 1947; Vagliano Cup 1947-8; Curtis Cup 1948; runner-up English Ladies' 1952

Her major achievement was in reaching the final of the British Ladies' Championship at Gullane in 1947, and there making a courageous fight against Mildred Zaharias, the famous American all-round athlete. They were all square after the first 18 holes both having taken 75 for the morning round. A good start to the afternoon enabled the American to win. Jacqueline Gordon was a finalist in the English Championship of 1952 and had an outstanding record in mixed foursomes tournaments.

Like many women players of above average height, she was prone to back trouble, and this was probably the reason for her premature retirement from competitive golf.

Gothenburg GC SWEDEN

Hovås, nr Gothenburg (Göteborg). 18 holes; 5,632 yd (5,150 m)

Göteborgs Golfklubb is Sweden's oldest, started in 1902 as a golf section of the Gothenburg Athletics Association and re-named in 1909. The first, very primitive course was at Arendal, and a second of 6 holes totalling 940 yd (860 m) was laid out at Sandviken in 1901. In 1902 the course was extended to 1,457 yd (1,332 m). As the area was needed for gravel extraction the golfers moved to the present site at Hovås, south of the city, in 1904. Six holes were used until 1907; gradual extensions later brought it up to 18 holes. All Swedish championships were played at Hovås until 1912, when Falsterbo was first used for a major competition. The last championship played at Hovås was in 1938 – it is too short and confined for the modern game.

A Scandinavian 72-hole foursomes medal championship is still held there each year, and the club, the fifth largest in Sweden with nearly 1,000 members, continues to produce first-class players. It is no coincidence that Swedish golf on any scale should have started around Gothenburg. Many descendants of Scottish mercenaries from the Thirty Years' War and of later Scottish immigrants have lived, and still live, in this city, which traditionally has had closer personal and business contacts with Scotland and England than any other part of the country.

Gourlay, Mary Perceval BRITISH

b. Basingstoke, Hampshire. English Ladies' 1926, 1929; Vagliano Cup 1931-3, 1939; Curtis Cup 1932, 1934; chairman LGU Executive Council 1957-9; president English Ladies' GA 1963-5.

Molly Gourlay's earlier competitive years were during the era dominated by Cecil Leitch and Joyce Wethered. After their retirement a bevy of powerful youngsters equipped with steel shafts were quickly on the scene. In the brief interlude between the change-over, Molly Gourlay won two English Championships. She was one of the most reliable and consistent strikers of her time, and her steady long game was backed up by uncommon ability on the greens. Besides her two English titles she also won the French Open three times, (1923, 1928-9) the Swedish Open three times (1932, 1936, 1939), and toured South Africa with the British team in 1933.

She has become an authority on the regulations and rules of the game, and as such is in demand as referee at major championships and tournaments.

Graffis, Herb AMERICAN

Herb Graffis has been at the centre of American golf for over half a century. He established *Golfdom*, a trade magazine, in Chicago in 1927, and he served as the editor of that magazine and the monthly *Golfing*, until their sale to *Golf* in the 1960s. His younger brother Joe was his partner in these and other ventures. It was the Graffis brothers who established the National Golf Foundation. They have been the joint recipients of many awards, including the Richardson Trophy and the annual award of the USGA Green Section. Herb has been president of the Golf Writers Association of America, president of the National Golf Fund, and a member of several USGA committees, an adviser to the PGA, and – without dispute – the funniest after-dinner speaker in American golf for some four decades. He collaborated with Tommy

Top, Tommy Horton using a modern putter with a goose neck

Above, Jacqueline Gordon during the English Ladies', 1952

Armour on the latter's remarkably successful book of instruction entitled *How to Play Your Best Golf at all Times*. Now semi-retired, Graffis lives at Fort Myers, Fla., from which retreat he issues from time to time to look in on the tournament scene and to dispense, in passing, a profundity here, an irreverence there.

Graham, John, Jr BRITISH

b. Liverpool 1877; d. 1915. Semi-finalist British Amateur 1900-1, 1905, 1908

Generally conceded to be the greatest amateur never to have won a championship, although he won almost every other event open to amateurs in those days. Jack Graham finished low amateur in the British Opens of 1904-7 and 1913. In the Amateur he reached the semi-finals four times.

As a schoolboy he was something of an all-round phenomenon; he captained his school at cricket and hockey, represented it at racquets, later played rugby for Liverpool, and was invited to play cricket for Lancashire. Bernard Darwin described him as far, far better at golf than most of those who won the championships.

He always played well in the amateur international matches that preceded the championship, playing 10 times for Scotland against England and only being beaten twice. His form continued into the early rounds of the Amateur, but he always faded away before the final. Graham did not have the temperament for the big occasion, and he was never happier than when playing an evening round at Hoylake after a day's work at his Liverpool office, slipping round the championship course in a low score which would take him about an hour and a half to compile. He had neither the temperament nor the time for championship golf, yet he hated to disappoint his admirers who confidently expected him to win everything for

Herb Graffis

which he entered. He did win the St George Challenge Cup twice, in 1904 and 1914, regarded then as a strokeplay test of national dimensions from the strength of the entry. The second time his two-round score was 146, the lowest ever recorded in that event and one that was not beaten until 1928. As a player he was courageous but not aggressive, so there was perhaps irony in his death leading his company of the Liverpool Scottish in one of the fiercest battles of World War I.

Grandfather GCC USA

Linville, N. Car. 7,300 yd (6,675 m)

In a high valley of the Blue Ridge Mountains near the town of Linville, below the rounded top of Grandfather Mountain, highest peak of the Blue Ridge range, and beside the Linville River, lies The Grandfather GCC, a new private course in Western Carolina. Below Grandfather Mountain the golf course snakes and turns through pine forests with rhododendron and laurel, and across mountain stream, offering great variety of scenic beauty and precision golf

Grandfather GCC – the 8th hole

shots. Like most mountain courses, Grandfather requires a familiarity with the uphill, downhill, and sidehill lies, and even though it is a course of unusual length from its back tees, perhaps the best hole is a modest 349 yd (319 m), the 8th. This is a right-to-left dogleg with a fairway that tilts to the left, directing the pulled or hooked drive towards

the Linville River, which runs parallel to the hole. Bunkers are placed on either side of the drive zone about 240 yd (220 m) from the tee, and the short-iron approach must clear another bunker to a spacious elevated, undulating, and very deceiving green. Ellis Maples, the designer, used natural features as he found them, including a number of boulders, much too difficult to remove. They are used as hazards. This high mountain country is cool enough to support bent grass, and it is blended with a mixture of Bermuda.

Grandfather is a super private club built to encourage the sale of real estate; the aim is for national membership for this is resort country. Not far from Grandfather is the Linville CC, which for many years was known for the excellence, friendliness, and familiarity of its caddies who, quite unselfconsciously, called members and guests of the Eseeola Lodge by their first names. One of the more endearing local stories tells of the caddie who was helping a lady play a round in the sixth flight of a state tournament. She had been in every trap and every creek and under every bush from the first hole to the 16th, and as they trudged towards the 17th tee the lady asked solicitously of the caddie, 'Aren't you getting tired?' 'No Ma'am,' he answered 'but I'm powerful homesick.'

Grand Slam

The achievement, also known as the

'Impregnable Quadrilateral', of Bobby Jones in 1930 when, in the same season, he won the Open and Amateur championships of the United States and Britain. It is quite without parallel and it is virtually certain that nobody in future will come near to such a feat.

The sequence of victories was the British Amateur, the British Open, the US Open and US Amateur. The details are as follows:

British Amateur Championship at St Andrews

2nd round	(Monday 26 May)	beat	S. Roper (Wollaton Park)	3/2
3rd round	(Tuesday 27 May)	beat	C. Shankland (St George's Hill)	3/2
4th round	(Wednesday 28 May)	beat	C. J. H. Tolley (R. and A.)	at 19th
5th round	(Thursday 29 May)	beat	G. O. Watt (Broughty)	7/6
6th round	(Thursday 29 May)	beat	H. R. Johnston (USA)	1 hole
7th round	(Friday 30 May)	beat	E. W. Fiddian (Stourbridge)	4/3
Semi-final	(Friday 30 May)	beat	G. J. Voigt (USA)	1 hole
Final	(Saturday 31 May)	beat	R. H. Wethered (Worplesdon)	7/6

British Open Championship at Hoylake, 18, 19, 20 June

291	R. T. Jones (Atlanta, USA)	70 73 74 75
293	L. Diegel (Agua Caliente, Mexico)	74 73 71 75
	Macdonald Smith (USA)	70 77 75 71
296	F. Robson (Cooden Beach)	71 72 78 75
	Horton Smith (Cragston, USA)	72 73 78 73
297	A. Compston (Coombe Hill)	74 73 68 82
	J. Barnes (Pelham Manor, USA)	71 77 72 77

US Open Championship at Interlachen GC

287	R. T. Jones	71 73 68 75
289	Macdonald Smith	70 75 74 70
292	Horton Smith	72 70 76 74
293	Harry Cooper	72 72 73 76
294	John Golden	74 73 71 76
297	Tommy Armour	70 76 75 76

US Amateur Championship at Merion Cricket Club 22-27 September

Having been the medallist in the qualifying rounds with a score of 142, one stroke better than George Von Elm (Rancho), Jones won the matchplay section as follows:

1st round	18 holes	beat	C. Ross Somerville (Canada)	5/4
2nd round	18 holes	beat	F. G. Hoblitzel (Canada)	5/4
3rd round	36 holes	beat	Fay Coleman (California)	6/5
Semi-final	36 holes	beat	Jess W. Sweetser (Siwanoy)	9/8
Final	36 holes	beat	Eugene V. Homans (Englewood)	8/7

years when Angelini and Casera were his main rivals. He won the 1950 Italian Open after a tie with Angelini and the 1954 Open after a tie with John Jacobs. He played regularly in European events including the British Open. He also took part in three Canada Cups and the American Tam O'Shanter tournament of 1952-3. Grappasonni started his career as a caddie in Rome, was later engaged as professional at Villa d'Este, and in 1966 took up the post at Olgiata in Rome. He was a classical swinger whose slightly excitable temperament occasionally let him down.

Gray, Albert Downing, Jr AMERICAN
b. Pensacola, Fla., 1938. Runner-up US Amateur 1962; Walker Cup 1963, 1965; runner-up Southern Amateur 1965; low amateur US Masters 1965

A graduate of Florida State University, engaged in insurance. In his two Walker Cup appearances Gray played four singles matches, three of them against Ronnie Shade, to whom he lost each time; when he finally got away from him, he beat Peter Townsend on the last green in the 'turn-round' last afternoon at Baltimore when the United States forced a tie.

Gray, Helen SEE HOLM, MRS HELEN

Great Harbour Cay GC BAHAMAS
Berry Islands. 18 holes; 7,010 yd (6,410 m)

Situated 160 miles east of Miami and roughly halfway between Nassau and Grand Bahama, Great Harbour Cay has its own airstrip and is easily accessible. Creating a golf course on this largest of the Berry Islands was relatively simple. A limestone island with its own topsoil, it has more

Grant, James A. AMERICAN
b. Hartford, Conn., 1942. Low amateur US Masters 1966; Walker Cup 1967

A graduate of the University of Houston, Grant turned professional in 1967.

Grappasonni, Ugo ITALIAN
b. Rome 1922. Italian Native Professional 1941, 1954-5, 1957; Swiss Open 1948, 1952; French Open 1949; Italian Open 1950, 1954; Moroccan Open 1953; Dutch Open 1954; World (Canada) Cup 1954-6

One of the best known of all Italian professionals, prominent in the postwar

Top, James A. Grant

Above, Downing Gray

change of scene and contour than many of the islands. The course designer, Joe Lee, has succeeded in giving it a special character and identity among the many Bahamian courses built in recent times.

The club and course were part of a $20 million development programme. The work was completed in less than a year and one of its unusual aspects was the method employed to grass the course: sprigs were gathered in Georgia and transported by sea barge to the island for planting within 72 hours of harvesting. The course opened with a spectacular one-day tournament in March 1969 attended by many famous names from the world of golf. The club's director of golf is the American, Gardner Dickinson.

Greece

Golf in Greece is developing slowly but surely, coming into focus as a significant attraction in a country that draws hosts of international tourists every year. Numbers of them now come to play golf at the country's courses, in Athens, Corfu and on Rhodes. Plans for several other courses are under study.

The Glyfada GC of Athens offers visiting golfers an all-grass all-year 18-hole course, built by the National Tourist Organization of Greece.

The island of Corfu in the Aegean Sea has the second 18-hole course in Greece, designed by Donald Harradine and built by the owners of the Grand Hotel Glyfada and the Xenia Hotel, assisted by the National Tourist Organization. It lies in the Ropa Valley, 10 miles from Corfu town and the new international airport.

The National Tourist Organization is now building a new 18-hole course on the island of Rhodes. This is yet another Donald Harradine design, the third full-length course in Greece, to be open to tourists at nominal fees at all times. The best months for golf in the mild, dry Athens climate are September to the end of June. Play is usually restricted to early morning and late afternoon during July and August.

On Corfu, which is quite unlike the other Greek islands, the weather cycle is different. There, heavy seasonal rainfall from late autumn to early spring limits reasonable golf weather to the remaining months, April to November. During that period, with virtually no summer rain, warm sunny days are ideal for golf.

Green

The whole course over which the game is played, not just the area commonly so called, which is, strictly speaking, the putting green.

The term 'green' survives as 'through the green' which, for the convenience of certain rules, includes all parts except the teeing ground, the putting greens and hazards.

Green, Charles Wilson BRITISH

b. Dumbarton, Dunbartonshire, 1932. Leading amateur British Open 1962; Walker Cup 1963, 1969, 1971, 1973; Scottish Amateur 1970, runner-up 1971; Eisenhower Trophy 1970, 1972

From the early 1960s the winner of innumerable tournaments and championships in the west of Scotland, and chosen for the Walker Cup match in 1963, Charlie Green, like all other Scottish amateurs of the period, lived under the dominating shadow of Ronnie Shade; it was not until the end of the decade that he commanded recognition more widely, although he played for Scotland for more than 10 years.

Then in the space of 12 months Green became, at almost 38, Scottish Champion, a title that seemed destined to elude him; played in the Eisenhower Trophy team; was a worthy member of only the second successful British Walker Cup side; and again reached the final in defence of his Scottish title. These achievements brought Green to the peak of his playing career, rewarding an unflagging perseverance and enthusiasm, although many believe he never played better than in the 1973 Walker Cup.

Very tall and with a fast swing that made his driving vulnerable, Green was pre-eminently a fine exponent of long iron shots. He had a tentative putting stroke, yet like many big men Green had a delicate touch about the greens. He was particularly adept with the wedge and sand iron, frequently from difficult lies and was a most resolute holer-out under pressure.

Greenbrier Golf and Tennis Club USA

White Sulphur Springs, W. Va. 6,500 yd (5,944 m); par 70

The Greenbrier Hotel with its surrounding facilities, tucked away in the mountains of West Virginia, is one of America's most magnificent resorts with an opulent, Colonial atmosphere. General Robert E. Lee used to go there frequently in the years following the Civil War, when the Greenbrier was famous for its mineral water. Today it has three courses nearly always in superb condition.

Of the three courses, the one most visitors prefer to play is called the Old White. It has more charm than the Greenbrier, the second course, and it is an altogether better test. It has an abundance of bunkers, trees, and water, and its holes have a pleasant aspect. Sam Snead, the host professional, has a great fondness for the course, considering Old White's first hole to be the best first hole in the country. And if it is not the best, it may well be the most difficult and frightening starting hole west of Prestwick. The 60-ft (18-m) tee is elevated a good way above the fairway, and the drive must cross Howard Creek to reach fair ground. It must also be kept to the left if a decent second to the green is to be had. The green is practically encompassed by deep bunkers. At 430 yd (393 m), this is a tough par 4, but after that the course lets the golfer catch his breath and sets very reasonable problems the rest of the way. It is one of those rare courses that ends with a par 3 – a scenic hole over water.

Greenhalgh, Julia BRITISH

b. 1941. Runner-up British Girls' 1959; British Women's Open Strokeplay 1974; Commonwealth Tournament 1963; New Zealand Ladies' Open 1963; Curtis Cup 1964, 1966, 1970; English Ladies' 1966; World Women's Amateur Team Championships 1970, 1974

A redoubtable match player who seemed

Green, the well-kept 18th at St Annes Old Links   Charlie Green

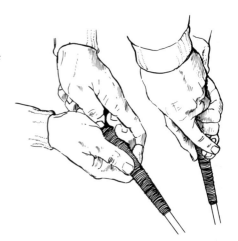

set at one time for the highest honours. On the strength of her promise as a junior, and of reaching the semi-finals of the British championship shortly after, Julia Greenhalgh accompanied the British Commonwealth team to Australia and New Zealand in 1963 where she again had a successful record. When she finally broke through in 1966, damage to her wrist soon kept her out of the game for some time, and she was slow to get back to her old eminence. In the Curtis Cup match of 1970, her losing the last two holes and the match to Mrs Dye, a result which changed the whole emphasis of the match, obscured the fact that she contributed as many points to the British team as anyone, $2\frac{1}{2}$ out of 4. Fate was not kind to her that year; because of a series of withdrawals she was pitchforked with little notice into captaining the British team for the World Women's Amateur Championship Team in Madrid, a difficult assignment since she was also competing in the event.

Greensome

A variation of the fourball game in which each player drives at each hole and then continues on a foursomes basis, each side having the choice of which drive to play. If A's drive is chosen, B plays the second shot. In America this variation is called a selected-drive foursome.

Gregson, Malcolm Edward BRITISH

b. Leicester 1943. Harry Vardon Trophy 1967; Schweppes PGA 1967; Ryder Cup 1967

After leaving Millfield School, Gregson turned professional in 1961 and soon became one of Britain's leading young players. A steady rise through Assistants' championships led to his first major victory, in the Schweppes PGA Championship at Hunstanton in 1967 in which he had final rounds of 67 and 65. This was the start of a memorable season in which he won the Daks, tied for the Martini and played in the Ryder Cup and World Cup. He won the Harry Vardon Trophy the same year and became a much-travelled tournament player in many countries throughout the world, although he has not since captured that same brilliance.

Grip

The part of the shaft which is held in the hands, and covered by leather or rubber to prevent the club from slipping. When applied to a player: the position of the hands on the club, one of the most important factors in technique, since it governs whether the clubface is presented square to the ball at impact.

Variations of grip, often decided by the size of the player's hands, include the Harry Vardon overlapping, the interlocking, the two-handed or baseball, and more rarely the grip of left hand below right as used by the South African Indian, Sewsunker Sewgolum.

Many comments have been made about the importance of the grip. Tommy Armour,

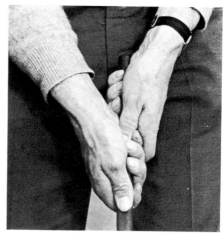

Julia Greenhalgh

Malcolm Gregson in the 1967 Alcan

Top and centre, two examples of the putting grip and, *below,* Mary Everard contriving a stroke with a make-shift grip

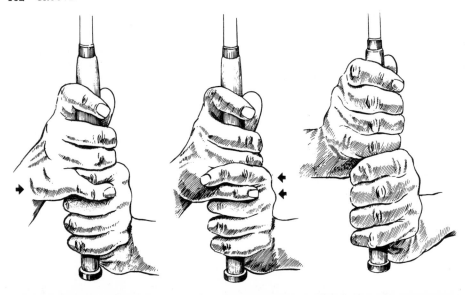

looking the beautiful L'Ancresse and Grand Havre bays. Organized golf, which has always thrived there, began in Guernsey with the formation of the club by 37 founder members in 1890. It received its Royal Warrant in June 1891; it played its first inter-island match against Royal Jersey in 1895; and there is a record of a professional match in August 1899 between Ted Ray and T. Boutell. Few of the old records, however, survived the German occupation during World War II, when the fairways were destroyed and German guns were sited on the greens. The clubhouse too was almost gutted by the end of the war. The club found it impossible to meet all the costs of restoration, but with the support of the authorities the course was fully in use once more at the beginning of 1949. Mackenzie Ross undertook the work of redesign.

Guilford, Jesse P. AMERICAN

b. Manchester, N.H., 1895; d. 1962. New Hampshire Amateur 1909, 1913; Massachusetts Amateur 1916, 1921, 1924; US Amateur 1921, semi-finalist 1916, 1932; Massachusetts Open 1919, 1929; Miami Invitation 1922; Walker Cup 1922, 1924, 1926

Known as the 'Siege Gun' because of his tremendous drives; the first American golfer known to hit the ball as hard as he could. Francis Ouimet, a close friend, credited Guilford with revolutionizing the game in the United States. He was brought up on a farm near to the Intervale Club and naturally turned to the game as a youngster. He won the New Hampshire Amateur at the age of 14 and, by the time he appeared for his first US Amateur in 1914, was a formidable player. Two years later, he had added some finesse to his short game and was able to advance to the semi-finals at Merion. He won the championship at St Louis in 1921 by eliminating George Von Elm, Dewey Webber, Jimmy Johnston, Chick Evans and Bob Gardner – two of them former champions and two of them future winners. The final against Gardner was remarkable because it pitted the two biggest hitters in the amateur ranks against each other. The victory was notable for Guilford's shy acceptance speech, in which he said 'If I am expected to give a speech, I am sorry I won the title'.

Guldahl, Ralph AMERICAN

b. Dallas, Tex., 1911. Western Open 1936-8; Ryder Cup 1937, 1939 (not played); US Open 1937-8, runner-up 1933; US Masters 1939, runner-up 1938

A strange up-and-down record, but in

for example, said, 'The basic factor in all good golf is the grip. Get it right and all other progress follows'; and from Gene Sarazen comes 'If I was tutoring a young player, I would instil in him the importance of the grip. If he hasn't got a good grip, he's got two chances; slim and none.'

Groove

American term describing a swing that will repeat itself without variation, an ideal all golfers seek but rarely achieve. Thus 'in the groove', 'a grooved swing'.

Gross Score

The player's score, before the deduction from it of his handicap, when it becomes net.

Ground Under Repair

An area of the course from which the player is allowed to remove his ball without penalty, usually a temporary concession occasioned by returfing, reseeding, repairs, damage from animals or machines. It is the responsibility of the club or tournament committee to mark the area clearly. Ground under repair is dealt with under Rule 32 of the Rules of Golf.

Guernsey GC, Royal CHANNEL ISLANDS

L'Ancresse, Guernsey. 18 holes

The Guernsey Links, home of the Royal Guernsey GC, enjoys a splendid situation on the extensive L'Ancresse Common at the northern end of the island of Guernsey, over-

Top, the driving grips: *left*, the Vardon overlap; *centre*, the interlocking; *right*, the baseball. The arrows indicate overlapping fingers

Above, the reversed grip being used by Sam King

Guldahl looked a certain winner of the 1937 US Masters, but Nelson made up 6 strokes on him at the 12th and 13th holes and overtook him. Guldahl was 2nd again in 1938, in a tie, but in 1939 he went one better, finishing the last 9 holes in 33 and overtaking Sam Snead in the process. He won one tournament in 1940 and showed moderately well in the Masters for another year or two but that was all. Such inconsistency of record gave rise to many explanations and his style was closely studied. Though he made a full pivot of the shoulders he moved the lower half of his body very little, keeping his feet firmly planted on the ground. Such a seemingly awkward style was made possible by his sledgehammer

action with the right hand which he allowed to slide down the grip as he completed the backswing. His wriggling at the address has been likened to a man squirming his way into a telephone box with a load of parcels in his arms. Once settled he drew back the clubhead with explosive speed and struck the ball what looked like an uppercut; but his concentration was tremendous and he never putted until he had outstared the hole.

Gullane GC SCOTLAND

Gullane, East Lothian. 54 holes (3 courses)

Whether Gullane or the area around Prestwick is the British centre from which the most rounds can be played in one day is open to question. However, there is no doubt

one spell when Guldahl won two US Open Championships in succession and one Masters, and was runner-up another year in each, he rose to heights attained by few golfers. He also won three consecutive Western Opens, then considered second in importance to the Big Three. A tall powerful man, his first tournament success came in 1932, and he was runner-up in the US Open the following year. Then his form collapsed and he came near to quitting the tour altogether in 1935. He was persuaded to continue after making some adjustments to his swing and putting in hours of practice. He came back to the top, winning 10 tournaments in the next five years. In winning his first Open at Oakland Hills he was one of only five competitors to finish below par and the first player not to go over par in any round of the Open; and his final 69 revealed one of his strongest points, his ability to preserve great accuracy through the green under pressure. The following year at Cherry Hills he became only the fourth winner to defend his title successfully, again earning $1,000 for first prize.

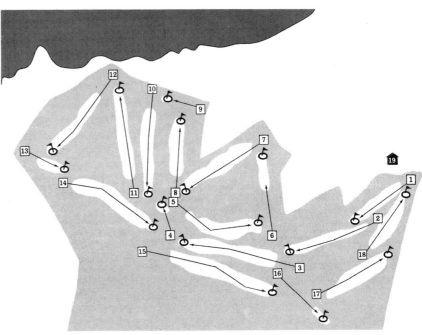

Top, Jesse P. Guilford

Above, Ralph Guldahl

Top, a view of the Gullane GC, and, *above,* the course plan that Gullane provides as good a golfing centre as anywhere in the world. The three courses run on either side of Gullane Hill – one of the most famous settings in golf, with views of distant Edinburgh, the Firth of Forth and the hills of Fife. This is incomparable golfing country with the finest turf. There is a little climbing to be done, but the game there has all the qualities of good seaside golf, its difficulty mainly determined by wind strength.

Golf at Gullane began with enthusiastic farmers who formed the first club, the East Lothian, around 1850. The present private club was founded in 1882, has prospered ever since, and has accommodated many events of national importance. Gullane and the name of Babe Zaharias are inseparable. It was there in 1947 that she became the first American to win the British Ladies' Championship, giving an almost flawless exhibition of her strength and power. Gullane's other British Ladies' Championships were those of 1897, when the Orr sisters were the finalists, and 1970, when Dinah Oxley beat Belle Robertson on the last green. Besides several Scottish Ladies' Championships, Gullane has also staged the Boys' Championship of 1965 and qualifying and pre-qualifying rounds for the British Open.

Gulmarg GC INDIA

Gulmarg, Kashmir. 18 holes; 6,760 yd (6,181 m); par 70

This course, 24 miles west of Srinagar at the Himalayan resort of Gulmarg ('flower meadow'), was laid out by a Colonel Sir Neville Chamberlain in the early days of British rule. At one time there were three courses here, two 18-hole and one 9-hole. Kashmir was one of the areas the British repaired to in the hot season, and at these times Gulmarg had a population of nearly 10,000, mainly Europeans, housed in cottages scattered over the basin. The long wooden clubhouse was near the 1st tee. No Indians were allowed.

Up to the end of World War II the Northern India Amateur Championship was played at Gulmarg in the middle of summer. Subsequently it moved to Delhi. More recently the Indian government decided to build a complete tourist centre at Gulmarg, fully equipped for both summer and winter sports. The plan included a luxury hotel and a completely new golf course up to international standards. Peter Thomson of Australia was entrusted with the latter task. His design envisaged an 18-hole and a 9-hole course that made the most of the magnificent mountain scenery (the

Khillanmarg Ridge and glacier form a backdrop; the 14,500-ft peak of Apharwat can be seen, and far to the north the 26,620-ft Nanga Parbhat) and at the same time cut out much of the climbing that used to be necessary. The old course had been laid 'against the grain', across the mountain spurs; the new course allows play to run mainly along the natural features. Hundreds of trees have been planted and snow-fed streams canalized into ponds and two small lakes. The surface of the greens is a close-weave mossy grass (Gulmarg is nearly six months under snow); it holds a pitch beautifully and yet is fast and true for putting. Unchecked sheep grazing in the past damaged the grass cover and the abundant alpine flowers. Thomson has fenced in the whole course. In future fairways will be mechanically cut; the rough will be a mass of mountain flowers.

Thomson's course has four par 5s, eight par 4s and six par 3s. The new hotel incorporates the clubhouse and has been sited so that it is possible to start a round either at the 1st or the 10th. One hole, the 8th, is over 600 yd (550 m) long, uphill most of the way, which may require three good wood shots to reach the green. But in a setting of such beauty, golf scores may not be the most memorable aspect of a visit to Gulmarg.

Gunderson, JoAnne see CARNER, MRS D. R.

Gunn, Watts AMERICAN

b. Macon, Ga., 1905. Georgia Amateur 1923, 1927; runner-up US Amateur 1925; Walker Cup 1926, 1928; US National Collegiate 1927; Southern Amateur 1928

Watts Gunn had a dazzling career as a young amateur, reaching the final of the National Amateur at his first attempt, aged 20. He had won the Georgia Amateur at the age of 18 and his consistently good play had impressed Bobby Jones, three years his elder, who prevailed on Gunn's parents to let him compete in the Amateur at Oakmont in 1925. He won his first-round match by 12 and 10, winning 15 holes in a row after being 3 down. The USGA was experimenting with the championship at the time and had qualified 16 for matchplay over 36 holes; the practice was not continued. Scarcely less incredible was his defeat of Jess Sweetser by 11 and 10 in the next round. In the final he found he was opposed to Bobby Jones, the only time two finalists in the championship have come from the same club, Atlanta. Gunn made a brave start against him and after reaching the turn in 35 was 1 up, but Jones had five 3s in the next 7 holes and won by 8 and 7.

Another example of his brilliance came in 1927 when he won the National Collegiate title, entered from Georgia Tech, in the course of which he had seven consecutive birdies. His record in Walker Cup matches is equally dramatic. He won 4 points out of 4, his margin of victory in the foursomes being 4 and 3 with his friend Bobby Jones, and 7 and 5; in his two singles the margins were 9 and 8 and 11 and 10. After his graduation from college in 1928 he devoted less time to competitive golf and was no longer in the national picture after 1930.

Watts Gunn

H

Haas, Fred AMERICAN
b. 1916

The first player to compete in both the Walker Cup and the Ryder Cup: he was in the 1938 American Walker Cup team at St Andrews and, after turning professional in 1945, in the 1953 Ryder Cup team at Wentworth. Moderately successful as a professional, he won four tournaments. He served on the PGA tournament committee in 1954-5.

Hagen, Walter Charles AMERICAN
b. Rochester, N.Y.; d. 1969. US Open 1914, 1919, runner-up 1921; Western Open 1916, 1921, 1926-7, 1932; French Open 1920; Ryder Cup 1921 (unofficial), 1926-7, 1929, 1931, 1933, 1935, (non-playing captain 1937); USPGA 1921, 1924-7; British Open 1922, 1924, 1928-9, runner-up 1923; North and South Open 1923-4; Belgian Open 1924; Canadian Open 1931

Hagen rose from the ranks of caddie to win two American and four British Open Championships, and the American PGA Championship five times. But it was his personality that wrote his name large across the pages of golfing history. Hagen was flamboyant and colourful, but his style of living made professionals aware of what was possible in their profession, so that the whole standard of living rose through his influence. The epigrams that have been attributed to him would fill a book. Not all of them would be true but he was prepared to accept them

even if they were not. They have formed a legend of gaiety, nerve, and approach to gamesmanship that is solidly entrenched in the history of the game.

No golfer could have a temperament better suited to the game. He could break his concentration between strokes, chatting nonchalantly to spectators, without losing his grip on a match. Indeed, it was his ability to project his personality in the course of a round that played such havoc with his opponents. Bernard Darwin wrote of him: 'His demeanour towards his opponents, though entirely correct, had yet a certain suppressed truculence; he exhibited so supreme a confidence that they could not get it out of their minds and could not live against it.'

So his real strength was in matchplay, and this was shown by his five victories in the PGA Championship at a time when these were decided by matches, in the later stages over 36 holes. Four of his victories were consecutive; in winning them he scored 22 victories over 36 holes against the best American golfers.

Hagen was no less effective in strokeplay. Like Sarazen he made his mark early. His first American Open was in 1913, the year of Ouimet's triumph. Almost unknown, he finished in a tie for fourth place, and the following year he won the first of his two titles. Suffering from a stomach upset due to a surfeit of lobster and oysters, Hagen nevertheless led the field with a record 68 over Midlothian, Chicago, and continued to lead throughout. His second victory, at Brae Burn in 1919, persuaded him to take the unprecedented step of giving up his job as professional at Oakland Hills and becoming the first full-time tournament professional.

Britain first saw him in 1920 when in an exhibition match with Jim Barnes they beat the pride of Britain, Abe Mitchell and George Duncan. In the Open he went almost unnoticed, finishing last but one in a field of 54, but before returning home he won the French Open. Like Sarazen, Hagen's career covers a wide span: he won the American Open first in 1914, and he finished 3rd 21 years later. It was in the 1920s that he enjoyed his greatest success, and it began with his victory in the British Open in 1922, the first American to hold both Open titles. The British at Royal St George's seemed to be his from the start and he was threatened only when George Duncan nearly caught him with a final 69. He won there again in 1928, but before that he was runner-up to Arthur Havers at Troon in 1923. It was there that he declined to enter the clubhouse for the presentation because

none of the professionals had been allowed near it during the week; instead, while thanking the officials for their many courtesies he invited the spectators over to the pub where he was staying. It was one of several incidents that highlighted efforts to raise the status of the professional in golf. At Hoylake in 1924 came his second victory in

the British after nearly failing to pre-qualify with a first round of 83. His fellow competitor in the first round was John Ball who had played in his first Open 48 years before.

In 1928 Hagen came to the British Open smarting from a defeat over 72 holes from Archie Compston by the margin of 18 and 17. Hagen had not had time to practice, having landed the previous day, and was out of form, but with typical resilience he put this behind him and went out to win the Open, for the second time at Sandwich. In this he must have been encouraged by the memory of Bobby Jones who, after losing to Hagen in an exhibition match by 12 and 11, went on to win that same year, 1926, the Opens of America and Britain. In winning the championship he played his best golf, not once taking six in the 72 holes. The Prince of Wales followed him on his last round and presented the Cup, beginning an acquaintance which lasted for many years. His fourth victory came the following year at Muirfield when he won by 6 strokes in a strong field which included the American Ryder Cup team and a good few others beside. Thus in eight appearances in the British Open between 1920 and 1929, he finished 53rd, then 3rd and 2nd once each, and four times 1st.

Hagen played in all the Ryder Cup matches until 1937. He was responsible for getting a team to come over to Wentworth for the first match in 1926, and the trouncing the Americans got on that occasion was

Fred Haas

Walter Hagen

compensated for 11 years later when Hagen captained the first American team to win on British soil, against a British team captained by J. H. Taylor. From 1927 when the first official Ryder Cup match was played Hagen acted as captain to the team until 1937.

In the 1930s, while continuing to compete in the US National Championships, Hagen devoted much time to world travel, and in this way he again showed himself the forerunner of the modern jet-age professional. He made several world tours, taking in South America, Australia, Japan, and even a safari in East Africa. On these trips he was usually accompanied by Joe Kirkwood, the famous trick golfer, with whom he would stage a show. The least impressive part of Hagen's game was his wooden club play, for he would usually expect to have one or two loose ones in a round, but he had great capacity for putting the bad shot behind him; and his short game, especially out of bunkers, was in the highest class. But it was as a putter that he was supreme, and so great a putter as Bobby Locke admitted that he based his putting on Hagen's game.

Hague GCC, The NETHERLANDS

The Hague (Den Haag). 18 holes; 6,649 yd (6,080 m)

The present Haagsche club course came into being after World War II but in its origins this is the oldest course in the Netherlands, dating from 1889 when Baron van Brienen van de Groote Lindt laid out 3 holes for his friends on his estate between The Hague and Wassenaar. J. D. Dunn, a nephew of Willie Dunn, extended the course to 9 holes, taking in part of a racecourse. In 1920 it was extended to 18 holes, the first to be so in Holland, by J. F. Abercromby, and a few years later was opened by an exhibition match between the two French players Arnaud Massy and Jean Gassiat. After the outbreak of World War II golf struggled on there, although the delightful old clubhouse was blown up by the Germans and an underground hospital and shelters were built in its place.

A few holes were marked out by Gerard de Wit, Holland's best-known professional, on nearby hockey fields. And when the members' clubs were threatened with destruction, a resourceful member of the committee had them transferred to the safe keeping of a bank.

A fresh start was made after the war on the site of the old Wildhoeve club at Wassenaar. Alterations were made under the guidance of Sir Guy Campbell and the club was opened in May 1947.

The course occupies spectacular dune country with steep gradients, fringed by willow scrub and buckthorn. Its plunging fairways are constantly changing direction and the greens have been placed to make the most of the many undulations. Traditional Scots golfers might regard it as 'the real thing' and the Continent offers no finer links course. It calls for great judgment and control, as has been well illustrated by the holding there of several Dutch Open Championships. Percy Boomer won three titles in a row from 1924 over the old course; the first championship over the reconstructed course was won by Jimmy Adams in 1949 who said afterwards that it was the toughest course he had ever had to master. In 1968 the club celebrated its 75th anniversary, and in 1972 by raising prize money to £12,000 it became associated with the British Professional Golfers' Associations. The Open attracted a first-class field, from which Jack Newton of Australia emerged the winner, after a close fight with Peter Oosterhuis.

Hahn, Paul AMERICAN

b. Charleston, S. Car., 1918

One of the tiny band of specialists whose exhibitions of trick shots with a multiplicity of weird equipment are delighting crowds throughout the world. Hahn was a full member of the USPGA and began his golfing life as a tournament player. The light-hearted patter which accompanies his act adds to the popularity he has enjoyed in many countries.

Halford Hewitt Challenge Cup

A cup played for by teams of 10 representing the old boys of 64 British public (endowed) schools. Founded in 1924 by Halford Hewitt, this is the world's largest golf tournament and is run by the Public Schools Golfing Societies in the form of a foursomes knockout competition, each match consisting of five games between two schools. The tournament takes place each April at the Royal Cinque Ports GC; half the field play the first two rounds at the neighbouring course of Royal St George's, Sandwich. Besides being one of the friendliest of gatherings it produces its own brand of competitive action. The tradition of foursomes play is well preserved here and cliff-

Top, the sand-dune course of The Hague GCC

Above, Paul Hahn giving one of his trick displays in London's Festival Gardens in 1951

hanging finishes are common. Eton, Harrow and Charterhouse (the founder's own school) have dominated the winners' list, but in recent years success has been more widely spread.

Haliburton, Thomas Bruce BRITISH

b. Rhu, Dunbartonshire, 1915. Ryder Cup 1961, 1963; captain PGA 1969

For many years holder of the lowest tournament round on the British professional circuit (a 61 at Worthing) and of the world record for two consecutive rounds in a tournament – 126 – in the same event. After turning professional in 1933, Haliburton, a quiet-spoken Scot, became a successful tournament player and a highly respected club professional at Wentworth. Though by no means a powerful striker, his game was finely controlled and he played a lot of his best golf when well past 40. His putting style is remembered for the pronounced rap he gave the ball. He played in the Ryder Cup in 1961, then won the 1963 *Yorkshire Evening News* tournament, coming from behind with final rounds of 69 and 66 to beat

Peter Thomson by 1 stroke. Largely thanks to this result he kept his place in the Ryder Cup team later that year in Atlanta.

Half, Halve

A half is scored on a hole when each side plays it in the same number of strokes. To halve also means to play a match that finishes all square.

Half Shot

A shot played with something less than a full swing. A shot not hit with full power.

Halmstad GC SWEDEN

Tylösand. 27 holes; Main Course 6,567 yd (6,005 m)

Tom Haliburton

The origins of Halmstad Golfklubb go back to 1925 when golf was first played on a primitive course laid out on land belonging to the local infantry regiment. During the Depression work started on the present course at Tylösand, a summer resort on the coast near Halmstad, with out-of-work youths as labourers and money put up by the government. The local authority presented the course to the club and still appoints a majority of the committee members. However, full freedom is given for the club to be run in the usual way. As might be expected Tylösand has sandy soil. The course is beautifully carved out among pine and broadleaved woods (pine forest was planted here several hundred years ago to bind the sand and stop it spreading inland). Eighteen holes designed by Rafael Sundblom of Stockholm were ready in 1938. A further 9 holes were added by Nils Sköld, also of Stockholm, in 1964. The wind is sometimes a factor to be taken into account here, although the trees give some protection.

A number of major competitions have been played at Tylösand since 1939. In 1947 an English team with Cyril Tolley, P. B. Lucas, J. J. F. Pennink, Alec Hill and A. H. Perowne (who also won the Swedish Open Amateur here in that year) played a Swedish side at Tylösand, the first organized match between the two countries. The two-yearly match between the British Isles and the Continent of Europe was played there in 1962 and the European Women's Team Tournament in 1969.

Hamilton, Robert AMERICAN

b. Evansville, Ind., 1916. Indiana Amateur 1936; Indiana Open 1938, 1942; North and South Open 1944; USPGA 1944, semifinalist 1952; Charlotte Open 1946; Nevada Open 1946; New Orleans Open 1948; Inverness Fourball 1949; Ryder Cup 1949

Winner of the USPGA championship in 1944, his first year on the professional tour, Bob Hamilton was 6th money winner for that season, although he played in only 11 tournaments. For the next five years he was a regular on the circuit and established himself as one of the best pressure players in golf. He was 3rd in the 1946 Masters and reached the semi-finals of the USPGA in 1952. His victims in the 1944 PGA included Byron Nelson – whom he beat in the final – and Jug McSpaden, the two finest players in the game at the time.

Hamilton GC NEW ZEALAND

St Andrews, Auckland. 18 holes

Hamilton GC owes a great deal to one man, H. T. Gillies, brother of Sir Harold

Gillies who is remembered as the founder of modern plastic surgery. After a small group of enthusiasts had started golf in Hamilton in 1896 and the club had been officially formed in 1903, H. T. Gillies ended the frequent shifts of site which had been a feature of the early days by discovering a piece of land on the western bank of the Waikato River and later buying it in 1912 at £8 an acre. Originally the property was a wilderness of gorse, blackberry and bracken but the excellent soil presented few drainage problems and, with the help of a little outside advice, Gillies undertook the design himself in the enthusiastic belief that the area could be developed into the best links in New Zealand. In 1920 the club staged the first of

many national championships held there, the Amateur, won by Sloan Morpeth, followed by the Open, won by J. H. Kirkwood.

Gillies implemented many of the old Scots principles in his design and, for those days, it was a demanding course at nearly 6,400 yd (5,850 m) with a good deal of rough. It says much for his skill that it was not until the early 1930s that alterations were found desirable. These consisted mainly of reducing the rough and adding to greenside bunkers, and had the effect of developing the parkland qualities of the course. With fuel restrictions in force during World War II, sheep replaced machinery. In 1934 the clubhouse burned down. Voluntary labour built a replacement; a new building was erected in 1956.

Bob Hamilton

Hamilton golfers have maintained the record of their predecessors – Gillies, a scratch player, Sloan Morpeth, Jack Black, and Norrie Bell. Bob Glading played out of Hamilton in winning the Opens of 1946 and 1947; Tim Woon, four times Amateur Champion, moved to Hamilton from Waitiriki. Walter Godfrey, now a successful professional, and Stuart Jones both won the Amateur at Hamilton, and Kel Nagle won the Opens of 1958 and 1967 there. One of the highlights in the distinguished history of Hamilton and its delightful course was the staging of the Women's Commonwealth Tournament, in 1971, the year that marked the centenary of golf in New Zealand.

Hamlin, Shelley AMERICAN

b. California. World Women's Amateur Team Championship 1966, 1968, 1970; Curtis Cup 1968, 1970; runner-up US Women's Amateur 1969

At her best in strokeplay, Shelley Hamlin first attracted attention by finishing 9th and low amateur in the 1966 Women's Open Championship. In the US Amateur Championship the same year she set a qualifying record of 143 which has not been equalled, nor has her final round of 70. Her 72 in each of the last two rounds of the 1968 World Team Championship in Melbourne was the lowest and helped the United States to victory. She turned professional in 1972.

Hanger Hill GC ENGLAND

One of several old courses buried by London's suburban sprawl. For many years it was one of the leading clubs of West London but building developments forced it to close in the early 1930s. It was notable for its connection with George Duncan who was professional there when he won the British Open in 1920. He served the club from 1907 to 1924, when he moved to Wentworth.

Hannigan, Frank AMERICAN

Assistant Executive Director of the United States Golf Association. A native of Staten Island who learned golf on that island's Silver Lake course, he graduated from Wagner College there in 1951, and worked as a general reporter for the Staten Island *Advance* before joining the outside world and the USGA in 1961. Very soon he established himself as one of the least insular young administrators in American sport. At the USGA he served first as Public Information Manager and then as Tournament Relations Manager before being appointed to his present position in 1969. Hannigan is that rare man in contemporary American sports – an intellectual with a flair for the practical and an easy, engaging manner. A low-handicap golfer, he plays his golf at Somerset Hills.

Handicapping

Golf is the only game in which the best player in the world can take on the worst and still have a real contest. This is because of its special system of handicapping which was introduced to act as the yardstick by which the competence of every golfer could be measured. Handicaps are largely a matter for amateur players, although when professionals compete with amateurs, they play off a stipulated handicap (usually scratch or plus two). When they play among themselves in unofficial matchplay, the match may be based on a mutually agreed stroke difference. For the average amateur golfer, however, his handicap is a matter for concern, pride, frustration and even of status.

There are many handicapping systems, all too intricate to explain in detail here. Each country is free to adopt any system it wishes and considerable variation exists. For instance, American golfers, more strokeplay conscious than most, are assessed on an average of their scores which they record for each round. In Britain, apart from the low handicap players in what is known as Category One, the system is more rough and ready because some players rarely, if ever, make a medal return, the only true basis of handicapping.

Nevertheless the fundamental principle of handicapping is nearly universal. Each course is given a standard scratch score (SSS) or course rating and each individual's handicap is the number of strokes needed to reduce his score for the round when playing well, by his standards, to the SSS figure. For instance, if the SSS for a given course is 70 and a player returns scores of 88, 87 and 89, he will probably be assessed as 18 handicap; if he returns three scores of 70, he will be given scratch.

If a player regularly returns scores lower than the SSS, he will then be given a plus handicap and, in handicap events, has to add that figure to his total for the round, although golfers in this category are usually rare and of international class. Otherwise, men's handicaps vary from plus 4 to 24 and women's handicaps from plus 2 to 36.

Handicaps are revised from time to time. Under some systems adjustments are automatic and if a golfer does not play for a long period his handicap can lapse altogether. In medal play the full handicap is deducted but for matchplay, or under the Stableford system, the allowance is a fraction of the whole. In matchplay it is three quarters of the difference of handicaps; under the Stableford system it is seven eighths; in foursomes matchplay it is three eighths of the combined total; and in Stableford foursomes it is seven sixteenths of the combined total. Where a fraction results from these calculations the nearest whole number is taken (the higher number in the case of a half: thus $3\frac{1}{2}$ becomes 4).

The reasoning behind this fractional handicapping is that the score returned by longer-handicapped players may contain a higher proportion of strokes spent at a few bad holes and this gives them an advantage in matchplay over lower handicapped players.

Players make mutual adjustments among themselves. They may introduce such refinements as bisques or play the Sunningdale system (doubtless known by other names as well): if the player becomes 2 up in a match, he concedes a stroke at the next hole and goes on doing so until the lead is reduced to 1.

No system is foolproof and handicaps are often abused, 'nursed' or exploited. They are also a ceaseless subject of conversation

Shelley Hamlin playing a wedge shot to the 4th green during the British Ladies' in 1968

Frank Hannigan

and criticism among club players. But when properly applied they work well and remain the framework within which a golfer can challenge any other and, theoretically at least, have an equal chance of victory.

Hanson, Beverly (Mrs Sfingi) AMERICAN
b. 1926. Curtis Cup 1950; US Women's Amateur 1950; USPGA 1955

Beverly Hanson attempted the American-British double but was defeated in the fifth round of the British in 1951 at Broadstone by Jeanne Bisgood. On her return to the United States she turned professional and was LPGA Champion in 1955. Her outstanding season was 1958 when she won the Vare Trophy, the Titleholders' Championship, and was leading money winner. Of tall, wiry build, she uses her exceptional height and reach to fullest advantage, and hits the ball tremendous distances.

Harbert, Melvin R. AMERICAN
b. Dayton, Ohio, 1915. Michigan Open 1937, 1942, 1949; Texas Open 1942; Ryder Cup 1949 (captain 1955); World (Canada) Cup 1954; runner-up USPGA 1947, 1952

Chick Harbert was a powerful figure in tournament golf for two decades. He was a strong, if sometimes wild, driver, and an outstanding matchplayer. The two USPGA finals he lost, to Jim Ferrier in 1947 and to Jim Turnesa in 1952, went to the 35th and 36th holes respectively. Although he did not complete his studies at Michigan State

University, he is an articulate man who served for four years on the PGA tournament committee in a difficult period, 1946-50, when an abortive attempt was made to stage a players' revolt. For two of those years he acted as chairman. In Michigan he reigned supreme, first winning the State's Open Championship as an amateur aged 22,

his score of 268 constituting at the time a record low score over four rounds. He won some half a dozen tournaments including the Texas Open when he beat Hegan in a play-off.

Harbour Town GC USA
Hilton Head Island, S. Car., 18 holes; 6,655 yd (6,085 m) par 71

In American terms, golf architect Pete Dye is an anachronism in an age of 7,000 yd courses and vast greens. He prefers to make courses short, tight, challenging, interesting and perhaps unusual. He has done all this on Hilton Head Island, off the South Carolina coast.

Harbour Town's greens are generally small, its fairways narrow, and its finishing hole is among the most challenging in American golf. This is a 458 yd (419 m) par 4 calling for two shots across the waters of Calibogue Sound to a smallish green. A lighthouse sits as a backdrop across another arm of the sound. Jack Nicklaus, who assisted Dye in the design, describes the course as having some features of Pebble Beach, Scioto, Merion and Pine Valley. Much of it though, is pure South Carolina with fairways lined with deep green magnolias draped with spidery Spanish moss. Dye insists on a naturalness in his courses. much as Donald Ross did.

At Harbour Town there are no elevated greens or tees; they are blended into the natural contours. Dye has brought a little bit

of Scotland into his design. Railroad ties (sleepers) have been used to shore up the faces of some bunkers, and in a number of places, vast untended areas of bare earth may be seen.

Hardman, Ronald Hoyle BRITISH
b. Bury, Lancashire, 1899. Lancashire Amateur 1923, 1927, 1930; semi-finalist British Amateur 1925; Walker Cup 1928

Harmon, Eugene Claude AMERICAN
b. Savannah, Ga., 1916. Florida Junior 1933; Club Champions' Tourney 1936; semi-finalist USPGA 1945, 1948, 1953; Metropolitan Professional 1946; Westchester Open 1946-7, 1969; US Masters 1948; tied 3rd US Open 1959

Although he had an excellent record in the championships Harmon was principally a club professional and gained the reputation of being a fine teacher and a fine developer of young professionals. Despite the time he devoted to his club jobs, he kept his game sharp enough to win the Masters in 1948 and to make several serious threats

in the US Open and the USPGA. He reached the semi-finals of the latter event three times. Harmon has three sons; all are first-class players and of them one was appointed to teach the king of Morocco.

Harper, Chandler AMERICAN
b. Portsmouth, Va. Virginia State Amateur 1930, 1933-4; USPGA 1950; Ryder Cup 1955; World Senior Champion 1968

Chandler Harper was only 17 when he won the Virginia Amateur Championship for the first time. He turned professional three years later and had a long career without any national success until he won the USPGA title in 1950. After gaining a place in the Ryder Cup team in 1955 at the

Beverly Hanson

Chick Harbert

Chandler Harper

age of 41, he concentrated on his work as resident professional at the Bide-a-Wee Club. He was World Senior Champion in 1968 and he set a USPGA record of 259 in winning the 1954 Texas Open.

Harradine, Donald Leslie BRITISH
b. Enfield, Middlesex, 1911

Donald Harradine's introduction to golf came through his stepfather, A. Hockey, who was professional at Harrods, the London department store. Harradine learned the skills of the trade including club-making and, through his stepfather, was given the job of reconstructing the course at Bad Ragaz, Switzerland, in 1930. He showed an obvious aptitude for the work and a liking for the Swiss air. He stayed as professional and greenkeeper before branching out on his own into construction, maintenance and design all over the Continent, although mainly in Switzerland where he made his home. After World War II he set up his own firm, and with notable exceptions such as the construction of the Swiss State Sports School, specialized as a golf-course architect. Of the courses he designed he is most proud of Varese in Italy, Glyfada in Greece, and Valbonne near Cannes.

A founder member of the British Association of Golf Course Architects, he has done good work in encouraging and raising the standard of greenkeeping throughout Europe.

Harriman, H. M. AMERICAN
First homebred golfer to win the US Amateur Championship. At Onwentsia in 1899 Harriman, of the Knollwood CC, White Plains, N.Y., beat Findlay Douglas in the final by 3 and 2.

Harris, John D. BRITISH
b. Chobham, Surrey, 1912

One of the first British course architects to see the possibilities beyond the confines of Europe, Harris claims to have worked on more than 300 courses throughout the world. He has been a low handicap golfer and is a civil engineer. He designed his first golf course when at the Nautical College, Pangbourne, Berkshire, when he was 17, but only turned full-time to golf-course design in 1957 after leaving the family firm. One feature of his design is his bunkers: he sets out to make them obvious and thus fair to the golfer, but also attractive by cutting them out of a graceful mound and filling them with fine white sand. He also believes in the prolonged tee which will adapt a hole to all categories of player. Some of his principal courses overseas are Tobago GC, Runaway

Bay in Jamaica, Royal Canberra, Fujipoka in Japan, and Wairakei in New Zealand.

Harris, Labron, Jr AMERICAN
b. Stillwater, Okla., 1941. Oklahoma Amateur 1962; US Amateur 1962; Oklahoma Open 1963; Walker Cup 1963; Robinson Classic 1971

A product of Oklahoma State University where his father was golf coach, Harris won the 1962 US Amateur, overcoming on his way to the final such players as Richard Sikes, Homero Blancas, and Billy Joe Patton. In the final he was 5 down to Downing Gray at lunch, but got back onto terms with better than par golf, and after a break at the 33rd hole to be introduced to

President Eisenhower, beat Gray by one hole. He turned professional in 1964 and started to compete while still studying for his degree in statistics. He achieved this, but knew some lean years before finally breaking through in 1971, when he won his first tournament and finished in the top 60 for the first time. In 1970 he collected his biggest prize – $34,000 for finishing 2nd in the Dow Jones Classic, more than he had won in the previous years put together.

Harris, Mrs Marley (Mrs A. D. Spearman) BRITISH
b. 1928. Commonwealth Tournament 1959, 1963; Curtis Cup 1962, 1964; British Ladies' 1961-2; Golf Writers' Trophy 1962; New Zealand Strokeplay 1963; Astor Princes Trophy 1964-5; English Ladies' 1964

Marley Spearman's rise to champion is a remarkable tale. She did not take up the game until a stage career ended when she was 22. Her introduction to golf came by chance. One day in 1950, after shopping in Harrods, her attention was caught by a

Top, H. M. Harriman

Above, John D. Harris

Top, Labron Harris

Above, Mrs Marley Harris

notice about the golf school run by this London store. She was curious and interested enough to take an instant lesson. From this grew a deeper fascination. So rapid was her progress that within two years she played in the English Ladies' Championship at Westward Ho!, an advance achieved by exceptional dedication and long hours of practice in the garage of her London home.

To a perfectionist attitude she added the achievement of an eminently sound game; its strength was her fairway woods aided by beautiful balance and poise that owed much to her serious training as a dancer. It demanded constant practice. As significant as her strokemaking ability was a will to compete and win that was deceptively strong in a person of great charm. She was for a time the best woman golfer in Britain.

She won her first British Ladies' title by beating Diane Robb by 7 and 6 at Carnoustie in 1961. She became the first person to defend it successfully for 30 years when she beat her friend and rival, Angela Bonallack, in a marvellous match at Birkdale by 1 hole. In 1964 she defeated Mary Everard by 6 and 5 for the English title at Royal Lytham.

In the 1964 Curtis Cup match at Royal Porthcawl she gave Britain an inspiring lead, winning both her foursomes matches with Mrs Bonallack and achieving two mighty halves against Barbara McIntyre and JoAnne Gunderson (Mrs D. R. Carner). Her record in strokeplay was equally impressive but, before her retirement from competitive golf, she also established a formidable record in foursomes events of various kinds. With her departure from the scene went also a sense of gaiety which has not been replaced.

Harris, Robert BRITISH
b. Dundee 1882. Walker Cup 1922-3, 1926; British Amateur 1925, runner-up 1913, 1923

Robert Harris was one of the best amateurs of his generation. Well known since the early days of the century, particularly round London, where he was a stockbroker, this Scotsman twice reached the final of the Amateur Championship, losing to two redoubtable opponents, Harold Hilton and Roger Wethered. He won the Dundee *Evening Telegraph* Cup, something of a forerunner to the Scottish Amateur Championship, and was exceedingly hard to beat round his home course at Woking where his rather short but accurate game, in which he hit the ball with draw from an open stance, was often devastating.

He was brought up at Carnoustie, wedded to the belief that one should 'learn it first and think about it afterwards'. Very much a player of pre-World War I vintage, people

were beginning to think he might never win the Amateur Championship but his year came at Westward Ho!, in 1925 when he was 43. His victory in the final over Kenneth Fradgley by 13 and 12 was exceeded in severity only by Lawson Little in 1934. Harris played a notable part in the early days of the Walker Cup. It was his eleventh-hour illness of 1922 which caused him to be replaced as player and captain by Bernard Darwin. In 1926 he beat Jesse Guilford in the singles by 3 and 1.

Harrison, Ernest Joe AMERICAN
b. Conway, Ark., 1910. Semi-finalist USPGA 1937; Bing Crosby Tournament 1939; Texas Open 1939, 1951; Mississippi Open 1940; Ryder Cup 1947, 1949, 1951; Western Open 1953; Vardon Trophy 1954; All American Open 1956; Tijuana Open 1958

Dutch Harrison won many tournaments in a career of nearly 40 years, was regarded as one of the finest American golfers, but never achieved victory in a major championship. He gained the Vardon Trophy in 1954 and tied for 3rd place in the 1960 US Open. In 1962 he was voted into the PGA Hall of Fame.

Harrison began as a caddie at Little Rock CC in 1925, chipping with a club fashioned from a cypress root, and turned professional in 1930. He played left-handed for two years, winning a local tournament, before changing to right-handed golf. After a long struggle he finally came into the limelight in 1939 by winning the Bing Crosby Tournament and the Texas Open and reaching the semi-finals of the USPGA. After three years as an Air Corps staff sergeant in World War II, Harrison rejoined the tour and became a consistent winner for the next 15 years, achieving more than one tournament victory in a number of them. He finished 4th

in the 1950 Open at Merion, a final round of 76 leaving him 1 stroke behind the three leaders.

It is recorded of Dutch Harrison that once, after playing with the Duke of Windsor in Florida, he slapped the prince on the back and exclaimed 'Attaboy, Dukie!'.

Hartley Brothers BRITISH
William Lister, b. Beckenham, Kent, 1904. Semi-finalist British Amateur 1930; Walker Cup 1932
Rex W. Walker Cup 1930, 1932

The Hartley brothers were prominent in British Amateur golf between the wars and in 1932 provided the only recorded instance of brothers playing in the same Walker Cup team.

Haskell, Coburn AMERICAN
b. Boston, Mass., 1868; d. 1922.

A nondescript player from Cleveland, where he had moved in 1892, Haskell was the inventor of the rubber-wound ball which replaced the old gutty and revolutionized the game. Haskell, believing that a better ball than the gutty could be found, experimented with a softer, more resilient substitute and found the answer when visiting a friend at the Goodrich Rubber Company's plant in Akron, Ohio. There he saw some thin rubber strips and had the notion of wrapping round them an elastic core under tension. He and his friend Bertram Work submitted their specifications to the US Patent Office in 1898 and, after a few modifications to the outside cover and the depth of the dimples, the advantages of the new ball became obvious. It flew a good 20 yd further than the gutty. Though a number of older golfers were slow to be convinced that its introduction was good for the game, the Goodrich Rubber Company brought it into production and gradually perfected it.

Its first great success was Walter Travis's victory in the US Amateur Championship of 1901 and the following spring it invaded England. John Ball was one of those responsible for persuading Sandy Herd to use it in the Open Championship at Hoylake which Herd eventually won by a single stroke from Harry Vardon who played the old ball. After that its reputation was assured.

Hassanein, Hassan EGYPTIAN
b. Cairo, 1916; d. 1957. Egyptian Open 1949-52; Italian Open 1949; Egyptian Matchplay 1951; French Open 1951; World (Canada) Cup 1955-6

Most famous of all Eygptian golfers and the best ever produced in the Arab world, Hassanein started his career as a barefoot

Dutch Harrison

caddie at the old Heliopolis sand course. From such humble beginnings he developed into a top-class international professional, successful in tournaments in Britain, the United States and at home in Egypt where he was equally adept on grass or sand.

In winning the Egyptian Open four times, he beat many of the leading British players and in the final of the 1951 Egyptian Matchplay Championship, he defeated the distinguished Australian, Norman von Nida.

As well as capturing the Italian Open at Villa d'Este and the French Open at Saint-Cloud, he reached the last day three times in the British Open Championship, including 1953 when he finished 17th behind Ben Hogan at Carnoustie. He played for Egypt in the Canada Cup at Wentworth and Washington, and in George May's World Championship at Tam O'Shanter, Chicago, on three occasions. He won the Desert Open every year from 1946 to 1956, except 1955 when he failed by 1 stroke in the annual 72-hole event at the Maadi Sporting Club course near Cairo.

His tragic death in 1957, the result of a kerosene cooking stove exploding as he primed it, deprived Egypt and the golfing world of a notable personality.

Havers, Arthur Gladstone BRITISH
b. Norwich, Norfolk, 1898. Northern Open 1921-2; British Open 1923; Ryder Cup 1926-7, 1931, 1933

Arthur Havers, now retired in his native East Anglia, was the first leader of the younger school of British professionals who took over from Duncan and Mitchell and were later to include Henry Cotton. A tall, free-swinging player noted particularly for the precision of his iron play, Havers had 'blooded' himself in the 1914 Open when only 16 and rapidly moved to the front after the war. He had the satisfaction of winning

the British Open at Troon in 1923 with one stroke to spare from Walter Hagen, the defending champion, and in a great last-round struggle proved that courage and determination lay behind a courteous and charming exterior.

Hawkins, Fred AMERICAN
b. Antioch, Ill., 1923. Oklahoma City Open 1956; Ryder Cup 1957; Jackson Open 1958; New Mexico Open 1961

Although one of the most consistent players on the circuit, Hawkins won only one tour event in some 15 years, the Oklahoma City Open of 1956. He was twice a quarter-finalist in the USPGA Championship, tied 2nd in the 1958 US Masters, and was the only American to win his singles match in the 1957 Ryder Cup. Hawkins was chairman of the PGA Tournament Commitee in 1955-6.

Hawtree, Frederick George BRITISH
b. 1883; d. 1955

After serving with the Royal Army Ordnance Corps during World War I, F. G. Hawtree formed the golf-course construction firm of Hawtree and J. H. Taylor (1922) which was subsequently responsible for 55 new courses, besides remodelling work that included Royal Birkdale's conversion to championship quality in 1932.

Hawtree began his work at Croham Hurst near London in 1912, when he became founder and later president of the British Golf Greenkeepers' Association. He interested himself in many organizations and led the way in dispelling the belief that golf was a rich man's game. He was co-founder with J. H. Taylor of the Artisan Golfers' Association (1921), and the National Association of Public Golf Courses. He was on the board of the Sports Turf Research Institute from its inception in 1929, served on the

English Golf Union council and executive committee 1938-55, and built Britain's first daily-fee public course at Addington Court in 1932.

The courses he designed or altered included Richmond Park, Ipswich, Pallanza (Italy), Båstad (Sweden), Royal Musselburgh, Royal Porthcawl, Rickmansworth Municipal and Royal Birkdale, together with public courses in London, Birmingham, Southampton, St Albans and Worthing.

Hawtree, Frederick William BRITISH
b. Bromley, Kent, 1916

After leaving Oxford in 1938, Fred Hawtree trained as a golf-course architect under his father F. G. Hawtree, but his career was halted by World War II during which he served in the Royal Artillery and was a prisoner of war of the Japanese. It was not until after the war that he made a name of his own, becoming one of Britain's best-known architects and eventually taking over the firm his father founded. He also preserved the family connection with the Artisan Golfers' Association, the National

Association of Public Golf Courses and the Sports Turf Research Institute. He served on the Golf Development Council, became editor of *The British Golf Greenkeeper*, was a founder member of the British Association of Golf Course Architects and wrote *Elements of Golf Course Layout and Design* and *Golf Courses* for the Country Landowners' Association.

He has designed over 70 courses in Britain and Continental Europe and has done major and minor work at 400 courses between 1946 and 1973; these include Royal Birkdale, Royal Liverpool, Hillside, Sandiway, Royal St David's, Burnham and Berrow, Lindrick, Bruntsfield and Portmarnock. Two of his most recent projects are

Hassan Hassanein, winner of the 1956 Desert Open

Fred Hawkins

F. W. Hawtree

36-holes at Foxhills, Surrey for Aer Lingus and a course for the Japanese near London.

Hazards

The Rules of Golf define a hazard as: any bunker or water hazard. Bare patches, scrapes, roads, tracks and paths are not hazards.

(a) A 'bunker' is any area of bare ground,

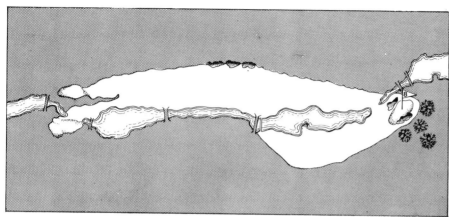

often a depression, which is usually covered with sand. Grass-covered ground bordering or within a bunker is *not* part of the hazard.

(b) A 'water hazard' is any sea, lake,

pond, river, ditch or other open water course (regardless of whether or not it contains water) and anything of a similar nature. All ground or water within the margin of a water hazard, whether or not it be covered with any growing substance, is part of the water hazard. The margin of a water hazard is deemed to extend vertically upwards.

(c) A 'lateral water hazard' is a water hazard or that part of a water hazard running approximately parallel to the line of play and so situated that it is not possible or is deemed by the committee to be impracticable to drop a ball behind the water hazard and keep the spot at which the ball last crossed the hazard margin between the player and the hole.

(d) It is the duty of the committee in charge of a course to define accurately the extent of the hazards and water hazards when there is any doubt. That part of a hazard to be played as a lateral water hazard should be distinctly marked. Stakes and lines defining the margins of hazards are not in the hazards.

Head

The shaped part of the club, attached to the shaft, which strikes the ball.

Head-up

The oldest and commonest fault in the game. The player, anxious to watch the flight of the ball, takes his eye off it too soon with the result that the ball is either missed altogether or mis-hit.

Heafner, Clayton AMERICAN

b. 1914; d. 1960. Ryder Cup 1949, 1951; runner-up US Open 1949, 1951

An ex-Army sergeant from North Carolina, Heafner gained a reputation for unpredictability and was also once described

as the angriest man in golf, but without winning a championship he made his mark in the US Open in more ways than one. He first came to the public eye in the Open of 1939 when he shot a third round 66, the lowest of that championship. It raised him into a tie for 2nd place at that stage, but his last round of 80 dropped him right out of contention. Heafner's first major tourna-

ment victory was in the Jacksonville Open of 1948 when he won a long duel of low scoring with the Open Champion, Lew Worsham. Worsham appeared to have won the tournament but called a penalty stroke on himself when the ball moved as he addressed it on the last green. After an 18-hole play-off which left them still level, Heafner won at the third extra hole. In the 1951 Open he was tied with Hogan with one round to play, but Hogan returned an unanswerable 67 in the final round and won by 2 strokes. Heafner played in two Ryder Cup matches and was unbeaten in four contests. In 1951 he halved with Fred Daly. In that match he was laid a stymie by the Irishman which is believed to be the last on record: stymies were abolished six weeks later.

Hebert, Junius Jay AMERICAN

b. St Martinville, La., 1923. Bing Crosby National 1957; Texas Open 1957; Lafayette Open 1958; Orange County Open 1959; Ryder Cup 1959, 1961, (non-playing captain 1971); USPGA 1960; American Golf Classic 1961; Houston Classic 1961

The USPGA Champion of 1960 and one of the best-liked players on the tour during the late 1950s and 1960s. A sound swinger he labelled himself a poor chipper and putter and it was this perhaps that kept him from reaching heights predicted for him. Jay Hebert enlisted in the US Marines in World War II, rose to the rank of lieutenant and was

Hazard *(centre)*: Bob Charles looking for his ball in a water-filled bunker during the 1968 Alcan

Above, Charles Crombie's cartoon on a golf rule concerning a hazard

Top, Water Hazard: the 8th hole at Nueva Andulucía, Spain

Clayton Heafner

wounded at Iwo Jima. After the war he attended Louisiana State University, graduated in 1948 and turned professional in the same year. After several years as a club professional, during which period he seldom competed, he became a full-time tournament player in 1956 and was a consistent money winner for the next decade. Besides his seven tournament victories he finished 2nd 16 times in his first 10 years on the tour. He was chairman of the PGA Tournament Committee in 1957-8 and 1963-4.

Hebert, Lionel AMERICAN

b. Lafayette, La., 1928. Ryder Cup 1957; USPGA 1957: Tucson Open 1958; Cajun Classic 1960; Memphis Open 1962

Winner of the 1957 USPGA Championship, the last year the event was settled by matchplay. His time on the professional tour roughly parallels that of his brother Jay. Lionel Hebert took a degree in music at Louisiana State University and was runner-up in the Louisiana Amateur before turning professional in 1950. The PGA

triumph was his first tournament victory, although he subsequently won other tour events and played for many more years. He was chairman of the PGA Tournament Committee in 1962-3.

Heel

That part of the face of a club nearest the shaft. 'Hitting it out of the heel' is a common fault: the ball does not travel as well as when hit out of the middle.

Hell

Perhaps the most notorious and certainly the most aptly named bunker in the world. It is situated on the 14th hole of the Old Course at St Andrews, where nearly all the bunkers are named, and guards the straight approach to the green. It has to be carried or skirted and although the hole is not quite so formidable as in the days of the hickory, it has claimed many distinguished victims, including Gene Sarazen when he might have won the 1933 British Open. Unlike most bunkers at St Andrews, Hell is unusually large, involving a big stroke, more often than not with wood, to carry over it. P. G. Wodehouse invented the metaphor, 'His spirits rose like a good niblick out of Hell Bunker'.

Helme, Eleanor E. BRITISH

b. 1887; d. 1967

Author, journalist and naturalist. Eleanor Helme covered women's golf for the *York-*

shire Post, the *Morning Post* and the *Daily Telegraph*. She was organizer of the British Girls' Championship from 1924 to 1938, when the competition was held under the aegis of the *Gentlewoman*, then of *Eve* and the *Bystander*. Her books on golf include *After The Ball*, *The Lady Golfers' Tip Book* and *Family Golf*.

She was herself a golfer of above average merit and played for England in international matches. With T. A. Torrance she won the inaugural Worplesdon Open Mixed Foursomes in 1921. Their opponents in the final were Joyce and Roger Wethered. She also reached the semi-finals of the 1924 British Ladies' Championship.

Henning, Harold SOUTH AFRICAN

b. Johannesburg, Transvaal, 1934. South African Open 1957, 1962; Texas Open 1966; South African PGA 1972

One of four golfing brothers, all professionals, he has enjoyed success in many countries. Henning turned professional in 1953 and went to Britain in the late 1950s. He won the South African Open Championship in 1957 and 1962 and tried his hand on the American circuit as early as 1960: but he found it hard and unrewarding at the start. He lost his inspired putting touch, with its stiff pendulum style and his game was in a depressed state; but from 1963, when he won £10,000 for holing in one during a tournament at Moor Park, Henning, one of the most popular professionals, enjoyed much greater success.

He won the Texas Open in 1966, tied for the Los Angeles Open of 1969, and generally found his visits vastly more profitable. He continued to play in Britain from time to time, finishing equal 3rd in the Open at St Andrews with Lee Trevino in 1970, 2 shots behind Nicklaus and Sanders. He won a number of Continental Open championships and represented South Africa many times in the Canada and World Cup, winning a handsome victory with Gary Player in Madrid in the autumn of 1965. He went into semi-retirement in 1972 but in November won the South African PGA Championship.

Herd, Alexander BRITISH

b. St Andrews, Fife, 1868; d. London, 1944. British Open 1902, runner-up 1892, 1895, 1910, 1920; British Professional Matchplay 1906, 1926, runner-up 1909

Somewhat overshadowed by the Big Three of his age – Vardon, Braid and Taylor – Sandy Herd was nonetheless a great golfer, and a man of character besides – downright, independent, uncompromising and lovable. In addition to winning the 1902 Open, in which in the nick of time he had the shrewdness to adopt the Haskell ball that had just made its appearance, he was 2nd four times. He represented Scotland against England 10 times between 1903 and 1913.

Herd came to Hoylake for the 1902 Open

Top, Junius Jay Hebert

Above, Lionel Hebert

Above, Harold Henning displays his trophy after winning the 1965 Canada Cup with Gary Player

disliking the new-fangled rubber-core ball, but in a practice round before the Open with John Ball, he received a practical demonstration of its qualities and was converted to its use. His victory was attributed largely to the new ball, for at that time he was not seriously looked on as a potential winner. The story of that championship was one of a battle between Herd and Vardon who started out with a brilliant 72, in spite of putting two balls out of bounds at the 1st. But the great man's putting let him down, and coming to the last hole, where he needed a 4 to tie, he took a miserable 3 putts. In 1895 Herd looked certain to be the winner but a rainstorm ruined his chances, and Taylor came in ahead of him after the storm had cleared.

Apart from bad luck, Herd was a shade too eager in temperament, hearing the bells of victory ringing prematurely and lacking a little of the dour patience that lets it come in its own good time. But he acquired the right temperament later in his career and won the British Professional Matchplay Championship at the age of 58. When nearly 70 he played four rounds in a major tournament at Moor Park in level 4s. He adopted the old-fashioned palm grip, sat well down to the shot, and was distinctive for the number and ferocity of his waggles. In his lifetime he claimed 19 holes in one: two of them when over the age of 60, and thirteen of them at Coombe Hill where he served as professional after being attached to the West Lancashire club, Portrush and Huddersfield.

Herd, Fred AMERICAN
b. St Andrews, Fife, US Open 1898

Winner of the first US Open Championship to be decided over 72 holes. Fred Herd, brother of Sandy, won in June 1898 over the 9-hole course of the Myopia Hunt Club, Hamilton, Mass., which meant that competitors had to play eight times round in two days. His score was 328 (84, 85, 75, 84).

Herron, S. Davidson AMERICAN
US Amateur 1919

Davy Herron defeated Bobby Jones by 5 and 4 in the final of the 1919 US Amateur at Oakmont, Pa. It was a notable performance on three counts. At 20, he was one of the youngest winners; he won playing over his own course; and he was one of the few to inflict such a heavy defeat on Jones, although this was before Jones's 'break-through'; Herron was 4 under 4s when he won.

Hezlet, Lieut. Col. Charles Owen IRISH
b. 1891, d. 1965. Runner-up British Ama-

Top, Fred Herd

Above, Davy Herron

teur 1914; Walker Cup 1924, 1926, 1928; Irish Open Amateur 1926, 1929, runner-up 1923, 1925

Charles Hezlet was in every sense a giant of golf. He was well proportioned, had a determined attacking style and could hit with plenty of power. His stance was the widest ever known in first-class golf. Al-

though he did not gain a title outside his native Ireland he made many international appearances. Later in life he was a valued and respected legislator.

Hezlet served in World War I, winning the DSO, and in the Royal Artillery in World War II. He came of a golfing family: his mother helped to form the Ladies' Golf Union; May and Florence Hezlet were his sisters.

Hezlet, May (Mrs A. E. Ross) IRISH
b. 1882. British Ladies' 1899, 1902, 1907, runner-up 1904; Irish Ladies' 1899, 1904-6, 1908, runner-up 1898

May Hezlet established herself in the forefront of women's golf by winning the Irish Ladies' and the British Ladies' Championships in 1899. She carried off the double in consecutive weeks and on the same course, Royal County Down. In the weekend between the two championships she celebrated her 17th birthday, and became the youngest winner of the Irish and British titles. Her record still stands.

She won two of her three British Championships at Royal County Down, and two of her five Irish Championships over that course. In four finals, all of which she won, she was opposed by her sister, Florence Hezlet (Mrs Cramsie). They met in the British in 1907, and three times in the Irish, in 1905, 1906, and 1908.

May Hezlet was one of the players in the historic match at Royal Cromer in 1905

when the best of the British golfers played the visiting Americans. Her opponent on that occasion was Margaret Curtis, one of the donors of the Curtis Cup.

Hickory
The wood from which the shafts of golf clubs used to be made. It was replaced by

Hickory: Max Faulkner using a hickory-shafted putter

steel (legalized by the Royal and Ancient in 1929). Bobby Jones, however, won all his championships with hickory-shafted clubs, including 1930, the year of the Impregnable Quadrilateral.

With hickory shafts golf was a different game. They had torsion: when swung they would twist as well as bend. They could also be trimmed by sandpapering to give exactly the sort of feel a player wanted. Hickory-shafted putters are still produced. The hickory is indigenous to eastern North America.

Hill, Dave AMERICAN

b. Jackson, Mich., 1937. Vardon Trophy 1969; Ryder Cup 1969, 1973; 2nd leading money winner 1969; runner-up US Open 1970

Although he turned professional in 1958 and joined the tour a year later, it took Dave Hill several years to become successful. He won occasional tournaments before 1969, but regarded that year as the end of a five-year slump and credited the change to an enforced two-month lay-off when his wife locked his clubs in a neighbour's garage.

After that he won the Memphis Open, the Buick Open and the Philadelphia Classic and at one stage was the only three-time winner for the year. More important in the long run, he won the Harry Vardon Trophy with a strokeplay average of 70.344 for 90 rounds. He played in the Ryder Cup match at Birkdale in the autumn of 1969 and had another good year in 1970 when he finished

2nd to Tony Jacklin in the US Open at Hazeltine. His openly expressed criticism of the course at the time resulted in a fine, nor was that the only occasion on which the sharpness of his tongue has landed him in trouble. Another somewhat lean spell was ended by his victory in the Monsanto Open in April 1972.

Top, Hickory: Tony Jacklin and Dave Marr (left) reconstruct for a TV network what golf looked like a hundred years ago

Above, Dave Hill

Hill, George Alec BRITISH

b. Northwood, Middlesex, 1908. Semi-finalist British Amateur 1936; Walker Cup 1936, (non-playing captain 1955); captain Royal and Ancient 1964-5

Ever since he emerged as a boy golfer, Alec Hill has been a well-known figure in British amateur golf. His performance in reaching the semi-finals of the 1936 British Amateur at Carnoustie, in which he lost to Jim Ferrier, was an important factor in his selection for England in 1936 and 1937, and for the Walker Cup team in 1936. The match was played at Pine Valley and was notable for a remarkable recovery by Hill and his partner, Cecil Ewing, in the four-somes match against H. L. Givan and George Voigt. Hill and Ewing were 7 down with 11 to play and all square on the 36th tee, having lost a hole in between. The match was halved after the Americans holed a tricky putt on the last green.

Hill, a holder of the DSO, did much hard work on committees of the Royal and Ancient. He was chairman of the Championship Committee in 1955 and in 1964 drove himself into office as captain of the Royal and Ancient, going on the same day to win the King William IV Medal, a unique achievement.

Hillside GC ENGLAND

Southport, Lancashire. 18 holes; 7,064 yd (6,459 m)

Hillside GC was founded in 1912 on land that has long since been used for building. It moved to its present home in 1923 and is one of the rich chain of courses along the Lancashire coast.

It lies sandwiched between Southport and Ainsdale and Royal Birkdale, and for many years suffered when comparisons were made, particularly with Birkdale. These were a little unfair as Hillside has always been a good test. In 1962 it staged the tournament in which Jack Nicklaus made his first appearance in Britain as a professional. From 1967, when the course underwent major reconstruction, it has been fit to rank with any of its championship neighbours.

The early holes, influenced as at Formby, though on the hooking side, by a railway running parallel, remain the same, but the course has gained much class by the stiffness of the inward half fashioned out of majestic dune country alongside Royal Birkdale. Much earth moving was necessary, but the cost of building the new holes, essentially seaside in character, was met by the sale of the plentiful supplies of sand that the area offers. Thus a new Hillside was born with the help of Fred Hawtree, who made skilful

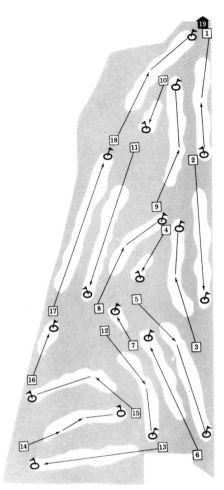

9, it is recognized as one of the country's main courses and is a regular venue for national and provincial tournaments.

The club also believes itself to be the home of the only other Ryder Cup. In 1933, Samuel Ryder, donor of the famous Ryder Cup, presented a cup, still played for, to Hillside for competition among the farming community of the region.

Hilton, Harold Horsfall BRITISH
b. West Kirby, Cheshire, 1869; d. 1942. British Open 1892, 1897, joint 3rd 1911; St George's Cup 1893-4; Irish Open 1897, 1900-2; British Amateur 1900-1, 1911, runner-up 1890-1, 1896; US Amateur 1911

Born the same year as the formation of Royal Liverpool, the club of which he became such a distinguished member, Hilton won two championships before he succeeded in winning the first of his four Amateurs.

Strokeplay was considered to be his strongest suit, but since he won four British Amateur Championships and the American Amateur Championship, he can hardly be said to have been lacking as a match-player. He was also runner-up three times in the British Amateur.

His victories in the Open came in 1892 when the event was extended for the first year to 72 holes, and in 1897 when it first visited Hoylake. On that occasion, he was 1 stroke behind James Braid at the halfway stage. Both had bad third rounds, Hilton taking 84; but it was his 75 in the final round that restored him to the lead. He passed the time waiting to see if Braid would catch his total of 314 by playing billiards, then came out to see Braid, needing a 3 to tie, strike a magnificent second which almost hit the flagstick but rolled too far past.

Hilton may have been overshadowed in his day by John Ball and Freddie Tait, both fine matchplayers, finding Tait in particular hard to beat; but he did not lack courage. There have been greater hitters of the ball, but not many, and very few brought to the game he adored so acute and lively an intelligence. He is also the only British player ever to have won the US Amateur, his victory coming at the 37th hole at Apawamis against F. Herreshoff. He did not stand above 5 ft 7 in, but he was powerfully built. He had an explosively fast swing, jumping onto his toes just before he began it. He looked like a schoolboy having a really good smack at the ball, but like all those who had learned to play at Hoylake, he had great control. He also had an extremely good touch with the putter, rolling the ball with topspin up to the hole.

He was a scientific player, with a deep

knowledge of technique; he was also a master of backspin, able to improvise shots which he perfected through long hours of practice. He was the author of several books, notable among them being *My Golfing Reminiscences*, and he was also for a time editor of *Golf Illustrated*.

Hilversum GC NETHERLANDS
Hilversum. 18 holes

Situated 1½ miles southeast of Hilversum and 20 miles from Amsterdam, the Hilversumsche GC was founded in 1910. It moved to its present home in 1917. The course was extended from 9 to 18 holes some 11 years later. This original layout has been altered several times. On the most recent occasion, in 1952, the British architect expressed the view that the alterations helped to bring the Hilversumsche into 'the forefront of modern courses'. All the reconstruction was carried out by the club's greenkeeping staff and completed in two years. Championships were then resumed there, the Dutch Opens of 1957 and 1962 being won by the British professionals John Jacobs and Brian Huggett.

The club has been unlucky with its clubhouses. Two were burned down; the replacement for the second was ready in time for the 1968 Dutch Open.

This is a typical Dutch inland course: the land is flat and sandy, the trees abundant.

Hindu GC ARGENTINA
Buenos Aires. 27 holes

The Hindu club was founded in 1916 although golf has only been included in its sporting activities since 1938, when 168 acres (68 ha) were bought on the site where the Don Torcuato GC had its 18 holes. There is a huge clubhouse composed of two buildings, and also apartments and many weekend houses owned by members at the new course.

Hirono GC JAPAN
Kobe. 18 holes; 6,950 yd (6,314 m); par 72

Built in 1932 in a suburban area that can be reached by car from Kobe in 30 minutes, Hirono has played host many times to major tournaments, both amateur and professional, in its 40-year history. The course was designed by C. H. Alison, the veteran English architect who had come to Japan earlier to lay out Tokyo GC's new course. When he was first guided over the site by the committee that had selected it he was struck by the resemblance of the scenery to parts of Scotland. On completion of the course he ventured the opinion that, both for scenery, and as a challenge to golfing skill, Hirono would stand comparison with

use of the great opportunity offered and soon Hillside was in demand for championships: the English Open Amateur Strokeplay Championship was held there in 1971; and later the same summer the new course was used for the first time for the pre-qualifying rounds of the Open Championship, only five players breaking 70 over the two days.

Hillside GC RHODESIA
Umtali. 18 holes

One of the oldest clubs in Rhodesia, Hillside lies 3,500 ft above sea level at Umtali in the mountainous Eastern Highlands. The club was formed in 1905 but the land was later taken over for industrial sites and in 1911 a number of members broke away and started building the present course which has remained very largely unaltered. A new clubhouse was built in the late 1920s and now serves some 250 active golfing members. Grass greens were first laid out in the early years of World War II. In 1958 the clubhouse was greatly increased in size for the Central African Championships. With an extremely tight and difficult tree-lined first

The course plan of Hillside GC

St George's Hill, Surrey, or America's Pine Valley. Suffice to say that no golfer who has played at Hirono has ever questioned its claim to have the finest layout in all Japan.

The terrain is generally flat, but there are many deep streams that criss-cross some of the fairways; also numerous ponds, large and small, that lend individuality and rich variety to the holes. Most of the holes are flanked on both sides by pine groves, and the rough is thick and heavy. The bunkers, of which there are many, are of the type that has come to be known to Japanese golfers as the 'Alison bunker', similar to those at Kasumigaseki CC in Tokyo – very deep, especially those guarding the greens.

The most interesting – also awe-inspiring – hole is perhaps the short one that calls for a carry of 160 yd (146 m) all the way over a pond to an elevated green close-guarded by bunkers. Unlike most Japanese courses, Hirono has only one *korai* green for each hole that is used the year round.

World War II was no kinder to Hirono than it was to so many other golf clubs in the country. The club was formally closed on the outbreak of war; one part of the course was turned over to agriculture and another part used as an airstrip by the military. Then at the end of the war there were hundreds of squatters growing food on the unused sections of the course. They refused to move and strenuous negotiations were necessary before the property was recovered for golf and restored to its immaculate pre-war condition.

Hitchcock, James BRITISH
b. Bromley, Kent, 1930. Dunlop Masters 1960; Ryder Cup 1965

Hitchcock, who learned his golf under Dick Burton at Coombe Hill, Surrey, where his father was greenkeeper, had much less success than his dedication to golf and his hard work in practice merited. His best performance was in the Dunlop Masters at Sunningdale in 1960. Four years later he had his best season in British tournaments and won a place in the Ryder Cup team.

Hobart GC, Royal AUSTRALIA
Seven Mile Beach, Hobart, Tasmania. 18 holes; 6,636 yd (6,068 m)

The founding of the Hobart Club dates back to the turn of the century. In 1916 it moved across the Derwent River to Rosny where it remained until its present location was found at Seven Mile Beach, a few miles out of the city.

The club's latest move was necessitated by the post-war development of Hobart's Eastern Shore which produced a dramatic

increase in land values. The site was selected because of many special characteristics, including a sandy soil, availability of water and gentle contours. The presence of a magnificent beach within a short distance and Hobart Airport nearby were added attractions. Royal Hobart's new course (the Royal Charter being conferred upon the Club in 1925) was officially opened on 12 October 1963, by the Governor, Sir Charles Gardiner, and was quickly recognized as a test fit for Australian Championships.

The 1968 Australian Amateur was won there by a Tasmanian, Roy Scott. This was followed in 1969 by the Australian Ladies' Championship and in October 1971 by the Qantas Australian Open, which produced a resounding victory for Jack Nicklaus. His driving down the avenues of blue gum trees was prodigious and led to a record victory margin of 8 strokes. His total was 269 (68, 65, 66, 70).

The club can also boast a number of extremely good players and a fine, modern two-storey clubhouse.

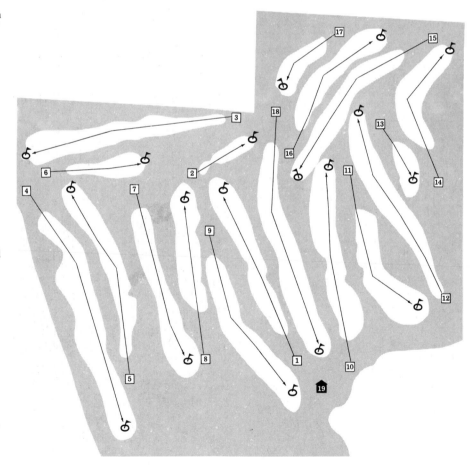

Top, Jimmy Hitchcock   *Above,* the course plan of Royal Hobart GC

Hogan, Benjamin William AMERICAN
b. Dublin, Tex., 1912. USPGA 1946, 1948;
US Open 1948, 1950-1, 1953, runner-up
1955, joint 2nd 1956; US Masters 1951, 1953,
runner-up 1942, 1946, 1954-5; British Open
1953

Hogan is regarded by many as the greatest
player of the modern era. Sarazen, who has
seen all the champions from Vardon to
Jacklin, said 'Nobody covered the flag like
Hogan'. Not a big man (he weighed only
138 lb when he was leading money winner in
1940), he was an extreme perfectionist and
a ruthless competitor. His control was
absolute, his dedication immense. He was
the finest stroke player the game has known,
a legend in his lifetime.

He is one of the four players (the others are
Sarazen, Player and Nicklaus) to have won
all four of the world's major titles and of the
four (with Jones, Sarazen and Trevino) to
have won the British and US Opens in the
same summer. In 14 consecutive US Open
Championships up to 1960, and the same
number of Masters to 1956, he was always
in the first 10, and 18 times was in the first 4:
a superb record of consistency. Hogan also
won 63 tournaments on the American
professional tour.

Golf to him was an intensely serious
business which he practised with a remarkable single-mindedness of purpose. It was
quite simply his profession and he wanted to
play it better than anyone has ever played it.
That he succeeded came as no surprise to
those who knew him. What makes his story
almost incredible was that one foggy morning
in Texas early in 1949 a terrible car accident
practically killed him. If he had not instinc-
tively thrown himself across his wife, Valerie,
to protect her, the steering wheel would
have impaled him. As it was, he lay there
for an hour and a half before an ambulance
arrived and then faced the 150-mile drive
to hospital in El Paso. He suffered multiple
injuries but he kept himself alive with the
same strong will that guided his golf, and was
discharged from hospital one month after
an operation. Though hobbling badly, he
was able to make the trip to England later
that year to captain the American Ryder
Cup team at Ganton.

There had been fears that he might never
play again but, after a gradual return,
Hogan filed an entry in January 1950 for
the Los Angeles Open as an 'experiment' to
see if he could stand the exertion of 72 holes.
The experiment worked; Hogan tied with
Snead for 1st place, and a few months later
accomplished an even more prodigious feat
by winning the US Open at Merion. He tied
with Mangrum and Fazio on 287, his victory

coming after a play-off in which he shot 69
to Mangrum's 73 and Fazio's 75. A year
later he made a successful defence of his
title at Oakland Hills, where his best golf
was brought forth by a feeling that the
architect had gone too far in the severity of
his bunkering and design. 'I vowed that I
would bring this monster to its knees' he said.

As far as major titles were concerned
1952 was a barren year, but this merely
hardened his resolve for 1953, when his
game reached a new peak. In that summer
he won the Masters, the US Open at Oakmont and the British Open at Carnoustie.
That was his first appearance in Britain and
he had needed a good deal of persuasion
before he undertook the trip. He did not

Two typical Ben Hogan shots

like travelling after his accident and stood to
lose more than he could gain but he had
won the Masters at Augusta with the lowest
score in the history of the event at that time,
scored another commanding victory in the
US Open, and something prompted him to try
for the hat trick, winning a victory that gave
him as much satisfaction as any in his career.

Typically, his preparation was immensely
thorough. He arrived two weeks before the
championship, largely to acquaint himself
with the small ball which he had never
played, analysed the course inch by inch,
came through the ordeal of the qualifying
rounds and, in the championship itself, won
by 4 strokes from Frank Stranahan, Dai
Rees, Tony Cerda and Peter Thomson.
Throughout, he was frustrated by his
failure to hole any telling putts. The greens
were heavy and he could not get the ball up
to the hole, but each round was lower than
the one before (73, 71, 70, 68), his 68 being
one of the finest final rounds ever played.
All week, he had been watched by enormous
crowds and, at times, they must have tested
even his powers of concentration.

Stewarding was not the art it has since
become but Hogan was impressed by the
knowledge and enthusiasm of the Scottish
crowd, and touched by their joy at his
success. All British golfers would have loved
to have seen him return more often but his
only other visit was for the 1956 World
(Canada) Cup at Wentworth where, in front
of even bigger crowds, he and Sam Snead
won for the United States and played an
historic first nine holes.

In the years that followed, the fates
taunted Hogan. In his quest to win the US
Open for the fifth time, once more than
Jones, he was more than once thwarted. The
end of 1953 would have been a good time to
retire from competitive golf, for a decline
was bound to set in; but golf was his life,
ambition still burned in him and, most important of all, he probably felt that he had
not yet attained perfection.

For a while his golf faltered, but in the
1955 US Open at the Olympic Club at San
Francisco his fifth victory seemed certain.
There remained only a play-off between
him and an unknown Jack Fleck who somehow had managed to equal the great man's
score over four rounds. Nobody gave Fleck
a chance the following day over another 18
holes but Fleck was round in 69. Hogan took
6 at the 18th, a shortish par 4, finishing 2nd.

A year later, Hogan failed to get the two
pars that would have enabled him to tie
with Cary Middlecoff. He continued to play
in the Open and Masters but, while his long
game remained marvellously controlled he

became plagued by his putting. His agony was pitiful to watch and he undoubtedly suffered on the fast greens at Augusta. On the Open courses, where there is more emphasis on driving, he remained in contention far longer.

In 1960 at Cherry Hills, at the age of 48, he came very close to denying Arnold Palmer his victory, going in the water twice at the last 2 holes. He never came so near again though there was one superb third round of 66 in which he came back in 30, when it seemed as if he might win the 1967 Masters. But, by then, he was beginning to be afflicted by aches and pains and was later operated on for a shoulder injury. He made one or two more appearances to test out his game but he would never have played in public unless certain that he could give lastingly of his best. The white cap, the cold stare, the cigarette, faded quietly out of the limelight. The man who never made any attempt to draw attention to himself either by his dress or actions, or to invite cheap adulation or publicity, retired to his home in Fort Worth.

Hogan's golf was his greatest form of expression and yardstick by which he wanted to be judged. Young golfers of his day, as well as his contemporaries, still talk of him with awe but though they may seek his standards, they never attain them. Hogan's name is a symbol of the limits to which a golfer can go in his search for perfection.

Holderness, Sir Ernest William Elsmie
BRITISH

b. Lahore 1890; d. 1968. President's Putter 1920-3, 1929; British Amateur 1922, 1924; Walker Cup 1923, 1926, 1930

Holderness was a shy, reticent civil servant and one of the most genuine amateurs who ever won a championship. Severe illness while at school caused him to finish his education privately and to take to golf. He played for Oxford for three years from 1910, and after World War I was, for a decade, one of a handful of leading amateurs in Britain. His job in the Home Office and at the Local Government Board kept him fully occupied, and at the time of his two Amateur victories he was hard at work advising the government on private members' bills. He practised golf in the evenings and at weekends (though not on Saturday mornings, when he had to go to his office). He gave up his holidays to play in the Amateur and for practice hit cork balls about his drawing room. Of slight build, especially compared with his two contemporaries, Roger Wethered and Cyril Tolley, Holderness was yet 'all wire and whipcord'. He seldom hit

the ball off line, and one reason for this was, in the opinion of a distinguished coach of those days, Fred Robson, 'that I never once saw him address the ball anything but perfectly'. He was also a fine iron player and capable of deep concentration, which made him a formidable match player. In the relaxed atmosphere of the President's Putter, which in those days attracted as strong if not as large an entry as the Amateur Championship, he was most at home, and won the first four events held, and a fifth in 1929. Anyone who can win two Amateurs in three years must be a quite exceptional golfer, but, although he was a dogged performer, his game did not suggest that he had a great love of the arena.

Hole
The units into which a course is divided; i.e. the part of the course from the tee to the putting surface. Most courses are made up of 9 or 18 holes.

More specifically, hole means the opening $4\frac{1}{4}$ in (107.9 mm) in diameter and at least 4 in (101.6 mm) deep cut in every green, into which the ball is played.

Holed Out
A ball is said to have been holed out when it has been struck into the hole.

Holland see NETHERLANDS

Holm, Mrs A. M. (née Helen Gray)
BRITISH

b. Glasgow 1907; d. Ayr 1971. Scottish Ladies' 1930, 1932, 1937, 1948, 1950, runner-up 1933, 1938, 1949, 1956-7; British Ladies' 1934, 1938; Curtis Cup 1936, 1938, 1948

Helen Holm's exceptional height made her distinctive in any gathering. She was a graceful swinger of the club, a fine iron

player, and particularly effective with the shorter pitching clubs. Like all outstanding women players she was a good putter. She won the British Ladies' Championship twice and the Scottish Ladies' five times, and earned 15 medals in her native championships over a period of 35 years.

Because she put her family first she did not play outside Scotland often; thus she did not go to the United States with the Curtis Cup team because her only son was then an infant.

She captained British teams against France and Belgium in 1949 and 1951, and Scotland in the Home Internationals in 1949. In the autumn of 1951 she had a thrombosis, and although it was thought her golfing days were over, she fought back courageously, and recovered sufficiently to win four more medals in the Scottish.

She played for Britain against the United States three times, against France nine times, and against Belgium once, and for Scotland in the Home Internationals for 13 years.

The first of her Scottish titles was gained at Turnberry in 1930. She did not defend the following year, but regained the championship at Cruden Bay in 1932, playing the longest 18 holes final to date, when she won at the 5th extra hole from Mrs George Coates. A year later she lost her title in the final at the 22nd hole to Miss M. G. Couper. Her third and fourth Scottish championships were won at Gleneagles, in 1937, and 1948, and her fifth at St Andrews in 1950 when her opponent in the final was 62-year-old Mrs Charlotte Beddows, who was also endeavouring to capture the event for the fifth time.

Holmes, Mrs J. C. (née Jean McClure)
BRITISH

b. Wanstead, Essex, 1923. British Ladies' 1946; runner-up English Ladies' 1966

Hole: the legendary Bobby Locke addressing a putt

Holed Out: David Marsh

An attractive, easy swinger, Mrs Holmes (then Mrs G. W. Hetherington) won the British Ladies' Championship at Hunstanton, beating Philomena Garvey in the final by 1 hole. She remained a top-class player for another 25 years, despite limited opportunity for play. She reached the final of the 1966 English Ladies' at Hayling Island, Hampshire, but lost to Julia Greenhalgh. Later she became an England selector.

Homer, Trevor Walter Brian BRITISH
b. Bloxwich, Staffordshire, 1943. British Amateur 1972, 1974; Eisenhower Trophy 1972; Walker Cup 1973

Trevor Homer achieved the distinction of gaining the 1972 British Amateur Championship at Royal St George's without previously having won anything of note – not even his county championship of Staffordshire. He had looked a promising player with a fine strong style for a number of years and was a regular competitor at the major amateur events but, having won his way through to the final at Sandwich, he played wonderfully well in beating Alan Thirlwell

by 4 and 2. His victory led to his selection for the British side against the Continent of Europe, the England team for the Home Internationals, the British Eisenhower Trophy team, and the Walker Cup team, all experience which equipped him for a good display in the 1974 US Masters and a second victory in the British Amateur at Muirfield. This places him in the distinguished bracket of those who have won the title more than once. Within six weeks he turned professional.

Hong Kong GC, Royal
Fanling, Hong Kong. 54 holes

A notice in the local press on 8 May 1889 announced: 'Gentlemen interested in the

Royal and Ancient game of golf are requested to attend a meeting to be held in the Hong Kong Club on Friday May 10th 1889 at 5 p.m. to consider the question of starting a golf links in Hong Kong or Kowloon.' Only 13 enthusiasts attended and, with the exception of Robert Murray Ramsay (then Hong Kong harbourmaster) and Gershom Stewart (later Sir Gershom and Member of Parliament for Hoylake), very few knew much about golf, but they formed the Hong Kong GC. Attempts to find a home on military land in Kowloon on the Mainland failed, but on 30 September 1889 government permission was obtained to use ground at Happy Valley on the Island. It was subject to flooding and was in constant use by the army and navy for polo, football and drill. However, money was raised to make greens and tees. One hole, the 8th, became known as 'Old Misery' on account of the pond which swallowed up balls, scarce at that time.

In 1890 the club easily won an opening match against the Argyll and Sutherland Highlanders. By 1891 membership had

risen to 100. In 1897 Queen Victoria gave permission for the club to be called Royal and negotiations were begun to obtain 16½ acres (6.6 ha) at Deep Water Bay to provide more facilities for ladies' golf, restricted at Happy Valley.

Deep Water Bay, where 9 holes were opened in 1898, is still a charming spot, accessible in early days only by launch. The idea of constructing a golf course at Fanling, 23 miles inland from Kowloon, came from E. R. Halifax, who used to walk over the hills with gun and dog, as recorded in the official history of Royal Hong Kong GC by T. F. R. Waters. Fanling had exciting possibilities and by 1911 a course had been laid out. In earlier days the club had its own Pullman car which, after breakfast had been served on the way up, was unhitched from the 'Taipo Belle'. Members were then run smartly up to the club in rickshaws: which, for the golfers, made a more romantic journey than today's ferry trip and car drive over the hills.

In 1912 a further 55 acres (22.26 ha) were acquired for golf and thereafter other additions were made to the courses and facilities, which eventually achieved a high degree of comfort and included accommodation for members. By 1923 membership had reached 800 and the club continued to thrive in three places – at Fanling; Happy Valley, where a new clubhouse was built in 1930; and at Deep Water Bay. But World War II brought inevitable changes.

By 1940 Fanling had two 18-hole courses and one 9-hole (called the Old, the New and the Eden, after St Andrews) and another 9 was contemplated. With the threat of war, however, the Hong Kong Government took over the course and clubhouse at Deep Water Bay, from October 1941. After the fall of Hong Kong, on Christmas Day 1941, the Japanese occupied both Deep Water Bay and Fanling, where most of the trees were cut down to provide fuel and the greens used for growing vegetables.

The work of rehabilitation needed in the postwar years was immense, and complicated by Fanling's position near the boundary with Communist territory. However, the Royal Hong Kong GC was soon restored to its former glory, a process that took a great deal of energy and money, although it resulted in the loss of Happy Valley after more than half a century. Today the club has three courses.

Honour
The privilege of playing first from the tee. In matchplay, the honour is decided by whichever player won the previous hole, or, if it

Top, Mrs Jean Holmes

Above, Trevor Homer

A scene at the Royal Hong Kong GC

was halved, the last hole to be won.

In strokeplay, the honour is taken by the player or side which last completed a hole in fewer strokes than the paired player.

On the first tee, the honour is taken either in the order of the draw, by the visitors in the case of a team match, by the toss of a coin, or, according to some customs, by the pair or player with the lower handicap.

In all cases, the honour may not be declined, although in matchplay a player has the option of recalling a shot if his opponent has 'stolen' the honour.

Honourable Company of Edinburgh Golfers (Muirfield) SCOTLAND

Muirfield, East Lothian. 18 holes
Muirfield, the third home of the Honourable Company of Edinburgh Golfers, has many claims. It occupies a noble setting on the shores of the Firth of Forth between Gullane Hill and North Berwick; it is the fairest, if not the best, examination of any championship course in Britain; its lay-out is classically simple and convenient; it has been the scene of more championships and international matches than any other course and is generally accepted as the home of the oldest golf clubs in the world.

From the researches of C. B. Clapcott, there are grounds for supposing that, if the Provost of Edinburgh presented a silver club for competition in 1744 among the Gentlemen Golfers of Edinburgh, as they were known in their earliest days, they must have existed before that time but the Honourable Company themselves take the minute recording the Provost's gift, dated 1 May 1744, as their real date of origin.

The Company was formed from a small and select number of enthusiasts under its president, Duncan Forbes of Culloden, who tried to prevent the Clan rising in 1745. It was largely because of his eminence that the silver club was presented by the Lord Provost, who decreed that it should be an annual challenge trophy. It was further stipulated that the winner should hold the title of 'Captain of the Golf' and that, with help, he should settle and determine under the conditions of play then in being 'all disputes touching the Golf among golfers'. The club was therefore responsible for the first set of rules, and in 1754 for the founding of the Royal and Ancient Golf Club of St Andrews whose first rules were almost verbatim with its own.

The Company played on 5 holes over Leith Links and in 1795 its members applied for, and were granted, permission by the Magistrates and Council of the City of Edinburgh to adopt their now familiar title

of the Honourable Company of Edinburgh Golfers. Leith Links was the official home until about 1830 when conditions of play became so difficult that the Company wound up its affairs; but in 1836 it was happily revived, using Musselburgh as its home until it acquired its present site further down the coast at Muirfield in 1891.

A year later the new course was used for the Open Championship which Harold Hilton won and is thus, apart from St Andrews, the senior club still in current use for the championship. In the early days, there were a certain number of derogatory remarks about the course, largely from the traditional lovers of St Andrews, Prestwick and Musselburgh. The Honourable Com-

pany, in leaving Musselburgh, took the championship away from an ancient home and Andrew Kirkaldy described Muirfield as 'an auld water-meadie'. It received other abuse but gradually it gathered a strong army of admirers and, after a series of changes, developed a far more seaside character as some of the sandhills became part of the course. Nowadays, it is bounded by a stone wall on three sides with the dunes and buckthorn to the north. It does not go right down to the sea and the fairways are much flatter than most seaside links but the holes are laid out in two loops of 9, a clockwise outer loop and an anti-clockwise inner loop. This makes it a wonderful 'watching' course and with no more than 3 consecutive

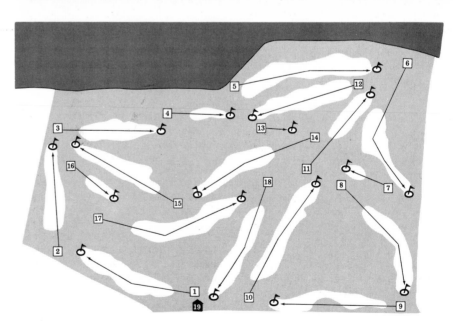

Top, the 8th green at Muirfield, home of the Honourable Company of Edinburgh Golfers; *above*, the plan of the course

holes running the same way, the golfer has a constantly changing battle with the wind.

Its reputation for frankness and honesty stems from the fact that all its hazards are visible and that its many beautifully constructed bunkers seldom allow a bad shot to escape. Bunkers are a great feature of the 8th, which lies alongside Archerfield Wood (this was the Graden Sea Wood of Robert Louis Stevenson's *Pavilion on the Links*), but the terror of the long 9th consists of a formidable drive and a fine second alongside the stone wall on the left. The 10th takes us away from the clubhouse and from the 11th fairway, looking out on the Forth, the Kingdom of Fife and the distant outlines of Edinburgh, the full scenic glories of Muirfield are realized. But, besides its aesthetic delights, Muirfield forms a considerable part of British golfing history.

Muirfield's Open Champions include Hilton (1896), Braid (1901 and 1906), Ray (1912), Hagen (1929), Perry (1935), Cotton, (1948), Player (1959), Nicklaus (1966) and Trevino (1972). In 1948 Cotton had a second round of 66 watched by King George VI; Player, despite starting the last day 8 strokes behind the leader and finishing with a 6, won the first of his major championship victories; Nicklaus, conquering the waist-high rough, joined the ranks of those who have won all four of the world's major championships; and in 1972, Trevino, watched by enormous crowds, 'stole' a remarkable victory by chipping in three times in the last 21 holes.

However, 1966 was not the only year when Muirfield's rough played its part. When Robert Maxwell won the Amateur Championship there in 1909, it was said that, if a player went off the fairway, his main consideration was to get back on it, often with a niblick.

Cyril Tolley won the Amateur at Muirfield in 1920, and in 1926, Jess Sweetser became champion. He was the second American to win the title and the first of a distinguished line of Americans to win in a year when the American Walker Cup team was in Britain. But in 1932 John de Forest (Count de Bendern) was victorious and in the year of the great Commonwealth tournament that marked the bicentenary of the Royal and Ancient in 1954, the Australian, Doug Bachli beat the American, Bill Campbell by 2 and 1 in the Amateur Championship which followed.

The Scottish Amateur Championship has been housed at Muirfield seven times and in 1967 it staged the first Scottish Strokeplay Championship. There have been other great international occasions and Muirfield shares

with Birkdale the distinction of being the only British clubs to have staged the Walker, Curtis and Ryder Cups.

Although hopes were high in 1959 of a home victory in the Walker Cup, the American team, which included 19-year-old Jack Nicklaus, destroyed them by winning all the foursomes on the first day. However, the seventh Curtis Cup match in 1952 ended a long run of American successes, and the 1973 Ryder Cup, the first to be held in Scotland, was another memorable occasion.

In between all these momentous events, however, Muirfield is very much a private members' club, a bastion of foursomes golf with a long tradition of Dinner matches: 36-hole contests, made and recorded at one of nine dinners held annually.

Hooman, C. V. L. BRITISH
b. 1887. Walker Cup 1922 (unofficial), 1923

Hooman played four times for Oxford University against Cambridge and represented England against Scotland before and after World War I. In the first official match against the United States he won a notable victory at the 37th against Jess Sweetser, who went on to win the US Amateur. Their match illustrated the informal nature of the contest in those years, for no provision had been made for a match finishing all square. While they played on, the advice of the two captains playing their single was sought; their decision was that for the future when two players had played 36 holes in such a match they had earned the right to an immediate drink. As Bernard Darwin, the British captain, later remarked: 'It was a point which I made clear to Bill Fownes when I was two up on the 35th tee.' The decision has been observed ever since, and Hooman remained the only Walker Cup player to win in extra holes.

Hooding the Club
An adjustment made with the clubhead in such a way that the normal effect of its loft is decreased.

Hook
A stroke which starts to the right of the direct line to the target and finishes to the left. For a left-hander, this is reversed. There are degrees of hook, including the quick hook which does not stay in the air for long. The hook is different from the pull, which is a stroke (often perfectly struck) in the wrong direction that travels straight or curving to the left of the intended line.
See also Draw.

Hopkins, John Jay AMERICAN
b. Santa Ana, Cal., 1893; d. 1957

Founder and president of the International Golf Association, which stages the annual World (formerly Canada) Cup matches. Hopkins, chairman of the board of General Dynamics, was a member of the PGA advisory committee and its chairman in 1957, also a member of the Ryder Cup committee, the US Senior Golf Association and the Royal and Ancient. He got the idea for the Canada Cup competition while watching the Ryder Cup matches at Pinehurst in 1951. He was an ardent golfer and belonged to Burning Tree, Columbia and Garden City GCs.

Horne, Reginald W. BRITISH
b. London 1908. British Professional Matchplay 1945; joint 2nd British Open 1947; Ryder Cup 1951; British Seniors 1960

Before scoring a surprise victory in the first postwar PGA Matchplay Championship at Walton Heath Reg Horne was scarcely known outside Hampshire, where he was professional at Romsey. A victory over Percy Alliss, however, changed his

The clubhouse at Muirfield

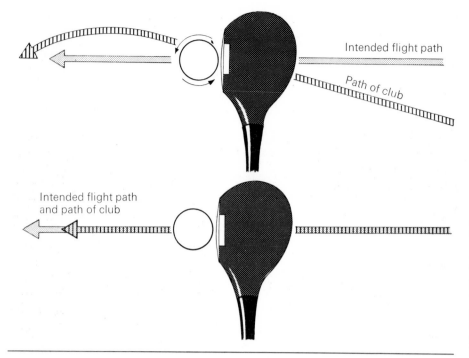

Intended flight path

Path of club

Intended flight path
and path of club

career. He moved to Hendon in London,
where he stayed till his retirement in 1972.
In 1947 he came very near to being Open
Champion. He led the field with only two
rivals to finish, but was beaten by Fred Daly
and tied with Frank Stranahan for 2nd
place.

Horton, Tommy BRITISH
b. Jersey 1941. British Professional Matchplay 1970; South African Open 1970;
Gallaher Ulster Open 1971; Penfold 1974

A young British professional whose hard
work at the game brought success after many
disappointments and near misses. After
tournament victories in Ireland and in
Newcastle in 1969, he moved on to his
finest performance in major competitions in
1970.

In February this Channel Islander
became the first non-South African to capture the South African Open, winning at
Royal Durban with a score of 285; and in
August he won the revived Professional
Matchplay Championship at Moor Park,
beating Ronnie Shade in the 18-hole final
by 3 and 2.

Always regarded as extremely unlucky
never to have gained a Ryder Cup place,
Horton continues the distinguished line of
Channel Islands golfers.

Hosel
The socket on iron clubs into which the shaft
is fitted.

Houghton GC SOUTH AFRICA
Johannesburg, Transvaal
A course made famous by one of South
Africa's greatest golfers, Sid Brews, and
by other distinguished players. In 1952
Brews, who was professional at Houghton,
won the South African Open title for the
eighth time; in the same year Mickey Janks
won the Amateur Championship and Mrs
Reggie Green won the South African
Women's Championship, thereby completing a notable treble for club members. The
foundation of the club goes back to the time
when golf was played on the Houghton
Ridge. When building began to encroach,
Johannesburg GC moved away to form a
separate club at Orange Grove. An area of
155 acres (63 ha) of the old course was
purchased which became Houghton Club.
The course, originally laid out by A. M. Cop-
land, has been maintained and improved to
the more exacting demands of first-class
play under the supervision of Sid Brews. One
example of several memorable championships there was the struggle between Gary
Player and Bobby Locke in the 1958 Open,

each breaking 70 in every round. Player fell
behind when he hit his ball at the 1st hole of
the final round into one of the many trees
which abound on this parkland course.

Hoylake see LIVERPOOL GC, ROYAL.

Hoyt, Beatrix AMERICAN
b. 1880; US Women's Amateur 1896-8,
semi-finalist 1900
The outstanding American woman player
in the 1890s. At the age of 16 she began a
run of three successive victories in the US
Women's Amateur. Her dominance in them
was complete, for in 1896 she led the qualifiers by 7 strokes, the next year by 6 strokes
and in 1898 by 8 strokes. The only close

Hook: a diagram showing, above, the flight
path of a ball when hooked and, below, the
correct path

Centre, Reg Horne with his 1960 British
Seniors' Trophy and replica

Above, Tommy Horton

Beatrix Hoyt

match she had in those championships was in the final of 1896, when she played a member from her home club, Mrs A. Turnure, of Shinnecock Hills, Long Island, and won by 2 and 1. The results of her medal scores, and the margins by which she won through to the matchplay stages suggests she was able to give her contemporaries a third over 18 holes.

Altogether, Beatrix Hoyt won the medal for the best score in the qualifying round five years in succession. Her reign as champion was ended in 1899 when she lost in the first round to Mrs Caleb Fox. The following year, in 1900, Miss Hoyt reached the semifinals of the National Amateur and there lost a prolonged contest, to Margaret Curtis, at the 20th. This was her last attempt in serious competition, and she retired from tournaments at the age of 20.

Since her victory in the 1896 US Women's Amateur, Beatrix Hoyt has had her own special place in the record books as the youngest winner of a major championship, at 16. This distinction is now shared with Laura Baugh, a Californian, who won the US Amateur in 1971.

Hsieh Min Nam TAIWANESE
b. Tansui 1940. Italian Open Amateur 1964; Japan (Kanto) Open 1968; Sobu Open 1968; Thailand Open 1972; Tokyo South 1968; leader Asia Circuit 1971, runner-up 1972

The only person who has won the individual titles in the World Amateur Team Championship (1964) and the World Cup (1972). His performance in Rome first brought him into prominence, particularly as he won the Italian Open Amateur as well. He turned professional shortly afterwards and made a good living playing the tournaments in the Far East. He rapidly became one of the leading players and made a name for himself in many countries.

His progress much enhanced the growing reputation of the professionals from Taiwan but the crowning glory came when Hsieh Min Nam and Lu Liang Huan won the World Cup together for their country in Melbourne in November 1972. In an event reduced to three rounds by the weather, they coped manfully with the difficult conditions – especially the fast greens – and won by 2 strokes with a total of 438. Like many golfers from the Far East, Hsieh's game is sound and solid rather than spectacular, but he is extremely successful at keeping the ball in play.

Hsieh Yung Yo TAIWANESE
b. Taipei 1934. Korean Open 1961, 1963;

Hong Kong Open 1963-5; Thailand Open 1965, 1969; China Open 1967-8; Japan (Crown) Open 1967; Singapore Open 1968, 1970; Philippines Open 1970; Japan (Kanto) Open 1971

Hsieh Yung Yo turned professional in 1960 and quickly became one of the most successful tournament players in the Far

East, leading the Far East (later the Asia) circuit on four occasions. He has also played many times for his country in the World Cup.

Huddy, Gordon BRITISH
Walker Cup 1961

After captaining Cambridge University, Gordon Huddy played for England in 1961 and 1962, and in the Walker Cup match of 1961. He was a semi-finalist in the British Amateur Championship at Portrush in 1960.

Hudson, Robert A. AMERICAN
b. 1887; d. 1974

A well-known sponsor and official who made considerable contributions to golf,

especially after World War II. He was largely responsible for the resumption of the Ryder Cup matches after the war and for many years staged the annual Portland Open. His generosity in these affairs was a byword among touring professionals. Hudson also staged the Hudson Cup matches in the Pacific-Northwest section as well as an

annual event among British golfers, the Hudson Trophy at South Herts GC in the North London suburbs. He was a member of the PGA Advisory Committee in 1946, serving as chairman in 1951 and won the golf writers' Richardson Award in 1947 and the Hagen Award in 1966.

Huggett, Brian George Charles BRITISH
b. Porthcawl, Glamorgan 1936. Dutch Open 1962; German Open 1963; Ryder Cup 1963, 1967, 1969, 1971, 1973; joint runner-up British Open 1965; joint 3rd 1962; British Professional Matchplay 1968; Harry Vardon Trophy 1968; Dunlop Masters 1970

Brian Huggett, the son of a professional golfer, graduated through Assistants' cham-

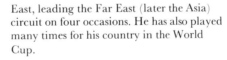

Top, Hsieh Min Nam

Above, Hsieh Yung Yo

Top, Gordon Huddy

Above, Brian Huggett

pionships to a leading position among professional golfers. His development was the result of much practice and competitive instinct that first proved itself when he finished equal 3rd in the 1962 British Open at Troon, behind Palmer and Nagle. Not very tall, he showed dogged determination. He was one of the first to welcome openly the change to the larger ball.

Huggett scored his first major victory on the British circuit in 1963 and thereafter was a consistent money winner. He finished joint 2nd in the 1965 British Open, 2 strokes behind Peter Thomson, and in 1969 played a memorable part in enabling Britain to halve the Ryder Cup at Birkdale. He won the PGA Matchplay Championship in 1968, beating John Panton in the final, and won the Dunlop Masters at Royal Lytham in 1970 with a final round of 65. He also played many times for his native Wales in the World Cup. Though 1973 was not one of his best years, he scored 3½ points out of 4 in the Ryder Cup at Muirfield and started the 1974 season well by winning the Portuguese Open.

Humewood GC SOUTH AFRICA
Port Elizabeth, Cape Province. 18 holes; 6,777 yd (6,197 m); par 74

The idea of a links course, in contrast to the inland Port Elizabeth Club, began to form in the late 1920s and in 1929 the services of the British course designer, Major S. V. Hotchkin, were engaged. Despite the rough terrain, bush and scrub, he quickly worked out the siting of the greens, with the result that an authentic links, of a type uncommon in South Africa, was evolved. A feature of Humewood is the shrewd bunkering. All except two of the bunkers, those on the right of the 18th fairway, were fashioned out of the windswept humps or depressions in the surrounding duneland. With the exception of the four short holes there are two routes to every Humewood green – the bold challenge or the safe line. The course places a premium on accuracy, audacity and intelligent play. It was constructed in the belief that there is more in the game than striking the ball long distances. The test is supplied by normally strong winds, tough rough, and clever lay-out, as was shown by the scoring in a number of championships, notably the 1952 South African Open when only the winner, Sid Brews, and D. Hay broke 80 in every round.

Hungary
No golf exists in Hungary at present but there seems no reason why the game should not return one day to a country which, between the two Wars, had thriving Open

Amateur and Ladies' Open Championships. These were all held at the Magyar Club, Budapest, the men's from 1920-39, and the ladies' from 1922-39. Hungary had another 18-hole course at Lillafüred, and one of 9 holes at Balatonfüred. Hungary's most famous golfer was Mrs Erzsebet von Szlavy who won the Austrian Ladies' Open title four times and the Hungarian title 15 times.

Golf has never been encouraged in Communist countries, but with activity stirring in Yugoslavia, for example, there seems some hope for the future in Hungary. In 1973 a British golf-course architect was approached about building a course there.

Hunstanton GC ENGLAND
Hunstanton, Norfolk. 18 holes

Hunstanton has a special place in British golf because it is the only championship course on the more than 400 miles of the east coast between Sandwich and Muirfield. It stands on a little strip of duneland between the banks of the River Hun and the shores of the Wash, and forms one of the principal golfing delights of East Anglia. It was not the first of the courses to be built in this region. The club scrapbook records an early captain as saying that a small party of enthusiasts met in the Golden Lion Hotel on 14 March 1891 because it was felt the time had come for Hunstanton to follow the example of Yarmouth, Cromer, Sheringham and 'other East Coast watering places' in having its own golf course.

George Fernie was given a wilderness of marram, rushes, and rabbit holes to try to build a course on. The first clubhouse, on the site of the present one, was the size of a shepherd's hut, although its facilities were reinforced by a notice saying that horses could be stabled and tea obtained at Melton's Farm. The club was still poor and money was urgently needed. It was a critical time, particularly since the Brancaster Club had been founded a few miles down the coast, and there were prophets of doom who foretold a speedy collapse in the face of its new and formidable rival. The club had a hard time persuading the inhabitants of Hunstanton to take an interest, but a Mr J. Thompson of Peterborough arrived to help put the club on its feet in the late 1890s. He provided £25 for the extension of the course to 18 holes. This was proudly recorded as proof that Hunstanton was a real golf course.

The change worked wonders. Hunstanton quickly built up a reputation for itself, staged the British Ladies' in 1914 that provided Cecil Leitch with the first of her victories, and ever since has been a regular

home for various championships.

Many years ago it was written that Hunstanton was a little overshadowed in public estimation by Brancaster, with which it has always been coupled and compared. But though there is still friendly discussion of this topic, nobody could question Hunstanton's qualities or the stern nature of its golf, which wends its way out to the 8th on the inland side, and returns in among the dunes.

Hunstanton's great moments include victories in the British Ladies' by Jessie Valentine (1958) and Michelle Walker (1972); an English Ladies' victory by Joyce Wethered (1922); the 1967 PGA Close Championship, won by Malcolm Gregson with a last round of 65; and the longest English Amateur Championship final, 41 holes in 1960 between Doug Sewell and Martin Christmas. It also housed the Brabazon Trophy in 1966 and 1973.

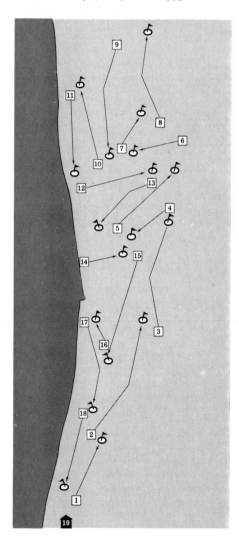

The course plan of Hunstanton GC

Hunt, Bernard John BRITISH

b. Atherstone, Warwickshire, 1930. Ryder Cup 1953, 1957, 1959, 1961, 1963, 1965, 1967, 1969, 1973 (non-playing captain); Vardon Trophy 1958, 1960, 1965; German Open 1961; French Open 1967

Son of a professional and brother of Geoffrey, who also played in the Ryder Cup match of 1963, Bernard Hunt has been one of the most consistent tournament players for more than 15 years. Blooded in the Ryder Cup match of 1953 and involved in its dramatic climax, he worked steadily in building up a repetitive method and became a devastating scorer particularly on the parkland type of course on which many professional events were played. He won many professional tournaments and in 1953 completed the outward half at Worthing in 28 strokes which equals the record for the lowest 9 holes in a British tournament.

Though not a handsome swinger, and one who would always play the percentage shot, he was equal 3rd in the British Open of 1960, 4th in 1964 and equal 5th in 1965. His great strength, however, lay in his ability to win money in ordinary professional events in which he was a much-respected figure and one whose conduct was always exemplary. In addition to his Ryder Cup appearances, he played several times for England in the World Cup. In 1971 he won the Arenzano Tournament in Italy and the Wills Tournament at Dalmahoy after a third round of 63. In January 1973 professional golf bestowed its highest honour on him, that of captaining the Ryder Cup team.

Hunt, Geoffrey Michael BRITISH

b. Atherstone, Warwickshire, 1936. Coombe Hill Assistants' Tournament 1962; Ryder Cup 1963

In spite of ill-health, Geoffrey was on the professional circuit long enough to win the Assistants' Tournament with a record score of 274, and win last place in the 1963 Ryder Cup team without having had a major success. In doing so, he and his elder brother, Bernard, became the first British brothers to play in the match since Charles and Ernest Whitcombe in 1935.

Hunter, William I. BRITISH

b. Forest Row, Sussex, 1892. British Amateur 1921, semi-finalist 1922; semi-finalist US Amateur 1921

One of Britain's most promising amateurs immediately after World War I. His early youth was spent at Royal Cinque Ports where his father, Harry Hunter, was professional. Willie had no great length, but there was a professional crispness about his iron play and he played with refreshing speed. The year he won his championship, Hoylake was burned up making length of small advantage. Hunter also had the fortune not to meet any of the members of a strong American pre-Walker Cup team, and to catch an exhausted Allan Graham in the final, but he played very well and found a wonderful touch on greens that were like ice. That it was no chance victory he showed by reaching the semi-finals of the US Championship later that year, defeating on the way Bobby Jones over 36 holes. Down most of the way, he hung on without ever letting Jones get away from him and in the end wore him down, winning by 2 and 1. A year later he looked likely to succeed in the defence of his title, but just when he looked like going 2 up with 3 to play against Holderness in the semi-final he missed a short putt, laid himself a stymie, and lost a hole he should have won. The same year he also won the St George's Gold Vase and captained an England team against the Scots. He then decided to give up his job as a postal clerk and moved to California in which area he won several tournaments (he turned professional in 1923). His two sons both played well, one of them, McGregor, becoming a successful professional.

Huntercombe GC ENGLAND

Nuffield, Henley on Thames, Oxfordshire. 18 holes

Huntercombe is perhaps the most famous of Oxfordshire's courses, perched on the hills above Henley near the village of Nettlebed. It has a peaceful breeziness all its own and was once the home of Willie Park, its architect. It is said that in 1896 a man called Palmer was returning to his house, Ewelme Park, from the 9-hole course on Peppard Common when his horse cast a shoe and while it was being re-shod, Palmer took out his mashie and played a few shots on Nuffield Common, which was then covered in gorse and heather and grazed by sheep.

The course was opened in 1901 by J. H. Taylor and Jack White. Park insisted that sheep should be allowed to graze in order to improve the fairways but he had to abandon his ideas for developing the surrounding area with houses. When he left for America in 1906, the Norwich Union Assurance Company took it over.

Park made excellent use of the ground and, in one respect, can be said to have anticipated the coming of the rubber-cored ball. Huntercombe has sandy soil, downland turf and an abundance of grassy hollows. For years these took the place of sand bunkers which, even today, are limited to a handful. As author of the slogan 'a man who can putt is a match for anyone' Park also designed large, awkward greens, most of which have been modified since except for the 8th with its characteristically severe double tier. Huntercombe, at the inclination of its members, has never sought championship status even of a modest variety, but it has always been a good test of control.

In 1925 when Huntercombe was put up for sale W. R. Morris, later Lord Nuffield, whose car factory was at Oxford, instructed his secretary to buy the club and, when asked how much he should offer, was simply told 'Buy it'. This was the beginning of his close link with the club. It was registered in the name of his wife who took a keen interest in the course and refused to allow any seedling trees to be pulled up, thereby ensuring its present character.

In 1963, Lord Nuffield gave the course to the members and the old clubhouse which was separated from the course by a main road was replaced by one on the far side of the course. Huntercombe has always had a close affinity with Oxford University golf

Bernard Hunt

Geoffrey Hunt

and many generations of undergraduates came to know Jim Morris, professional there from 1921 to 1964.

Huntingdale GC AUSTRALIA

nr Melbourne, Victoria. 18 holes; 6,963 yd (6,367 m)

Huntingdale's affiliations with golf go back, indirectly, to 1896, when the Surrey Hills GC was established. The present club was opened on 10 June 1924; the Prime Minister of Australia, later Viscount Bruce of Melbourne, hit the first ball. The club flourished: a one-day competition once attracted 693 entrants. In 1938 new land was found and the present course took shape from a mass of poorly drained, tangled woodland. Charles Dempster achieved wonders in drainage and C. H. Alison, the English architect, designed the lay-out.

The combination was a great success. The club moved in in 1941 and the name Huntingdale was adopted. Then, because of Japan's entry into World War II and the threat of an invasion of Australia, the clubhouse of the old Eastern GC – an asset Huntingdale was in the process of selling – was taken over for use by a school evacuated from Melbourne. This left the new Huntingdale in an awkward financial position – the clubhouse had been sold but the contract had not been finalized. However, the sacrifices and determination of the debenture holders prevented Huntingdale from foundering and when the Armistice came the clouds of doubt were rolled away.

At the completion of the 12-year plan in 1953 the club had paid back all the money borrowed. It began a period of development and prosperity that has never been halted. The course has a fine reputation in an area renowned for good golf. In 1957 it accommodated the Australian Professional Championship in which the hitherto little-known Gary Player defeated Peter Thomson in the final by 2 holes.

Hurd, Mrs J. V. see CAMPBELL, DOROTHY IONA

Hutchings, Charles BRITISH

b. Devon 1849. British Amateur 1902

One of the oldest winners of the British Amateur at the age of 53, Hutchings took up golf when 33. He suffered greatly from rheumatism, but it was said of him that 'the worse he aches the better he plays'. His swing was somewhat stiff, but he was a most redoubtable putter. He once backed himself to go round Hoylake in 85 with a single club and completed the course in 81. His victory over Sydney Fry in the final of the Amateur at Hoylake was the first championship to be won with the new rubber-cored ball, a few months before the Open Championship over the same course.

Hutchinson, Horace George BRITISH

b. London 1859; d. London 1932. British Amateur 1886-7, runner-up 1885, 1903; captain Royal and Ancient 1908.

The name of Horace Hutchinson is forever linked with the Royal North Devon Club at Westward Ho! At the age of 16, he committed 'the blazing indiscretion' of winning the scratch medal of the club's autumn meeting and, by the rules of the club (which were altered the following year) became captain and thus presided over the meetings for 12 months. A few years later, he played top for Oxford in the first university match and reached the final of the first three British Amateur Championships – winning two of them. In 1886, he beat Henry Lamb at St Andrews by 7 and 6, and in 1887 achieved his greatest performance, defeating John Ball by one hole over Ball's own course at Hoylake.

He also had a reputation as a golfer who could play the most incredible shots out of the most incredible places. 'For a ball down a drain or on a roof or in the branches of a tree, there has been nobody quite like him. With that very loose style of his, he appeared to be able to swing the club in any plane or direction.'

While on vacation from Oxford he often had as his caddie a young Northam lad who was employed in the Hutchinson home. His name was John Henry Taylor who, in a famous career, became the first Englishman to win the Open Championship and, in his retirement, was made president of the Royal North Devon Club.

Hutchinson was almost certainly the first really good golfer that Taylor saw and it is possible that Hutchinson had considerable influence on him. Hutchinson won numerous club medals and in 1908 had the distinction of being elected the first English captain of the Royal and Ancient. Besides being an outstanding player, he was one of the first writers on the game.

He wrote with the lazy charm of a natural essayist, at a time when there was no other writing on golf worthy of the name, except Sir Walter Simpson's *Art of Golf*. Among his publications were *Golf* in the Badminton Library series, *The Book of Golf and Golfers*, and *Fifty Years of Golf*. He was a pioneer of the game in many directions and an outstanding figure on its courses.

Hutchison, Cecil Key BRITISH

b. London 1877; d. 1941

An Old Etonian who served in the Coldstream Guards, Hutchison was a fine amateur golfer who won many medals at North Berwick, Royal St George's, Royal Mid-Surrey and Huntercombe; he played for Scotland on many occasions and reached the final of the British Amateur Championship in 1909 at Muirfield, where he lost on his own course to Robert Maxwell by one hole.

He played much of his golf in East Lothian and at St Andrews. Later he was remembered for his work as a golf-course architect, helping James Braid in the construction of Gleneagles and reconstructing the Old Ailsa course at Turnberry before World War II.

Hutchison, Jock AMERICAN

b. St. Andrews, Fife, 1884. 2nd US Open 1916, tied 2nd 1920; 3rd 1919, 1923; USPGA 1920, runner-up 1916; Western Open 1920, 1923; British Open 1921, 4th 1922; North and South Open 1921; US Professional Seniors' 1947, tied 1st 1946, runner-up 1942, 1951

With Walter Hagen and Jim Barnes, Hutchison ranked as America's finest player in the decade preceding the emergence of Bobby Jones in the early 1920s. Besides his two major victories in the PGA Championship of America and in the British Open, he had for years a fine record in the US Open, and won many lesser tournaments. He was a nervous, talkative player who was capable of great scoring bursts and whose skills were so enduring that he was able to shoot a 66 at the age of 66, and even in his 80s was hitting the ball solidly. If he ever had a St Andrews swing, it was much modified by the time he returned to Britain; his swing then was rhythmical but with the suggestion of being put together in three pieces.

Following the example of dozens of his countrymen, Hutchison arrived in the United States from Scotland in the early years of the century and settled in the Pittsburgh area. After several years of winning the Western Pensylvania Open and performing creditably in the US Open, he made his mark in 1916, finishing 2nd in both the Open and the PGA Championships. Although World War I brought a halt to the championships, he showed he was ready to pick up where he had left off by winning the Patriotic Open in 1918 by 7 strokes. In the 1920 PGA Championship he failed to qualify in the first instance but got into the tournament as an alternate and went on to win. He came close that year to scoring a double by winning the US Open, but a missed putt on the 69th lost him the chance

to tie with Ted Ray and he finished in a four-way tie for 2nd.

In 1921 the British Open was held at St Andrews and Hutchison saw his chance to combine business with pleasure. He sailed to Britain early in the year and while staying with relatives played the Old Course dozens of times in preparation. He opened with 72, in the course of which he nearly had two consecutive ones. He holed his tee shot to the 8th, and at the 9th, with plenty of run on the fairways, his drive reached the green and the ball missed the hole by inches. He held on with a 75 in the second round, but a third-round 79 put him a stroke behind the British amateur, Roger Wethered. A final 70 brought him into a tie and he won the play-off by 9 strokes. Spectators were astounded by Hutchison's pitching and by the amount of backspin he could impart to the ball; as a result deeply scored irons, such as Hutchi-son was using, were later made illegal. It was the first American victory in the championship. Although he continued to play well for 30 years, Hutchison's last good tournament year was 1923. After leading

the US Open for 36 holes he dropped back with an 82 and finished 3rd behind Bobby Jones. From 1928 Hutchison took little part in tournaments until he started playing in the USPGA Seniors which was started in 1941. He put together a remarkable run in this event, winning once, tying once for 1st, and never being lower than 3rd in eight years. In 1951 when he finished runner-up, he was 67. Hutchison, who weighed only 140 lb, was a highly strung golfer who bounded forward after each shot. Between shots he talked, chuckled, twiddled his thumbs and waved his arms to dry the perspiration which flowed freely. He had a theory for everything and was more than willing to discuss any aspect of the game. For many years after 1963 he was paired with another octogenarian champion, Freddie McLeod, in opening the proceedings at the Masters tournament. He moved from the Pittsburgh area to Chicago during the first war and remained at Glen View CC for the rest of his career.

Hutt GC NEW ZEALAND
Lower Hutt, nr Wellington. 18 holes

Before the Hutt Golf Club, the third to be formed in New Zealand, was founded in 1892, the Valley of the Hutt was the scene of an historic encounter in 1846 when Imperial forces repulsed an attack by Wanganui Maoris in one of the major clashes of the European settlement. In remembrance of the past, three holes at the Hutt are still named 'Boulcott', 'Stockade' and 'Buglers', the last after the bugler boy who, his right hand severed, sounded the alarm with his left.

The man responsible for getting golf going at Hutt was David B. Howden, the younger brother of C. R. Howden who is regarded as the father of New Zealand golf. By 1895 the Otago and Christchurch Clubs agreed to Hutt's holding the third Amateur Championship, although there was some doubt whether the course was in good enough order. In 1908 the club purchased 108 acres (44 ha) of river flats north of the Hutt township. The ground, though mainly flat and covered with gorse and a certain amount of surface stone, also had some undulation and was reckoned suitable for golf, but its future was fraught with difficulty.

To begin with, some members chose not to continue at the new site where the full lay-out was not completed until 1921, and then only in rudimentary fashion. A tree-planting programme was carried out using pines and gums, but disapproval of the original lay-out caused alterations to be made in 1929 which were then extensively

damaged by flood and financial famine.

In 1931, the Hutt River overflowed as it had done several times before and for some years playing conditions remained indifferent, although the standard of play in the club at that time was unrivalled. World War II left its mark on the Hutt and in 1947, just when recovery was gathering momentum, more flooding took place and fire ruined the men's locker room. From that point the future grew clearer and brighter.

The River Board took action, membership passed 500 within 10 years, more tree planting took place and much-praised course alterations were carried out in 1966 following a report by J. D. Harris. The luck of the Hutt has turned.

Hyndman, William, III AMERICAN
b. 1915. Runner-up US Amateur 1955; Walker Cup 1957, 1959, 1961, 1969, 1971; Eisenhower Trophy 1958, 1960, runner-up British Amateur 1959, 1969-70.

A supremely elegant player who was one of America's leading amateurs for more than 15 years. He played with distinction in the first World Amateur Team Championship for the Eisenhower Trophy at St Andrews in 1958, and again two years later at Merion when America won commandingly. But, however well Hyndman played in championships, someone always seemed to play just that little bit better.

He suffered from the greatness of Harvie Ward in the 1955 final of the US Amateur and, after the Walker Cup match of 1959 at Muirfield, went down to Deane Beman in the British final at Sandwich. He was a regular competitor in Britain during the 1960s and reached the final two years running in 1969 and 1970. On both occasions he lost to Michael Bonallack, their meeting in 1970 at Newcastle, Co. Down, being the first repeat final in the history of the event.

His collapse in the afternoon, having ended the first round 1 up, was a disappointment but his reaching the final at the age of 55 was a wonderful performance which guaranteed his selection for the 1971 Walker Cup team at St Andrews. Although he could not prevent a British victory on the second day, he had a good singles record in the event including victories over Frank Deighton, Doug Sewell, and David Frame. He will be remembered as a kindly but formidable opponent with a classical style.

Top, Jock Hutchison

Above, Bill Hyndman

I

Iceland

Golf in Iceland is limited to four months from the beginning of June to the end of September, although occasionally the season lasts a little longer. Despite this, and the fact that both seaside and inland courses have rather soft fairways and greens that are not yet quite of international standard (though improving rapidly), Iceland entered a team for the first Eisenhower Trophy at St Andrews in 1958 and again in 1970. It also sent a side to the World Senior Championship in 1970. Iceland also competed in the Scandinavian Championship in Denmark for the first time in 1972 and regularly takes part in the European Team Championship.

Golf started in Iceland in 1934 when Gunnlaugur Einarsson, a Reykjavík doctor, founded Golfklúbbur Íslands (the Golf Club of Iceland) with his colleague, Dr Valtýr Albertsson, and a group of prominent citizens. In 1937 the club moved to a new 9-hole course and pleasant clubhouse at Öskjuhlídh in Reykjavík, where it remained until 1962.

After two new clubs had been founded, the Akureyri in 1936 and Golfklúbbur Vestmannaeyja (Westman Islands GC), the Golf Club of Iceland changed its name in 1946 to Golfklúbbur Reykjavíkur. Together these three clubs formed the Golf Union of Iceland in 1942, which is part of the Icelandic Athletic Organization. This also marked the beginning of the Iceland Amateur Championship, which was played for the first time in Reykjavík. In 1946 it changed from matchplay to strokeplay and has retained this form ever since.

In 1962 the Reykjavík club made another move, to the present site at Grafarholt, five miles north of the city. The new 6,562-yd (6,000-m) course had 18 holes and a par of 69. By this time the game was beginning to enjoy increasing popularity and two more clubs emerged in 1964. These were the Sudhurnesja club in Keflavík and the Ness club in Reykjavík; more have followed since, making 10 courses in 1972 with a total membership of 1,100. Like Reykjavík, Akureyri has an 18-hole course.

Dr Gunnlaugur Einarsson, to whom golfers in Iceland owe a great deal for his pioneering efforts and contribution to the game, died in 1972.

Impact

The period of contact between clubface and ball.

In

The holes of the second 9 of a course as opposed to 'out', the holes of the first 9.

India

The story of golf in India before 1947 forms part of the social history of the British Raj, from the early 19th century to Indian Independence, so that there could be said to be a British period followed by an Indian period of golf (before Independence Indians were neither admitted as members of golf clubs, nor generally allowed to take part in golf tournaments). Nevertheless, golf is as much a part of the British legacy bequeathed to India as parliamentary institutions, electric trams, cricket, or the skirl of military bagpipes.

Only eight years after Napoleon's death, the oldest golf club in the world outside of Britain was founded in Calcutta in 1829. And the history of Indian golf is largely the history of that enduring institution, the Royal Calcutta GC. As the British sphere of administration and influence spread, from Kashmir to Kanya Kumari, and from the shores of the Arabian Sea to Assam, golf clubs and courses were established wherever a patch of grass grew, and in many places where it did not.

Queen Victoria had been on the throne

India: Australian Stewart Ginn *(top)* playing off the 8th tee in the 1973 Indian Open, the Barah Khamba Lodhi tomb in the background

Centre, on the last day of the same Open bees invaded the course and fires had to be lit to keep them away

Above, I. S. Malik and his son, Ashok Malik, who both played for India in the 1958 World Amateur Team Championship

only five years when the second golf club was founded, in 1842 – Royal Bombay, no longer in existence. Thirty-four years later Bangalore, in South India, started a golf club in 1876; shortage of water meant it had browns only, no greens. This was followed in 1878 by the Shillong club in Upper Assam, nearly 2,000 miles northeast in the eastern Himalayas. Ahmedabad, India's textile city, capital of Gujerat State, founded one in 1884, and two years later the Madras Gymkhana Club opened a golf section; like Bangalore and Ahmedabad it had browns not greens. In 1887 a club appeared in the dusty army cantonment of Bolarum, a suburb of Secunderabad. Thus golf had been played in India for several decades before it took root in the United States and continental Europe. Before the end of the 19th century India had nearly a dozen golf clubs, three of them 'royal': Royal Calcutta; Royal Bombay; and Royal Western, Nasik, which, like Royal Bombay, no longer exists.

In 1892 the first Amateur Golf Championship of India, a 54-hole, strokeplay event, was played over the Dum Dum course, Calcutta, and won by J. F. MacNair. After 1898 the championship was decided by matchplay. The first Indian to appear in the All-India Amateur Golf Championship was a Sikh, Sardar I. S. Malik, a father figure of Indian golf who in 1946, on the eve of Independence, became the first Indian member of Royal Calcutta. His elder brother, Sardar H. S. Malik, was the first Indian to get a golf Blue at Oxford, in 1914; the second was Rajkumar Pitamber, of Nepalese origin, who became India's amateur captain. Malik's son, Ashok, has won the All-India five times, followed by Major P. G. Sethi (four-times winner), India's outstanding power golfer, who finished 6th in the 1966 Eisenhower Trophy match at Mexico City. Ashok Malik and P. G. Sethi have represented their country in every Eisenhower Trophy event from the start in 1958 to 1968, the last year India sent a side.

Encouraged by India's golf patron, Peter Thomson of Australia, the Indian Golf Union staged the first Indian Open in 1964 in Delhi, appropriately won by Thomson. The 1965 Indian Open, in Calcutta, was won by Sethi, with Thomson also in the field. Alternating between Delhi and Calcutta, the Indian Open became an official part of the Asia Golf Circuit in 1970; in 1971 the total prize money was $180,000 for the nine events in nine countries. The 1972 Indian Open, at Royal Calcutta, drew a record 111 professional entries and was won by 21-year-old Brian Jones of Sydney,

Australia, in his first major tournament.

The Indian Golf Union, the governing body of golf in India, had 85 member clubs in 1972, with thousands of men and women golfers. Despite shortage of golf balls and clubs, the rising costs of greens, course maintenance, and water problems, the game is flourishing throughout the country. Perhaps

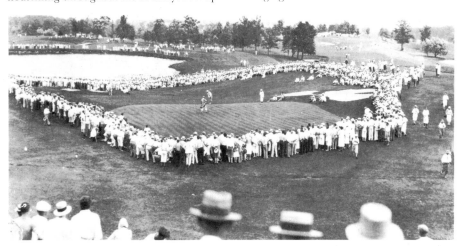

the most significant single factor helping the expansion is the encouragement given by the armed forces. Whereas each army cantonment, air force station or naval base used to have its fields for the traditional cricket, hockey, football and polo, the last-mentioned has tended to give way to a golf course, laid out over the nearest open ground regardless of rocks and bare earth. Today the Indian armed forces boast of golf played 11,000 ft up at wind-blown Leh in the western Himalayas, and from the desert plains of Kutch and Rajasthan to the jungle hills of the Indo-Burmese border. Even during the 1971 hostilities, the general officer commanding one of the most critical forward areas on the Kashmir front made sure that a 9-hole course was maintained not far from the headquarters mess.

As elsewhere, golf in India has been played mainly by the more affluent members of society. However, years ago the IGU established a number of schemes to benefit caddies and assistant professionals. Employment is provided for thousands of groundsmen and workers on courses throughout India.

In 1969 India was invited to send two professionals, Shadi Lal of Delhi and Ruda Valji, to play in the World Cup at Singapore. Then in 1971 came the Wills Open, a commercially sponsored event for caddies and professionals.

In Play
A ball is 'in play' as soon as the player has

made a stroke on the teeing ground. It remains in play as his ball until holed out, except when it is out of bounds, lost or lifted, or another ball is substituted in accordance with the rules or local rules.

In-to-out
Swinging the club in such a manner that at impact the clubface is not travelling towards the hole but to the right of the aiming point. In America, inside-out is the more usual term.

Interlachen CC USA
Minneapolis, Minn.

The city of Minneapolis has had an unusual number of national championships awarded to its eight courses, and the Interlachen Club remains memorable as the site of Bobby Jones' US Open victory in 1930, the third side of what George Trevor called the Impregnable Quadrilateral. Jones, who had won the British Open at Hoylake hardly three weeks earlier, and, before that, the British Amateur at St Andrews, completed this Grand Slam of golf by winning the US Amateur at Merion in September.

Interlachen was opened for play in 1911 but was redesigned and rebuilt by Donald Ross in 1919. It is not perhaps a typical Ross course, although characteristics of the noted man's work (such as the crown green) are recognizable.

Old Interlachen hands often insist on pointing out the site of the famous 'Lilypad Shot' at the 9th hole, possibly even the exact lilypad on which Jones' half-topped second in the second round in 1930 is now believed by thousands to have hit and skipped across the water hazard, saving him vital strokes. The correct account of this supposed incident appears in Jones' own excellent writings.

It was at Interlachen that Patty Berg

History in the making – Interlachen CC in 1930

played her first golf and in 1935 her first national championship. At the age of 17 she was beaten 3 and 2 in the final by Glenna Collett Vare who won her sixth and last title that day.

International Match for the Curtis Cup

The origin of the Curtis Cup goes back to 25 May 1905 when seven Americans, entered for the British Ladies' Championship at Royal Cromer, met a team of leading British players in a friendly match before the championship. The composition of the sides is of interest, for those taking part comprised the cream of talent from both sides of the Atlantic.

British	American
Miss C. Dod (England)	Miss G. Bishop
Miss M. Hezlet (Ireland)	Miss M. Curtis
Miss M. A. Graham (Scotland)	Miss M. B. Adams
Miss E. C. Neville (England)	Miss H. Curtis
Miss F. Hezlet (Ireland)	Miss Lockwood
Miss A. M. Glover (Scotland)	Miss Griscom
Miss D. Campbell (Scotland)	Mrs J. T. Martin

The visitors' only point was gained by their champion, Miss Bishop, and that after two extra holes, but the result in no way detracted from the enjoyment of the occasion; the two sisters on the American side, Harriot and Margaret Curtis of Manchester, Mass., had a great desire to arrange regular matches of this kind.

It was not until 1924, and again in 1927 and 1929, that American, British, and French officials seriously discussed the subject of international matches, but nothing came of it because of the difficulties of financing such events.

On May Day, 1930, there was another 'unofficial' match between American and British players on the Old Course at Sunningdale. From the tremendous interest it aroused the LGU was encouraged to go ahead with plans for official fixtures, and opened an International Match Fund. The USGA responded in 1931 by assuming financial and administrative responsibilities for its side.

The Curtis Cup, offered by the Curtis sisters, was first played for in 1932. It is a simple silver bowl of a design made famous by Boston's master silversmith Paul Revere. The inscription on it says it was presented 'To stimulate friendly rivalry among the women golfers of many lands'.

By 1958, long established as the premier trophy in women's international golf, the Curtis Cup was thought by its donors to be too insignificant, and they offered to replace it with a larger cup, but the USGA and

LGU had no desire to change it, for by that time it had become a symbol of the best of sportsmanship and the best of golf on both sides of the Atlantic.

The first official match between Britain and America was held on the East Course of the Wentworth GC, Surrey, on 21 May 1932 and consisted of three foursomes in the morning and six singles in the afternoon.

There were four matches before the outbreak of World War II in Europe brought play to a halt, and there was a gap of 10 years from 1938 to 1948.

In 1950, at the request of the Americans, the foursomes and singles were extended to 36 holes. From then until 1964 this was the format of the matches; in that year, the games were reduced to 18, but the match continued as a two-day event, with three foursomes and six singles each day.

The 18 matches held from 1932 to 1974 have resulted in 14 American victories, 2 British victories, and 2 draws. See p. 437 for results.

International Match for the Walker Cup

The biennial match between the amateurs of the United States and of Great Britain and Ireland, played alternately in Britain and America. The series started at a time when British and American players began to take each other's championships seriously. In 1920 Bob Gardner reached the final of the British Amateur Championship at Muirfield and Cyril Tolley, Roger Wethered and Tommy Armour challenged for the US Amateur at Roslyn, New York.

In the meantime, representatives of the USGA had accepted the invitation of the Royal and Ancient Golf Club to confer on the rules. Among the delegation was George Herbert Walker of the National Golf Links of America club, a keen advocate of the game and president of the USGA in 1920. On returning to the United States, the Executive discussed the possibility of holding international matches. The idea so appealed to George Walker that at a meeting of the committee in the Links Club, Manhattan, on 21 December 1920, he outlined his plan for an international championship and offered to present a trophy. When the newspapers got hold of the story, they called it the 'Walker' Cup and though Walker was embarrassed by this, the name has persisted. In 1921 the USGA invited all countries interested in golf to send a team to compete for the trophy. No country accepted that year but in the spring of 1921 William C. Fownes Jr, who had twice assembled a team to play against Canada, got together a third

which he took to Hoylake, where they defeated an informal British team by 9 matches to 3 on the day before the British Amateur. The American team included Ouimet, Jones, and Evans; the British, Tolley, Wethered, Holderness and Tommy Armour, who later played against Britain in the Ryder Cup.

The following August the R. and A. sent a team to compete for the Walker Cup at George Walker's home club. The idea was to play four foursomes the first day and eight singles the second. Robert Harris was appointed to captain the British team but he fell ill before the match. His place was taken by Bernard Darwin who was travelling with the team to report the match for *The Times*. This was hardly a role which Darwin can have anticipated but he won his match against Fownes by 3 and 1.

This match was also notable for Hooman's defeat of Jess Sweetser at the 37th, the only extra-hole match ever played in the Walker Cup; and for the fact that every member of the American team won the American Amateur Championship at some time.

With further matches in 1923 and 1924, the Walker Cup became established as a contest that players on both sides of the Atlantic were desperately anxious to take part in, and though it was decided in 1924 to meet in alternate years thereafter, interest grew enormously. The only disquieting factor from the British point of view was that American victories became a trend impossible to arrest after the close results at St Andrews in 1923 and 1926. The regular interchange of visits, however, has produced nothing but friendliness and pleasure; if it is said, and occasionally with truth, that international matches do more harm than good, the contrary can be said of the Walker Cup.

Emphasis in the Walker Cup has, of course, always been on the team, but individual performances form an important part of its story. In five singles matches, Bobby Jones was victorious each time, beating Tolley by 12 and 11, T. P. Perkins by 13 and 12, and Roger Wethered by 9 and 8. This, his second match with Wethered, took place at Sandwich, the first time that St Andrews was not the British venue. Supporting Jones on many occasions were Francis Ouimet and Jess Sweetser. However, because of the one-sidedness of the matches, it is the isolated victories of some of the British that tend to attract attention. Tony Torrance and Leonard Crawley undoubtedly belong in this category: Torrance because of three victories and a halved match out of five singles; Crawley because his victory over Voigt in 1932 at Brookline was the only British win in the entire match, and also

Opposite, The Indian Open at Delhi

land was found at Otatara across the estuary from Invercargill for a new course that came into its own when the borough reduced Queen's Park to 9 holes and adopted it as a municipal course. By 1924, 18 holes were in play at Otatara. Although it was before the days of full watering, the grass lasted well in summer and many compliments were paid the course, by Gene Sarazen among others. It was lengthened in 1938 from its modest 6,000 yd (5,486 m) and after World War II it became recognized for national events. The women led the way by staging the NZ Ladies' Open there in 1949, returning in 1958 and 1970. In the club's jubilee year of 1960 the NZ Amateur and Open championships were both held there; Peter Thomson won the latter. Events of this kind confirmed Otatara as a fine championship test, in a setting of great beauty.

Inverness Club USA
Toledo, Ohio

Inverness is steeped in old-country tradition. When the citizens of Toledo decided in 1903 to have a golf club, they wrote to the capital of the Highlands and asked the Inverness Club if they could use its name. The generous Scots not only gave that permission but offered the Americans permission to use their club's own seal. The club managed with two unexceptional 9-hole courses until 1919 when Donald Ross, a Scot who had become America's premier golf architect, laid out a new 18.

In 1920 the club was host to the US Open with Harry Vardon and Ted Ray on hand. Ray won it with a total of 295, cutting the corner of the 7th hole, a short dogleg par 4, on all four rounds and picking up a birdie each time. (This required a carry of 275 yd.) Vardon, Jack Burke, Sr, Leo Diegel, and Jock Hutchison all tied for 2nd a stroke higher. Vardon seemed to have the championship secured until a severe thunderstorm off Lake Erie overtook him 7 holes from home and blew him into a string of bogeys. This event is also memorable because Bobby Jones, Gene Sarazen, Tommy Armour, Leo Diegel and Bill Mehlhorn were all playing in a US Open for the first time. Jones was paired with Vardon in the qualifying rounds.

The 1931 US Open at Inverness was also quite memorable. Billy Burke and George Von Elm, who had tied at 292, had to play 144 extra holes to decide the winner. Burke won the marathon by a stroke. The 1957 US Open was held at Inverness, and it too ended in a tie: Dick Mayer defeated Cary Middlecoff, the defender, in an 18-hole play-off. The course was revised for the 1957

Open by Dick Wilson, and it now presents a rolling, open face by American standards, with comparatively few trees. The greens are very exacting. It is no longer any use trying to cut the corner at the 7th. The hole is 20 yd longer now, and nobody can drive the ball high and far enough to clear the trees which now have half a century of new growth on them. In 1973 the club was host to the US Amateur Championship.

During the 1920 Open, for the first time anywhere, the whole Inverness clubhouse was thrown open to the professionals. For the first time at a championship, the professionals changed in the locker room, ate in the club's restaurants, and entered by the front door. In appreciation, Walter Hagen

took up a collection from his colleagues, and they bought a handsome clock to present to the club. It still stands, keeping good time, in the main foyer with the following inscription engraved on a brass plate:

> *God measures men by what they are*
> *Not what in wealth they possess.*
> *This vibrant message chimes afar*
> *The voice of Inverness.*

Inwood CC USA
Inwood, Long Island, N.Y.

The first professional at Inwood, which was founded in 1901, was a Scot named Herbert Martin. At the end of his first season he resigned and took up the more lucrative occupation of driving a carriage

for hire at neighbouring Far Rockaway. He should have stuck to his first job, for this club was to prosper greatly and golfing history lay in its future.

In 1923 Bobby Jones won his first US Open at Inwood, starting a run of 13 national championships on both sides of the Atlantic. Here also, two years earlier, Walter Hagen began his sequence of five out of seven USPGA titles, and the visitor can see where 'The Haig' forced the club to plant trees to keep the field from taking short cuts to the greens. Also visible is the spot in the rough to the right of the 18th fairway from which Jones made one of the most memorable shots of golf history, a shot comparable in every way to his winning shot

Top, the 6th hole at the Inverness club

Above, the 18th hole at Inwood CC, Bobby Jones on the green

because an overstrong second shot of his to the 18th dented the Walker Cup as it stood on display.

The Americans scored a 'shut-out' at Pine Valley in 1936, winning by 9 matches to 0. Then in 1938, Great Britain and Ireland won for the first time, a victory that was infinitely reviving to their spirits. It is possible that without it, the Americans might not have thought it worthwhile continuing the matches after World War II. Realizing that postwar conditions made it difficult for the British to travel to the United States, the Americans journeyed to St Andrews in 1947. Although their victory started the familiar trend again, the Walker Cup's future was assured.

The 1947 match brought the first appearance of Joe Carr who, by playing in or captaining the next 10 British and Irish sides, set up a record playing span that lasted 20 years, and was equalled only by the American Bill Campbell who did not take part in all the matches during that period. It was also marked by the emergence of Ronnie White, who beat F. Kammer, Willie P. Turnesa, Charlie Coe and Dick Chapman in his four singles, the last in 1953 at Kittansett. It was here that James Jackson, playing with Gene Littler against Roy Mcgregor and Jimmy Wilson, discovered he had 16 clubs in his bag on the 2nd fairway. The penalty in those days was disqualification but the British captain, Tony Duncan, said his team wished to win points only on its play of the game; the penalty was modified to 2 holes and the American pair went on to win. The British were eternal optimists in their Walker Cup meetings and more than once had thoughts of victory dashed cruelly. Obvious examples were 1957 and 1959 (the latter was the year Jack Nicklaus took his place in the American side). Then 1961 brought another crushing defeat for the British and a change to playing the match in the form adopted by the Ryder Cup, four series of 18-hole matches with foursomes and singles each day.

Since that day the British teams have gone at the Americans with renewed vigour and skill. In 1963 it needed a fine second-day recovery to enable the Americans to win the match and in 1965 in Baltimore Britain

achieved a tie. Clive Clark had to hole a putt of 33 ft to halve the match for the British.

In 1969 in Milwaukee the British again came close. Then in 1971 they achieved their second victory, again at St Andrews, with a tremendous finish on the last afternoon, a time in the past when they have usually allowed good positions to slip. There were understandable scenes of jubilation that night, 50 years after the end of the first unofficial match. Earlier in the week, the R. and A. held a celebration dinner to which every living person who has taken part in a Walker Cup match was invited. Those who had to refuse did so with the utmost regret because the Walker Cup has done so much to preserve the traditions of amateur golf and to promote friendship and goodwill among the golfers of Britain and Ireland and the United States.

America regained the Cup in 1973 but it was another close result despite the fact that the British did not win a foursomes match. See p. 429 for results.

Invercargill GC NEW ZEALAND

Otatara, nr Invercargill. 18 holes; 6,511 yd (5,954 m)

Golf in Invercargill owes its origin mainly to the Scots who came in large numbers to that town about 1900. A. M. Howden, son of C. R. Howden, known as the father of New Zealand golf, laid out 9 holes at Queen's Park, later extended to 18. In 1911

Top, the British and American teams for the first Walker Cup match in 1922

Above, the victorious British Walker Cup Team of 1971 show the trophy

Opposite, Tony Jacklin

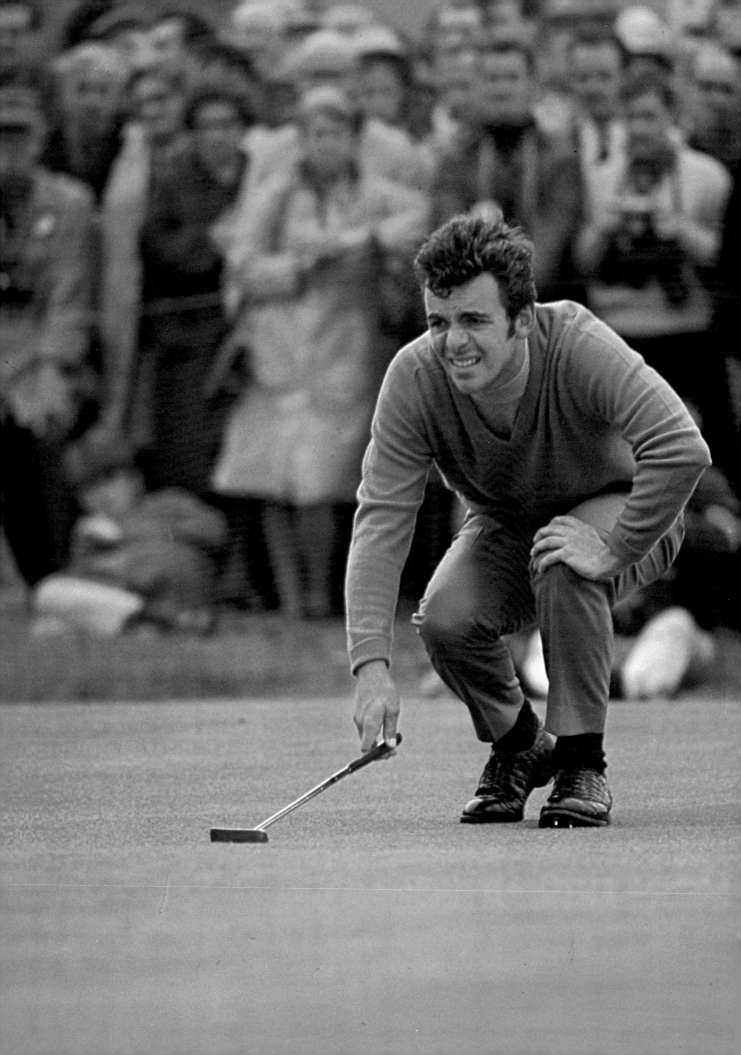

from the sand on the 17th at Royal Lytham in 1926. This one at Inwood, a no. 2 iron that finished 6 ft from the flag, beat Bobby Cruickshank on the final hole of their play-off.

Inwood is a golf course where, as on the classic courses of Britain, nature and man combined to bring about a beautiful, varied, and always interesting ground to test adaptability and strokes – and, in places, the nerve. At Inwood there are seaside, or harbourside, holes along Jamaica Bay, with a change frequently to inland golf. There are significant trees, but some holes are open to the wind. Few old courses have remained exactly as they were, and Inwood is no exception, but the golfer still has the feeling there that he is on the course the great men played.

Iran

When Prime Minister Amir Abbas Noveyda inaugurated the new 18-hole grass course at the Imperial CC in Teheran in October 1970 before an elite gallery of Iranian government officials and club members, he ushered Iran into the world of modern golf and international golf tourism. Until then Iran, ancient Persia, had only a primitive rock and sand course at the Imperial CC and several sand courses scattered among oil-company properties in the southwest part of the country in the region of Abadan, Ahwaz, and Agha Jari. There was also one on Kharg Island in the Persian Gulf.

The new Imperial CC course, which replaces the old sand course, has been developed under a British resident professional, Jack Armitage, once assistant to Archie Compston at Wentworth. The course was inaugurated with 10 permanent holes in play; the remaining 8 were opened during 1972.

The course is situated just below the Royal Teheran Hilton Hotel, overlooking the city, with the Elburz Mountains for a backdrop. It lies spaciously over 180 acres (73 ha) of undulating land; and, in keeping with the altitude where the thin air adds 10-15 per cent more distance to a golf shot than at sea level, the course is long: 7,200 yd (6,582 m), with par-5 holes running to 600 yd (550 m). With long tees, the design provides both a valid test for the high-calibre player and a pleasant social round for the average golfer. The fairways are Kentucky Blue grass, the greens Pentcross Bent.

Golf in Iran was further encouraged by the construction of an 18-hole par-3 grass course in the ancient capital of Persepolis, opened in October 1971 as part of the widely publicized celebration of the 2,500th anni-

versary of the founding of the Persian Empire by Cyrus the Great. Jack Armitage designed the course.

A major golf development is planned as part of a large urban programme for a site on the shore of the Caspian Sea, north of Teheran. The landlocked Caspian lies 93 ft (28 m) below sea level, with a subtropical shoreline climate.

Golf plans entail an 18-hole, 7,000 yd, par-72 course, with Bermuda grass fairways and Pentcross Bent greens, and a par-3 9-hole course, a driving range and putting green. Construction began in 1973. Peter Alliss, Dave Thomas and Partners Ltd, of London, are the course architects.

The sand courses in the southwest, near the head of the Persian Gulf, still function. These, however, are privately owned by the oil companies, run primarily for their staff and guests. Visitors to that part of Iran are usually welcome to play as guests; but these courses, all sand, should not be considered in terms of holiday golf for the average tourist.

The Iran National Tourist Organization is studying the possibility of building more courses in the country. Though starting late and moving slowly, Iran has taken a modest but promising place on the world golf map.

The best time for golf in Iran is from early spring to late autumn. In Teheran it is possible to play well into December and begin again perhaps as early as February, depending upon the winter snows. During the hot summer months play is restricted normally to early morning and late afternoon, as in other Middle East countries. In the southwest, on the sand courses, play is all year round.

Iraq

Golf once had a foothold in Iraq, largely through resident British interest and activity in Baghdad, where there was a 13-hole sand course at the Baghdad GC which was founded in 1925. The course measured 6,065 yd (5,546 m) and had a par of 72 for 18 holes, playing some holes twice. Now, however, that course is more or less abandoned, local interest having declined since the revolution and economic reform in the country that began in 1958.

The Iraq Petroleum Company still has an 18-hole 6,000 yd (5,486 m) sand course at Kirkuk in the northern oilfield area where the Kirkuk GC was founded in 1933. And near Basrah, at the head of the Persian Gulf in southern Iraq, the Basrah Petroleum Company runs the Barjisiyah GC which was founded in 1951. This is an 18-hole, 6,200-yd (5,670-m) sand course.

As with all oil-company courses in the

Middle East, the Kirkuk and Barjisiyah courses are primarily for company staff. Visitors, however, are welcome.

Irons

Clubs with metal blades for heads. They comprise well over half of the normal set and are graduated according to loft from 1 to 10, plus the wedges and sand irons. The no. 1 iron is a rarity on account of its straight face, but top-class professionals can obtain great distance with it and often use it for driving when extra control is demanded. Irons also vary in lie as well as loft, lie being the angle between the face and the shaft; this determines how it sits on the ground to suit players of different height and style.

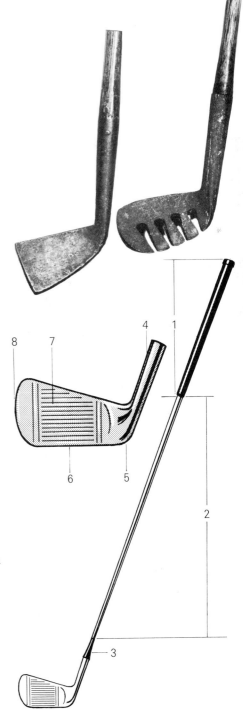

Top, an iron of 1700 (right) and a rake niblick

The nomenclature of the iron:
1 grip, surmounted by plug: 2 shaft: 3 ferrule:
4 neck or socket: 5 heel: 6 sole: 7 face with corrugation: 8 toe

Irons are usually employed when a player is in range of the green and are graded so that a good player, in normal conditions, knows how far each iron can be hit. The modern iron clubs, particularly the wedge and sand iron, have made the game easier. In the early days irons were rare and evolved gradually.

Women's Open Strokeplay 1969; British Ladies' 1973, runner-up 1969

Technically one of the soundest British golfers since World War II. The somewhat erratic nature of Ann Irvin's golfing career reflects the varying intensity of her desire to compete rather than any flaw in her game. The proudest moment of a career that

the finest phase of her career. That the Curtis Cup match the following year hung in the balance until the last hour was in large measure due to her.

It seemed now as though her career was approaching its height, but in the Amateur Championship the same year she was taken ill in the early stages and had to withdraw.

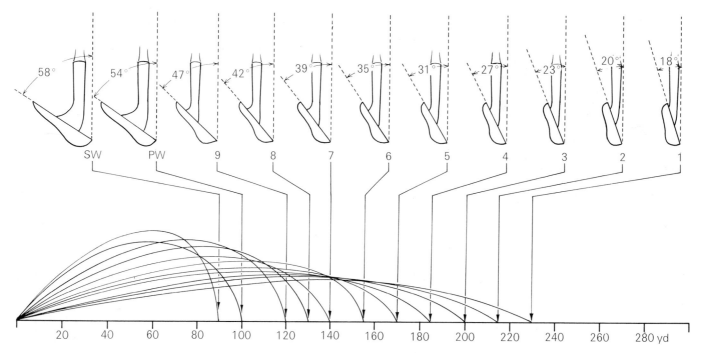

The earliest types were the crude-looking 'Carrick' irons. They were deep in the blade and were used to hack the old feathery ball, which was susceptible to cutting or tearing, from rough places such as tracks and ruts. Hence the rut iron and track iron. Then came the cleek with the advent of the gutty ball which Allan Robertson realized could be easily adapted to use with irons; the niblick, introduced by Tom Morris for short pitches; and the mashie, of which J. H. Taylor was the master. The mashie was the equivalent of the modern no. 5 iron.

It was the Americans who developed the more lofted irons, the wedges. These suited their conditions better. With the adoption of steel shafts, however, matched sets of irons became the fashion; players now carried more than just a jigger, cleek, mashie and niblick, and numbers replaced names.

Irvin, Ann Lesley BRITISH

b. Lancashire 1944. Curtis Cup 1962, 1968, 1970; European Women's Team 1965, 1967, 1969, 1971; Commonwealth Tournament 1967; English Ladies' 1967, 1974; British

suffered from interruption was her performance in the 1968 Curtis Cup match when, playing at the top of the British team at Newcastle, Co. Down, she won 3½ points out of 4 and was throughout the mainstay of her side. Whenever she was available, she was too good to leave out of any team, but uncertain health made her a doubtful risk for a world-wide trip, and certainly cost her her place in the 1968 World Cup team. A compact figure with small hands in the tradition of that world-class golfer, Marlene Streit, her orthodox swing was grooved and firm from an early age, and she put more power into her shots than many larger women. She also possessed a fine determination and concentration which set her apart from the less serious section of women's golf.

Although she formed part of the 1962 Curtis Cup team, it was not until 1967 that she won the championship title that her play suggested she would win much sooner. That year when she defeated Mrs A. Pickard (Margaret Nichol) in the final of the English Ladies' at Alwoodley it was felt that justice had at last been done, and she entered upon

In the 1969 Amateur at Royal Portrush she came as near to winning the title as she had ever done. Her way was barred by the indomitable figure of Catharine Lacoste who fought back from 4 down with 7 played to win the match on the 17th green. However, her patience was at last rewarded when she won the 1973 Championship at Carnoustie, beating Michelle Walker who was trying to win for the third successive year.

Irwin, Hale AMERICAN

b. Joplin, Mo., 1945. US Open 1974

A one-time college footballer of note and graduate of Colorado, Hale Irwin achieved eminence by winning the 1974 US Open at Winged Foot with a score of 287. His victory was not quite as surprising as some in the past because he had twice won the Heritage Classic, was 4th in the 1974 US Masters, and had made steady progress on the Tour. But it was generally thought that Nicklaus, Player, Weiskopf or Miller would be in their element at Winged Foot on a course the USGA had prepared with characteristic thoroughness.

Irons – the approximate distance achieved by the average golfer

As it was, the bespectacled Irwin, a sound rather than a spectacular golfer, played best of all and deservedly won in the end by 2 strokes from the even less well-known Forrest Fezler.

Israel

Israel has one golf course. This is an all-grass

18-hole course of approximately 6,600 yd (6,035 m) and par 72, at the Caesarea GCC, about 25 miles north of Tel Aviv, along the coastal highway linking that city with Haifa. The Caesarea course was built in 1960-1 on seaside dunes which for centuries have covered the ruins of the ancient city of Caesarea, an important port 2,000 years ago

Ann Irvin

under Herod the Great. Here, as elsewhere throughout the arid Middle East, where sand predominates and fresh water is a precious commodity, it was necessary to install an irrigation system and to introduce a combination of imported grass seed and fertilizers to grow and maintain fairway turf and putting greens on soil spread over sand. The course was opened in 1961 when Sam Snead played an exhibition match of contrasting styles with Harry Weetman.

Visitors are welcome to play at Caesarea where the Mediterranean climate permits all-year play. The most favourable weather generally is in spring and autumn when there is little if any rain and the temperature is more comfortable than in the hotter summer months. Seasonal rains make the winter months somewhat undependable; otherwise the weather then is good for golf.

The clubhouse overlooks the Mediterranean, and has good facilities.

Istanbul GC SEE TURKEY

Italy

Forty courses were in use in 1970 but most of them are open only from March to November because of the rigours of the winter climate in northern Italy where they are situated. Because the Mediterranean has no tides, Italy does not possess links-type courses associated with dunes, except perhaps Venice which is laid out half in dunes and half in pine woods. The view is sometimes expressed that golf as it developed in Britain was first played on the Continent in Rome by Scottish officers who had followed Bonnie Prince Charlie into exile. Italian courses generally are kept in impeccable order to satisfy the requirements of one of the most fastidious golfing publics in the world. The clubhouses of courses like Barlassina, Monza, Turin, Padua and Olgiata are almost palatial, and good taste and quality often compensate when size is lacking.

Two of the 40 courses are par 3 and three Clubs (Turin, Monza and Olgiata) have two courses, 18 and 9 holes. Those three and five others – Acquasanta, Villa d'Este, Venice, Ugolino (Florence) and Biella – are outstanding and are listed separately under the name of the club. Several others are worthy of note: San Remo was where, in 1935, Percy Alliss set a record low figure of 262 for a national championship, a figure lowered in 1970 by Lu Liang Huang in the French Open at Biarritz; Rapallo, Garlenda, Bologna, Carmate, Padua, Barlassina, and Menaggio, one of the prettiest courses and

the second oldest in Italy (1906).

There are eight mountain courses, open for the most part only during the three summer months. Spectacular examples of these are Sestriere, 6,000 ft above sea level, where Henry Cotton won the Italian Open in 1937, and Courmayeur on the edge of the Entrèves glacier, with Mont Blanc in the background making the most towering drive look puny. Golf is mostly restricted to that part of the country lying north of Rome. South of the capital, apart from some new Sardinian ventures and a course on the Ionian Sea, Italy is, or was until recently, a golfing desert, but there are signs that this is changing.

J

Jack, Robert Reid BRITISH
b. Cumbernauld, Dunbartonshire, 1924. Scottish Amateur 1955; British Amateur 1957, semi-finalist 1956; Walker Cup 1957, 1959; Eisenhower Trophy 1958; joint 5th British Open 1959.

A light-weight, compact golfer with a classical, fluent swing. Jack's time at the top was comparatively brief, but, in his lovely style and his ceaseless search after perfection, he left his mark. The year 1957 was the peak of his career. He won a most convincing victory in the British Amateur at Formby and later took part in a dramatic match at the top of the British Walker Cup side. Standing 5 up at lunch on Billy Joe Patton, he raised hopes of an overall British victory, but, after a faltering start to the second round, he was subjected to a stream of heart-breaking recovery shots by the wayward but always resilient Patton, and lost the match on the last green. Two years later Jack had his revenge at Muirfield by defeating Patton in the Walker Cup match, but it was a hollow revenge for the United States had already assured themselves of

Reid Jack

victory. On Scottish links Jack was always formidable, showing real class in a wind or from a tight lie. In the 1959 Open at Muirfield he finished in a tie for 5th place, which equalled the best finish by a British amateur in that event since the war; a year later at St Andrews he finished tied 15th, 2nd amateur to Guy Wolstenholme. He has won several medals at the Royal and Ancient, but was unable to devote enough time to the game in the 1960s to remain in first-class company.

Jacklin, Anthony BRITISH
b. Scunthorpe, Lincolnshire, 1944. British Assistants' 1965; Dunlop Masters 1967, 1973; Pringle Tournament 1967; Ryder Cup 1967, 1969, 1971, 1973; Jacksonville Open 1968, 1972; British Open 1969; US Open 1970; Lancome Tournament 1970; Viyella-PGA 1972; Italian Open 1973

Tony Jacklin was the man who brought a new pride to British professional golf; a player capable of beating the best in the world, who became the first British-born double champion since Ted Ray in 1920. His victory in the British Open in 1969 ended the longest period in the championship's history without a British winner – 18 years from the time Max Faulkner won at Portrush in 1951. By so doing, Jacklin set new standards for young British professionals, convincing them that the Americans were not invincible and showing the financial rewards that can be gained. The fortune he has accumulated far exceeds that made by any other British player. Before him, nobody had been able to exploit the growing market in Britain but through his golf, which set him apart, and because of his positive personality, he became a national hero overnight.

As a boy Jacklin sold papers outside the steelworks in Scunthorpe where his father drove a locomotive. His father took to the game late in life and became very keen, but he was opposed to the idea of his son turning professional. Tony, however, after a short amateur career in which he played for the England Boys' team, joined up with Bill Shankland at Potters Bar GC, Middlesex, in November 1961 when he was 17 and never for a moment had cause for regret.

Like many assistants, he found his early training heartbreakingly long, but gradually his tournament career took shape. In 1964 he accepted an offer to play the winter tour in South Africa; he had his first taste of American golf at the Carling Open tournament at Pleasant Valley, Ark., in 1965; and, on his return home, won the Assistants' title at Hartsbourne CC, Hertfordshire.

Technically his swing was still a trifle fast and unreliable but competitively he was wasting no time proving himself. At the end of 1966 he represented England in the World Cup in Tokyo, and the following spring played in his first US Masters where he outscored his partner, Arnold Palmer, in one round.

The effect upon Jacklin of being paired with his self-confessed hero was immense. It showed that he had a definite liking for the limelight and thereafter his progress was rapid. Later that summer he won his first major tournament, the Pringle at Lytham St Annes. He finished 5th in the British Open at Hoylake, engaged the McCormack organization to manage his affairs, and in September won the Dunlop Masters at Sandwich with a last round of 64 that included a hole in one at the 16th. His aggregate for the four rounds was 274.

This was an undoubted turning point in his life but of even greater significance was his victory in the Jacksonville Open when he rejoined the American tour in 1968. It was the greatest achievement by a British golfer for years and the prelude to his historic success in the British Open in July 1969. British crowds had grown accustomed to greeting overseas winners of their championship and there were memorable scenes as he played the last few holes. Those who had watched Jacklin blossom into a champion were impressed by the technical improvement that accompanied his success, particularly the way he had learned in America the proper part that the legs play in the swing. This gave it an unhurried control that added authority and conviction to his game under pressure. His total of 280 was two better than Bob Charles, and the acclaim he received was the reward for years of dedication and hard work, but nobody expected him to follow this triumph so quickly with the even more difficult task of winning the US Open.

The Americans recognized the impact he had made in their country but were hardly ready to salute him as their champion as well. In difficult weather conditions, however, and on a course that drew unfavourable comments from many leading players, he began and ended the championship with a birdie, became only the second man to shoot four sub-par rounds in the US Open, and led from start to finish. From the moment that he returned a first round of 70, compared with a 79 by Palmer, an 80 by Player and an 81 by Nicklaus, he managed the Hazeltine National course at Chaska, Minn., better than anyone, compensating for the inevitable mistakes with a spell of putting far more inspired than anything he had experienced in a long while. He led by 4 strokes after 54 holes and in the last round, apart from an uneasy passage at the 7th and 8th, was always in command. At the 9th, he holed from 30 ft for a birdie 3 after driving into the rough, the ball hitting the back of the hole and jumping in the air before disappearing. With the aid of some more

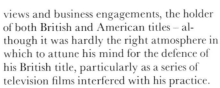

resolute holing out, he widened the gap, finally holing from 30 ft on the 18th for another birdie. He thus became the first British player to win since Ted Ray in 1920, and his winning margin of 7 strokes has only been exceeded by Jim Barnes in 1921.

With his fortune assured, Jacklin returned home to all manner of celebrations, inter-

views and business engagements, the holder of both British and American titles – although it was hardly the right atmosphere in which to attune his mind for the defence of his British title, particularly as a series of television films interfered with his practice.

The omens were not propitious but once again Jacklin startled everyone, this time by playing the first 9 holes of his opening round at St Andrews in 29 and starting home with a birdie. He was all set for a score in the low 60s when a violent storm washed out play for the day just as he had hit his second shot at the long 14th into an unplayable spot in a gorse bush on the right. The next morning he finished in 67 and maintained a stout defence of his title, finishing only 3 strokes behind Nicklaus and Sanders, but, without the storm on the first evening, he might well have won again.

He was awarded the OBE for his services to golf and, not surprisingly, won the 1970 British Golf Writers' Trophy as the person who had done most for British golf. For Jacklin 1971 was a difficult year, although

Tony Jacklin – a series of studies

he did well to finish 3rd in the British Open at Birkdale without being on his game, but in 1972 he won the Jacksonville Open for the second time and in the Open at Muirfield in July was yet again very much in the running for victory. As he and his partner, Lee Trevino, approached the 17th green in the last round, he seemed the most likely winner, but Trevino holed his third devastating chip in 21 holes; Jacklin, after a weak chip, took 3 putts, and a 5 at the 18th cost him 2nd place to Jack Nicklaus.

Jacklin spent the rest of the 1972 season in Britain, winning the PGA championship at Wentworth and later playing a truly memorable match with Trevino in the Piccadilly Matchplay Championship. He then went on to win the Australian Dunlop tournament in Melbourne and in the spring of 1973 captured the Italian Open Championship in Rome.

Having become, with the blessing of the other British players, the first British golfer to receive regular appearance money for tournaments, at home and on the Continent, his play for most of the remainder of the summer lacked the brilliance that everyone, perhaps unjustly, had come to expect although he ended on a high note. Jacklin's golf, however, has never been known for its consistency. It has brought him fame and wealth simply because, when the mood is on him, he is capable of being as good as anyone in the world.

Jackson, Barbara Amy Bridget BRITISH b. Birmingham 1936. British Girls' 1954; English Ladies' 1956, runner-up 1958; Curtis Cup 1958, 1964, 1968; runner-up British Ladies' 1964; Canadian Ladies' Open 1967

For many years after becoming British Girls' Champion in 1954, Bridget Jackson was one of Britain's leading women golfers. She won the English Championship in 1956 at Hunstanton, beating Mrs Ruth Ferguson in the final by 2 and 1 and was runner-up to Mrs M. Bonallack (Angela Ward) at Formby in 1958. She also had a formidable record in foursomes events. She had plenty of power but never became a reliable driver.

She won the Australian foursomes with Janette Robertson (Mrs Innes Wright) in 1955. Probably her finest performance was in reaching the final of the British Ladies' Championship at Prince's, Sandwich, in 1964 although this ended sadly. She missed a short putt to beat Carol Sorenson of America on the last green before losing at the 37th. Bridget Jackson later played a notable part in administrative work, became chairman of the English Ladies' Golf Association and

captained the British team in the 1973 Vagliano Trophy event.

Jackson, James G. AMERICAN
b. 1924. Leading Amateur US Open 1952; Missouri Amateur 1954; Trans-Mississippi Amateur 1954-5; Walker Cup 1953, 1955

Jacobs, John Robert Maurice BRITISH
b. Lindrick, Yorkshire, 1925. Ryder Cup 1955; Dutch Open 1957; South African Matchplay 1957

A regular British tournament player for many years whose best achievements were his victory over Gary Player in the South African Matchplay final by 2 and 1, and his Ryder Cup performance in 1955 at Palm Springs. Jacobs and Johnny Fallon won the top foursome for Britain, and in the singles he beat Cary Middlecoff, US Masters Champion at the time, by 1 hole. This was a unique performance by a British player in his first match in America, and one that made it surprising that he never played again. It was also surprising that Jacobs never won a major tournament in Britain, though he often came close to it.

Since then Jacobs has become one of the leading teachers of the game and a highly respected figure. He has established a series of golf centres where his services are in constant demand. He became coach to a number of international sides, notably the victorious British Walker Cup team of 1971. Later that year he was appointed tournament director of the British PGA and was responsible for injecting order, new wealth, and new life into the professional circuit. Jacobs has also made instructional films and done commentaries for television.

Jacobs, K. Thomas AMERICAN
b. Denver, Colo., 1935. US Junior Amateur 1951; runner-up US Open 1964; Ryder

Cup 1965; runner-up US Masters 1966

A steady rather than a spectacular performer, although in winning the Utah Open in 1963 he scored a 62. Tommy Jacobs played well on the big occasions. His best finish in the US Open was as runner-up to Ken Venturi at the Congressional club in 1964, in the course of which he scored a 64 in the second round, equalling the lowest round in the championship at that time. This earned him a place in the 1965 Ryder Cup team that visited Britain; he won three of the four matches in which he played. In 1966 he figured in a three-way play-off with Jack Nicklaus and Gay Brewer for the US Masters after 17 players had either held or shared the lead during the tournament.

Jamaica
Golf has probably been played longer in Jamaica than anywhere else in the West Indies. The Manchester Club at Mandeville claims in fact to be one of the oldest golf clubs in the world outside Scotland, with a founding date of 1868. Of the dozen clubs in the island the best are probably Cayamanas

and Constant Spring. The latter lies a little north of Kingston and was laid out in 1931 by a Canadian, Stanley Thomson, over land that used to be a sugar plantation. Ruins of its cane mill can still be seen between the 9th and 10th fairways. Another Kingston club is the Liguanea, founded in 1908. Golf on the island is governed by the Jamaica Golf Association, based at Kingston.

The Jamaica Open Championship began in 1953. Winners have included Antonio Cerda and Roberto de Vicenzo (twice).

James, Louis N. AMERICAN
b. 1882

James was US Amateur Champion in 1902 at Glen View, Chicago, when a new system was introduced of qualifying 64 places. James squeezed in with the highest score of 94 but, two months short of his 20th birthday, reached the final where he beat Eben M. Byers.

Jameson, Betty AMERICAN
b. Norman, Okla., 1919. Women's Trans-Mississippi Amateur 1937, 1940; US

Top, Bridget Jackson putting on the 18th green of the Blue course at the Berkshire GC

Above, James G. Jackson

Top, John Jacobs

Above, Tommy Jacobs playing in the 1965 Ryder Cup

Women's Amateur 1939-40; US Women's Open 1947, runner-up 1946

After winning the Women's National Amateur at Wee Burn in 1939 and successfully defending her title at Delmonte, Cal., the next year, she was co-medallist in 1941 at Brookline, but was unexpectedly beaten by Janet Younker by 1 hole in the first round.

Betty Jameson won the second American Women's Open Championship in 1947 at Starmount Forest CC, Greensborough, N. Car., with a total of 295 and 6 strokes to spare, having been runner-up to Patty Berg in the first Championship in 1946.

One of the 'Big Four' during the early days of the women professionals, she won

Top, Louis James

Above, Betty Jameson

over $91,000 in prize money between 1948 and 1965.

Jamieson, Andrew, Jr BRITISH
b. Glasgow 1905. Glasgow Amateur 1925, runner-up 1926; semi-finalist British Amateur 1926; Walker Cup 1926; Scottish Amateur 1927, runner-up 1931

Jamieson, a neat and efficient golfer who played many times for Scotland, is remembered primarily for beating Bobby Jones in the 5th round of the 1926 British Amateur Championship at Muirfield without Jones winning a hole.

January, Don AMERICAN
b. Plainview, Tex., 1929. Apple Valley Clambake 1956; Dallas Open 1956; Valencia Open 1959; Tucson Open 1960, 1963; St Paul Open 1961; Ryder Cup 1965; Philadelphia Classic 1966; USPGA 1967, runner-up 1961; Tournament of Champions 1968, Greater Jacksonville Open 1970

A consistent winner on the tour since the mid-1950s, when he turned professional after serving in the US Air Force. January had won many amateur tournaments and had been a member of the championship North Texas State golf teams of 1950, 1951 and 1952 with Billy Maxwell and Joe Conrad. His first victory as a professional came in the Dallas Open of 1956 when he holed a bunker shot for an eagle on the 72nd hole. He made several good showings in the US Open, USPGA and Masters over the next few years, the best being in 1961 when he was runner-up to Jerry Barber in the USPGA. In 1961 he won $50,000 for a hole-in-one at Palm Springs but two years later when he 'aced' the same hole, he collected only $100. The highlight of his career came with his victory in the USPGA Championship of 1967 after a play-off with Don Massengale (69 to 71). They had tied with 281. This qualified him for the Tournament of Champions which he won in 1968. In 1971 he finished in the top 10 in eight of his 22 starts and in the top 5 five times. He was a member of the USPGA tournament committee in 1960-1 and served as chairman the following year.

Japan

The first golf club in Japan was formed in 1901 with a 9-hole layout built on the slopes of Mount Rokko, not far from Kobe, by a group of foreign residents of that city, mostly English, with a sprinkling of Scots no doubt, who needed exercise but found the native sports of judo and kendo (fencing) too strenuous, or were moved by nostalgia for the old country. The prime mover was an

English tea merchant named Arthur Groom who served as the club's first honorary secretary. Shortly after formation the club placed an advertisement in a Kobe newspaper inviting people interested in golf to join. Of the 170 who responded 7 were Japanese; but there is no record to show that any of the 7 ever played the game.

According to an early record reported in S. Setsu's exhaustive work on the history of golf in Japan (published in 1960), two Japanese living abroad had taken up golf some five years before the first spadeful of earth was turned at Rokko. Y. Mizutani (later Vice Admiral), who was sent by the navy to study in Britain in 1896, was persuaded by two American students in the

college to join them in the game at Blackheath in London; the story, as he told it, was that he played with gutta-percha balls and a 'full set' of clubs consisting of a driver, mashie and putter.

The second Japanese to take up golf in a foreign country was Ryoichiro Arai, a silk merchant who went to New York in 1876 and lived there until his death 60 years later. He was introduced to golf while on holiday at Pinehurst in 1901; and it seems that the bug bit so hard that he not only became an ardent golfer but urged other Japanese businessmen in New York to join him on the courses. Most prominent among his early pupils were Messrs Murai, M. Tanaka and Jinushi of Nippon Toki's office who took up the game in 1903. These men and a few others like them, became, on their return to Tokyo, the pioneers of golf in Japan in the early years.

Another disciple was Shin Inouye, manager of Mitsui Bussan's New York office. A champion tennis player in college, his golf improved with such giant strides that he not only won the club championship of Haworth

Don January playing in the 1965 Ryder Cup Match at Royal Birkdale

GC in nearby New Jersey but became in 1918, on his return to Tokyo, the first Japanese ever to win the Japan Amateur Championship, thus breaking the monotonous string of victories by foreigners.

The first golf club in the Tokyo area was formed in 1906 by foreign residents of Yokohama, starting with a 9-hole layout inside a racecourse in the suburb of Negishi. Soon extended to 18 holes, the club held the first 'Interport' match with Rokko in 1907.

Japan's first public course was built in 1911 at Unzen spa in the hills behind Nagasaki. As Japanese golfers were very few, especially in Kyushu, most of the play at Unzen was by foreign businessmen living in Nagasaki and others who brought their families from Shanghai for a holiday during July and August. The course has become quite popular in recent years, especially in the spring because of the multi-hued azaleas which beautify the whole course. But a player here should start with a good supply of balls because a few may be lost to crows who wait at strategic spots, ready to pick up a ball even before it comes to rest. Some have been seen catching a ball in flight.

The first golf club formed by Japanese for Japanese was the Tokyo club started in 1914. The course was laid out in the suburb of Komazawa which was largely farmland in those days. The design was entrusted to an American named Brady, then captain of the Negishi Club, and a Scots veteran named Colchester. The chief promoter in this

project was Junnosuke Inouye, then president of Yokohama Specie Bank, later Finance Minister, who had become addicted while serving in London. He was supported by some 30 leaders in business and financial circles, most of whom had learned the game abroad; but a few, complete strangers to golf, were induced to lend their names and titles to enhance the club's prestige. It was in consideration of these 'sleeping' members who never used the club's facilities that it was decided to charge green fees in addition to initiation fees and annual dues since it would not be fair, the organizing committee felt, to compel non-users to share the burden of operating costs. This practice of charging fees each time a member plays is still widely followed in Japan.

As Tokyo grew in size, the surrounding farms gradually turned into residential sites. So in 1932 Tokyo GC moved to Asaka 20 miles to the north of the city and employed C. H. Alison of England who produced a magnificent layout. As an experiment bent grass was used for the fairways and greens;

but it was found that it could not take the midsummer heat, and two years later it was replaced by *korai* for the fairways. But worse was to come. In 1940, as the war clouds darkened over the Pacific, the military took over the club with all its facilities, necessitating another move, this time to a remodelled public course next door to Kasumigaseki CC, which it closely resembles in contour and scenery.

The 1920s and 1930s brought a steady growth in the number of golf clubs in the country; by the outbreak of war there were 60. Most popular among them were Koga near the city of Fukuoka in Kyushu; Hirono, Ibaraki and Inagawa in the Osaka-Kobe district; and Abiko, Sagami, Kasumigaseki, Koganei and Kawana in the Tokyo area. But the outbreak of war not only put a stop to further construction but forced many already in existence to be turned into vegetable plots or military installations. As the military frowned on golf as a Western sport, only the real die-hards continued playing through the war years, and that almost furtively. The last Eastern Japanese Amateur held before the war was permitted only under the sponsorship of the Welfare Ministry with participation limited to golfers of 40 and older. The winner received, not a silver trophy, but a certificate of commendation signed by the Welfare Minister.

The end of the war in August 1945 seemed to sound the death knell for golf in Japan. For within a month or two of the landing of the Allied Forces, all but a handful of the 60 golf clubs were requisitioned for their exclusive use. In the Tokyo area, for instance, only two of the nine clubs were left in Japanese hands.

With the end of the Occupation in the spring of 1952, all requisitioned clubs were returned to their Japanese owners. That is not to say that Allied personnel were deprived of golfing privileges, for several of the clubs continued to 'play ball' with them. Kasumigaseki CC, for instance, extended temporary membership to 300 US Air Force golfers which enabled them to enjoy the game with the same rights and obligations as those of Japanese members but without payment of the initiation fees of 1.5 million yen. The relationship was continued until June 1969 when a golf course for exclusive use of the Air Force was constructed by the Japanese Government at Camp Tama, a former army ordnance depot.

As Japan's golfing population increased during and after the Occupation, many new courses came into being, some literally carved out of mountainsides. But the event that really sparked the golf boom that has

Japanese golfers: *above left,* Isao Aoki on the 8th fairway at Nueva Andalucía in the World Cup of 1973; *above right,* Tohru Nakamura on the same course and, *top,* Masashi Osaki in the US Masters, 1972

astounded even the Japanese was the surprising victory of the Japanese team in the Canada Cup matches of 1957 played over the East Course of Kasumigaseki CC, 'Pete' Nakamura winning the individual cup with a score of 274 and the team championship with his partner Koichi Ono. With the home team having a comfortable margin at the end of the third round, nearly 10,000 fans came from Tokyo and its environs to witness the home team's victory on the final day.

That was but the first of numerous big international golf events staged in Japan Next came the match between Japan's 'Pete' and Bob Rosburg of America, for the filming of Shell's 'Wonderful World of Golf' TV series; Rosburg, playing on *korai* greens for the first time, beat 'Pete' by outputting him. Such well-known foreign stars as Hagen, Kirkwood, Sarazen, Snead, Palmer, Nicklaus, Player, Thomson and Jacklin have visited Japan to compete in competitions and to hold exhibitions and clinics.

In 1967 there were 10 major tournaments with prize money totalling 60 million yen. In 1972, some 50 big events covered a 7-month season that began with the last leg of the Far Eastern Circuit in April. The total offered in 1972 was in the neighbourhood of 300 million yen with a first prize of one million yen. For Japanese professionals, many of whom have graduated from the caddie ranks, that is quite a windfall. In 1970 Japan produced its first 10-million-yen winner in Takaaki Kono; but he was topped in 1971 by the up-and-coming 'Jumbo' Ozaki who earned nearly 18 million yen in cash plus three cars. Ozaki is said to be capable of matching drives with Nicklaus.

According to the Japan Golf Association, organized in 1924 with Mitsujiro Ishii as president – later Deputy Premier and President of the Diet and still an enthusiastic

Japan: the Yomiuri CC

golfer with a 10 handicap – the number of golfers in the country was estimated in 1972 to be about 5 million, of whom 3 million play an average of one round a month. To accommodate this number, there are 600 courses already in operation from the southern tip of Kyushu to Hokkaido in the north. The end is not in sight, for some 80 new courses were under construction in 1972. Even then, it is suspected, not a few players will have their golf confined to driving ranges. Some 360 clubs are affiliated with the Japanese Golf Association.

Jenkins, Dan AMERICAN
b. Fort Worth, Tex.

Sports writer in the sophisticated vein, chiefly associated with *Sports Illustrated*, an American magazine of which he is an associate editor. After attending Texas Christian University, he worked as a columnist and later as sports editor of the *Fort Worth Press* and the *Dallas Times-Herald*. He is the author of several humorous books on golf and also of *Semi-Tough*, a best-selling novel about professional football.

Jenkins, J. L. C. BRITISH
b. Glasgow 1883. British Amateur 1914; 8th British Open 1914.

Jenkins won the British Amateur championship by beating Charles Hezlet in the final at Sandwich by 3 and 2. He played for Scotland several times and in the forerunner to the Walker Cup in 1921.

Jersey, Royal CHANNEL ISLANDS
Grouville, Jersey. 18 holes

Jersey is a small island with only two 18-hole golf courses, Royal Jersey and La Moye, but its name has a special place in golfing history. Within a stone's throw of the Royal Jersey Club at Grouville, Harry Vardon and Ted Ray, both winners of the United States and British Open championships were born and, so to speak, founded the 'Jersey School' of professional golfers which included such names as the Gaudins, the Renoufs, the Boomers, the Le Chevaliers and, more recently, Tommy Horton.

The Boomers' names are more closely linked with La Moye, which occupies a spectacular setting on a western headland of the island, but Vardon and Ray belonged to Grouville. They owed their development as golfers to the opportunity they had of playing over the links of Royal Jersey which was founded in 1878 when Vardon was eight years old. F. W. Brewster was the prime mover in persuading seven others to subscribe a guinea to become founder members and the following year Queen Victoria

granted to the Club the style of 'Royal'.

The course lies on gently undulating ground that takes the golfer out along the curve of Grouville Bay towards the picturesque harbour at Gorey, huddled beneath the castle of Mont Orgueil. During World War II, the Germans occupied the coast, causing no little harm to the course, but the scars have healed and, as the holes move inland, their change of character provides a pleasant contrast.

Jigger
An obsolete iron club with a narrow blade. It has no equivalent in the modern set but had roughly the loft of a no. 4 iron and was mainly used for recoveries from bad lies and for chipping.

Jockey Club, The ARGENTINA
Buenos Aires. 36 holes

Situated in San Isidro, some 15 miles from the city, both courses (Red and Blue) were designed by the British architect, Alister Mackenzie, and were inaugurated in 1935. The club, founded in 1882, has 7,000 members of whom more than 1,000 play golf. As its name suggests, it is principally concerned with horse racing. The racetrack and polo fields lie next to the golf courses.

Johannesburg GC, Royal SOUTH AFRICA
Johannesburg GC, Transvaal. 36 holes; (2 courses); East Course 7,283 yd (6,660 m); par 74

Before the club settled in its present site beyond Orange Grove it was obliged to move at least four times from the day it started in 1890, when the town was only a rough mining camp. It was in 1906 that the land was purchased that gave the club its permanent home; the sum of £2,000 each was contributed by Sir Lionel Phillips and by two mining magnates, Sir Abe Bailey and Sir George Farrar. The course, laid out by Laurie Waters, a young golfer from St Andrews, Scotland, with a flair for construction, was a big advance on anything attempted previously, and for the first time grass greens were laid. One of them, the 3rd on the West, still survives as a testimony to his work. The creation of a second course, the East, which became the championship test, began in 1933 and was the work of R. G. Grimsdell, the club professional at the time. It is laid out in somewhat rolling country. There is a valley with a stream flowing through that is featured at several holes and a wide variety of trees, many of which determine the line of play. The course provides a high standard of championship test. It is very long but not unduly so at the altitude of the Rand. Long two-shotters abound, calling for every club in the bag. Of many championships held there one of the most memorable was the victory of the amateur Denis Hutchinson in the South African Open of 1959 after a tremendous battle with Gary Player.

Jöhncke, Claes SWEDISH

b. 1941. French Junior 1959; Swedish Junior Open 1961; British Isles v. Continent of Europe 1962, 1966, 1968, 1970, 1972, 1974; Eisenhower Trophy 1962, 1964, 1966, 1970; Scandinavian Open Amateur 1967, 1969

The best of the younger generation of Swedish golfers. An elegant player, Jöhncke is better at strokeplay than matchplay (he was Swedish Amateur Strokeplay Champion seven times between 1963 and 1969). He has twice been Sweden's Golfer of the Year, in 1967 and 1969. He went to work in America, but retained his place in the Continental team in 1974.

Johnston, Harrison R. AMERICAN

b. Minnesota 1896. Walker Cup 1924, 1928, 1930; US Amateur 1929

Jimmy Johnston was one of the top amateurs in the United States through the 1920s, despite the fact that he had been shell-shocked during World War I and on that account had to fight tension and nerves. These went so far as to cause him trouble in lining up the club behind the ball at the address. As late as 1929 when he beat Dr O. F. Willing in the final of the US Amateur he took 43 for the first 9, but he was not afraid of meeting the best. In the 1921 US Amateur he beat Francis Ouimet in an early round and in the following year Tommy Armour. Then in 1927 Johnston was again in the last 8 of the US Amateur. In 1928 in the last 8

Harrison R. Johnston

Bobby Jones routed him by 10 and 9, but Jones had to go to the last green against him in the British Amateur of 1930 after being 4 up with 5 to play. Johnston was victorious in all his Walker Cup matches.

Jolly, Herbert C. BRITISH

Ryder Cup 1926-7; semi-finalist British Professional Matchplay 1928

One of the famous group of Channel Islanders who made such an impact on British golf. His career was affected by World War I, in which he served in the infantry. Afterwards he soon made his mark in tournament golf, his biggest triumph being victory over Walter Hagen in the final of the first *Yorkshire Evening News* tournament in 1923. He won that event again in 1930 and was twice runner-up.

Jones, Ernest BRITISH

b. Manchester 1887

Ernest Jones will ever be remembered for his oft-repeated dictum – 'Swing the clubhead'. Doubtless he could have been a sound tournament player – the loss of a leg on Vimy Ridge in World War I stopped any ambitions in that direction – but he was spared to be a fine club professional and one of the greatest coaches the game has produced. During the 15 years he spent at Chislehurst GC in Kent, he built up a big reputation as a teacher. In 1924 he emigrated to the United States where he entered

upon the most noteworthy and profitable period of his career.

Jones, Robert Trent AMERICAN

b. Ince, Lancashire, 1906

In the more than 40 years that he has been in business, Robert Trent Jones has become probably the best-known golf course architect in the world. His courses can be found everywhere – in the South Sea Islands and the Caribbean, in North America and North Africa, on the southern coast of Spain and the southern coast of Alaska, in Switzerland and Japan, in England and in Colombia.

Jones has designed or remodelled over 300 courses, and they include some of the most renowned and most controversial in the world. During one five-year period in the 1960s, the US Open Championship was played each year on golf courses either designed from the beginning by Jones or remodelled by him. Among the courses he has built outside continental United States are Dorado Beach and Cerromar Beach, Puerto Rico; Cotton Bay Club, Eleuthera in

A watercolour by Richard Elms of the 12th hole of the Spy Glass Hill course, one of Robert Trent Jones's many architectural achievements

the Bahamas; Mauna Kea in Hawaii; the Geneva GC, Switzerland; Costa Smerelda Golf Course, Sardinia; Karuizawa Golf Course, Japan; Moor Allerton GC, Yorkshire; and Sotogrande, near Cadiz, Spain. His American achievements include The Dunes, Peachtree, Hazeltine, Bellerive, and Spyglass Hill. He has remodelled Oakland

Hills, Olympic, the CC of Detroit, Sea Island, Southern Hills, Mid-Ocean, Winged Foot, and the first 9 at Congressional.

Jones, a friendly man with a pleasing personality, is sensitive to criticism, and his designs have won him a good deal of it. If there were such a thing as a typical Jones course, it would be quite long – 7,000 yd or more from the back tees – with long, narrow tees, many doglegged holes, and huge, undulating greens with a number of pin locations. His bunkers are flared, and they have an artistic look to them.

Jones was born in England in 1906. His parents arrived in the United States when young Trent was 4, and settled in Rochester, N.Y. Trent became a rather good teenage golfer, but at 19 he developed a stomach ulcer and gave up serious competition. He turned to golf-course architecture, preparing himself at Cornell University where he took an odd assortment of courses that did not lead to a degree but did lead to his current fame – agronomy, engineering, and landscape architecture, plus an additional course in sketching at the Rochester Art School.

Jones' first course was Durand-Eastman Park in Rochester, which he built on swampland. Stanley Thompson, a Canadian who was a well-known golf course architect of that period, was impressed with the design and persuaded Jones to form a partnership with him. It lasted about 10 years, until Thompson's death, and Jones then went on his own in the early 1940s. With the postwar era came the great expansion in golf, and Jones has been in the vanguard of the golf architects. His is a big concern employing perhaps 25 people – landscape architects, engineers, draftsmen. His main office is in Montclair, N.J., a suburb of New York, where he has a staff of 13, including his son Rees. Half a dozen others, including another son Bob, are in his California office in Palo Alto.

Jones, Robert Tyre, Jr AMERICAN

b. Atlanta, Ga., 1902; d. Atlanta 1971. Southern Amateur 1917, 1920, 1922; Walker Cup 1922, 1924, 1926, 1928, 1930 (captain 1928, 1930); US Open 1923, 1926, 1929-30, runner-up 1924, 1925, 1928, joint 2nd 1922, joint 5th 1921; US Amateur 1924-5, 1927-8, 1930, runner-up 1919, 1926, semi-finalist 1920, 1922; British Open 1926-7, 1930; British Amateur 1930

To the question 'How great was Bobby Jones?' the answer is usually given: 'Look at the record'. It is a record without parallel. An amateur, he won in the space of eight years, from 1923, 13 of the world's major titles – the US Amateur five times, the US Open four times, the British Open three times and the British Amateur once. He achieved this before he was 30, and in his last competitive year in 1930 he won the Open and Amateur titles of both countries – the Grand Slam of golf as it has been called. In his 11 US Open performances, starting in 1920, he finished, in addition to his four victories, three times 2nd, once tied 2nd, tied 5th, tied 8th, tied 11th. In the five American Amateur championships which he won, he defeated his opponents in 10 semi-final and final matches over 36 holes by an average margin of 9 and 8. He played in five Walker Cup singles matches, his average winning margin being 8 and 7.

As well as being a superb golf stylist, Jones was also one of the most highly educated men ever to have played the game successfully. He held degrees in engineering, literature, and law, graduating at the Atlanta School of Technology and subsequently at Harvard. He wrote lucidly and deeply about the game. The high example of sportsmanship he set, without any loss of competitive spirit, was reflected and has been perpetuated by the US Masters tournament on the course at Augusta which he was chiefly responsible for creating.

Bernard Darwin's judgment of his game was aptly phrased: 'Harry Vardon and Bobby Jones combined exquisiteness of art with utterly relentless precision in a way not given to any other golfer.' His artistry and the simplicity of his method, combined with his modesty and quietness, were immediately attractive to people. His boyish good looks, the directness of his eyes, and the air of gravity that hung around him reflecting the struggle he had gone through to obtain self-mastery, all combined to make him a magnetic personality.

Jones showed early promise. He was just nine when he won the junior championship at his club, East Lake, and he was 14 when he won his first Georgia State Amateur Championship. A year later he won the Southern Amateur and in 1919 was runner-up in the Canadian Open and the US Amateur. His style was based on that of the professional at East Lake, Stewart Maiden, a Scot who had emigrated from Carnoustie. Jones, a born imitator, did not need lessons, and it was only later that he sometimes went back to his boyhood idol for a check-up. Although sturdily built, his style was lithe and smooth with a drowsy, rhythmic grace. The swing was upright with a full shoulder turn.

He played in his first Open Championship at the age of 18, finishing in a tie for 8th place. In fact so great was his promise that the public expected him to start winning everything at once, and the years of disappointment that preceded his phenomenal years of success were made harder to bear by the interest his appearances aroused. Thus for seven years from the age of 15 he played in 10 major championships without success. He first visited Britain in 1921 where he lost in the fourth round of the Amateur and first came to know St Andrews. Though he later grew to love the course above all others, he was at first so maddened by its subtleties that he tore up his card in the fourth round of his first British Open. Many years later, in 1958, he said that, if he were allowed only one course on which to play golf in the whole world, he would choose the Old Course above all others.

Although always considerate to others and later a model of good behaviour he was prone to fits of anger when young; he hid a naturally fiery temper which broke out when he failed to satisfy his own standards of perfection and which he took some years to master.

In 1925, having tied for 2nd place the year before, he won the US Open after a play-off against Bobby Cruickshank, and this unlocked the floodgates of his unique success. In 1926 he returned to Britain; after being beaten in the fifth round of the Amateur, and having won his Walker Cup single against Cyril Tolley by 12 and 11, he decided to stay on for the Open. To play in this he had to qualify and, in so doing, scored his famous 66 at Sunningdale, which has been described as coming as close to a flawless piece of golf as anyone is likely to get. He visited one bunker and holed one long putt, otherwise he hit every green, 10 of them with the no. 2 iron or with a wood, and took 33 putts involving nothing much more than tap-ins. At Royal Lytham he won his first British championship, in spite of taking 39 putts in the final round. He shook off Al Watrous only by striking a mashie niblick out of a bunker at the 17th to the green, an historic stroke that won him the title and caused a plaque to be placed in the wall of the bunker.

His second British victory the following year at St Andrews was less of a stuggle; he swept serenely through the field winning by 6 strokes with a total of 285. He led all the way thanks to an opening 68 which set a new record and contained six putts of more than 100 ft (30 m). Over the same course in 1930 he at last secured the British Amateur victory which had eluded him for nine years and of which he said: 'There has been nothing in golf I wanted so much.' His defeat of Cyril Tolley at the 19th in the fourth round was watched by 12,000, and in the final he beat Roger Wethered by 7 and 6.

It was only the first leg of his Impregnable Quadrilateral, but it was also, because of the 18-hole matchplay, the one that had caused him the most trouble. His victory in the British Open at Hoylake was as much a triumph of character as of skill for he was not at the top of his form. Asked on his way back to the United States whether he thought he had ever played worse so successfully, he replied that he thought not. In the third round he lost 8 strokes to par in the first 3 holes, and in the fourth he took 7 at the 8th, 5 of them after being almost green high in 2. That championship cost him much and those closest to him saw that the strain on him was taking too high a toll. He had subdued a fiery temper, but he could not subdue his silent sufferings; he lost sometimes 14 lb in weight during a championship and often dare not wear a necktie lest it should make him physically sick. But two triumphs still lay ahead – the American Open came first which he won in temperatures above 100 °F. It was in the second round that he made the famous so-called lilypad shot. According to O. B. Keeler, his faithful chronicler, the ball skidded on the surface of the water and covered the remaining 20 yd to the far side of the lake in that fashion. It was at the end of that championship that he took the decision to give up competitive golf. Through the last of the four championships he was, according to Keeler, 'incomparably brilliant and incredibly sloppy by turns', and in the final he beat E. V. Homans by 8 and 7. It was typical of the margin of defeat he had time and again inflicted on opponents over 36 holes; at that distance it was extremely rare for anyone to hold him, one notable exception being George Von Elm in the 1925 final of the US Amateur. This was the end; the man who had been a national champion for eight years, retired at the age of 28.

Jones played for the United States in five Walker Cup matches. His great superiority can be judged by the margin of three of his five singles victories: over Cyril Tolley by 12 and 11, over T. P. Perkins by 13 and 12, and over Roger Wethered by 9 and 8. After he had retired, he played now and then in public for some good cause, one of which was establishing the popularity of the US Masters tournament which began in 1934; but, with the keen urge of competition removed, something had gone from his game for ever; he could not really play without the itch of ambition. Once he had retired, he made instructional films and wrote articles, and through his inspiration the Masters

tournament, his favourite golfing child, rose to be one of the major golfing events. Jones saw service with the US artillery in the war, rising to the rank of lieutenant-colonel, and a visit to Britain enabled him to renew his acquaintance with the Old Course at St Andrews. During the 1950s he began to suffer from a muscular disease, the result of

an operation, which eventually reduced him to a complete cripple. The hands which had wielded a golf club with more delicacy and effect than any golfer of his age took minutes to light a cigarette. But he was still able to journey to Britain in 1958 to inaugurate the first World Amateur Team Championship for the Eisenhower Trophy, and to receive

Top, Bobby Jones with the four major trophies, 1930

Above, Bobby Jones – a portrait

the freedom of the Burgh of St Andrews at a most moving ceremony which those present remember as an unforgettable occasion. He bore his illness with incomparable courage, and the slow destruction of his body could not dim his mind or impair his courtesy. When it became too difficult for him to watch the Masters, he continued to hold court in the little white villa alongside the 10th tee at Augusta, where the golfing celebrities of every age came to visit him and to tell him, what he still passionately wanted to know, every detail of the golf outside. When he died in the winter of 1971, after a cheerful acceptance of illness which impressed those who knew him no less than his triumphs as a golfer, he was acclaimed by every generation and in many countries outside his own, although the final year of his golfing career was more than 30 years behind. A service commemorating his life was held in St Andrews, the city which outside the United States shared most in his golfing life.

Jones, Stuart Gwyn NEW ZEALANDER

b. Hastings, N. Island, 1925. NZ Amateur 1955, 1959, 1961-2, 1964, 1966, 1971; Eisenhower Trophy 1958, 1960, 1962, 1964, 1966, 1970, 1972; Australian Foursomes 1963; NZ Watties Tournament 1965; Canadian Amateur 1967; Spalding Masters 1970

Stuart Jones, a fine rugby player, was badly burned by a geyser in 1947. During his convalescence at Rotorua, he took up golf and became the best and most consistent New Zealand amateur of his generation. By 1949, he was scratch and in 1953 he won the North Island title at Napier. From then on he was the backbone of the New Zealand side. He won his first NZ Amateur title in 1955, and in 1958 began the first of a remarkable sequence of appearances for his country in the World Amateur Team Championship; between 1958 and 1972, his only omission was in 1968 when the event was held in Melbourne. He won back his place in 1970 when his country finished 2nd in Madrid and the following year won the New Zealand Amateur for the seventh time.

Jones also won the Canadian title in 1967. In the final he beat his fellow countryman, Ross Murray, with whom he had won the Australian Foursomes in 1963.

Such remarkable consistency over a long period is testimony of a sound, easy style and a strong, competitive desire. At his best, he was a match for anyone: in 1965 his 270 led the field in the NZ Watties Tournament ahead of such mighty professionals as Thomson and Nagle; and in 1971 in a tournament at Bridge, Pa., he went round in 60. Jones is a member of the Hastings Club.

Jönköping-Huskvarna GC SWEDEN
Jönköping. 18 holes; 6,059 yd (5,540 m)

Jönköping-Huskvarna Golfklubb has a first-class course not far from Ryfors, the site of Sweden's earliest private course. The town, at the southern end of Sweden's second largest and Europe's fourth largest lake, is the centre of the South Swedish Highlands, with abundant snow in winter and rain during the summer. Several championships have been played there. In 1967 the European Junior Golf Team Championship was held at Jönköping with 10 nations participating, Spain were the winners.

Jurado, José ARGENTINIAN
b. San Martin, Buenos Aires, 1899; d. 1972. Argentine Open 1920, 1924-5, 1927, 1929, 1931; runner-up British Open 1931

The first of the great Latin golfers, Jurado was also the first Argentinian professional to make a name for himself as a tournament player. He was a popular figure, particularly in Britain, where he had a fine record in the British Open. In 1926, he tied 8th at Royal Lytham. In 1928 he led the qualifiers and finished 5th at Sandwich. In 1931 he was runner-up to Tommy Armour at Carnoustie. Coming to the 72nd hole in that championship, he needed a 4 to tie although he was not aware of it. Had he been aware, he might have gone for his second over the burn instead of playing short, for his drive was good. His score was 297 to Armour's 296.

Jurado was the favourite of the crowd throughout. The Duke of Windsor, then Prince of Wales, watched a great deal of his play in that championship and was not the only one to be attracted by the small, dapper figure with an agreeable smile, a swing as fast as greased lightning and a dashing, pleasant way with him.

In 1939 he captained a side of Argentinian professionals on a tour to Europe.

Kahkwa Club USA

Erie, Pa. 18 holes; 6,800 yd (6,218 m);
par 72

The Great Depression of the 1930s had a devastating effect on any number of golf and country clubs in the United States, and though the general economic situation may not have been good for the members of the Kahkwa Club, it did leave a number of them with some leisure time. It must have been an inspiring, if strange, sight to see these members, aided by caddies, digging holes and planting saplings.

This programme changed the character of the course tremendously, for when it was originally laid out by Donald Ross in 1917, it was wide open, resembling the popular conception of a British links. Now that the trees have matured, anyone who can conquer Kahkwa must be able to play with accuracy, for they border every fairway as the 6,800-yd course wanders over small hills and valleys. It has been the site of two major tournaments, the 1958 Women's Western Open and the 1971 US Women's Open.

Kahkwa traces its history to the early 1890s when it was established as a country club. In 1899 the Erie GC was organized, and many members of Kahkwa also became members of Erie. The city was expanding into the areas where the two clubs were situated, and so in 1915 they joined together, purchased the property where Kahkwa is now located, and began building a new course.

Charley Hymers, a Scot from Carnoustie, was the club's first professional. Both Lionel and Jay Hebert have served as professionals at Kahkwa.

Kammer, August Frederick, Jr AMERICAN

b. Brooklyn, N.Y., 1912. Runner-up Michigan Amateur 1940, Detroit District Amateur 1945-6; semi-finalist US Amateur 1946; Walker Cup 1947

Kanawaki GC CANADA

Caughnawaga, Que. 18 holes; 6,645 yd (6,076 m); par 70

The club derives its name from Kahne-wake, an Indian word meaning 'at the rapids', and the name of the mission founded in 1676 at the foot of the present Lachine Rapids on the St Lawrence River. For the club is situated in the Caughnawaga Reservation of the Iroquois Indians, opposite those rapids, about 10 miles from central Montreal. Although not itself an old club, Kanawaki is an offshoot of the Outremont GC founded in 1902, on the northern slope of Mount Royal in Montreal. The spread of the city meant that this club had to be abandoned about 15 years later.

Much of the club's land has been reclaimed from the original swampy, scrub waste. As a result, the fairways are renowned for their soft and springy turf, especially in the lower areas where the rich, black loam produces a grass that feels like a deep carpet underfoot. The terrain has an easy-rolling contour and a wealth of woods, with here and there stately elm trees dotting the fairways. Contributing to the pleasure are the Indian boys from the nearby village who serve as caddies. They are unusually capable and helpful at their task, and their keen vision – or perhaps it is their hunting instinct – makes them uncanny in finding stray balls. Only once has the Canadian Open Championship been played at Kanawaki. In 1929 it was won there by Leo Diegel with a score of 274. It has twice been the venue of the Canadian Amateur Championship. The 1953 British Walker Cup players competed on the second occasion on their way to the matches against the United States team in Massachusetts.

Karen CC KENYA

nr Nairobi. 18 holes; 6,839 yd (6,254 m)

Karen CC and course occupy land that used to be a coffee farm belonging to the celebrated writer Baroness Karen von Blixen (Isak Dinesen), who later allowed the club to adopt the centre portion of her coat of arms as the centrepiece of their flag. In her book, *Out of Africa*, she described how in 1931 she left the farm where she had lived

for more than 20 years and, for financial reasons, allowed the property to be taken over for the building of a residential estate. The golf course came later, in 1938, with 9 holes which had grass greens from the outset. A further 9 holes were laid out in 1934.

The prime mover in Karen's development was J. R. Martin who brought in Bradley grass for the greens although, as at Muthaiga, the club gradually replaced this with another species.

With the growth of Karen as an outlying suburb of Nairobi, membership increased rapidly. Facilities now include bowls, lawn tennis, and swimming and total membership is about 850. The course, 6,200 ft above sea level, is well up to championship standard; indeed, many rate it the best in Kenya. It was also the first course over which in 1950 the Kenya Amateur Championship was played on grass greens. Karen has produced a good proportion of winners of this championship and its members have won the Coronation Trophy, the unofficial strokeplay championship of Kenya, on seven occasions.

Karlovy Vary GC CZECHOSLOVAKIA

Karlovy Vary (Carlsbad). 18 holes

The town of Karlovy Vary bears the name of Charles IV of Bohemia, who founded the spa in about 1360. The spa, with its 12 thermal springs from which flow three million litres of mineral water daily, still functions, and it is also the setting for one of the country's best-known courses. The original course emerged out of the Gentlemen's Fencing Club in 1904, with 9 holes laid out in the Imperial Park in the valley of the River Teplá, over which the golfer had to play five times in a round. In 1930 a new site was found a few miles out of the town with glorious views over the Doupovské hills, the forests of Slavkov, and the Krušné Hory (Ore Mountains). The designer was C. Noskowski and Czechoslovakia's first 18-hole course was opened in 1935.

The restoring of the course after its demolition during World War II was the work of a handful of local enthusiasts who used to take the air by walking over the derelict ground, by then much overgrown with pine and scrub. Many of the pre-war inhabitants of this region (the old Sudetenland) had gone to Germany after the war, but a small group of those who remained, reinforced by golfers from Prague, set about reclaiming fairways and bunkers. Until the authorities began to help with money and machinery about 1950, the course had been maintained with three pre-war fairway mowing units and one handmower for the greens. Every member

August Frederick Kammer Jr

Opposite, Kawana GC

was responsible for mowing one green and one of the leaders of the group, Otto Rezac, maintained the fairways with the help of an old tractor. The devotion of these few saved the club and today Karlovy Vary and Mariánské Lázně (Marienbad) are the two leading courses in Czechoslovakia, the former still upholding Henry Cotton's opinion of it as one of the most beautiful on the Continent.

The lay-out is somewhat hilly and strenuous. The fairways, linked by birch and pine, are mostly narrow. Rainfall is small and the soil light. The club, re-formed in 1948 under a state scheme for physical culture, thrives today as a popular port of call for visitors from all parts of Europe.

Karuizawa GC JAPAN
Karuizawa. 18 holes; 6,726 yd (6,150 m); par 72

Karuizawa GC lies close to the summer resort town of Karuizawa in the highland region of Nagano Prefecture, some 1,500 ft above sea level. It can be reached by train from Ueno Station in central Tokyo in about 2 hours. A 9-hole course was first constructed in 1921 at a spot quite close to the town. As the years went by the members grew unhappy with its limitations and in 1930 it was decided to move to the present site. With one of the club's members, Yuji Kodera, placed in complete charge of design and construction, 9 holes were completed by the summer of 1931; and all 18 holes were opened the following July. The club was closed for the duration of World War II; then from the end of the war to the spring of 1952, it was taken by the Allied Forces for their exclusive use.

The longest hole, the 14th, measures 596 yd (545 m) and calls for a long carry from the tee over a slightly undulating fairway. The short 12th is only 128 yd (117 m); but is water all the way from tee to a green further guarded by bunkers on three sides. The 11th hole of 392 yd (358 m) has a sharp dogleg to the right, with a pond on the right side of the bend; and an ambitious player who goes for the short cut over the pond, even if successful, still faces a difficult second to a highly elevated green which is double tiered. The only other hole with a dogleg is the 5th of 568 yd (519 m).

Unlike other courses in Japan, where the fairway grass is the native *korai*, Karuizawa uses creeping bent – this is made possible by the cooler highland climate. Although most of the course is quite flat, some of the holes have enough undulation to break the monotony. The trees that line both sides of the fairways are mostly larch and white birch, which add much to the beauty of the setting.

The club is surrounded by three mountain ranges – Asama-yama, Hanare-yama and Tokkuri-yama – so that the scene from the various tees presents an interesting variety of distant backdrops. A player looking for more excitement than is provided by the ponds and bunkers should play here on the occasions when Asama-yama, a very active volcano, spouts smoke and red-hot ashes.

The season is from April to November. In the months of July and August, the course gets very heavy play by members who come to Karuizawa at weekends to escape Tokyo's murky heat. Visitors are allowed only on weekdays, and then only when introduced or accompanied by a member. The best time for play is in September.

Kasumigaseki CC JAPAN
36 holes; East (Championship) Course 6,933 yd (6,340 m), par 72; West Course 6,660 yd (6,090 m), par 72

No doubt the best known, especially to foreign golfers, of the hundreds of golf clubs scattered throughout Japan, Kasumigaseki CC was started in 1929 by a group of prominent businessmen who 'defected' from an older club in protest against what they considered too restrictive membership requirements and undemocratic management. The East course was laid out in a heavily wooded area about 30 miles west of Tokyo in Saitama Prefecture. Within a year of its opening the club's membership reached 300, so it was decided to add another 18 holes in the land immediately adjoining. This, named the West Course, was completed in 1931. As might be expected, scarcity of land in Japan was – and still is – the major obstacle to golf-course construction. Fortunately for Kasumigaseki virtually all the land covered by the two courses belonged to one family who foresaw in this project not only economic benefits to the impoverished villages, but cultural and educational stimuli as well.

Both courses are quite flat. And with the exception of the 13th hole on the East, where a huge bunker leaves only 20 yd of fairway between its edge and the tree-lined rough, all the fairways are more than wide enough. The East Course, in particular, is heavily bunkered; and some of those around the greens are not only deep but are topped off by mean, protruding lips. The huge trees, many of which were said to have been over 100 years old at the time of construction, are mostly red and black pine, with a sprinkling of crytomeria and maple, and of course, cherry trees and wild azalea bushes which brighten the scenery through April and May. As with all but a few older highland courses in Japan, all 36 holes have two greens – one for summer with native *korai* grass which turns brown with the first heavy frost, and the other with evergreen bent grass for winter use.

The prize hole of the East is the 185-yd (169-m) 10th, which calls for a carry of 145 yd (133 m) to the far shore of a pond graced by several pine trees and a huge crytomeria on the far right that keeps growing, to the chagrin of chronic slicers. Gene Sarazen has expressed the view that this hole would rank among the world's top par 3s. A feature of the West is the dogleg 5th hole of 359 yd (328 m) where a player standing on the tee on a clear winter day aims his drive for the snow-capped peak of Mount Fuji; if the shot is true he is clear of the bunker at the bend and is in an ideal position for his second shot.

Kasumigaseki has been the venue of all the major golfing events of Japan, both amateur and professional, several times over. But the one that gave it world prominence was the Canada Cup matches of 1957 which, to the surprise of everyone including the Japanese, was won by the Japanese team of 'Pete' Nakamura and Koichi Ono. Other professionals, Jack Burke, Ken Venturi and the Big Three of Nicklaus, Palmer and Player, all played exhibition matches on the East Course. And in more recent years, America's 'People-to-People Golf Team' sponsored by the State Department played here on two occasions in friendly matches against an equal number of the club's members – men playing the East Course and the ladies the West.

The architect of this masterpiece was Kinya Fujita, a rank amateur as golf architects go, for Kasumigaseki was his first effort. A lover of the beauty and harmony of nature and a man of many vigorously pursued hobbies, he probably took up golf-course architecture as just one more pastime since it fitted nicely with the game he excelled at. At one time or another he held every important post in the club – honorary secretary, club captain, board chairman – and was club champion three times. He died in April 1970 addressing a meeting at the club he had founded and nurtured. In April 1973 the club held an anniversary tournament in his honour in which his five sons took part. His aged widow was able to attend the ceremony at the 19th in which Kasumigaseki paid tribute to the founding member to whom it owed so much.

Kawana GC JAPAN
Kawana. Oshima Course 5,711 yd (5,222 m),

par 70; Fuji Course 6,691 yd (6,118 m)

Kawana's founder, Baron Kishichiro Okura, returned from England with the dream of reproducing in Japan the kind of green pastureland he had seen surrounding the country estates of his English friends. After some search he purchased nearly 500 acres (202 ha) of what appeared to be suitable land on a high promontory in Izu Peninsula, famous for its hot springs. The design of the course was entrusted to his friend of London days, Komei Otani, who had learned his golf as a student in England. Completed in 1928, it was named Oshima Course because of the offshore view of Oshima Island with its ever-smoking volcano. The names given to some of the holes are truly descriptive of their character. The 4th, 'Good-bye', calls for a tee shot over a little of the Pacific Ocean to a fairway bending sharply to the left.

The 6th, a short hole, 'S.O.S.' is only 147 yd (134 m); but tee and green are separated by a ravine fully 100 yd (91 m) wide and just as deep; and the crossing is by a suspension bridge that sways with the wind. The 17th, 494 yd (452 m) long and aptly named 'Champs Élysées', has the only fairway that is wide, straight and fairly flat. The Oshima Course, in short, is extremely interesting and fairly easy for the experienced golfer; but the beginner will probably not be able to appreciate its beauty because of the many awesome features.

The Fuji Course immediately adjoining the Oshima was laid out by C. H. Alison, the English architect, in 1936 and was so named because Mount Fuji soars above an inlet of the Pacific and the Hakone Range beyond the peak is best viewed from holes 11, 12 and 13, which cover the tip of the promontory high above the breakers. Like the Oshima, Fuji has plenty of undulations and dogleg holes, but without its frightening pitfalls.

Truly a championship course, Fuji was the site of the third World Amateur Golf Team Championship (Eisenhower Trophy) with all teams quartered in the hotel that serves the two courses. On that occasion, a member of the American team remarked that Fuji might well be called the 'Pebble Beach of the Orient' because of the striking similarity of features.

Kawana Hotel has 130 rooms that can accommodate up to 300 guests, with fully modern facilities. The courses are operated under a quasi-membership system, but full playing privileges are extended to all guests of the hotel. Kawana is two hours by train from Tokyo, with a 15-minute taxi ride at the end.

O. B. Keeler

Keeler, Oscar Baun AMERICAN

The Atlanta sports writer who became famous as the chronicler of Bobby Jones's feats on the golf course. Keeler gave up his job as a railroad clerk and went into the newspaper business at about the same time as Jones was coming into prominence as a golfer. In fact, the first tournament Keeler covered was the 1916 Georgia Amateur, which was won by Jones and led to his entry into national championship competition.

Keeler not only covered all the tournaments in which Jones played, he was also a close friend, and the two travelled and stayed together at almost every championship. Although Jones did not need any written assistance in becoming a champion, he was nevertheless always the first to admit he owed Keeler a great deal – as a friend and counsellor as well as biographer. Keeler's efforts on Jones's behalf over the years led many persons to refer to him as Jones's Boswell; some of his fellow writers jokingly carried the comparison a step further and referred to Boswell as Samuel Johnson's Keeler. Keeler was a charter member of the Golf Writers' Association of America and served as one of its first presidents.

Keiser, Herman AMERICAN

b. Springfield, Mo., 1914. Iowa Open 1939; Miami Fourball (with Chandler Harper) 1942; Knoxville Invitation 1946; Richmond Invitation 1946; US Masters 1946; Esmeralda Open 1947; Ryder Cup 1947; Ohio Open 1949, 1951

Keiser turned professional in the 1930s and made several pre-war appearances on the tour. After US Navy service that included 30 months at sea he rejoined the circuit and soon scored a major surprise by winning the Masters. In that event Ben Hogan had a chance of victory, but took three putts from 12 ft on the last green and

Herman Keiser during the US Masters, 1970

finished 2nd. This victory helped gain Keiser a place in the 1947 Ryder Cup team.

Kelowna GCC CANADA

Kelowna, B.C. 18 holes; 6,103 yd (5,580 m); par 72

The Okanagan Valley in the interior of British Columbia is favoured with a dry temperate climate which makes it a renowned fruit-growing area. It further benefits from a golfing season that extends throughout nine months of the year, some three months longer than in most other parts of Canada. The Kelowna course in the heart of this district was developed in a manner typical of many of the courses in smaller centres of population of western Canada. Natural rainfall being insufficient to support a good growth of grass, and artificial watering being beyond the means of the infant club, it began in 1920 as a 9-hole course with sand greens. A decade later it was enlarged to 18 holes, but still on the same basis. Not until 1938 was an underground watering system introduced, permitting the installation of grass greens. After another 25 years automatic watering of tees, greens and fairways was achieved. The result is a course universally admired for the grooming of its lush turf, and providing the most discriminating golfer with challenging golf in lovely surroundings.

Kennemer GCC NETHERLANDS

Zandvoort. 18 holes; 6,795 yd (6,213 m)

The present Golf and Country Club, one mile east of Zandvoort and seven miles southwest of Haarlem, was founded by G. J. van der Vliet in 1928. Previously there had been a 9-hole course with a converted manor for a clubhouse some 10 miles north of the present location. The Zandvoort course was one of the many creations of Harry Colt, the English architect, and

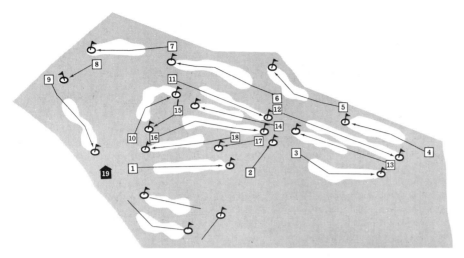

quickly acquired a reputation befitting one
of the oldest clubs in the Netherlands. It
housed its first Dutch Open Championship
in 1933. In 1942 the club and clubhouse
were taken over by German occupation
forces and in the next few years everything
to do with golf was forgotten. Reinforced-
concrete gun sites and anti-tank ditches
replaced greens and fairways. In 1945 rehabilitation was undertaken with vigour by
the local people, but it was not until 1963 that
everything was restored to its former splendour. Great care was taken to preserve as
many of Harry Colt's original concepts as
possible, but in 1970 the championship tees
were redesigned in readiness for the Dutch
Open the following summer.

Kennemer has always had a close link with
the Dutch Amateur and Open championships. It is also proud of two paintings of
the early 17th century; in one of them a
boy holds what is very definitely a 'modern'
golf club. Elsewhere in the clubhouse are two
oddly shaped *kolven* or clubs of the type used
in the centuries-old Dutch indoor version of
golf still played in the district.

Kenya

Although golf in Kenya, or British East
Africa as it was then known, dates from 1906
in Nairobi, and 1911 in Mombasa, it is, for
every practical purpose, a post-World War I
growth. Two factors contributed: a considerable increase in the playing population
in the early 1920s, and the greater availability of cheap and reliable motor vehicles.
This enabled people to become more mobile
and to attend urban or rural clubs regularly,
the former in the evenings and the latter at
weekends when farming conditions permitted. In the larger centres of population,
Nairobi, Mombasa and, in due course,
Nakuru, clubs flourished and, year by year,
more and more district clubs were formed to
cater for a number of sports often including
lawn tennis, cricket and rugby.

Before World War II there was a time of
golfing consolidation and development
which witnessed the growth of an open
fixture list, the formation of the Kenya Golf
Union and East African Ladies' Golf Union.
The former inaugurated a school coaching
scheme that had success with boy golfers.
Open Amateur championships were established in all three East African territories.
There was a hiatus between 1940 and 1945
and then, with another population influx
after World War II, golf again got under way.

With very few exceptions, putting surfaces were 'browns', Karen being one of the
few clubs to have grass greens from the
start; but in the late 1940s experiments

Top, the course plan of Kennemer GCC: the
three unnumbered holes are for practice

Above, 'The Young Golfer'. a Dutch panel of
c.1635 in the Kennemer GCC

began to prove the feasibility of grass for putting surfaces, mainly runner grasses of the Bradley and Cape Royal strains. Today only two or three of the smaller 9-hole courses, with too few members to bear the expense, use 'browns'.

Perhaps the most important development, however, has come about since the achievement of self-government. By the time of Independence, many clubs where golf had hitherto been predominantly a sport of white settlers had already opened their doors to people from all communities.

This coincided with a marked interest in golf by the Asians and Africans. Two Kenya-born Asians, Mohamed Rajab and Osman Amber, went to Rumbereck Academy at Malakal in the Sudan where they had coaching from an Egyptian professional and showed exceptional aptitude for golf. On their return in 1959 they interested others in the game. Today golf has become a truly national game. Africans took the Amateur championships three times in four years up to 1972.

The emergence of a top-class African professional only seems to be a matter of time. Golf is now established as an all-community game and grows in popularity all the time.

Killarney GC IRISH REPUBLIC
nr Killarney (Cill Áirne), Co. Kerry.
36 holes; Mahony's Point 6,734 yd (6,158 m), par 72; Killeen 6,732 yd (6,156 m), par 72

Although golf was played in Killarney from 1891, interest was lukewarm until, in the late 1930s, Valentine, Viscount Castlerosse, later 6th Earl of Kenmare, inherited the family property facing Lough Leane, the largest of the four lakes of Killarney. For many years Castlerosse had been an outstanding gossip columnist in London's Fleet Street, but he was also a keen competent golfer who had long nourished an ambition to build a championship course at the famous County Kerry resort.

He engaged Sir Guy Campbell as architect and with encouragement and advice from Henry Longhurst and the local expert, Dr Billy O'Sullivan, the dream became a reality beyond, perhaps, even his own expectations – although he did not live long enough to savour it fully. So healthily did the close-knit, lush grass flourish – it was almost of seaside texture – that, within three years, all was ready for a championship. When the local hero Dr O'Sullivan won the Irish Open Amateur there in 1949, the subsequent celebrations were memorable. Since then it has been the scene of two more

Amateur championships, three Irish Ladies' championships, the home internationals – both men's and women's – and a big sponsored event.

Tourists flocked to Killarney and when in 1970 their numbers reached 27,000 it became clear that the only way to preserve the course was to build another one. Instead of having two distinct courses, old and new, the two were blended. On the West side is the Mahony's Point course named after the peninsula on which the clubhouse is built, while Killeen is the name given to the other. The lengths of the two courses have skilfully and deliberately been made almost identical, the outstanding holes of the original lay-out being cleverly distributed between the two. The most famous is the short 18th on Mahony's Point, 202 yd (185 m) from the championship tee and 20 yd shorter from the medal tee. A small inlet of the lake cuts in front of the tee and extends to the edge of the green that is tightly shut in on the other three sides by giant rhododendrons and pines, with a shallow bunker skirting the left of the green. It has a strong claim to be one of the most dramatic holes in Europe.

Killeen contains the lovely short 6th with its green by the lakeside, followed by the tightly guarded green of the long 7th, and the 8th where the approach lies through a deep valley. Killarney was chosen for the 1973 European Amateur Team Championship, but because of the troubles in Northern Ireland, the venue was changed to Portugal.

King, Michael G. BRITISH
Walker Cup 1969, 1973; tied 1st Lytham Trophy 1973

A leading boy golfer, Michael King quickly made his mark at senior amateur level, playing for England from 1969 to 1973 and winning a place in the 1969 and 1973 Walker Cup teams. Victory in a major event

eluded him until he tied with S. G. Birtwell in the Lytham Trophy.

King, Samuel Leonard BRITISH
b. Sevenoaks, Kent, 1911. Ryder Cup 1937, 1947, 1949; tied 3rd British Open 1939; British Seniors' 1961-2

No man was ever more entitled to be called a yeoman golfer than Sam King, whose father had been a charcoal burner in the Weald of Kent, and whose love of wildlife was at least as intense as his love of golf. He was one of Britain's leading professionals for a long time, finishing in the first 10 of the British Open nine times and maintaining his game at a high peak until he was well past 50.

King James VI GC SCOTLAND
Moncreiffe Island, Perth. 18 holes; 5,923 yd (5,416 m); par 69

This club may be unique on several counts: named after King James VI of Scotland and I of England, its course occupies an entire island, not merely in the middle of a major tidal river but in the centre of a busy city, the one-time capital of Scotland. The club owes its existence and name to the Rev. Charles Robertson, famous throughout Scotland as 'Gowfin Charlie', a man of great culture and wit who, having been ordained to the ministry, declined the only 'call' he ever received because it would interfere with his passion for golf. On 22 December 1858 Gowfin' Charlie and four other North Inch golfers gathered in the St John's Inn to form a club. Elected first captain, he chose the name 'to commemorate the tradition that not only had the last of the Scottish Kings played golf on the Inches of Perth, but had also a fine care for the game'.

By the 1890s golf on the North Inch had become hazardous, with grazing cattle, an

Michael King in action during the final of the 1972 Sunningdale Foursomes

Sam King

influx of cricketers and pedestrians, and a lease of the whole of Moncreiffe Island was acquired from the city. Tom Morris laid out the course (with a kindly thought for the addicted slicer on the riverside holes) and it was opened on 19 July 1897. Moncreiffe Island may not appeal 'to those sportsmen who prefer to do their golfing and mountaineering together' but it is a good test and has splendid surroundings, plenty of fresh air coming up from the Carse o' Gowrie and the broad stretches of the Tay. Always great matchplayers, the members of 'King Jimmie' claim two unusual records: on 28 April 1884 they went to Belfast for what is believed to be the first golf match ever played in Ireland, and beat the Belfast club

by 37 to 8; and in a 27-a-side match against the Forfar club, all matches played to a finish, in April 1899, they won by 150 holes.

King's Inn and GC BAHAMAS

Freeport, Grand Bahama Island. 36 holes, Emerald and Ruby Courses

The Emerald and Ruby Courses of the King's Inn and GC present a twin challenge of roughly equal popularity, but it is the Emerald that has championship qualities. It was the creation of Dick Wilson, who, with his partner and successor, Joe Lee, was responsible for so much fine work in the Bahamas. The course weaves a pleasant path through a few hundred acres of real estate round the hotel resort. Along its 7,000-yd

(6,400-m) length, tall pines, large bunkers and colourful bushes present the main hazards, but there is also water to contend with. One of the most famous holes in the Bahamas is the 9th, which is surrounded by water. Although a par 5, it poses a stiff, but richly rewarding challenge to the player who attempts to get home in two. In the inaugural Bahama Islands Open, in 1970, it made an admirable 18th hole, the two 9s having been reversed for the event, which ended in victory for Doug Sanders.

Kingston Heath GC AUSTRALIA

Cheltenham, Victoria. 18 holes; 6,797 yd (6,215 m)

Kingston Heath GC lies in the 'sand belt'

some 16 miles southeast of Melbourne. It was originally known as the Elsternwick club after its first site. The present course opened in 1925. D. Soutar, the Sydney professional, designed the lay-out and Dr Alister Mackenzie advised on the bunkering.

With many tree-lined fairways, deep bunkers and well-contoured greens, Kingston Heath has always been a fine test. In 1938 it was approved by the Australian Golf Union for the staging of national championships. Since then it has accommodated the Australian Opens of 1948, 1957 and 1970, the Australian Amateur of 1963, and many of the Victorian championships. The large Colonial-style clubhouse was modernized as part of extensive alterations in 1967. The course now has its own water supply from two bore holes on club property.

Kirby, Dorothy AMERICAN

b. Atlanta, Ga., 1919. Titleholders' Champion 1941-2; Curtis Cup 1948, 1950, 1952, 1954; US Women's Amateur 1951, runner-up 1939, 1947

Although one of the most consistent amateurs, Dorothy Kirby did not win the US Women's National Amateur until 1951, the third time she reached the final. She had been runner-up to Betty Jameson in 1939 and to Louise Suggs in 1947.

Kirkaldy, Andrew BRITISH

b. Fife 1860; d. St Andrew's, Fife, 1934. Runner-up British Open 1889, tied 2nd 1879

One of the best who never won the Open, and a redoubtable matchplayer. Andrew was the last survivor of three golfing brothers, the other two being Jack and Hugh. His father was a miner who fought in the Crimean war. Andrew himself fought at Tel-el-Kebir in the Egyptian campaign, before returning to St Andrews. There he soon made a name for himself in matchplay, displaying a fine courage and plenty of dourness. His most famous match came as a direct result of losing the play-off in the Open, for he at once challenged Willie Park to a 72-hole match over four greens, which he won by 8 and 7. Another famous match was the foursome in which, partnered by his brother Hugh, they lost 12 and 11 over four rounds to the diminutive combination of Ben Sayers and David Grant.

For a time Kirkaldy was professional at Winchester, Hampshire, but not for long: perhaps it was too genteel a town for his caustic, old-soldier's tongue. After losing a rare challenge match to an up-and-coming golfer called J. H. Taylor he returned to his beloved St Andrews and he was pro-

Top, Sam King (on the left) in the replay round of the 1961 British Seniors' Golf Tournament at the Hill Barn GC, Worthing

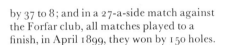

Above, Dorothy Kirby

fessional to the Royal and Ancient from 1920 to 1934. At one time or another he beat Taylor and Braid over the Old course, but gradually the Triumvirate became too strong for him. He lingered on long enough to tee up the ball at the driving-in ceremony both for the Prince of Wales and the Duke of York. He wrote a book, *Fifty Years of Golf*.

Kirkaldy, Hugh BRITISH

b. St Andrews, Fife, 1865; d. 1897. British Open 1891, tied 2nd 1892

The younger brother of the illustrious Andrew Kirkaldy, Hugh won the Open Championship in 1891, the last to be decided over 36 holes, beating the brothers Andrew and Willie Fernie by 2 strokes. In 1892 he tied 2nd with John Ball and Sandy Herd and in 1893 was 4th, 4 strokes behind the winner. A few days later he won a tournament at Musselburgh, with 158, in bad weather. Two years later, however, he made his last appearance in the Open. In 1896, just before he contracted his fatal illness, he played and beat J. H. Taylor, Open Champion in 1894 and 1895, in a two-day match at Silloth. Soon after he was stricken down and a fine young player, who once did 33 for the first 9 at St Andrews, was lost. His fine, slashing swing appealed to spectators.

The putter with which he won the Open became the first President's Putter, the annual trophy of the Oxford and Cambridge Golfing Society. It was bought from Hugh at St Andrews and hangs in a case in the clubhouse at Rye. The putter originally cost four shillings.

Kirkwood, Joseph H. AUSTRALIAN

b. Sydney, N.S.W., 1898. Australian Open 1920; New Zealand Open 1920; 4th British Open 1923, tied 4th 1927, tied 4th 1934; California Open 1923; Houston Open 1923; Illinois Open 1923; Canadian Open 1933

Besides being an excellent tournament player, Joe Kirkwood became the leading trick-shot artist of his age. He is said to have been persuaded to the act by Walter Hagen with whom he collaborated in many of the hundreds of exhibitions staged by the great golfer. The formula was to put on a show at any town on the road to the tournament they were heading for, and to make no charge for their appearance other than collecting the gate money. Kirkwood's most celebrated act was to borrow a watch from the audience, tee up a ball on the face of it, and drive it off. Once while doing that he holed his drive of about 250 yd. He hit balls suspended by a piece of string, he pretended to be a beginner, he hit balls which he ran forward and caught, besides hitting sliced and hooked shots to order.

Kirkwood was only 23 when he won both Open championships 'down under' and this fired him with the desire to travel. He travelled to Britain, defeated Vardon and Havers at extra holes in the same day in the first tournament he played in the country, and was a regular contender for the British Open for several years. Conjuror though he was with the ball and a fine stroke maker, he lacked the winning touch and more than once had his chance to win but could not take it. This may have been a question of temperament, but it is Henry Cotton's opinion that his rather jerky swing and light grip of the club let him down in moments of extreme pressure. From Britain he moved to the United States and at once began winning good tournaments, but his series of exhibitions across the country with Hagen were no doubt more profitable for him, and over the years he developed a fluent patter to accompany his highly polished act. In 1930 he returned to Australia on tour and in 1937 undertook a world tour with Hagen. He estimated that in all he played 6,470 different courses throughout the world. On Christmas Day 1960, when he was 63, he went round his home course in 62.

Kirouac, Mrs Martha (née Wilkinson) AMERICAN

Mexican Women's Amateur 1969; Curtis Cup 1970, 1972; US Women's Amateur 1970, semi-finalist 1971; World Women's Amateur Team Championship 1970

Having defeated Cynthia Hill by 3 and 2 in the final of 1970 US Women's Championship, she went on to play a leading part in America's victory in the Espirito Santo Trophy in Madrid in 1970. Paired with Catherine de Prado (formerly Lacoste) in the final round, she made up 3 strokes on her, giving her country victory by 1 stroke.

Kite, Thomas, Jr AMERICAN

b. Austin, Tex., 1950. Walker Cup 1969, 1971; runner-up US Amateur 1970; Eisenhower Trophy 1970; semi-finalist British Amateur 1971

Tom Kite made a name for himself in amateur golf while still at the University of Texas. His most successful year was 1970 when he was runner-up by a stroke to Lanny Wadkins in the US Amateur, the third time that season that he had lost to Wadkins. Kite lost the Eastern Amateur in a play-off to Steve Melnyk, but was a member of America's victorious Eisenhower Trophy team in Madrid in 1970 and played in the Walker Cup team for the second time in May 1971 at St Andrews. Although the

Andrew Kirkaldy

Top, Mrs Martha Kirouac

Above, Tom Kite, Jr

Americans lost, he had a good record and then reached the semi-final of the British Amateur, losing on the last green to Jim Simons. He later turned professional.

Kittansett Club USA
Marion, Mass.

Kittansett, scene of the 1953 Walker Cup

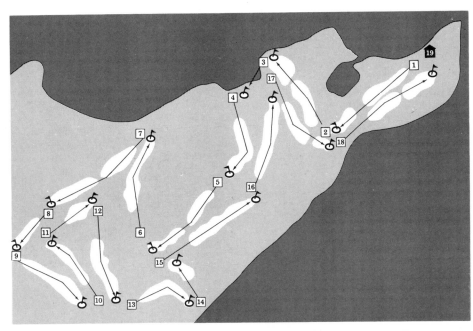

may have been, collectively, the most talented contingent brought together for a Cup competition. Included were the winners or future winners of nine US Amateurs, five British Amateurs, and two US Opens. And if Charlie Yates, the non-playing American captain is included, there is another British Amateur champion.

match, is usually thought of as being on Cape Cod. It is, in fact, on the mainland side of Buzzards Bay, about 10 miles northeast of New Bedford, the famous old whaling port. Kittansett, however, shares many of the excellences of Oyster Harbor and the other top Cape courses. Kittansett is on a neck of land which, when settled in 1639 by colonists from England, was covered with scrub oak and sand dunes, and inhabited by Indians of the Seppecan tribe. Everything but the Indians remains. Architecturally, this is a most appealing course, primarily because nature has, as it were, been the chief designer. It is not entirely linksland or duneland, but there is enough of that for it to be called a Scotsman's type of course – full of wind, sand, and tough seaside rough. It has a nice irregular routing, and it asks the golfer to play a wide assortment of tee shots, some thrusting irons and some delicate ones. There is a comfortable small clubhouse and a comfortable small membership to welcome the visitor.

The two groups of players involved in that pleasant Walker Cup meeting at Kittansett

The course plan of Kittansett Club

George Knudson hitting his 2nd shot to the 18th green in the final round of the 1968 World Cup

Knock-out
The normal form of matchplay competition in which the defeated player or side takes no further part in the tournament. This term is not used in America.

Knoll GC USA
Boonton, N.J.

The Knoll has passed through many vicissitudes since it was opened with a great flourish as a millionaire's playground just before the market crash in 1929 sent the world into the Great Depression. The property now is owned by Bloomfield College, but the course can still be played by visiting golfers. It ought to be played by all who love golf and can find the time for a day's expedition from New York. The Knoll is only an hour from Times Square.

The course was designed by Charles Banks who had earlier been an associate of Charles Blair Macdonald. In recent years it has largely been forgotten, but it used to be discussed and praised whenever golfers met. By contemporary standards, some of its holes are short, but they are nonetheless demanding. As recently as 1954, the Metropolitan Open, one of the country's most important events, was played there with no one in a vast field breaking 290.

Banks was not reticent about moving around great quantities of earth to give his green areas and other features an imposing look. This is a big course, with considerable fairway contouring and interestingly moulded greens, many of them on two levels. It has always been one of Gene Sarazen's favourites.

Knuckles
Used to describe the types of grip, mainly of the left hand; the number of knuckles seen by a person standing opposite the player at address. A player can show one knuckle, two knuckles or three knuckles. A four-knuckle grip is virtually impossible.

Knudson, George CANADIAN
b. Winnipeg, Man., 1937. Coral Gables Open 1961; Portland Open 1963; Caracas Open 1964; Fresno Open 1964; Phoenix Open 1968; Tucson Open 1968; Robinson Open 1970; joint runner-up US Masters 1969

One of the four Canadians who have won on the American professional tour, since he joined it in 1961. Knudson's best year was 1968 when he won two tournaments back to back and took home $70,000. He was also top individual scorer in the World Cup in which Canada finished first.

In 1969 he was equal 2nd in the Masters, 1 stroke behind the winner.

Kocsis, Charles AMERICAN
b. Newcastle, Pa., 1913. Michigan Amateur
1930, 1933-4, 1937, 1948, 1951; Michigan
Open 1931, 1945-6; Detroit District
Amateur 1932; US National Collegiate
1936; Walker Cup 1938, 1949, 1957;
Chicago Amateur 1944; runner-up US
Amateur 1956

One of the country's best amateurs for
three decades, during which he won the US
National Collegiate, was runner-up in the
US Amateur and played in three Walker
Cup teams. Chuck Kocsis first attracted
national attention in the 1930 US Amateur
(his high-school principal sent in his entry)
when, at the age of 17, he beat Francis
Ouimet in the first round. The next year he
beat Tommy Armour, the British Open
Champion, in a play-off to win the Michigan
Open. He later attended the University of
Michigan and won three Big Ten titles in
addition to the National Collegiate. Kocsis is
one of 12 children of a Hungarian immigrant. Sam, one of his six brothers who were
all golfers, won the 1955 US Public Links
Championship.

Kodaikanal GC INDIA
Kodaikanal, Tamil Nadu State. 18 holes;
5,475 yd (5,006 m); par 66
Some 325 miles south by rail from Madras
is a station with the Tamil name of Am-
mayanayakkanur, or Kodaikanal Road.
Fifty miles from there by road is the hill
station of Kodaikanal, on the eastern flanks
of the Palni Hills. The golf course is a scenic
joy. Nutmeg, cinnamon and the pepper-vine
grow wild. The course is laid out over
natural grassland among forests of pine,
eucalyptus, acacia and wattle. A stream
criss-crosses the course and provides a natural
hazard to the 1st, 5th, 8th and 18th holes.
At present there are only 'browns' of

rolled sand, but with the Indian Government's interest and investment in tourism,
the club hopes to receive a grant both to
convert the present browns to greens and to
make the course of championship length.
The rolling wooded country provides
many challenging holes, only one of which,
the 307-yd (281-m), par-4 16th, is flat. The
fairways are on the whole good, but because
of the shallow subsoil and the hilly nature of
the ground, heavy rain is apt to pit them at
times, so that local rules permit preferred lies
on the fairways. Kodaikanal, with an
equable climate throughout the year, with
temperatures seldom exceeding the 70s
Fahrenheit, has the reputation of having
'the second-best climate in the world'.
December and January nights have slight
frost, average rainfall is not heavy, providing
year-round golf in a perfect setting.

Köln-Refrath GCC WEST GERMANY
Refrath. 18 holes; 6,745 yd (6,168 m);
par 72
Refrath is situated about 10 miles from
Cologne in the heart of the Königsforst, an
area of pleasant woodland surrounding the
city. Most of the fairways are carved out of
woodland and include a number of doglegs
requiring long, straight shots. Since the fairways are soft most of the time, there is little
run on the ball. There are only slight undulations but use is made of a few water
hazards. The five par-5 holes must be considered easy par holes, but difficult birdies.
This is one of the oldest clubs in Germany;
its membership includes many foreign diplomats from neighbouring Bonn.

Kono, Takaaki JAPANESE
b. Hodogaya, nr Yokohama, 1940. Kanto
Open 1967, runner-up 1970; Brazilian Open
1968; Japanese Open 1968; Malaysian
Open 1969; Japanese Dunlop Tournament
1969; Singapore Open 1972; Tournament
of Champions 1971-2
Perhaps more than any other professional
in Japan, Takaaki Kono, together with his
younger brother Mitsutaka, was predestined
to follow a golfing career. For not only were
they born a stone's throw from the Hodogaya club, but their father was associated
with the club from its very beginning and
was in 1972 still its assistant manager. The
story goes that their teeth were cut on golf
balls and that they learned to shout 'Fore!'
before they learned to cry 'Mama!' One
thing is certain, that they started caddying
as soon as they were strong enough to lift a
golf bag. Strangely, the younger Mitsutaka
jumped off first in the professional tour,
winning the Japanese professional cham-

pionship twice before his elder brother won
the Japanese Open in 1968. Kono is well
travelled; he has been four times in the
Japanese World Cup team, the last occasion
being in 1972. His record in the US
Masters, in which he has also played four
times, is exceptional for a non-American. In
1969 he finished 13th and the next year went
one better. Kono was named outstanding
professional athlete of the year in 1967 and
1968 by Japanese sports writers.

Korea
Golf in Korea dates from about 1920 but it
was not until the present Seoul CC was
founded in 1931 that the country had an
18-hole course. The club suffered badly
during World War II and later during the
Korean War, but it was successfully restored
and is now one of the very best in the Far
East. Some people even consider it the finest
in Asia with its pinewoods, sandy soil and
undulating ground. There are now a few
other clubs in South Korea. The Korean
Open forms part of the lucrative chain of
tournaments on the Far Eastern circuit and
South Korea now regularly enters a team
for the World Cup.

Krefeld GC WEST GERMANY
Krefeld-Linn. 18 holes; 6,840 yd (6,254 m);
par 73
When the Krefelder Golfklub was
founded in 1930 it had to be content with a
9-hole course not far from the city centre.

Chuck Kocsis

Takaaki Kono

Shortly after, the land had to be given up and the club was closed. The committee found a new area at Krefeld-Linn, an outlying suburb. The new course came into existence in 1940. The fairways are mostly wide open, with only a few holes restricted by trees. The six par-5 holes, not too easy in fine weather, become even more of a prob-

lem when the wind blows across this generally flat area with a strength similar to that at the seaside. The par-4 holes average 385 yd (352 m) and present no particular difficulty to the straight hitter, but the rough can be thick. Greens are on the large side and well groomed. Several doglegs add to the interest. Krefeld is a purely industrial town dealing in velvet and silk, to which only the purposeful traveller will find his way, but there is an attractive clubhouse, converted from an old farmhouse.

Kroll, Ted AMERICAN
b. New Hartford, N.Y., 1919. Ryder Cup 1953; runner-up USPGA 1956; tied 2nd US Open 1960; Canadian Open Champion 1962

Kroll turned professional before he was 18, but did not begin playing in tournaments full-time until 1950. The delay was partly due to World War II, in which he served as an army sergeant and was four times wounded. When he started to compete he soon made up for lost time; he won his first tournament in 1952, and also two others

Ted Kroll

which secured him a place in the 1953 Ryder Cup team. Thereafter, he earned a great deal of money in a few years, his only bad one being 1957, the year after winning the George May World Championship, when he was busy with exhibitions resulting from that victory which was worth $50,000. Kroll built up a reputation as a diagnostician and many a professional has consulted him when his game has gone off.

Kundale GC INDIA
High Range, Kerala. 9 holes; 2,266 yd (2,072 m); par 34

This little golf course at Top Station, 18 miles from Munnar, is set among tea gardens in delightful hill country some 120 miles east of the historic port of Cochin. Kundale was first opened by tea planters in 1918 as a social club. It was not until 1926 that the golf course came into being. From 1934 it was enlarged into a 12-hole course which continued until World War II. Membership then dropped and when four or five holes were lost with the opening of the Sethuparvathipuram Dam, the course ceased to exist.

Little effort was made to reopen it until 1956. Then N. S. Cole, the present chairman, took the matter in hand and opened a 9-hole course in collaboration with J. Jackson, club secretary at that time. The course has gradually been improved and work continues under the secretaryship of K. M. Cariappa: eventually there will be putting greens as well as browns at every hole. Play should then be possible in any weather.

The club is private with no external affiliations. Membership in 1972 was between 80 and 90.

Of the 9 holes, 7 are par 4s, the 9th being 337 yd (308 m). The 285-yd (251-m) 6th doglegs left over the confluence of two streams; the short par-3 2nd and 8th require great accuracy across a menacing ravine. Two old roads run through the course and serve to mark the out-of-bounds.

The course is in a valley overlooking the hydro-electric dam. There are eucalyptus and acacia trees and the turf is mainly kikuyu grass. It forms an almost impossible rough to get out of and local rules permit a free lift.

Two wildlife sanctuaries, Rajamallay and Eruvikulam, lie only 25 miles from Kundale. There is wild game on the estates surrounding the club, but it is active mainly at night. From the course wild elephants can be seen swimming in the dam. Occasionally they invade the golf course and happily blow sand over each other in the bunkers.

Kuwait see DESERT COURSES

Kyle, Alexander Thomson BRITISH
b. Hawick, Roxburghshire, 1907. Walker Cup 1938, 1947, 1951; British Amateur 1939; runner-up Brabazon Trophy 1952; World Seniors' Team Championship 1969

A Border Scot by birth and a Yorkshireman by adoption, Alec Kyle was twice Yorkshire Champion (1935 and 1936) and one of the leading British amateurs for a time. He was a member of the victorious British Walker Cup team at St Andrews in 1938, his singles victory over Fred Haas by 5 and 4 eventually sealing America's fate. The following year he won the British Amateur Championship at Hoylake. In the last eight he beat Jimmy Bruen, about the most formidable opponent anyone could have in those days, on the last green and in the final accounted for Tony Duncan by 2 and 1 in a capital match played at a delightfully brisk pace. In 1951 Kyle won his Walker Cup single against W. P. Turnesa, was in the British touring side in South Africa in 1952, played for Scotland until 1953, was runner-up in the Yorkshire Championship in 1959, and represented Britain in the first World Senior team championship at St Andrews in 1969.

Kyle, Denis H. BRITISH
b. St Andrews, Fife, 1897. Walker Cup 1924

Denis Kyle, a holder of the OBE, represented Scotland against England in the 1920s and 1930s.

L

Lacey, Arthur J. BRITISH
b. Burnham, Buckinghamshire, 1904.
Belgian Open 1931-2; French Open 1932;
Ryder Cup 1933, 1937 (non-playing captain
1951)

Arthur Lacey, son of a greenkeeper, kicked
his infant heels on the Burnham Beeches
course. He grew up a natural golfer, cheerful
in disposition, but perhaps lacked the drive
and concentration which would have taken
him to the heights. He was, however, a fine
player and a valuable member of the PGA
Executive for many years, being chairman in
1949 and 1951. Lacey now lives in the
United States, adopted country of his
brother Charles, who finished 3rd in the
1937 British Open at Carnoustie.

Lacoste, Catherine (Mrs J. de Prado)
FRENCH
b. Paris 1945. French Ladies' Open 1967,
1969-70, 1972; US Women's Open 1967;
French Ladies' Close 1968-9; British Ladies'
1969; US Women's Amateur 1969

Catherine Lacoste's father is the famous
tennis player René Lacoste; her mother, as
Mlle Thion de la Chaume, won the British
Ladies' Golf Championship. Catherine has
been a champion in her own right and one
of the most brilliant players of her age. By
winning the United States Women's Open
in 1967 she did what no other foreigner had
achieved before; she was also the first
amateur to win it and the youngest player.
In 1969 after a runaway victory early in the
season in the Spanish Championship she
went on to win the French Open, the
British, which had always eluded her, and
the American championship.

It was in the world championship for the
Espirito Santo Trophy that Catherine
Lacoste first became prominent. In 1964 the
event was held for the first time in Paris.
Catherine Lacoste was 19 at the time, and
although showing exceptional promise, had
achieved little beyond being Junior Champion of France. It was largely thanks to her
that France won this inaugural championship, for her play was inspired and she tied
for 1st place in the individual scoring with
Carol Sorenson who had just won the British
Women's Championship. Her subsequent
record in this event is without parallel.

Together with her two team mates, Claudine
Cros and Brigitte Varangot, she played in
every championship until her retirement in
1970, finishing 3rd twice in the individual
and at Melbourne in 1968 finishing top on
her own.

Catherine Lacoste learned her golf at
Chantaco, the course at the foot of the
Pyrenees which belongs to the Lacoste
family. She had occasional lessons from Jean
Garaialde, but her natural swing needed
little alteration, and she had in her father an
expert in the technique of hitting a ball on
whom she could call when things went
wrong. As a child she won almost everything
for which she entered but her success in
national golf was not immediate because of

Catherine Lacoste, *top* with the British Ladies'
Cup in 1969 and *above* in the Open Foursomes
at Sunningdale

the quality of women's golf in France at the
time. She first became Ladies' Open champion of France in 1967, and again succeeded
in defeating her old rival, Brigitte Varangot,
in the Close championships of 1968 and 1969.

By that time, she had already performed
other prodigious feats. In 1966 in winning the
Astor Trophy medal at Prince's, Sandwich,
ahead of a strong British entry, she scored a
record 66 which stands as one of the most
remarkable rounds of golf ever played by a
woman. Then in 1967 came her triumph in
the United States. It was all the more impressive because she had made the trip
alone, indeed in defiance of her colleagues
who were playing in the European team
championship. In a field that included the
leading American women professionals she
was almost ignored, but a second round of
70 raised her into the lead by 5 shots and she
won the championship by a margin of 2. In
spite of this, her achievements in the amateur
field were far from complete. Her ambition
to win the British Championship as her
mother had done was repeatedly frustrated,
even though on two occasions she led the
qualifying scores. In 1969 the championship
was held at Portrush, up the Irish coast from
Royal County Down where 23 years before
her mother had won the title. This time
Catherine took her mother with her and
practised intensively for a week beforehand.
In spite of being 4 down to Ann Irvin in the
final, she recovered and won her first British
title. She had already won the Spanish and
the French again that year, and had now to
decide whether to go for the 'grand slam' by
attempting to win the US Amateur, the only
important title that still eluded her. It was a
decision not lightly taken. The constant
strain of being expected to win was taking its
toll, even though she was only 24, and the
American championship was being held in
Texas at the hottest time of the year.

Catherine Lacoste never lacked determination, and in temperatures above 100°F
almost all the week, she beat Anne Quast
(Mrs Welts), having once again been 3 down
at one stage of their semi-final. The following
year she married and withdrew from top
competitive golf, though she decided to play
once more for France in the Espirito Santo
Trophy match six weeks after her marriage,
in Madrid, where she was making her new
home. It was a calculated risk she took in
playing and all the week she was struggling
to find her true game. In the final round she
bore the full burden as she and the last
American competitor fought it out to decide
which country would win the trophy. In the
end Mrs Lacoste de Prado's lengthy absence
from competitive golf told and the 3-stroke

lead she held with 9 holes to play against Matha Wilkinson slipped away.

As a striker of the long irons and as a long straight driver, Catherine Lacoste probably had no equal since Babe Zaharias. She was one of the few women in golf to use a no. 1 iron regularly with great effect. She could be equally devastating in stroke or matchplay, but medal scores more surely reflected her genius for the game. She had a splendid temperament, playing with zest and boldness and nearly always responding to a challenge. Ambition and fearless expression of her opinions sometimes gave offence to those round her, but she knew how to make full use of those qualities that make a champion and with which she was well endowed.

Lacoste, Mrs René SEE CHAUME, SIMONE THION DE LA

Laffoon, Ky AMERICAN
b. Zinc, Ark., 1908. Runner-up Canadian Open 1934, tied 2nd 1948; semi-finalist USPGA 1937; tied 4th US Masters 1946

Laffoon, of Irish-French-Cherokee an-

Ky Laffoon

cestry, was one of the top professionals on the circuit in the 1930s, his best year being 1934 when he won four tournaments and the Radix Cup, forerunner of the Vardon Trophy. Laffoon continued to follow the tour more or less regularly until 1950 and retained his skills to a large degree over a 15-year span. For example, he was runner-up in the 1934 Canadian Open and still good enough to tie for 2nd in the same event 14 years later. Altogether he won about a dozen major tournaments. In addition to playing good golf (despite a loop in his swing), Laffoon wore canary-yellow socks and sweaters, chewed tobacco and gave way to occasional outbursts of temper. He was tied with Tony Manero after three rounds in the 1936 Open, but finished tied 5th after shooting a 74 while Manero was scoring a 67.

Lahinch GC IRISH REPUBLIC
Lahinch (Leacht Uí Chonchubhair) Co. Clare. 18 holes, 6,363 yd (5,818 m), par 71; 9 holes, 3,212 yd (2,937 m), par 36

A linksland course in the village of Lahinch on Liscannor Bay. Golf was started in Lahinch, as it was in many other older centres in the country, by the army; in this case the Black Watch, who began on Limerick racecourse in 1891 and then moved to the genuine golfing country along the coast. Old Tom Morris laid out the course which was opened in 1893, and, having made best use of the ridges, grassy hollows, and sandhills, pronounced it to be 'as fine a natural course as it has ever been my good fortune to play over'. In spite of this Dr Alister Mackenzie was engaged in 1927 to modernize the course and he built some fine new holes in an adjoining stretch of the dunes.

Lahinch contains a number of outstanding holes, notably the 4th where the drive is up a steep hill between towering dunes, the 14th which has the narrowest possible entrance to the green, and the testing finish of the 17th and 18th, with the road to Liscannor bordering the fairway on the left. The two most famous holes are the 5th (Klondyke) and the 6th (The Dell). Neither is a good hole from the modern standpoint, somewhat blind among the dunes, but to suggest any modification is to utter heresy.

Lahinch is the home of the oldest of the provincial championships, the South of Ireland, started in 1895. The Close, too, has been staged there four times. The professionals have pitted their skill against it in the Irish Dunlop tournament and the women have paid three visits for their national event. Above and beyond any statistics, Lahinch eats, drinks and breathes golf, and has become so popular with visitors that in 1967 it was decided to add a 9-hole course to offset the growing traffic on the main one.

Such is the interest in the game in the village that Lahinch could be termed the St Andrews of Ireland; and the Lahinch caddies are famous, even from their tenderest years, for their knowledge of the course and their wisdom in club selection. The story is told of Tom O'Donnell, a former president of the Golfing Union of Ireland, who one day engaged a lad whose father had been O'Donnell's caddie for many years. After hitting his drive at the first, O'Donnell asked the boy for the wedge, a club with which, to put it mildly, he was erratic. As he walked up to the ball he saw the boy holding out the 9-iron. 'No thanks, Jimmy, I'll take the wedge.' The boy continued to hold out the other club with a mulish look on his face and said in his rich Clare accent, 'My father said I was not to give Misther O'Donnell the wedge.'

Laidlay, John Ernest BRITISH
b. 1860; d. 1940. British Amateur 1889, 1891, runner-up 1888, 1890, 1893; runner-up British Open 1893

Perhaps one of the two best tributes to John Laidlay's skill is that of Bernard Darwin who once wrote, 'Thus, strive as I will, I cannot wholly convince myself that young golfers of today stare with quite such reverential eyes at Mr Tolley and Mr Wethered as I did when, as a small boy, I first beheld Mr Mure Fergusson and Mr Horace Hutchinson, or, at a later date, Mr John Ball and Mr Laidlay.'

The other is contained in one of Horace Hutchinson's books, in a story of Sir Alexander Kinloch who once exclaimed at a general meeting of the Royal and Ancient: 'What's the good of all this talk about first-class players? There are only three first-class amateurs, Johnny Ball, Johnny Laidlay and Horace Hutchinson.'

Laidlay was one of the two most conspicuous Scottish amateurs of his day and was also described as a player of genius, a very unorthodox genius. He was particularly gifted as an iron player, rivalled J. H. Taylor with a mashie, and was a very fine putter with a little lofted cleek, a relic of his boyhood days at Loretto school.

Laidlay had an outstanding record in the early days of the British Amateur and in the early international matches between Scotland and England, when he invariably had to take on such players as Ball and Hilton.

His victory in the 1891 Amateur came after a final against Hilton at the 20th hole; his success in 1889 had come after a close match with Balfour-Melville, a fellow member of the Honourable Company. Laidlay was runner-up on three occasions, twice to John Ball. His performance in finishing 2nd in the 1893 British Open, two strokes behind Willie Auchterlonie was a further mark of his class.

La Galea GC SEE REAL SOCIEDAD DE GOLF DE NEGURI 'LA GALEA'

Lake Karrinyup CC AUSTRALIA
Balcatta, W. Australia. 18 holes; 6,523 yd (5,965 m)

Lake Karrinyup CC, about 12 miles from

Perth, was founded in 1927 by a few golf enthusiasts who acquired 365 acres (148 ha) of undulating, heavily forested country around a lake. Dr Alister Mackenzie and Alex Russell, who had worked together at Royal Melbourne, were engaged as architects. Russell first went to Perth in February 1928 and the course was opened for play in May 1930. The clubhouse was completed later. During World War II, when it was requisitioned by the services, the course almost reverted to bush. However, it regained much of its old character and has twice accommodated the Australian Amateur and the Australian Open: the last one, in 1968, was won by Nicklaus. A new clubhouse was opened in 1972.

Lakes GC AUSTRALIA
Sydney, N.S.W. 18 holes; 6,833 yd (6,248 m)

The original course of the Lakes GC was opened on 12 April 1930, but in 1968 it was bisected by a new expressway, which meant a complete reconstruction. The American architect, Robert Von Hagge, carried out this work making full use of the many natural lakes that give the course its name and main character. The course was ready in June 1970. The club was the first in Australia to install a fully automatic watering system. In May 1971 a new two-storey clubhouse of circular design was opened. Centrally sited, it gives views over the entire area of the course.

In 1934 the club sponsored the first international golf tournament held in Australia, The Lakes International Cup, and in 1936, 1952 and 1954 it also staged the match between Australia and a team of professionals from the United States. The first two Wills International tournaments in 1961 and 1963 were held there, and in 1964 the first Australian Open Championship.

La Mandria GC ITALY
Turin (Torino). 18 holes; 6,775 yd (6,195 m); par 73

John Morrison designed this in 1956 as a 9-hole course; another 9 holes were added 10 years later, the work of John Harris. La Mandria has several of the features of a good American inland course – undulating greens and clever use of water hazards. Before modernization, the land was rather flat, but now the 3rd, 9th, 16th and 17th, and in particular a very good double dogleg, the 12th, are of a high standard. The club was host to the European Men's Team Championship in 1967.

La Manga Campo de Golf SPAIN
Costa Blanca. 36 holes; North Course 6,125 yd (5,601 m); South Course 6,510 yd (5,953 m)

La Manga, some 55 miles south of Alicante and about 15 miles north of Cartagena, is one of the latest of several developments that have turned the east coast of Spain into a thriving tourist area.

La Manga was the first course in Spain to be built as a 36-hole layout. It was opened in the summer of 1972 and later held an inaugural tournament in which its director of golf, Gary Player, took part. The site lies in a shallow valley, a mile or two from the sea and was laid out by the American architect, Robert Dean Putman from California, who overcame the shortage of natural features in

La Manga Campo de Golf, a view from the hill above the clubhouse

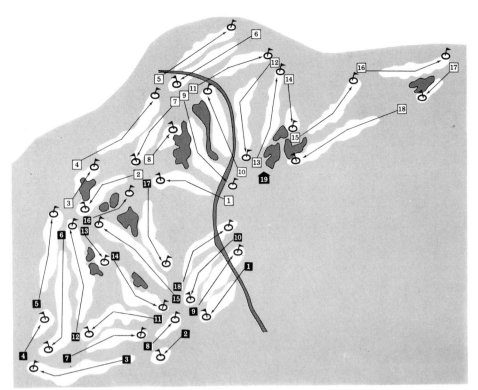

one of the hottest parts of Spain by planting 3,000 palm trees and sinking 14 interconnected lakes. The South Course is the championship test and in 1972 was agreed as the setting for the Spanish Open Championship for five years.

Lamaze, Henri de FRENCH

b. Dordogne 1918. French Close Amateur 1947-51, 1953, 1955-8, 1961-2, 1966, 1971; French Open Amateur 1947-50, 1954-60; Italian Open Amateur 1955, 1958; semifinalist British Amateur 1966

At a time when there was meagre opposition in his own country Henri de Lamaze reigned supreme. Just after World War II when his enthusiasm for the game caused him to practise long hours there were only one or two first-class players in the country; yet his total of 25 French championships spread over about 15 years could have been achieved only by a player of high class with a stubborn determination to succeed. The wonder is that with such a record he was content to play most of his golf in his own country. He won twice over the years in Italy and he made occasional visits to the British Amateur, where for years he failed to do himself justice. Then at the age of 48 on the toughest of courses, Carnoustie, he reached the semi-finals and was beaten by the eventual winner, 18-year-old Bobby Cole from South Africa. An even more remarkable revival was his French Close Amateur victory in 1971.

Lamaze seemed to hit the ball flat-footedly and without much action of the hips, but he hit few loose shots and was an outstanding putter.

Laminated

The heads of nearly all modern wooden clubs are of laminated-block construction; each layer is placed at right angles to the one before (maple and beech are chiefly used). The results are more consistent, less prone to moisture changes, than some of the old wooden heads – such as those of persimmon.

Laney, Al AMERICAN

b. Pensacola, Fla., 1896

Al Laney is in the first rank of American sports writers. Although he is best known for his tennis and golf writing, he has covered nearly all sports at one time or another. He began his career in journalism on the Pensacola *Journal* and later moved on to the Dallas *Dispatch* and Minneapolis *News* before serving in the American army during World War I. He saw action in the 308th Infantry of the 77th Division – the unit to which the famed 'Lost Battalion' was attached – and was wounded. Back in the United States, he worked for Associated Press in Atlanta – it was then that he formed his enduring friendship with Bob Jones – but he was drawn back to Europe, and in 1925 he joined the Paris *Herald*. He served as night editor and also covered the great golf and tennis events in Europe for the *Herald's* rich American uncle, the *New York Herald Tribune*. In the middle Thirties he went back to the United States and wrote about sports there for the *Herald Tribune*, but he seldom missed the great May, June, and July sports events in Europe. (He and O. B. Keeler were the only American newsmen who were on hand for the first two tricks in Jones's Grand Slam, at St Andrews and Doylake.) Laney's transatlantic commuting was ended by the outbreak of World War II, and from that time, until the *Herald Tribune* closed down in 1968, he was a member of the sports staff of that paper, based in New York.

Laney is the author of a number of books, including the well-known *Paris Herald*, *Golfing America*, *Covering the Court*, and *Prep Schools*. Kindly and soft-spoken, although a man of considerable inner fire and fibre, Laney has long been one of the most respected and best-liked American newspapermen, and one of the few truly distinguished writers on sports. An admirer of Bernard Darwin, he writes a calm and observant prose with a good measure of human warmth.

Langley, John Douglas Algernon

BRITISH

b. Northwood, Middlesex, 1918. Walker Cup 1936, 1951, 1953; English Amateur 1950, runner-up 1936; *Golf Illustrated* Gold Vase 1952-3

A brilliant boy golfer, John Langley was picked for the 1936 Walker Cup team while still at school and was awarded his Blue at Cambridge on the first day of his first university term. His selection for Britain owed much to his performance in reaching the 1936 final of the English Amateur at Royal Cinque Ports. His victory in the event came in 1950, also at Deal. After playing again in two Walker Cups, and winning the *Golf*

Top, the course plan of La Manga

Above, Henri de Lamaze

Illustrated Gold Vase twice in the early 1950s, he played practically no competitive golf. However, he returned to the golfing scene to be chairman of the British selectors in 1967-9.

Lassen, E. A. BRITISH

b. Bradford, Yorkshire, 1876. British Amateur 1908; runner-up 1911; Yorkshire Amateur 1900, 1908-9, 1913-14

Laurel Valley GC USA

Ligonier, Pa.

Set in the foothills of the Allegheny Mountains, some distance east of Pittsburgh, Laurel Valley was built by Dick Wilson early in the 1960s. It occupies land that was formerly a hunting preserve of the very wealthy Mellon family, and its membership is studded with US Steel executives and other millionaires, including Arnold Palmer who grew up in the town of Latrobe only a few brassie shots away.

The course has a very pretty look to it as it drops away from high, hilly land and, after wandering through a valley, returns to a tasteful, smallish clubhouse set on a plateau at the foot of a higher ridge. It is good and interesting, as all Wilson courses are, but it is not a 'big' course. Although it measured 7,090 yd (6,483 m) for the 1965 USPGA Championship, won by Dave Marr, it had to be tightened up considerably to test the long-hitting modern professionals. In recent summers, Laurel Valley has been host to a tour event called the PGA Team Championship, a four-ball tournament that has twice been won by Arnold Palmer and Jack Nicklaus.

Lausanne GC SWITZERLAND

Lausanne. 18 holes; 6,920 yd (6,328 m); par 72

Situated a mile or two north of the city on rising ground, the course commands views of the Lake of Geneva (Leman) and, on the far side, of the Savoy Alps. It covers undulating country on the edge of large spruce forests in the Jorat region. The first 9 holes on the higher part of the course are perhaps more open and make their length felt with drives to rising fairways. Leaving the clubhouse area again for the second time the course plunges down at the 12th with a narrow approach to the green through a corridor of trees, regaining height at the next hole and then rejoining the area of the earlier holes. The course was started in 1921 by a local resident who with his own hands cleared the ground for the 2 holes he had in mind; friends helped him to increase the number but it was 1932 before the full 18 holes were in use. Between 1940 and 1945 9 of the holes were given up to potato growing, and in 1960 major reconstruction of the course was undertaken. Since then it has been reckoned Switzerland's leading championship course and in 1971 the European Team Championship was held there.

Laval-sur-le-Lac GC CANADA

Laval-sur-le-Lac, Que. 18 holes; 6,555 yd (5,994 m); par 72

The luxurious and hospitable Club Laval-sur-le-Lac is the premier French club of the Montreal area. Renowned for its cuisine, it is a club where nothing for comfort and well-being is overlooked. The manicured course is the epitome of the parkland variety, set in a veritable arboretum. The beautiful trees include superb maples, elms and oaks, to which have been added groups of white pine, blue spruce, Norwegian maple, silver birch and weeping willow, together with hundreds of decorative and sweet-scented shrubs.

It seems almost sacrilege to dig a divot from the immaculate turf. One could imagine that 'Capability' Brown might suddenly appear from behind a tree to administer a reprimand, except that at Laval it would more probably be the great Le Nôtre. But, if the course seems a trifle artificial to those accustomed to testing their golfing skills against more rugged features, it does demand a good standard of golf and has a soothing and infectious charm.

It was at Laval in 1951 that Marlene Streit sprang into national prominence at the age of 17, winning the first of the nine Canadian Ladies' Open Championships she was to acquire during the ensuing 18 years The second playing of the World Cup (then the Canada Cup) matches took place at Laval in 1954, when they were won by the Australian team of Peter Thomson and Kel Nagle who averaged 2½ strokes under par per round for the eight rounds they played between them. In winning the Canadian Open Championship of 1962 Ted Kroll, of Fort Lauderdale, Fla., had precisely the same average score. Laval-sur-le-Lac is well worth the 20-mile drive from Montreal to the western tip of Île Jésus in the Rivière des Mille-Îles.

John Langley

The 18th hole of Laurel Valley GC

Lawrence, Joan B. BRITISH
b. Kinghorn, Fife, 1930. Scottish Ladies' 1962-4, runner-up 1965; Vagliano Cup 1963, 1965; Curtis Cup 1964

Three Scottish championships in succession, and four consecutive finals in that event are testimony to Joan Lawrence's consistency, and few women have equalled her ability to get down in 2 from a range of anywhere within a hundred yards of the pin. Her Scottish victories were obtained at Dornoch in 1962, Troon in 1963, and Gullane in 1964, and she relinquished the title to Mrs Belle Robertson in the final of the championship at Nairn in 1965.

She began a long career for Scotland in 1959, uninterrupted until 1971, when her appointment as captain of the British Commonwealth team prevented her from taking part in the Home International matches. She was vice-captain of the Curtis Cup team in 1970, and captained Scotland in the European Team Championship of 1969.

Lawrie, Charles Dundas BRITISH
b. Edinburgh 1923. Semi-finalist Scottish Amateur 1955; non-playing captain Walker Cup 1961, 1963

A gifted player of many games, Charles Lawrie had the ability to perform well in golf with a minimum of practice. He was, however, a regular competitor in championships and he had a playing career in which, besides reaching the semi-final of the 1955 Scottish Amateur, he was a leading member

Charles Lawrie

of several Scottish sides, and had an outstanding record in foursomes competitions. Besides being non-playing captain of the 1961 and 1963 Walker Cup teams, he led Scotland in 1960 and at Portmarnock in 1961, when the Scots won all their matches and all 10 singles against England.

Lawrie's competitive career has been followed by notable service in golf administration: chairman of the Royal and Ancient selectors, 1963-7; member of the committee on amateur status; chairman of the committee responsible for running all the R. and A.'s championships, including the Open, which were eminently successful under his direction. He is now a leading golf-course architect, one of his current major projects being 36 holes on the Duke of Bedford's estate.

Lawson, Estelle see PAGE, MRS JULIUS A., JR

Lebanon

Although some golf has been played in the Lebanon almost as long as in Egypt, it is only in recent years that the country has become involved in the international game, in a modest but promising way, as Beirut grows into the golfing centre of the Middle East.

Before 1967 there were only three courses in the country, each of 9 holes, two grass and one sand. The Beirut Sporting Club dated back to the 1920s when the American representative in Lebanon and Syria, then under French mandate, was important in introducing the game to the Levant. Its sand course, abandoned in 1965, was not only devoid of grass, but failed even to be good of its kind: the addicts who played it, mostly resident foreigners, did so for the want of anything better. Occasionally invited guests could play at the Zahrani CC course near Sidon, 30 miles south of Beirut, run by Tapline (Trans Arabian Pipeline Co.), or at the Iraq Petroleum Company's Ras El Lados Club course near Tripoli, 50 miles north, both primarily for company staff. The Zahrani course was built in 1956-9 near the Mediterranean terminus of the 1,100-mile pipeline that starts in Saudi Arabia. Ras El Lados was built in the late 1940s at the Tripoli end of the pipeline from northern Iraq.

Now Lebanon, one of the smallest of the Arab states, has acquired two new courses, opened in 1966-8. Both are available to tourists, who are welcomed enthusiastically. They are run by the GC of Lebanon in suburban Ouzai, five miles from central Beirut, and the Delhamyeh CC near Damour, 15 miles south of Beirut, a mile above the coast road to Tyre and Sidon. Though only of 9 holes each, the fact that these courses are all grass, including the

greens – rare in this part of the world – makes them attractive. They are valid and rather difficult, largely because the terrain seldom provides a level stance.

The best golf weather is from March to December, with spring and autumn most favourable. In July and August midday heat restricts play to early mornings and late afternoons.

Le Blan, Nanette (Mrs R. Thion de la Chaume) FRENCH
b. 1908. Runner-up French Ladies' Close 1926; British Ladies' 1928

The second French player to win the British Ladies' Championship, Nanette Le Blan was in three Vagliano Cup teams in the 1930s.

Lees, Arthur BRITISH
b. Sheffield, Yorkshire, 1908. Dunlop Masters 1947; Ryder Cup 1947, 1949, 1951, 1955; Penfold Tournament 1951, 1953; British Seniors' 1959

Throughout the 1950s Arthur Lees was one of the leading British tournament professionals with a good record in the Ryder Cup which included singles victories over Porky Oliver and Marty Furgol both in America. He also won his foursomes in 1949 and 1951. He was an extremely steady player with a deadly short game who, on his appointment as professional at Sunningdale, had some remarkable records of scoring in the matches – invariably for highish stakes –

which he often arranged and in which he was very successful.

Leeward and Windward Islands see MONTSERRAT

Legrange, Cobie SOUTH AFRICAN
b. Boksburg, Transvaal. Dunlop Masters

Arthur Lees

1964, 1969; tied French Open 1964, runner-up 1965; Wills Masters (Australia) 1964

One of the young South Africans who challenged Gary Player's position as the country's leading player, although he has never won the South African Open. Legrange began to travel and was a well-known figure in many countries, winning a number of tournaments. He has great application rather than great natural ability, but by 1972 he had faded from all except the South African scene. While playing in Britain he developed a pronounced hesitation in taking away the club on the backswing.

Leinborn, Lennart SWEDISH

b. 1919. Swedish Strokeplay 1953; Scandinavian Open Amateur 1957, 1960, 1963; Swedish Close Amateur 1958, 1961, 1964; Eisenhower Trophy 1960; European Amateur Team Championship 1961; Europe v. British Isles 1962

Leinborn turned seriously to golf when too old to play ice hockey. He played 15 times for Sweden between 1953 and 1964, and took his first Scandinavian Open Amateur Championship in 1957 at the age of 38. He has a stylish swing and plays bravely, though wisely.

Leitch, Charlotte Cecilia Pitcairn
BRITISH

b. Silloth, Cumberland, 1891. French Ladies' Open 1912, 1914, 1920-1, 1924; British Ladies' 1914, 1920-1, 1926; English Ladies' 1914, 1919; Canadian Ladies' Open 1921

Cecil Leitch's debut in the British Ladies' Championship on the Old Course at St Andrews in 1908 was the beginning of a fresh era in women's golf. She reached the semi-finals of this event, which was her first attempt in serious competition, and her outstanding power and authority with woods

and irons set fresh standards. But it was not until 1914 that she gained her expected position as leading player in Britain, by winning the British Championship and the English title.

World War I intervened, but when competition was resumed, she retained her ascendancy and kept her titles, winning the British in 1920 and 1921 and the English in 1919. She won her fourth British at Harlech in 1926, and so had the unique distinction of collecting a British Championship in each of the four Home Countries. Altogether she won 12 national titles, two English, the French Open five times, and the Canadian Open. Her victory in the 1921 Canadian Open at Ottawa was exceptional for the margin of 17 up and 15 to play by which she defeated Miss M. M'Bride.

Her matches with Joyce Wethered focused attention on women's golf so that it became front-page news, and their homeric battles did much to increase the popularity of the game, and radically uplifted the quality of play so far as women were concerned.

Cecil Leitch and Joyce Wethered first met in the final of the English Championship at Sheringham, Norfolk, in 1920, when Miss Wethered scored a shock victory. In 1921 Miss Leitch gained her revenge by defeating her great rival twice, when they met in the final of the British at Turnberry and the French Open at Fontainebleau. They met again in the finals of the British at Princes in 1922, and at Troon in 1925. In both these contests Joyce Wethered prevailed. Their greatest battle was prolonged over 37 holes at Troon. The only time these two giantesses met in a championship before the finals was at Portrush in 1924, when they played in the sixth round, and started off by halving the first 7 holes: this was in the British, subsequently won by Miss Wethered.

Miss Leitch had to defer her arrival in the English team until 1910, because of the rules governing residential qualification. They were amended to let her in. In the Home Internationals between 1910 and 1928, she played in 33 matches, winning 29 and halving one.

Lema, Anthony David AMERICAN

b. Oakland, Cal., 1934; d. 1966. Runner-up US Masters 1963; Ryder Cup 1963, 1965; British Open 1964; World Series Tournament 1964; Carling World Tournament 1965; World (Canada) Cup 1965

The glamorous and prosperous world of modern American professional golf was a far cry from Lema's humble beginnings on the San Francisco waterfront. A caddie at 12 and a marine in the Korean War, Tony

Lema experienced a tough upbringing. After becoming an assistant at the San Francisco GC, joining the tour in 1958 and then suffering two discouragingly unsuccessful years, he rapidly became a challenger to the supremacy of Arnold Palmer and Jack Nicklaus. He wrote in his book on those early years on the tour, 'I moved like a zombie

from city to city', but his talent was undeniable; in 1962 he won his first major tournament and in 1963, the year in which he was nosed out of the US Masters by a sterling finish by Jack Nicklaus, he finished 4th in the money list.

Lema, a lover of the high life, came as near as any contemporary golfer to being another Walter Hagen. He often conveyed the impression of a man simply enjoying himself; he was also a tall, handsome figure endowed with a swing which was a movement of rhythm, grace and beauty.

He was the antithesis of those who based their golf on power alone but, like Hagen, he tried much harder than legend would have us believe and was always likely to win when big money was at stake. The best example was in July 1964, shortly after he had captured three major American tournaments in the space of a few weeks, when he won the British Open at St Andrews. It was without doubt one of the most remarkable victories in the championship's history for Lema had never previously played golf in Europe and allowed himself only about 36 hours in

Cobie Legrange

Tony Lema driving in the 1965 Piccadilly matchplay championship at Wentworth which to acquaint himself with the Old Course, which many believe takes years to fathom. For a man conditioned almost entirely to American courses, the manner in which he adapted his game was indicative of a great skill.

He showed rare judgment and control of the little shots into the greens which have no parallel in America, putted marvellously on greens which had baffled many distinguished overseas challengers of the past, and drove superbly – particularly on the first day when gale-force gusts blew from the west. He opened with a 73 and then with a succession of 3s around the famous Loop in the next three rounds consolidated his challenge. The crux of the whole championship came on those holes on the final morning when he passed Jack Nicklaus on the 13th green and became aware that Nicklaus was in inspired form. Nicklaus holed the course in 66 and sustained this brilliance with a fourth round of 68 – the best scoring in the last two rounds that the championship has seen – but Lema was in no way dismayed. Rounds of 68 and 70 gave him a total of 279 and his victory by 5 shots was, at the time, the biggest since the war, except for Palmer at Troon in 1962.

Lema never won a major title in the States and his British Open performance was without question the high point of his career which was so tragically shortened. He continued to be one of the leading figures in American golf for the next couple of years, made a brave defence of his title in 1965, represented the United States in the Canada Cup in Madrid the same summer and a week or so later was involved in his famous match with Gary Player in the Piccadilly Matchplay Championship at Wentworth. This is remembered for Lema's defeat at the 37th hole after being 7 up on the 20th tee, but it is remembered also for the quiet dignity with which he accepted what must have been a bitter disappointment. It seems almost certain that Lema was destined to win many major titles but, just as he was nearing the height of his powers, he was killed when the private aircraft in which he was travelling, crashed on landing at a course near Lansing, Ill. His wife, Betty, and his companions were also killed.

Leonard, Stan CANADIAN

b. Vancouver, B.C., 1914. Canadian PGA 1940-1, 1950-1, 1954, 1957, 1959, 1961 tied 1962; Greater Greensboro Open 1957; Tournament of Champions 1958; Western Open 1960

One of the better-known Canadian tournament professionals, Stan Leonard made a name for himself on the American circuit although he did not start playing there until 1955 when he was already over 40. Altogether he won three tournaments and was a most consistent player, particularly in the US Masters at Augusta. He tied for 4th place in 1958 and 1959 and from 1957 to 1961 was never lower than 15th.

Leonard played in the first Canada Cup in 1953 and thereafter played for Canada in the event six times. He formed a formidable partnership with Al Balding and in 1954 won the individual title, later tying with Peter Thomson in Melbourne in 1959.

Leven Golfing Society SCOTLAND

Leven, Fife. 18 holes; 6,425 yd (5,875 m); par 70

An amalgam in 1957 of the Innerleven GC (1820), the Leven GC (1846) and the Leven Ladies' GC (1891) although golf had been played on the 'sweet banks' of Dubbieside, for at least a century before it became organized. Its Standard Assurance Gold Medal is claimed to be the oldest Open amateur trophy in the world. Innerleven's original links lay between the sea and village gardens, where the 'wives', it is recorded, were the terror of all players, one of them being 'a virago of priceless value'. When a certain sheriff, resplendent in his tartan golfing uniform, ventured into her cabbage patch 'he was received with genuine warmth'. Her explanation to the neighbours for this picturesque outburst was simply 'A muckle lauddie reiving at my rizzers' (A big lad scratching among my cabbages).

In 1852 the Standard Assurance Company of Edinburgh became owners of the Lundin estate and proved fairy godmothers to the golfers and the district. The arrival of the railway and development of Methil harbour for the coal trade made Dubbieside untenable and in 1867 Innerleven also moved to Scoonie, the home of the new Leven club, and the Leven Thistle club was formed for artisans. The course was extended to 18 holes and in 1868 Young Tom Morris of St Andrews won the first tournament with 170 for 36 holes. The Standard continued to fight the club's battles and in 1870 presented their gold medal for open competition among 'the members of Innerleven, Leven and Lundin Links golf clubs and such other clubs as the Captain and Council of the Innerleven Club shall approve,' but 'makers of clubs or balls or professionals' were barred.

It was on Innerleven's course, according to Sir Robert Anstruther, that sand boxes were first provided on tees: previously caddies had to carry boxes of wet sand slung round their necks.

Lewis, Jack AMERICAN

b. Florence, S. Car. South Carolina Amateur 1964; semi-finalist Western Amateur 1966; Walker Cup team 1967; North-South Amateur 1968; Eisenhower Trophy 1968

Another product of Wake Forest University where in 1968 he won the Arnold

Palmer Athlete of the Year award. Three years running Lewis was Carolina's junior champion; he was a regular performer for five years in the US Amateur in which his best finish was 7th. He turned professional in 1969, but has had to wait for success to come. In 1972, no doubt on the strength of their association with Wake Forest, Lewis was invited by Palmer to partner him in the USPGA team championship when his original partner, Jack Nicklaus, had to withdraw.

Libya

Libya has four golf courses, all sand, two 18 holes, two 9; three of them open to visitors. The 18-hole courses are both in Tripoli, largest city in the country: Tripoli GC (6,224 yd, 5,691 m); and Tajura GC (5,500 yd, 5,029 m). The 9-hole courses are at the Benghazi GC, in Libya's second city, and at Brega on the Mediterranean coast halfway between Tripoli and Benghazi. The Brega course was built by Esso for company staff and their invited guests.

The Libyan Golf Federation, which has

Jack Lewis

sent teams to the World (Canada) Cup and Eisenhower Trophy tournaments, is trying enthusiastically to develop golf in the country, seeking government support for a grass course. Until this materializes Libya cannot be included among golf holiday countries, despite excellent weather.

Lie

The situation in which the ball comes to rest. A 'good lie' is one where the ball 'sits up' on nice, springy turf; a 'bare lie' where it rests on turf worn or pounded hard; and a 'bad lie' when it nestles in a depression and may not be fully visible. It is a fundamental rule of golf that the ball should be played 'as it lies'.

The word is also used to describe the angle between the horizontal and the centre line of a club's shaft. This all-important angle helps the golfer to make a correct swing. Too small an angle is likely to produce a pushed or sliced shot, while too large an angle will give a pulled or hooked shot.

Lindrick GC ENGLAND

Worksop, Nottinghamshire. 6,578 yd (6,015 m); par 71

A course famous as the scene of Britain's

only Ryder Cup victory since the war, but also long known to connoisseurs of the game. Laid out on Lindrick Common astride the Sheffield-Worksop road, it is moorland in character with fine natural turf and well broken up by gorse. Formed in 1891 as a 9-hole course, it had handicaps ranging up to 45, and one competition was won with a net 29. A historic touch is provided by the 4th hole. The 'cockpit' green, guarded by the little Ryton River, used to be the scene of cockfighting; it was conveniently placed near the border of three counties – Yorkshire, Derbyshire and Nottinghamshire, and enabled those taking part to escape across the county border if threatened by the arm of the law. It is not otherwise a particularly distinguished hole, but it is fun to play. The opportunity to score lies in the first half which is shorter by some 340 yd (311 m) than the second 9. The 12th runs parallel to the main road, and once that is crossed to the 13th tee the sense of restraint imposed by the gorse diminishes and the golfer can hope to open his shoulders. But the finishing holes, over rising ground which catches the wind, can be tough and have been the graveyard of many a good score. The long, par 3 that comes back to the clubhouse makes a grandstand finishing hole. It was thanks to the good offices of Sir Stuart Goodwin, a Yorkshire industrialist and a benefactor to the game, that the 1957 Ryder Cup match was held there and it was followed in 1960 by the Curtis Cup match.

Line

The direction in which the player intends the ball to travel after it is hit. In most cases, the correct line is a straight one. It often happens, however, that the line is different for two players, particularly if one is a longer hitter than the other. Speed of the ball and the amount of borrow are the factors that govern the line of a putt.

Links

A term surrounded by some doubt and controversy. In his *History of Golf*, Robert Browning said, 'There is a modern tendency to restrict this term to the natural seaside golf country among the sand dunes, and it is frequently suggested that the word has been

Lie, of a club: the angle between the sole and the shaft, indicated by the arrows in the diagram

Above, the 'cockpit' green of the Lindrick GC

Line: *top,* a pensive Sally Barber studies the line of her putt

applied only to courses of this traditional type. But I can find no support for this contention. The noble expanse of turf on which the Royal Eastbourne course is laid out was known as "The Links" long before anyone thought of playing golf over it, and it is high up on the downs.'

A similar stretch of down at Cambridge was long known as 'The Links' although nobody ever thought of playing golf there.

Nevertheless, in modern usage the term tends to be taken to mean the sand-dune country of little use except for golf that lies between the sea and more fertile areas; 'links' type golf is generally thought of as that found only on traditional seaside courses.

Linskill, W. T. BRITISH
b. Tynemouth, Northumberland, 1855; d. St Andrews, Fife, 1929

The man best remembered for starting the Oxford v. Cambridge match in 1878 and for introducing golf to Cambridge when he came up from St Andrews in 1873. It was, of course, an obvious thing for a St Andrean to do – he was also the founder of the Cambridge University GC in 1875 at a time when Coldham Common was in use.

Linskill was the club's first president, captain, and for many years Honorary Secretary; he was a member of the Royal and Ancient, an original member of the Oxford and Cambridge Golfing Society and a great St Andrews character.

Lip
The edge of the hole on the putting green. A putt that grazes the hole without dropping is said to have 'lipped the hole'.

Liphook GC ENGLAND
Liphook, Hampshire. 18 holes; 6,277 yd (5,740 m); par 70

One of a group of courses not far from London blessed with sandy soil, heather and conifers. These blend to produce a subtle, largely natural course of considerable charm. Designed by A. C. Croome and T. Simpson in 1921, the course lies just off the London-Portsmouth road which is crossed for all except 8 holes. Five short holes help to emphasize the comparative shortness of the course but they contain much quality – notably the 7th and the 11th. The same is true of some of the shorter doglegs, such as the 14th and 15th. A new clubhouse replaced the old sheds after World War II and stands overlooking the steep opening and finishing holes. The club is traditionally linked with the Royal Navy, being within easy reach of the Portsmouth division. The rest of the course undulates gently, and the springy

turf makes easy walking. The English Ladies' Championship was held there in 1963 and the English Girls' in 1971. It was the boast of one of the designers, Tom Simpson, that the difficulty of the approach to the greens at Liphook would for ever defeat any improvements in the manufacture of the golf ball.

Lister, John NEW ZEALANDER
b. Temuka, S. Island, 1947. NZ Professional 1971

Lister became the first New Zealand professional after Bob Charles to seek his living on the professional circuit in America. Although he won the South Canterbury strokeplay championship in 1965 and played for his state in the Freiberg Trophy, he had limited success as an amateur, but enough to persuade him to turn professional in 1967. He began to travel and soon made an impact, winning two tournaments in Australia in 1969 and two in Britain in 1970. In 1971 he became PGA Champion of New Zealand at Mount Maunganui, winning by 8 strokes with a total of 30 under par.

He first went to the United States in 1970 and has since done well enough to suggest that he may one day be successful in the big league. His brother played rugby for the All Blacks.

Little Aston GC ENGLAND
Sutton Coldfield, Warwickshire. 18 holes

Little Aston, in a setting of green seclusion on the northeast fringe of Birmingham, is commonly recognized as one of the finest inland courses in Britain and certainly one of the main championship centres in the Midlands. It typifies parkland golf at its best and always seems to be immaculately prepared for the many major events which it houses. These have included two English Amateur Championships, the English Open Stroke-

play Championship of 1970 and several important professional events but, for all its obvious qualities as a modern test of golf, the club itself is not as old as some of its neighbours around the Midlands. In fact, it was founded in 1908 when a few members of the Sutton Coldfield Club decided to break away and find a home of their own.

They did not have to look very far for an ideal site because Little Aston Park, an old deer park, had a profusion of forest trees, a free-draining soil and a fine, weed-free turf. The construction work, carried out to the design of Harry Vardon who did surprisingly little work as a golf-course architect, was therefore relatively easy even in the days before heavy machinery; but it owed much to the loan of horses and carts from local farmers.

The first professional, named Butchart, was replaced in 1910 by Mart Lewis who served as Professional/Greenkeeper for the next 40 years. Throughout World War I, maintenance was left to two elderly men, some sheep and a group of members who mowed the greens. Brewery horses were also

Top, Liphook GC, a view of the 5th green

Above, John Lister

used, on the condition that they ended their days at Little Aston.

Peace brought a renovation and a slight redesign of the course involving the 1st, 9th and 14th, where new cross bunkers were introduced. The drought of 1921 gave rise to fires on the course, but silver birch seeds from as far away as Streetly settled on the sparse patches and a new species of tree was added which has given Little Aston much of its present character and beauty.

Little Aston moved steadily towards championship status and in its first championship, the English Amateur of 1927, it was appropriate that the finalists, Phil Perkins, the winner, and Jack Beddard were both Midland men. Then in 1937, Sam King won the *Daily Mail* Professional Tournament and Henry Longhurst gave one of the first broadcasts on golf from a commentary point between the 4th and 7th greens.

After World War II the club became a popular and regular setting for the Dunlop Masters. One of the local members, John Beharrell, became the youngest winner of the British Amateur Championship at Troon in 1956. Nor must the performances of the club's current professional, Charlie Ward, who succeeded Lewis, be overlooked. He was a member of three Ryder Cup teams and a leading tournament player for many years.

Little Aston, however, remains essentially a member's club. Members obviously take pride in the present reputation of their course and the traditions of the early days have been faithfully maintained. They no longer come on bicycles or walk from Streetly station as they did before the advent of buses; and nobody can quite emulate Lt Colonel C. F. Fiddian-Green who used to arrive at the club in a carriage drawn by two horses with coachman and flunkey in scarlet coats, top hats and cockades. They perhaps would not know the course surrounded now by a private housing estate but to many generations Little Aston has proved a perfect retreat from the city.

Little, William Lawson, Jr AMERICAN
b. Newport, R.I. British Amateur 1934-5; Canadian Open 1936; US Amateur 1934-5; Walker Cup 1934; US Open 1940; Los Angeles Open 1940; Texas Open 1941

One of America's great amateurs who turned professional and won his country's Open championship. His double victories in the Amateur championships of both countries remain a unique achievement, involving the winning of 31 consecutive matches against the best of both nations. A tremendously powerful hitter with a shut-face swing, he had also a deft touch round the

greens; he made a formidable opponent with his capacity to exude pugnacity, and, for a time, he swept all before him. He was too squarely built and too explosive in his stroke-making to be a pretty golfer to watch, but he had tremendous speed of hand and an immense determination. Henry Cotton wrote of him that when he first saw him play he had a hooker's grip of three or four knuckles – he was also carrying 23 clubs in his bag – but he later adjusted his grip.

On the strength of reaching the semi-finals of the 1933 Amateur he was chosen for the Walker Cup the following year and his success in that match could hardly have been more complete. He won his foursome with Johnny Goodman against Roger

Wethered and Cyril Tolley by 8 and 6, and his single against the latter by 6 and 5. The golf he played in the final of the Amateur at Prestwick later that year was perhaps as good as he ever played in his life. He won by 14 and 13, a record margin in the championship, finishing off a locally born Scot, J. Wallace, as his supporters were still flocking onto the course to watch the match. Little went round Prestwick in 66 in the morning and of the 23 holes he played altogether, 12 were threes. Bernard Darwin, who was not given to superlatives, described it as 'one of the most terrific exhibitions in all golfing history'. The match was over at 2.10 p.m. at which point Little was an average of 13 over 3s. His drive to the 18th (260 yd) pitched

Top, the 3rd fairway and green of the Little Aston GC and below, a view across the lake to the 17th green

close to the hole and ran on to finish 6 yd behind it.

His victory in the following year was in sharp contrast. Dr Tweddell, though 5 down after 11 against him, in the final, put up a magnificent resistance; he was back to all square by the 30th and lost only on the last green. In 1936 Little turned professional and at once won the Canadian Open. In an exhibition tour he was frequently matched against Jimmy Thomson, then considered one of the longest hitters in America. Thomson was reckoned slightly the longer but there was not much in it. In the 1939 US Open Little had started with a 69 but slipped with a last round 81; the following year he tied first with Gene Sarazen who, in his 38th year and 20 years after winning his first Open, lost the play-off to Lawson Little's 70. This was the championship in which six competitors were disqualified for starting ahead of schedule because a storm was brewing.

Littler, Gene Alec AMERICAN

b. San Diego, Cal., 1930. US Amateur 1953; Walker Cup 1953; San Diego Open 1954; Ryder Cup 1961, 1963, 1965, 1967, 1969, 1971; US Open 1961; Canadian Open 1965; World Series 1966; runner-up US Masters 1970

When Gene Littler won the US Amateur Championship in 1953 he was hailed as the likely successor to Hogan as the outstanding golfer of the next generation. The founda-

tion for the claim was that Littler's swing was a perfect expression of pure orthodoxy in outline, of an effortless rhythm, and of freedom from any kind of idiosyncrasy. It was a completely unselfconscious movement and has always remained so.

Littler might have been born playing golf for no one, with the possible exception of Snead, has ever made the process of striking a ball look simpler or more natural. Indeed, it is so quiet that he might be a man taking practice swings in front of a mirror. He is a perfect model for any golfer to study in the relaxed approach to every shot, the stance taken so easily, the pace of the takeaway and, above all, the completely unhurried start to the downswing. Watching him can

be almost hypnotic and it seems inconceivable that he could ever produce a false stroke, but after a remarkably successful start to his professional career in 1954 Littler endured several lean years. It was as if, having played golf so brilliantly and easily since boyhood, he had suddenly become aware of its difficulties, but for the last decade he has been one of the most consistent golfers in history.

By nature Littler is a modest, gentle and pleasant person, always the same in success or defeat; in fact at times he seems unaware, almost uncaring of the beauty his golf creates, and has perhaps lacked the fire in his temperament and the consuming ambition necessary for the supreme achievements commensurate with his talents.

In 1961 he was US Open Champion; he has won a score of major PGA tournaments besides, and over $800,000 in prize money. Only a handful of golfers have won more. And he played in every US Ryder Cup team from 1961 to 1971. These are substantial rewards but somehow less than adequate for a man so gifted. Three or four more major championships should have come his way but the closest approach was at Augusta in 1970 when, after a play-off for the Masters, he lost to Casper, a boyhood rival from the great golfing nursery of San Diego.

The reason why Littler has not commanded the world scene to a greater extent probably lies in a personality that is essentially retiring. Year after year he will play the tour as much as is necessary to make a substantial income and maintain his position among the leading players; then, at every reasonable opportunity, he will hasten home to La Jolla, his wife, Shirley, two children and vintage cars. The hobby of collecting ancient cars, particularly Rolls-Royces, and working on them himself, seems closer to his heart than grinding round the tournament circuit. It has always seemed that Littler is one golfer who has his priorities right, who knows what he wants from life and is not to be deterred from its pursuit.

In 1972 he contracted what was feared to be a malignant cancer and was ill for some time but happily he made a complete recovery and in 1973 won a major tournament on the American tour.

Liverpool GC, Royal ENGLAND

Hoylake, Cheshire. 18 holes; Medal Course 6,702 yd (6,128 m); par 72

One of the oldest and most historic courses in all Britain – in England only Royal Blackheath and Royal North Devon are older – which became the venue for several new events. The first Amateur Champion-

William Lawson Little Jr

Two studies of Gene Littler

ships was held there in 1885 and so was the first English Amateur Championship in 1925. Hoylake was the scene of not only the first international match between England and Scotland but of the first match between Britain and the United States, and of the Home International matches between the four countries. It was at Hoylake that the rubber-cored ball burst upon the British scene in 1902.

The popularity of the club arose from the pre-eminence of three of its players in those early years. Between them John Ball and Harold Hilton won three Open championships and 12 Amateurs. The third figure, Jack Graham, although he won no championship, was hardly less distinguished in reputation. Appropriately enough, Ball was the first Englishman to win the Open Championship when he went to Prestwick in 1890. His eight victories in the Amateur extend from 1888 to 1912, the formative period in English amateur golf.

The sandy stretch of turf on the shores of the Dee estuary was originally a rabbit warren used occasionally as a racecourse. The club was formed in 1869 at a meeting called by J. Muir Dowie, the first captain. Its headquarters were across the road in the Royal Hotel owned by John Ball's father, and the first professional was Jack Morris, son of George who designed the first 9 holes, and nephew of Old Tom. Jack remained there for 60 years, a much-respected outpost of Scotland in a very English club. The course was extended to 18 holes in 1871 and the clubhouse moved to its present site in 1895.

There is little resemblance between the original few holes, pitted with rabbit scrapes, dotted with racecourse posts, surrounded by rushes, and the giant championship test of today with its fine quality greens which led to the oft-quoted remark: 'The man who cannot putt at Hoylake cannot putt.'

Today the flat expanse of the opening and closing holes is hemmed in by housing but if there are lovelier courses than Hoylake few will make greater demands on the player's skill and courage. One reason for this is the abundant and controversial out-of-bounds. Some of it occurs at the boundaries of the course and some within the confines, owing to the erection of artificial banks or 'cops'. The famous Dowie hole (7th) has an out-of-bounds bank lining the left-hand side of the green. The 1st hole has become one of the most testing ones in championships thanks to an out-of-bounds bank extending all the way down the right side. The 16th is a similar hole played in the opposite direction; the 17th has the railing nearly as close to the green as in the case of the 7th. These and

other features test the nerve of every player, and although the ball is hit ever-greater distances, the finish, one of the longest in golf, still can be tough in a wind. But the emphasis on length is decreasing, and the shift now is on the difficulty of the opening holes, specially since the reshaping of the 3rd and 4th.

When the Open Championship first came to Hoylake, hopes were high that victory would go to one of its members, for both Ball and Hilton had won the title before. Hilton, generally reckoned the better stroke player of the two, had difficulty in shaking off James Braid, but with two putts for victory on the last green, he got the second one in 'through the back door'. The Triumvirate of Vardon, Taylor and Braid had little success at Hoylake. In 1902 Alex Herd, having been converted to the new rubber-cored ball by John Ball who had seen the Amateur won with it on the same course a few months before, got the better of Vardon in the final round, and five years later it was the turn of Arnaud Massy, brought over from Biarritz; he became the first foreigner to win the championship. Only in 1913 did J. H. Taylor, playing one of the great rounds of his life in a gale, win his last Open. He was in the field 11 years later when Walter Hagen won his second title and began a run of American victories which was not to be broken until 1934. In 1930 Jones scored the second leg of his Grand Slam there, a victory almost as emotional as that of Roberto de Vicenzo 37 years later, who moved the great crowd by saying he had given up hopes of an Open title and had come over that year only to see his friends.

With the tendency to reduce the number of championship courses for the Open, doubts have been raised about the suitability of Hoylake because of difficulties of accommodation and of car parking; but as to the suitability of the course there can be no doubt. Its short holes, two of them short and

two long, make as fine a quartet as any in the country, and anyone finishing with four 4s will be more likely to make up ground than to lose it. The quadrilateral bounded by the 1st and 16th holes, and marked by cops, provides a rare example of out-of-bounds within a championship course, and at least eight holes present out-of-bounds problems. At only one hole, the 9th with its punchbowl green, is the player given any respite.

In 1969 the club appropriately celebrated its centenary by holding the Amateur Championship. It was won by Michael Bonallack, his fifth victory in the event, and for the second year running he defeated Bill Hyndman of the United States in the final. This echoed Joe Carr's 1953 victory over the same course: he was another of the greatest amateurs of postwar Britain and Ireland and he also defeated an American, Harvie Ward, in the final. In the centenary year the captain of the club was Selwyn Lloyd, a former cabinet minister who was shortly to become Speaker of the House of Commons.

Liwai, Jacqueline (Mrs Barney Pung)
AMERICAN
US Women's Amateur 1952; runner-up US Women's Open 1953

First Hawaiian to win the United States Women's Amateur Championship. This she did in 1952 at Portland, Ore. by defeating Shirley McFedters by 2 and 1 in the final. This was on her third visit to the mainland, her previous visits being in the 1946 and 1948 Amateur Championships.

In the 1952 championship Mrs Pung who learned her golf on a public course out-hit her rivals by 40 to 50 yd from the tee, and this considerable advantage in power was the main factor of her success.

In January 1953 she turned professional, and later that year tied with Betsy Rawls

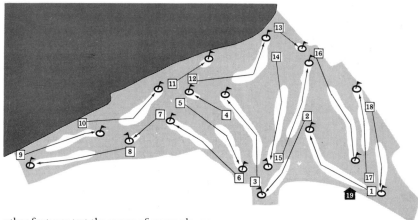

The course plan of the Royal Liverpool GC

for 1st place in the US Women's Open Championship at Rochester CC, N.Y., with a score of 302, but lost on a play-off.

The 1957 US Women's Open Championship at Winged Foot, Mamaroneck CC, N.Y., was a major tragedy for the Hawaiian. Mrs Pung scored 78, 75, 73, 72, for a leading total of 298. Although her fourth round total of 72 was given correctly, she was too excited when checking her card to notice that a 5 instead of a 6 had been put down as her score for the 4th hole. The error imposed a penalty of disqualification. Sympathetic officials and onlookers made a collection for Mrs Pung to alleviate her financial loss, but this could not compensate her for loss of the title.

Lloyd, Joe

An English professional who worked at the Essex CC, Manchester, Mass., in the summer, and at Pau in France in the winter. He won the US Open Championship in 1897 at the Chicago GC. Out of a field of 35, he scored 83-79 (162).

Locke, Arthur d'Arcy SOUTH AFRICAN

b. Germiston, Transvaal, 1917. South African Amateur 1935, 1937; South African Open 1935, 1937-40, 1946, 1950-1, 1955; Irish Open 1938; New Zealand Open 1938; Vardon Trophy 1946, 1950, 1954; Canadian Open 1947; 2nd leading money winner US Circuit 1947; British Open 1949-50, 1952, 1957, runner-up 1946, 1954; Tam O'Shanter All-American Tournament 1950; French Open 1952-3; Dunlop Masters 1954; Egyptian Open 1954; Swiss Open 1954; 3rd US Open 1947, 1951

Bobby Locke ranks with Hagen, on whose method he drew, Jones, and Palmer as the greatest putter of any age. This combined with a wonderful temperament built him a record of achievement which, had he pursued his career in the United States, must surely have given him a place among the all-time great players. As it was, in his brief visits to the United States he achieved enough to suggest that the Masters and Open titles must have come his way had he persisted. But his relationship with American golf was generally unhappy and, at the height of his career, he turned to Britain as his happy hunting ground. He and Peter Thomson between them dominated the game whenever they landed in Britain. A hat trick of Opens for Locke was interrupted only by Max Faulkner in 1951, and Locke became the first player since the Triumvirate to record four Open victories. Not until later was he overtaken in this by Peter Thomson. It must remain one of the regrets of the game that by the time American interest in the

British Open had revived with the advent of Palmer in the late 1950s, his reign was over.

Locke never commanded the length that has become fashionable in the age of Nicklaus, but he had wonderful control of his long game which was played with a pronounced draw, and his short game was second to none. He made popular in Britain the use of the wedge and became a byword for saving a stroke round the green. His preparation for the putt was detailed and methodical, but the stroke made with a rusty-bladed, hickory-shafted putter was quickly executed, the clubhead again being taken back within the line of flight. Contrary to modern theory Locke was not a believer in much practice, but he had a passion for

Three studies of Bobby Locke

the game and felt it necessary to play at least nine holes a day, which he frequently did with amateurs.

His ability to score well, and to score well without necessarily playing well, owed much to a methodical approach. He never allowed himself to be rushed, and this extended even to his rhythm of life off the course. The worse the weather, the more deliberate he seemed to become. He was frequently blamed for slow play, yet this never arose from wasted time, and the three hours and a quarter which he normally took to complete a round does not seem long by the standards of the 1970s. Whatever his secret thoughts, he set a standard of behaviour on the course which was an example to the younger generation. He was always carefully turned out, at the height of his career in plus-fours until they began to affect his circulation, and in a white cap which became familiar on courses throughout the world.

Locke was born of Irish parents who had emigrated; his earliest success was at the age of 14 in the Transvaal Junior Championship, and within three years while still a slender stripling he had won the South African Open and Amateur titles. By the age of 20 he had won everything worth winning in his own country, and shortly afterwards turned professional. He had visited England first in 1936, losing in the first round of the Amateur Championship, but picking up a number of smaller events and finishing leading amateur in the Open, in a tie for 8th place. On his return as a professional two years later he won the Irish Championship, and the following year played one of the most remarkable rounds at St Andrews ever recorded in the British Open. His opening round of 70 contained an 8 at the par-5 14th, but he finished with a birdie and two pars. It was an early example of his unshakeable temperament, of the ability of the great player to put the bad stroke or the slice of bad luck behind him at once. Ten years later when he won his first British Open at Sandwich his first round of 69 contained a 7 at the 14th; and the following year, when he successfully defended his title at Troon, he followed a 6 at the short 5th hole with four birdies in the next 6 holes. In South Africa he reigned supreme and for 20 years was undefeated there over 72 holes, and only his frequent trips abroad limited his South African open victories to nine. On the outbreak of war, he joined the South African Air Force, got his wings as a bomber pilot, and served in the Middle East. Finishing joint runner-up in the first British Open after the war, he showed that hundreds of hours of active service flying had not reduced his skill. Indeed, he was now entering on his best phase. In 1947 he made his first trip to the United States accepting an invitation from Snead who, on a visit to South Africa the previous year, had lost 12 of a series of 16 matches to Locke. In America against the toughest opposition which included Hogan, Nelson, and Snead, Locke more than held his own. His record in that country is worth elaborating because it shows more clearly than anything else his great ability. In 1947 he finished 15th in his first tournament on American soil, the Masters, and of the other 12 strokeplay tournaments in which he took part he won no fewer than six, finished 2nd in two others, and was never lower than 7th. Only in the USPGA Championship did he fail, being eliminated in the first round. He was 2nd leading money winner with $24,000. It is an astonishing record and the following year he was not far behind it. This time he stayed for 25 tournaments; he won only two of them, but was runner-up five times and only three times throughout the season failed to get into the first 10. For the second year running he was 4th in the US Open and finished 4th leading money winner. In 1950, during a brief visit to the United States, his victory came in the Tam O'Shanter, during which a difference of opinion with Lloyd Mangrum, the runner-up, did not improve his feeling toward golf in that country.

Locke's four victories in the British Open all started with a round of 69; during the first of them came the incident of Harry Bradshaw, his nearest rival, playing out of a broken bottle. In 1952 at Royal Lytham Thomson finished 2nd to him and after Hogan's victory the next year won three years in a row; but in 1957 Locke came back and beat him at St Andrews. By this time, he

had put on much weight and was a very different figure from the lithe young amateur who had come over before the war. Locke always said that he would not continue playing to a ripe old age. His last Open victory came in his 40th year; three years later he was involved in a road accident which kept him in hospital for several months, impaired his sight, and accelerated the speed with which he passed from the scene, although within 18 months he was back playing as a senior competitor still in love with the game. He was made an honorary member of the R. and A.

Loft

The degree of slope on the face of a club which varies the distance and trajectory that can be achieved with each. *See* Irons, Woods.

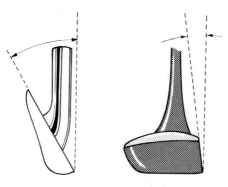

Loft: the angle made by the vertical shaft and the face of the club

London Hunt and CC CANADA
London, Ont. 18 holes; 7,168 yd (6,554 m); par 72

Although it was opened for play only in 1960, there are many who consider that the London Hunt course provides the finest test of golf to be found anywhere in Canada. Certainly it offers almost every golfing feature that the keenest player could wish to encounter. It has great length for tournament play, but because of unusually long tees can be shortened by as much as 800 yd (732 m) for ordinary play. It has giant, rolling greens, several ponds, streams and gullies, not to mention strategically clever bunkering, all set in its undulating and wooded terrain by the banks of the Thames River. The American golf architect Robert Trent Jones was at his best in designing this heroic course. It was formed solely as a riding club in 1885 and golf was added to the facilities 15 years later. It first built a 9-hole course which continued until the early 1920s. Then the University of Western Ontario established itself on the site and permitted the club to enlarge its course to 18 holes. The result was to survive for the

next four decades. The club played host to the Canadian Amateur Championship during this period and in 1954 to the first playing in Canada of the American Golf Cup Team Matches between amateur teams representing Canada, the United States and Mexico.

The present course was the venue of the 1970 Canadian Open Championship which was won by Kermit Zarley, of Houston, Tex., with a score of 279. Unquestionably the club's most famous player has been C. Ross Somerville, six times Canadian Amateur Champion. John B. Nash is another of the club's prominent players. He won the Ontario Amateur Championship three times, the Senior Championship of Canada, and on two occasions the Canadian Seniors' Golf Association Championship.

Longhurst, Henry Carpenter CBE BRITISH
b. Bromham, Bedfordshire 1909

By his unique ability to write and talk amusingly about golf, the name and voice of Henry Longhurst have become better known throughout the world than most of the great players. His weekly articles in the *Sunday Times* – he went 21 years without missing a Sunday – were a watchword and in the realms of radio and television broadcasting he was a pioneer.

His interest in golf was roused by his prep school's nearness to the Royal Eastbourne GC; he later joined the Bedford GC, captained Cambridge University and won the German Amateur in 1936. By this time modest beginnings as a golf writer had blossomed into his appointment with the *Evening Standard* and it was also a period when he began to think about the first of his many books. Not all were about golf; indeed, as a great observer of life, he has had a profound interest in many things far removed from the game. With a belief of going everywhere and doing anything once, he is much travelled and has shown himself a man of many parts. He was for two years in politics, serving as Member of Parliament for Acton, and was author of a book on oil for which Churchill wrote the introduction. Happily, however, Longhurst never strayed far from golf and by the charm and wit of his writing, commentating and after-dinner speaking has given untold pleasure.

Loop
A peculiarity of certain swings which are not formed in a consistent plane but deviate inside or outside the line on either backswing or downswing, or both. James Bruen, Gay Brewer and Miller Barber are examples of players with famous loops.

Loop, The
The famous part of the Old Course at St Andrews out by the 7th, 8th, 9th, 10th, 11th and 12th which form a little loop at the end of the course.

Loose impediments
A term denoting natural objects not fixed or

member, and it is not much easier for anyone else. Memberships are passed on as family legacies, and they are even more rare than professional football tickets. The waiting list is usually around 300.

The Los Angeles CC has two golf courses, the North and the South, both hemmed in by expensive real estate. The North Course

growing and not adhering to the ball. It includes stones not solidly embedded, leaves, twigs, branches and the like, dung, worms and insects and casts or heaps made by them.

Los Angeles CC USA
Los Angeles, 36 holes; North Course 6,780 yd (6,200 m), par 72; South Course 6,520 yd (5,962 m)

Two clubs within a brassie shot of one another could well be the wealthiest in the United States. One is the Los Angeles CC, which owns about a mile of Wilshire Boulevard, and the other is Hillcrest CC. Both are inconspicuously dotted with oil wells and both are very exclusive and very private. In 1967 the assets of the Los Angeles CC were said to total $45 million.

The Los Angeles CC has had a long-standing policy of non-admittance to movie actors. One famous star is supposed to have bought a house along one of the fairways with the hope that he would be extended an invitation to become a member, but if that was his intention, he was disappointed. It was impossible for that star to become a

is on rolling land, beautifully planted, with fine fairways and greens and many big trees. Through an occasional opening in the trees, the player can look over the Los Angeles basin with its pastel-coloured buildings glistening in the Southern California sun. The North Course measures 6,780 yards with a par of 72, and although it is an excellent test, the membership shuns opening the course to 'outside' tournaments. It was the site of the Los Angeles Open in the mid-1930s, but the members felt that the event ruined their course, and so it was not invited back. Some years ago a proposal to host the US Open was put before the membership, but it was rejected.

As for the South Course, it is laid out over flattish land, and is considerably shorter than the North. It is very popular with the older members.

Both the South Course of the Los Angeles Country Club and the Hillcrest CC's one 18-hole course occupy part of the old Twentieth Century-Fox movie lot. Like the Los Angeles CC, Hillcrest is surrounded by houses in the $500,000 range. The course

itself is slightly rolling dotted with eucalyptus trees, and is somewhat old fashioned in style with rather small greens. It measures 6,172 yd (5,644 m) for normal play, 6,520 from the championship tees, and it is tight. It has out-of-bounds on 12 holes, and water on three. Unlike the Los Angeles Country Club, Hillcrest's membership includes many actors, among them Jack Benny and Danny Kaye.

Los Lagartos GC COLOMBIA
Bogota. 27 holes

Founded in March 1936, Los Lagartos is one of the most important clubs in Colombia. It is the headquarters of the Caribbean golf circuit which is held each winter and is attracting an increasing number of overseas players. The grounds contain a beautiful lake where water skiing is practised; tennis courts and a swimming pool complete the picture of a modern country club.

Lost Ball
A ball is lost if it is not found and identified within five minutes of the player(s) or caddies beginning a search for it. Five minutes is the maximum time allowed for search but the player can declare a ball lost before that time is up or without even going to look for it.

Lucas, Percy Belgrave BRITISH
b. Sandwich, Kent, 1915. Walker Cup 1936, 1947, 1949 (captain 1949); Berkshire

Trophy 1947, 1949; Prince of Wales Cup 1947; St George's Grand Challenge Cup 1947; President's Putter 1949

Commonly regarded as the most handsome left-handed swinger in the history of golf and certainly one of the best amateurs who have played that way. He had a brilliant career as a boy and was selected for the

Los Angeles CC

Laddie' Lucas driving from the 4th tee at Rye GC

Walker Cup side at Pine Valley in 1936. During World War II he won the DSO and DFC serving with the Royal Air Force. 'Laddie' played again in 1947 when he won his foursome with Leonard Crawley and was captain two years later, but he played very little competitive golf after that although he remained active in a non-playing capacity. He also served for a while as a Member of Parliament.

Lucayan/Shannon Complex BAHAMAS
Grand Bahama Island. Lucaya CC, 18 holes, 6,805 yd (6,222 m); Shannon GCC 6,700 yd (6,126 m)

The Lucaya CC and the Shannon GCC form a delightful complex on the island of Grand Bahama which has developed rapidly in recent years as a thriving golfing centre. Although not the oldest course on the island, Lucaya, designed by Dick Wilson and opened in 1964, can be said to have launched Freeport's boom and gained fame, first under Craig Wood, former US Open and Masters champion, and then, after his death in 1968, through the energies of Harry Obitz and Dick Farley.

Obitz acted as golf consultant and Farley as director of golf for the Grand Bahama Development Company Ltd who operate the complex. Lucaya is a demanding course which housed the 1971 Bahama Islands Open, won by Bob Goalby, though it is extremely popular among its many visitors and members. Obitz and Farley were also responsible for the twin spur of the complex at Shannon which was opened in December 1970.

Situated a little further out of Freeport than Lucaya, Shannon is the more beautiful of the two courses. It was designed by Joe Lee and demonstrates the abundant local water supply. Incredibly enough, it was cleared from a dense forest on a base of white coral and prepared ready for golf in the space of eight months. This could only have been done in a constantly mellow climate, but with the supplement of thousands of tons of sand mixed with soil, the fairways quickly looked long established.

Lucerne GC see DIETSCHIBERG GC

Lu Liang Huan TAIWANESE
b. Tamsui 1936. Hong Kong Open 1959; Philippines Open 1965; China Open 1966; World (Canada) Cup 1966, 1972; Thailand Open 1970; runner-up Asia Circuit 1971; runner-up British Open 1971; French Open 1971; Japan (Crown) Open 1972; Panama Open 1972

One of the best players to come out of

Taiwan. He started golf as a caddie but had opportunities to play and developed so well that he turned professional in 1955 at a time when golf was really beginning to boom in the Far East.

Lu Liang Huan represented his country in the Canada Cup at Wentworth in 1956 and quickly established himself as a fine competitor. His swing is controlled rather than powerful, well suited to the courses on which he was raised; but, after steady success in the Far East during the 1960s, in which he twice headed the Order of Merit table, he won one of the exempted places for the 1971 British Open and caused a great impact by almost winning the title. In the end, he finished 2nd, 1 stroke behind Lee Trevino with whom he played the final round but he was, in many ways, the hit of the championship, universally adopting the name of 'Mr Lu' and becoming instantly recognizable by his soft, trilby hat which he seemed to be forever raising.

His performance was undoubtedly the finest that an Oriental player had achieved in a European or American championship and he quickly earned invitations to many of the European tournaments that followed. He won the French Open at Biarritz with a total of 262 and only just failed to beat Jack Nicklaus in the first round of the Piccadilly Matchplay Championship at Wentworth in October.

In the 1966 World Cup Taiwan, with 'Mr Lu' much to the fore, announced itself as a rising force in world golf. This was amply confirmed in 1972 at Melbourne when 'Mr Lu' and Hsieh Min Nam won a glorious victory with a three-round total of 438, 2 strokes better than Japan.

Lund Academic GC SWEDEN
nr Lund. 18 holes; 6,616 yd (6,090 m)

Lunds Akademiska Golfklubb is so called

because the land belongs to the University of Lund and students have certain privileges. In fact the history of this area goes further back even than the founding of this seat of learning in the Middle Ages. The Viking chieftain Glom had his fortress near the 4th green from where he could see his ships returning home after plundering Britain and Ireland more than a thousand years ago. Even the fairways have a history here. The 8th is still like a huge washboard. According to tradition, the ancient farmers were always assured of some sort of crop: in wet years the raised parts of their land were certain to yield harvests, in dry years they had the sunken parts to rely on.

The course is laid out in two loops, each with its own character. They are separated by the Gloms brook, which forms a small lake and bird sanctuary. The old grazing meadows are also of great interest as they contain several rare and protected plants. The rough on this course must therefore not be cut before seeding, which means after midsummer.

The Swedish Amateur Matchplay championship has been played at Lund twice (1961, 1967) on both occasions before seeding.

Lunt, Michael Stanley Randle BRITISH
b. Birmingham 1935. *Golf Illustrated* Gold Vase 1958; Walker Cup 1959, 1961, 1963, 1965; runner-up Brabazon Trophy 1961; British Amateur Champion 1963, runner-up 1964; Commonwealth Tournament 1963; Eisenhower Trophy 1964; English Amateur 1966, runner-up 1962; non-playing captain of England 1972-4

Son of Stanley Lunt, English Amateur Champion in 1934, Michael Lunt had a distinguished career as an amateur golfer. He and Michael Bonallack are the only Englishmen who have won both the English and British titles, and Lunt became the first British player since Roger Wethered in 1923 to win the British Amateur Championship in a year when the field included a visiting American Walker Cup team.

In the 1963 final at St Andrews he beat John Blackwell by 2 and 1 but it was in the previous rounds that he had shown his competitive powers by beating the Americans, Chris Blocker, now a successful professional, Richard Davies, the defending champion, and Ed Updegraff. All meant pressure of one sort or another for Lunt but nothing quite exceeded the putt of 6 ft which he holed on the last green of his semi-final with Updegraff.

The following year it looked as if he would become the first player since Lawson Little

Lu Liang Huan

to defend his title successfully but he faltered on the last few holes against Gordon Clark and lost at the 39th in the longest final in the history of the championship. In the English final in 1966, however, he was the hero of a gallant recovery, beating Dudley Millensted by 3 and 2 after being 5 down on the 25th tee. In 1962 he lost to Michael Bonallack at Moortown by 2 and 1. Lunt played a notable part in the historic British victory in the Eisenhower Trophy in Rome in 1964.

In Walker Cup matches he was less successful but uncertainties of driving always rendered him vulnerable and inconsistent. His great power often carried him into all sorts of trouble but he had an undoubted flair for recovery, was one of the best pitchers

in the amateur game, and a superb approach putter and holer-out. He was awarded the British Golf Writers' Trophy in 1963.

Luxembourg

Golf in the Grand Duchy of Luxembourg is confined to the Golf Club Grand-Ducal de Luxembourg which was founded in 1935 at a place six miles from the city. The course was designed by the Dutch architect, Major Simons, but, though not long by modern standards – 6,345 yd (5,802 m) with a par of 71 – its wooded surroundings demand accuracy and control.

From modest beginnings, the membership has now risen to around 500 and includes players not only from Luxembourg but also

Michael Lunt

from France, Germany, Belgium and a number of Americans with business in Luxembourg.

Each July the club holds the Luxembourg International Amateur Championship for Ladies and Men (matchplay) and in 1971 there were over 100 entrants. The Men's championship in the last five years has been won by entrants from Austria, Germany, America and Portugal and the Ladies' event by players from Austria, Germany and Belgium.

Lyon, George Seymour CANADIAN

b. Richmond, Ont., 1858; d. 1938. Canadian Amateur 1898, 1900, 1903, 1905-7, 1912, 1914; Olympic Games Golf Champion 1904; runner-up US Amateur 1906; runner-up Canadian Open 1910; Canadian Seniors' 1918-23, 1925-6, 1928, 1930; North American Seniors' 1923, 1930-2

A versatile athlete, excelling at cricket, tennis, baseball, football, rowing and curling, George Lyon first played golf at the age of 38. Two years later he won the first of his eight Canadian Amateur Championships. His golfing career extended over more than 40 years, and from the age of 69 until he died in his 80th year he scored his age at least once in each year.

A man of unusual strength he delighted, until over 60 years of age, in demonstrating his prowess in walking on his hands. His peculiar style at golf featured a swing so flat the club went around behind his back rather than over his shoulder. This may have been due to his earlier participation in cricket, a sport in which he served on no fewer than eleven Canadian teams in international competition and in which as a batsman he established the Canadian record of 238 not out.

Lyon's most exceptional victory was at the 1904 Olympic Games at St Louis, Mo., which, unusually, included a competition at golf. There he won the title for Canada, defeating by 3 and 2 in the final the reigning United States Amateur Champion, H. Chandler Egan, who had eliminated the holder that year of the British Amateur Championship. At the dinner following his victory Lyon had the energy to walk the length of the dining room on his hands, while his opponent in the finals, who was half his age, was said to be too fatigued to attend the festivities.

Lytham and St Annes GC, Royal

ENGLAND

St Annes-on-Sea, Lancashire

Royal Lytham and St Annes, one of the chain of fine courses on the Lancashire coast,

has been host to all the major British and English championships. Possessing the characteristics of traditional British seaside golf, though long since hidden from the sea by suburban houses, it is a demanding test which has featured regularly on the Open Championship rota since 1926.

It was there that Bobby Jones won the first of his three British Open titles and there in more modern times that Tony Jacklin ended the drought of home victories in 1969. However, the present site of the club is not the original. The first clubhouse consisted of one room in the St Annes Hotel and a letter sent to the local gentry and dated 23 February 1886 stated that suitable 'links' could be obtained close to St Annes Station.

To reach the first tee, members walked along the length of the Blackpool-side platform, over the level crossing and climbed the fence. The membership increased and it was not until the Annual General Meeting of 1892 that it was made known that security of tenure could not be obtained.

Though nobody seemed to be in any hurry, the course known today was reported to be 'very good ground' and by late 1896 and early 1897 the new clubhouse and links were in full use, and by September 1903 the register of men members was full at 556. Lady subscribers totalled 195. In addition, the present Dormy House was opened in 1912 and has provided warm and friendly shelter for legions of golfers ever since.

Four men were principally concerned in fashioning the links which brought the club the prefix 'Royal' in 1926: W. H. Fowler, Harry Colt, Tom Simpson and George Lowe, the club's first professional. Before the Open of 1952, C. K. Cotton undertook a certain amount of redesign but very early in its history, the course became a favourite and worthy stage for championships.

Royal Lytham and St Annes – the Bobby Jones plaque

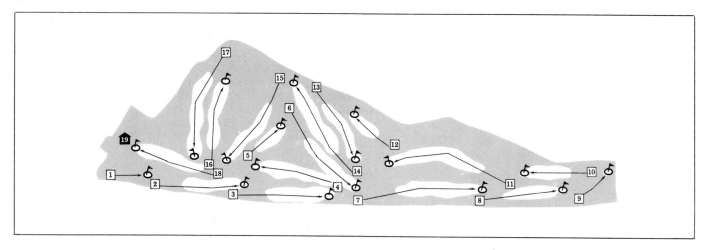

The inaugural British Ladies' Championship was played on the old site in 1893 and won by Lady Margaret Scott; it returned in 1913 and again in 1948, when the American Louise Suggs beat Jean Donald in floods of rain.

English Ladies' Champions include Cecil Leitch in 1919, Joyce Wethered in 1921 and Marley Spearman in 1964. It is, however, the frequency with which the Royal and Ancient GC have chosen Lytham for the Open Championship that really reflects its quality as an examination of world-ranking golfers.

Lytham's first Open has a special place in history for it provided Bobby Jones with a victory which was clinched with a famous stroke at the 17th. Partnered by Al Watrous, another American, on the final day, he lost his lead in the third round with a 73 to Watrous's 69. In the final round he dropped strokes in an outward half of 39, largely on the greens, and is reported to have said to an accompanying official, 'my golf is terrible'. He was still 2 behind Watrous with 5 holes to play but the pair were level with 3 to play, although with Watrous on the 17th green in 2 and Jones bunkered from his drive, it was Watrous who looked the more likely champion.

Jones was on the left of the dogleg hole with no sight of the green which was 170 yd or more away but the ball lay clean and with a mashie iron, now a sacred relic reposing in the clubhouse, he hit a staggering recovery. Watrous took 3 putts, Jones got down in 2 and with Watrous bunkered at the 18th, Jones finished with a 4 for a 74 and a total of 291, the winner by 2 shots.

A commemorative plaque in the bunker marks the spot to this day. There is one other little postscript and that is that Walter Hagen, needing a 2 to tie with Jones, sent his caddie forward to remove the flag at the 18th before playing his second, but though the shot pitched near the hole, it ran through the green and he took 4 more.

Royal Lytham had to wait a long time to stage another Open but in post-war years it found more frequent and deserved favour. Bobby Locke won in 1952 with 287 and Peter Thomson beat David Thomas in a play-off in 1958, after they had tied, in wonderfully calm conditions, with a score of 278. In the play-off, Thomson returned 139 to win by 4 shots. In the last round Brown, O'Connor and Ruiz all lost possible chances of victory, each failing to get his four at the last hole.

In 1963, with Arnold Palmer defending, there was another tie, this time between Bob Charles and the American Phil Rodgers. In a week in which Charles putted magnificently and so became the first left-hander and the first New Zealander to win the Open, he won what proved to be the last 36-hole play-off by 8 strokes.

The year 1969 will be remembered with pride in British hearts as the year in which Tony Jacklin became the first British player to win for 18 years. Jacklin's eminently steady play for the first three rounds earned him a 2-stroke lead by Friday night and his last round was a triumph.

He covered the first 9 which move out close to the railway as far as Ansdell station in 33 and with a championship now more or less a duel between him and Bob Charles, he played the harder back 9 with its formidable finish without alarm. Jacklin, swinging beautifully, finished in 280 amid scenes of unashamed, patriotic delight, 2 shots ahead of Charles.

America won the 1961 Ryder Cup at Lytham, the first to be decided by 18-hole matches.

The club has also seen its share of historic moments in amateur golf. Lawson Little,

Amateur champion of America and Britain in 1934 and 1935, beat Dr William Tweddell by 1 hole in a titanic struggle in 1935, and 20 years later a relatively unknown American serviceman, Joe Conrad, beat Alan Slater by 3 and 2.

Of great significance to amateur golf was the club's decision to found the Lytham Trophy in 1965. The club has been blessed with a devoted band of committee members whose organization of championships and tournaments is most efficient and the Lytham Trophy, 72 holes of strokeplay, quickly established itself as one of the main amateur events in Britain.

Top, the course plan of Royal Lytham and St Annes GC and the short 9th from the tee

M

Macbeth, Mrs Allan see DODD, MURIEL

MacCann, Mrs P. G. see SMYE, CATHERINE

Maccauvlei GC SOUTH AFRICA
Vereeniging, Transvaal. 18 holes; 6,847 yd (6,261 m); par 74

Built in 1926 on a vast stretch of sand adjoining the Vaal river, Maccauvlei has all the seaside characteristics of a links, although lying 400 miles from the coast and at an altitude of 5,000 ft. The course has been a favourite for championships ever since it staged its first South African championship in 1927, within a year of its completion. The natural site has remained much as it was in its original state. Flocks of guinea fowl sometimes intrude upon the fairways and the harsh cry of francolins can be heard. Occasionally a glimpse may be caught of antelopes taking their ease on the edge of the forest. The course was designed by H. G. Peck, professional at Royal Johannesburg, and formerly of Felixstowe, England, in collaboration with A. F. Tomsett. The course was visited and highly praised by the British team that went to the Union in 1927 under the captaincy of R. H. de Montmorency. Another distinguished visitor was Roger Wethered in 1948, who described Maccauvlei as the 'St Andrews of South Africa'.

M'Clure, Jean see HOLMES, MRS JEAN

McCormack, Mark AMERICAN
b. Chicago, Ill. 1931

Famous as the manager of the Big Three in modern golf – Arnold Palmer, Gary Player and Jack Nicklaus. Business managers for sporting personalities had already been tried, but McCormack, employing up-to-date business methods, brought a new dimension to the work. In this he was helped by the explosion of golf in the United States at the beginning of the 1960s brought about by the development of television. McCormack made his fortune from it and at the same time greatly increased the earning power of his clients. The names on his books began to include such as the French skier, Jean-Claude Killy, ranging through all kinds of jobs to Jean Shrimpton, a model.

Of Irish origin, McCormack went to school in Chicago, then graduated from William and Mary College in 1951. He took his law degree at Princeton in 1954 and joined a firm of Cleveland lawyers. He is a good golfer who has played in both the British and US Amateur Championships, as well as once in the US Open. As the limelight increasingly fell on the stars of sport, McCormack was able to expand their earning power by coordinating a programme of television appearances and exhibition matches and by selling their fame to the advertisers.

The danger inherent in such a system is that where the opportunities to make money come so easily a star may become diverted

Mark McCormack

from pursuing the excellence of his game. This was given as one of the reasons for a relative loss of form by Palmer in the mid-1960s. Nicklaus, when he had made a fortune, decided to run his own show, and Bruce Devlin also broke away as his interest in golf-course development increased. But generally the arrangement worked successfully for both sides, thanks to the personality of the manager and the looseness of the agreement with his clients. British players who joined his organization included Tony Jacklin, Clive Clark, Peter Townsend, and Peter Oosterhuis. McCormack has made use of every modern business technique and flies hundreds of thousands of miles each year maintaining contact with offices in London, Tokyo, and Johannesburg. A man of great energy he turned his hand to publishing, producing a *Golf Annual* and a weekly British paper *Golf International*. He has also done commentaries on televised golf.

McCready, Samuel Maxwell IRISH
b. Belfast 1918. RAF Champion 1947;

Jamaican Amateur 1948; British Amateur 1949; Walker Cup 1949-51

McCready was an all-round sportsman, good also at cricket, rugby, boxing and badminton. Strong, well-built, an extrovert, and one of the most powerful drivers of his day, he reached the heights at Portmarnock in 1949. In a tremendous final of the British Amateur, he defeated Willie Turnesa of the United States, who had won the title in 1947 at the 35th hole, thereby interrupting a run of five American victories. McCready was in the cigar business (hence his Jamaican championship), and frequent absences from Britain limited his number of successes. He now lives in South Africa.

McDermott, John J. AMERICAN
b. Philadelphia, Pa., 1891; d. 1971. Runner-up Metropolitan Open 1910; US Open 1911-12, runner-up 1910; Philadelphia Open 1912; Western Open 1912; tied 5th British Open 1913; Shawnee Open 1913; North and South Open 1914

Three years after the successful defence of his US Open title this brilliant player was out of the game, a victim of mental illness. So bright was the flame within him that, in the opinion of many, he burned himself out trying to prove himself the best. In one season he raised himself to championship class and became the first home-bred American to win the US Open. Then after five short years he was gone. A small man, he had a flat swing, used extra long clubs, and was one of the first to perfect the use of backspin. In his first US Open in 1909 McDermott finished 48th, but his fiery determination was rewarded the next year when he tied 1st on 298 with the Smith brothers, Alex and Macdonald. He lost the play-off by 6 strokes to Alex and vowed to correct the situation the following year. This he did but only after another three-way tie, this time with Mike Brady and George Simpson, a play-off which he won by 2 after a round of 80. In 1912 he won outright, overtaking Brady in the final round. McDermott, wishing to prove that that victory was no accident, took part in the British Open; his best finish was a tie for 5th in 1913. He had beaten Vardon and Ray earlier the same year in the Shawnee Open.

Macdonald, Charles Blair AMERICAN
b. Niagara Falls, N.Y. 1855; d. 1939. US Amateur 1895, runner-up 1894 (unofficial); semi-finalist 1897-9

One of the early pillars of golf in the United States, and one of its most controversial figures. He founded the Chicago GC; he designed and built several courses of which

the best known were the National Golf Links of America and Mid-Ocean. A new country likes to play the game in a new way, whereas Macdonald had been brought up in the old Scottish ways for which he felt a fierce loyalty. This fierceness derived from an idealistic and almost emotional streak, but it was tempered by great shrewdness and joviality. He hated – there was no better hater – people who asked questions about the rules and argued about fairness when he took the line that perfect justice would make a dull and dreary game. This one man, with a few like-minded friends in the Links Club of New York, controlled a whole continent of golfers of totally different outlook and upbringing by sheer, formidable force of character.

Macdonald left Chicago for St Andrews in 1872 to live with his Scottish grandfather and attend St Andrews University. He returned bitten by the game, having watched Young Tom Morris and other giants of those early days, but attempts to interest his friends met with only limited success. Asked in 1892 to lay out a 7-hole course, he designed what became the home of the Chicago club at Belmont and afterwards at Wheaton.

Stories about him are legion. On the final day of the Unofficial 1894 US Amateur, for example, he went to bed at five, and having beaten Charles Sands by 12 and 11, he is said to have played the remaining holes with a friend who was following the final. His enduring monument is the National

Links. He brought back from Europe surveyors' plans of several famous holes to be copied. From 1911 on he became 'president, founder and autocrat' of the club which gained a reputation for being over strict in its observance of the rules and a place where women were unwelcome. But he was unyielding in his devotion to the game and its traditions.

Macfarlane, William BRITISH
b. Aberdeen 1890; d. 1961. Semi-finalist USPGA 1916; US Open 1925

Willie Macfarlane was one of the smoothest swingers in the game. He was far from a sturdy man and his graceful swing might best be described as neat. He was an excellent middle and short iron player. He was a steady tournament winner from the end of World War I to the mid-1930s (he won 19 tournaments between 1922 and 1936), although he played far fewer events than many of his contemporaries. He was a quiet, pleasant man who enjoyed playing for the fun of it and who did not really like tournament competition. In the 1925 Open at Worcester, Mass., Macfarlane and Bobby Jones, with whom he tied, were two of seven who had a chance for the title coming to the last hole. Macfarlane's final putt, 1 ft in length, was in a divot mark but he holed it with a mid-iron. The first 18 holes of the play-off were close all the way; in the second round Jones opened up a lead of 4 strokes, but Macfarlane came back in 33 and won by a stroke.

MacGregor, Roy C. BRITISH
Walker Cup 1953

Roy MacGregor played for Scotland from 1951 to 1954.

McHale, James B., Jr AMERICAN
b. Stockton, Cal., 1916. Philadelphia Open

1948; runner-up Western Amateur 1948; Walker Cup 1949, 1951; semi-finalist British Amateur 1950; National Mixed Foursomes 1954; Colonial Invitation 1956

One of the country's best amateurs in the decade immediately following World War II. McHale was a member of two Walker Cup teams, a semi-finalist and a quarter-finalist in the British Amateur and a quarter-finalist in the US Amateur. In the 1947 US Open at St Louis, Mo., he set scoring records of 30 for 9 holes and 65 for 18 holes, although he eventually slipped to a tie for 23rd. He was a professional for a brief period early in his career.

McIntire, Barbara AMERICAN
b. Toledo, Ohio, 1935. Runner-up US Women's Open 1956; Curtis Cup 1958, 1960, 1962, 1964, 1966, 1972; US Women's Amateur 1959, 1964; British Ladies' 1960

One of the triumvirate of women who dominated amateur golf in the United States in the 1950s and 1960s. That she was able to hold her own in the company of JoAnne Gunderson and Anne Quast is an indication of her quality. She conveys the impression of being a 'made' golfer rather than a natural swinger of the club, but the soundness of her mechanical-looking style has been proved by her successes. The stillness of her head and body when she putts is an object lesson, and it is hardly necessary to add that her skill with a putter is exceptional. Her swing is also clearly of the enduring kind for in 1972, after a highly successful competitive preceding year, she returned to Britain as one of the US Curtis Cup team. Her first appearance in Britain had been in 1960 after winning the US Amateur the year before at the Congressional club, Washington. From the match at Lindrick in 1960 she went to Royal St David's and won the British Championship, defeating Philomena

Charles Blair Macdonald

James B. McHale Jr

Barbara McIntire

Garvey by 4 and 2 in the final; and thus she became the fourth American woman to do so. In 1964 she returned to Britain, again as US Champion, but her attempt to repeat the double ended in a second-round defeat by the young Catherine Lacoste. She lost the play-off for the US Open in 1956 against Kathy Cornelius, returning 82 to 75.

McKenna, Mary IRISH

b. 1950. Irish Ladies' 1969, 1972, runner-up 1968; Curtis Cup 1970, 1972, 1974; World Women's Amateur Team Championship 1970

One of the longest drivers in the women's game, Mary McKenna makes full use of her tall, powerful body. It was some time before her driving reached the same class as the rest of her game, but when it did she was a match for anyone. This was specially true in the 1972 Curtis Cup match when, inspired by her foursomes partner, Michelle Walker, she outdrove her singles opponents by scores of yards, winning 3 out of 4 matches. In the summer of the same year she visited the United States, winning the important

Broadmoor Invitational tournament. Miss McKenna worked at the time as a clerk for the Bank of Ireland.

Mackenzie, Ada Charlotte CANADIAN

b. Toronto, Ont., 1891; d. 1973. Canadian Ladies' Open 1919, 1925-6, 1933, 1935; Canadian Ladies' Close 1926-7, 1929, 1931, 1933; semi-finalist US Women's Amateur 1927

Ada Mackenzie, a great advocate and exponent of matchplay, dominated women's golf in Canada for many years and compiled a brilliant record. She also became well known abroad; she competed in three British and two Scottish championships, and was a semi-finalist in the US Amateur. Her

victories in lesser tournaments were numerous. Always one to encourage girls' golf, she was instrumental in launching the first girls' championship in Canada. She also has to her credit the founding of the only women's club in Canada, the Ladies' Golf and Tennis Club. Her younger friend and successor as the eminent woman golfer, Mrs Marlene Stewart Streit, owes much to her for inspiration and constant encouragement. Together they were the first two women to be elected to Canada's Golf Hall of Fame.

Mackenzie, Alexander (Alister) BRITISH

b. Normanton, Yorkshire, 1870; d. Santa Cruz, Cal., 1934

One of the greatest of golf-course architects, Mackenzie was responsible for such contrasting masterpieces as Cypress Point, the Augusta National, and Royal Melbourne. There was a touch of genius about the use he made of natural features. He believed the architect's job to be one of making the golfer think before playing a shot, and he preferred a course that was what he called strategic to one that was merely penal. Although he designed and redesigned dozens of courses in Britain he is almost better remembered abroad. He did fine work in Australia and New Zealand, the West Course of Royal Melbourne being an outstanding example. In 1925 he set out for the United States.

In Cypress Point, overlooking the Pacific south of San Francisco, Mackenzie made good work of one of the most enviable sites in the whole world of golf. It was the impression that this course made upon Bobby Jones that decided him to ask Mackenzie to help him at Augusta, and this in itself is a mark of the qualities Mackenzie showed both as man and architect. That course was opened in 1931, but the great tournament with which it is associated began only in the last year of Mackenzie's life.

Mackenzie trained as a doctor after attending Cambridge University and getting degrees in medicine, chemistry and natural science, a record of learning that would appeal to Jones himself. As a young doctor Mackenzie was already interested in golf, being a founder member of the Alwoodley club and its honorary secretary until 1912. During World War I, in which he started service as a surgeon, he developed an interest in camouflage which had its origins in his early passion for outdoor life. His open-air pursuits included stalking, yachting, shooting and fishing. During that war he transferred to the Royal Engineers and gave a demonstration before King George V in Hyde Park on camouflaging trenches.

After the war he gave up medicine to become a course architect because he put health and happiness first and was convinced of the extraordinary influence on health of pleasurable excitement, specially when combined with fresh air and exercise. 'How frequently', he wrote, 'have I with great difficulty persuaded patients who were never off my doorstep, to take up golf, and how rarely, if ever, did I see them again in my consulting room. Many of the greatest politicians, thinkers and business men conserve their health and mental powers through golf, and I hope to live to see the day when there are crowds of municipal courses, as in Scotland, cropping up all over England.'

Mackenzie wrote *Golf Architecture* in 1921, and made occasional return visits to Britain to watch championships and to play at St Andrews, where he was a member of the R. and A. (Since his death he has generally been known as Alister Mackenzie, the form used in his obituary, rather than Alexander, or the other two Gaelic variants of the name, Alastair or Alasdair.)

Mackenzie, Keith Roderick Turing
BRITISH
b. 1921

Keith Mackenzie took up his appointment as secretary of the Royal and Ancient GC in September 1967 at a time when the task of running the club's affairs and, more particularly, its championships, was greater than it had ever been. The success of recent Opens owes a great deal to his work and he quickly became a respected figure in the game who, on several visits abroad, persuaded many leading overseas players to visit Britain.

With the background of a commission in the 6th Gurkha Rifles (he is a holder of the MC), a career in Shell, and a low handicap at

Mary McKenna

Keith Mackenzie

the game, his powers of organization and management soon became evident; equally important, he has combined a friendly manner with a sense of firmness and purpose, qualities essential to the post.

Mackenzie, Roland Redus AMERICAN

b. Washington, D.C., 1907. District of Columbia Amateur 1924; Middle Atlantic Amateur 1925, 1948; Walker Cup 1926, 1928, 1930; semi-finalist US Amateur 1927; Maine Amateur 1930

A protégé of Fred McLeod who became one of the country's best amateurs in the 1920s. He was a low qualifier in the US Amateur at the age of 18 and, two years later, reached the semi-finals. Roland's father, Albert R. Mackenzie, was a good golfer who interested his son in the game quite early. The son quickly became proficient and was good enough to reach the final of the Middle Atlantic Amateur at the age of 16. And the man who defeated him in the final was his father. In his first attempt at the US Amateur, in 1924, Mackenzie attracted immediate notice despite losing in

the first round. He was 8 holes down to George Von Elm after 23 and rallied to square the match – only to lose at the 37th. Although he won five out of six matches in Walker Cup play, his most memorable shot was a bad one. It occurred in 1926 at St Andrews when he and Bob Gardner saw their lead over Eustace Storey and W. G. E. Brownlow vanish with 2 holes to play. Then, at the Road Hole, Mackenzie badly topped a shot that rolled all the way to the green. Thereupon, Gardner holed a great putt to win the hole and the match.

Mackenzie Ross, Phillip see ROSS, PHILLIP MACKENZIE

Mackenzie, Walter Willis BRITISH

b. Edinburgh 1893. Walker Cup 1922-3; Scottish Amateur 1924

Mackenzie reached the fifth round of the British Amateur in 1921, and the sixth round in the two following years. He won his single when he played against the United States in 1922, and was Scottish Amateur Champion in 1924.

Mackey, Lee, Jr AMERICAN

A young Alabama professional who startled the golfing world in 1950 by shooting a record 64 in the first round of the US Open – and at Merion of all places. Mackey, who was unemployed at the time, needed an 81 the next day and went on to finish with rounds of 75 and 77 for 297 and 25th place. Although he never again gained the national spotlight, his brief moment of glory was enough to make him a household word among golf fans for many years.

McKinlay, Samuel L. BRITISH

b. Glasgow 1907. Walker Cup 1934; semi-finalist British Amateur 1947

One of the few professional journalists and writers in the game to establish a career in the sport at the top level, Sam McKinlay played in the 1934 Walker Cup match. He also twice reached the semi-finals of the Scottish Amateur Championship (1927 and 1929), once in the British Amateur (1947), and represented Scotland in eight years between 1929 and 1947. Not a long hitter, McKinlay had an exceptionally effective short game and an uncanny liaison with an old rusty-headed, wooden-shafted putter, which he used with a smooth, measured stroke.

M'Lean, Jack BRITISH

b. Glasgow 1911; d. Gleneagles, Perthshire, 1961. Irish Open Amateur 1932-3; Scottish Amateur 1932-4, runner-up 1935; leading amateur British Open 1933-4; Walker Cup

1934, 1936; runner-up US Amateur 1936

Only three British golfers have reached the final of the US Amateur – Harold Hilton, who won the title, Phil Perkins and Jack M'Lean who were beaten. In 1936, at Garden City, New York, M'Lean was deprived of the title by Johnny Fischer in a celebrated climax. M'Lean, 1 up with 3 to play, was prevented from becoming 2 up by a stymie, and having halved the 35th in birdies, lost the 36th and the first extra hole, also to birdies. M'Lean has been described as 'the first of the full-time amateurs'. Golf was his life. Jobs as a representative of a sports goods company and then of a whisky manufacturer allowed him to devote much of his time to the game. He and Hector Thomson, friend and arch-rival, dominated Scottish golf in the 1930s; his record in the Scottish Amateur was unsurpassed until Ronnie Shade recorded five consecutive victories some 30 years later.

M'Lean was not physically strong, but he more than made up for this in accuracy, particularly with the irons. Opponents who outdrove him often found themselves looking at M'Lean's second shot distractingly near the hole before they had played their own. Although M'Lean changed his occupation when the authorities made it clear that a player could not retain his status while with a sports company (a rule that has since been modified), he turned professional towards the end of 1936. He served with the Royal Air Force during World War II and after being invalided out resumed his club job at Buchanan Castle, subsequently moving to Worthing and the RAC club at Epsom. In 1951 he was appointed professional at Gleneagles and held the post for the last 10 years of his life.

McLeod, Frederick Robertson AMERICAN

b. North Berwick, East Lothian, 1882. Western Professional 1905, 1907; US Open 1908, tied 2nd 1921, tied 3rd 1914; runner-up North and South Open 1917; runner-up USPGA 1919; St Petersburg Open 1924; Maryland Open 1927; USPGA Seniors' 1928

McLeod emigrated from Scotland to the United States in 1903. Despite his small size he soon showed himself to be an excellent golfer and was one of the most respected men in the game for more than 50 years. In 1908 he became US Open Champion at Myopia, a course that in those days yielded pars and birdies grudgingly; McLeod started the tournament weighing 118 lb and finished at 108 . He tied for the title with Willie Smith at 322, then beat him in a play-off, 77 to 83.

Top, Roland R. Mackenzie

Above, Lee Mackey, Jr

In all, McLeod played in 20 US Opens and finished in the top 10 eight times. He led after three rounds in 1911, but finished with an 83 and ended in 4th place. In 1914 he closed with a 71 and tied for 3rd and in 1921 he tied for 2nd with Walter Hagen, 9 strokes behind Jim Barnes. He made up for his lack of size with a fine short game and

was an outstanding bunker player, using a no. 9 iron even after the wedge became popular. He became professional at Columbia in 1912 and remained there throughout his career. In later years he and Jock Hutchison were by tradition the first pair off the tee each April in the US Masters at Augusta.

McNamara, Thomas L. AMERICAN
b. 1882; d. 1939. Runner-up US Open 1909, 1912, 1915, tied 5th 1910; North and South Open 1912-13; Western Open 1915

The first homebred American professional to threaten seriously the domination of the Scottish and English professionals who emigrated to the United States. His 69 in the

1909 Open was the first score under 70 in that event. McNamara held the lead after three rounds that year at Englewood, N.J., but his final 77 left him 4 shots behind George Sargent. In 1912 he scored another 69, this time in the last round, but failed by 2 strokes to catch Johnny McDermott. In 1915 he lost by a stroke to Jerry Travers. McNamara was not a long hitter, but overcame the lack of distance through deadly putting.

McRuvie, Eric Alexander BRITISH
b. Leven, Fife, 1909. British Boys' 1926; leading Amateur British Open 1931; Irish Open Amateur 1931; Walker Cup 1932, 1934

In 1934 at St Andrews won his Walker Cup foursome with Jack M'Lean and halved his single against Jack Westland.

McSpaden, Harold AMERICAN
b. Rosedale, Kan., 1908. Runner-up USPGA 1937, semi-finalist 1940, 1946; Canadian Open 1939, runner-up 1940, 1945

One of the stars of the professional tour during the 1930s and a major figure in American golf during World War II, when he and Byron Nelson became known as the Golddust Twins. Apart from a couple of moderate showings in the US Open, 'Jug' McSpaden had made little headway until 1934, when he won several small Midwestern tournaments. During a brief span in the winter of 1934-5, he won three tournaments, a pro-am event and a driving contest, and people suddenly were taking notice. He continued to win a tournament or two each year for the next decade (he won more than 20 professional tournaments from 1934 to 1945). Then, in 1944, he suddenly burst forth, winning almost everything Nelson did not. His performance was all the more impressive because Nelson was dominating the game during that period in a manner not seen before or since. In one tournament, for example, McSpaden scored three consecutive 66s, but still finished 2nd to Nelson. Although McSpaden obviously could score, he was perhaps better at matchplay. He won the San Francisco matchplay tournament once and in the USPGA Championship he was runner-up once, a semi-finalist twice, and a quarter-finalist twice. After his playing career ended McSpaden confined himself to running a course in Kansas City.

Madeley, J. F. David IRISH
b. 1938. North of Ireland (Amateur) Open 1962-3; Walker Cup 1963

David Madeley represented Ireland in

Home Internationals in 1959-62 and 1964.

Maiden, Stewart AMERICAN
b. Carnoustie, Angus, 1886; d. 1948

Although he played little tournament golf, Stewart Maiden's fame is secure as the teacher of Bobby Jones, Alexa Stirling and other Atlanta prodigies. Maiden and his brother James, who were related to the famous Smiths of Carnoustie by marriage, followed their example and emigrated from Scotland to the United States around the turn of the century. James became professional at East Lake in Atlanta and Stewart succeeded him there in 1908. Although Jones did not actually copy Maiden's swing, he followed him round as a youngster and soon developed one strongly resembling it. Maiden had a knack of spotting what flaws there were in Jones's swing and more than once the champion called on Maiden to straighten out some hitch. This Maiden usually was able to do in very few words. Maiden, often called 'Kiltie' by his friends, also served as professional at Peachtree in Atlanta and at St Louis, and ran a golf studio in New York. The swing that was typical of this 'Forfarshire School' was rounded, smooth and upright.

Maidstone GC USA
Long Island, N.Y. 18 holes

Maidstone is situated on the south shore of Long Island, near the summer colony of East Hampton, an area that bears a strong resemblance to the linksland of Scotland on which the game as known today was developed. It is one of the few clubs in the United States laid out over sandy duneland where winds from the sea can influence play so decidedly.

Maidstone, however, is much more than simply a golf club. It is strong in family influence and has, among its facilities, 21 grass tennis courts, a swimming pool, and cabanas facing the Atlantic Ocean. It is the middle 8 holes that give the course its character, and these run alongside and through the dunes, just out of reach of the surf. The course starts on top of a dune, moves downhill to Hook Pond, a tidewater pool sunk down in the dunes, then swings outward to the sea before turning back to circle Hook Pond once more. Finally it heads up the face of the dunes to the clubhouse. Among the more memorable holes are the 7th, a dogleg around Hook Pond on the fairway's edge with dunes flanking the left side; the 8th, a blind par 3 made all the more difficult by a constant wind from the sea; and the 13th, a par 5 into the wind directly towards the sea, with trouble lurking in the dunes.

Top, Frederick R. McLeod

Above, Harold McSpaden

Tennis was the principal game at Maidstone when it was begun in 1891. Three rough golf holes were laid out in 1894, and six more were later added. Then in the early 1920s, Willie and John Park were brought in to bring the course up to date. In succeeding years the club expanded to 36 holes, but it was financially troubled in the mid-1930s, and after World War II it cut back to one 18-hole course and a short 9-hole, enjoyed mostly by the older members. The design of the Parks' course is at the base of the present 18.

Until 1905, Sunday golf was forbidden at Maidstone because of a clause put into a land lease by Dr Everett Herrick, Maidstone's first president. The club bought the land in 1905, thus ending the Sunday ban, but Herrick was also a teetotaller, and he bequeathed $7,500 to Maidstone on the provision that drinking would forever be forbidden. If the ban were broken, the money was to go to the East Hampton public library. With the repeal of Prohibition, an anonymous member sent the club a check for $7,500, and eventually the bar became as well stocked as the library.

Malawi

The Golf Union of Malawi was formed in 1929 as the Nyasaland Golf Union and has been affiliated to the Royal and Ancient GC since its earliest days. The first 9-hole course with sand greens ('browns') was opened at Blantyre on Easter Monday, 1911, and was followed by 9-hole courses at Limbe and Dedza, the only clubs in existence when the Union was formed. There has been no course at Dedza for many years but there are now seven clubs affiliated to the Union: Blantyre, Lilongwe, Limbe, Mulanje, Mzuzu, Thyolo and Zomba. The Golf Club of Chipata in Zambia also pays an affiliation fee, and a new private hotel on the southern

shore of Lake Malawi, the Club Makakola, is building a course.

The courses were all largely planned and built by local enthusiasts over the years, some of them (particularly Thyolo, Mulanje and Mzuzu) by very small groups; Mzuzu was, in fact, hacked out of the bush in the late 1960s by about 15 golfers. All the courses are of 9 holes but the government has made land available to extend Lilongwe to 18. All have sand greens except for Limbe, which was, at one time, said to be the longest course in Africa.

Malaysia

Golf thrives in Malaysia, a federation that includes the states of Sabah and Sarawak, as it does elsewhere in the East. The country's senior clubs, Perak at Taiping and Royal Selangor in Kuala Lumpur, date back to 1888 and 1893, but many courses were damaged by the Japanese during World War II, and expansion really began only about 1953. Previously, players came mostly from the European and other expatriate communities but since then Asians have taken to the game enthusiastically, the largest single incentive probably being political. Royal families, prime ministers and many other government and public figures have become golfers, mixing freely with members. Thousands have taken up the game and new clubs have been springing up all over the country. In 1962 the Malaysian Golf Association, with its headquarters at Kuala Lumpur, had 18 clubs affiliated to it; in 1972 the number had risen to 36 with a dozen or more about to join.

Interest has also been aroused by increasing the number of professional tournaments. The Malaysian Open Championship, held each year since 1962 at Royal Selangor, is now part of the rich and expanding Asian circuit. In nine years to 1970 prize money

rose from 22,500 to 75,000 dollars, attracting players of world class. An indication of the game's growth was the decision, later cancelled, to hold the 1974 World Amateur Team Championship at Kuala Lumpur.

Apart from Royal Selangor and Perak, the most notable clubs are the Penang Turf Club and the Ayer Keroh CC in Malacca.

Malta GC, Royal MALTA

The Marsa. 18 holes; 5,377 yd (4,917 m)

Golf was first played in Malta in the 1890s but the first 9 holes of the present course were officially opened in 1905 and the second 9 in 1925. The course is the centre of a sports compound which forms part of the United Services Sports Club and, though comparatively short and laid out on ground that elsewhere might not be considered very suitable for the game, provides a good as well as the island's only test.

Manero, Tony AMERICAN

b. New York 1905. US Open 1936; Ryder Cup 1937; semi-finals USPGA 1937

A good, sound player, if not a great one, and the surprise winner of the 1936 US Open with a record score for those times of 282. Manero finished brilliantly in 67 at Baltusrol, ahead of Harry Cooper who had also beaten the old Open record of 284 and who was in the clubhouse being congratulated as the apparent winner. Although Manero was described as unknown, he had grown up in Westchester County along with Sarazen, the Turnesas and other leading golfers of Italian descent, and had done quite well in that area in the winter tournaments in the south. He reached the last eight of the USPGA as far back as 1929, competed in four Opens, and had won several minor tournaments before his outstanding victory in 1936. Between 1929 and 1941 he won a total of 13 tournaments.

Mangrum, Lloyd Eugene AMERICAN

b. Trenton, Tex., 1914; d. 1973. Pennsylvania Open 1938; runner-up US Masters 1940; Argentine Open 1946; US Open 1946, runner-up 1950; Ryder Cup 1947, 1949, 1951, 1953 (captain 1953); All-American Open 1948; World Tournament 1948

Mangrum was a cool, tough competitor, essentially a money player, an ice-cool putter. His long game was unspectacular but within 20 yd of the green he was deadly. Sensitive touch allied to a clear and inventive mind made him a brilliant recovery artist. In putting he used a variation of the interlocking grip with a pronounced shoulder movement, and at his peak would go for weeks without three-putting. He came of a

Part of the course of the Royal Malta GC

either, but I manage to drive through without being arrested.' He appeared indifferent alike to fame and authority, but he successfully replaced Hogan as captain of the 1953 Ryder Cup team, though losing a fine match himself to Eric Brown on the 36th green. He won six out of eight Ryder Cup matches. His record 64 in the 1940 Masters stood until later equalled by Nicklaus and Bembridge.

Manila GCC PHILIPPINES
Makati, Rizal. 18 holes; 6,786 yd (6,205 m)

The Manila GCC was formed in 1901 as the Manila GC at Caloocan in Rizal Province. Immediately after World War II it was transferred to its present site at Makati. Since then, major improvements have been made to both courses and clubhouse; the greens were enlarged and the tees elongated with the result that the original lay-out, designed by Andy Black, an American from Nebraska, now enjoys championship status.

Apart from a good many local tournaments, the most notable occasions were two matches in Shell's Wonderful World of Golf series and interport matches with Hong Kong and Singapore. The holes are all named after indigenous trees.

Manor House Hotel GC ENGLAND
Moretonhampstead, Devon. 18 holes; 6,260 yd (5,724 m)

Hotels with their own golf courses are not uncommon, but rarely do they possess the charm and quality of this one on the edge of Dartmoor. Like Turnberry and Gleneagles, it is a member of the British Transport Hotels Group. The course started as the property of the old Great Western Railway who bought the land on which it stands in the hope of developing it as a country hotel. Designed by J. F. Abercromby, who made good use of the natural hazards, it was opened in 1930 but received insufficient maintenance and failed as a result to become attractive. At times during the 1950s there were fewer than a dozen annual subscribers, and it was not until the hotel decided, under the direction of Frank Hole, to improve the quality of the golf that new life was instilled into the place. James Alexander, the group's course superintendent, revised the lay-out and gave the course a fresh identity by adding more than 500 yd and giving the good player something to think about without dismaying the less gifted. The setting, 700 ft above sea level, is glorious. The course, set snugly in the hotel grounds, provides a distinct contrast. The last 9 are better suited to the golfer seeking a little exercise after tea, but it is the first 8, conceived with a subtle blend of malice and

golfing family; his elder brother, Ray, tied 4th in the 1935 US Open. Lloyd began to make a name for himself before World War II and was picked for the 1939 Ryder Cup match which was never played. In 1943 he went into the army and took part in the Normandy invasion. In 1945 he was wounded, but before returning home to win the first postwar Open, he won the US Army Golf Championship in Paris and the British G.I. Championship at St Andrews. In the Open at Canterbury the war hero drew a vast crowd. After 18 holes of the play-off he was level with Nelson and Ghezzi and with 6 to play in the second extra round Mangrum was 3 behind Ghezzi and 2 behind Nelson. But he finished with three birdies in a rainstorm and won by 1 stroke. His most successful year financially, 1948, owed much to his winning $22,000 out of a record $48,000 in a single week, by capturing the All-American tournament and the World Championship in the Tam O'Shanter event, at the club to which he was attached.

Mangrum's name was linked with penalties. Leading the field in the second round of the 1948 US Masters he imposed a penalty on himself because his ball moved in the rough as he addressed it. In the 1950 US Open play-off he was penalized 2 strokes at the 16th because he picked up his ball to remove a fly. His reaction was typical – a shrug of the shoulders and an admission that he never read the rule books. 'I don't know the traffic regulations of every city I get to

Top, Tony Manero

Centre, Lloyd E. Mangrum and *above,* as captain of the Ryder Cup team in 1953, with the trophy at Wentworth GC

cunning, that gives Moretonhampstead its character. These are centred round the fast-flowing River Bovey, which winds through a green, tree-lined valley and sets some engaging problems. Even the most accomplished player is pleased to keep his ball above water if he attempts all the shots.

Mar del Plata GC ARGENTINA
Buenos Aires. 18 holes

Built in 1900 in sandy, hilly country facing the Atlantic Ocean. The course was designed by the first Argentinian professional, Juan Dentone. Its members in those days were mostly executives of the Argentinian Southern Railways. With no bulldozers available, camels were used for much of the construction work. It is generally regarded as one of the best courses in Argentina.

Mariánské GC CZECHOSLOVAKIA
Mariánské Lázně (Marienbad). 18 holes

In the past great composers, poets, playwrights and other men of genius were attracted to the spa town of Mariánské Lázně by the lyrical charm of the surrounding

countryside. But the spa is also known as the home of one of Czechoslovakia's most famous courses, opened in 1904. The course owed its design largely to an English professional who was staying at Karlovy Vary (Carlsbad) and who was called in to advise. It was officially opened in 1905 by King Edward VII, a frequent guest at the spa. It was a noteworthy

social occasion, at which the British monarch signed the visitors' book with a gold pen. He was made a founder member of the club, returning regularly in after years. The course, a little way out of the town on the road to Karlovy Vary, began as 9 holes but was increased to 18. Although it stands 2,100 ft above sea level, it is mostly flat with

Top, the 3rd green of the Manor House Hotel GC and, *above,* the approach to the 5th

all the characteristics of natural parkland golf. Because of the composition of the sub-soil, the fairways and greens allow little run on the ball, and the game is therefore greatly influenced by the weather. But it is a soothing course to play and conditions did not stop Henry Cotton from setting a course record of 68 before World War II.

Marker

A scorer in strokeplay appointed by the tournament committee to record a competitor's score. He may be a fellow competitor or a 'substitute' brought in when the numbers are odd or if another competitor is forced to retire. Scorer, or scorekeeper, are the American terms.

A marker is also a small disc used by a player to mark the position of his ball when he lifts it from the putting green.

Marks, Geoffrey BRITISH

b. Hanley, Stoke on Trent, Staffordshire, 1938. Walker Cup 1969, 1971

A leading boy golfer and also a keen cricketer Marks later graduated to international level and played in the Walker Cup matches of 1969 and 1971. He was a semi-finalist in the 1968 British Amateur at Troon, won the Scrutton Jug in 1967 (awarded for the best aggregate in the

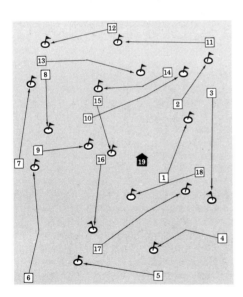

Brabazon and Berkshire Trophies) and has been a real force in Midland events for some years.

Marr, Dave AMERICAN

b. Houston, Tex., 1933. Joint runner-up US Masters 1964; Ryder Cup 1965; USPGA 1965

The course plan of the Mariánské GC

A fine swinger though not a particularly powerful one, Dave Marr, having turned professional in 1953, joined the tour in 1960 and for five or six years was one of the leading American players. After finishing 2nd with Nicklaus in the Masters of 1964 which Arnold Palmer won, he became USPGA Champion at Laurel Valley in the following year, beating Casper and Nicklaus into 2nd place with a total of 280 – the high point of his career. To emphasize his good form in 1965, he also won three tour events and was given the PGA Player of the Year award. A popular figure in American golf, he has shown himself an able television commentator. He was a member of the USPGA championship committee in 1963-5

and chairman in 1964-5.

Marsh, David Max BRITISH

b. Southport, Lancashire, 1934. Walker Cup 1959, 1971, 1973 (captain); English Amateur 1964, 1970; captain of England 1968-71

A distinguished university golfer at Cam-

Top, Geoffrey Marks

Above, Dave Marr

bridge, Marsh was picked for the Walker Cup team in 1959 but did not play. Thereafter he was lost to competitive golf until he qualified as a doctor. He won the English Amateur at Hollinwell in 1964, beating Rodney Foster in the final by 1 hole having been 4 down after 13 holes in the morning. He reached the semi-finals at Royal Lytham in 1966 and won again in 1970 when he beat Geoff Birtwell at Royal Birkdale by 6 and 4, again after being 4 down in the morning. This earned him a place in the 1971 Walker Cup side at St Andrews where he hit the winning stroke for Britain, a wonderful 3 iron to the 17th green. His 4 made him 1 up on Bill Hyndman and gave his side the half point they needed for victory.

Marsh, Graham AUSTRALIAN

b. Kalgoorlie, W. Australia, 1944. New Zealand Watties Tournament 1970; Swiss Open 1970, 1972; Indian Open 1971, 1973; New Zealand Spalding Masters 1971; German Open 1972; Scottish Open 1973; Thailand Open 1973

Marsh started playing at the age of eight and, by the time he was 18, was down to scratch. He represented Western Australia as an amateur for six successive seasons but, on winning the Western Australian Amateur Championship in 1967 and finishing runner-up in the Australian Amateur, he gave up a career as a schoolmaster and, on the advice of Peter Thomson, turned professional.

David Marsh driving during the Sunningdale Foursomes, 1972

In 1970 his first tournament victory came in New Zealand and he finished runner-up to Bob Charles in the New Zealand Open. In Europe he also had conspicuous success with major victories in 1971; and he qualified for a place in the British Open in 1972 by his overall performance in the Far East.

Two weeks later he won his second Swiss title at Crans with a total of 270 and the following Sunday added the German title with a total of 271. These performances were unmistakable signs of his class but his play in the Far East a few months later, when he topped the Order of Merit there, confirmed him as one of the best players in the world outside America. Besides winning the Indian and Thailand Opens, he was consistently in the first 4, won a good deal of money in Japan and, on his trip to Europe in the summer of 1973, won the Scottish Open Championship at St Andrews – showing great adaptability in keeping the big ball low in the wind. At that time he had never played in America and had no plans to do so, which showed how much money there is to be won in other parts of the world.

A cheerful and popular figure, Graham Marsh comes from a distinguished sporting family; his brother, Rodney, has played cricket many times for Australia.

Marston, Maxwell Rolston AMERICAN
b. 1892. Walker Cup 1922-4, 1934; US Amateur 1923, runner-up 1933, semifinalist 1915

One of the country's leading players over a long period, he reached the final of the US Amateur in 1933, 18 years after he first reached the semi-finals. He first played in the Amateur in 1914, losing in the first round by 1 hole to Francis Ouimet, the eventual winner. The next year he missed a 2 ft putt to win on the 36th green against

Bob Gardner, then lost on the 37th. In 1916 he adopted the Vardon grip and his game improved to the extent that he won six invitation tournaments that year. Marston served in the US Navy in World War I, then, in 1919, moved from New Jersey to Philadelphia. He continued to win invitation tournaments by the handful and on one occasion did 6 holes in level 3s to win his match. In the 1923 Amateur Marston defeated Bobby Jones in the second round, then beat the defending champion, Jess Sweetser, in the final with the help of two stymies. The following year he was trounced by George Von Elm, 7 and 6, in the semifinals. Marston's record in the Amateur over the next eight years was patchy, but in 1933 he went all the way to the final after having to qualify in a play-off. He played in four Walker Cup teams, winning five out of eight matches.

Martin, Bob BRITISH
b. St Andrews, Fife, 1848. British Open 1876, 1885, 2nd 1875, 1887

One of the luckiest champions in the history of the event, but a formidable player nonetheless. His first victory came when after a tie with David Strath at St Andrews, both having scored 176 for the two rounds, Strath refused to play off because there had been a complaint against his play in the championship and a decision had not been reached by the committee of the club. The complaint had been that Strath had played

to a green before the players ahead had moved off it and had struck a spectator. Martin's second victory came about only because David Ayton, who came to the 17th at St Andrews 5 strokes ahead of the field with 2 holes to play, took 11, two of them from the road itself.

Martin, James IRISH
World (Canada) Cup 1963; Piccadilly Medal Tournament 1964; Ryder Cup 1965

A consistent player with a limited long game, but a beautiful touch with wedge and putter when the mood is on him makes up for his lack of length. Jimmy Martin won the Turnberry-BOAC pro-am foursomes with Roddy Carr in 1970.

Martin, G. Noel IRISH
b. Portrush, Co. Antrim, 1893. Irish Open Amateur 1920, 1923; British Army 1928; Walker Cup 1928

G. Noel Martin, a holder of the DSO and MC, twice won the North Indian Championship.

Mashie
An obsolete hickory-shafted iron club with approximately the loft of the no. 5 iron. As with other old golfing terms, it is linked with Scottish domesticity. The mashie does not resemble the instrument used for mashing potatoes, but took its name from its effect on the ball when entrusted to unskilful hands.

Graham Marsh putting at Delhi in the 1973 India Open

Maxwell R. Marston

James Martin

A mashie niblick, with slightly more loft, was also in common use in the old days.

Massy, Arnaud FRENCH

b. Biarritz, Basses-Pyrénées, 1877; d. 1958. French Open 1906-7, 1911, 1925, runner-up 1908, 1910, 1926; British Open 1907, runner-up 1911; Belgian Open 1910; Spanish Open 1912, 1927-8

Massy's success was a story of remarkable application and strength of character for at the turn of the century when he started to learn, it was extremely rare for a Frenchman to play golf. He trained in his spare time and set sail for North Berwick in 1902, by which time he had secured backing from wealthy supporters. When he reached Scotland he was left-handed, simply because he had been given a left-handed set, but practising hard at North Berwick he learned to play right-handed. His first appearance in the British Open was in 1905 when he finished 5th; a year later he was joint 6th and his talent left no doubts. From Basque forebears he inherited an excellent eye. He held himself like a Grenadier and made the most of his mighty chest, playing with a fine, ferocious gaiety that made him a most attractive golfer. His club gave a 'pigtail flourish' at the top of the backswing, and in his pitch shots he seemed to lift the club up almost vertically and caress the ball onto the green. He was at his best in a wind; it was blowing hard when he finished ahead of the Great Triumvirate at Hoylake in 1907, and in doing so became the first foreigner to win the title. In the year he tied at Royal St George's with Vardon he proclaimed his famous prayer that the wind would blow hard enough to uproot all the trees in Sandwich. He returned to France, became professional at Chantaco, and after World War I he won a number of championships in Spain.

Masters Tournament SEE US MASTERS TOURNAMENT

Match

A contest between two players or two sides which is determined by the number of holes won and lost. Matchplay is a tournament or championship conducted under the rules of match rather than those of strokeplay. It was the original form of the game.

Mauna Kea Beach Hotel GC HAWAII

18 holes; 6,900 yd (6,310 m); par 72

Hawaii, the biggest island in the mid-Pacific archipelago, has five volcanoes. Kea, the white mountain, is the tallest, rising nearly 14,000 ft above an emerald plain. Between that peak, snow-capped much of the year, and the froth-covered lava rocks of the Kona coast, lies the Mauna course, built on some 230 acres (93 ha) of gently rolling land once part of the Parker Ranch, a vast expanse owned today by Richard Smart, a descendant of the legendary Kamehameha I.

The golf course and the Mauna Kea Beach Hotel were developed by Laurance S. Rockefeller in the mid-1960s. The course, designed by Robert Trent Jones, can be stretched to 7,144 yd (6,532 m), but plays more comfortably at around 6,900 yd. Its tees average about 75 yd (69 m) in length, which gives it remarkable versatility. For instance, from the same general teeing area, Mauna Kea can be played at 6,300 yd (5,760 m).

The 3rd hole is a prime example of the course's flexibility. This is a par 3 that resembles the 16th at Cypress Point, but at Mauna Kea the carry over water can range from 133 to 200 yd (122 to 83 m), depending on which of several tees is used. The back tee is on a promontory of volcanic rock extending 30 ft (9 m) over the ocean. The 11th, another outstanding hole, is framed by kiawe trees, and behind the green the ground drops dramatically 100 ft to a ragged shoreline battered by the surf. Mauna Kea is dotted with other strange flora – rainbow shower, wili-wili, epiuma, monkey pod, African tulip, banyan, as well as the more familiar coconut palm.

Maxwell, Robert BRITISH

b. Edinburgh 1876. British Amateur 1903, 1909.

One of the few amateur golfers who could ever call himself a match for John Ball in the era of the latter's eight championships. The two championships Maxwell won were both at Muirfield, one of his clubs, and indeed he was not interested in travelling far afield in search of glory. He was for all that a fine,

powerful golfer, whose game enriched the vocabulary of the game. His forcing shot with the long irons – his favourite stroke – came to be called a dunch, though it was far more effective than the modern sense given to the word; in spite of his great power he had a most delicate stroke out of bunkers which became known as the 'pussy-cat shot'. Once in the ring he was a dour fighter; he took part in early international matches playing top for Scotland against England, in which position he won five games out of seven against the Amateur Champion of most of those years, John Ball. In winning his second championship at Muirfield in 1909 he finished 3, 4 to defeat C. K. Hutchison – hard enough scoring today but much harder at that time.

Maxwell, William J. AMERICAN

b. Abilene, Tex., 1929. US Amateur 1951; runner-up French Amateur Open 1952; Mexican Amateur 1953; Mexican Open 1956; Ryder Cup 1963

A successful touring professional for many years following victory in the 1951 US Amateur. Except for one year, Billy Maxwell was among the leading money winners for a decade after joining their ranks in 1954. His record is all the more remarkable because he was a short hitter by modern tournament standards, and has admitted that his lack of length more than once gave him a feeling of inferiority. However, he made up for this deficiency by being an excellent putter

besides being very good with the short irons. He once played through four consecutive tournaments without taking three putts. Thus, although he fell short of victory in a major professional championship, he finished joint 5th in three of them, the Masters in 1962, the US Open and PGA championships in 1963. His best stretch as

An ordinary mashie (left) of 1870-80 and a deep-faced mashie of 1900

William J. Maxwell

a professional came between 1961 and 1962 when he won four tournaments, and earned a place in the Ryder Cup team. He won seven tournaments between 1955 and 1962 in addition to the Mexican Open. He was still competing on the tour in 1971.

May, George Storr AMERICAN
b. Windsor, Ill., 1891; d. 1962

One of golf's most colourful entrepreneurs who helped the game into the big-money class. It was more than mere coincidence that the leading money winner of the year usually was the man who won May's rich 'world' championship at Tam O'Shanter near Chicago. May, a wealthy president of the George S. May Co., business engineers, began his All-America Tournament in 1941 and also invited a few amateurs to compete. In 1942 the amateur event was separated and in 1943 a professsional women's competition was added. A winner-take-all event, which was to evolve into the 'world' championship, capped the carnival week for the first time in 1947 and before long the winner was collecting $50,000 plus an option of an additional $100,000 for playing exhibitions. More than one man who decided to play the exhibitions found it hard a year or two later to get back into the tournament groove. May embellished the show with clowns, 'masked marvels' and door prizes and insisted that the players should wear numbers to help the gallery identify them. Ben Hogan, among others, refused to wear the numbers, but the show went on. May was a member of the USPGA advisory committee for several years and served as chairman in 1954, but by 1958 he and the USPGA failed to agree on who was to get entry fees for his events, so he cancelled the tournaments.

Mayer, Dick AMERICAN
b. Stamford, Conn., 1924. New York Amateur 1947; Eastern Open 1953; Kansas City Open 1955; *Philadelphia Daily News* Open 1956; US Open 1957, tied 3rd 1954; Ryder Cup 1957; New Orleans Open 1965

Blond, handsome Mayer had been steadily improving on the professional tour for several years before his Open victory in 1957, and it seemed likely that he would continue. However, the ensuing exhibition and other commitments not only kept him away from many tournaments, they also reduced his efficiency. Tendon trouble and a broken elbow in 1960 compounded his difficulties and, although he had moderate success in 1963, he never again reached his 1957 level of efficiency. Mayer grew up in Greenwich, Conn., where he excelled as an all-rounder in sport. After four years in the

army he played top amateur golf while working in his father's car business and for a New York investment firm. He joined the tour in 1950 and had won four tournaments before 1957 when, in addition to the Open, he won the Tam O'Shanter World Tournament and finished leading money winner. In that Open he holed from 10 ft on the 72nd green at Inverness, which gave him the lead, but Cary Middlecoff finished strongly with 68 to tie him. Mayer won the play-off by 7 strokes with a round of 72. After staying away in 1964 he returned to the tour the following year and had one final moment of glory when he holed a 35 yd-wedge shot on the 72nd green to win the New Orleans Open and $20,000. In 1962 another big shot – a hole in one in the Palm Springs Classic – brought him $50,000.

Mayfair GCC CANADA
Edmonton, Alta. 18 holes; 6,632 yd (6,064 m); par 70

This course offers a unique escape from urban bustle, so complete that the golfer might imagine himself to be many miles from, instead of readily accessible to, a large city. Picturesquely located on the curving south bank of the North Saskatchewan River, the course provides excellent golf. It was officially opened in May 1922 by Lord Byng of Vimy, then Governor General of Canada. Some six years later it was extensively revamped and perfected by Stanley Thompson, the Canadian golf architect. Hewn from virgin forest, it remains heavily wooded. The fairways which wind their undulating way through the trees to good greens provide stimulating, although not difficult golf. The 1946, 1961 and 1968 Canadian Amateur Championships were played at Mayfair, as was the 1958 Canadian Open Championship, won with a score of 267, and the 1963 Canadian Professional

Golfers' Association Championship, won by Al Balding with a three-round total of 202. Bobby Locke scored 63 in an exhibition round, a figure that was established as the course record when Bob Wylie of Calgary equalled it in the qualifying round of the 1960 Alberta Amateur Championship.

Meadow Brook Club USA
Long Island, N.Y. 18 holes

Of the many new courses that have gone up in the suburban reaches of New York City since World War II, the Meadow Brook Club's new 18 in Jericho, Long Island, is certainly among the best, if not actually the best. There was nothing particularly wrong with the club's old course in Old Westbury – it was there in 1895 that Mrs C. S. Brown won the first US Women's Championship – but after Robert Moses, New York City's Park Commissioner, announced that he would have to take over the land for one of his parkway extensions, Meadow Brook had no choice but to build a new course.

Meadow Brook chose Dick Wilson, then at the top of his fame, to design its new course. After inspecting 20 sites, Wilson selected the one he wanted in October 1953. George Heron, a Scot who had left Stoke Poges to become the professional at Meadow Brook in 1922, performed with his usual efficiency in a new role – superintendent of the new course. The course was opened in the spring of 1955. The club professional at that time was Shelley Mayfield, a young man from Texas who had played the tour with distinction.

The new Meadow Brook has already had to revise and re-arrange some of its holes because of further highway construction. From the start, however, the course has looked as if it had been around for decades, so well do Wilson's holes fit the rolling, wooded land. From the back tees, the course is over 7,100 yd (6,490 m) in length, and since it plays at least that long, the big hitter enjoys a definite advantage as long as he maintains a reasonable degree of accuracy.

Medallist
The player with the lowest qualifying score for a matchplay tournament or championship. He receives a medal for this achievement. A predominantly American expression.

Medal play
A tournament or championship conducted under the rules of medal play as distinct from matchplay. The winner is the player returning the lowest total or, in handicap events, the player with the lowest net total. Nowa-

Dick Mayer

Opposite, Lu Liang Huan

Overleaf, Skating Scene on the Scheldt – a painting in the Royal and Ancient GC

vised work on the new holes was solely responsible for the design and lay-out of the East Course. It was opened in 1932 and gives Royal Melbourne a superb pair of courses where good driving is imperative in order to allow players a chance of negotiating the many demanding second shots.

A composite course of both East and West (this ensured that no neighbouring roads had to be crossed) confronted the World (Canada) Cup in 1959 and 1972; the World Amateur Team Championship for the Eisenhower Trophy in 1968, for which occasion the present modern clubhouse was completed; and the 1972 World Cup which was reduced from 72 to 54 holes because of bad weather.

Two events of this kind, bringing together the best players of the amateur and professional worlds, are a rich and proud part of the club's history: the first because it resulted in a famous victory for the Australians, Kel Nagle and Peter Thomson (the latter learned his golf just down the road); the second because of a dramatic finish between the United States and Britain.

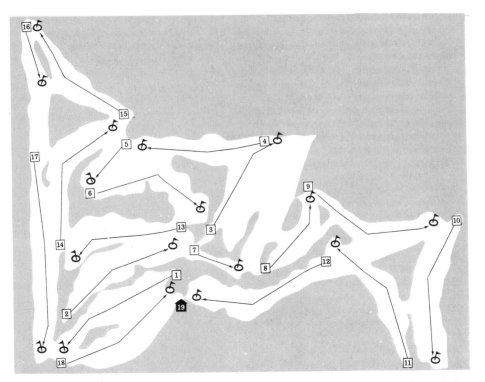

Melville, John Whyte BRITISH
b. 1797; d. 1883

The only man to have been nominated to be captain of the Royal and Ancient Golf Club a second time. He first held office in 1823. He was nominated in 1883 but died before he could drive himself into office again. The office was left vacant that year in his memory. He was the father of the novelist George John Whyte-Melville. Old Whyte Melville, though no great performer, loved the game and was a well-known figure for many years at St Andrews.

Mena House Course EGYPT
Cairo. 9 holes; 5,800 yd (5,303 m); par 69 (for 18 holes)

All grass, including grass greens, but thin and poorly maintained. The course is picturesquely situated by the Pyramids, immediately adjoining the Mena House Hotel, known throughout the world in the years gone by as a famous winter haven for international tourists.

Merion GC USA
Ardmore, Philadelphia, Pa. 18 holes

One of Merion's many claims to fame is that it has hosted more USGA events than any other club – 13 in all. The first of these was the 1904 Women's Amateur, and the most recent the 1971 Open. Another of the club's distinctions is that it is more closely linked with the career of Bobby Jones than any other championship venue in America.

It was at Merion that Jones made his debut in national competition in the 1916 Amateur at the age of 14 – he won two matches – and it was at Merion that he won his first Amateur (in 1924) and his last Amateur (in 1930). His triumph in the 1930 US Amateur completed his Grand Slam of the four major championships.

Since 1924, Merion has made its home in Ardmore, a suburb of Philadelphia, a dozen or so miles west of Independence Hall. Until comparatively recent times, the club's official name was the Merion Cricket Club, for from its founding in the middle of the 19th century until the turn of the 20th, cricket was the chief interest of its members.

Top, the course plan of the Royal Melbourne GC

Above, the 6th green on the West Course at Royal Melbourne and, *top right,* the well-trapped 5th

days in America this is more commonly
called strokeplay.

Medinah CC USA
Chicago, Ill. 18 holes

Many golfers of the Chicago district rate
Old No. 3 at Medinah, as they call it, the
toughest course in that area and among the
toughest in the world. Like most other golf
subjects, that is arguable, but in playing No.
3 there is no harm in assuming it to be true.

Cary Middlecoff needed 286 strokes
there to win the 1949 US Open – the one
Ben Hogan missed because of his accident –
when No. 3 was not at all tricked up.
The course is quite a bit up and down,
and dense woods border every hole
except the first and last. The trees edge
in very close, making the fairways seem
narrower than they actually are. There are
nine doglegs; water has to be crossed three
times and avoided twice. They say that the
17th, a 204-yd (187-m) par 3, is the hardest
hole. The tee shot, from a series of terraces, is
across an arm of Lake Kadijah and over a
large frontal bunker to a green enveloped in
more sand. This is the hole on which Sam
Snead spoiled his chance in the 1949 Open
when, in the last round, he took 3 to get
down from just off the edge of the green.
Some members contend that the 7th, a
599-yd (550-m) dogleg with a slew of
bunkers, is even more difficult.

Situated 20 miles due west of Chicago's
Loop, the Medinah club was originally built
as a private playground for the Shriner
organization. Its clubhouse, large and
mosque-like, shows the Near Eastern
influence. There is a story that some of the
bunkers were built in the shape of camels to
carry out the theme, but if they were, the
camels have now lost their shape.

Mehlhorn, William E. AMERICAN
b. 1898. 3rd US Open 1924, tied 3rd 1926;
Western Open 1924; runner-up USPGA
1925; semi-finalist 1936; Hawaiian Open
1928; Texas Open 1928; Ryder Cup 1927

Wild Bill Mehlhorn was one of the most
colourful members of the touring troupe in
the 1920s and a man who, when he was
making a few putts, was capable of great
scoring bursts. Whatever a golf star is supposed to look like, Mehlhorn did not.
Bernard Darwin once said he looked like a
hod carrier for the champion bricklayer. But
appearances were deceptive for Mehlhorn
was a good golfer. Ben Hogan once called
him one of the finest tee-to-green players he
ever saw. In 1929, for example, Mehlhorn
won the El Paso Open with 271 – a record at
that time – and then followed this with

277 and victory in the Texas Open, in the
course of which he had two 66s, two 67s, a 68
and a 69. He finished 5th or better in the
US Open five times, and between 1921 and
1929 he won 14 tournaments in addition to
those listed above.

Melbourne GC, Royal AUSTRALIA
Melbourne, Victoria. 36 holes; West Course
6,588 yd (5,997 m); East Course 6,642 yd
(6,073 m)

Royal Melbourne, the pride of the many
courses on Melbourne's famous 'sand belt',
provides some of the best inland golf to be
found anywhere in the world. Founded in
1891 through the initiative of William Knox
and J. M. Bruce, it is the oldest golf club in
Australia with a continuous existence under
the same name, and owes its origin to a meeting at Scots Hotel, Collins Street, on 2 May
1891. Eighty members enrolled in the first
few days, one of the first being an old
Scottish golfer, T. J. Findlay, who had
arrived 10 years earlier with six sets of clubs,
a supply of balls and an implement for
cutting holes. On 29 June 1891, the meeting

accepted the offer of an area for a course,
only a few minutes from Caulfield Station,
and a newly erected brick clubhouse for
30 shillings a week. Work started on the
course and it was opened on 4 July 1891 by
J. M. Bruce who, wearing a scarlet coat with
gilt buttons, knickerbockers, and a Tam
o'Shanter, the official club costume, hit the
first ball. Towards the turn of the century,
however, building at Caulfield caused the
club to look elsewhere.

An alternative site was found in the
Sandringham area, only a stone's throw
from the sea. Construction work presented
many problems and took about three years.
A thick growth of scrub and ti-tree had to be
removed before the ground could be
ploughed but, because it is so close to the sea,
the soil has a rich, sandy base giving fairways and greens of superb pace and texture.
It also accounts for Royal Melbourne's renowned fairway and greenside bunkers
which are large and deep.

The Lieutenant-Governor, Sir John
Madden, opened the new course on 27 July
1901. Sir John excelled himself in his speech,
but when it came to driving the first ball, he
performed less gracefully. As Royal Melbourne's official history relates, 'He was
not endowed with any great faculty for the
game nor had he made any attempt to
remedy by art his natural infirmities as a
golfer.' He is recorded as announcing that he
had never played the game before. In top
hat and tail coat he hit an air shot which, to
make matters worse, the camera caught for
posterity.

The course was soon in use for Australian
championships and quickly gained the reputation of a wonderful test of golf. In October
1926 Dr Alister Mackenzie arrived, at a fee
of 1,000 guineas, to suggest major alterations
to the existing course, subsequently known as
the West Course. Alex Russell who super-

Opposite, Royal Melbourne GC

Top, Medinah CC

Above, William E. Mehlhorn

vised work on the new holes was solely responsible for the design and lay-out of the East Course. It was opened in 1932 and gives Royal Melbourne a superb pair of courses where good driving is imperative in order to allow players a chance of negotiating the many demanding second shots.

A composite course of both East and West (this ensured that no neighbouring roads had to be crossed) confronted the World (Canada) Cup in 1959 and 1972; the World Amateur Team Championship for the Eisenhower Trophy in 1968, for which occasion the present modern clubhouse was completed; and the 1972 World Cup which was reduced from 72 to 54 holes because of bad weather.

Two events of this kind, bringing together the best players of the amateur and professional worlds, are a rich and proud part of the club's history: the first because it resulted in a famous victory for the Australians, Kel Nagle and Peter Thomson (the latter learned his golf just down the road); the second because of a dramatic finish between the United States and Britain.

Melville, John Whyte BRITISH
b. 1797; d. 1883

The only man to have been nominated to be captain of the Royal and Ancient Golf Club a second time. He first held office in 1823. He was nominated in 1883 but died before he could drive himself into office again. The office was left vacant that year in his memory. He was the father of the novelist George John Whyte-Melville. Old Whyte Melville, though no great performer, loved the game and was a well-known figure for many years at St Andrews.

Mena House Course EGYPT
Cairo. 9 holes; 5,800 yd (5,303 m); par 69 (for 18 holes)

All grass, including grass greens, but thin and poorly maintained. The course is picturesquely situated by the Pyramids, immediately adjoining the Mena House Hotel, known throughout the world in the years gone by as a famous winter haven for international tourists.

Merion GC USA
Ardmore, Philadelphia, Pa. 18 holes

One of Merion's many claims to fame is that it has hosted more USGA events than any other club – 13 in all. The first of these was the 1904 Women's Amateur, and the most recent the 1971 Open. Another of the club's distinctions is that it is more closely linked with the career of Bobby Jones than any other championship venue in America.

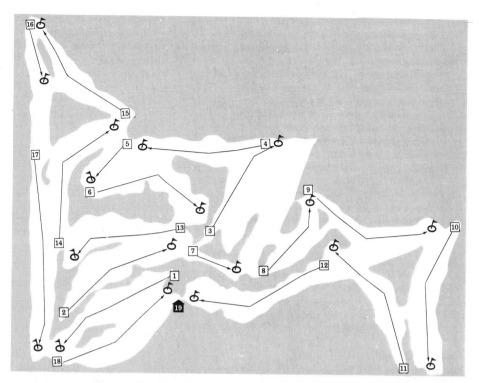

It was at Merion that Jones made his debut in national competition in the 1916 Amateur at the age of 14 – he won two matches – and it was at Merion that he won his first Amateur (in 1924) and his last Amateur (in 1930). His triumph in the 1930 US Amateur completed his Grand Slam of the four major championships.

Since 1924, Merion has made its home in Ardmore, a suburb of Philadelphia, a dozen or so miles west of Independence Hall. Until comparatively recent times, the club's official name was the Merion Cricket Club, for from its founding in the middle of the 19th century until the turn of the 20th, cricket was the chief interest of its members.

Top, the course plan of the Royal Melbourne GC

Above, the 6th green on the West Course at Royal Melbourne and, *top right,* the well-trapped 5th

Above, Merion GC, the 11th hole

In the late 1890s, a golf course of no particular merit was built near the club's headquarters in Haverford, and shortly afterwards a slightly less rudimentary lay-out replaced it. In 1910, recognizing that these facilities were now outmoded, the club purchased land for a new course – an L-shaped plot of 127 acres (51 ha) which held the remains of an abandoned farm and a worked-out stone quarry. This land had a number of shortcomings. The soil was on the clayey side; the terrain was bumpy and almost totally lacking in handsome trees and shrubs; two small brooks meandered through the property, but that was the extent of the water. Nevertheless, the course that emerged was both a challenging and a charming one. This was due to the high talent – perhaps the genius – of Hugh Wilson, a young Princetonian the building committee had sent to Britain to study the famous courses and who, upon his return, took over the responsibility of laying out the new course, which was completed in 1912. This came to be called the East Course after a second 18 was added in 1914. This latter course, the West, also designed by Wilson, is a pleasant lay-out but it is shorter and appreciably easier than the East.

Hugh Wilson, working in partnership with the club's renowned greenkeeper, Joe Valentine, effected some striking improvements in the East Course, which he revised steadily until his death in 1925. The firm of Toomey & Flynn then finished the job. Since 1930, only minor changes have been made. As a result, Merion is an exceedingly short course compared to the 7,000-yarders over which most of the Opens have been held in the last decade. At 6,544 yd (5,984 m), it is, in fact, the shortest course on which the championship has been played since World War II. However, long-hitting by itself means less at Merion than at most American courses. The key to playing it well is placement of the tee shot, for the greens, which are small and hard-surfaced, are difficult to hold unless the golfer comes into them from the best possible angle.

Merion will yield to brilliant golf, but low scores do not come easily there. Olin Dutra's winning total in the 1934 Open was 293 (76-74-71-72). In the 1950 Open, Ben Hogan's 287 (72-69-72-74) was good enough to earn him a tie with Lloyd Mangrum and George Fazio, whom he defeated in the play-off with a 69. In the 1971 Open, before his clear-cut victory in the play-off, Lee Trevino tied with Jack Nicklaus at 280 – even par – a much higher figure than many experts had predicted. A number of these experts had been beguiled by the 269 Nicklaus had compiled at Merion in the 1960 Eisenhower Trophy match when he put together a 66, a 67, and two 68s. Nicklaus himself has said that he doubts that he has ever hit the ball as consistently well over 72 holes as he did in that tournament, but he is the first to point out that his scoring was possible only because Merion was not set up to play anything like as severely as it does for the Opens. The fairways were wider, the rough was milder, the pin positions far easier, the speed of the greens far slower, and, on top of all this, four days of wet and heavy weather took most of the fierceness out of the course.

On the other hand, the reason why Merion kept most of the long-hitting modern players at bay in the 1971 Open was that it was in perfect shape for the event, thanks to the ministrations of Richie Valentine, who succeeded his father as the course greenkeeper, or superintendent, as the post is called today. For example, to get the greens to a properly fast speed, Valentine did the following: three weeks before the tournament he gave the greens a top dressing of sand an eighth of an inch deep; two weeks before the tournament, he top-dressed them with sand again, also an eighth of an inch deep; a week before the tournament, he began cutting them to five thirty-seconds of an inch; and during the tournament his crews cut the greens twice each morning, the second cutting criss-crossing the first. Valentine also produced a wonderfully lush growth of rough. Without fast greens and thick rough, Merion, for all the implicit strategic niceties of its holes, could not hope to stand up to the present professional brigade.

The most famous hole at Merion, the 11th, is representative of the spirit of the whole course. To begin with, it is a short par 4 of only 370 yd (338 m). There is, however, a lot for the golfer to take into consideration. The drive is downhill to a narrow fairway crossed by Baffling Brook. The brook then swings out alongside a stand of trees off to the left of the fairway, breaks back sharply in front of the green, and then breaks again along the right-hand side of the green and around to the back of it. The shot to the green, be it a no. 9 iron for the professional or a 4 iron for the average golfer, is at one and the same time a tartar and a treat. There are many other such shots on Merion, and, fittingly, a good percentage of them are to be found on the closing 5 holes, four difficult 4s broken up by the 17th, a rugged par 3. (Incidentally, the second and last of the two par 5s is the 4th.) This quiet auditing

of a golfer's skill takes place in a parklike setting that looks lovely in the spring when the very green fairways are set off by the numerous bunkers, the famed 'White Faces of Merion'.

Method
The manner of a player's striking and swinging. No two players swing alike but the ideal requirements of any method are reliability and repetitiveness.

Metropolitan GC AUSTRALIA
nr Melbourne, Victoria. 18 holes; 7,000 yd (6,400 m)

This club and Royal Melbourne have the same origin. In 1901 a group of members of the Melbourne club, founded in 1891, set up on their own at Sandringham where Royal Melbourne now is. The remainder stayed on at Caulfield, and in 1906 formed the Metropolitan club on 147 acres (59 ha) of fresh land, in the suburb of Oakleigh. It has become one of the best known of Melbourne's belt of courses and has undergone only one important change in the last 60 years.

In 1962 new land had to be found for 4 holes which had been given up for school building. Dick Wilson, the well-known American architect, effectively merged the old with the new and maintained the course's championship standard.

The Metropolitan has produced distinguished champions in Gene Sarazen and Peter Thomson who won his first Australian Open there; Thomson and Kel Nagle both won professional titles on the course. Three good amateurs have won their titles at Metropolitan: Jim Ferrier in 1936 before turning professional, Doug Bachli and G. R. Hicks.

Metz, Dick AMERICAN
b. Arkansas City, Kan., 1909. Southwest Open 1931; runner-up US Open 1938; Ryder Cup 1939; semi-finalist USPGA 1939

One of those good players who never quite achieved his breakthrough in the major championships. He was, however, a big winner on the tour in the 1930s and still capable in his fifties of giving anybody a good run for his money. He had more than 15 tournaments to his credit. Metz had his best year in 1939, when he won six tournaments, tied for 7th in the US Open, reached the semi-finals of the USPGA and was picked for the Ryder Cup team. In those days he was called Handsome Dick Metz: with his black, wavy hair and dark complexion he was a natural for the lead in a

Hollywood Western. He was runner-up in the 1938 US Open and finished in the top 10 of that event nine times in a period of 23 years. As late as 1958, when he was 50, he shared the first-round lead and was able to hang on and tie for 7th. In 1938 he went into the last round with a 4-stroke lead over Ralph Guldahl, but wound up 6 shots behind, Guldahl finishing in 69 while Metz was faltering. He won the USPGA Seniors' in 1960, and that same year, as proof of his durability, he won the Texas PGA Seniors', 29 years after taking the Texas PGA title.

Mexico
Mexican golf has made rapid advances in the last 20 years. The main golfing centre is Mexico City, although Roberto de Vicenzo, whose brother is professional there, rates the Monterey and Guadalajara courses very highly. The game received a big fillip from the achievements of Mexican-born Lee Trevino or 'Super Mex', and from the staging of the World Amateur Team Championship in 1966 at the Club de Golf Mexico. Eight years before, the World Cup was held in Mexico City and won by the Irish pair, Harry Bradshaw and Christy O'Connor, who made light of playing at such a high altitude.

Mexican golf dates from 1897 when 9 holes were constructed in the Mexico City suburb of Puebla. The San Pedro club was founded by a group headed by an American, William Townsend, from Louisville, Ky. In 1907 the Mexico City CC came into being. Willie Smith, the 1899 US Open Champion, served as professional until his death in 1915 when the clubhouse was shelled during an uprising. Government troops tried to oust the rebels but when Smith was found hiding in a cellar, he was in a critical condition. It was some time before building golf courses was again considered, but in 1923 the

Dick Metz

Chapultec club was founded and designed by Alex Smith. Following the Tampico oil boom a number of new courses were opened to cater for the influx of foreign, golf-minded oil workers. In spite of this the country's most famous club, the Club de Golf Mexico, dates only from 1947. Its 36 holes were an obvious choice for the World Cup and the World Amateur Team Championship.

The Mexican Open Championship which now forms part of the Caribbean circuit holds a respected place in the calendar and has maintained a distinguished list of winners since Al Espinosa won four successive titles from 1944. The same is true of the Mexican Amateur Championship which has a strong roll of winners. Mexico's participation, from 1952 until it was discontinued, in the Americas Cup, a team event for amateurs (the United States and Canada completed the triangle), helped to raise playing standards. In 1970 the leading individual scorer in the World Team Championship in Madrid was a Mexican, Victor Regalado, with a four-round total of 280. The Mexican team finished 5th, as in 1962 and 1966. On the professional side the Mexican pair, R. Cazares and Tony Cerda, who was born in Argentina, finished 3rd in the 1967 World Cup.

Micklem, Gerald Hugh BRITISH

b. Burgh Heath, Surrey, 1911. Semi-finalist British Amateur 1946; English Amateur 1947, 1953; Walker Cup 1947, 1949, 1953, 1955 (non-playing captain 1957, 1959); President's Putter 1953; President English Golf Union 1965-6; President European Golf Association 1967-9; captain Royal and Ancient 1968-9

Gerald Micklem's contribution to golf has been vast both as player and later as administrator. There is hardly a committee on which he has not served or a cause to which he has not given support. He never regarded the many offices he has held as sinecures but as opportunities to lend his influence to some neglected aspect of the game.

In the first of his English championship finals he defeated Charlie Stowe by 1 hole at Ganton; his second victory was over Ronnie White, generally reckoned to be the best amateur in Britain at the time and a member of Royal Birkdale where the championship was played. In 1948 he won the *Daily Telegraph* Foursomes with Charlie Ward. His four Walker Cup appearances included a foursome victory with John Morgan at Kittansett over Charlie Coe and Bill Campbell and a singles match the same year, 1953, in which he took Gene Littler to the 33rd hole.

Educated at Winchester and Oxford

where he won a Blue, he served with the Brigade of Guards in World War II. He gave up stockbroking after the death of his father and devoted himself full-time to the better running of the game. His work for the Royal and Ancient included chairmanship of the Selection Committee, the Championship Committee, and the Rules of Golf Committee. He has been a crusader in the cause of true amateurism and against slow play, and was a prime mover in the attempt to find one size of the ball for the world. Many now well-established professionals turned to him for advice before embarking on their careers and he has shown great understanding of the problems of young players. His wide interests are reflected in other posts he has held, such

as Chairman of the Golf Foundation and of the Golf Development Council, president of the Oxford and Cambridge Golfing Society and of the Public Schools Golfing Societies, and vice-president of the British Professional Golfers' Association. Micklem, who holds the CBE, has received the British Golf Writers' Award, and in the United States the Bobby Jones and Walter Hagen awards.

Middlecoff, Dr Cary AMERICAN

b. Halls, Tenn., 1921. North and South Open 1945; US Open 1949, 1956, runner-up 1957; Ryder Cup 1953, 1955, 1959; US Masters 1955; Western Open 1955; Vardon Trophy 1956; Memphis Open 1961

For several years an outstanding amateur

in the Tennessee area, Middlecoff was trained to follow his father and two uncles into the dental profession. While training as a dentist before going into the US Army in 1943, he won the North and South Open, the only amateur ever to have done so. He was invited to join the first Walker Cup team after the war, but declined on the grounds that he was contemplating turning professional. He did so the following year, in 1947, and won the third tournament he played in as a professional, the Charlotte Open. He rose rapidly to the top, finished 7th in the order of merit, and a year later in 1949 won the first of his two US Opens. For the next seven years he won at least one tournament a year – in 1955 he won six – and was not once out of the top 10 money winners.

In defence of his 1956 Open title Middlecoff scored 68 in his two closing rounds, equalling the record set by Sarazen for the last two rounds in 1932 – but lost the play-off to Dick Mayer by 79 to 72. Middlecoff was a magnificent long driver and very competent round the greens, but he gained a reputation for slow play, especially in sizing up his

Gerald Micklem with *(top)* his English Amateur Championship Trophy in 1953

Cary Middlecoff during the 1970 Masters Tournament

putts; he was also a bit of a fidget, and being over 6 ft tall, he was not destined to stay long in the game. In the early 1960s his back began to give him trouble. He was an intelligent golfer, much versed in theory, and wrote a number of books on the advanced theory of the game. His attitude of perfectionism towards the game accounted in part for the slowness and deliberation of his play. His lowest competitive round was a 62 in 1953 and his lowest four-round total 264. His best performance in the USPGA championship was the semi-finals in 1954 and the last eight in 1952. He was chairman of the USPGA tournament committee in 1953-4.

Mid-Surrey GC, Royal ENGLAND

Richmond, Surrey. 18 holes; 6,385 yd (5,838 m); par 72; Ladies' Course 5,530 yd (5,057 m); par 72

In 1892 when the Mid-Surrey club was formed on the edge of Kew Gardens, the setting was one of rural peacefulness. London was a pleasant carriage ride away and the suburbs had not begun to eat their way into the surrounding counties. Today, as the club cowers beneath one of the glidepaths to London's Heathrow Airport, evidence of the modern world is everywhere apparent, but the club remains a notable retreat, easily accessible from central London. The Mid in the name is an abbreviation for the county of Middlesex which lies over the nearby Thames. The river has been known to overflow onto the 9th fairway. The course is bounded by the river, Kew Gardens, and more recently by Richmond Athletic Ground. It is park golf, flat and rather dull looking from a distance, but always good fun and never easy. Good use has been made of the groups of stately trees, including some handsome specimens; outstanding among them is a cedar which was once described by a passing caddie to an American (who had no reason to doubt him) as having been planted by William the Conqueror when he was mayor of Richmond. A number of bumps and hollows introduced by J. H. Taylor about 1910 added features to the scene, and these together with the raising of some greens and the placing of well-defined bunkers, effectively break up the flatness. The 6th hole is a specially fine 2-shotter, leading to a teasing little shot to the short par-4 7th. The second 9, a good deal longer than the first, includes some testing finishing holes, one of them, the 16th, a tight long par 3.

The club owes its origins to a group who broke away from the old Richmond club, where there was no provision for women, and moved to the present site. The original

course was laid out by Tom Dunn, professional at the Richmond club, and the first place of assembly was a room in the Tulip Tree public house. In 1895 a new clubhouse was opened on the present site while the women had sole use of a nearby farmhouse. With the appointment shortly after the turn of the century of Peter Lees, a greenkeeper from Scotland, the greens earned the reputation of being among the best in England. Lees was a stern disciplinarian who never allowed his men to work in a jacket, on the grounds that if they were doing their job properly they would be warm enough without one. In 1913, the Suffragettes, during their campaign for women's votes, dug up some of the greens on the women's course. The greenkeeping staff patrolled the two courses by night until votes were granted.

The engagement of J. H. Taylor as professional was the start of one of the club's most valued associations. He held the post for 47 years, and was succeeded by Henry Cotton. Jimmy Adams and David Talbot have helped to maintain its proud pro-

fessional tradition. The club became Royal in 1926, the year in which the Prince of Wales accepted the captaincy. It has been host to a wide variety of events, including the 1946 English Championship. The Ladies' Course, one of the foremost in women's golf, was founded along with the other in 1892, and lies inside the main course. Modernized by Taylor, also in 1910, it contains some first-class holes which were brought into use in the PGA championship held there in 1961. Mid-Surrey is, however, essentially a members' club, characterized by their annual competition, the Antlers, a foursomes medal event with a wide appeal.

Miguel Brothers, The SPANISH

Angel, b. Madrid 1929. French Open 1956; World Cup Individual Trophy 1958; Spanish Open 1961, 1964; Agfa Gevaert Tournament 1966
Sebastián, b. Madrid 1921. Spanish Open 1954, 1960, 1967; World Cup 1963

The two brothers first gave Spain a reputation in golf outside its own frontiers and their careers remained inseparable. Both

A scene on the 18th green of the Royal Mid-Surrey GC during the 1968 PGA Close Championship

followed a similar pattern they were not alike in temperament. Angel had a classic swing reminiscent almost of Hogan in its compactness and tempo; this was all the more remarkable in that he had no instruction but picked the game up as best he could at his home club. His was the more fiery temperament and his list of successes might well have been longer if he had not had several years of bad health at the time when his powers were at their height. Sebastián was easier going, a more timid player to use his own assessment, but a player of great consistency. Thus whereas Angel had the lower finish of the two in the British Open, 4th in 1957, Sebastián played with great steadiness in the same event. He never

threatened to win it, but in all the years he competed in it he never failed to qualify, and in the later years he could be relied on to finish in the first 10 with almost unfailing regularity. His lowest finish was tied 6th in 1967.

Home successes for the Miguels included Angel's five victories in the Spanish National Close Championship and Sebastián's seven in the Spanish Professional.

In 1958, the year that Angel won the World Cup individual title after a sudden-death play-off with Christy O'Connor, he and Sebastián finished 2nd to Ireland in the team event, and only a scorching last round by the United States pair in 1963 prevented Sebastián, partnered by Sota, from winning

started in the humblest way as caddies at the Madrid club of Puerta de Hierro; both visited Britain for the early part of each season, travelling by train in the early 1950s and living in small lodging apartments. Since 1954, when Sebastián stole a march on his elder brother by first winning the Spanish Open, they visited Britain for three or four months every year up until 1968. Everywhere they were worthy ambassadors, and even now that they have retired from the game and have important club posts, Sebastián at Andalucía Nueva and Angel at Los Monteros, it is doubtful whether there is proper appreciation of their work in breaking down the narrow national boundaries of Continental golf. Though their careers

the event. Sebastián took part in five US Masters, but in those days although his short game was immaculate and he seldom missed a fairway he had not enough length to match the Americans. Nevertheless his persistence among the top players kept the door open for the growing number of Spanish professionals, led by Sota and Barrios, who have since made Spain the leading Continental golfing country.

Millensted, Dudley BRITISH
b. 1942. Joint winner English Strokeplay 1965; runner-up English Amateur 1966; Berkshire Trophy 1967; Duncan Putter 1967; Scrutton Jug 1967; Walker Cup 1967

Millensted turned professional in 1967 after announcing his intention at the Commonwealth Tournament, following his only Walker Cup appearance.

Miller, Allen L. AMERICAN
b. San Diego, Cal., 1948. Trans-Mississippi Amateur 1969-70; 3rd US Amateur 1969; Walker Cup 1969, 1971; Canadian Amateur 1970

Angel Miguel, *top*, and *above* on the 13th fairway during the 1967 Agfa-Gevaert Tournament at Stoke Poges

Top, Sebastián Miguel

Above, Dudley Millensted

Allen L. Miller

As a member of the 1969 Walker Cup team, Miller won two key singles on the last green, and two years later at St Andrews his two singles again finished on the last green. In 1970, besides his success in the Canadian Amateur, he also won the Trans-Mississippi for the second time, the Southeastern, and the Northeastern, and was low amateur in the Monsanto Open at his home town of Pensacola, Fla. A graduate of Georgia University, he turned professional in 1971.

Miller, John L. AMERICAN

b. San Francisco, Cal., 1947. Southern Open 1971; tied 2nd US Masters 1971; 2nd Bob Hope Desert Classic 1972; Heritage Golf Classic 1972; tied 2nd British Open 1973; US Open 1973

Miller early acquired a reputation for blowing hot and cold, for following a bad round with a good round, and of being a good contender on the big occasion. This impression was confirmed in his US Open victory, in which he followed a third-round 76 with a final 63 which left the rest of the field struggling. It is the lowest round ever played in the British or US Open championships. Another 63, in the Bob Hope in 1972, had raised him to 2nd place with Nicklaus. In 1970 he scored a 61 in the third round of the Phoenix, and he has had three competitive 65s. Miller is one of the personalities of the yonger generation – a blond, lanky 6-footer, gaily dressed, assured, with a high, upright swing and pronounced follow-through. A Mormon of abstemious habits he strides freely along the fairways with an air of dedicated, almost detached, purpose.

Miller had already made a name for himself in his home state of California when at the age of 16 he qualified for his first US Open at the Olympic Club while still a sophomore at Brigham Young University. He attracted more than local interest with a 70 which kept him in the picture and he finished 8th. Three years later, after graduating in physical education he turned professional, having as an amateur won the junior championship in 1964 and obtained all-American honours. Two final rounds of 68 in the 1971 Masters brought the event to life and gave him the confidence to stay with the star players. In winning the US Open he said that he had always reckoned to do well in the big events because he felt that the pressure on the stars was greater then than at any other time, whereas for him it was less. In 1972 he finished 7th in the US Open and had won a few dollars short of 100,000 by the end of the season. His victory in the Heritage followed a pattern which was becoming familiar in his play: 71, 65, 74, 65,

although changes of weather accounted for some of the irregularity. Thus his final rounds in the three events he had won up to and including the Open were 67, 65, 63. Always a flair player, his record in 1972 and 1973 showed that he has learned to restrict the effect of his bad rounds. He made it clear that his US Open victory was no flash in the pan by remaining in contention in the British Open the following month until the last 9 holes and by having a marvellous season in 1974, winning the first three tour events, adding five more, and breaking the money winning record.

Mills, Ralph Peter BRITISH

b. Virginia Water, Surrey, 1931. Coombe Hill Assistants' Tournament 1951, 1955; semi-finalist British Professional Matchplay 1956; Ryder Cup 1957

Milton, Mrs J. SEE PATERSON, MOIRA

Milwaukee CC USA

Milwaukee, Wis. 18 holes; 6,716 yd (6,141 m)

Charles Blair Macdonald, who introduced golf to Chicago, might also claim responsibility for bringing it to Milwaukee, for in 1894 three Milwaukeans played the Chicago GC and became so enthusiastic that on the way home they organized a committee to form a club of their own. The result is the Milwaukee CC which runs over rolling land along the brown, silty waters of the Mil-

Top, Johnny Miller

Centre, Peter Mills

Above, Milwaukee CC

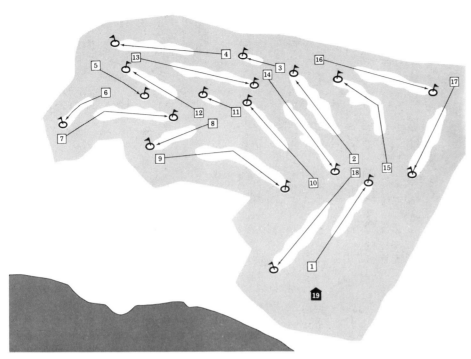

The course plan of Minikahda GC

waukee River. It is probably the top club in Milwaukee, and its 440 members include many of the city's leading citizens. It has been at the same site since 1909, but the present course was not built until 1929 and the clubhouse two years later. Swimming was added in 1957, and at that time a tunnel was dug from the locker room area to the pool, supposedly to keep members away from the front of the clubhouse windows on on their way to a swim.

The course was designed by the British architects, Colt and Alison. It begins on a high hill next to the clubhouse and immediately drops to the fairway far below. From there it moves around the perimeter of the property with a series of fine, long par 4s and two short par 5s. The first 9 finish with a 332-yd (304-m) par 4 to an elevated green, an excellent drive-and-pitch hole. The river swings behind the 11th green, and the 145-yd (133-m) 12th plays across the river as does the 14th. The drive on the 18th must carry the crest of a hill studded with bunkers on the left, leaving a mid-iron to a two-tiered green. This sturdy finishing hole had a good deal to say about the winning and losing of the Walker Cup match held there in 1969.

Minikahda GC USA
Minneapolis, Minn.

When golfers think of Minneapolis, they think of Interlachen because that is where Bobby Jones won the third trick in his Grand Slam – the US Open – but Jones also won

another national championship at another Minneapolis club, Minikahda. That was the 1927 US Amateur. Chick Evans, that other outstanding amateur, won the US Open at Minikahda in 1916. At the time of Evans's victory, cornfields lay close by the course, but all that is changed now. The course itself has changed, too, but the 72-hole score of 286 which Evans posted remains out of reach of all but the very best golfers. Evans was still good enough to be finalist to Jones at Minikahda 11 years later.

The last event of importance to be held on the course was the Walker Cup match of 1957. The United States won that match 8-3, but it was much closer than the score indicates, and at one point in the second day the British were in front. Billy Joe Patton, after standing 5 down to Reid Jack at lunch, sparked off an American recovery by winning those 5 holes back by going out in 32 in the afternoon. Patton eventually won that top single by 1 hole.

Mississaugua GCC CANADA
Port Credit, Ont. 18 holes; 6,820 yd (6,236 m); par 70

The challenging course takes full advantage of its setting. It makes a complete sweep of the Credit Valley, on several occasions playing across the river which flows through it. The greens average about 7,500 sq ft (700 m²) in area and present no great problem. The premium at Mississaugua is on length and accuracy from the tees, which

are required in order to allow the greens to be attacked from the proper angle. The first championship of the Canadian Professional Golfers' Association was held there in 1912 when it was won by Charles R. Murray. The course has never failed to produce a worthy Canadian Open Champion on all five occasions the tournament has been played over it. In 1931 it was Walter Hagen, who tied with Percy Allis and then beat him with a score of 141 in a 36-hole play-off. His prize was a mere $500 from a total purse of $1,500. In 1938 the winner was Sam Snead. He tied with Harry Cooper with a score of 277, remained tied with him at 67 after an 18-hole play-off, and finally triumphed by 5 strokes over a further 9 holes. The 1942 event produced Craig Wood as champion with a score of 275; 1951 Jim Ferrier with 273; and 1965 Gene Littler also with 273, 1 stroke less than Jack Nicklaus. The club's situation is an historic one. It is on the site of an Indian village of the Mississaugua branch of the great Ojibway nation. It was visited in 1795 by Governor Sir John Simcoe and his party as they paddled up the old Credit River. Within sight from the present clubhouse were the tribal burial grounds, and many Indian relics found in the vicinity have been contributed to the Ontario Museum. Fortunate indeed were the members of the former Highland GC in Toronto when they founded the Mississaugua in 1905.

Mitchell, Abe BRITISH
b. East Grinstead, Sussex, 1887; d. 1947. Runner-up British Amateur 1912; British Professional Matchplay 1919-20, 1929; Ryder Cup 1929, 1931, 1933

Often described as the best golfer who never won a British Open, Mitchell was a glorious striker of the ball who won three Matchplay Championships. With George Duncan he inherited the throne vacated by the Triumvirate after the war, but lacked something of their indomitable stonewall quality and love of fighting. A retiring, gentle soul, he was a powerful hitter, his feet rooted to the ground as he swung the club with a pair of massive hands. Horace Hutchinson 'discovered' this gentle gardener son of the golfing clan at Ashdown Forest. He played for England against Scotland in 1910, and in the semi-final of the Amateur lost to John Ball. They met again in 1912 in an historic final at Westward Ho!, Ball winning the last of his eight titles at the 38th after Mitchell had missed from 4 ft for the match at the 36th. In 1913 Mitchell turned professional and in the last Open before the war finished joint 4th. In all he finished in the first 6 five times. After the war he and Duncan appropriately tied the first major tournament, and at Deal in 1920 he lost a chance to win the Open. In the lead by 6 strokes after two rounds, he started the final round disastrously and finished in 84, Duncan the winner making up 13 strokes on him. Of that day Bernard Darwin wrote: 'If Mitchell had won that time he might have won again and again for he was a truly magnificent golfer armed at all points.' His third matchplay victory came in 1929 and made sure of his place in the Ryder Cup team. He was beaten 9 and 8 by Diegel, but won the three foursomes in which he played, and avenged his earlier defeat in the singles by beating Dutra by the same margin in 1933.

Mixed Foursomes

One in which each pair consists of a man and a woman.

Miyamoto, Tomekichi JAPANESE

b. nr Rokko 1902

Miyamoto's position as the elder states- man of Japanese professional golf is undis- puted. In the early days when competition was not so fierce and the rewards not so lucrative, Miyamoto won the Japanese Open Championship six times, the Pro- fessional Championship four times, and innumerable lesser events. His home was not far from Rokko where the first Japanese course was built, opening one year before he was born, and where he learned the game as a caddie, starting when he was 11 years old.

After turning professional he was associ- ated with the Ibaraki CC near Osaka until the outbreak of World War II. Invited to the Hawaiian Open Championship in 1929, he was the first Japanese professional to play overseas. Two years later he received an invitation from the professional director, Bob Harlow, to visit the United States, in company with two other Japanese pro- fessionals, Yasuda and Asami. They went from end to end of the country playing most of the leading professionals of the day, including Walter Hagen, Joe Kirkwood, Gene Sarazen, Horton Smith, and Tommy Armour.

Moe, Donald K. AMERICAN

b. 1909. Oregon Amateur 1928, 1937, runner-up 1927, 1929, 1933; runner-up Pacific Northwest Amateur 1928, 1937-8; Western Amateur 1929, 1931; Walker Cup 1930, 1932; runner-up Canadian Amateur 1953

An outstanding amateur from the Pacific Northwest who won two Western Amateurs, the first when he was only 19, and was a

member of two Walker Cup teams. Moe played perhaps the best golf of his career during the 1930 Walker Cup matches at Sandwich. In his singles match against Stout, Moe went out in 32 only to find himself 1 down to Bill Stout, who had six 3s on his card. Moe was 4 down after 18 holes and 7 down after 21, then staged a great rally to win on the 36th. He had a 67 for the final 18. He was out of competition during the mid- 1930s because of illness.

Moffitt, Ralph Lawson BRITISH

b. Ryton, Co. Durham, 1932. Tied 1st Dunlop Masters 1963, runner-up 1962-4; runner-up British Professional Matchplay 1961; Ryder Cup 1961

In 1961 Ralph Moffitt played six con- secutive tournament rounds in 67 apiece.

Mohammed Said Moussa EGYPTIAN

b. 1933. Desert Open 1955; Egyptian Open 1958, 1960-2, 1964-6, 1969-73

Known popularly at home and abroad as 'Doche'. Mohammed Said Moussa won the Desert Open Championship at the old Maadi sand course near Cairo in 1955, beating Hassan Hassanein by 1 stroke. He has achieved 12 victories in the Egyptian Open and represented his country 13 times in the World (Canada) Cup, beginning in 1957 at Tokyo and including 1971 at Palm Beach Gardens. At present head profes- sional at the Alexandria Sporting Club, he is clearly the best Arab golfer in the world

today. However, his foreign tournament play is limited by Egyptian travel and foreign exchange restrictions.

Mombasa GC KENYA

Mombasa. 9 holes

Mombasa GC, the second oldest in Kenya, was formed in 1911 with a com- mittee consisting of a company director and two bank managers. They obtained from the Government a grant of land running alongside the channel to Kilindini Harbour, and showed such obvious enthusiasm that would-be members helped clear the neces- sary bush and scrub in order to build a course.

Three holes were ready that same year and a full 9 with 'browns' was completed by 1912. The course is still only 9 holes but there are alternate tees and, since 1960, grass greens of a Mozambique strain (originally imported by the Nyali GC). This justifies its claim to be among the best in Kenya.

Monsheim GC WEST GERMANY

18 holes; 6,870 yd (6,282 m); par 72

A recent addition to Germany's new 18-hole courses, Monsheim is situated about 25 minutes from the centre of Stuttgart, home of Daimler-Benz. It occupies farming country with gently sloping hills, bordering here and there on dense forest. Most of its fairways are wide open, making the approach to the fairly large greens easy. The chief difficulty lies in well-placed bunkers and in the rough which is usually high and thick. The course continues to mature and may yet achieve championship standard. A particularly tricky hole is the 12th where a small lake lies beside the green. The short 8th also poses a problem at the forest edge with steep sloping ground to either side of the green. Many trees have been planted

Donald K. Moe

Ralph Moffitt

which will in time provide a more scenic background. There is no public transport to the course and a car is required, but the clubhouse is comfortable and commands a fine view over the course.

Montreal GC, Royal CANADA

Île Bizard, Que. Blue Course 18 holes, 6,740 yd (6,163 m), par 70; Red Course 18 holes, 6,730 yd (6,154 m), par 71; The Nine 9 holes, 3,185 yd (2,912 m), par 35

Founded in November 1873 as Montreal GC, the club is the oldest in North America. In 1884 Queen Victoria granted it permission to assume the prefix 'Royal'.

The club's present site on an island close to the Island of Montreal, which it has occupied since 1958, is the third in its history. Its two championship courses as well as the 9-hole course were designed by the American golf architect Dick Wilson. They feature huge, raised greens of interesting shape, strongly bunkered on either side of their narrow entrances but quite open towards the back and behind. Their surfaces, seeded with bent grass, are exceptionally true. Unusually long tees permit the courses to be played several hundred yards shorter than their championship lengths. Strong winds from the nearby Lake of Two Mountains regularly add to their difficulty. No major tournament has yet been played over them, except the 1965 championship of the Canadian Professional Golfers' Association when the winning score totalled 5 over par for three rounds played mainly from forward positions on the tees, although in wet weather. From the clubhouse veranda the sweeping view of golf extends excitingly almost as far as the eye can see.

The first 23 years of the club's existence were spent on Fletcher's Field on the eastern slopes of Mount Royal, now in the heart of Montreal. There the members repaired each Wednesday and Saturday to play. In 1876 the club began a series of inter-club matches with Quebec GC in Quebec City which had been formed the year before. They have been played continuously since, except for war years. In 1881 the club brought from England the first professional to move to North America, W. F. Davis of Hoylake. He was given his passage and his wages were £1 a week. He also received all that he could earn for making and repairing clubs and balls. His tariff included 2s 6d for a clubhead, 2s for making a shaft and 4d for making up a ball. For teaching beginners his charge was one shilling a round of 9 holes, one-third of which had to be returned to the club. Coupled with his duties as professional he had charge of the greens and was expected to do the manual work.

By 1896 the club was forced by increasing membership and crowded conditions to move to Dorval on Lake St Louis, 10 miles from the centre of Montreal, where it was to remain for over 60 years. The area was known as 'Dixie' from the name of the nearby railroad station. There a 12-hole course was developed. It was later extended to 18 holes, and then in the early 1920s expanded to two fine 18-hole courses. They were designed by Willie Park Jr, of Musselburgh, and they measured 6,453 yd (5,901 m) and 6,527 yd (5,968 m) in length. A number of historic events occurred there. In 1898 there began inter-club competition with The Country Club of Brookline, Mass., which has been played ever since, except for war years. This competition is believed to constitute the oldest continuous series of international golf matches anywhere in the world. Harry Vardon played a round at the club in 1900, as did the Prince of Wales in 1917 and 1927. The Canadian Seniors' Golf Association was formed at meetings held at the club in 1918, W. R. Baker, CVO, of Royal Montreal being its founder and president. The Canadian Open Championship and the Canadian Amateur Championship were contested over the club's courses many times in their early years. But pressure of urban development eventually obliged the club to move again. And so the present ground on Île Bizard was acquired in 1956, and work completed two years later.

From its inception the club has been the premier golf club in Canada. With a membership of more than 1,600 it is also the largest. Mindful of the position of leadership thrust upon it by history, the club has always been found in the forefront of the development of golf in Canada. It celebrated its centenary in due style in 1973 by inviting teams from every 'Royal' club in the world to take part in a stableford competition.

Montserrat

The island of Montserrat, in the Leeward and Windward Islands, boasts a course that is generally accepted as one of the best in the British West Indies. The Belham River Valley GC has an 11-hole course which provides two 9-hole loops. It commands wonderful views: the Caribbean to the west, a 1,000-ft hill to the south, and to the north another of 600 ft and views towards a mountain range rising to 1,000 ft. Beautiful tropical trees line the fairways: a dozen different kinds have been counted beside the first 250 yd (230 m) of fairway at the first hole. The course is well watered by the Belham River which meanders through it, crossing the fairways five times. It provides enough water for green fairways and excellent Bermuda-grass greens throughout the year. The Old Course, 3,200 yd (2,925 m) for 9 holes, is a fine test with a magnificent second hole of 575 yd (526 m). The New Course, 3,042 yd (2,782 m) for 9 holes, cuts out nos 3 and 4 holes on the Old, and has separate tees and greens so that only the 1st, 7th and 8th holes are identical on the two courses. The New is the easier of the two and was laid out to avoid climbing. The clubhouse is a 200-year-old building, originally designed as a cotton gin by a British planter. The course, running from sea to mountain, was the work of Edmund Alt.

Monza GC ITALY

Milan (Milano). 18 holes, 6,900 yd (6,309 m), par 72; 9 holes, 3,400 yd (3,109 m)

Situated in what was once a royal park, Monza was designed as an 18-hole course by an Englishman called Blandford before World War II. It was modernized in the early 1960s and another 9 holes added.

Moody, Orville AMERICAN

b. Chickacha, Okla., 1933. US Open 1969; World Series of Golf 1969

A player who has never taken a lesson in his life and who is not a believer in regular practice, Orville Moody surprised everyone

by his victory in the 1969 US Open at Houston.

Son of a golf-course superintendent, Moody won the Oklahoma State Scholastic Golf Championship. He was offered an athletic scholarship to the University of Oklahoma but left college shortly after enrolling in 1953 and enlisted in the US

Orville Moody

Army. During his 14-year service career he won three Korean Opens and was All-Service Champion in 1962. He left the army and qualified for his player's ticket from the USPGA in 1967 and decided to give himself a two-year trial on the tour.

In 1968 he won a mere 12,950 dollars but, taking a week's vacation before the 1969 Open, he proved himself to the world at the Champions' Club at Houston. After opening rounds of 71 and 70 he moved into 2nd place with a round of 68 and then, as others encountered all manner of trouble, returned a final 72 for a total of 281 and victory by 1 stroke from Beman, Geiberger and Rosburg.

A superb driver and a reliable cross-hand putter, Moody won the unofficial World Series of Golf later in the year and was elected Player of the Year, winning a total of just over $79,000.

Moor Park GC ENGLAND

Rickmansworth, Hertfordshire. 36 holes; High 6,652 yd (6,083 m), par 71; West 6,011 yd (5,469 m), par 69

Before World War II Oxhey, Sandy Lodge and Moor Park formed a distinguished golfing triangle in the relative peacefulness of Hertfordshire countryside on the outskirts of London. Oxhey has long since been submerged by suburban housing – indeed the whole area is rather more urban than rural – but Sandy Lodge and Moor Park, separated by a railway, have survived. Moor Park represents the best of parkland golf and has long been popular as a setting for professional tournaments. The two courses lie over pleasantly undulating country with a number of fine old trees lending character to the golf. The High with its well-guarded greens is the better of the two, or to be more accurate, the best of the three, since the adjoining Rickmansworth Municipal is maintained by the same staff.

Moor Park's history is older than the game itself. Fragments of Roman tiles found in 1935 near the present clubhouse suggest that there had been a Roman villa here until the 5th century A.D., and records of the Manor of More go back to 1200. In 1470 the Archbishop of York acquired the property and under Henry VIII it came into the possession of Cardinal Wolsey. After his downfall the estate was seized by the King and Catherine of Aragon stayed there during her divorce proceedings. The present mansion was built in 1678, some believe by Christopher Wren or one of his pupils. Golf was first played there in 1923, although it did not become a members' club until 1937 when the Rickmansworth Council bought

350 acres (142 ha) and granted a 40-year lease to the club. The clubhouse with its high Grecian portico has been a familiar landmark in the golfing world for years but the West and High owe their origin to the design of H. S. Colt who laid them out to suit all tastes. The club has a huge membership including separate social and tennis

sections, and has in more recent times taken over the running of the Carris Trophy, one of the country's leading boys' events, founded in 1935 by the late Austin Carris in memory of his son. The High is a regular home for county championships. During World War II the Allied airborne Arnhem operation was planned from the clubhouse.

Moor Park GC: *top,* the 18th on the High Course and, *above,* looking up the 16th fairway and across the 17th green

Moortown GC ENGLAND
Alwoodley, Leeds, Yorkshire. 18 holes;
6,604 yd (6,039 m)

Moortown, Sand Moor, Alwoodley, and
the site of the old Moor Allerton lie close
together just off the main Leeds-Harrogate
road. Alwoodley is the senior of this distinguished quartet but Moortown, founded
in 1909, is only a year younger. With a
notable history of tournament and championship golf, it is one of the best-known
courses in England. It also has the distinction of having been designed by Alister
Mackenzie when he was honorary secretary
at Alwoodley.

Although the encroachment of building
has long since robbed the club of fully rural
surroundings, the springy turf is the basis of
a fine test of inland golf with emphasis on
straight driving and keeping the ball in play.
The ingredients are varied, including moorland, woods, heather and streams. The start
is long, the first 3 totalling more than
1,300 yd (1,190 m). Five short holes redress
that balance, of which the 8th, built on rock
with trouble on both sides, and called

long been recognized as a championship
course for amateurs. Frank Pennink won the
English Amateur there in 1938. Twenty-
four years later Michael Bonallack won his
first English title there, and tied with
Rodney Foster when the Brabazon Trophy
was held at Moortown for the second time
in 1969. Mrs Frances Smith retained her
title as English Champion there in 1955; it
has also acted as host to the Boys' Championship in 1934, 1958, 1966, and 1972.

Moran, Frank BRITISH
Frank Moran may justly be termed the
doyen of British golf writers. He began
reporting the game in 1911 and for more
than half a century delighted readers of
The Scotsman, not only by his day-to-day
reports, but also by his weekly articles, full
of humour and warmth, with many nostalgic references to the past. The lore of the
game shone in every sentence he wrote. He
is a great raconteur, and had a fund of stories
to sprinkle his speeches with at dinners and
other functions. His tenure of the presidency
of the Association of Golf Writers has been

Chicago Amateur 1937; Illinois Amateur
1940

The most formidable player in the Southwest and one of the country's best amateurs
in the early 1930s. In 1932 he tied 2nd in
the Texas Open against the stars of the
professional tour; the next year he finished
7th in the US Open at North Shore. He
won all his four matches in the Walker Cup.
In the late 1930s he moved to Illinois where
he became a successful businessman. He
turned professional in the early 1960s,
although past 50, saying, 'Better late than
never – I always wanted to be a golf professional'. For all his ability, Moreland
never advanced beyond the fifth round of
the US Amateur; that was in 1936 when he
lost to the eventual winner, Johnny Fischer.

Moretonhampstead SEE MANOR HOUSE
HOTEL GC

Morey, Dale AMERICAN
b. 1919. Indiana Amateur 1943-4; Southern
Amateur 1950, 1964; Indiana Open 1951,
1953, 1957; runner-up US Amateur 1953;

Western Amateur 1953; Walker Cup 1955,
1965; New Orleans Amateur 1957; North
and South Amateur 1964

One of the country's leading amateurs for
almost three decades, Morey was a high-
school basketball star at Martinsville, Ind.
in the late 1930s and won the Indiana High
School title in 1937. He attended Butler,
then graduated from Louisiana State. He
was a professional for a brief period, then
regained his amateur status and first made
his mark in top amateur golf by winning the
Southern Amateur in 1950. In the 1953 US
Amateur Morey birdied the 34th and 35th
at Oklahoma City to bring Gene Littler
back to all square, but lost to a birdie on the
36th. After a period of relative inactivity

'Gibraltar', is outstanding. The course has
recently been redesigned taking in more
woodland.

The club's reputation first extended
beyond the Yorkshire borders with the
staging in 1929 of the first Ryder Cup match
to be held in Britain. Moortown has seen
many other professional events and has for

perpetuated as a mark of the esteem in
which he is held by his fellows.

Moreland, Gus AMERICAN
b. June 1911. Houston Invitation 1930-1;
Texas Amateur 1932-3; Trans-Mississippi
1932-3; Western Amateur 1932; Walker
Cup 1932, 1934; Mexican Amateur 1934;

Moortown GC, the 15th hole

Gus Moreland

Morey came back in 1964 by winning the Southern and the North and South; he also reached the quarter-finals of the US Amateur as he had done in 1954, and was picked for the Walker Cup team 10 years after his first appearance in it. He played fairly regularly in the British Amateur.

Morfontaine GC FRANCE

nr Senlis, Oise. 18 holes, 6,450 yd (5,898 m), par 72; 9 holes, 2,800 yd (2,560 m), par 36 (private course)

Although not considered long enough to stage the French Open Championship or other matches of full international standing, it is probably the best-loved course in the whole Paris area, differing from the majority of them in the nature of its surroundings. Morfontaine has need of few bunkers because the fairways are exceptionally narrow and the rough is almost exclusively heather on a sandy subsoil. This, together with the presence of pine trees and boulders, gives more the impression of a seaside course. Such hazards make up for the comparative shortness of the course, and fairways with little run on them help to stiffen the test. The main course was the creation of Tom Simpson, the British architect. The 9-hole course lies in the property of the Duc de Gramont. Women's championships have frequently been held there, and in 1971 Mrs Catherine de Prado (née Lacoste) playing in the final against the British golfer, Miss Denison-Pender, went round in 62 with only one short putt not holed out. She stood 9 up and naturally went on to win the championship.

Morgan, John Llewellyn BRITISH

b. Llandrindod Wells, Radnorshire, 1918. Welsh Amateur Close 1950-1, runner-up 1952; Walker Cup 1951, 1953, 1955

After four years as a professional Morgan was reinstated as an amateur, and later became the first Welshman to play in the Walker Cup match. His first appearance was in 1951, after successfully defending his title as Welsh Champion. In the 1953 Walker Cup match in the United States, in which he won both his matches, he putted so well during the foursomes that his partner Gerald Micklem never needed more than a tap-in to hole out for 33 holes.

Morgan, Wanda BRITISH

b. Lymm, Cheshire, 1910. English Ladies' 1931, 1936-7; Curtis Cup 1932, 1934, 1936; British Ladies' 1935, runner-up 1931; *Daily Graphic* National Tournament 1941-2; Sunningdale Foursomes 1948; Worplesdon Foursomes 1948

An outstanding player of the 1930s, during which she won one British and three English Championships; she also represented Britain in the Vagliano Cup in this decade, was seven times Champion of Kent in the period 1930-53, and played in eight Home Internationals, 1931-53. Wanda Morgan was prevented from gaining further distinction when she joined the Dunlop sports company as a sales representative. In that capacity she was an unfailing source of encouragement and help to players young and old. She came to the fore in the English Ladies' at Broadstone in 1929 by reaching the semi-finals, and was promptly dubbed one of the 'Kent Kids' – the other being Diana Fishwick (Mrs Critchley) with whom she subsequently was paired several times in foursomes for Britain. She won her British title in 1935 at Royal County Down, defeating another distinguished young golfer, Pam Barton, by 3 and 2 in the final. A fine wooden club player and outstanding with irons, Wanda Morgan was less confident close to the hole, continually experimenting with new putters and methods.

Morocco

Islamic in religion and culture, with a golfing history of some 50 years, Morocco leads the way in golf among the Arab nations, primarily because of King Hassan II's strong participating interest in the game. Bordering the North Atlantic and boasting an annual 300 days of sunshine and year-long golfing weather, Morocco has 13 courses. They are situated in Agadir, Casablanca, Fez, Marrakesh, Meknes, Mohammedia, Rabat, Skhirat, and Tangier. Five of the courses are 18 holes, all are grass, and nine are generally open to visitors at nominal green fees. Tourists are encouraged for King Hassan's enthusiasm for golf is not purely a personal matter. He also has a business eye on the international tourist market. With that in mind, he commissioned Robert Trent Jones to design a 45-hole complex at the Royal Golf Club Dar-es-Salam near Rabat, the nation's capital, suitable both for major international events as well as for holiday golfers. It includes the Red Course, whose full length is 7,500 yd (6,858 m), and was opened in 1971 for the first Moroccan Grand Prix. The Moroccan Golf Federation, led by the King's brother, Prince Moulay Abdullah, conducts an active programme of amateur and professional promotion, including a free training programme for juniors.

For a time the professional at Marrakesh was the famous Frenchman Arnaud Massy, the first overseas winner of the British Open.

The course plan of the Royal GC of Dar-es-Salam, near Rabat in Morocco

Morris County GC USA

Morristown, N.J.

The ruthless march of the bulldozers through private and public property has threatened and destroyed some of the best American golf clubs near metropolitan centres. Some clubs have been able to come to terms with 'progress', and one of the happiest of these is Morris County on Punch Bowl Road, a leafy oasis on the outskirts of Morristown not far from New York City. The club is an institution of historic interest, for when it came into being during the game's formative years in the United States, it was organized as a golf club exclusively for women. Although it could not quite make a go of it that way, the distaff influence is still strongly felt there. The second US Women's Amateur Championship was held at Morris County in 1896, and again in 1905. The men's Amateur was held there in 1898.

Built with women's play in mind, the course has been revised to meet modern conditions down through the years. Its members are devoted both to their club and

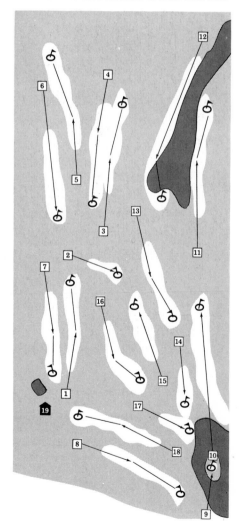

to the game of golf, and in recent years have been in the forefront in the promotion of junior golf. The professional at the club is Walter Kozak, and both he and his wife are regular subscription-paying members. If this is not actually unique, and it may be, it is rare enough to indicate something about the club.

Morris, John Ogilvie Fairlie

Younger brother of Young Tom Morris, J. O. F. Morris, named after Colonel John Ogilvie Fairlie who was responsible for Old Tom's going to Prestwick, was a fine golfer. He finished 3rd in the Open Championship of 1878 and joint 4th 1876, but was somewhat overshadowed by the rest of the family. Old Tom also had a third son, but he was a cripple from birth and never took part in competitive golf.

Morris, Tom (Old) BRITISH

b. St Andrews 1821; d. St Andrews 1908. British Open 1861-2, 1864, 1867

Old Tom, as distinct from his equally famous son, Young Tom, was one of the

Old Tom Morris, a portrait by Sir George Reid, 1903

pioneering Scots of professional golf, belonging to the romantic era of St Andrews when Allan Robertson, generally regarded as the first of the great players, was at the height of his powers. Even around the turn of the century, when golf was little known outside Britain, Tom Morris was described as 'known, it may be said without contra-

diction, in each of the four continents of the globe'.

Old Tom was a character and an institution. His beginnings were humble. His father was a letter carrier, living in North Street where Old Tom was born, but later he turned to carrying clubs. It was natural that any youngster living in St Andrews should take to knocking a golf ball about and Old Tom was 10 or 12 when he started. He did so with his left hand below his right, although he soon turned to more conventional methods. It was intended that he should become a carpenter, but at Sandy Herd's suggestion he was apprenticed to Allan Robertson as maker of clubs and balls, serving under him for five years as apprentice and for five as journeyman.

Gradually his game developed as well and Robertson found himself having to cut down his stroke allowance alarmingly until they played level. Old Tom, indeed, had his backers ready for a challenge match with Robertson, who understandably was never disposed to accept, and there are reports that Old Tom beat him twice in unofficial

Young Tom Morris, wearing the British Open Championship Belt

matches, but it was rather as partners that they took the golfing world by storm.

The great match of the time took place in 1849 between Robertson and Old Tom and the two Dunns from Musselburgh. It was played over Musselburgh, St Andrews and North Berwick, the St Andrews pair contriving a desperate recovery at North

Berwick, winning by two holes after being 4 down with 8 to play.

A dispute over the use of the new gutty ball is said to have severed their business connection. For about three years Old Tom was in business as a club and ball maker on his own account but in 1851, at the age of 30, he accepted an invitation to become custodian of the links at the newly formed club at Prestwick.

During this period Robertson died (1859) of jaundice, the Open Championship began (1860) and Old Tom showed himself to be the best player in the country. It was fortunate for him that the start of the championship coincided with his best days; nevertheless he won the title four times and was only dethroned by the sheer brilliance of his own son. Whether Young Tom's rise irked his father or was a matter for intense pride is hard to say, but the old man was once moved to remark in later years, 'I could cope wi' Allan mysel' but never wi' Tommy.'

From the time of his first victory, Old Tom was subjected to repeated pleas to return to St Andrews. For some while he held out, preferring Prestwick's 12-hole course, but in 1865 he succumbed and went back to the 'auld grey toon', where he was appointed greenkeeper to the Royal and Ancient, holding the position until he retired in 1904 and then carrying on in an honorary capacity until his death in 1908.

His funeral was an occasion for universal mourning in St Andrews where he was a familiar figure with characteristic attitudes. When his hands were not in his pockets, he was either grasping a club or filling his pipe in a manner as unmistakable as his grey beard. His golf and his strictly temperate life had a good effect on his fellow professionals and his successors. His shop beside the 18th green which he helped to shape, the many tales about him, and his portrait which hangs in the Royal and Ancient Golf Club are perpetual reminders of him and of his noble influence on the game.

Morris, Tom (Young) BRITISH

b. St Andrews, Fife, 1851; d. St Andrews 1875. British Open 1868-9, 1870, 1872

Certain records in golf, it is safe to say, will never be broken, and the achievement of a son succeeding his father as British Open Champion is almost certainly one of them. In 1868 when Young Tom Morris captured the title won by his father the year before, he started an unequalled succession of victories, and it is round these two Scots that most of early championship history is based. Young Tom was born at St Andrews and soon revealed his gifts. At the age of 13 he won an exhibition match at Perth against another boy for a prize of £5; three years later he won a professional tournament at Carnoustie, defeating Willie Park and Bob Andrew in a play-off. The same year he finished 4th behind his father in the Open, but in 1869, after winning another tournament at Leven, he beat Old Tom into 2nd place in the Open, with the incomparable score of 154.

The margin of his Open victory was 12 strokes in 1870 over R. Kirk, also of St Andrews, an enormous gap to have opened up over 36 holes. In that year he covered three rounds of Prestwick's 12-hole course in 149 strokes, a score never equalled even by Vardon, Taylor, or Braid so long as the gutty ball was in use. Tom's last round was 47, or 1 under 4s. That third victory entitled him to the custody of the championship belt which now rests in the clubhouse of the Royal and Ancient, and caused the suspension of the event for one year until, in 1872, it was revived at Prestwick where Young Tom won for the fourth time. Comparison of scores and players is difficult but his outstanding performances established his clear supremacy over his contemporaries. It has been said that his style lacked classic smoothness, but the great power which his broad shoulders generated gave him the rare gift of squeezing the ball out of the bad lies which abounded, and there was no weakness throughout his whole game. Once he proved himself the master of Davie Strath and Jamie Anderson playing their better ball; and on another occasion he played nothing but singles for a whole week at St Andrews, backing himself each round for 83 and winning every time, then lowering his target to 81 and 80.

In 1874 he finished second in the championship, but his short career was nearing its end. At the end of a foursome match in September, 1875, in which the two Morrises gained revenge for a previous defeat by Willie and Mungo Park, Young Tom was handed a telegram telling him that his wife was dangerously ill. There being no trains, he accepted the loan of a yacht, but before it had cleared North Berwick Harbour another message was received that it was too late. His wife and newborn baby were dead. The first of the great champions never recovered from the shock, for he was devoted to his wife to whom he had been married for only a year. He played one more notable match, against a certain A. Molesworth of Westward Ho!, who was misguided enough to believe he could beat anyone on receipt

of a third. Young Tom's victory by 9 and 7 over two rounds a day for three days, a great portion of the match played in snow, was the last confirmation of his supremacy. On Christmas Day at the age of 24 he died, it is generally considered, of a broken heart. A memorial marking his last resting place in St Andrews Cathedral bears the inscription: 'Deeply regretted by numerous friends and all golfers, he thrice in succession won the championship belt and held it without rivalry and yet without envy, his many amiable qualities being no less acknowledged than his golfing achievements.'

Moselem Springs GC USA
Fleetwood, Pa. 18 holes; par 70

Moselem Springs, built in 1964 by George Fazio, lies in wooded mountainous country in a natural setting of knolls, valleys of various sizes, streams, and ponds. Because of its scenic assets and its first-class design, the course is a pleasure to play. When Fazio was asked to lay out the course, he found the situation ideal: terrain perfectly suited to his purpose and ample acreage. He made full use of all the advantages offered by nature, and the result is an intriguing course, far more difficult than it appears to be, particularly on the second 9 where the holes run closer to the mountain slopes. The US Women's Open was played there in 1968 when the course was only four years old, and it was generally considered a memorable golfing experience.

Mowbray GC SOUTH AFRICA
Mowbray, Cape Province

Built among the sand and bush of the Cape Flats in 1910, the course was enlarged and brought up to championship standard in 1923. After the installation of water on the greens the course staged in 1932 its first

South African Open Championship. In the Western Province Championship there in 1936 new professional and amateur records were set by Alf Padgham (64) and Otway Hayes (67) respectively. The Open returned there in 1960 and 1971.

Muirfield see HONOURABLE COMPANY OF EDINBURGH GOLFERS

Muirhead, Desmond AMERICAN
Muirhead is a brand-new version of the old American success story. Born in Britain and educated at Cambridge, he went into town and city planning after World War II, eventually settling in western Canada. Since many of the new resorts and retirement

Top, the memorial to Young Tom Morris

Above, Moselem Springs GC

communities for 'senior citizens' required an 18-hole golf course as a focal point, Muirhead gradually moved more and more into golf-course design. In the 1960s and early 1970s, operating from headquarters in southern California, he continued his work in town planning and built courses in Massachusetts, New Jersey, Connecticut, Florida, Ohio and elsewhere. A genial man who wears a big black beard of the type that flourished during the Civil War, Muirhead built many courses on which Gene Sarazen served as his consultant. For a while, too, he was associated with Jack Nicklaus.

Mulligan
Slang for a friendly arrangement whereby a player has the option of a second drive from the first tee. It is largely an American habit. Not, of course, practised in serious competition.

Munich GC WEST GERMANY
Strasslach, nr Munich (München). 18 holes; 6,650 yd (6,080 m); par 72
Lying on both sides of the Munich-Bad Tölz road against a background of the Bavarian Alps, this 18-hole course of the Münchener Golfklub is gently undulating with wide fairways. It is ideal, perhaps, for the higher-handicap player since it is not an exacting test and employs a high-class teaching staff. Junior championships have been played on it, but it was primarily designed to meet the growing demand for golf in the Bavarian capital. Munich has a second course, of 9 holes, at Thalkirchen.

Municipal Course
A public course run by a local authority on which anyone may play on payment of a green fee. Two of the great Scottish championship courses, Carnoustie and St Andrews, are run by the town councils, the latter course in conjunction with the Royal and Ancient GC. Though not strictly a public course, Pebble Beach in California does not restrict those who can play there.

Murphy, Robert J. AMERICAN
b. Brooklyn, N.Y. 1943. US Amateur 1965; Walker Cup 1967; Eisenhower Trophy 1966; Philadelphia Classic 1968; Thunderbird Classic 1968; Greater Hartford Open 1970; Australian Wills Tournament 1972
After becoming the first winner of the US Amateur to be decided by strokeplay in 1965 at Tulsa, Okla., Murphy turned professional, winning two tournaments back-to-back in his first year (1966) and becoming

the first 'rookie' to win more than $100,000 in his opening year. Although 1969 was not such a good year for him, he finished only 2 strokes behind the winner of the US Open, Orville Moody, and in 1970 finished in the top 10 in the order of merit.

Murray, Stuart W. T. BRITISH
b. Paisley, Renfrewshire, 1933. West of Scotland Amateur 1958; Scottish Amateur 1962, runner-up 1961; Walker Cup 1963
A heavy, powerful golfer who made a reputation in strokeplay in the West of Scotland. He played for the British team against the Continent of Europe in 1958 before he was picked for Scotland in the Home Internationals. Murray won his single against the Continent by striking a

Top, Robert J. Murphy

Above, Stuart Murray

2 iron to 2 ft against Franco Bevione at the 36th hole. He played with distinction at the head of the field in the 1963 Walker Cup match. He turned professional later that year, but he had left it a little late to hope to shine as he had done as an amateur and settled down at the Northamptonshire Club, later moving to Hendon.

Musselburgh GC, Royal SCOTLAND
Prestonpans, East Lothian. 18 holes; 6,284 yd (5,746 m); par 70
Modestly accepting 1774 as its foundation date, based on the presentation of its famous 'Old Cup', this club among its other distinctions could probably claim to have staged the first annual competition for women, the notable fishwives of Musselburgh. *The Statistical Account of Scotland* gives the club as founded in 1760 and the first surviving minute is dated 1784, but the Old Cup is there to prove that it was presented in 1774.
A minute of 1810 reads: 'The club to present by subscription a handsome new creel and skull [the smaller fish basket attached to the large creel] to the best female golfer who plays on the annual occasion on the 1st January next, to be intimated to the Fish Ladies . . . Two of the best Barcelona silk handkerchiefs to be added to the above premium of the Creels.' *The Statistical Account* (1795) describing these remarkable women states: 'As they do the work of men, their manners are masculine and their strength and activity is equal to their work. On holidays they frequently play at golf; and on Shrove Tuesday there is a standing match at football between married and unmarried women, in which the former are always victors.'
The original Musselburgh course was of 7 holes: in 1833 an eighth was added and, soon after, a ninth, giving a total distance of 2,850 yd (2,606 m) and a par of 39. As the three holes of 400 yd (366 m) and over were all par 5, this is an indication that the feather ball could be hit substantial distances and played accurately. This course was shared with the Honourable Company of Edinburgh Golfers, the Bruntsfield Links and (now) Royal Burgess Clubs, these having fled from encroachments on the links at Leith and Bruntsfield. But in the 1890s they all departed for pastures new and there was slight acrimony when, with the Honourable Company's move in 1891, Musselburgh ceased to be listed as an Open Championship course. But Royal Musselburgh (the coveted prefix came in 1876 when the Duke of Connaught became for many years president of the club) was itself

cramped and in 1924, with the cooperation of the Coal Industry of Scotland Welfare Organization, moved to the estate of Prestongrange where the mansion house provides one of the most impressive club-houses in Britain. The course laid out by James Braid – Harry Vardon, Sandy Herd, J. H. Taylor and Braid opened it with an exhibition match – was slightly altered by Mungo Park soon after World War I.

Musselburgh, apart from possessing the oldest cup, has a remarkable record as a 'cradle'. The early *Statistical Account* noted: 'The golf, so long a favourite and peculiar exercise of the Scots, is much in use here. Children are trained to it in their early days, being enticed by the beauty of the links and the sea, and excited by the example of their parents.' Moreover, the club minutes record annually the gift of golf balls for the scholars of the local school.

Its links (unlike some others in Scotland) is now safe from the fate of which the Account gave dire warning: 'The inhabitants had need to watch over this precious field for health and exercise lest in some unlucky period the Magistrates and Council should be induced to feu it out, on pretence of increasing the revenue of the town . . .' Even then, nearly 200 years ago, 'development' was threatening the environment.

Muthaiga GC KENYA

Nairobi. 18 holes; 6,711 yd (6,137 m)

Situated three miles from the centre of Nairobi in the suburb of Muthaiga 5,500 ft above sea level, the course began as a 9-hole adjunct to the Muthaiga CC in 1913 when a professional was engaged and greens planted. These were watered by gravity from the club's overflow system, but when World War I came the piping was commandeered and the course was taken over by a tented field hospital with the result that the course was neglected. For all practical purposes, the history of the course dates from 1927 when it was extended to 18 holes, a clubhouse was built, and Harry Kinnell engaged as professional.

In 1942 the club bought the land on which the course lay, and in 1949 grass greens were planted under the supervision of Alex Kinnell, who had succeeded his brother when the latter left for the United States in 1931. Having its own bore holes, the club was able to cope with tee and green watering; it installed fairway watering about 1969. Club membership is limited to 600. In 1967 it was the venue for the first Kenya Open Championship, which owed much to the encouragement of Peter Thomson. The club has a good record in Open events and provided the youngest winner of the Kenya Amateur in David Farrar at the age of 19 in 1967. In 1933 R. D. England had the distinction of winning not only the Amateur but also the Kenya Lawn Tennis Championship and the doubles with his son, Jack. The latter became Kenya Amateur Champion, on his own course, exactly 30 years later. Not the least of Muthaiga's notable members was Lord Delamere. He was so attracted by the course that he took up the game with enthusiasm in the 1920s, and almost as rapidly as he made that decision he became the club's president. He was instantly recognizable on the course by his entourage which consisted of one servant carrying his box of cigars, another a box of balls, and a third his fieldglasses. In addition he had a caddie and forecaddies.

Myopia Hunt Club USA

South Hamilton, Mass. 6,353 yd (5,809 m); par 72

In its early years in the United States, golf often was an added attraction at clubs formed for other purposes. This was certainly the case at the Myopia Hunt Club, where even today golf is missing from the club name.

Myopia's founding was based on the possibility that baseball might become a prominent amateur sport. In the winter of 1879 a number of leading sportsmen of Boston decided to build a club where they could play baseball, tennis, the new game of polo, and perhaps engage in horse racing. Most of them wore glasses, and so they named their group the Myopia Club. Gradually, interest in all those sports faded, and in 1883 the members turned to fox-hunting. The club then evolved into the Myopia Fox Hounds. It was formally incorporated as the Myopia Hunt Club in 1892, and two years later golf was first played over the grounds.

The original course was of 9 holes when the US Open was played at Myopia for the first time in 1898. Three more Open Championships were played there – in 1901, 1905, and 1908 – but just when the club acquired more property and expanded the course to 18 holes is not known. As with Merion, the original architect was a club member: Herbert Leeds, an excellent amateur golfer who had played many courses both in the United States and in Britain. Leeds's design stood up until the mid-1950s when Myopia was modernized, although it still retains much of its original concept. Today it is a comfortable course of 6,353 yards, par 72, with 150 members with voting rights and another 150 without. The hunt is still active with 80 members, although they drag hunt now rather than chase a live fox. The pack now numbers 22 couples.

In recent years Myopia has begun to diversify, as it did in the beginning. It has an active tennis programme, and a swimming pool was added in 1966. Even polo has been restarted. Those myopic founders were strangely far-sighted.

Nagle, Kelvin D. AUSTRALIAN
b. Sydney, N.S.W., 1920. New Zealand
Open 1957-8, 1962, 1964, 1967-9; Australian
Open 1959; British Open 1960, runner-up
1962; French Open 1961; Canadian Open
1964; runner-up US Open 1965; World
Seniors' 1971

Although he developed late as a golfer,

Kel Nagle's record of five major national
championships and narrow failure in the US
Open confirm him in the front rank of world
golfers. One of the game's most popular
figures, he was once described by a close
friend as a man 'in whom there is no
malice'. His style is solid and consistent
rather than classical, but his short game has
enviable qualities.

Nagle was 15 when he became assistant
to Tom Popplewell at the Pymble Club near
Sydney, and like many a champion, he
came up the hard way. In the years of
depression before World War II Nagle had
to be content with collecting balls on the
practice ground. He had to wait longer than
two years for admission to the Australian
PGA because that body decided it had
enough assistants. Then came the war
during which he served in New Guinea.
Shortly afterwards Norman von Nida,
Ossie Pickworth, Eric Cremin, and later the
youthful Peter Thomson, provided stiff
opposition but in 1949 Nagle won the
Australian Professional Championship and
in 1954 formed a winning partnership with
Thomson in the second World Cup competition. This was the making of him, but it was
not until after his second victory in that
event, in 1959, that he approached the
height of his powers. He climbed the
pinnacle the following year, 1960, by his
victory in the Centenary British Open at
St Andrews when he held off Arnold Palmer
who, though playing his first British Open,
was then the world's most formidable golfer.
It was an historic occasion. The entry was
the strongest for years and Nagle, in his
40th year, had not hitherto achieved anything comparable; but in a tense climax his
calm good sense and plain, straightforward
thinking prevailed. A lead of 4 had dwindled
to 2 in the final round and when Palmer
birdied the last hole, Nagle needed two 4s to
win. Having played short in 2 at the 17th he
was left with a 10-ft putt for his 4, with
cheers for Palmer's birdie ahead ringing in
his ears. His holing of it was one of the great
competitive putts in the championship's
history. His putting had been inspired from
the first round which put him in the lead,
and his steady nerves justified his reputation
as a 'good front runner'. His total was 278
(69, 67, 71, 71).

In the next 10 years he became one of the
most reliable professionals and he soon
developed the knack of winning, especially
in Britain where he became a regular
visitor. Two other achievements stand out.
In 1962, although Palmer was in quite
irresistible form, Nagle's placid nature
enabled him to stay with him over 36 holes,

facing difficulty from the crowd and
Palmer's brilliance with equal composure.
In 1965 he tied Gary Player for the US
Open at Bellerive, St Louis, on a course that
demanded great patience and in great heat.
He lost the play-off 71 to 74, but it was the
nearest any Australian has come to winning
that event. His victory over Boros in the
1971 World Seniors' Championship was
another mark of his enduring skill. He won
the British Senior title again in 1973 at Elie.

Nairn GC SCOTLAND
Nairn. 18 holes; 6,525 yd (5,966 m); Newton Course 9 holes

One of the fine northern courses of Scotland, Nairn lies along the southern shores of
the Moray Firth. Though golf is generally
regarded as having been played at Dornoch
since an early date, the Nairn club dates
only from 1887. It is a fine example of
traditional seaside golf, the holes going
straight out and back along a narrow neck of
land within view of the sea, and, with luck,
gorse in bloom providing a contrast with the
dark of the pines. It was laid out by Archie
Simpson, who was professional at Royal
Aberdeen, and subsequently both Old Tom
Morris and James Braid made alterations.
It has long been a regular choice for Scottish
championships. The Scottish women first
took their championship there in 1910; their
lead was followed later by the professionals
but it was not until 1954 that the Scottish
Amateur was first held there.

With its views across the water to the
Black Isle or westward to the peaks about
Strath Conon, Nairn has an engaging
beauty, but the natural quality of the golf is
the main reason for its steadily increasing
fame. Among the many fine players Nairn
has produced, Major David Blair is the best
known. The course has an unusually high
number of country members, and gains
further recognition from the Open tournament, dating back to 1907, held every
August.

Nairobi GC, Royal KENYA
Nairobi. 18 holes; 6,901 yd (6,310 m)

Nairobi GC (it did not receive the Royal
warrant until 1935) was formed in 1906
when a 9-hole course was begun near the
King's African Rifle lines, the troops providing a convenient reserve of caddies. By
1907 it was fully operative and had a
changing room of corrugated iron with floor
space of only 16 by 12 ft, although the early
records speak of a spacious rack for bicycles
as well.

These early records, dated 1908, indicate
that civil servants were the prime movers in

Kel Nagle; in the lower picture playing in the
1960 British Open at St Andrews

getting things started and that the same committee appears to have carried on until the first Annual General Meeting in 1910 when the Governor of the colony was elected captain. A club championship was inaugurated in 1910 and lady members admitted in 1916.

In 1911 a new clubhouse was built at a cost of £187 but in 1922 the Commissioner for Lands requested that the building be removed and a third clubhouse erected. At the same time, course extensions to 18 holes were undertaken and completed to coincide with the opening of the new clubhouse.

Progress was rapid after World War I. The club, having been semi-dormant during hostilities, took a leading part in the development of the game of golf with two outstanding personalities as administrators. They were A. C. Tannahill and Major J. D. Leonard, both in turn captain and president. They played a vital part in bringing the Golf Union of East Africa into being in 1923; it was re-formed in 1928 as the Kenya Golf Union and has grown in influence and prestige ever since.

These two were also instrumental in inaugurating the Easter tournament in 1924. This became the most prestigious inter-club event and retains its popularity today. The Easter weekend draws golfers from all over the country and the occasion is taken to hold the Annual General Meeting of the Kenya Golf Union at the same time.

The first Kenya Amateur Championship was held at Nairobi and nine others have followed there; the title had been won by Nairobi or RNGC members seven times by 1971. The club at one time had sufficient land to have 27 holes but the so-called Jubilee Nine were sold in 1971 to the Nairobi City Council for housing.

This provided funds for much-needed development of the course and for a fairway watering system to be added to that of the greens and tees. The club was one of the first to extend its membership to all communities and continues to house important championships. The course, three miles from the centre of Nairobi, is well lined with trees and in September and October the fairways are brightened by the jacarandas in full bloom. The clubhouse veranda looks out across the Athi Plains, and from it, on a very clear day, the volcanic outline and snow-capped 19,565-foot peak of Kilimanjaro are visible.

In 1957, Walter Gitari, in winning the caddies' championship, did so with four borrowed clubs – a brassie, nos 4 and 8 irons, and a putter. He had a perfect round, scoring 18 straight pars.

Nap

A feature of certain grasses used in putting greens that can affect the behaviour of the ball. It is particularly common with broad, coarse-bladed grasses in hot climates where growth is fast and less sturdy varieties would not survive. In extreme cases, the surface of the green resembles an upturned brush and has to be 'read' most carefully in order to predict how the ball will react.

Nassau

Three matches in one. A point is allotted for the result of the first 9 holes of a match, another for the second 9, and another for the overall eighteen. A dollar Nassau therefore means a dollar on the first 9, a dollar on the second and a third on the match.

Nassau GC BAHAMAS
Nassau, New Province Island. 18 holes; 6,812 yd (6,229 m)

Although golf was played in the Bahamas as early as the 18th century, it was only in the late 1920s that it began to take root. At that time a 9-hole course with sand greens was laid out in the grounds of Fort Charlotte. This proved popular, but it was not until Charles Munson of the Munson Shipping Line leased land three miles west of the town that the Nassau GC became established. Golf in the island then began to be played all the year round.

The original 18-hole course, designed by Devereux Emmet, was bordered by the beautiful Cable Beach, and recently underwent changes when it was taken over as part of the Sonesta Beach Hotel and Golf Club complex. Carved out of Prospect Ridge, with its stately colonial and Spanish-style villas and mansions, the course threads its way round eight lakes and has many bunkers. It has regularly been the scene of tournaments and international events. The new $15-million development allowed for a second 18 holes and clubhouse, 100 electric carts, and a complete watering system pumping 100,000 gallons a day onto the course. Also planned were tennis courts, riding stables, and hockey pitches.

National Golf Links of America USA
Southampton, Long Island, N.Y. 18 holes; 6,650 yd (6,081 m)

'The National' is situated on Sebonac Bay near the tip of Long Island, a few miles from Southampton. Membership is composed today, as always, of the well-to-do and socially prominent who summer in that area. They are properly enthusiastic about their course – the more so since the installation of a watering system prevents fairways from burning out during dry summers – but, when all is said and done, the National is no longer in the national consciousness as once it was and still should be. This is regrettable for two reasons: little altered since it opened for play in 1911, the course is a fascinating challenge still for even the best modern golfers, although it is relatively short; and, since it is so unchanged, it is nothing less than a living museum, for it was the first great course to be built in the United States, and as such it served to educate a whole continent of keen but untutored golfers in the subtle art of golf architecture.

The man behind the National was Charles Blair Macdonald, a Chicago financier who had learned golf as a student at St Andrews University – well enough to win the first US Amateur Championship, in 1895. A few years before, he had built the country's first 18-hole course for the Chicago GC. A man who liked to win, Macdonald designed the course so that the holes followed along the perimeter of the plot in a clockwise direction, for this meant that golfers who hooked were constantly in danger of going out of bounds, while Macdonald, a chronic fader, had no such worries. Having learned golf at the cradle of the game, he was continually vexed by the failure of his countrymen to perceive how little they knew about golf and golf courses, and how much he did.

His strong desire to correct this defect was a main reason for his building the National, but there was a lot more to it. The idea first came to him in 1901 when the British magazine *Golf Illustrated* ran a series 'The Best Hole Discussion', in which its readers submitted their candidates for the best holes of varying lengths in the British Isles. Why not build a course in the United States which would feature holes modelled after the outstanding holes in the old country? A born salesman, Macdonald persuaded 70 men to put up one thousand dollars each. Work did not start until 1907 and the course did not open for play for another four years, but the National turned out to be a tremendous success in every respect. British authorities such as Horace Hutchinson, Ben Sayers, Harold Hilton and Bernard Darwin enthused over it, and as often as not they liked Macdonald's versions of the Alps, the Eden, the Road and the Redan holes and others at least as much as they did the originals. American visitors loved the course, too; it took them a little time to understand why Macdonald had dispensed with such artificial concoctions as chocolate-drop mounds and cross-bunkers that spanned the width of the fairway, but in time they absorbed the lecture in strategic design that

lay unfolded before them. They returned home and tried to bring their courses up to this new standard.

The National has been host to only one significant event, the first Walker Cup meeting in 1922: another important event there might call attention once again to this historic course. For a friendly round of golf few courses in the United States still can equal it. It begins unimpressively with two short par 4s – the opening hole is only 320 yd (293 m) and the second 271 yd (248 m) from the championship tees. Then slowly the course begins to stretch out, although total yardage for the first nine is only 3,227 (2,951 m) from the championship tees. The second 9 is longer and also appreciably more scenic, for the last 7 holes wend their way beside Sebonac Bay. The course sets a fine variety of problems. For example, unlike nearly all the American courses of the past 40 years, its fairways are replete with dips and hollows and ripples, and to score well a man must be adept at playing from a variety of lies. The landing area for the drive on many holes is on the tight side, and in the green area the bunkering can be stringent. All in all, a charming, evocative and stimulating course, and if there is a fresh wind, no pushover even for a Palmer or a Nicklaus.

Macdonald, after his triumph with the National, was besieged with requests to build similarly sensational courses elsewhere. He built some splendid courses (among them Yale, Mid-Ocean, Piping Rock, and Lido)

but none of them really approached the National in technical skill or in the spirit of golf it projects. The National is an inspired piece of work, and very few golf courses are.

Nelson, John Byron, Jr AMERICAN

b. Fort Worth, Tex., 1912. Ryder Cup 1937, 1939, 1947 (non-playing captain 1965); US Masters 1937, 1942; US Open 1939, joint runner-up 1946; USPGA 1940, 1945, runner-up 1939, 1941, 1944; French Open 1955

Nelson's fame is less than some other great American golfers because his comparatively short spell at the top coincided with World War II, but his achievements in scoring were as fine as any in the history of the game. The probability is that he would have won more than five major championships had not the war ended all major championships except the USPGA; for his record of scoring in 1944 and 1945 was one of sustained brilliance that has never been equalled. It has been said that because of the absence of others on war service and because the USPGA relaxed certain rules about the number of clubs carried and preferred lies, Nelson had things easier during that spell. But to have sustained rounds under par for so long entitles him, apart from his other achievements, to be considered among the greatest players of all time.

He was born in 1912 at Fort Worth and worked his way up from the caddie ranks just as Ben Hogan did, and from the same birthplace. He turned professional in 1933;

four years later came his first major triumph when he caught up 6 strokes at 2 holes in the final round at Augusta on Ralph Guldahl to win his first Masters. In winning the US Open two years later he had to go 36 holes in the play-off for at the end of 18 he was still tied with Craig Wood, although Shute had been eliminated. He owed his lead, which he never relinquished, in that final 18 to holing his no. 1 iron shot to the 4th for an eagle 2, whereas Wood took a par 4. In addition that year he won the North and South, the Western, and the Vardon Trophy, being runner-up in the USPGA. In the Masters of 1942 he won again on a play-off, this time in an epic match against Ben Hogan. Nelson gained 5 strokes on him in 11 holes and was 6 under par in doing so; yet he won only by 1 stroke. In 1944 Nelson won 13 of the 23 events for which he entered and was leading money winner with a record total of $37,000. The following year at the age of 33 he won 11 official professional tournaments in succession, one of them a four-ball. Of the 31 tournaments he played in that year, he won 18, was second seven times and never finished lower than 9th. He achieved a stroke average of 68.33 and scored at one stage 19 straight rounds under 70. It has been estimated that he was a total of 320 under par for the tournaments in which he played, and that his total prize money of about $60,000 would have been, in the context of modern golf, about $600,000 for the same number of

victories. His four-round total of 259 on the par-70 course at Broadmoor was a USPGA tournament record until beaten by Mike Souchak with 257 in 1955.

Nelson, although the same age as Hogan, had reached the climax of his career while his fellow Texan was still climbing upwards. In 1947, after losing this time in another three-way play-off for the Open title, Nelson virtually withdrew from competitive golf. He was not constitutionally a strong man. Being a 'free bleeder' – he once said it took his blood 12 minutes to congeal compared with two and a half for normal people – he was barred from active service in the war, and the tournament circuit at the pitch he played it took a premature toll of his physical condition. He is in any case a fine teacher with deep understanding of the game, and when television came his Southern drawl was soon recognized as an asset by the golf-conscious American Broadcasting Corporation. But before he gave up competitive golf completely he left behind for the postwar generation one last example of his artistry. In 1955 he played in the British Open at St Andrews. It was not his only appearance; in 1937 he visited with the American Ryder Cup team, and staying on for the Open finished 5th to Cotton at Carnoustie. The second time he was in the autumn of his career and did not score well, but he crossed to Paris and won the French Open with a dazzling display of iron play.

His long spell of low scoring led people to think he was some kind of machine. In fact he was, according to contemporary reports, an adventurous player, attempting unexpected shots with the longer irons, of which he was a master. He did not have an outstanding reputation as a putter, but he was a magnificent driver, able to manoeuvre the ball to within a few yards of where he wanted it. Well over 6 ft in height with huge

hands, he relied more on controlled sway than pivot for his power, and hit the ball with a pronounced dip in his swing, as did Cary Middlecoff and other tall men. He played in two Ryder Cup matches 10 years apart: 1937 when he lost his single to a newcomer, Dai Rees, and 1947 when at Portland, Ore., he beat Arthur Lees. In 1974 he won the Bob Jones Award for his outstanding contribution to the game.

Net Score
A player's score when his handicap has been deducted.

Netherlands
Golfers have long argued about the origins of their game and it seems that nobody will ever produce an answer to satisfy everyone. The real point at issue is whether a game played centuries ago in Holland is a true forerunner of golf, or just a game bearing a strong resemblance. The game was *kolfspel*, so called because it was played with a club (*kolf*, plural *kolven*, in Dutch; the verb *kolven* means 'to play *kolfspel*'). Early Dutch painters show several forms of *kolfspel*, particularly one played on ice and another, still common today, played in an enclosed space. A portrait that hangs in the Kennemer GCC, 'The Young Golfer', 1635, unmistakably shows a lad holding a golf club, or something closely akin to it. However, S. J. H. van Hengel, whose diligent and valuable research is reported in a booklet *Early Golf History and Development* (1971), makes no claim 'to prove conclusively where golf came into its own' nor does he claim to establish when the present indoor version of *kolfspel* started.

Doubt may surround the early days of *kolven* or proto-golf in Holland, but the modern part of the story dates precisely from 1893 when the Haagsche GC was founded at The Hague. The Golf Club 'De Pan', originally the Doornsche GC, followed at Utrecht in 1894. Then came the Rosendaelsche club at Rozendaal near Arnhem in 1896, the Kennemer club and one at Hilversum in 1910.

The Dutch Open Championship was started in 1919. Two years later the Dutch International Amateur and Ladies' championships got under way. Play came to a standstill during the German occupation of World War II and several courses suffered damage. The worst affected were those along the coast at Domburg, The Hague, Noordwijk and Kennemer where the Germans built fortifications as part of their *Westwall*. The Haagsche GC moved from Waalsdorp to nearby Wassenaar but the

other three clubs rebuilt their courses at great expense over a number of years and gradually Dutch golf found its feet again.

Golf now thrives in the Netherlands and the number of courses, 22 in 1971, continues to rise. New projects include a fine seaside lay-out at Noordwijk, public courses at Amsterdam and Haarlem, and an ambitious 27-hole scheme north of the latter city. Many Dutch courses have great quality and variety; those at The Hague, Kennemer and Noordwijk occupy some of the grandest dune country in the world.

The best-known Dutch players over the years have been the professionals Gerry de Wit, Martin Roesink, and Joyce de Witt Puyt.

Byron Nelson making his victory speech after the 1965 Ryder Cup Match

Top, Mrs A. E. Eschauzier of the Netherlands in the European Ladies' Team Championship of 1971

Above, Jack Francis Neville

Neville, Jack Francis AMERICAN

b. St Louis, Mo., 1893. Walker Cup 1923

Jack Neville, a former Californian Amateur Champion, played in the Walker Cup at St Andrews in 1923, but he is best remembered as the man who, with Douglas Grant, was responsible for designing Pebble Beach, scene of the 1972 US Open and one of the most renowned courses in the world. Although neither Neville nor Grant had much experience of designing golf courses when commissioned by Sam Morse, head of the Del Monte Properties, it is doubtful whether anyone could have made better use of an exceptional opportunity. The result, a mixture of superb ocean holes and a contrasting stretch largely inland in character, forms a lasting memorial to its designers. Few changes have been made over the years but Neville, who did little other work in this field, was consulted about minor alterations for the US Open of 1972. Neville also designed the Bel-Air course, Los Angeles.

Newcastle GC AUSTRALIA

Fern Bay, N.S.W. 18 holes; 6,600 yd (6,035 m)

The Newcastle GC was formed in 1905 and moved to its present site in 1915, when its professional was Fred Popplewell. Two hundred acres (81 ha) of sand-based land was bought, but the second 9 holes, designed by Eric Apperley, did not come into play until 1936. The present clubhouse was opened in 1971.

Newell, Ursula Bridget Constance BRITISH

b. Eldwick, Yorkshire, 1911; d. Turnberry, Ayrshire, 1937. Runner-up British Ladies' 1936

Runner-up to Pam Barton in the British Ladies' Championship at Southport and Ainsdale in 1936, by which time she had become one of the most consistent players in England, having reached the last eight of the British in 1935 and of the English in 1935 and 1936. She was a reserve for the 1936 Curtis Cup match, and after playing for Britain against France and in the Vagliano Cup against the Continent she went to Turnberry to compete in the British championship. She had been complaining of a bad throat which continued to trouble her. Her death came suddenly and the Home Internationals, which preceded the championship and in which she had played the previous year, were cancelled in remembrance of her. The daughter of a judge, she had herself qualified as a barrister and was the youngest magistrate in England. Her personality was gay and vivacious, and her golf was forceful

and inspiring to her contemporaries.

Newport CC USA

Newport, R.I. 18 holes

Most golfers have probably read somewhere that the first US Open Championship was played at Newport, Rhode Island, and was won by a young Briton named Horace Rawlins. They may not know that the first US Amateur Championship was played at the same time, or that this is the same Newport where the first 34 US Lawn Tennis Championships were held, not to mention the place from which so many yachts have set hopefully forth to race for the America's Cup. All four of these momentous sporting events had their start in Newport, long the resort of the affluent society.

The ground on which the first American golf championships were played in 1895 was said to be the first 9-hole course on the American side of the Atlantic, a highly disputable assertion. There is no doubt about the championships, though. There were 11 entries for the Open and 32 for the Amateur which was won by Charles Blair Macdonald. The Amateur was the important one; the Open was just an afterthought. Newport society today is neither so affluent nor so exclusive as it was then. Some of the old families are struggling along on only a dozen or so servants, and some of the old palaces are closed or open for inspection on payment of a fee. The 9 holes of that original championship course are no longer identifiable. The present course, set back a little from the shoreline, swings past the famous Bailey's Beach, where society swims and suns, and out towards Narragansett Bay. The club is a comparatively modest place. The course, though not among the great ones, presents a nice comfortable test.

New South Wales GC AUSTRALIA

La Perouse; Sydney. 18 holes; 6,667 yd (6,096 m)

Not far from Sting Ray Harbour, where Captain Cook anchored in the *Endeavour* on 29 April 1770, the New South Wales club came into existence at Cape Banks, La Perouse, near Sydney on 23 June 1928. It was opened by the Governor-General, Lord Stonehaven, some years after a group of stalwarts saw the possibility of turning a wilderness of dense scrub into one of Australia's finest links, similar in character to some of the British seaside courses where the game began. At La Perouse the golfer is always within sight and sound of the sea around Botany Bay, that cradle of Australian history; but the club hardly seemed to have had time to become established when in

1942 the links and clubhouse were requisitioned for the nation's defence. By February 1946, when the course was handed back, members faced a similar task to that faced by the pioneers of the 1920s, but enthusiasm won through again. Major alterations were completed late in 1951, and shortly afterwards the course, differing greatly from its pre-war lay-out, was awarded championship status. Among the golfers who learned to play there was Bruce Crampton who went on to make a name for himself in the United States.

New Zealand

Just how many countries owe the founding and fostering of their first golf club to the influence of the British, and in particular the Scots, is hard to say, but it is many. Certainly the father of New Zealand golf, Charles Ritchie Howden, was an Edinburgh Scot who emigrated and worked on sheepruns in Otago. Legend has it that golf was fitfully played during the 1860s, but the first verifiable date was September 1871, when Howden, by then in business in Dunedin, where he later started the New Zealand Distillery Company, took the chair at a meeting at Wains Hotel and was elected captain of the Dunedin club, later called the Otago.

Although one of the first duties of the committee was 'to provide the necessary playing material for members until regular supplies could be obtained', interest and activity quickly built up so that members mustered 'in pretty good force' to compete for the club's Silver Cup. Other early trophies still preserved by the Otago club were the St Andrews Cross and the Bruntsfield Medal. In March 1872, golfing activity was also reported in Christchurch, where 'materials' were awaited by the next San Francisco steamer. A year later the Christchurch became New Zealand's second club, thanks primarily to the bearers of two more Scottish names, Messrs Duncan and Jameson. But its days were numbered for other sports interfered with the game at Hagley Park and cattle damaged the greens. With the Dunedin club running into similar difficulties, neither club could continue and organized golf lapsed in New Zealand for almost 20 years.

It was what G. M. Kelly, in his centennial history, *Golf in New Zealand*, called the 'false dawn', but under the influence of new settlers Christchurch, with its strong English community, led a revival in 1891. Three of its members, W. T. Charlewood, Professor F. H. Haslam, and Dr George Gosset, had learned their golf at Westward Ho!, and

was about to begin junior year in high school when a car accident left him with multiple injuries to his pelvis, spleen, liver and one kidney. He was told he would never walk again but like Ben Hogan, from whom he received two inspirational letters, he not only walked again but became a champion. He won two high-school golf titles and went to college in Texas on a football scholarship as none was available for golf.

Nichols turned professional in 1959, joined the tour in 1960, and showed steady improvement until in 1962 he won two tournaments, tied 3rd in the United States Open and finished 6th in the USPGA. He rounded off 1964 with a $35,000 1st prize in the Carling Open. He lost the US Masters by 1 stroke to Gay Brewer in 1967 and the same year at Houston scored 4½ points out of 5 in his first Ryder Cup match. The following year he won the USPGA Team Championship with George Archer. A most consistent player, he won 1st prize, worth $60,000, in the Dow Jones Tournament of 1970. He won seven tournaments in 1962-70 and finished seven times in the first 10 in

Christchurch became distinctly county in flavour. When golf revived at Dunedin in 1892, many survivors of the 1870s helped to reform the Otago club, and the same year North Otago and the Hutt clubs came into existence. In 1893 a national championship was inaugurated, the second such event in any British possession, and for many years 'the four senior clubs' assumed the right to organize it.

Thereafter, development came with a rush. In 1894 golf began at Auckland, Wanganui, Timaru and Poverty Bay. The year 1895 brought a start at Manawatu, Napier and Wellington. By the time the New Zealand Golf Association was formed in 1910, the game was firmly entrenched in other areas too, and was becoming specially popular among the ladies; affiliation with the British LGU came in 1905. By 1929 clubs affiliated to the NZGA totalled 129, with special progress having been made in the North Island, and this expansion reflected generally the prosperity of New Zealand after World War I. Even the Depression had little effect on golf and just before World War II, the number of registered golfers totalled nearly 29,000 at 328 clubs. During the war membership of the Association fell to its lowest since the 1920s, as courses deteriorated through shortage of staff and as the nation responded to the Japanese threat.

For those who managed to continue playing the supply of golf balls was a problem, but the game soon regained its popularity

when fighting ceased. Just before New Zealand golf celebrated its centenary in 1971 and staged the Commonwealth Tournament, there were more than 330 clubs, about 66,000 male golfers and more than 35,000 women. Such development was helped by a growing tournament circuit and by increased coverage on television. As interest in the championships intensified, so world-class champions began to emerge. Bob Charles won the 1963 British Open and later John Lister began to make his mark. The sending of teams for the Eisenhower Trophy and the Commonwealth Tournament produced strong competition among the amateurs; their efforts were rewarded when Britain and New Zealand tied for the Commonwealth title in Canada in 1967, and New Zealand finished runners-up in the World Amateur Championship in Madrid. With this kind of encouragement behind them the future of New Zealand golf is assured, drawing strength from one of the oldest golfing heritages in the world.

Niblick
An old-fashioned iron club with more loft than a mashie. Used mainly for recovery play and pitching.

Nichols, Bob AMERICAN
b. Louisville, Ky., 1936. Carling Open 1964; USPGA 1964; Ryder Cup 1967; runner-up US Masters 1967; Canadian Open 1974
Bob Nichols, good at football and golf,

New Zealand: the course in the Tangariro National Park, North Island

Top, Niblick 1880-90

Above, Bob Nichols

1971 tournaments. He is head professional at Firestone CC, Ohio.

In 1962 Nichols received the Ben Hogan Award for his courageous recovery from severe injuries.

Nicklaus, Jack William AMERICAN

b. Columbus, Ohio, 1940. US Amateur 1959, 1961; US Open 1962, 1967, 1972, runner-up 1960, 1968, 1971; US Masters 1963, 1965-6, 1972, joint runner-up 1971; USPGA 1963, 1971, 1973; World (Canada) Cup 1963-4, 1966-7, 1971, 1973; Australian Open 1964, 1968, 1971; British Open 1966, 1970, runner-up 1964, 1967-9, 1972, joint runner-up 1968; Ryder Cup 1969, 1971, 1973

The greatest contemporary golfer. The recital of his championship successes alone points to that, since he is the only one to have won the Big Four events twice (the US and British Opens, the USPGA Championship and the Masters). He has added a third US Open victory, a third PGA title, and a third and fourth victory in the Masters, giving him a total of 12 major professional titles. The total of his major tournament victories, 1962-73, is 40. Only Hogan, Sarazen and Player have won the Big Four once. Before turning professional Jack Nicklaus won the National Amateur twice. As he searched for new peaks to climb he espied the possibility of winning all four big titles in the same year, something that to anyone else would be quite unthinkable. His failure in 1971 and 1972 to achieve that ambition did not lessen his reputation. Not the least part of his claim to greatness lies in the number of high finishes he has had in those major events he has not won, and to these he added steadily in those two years, while at the same time he continued to win the money, setting a new record in 1972 of $330,000 from only 19 tournaments.

An outstanding record as an amateur soon caused him to be compared with Bobby Jones who was his boyhood idol. It is enough for any man to be the greatest in his own age and nothing is gained by weighing the merits of one against the other. It is enough to remember Jones's assessment of him in the Nicklaus book, *The Greatest Game of All*: 'I think it is completely safe to say that there has not yet been a more effective golfer than Jack Nicklaus.' In the brilliance of Nicklaus's scoring and in the distance he hits the ball most people will echo that other characteristically cautious remark of Jones, made when Nicklaus toured the Masters course in a record-equalling 64: 'He plays a kind of golf with which I am not familiar.' Born in Columbus, the son of a pharmacist, his early

years as an amateur foreshadowed his future. He first qualified for the US Amateur at the age of 15 and began winning his state championship, Ohio, one year later. He was 19 when in 1959 he became the youngest winner of the US National Amateur for 50 years in one of the best finals against the holder, Charlie Coe, that the old championship had ever witnessed. That opened the floodgates. It was said that he lost only one match out of the 29 played, against the best amateurs, that year. He had already won both his matches in the Walker Cup in Britain earlier that season, and joined the celebrated list of winners of the Royal St George's Gold Challenge Cup. The following year he almost won the US Open, Palmer beating him only over the last few holes. In the autumn of the same year he achieved one of the most astonishing feats of his lifetime while taking part in the World Amateur Team Championship at Merion. In wet and windy weather he scored 66, 67, 68 and 68 for a total of 269, fewer by 18 strokes than Hogan's winning score there in 1950. It was 13 strokes better than anyone else in the tournament and it helped the American team to victory by 42 strokes over the Australians. By now the world of amateur golf was at his feet and it became clear that if he turned professional he would soon be among the leaders, though just how soon no one saw clearly.

For some time Nicklaus had been saying that if he could make enough money in insurance he would remain amateur, but after Merion and another victory in the US Amateur in 1961 he found the attraction of an increasingly lucrative professional career irresistible. He was helped in this decision by the presence on the scene of an impresario, Mark McCormack, who was already powerfully enlarging Palmer's earning capacity. As an amateur Nicklaus had formed the habit of playing in professional events and this eased the change-over to their ranks. Even so, the rapidity of his rise was astonishing. In his first professional year he won the US Open, defeating in a play-off Arnold Palmer, the man who had blazed the trail into the 1960s and who through the next decade was to be his friend and chief rival. His victory was more impressive because it was at Oakmont, one of the most testing courses in the country. On putting surfaces that are notoriously fast and deceptive Nicklaus took 3 putts only once in 72 holes. He finished the season 3rd in the money list; the following year he was 1st, the second man at that time to win more than $100,000 in a season. He was still only 23.

That same year, 1963, the Masters and

USPGA titles fell to him for the first time. He won the PGA title in Dallas in boiling heat shortly after flying back from the cool weather of Scotland and Lancashire. Since the Masters was Jones's creation it gave Nicklaus special pleasure to win at Augusta. His powerful game was well suited to the course where extra length, especially in driving, is an advantage. He won again in 1965 and in the following year, in gaining his third victory, he scored the 64 that equalled Lloyd Mangrum's record for the course. But Nicklaus had to wait three years after winning the third of the Big Four before completing the Slam by winning the British Open in 1966. His victory was all the more complete because Muirfield was playing short and he used his driver only 17 times in the four days. In 1967, after failing to make the cut in attempting to defend his Masters title, he won his second US Open with a record low total for the event of 275. It developed into a duel with his old rival Arnold Palmer, but a final 65, which equalled the lowest final-round score (at that time), gave Nicklaus victory by 4 strokes.

There followed a period of frustration. He

Jack Nicklaus

played, as the table shows, in 12 Big Four events and failed to win one of them. He continued to add to his reputation by the number of high finishes he put in, and he continued to amass a fortune by winning tournaments, but he also had some serious reverses, such as failing to qualify in the 1968 PGA Championship. In the 1970 US

Open he finished in a tie for 49th place, the lowest position he has ever filled in a major championship. But it was darkest before the dawn. At the British Open the same month he broke the spell, winning in a play-off against Doug Sanders who had missed from a yard or so for the title on the last green of the final round. Nicklaus's game was now ready to enter on its finest phase, the full flowering of a great talent. His technique has remained much as it was taught him in his schoolboy days by Jack Grout of the Scioto CC. He addresses the ball with a slightly open stance, the head perfectly but not rigidly still, allowing the right elbow to ride a little high on the back-swing in order to give him a full wide arc. The main source of his great power, which is the cornerstone of his pre-eminence, derives mainly from the force in his hips and legs and the use he makes of that, anchored to perfectly synchronized footwork in coming into the ball. His hands are on the small side and he has always used the interlocking grip. This talent is harnessed to a massive concentration and determination which enables him almost to dominate any course on which he sets out. Yet with that goes a detachment that is in contrast to the dedicated attitude of Player and with Palmer's sheer love of playing. Nicklaus is deliberate in his shotmaking, playing no stroke until he is absolutely ready to do so and sure of what he is trying to do. The effect is to make him one of the slower players, yet between shots he moves his powerful frame at a brisk pace down the fairway.

As the pressure of fame increased, and with material success now assured, he began to pace himself, cutting down the number of events for which he entered each year to about 20, and making special preparation for those in which he decided to play. At the same time – for he had always recognized that there was more to his career than smiles at the bank – he began to look around for new fields to conquer. In 1971 he won the PGA Championship which, for a change, was held in January, in Florida, not far from his new home where he had brought his wife and four children (now five). It was this change of date as much as anything that gave rise to the idea of his winning all four major events in one year. Hitherto, one of the biggest handicaps to winning all four was that the PGA followed close on the heels of the British and gave American competitors little time to prepare adequately for either. Nicklaus failed in his grand design for 1971 because Charles Coody slipped in ahead of him in the Masters. But in the same

autumn Nicklaus had a fantastic success, winning not only the Australian Open for the third time, but two other tournaments for which he had a grand total of 33 under par. He returned to the States to take part in the World Cup, this time with Trevino. In the third round he returned a 63, which put the United States safely ahead, won him

the individual trophy, and was one of the best – albeit slowest – rounds he ever played. The target of the Grand Slam in one year once again seemed a possibility for 1972, because for the second year running the four events were to be played on courses to his liking. He won the Masters after an opening round that gave him a lead he never surrendered. He also won the US Open at Pebble Beach, a course of which he was specially fond and on which he had won one of his Amateur titles. The stage was set for the third leg at Muirfield, where he had won his first British Open and broken through to the affection of the British public. Here he failed by 1 stroke to beat Lee Trevino in one of the great dramas of the oldest championship, a brilliant last round of 66 just failing to make up the necessary ground. With the incentive now missing he performed only moderately in the USPGA Championship, but he showed his resilience by winning three big tournaments before the end of the season, bringing his total up to seven for the year. His other ambition, to win an unassailable number of major cham-

pionships, advanced powerfully in those two years, and at the same time he strengthened his record of finishing in the first three. His victory in the PGA Championship of 1973, another prolific year for him, gave him a total of 14 major titles, two of which were Amateur Championships – one more than Jones accumulated.

Two changes were apparent in the man himself in those tumultuous years of his career. In 1970 he ended his association with McCormack and set up in business with another partner. He admitted to finding in business a new challenge, and when not competing was to be found more often at his desk than out fishing, which is one of his favourite hobbies. About that time there came also a change, more gradual, in his personality. There became apparent a better-groomed, a more personable Nicklaus, with a hair style far removed from the crew-cut of the tubby Ohio college boy of only a decade before. His not always easy personality, which in the early years had suffered from being in the shadow of Palmer's magnetism, had come to full

Above, Jack Nicklaus during the 1973 Ryder Cup and, *right,* during the 1973 British Open at Troon

fruition. He had won through to the hearts of the public in every country on sheer merit, coupled with plain dealing and a sense of proportion. Although Nicklaus had been dominating golf for years he became eligible to compete in the Ryder Cup only in 1969, when he played a principal part in the overall tie by halving his match with Tony Jacklin. It was not the least of the steps that brought him full recognition in Britain.

The following table gives Nicklaus's record in the Big Four events since turning professional in 1962:

	US Open	British Open	US Masters	US PGA
1962	1	t32	t15	t3
1963	mc	3	1	1
1964	t23	2	t2	t2
1965	t32	t12	1	t2
1966	3	1	1	t22
1967	1	2	mc	t3
1968	2	t2	t5	mc
1969	t25	t6	t24	t11
1970	t51	1	8	t6
1971	2	t5	2	1
1972	1	2	1	t13
1973	t4	4	t3	1

t = tied   mc = missed cut

Of the 48 championships of the Big Four in which he played up until 1974, he finished 1st 12 times and 25 times finished in the first 3. He has missed the cut only three times,

never in the British Open. Out of 48 appearances he has only 12 times failed to finish in the first 10. His performance as an amateur should also be taken into consideration: he won two US National Amateurs and was runner-up in the US Open in 1960.

Nigeria

Most of Nigeria's 17 golf clubs have a small membership, and all except three are of less than 18 holes, but interest in the game is slowly growing, especially in the capital, Lagos. The Ikoyi club in Lagos is the largest and oldest in the country. In 1933 the golf section of the club moved from Lagos racecourse, and in 1936-7 the course was increased to 18 holes from 12. A year later the Lagos GC and the Ikoyi club amalgamated to form the Ikoyi Club 1938, sharing a new clubhouse. Membership of the golf section numbers almost 1,000, of whom about 370 are women members; the club provides a variety of other interests including swimming, squash, judo, badminton, and snooker. The course, 6,100 yd (5,578 m) in length, is flat but strategically placed trees here and there provide some hazard. The lies are sandy and the greens are 'browns' made of oiled sand. In 1972, before staging the Nigerian Open Championship for the third year running, alterations were carried out which made the course more compact and increased the number of doglegs.

Nineteenth

The club bar; or, less frequently, the first extra hole of a match that was undecided at the 18th.

Noordwijk GC NETHERLANDS

Noordwijk aan Zee. 18 holes; 7,000 yd (6,400 m)

The Noordwijksche GC has one of the most exciting new courses to be built in Europe for many years. A classic duneland seaside course right on the North Sea coast between Kennemer and The Hague, it was built by the British architect, Frank Pennink. Nine holes were opened in May 1972, and the other 9 a few months later. But the club itself dates back to the day in 1915 when three elderly gentlemen, during a heavy drinking session, decided to make themselves a course at Noordwijk and each contributed £1,000 to help things along. A year later 9 holes were ready and in 1923 the course, pine-fringed and inland in character, was made up to an attractive 18. It was the scene for one or two early Dutch championships, but in 1943 it was ruined by the

Germans during World War II, and after the Liberation in 1945 only the first 9 holes could be used. The area of the second 9 was destined for town expansion, and in 1950 the municipal authorities made approaches to take over the whole course. From 1952 until 1969 there were endless negotiations, culminating in the invitation to Frank Pennink to build his new course a mile or two to the north of the old. This was a great breakthrough for the club. The new course could easily become one of the best in Europe. The old course was used as a training ground for 'non-handicap' golfers until it was eventually developed as a recreation centre.

Northamptonshire County GC ENGLAND

Church Brampton, Northamptonshire. 18 holes; 6,462 yd (5,909 m)

The club, situated in pleasant rural surroundings on either side of the main London railway line and offering a variety of gently undulating, inland golf, is one of the best in the Midlands. It was founded in 1909 on land acquired from Lord Spencer, and the course was laid out by H. S. Colt who designed so many British courses of that period. It is a tribute to his work that very little alteration has been needed, although James Braid, who took part in the club's inaugural match, returned to make suggestions for course improvements. These were connected mainly with updating the holes and bunkering, and they more than maintained its reputation as a challenging course. Recognition of this came in 1966 when the club staged the County Champion of Champions Tournament and, in 1971, the British Youths' Championship, won by Philip Elson.

North Berwick GC, The SCOTLAND

North Berwick, East Lothian. 18 holes; 6,317 yd (5,776 m); par 71

Because of its beautiful views over the Bass Rock and the North Sea, its splendidly kept course and numerous hotels, North Berwick has for generations attracted golfing families and those to whom golf is a recuperative rather than a deadly serious affair. Many statesmen and politicians have been among its devotees: A. J. Balfour, later Prime Minister, for example, was captain in 1891-2. In the club's annual sponsorship of the Scottish Boys' Championship is reflected its encouragement of the young. The original club (1832) was an exclusive coterie of gentlemen whose clubhouse was a tent; but in 1879 the New Club was formed by professional men and others with a handsome clubhouse, and only in 1963 did the

Jack Nicklaus putting on the 17th during World Cup Golf at Nueva Andalucía in 1973

two combine as the North Berwick Club.
The course evolved slowly, with some
alterations in 1930 by Sir Guy Campbell,
and possesses two of the most notable holes
in golf – the 14th (Perfection) with the sea
seeming too close to the green for comfort,
and the short 15th (Redan). Copies of these
two have been made in the National Golf
Links of America. This course may also
claim to have seen the only instance of a golf
shot deliberately killing a rabbit. In 1867, it
is recorded, 'Roberts, stationmaster at
Dirleton, playing with J. Whitecross from
the Gate to Point Garry In (17th), saw a
rabbit sitting on top of the rock of the
quarry, and said he would have a shot at it.
He was playing from about 70 or 80 yards
off, and struck the rabbit on the head,
killing it instantly.' That was in 1867, the
year that saw the presentation of the oldest
trophy for junior golfers, the Elcho Medal.

North Carolina, CC of USA
Sanford, N. Car. 18 holes; 6,900 yd
(6,309 m), par 72; 9 holes

The Country Club of North Carolina is
among the newer golf courses in the sandhills near Pinehurst, an area that may have
been at the bottom of some prehistoric sea
but is now better known for mild winters
and much golf. This is an ultra-exclusive
club with an initiation fee of $10,000. The
club tries to maintain a national membership, but the bulk of the members are from
North Carolina. Its 27 holes weave among
thick stands of dark blue-green longleaf and
loblolly pines, and along the banks of lakes
that border 7 of its holes. It has been the
venue for the Southern Amateur, the
Carolina Amateur, the Carolina Open, and
the Atlantic Coast Conference Championships. Sanford, a major brick-producing
centre of the eastern United States, is a mile
or two down the road, which gives the
members the opportunity to boast that their
contemporary clubhouse was built with
North Carolina brick.

North Devon GC, Royal ENGLAND
Westward Ho!, Devon. 18 holes; 6,639 yd
(6,071 m)

The oft-quoted remark 'this spot was
designed by Providence for a golf links' is
reputed to have been said by General
Moncrieffe to Mr Gossett, vicar of Northam
and founder of the club at Westward Ho!
The club, which came into being in 1864 as
the North Devon and West of England GC,
became the Royal North Devon GC in
1867. It celebrated its centenary in fitting
style with a picturesque foursome between
Christy O'Connor and Max Faulkner,

suitably attired and using a gutty ball, and
two present-day professionals, Brian Huggett
and Peter Alliss.

The club's early days were closely linked
with the amateur golfers of Royal Liverpool
and the Royal and Ancient. Its own early
stalwarts included the Molesworths,
J. A. T. Bramston and, in particular,
Horace Hutchinson. In more recent years
the Scott brothers, Osmund, Dennis and
Michael, have left their names innumerable
times on the club's medal boards; Michael
remains the oldest winner of the Amateur
Championship – in 1933 at the age of 54.

John Henry Taylor, who was born at
Northam, first learned his golf by caddying
at Westward Ho! and went on to win five
Open Championships, returning in his
retirement to become club president in 1957.

The course was redesigned by Herbert
Fowler in 1908, and has changed only in
minor details since then. The first 3 and the
last 2 holes are played over comparatively
flat land, intersected by ditches and the
burn; on a first visit they are frequently
regarded as dull and uninteresting, but, as
with the whole course, they take a deal of
knowing and playing. The 4th, over the
famous sleepered Cape Bunker, takes the
player into real sandhill country, along the
shore of Bideford Bay and inland from the
Pebble Ridge. Of the next 9 holes, perhaps
the 6th is the most immediately attractive,
but all are good. After the turn the next 3
holes lie through the Great Sea Rushes,

which are the graveyard of many balls and
the ruin of many scores. The 13th, back on
flatter ground, is 'made' by the plateau
green, and the 14th and the 16th together
with the 5th and 8th make up as fine a
quartet of short holes as any in the country.

With something of St Andrews in its
design, Westward Ho! has many devotees,
although nowadays, largely because of the
distance from London, it sees no major
championships.

In the past it was the scene of a famous
British Amateur final between John Ball and
Abe Mitchell in 1912, won by the former at
the 38th hole; in 1925 Robert Harris won,
beating K. F. Fradgley by 13 and 12, and
in 1931 Eric Martin Smith defeated John de
Forest by 1 hole. The British Ladies'
Championship was played there in 1900 and
1910 and won by Miss Adair and Miss
Grant Suttle respectively. The English
Ladies' Championships of 1925, 1933 and
1952 were won by Miss D. R. Fowler, Miss
Dorothy Pearson and Miss Pamela Davies.
The Oxford v Cambridge University match
was played at Westward Ho! for the only
occasion in 1938 and won by Cambridge.

The only major professional event played
there was the *Daily Mail* Tournament of
1920, won by George Duncan with 291 for
four rounds.

North Hants GC ENGLAND
Fleet, Hampshire. 18 holes; 6,231 yd
(5,698 m)

The Country Club of North Carolina

A connoisseur's course in the heather and pine belt beyond the outskirts of Greater London, just off the London-Southampton road. The course is pleasantly undulating, with springy turf in a peaceful setting which includes birch trees and rhododendrons. On the outward half the short 8th, 123 yd (112 m), can cause a deal of trouble for the

King Charles I is said to have played. Some 130 years later in 1770 landowners called Brandling, dating back to the 15th century, built Gosforth House and laid out the park in which the Northumberland club now has its home. Part of the park was taken over for golf in 1898 and owes its design to H. S. Colt who was called in in about 1911

and today there are seven courses in Norway, five with 9 holes and Oslo and Stavanger with 18. Interest is growing, particularly in Oslo, and the British architect, Frank Pennink, has recently been consulted about the possibility of more courses.

The playing season is short, usually from May until the snows come in late autumn, but many golfers practise and train indoors in an organized manner throughout the winter. This has produced many encouraging results, the most notable being Norway's excellent performance in finishing 3rd behind England and Scotland in the 1971 European Team Championship in Switzerland.

Nose
The toe of the club, the part furthest from the shaft

Notts GC ENGLAND
Hollinwell, Kirby in Ashfield, Nottinghamshire. 18 holes; 6,931 yd (6,337 m)

The course lies in the industrial Midlands where land for golf is now scarce, but ever since 1887 when the Rev. A. H. Baynes invited all those in Nottingham interested in golf to meet him in his house, it has been a respected name in English golf, as one of the longest and toughest of inland courses. Only five attended that meeting but the good vicar was persuasive enough to get the game started on what was then the Recreation Ground, and after a move to Bulwell Forest, where the club's most famous professional, Tom Williamson, was engaged on a month's trial, the club found its present home in the valley below the main Nottingham-Mansfield road about the year 1898. The choice of land was largely a matter of chance though its discoverer, Charles Robert Hemingway, certainly had an eye for golf. He stumbled upon it while surveying a site on behalf of the former Great Central Railway for a tunnel, and was so enthusiastic about its possibilities that he overcame all opposition to it in the club, and the lease of the land was obtained. Willie Park was engaged as architect and the course quickly gained a reputation as one of great challenge. The first 2 holes set off in an opposite direction to the rest, but the 3rd returns to the clubhouse and the rest of the round strikes a contrast between the early lower holes, sometimes between trees, and the sterner holes after the turn which means a long haul up to exposed fairways until most of the height is lost in a long downhill short hole. Common to the whole course is the springy moorland type of turf. The course

green is shaped like a figure-of-eight and is guarded by fiendish bunkers. But the course is renowned for its tough finish, the last three holes having caused the ruin of the card of many an international player, especially in the Hampshire Hog, the annual open amateur event with a distinguished list of winners. The 17th was designed to resemble the Road hole at St Andrews. The course, which was opened in 1904 by Princess Alice of Teck, was laid out by James Braid with a length of 5,500 yd (5,029 m) and a bogey of 78. The land belonged to the Calthorpe family; the club's first president was Lord Calthorpe, and the present one is his grandson, Sir Richard Anstruther-Gough-Calthorpe. In the late 1920s the course was redesigned by a Scots captain, L. J. Torrie, who increased it to its present length.

Northumberland GC ENGLAND
High Gosforth Park, Newcastle upon Tyne. 18 holes; 6,438 yd (5,887 m); par 72

Golf courses built close to racecourses are not uncommon but the Northumberland club, bordering the old main road to Scotland, is a prime example of that combination in Britain. The setting is an 18th-century deer park whose trees mask the proximity of industrial Newcastle; and the golf blends well with the neighbouring racecourse entering it at the 3rd and leaving it after the 17th. Not far away is the sea and four miles to the north is Shieldfield where

and returned in 1924 after James Braid had suggested changes in 1920. It quickly obtained a local reputation as a course of beauty and quality, and in 1938 staged the *Daily Mail* Tournament. After World War II it became recognized as a course of championship standard. Philip Scrutton won the Brabazon Trophy there in 1955 with a total of 283, and within the space of 10 years from 1963 it played host to the English County Championship finals, the Teachers Seniors' Championship, the British Youths' Championship, the Dunlop Masters and the English Championship, the last two events within a few months of each other in 1972.

Norway
Norwegian golf began in Oslo in 1924 with the founding of the Oslo Golfklubb which has played a leading role ever since. It started as a 9-hole course with sand greens and a local rule that allowed golfers to smooth the line before putting, and, though now 18 holes, occupies more or less the same site as before. The course, which is 6,700 yd (6,126 m) from the back tees, has been the heart of competitive golf in Norway. It housed the 1963 European Junior Team Championship, a number of Scandinavian Open Matchplay Championships and most of the Norwegian championships, but interest has been alive for some while in other areas, too. The Norwegian Golf Union (Norges Golfforbund) was founded in 1948

The restricted approach to the short 8th of the North Hants GC ranks high on the list of British inland ones, having housed the English Championship of 1935 and 1964, the Brabazon Trophy, Britain's premier amateur strokeplay event, in 1959, the Dunlop Masters of 1957 and other professional events. In that Dunlop Masters, Eric Brown established a record of 64, a score not approached in the John Player Classic of 1970 at Notts when Christy O'Connor won what was at that time a world record 1st prize of £25,000.

Novak, Joe AMERICAN
b. Butte, Mont., 1898

Novak became professional at the Helena Town and Country Club at the age of 16 and later served in San Francisco and Spokane before settling in southern California. He took the job as professional at Bel-Air in Los Angeles in 1927 and remained there for the rest of his career. Novak joined the Professional Golfers' Association in 1919 and served in many capacities, both at the regional and national level, before becoming PGA president in 1949. He served until 1952, then became honorary president until 1955. Besides being author of several books and articles on instruction, Novak was a pioneer in giving golf lessons over the radio. He also earned a degree from Loyola Law School in his spare time.

Nueva Andalucía GC SPAIN
Marbella. 18 holes

One of a number of new courses built since the late 1950s around Marbella, an area hitherto unknown for golf. Golf Nueva Andalucía was founded in 1968 and is part of an elaborate development that includes bungalows, apartments and a bull ring. The course, which lies just on the inland side of the main coast road, was designed by Robert Trent Jones and is full of subtle terror. There is no undue emphasis on length but water, in the shape of lakes and streams, is a feature at 12 of the holes; the well-guarded greens are small and fast, and the 13th, 14th and 15th holes curve gently through the olive trees.

The Spanish Open Championship was held there in 1970 and the World Cup Tournament in 1973. Sebastián Miguel, famous among Spanish golfers, became the club's first professional.

Nuwara Eliya SRI LANKA
Nuwara Eliya. 18 holes; 6,064 yd (5,545 m)

Situated in magnificent countryside at an altitude of 6,200 ft, Nuwara Eliya or, as it soon became anglicized, 'Newraylia', is 115 miles by road from Colombo and 45 from the ancient capital of Kandy. From the club, which was described in Murray's *Handbook*

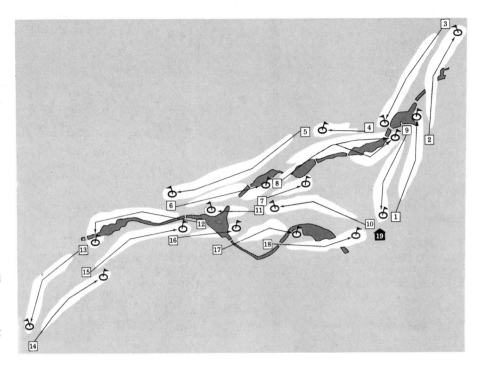

of India, Ceylon and Burma, as the finest in the East, a bridle path leads to Pidurutalagala, the highest mountain in Sri Lanka (Ceylon) at over 8,000 ft. Four miles away is the Sita Eliyah temple which commemorates the venerated Hindu epic of Rama and Sita. Here, in 1888, six years after Royal Colombo, the club was founded for the British administration which used to move up in summer to the cool heights from Colombo's steamy coastal humidity. The Amateur Championship of Ceylon was first played at Nuwara Eliya in 1891, and thereafter alternated annually with Royal Colombo.

Special Cumberland turf had been imported from England for the grounds of the adjacent Queen's Cottage, the official residence of the Governors. In time this seeded and spread over much of the course, providing excellent fairways. The course, open and rather moorlike, is thickly dotted with bushes of crimson rhododendron and stands of cypress, golden wattle, and the numerous kina trees, which resemble a stone pine. In the rough can be seen a species of pink hyacinth orchid and the Ceylon gentian, with flowers of perfect sky-blue. A stream runs through the course, guarding some of the greens. The 374-yd (342-m) 12th is the most difficult on the course. With sloping lies and a carry over two hollows, the attack to the elevated green, well guarded by bunkers, makes a very complex hole. The 207-yd (189-m) 13th's uphill finish is compensated

for by the view from the 14th tee across to Mount Pedro, although thick cloud or mist frequently hangs over it. Here, too, can be heard the whoop-whoop of the large wanderoo monkey and the call of the jungle fowl.

Nyali GC KENYA
Nyali, Mombasa. 9 holes; combined length 6,438 yd (5,886 m)

Nyali is a proprietary club, membership by invitation, that started in 1959 through the efforts of Nyali Ltd, owners of the land, and is situated on the mainland. Much work was done in grubbing out coral and planting good fairways, and in experimenting with a strain of Mozambique grass, known locally as Polana grass, which is well suited to the light soil and sea air. Peter Thomson was much impressed by the course and greens when he played an exhibition match there some years ago with David Thomas and two local players. Shortly afterwards plans were drawn up for a full 18 which could become one of Kenya's finest courses.

The course plan of Nueva Andalucía GC

O

Oak Hill CC USA

Rochester, N.Y. 18 holes; Championship
Course 6,900 yd (6,309 m); par 70

Among the qualities looked for in a golf
course worthy of a United States Open
championship is a strong set of finishing
holes where the title can be won by bold and
imaginative play or lost by timid, indecisive
strokes. The last 3 holes of the East Course at
Oak Hill comprise one of the strongest
finishes in American golf – three brutally
hard par 4s requiring well-placed tee shots
followed by long or medium irons to well-
protected greens.

The 16th is 441 yd (403 m) with a fairway
sloping to the left. Thick stands of oak,
maple, and evergreens line the right side, and
anyone hitting into them must almost surely
sacrifice a shot. The 17th normally plays as a
par 5 and as such is not too terrifying, but as a
4 to a length of 460 yd (421 m) the drive needs
careful placing. Two bunkers pinch the
entrance to the green and it is easy in clearing
them to roll over the green, as Ben Hogan did
in the 1956 Open, losing his chance to tie
Cary Middlecoff by taking three more to get
down. As for the 18th, it is 450 yd (411 m) in
length with a fairway bunker on the right
and a deep chasm which extends just to the
edge of the plateau green. The really
powerful hitter can pick up considerable
yardage by driving over the fairway bunker
but is then left with a downhill lie. Though
the 3 finishing holes may be the most difficult
on the course, the best are probably the 6th
to the 9th. This stretch is again a series of
par 4s, each over 400 yd but each posing a
different problem. The finest of them might
well be the 6th, 440 yd (402 m) in length
with a creek running along the right side
until it swerves left and cuts across the fairway just short of the green. A line of willows
borders the fairway on the right, and the tee
shot must be placed to avoid the water and
the trees. The rough is always kept heavy on
the left.

Oak Hill was originally designed by
Donald Ross and later remodelled by Robert
Trent Jones, who lengthened it and added
some of his own hallmarks, such as the flared
white bunkers that guard the greens and
flank most of the fairways in the driving
zone. The course has been the scene of two

US Opens, in 1956 when Middlecoff won,
and in 1968 when Lee Trevino on his way to
victory tied the record low Open total of
275. The club name derives from the hill
where the brick Tudor-style clubhouse
stands overlooking the course. Known as the
Hill of Fame, it is studded with oaks, many
of them dedicated to prominent golfers.

Oakland Hills CC USA

Birmingham, Mich. 18 holes; 6,600 yd
(6,035 m)

Oakland Hills, on the outskirts of Detroit,
is not a beautiful course in the generally
accepted sense of pretty vistas, but it is
loaded with intriguingly formidable golf
holes. For the members it plays around

Top, Oak Hill CC

Above, Oakland Hills CC

6,600 yd, but from the championship tees it is more than 300 yd (275 m) longer. The land is rugged and rolling and most of the greens are very well protected, which makes it under normal conditions no easy scoring course. The United States Open Championship has been held there four times, and one of them will be remembered as long as golf is played. In 1951 the USGA, after considerable soul-searching, had gone perhaps too far in its effort to put par back on the pedestal from which it had been toppled by greatly improved implements, the perfect grooming of fairways, and the virtual disappearance of that fierce rough once known on championship courses. After 54 holes no score below the par of 70 had been recorded. At the end, only two such rounds had been returned, a 67 by Ben Hogan which won him the third of his four US Open titles, and a 69 by Clayton Heafner, the runner-up. The man in charge of the drastic renovation of the course was Robert Trent Jones, and the publicity that accrued to Jones from that tournament was undoubtedly the springboard that vaulted him to national attention and eventually led to his becoming an international figure. The critical change he made was to fill in all the obsolete bunkers and to replace them with new ones cut into the edge of the rough 240-260 yd (220-238 m) from the tee. When the USGA set up the course for the Open with the narrowest fairways ever – in places some were hardly 25 yd (23 m) wide – the players were confronted by the most severe test of driving any Open field had undertaken. Most of them panicked, taking fairway woods or irons off the tees, and finding themselves as a result with approaches too difficult to bring off successfully. Bogey followed bogey, but Hogan, grim and silent, kept working and reduced his scores round by round: 76, 73, 71, 67. He was to do the same thing in winning the British Open two years later. He himself called that final round his finest in golf, and others have rated it the best single round ever played in a championship.

In accepting the trophy Hogan made a historic remark: 'I am glad that I finally was able to bring this monster to its knees.' No one is likely to find Oakland Hills such a monster as it was that year. Hogan's winning score was 287, as against 281 when Ralph Guldahl won in 1937 and the 281 of Gene Littler in 1961. Back in 1924 Cyril Walker's winning 297 had been 3 strokes better than Bobby Jones's 300 in 2nd place.

Al Watrous, for many year the professional at Oakland Hills, was replaced by Mike Souchak. Presently Al Mengert holds that position.

Oakmont CC USA
Oakmont, Pittsburgh, Pa. 6,800 yd (6,218 m); par 71

Oakmont is not a pretty course. The visitor will not be distracted by flowering bushes, stately trees, or shimmering water hazards. On the contrary, Oakmont is bisected by an awful scar – the Pennsylvania Turnpike separates 11 holes on the clubhouse side from 7 holes starting at the 2nd. But then, a pretty Oakmont would be incongruous. It is not intended to arouse feelings of warmth and affection. Oakmont is all golf – and very harsh golf at that. It is a severe test of nerve which, of all the courses associated with the US Open and Amateur championships, traditionally produces the highest scores. Laid out in 1903 by H. C. Fownes and named after the town of Oakmont, a suburb of Pittsburgh, the course was nurtured by his son, William, an important and unusual figure in American golf in that he was both a wonderful player (Amateur Champion in 1910) and an influential administrator of the game (USGA president in 1926 and 1927).

Oakmont is not long by modern championship standards. Its difficulty has to do with the vast expanses of sand near its target areas (some 187 bunkers) and the legendary Oakmont greens. They are, perhaps the world's fastest: Michael Bonallack, during the 1969 US Amateur, pronounced them the fastest in his experience. These greens are absolutely essential to the Oakmont heritage,

and great care is taken to see that they retain their character. Some Oakmont members talk reverently of a great strain of south German bent grass, but agronomists scoff at this and attribute the quality of the greens to inspired management. The greens are shaved at 3/32nds of an inch all the time and they are not overwatered. The members do not mind if their greens lose some colour so long as they putt true and fast. When they are at their best, as they invariably are for a national competition, they add dimension to the game which then becomes one of sensitive touch and nerve. The slightest twitch may cause the most horrifying result. Every Oakmont championship arouses new tales of anguish. Harry Cooper, runner-up to Tommy Armour in the 1927 Open, vows he putted into a bunker off the 17th green. Phil Rodgers, who finished only 2 shots behind in the 1962 Open, took 4 putts on the 10th green. That 10th green is one of several – including the 1st and 12th – which add the demoniac touch of canting from front to back.

Oakmont's 15th, a par 4 of heroic proportions, is often cited as the course's best. It can be stretched to more than 450 yd (411 m), the green is 65 yd (59 m) long, and the bunker to the right of the green is fully 95 yd (87 m) long by 15 yd (14 m) wide. (That bunker is not Oakmont's largest.) The 18th hole may be even better. Played at 460 yd (421 m) for the US Open, it becomes as hard as a hole can be without going beyond the

The 'Church Pews' at Oakmont CC

pale and into the realm of the unfair, where there is no particular advantage in being the best player in the world. That is to say, the hole can be played – as Nicklaus did in the fourth round in 1962 when, after a colossal drive, he hit an 8 iron shot that seemed to go storeys high and settle down instantly when it struck the green 15 ft from the hole. He did not get the putt that would have won for him. Next day he beat Palmer in the play-off for his first professional victory in a championship that seems more significant as the years go by. The score at which he and Palmer tied, 283, was the same aggregate that Ben Hogan compiled in winning the 1953 Open there by 6 strokes. That was a vintage year for Hogan, for he also carried off the US Masters and the British Open.

When the US Open returned there in 1973, Oakmont joined Baltusrol as the only venue to entertain the event five times. The championship was remarkable in that Johnny Miller returned a 63 in the final round, the lowest round ever recorded in the US Open. A violent tropical storm on the eve of play had taken much of the terror out of the notoriously fast greens. Oakmont has, in addition, been the site of four US Amateurs and of the USPGA Championship. Through the years the spirit of the Fownes family has been carried on by an unusual number of very able players who have been associated with the club. These include Sam Parks, now an executive in a Pittsburgh steel firm, who astonished everyone by winning the 1935 Open over the course. The club's professional, Lew Worsham, was himself Open Champion as the conqueror of Sam Snead in 1947.

Observer

A person appointed by a tournament committee to answer questions of fact and to report any breach of rule.

O'Connor, Christy IRISH

b. Galway 1924. Ryder Cup 1955, 1957, 1959, 1961, 1963, 1965, 1967, 1969, 1971, 1973; British Professional Matchplay 1957; winner World (Canada) Cup 1958; Vardon Trophy 1961-2; tied 2nd British Open 1965, tied 3rd 1958, 1961; John Player Classic 1970

O'Connor has been one of the best and most consistent professionals on the British circuit since the late 1950s. Like so many of his countrymen he is a natural player, blessed with a beautifully free, rhythmic swing. It is also strong and graceful with just a hint of looseness about the action, but ideal in the winds in which he was raised. Practice as a boy on the sands of Galway developed in him a lovely late swing through the ball. His

golfing life began as a caddie; he turned professional in 1951, competing only in Ireland. His first British Open was in 1951 at Royal Portrush. He did not compete outside Ireland until he went to Llandudno in 1954 where he gave notice of his ability by losing to Henry Cotton at the 23rd in the Penfold semi-finals. The following year he again

fared well in the same tournament and made his debut in the Ryder Cup, the first of a long unbroken run of appearances that included a 7 and 6 victory over Dow Finsterwald as a contribution to the British victory at Lindrick. By 1958, when he and Bradshaw recorded their remarkable victory for Ireland in the Canada Cup at a high altitude in Mexico City, he had gained a reputation as a fierce competitor and a strong finisher with a particular ability to land the big-figure cheques. He had been the first on the British circuit to pick up a four-figure cheque and became in 1970 the first on the home circuit to win a five-figure cheque – a £25,000 reward for 1st place in the John Player Tournament. In the 1956 Dunlop Masters at Prestwick he made up 6 strokes on Eric Brown in the last round to win, and in the same tournament four years later it took a 66 from him to beat the amateur, Joe Carr, and save the professionals' pride. He played the last 23 holes of that tournament at Portmarnock in 83. Apart from his achievement in the Canada Cup he did not enjoy much success abroad, but his consistency endured, and after missing 1st place in the 1958 British Open by a single stroke he built up as good a record in that event as any other current player in these islands. Even though beset by aches and pains he was still a force in the early 1970s, and set up a new Ryder Cup playing record with ten consecutive appearances.

Olgiata GC ITALY

nr Rome. 18 holes, 6,930 yd (6,336 m), par 72; 9 holes, 3,170 yd (2,899 m)

An outstanding championship course 12 miles north of the city, the Circolo Golf Olgiata has an international reputation through its staging of the World Amateur Team Championship in 1964 and the World Cup in 1968. Designed by C. K. Cotton in

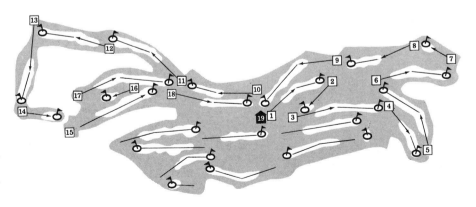

Top, Christy O'Connor in the 1967 Alcan Golfer of the Year Championship and, *centre*, missing a short putt on his way to victory in the 1970 John Player Classic

Above, the course plan of Olgiata GC

1958 it lies within a luxury residential estate. Oaks and elms abound on this well-balanced park course. The start is tough with a difficult par-3 2nd and a 3rd hole which except in the summer may be out of reach of two woods. It is not unusual for strokes to be dropped at each of the first 3 holes. Of the middle holes the 10th is one of the subtlest. The 16th is a most picturesque par 3 and on either side of it are two par 5s which can be reached in two by the long hitters, thus making the finish a suitably testing one. The 18th green was redesigned as an *hommage gracieux* to Cotton by a colleague, Tom Simpson, and was one of his last layouts.

Oliver, Edward AMERICAN

b. Delaware 1916; d. 1961. Bing Crosby Tournament 1940; Phoenix Open 1940; Western Open 1941; runner-up USPGA 1946; runner-up Canadian Open 1947; Ryder Cup 1949, 1951, 1953; Texas Open 1947; runner-up US Open 1952, tied 3rd 1947; runner-up US Masters 1953

'Porky' Oliver was a familiar figure on the tournament circuit for 20 years and a winner of several tournaments, although he is best remembered as a hard-luck player because of his numerous 2nd-place finishes, including the three biggest events in American golf. Altogether he was runner-up in some 20 tournaments, but it was his misfortune in the 1940 US Open that is best remembered. On that occasion Oliver and Dutch Harrison – both very much in contention – together with

Johnny Bulla teed off in the final round before their scheduled starting time and were disqualified. Their excuse was that they wanted to beat a threatened rainstorm, but this did not materialize. Oliver scored 71 which tied Sarazen and Little for 1st place, but his disqualification was complete.

That was as close as he came to winning one of the big championships. In 1946 he eliminated Byron Nelson on his way to the final of the USPGA against Ben Hogan. He was 3 up on Hogan at lunch, but in the second round of the final Hogan went out in 30 and won by 6 and 4. In the 1952 Open Oliver stayed among the leaders all the way but failed to close the gap on Julius Boros, who won by 4 strokes. In the 1953 Masters Oliver ran into Hogan once more and found him again at his best, for Hogan's total of 274 set a new record for the tournament. Hogan's third round of 66 was only 1 stroke better than Oliver's and together they had a better ball of 60. In spite of these frustrations Oliver was a steady money winner, being successful in 10 events on the American tour. Oliver was one of the most popular of professionals with the gallery and with his fellow professionals. When it became known that he was dying of cancer in 1961 there was a great surge of sympathy from all over the nation.

Olivos GC ARGENTINA

General Pacheco. 18 holes and 9 holes

Founded in 1916 at Olivos, this club moved in 1951 to General Pacheco, about 25 miles from Buenos Aires. It has housed the Argentine Masters every year since 1960. The lay-out of this parkland course with its abundant trees is compact. It was the scene in 1972 of the Eisenhower Trophy event.

Olympia Fields CC USA

Matteson, Ill. 36 holes

When it opened in the mid-1920s, Olympia Fields was one of the wonders of the golf world. The club had four 18-hole courses that meandered through its vast wooded preserve some 30 miles south of Chicago. The huge clubhouse had a dining room that could seat 800 and a grill room that could seat 600 more. There were other conveniences, such as a private hospital, an ice-making plant, and a dance pavilion. In recent times these facilities have been reduced to more normal proportions, but the club retains two of its courses and all of its class.

Over the years, Olympia Fields' North Course has been the scene of four national championships. Two of these ended in ties, one of which produced a new member for the select and limited company of golfers who beat Bob Jones. This was Johnny Farrell, who defeated Jones in a 36-hole play-off in the 1928 US Open. It was there that Walter Hagen won the second of his four straight USPGA championships in 1925, and it was there that Jerry Barber defeated Don January for the PGA title in 1961 on the strength of one of the most incredible exhibitions of putting in tournament history.

Olympic Club USA

San Francisco, Cal. 36 holes; Lakeside 6,727 yd (6,151 m) and Ocean

Trees – majestic pines, cypress and eucalyptus – dominate the Lakeside Course at Olympic. They are never removed from the player's sight or consciousness. The course has about 30,000 in all; every hole seems an island carved out of a forest. The trees, some of which are now 100 ft high, are the product almost entirely of planting begun in this century. This site was largely sand dunes, nearly treeless, lying between Lake Merced and the Pacific Ocean, half a

Edward Oliver

The 14th hole of Olympia Fields GC

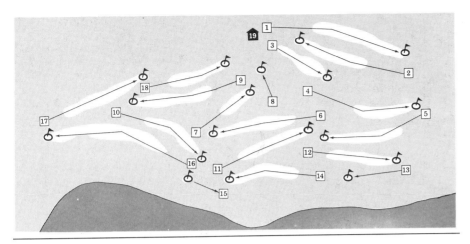

associated with the Eastern championship venues, Oakmont and Merion in particular.

With its background of dark green flora and its frequent mists from off the ocean, Olympic seemed a proper setting for the most painful disappointments in the careers of Ben Hogan and Arnold Palmer. Hogan was robbed of his ultimate ambition, a fifth US Open title, by the unknown Jack Fleck in 1955. Palmer, on the verge of what might have been his most illustrious triumph, kicked away a 7-stroke lead with 9 holes to play. He had to make a remarkable recovery from heavy rough at the 18th to force a play-off, which he lost, against Billy Casper. Hogan and Fleck tied at 287, Casper and Palmer, 11 years later, at 278. The difference should be attributed mainly to a more sensible playing arrangement. Olympic's turf and climate encourage the growth of a truly frightening rough, an element revered by the USGA for its Open. In 1955 the rough was allowed to get out of hand to the point where it became virtually unplayable. In 1966, though it still represented a dire threat and placed a high premium on accuracy, some advance from it was possible. Two other points deserve mention: (1) the 18th hole, only 337 yd (308 m), is the best hole for spectators in American champion-ship golf, the tiny green sitting at the bottom of a horseshoe hill so steep that it affords a place for everyone who wants to see; (2) Olympic has been found to be the fastest-playing course of those in regular use by the USGA. In the final round of the 1966 Open Casper and Palmer were round in $3\frac{1}{2}$ hours – a veritable foot-race in American golf.

One Boat GC ASCENSION ISLAND
9 holes; 2,232 yd (2,041 m)

Golf is played in a variety of settings throughout the world and on a variety of courses. By no means all are blessed with the refinements of manicured greens and watered fairways that many take for granted; but that has not stopped golf's pioneers from introducing the game to remote corners or prevented enthusiasts from enjoying its unique pleasures in unusual circumstances. Such is the case with the One Boat GC on the British island of Ascension, in the South Atlantic, where the terrain is composed of extinct volcanoes that have scattered vol-canic debris everywhere over the surface. The idea of clearing it in order to make a golf course would not have occurred to very many but, following a preliminary survey in 1960, a small band of enthusiasts started work in 1969 with this aim in view. So rapid was progress that it was officially opened on July 27 that year.

mile away. Despite its proximity the sea cannot be seen from Lakeside. Olympic's other course – the Ocean – contains a few breathtaking oceanside holes, but it is not suitable for grand events.

The strong natural feeling of the Lakeside Course is due in part to the omission of bunkers. There is only one fairway bunker, to the left of the fairway on the 6th; nor is the greenside bunkering specially menacing.

There is a tendency to overpraise particu-lar holes on estimable courses by those who prefer specific or simple keys to good design. This is true of Olympic where the 3rd hole, a short one of something over 200 yd (183 m), is invariably included in compendia of great holes. However, the dominant feature is the

view it affords of San Francisco and of the Golden Gate Bridge from its elevated tee. The hole itself calls for a rather long poke downhill to an open green. It is in the par 4s that lies the strength of Olympic and its validity as a test of the finest players. They are admirably varied, but the overall im-pression is of a series of very demanding and beautiful 2-shot holes. Seven of them can play at 420 yd (384 m) or more: honest yards because the moist San Francisco climate limits both carry and roll. Indeed when set up at its full length, it is amply long. The greens are small, and neither heavily con-toured nor difficult to gauge. If the course has a failing, it may be that these greens never seem to attain the speed and firmness

Olympic Club – the course plan and the 3rd hole on Lakeside

Rocks of all shapes and sizes, anything, in fact, up to large boulders, were removed from the areas designated as fairways, the boundaries of which are marked with posts. Greens, called 'browns', were smoothed out and covered with sand, and strategic bunkers dug. As on most grassless courses a local rule allows players to improve their lies without penalty. Rocks, stones and boulders constitute the main hazards but live hazards exist as well in the shape of wild goats which have been known to chase lone golfers back to the safety of the clubhouse.

They have not, however, deterred the growth of the game for, in the first six months of its existence, One Boat's membership rose from 39 to 121 and by the autumn of 1971 had increased to 170.

Ono, Koichi JAPANESE

b. Dairen, Manchuria, 1919. Japanese Open 1955; Japanese Professional 1955; World (Canada) Cup 1957; runner-up Korean Open 1963; Kanto Professional 1958, 1959, 1963; runner-up Indian Open 1970

Ono started his career as a caddie at the Dairen GC, most of whose members were Japanese businessmen and officials stationed in Manchuria. He showed such promise in the game that he was brought over to the Hodogaya GC in the mid-1930s, and has been associated with that club ever since. He partnered Nakamura in Japan's victory in the Canada Cup contest in 1957 and was placed 5th in the individual list in a week that was a turning point in the history of Japanese Golf. Although he still competes in major tournaments, his best days were those before the advent of the lucrative international circuit in the Far East. He has twice won the Professional Seniors' Championship.

Onsham, Sukree THAI

b. Prachuap Khiri Khan 1944. 2nd Dunlop International (Australia) 1972; 3rd Japanese Open 1972; 2nd Malaysian Open 1972; 2nd Wills Masters (Australia) 1972

Only 5 ft 3 in tall and weighing about 110 lb, Sukree Onsham is probably the world's smallest playing professional. He is also the best player ever produced by Thailand where, as a carpenter's son, he started caddying at the age of nine. It took him 10 years to save up enough to buy a secondhand set of clubs and he was 21 before he owned a pair of golf shoes, but he made his way to Bangkok, turned professional in 1967, and was engaged as assistant at the Royal Bangkok Sports Club.

His tournament aspirations were naturally centred upon the Far East circuit which was

gathering force at that time and he soon became a steady money winner. He has made regular appearances in Japan and Australia. His first major victory still awaits him, but he had an outstanding moment in the 1969 World Cup in Singapore when he led the individual event with three holes to play. He finished equal third but gained enough success in the Far East in 1970 and 1971 to be invited to the US Masters at Augusta. Despite his size, he hits the ball a surprising distance with clubs longer than standard.

Onwentsia Club USA

Lake Forest, Ill. 18 holes; 6,520 yd (5,962 m); par 72

Onwentsia, an Indian name meaning 'a meeting place for braves and squaws', was originally planned as a typical British seaside course with virtually no trees. Lying over rolling land on a bluff above the lake, it remains essentially the same today as it was when it was founded in 1895, although some trees have been added. Many of the numerous cross-bunkers have been eliminated, although some reminders of them remain in the form of ridges running bewilderingly across the line of play. It is a beautifully kept course and the greens are always fast. The golf shop at Onwentsia is one of the few places in the United States where it is possible to have a set of clubs made by the resident professional. The enterprising Hubby Habjan, who also directs the PGA's Caribbean tour, is an accomplished clubmaker, a rare talent today, particularly in a young man. But Onwentsia is a club whose members include the Armours, the Swifts, the Cudahys, the Palmers of the meat-packing industry, and the McCormicks of *Chicago Tribune* fame. Hobart Chatfield-Taylor was the club's first president, and H. J. Whigham was among the first members. Whigham, a son-in-law of Charles

Blair Macdonald, was the US Amateur Champion in 1896 and 1897. Robert A. Gardner, twice an amateur champion and member of four Walker Cup teams, was a member, and so was Edith Summings, the 1923 US Women's Amateur Champion. Also of that company is John D. Ames, a former president of the USGA.

Oosterhuis, Peter A. BRITISH

b. London 1948. Walker Cup 1967; Agfa-Gevaert Tournament 1971; Piccadilly Medal 1971, 1973; Ryder Cup 1971, 1973; Sunbeam Electric Tournament 1971; Vardon Trophy 1971-4; Penfold-Bournemouth Tournament 1972; British PGA Champion 1973; French Open 1973, 1974; runner-up British Open 1974

Peter Oosterhuis, one of the tallest of the world's leading golfers at 6 ft 5 in, turned professional after a promising start in amateur golf. He was captain of the England Boys' team, won the British Youths' Championship in 1966 at Dalmahoy, and the following summer capped some fine performances at the senior level by being picked for the Walker Cup team while still a schoolboy at Dulwich College – a unique achievement.

His decision to turn professional in November 1968 followed a short spell in a city office in London and reflected his obvious love of the game, but nobody was quite prepared for the impact he was to make so quickly. He became a steady money

Peter Oosterhuis driving at the dogleg 18th at Wentworth

Sukree Onsham

winner from the start, won his first professional victory, the South African General Motors Open, in 1970, made consistent progress throughout the remainder of that year both in Britain and elsewhere, and for the next four summers was leading British professional on the home circuit. No British player has ever made a more successful transition from amateur to professional.

In the 1971 Ryder Cup in St Louis he scored singles victories against Arnold Palmer and Gene Littler and partnered Tony Jacklin in the World Cup in Florida. He has always been a great supporter of the tournaments in South Africa where he met his wife, Ann, and in 1973, following a victory over Gary Player in the Piccadilly Matchplay Championship at Wentworth the previous October, won a notable victory in a similar matchplay event, sponsored by Rothmans.

In this he beat Harold Henning, Bobby Cole and Player. This was further proof of his progress towards being one of the world's best players but his most striking achievement was in finishing 3rd in the 1973 US Masters after leading with a round to go. It was not until the 15th hole in the last round that Tommy Aaron finally got away from him, but he impressed everyone with his golf and pleasant manner.

Oosterhuis, very much a perfectionist, has been vulnerable to the sort of damaging stroke that cost him the John Player Classic on the 35th tee at Turnberry in 1972, but he

Peter Oosterhuis

is an exceptionally good putter, a fine iron player and a wonderfully good competitor; ideally cast to the life which has made him a far richer man than working in a City of London office. He had an outstanding year In 1973, winning the Vardon Trophy for a record third year in a row but he failed to gain his card for the USPGA tour – although

it was unfortunate the week coincided with the birth of his son and followed another hectic Ryder Cup match in which he again shone. His outstanding performance in 1974 was in finishing runner-up to Gary Player in the British Open at Lytham.

Ootacamund GC INDIA
Ootacamund, Madras State. 6,207 yd (5,676 m); par 72

The Nilgiris ('Blue Hills') of southwest Madras are the setting for the hill station of Ootacamund – 'Ooty' to the British. Here, about 12°N, are trout-filled streams and rolling hills planted with tea bushes and Australian blue gum. It is not only the sign 'Charing Cross' at the busy traffic intersection, nor the flower-decked cottages, that recall the British legacy, but the startling sight of the Wenlock Downs over which the testing Ooty course lies. It could have been transplanted straight from the Sussex downs, complete with yellow-flowered gorse.

In 1896 the Nilgiri club was founded and joined the inevitable local gymkhana club. Golf had been introduced into the Nilgiris from Bangalore by a Colonel Ross Thompson of the Royal Artillery at the turn of the century. By trial and error 15 holes were finally laid out on a part of the Wenlock Downs. 'The holes start from the eastern end of Cockey's course, which is by no means level ground, and are laid over some rather broken country.' Though no golfer, Sir Frederick Price, a distinguished British administrator, gives a fairly accurate description in his *History of Ootacamund* (1908). Ooty, a holiday resort course, is the venue for the Southern India championship during May. Under a veteran Nilgiri Scot, Norman Hamilton, major changes were made in the 1960s. Nine holes are blind and use has to be made either of guideposts or of a nimble *agewalla* (forecaddie) for a line to the greens. The gruelling long 5th has a difference of altitude of as much as 200 ft (61 m), but the reward is the magnificent view clear across to distant hill ranges. The Ootacamund course follows the soft contours of downland ringed with gorse and, in the hollows, thick, scented *sholas* (copses) of eucalyptus, oak, rhododendron and fir. The combination of light and air at 8,000 ft is almost intoxicating. At the 13th green, twice a day, there comes the baying of foxhounds and beagles at feeding time in the nearby kennels of the Ootacamund hunt. Otherwise the only sounds to be heard are the thwack of club on ball and the ceaseless birdsong. Playing the 7th across a wooded ravine provides a view of an old country road winding past a stream where goats graze. The scene has changed

little since the days when the saddleback ibex, now rare, used to roam freely over this ancient homeland of the aboriginal Todas.

Oporto GC PORTUGAL
Espinho, Douro Litoral. 18 holes; 5,269 yd (4,818 m)

Situated 10 miles south of Oporto, the club is the oldest in continental Europe outside France. It was started in 1890 by a group of British players, mostly port-wine shippers, who called it the Oporto Niblicks club. The first 9 holes were just south of Espinho and were called the 'St Skeff Links' after C. N. Skeffington, the club's first president. The carry over the main Oporto to Lisbon railway line at one of the holes was regarded with trepidation by certain members who were said to have to fortify themselves with port before undertaking the shot. The course measured 2,027 yd (1,853 m) and was rough enough to warrant handicaps ranging from scratch to 50. Golf was played at two other places near Oporto between 1895 and 1905: a 9-hole course at Matosinhos, and a 5-hole course near Castelo de Queijo. One hole at Matosinhos consisted of a drive over a wall into a small field, and the golf at both was rough and did not survive. But the Niblicks continued to thrive and in 1900 moved its 9 holes to the present site. Soon the title of 'Niblick' was dropped and the first annual meeting of the Oporto GC was held in March 1901, in a wooden hut by the first tee. The main part of the present clubhouse was built in 1910. In 1917 a proposal to admit women was defeated on the grounds that it would be unchivalrous to ask them to pay a subscription, but the club relented in 1932 when female relatives of members were admitted.

In 1921 the number of members exceeded 100, although it was only in the previous year that the first Portuguese was elected to the club. The course was extended to 18 holes in 1934, with further improvements and a lengthening in 1955-8, part of them by Mackenzie Ross. On the 50th anniversary of the club in 1940 the first club captain, A. C. Kendall, was appointed. It was another eight years before the first Portuguese became a member of the committee.

Oppenheimer, Raymond Henry BRITISH
b. London 1905. Worplesdon Foursomes (with Joyce Wethered) 1932

Although better known in recent years for his outstanding contribution as an administrator and selector, Oppenheimer's judgment and knowledge in these matters was undoubtedly strengthened by his having been a golfer of international class. After

playing for Oxford for four years from 1925 to 1928, he won a place in several England sides and was unlucky not to be selected for the Walker Cup. He partnered Joyce Wethered to victory in the Worplesdon Foursomes of 1932 and played with Bobby Jones in the first two rounds of the 1930 British Open at Hoylake, the second leg of the Grand Slam. He played a good deal with Bobby Jones in those days and his admiration for him influenced his own beliefs in the importance of technique, of which he acquired a profound knowledge.

In an attempt to improve the haphazard methods of selection that prevailed between the wars, he took an increasing interest in the administrative side of amateur golf and in the encouragement of young players. He regarded strokeplay as the more reliable means of assessing a player's ability and, with Gerald Micklem, was responsible in the early 1950s for raising the standard of British golf by the introduction of long-term planning and coaching programmes. While Chairman of the British selectors he travelled thousands of miles in his search for talent and, by so doing, established a much closer relationship between selector and player. He captained the 1951 Walker Cup team and served a long period on the British and English selection committees and has been chairman of both.

He was also president of the English Golf Union in 1962 but once the principles which he encouraged had been adopted, he turned his lively mind to his other consuming

interest, the breeding of bull terriers.

His great love for St Andrews, where he won many of the Royal and Ancient Club's medals, originated in childhood golfing holidays spent there with his father. He has also taken a lifelong interest in university golf through the medium of the Oxford and Cambridge Golfing Society, and of the League, a private club founded by him which for years gave undergraduates the chance to play against some of the best amateurs in the country. For his services to the game he was awarded the CBE.

Orange GC AUSTRALIA
Duntryleague, N.S.W. 18 holes; 6,609 yd (6,043 m)

The club at Orange, the 'Cherry Blossom City', was inaugurated early in the 1900s, although golf was played elsewhere in Orange before the club had borrowed £25,000 to purchase 141 acres on the Duntryleague Estate (57 ha). John Irving came from Canberra as the first professional and supervised the construction of tees and greens on a course which was adorned with few trees apart from large pines. Some trees were planted at that time but it was not until 1950 that, with the object both of adding beauty to the course and adding more feature to the golf, a tree-planting programme was undertaken under the direction of Ilmar Berzenz. Today the club can boast 10,000 trees. The original clubhouse was a small room in what is now the Duntryleague Country Club guesthouse; after the war an army hut served as clubhouse until the existing one was built. The lush fairways of African couch grass were grown from a 4-ft square patch planted as an experiment in 1948. This grass was given to Bathurst GC by the greenkeeper of Elanora in Sydney. It had not thrived at Bathurst, but was a great success at Orange. The first club championship was held in 1908, and during the 1950s and 1960s exhibition matches were played by Bobby Locke, Norman von Nida, Arnold Palmer and Bruce Devlin. In 1960 during the playing of the Wills International Golf Marathon, Peter Thomson was lowest scorer in the third round there with 66.

Orcutt, Maureen (Mrs J. D. Crews) AMERICAN
Runner-up US Women's Amateur 1927, 1936, semi-finalist 1933; Canadian Women's 1930-1; Curtis Cup 1932, 1934, 1936, 1938; US Women's Senior 1962, runner-up 1963

A prolific winner of regional championships, Maureen Orcutt appeared in four Curtis Cup matches. She was Mrs Crews

before the dissolution of her marriage. In addition to her appearances in national championships she won the North and South Women's three times, the Eastern seven times, the Women's Metropolitan eight times, and the New Jersey State Matchplay Championship eight times. She

was three times the lowest scorer in qualifying for the National Amateur, and she lost the 1936 final to the 19-year-old English girl, Pam Barton. Her appearances in the first four Curtis Cup matches included three foursome and two singles victories. Maureen Orcutt covered the leading golf championships and women's events for the *New York Times*.

Örebro GC SWEDEN
Örebro. 18 holes; 6,409 yd (5,860 m)

Nine holes were first laid out in 1939, with extensions later. Örebro Golfklubb is regarded as having the best inland course in Sweden and is frequently used for championships, more so than any other in the country. It has all the characteristics of a first-class golf course with great variety and it is absolutely necessary for the player to think his way round. It is conveniently situated near the E3 road from Gothenburg (Göteborg) to Örebro.

Orr, Edith C. BRITISH
British Ladies' 1897

Edith Orr defeated her elder sister by 4 and 3 in the final of the British Ladies' at Gullane, this being the first time two sisters had met in the final, and the first visit of the event to Scotland. A third sister also competed and reached the fourth round. In reaching the final Miss Orr won three of her matches in 11 holes and two more in 16; only by Maud Titterton (Mrs Jock Gibb) was she taken to the 18th in the semi-finals.

Raymond Oppenheimer playing in the President's Putter

Maureen Orcutt

She was reported as having an excellent style, and as being a strong driver, accurate iron player and deadly putter. The first club the Orr sisters had joined was North Berwick Ladies earlier in the same year. They did not compete again after that championship. The reason is said to have been that their father, a man of strict principles, refused to permit them to take part in any further competitive events because he had discovered that bets had been placed on the results of matches in the championship.

Östersund-Frösö GC SWEDEN
Östersund. 18 holes; 6,398 yd (5,850 m)
A famous winter resort, Östersund, near the geographical centre of Sweden, is also known for its golf. Östersund-Frösö Golfklubb has a course on the island of Frösö in Storsjön, a lake. The scenery is breathtaking; the course is built on slopes above the lake with snow-clad mountains surrounding it. The area is famous for its ancient history and romantic songs. Lately an added attraction has been its Midnight Sun Golf Tournament, starting at midnight on Midsummer Eve and combined with a sumptuous *smörgåsbord* supper.

O'Sullivan, Dr William M. IRISH
b. Killarney, Co. Kerry, 1911. Runner-up Irish Close Amateur 1940; Irish Open Amateur 1949, runner-up 1936, 1953
When 'Docther Billy'o', as he is known affectionately throughout his native Kerry, won the Irish Open Amateur Championship on his own course in 1949, he was carried shoulder high through the town headed by the local band and bonfires blazed on the surrounding hills – a tribute to Killarney's most famous player. He was one of the small, dedicated group, headed by the landlord, the Earl of Kenmare, better known as Lord Castlerosse, who were determined that Ireland's universally known beauty spot should have a golf course of championship quality. Having taken a leading part in the planning, it was fitting that he should win the first important event there three years after the opening of the course.
A powerful athlete who had only just missed selection as Ireland's rugby out half, his hitting was legendary and his method of attacking the ball unique. The split second before unleashing his backswing he widened his stance by moving his right foot some 8 in further to the right, thus widening the arc of his swing, but while this looked perfectly natural for him, none of his contemporaries, nor for that matter any other first-class player, has attempted to emulate that movement. The results were almost sensational,

for nobody could hit the ball further than he did at his peak, and his feats in this respect were the joy of his faithful local followers.
Although his putting was not of the most consistent, he backed up his siege-gun driving with iron play of fine quality. He played 12 times for Ireland from 1934 in the Home Internationals, and in 1949 came very close to Walker Cup selection. When he retired from the international scene he became an important figure on the administrative side. He was president of the Golfing Union of Ireland in 1958-60 and did much to ensure the success of the Canada Cup meeting at Portmarnock in 1960.

Otago GC NEW ZEALAND
Dunedin, S. Island. 18 holes
New Zealand golf began in Dunedin and the Otago GC (Balmacewan) can claim a link with the earliest days. In September 1871 the Dunedin club was formed (*see* New Zealand), but by 1876 deterioration in the course and the burning down of the original clubhouse caused golf to vanish from the scene. It reappeared in 1892 with the establishment of the Otago club. Although the founder, C. R. Howden, and his friends supplied an element of continuity, Otago makes no claim to be a revival of the old Dunedin club. However, some of the trophies presented in 1872 to the latter club – the first in the southern hemisphere – are still played for today. In this sense the Otago club can claim a hundred years of golf.
In 1892 the Otago course was at Roslyn, with a room at Roslyn Hall used as a clubhouse, but a new site had to be found in 1895, and after a great deal of negotiation the club became the owners for £1,650 of an 18-hole course at Balmacewan. Its qualities as a course soon became evident and it played a notable part in the history of New Zealand golf and of its championships. Set on heavy subsoil in the long basin behind the western ridge of Dunedin, it provides attractive golf, although in 1919 it was once described as a 'beastly course', and it took some time for criticism to be lived down. Alterations made in 1948 and 1953 lengthened it considerably and gave it a stern new front. Talk of a proposed move to the sand dunes of Brighton in the face of the threat of suburban encroachment came to nothing. Today, with its modern clubhouse, Otago is proud of its traditions and of its place in the nation's golfing history. It has staged many championships, and the one match in the 1928 New Zealand Amateur has gone into the record books. It was in a 36-hole quarter-final match that Jack Black of Wellington beat Chris Wight of Dunedin

at the 37th hole after having been 9 down at lunchtime.

Ottawa GC, Royal CANADA
Hull, Que. 18 holes, 6,285 yd (5,747 m), par 71
Although not of modern championship class, the course is as pleasant as may be found anywhere and is a constant delight to play. Built on two main levels, and with a gully running through it, the rolling terrain provides few level fairways. Thus a considerable variety of lies and stances are encountered, which helps to explain why the official course record is 69. It was here that the revered Charles R. Murray in 1906 and 1911 scored his two Canadian Open Championship victories. But it is for amateur competition that the course is best suited. The Canadian Amateur Championship has been contested at Royal Ottawa on seven occasions, including its first playing in 1895. Ottawa GC, as it was then called, was first located in 1891 in the Sandy Hill district, now in the heart of Canada's capital city. It moved a few years later out to Chelsea Road where it had 9 holes. Within 10 years an offer to purchase the club's land for more than twice its cost was shrewdly accepted by its directors. This enabled the club to buy sufficient fertile farmland on Aylmer Road on the Quebec side of the Ottawa River for a full 18 holes. Later acquisitions have increased the club's property to more than 300 acres (121 ha), accessible in a few minutes by road from Ottawa. The Duke of Connaught, then Governor General of Canada, himself an avid golfer and a member of the club, was instrumental in 1912 in having 'Royal' added to its name. Fires have twice razed the clubhouse, the second time in 1930. But after each disaster a finer building has risen from the ashes, so that the club now has one of the most gracious and comfortable clubhouses in the country.

Ouimet, Francis D. AMERICAN
b. Brookline, Mass., 1893; d. Newton, Mass., 1967. US Open 1913; joint 5th 1914; French Open Amateur 1914; US Amateur 1914, 1931, runner-up 1920; Walker Cup 1922, 1923-4, 1926, 1928, 1930, 1932, 1934, non-playing captain 1936, 1938, 1947, 1949; semi-finalist British Amateur 1923
Ouimet distinguished himself by winning one of the most momentous championships of all time – the US Open at Brookline in 1913. An amateur of 20, unknown outside the state of Massachusetts where he was born, he tied with two outstanding British professionals of the day – Harry Vardon and Ted Ray – and won the play-off. The follow-

ing year he won the US Amateur and 17 years later, when he was thought to be past his best, he repeated that victory. In between, his golf was distinguished more for its solid consistency than for the brilliance which had marked his arrival in the front rank, but because of the importance of that Open victory and because of his courtesy and friendliness towards British golfers, his name stands high among the great ones of that period.

Ouimet's victory cannot be said to have marked the end of British domination of American golf, for in 1920 Ray won the title with Vardon joint 2nd; nor can it be said exactly to have put golf on the front page there, for the powerful press of New York

almost ignored his victory. As much as anything it was his personality that made such an impression, making golfers in that country aware of the possibilities for all and any of them. Unassuming and modest, Ouimet was a complete amateur, not belonging to the country club set, but working in Boston, caddying for a few dollars a day and playing on the course which lay across the road from his home. He had entered that championship with diffidence, in response to the efforts of the USGA to build up the entry, and in order to get a closer look at Vardon. The better-known Americans failed in their challenge to the British couple and only Ouimet was left in contention. A slender chance, for with 4 holes to play he needed to finish in 1 under the par of 15 to tie them, but he took only 1 putt on each of the last four greens, holing an awkward one on the 17th for his birdie. The play-off was something of an anti-climax. By all the laws the boy ought to have cracked, but he played steadily and allowed the others to defeat themselves. He won by 5 strokes from Vardon and 6 from Ray. Bernard Darwin,

who was marker in the play-off, was so struck by Ouimet's courage that he found himself hoping that he would win.

In the following year Ouimet was the centre of great interest on his visit to Britain but in the strange conditions he suffered a complete loss of form. He finished well down the list in the *Golf Illustrated* Gold Vase and was beaten in the second round of the Amateur, but he took back with him a useful lesson in the art of iron play in wind. Ouimet adopted the interlocking grip and from a narrow stance used an upright swing. From Harold Hilton he learned the punch shot that stood him in good stead afterwards. Gradually his confidence returned. He won the French Amateur Championship, finished joint 5th in the US Open; victory in the US Amateur fulfilled his dearest ambition, and he came to it as Bobby Jones was to, after victory in the Open. Altogether, including his second victory in 1931, Ouimet reached the semi-finals nine times, and in 1920 was beaten in the final by Chick Evans.

No man has had stronger associations with the Walker Cup. He started with a remarkable recovery in 1923 in which the Americans scraped home by a single point, and in which Ouimet halved a magnificent match against Roger Wethered with a birdie at the 36th hole. From that year he took part in all seven matches until 1949, captaining the team on the last six occasions. For many years he was a committee member of the USGA and was prominent in golf administration and legislation in America. In 1951, in recognition of his services to the game and of his friendliness and long association with Britain, he was elected captain of the Royal and Ancient GC, the first person not of British nationality to hold that office.

Out
The holes of the first 9; the holes of the

second 9 are variously known as 'in', 'back' or 'home'.

Out-to-in
Swinging a club in such a manner that at impact the clubhead is not travelling straight towards the hole but to the left of the aiming point. In America the expression 'outside-in' is preferred.

Oxford and Cambridge Golfing Society
The Oxford and Cambridge Golfing Society, better known simply as the Society, was first conceived in 1897 after R. H. de Montmorency, then captain of Oxford, had invited a team of former University players to come down and play a match against Oxford and dine afterwards at the Gridiron Club. During the dinner, the suggestion was made and later adopted to form a club from both universities. On 23 March 1898, the Society was formally constituted with Horace Hutchinson as president, John Low, captain, Arthur Croome secretary and de Montmorency as treasurer. The original committee included Eric Hambro and H. S. Colt, the well-known golf course architect.

The first match, in which Bernard Darwin took part, was played in June 1898, against Royal St George's. From this a full fixture list of matches (usually foursomes) and tours quickly developed. In 1903 a visit was made to the United States, often regarded as a forerunner to the Walker Cup; in 1923 the Society entertained an American team at Rye; and in 1911 beat a team of professionals that included Vardon, Taylor and Braid.

One of the main objects of the Society is to foster and encourage golf at Oxford and Cambridge whose players over the years have made a notable contribution to British sides. The Society has had a representative in nearly every Walker Cup match and can claim a long list of other inter-

A portrait of Francis D. Ouimet in his captain's coat of the Royal and Ancient GC

Oxford *v* Cambridge at Rye, 1967

nationals. However, the Society is best known by the public for its annual meeting for the President's Putter which takes place at Rye in January in a variety of weathers.

The original putter presented by John Low belonged to Hughie Kirkaldy, who won the Open at St Andrews in 1891, and was bought from him by John Boger. The winner of the tournament attaches the ball which he played in the final to the shaft of the club by a silver band. The winner is further rewarded by the presentation of a specially struck silver medal. The number of winners of the Putter, however, has made it necessary for a second putter to be added in order to accommodate the balls and both hang in the clubhouse at Rye, the club which long ago 'adopted' the Society and made it welcome.

The history of the Society up to 1948 is set out in *The Oxford and Cambridge Golfing Society 1898-1948*, edited by Eric Prain. The Society's famous players over the years include Roger Wethered, Cyril Tolley, Leonard Crawley, Sir Ernest Holderness, Frank Pennink, Bobby Sweeny, Laddie Lucas, Gerald Micklem, John Langley, Gordon Huddy, Alec Shepperson and David Marsh.

Oxley, Dinah BRITISH

b. Dorking, Surrey, 1948. British Girls' 1963, runner-up 1966; English Girls' 1965, runner-up 1966; Curtis Cup 1968, 1970, 1972; Worplesdon Foursomes (with J. Dudok van Heel) 1968; runner-up British Strokeplay 1969; French Girls' 1969; Wills Ladies' Matchplay 1969-71; British Ladies' 1970, semi-finalist 1969; English Ladies' 1970, 1971, runner-up 1968; World Women's Amateur Team Championship 1970

One of the outstanding shotmakers in postwar British golf, Dinah Oxley had an outstanding career as a junior, winning both girls' championships before she was 17 (the British Girls' while still only 14). Her career had ups and downs, but reached its full flowering in 1970 when she won the British and English championships and had numerous other successes. At her best there was no holding her until the arrival on the scene of Michelle Walker. Her classical swing with a wide arc and hands high at the top of the backswing was responsible for towering, majestic strokes and accurate iron shots into the green. She suffered the handicaps of the perfectionist and she needed constant reminders of how good she was. Matchplay was her strongest point, especially in single combat when, given a good start, she was capable of outclassing any opponent, but she had a number of minor achievements in strokeplay, including the 1968 Astor Salver.

Dinah Oxley

Oyster Harbors Club USA

Cape Cod, Mass. 18 holes; 6,770 yd (6,191 m); par 72

Cape Cod is an appendage of Massachusetts, jutting into the Gulf Stream, whose warming waters give it a climate much more mild than the rest of the state, and golf can be played there the year round. Oysterville is a small resort village on the southern coast of the Cape. It is the home of the Oyster Harbors Club, a pleasant though testing course, whose members have included some of the best-known players in American golf and politics. It was the favourite course of Francis Ouimet; Dick Chapman was a member, and so was Johnny Fischer – all of them United States Amateur Champions. This was where the Kennedy boys learned to play, and where Joseph P. Kennedy, father of the clan and once Ambassador to the Court of St James, had a standing date to play every Tuesday afternoon when he was in Hyannis, a neighbouring village.

The course itself is one of the finest of Donald Ross's creations, set on an island in the harbour and bearing a strong resemblance to Pinehurst. It is built on sandy soil, and its fairways weave through a heavy growth of scrub pine, although the trees have twice been thinned by hurricanes that occasionally rip across the Cape. For a number of years it was the site of the Massachusetts Open when the tournament drew some of the great players of New England. Jug McSpaden won it four years running.

Oyster Harbors was built in the mid-1920s as a member-owned club, and through the years it became quite exclusive. In the late 1960s, it was bought by a few Cape Cod residents, including Felix du Pont and Paul Mellon, neither of them golfers. The old cavernous clubhouse was demolished, and then some of those who came to play Oyster Harbors had nowhere to stay. Gradually the members again asserted an influence on management, and the club began a rejuvenation. The golf course, though, has remained untouched, and it is still so pleasure-giving that the members say that if they had to limit themselves to one golf course for the rest of their lives, this would be it.

Ozaki, Masashi JAPANESE

b. Tokushima Prefecture 1947. Japanese Professional 1971; Asahi International 1972; Kanto Open 1972; New Zealand PGA 1972; runner-up Tournament of Champions 1972

Ozaki's athletic career started in baseball; he left school a star pitcher, having carried his school team to the National High School Championship in his final year. After graduating he was signed up with a team in the professional league for a bonus of 10 million yen, but he hardly fulfilled his promise, and after two years with only a moderate record, he turned from baseball to golf, becoming professional in 1969. In his short time in professional golf he has already made his mark. In 1971, only his second year as a professional, his prize winnings were more than 17 million yen. In 1972, he was already past the 10-million-yen mark shortly after the season had reached the halfway mark. Because of the tremendous distance he gets off the tee, he is generally called 'Jumbo' Ozaki. He is also conspicuous for the colourful clothes he wears on the course, and he is always sure of a following. He has been called for this reason the 'Doug Sanders' of Japan. He has played in the US Masters.

Pacing

A modern practice that enables the player to know the length of any shot he has to play. He keeps a set of notes marking the paced-out distances from particular landmarks to the centre of a given green and then calculates any difference. He may also note the length of certain carries from the tee. Pacing is now an accepted practice although it offends those who believe that judgment of distance is part of the game. Players usually do their pacing during practice or, an increasingly popular custom, receive the information set out on specially printed cards.

Padgham, Alfred H. BRITISH

b. Surrey 1906; d. 1966. British Professional Matchplay 1931, 1935, runner-up 1940; Ryder Cup 1933, 1935, 1937; British Open 1936, runner-up 1935, 3rd 1934

In the days before national champions tried to project themselves as national figures, Padgham was one of the quiet champions of British golf following in the footsteps of an even quieter one, Alf Perry. Yet there was nothing unobtrusive about his string of successes in the mid-1930s. In 1935 he had won the second of his British Matchplay Championships, defeating Percy Alliss in the final, and he won three tournaments in 1936 before coming to the Open in a blaze of glory. There were signs of his long game beginning to wilt, but he continued to score well and his putter, which had performed prodigies for him, did not let him down for he holed from 12 ft for a birdie to win the championship. His swing was short and effortless but he drove a long ball, and his iron play was usually most accurate. In contrast to his drowsy rhythm in the long game his putting was ungainly to look at: he adopted an upright stance with his huge hands held well away from the body and struck the ball almost as if he were playing a short chip. Padgham's family had strong associations with Royal Ashdown Forest and he was an apprentice there for some years. In his great year, 1936, he was elected captain of the Professional Golfers' Association. On the course he gave an impression of almost bovine serenity, but he was a shrewd and observant man. In a wartime Matchplay Championship in 1940 he was runner-up to

Henry Cotton at Royal Mid-Surrey where he had won his other two matchplay titles.

Page, Mrs Julius A., Jr (née Estelle Lawson) AMERICAN

US Women's Amateur 1937, runner-up 1938, semi-finalist 1941, 1947, 1951; Curtis Cup 1938, 1948

Mrs Page had the edge over her rival, Patty Berg, when they met in the 1937 final of the National Women's Amateur at Memphis and won by 7 and 6. When they met next year at Wilmette, however, Patty Berg was successful by 6 and 5.

Undoubtedly World War II deprived Mrs Page of further honours but she played in two Curtis Cup matches, the last before, and the first after hostilities. From these games Mrs Page gained 3 points, both singles, and a win in the foursomes in 1948.

In the Women's North and South Amateur at Pinehurst in 1950 she played the last two days of the event with acute appendicitis, and after losing the final by 3 and 2 to Pat O'Sullivan, drove home to Chapel Hill, N. Car., and was later that day admitted to hospital for an emergency operation.

She has been the dominant figure in North Carolina women's event for more than 20 years, but without ever letting her domestic and social life suffer thereby.

Pakistan

The origins of golf in Pakistan date back to the days before the partition of the Indian subcontinent when the game was patronized largely by the British. Of the small number of Indians who had the opportunity to play very few were Muslim. Thus after Partition in 1947 and the departure from the new state of Pakistan of many non-Muslims, the membership of all golf clubs fell and a number closed down altogether. It was left to a handful of Pakistani players to keep the game alive. This they did and their keenness not only kept the clubs going but attracted more of their countrymen to the game. Golf increased considerably in popularity.

In February 1960 the Pakistan Golf Union was formed with a view to promoting still further the interests of the game, and to help member clubs in the maintenance of a uniform handicap system, interpretation of the Rules of Golf, assisting in the lay-out and upkeep of courses and maintaining a link with other golfing countries as a means of fostering friendship.

Frank Pennink was one overseas golf-course architect who did a lot of work for a time in Pakistan in the 1960s and there are now seven 18-hole and eight 9-hole courses

in the country. Before the establishment of the Pakistan Golf Union there had been only four 18-hole and three 9-hole courses; 18-hole courses are now to be found at Abbottabad, Islamabad, Karachi, Lahore Gymkhana, Pakistan Western Railway in Lahore, Peshawar, and Rawalpindi; there are 9-hole courses at Bhurban Services GC, Kohat, Lyallpur, Multan, Nowshera, Quetta, Sialkot and Tarbela.

All the courses, except Bhurban, remain open throughout the year and all have grass greens except Karachi and Quetta which have sand-browns or 'chocolates'.

As the popularity of the game has increased, the standard of play has also risen. Pakistan has entered teams at intervals for the World Amateur Team Championships, and the Asia Amateur Men's Team Championship, and Pakistanis have competed in the Amateur Championship of Sri Lanka (Ceylon).

Palabora GC SOUTH AFRICA

Phalaborwa, Transvaal. 18 holes; 6,640 yd (6,072 m); par 71

In a remote area of the eastern Transvaal, where the great complex of the American Palabora Mining Co. operates, confusingly, at Phalaborwa, is a comprehensive recreational centre that includes a first-class, unique golf course. Unique because the course was carved out of what was part of the Kruger National Park, one of the great wildlife reserves of the world. When the ground for the golf course was taken over it teemed with game and this had to be cleared before work could begin. A fence was erected leaving an open gap through which an army of Africans beating tin buckets and tom-toms carried out a great game drive. Masses of buck and big game, including two leopards, were driven through the gap. The fence was closed but the game were reluctant to go. The next morning it was breached in 27 places and further drives had to be conducted until the ground was cleared. But wild animals are not easily displaced from their territory and during construction there were times when workers had to jump for the top of the bulldozer to avoid angry buffalo. Nor do stiff barbed-wire fences confine elephant and buffalo who break through for the greener pastures of fairways, stately giraffe step over the wire, and a permanent official is kept at work making repairs. Lions keep out of the way of the golf in daytime but, being nocturnal by habit, they frequently leave the remains of their kills to be cleared away by the greenkeeper in the morning. Golfers have to be wary, however, and one four-ball group, looking back at a bunker they had just passed, saw lions lying in the sand. Sometimes elephant and buffalo on the course have halted play; it was deemed necessary to shoot two obdurate elephants and three buffaloes that dangerously resisted attempts to drive them off.

Palabora is probably the only course in the world where players may on occasion see big game and varieties of buck grazing on the far side of the fence lining several of the fairways, and the five excellent water features often have spoor marks round them, telling of nightly visitations. The course is at an elevation of about 1,300 ft, and has a plentiful supply of water from about $9\frac{1}{2}$ miles of underground piping.

Palm Beach Gardens see PROFESSIONAL GOLFERS' ASSOCIATION OF AMERICA

Palmer, Arnold D. AMERICAN
b. Latrobe, Pa., 1929. US Amateur 1954; US Masters 1958, 1960, 1962, 1964; US Open 1960, runner-up 1962, 1966-7; British Open 1961-2; Ryder Cup 1961, 1963, 1965, 1967, 1971, 1973 (captain 1963)

There is a natural law in games by which, periodically, a genius arises and sets the standard of achievement perceptibly higher than before. He forces the pace; the rest have to follow as best they can, and end by squeezing out of themselves just that little bit more than they would have believed possible. Such a leader was Arnold Palmer, the symbol of modern professional golf and

the hero of the golfing world. It is safe to say that nobody in history has made more money from all aspects of golf although, in a sense, he was fortunate in that his career coincided with the astonishing boom the game underwent in the late 1950s and early 1960s.

He benefited from the rapid change but, in many ways, he was the person responsible

for it. Without his example, his heroic golf, his friendliness and his ambition, the transition might not have been as spectacular. His name was on more lips than that of any golfer and has remained in constant respect through the attractive and always positive personality of the man. Palmer's ambition and dedication goes far beyond the mere acquisition of dollars and was forged very largely by the influence of his father who, after working in the Pennsylvania steelmills, became professional at the small Latrobe CC. From an early age, he instilled into his son the importance of respecting the game's traditions and has remained his only teacher.

Palmer has also inherited a good deal of his father's humour and strength as well as the belief that no one can play good golf without a good grip. His huge hands maintained a firm hold and were the basis of the characteristically strong game that developed. Palmer gave everything and attempted everything, or so it seemed, with every shot. Sometimes the results were fatal but, at his height, his flair for recovery from the most unlikely and unpromising places knew no limits; and he identified himself with spectators until, at the end of a round, they felt that they too had taken part.

Nobody, apart perhaps from Walter Hagen, had quite this same appeal and certainly nobody ever had such a following. American crowds had eyes only for Palmer; and Palmer was the player organizers wanted for clinics, exhibitions and for the

endorsement and advertisement of their products.

The first impression of Palmer's power play came in 1954 when he won the final of the US Amateur Championship against Bob Sweeny in Detroit but, having turned professional and won the Canadian Open in 1955, the first of his major championship victories came in the 1958 US Masters. Although not one of his most dramatic wins, it was the signal of what was to come.

He finished 1958 as leading money winner but it was in 1960 that his full competitive powers turned doubters into disciples. In the spring he won the Masters for the second time in three years, showing his capacity for finishing strongly under severe pressure. Ken Venturi was already being spoken of as the winner when Palmer came to the last 3 holes needing 3 birdies to win. His putt for a 2 on the 16th is said to have leaped in the air before going in; and then, after holing from 10 yd for a 3 on the 17th, he hit a superb second to the 18th and holed from 5 ft for victory.

His first and, as things have turned out,

his only victory in the US Open the same June was even more dramatic. After 54 holes on the Cherry Hills course in Colorado he was 7 strokes behind the leader, Mike Souchak, but he mastered the outward 9 in the last round in 30 with 6 birdies in 7 holes, and finished in 65.

A few days later, he won the Canada Cup

Arnold Palmer

Arnold Palmer, *above,* at impact and, *right,* showing characteristic reaction at Portmarnock for the United States with Sam Snead and then went on to St Andrews to play in his first British Open. Only Ben Hogan had achieved the feat of winning the Masters and the two Opens in the same year and Palmer was anxious to join him. His failure to do so can be attributed to taking 3 from just short of the 17th green in the third round and 3 from the Valley of Sin at the 18th but, despite being frustrated by holing few putts on the huge greens, he came 2nd and it needed a brave finish by Kel Nagle to hold him at bay. None the less, his presence was of greater significance than that of any other competitor. His continuing influence restored the British Open to its exalted position as one of the world's major championships. By his example, he persuaded other American players of its importance and, greatly helped by the R. and A.'s admirable staging of the event, its prestige has been maintained.

It was therefore fitting that Palmer should dominate the event for the next two years. At Birkdale in 1961, the year that a storm washed out the Friday's play, he was the central figure. His father had always impressed upon him the importance of being able to play any shot at will, and that week he had reason to be grateful for such wise grounding. His play for the first 6 holes of the second round in a tearing wind in 3 under par was almost beyond belief and is still regarded by him as one of his best performances; in such weather, there were bound to be anxious moments but he was the worthiest of winners, beating Dai Rees by 1 stroke with a total of 284.

The following year the conditions at Troon were very different. The course was baked hard and the ball ran and bounced with almost uncontrollable fury. Palmer obviously did not like the way the course played but he has always responded to a challenge and met that particular one with golf that he has never bettered. He failed to get off to a good start in any round but he played the back 9 commandingly each day, particularly the dangerous 11th by the railway, and, on the last day amid wild crowd scenes which might have had a disastrous effect, he set the lowest aggregate in the history of the championship (276) at that time. This beat Kel Nagle by 6 strokes, the rest by 13, and meant that his talent for holing awkward putts has seldom been equalled.

In the spring of 1962 Palmer had won the Masters yet again, this time after a play-off with Player and Finsterwald, but in June he had lost a play-off with Jack Nicklaus in Nicklaus' first appearance in the US Open as a professional. This was a significant

meeting since it was the first warning of the mighty challenge that was to come from Nicklaus, and the first sign of the emergence of the Big Three – Palmer, Nicklaus and Player.

Palmer's defeat by Nicklaus did not stem his success for he won the US Masters for a record fourth time in 1964. However, a man whose nature it is to be bold and to attack is bound to have his failures; and, as with his successes, they too were spectacular. In the 1960 USPGA Championship at Akron, Ohio, he took 8 at one hole in the third round and this championship remains the one major event he has never won. In the 1961 Masters, needing a four at the 18th to beat Gary Player, he bunkered his second shot with a no. 7 iron and, worse still, took 4 more to get down. Coming at the very height of his powers, it was a surprising lapse, but the most tragic failure of all was in the 1966 US Open at the Olympic Club in San Francisco when he dropped 7 strokes to Billy Casper over the last 9 holes of the final round, and lost a play-off the following day, as Ben Hogan had done on the same course in his most bewildering failure in 1955.

Rounds of 71, 66 and 70, followed by a brilliant outward half of 32 in the final round, seemed to have drained all challenge and interest but Palmer had an eye to beating Hogan's 1948 Open record of 276. He tried to force the course instead of consolidating his victory and his tactics proved disastrous. In the end, he might easily have lost without going to a play-off in which he again faltered on the last 8 holes after leading by 2 strokes at the turn. This was a terrible defeat to bear and Palmer has never been the same again.

He became the first person to win a million dollars in official prize money and, in fact, his long game built up a consistency which it had never possessed even in his most successful days. Palmer has preserved his zest for golf in a remarkable way but the growing inability to hole putts he used to gobble, and trouble with a hip, has deprived him of further major championships. In 1970, he failed to win an individual event on the American tour for the first time since 1955 (he has won more than 60 tournaments altogether on the American professional circuit), but he finished 5th in the official money list, and in 1971 he won the Bob Hope Desert Classic over 90 holes as well as the Westchester Classic. Another barren year as far as victories were concerned was 1972, but in 1973 he again won the Bob Hope Desert Classic and in the US Open finished equal 4th having on the 11th green on the last afternoon missed a shortish putt

to tie the lead; and he qualified for the Ryder Cup team once more.

Ably guided by Mark McCormack who started managing his business affairs in 1960, he built up his financial empire to vast proportions and was the first golfer to fly his own plane to tournaments; but wealth and success never altered him. He was always helpful and approachable to the Press, highly regarded by his fellow professionals and worshipped by a great host of admirers.

In 1971, he was presented with the Bob Jones Award by the USGA for 'distinguished sportsmanship'.

Palmer, Johnny AMERICAN
b. Eldorado, N. Car., 1918. Western Open 1947; Ryder Cup 1949; runner-up USPGA 1949; Canadian Open 1952; Colonial Invitation 1954; Mexican Open 1954

After turning professional in 1938 and serving for $2\frac{1}{2}$ years in the US Air Force, Johnny Palmer, who grew up in the caddie ranks, became a most consistent player on the American circuit. From 1946 to 1951 he averaged over $13,000 a year – good money in those days – a figure beaten only by Hogan, Snead, Middlecoff, Demaret, Mangrum and Ferrier. Major championship victories eluded him but, with a fine short game, he won the Canadian and Mexican titles.

Pals GC SPAIN
Pals, Gerona. 18 holes; 6,825 yd (6,241 m); par 73

The most important golf club on the Costa Brava, though by no means the oldest. Nine holes were opened in 1966 in a pine forest leading down to the Mediterranean from close to the Gothic city of Pals. These first 9 holes, designed by Fred Hawtree, were narrow with small greens, a much greater test of accuracy than of power, as

Johnny Palmer

they moved back and forth between umbrella pines. The second 9, more open in character and providing a greater challenge, were also designed by Hawtree and opened in 1970. That year the club staged the Spanish Open Amateur Championship – hitherto it had been the venue only of the Spanish Junior Championship. The course has many of the features usually associated with the celebrated Spanish architect, Arana; fairway trees and narrow well-defined greens guarded by distinctive bunkers with open ground behind them. The two 9s have been interwoven, giving a good balance to the whole. Because of the mild climate the course has never been closed. The Costa Brava motor road has brought the course within a two-hour drive of Barcelona. It also forms a natural outlet for the golfers among the two million tourists who invade this part of Spain every year. In particular it serves the coastal resorts of Palafrugell, Calella, Palamos and Llafranch in the Bay of Pals.

Panton, John BRITISH

b. Pitlochry, Perthshire, 1916. Scottish PGA 1948-51, 1954-5, 1959; Ryder Cup 1951, 1953, 1961; Vardon Trophy 1951; World (Canada) Cup 1955-66; British Professional Matchplay 1956, runner-up 1968; Teachers' British Senior Professional 1967; World Senior Professional 1967; Pringle Senior Professional 1969

Together with Eric Brown, John Panton dominated Scottish professional golf for the best part of 20 years after World War II. He captured the Scottish and Northern Open championships seven times each and won a host of lesser events in his native Scotland. In addition to his World and Ryder Cup appearances he also won five major official tournaments in the early and middle 1950s, culminating in his most prestigious success, the 1956 Professional Matchplay event.

The strengths of Panton's game were his masterly long-iron shots and the touch he acquired and maintained in his approach putting. But his driving was erratic and his holing out uncertain, the two flaws in an otherwise complete armoury of stroke-making, in which his ability to 'manufacture' shots was outstanding.

Perhaps above all Panton had a swing and a method that were made to last, despite the fact that in physique he was never less than portly. Taciturn by nature, Panton let his game speak for him and its qualities of endurance were underlined when, at the age of 53, he finished equal 9th in the 1970 British Open Championship, having returned the lowest last round and won £1,200, the biggest single prize of his long career.

When Panton, in 1966, reached his golfing seniority he took on a new lease of tournament life. He twice won British Seniors' championships and in 1967 beat Sam Snead by 3 and 2 over 36 holes in the World Seniors' final at Wallasey.

Par

'Par' is the score that an expert golfer would be expected to make for a given hole. Par means errorless play without flukes and, under ordinary weather conditions, allows 2 strokes on each putting green.

Par is based on yardage recommended by the various governing bodies of the world. It should be emphasized that par applies to each individual hole and is governed by the length of this hole and not, necessarily, by its difficulty. Difficulty is taken care of under the heading of Standard Scratch Score in Britain and elsewhere, and Course Rating in America.

Paraparaumu Beach GC NEW ZEALAND

Paraparaumu, N. Island. 18 holes; 6,428 yd (5,878 m)

Paraparaumu Beach, as its name suggests, is a true seaside course, exposed to all winds and situated on a sandy belt in fine, rolling country. The club itself was not formed until 1949 when Alex Russell of Melbourne designed the course and the foundation committee of S. Paterson, D. O. Whyte, J. H. Francis, W. G. Horne and W. B. Brown was responsible for creating the facilities that exist today. Although a relatively young club, its reputation spread fast and over the years it has been host to many major tournaments including three New Zealand Opens, the New Zealand Mens' and Ladies' Amateur championships, the Freyberg Rosebowl Tournament and the North Island Championship.

For many years also it has been the scene of the Caltex Tournament. Peter Thomson and Kel Nagle have helped to increase the club's stature by returning each year to play in a place they both enjoy very much.

Park, Mungo BRITISH

b. Musselburgh, Midlothian. British Open 1874, 3rd 1875, joint 4th 1876

John Panton

Paraparaumu Beach GC, the 1967 New Zealand Championship in progress

Although overshadowed by his brother Willie Park Sr and his nephew, Willie Jr, Mungo was a champion in his own right and contributed to that talented family's tally of seven Open Championships. But for having been a sailor until he was past his prime he would no doubt have won the title more than once for his winning score at Musselburgh, 159 for 36 holes, was the lowest since Young Tom Morris's last victory four years earlier. Mungo had the family skill in putting, and took part in many of the challenge matches of the period.

Park, Willie, Jr BRITISH

b. Musselburgh, Midlothian, 1864; d. 1925.
British Open 1887, 1889

A member of the old Scots school of professionals, Park was brought up surrounded by the traditions of the game since his father, Willie Park Sr, won the first British Open in 1860 and also those of 1863, 1866 and 1875; and his uncle, Mungo Park, was champion in 1874.

At the age of 16, Willie Park Jr went for four years as professional/greenkeeper to Ryton before returning to his native town to start business as a club and ball maker. He won his first tournament at the age of 17 at Alnmouth against one of the best fields available, and triumphed again in 1886 in one of the first events at Troon. Coming in late, he returned 148 for two rounds.

These were undeniable indications of his class and in 1887, having finished joint 4th in

1884, he won the Open Championship at Prestwick with a total of 161. A little later, he played havoc with the course record at Alnmouth but perhaps his finest performance came in 1889 when he won the Open Championship for the second time at Musselburgh. Andrew Kirkaldy was thought to be in an unassailable position with 155 but Park, having to finish almost in the dark, made up 2 strokes in the last 3 holes to tie. Play-offs in those days were not considered a matter of undue urgency and three days passed before Park and Kirkaldy set forth to decide the issue but the play-off was an anticlimax. Park, always the steadier, won by 5 strokes.

Park was also an unashamed lover of the challenge match and a few months later offered to play anyone for £100 per side over four greens. Kirkaldy took up the gauntlet and came out on top by 8 and 7, not a large margin over 144 holes that produced some wonderful golf.

In 1896, Park, the most imperturbable of golfers, won a notable match for the same sum against J. H. Taylor, the Open champion of 1894 and 1895. His most famous match, however, is generally considered to have been that against Harry Vardon in 1899, which in some sense was a test of driver v. putter. Park was perhaps the first of the deadly putters and the remark 'a man who can putt is a match for anyone' is attributed to him. Although he had a deliberate style with the long game and was powerful as

well as accurate with his irons, his putting was his great strength and his favourite putter, 'Old Pawky', became almost as famous as its master; but when he and Vardon came to Ganton for the second half of the match, Vardon had built new tees which made the course longer and Park was never able to live with him.

About this time, Park became the first in a subsequently long and distinguished line of golf-course architects. It was an art in which he was obviously gifted and several famous courses (Sunningdale Old, West Hill, Huntercombe among them) are memorials to him. He set standards which others followed, and later undertook a good deal of work in America and Canada. After a long spell overseas, he died of a nervous complaint in Edinburgh in 1925.

Park, Willie, Sr BRITISH

British Open 1860, 1863, 1866, 1875

Willie Park, a member of a great Scottish golfing family whose name was synonymous with Musselburgh, has the distinction of being the first Open champion in the history of golf. At a time when he and Old Tom Morris had a glorious struggle for supremacy and repeatedly challenged each other to big money matches, Willie Park won the first championship at Prestwick in 1860 from a field of eight and later three more victories.

Although a brilliant shotmaker and a daring player, he was also a fine putter and

Willie Park Jr *(centre)* in the Grand Challenge Match of 1890 with, third from the left, Andrew Kirkaldy at St Andrews

is said to have learned the art by practising over the four 'baker's holes' at Musselburgh, so called because the local baker, who used to sell his pies to hungry golfers, often engaged in putting matches. Park's record for the course was 5 and he was to be seen there most evenings as a boy. Later he was to pass on his skill to his son, Willie Park Jr.

Parks, Sam AMERICAN
US Open 1935

Having only a short time before joined the professional ranks from college and the amateur game, Parks caused a major surprise by winning the 1935 US Open at Oakmont. A likeable and retiring professional in the Pittsburgh area, he had played many times at the host club, and his knowledge of the course undoubtedly influenced his victory. He was the only player to break 300 on a course of many furrowed bunkers and lightning-fast greens. His total was 299 (77, 73, 73, 76). None of the 20 leaders broke 75 in the last round.

Parks grew up in Pittsburgh and learned the game as a youngster from Gene Sarazen. He was a star player on the Pittsburgh University team before deciding to turn professional.

Parkstone GC ENGLAND
Parkstone, Dorset. 18 holes; 6,202 yd (5,671 m); par 70

Parkstone, only a short distance from the holiday centre of Bournemouth, began its association with golf in 1910 when the famous old professional, Willie Park, laid out the course on land owned by Lord Wimborne. Seventeen years later this land was acquired by the Parkstone GC Co. who added to it and made alterations under the supervision of James Braid and Reggie Whitcombe; the latter won the British Open in 1938 and was professional at

Sam Parks

Parkstone GC – Peter Alliss seen putting

the club until his death in 1957. Three years later the course was sold to the members. By this time Parkstone had become one of the best courses in the West of England and certainly one of the most scenic, with views over the Purbeck Hills and Poole Harbour. In the opinion of Peter Alliss, who succeeded Whitcombe as professional, the course, skirted by ornamental lakes and on a sandy subsoil, is one of the best training grounds to be found. Gorse, heather, pine and silver birch add to its beauty and to its golfing distinction. Besides its proud connection with two such eminent club professionals, it produced Ernest Millward, English Amateur Champion in 1952, two British Curtis Cup players and captains, Jeanne Bisgood and Mrs Maureen Garrett, and also Barbara Dixon, winner at her first attempt of the English Ladies' Championship in 1969.

Pascoe, Amy Bennett BRITISH
British Ladies' 1896

Amy Pascoe's victory in the British championship at Royal Liverpool was her outstanding performance. About three thousand spectators followed her final against Lena Thompson whom she defeated by 3 and 2. Two years before when Miss Pascoe followed the play in the Ladies' Championship she had been only a beginner. The following year, 1895, she had played in the championship at Portrush in borrowed clothing which included a man's red coat, her luggage having been lost on the journey. In an age

when competition was not at all serious, Miss Pascoe astonished her friends by practising intensively and by having much professional tuition. She played with tremendous concentration and her style was wholly artificial. Photographs of her in action show her right elbow pointing skywards at the top of the backswing. She represented England against Ireland in 1895 and 1901 and was the first captain of the Surrey Ladies' county team in 1900. During 1898 she held the women's records of Woking (96), Wimbledon (73), Great Yarmouth (86), Surbiton (88), Bushey (88), and Ranelagh (78). It is hardly surprising that she was considered stronger in medal than match-play. A firm nerve and dogged resolution brought their rewards.

Paterson, Moira (Mrs John C. Milton) BRITISH
b. 1923. Runner-up French Ladies' Open 1949; runner-up Scottish Ladies' 1951; British Ladies' 1952; Curtis Cup 1952

Moira Paterson won the British championship at Troon after the longest final in that event. Twice five down she fought back to take the title at the 38th hole against Frances Stephens. In 1951 she toured South Africa with a British team.

Patton, William Joseph AMERICAN
b. North Carolina 1922. North and South Amateur 1954, 1962-3; 3rd US Masters 1954; low amateur US Open 1954, 1957;

Walker Cup 1955, 1957, 1959, 1963, 1965 (captain 1969); Eisenhower Trophy 1958, 1962; Southern Amateur 1961, 1965; semi-finalist US Amateur 1962

The record is less impressive than the man. Few amateurs in any country of the world made quite the same impact as Billy Joe Patton. This was because he was a man who responded to the big occasion and who was capable of flair. He has been a golfing warrior. Possessed of one of the fastest swings in first-class golf he inevitably hit many loose shots; when out of form and timing he could play downright badly, but thanks to his great strength and speed of clubhead he could engineer marvellous recoveries, which were useful in strokeplay and sometimes devastating in matchplay. Nowhere was this better illustrated than in the Walker Cup matches, and particularly those of 1957 and 1963, in both of which he was largely instrumental in extricating his country from an awkward position. In 1957, 5 down at lunch to Reid Jack in the top match with the contest evenly poised, he saved himself at least four times after driving into rough or trees and either halved or won holes he looked likely to lose without being on the fairway. The year 1965 was his last appearance as a player in the matches, in which he scored 11 points out of 14, but he captained the 1969 US team at Milwaukee which was also engaged in a close finish.

Such genius for matchplay did not prevent his scoring well in strokeplay. With his uncertain driving and because he was for much of the time little more than a weekend golfer, his medal play was unpredictable, but in one remarkable year, 1954, he finished 3rd in the Masters to Snead and Hogan, and led the field with a first-round 69 in the US Open. He led in the Masters at the halfway stage, and regained the lead in the last round, when he was playing with Hogan, by

holing his tee shot to the 6th hole. He was still contesting the lead at the 12th, but found the challenge of trying to get up in 2 at the 13th irresistible and, failing to make it, ran up a 7. At the address Patton's whole powerful frame was tensed as though against some explosion, and he used a waggle that gave full notice of what was to come. He was educated at Wake Forest College, made famous by Arnold Palmer and the home of several first-class golfers.

Pau GC FRANCE
Pau, Basses-Pyrénées. 18 holes; 5,950 yd (5,441 m); par 70

Situated below the town beside the river Gave de Pau, this is the oldest course on the continent of Europe. The idea of playing golf in that area is said to have come first from Scottish officers convalescing there after the Peninsular War against Napoleon. When the course was opened in 1856 it was supported by the considerable British colony in the spa town. The names of the Duke of Hamilton and Colonel Hutchinson, father of Horace Hutchinson, are associated with the club's early days; its extension from 9 to 18 holes and from one room in a nearby inn as the original clubhouse to a separate building owed much to Sir Victor Brooke, the father of Lord Alanbrooke. The clubhouse today retains several features that recall its British origins. The walls are lined with the winners of club competitions, the oldest of them going back to its early years, and most of those names are British. The bridge room is furnished in Edwardian style with British furniture, and the signpost leading to the club is still printed in English. The course itself is flat, but there are many trees, in particular pines; the rough is thick and lush and a ball is easily lost.

Peachtree GC USA
Atlanta, Ga. 18 holes; 7,000 yd (6,400 m)

Mention of golf in Georgia used to bring Atlanta and Bobby Jones first to mind. Today the name of the State probably calls up for most people the Masters tournament in Augusta. At the same time, there is much fine golf on the many fine courses in Atlanta, and one of the best of these is the Peachtree GC.

Bob Jones had a big hand in building Peachtree. It was constructed shortly after World War II, and Bob, then in excellent health, hit hundreds of shots in assisting Robert Trent Jones, the architect, to arrive at the right golf values for the layout. As with most Trent Jones courses, Peachtree can be stretched beyond 7,000 yd by moving the tees back, but no one should play the

tiger tees unless he is a real tiger. The course starts with a 385-yd (352-m) par 4, then swings into a 555-yd (507-m) par 5 on which there are no bunkers and no need of them. From there on, the course never lets up. A good many of its tees are elevated, which helps the average golfer; a good many of its greens are crown greens, which helps him not at all.

The clubhouse has a real *Gone with the Wind* air about it and it is, in truth, an antebellum Southern mansion. Legend – perhaps best not mentioned around the club – has it that General Sherman made this his headquarters during his hours of ease while marching through Georgia.

Pebble Beach Golf Links USA
Pebble Beach, Cal. 18 holes; 6,832 yd (6,247 m); par 72

Despite its official name, Pebble Beach is not really a golf links. It is not built on linksland but on high-cliffed headlands which tower above Carmel Bay. Apart from this, everything commonly said about Pebble Beach is true. It is probably the most spec-

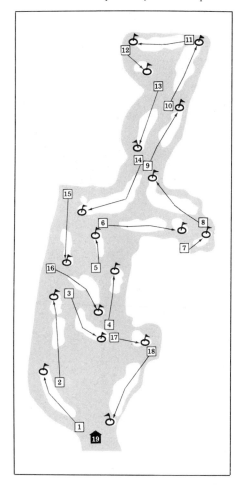

William J. Patton

Pebble Beach, *above*, the course plan and, on the next page, the short 7th hole

tacular golf course in the western hemisphere – maybe in the world.

Pebble Beach is situated on the Monterey Peninsula, which projects into the Pacific about 125 miles south of San Francisco. Almost all of the peninsula is owned by the Del Monte Properties Company which began in the resort field by building and operating the Del Monte Hotel, one of those huge, wooden, veranda-lined pleasure domes that shot up across America after the Civil War. The Del Monte aspired to be 'the Newport of the West', and towards this end it offered along with other delights one of the first golf courses in the West: the Del Monte GC. When a former Yale football captain named Sam Morse assumed command of Del Monte Properties in the second decade of this century, he was quick to realize that the day of the Del Monte Hotel and Victorian vacationing had passed. He therefore gave high priority to creating improved, up-to-date golf facilities on the peninsula. Work on Pebble Beach, the first new course, began in 1918, and after Pebble Beach had made the peninsula synonymous with golf,

Cypress Point, the Monterey CC, and Spyglass Hill were later added, in that order.

The land for Pebble Beach (much choicer than would normally be given to a golf-course architect to work with today) was acquired by Morse from the Chinese fishermen who had built a village along Carmel Bay. To lay out the course, Morse hired Jack Neville, with Douglas Grant as consultant, both former California Amateur Champions. Neither had much experience in golf architecture, but it is to be wondered whether H. S. Colt, Donald Ross, C. B. Macdonald, and Alister Mackenzie, working in concert, could have handled the land with comparable boldness and such sureness of instinct.

Eight of the holes at 'Pebble' are set along

the rocky shore of Carmel Bay: the 4th, 6th, 7th, 8th, 9th, 10th, 17th, and 18th. Some golfers – Jack Nicklaus, for one – have a high opinion of the interior holes, but when most people think of the glories of Pebble Beach, they have the seaside holes in mind. The first of these, the 4th, is a drive and pitch of only 325 yd (297 m), but the fairway is edged along the right by 50-ft cliffs that fall to a thin, pebbled beach – that is, when the tide is out. On the 6th, a 515-yd (471-m) par 5, a low-handicap golfer can get home in 2 if he has the nerve to aim his second over the elbow of the bay that cuts in below the steeply rising headland on which the green is perched. The 7th, 120 yd (110 m), is one of the most photographed golf holes in the world. It is usually shot from the elevated tee, with the spray of the pounding surf flying up behind the bunkered green.

Three par 4s follow, the 8th (425 yd, 389 m), the 9th (450 yd, 411 m), and the 10th (436 yd, 399 m). They are without a doubt the hardest trio of consecutive par 4s in golf. The 8th begins unpromisingly with a blind tee shot up the side of a hill. When the

tee shot is placed properly, the golfer will find his ball safely short of the precipice that drops well over 100 ft into Carmel Bay. Then, all that the golfer has to do is to take a long iron or wood, depending on the wind, and crack the ball 180 or 190 yd across a wide inlet of the bay to a tiny green that sits just beyond the cliffs on the far shore. The golfer who is not up to that can take an alternate route that trails around the inlet, off to the left. On both the 9th and 10th, the fairway follows close along the cliffs, which are on the right, and the greens are also set close to the cliffs. Both holes are exposed to the winds off the water, both are filled with stern undulations, and, on top of this, both seem to play longer then their length. They

would be extremely difficult to reach in 2 without the added anxiety that the sense of impending disaster imposes on the golfer. If he gets by the 8th, 9th, and 10th in good shape, he should be able to return a respectable score.

The 17th is a one-shotter of 218 yd (199 m), rocks and water along the left, a wide trap protecting the left half of the green, where the pin is generally set in tournament play. The 18th, 548 yd (501 m), is considered by many cognoscenti to be the best finishing hole in golf. From tee to green, the hole traces a gentle curve of the bay – here it is on the left. To add a fillip of interest, out-of-bounds markers patrol the right side of the fairway, which is not too wide to begin with. Breaking up the sweep of the fairway are a few isolated pines which, mysteriously, always seem to be blocking the direct route to the green. Some days, when a strong cross wind comes off the sea, a golfer, to be sure of staying in bounds, must aim his first two shots out to sea and calmly count on the wind to blow the ball back onto the fairway.

Pebble Beach is the course on which the fourth round of the annual Bing Crosby tournament is played. It was the venue of the 1929 US Amateur which Jimmy Johnston won. (Johnny Goodman eliminated Jones in the first round.) Two later Amateurs were played there, in 1947 (Skee Riegel's year) and in 1961 (when Nicklaus won the title for a second time). In 1972 Pebble Beach was the scene of the US Open won by Jack Nicklaus.

Penalty Stroke

A stroke added to a player's score for a hole or a round under the penalty clauses in the Rules of Golf – i.e. lost ball, out of bounds, accidentally moved, etc.

Penina GC PORTUGAL

nr Portimão. 18 holes; 6,889 yd (6,300 m)

Situated three miles west of Portimão, which used to be a quiet fishing town, Penina was the first of the golf projects in the Algarve. Henry Cotton, who has since made his home there, first saw the site in November 1963 and was undeterred by its muddy, waterlogged condition. Today's results justify his confidence and judgment as an architect.

The course took two years to construct once the elaborate drainage programme was completed and in June 1966 it was ready for play a few months ahead of its luxury hotel, which soon began to attract golfers from all over the world. Cotton had thousands of trees planted to mask the natural flatness of the course and to absorb excess moisture from the ground. As many of the trees grew 50 ft in five or six years, the success of this policy was soon apparent. The course, which can be stretched to 7,500 yd (6,860 m), is always in perfect condition: the local labour market enables Penina to be weeded by hand and not a drop of weedkiller has been used. The course is also fertilized eight times a year.

The European Women's Team Tournament was held there in 1967 and the European Men's event in 1973.

Peninsula GC AUSTRALIA

Frankston, nr Melbourne, Victoria. 36 holes; North Course 6,458 yd (5,905 m); South Course 6,666 yd (6,095 m)

The Tower House was built in 1922 and shortly afterwards became the Tower House GC with 13 holes and other amenities, including boating for the holidaymakers visiting Frankston. In 1924 it became a private country club, changing its name to Peninsula at the beginning of 1925. Later the course was extended after World War II. In 1960 when the new freeway took a slice

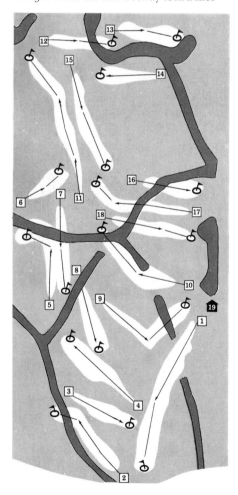

The course plan of Penina GC

off the west side, a new site had to be found. A move was made in 1964 to an area so thickly wooded in places that the men clearing it could not see each other at a distance of 10 feet. Two courses were made. The South measures 7,357 yd (6,727 m) off the back tees. The North was opened first, in April 1967. The most significant feature of the golf, apart from the severe length of the South Course, are the greens. There is a fine clubhouse, a bowling rink, putting greens, tennis courts, and an Olympic-size swimming pool. Considering the difficulties involved, the cost of building the courses – just over $A100,000 – was remarkably cheap.

Pennink, John Jacob Frank BRITISH

b. Delft, Netherlands, 1913. West of England Open Amateur 1935; English Amateur 1937-8; Walker Cup 1938

Frank Pennink showed early promise in boys' golf and as a member of three Oxford University teams from 1933. He graduated to international golf in the 1930s by virtue of winning the English Amateur two years running. In the 1937 final he beat Leonard Crawley by 6 and 5 at Saunton and in 1938 accounted for S. E. Banks by 2 and 1 at Moortown. He was one of the victorious 1938 Walker Cup team and won a vital foursomes match with Leonard Crawley. After World War II he regained his place in the England side. On his retirement from serious competition he played a valuable part in the game's administration. He served on several committees of the Royal and Ancient GC and in 1967 was president of the English Golf Union. He also distinguished himself in other fields. He was golf correspondent of the *Sunday Express* and *Daily Mail*, author of a best-selling Golfer's Companion and later a successful golf-course architect in the firm of Cotton (C. K.), Pennink, Lawrie and Partners. With his natural sympathy for the game and an intimate knowledge of golf abroad, he was well suited to the work and has built courses in more than 20 countries.

Perkins, Thomas Philip BRITISH

b. Birmingham 1904. English Amateur 1927, runner-up 1928; British Amateur 1928; runner-up US Amateur 1928; Walker Cup 1928; tied 2nd US Open 1932

A remarkable career, starting with victory in the Warwickshire Amateur Championship which he won for nine consecutive years from 1921, and ending with victory as a professional in the United States in the Ohio Open. With Dr William Tweddell, a contemporary, he was responsible for bringing amateur golf in the Midlands into the limelight. He was not an easy player to watch,

having an inelegant swing and taking his time over every shot, but he was most dogged and effective and never better than the time he beat Roger Wethered in the final of the Amateur Championship. At one time his game became painfully slow, and history was made in the championship the following year at Sandwich when the match behind him asked to be allowed through on the grounds that Perkins and his man had lost two holes on the match ahead of them. The publicity was not favourable to Perkins and he failed in his attempt to defend his title, although a strong favourite to do so.

In 1928 in his solitary appearance in the Walker Cup match before turning professional Perkins played top, but had the misfortune to meet Bobby Jones at his greatest and was beaten by 13 and 12; later in the US Championship, after playing brilliantly to reach the final, he lost again by double figures. But as Bernard Darwin wrote later: 'At that time the best of golfers might lose to Jones by double figures and leave the course without a stain on his character.' He moved to the United States at the beginning of the 1930s and turned professional there in 1932. The same year he seemed certain to have tied for 1st place in the US Open with Bobby Cruickshank, but Gene Sarazen, who was British Open Champion that year, came storming home in 66 at the Fresh Meadow CC, which gave him a clear victory. That round was the last 18 of Sarazen's famous 28 holes in 100 strokes. Perhaps no one has ever been runner-up in a US Open with more honour.

Perowne, Arthur Herbert BRITISH

b. Norwich, Norfolk, 1930. Walker Cup 1949, 1953, 1959; semi-finalist British Amateur 1953, 1955; Berkshire Trophy 1958; Eisenhower Trophy 1958; English Open Amateur Strokeplay 1958

After a distinguished beginning in boys' golf, Arthur Perowne blossomed into one of the best amateurs in Britain over a period of about 10 years and became the finest player ever to come out of East Anglia. He had a handsome though wonderfully simple style and gained a place in the 1949 Walker Cup team at the age of 19. A gentle nature prevented him from becoming the hardest of competitors and his championship record as a result did not quite do him justice, but he had an enviable record for England, for whom he played 54 matches, and in 1958 won the English Strokeplay title at Royal Birkdale. This was his outstanding performance. On a great golf course playing its full length, his 72-hole total of 289 gave him victory by 3 strokes from Alec Shepperson, a

victory characterized by straight driving and superb fairway wooden club play. After playing in the 1959 Walker Cup match at Muirfield, he faded from the tournament scene but in Norfolk, where he farms, he has remained virtually unbeatable, particularly at Brancaster where he now plays most of his golf.

Perry, Alfred BRITISH

b. Coulsdon, Surrey, 1904. Runner-up British Professional Matchplay 1932; Ryder Cup 1933, 1935, 1937; British Open 1935, tied 3rd 1939; Dunlop Metropolitan 1938

Chiefly remembered for his somewhat surprising victory in the British Open at Muirfield in 1935. Perry followed Cotton as champion and, in many ways, was his anti-thesis, but his victory, for all that, was thoroughly convincing and deserved. Although an inelegant player with a curious right-hand grip, he had a basically sound swing and a wonderful short game. After the first round at Muirfield, Perry's 69 left him 1 stroke behind Cotton, on whom most of the attention was naturally centred, but Cotton's putting began to fail him and, after a moderate second round of 75, Perry equalled Hagen's record of 67 in the third. This put him a stroke ahead of Charles Whitcombe and the road to victory was open. He began the final round with what might have been a disastrous 6 but it did not disturb him. He got a birdie at the 2nd and, the nearer he got to home, the more freely did he let out at his long second shots, standing a long way from the ball but displaying the usual glorious roundness and freedom in his swing.

He went for the hole all the time and at the 14th, disdainful of the consequences, he found the green with a spoon shot out of a bunker. He hit another spoon shot onto the green at the 18th, finished in 72 and won by 4 strokes from Alf Padgham. It was his only major victory but it is doubtful if the golfing public ever gave full credit to his game.

Persimmon

A hard American wood used for the heads of wooden clubs. The wood is that of the date-plum tree but it is nothing like as commonly used as it was.

Peru

Peru has no more than some dozen courses, most of them in or near the capital, Lima, but several are of top quality, including the Los Inkas Country Club. The game is growing in popularity and teams from Peru have taken part in the World Amateur Team Championships and the World (Canada) Cup. Hugo Nari, professional at Huampani GC in Lima, has played in the World Cup on a number of occasions, but so far no Peruvian player has made a notable repu-tation in tournaments abroad.

Peters, Gordon Buchanan BRITISH

b. Barrhead, Renfrewshire, 1910. Walker Cup 1936, 1938

Peters allied great natural ability with wooden clubs to a swash-buckling approach to the game which worked for him more successfully in matches than in medal play. He lost only one of the four games he played in two Walker Cup matches, three times reached the last eight both of the British Amateur (1936-7, 1939) and of the Scottish Amateur (1934-5, 1939) championships, and he represented Scotland continuously from 1934 to 1938. He is to be remembered not least for his rendering with the Ameri-can, Charlie Yates, of 'A wee deoch an doruis' from the steps of the Royal and Ancient clubhouse after Britain's first Walker Cup victory in 1938, and for his cryptic acknowledgment of praise offered him for a fine shot played in a crisis: 'Aye, trembling with bravery'.

Philippines

This country has been one of the main pioneering forces in Far Eastern golf and today the game is booming there. It started with the founding of the Manila GC not long after the Spanish-American War of 1898-1901. In 1972 there were about 60 courses and 80,000 golfers. There are some-thing like 200 professionals, the most notable being Ben Arda, Celestino Tugot and Eleuterio Nival. As in so many other coun-tries, one of the main reasons for the game's dramatic advance has been the influence of major tournaments. The Philippines Open Championship, which was the premier tour-nament in the Far East when it began in 1935, was won by Norman Von Nida in 1938 and in 1940 the first Americans, Al Zimmerman and 'Jug' McSpaden, took part. Since then, the championship has gained in popularity and wealth, and the modern field contains some of the best players in the world. The Republic of the Philippines Golf Association forms part of the Asia Golf Confederation.

Phillips, Frank AUSTRALIAN

b. 1932. New Zealand Professional 1955; Australian Open 1957, 1961; Singapore Open 1961, 1965; Hong Kong Open 1966

Frank Phillips has been a regular touring professional for many years, notably in

Australia, New Zealand, Britain and the Far East. He has not had spectacular success but is recognized as a fine player in all sorts of conditions. He has represented Australia in the World (Canada) Cup and is a 'keep fit' campaigner.

Phillips, Kathryn BRITISH

b. Bradford, Yorkshire, 1952. English Girls' 1968; Curtis Cup 1970, 1972

The first left-hander to play for Britain in the Curtis Cup match, Kathryn Phillips acquired a reputation as a most determined player and a beautiful putter. She had little length, and it was on these grounds that she did not get a game against the United States when she visited Brae Burn with the 1970

Arthur Perowne during the British Amateur Championship of 1953

Frank Phillips

team. At that time she had won the English Girls' Championship in 1968, and been runner-up the following year; she had also won the Scottish Girls' Strokeplay Championship two years running, and been runner-up in the French Girls' Championship. She had also earned her place in the Curtis Cup team by finishing high in the trials earlier in the year. She retained her place largely on the strength of being included in the team for the Vagliano Trophy at the last moment and performing well, and for being unbeaten in the Home Internationals. At last in the singles on the first afternoon of the 1972 match she broke her duck, and won her first Curtis Cup point.

Picard, Henry C. AMERICAN
b. Plymouth, Mass., 1907. Ryder Cup 1935, 1937, 1939; Argentine Open 1937; US Masters 1938; USPGA 1939, semi-finalist 1938, 1950

Picard was one of the outstanding golfers of the 1930s and his swing was one of the finest in the game. Besides winning two of the big four championships, he was successful in about 30 other tournaments in the 20 years of his playing career which began in 1925. His best finishes in the British and US Opens were 6th in 1935 and tied 6th in 1936 respectively. He experimented a good deal with his swing, but not to the extent of damaging it. In general his game was conservative; he was a fine long-iron player but seldom went for the difficult shot unless circumstances dictated. He moved from New England to Charleston when a young man, and there had his first successes.

In 1935 he became professional at Hershay, Pa., and almost immediately came to the fore, winning six tournaments in the same year, two of them in partnership with Johnny Revolta. He was clearly going to win a major title soon, and this happened in 1938

when he won the US Masters by 2 strokes with a score of 285. The following year he reached his peak, defeating Byron Nelson in the final of the USPGA Championship with birdies at the 36th and 37th. He also won five other tournaments, was leading money winner, and was selected for his third Ryder Cup match. To the general disappointment he began to curtail his appearances in 1940. When in 1942 war stopped the tour he virtually retired from competition, later taking a job at the Canterbury club. His last attempt at a major title was to reach the semi-finals of the USPGA in 1950.

Pick and Drop
Picking a ball out of a ditch or a puddle, etc and dropping it on a playable lie behind, or as otherwise allowed under the Rules or Local Rules.

Pick-out
The act of picking the ball out of an unplayable lie. The term is not used in America.

Pickworth, H. O. AUSTRALIAN
b. 1920; d. 1969. Australian Open 1946-8, 1954; Australian Professional 1947, 1953, 1955, runner-up 1951; Irish Open 1950

Ossie Pickworth was the leading Australian professional for some years. He suffered from the fact that, when he was in his prime, prize money was comparatively small and there were few tournaments, even

in his own country, where Norman Von Nida and Eric Cremin were his contemporaries.

He was a wonderfully easy swinger and a player who enjoyed considerable success, winning the Australian Open four times, the Australian Professional Championship three times, and doing well on his visits to Britain. Among his victories was the old Irish Open Championship in 1950 at Royal Dublin. He also took part in the first Canada Cup event in Montreal in 1953. While he was professional to the Royal Melbourne Club, a post he held for many years, he won a large prize in a lottery and severed all connections with the game. In his latter years he ran a pub.

Pim, Dorothy SEE BECK, MRS JOAN B.

Pinehurst CC USA
Pinehurst, N. Car. Five 18-hole courses

When a golfer speaks of Pinehurst, he can mean one of two things: he may be referring specifically to the championship course, the No. 2, or to the resort as a whole, which has been a centre of American golf since the turn of the century. Pinehurst was actually established in 1895. Its founding father was James W. Tufts, a native of Medford, Mass., who was the president of the American Soda Fountain Co. A man who was vulnerable to illness during the harsh northern winters, Tufts had the idea of setting up a health resort to which people of moderate means could go in the cold months. Writing off Florida as too far away, he found what he wanted in the Sandhills sector of North Carolina where the climate is mild and dry in winter and the air is filled with the invigorating aroma of the longleaf pine. Tufts purchased 5,000 acres of cut-over timberland, made a village green in true New England fashion, and opened his spa. From the beginning, the people who went to Pinehurst clamoured for a chance to play golf, the new international rage, and in 1898 Tufts acceded and built a 9-hole course. The next year the second 9 was finished. This was the course that Harry Vardon played (in 71 strokes) on his historic tour of the United States in 1900.

In the summer of 1900, Donald Ross, a young professional from Dornoch in Scotland, arrived in Pinehurst to take up his duties. Ross was a fine player and a gifted instructor, but it was as a course designer that he was destined to make his mark on American golf. As the game's popularity grew, Pinehurst needed increased facilities, and Ross was kept busy. In 1900 he laid out the first 9 holes of the No. 2 course. In 1907 he completed the No. 2 course, which

Kathryn Phillips

Henry C. Picard on the 17th tee during the 1970 US Masters at Augusta measured 5,860 yd (5,358 m). In 1910 the No. 3 course was ready. Shortly after the close of World War I, the No. 4 course was completed, giving Pinehurst the distinction of being the first golf resort in the western hemisphere to offer its patrons 72 holes. (In the early 1950s, not long after Ross's death, still another 18 holes – the No. 5 course –

were constructed. The designer was Richard S. Tufts, a grandson of the founder.)

Donald Ross's masterpiece is either Seminole or Pinehurst No. 2. In the mid-1930s, when the improvement in grass strains allowed Pinehurst to replace its old dirt greens with grass greens, Ross decided that this was the time thoroughly to remodel

No. 2. It was extended to over 7,000 yd (6,400 m), which was significant, but the high point of the revision was the beautifully subtle contouring that Ross did in the green areas. (Pinehurst No. 2 is considered by many as the best 'chipping course' in the United States.) For the rest, from the beginning Ross had the ability to design holes that gave the average golfer sufficient leeway for error but gave the low-handicap golfer all he could handle. His holes, sparingly bunkered in the green area, have a nice, unforced look about them and quiet character. Any list of the best holes on Pinehurst No. 2 would include: the 1st, a 414-yd (379-m) par 4, that may be the best 19th in the country; the 5th, a 438-yd (401-m) dogleg that demands a well-placed drive and an accurate middle-iron; the 13th, a par 4 that measures only 378-yd (346-m) but is very touchy, the landing area being narrow and the green area a tight plexus of sand and undulation; and the 18th, yet another formidable par 4, some 438 yd (401 m) in length – nearly all of them up a gradual slope.

Pinehurst reached its peak in the 1920s and 1930s when during the height of the season – mid-March to mid-April – a thousand rounds a day were played there. Pinehurst 'regulars' poured in from all corners of the country, many of them putting up at the huge old Carolina Inn or the cosier Holly Inn. Except on the practice range, Maniacs' Hill, the pace of life was slow and gentle, and an almost Edwardian atmosphere pervaded the resort. This changed hardly at all during those periods when big tournaments were staged at Pinehurst. The North and South Amateur, inaugurated in 1901, is still played each spring, but the North and South Open, inaugurated in 1903 and at one time surpassed by only the US Open and the Western Open in importance, was terminated in 1951. In 1951, Pinehurst was the scene of the Ryder Cup match and in 1962 of the US Amateur.

In late 1970, 75 years after Pinehurst was established, it was sold by the Tufts family to the Diamondhead Corporation, a rich land development company.

Pine Tree GC USA
Delray Beach, Fla.

During the last phase of his notable career, Dick Wilson, who got his start in golf architecture as an errand boy for Toomey & Flynn when that firm was remodelling Merion in the 1920s, made his home and his business headquarters in Delray Beach. Wilson accepted occasional jobs in other parts of the country, but mostly he worked

Pinehurst CC, *top,* the course plan and, *above,* the clubhouse and course

fairly close to home. Among the excellent courses he built in Florida were the Blue Course at Doral; Bay Hill, outside Orlando, which Arnold Palmer now owns; and the two PGA courses at Palm Beach Gardens. There is little doubt, however, that Wilson's best Florida course is Pine Tree, in Delray Beach, which was opened in 1961 and became his home club.

From the back tees, Pine Tree is well over 7,000 yd (6,400 m) long. It is also heroic in its proportions and from its back tees it is much too much for anyone except a scratch golfer. On most of the holes the approach shot must be flown all the way to the green, since wide bunkers almost invariably block the entrance. The greens are rather shallow, too, and severely bunkered at the sides and rear. When Ben Hogan made his first visit to Pine Tree, a fairly heavy wind was blowing directly into his face on the first hole, a par 4 of some 435 yd (398 m) to a slightly elevated green. After a good drive, he still needed a 3 wood to get home. Hogan was round in 73 that day, and wrote in the club's guest book that he considered the course the best he had ever played. From the middle tees it is a considerable test, too, for the greens are hard to hit unless the drive is placed on the correct side of the fairway and sent a good distance. The course is invariably in superb condition.

Pine Valley GC USA

Clementon, N.J. 18 holes; 6,765 yd (6,188 m)

Among the stable anecdotes in golf is one about Eustace Storey, the English amateur, on his first visit to Pine Valley. Standing on the tee of the second, a 367-yd (336-m) par 4, Storey's gaze took in the long carry over sand to the distant fairway, the thick woods framing the full hole, the dozen or so bunkers patrolling the right edge of the fairway, and the sudden 45-degree slope of sand and bushes rising between the fairway and the plateau green. Storey flicked a speck of dust from the corner of his eye. 'I say,' he said to the men in his foursome, 'do you people play this hole or do you simply photograph it?'

The second is one of the most dramatic holes at Pine Valley, but every hole has a distinct personality and makes an immense visual impact. This awesome course was conceived by George Crump, the owner of the Colonnades Hotel in Philadelphia, some 20 miles away. In the winter of 1912, Crump, an ardent and able golfer, began to carve his holes from the untouched forests of western New Jersey in an area where the land is reminiscent of seashore, the soil being extremely sandy and twisting in all varieties of

whorls and volutions. Totally obsessed by his project, Crump made his headquarters at the site, living first in a tent and later in a bungalow.

There was an immense amount of work to be done. Before the course was completed, for instance, 22,000 stumps had to be extracted. Along with his tenacity, Crump had a sound sense of what makes for an arresting golf hole. In addition he had the gift of originality, and in the end this was the difference between the creation of a very good course and a great one. He was fortunate, too, in that H. S. Colt, the accomplished British architect, travelled to Pine Valley in the summer of 1913 and worked with Crump during a brief but critical period in the preparation of the course plan. By the summer of 1914, Crump had roughed out 11 holes. By 1916, 14 holes were ready for play. Crump was still at work on the final four holes (the 12th, 13th, 14th, and 15th) when he died in the winter of 1918. Grinnell Willis of Morristown, N.J., a close friend of Crump's, put up the necessary money to finish construction of the course, and the work on the last four holes was directed by Hugh Wilson, the architect of Merion, and his brother Alan.

From the day of its unveiling, Pine Valley has been known as the most difficult course in the world. It may be. It keeps coming at the golfer with no let-up. This pressure and the severity of its hazards finally overwhelm most people. It really does take a first-class player to keep flying his tee shots straight enough to stay out of the woods and far enough to clear the sandy wastes between the tee and the fairway. These stretches are punctuated liberally with Scotch broom, poverty grass, scrub oak, mountain laurel, German heather, beach grass, wild hawthorn, and other flora. Once a golfer becomes entangled with them, more often than not he will end up with a 10 or an 11 for his troubles, not just a 6 or a 7.

Occasionally, however, certain golfers have managed to avoid all the pitfalls at Pine Valley and bring in a fine score. In 1922, George Rotan, a Walker Cup player from Texas, achieved a minor miracle when he got round in 70. This remained the course record until 1939 when Ed Dudley, a Ryder Cup star of that period, scored a 68. Few statements can transmit the perils of Pine Valley more succinctly than the footnote that Dudley followed his record round with a 77 and then with an 85. Woody Platt, a talented amateur from the Philadelphia area, once was in an unbelievable position to shatter all records for the course. He birdied the 1st, holed his approach on the 2nd for an

eagle, had a hole-in-one on the short 3rd, and then birdied the 4th, a par 5. Six under par after 4 holes, Platt went into the clubhouse, which stands close by the 4th, to steady himself. He never came out to finish his round.

Though Pine Valley's reputation as the most difficult course in the world is no doubt deserved, it is in a way unfortunate. The course has other, and superior, claims to fame. Many of its admirers believe that it contains more classic holes than any other course in the world. The seven holes they usually name first are: the 2nd; the 3rd, 185 yd (169 m) to a low green surrounded by sand; the 5th, a 226-yd (207-m) par 3, a full driver from an elevated tee across a ravine to an equally elevated green; the 7th, 584 yd (534 m), on which the player's second shot must carry Hell's Half Acre, a small desert that interrupts the fairway; the 13th, 446 yd (408 m), a dogleg left to a peninsular green jutting above a long expanse of sand; the 14th, a calendar par 3, the tee perched high and the sunken green sitting beyond a bright blue pond; and the 15th, 603 yd (551 m), embracing a long carry over water off the tee and then a steady climb up an ever-narrowing fairway to a green that no one has ever come close to reaching in 2. (The yardages above are from the back tees.)

Since 1929, Pine Valley has been an incorporated borough, and a number of members have built homes there. At about that time, John Arthur Brown, a Philadelphia lawyer and a man of limitless devotion to Pine Valley, became president of the club and was still fulfilling this function in the early 1970s. The club has hardly changed in its lifetime. Women still are permitted to play only on certain days, and the old pebbledash clubhouse is, except for a small changing room, off limits to them. Since there is no walking room for spectators on this course where practically each hole is a tight, isolated entity, Pine Valley has been the scene of only one major competition, the Walker Cup match of 1936. The club's most important fixture is the annual Crump Cup.

Pin High

A ball is pin high when it comes to rest at a point level with the hole for distance.

Pirie, Alexander Kemp BRITISH

b. Aberdeen 1942. Walker Cup 1967; Northern Open 1970

A leading Scottish amateur, and the greenkeeper at Hazlehead, Aberdeen, Sandy Pirie won a place in the 1967 British Walker Cup team. He has represented Scotland for several years in Home Inter-

nationals and the European team championship, and reached the finals of the 1972 and 1974 Scottish Amateur Championship, losing in 1972 to Hugh Stuart.

Pitch

A shot of varying length in which the ball is lobbed or lofted into the air. It is often not a full shot, usually one of 100 yd or less.

Pitch and Run

A shot so played that part of the desired distance is covered by the roll of the ball after it has pitched.

Pitch Mark

The depression on the ground caused by a ball when it pitches. In America known as ball mark.

Platt, J. Wood AMERICAN
b. Philadephia, Pa., 1899; d. 1959

One of the nation's leading amateur golfers for more than 40 years. Platt was good enough to reach the US Amateur semifinals in 1919 at the age of 20, and was still

winning senior tournaments 38 years later. Platt was a member of the American team that, in 1921, met the British in what was the forerunner of the Walker Cup matches. Although Platt won many tournaments in the Philadelphia area and elsewhere, he is best remembered for a round he never finished at Pine Valley (see p. 302).

Platts, Lionel BRITISH
b. Sheffield, Yorkshire, 1934. Assistant Professionals' 1961; Coombe Hill Assistants' 1961; Braemar 7-club Tournament 1964; joint winner Swallow-Penfold 1965; Ryder Cup 1965

A strong Yorkshireman with a fine swing and a good nerve on the green, which gave

him a taste for playing for money. He won the only 7-club tournament to be held in windy conditions at Turnberry, and several other tournaments in the north. Platts more than once distinguished himself in the British Professional Matchplay Championship, being leading qualifier three years in succession from 1959; in the 1965 Matchplay he won four matches at extra holes before going down to Neil Coles at the 19th in the final. He won the 1969 Wentworth Foursomes with B. Cawthray.

Play Away

The order by the starter to begin play. To this day, the starter on the Old Course at St Andrews bids everyone 'play away, please'.

Play Club

An ancient driver.

Player, Gary SOUTH AFRICAN
b. Johannesburg, Transvaal, 1935. South African Open 1956, 1960, 1965-9, 1972; Australian Open 1958, 1962-3, 1965, 1969-70; British Open 1959, 1968, 1974; US Masters 1961, 1974, runner-up 1962; USPGA 1962, 1972, runner-up 1969; US Open 1965, runner-up 1958

One of the best and most successful of all modern professionals; a player who, as a young man, took the brave step of tackling the American circuit in an attempt to make his fortune and quickly became the first non-American to make a lasting impact. He became the first South African to win the US Open, the first non-American to win the Masters and belongs to the select group of four who have won the four major titles of the world.

His story is one of dedication and determination. He turned professional in 1952 and first showed signs of wanting to become a leading tournament professional by going

---

Top, Sandy Pirie

Above, Pitch: Jack Nicklaus plays a pitch shot

Top, J. Wood Platt

Above, Lionel Platts

A lofted play club of 1830

to Britain in 1955. His small size and a number of technical faults hardly suggested that he would achieve his ambition but, from the time that he won the Dunlop tournament at Sunningdale the following year, it was obvious that he was a supreme competitor.

He ironed out a number of flaws, particularly his grip, and with long hours of practice and a strong urge to develop himself physically by means of diet and daily exercise, a regime he has maintained throughout his career, built up a sound, repetitive swing. His new-found strength enabled him to hit the ball far enough to match the leading Americans.

Player travelled to the United States for the first time shortly after his victory at Sunningdale and in 1958 finished 2nd in the US Open in Oklahoma, 4 shots behind Tommy Bolt. He then competed each year for the British Open and in 1959 won the title at Muirfield despite taking 6 at the last hole. At the time, the situation looked as though it would prove disastrous and Player was the picture of dejection until his nearest challengers, Flory Van Donck and Fred Bullock, failed to sustain their pressure. Player had begun the day 8 strokes behind Bullock.

It was a long time before Player came as near to winning the British Open after that. In 1961 and 1965, he withdrew; in 1962 he failed to qualify for the last day; and in 1964 he finished 13 shots behind Tony Lema.

There was a time, too, when his outspokenness lost a few friends, but, whatever others' feelings were towards Player – and later he became universally popular – everyone admired his golf and the remarkable way in which he triumphed over what appeared to be insurmountable hurdles.

Player's first golden year was 1961 when he won the US Masters and finished as leading money winner. The Masters was the second of his great ambitions to be realized, although right up to the final hole it looked as though Arnold Palmer was going to win for the second successive year. Coming to the last hole needing a par 4 to win, Palmer bunkered his second, came out too strongly and took 3 more to get down.

Player was by now a considerable force and he clearly loved the pace of life in the States and the attention Americans pay to a winner. Contracts were already accruing and more followed as a result of his victory in the 1962 USPGA Championship at Aronimink GC, Pa. This was the third leg of the modern 'quadrilateral'. Before the tournament he was depressed, recounting later in his book *Grand Slam Golf* how he

called his manager, Mark McCormack, and told him that he 'didn't think he could continue this ridiculous life'. His failure to qualify in the British Open at Troon had been a bad blow and, for the first and perhaps only time, the endless travelling was getting him down.

The sight of a marvellous course with lush green fairways, the sort he always preferred, inspired him, however, and with growing confidence he beat Bob Goalby by 1 stroke with a total of 278.

His victory in the US Open at Bellerive in 1965 after a play-off with the Australian, Kel Nagle, was the final confirmation of his greatness and yet another reminder of the dominance at that time of the Big Three.

Player, Palmer and Nicklaus, all managed by McCormack, were acclaimed throughout the golfing world and, as a result of their skill, amassed large fortunes.

Player, however, was always loyal to his own country and loved nothing better than to retreat there with his family. He bought a farm and often used to speak of it when abroad, but golf was still uppermost in his life and 1965 saw two other outstanding performances. He and Harold Henning won a resounding victory for South Africa in the Canada Cup in Madrid and the following week he beat Tony Lema at the 37th hole in the Piccadilly Matchplay Championship at Wentworth in a match which, as long as the game is played, will be quoted as an example

of a great recovery. At the 19th hole in the afternoon, Player went 7 down but, in an exhibition which exemplified his sterling qualities of courage and tenacity, he caught a bewildered Lema and finally beat him. The following day, he won the final against Peter Thomson to complete a triumph that surpassed anything he had done in Britain since the Open of 1959; then, to silence any remaining doubters, he won the British Open a second time in 1968 at Carnoustie. He beat Nicklaus and Bob Charles by 2 strokes and in the last round almost holed his wooden club second at the 14th.

In the USPGA Championship of 1969 in Dayton, Ohio, he was the target of anti-apartheid demonstrations. At the start of the

Gary Player, the unmistakable gesture indicating that another putt has been holed

A determined Gary Player in the World Cup at Nueva Andalucía in 1973

Opposite, Jack Nicklaus

1970 season, bodyguards were employed to shield him from over-forceful expressions of dislike of South African policies. Player's personal reaction to demonstrations was commendably calm, underlining the spirit of a remarkable person wholly dedicated to his sport.

Player's latest major victories came in the 1972 USPGA Championship when he won at Oakland Hills with a total of 281, the Masters and the British Open of 1974. The latter came after a major operation about eighteen months before and many believe it was his finest performance of all. He led from start to finish at Lytham, in the first championship to be played with the big ball, and eventually won by 4 strokes in conditions which were difficult throughout. It was his eighth major championship victory.

Playing the Like
British expression, not used in America, for playing the stroke that gives the player or his side the same number of strokes as his opponent(s) have already taken.

Playing the Odd
British expression, not used in America, for playing a shot when a player or his side have already played the same number as those already taken by the opponent(s).

Playing Safe
Avoiding risk by making sure of keeping the ball 'in play' rather than attempting a brilliant shot and accepting what may be dire consequences.

Playing out of Turn
Playing a stroke when it should have been your opponent to play first; or in a foursome when it should be your partner's turn.

Playing the Wrong Ball
Playing a shot with a ball that is not the one a player began the hole with and is still in play.

Play-off
When two or more players finish equal at the end of a strokeplay competition further play may be needed to decide an outright winner. This is done by means of a play-off sometimes over a given distance, such as 18 holes, or by sudden death, when play is continued until one player wins a hole.

Plugged, Plug
A plugged ball is one that pitches and remains embedded in its own pitch mark. Common on soft, wet ground or in the faces of bunkers.

Plus Handicap
A handicap better than scratch. A 'plus' player adds his handicap to his total instead of subtracting it. Nowadays, plus men are much rarer than formerly.

Poland
Before World War II there were golf clubs in the capital, Warsaw, and Katowice, but there were no signs of a revival afterwards until in the 1960s Frank Pennink, the British course architect, designed a 9-hole course in a park outside Warsaw at the invitation of the diplomatic corps. The park is shared by the diplomatic corps and the Polish Ministry of Science; 5 holes are set among trees and 4 through an apple orchard.

Pook, Mrs A. D. see CHADWICK, ELIZABETH

Porter, Mrs Mark see GERMAIN, DOROTHY

Porter, Ruth BRITISH
b. Chesterfield, Derbyshire, 1939. British Girls' 1956, runner-up 1957; English Ladies' 1959, 1961, 1965; Curtis Cup 1960, 1962, 1964; runner-up Australian Ladies' 1963; Commonwealth Tournament 1963; World Women's Amateur Team Championship 1964, 1966

Ruth Porter came to prominence in 1956 with her victory in the British Girls' at Seaton Carew; in 1957 she lost in the final to Brigitte Varangot in defence of her title. The first of her three championship victories in the English Ladies' caused something of a surprise for she beat Mrs Frances Smith in the final, but by her subsequent victories she showed this to be no flash in the pan. Ruth Porter had not the length to compete on American championship courses, but her steadiness, and the excellence of her chipping and putting, made her an esteemed and difficult opponent to beat in British and English teams.

Porthcawl GC, Royal WALES
Porthcawl, Glamorgan. 18 holes; 6,658 yd (6,088 m); par 72

In 1891 when Porthcawl was none too prosperous a port and not yet much known as a seaside resort, a meeting of businessmen in Cardiff, concerned in the main with the export of coal, decided to form a golf club. At that time golf was not popular in this area of South Wales, but as a result of the meeting 9 holes were laid out on Locks Common by the professional from Westward Ho! In 1895 another 9 were added on the present ground and in 1913, four years after the club became 'Royal', H. S. Colt submitted plans for further improvements.

World War I delayed the adoption of these until 1919. Then in 1934 Tom Simpson advised on alterations before the holding there of the British Ladies' Championship in which Mrs A. M. Holm (Helen Gray) defeated Pam Barton, then only 17, in the final.

Steadily Porthcawl came to be regarded as the premier club in Wales. It has all the qualities of true links golf: the sea is in sight all the time, which is not true of many links, there is a pleasantly undulating character about the holes, and the wind is felt everywhere. The start is glorious with the first 3 holes hugging the wide margin of the foreshore, and the 2nd forming the toughest par 4 on the course, with its greens guarded by

bunkers and its proximity to the beach. The pebbles are not out of bounds, but this is usually small compensation. The inland holes rise to a high plateau and without losing sight of the sea introduce gorse and heather, so that it is one of the most varied of championship links. The 7th, tucked into the most inland corner, is one of the shortest in championship golf, although at 125 yd (114 m) it is a few yards more – but a good deal less perilous – than the Postage Stamp at Troon. Any wind off the Bristol Channel – there usually is one – turns such holes as the 10th, 13th and the plunging 18th, into vigorous par 4s, but the same wind gives a helping hand at three of the longest holes.

The course has seen countless Welsh championships of various kinds as well as the occasional professional tournament, notably the Dunlop Masters of 1961 when Peter Thomson showed his supremacy with the small ball in wind by cantering home 8 strokes ahead of the field. The weather can be vicious, as it was for the home internationals in 1970 when golf was next to impossible, or in 1968 when for the first time

Opposite, Peter Oosterhuis

Ruth Porter

the university match went to Wales. On the other hand the weather was memorably good for the Curtis Cup match in 1964, the club's most international occasion producing a tight match in which the Americans prevailed by 10½ matches to 7½. It was a proud day for the club when the British Amateur paid its first visit in 1951, and more architectural advice was called for, this time from C. K. Cotton. Albert Evans, a respected name in Welsh golf, delighted his countrymen by reaching the semi-finals, but he could not prevent an all-American final in which Dick Chapman beat Charlie Coe. When the event returned in 1965 the American challenge was led by Hyndman and Campbell, but nothing was to stop Michael Bonallack from winning his second title, not even the fact that Clive Clark was 6 up on him after 13 holes in the final. In 1973 the championship was won by the American Richard Siderowf.

Portmarnock GC IRISH REPUBLIC

Portmarnock, Co Dublin. 18 holes; 7,093 yd

One of the great Irish courses; not perhaps as spectacularly beautiful as Newcastle, Rosses Point or Ballybunion but better known on account of the championships and international events it has housed. Bobby Locke paid it the compliment of rating it among the finest courses in Europe and certainly there is none fairer anywhere.

Situated a comfortable bus ride north of Dublin, its great occasions have always attracted huge crowds although in the early days when the final approach was by water, it wouldn't have been so suitable. It was discovered, in fact, by two gentlemen called Pickeman and Ross taking a boat from Sutton in 1893 and rowing across to the point of Portmarnock peninsula where they obviously liked what they saw. By Christmas a club was formed and though the early days were a little primitive, Portmarnock soon became a name for Irish golfers to recall with pride.

With all the qualities of a true seaside course, it has been a regular venue for Irish championships and gradually won even wider acclaim. Sam McCready won the British Amateur championship there in 1949 and in the 1960 World (Canada) Cup Arnold Palmer made his first appearance in Europe. But nothing ever quite matched the 1959 Dunlop Masters and Christy O'Connors narrow victory over Joe Carr, who has played so much of his golf on the links. As famous as O'Connor and Carr is the Club's professional, Harry Bradshaw.

Portrush GC, Royal NORTHERN IRELAND

Portrush, Co. Antrim. 36 holes

One of the great seaside courses of the British Isles, Royal Portrush lies in an enchanting setting on the north coast of Antrim, about 60 miles northwest of Belfast. The small town of Portrush owes much of its prosperity and fame to golf and to the golf club which was formed in May 1888. It was known first as the Country Club and became the Royal Country Club in 1892 when the Duke of York was patron. In 1895 it changed to its present name. Portrush did not have to wait long for recognition. The Irish Open Amateur Championship was inaugurated there in 1892, the British Ladies' Championship was held there in 1895, and the Irish Professional in 1907. The club's first professional tournament, however, took place in 1895 when the club's first professional, Sandy Herd, beat Harry Vardon in the final, the year before Vardon won the first of his six Open Championships.

Since then, Portrush has long been regarded as a great test of a golfer's skill and, had it been more suitable in other respects for staging a modern Open Championship, it would almost certainly have held more than the one it did in 1951. This was the occasion of Max Faulkner's victory, the last by a British player until Tony Jacklin won in 1969, and it gave Peter Thomson his first Open Championship appearance; he finished equal 6th. It is rather more surprising perhaps that the British Amateur Championship has only been held there once, in 1960; it produced a memorable climax with the crowning of Joe Carr as champion for the third time.

The women have been consistently loyal to Portrush and their champions include Lady Margaret Scott in 1895, Rhona Adair in 1903, Dorothy Campbell in 1911, Joyce Wethered in 1924, Pam Barton in 1939 (the last championship in which she played), and Mrs G. Valentine (Jessie Anderson) in 1955.

Mrs Valentine beat the fine American player, Barbara Romack, by 7 and 6. In 1969 Portrush provided Catherine Lacoste with victory in the British which had so often eluded her. She won by 1 hole after being 4 down after 7.

There are two 18-hole courses at Portrush, the Dunluce or Championship, and the Valley. The Championship Course, as it can be seen today, is the result of redesigning by H. S. Colt whom Bernard Darwin once described as, 'having built himself a monument more enduring than brass'.

The natural break of the ground and a frequent change in direction give the holes a compelling quality and challenge which is increased by the great beauty of their setting. As the course comes in view round a curve in the Antrim coast road, it provides an unforgettable sight with green fairways blending with the dunes and the great headland of Inishowen contrasting vividly with the low line of the Skerries and the sea beyond.

Portugal

The British were responsible for the introduction of golf to Portugal whose first course was at Oporto. Until 1929, which ends the first period of Portuguese golf, the game was played sporadically on various courses of 9 holes or even fewer. Two existed from about 1895 to 1905 at Matozinhos (9) and Castelo do Queijo (5); Miramar started in 1925 with 6 holes and sand greens; and the Lisbon Cricket Club, having begun on the same scale in 1905, constructed a new 9 at Carcavelos in 1917.

The second phase of Portugal's history revolves around the birth of the Estoril Club in 1929. The year 1930 brought the first Portuguese Open Amateur Championship and this and practically all the other Portuguese championships for the next 40 years took place at Estoril. Mackenzie Ross, the Scottish architect, constructed a new 18-hole

Royal Porthcawl GC, the 1st hole

course at Estoril in 1938; he had designed one at Vidago and another in the Azores around 1936. In 1940 the first international match between Portugal and Spain was contested for a cup presented by the British Ambassador in Portugal, Sir Walford Selby; the Portuguese team was made up of four British and four Portuguese golfers.

Also in 1940 the Portuguese Golf Federation was set up. The first Portuguese Open Championship was in 1943, and thereafter Portuguese teams were regular participants in European competitions and other international events. Today Portugal boasts more than a dozen courses with the promise of more to come, but the third important phase in the history of Portuguese golf has centred upon the recent elaborate development of certain areas in the Algarve, where splendid courses such as Penina, Vale do Lobo and Vilamoura have helped promote a thriving tourist industry and enhance Portugal's reputation as a golfing country.

Pott, John AMERICAN
b. Cape Girardeau, Mo., 1935. Dallas Open

1960; West Palm Beach Open 1960; Southeastern Professional 1962; Waco Turner Open 1962; American Golf Classic 1963; Ryder Cup 1963, 1965, 1967; Bing Crosby National 1968

A long-hitting regular member of the professional tour since the late 1950s and one of its steadiest money winners. Although Pott has won some tournaments on the tour, he seemed capable of doing even better. He was seldom far from the top as he proved by winning more than $33,000 in 1961 and more than $50,000 in 1965 – without a tournament victory in either season. Pott was a member of the Louisiana State University team that won the national title in 1955. He turned professional in 1956 and has gained stature every year since.

He made a steady income from the tour from 1966 to 1970, his best being victory in the 1968 Bing Crosby National and second place in the 1969 West End Classic, which moved him into the top 60 for the year and gave him qualifying exemption for 1970 but he gained little from it and in 1971 made only about $22,000.

Pot Bunker
A small, deep bunker shaped rather like a pot. The Old course at St Andrews can supply many examples.

Practice Swing
Any swing taken by a player during a round without the intention of striking the ball.

Prado, Mrs de SEE LACOSTE, CATHERINE

Prairie Dunes CC USA
Hutchinson, Kan. 18 holes; 6,530 yd (5,931 m); par 70

Prairie Dunes Country Club is America's great unknown course. Situated within striking distance of a major population centre, it would be as celebrated as Merion, Pebble Beach, or Oakmont. Prairie Dunes, however, is the jewel of Hutchinson, in central Kansas, with less than 50,000 population, and the course has been exposed to relatively few of the great players and others whose opinions influence the public mind. The wonder of Prairie Dunes is its kinship to the links courses of Scotland. It lacks sea, but its sandhills were formed in the same way as those of the links courses by the wind blowing over the water (the Arkansas River in this case) and building up the dunes. It also has waist-high native grasses, very severe natural rough created by a thick, prickly indigenous plant called yucca, dense thickets of wild plum, and constant winds that sweep across the Kansas prairie.

Prairie Dunes is less than 6,600 yd from the back tees, but Jack Nicklaus has played it 9 times and never bettered 71. In 1958, Nicklaus, then a pudgy 18-year-old, beat Deane Beman in the final of the Trans-Mississippi Amateur at Prairie Dunes. The course's other exposure to tournament publicity came through the 1964 US Women's Amateur Championship, when Barbara McIntire won the second of her USGA titles.

Prairie Dunes is the creature of the Careys, a prominent local family who have presided over the Carey Salt Mine at Hutchinson. Emerson Carey Jr was a member of the USGA Executive Committee during the 1950s. He tells how Perry Maxwell, the architect selected by himself and his brother William, took two weeks exploring the sandhills north and east of Hutchinson before settling on the present site. Nine holes were opened in 1937. The second nine, laid out by Preston Maxwell – the son of Perry Maxwell – opened in 1957. Carey says that before any layout or construction had begun, Perry Maxwell observed, 'There are 118 golf holes here. All I have to do is to eliminate one hundred.'

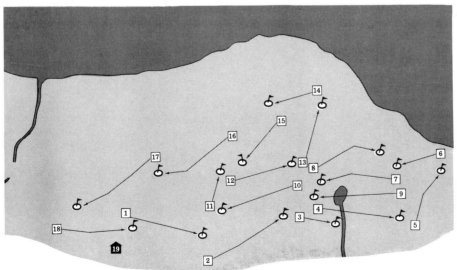

A view of the 5th green Royal Portrush GC and its course plan

Preferred Lies

Usually a winter rule whereby the committee allows players to select a lie (within close limits) either to preserve the fairway or because the likelihood of finding a reasonable lie is slim.

President's Putter

The annual matchplay tournament of the Oxford and Cambridge Golfing Society played at Rye, Sussex, each January. It was started in 1920 and has since become one of the most famous competitions in the world, partly because in its early days its entry compared in strength to that of the British Amateur, and partly because, with an increasing emphasis on professional stroke-play events, it upholds the true spirit of golf.

There have been times when snow and frost have made the public feel that the Putter is an act of winter madness but, though the meeting is equally a reunion, the golf is always sternly contested. The Putter, too, has produced a string of distinguished winners, including Ernest Holderness, Cyril Tolley, Roger Wethered, Leonard Crawley, Gerald Micklem, 'Laddie' Lucas, Tony Duncan and Michael Attenborough.

Two putters, one of them the original used by Hughie Kirkaldy when he won the Open championship in 1891, hang in a glass case in the Rye clubhouse. The winner has the ball he used in the final attached to the shaft. The winner's silver medal bears the inscription *Primus inter pares*, freely but aptly translated by Arthur Croome, the Society's first Secretary, as 'he was rather lucky to win'. *See also* Oxford and Cambridge Golfing Society.

Press

To strive to hit the ball excessively hard in an attempt to get extra distance, but at the expense of control; it is often disastrous.

Press also means to double the bet on the 9-hole section of a Nassau after becoming 2 down or, according to other interpretations, to begin another match for a halved stake when a bad start has been made and winning the original bet is unlikely. In America the number and variety of pressed bets (or 'presses') in a match can be almost endless.

Preston Trail GC USA

Dallas, Tex. 18 holes; 7,031 yd (6,429 m)

For a number of years, the International Business Machines Corp. sent a huge digital computer around the United States following the professional tour, ingesting a staggering amount of information and storing it within its magnetic-tape memory. Then when the 1969 season was completed, the

mechanical brain was asked to tell all: what, for instance, were the most difficult golf courses, in terms of average scores in relation to par, it had visited during the year? The most difficult, the computer reckoned, was the Champions GC in Houston; the second most difficult was Preston Trail in Dallas.

The club seems to be living up to its purpose, for it was built to give Dallas a truly great golf course. There is little doubt that it is a good one, and it may yet become a great one. As is true of most new courses, Preston Trail, which was built in 1962, is long. Its opening holes are intimidating; by the time the 4th is reached, the golfer has covered 1,390 yd (1,271 m). The first 9 are the more difficult, one reason being the severity of their two par 3s: the 4th is 212 yd (194 m) and the 8th is 238 yd (218 m). The 368-yd (336-m) 2nd and the 357-yd (326-m) 17th are the only par-4 holes under 400 yd.

Ralph Plummer, who designed so many fine Texas courses, was the architect, with shrewd assistance from Byron Nelson. The annual PGA tournament at the club is called the Byron Nelson Classic in his honour.

Prestwick GC SCOTLAND

Prestwick, Ayrshire. 18 holes; 6,571 yd (6,009 m); par 72

Prestwick holds a special place in the history of British golf because it is the birthplace of the Open Championship. Not only was the championship held there for the first 12 years of its existence, but the idea of it originated with the club itself. Because of its limited length and short finish, because of the lack of space for car parking, practice, and all the trappings of a modern championship, the course has not been used for a British Open since 1925 or for an Amateur since 1952. In a sense it may be described as a museum piece. It has retained perhaps better than any other course the basic

features of golf as it was originally understood – small, hidden greens guarded by humps and hollows, blind shots over towering dunes, a burn, a wall, and bunker faces lined with sleepers (railroad ties). In the clubhouse have been preserved the original documents relating to the early Open Championships, the scraps of paper – they were little more – on which were recorded the scores of the handful of competitors, and the masculine dignity of the earlier clubs has been to a certain extent retained. That is not to say that Prestwick has outlasted its usefulness. The reverse is true; it is still widely appreciated even by those who are not members for the novelty of experience in playing it, for its natural surroundings, and for the seaside quality of its turf and greens. Meetings such as the Army Championship and the Seniors' Championship have been held there recently, and it is regularly visited by societies. To that extent it has no need to lean upon the past, yet the past is all around it. 'It has', the veteran writer Frank Moran, has said, 'the unmistakable atmosphere of a shrine.'

Top, the President's Putter held by the 1970 President of the Oxford and Cambridge Golfing Society, Alan Cave; on his left David Marsh and right, Donald Steel

Above, play in progress at Rye GC for the 1961 President's Putter

The course was opened in 1851 on common land where golf had been played for years and consisted of 12 holes, with three rounds constituting the Open Championship test. Six more holes were added in 1883. It is 60 years since Bernard Darwin wrote of it 'A man is probably less likely to be contradicted in lauding Prestwick than in singing the praises of any other course in Christendom', and the course has changed little since then. The railway line runs the entire length of the first hole on the right, near enough for snorting engines in the days of steam to shower the golfers with cinders. A fine hole at which to score a 3, as John Ball found in his defeat of Freddie Tait at the 37th in the last championship before the

an unforgettable feature of the course. Ahead lie exciting features in the form of the Pow Burn and the Himalayas, the latter a high range of dunes giving a blind shot to the green at the 5th. Specially notable on the inward half is the 13th, Sea Hedrig, a fine 2-shotter with a pawky green obliquely set among the humps and hollows. The four finishing holes are less easy than their length suggests; they include a narrow drive between trouble at the 15th, and another blind shot over the Alps at the 17th. The finish may emphasize the impossibility of holding an Open Championship there again, now that it has reached such huge proportions, but in an age when there is a danger that courses will become more and

Macdonald Smith to take advantage of a 5-stroke lead in the last round. West of Scotland crowds have a reputation for unbridled enthusiasm; the thousands who swarmed round in pursuit of Smith destroyed his chance, and were a decisive factor in opening the championship committee's eyes to the handicaps of Prestwick, as simply a watching course. In the Amateur field John Ball won at Prestwick, just as he had startled Scotland and the professionals by becoming the first amateur to win the Open there. That was followed by Hilton's victory in 1911. The Prestwick crowds had their saddest moment in 1934 when Lawson Little played golf of such brilliance that he gave the crowds little chance to watch their

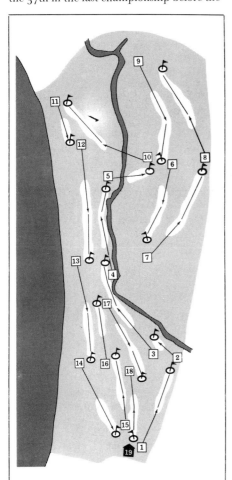

20th century, or as Lawson Little did, piling on the agony of yet another 3 against the unfortunate Mr Wallace in the 1934 Amateur. The Cardinal bunker at the 3rd is notorious for its cavernous proportions and for the black boards that shore up the fine sand of its face. It may have lost something of its fierceness in these long-hitting days but it is

more standardized the golfer comes in feeling he has had a fresh experience.

The club is associated with great names and stirring occasions in golf, for which perhaps a parallel may be found across the Atlantic in Merion Cricket Club. Old Tom Morris was at his most formidable in the years when he was employed as greenkeeper at £25 a year, although he won the fourth of his Opens after his return to St Andrews. Vardon won three of his titles there, and James Braid one of his in spite of nearly wrecking his chances by failing to get out of the Cardinal bunker and taking 8. The last Open to be played there was won by a naturalized American, Jim Barnes, but it is better remembered for the failure of

local hero against whom he was playing, dismissing him from the final by the record margin of 14 and 13.

Prestwick St Nicholas GC SCOTLAND
Prestwick, Ayrshire. 18 holes; 5,801 yd (5,304 m); par 68

Originally the Mechanics' Club, created four months after the 'Old' Prestwick club, on 3 November 1851, with Tom Morris heading the 28 members, the early history of St Nicholas (the name of Prestwick's patron saint was adopted in 1858) reflects the basic differences between early golf in the east and west of Scotland, and also sweeping social changes. Golf had certainly been played in Ayrshire from early times (there is a refer-

Above, the course plan of Prestwick GC and *right,* a view of the Cardinal Bunker at the 3rd

ence in the 16th century), but records of organized golf at Prestwick do not begin until about 1840 when the Earl of Eglinton regularly took parties to play on the natural links. Tom Morris had come from St Andrews as greenkeeper to the Prestwick Club in 1851 and through meeting golfers who were not members of the exclusive 'old' club conceived the idea of another club for artisans: hence the name 'Mechanics', which soon became a misnomer. To Tom Morris's many achievements may thus be added that of creating one club while employed by another: moreover both clubs shared the original course. St Nicholas must also be the only club that has found a new course and lost it immediately after its opening competition. This was in 1877 when because of congestion on the old links, St Nicholas was given five months to find new ground. This was done and a course laid out, but two days before the opening the club learned that neither the tenant nor occupant had the right to sublet: through the cooperation of the landlord's factor the competition was held – and the course forthwith vacated. But within weeks yet more new land was found for a 9-hole course, soon extended to 12. From 1893 this became the Ladies' Course, the first such 'long course' in Scotland; women had previously been relegated to putting and 'short courses'. In 1892 St Nicholas moved for the third time, because the membership had grown to 195, to the present course between the railway line and the sea with the blue hills of Arran as a backdrop. The course is basically as laid out by that Prestwick stalwart Charlie Hunter.

Pretty
A now largely obsolete word for the fairway.

Preuss, Phyllis AMERICAN
b. Detroit, Mich., 1939. Runner-up US Amateur 1961, semi-finalist 1962; semi-finalist British Ladies' 1964; low amateur US Women's Open 1968-9; Women's Southern Amateur 1968

In women's golf there has been only a slight movement from the amateur to professional ranks. Phyllis, or Tish, Preuss was one of the stalwarts of the US Curtis Cup team through the 1960s, reflecting all that is best in those matches and representing her country in 1962, 1964, 1966, 1968, 1970.

Price, Charles AMERICAN
Charles Price has been one of the outstanding golf writers in the United States over the past 20 years. He is perhaps best known as the author of *The World of Golf* and as the editor of *The American Golfer*, an excellent

anthology of selections from the magazine of that name which, unfortunately, perished during the Depression. Price collaborated with Bob Jones in preparing *Bobby Jones on Golf*, a first-rate collection of the articles on golf instruction which the young Jones had written for an American newspaper syndicate.

A native of Washington, D.C., Charles Price is a proficient golfer. One winter, soon after the end of World War II, he played on the professional tour from the West Coast to the East, travelling with his old friend Lew Worsham. He has won the Golf Writers' Championship at Myrtle Beach. Price has written articles for many magazines, but he is most closely identified with *Esquire* and *Golf*. He was the first editor of the latter and still contributes a sprightly monthly essay. A congenial man and a good judge of branch water, he currently makes his home at Hilton Head Island, S. Car., where he acts as Director of Golf for the Harbour Town links.

Price, Elizabeth (Mrs Price Fisher) BRITISH
b. London 1923. Runner-up English Ladies'

1947, 1954-5; Curtis Cup 1950, 1952, 1954, 1956, 1958, 1960; Danish Ladies' Open 1952; Astor Salver 1955-6, 1959; Daks Tournament 1957; British Ladies' 1959, runner-up 1954, 1958, semi-finalist 1950, 1957; Portuguese Ladies' Open Amateur 1964

Rhythm and accuracy were the keynotes of a game that kept Elizabeth Price at the top for more than a decade. Her presence in six Curtis Cup matches strengthened British teams at a time when they were more than holding their own against the Americans. Her successes pointed to the value of a swing without great power but which never seemed to vary and landed her in less trouble than almost any of her contemporaries. She was

also possessed of an unshakeable temperament. This made her an easy foursomes partner in such events as the Kayser Bondor foursomes in which she and Mrs Marley Spearman (Mrs Harris) tied in 1958.

After her marriage she lived in Portugal for a time, and in 1968 on her return to Britain she gave up her amateur status for three years. In 1974 she succeeded Enid Wilson as women's golf correspondent of the *Daily Telegraph*.

Prince's GC ENGLAND
Sandwich Bay, Kent. 18 and 9 holes; 6,843 yd (6,257 m); par 73

The youngest of the three distinguished courses in the area of Sandwich and Deal,

Top, Phyllis Preuss

Above, Charles Price

Elizabeth Price

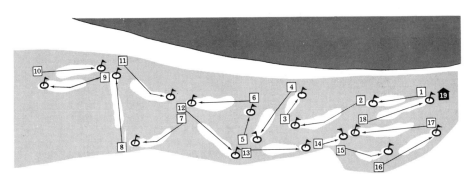

The course plan of 18 of Prince's GC's 27 holes

Prince's came into existence in 1906; its subsequent history has been easily the most turbulent of the three. In an area that was until recently considered remote, Prince's was the remotest of the three. Its championship history is brief; it could tell a far longer story of flood, wars, and financial crises. Yet it is a course of true links quality, and if its charm is less obvious than other seaside courses, it is nonetheless real to those who take the trouble to acquaint themselves with it.

Prince's consists of 27 holes, all of championship quality. The normal championship course is the Blue, and by ringing the changes with the other 9 holes, the 18-hole Red Course is brought into existence.

It was not for nothing that Bernard Darwin, savouring in his mind a day of sunshine and light breeze, wrote of this corner of Kent: 'It has for me something that no other spot, not even perhaps St Andrews, can quite equal. The larks seem to me to sing a little louder and more cheerfully there and the grass to have a more poignantly delicious taste of garlic. I am sure that no other cliffs are shining quite so white as those beyond Pegwell Bay. . . .'

There is an immediate sense of space caused not only by the large putting green and practice ground. Each hole seems an adventure into some uncharted ground; and the adventure is not to be made easy. There is a character and sternness about Prince's that is reminiscent of Carnoustie. Prince's imposes the subtle test of natural hazard – there are very few bunkers – and delicate judging of distance in a bewildering landscape of gentle dunes and greens that welcome only the most accurate of strokes.

Prince's features were not always so unpronounced. The links as laid out by Sir Harry Mallaby-Deeley and P. M. Lucas (the first secretary of the club and father of the Walker Cup player, 'Laddie' Lucas) in 1906 and opened a year later, was dominated by the towering range of dunes, known as the Himalayas, which ran like a spine down the centre of the course. But Prince's stands at the gateway to England from the Continent, and in both world wars it became one of the earliest war casualties. In the first war the area became a section of coastal defence with a rifle range, and after re-establishing itself between the wars it was turned in World War II into a battle training area. It nearly became a permanent firing range, but in the end it was bought by an Australian financier, Mr (later Sir) Aynsley Bridgland, one of those late converts to the game, and on that account all the more zealous in its cause. The one Open Championship held there was won by Gene Sarazen in 1932, making a double with the US Open which he had won again the same year. He led all the way at Prince's and his victory gave rise to one of the best stories ever told about a caddie – his 'partnership' with Skip Daniels. The Amateur Championship has not been held there, one explanation of this no doubt being the proximity of much-loved Royal St George's, but when Sir Aynsley Bridgland had restored the course, it began to attract attention. The 1956 Curtis Cup, of glorious memory for British supporters, was held there, and in the 1960s, it attracted two professional tournaments, neither of which, it should be noted, returned there.

Prince's is also the home of the Astor trophy, a medal tournament for women which gave Catherine Lacoste the chance to play one of the greatest rounds of her life, holing the course in 65.

Professional

One who teaches golf, or derives a living from the game.

Professional Golfers' Championship of America

One of the four major world championships making up the modern Grand Slam, although less widely publicized than the other three events, the US and British Opens and the US Masters. The PGA is easily the oldest and most important of the events that make up the rich American PGA tour. It was first held in 1916, the same year as the formation of the association. Each winner of the championship receives life exemption from pre-qualifying for any of its tournaments. This privilege is highly prized because of the added strain pre-qualifying puts on competitors and the few places open compared to the number seeking to fill them.

The first winner was Jim Barnes who successfully defended his title three years later after the competition had lapsed in the war years of 1917 and 1918. In the early days when the championship was decided by 36-hole matches the supremacy of Walter Hagen and his rivalry with Gene Sarazen helped to set the event on its feet. Between 1921 and 1927 Hagen won five times and Sarazen the other two. Starting in 1924 Hagen had 22 consecutive victories over 36 holes against the pride of American professional golf, a tribute as much to his ability to assert himself over an opponent as to his skill. He was in addition a great fighter, and on his way to victory the following year he won matches at the 39th and 40th holes. When his long run came to an end at the hands of Leo Diegel in 1928, he said he was sorry but he had left the trophy in a taxi back in 1925. It was later recovered and handed to Diegel, who went on to beat Sarazen by 9 and 8 and Espinosa by 6 and 5 in the final. In those years it was not uncommon for players to repeat their victory in the championship, not only the great names but winners like Paul Runyan whose first victory in 1934 over Craig Wood was at the 38th, which equalled the longest final recorded. Four years later he defeated Sam Snead by 8 and 7 in the biggest victory and shortest match in the history of the event. Great matches of that era included Sarazen's defeat of Hagen at the 38th in the 1923 final.

Hagen squared an uphill fight by winning the 35th and getting a half at the 36th from out of a bunker. In winning the 38th Sarazen had to play out from a cluster of crayfish mounds. Another memorable final was Tommy Armour's defeat of Sarazen on the last green in 1930, holing from 14 ft. The championship is open to foreign-born players only when they are full members of the American PGA. Armour was the first foreign-born winner since Hagen had taken over in 1920. Subsequently, two other non-Americans won the title, Jim Ferrier of Australia in 1947, and Gary Player of South Africa, who won in 1962 and again in 1972.

In 1958 the championship switched to strokeplay. It was the last stronghold of matchplay which was rapidly going out of fashion at the time because television needed a form of golf that ran a fixed length for the placing of cameras, and because professionals found the two rounds a day hard going and were sensitive to a personal defeat. But with the passing of matchplay something went out of the event. Only Arnold Palmer among the giants had failed to win the title at least once – he was three times joint runner-up – but after the war, from 1950 on, Sam Snead, who won the event three times in all, was the only golfer to win it more than once until Nicklaus's second victory in 1971. In the second half of the 1960s the legend grew up that winners of the championship were destined to have a lean time in the year that followed, a feeling that had some foundation in the subsequent performances of such as Geiberger, Marr, Nichols, and January, but victories in the early 1970s by Nicklaus (twice) and Player restored the event's prestige. When Nicklaus won his second title in 1971 the championship was played over the PGA's own new course at Palm Beach Gardens, Fla., and to give the occasion special emphasis as the first of the Big Four in the season, it was held in February. Previously it had been held in July following

close on the British Open, which had made it difficult to win both. The February date gave substance to Nicklaus's vain bid that year to win all the Big Four in one season. His third victory in the event in 1973 gave him his 14th major championship title, one more than Bobby Jones acquired. Another factor which has revived the reputation of the event has been the decision in recent years to find courses worthy of so important a tournament. Played on a different course almost every time and in a different part of the country, it is considered by professionals as one of the fairest as well as one of the toughest tests. For years it led the way in prize money and although it has been overtaken by some giant sponsored tournaments, its prize of more than £200,000 is well above the average. *See also* Professional Golfers' Association of America.

Professional Golfers' Association of America

In the beginning, the professional golfer was generally unwelcome in the clubhouse. His name in tournament records was not preceded by 'Mr' as in the case of amateurs. Today the club professional may be a college graduate, and certainly a combination of businessman-merchant-teacher-public relations representative, with a shop stocked with clothing as well as golf equipment. He may have an income greater than that of some of his clients. The other kind of modern professional – the tournament

player – could be a millionaire if, for instance, his name were Arnold Palmer or Jack Nicklaus.

The changes in the professional's status are traceable partly to the leadership of the Professional Golfers' Association of America and partly to the vast growth of golf and its attraction of new types of young men to compete for its financial rewards.

The PGA was founded in 1916 in New York, largely through the encouragement of businessmen and amateur golfers, notably Rodman Wanamaker of Philadelphia. It was modelled after the PGA of Great Britain – in fact, its creation was deferred while the organizers waited to receive the British body's constitution and by-laws.

Headquarters were first in New York, later in Chicago. In addition, from 1945 to 1962 the PGA was associated with a golf course as the PGA National GC in Dunedin, Fla., a sort of winter golfing haven for its members; and in 1956 the office was moved from Chicago to Dunedin. Since 1965 the PGA's headquarters have been in the new PGA National GC in Palm Beach Gardens, Fla., with an executive director and staff of 41. The club and its three courses are privately owned and controlled by a land-development company, to which the PGA lent its name and prestige.

The PGA has about 6,900 members. They are divided into 37 geographical sections, many of them subdivided into local chapters. National policy is shaped by delegates to the annual meeting and by the Executive Committee, all 17 members of which give their services free. There are four major departments organized under the PGA, dealing with public relations, education, general business and the tournament programme. The PGA's many Business Schools throughout the country reflect the character of the modern professional and help members to improve their talents, and qualify new members. Throughout the 37 sections educational forums and clinics seek to raise standards; merchandise shows attract the golfing public. The national PGA conducts a continuing campaign of public relations, including publication of a national magazine. There is a PGA brand of golf clubs and balls. Relief and benevolent funds administered by the national organization reflect the professionals' fraternal concern.

The tournament circuit – the Tour – is a phenomenon of sport. Its seeds were sown in the early 1920s, with Walter Hagen, Jim Barnes, Jock Hutchison, Tommy McNamara, Bobby Cruickshank as some of the chief performers. Later, the schedule grew under the management of Bob Harlow

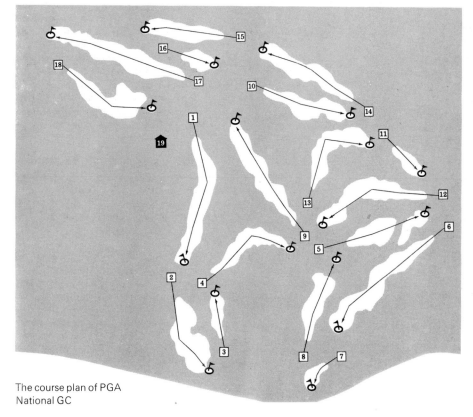

The course plan of PGA National GC

and Fred Corcoran. In 1972 it consisted of 46 major and 22 minor tournaments, for prize money totalling $7·5 million. It is a year-round, nation-wide tour.

The Tour now is conducted by a semi-autonomous corporation, the PGA Tournament Players Division (TPD). This was created in December 1968 to heal a breach.

The tournament players had separated from the PGA and formed their own organization, which lasted a few months until the TPD was born. Chief peacemakers were Leo Fraser as PGA President and Gardner Dickinson Jr, as head of the players' group.

The TPD is governed by a Policy Board of 10: four players, the three national PGA officers, and three prominent businessmen who serve as independent directors. Its affairs are administered by a Commissioner and staff with offices in New York and by a 10-man Tournament Staff in the field. The TPD is responsible for all events on the PGA Tour except the following, which are conducted by the PGA administration: the PGA Championship, Ryder Cup Match, PGA Club Professional Championship, PGA Seniors' Championship and World Series of Golf. The Tournament Players Division is a non-profit organization of 430 members; PGA members who do not belong to the TPD may also play in its tournaments. The Tour is the showcase of professional golf. There were 27 tournaments scheduled for American television in 1972, some indication of the profound influence the players exert on the game. A number of fundamental changes in the Rules of Golf arose from the crucible of the tour, including the right to clean the ball and to repair ball marks on the putting green.

Most of the new players go to the tour from colleges rather than golf shops. Unless they are PGA members, they can qualify only through an annual test – a 72-hole regional try-out leading to a 108-hole finale. In 1971, 357 players competed for 23 places. The money hazards of the tour are considerable. In the typical weekly major tournament (with a purse of at least $100,000), only 70 and ties receive prizes out of an average entry of 275. But the rewards can be vast. In 1971, 32 players won at least $70,000 each in prize money, not counting income from endorsements, exhibitions and other sources. A distorted sense of values and a preoccupation with money can result, typified by a certain caddie in a $250,000 tournament. He worked for the winner, who won $50,000 and paid the caddie $1,500 – and the caddie complained bitterly, and publicly.

Pull
Often a well-struck straight shot but in the wrong direction, left of the intended line. Not to be confused with a 'hook'.

Pung, Mrs Barney see LIWAI, JACQUELINE

Push
The opposite of pull; a shot which can be well struck and straight but in the wrong direction and right of the intended line.

Push Shot
A stroke with an iron designed to achieve distance but with the ball kept low to the ground. Popular in the days of hickory, it

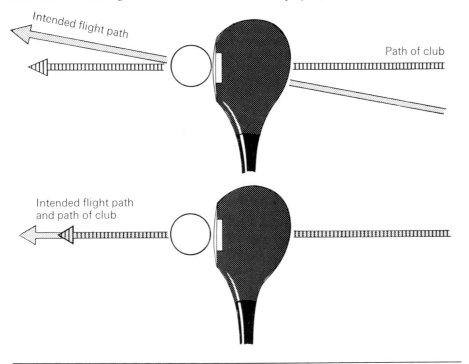

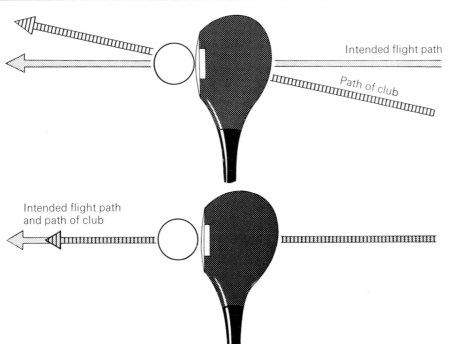

Pull, *above,* is the opposite of push, *below;* in the former, the ball travels to left of the target, in the latter to the right

was executed by keeping the weight on the left side and hitting the ball with a sharp, descending blow, pushing the hands at the ball. Very effective in the wind.

Putting
The part of golf taking place mainly on the putting green in which the ball is not made

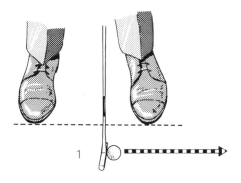

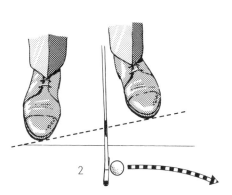

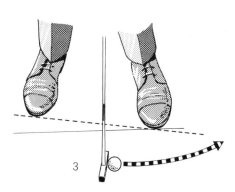

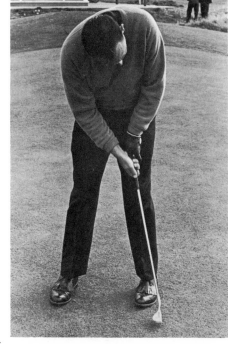

to fly but is rolled towards the hole with the purpose of 'holing out' or leaving the ball near enough to the hole to achieve this with the next stroke. The instrument almost exclusively used is the straight-faced and specially designed club called a putter (which has taken thousands of different forms): there have, however, been many cases of players using other clubs for putting, notably a no. 2 or 3 iron.

Putting is a game within a game in that a good player's score of, say, 69 may consist of 34 putts, or roughly half. Whatever the level of play, the success of a round depends very largely on the putting. This was apparent in the very early days of competition and gave rise to Willie Park's famous remark 'A man who can putt is a match for anyone'. It has since been proved over and over again to the point that many people believe that putting plays an entirely disproportionate part in the game.

At first sight, putting appears child's play but when the pressures build up to a peak

Putting: 1. square stance for a straight putt: 2. the stance for a putt that is to break to the right: 3. for a putt that is to break to the left

Putting styles: *top*, Bill Hyndman: *top right*, Billy Casper; *above*, Bob Rosburg, *above right*, Michael Bonallack

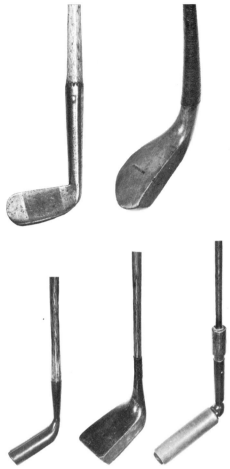

had two putters, a driving putter for playing low shots along the fairway, and a green putter for use nearer the hole. Today, most golfers carry only one putter but its use is not confined solely to the putting green. Its use off the putting green can be very effective; it is then known as a 'Texas wedge'.

Putting Green

The specially prepared part of every golf hole on which the hole is cut and the putting takes place. Ideally, greens have beautifully smooth and fast surfaces but this depends very largely on the type of grass, the climate and other factors. Greens vary enormously in size (there are no limits) and in their undulation. Their care is a specialized and costly job, the responsibility of the head greenkeeper (he has different titles in different parts of the world). In the early days of golf, however, nature was regarded as the greenkeeper. Players had to take the links as they found it; greens received no attention and it was a long time before anyone conceived the notion that greens should be mown or even rolled.

where everything may depend on the ability to hole two putts of a yard, it can take on an importance of appalling intensity. It can wreck nerves, ruin careers and destroy the balance of sane, intelligent men. Sufferers of putting ills resort to any method or gimmick that offers hope of relief.

In the days of the feathery ball, the golfer

Putting styles: *top*, John Cockin; *above*, Jack Rule

A selection of putters from the past — first row, 1700, 1770; second row, barrel-faced 1910, Gassiat 1920 and roller 1930

Qantas Australian Open Championship see AUSTRALIAN OPEN CHAMPIONSHIP

Qatar see DESERT COURSES

Quail High
A ball hit so that it flies at the height of the quail: not far off the ground.

Quaker Ridge GC USA
New York. 18 holes

Quaker Ridge, a broad strip of beautifully wooded land just north of New York City, was a summer vacation centre for wealthy New York families in the 1880s. Now the whole area is filled with suburban homes and golf courses, one of the most rewarding of which takes its name from the ridge.

The Quaker Ridge Golf Club lies just across a tree-lined suburban lane from Winged Foot. Compared to its illustrious neighbour, Quaker Ridge is obscure, but it possesses a course designed by A. W. Tillinghast, which any connoisseur would rate among the best in the Northeast. Few courses in the entire country have as many

1928 to win the US Open in a play-off with Bobby Jones.

A few years ago, a group of prominent golfers, among them winners of many national titles, were asked to pick what they thought were the best 18 holes from the 350 or more courses in the New York metropolitan area. Twenty of them chose holes from Quaker Ridge and six of its holes appeared on the ballots.

Quast, Anne see SANDER, MRS ANNE

Quebec GC, Royal CANADA
Boischatel, Que. 18 holes, 6,650 yd (6,081 m), par 72; 18 holes, 6,448 yd (5,896 m), par 72

The second golf club to be formed in North America followed by only two years the Royal Montreal GC, with which its early history is closely linked. Quebec GC was formed in 1875, and in 1933 it became 'Royal' by permission of King George V. Its members first played on the heights of Cove Fields, which crowned the St Lawrence River close by the ancient Citadel of Quebec. A more magnificent location in which to enjoy golf could hardly be imagined. There in 1876, in the first year of the club's since unbroken series of inter-club matches against Royal Montreal, the second of these historic contests took place. When the Plains of Abraham became a National Park, new ground for the course had to be sought. Accordingly, in 1914 the club moved

on the heights of Boischatel, overlooking the Island of Orleans in the St Lawrence River, with the Laurentian Mountains in the background. Willie Park Jr, of Musselburgh, who shortly before had completed Royal Montreal's expanded courses, was engaged to build a championship 18-hole course. How much of the work he was actually able to carry out himself is a matter of doubt, for he died in May 1925. Some forty years later a second 18-hole course was added. Tightly wooded and undulating, both courses offer golf at its best, in charming surroundings where French is the prevailing tongue.

Quick, Smiley Lyman AMERICAN
b. Centralia, Ill., 1907. Amateur Public Links 1946; runner-up US Amateur 1946; Walker Cup 1947

A colourful golfer who played the game in a vigorous style that matched his personality. He came close to scoring a rare double in 1946 when he won the Public Links title and only missed becoming US Amateur Champion when he missed a short putt at the 37th in the final against Ted Bishop. Quick began as a caddie at the age of seven and played his first round two years later. During the next 30 years his many occupations included being a trapeze artist, with golf thrown in wherever possible. Herbert Warren Wind wrote of him: 'He was short and heavy-muscled and looked more like a marathon runner than a golfer. He did not suffer from an inferiority complex.' Quick played in the 1947 Walker Cup match, winning his single, and turned professional the following year. Between then and 1960 he won the California Open twice and three other State championships.

Quitting
Failing to carry a stroke through to its correct or natural conclusion. The result is nearly always a poor stroke or, just as commonly, a poor putt. A flinch caused by a feeling that the ball may go too far or, more often, the effect of nervousness. Many important putts have been missed through 'quitting' on the stroke.

holes of such real character. There in 1936 Byron Nelson, then a slim, young assistant at Ridgewood, just over the Hudson River in New Jersey, won his first major title, the Metropolitan Open, at a time when the event was rated just behind the US Open and the Western Open. From this course Johnny Farrell went to Olympia Fields in

to a large farm set in the picturesque surroundings of Montmorency Falls near the historic Kent House just outside the city. Eighteen beautiful holes were constructed on leased land which, however, the club was never able to purchase. Wanting land in full ownership, the club moved again in 1925, this time to a tract of richly timbered land

Quaker Ridge GC – the 16th hole

R

Ragan, David, Jr AMERICAN

b. Daytona Beach, Fla., 1935. Ryder Cup 1963; runner-up USPGA 1963

Runner-up to Jack Nicklaus in the 1963 USPGA championship and a member of the Ryder Cup team that year. Ragan scored his first tour victory in 1959, improved his position on the money list steadily through 1962 and had seven other victories in his career. After his successful 1963 season, his game fell into decline. Ragan won the Florida Open and Southern Intercollegiate while attending the University of Florida and, encouraged by this showing, joined the tour late in 1956. He was backed by a group of Daytona Beach businessmen, including his father, a dentist.

Rangoon GC BURMA

Danyinggone. 18 holes; 6,984 yd (6,386 m); par 72

Founded in 1907 the club is at Danyinggone, 16 miles out of Rangoon on the city's circular railway. The small station is opposite the club. Rangoon GC, whose first captain was G. Ballance, was affiliated to the

Royal Calcutta and the Amateur Championship of Burma was played during the popular Puja festivities of Bengal to attract Europeans from Calcutta. The first championship was held in 1916 and won by W. H. L. Cabell. The club remained exclusively European until the end of World War II when the rule barring non-Europeans

David Ragan

was abandoned. During the war the old clubhouse was occupied by the pilots of General Chenault's Flying Circus up to the Japanese occupation of 1942 when the building was burned down. Between 1947 and 1952 the clubhouse was no more than a bamboo affair, but in 1952 the present clubhouse was built, a single-storeyed, sprawling brick structure with comfortable changing rooms.

The course is flat and the fairways are lined with small trees. In order to conserve the course, preferred lies are allowed the year round except during championships. The longest hole, the 12th, is more than 600 yd (550 m). Water hazards are formed by small *chaungs* or waterways and natural inlets, running across several fairways and in front of the 13th green. A course record of 66 was set in 1971 by Mya Aya.

Ransom, Henry AMERICAN

b. Houston, Tex., 1911. Tied 5th US Open 1950; Ryder Cup 1951

After many years as a club professional, Ransom joined the tournament circuit after World War II when in his mid-thirties, winning a dozen tournaments in more than a decade. He later developed a reputation as a teacher. Ransom's most successful season was 1950; this included victory in George May's World tournament. When Ransom had his fast swing in the groove, he was capable of shooting quite low scores, an example of which was his feat of eight

birdies in the last 11 holes to win the Illinois PGA in 1948.

Rap

A method of striking a putt. It is a short, decisive blow rather than a free-flowing stroke; positive rather than delicate. It is generally thought of as a fairly modern term

Henry Ransom

but Walter Travis, American Amateur Champion in 1900–1, 1903, and one of the best putters of all time, once said that he visualized the putting stroke as an attempt to drive an imaginary tack into the back of the ball.

Ras el Lados GC LEBANON

Tripoli. 9 holes; 5,920 yd (5,413 m); par 70 (18 holes)

Situated outside Tripoli, 50 miles north of Beirut on the Mediterranean. Ras el Lados is at sea level and is run by the Iraq Petroleum Co. as a private course for company staff and guests invited by a member.

Ravenscroft, Gladys (Mrs Temple Dobell) BRITISH

b. Rock Ferry, Cheshire, 1888; d. 1960. British Ladies' 1912; runner-up French Ladies' Open 1912; US Women's Amateur 1913; runner-up English Ladies' 1919

Gladys Ravenscroft was the first English and second British-born golfer to win the American championship, defeating Marion Hollins in the final at Wilmington by two holes. She was big in every sense of the word – tall, well built, striking looking, generous hearted. She played for fun but was a splendid competitor. Natural advantages of height and reach gave her power without undue exertion, and like most of her contemporaries she could hole out the ball with dexterity. She was Cheshire Ladies' Champion seven times between 1912 and 1930.

Rawlins, Horace BRITISH

US Open 1895; runner-up 1896

The youngest person ever to win the US Open. He took the first title in 1895 when, as a young English professional recently arrived to be assistant to the Newport (R.I.) club, he beat a field of 10 professionals and one amateur. He was 19 and had a total of 173

Horace Rawlins

(91, 82) over the 9-hole course at Newport. In 1896 he was runner-up 3 strokes behind the winner, Jim Foulis.

Rawls, Elizabeth Earle AMERICAN

b. Spartanburg, S. Car., 1928. US Women's Open 1951, 1953, 1957, 1960, runner-up 1950; Eastern Women's Open 1952-3;

Western Women's Open 1952, 1959; Tampa Women's Open 1954, 1956-8; LPGA 1959

Betsy Rawls holds the unique distinction of having won the American Women's Open four times, the first of them in her first year as a professional, 1951. In her first clash with the professionals she had finished 2nd in the Women's Open, 1950, 9 strokes behind the winner, Babe Zaharias. She was leading money winner in 1952 and 1959: it is an indication of the size of the tour at that time that her earnings in the latter year were under $27,000, in spite of winning 10 tournaments. She was appointed president of the LPGA in 1961 and 1962.

Ray, Edward BRITISH

b. Grouville, Jersey, Channel Islands, 1877; d. 1943. Runner-up British Professional Matchplay 1903, 1911-12; British Open 1912, runner-up 1913, joint 1925; US Open 1920, 3rd 1913; Ryder Cup captain 1927.

Ted Ray's early career coincided with the reign of the Great Triumvirate and, in some ways, he was overshadowed by them. These were difficult circumstances in which to have to make a name as a player, but he gave James Braid a hard run in the first final of the Matchplay Championship at Sunningdale in 1903 and was frequently well up the list in tournaments for the next eight years or so. He was a huge, lumbering figure of a man with a pipe invariably clenched between his teeth, a trilby hat on his head and a philosophy reflected in the advice he

once gave a golfer who wanted to hit the ball further: 'Hit it a bloody sight harder, mate.'

This made Ray prone to the wild, disastrous shot because he also swayed and heaved in a manner no teacher would recommend – but handsome was as handsome did. His game lasted well and though his style was unorthodox, it had the saving

grace of rhythm; he developed a fine skill at recovery and always possessed a delicate touch on the greens. These were the qualities that made him an outstanding player.

In 1911 and 1912 he lost successive finals of the Matchplay Championship to Braid and Harry Vardon. Then in 1912 his turn came to win the British Open at Muirfield with a total of 295, a victory that gave him understandable pleasure. During his year as champion he was consistently successful, but in 1913 Taylor beat him into 2nd place at Hoylake. That same year he took the bold step in those days of travelling to the United States where he, Vardon and Francis Ouimet tied for the American Open at Brookline. Ouimet's victory in the play-off at the age of 20 has long been one of the most famous in the history of golf. Ray returned to the States after the war to win at Inverness, with a score of 295, the same as at Muirfield. Until Tony Jacklin won the US Open in 1970, Ray remained the last British player to win the title. These two and Vardon are the only British players who have won both Opens. This gives Ray a special place in the records. It is not his only link with Vardon. They were born within a mile of each other on the little island of Jersey and Ray followed Vardon as professional at Ganton in Yorkshire.

Ray moved to Oxhey when that club started in 1912, his victory in the Open giving it immediate recognition. He remained there for the rest of his life, serving

the members in his kindly way and confirming his reputation as one of the game's most popular figures, and a skilled exponent at billiards.

Real Club de Golf 'El Prat' SPAIN

Barcelona. 27 holes; Championship Course 6,529 yd (5,970 m)

'El Prat' is set delightfully on the Catalan coast among the umbrella-shaped pines, known as *sombrillas*, near Barcelona Airport a little way south of the city. The best course in that part of Spain, it was designed by the leading Spanish architect, Javier Arana, and opened in 1954. It quickly gained a reputation for itself, the Spanish Open, won by Peter Alliss, being first held there in 1956. The start is not long but the first three holes and the 4th green are tightly enclosed by trees and form a nice contrast with the 5th and 6th; the 7th, 8th and 9th, running hard by the sea and returning to the clubhouse, are as different again. The 10th, 11th and 12th form another menacing, tree-lined loop, the next four offer a little more freedom, although all are demanding in their own way, and then the short 17th and 18th return to the setting in which the round began.

The club has housed the Spanish Amateur Championship on several occasions and, besides 1956, the Spanish Open Championships of 1959, 1963 and 1971. These were won by Peter Thomson, Ramón Sota and the 18-year-old Dale Hayes respectively. In addition to the championship course there is a separate 9-hole course and an ample practice ground.

Real Club de la Puerta de Hierro SPAIN

Madrid. 36 holes; Championship Course 7,042 yd (6,439 m)

This is the oldest club on the Spanish mainland. It was founded in 1904 under the name of the Madrid Polo GC. Later, King Alfonso XIII gave the land that has been its home ever since. The club is situated only a short distance from the centre of Madrid near the university.

The first Spanish Open Championship was played at the old Madrid Polo GC course. All subsequent Spanish Opens until 1942 were held at the present course. During the Spanish Civil War the course was fought over and almost completely destroyed. It was restored after the war by Tom Simpson. Later John Harris did some redesigning and made it up to 27 holes. Much of the course is undulating. It is a fine test and in 1970 was the scene of the United States victory in the World Amateur Team Championship for the Eisenhower Trophy. It is also one of the three courses on which the Madrid Open

Betsy Rawls

Ted Ray

Championship, started in 1968, takes place each year. The opening hole is an invigorating experience – a short hole usually requiring wood to the other side of a deep valley crossed by a wooden footbridge. In summer heat the course's length can be daunting for the holes sprawl over a wide area, but there are several holes of fine quality. The old polo ground makes a magnificent practice area.

Real Sociedad de Golf Neguri 'La Galea' SPAIN

Algorta, nr Bilbao. 18 holes; S.S.S. 72

Founded in 1911, this is the third oldest club in Spain although the present course, easily the best in the north of the country,

was opened only in 1960. 'La Galea' is situated about 10 miles from Bilbao and was designed by Javier Arana in two distinct parts: a pleasant, open section down towards the sea and the rest carved through the tall, handsome pines which set a fine yet fearsome test of control. The club, in both its old and new settings, has housed a great many Spanish championships. In 1966 it held the biennial match between the amateurs of Great Britain and Ireland, and those of the Continent of Europe.

Real Sociedad Hipica Española Club de Campo SPAIN

Madrid. 27 holes

This course is situated on a hill a little

way out of Madrid and commands a fine view of the city and the neighbouring countryside which was the scene of fighting during the Spanish Civil War. The club was founded in 1932 though the present course was not laid out by Javier Arana until 1956; it is a notable test and has been the setting of several international events including the Canada Cup, which Gary Player and Harold Henning won for South Africa in 1965, and the 1970 World Women's Team Championship in which the United States won a narrow victory over France.

The opening drive is a most inviting one to a fairway over 100 ft (30 m) below and the first half is laid out on ground of unusual undulation. The short 9th returns to within a few yards of the club's front door and the fine homeward half maintains the rolling nature, dropping to a point near the polo ground and tennis courts and later circling back to a raised plateau green at the 18th.

In addition to the main course, which measures over 7,000 yd (6,400 m), there are a separate 9 holes, opened in 1964, to complete the facilities of the biggest sporting complex in Spain.

Rees, David James BRITISH

b. Barry, Glamorgan, 1913. British Professional Matchplay 1936, 1938, 1949-50, runner-up 1953, 1967, 1969; Ryder Cup 1937, 1947, 1949, 1951, 1953 (captain 1955, 1957, 1959, 1961, 1967); Belgian Open 1954; Vardon Trophy 1955, 1959; runner-up British Open 1961, joint runner-up 1953-4; British Senior Professional 1966; captain PGA 1967

Dai Rees, son of a professional, inherited a remarkable zest and enthusiasm for the game which, together with an urge to keep fit, has enabled him to play tournament golf for more than 40 years. During that time he became one of the leading names in British professional golf, captained the only successful British Ryder Cup team in modern times, and received the CBE for his services to the game.

His career began as an assistant in his native Wales but he did not have to wait long before making his mark, winning the *News of the World* (now the British Professional) Matchplay Championship at Oxhey in 1936 when he beat Ernest Whitcombe in the final after being 5 down with 14 to play. This earned him a place in the 1937 Ryder Cup match at Southport and Ainsdale in which he halved his foursome with Charlie Whitcombe, the British captain, and won his single against the redoubtable Byron Nelson by 3 and 1.

This marked the beginning of a remark-

Top, the Real Club de la Puerta de Hierro, looking back from the first green to the clubhouse during the 1970 Eisenhower Trophy and, *above,* the Madrid skyline beyond the course of the Real Sociedad Hipica Española Club de Campo

able sequence of appearances in the Ryder Cup, culminating in his captaincy of the British side in the historic victory at Lindrick in 1957. Success was attributable in no small part to Rees's example and optimism since it came after he and Ken Bousfield had been the only British foursomes winners. Their rally in the singles, in which Rees beat Ed Furgol by 7 and 6, was heroic.

Rees is an expressive person and one of rare and assertive spirit, with confidence in his ability to achieve things. It was the basis of his approach to life and to golf. It showed in his swing which was fast, natural, aggressive and rhythmic. Though a small man, a free wind-up of the shoulders and a two-handed grip on the club was controlled and

orthodox enough to give him the longest playing career of any British professional in modern times.

He retained a youthful enthusiasm until long after he became a senior and played some of his most successful golf during the 1960s. It was as though the Ryder Cup victory gave him a new lease of golfing life. His temperament thrived on playing a leading role, as he so often did in the Matchplay Championship. However, despite winning almost every other event in Britain, the Open always eluded him, as it did Sam Snead in the United States. Rees finished the last round of the 1946 Open at St Andrews with an 80 to end 5 strokes behind Snead, and came close on more than one subsequent occasion: he was joint runner-up in Hogan's year at Carnoustie. In 1954 he might have won at Birkdale but at the last hole a fine, bold 4 iron ran through the back of the green; Rees could not get down in 2 and Peter Thomson finally won his first Open by a single stroke. Seven years later on the same course Rees again lost by 1 stroke – this time to Arnold Palmer.

Although he continued to play a prominent part in British professional golf, Rees never again came as near to winning the British Open.

One of his outstanding performances was in reaching the final of the Professional Matchplay in 1969 (the last under the *News of the World* name) – 33 years after reaching his first. This reflected his two exemplary virtues: unflagging enthusiasm and his determination never to stop trying on any shot, whatever the occasion.

In later years Rees, always a ready and amusing talker, did valuable committee work for the PGA and was the association's captain in 1967. He received other honours in addition to the CBE. He was awarded the Golf Writers' Trophy in 1957, was BBC Sportsview Personality the same year, and in 1971 received a presentation from his own club, South Herts, in the northern suburbs of London, after he had served for 25 years as its professional.

Reid, John BRITISH
b. Dunfermline, Fife, 1840; d. Yonkers, N.Y., 1916

Generally regarded as the 'Father of American Golf'. Although he had known of the game as a young man in Scotland, Reid had never played it until 1888, when, with clubs brought from St Andrews by his friend Robert Lockhart, he and other friends first played the game on a crude, 3-hole course laid out in a pasture across the street from Reid's home. The St Andrew's GC was formally organized in November 1888, at a dinner at Reid's home. Reid was elected president. The club was moved to another part of the pasture during that first year, then later twice more before reaching its present site at Mt Hope. At one of the later locations, the 'clubhouse' was a large apple tree, and the small group became known as

the 'Apple Tree Gang', a name that has endured to the present day.

In December of 1894, Reid was one of nine men who met to form the United States Golf Association and he and Charles B. Macdonald drew up the first constitution and by-laws. He served nine years as president of St Andrew's and, although he held no office in the USGA, was a strong force in American golf until his death. His sons, John Jr and Archie, also became prominent in golf circles.

Revolta, John AMERICAN
b. St Louis, Mo., 1911. USPGA 1935; Western Open 1935; Ryder Cup 1935, 1937; Texas Open 1944

Revolta was a caddie at the age of 12 and Wisconsin Caddie Champion at 14. In 1929 he turned professional and soon established himself among the best golfers in the Wisconsin-Minnesota region. Revolta beat the best ball of Gene Sarazen and Tommy Armour when they were touring the area early in the 1930s; friends then urged him to venture his obvious talent on the tournament circuit. He achieved victory in the 1933 Miami Open, and for the rest of the decade was one of the most consistent winners in the game; he was leading money winner in 1935.

In 1934 Revolta won four tournaments, and the next year he went all the way to the top – at the age of 24 – by winning the USPGA and Western Open, earning the reputation in the process of being a fine bunker player and putter. In beating Walter Hagen in the first round of the PGA and in his victory over Armour in the final, Revolta displayed a phenomenal short game.

Revolta continued to win tournaments until World War II interrupted the tour, and when the war ended he chose to devote most of his time to his job at the Evanston GC, a post he held from 1937 until 1966. He played

Dai Rees

John Reid

John Revolta

Opposite, Pebble Beach Golf Links

portions of the tour through the 1940s, but, although only in his thirties, he never achieved anything like the success of those early years on the circuit. When he was at his best he was splendid and at one time held 17 different course records in Wisconsin and Minnesota. His 270 in winning the 1931 Minnesota Open equalled the record for a 72-hole event.

Rhodesia
Rhodesia's climate is ideal for outdoor living and golf is a popular pastime among the white population. Bulawayo GC, founded in January 1895, a year or so after the European occupation of Matabeleland, is the oldest in the country. The Salisbury GC (now Royal Salisbury) followed in 1899 in the city which today can be regarded as the centre of Rhodesian golf. Of the more than 70 courses in the country, 12 lie within a 20-mile radius of Salisbury and provide admirable golf in a variety of settings. But by no means all the golf is confined to urban centres such as Salisbury, Bulawayo, Gwelo and Umtali.

Some of the most spectacularly beautiful country is to be found in the Eastern Highlands, an area that makes Scotsmen feel very much at home, and one of the most attractive courses is to be found at Troutbeck. Its 9 holes, created by Major MacIlwaine who once played rugby for England, are set against the background of a trout-filled lake, the Troutbeck Inn and glorious mountains.

Another short course in an equally majestic setting is at Chimanimani, a simple reminder of the enthusiasm and enterprise of golfers even in sparsely populated areas. The Leopard Rock course provides more interesting entertainment in the steep Vumba mountains outside Umtali while the course at Turner and Newell's vast asbestos mine at Shabani, though also somewhat remote, is a fine full-scale test.

There is a short season of professional golf tournaments closely linked with the expanding circuit in South Africa and this affords Rhodesian golfers the chance to see some of the world's leading players. Hagen, Locke, Snead, Casper, Bolt, Rees, Player, Palmer and Oosterhuis have all played in Rhodesia at various times, and national teams have played in the Eisenhower Trophy and the Women's World Team Championships.

Rhythm
The tempo of a golf swing; the smoothness, fluency and speed that influence the striking and timing of shots. It is an elusive quality which good players prize most and strive hardest to preserve. Bad rhythm nearly always produces a bad stroke. Rhythm is a pattern of recurrence.

Rice, Henry Grantland AMERICAN
b. Murfreesboro, Tenn., 1880; d. 1954
One of the world's best-known sports writers who was devoted to golf. He wrote about the game throughout his career, was a capable player himself, and was always on the scene for the major tournaments. He was also the editor of the *American Golfer* and of the Spalding Golf Guides for many years. Rice began playing golf at Nashville in 1909 and he approached it as he did everything else in life. As he wrote in his autobiography: 'You are meant to play the ball as it lies, a fact that may help to toughen your own objective approach to life.' And later: 'A man's true colours will surface quicker in a five-dollar Nassau than in any other form of peacetime diversion that I can name.' Rice not only wrote about all the great players of the game for more than 40 years, he played golf with most of them, as well as with baseball players, football stars, actors, famous authors and captains of industry. Through his fame as a writer and his warmth of personality, he contributed immeasurably to the growth of the game in the United States.

Richardson, William D. AMERICAN
b. Milwaukee, Wis., 1885
William Richardson, one of the leading golf writers in America, covered the game for the *New York Times* from 1921 to 1947. Richardson attended the University of Wisconsin, where he was the coxswain of the varsity crew. In World War I he served as an infantry captain. Richardson was admired equally for his journalistic skill and his high personal qualities, and when his colleagues in the Golf Writers' Association of America decided to establish an annual award to

someone in golf who had made an outstanding contribution to the game, it was entirely fitting that it was named after him: the Richardson Trophy.

Riegel, Robert H. AMERICAN
b. New Bloomfield, Pa., 1914. US Amateur 1947; Walker Cup 1947, 1949; runner-up US Masters 1951
Up to 1946 when he won the Trans-Mississippi and was a medallist in the US Amateur, Riegel's chief claim to fame as a golfer had been victory in the 1942 Florida Amateur. In 1947 he beat Johnny Dawson in the final of the US Amateur and was chosen for the Walker Cup team, and again two years later, winning 4 points out of 4. Towards the end of 1949, after another victory in the Trans-Mississippi, he turned professional and in the 1951 Masters set the pace with a final score of 282; but Hogan, still out, played the last 9 in better than par and finished with 280. After working as a professional in Tulsa, Riegel returned to his native Pennsylvania in the early 1950s.

Riley, Polly AMERICAN
b. Fort Worth, Tex. Runner-up US Women's Amateur 1953, semi-finalist 1965; Curtis Cup 1948, 1950, 1952, 1954, 1956, 1958 (non-playing captain 1962)
Although up to 1970 Polly Riley had made 25 consecutive appearances in the US Women's Amateur, victory eluded her. The nearest she came was in 1953 when she reached the final, but an outstanding round of 73 by her opponent, Mary Lena Faulk, left her down at lunch and she was beaten after hanging on grimly by 3 and 2. She won the Women's Southern Amateur six times, the Western Amateur twice, and the Trans-Mississippi twice. It is as a Curtis Cup player that she will be best remembered, especially in Britain; she represented her country six

Opposite. 'The Trophies' at the Royal and Ancient GC

William D. Richardson

Robert H. Riegel

times from 1948, largely on the strength of the number of regional championships she won. She won the first four singles in which she played, including an overwhelming defeat of Elizabeth Price. In the 1956 match at Prince's she came up against Frances Smith in her most determined mood. Each had an unbeaten record in four singles

matches to that point, but it was Mrs Smith who maintained hers, defeating Miss Riley on the last green and in doing so winning the contest for Britain. Two years later at Brae Burn they met again, the Englishwoman again being successful in holding onto a 1-up lead at the last hole and ensuring the first tied match by any British team in the United States. In 1962 Miss Riley had some measure of revenge, for the two met again as non-playing captains at Broadmoor, and the American team enjoyed an overwhelming victory.

Ringer Score

The cumulative score based on a player's best performance at each hole on a given course over a given period of time. Also known as an eclectic score.

Riverside CC CANADA

Saskatoon, Sask. 18 holes; 6,540 yd (5,980 m); par 70

The term 'inland links' may seem to be a contradictory one, but it aptly describes the Riverside course situated on the east bank of the South Saskatchewan River, some six miles south of Saskatoon. Its soil is of sandy texture such as is found by the seashore, and strong prairie province winds, often rising to a force of 45 mph, sweep across the course most of the time. Fortunately the rolling fairways are of ample, even generous, width The original design was by William Kinnear, who was born in Leven, Scotland, and per-

haps the only criticism of it is that it requires no fewer than six blind shots to greens. The club has witnessed the 1964 Canadian Amateur Championship; the 1967 Canadian Ladies' Open Championship, which was won by Bridget Jackson of England; and the 1968 Senior Championship of Canada.

Riverside GCC CANADA

St John, N.B. 18 holes; 6,300 yd (5,760 m); par 71

Overlooking the beautiful Kennebecasis River in New Brunswick, half a dozen miles from the centre of Canada's major winter seaport on the Bay of Fundy, is this scenic, tree-lined course. Its championship qualities have been proven in several national tournaments. It was the scene of the Canadian Open Championship in 1939, the Canadian Amateur Championship in 1949 and 1963, and the Canadian Ladies' Open Championship in 1948 and 1960. In all of these the course has commanded justifiable respect for the accuracy it demands. Many of the holes are wooded and narrow. Others are either hilly, tightly bunkered or provided with small greens. The regret is that such a good course should finish weakly. Its downhill, 220-yd (201-m) 18th hole is notorious for failing to settle a closely fought match.

Riviera GC USA

Beverly Hills, Los Angeles, Cal.

In the golf-conscious area round Los Angeles, the first club in time was the Los Angeles CC, built in 1899. But the Riviera club course, designed 25 years later in the Santa Monica Canyon, is better known and has been more highly praised. George C. Thomas Jr was the architect responsible for the excellent design, and Bill Bell was in charge of construction. In 1948, when Riviera measured 7,100 yd (6,492 m), Ben Hogan's winning score of 67, 72, 68, 69 for a total of 276 was 5 strokes lower than the record for the US Open, and stood for 19 years until Jack Nicklaus returned 275 at Baltusrol in 1967. These figures may be deceiving. Riviera is deserving of the praise it has had, for it is a very exacting course with tight fairways and several noteworthy holes. Hogan himself has chosen as one of the finest he has played anywhere the 2nd, a par 4 of 460 yd (420 m) where the approach is played across an undulating fairway to a narrow closely bunkered green below the handsome clubhouse. In contrast is the 10th, only a little over 300 yd (274 m). The Los Angeles Open, now generally played at the Rancho municipal course and at Brookside in Pasadena, was three times lost at this innocuous-looking hole with its single

narrow opening to a tricky green.

Riviera is still to a certain extent the favourite playground of the movie colony. It is expensive and strictly private, and the club likes a visitor to be accompanied by a member.

Robb, Diane SEE FREARSON, MRS DIANE

Robb, James BRITISH
b. Dunfermline, Fife, 1878. British Amateur 1906, runner-up 1897, 1900

Although not a native of St Andrews, Robb took his first steps in the game on the Old Course and scored his first competitive success by winning the junior medal of his school, Madras College. After reaching the final of the Amateur at his second attempt he moved to the West of Scotland and gained international honours five years later.

Robbins, Hillman AMERICAN
b. Memphis, Tenn., 1932. US National Collegiate 1954; North and South Amateur 1956; Interservice 1957; Colonial Invitation 1957; US Amateur 1957, semi-finalist 1955; Walker Cup 1957

Robbins crowned an outstanding amateur career by winning the US Amateur in 1957. He was considered to be a really good prospect when he turned professional in 1958, but he was unable to find himself in that sphere and soon rejected it in favour of the life of a club professional. In the final of the 1957 Amateur he defeated Bud Taylor, 5 and 4.

Robertson, Allan BRITISH
b. St Andrews, Fife, 1815; d. 1859

In the years before the first Open Championship in 1860 when St Andrews was imperceptibly establishing itself as the headquarters of the game, Allan Robertson was the dominant figure among the artisans of the game in that city. He was by common consent the supreme golfer of his age, at least until he handed over to the Morrises, and it was not surprising that the legend sprang up that in foursome challenge matches he had never been beaten. He died the year before the first Open Championship so that his name is not entered on the roll of honour, but it is said that the championship arose out of a desire to find out who ruled the roost once the matter had been thrown into doubt by Robertson's death.

The Robertsons had been makers of clubs and balls for many years when Allan took over the shop that overlooked the 18th green at St Andrews. With his assistant, Tom Morris, he turned out feather balls of the highest quality. In 1844, the year before the

Polly Riley

first gutty was made, his output was 2,456, a high figure considering that the making of them was a tedious process and that ball-makers did not reckon on producing more than four a day. He fell out with Old Tom over the use of the new-fangled 'gutta' ball, Tom setting up in business on his own, but on the links they buried their differences and partnered each other in many notable victories.

The most famous of these was over the Dunn brothers from Musselburgh, the contest being decided over three courses, each of 36 holes. North Berwick was the deciding match and amid scenes of explosive rivalry from the crowds the St Andrews pair won the last two holes of the 108-hole match. Robertson was by no means on form but Morris was a tower of strength, and an error of judgment by their Musselburgh opponents at the last hole but one let them in. Most of the clubs used in those days, and manufactured in Robertson's workshop, were wooden, the irons being reserved for specific tasks such as getting out of ruts. Allan is credited with having pioneered the use of the irons for more precise approach work from the fairways and in the short pitches round the green, but it was some years later that Young Tom Morris set the fashion in it. Robertson's robust, stocky figure was a familiar sight at St Andrews, and although he was never professional to the Royal and Ancient, the club recorded on his death its appreciation of him both as a

player and as one who was ever ready to 'promote the comfort of all who frequented the links'. He was buried in the graveyard of St Andrews cathedral and a monument to him stands in the city.

Robertson, Mrs I. C. (Belle McCorkindale) BRITISH

b. Argyll 1936. West of Scotland Ladies' 1957, 1964, 1966; runner-up British Ladies' 1959, 1965, 1970, semi-finalist 1971; Curtis Cup 1960, 1966, 1968, 1970, 1972, (captain 1974); World Women's Amateur Team Championship 1964, 1968; Scottish Ladies' 1965-6, 1971-2; British Women's Strokeplay 1971-2; New Zealand Ladies' Open 1971

Mrs Robertson took over the role of leading Scottish amateur golfer in succession to Janette Robertson and maintained it in spite of a hat trick of victories in the Scottish championship by Joan Lawrence during her reign. Her first appearance in the Curtis Cup was at Lindrick in 1960; at that time she was relatively inexperienced for her early golf had been mostly played in the delightful but inaccessible links of Machrihanish, Argyll. Her swing has a pronounced sway which tends to make her hook under pressure, but in the mood she is capable of the highest class of golf. She showed this notably when she was in Mexico captaining the British team in the World Women's Team Championship and returned a 68, the lowest of the championship. Twice when the

British Ladies' Championship visited Scotland she got to the final, but in 1965 she lost to Brigitte Varangot at St Andrews and five years later to Dinah Oxley at Gullane. One of her most successful years was 1971 when she won the Scottish for the third time and the Strokeplay Championship for the first time; she had also a most successful tour of New Zealand after the Commonwealth Tournament, winning the New Zealand Ladies' Open Championship.

Robertson, Janette (Mrs Innes Wright) BRITISH
b. Glasgow, 1935. British Girls' 1950, runner-up 1951; Curtis Cup 1954, 1956,

1958, 1960; semi-finalist British Ladies' 1955; New Zealand Ladies' Open Strokeplay 1955; Commonwealth Tournament 1959; Scottish Ladies' 1959-61, 1973, runner-up 1958; Worplesdon Foursomes (with Innes Wright) 1959

The British Girls' Championship that she won in 1950 was the first competitive event for which Janette Robertson had entered, and she at once impressed onlookers with the versatility and control of her iron play, which was exceptional for a 15-year-old. She played for Scotland for 14 years out of 16 between 1952 and 1967; she was more to be feared when playing for a team than when playing for herself. She was a popular and much respected member of British sides that went to the United States, Australia and New Zealand, and the continent of Europe. She had a notably successful time in New Zealand. Always trimly turned out, she made an attractive winner at Worplesdon with a partner who was to become her husband.

Robson, Frederick BRITISH
b. Cheshire, 1885. Ryder Cup 1927, 1929,

Allan Robertson – his gravestone commemorates his greatness as a Scottish golfer

Mrs I. C. Robertson during the 1972 Curtis Cup

Janette Robertson

1931; tied 2nd British Open 1927

Apart from his undoubted skill as a player, Robson was one of the finest clubmakers of his day and so renowned for his coaching that patrons frequently took him with them to championships, to have the benefit of his advice on the spot. He was for a time official coach to the British Walker Cup team. A well-loved man with a pleasant manner, Robson was for many years professional to the Addington club, being succeeded there by his son Robin, who inherited his father's skill at clubmaking.

Rochester CC USA

Rochester, N.J. 18 holes

Walter Hagen has told how, when he was 12 years old and in the seventh grade of school in suburban Rochester, near the Country Club where he had recently begun to caddie, he looked out of the window one day and saw a couple of golfers passing down a fairway carrying their own bags. He said he could not stand it, so when the teacher's back was turned he jumped out of the window and ran to the club. That was the end of Hagen's schooling, but not of his education. Hagen made this club famous, for it was here that he learned to play golf just about as well as anyone had ever learned anywhere. Hagen, of course, would have learned well on any course, but this was a particularly good one for the purpose because it presented very nearly every type of golf shot that is likely to come up in either social or competitive play.

It still does, since the course has kept pace with improved equipment and the means of growing turf have improved. The club's neighbour, Oak Hill, has attracted more attention because it was there that the US Open was held in 1956 and 1968, but the Country Club still is a quality course and a nice one to play. The US Women's Open and Amateur Championships have been held there, and the 302 at which Betsy Rawls tied with Jacqueline Pung in 1953 was a good representative score.

Rodgers, Philamon Webster AMERICAN

b. San Diego, Cal., 1938. Los Angeles Open 1962; Tucson Open 1962; runner-up British Open 1963, tied 3rd 1962; Buick Open 1966; Doral Open 1966; runner-up USPGA Matchplay 1971

After a fine amateur career Phil Rodgers made an impressive debut as a professional, although somewhat overshadowed by the emergence of Jack Nicklaus. He spent a year in the University of Houston golf team, winning the only three tournaments for which he entered, including the US National

Collegiate, and it soon became evident that he was a player of considerable talent, despite his temper, which was also considerable. Paul Runyan once said he was worried about Rodgers's temper: 'He is one of the few players who can make his anger work for him.' He also said that Rodgers at the age of 16 knew more about the golf swing than any youngster he had seen. After service in the US Marines, Rodgers turned professional in 1961. In the next 18 months he won three tournaments, almost $50,000, and came close to winning both the US and British Opens. He tied 3rd in the British when Arnold Palmer won with a record score in 1962, and in 1963 he earned a play-off with Bob Charles at Royal Lytham, which he lost over 36 holes, the last play-off at that length.

Rodgers made substantial money in 1964 and 1965 without winning a tournament, but he trimmed his weight from 200 to 170 lb, and by 1966 he was winning again. He made a good run at the British Open again that year, coming home at Muirfield in 30 in the third round which put him briefly into the lead. In 1971 he finished six times in the

top 10 despite two or three bad finishing rounds, and was runner-up in the inaugural US Matchplay Championship, losing the final at the North Carolina CC.

Roll

A tendency to turn the shoulders too much in a horizontal plane. One of the most common faults is to roll the right shoulder out horizontally at the beginning of the downswing, throwing the swing out of line and making it 'out-to-in'.

Rolland, Douglas (J. E. Douglas Stewart) BRITISH

b. Elie, Fife, 1860; d. Farnborough, Hampshire, 1914. Joint runner-up British Open 1884, runner-up 1894

One of the uncrowned kings of the game, a player who never won a championship but who was regarded as perhaps the greatest golfing genius of his time. From the age of 13 he worked for several years as a stone-mason, a job which probably accounted for his great strength. Six ft tall and with a chest measurement of $41\frac{1}{2}$ in, his physique was tremendous. According to Bernard Darwin, he hit the ball distances it had never been hit before, often with clubs he had borrowed. He was, it seems, as casual and reckless as his golf, but 'wherever he went he was loved, admired and forgiven – an irreclaimably dashing dog that nobody could withstand'. He learned his golf at Earlsferry, or Elie as the course is now known. In 1883 he took up the challenge of John Ball for a match on a home-and-home basis at Earlsferry and Hoylake. Rolland, 9 up at Earlsferry, went on to win by 11 and 10, and the next day won another match by 1 hole after being 5 down with 6 to play. This no doubt prompted him to turn professional but not until after he had finished joint 2nd with Willie Fernie in the 1884 Open at Prestwick,

Top, Rochester CC – one of the greens

Above, Phil W. Rodgers

4 strokes behind Jack Simpson. In 1887 he accepted the post as professional at Malvern and later at Rye, Limpsfield, and Bexhill. He finished 2nd again in the Open 10 years later, this time as a professional at Sandwich. The Saturday before the championship he beat Willie Park in a challenge for £50, and after the championship he defeated Horace Hutchinson, Willie Auchterlonie, F. G. Tait, and J. H. Taylor, the champion, in a professional/amateur tournament. He was not seen much thereafter, because of ill-health. He settled in the United States for a few years, but later returned to Britain.

Romania SEE RUMANIA

Romack, Barbara Gail AMERICAN
b. Sacramento, Cal., 1932. Canadian Ladies' Open 1953; Curtis Cup 1954, 1956, 1958; US Women's Amateur 1954, runner-up 1958; runner-up British Ladies' 1955

Barbara Romack's outstanding season as an amateur was 1954 when she won the US Women's at Allegheny, Pa. It was noteworthy because a series of thunderstorms prolonged the final against Mary Wright for $29\frac{1}{4}$ hours. The final began on a Saturday morning and ended on Sunday afternoon when Miss Romack won by 4 and 2. The following year she made a bid for the double by competing in the British Amateur, but in rough weather at Royal Portrush she lost the final to Mrs George Valentine (Jessie Anderson). Three years later she was

runner-up again in the US championship at Wee Burn, Darien, Conn., losing by 3 and 2 to Anne Quast (Mrs Decker) who played the last 7 holes of the match in 4 under par. During the autumn of 1958 Barbara Romack joined the professional ranks, but her career there was hampered by ill-health and injuries. She scored 3 points out of 5 in matches against Britain.

Rosburg, Bob AMERICAN
b. San Francisco, Cal., 1926. Vardon Trophy 1958; Ryder Cup 1959; USPGA 1959; runner-up US Open 1959, tied 2nd 1969

Bob Rosburg graduated from Stamford University in 1948. He turned professional in 1953 and with a marvellous putting stroke rather than a classical golf swing fashioned a successful career on the circuit. The highlight was his victory in the 1959 USPGA Championship at Minneapolis, where his total of 277 beat Doug Sanders and Jerry Barber into joint 2nd place.

This, together with his winning the 1958 Vardon Trophy, earned him a place in the 1959 Ryder Cup match at Palm Desert where he won both his matches. For some time he was active in administration – member of the USPGA tournament 1958-61, and chairman 1959-61 – and he was not particularly prominent as a player in the 1960s. Nevertheless he finished joint 2nd with Deane Beman and Al Geiberger in the 1969 US Open at Champions, Houston, 1

stroke behind Orville Moody. Rosburg's performance at 42 must have surprised even himself but, in fact, having played a superb bunker shot at the 72nd hole, he missed a very short putt that might have made him champion. He maintained his game well, and in February 1972 won the Bob Hope Classic.

Rosendaelsche GC NETHERLANDS
nr Arnhem. 9 holes

The Rosendaelsche GC, a little way out of Arnhem on the Apeldoorn road, takes its name – in suitably archaic spelling – from Rozendaal where the house of a religious order once stood. It is a beautiful course with a great variety of trees to give added interest to the golf. The club was founded in 1896, which makes it one of the oldest in the Netherlands, but it was not until 1906 that it moved to its present site when Mr de Court van Krimpen laid out the existing course on his own land. Despite being only 9 holes, the Dutch Amateur Championship has been staged at the Rosendaelsche. The club has about 400 members, the considered limit for a 9-hole course.

Ross, Mrs A. E. SEE HEZLET, MAY

Ross, Alec BRITISH
b. Dornoch, Sutherland. North and South Open 1904, 1907-8, 1910, 1915; US Open 1907

Alec Ross, son of a Dornoch stonemason, was slightly eclipsed by the renown of his elder brother, Donald, who built over 500 courses in the United States. However, Alec followed his brother to America in 1900 and became well known in his own right.

In 1903 he was appointed professional at the Brae Burn Club and spent his winters as assistant to Donald at Pinehurst. In 1907 he won the US Open in 302 from Gilbert Nicholls at the Philadelphia Cricket Club, an event in which he also finished five times in the top 10. He was Massachusetts Open Champion six years in succession, and won the North and South Open at Pinehurst five times.

Through his visits to Pinehurst, where rich men from northern cities loved to go, he was appointed professional at the Detroit GC by a millionaire, Horace Rackham, to whom Ross gave his first golf lesson. This was the beginning of a friendship with Rackham who provided Alec with a trust fund in his will and also the beginning of a long association with the Detroit club which lasted from 1916 until 1946. It was appropriate that Alec Ross specified in his will that his ashes should be scattered at Detroit GC.

Barbara G. Romack

Bob Rosburg

Ross, Donald BRITISH
b. Dornoch, Sutherland, 1873; d. Pinehurst, N. Car., 1948

An emigrant Scot who worked in the United States and was responsible for designing over 500 courses in that country, including such distinguished ones as Seminole (much admired by Ben Hogan), Pinehurst, Oak Hill, Kahkwa, Brae Burn, Seaview, Scioto, Inverness, Interlachen, and Detroit. He had learned in his native Dornoch what challenging golf really meant, and this influenced him greatly in his design. Pinehurst No. 2 Course, which he revised in the mid-1930s, is widely regarded as offering the most exacting test of chipping in the United States, for it contains many of the Dornoch-style crown greens, slopes, and run-ups. The group of Scottish golfers who emigrated to the United States at the turn of the century had an important influence on the development of golf there, and perhaps none made a greater impact than Ross.

The son of a stonemason, he began his working life as a journeyman carpenter but his main interest was golf and, after a period under Old Tom Morris at St Andrews and later as professional/greenkeeper at Dornoch, he emigrated to the United States, landing in Boston in 1898 with two dollars in his pocket. Although in doing so he was following the example of other Scottish professionals, it was a bold step; in taking it he was largely influenced by Robert Wilson, a Harvard professor who, in summers spent at Dornoch, had come under the spell of the game. Donald was later followed by his younger brother, Alec. When Ross arrived Professor Wilson came to his aid and found him an appointment as professional at the Oakley CC in Watertown, Mass. After his appointment by James W. Tufts in 1900 as professional at his new course in Pinehurst – an association which lasted for 48 years – Ross developed the principles and practice which were to make him an outstanding course architect in American golfing history. Ross's fame spread from Pinehurst, where new holes were designed by him and Frank Maples, and by 1910 he had severed all his professional connections except those with Pinehurst.

Donald Ross never forgot his early days at Dornoch or his training under Old Tom who had designed 9 holes there, an event which no golf-minded boy was likely to forget. Ross set up his home in Pinehurst and in later years became a director in the company which until recently operated the resort.

Ross, Philip Mackenzie BRITISH
b. Edinburgh 1890; d. 1974

Mackenzie Ross's interest in golf was aroused at an early age by his father who once reached the last eight of the British Amateur and one year finished 13th in the Open at Musselburgh, where Mackenzie Ross himself used to play frequently while a schoolboy at Loretto. He served for six years from the first month of World War I, finishing up with the British Military Mission to Siberia; but, on returning to civilian life, he was keen to have a varied and open-air job and, with the help of Tom Simpson, gradually became one of the world's leading golf-course architects.

The seeds, however, were sown in a rather unusual way for, after winning the Cruden Bay Open tournament which Tom Simpson refereed, Mackenzie Ross was standing admiring Simpson's new Rolls Royce. Mackenzie Ross remarked that it would look better if he placed the front numberplate below the cross bar instead of above it. Simpson had the alteration carried out and remarked that, if Ross noticed things like that, he would make a good golf-course architect. Later he took him on as a pupil for one year and then as a partner in the firm of Simpson and Ross.

While he was with Simpson, Mackenzie Ross did practically all of the lay-out work and quickly gained a reputation for his designs. He carried out a good deal of work on the Continent, in the Azores and in France, Spain, and the Canary Islands as well as in Britain. If he had to be remembered for his work on one course alone, it would undoubtedly be his restoration of Turnberry on the Ayrshire coast in Scotland. During World War II this had been used as an airfield and many felt that golf at Turnberry had gone for ever. They failed to see how concrete runways could ever be fairways again but, with skill, patience and the help of mechanical equipment, which can be monsters of creation as well as destruction, Mackenzie Ross worked what, in those days, was a minor miracle.

Also in the postwar period he designed Southerness on the northern shore of Solway Firth. In his own view this, together with Turnberry, Estoril near Lisbon, and the Royal Golf Club des Fagnes at Spa, ranked as the best of his work. Mackenzie Ross's other major designs or redesigns include:
British Isles Alnmouth, Balmoral (Belfast), Bangor (Co. Down), Carlisle City, Castletown (Isle of Man), Cramond (Edinburgh), Hythe (Southampton), Longniddry, North Berwick (Burgh Course), Royal Guernsey (Channel Islands)
Belgium Royal Antwerp
France Amiens, Deauville, Hardelot, Le Touquet, Mazamet
Portugal and the Azores Estoril, Furnas, San Miguel, Vidago
Spain and Canary Islands Costa Brava, Las Palmas, Málaga, Maspalomas, Santa Cristina de Aro

In 1972 he was elected first president of the British Association of Golf Course Architects.

Ross-on-Wye ENGLAND
Ross-on-Wye, Herefordshire. 18 holes; 6,575 yd (6,012 m)

The present course was created out of thick woodland on the edge of what is now the motorway to Birmingham. It lies outside the graceful town of Ross-on-Wye where golf was first played at the turn of the century on the old racecourse at Weirend. The architect, C. K. Cotton, expressed some initial doubts, but the course that was finally built showed that forest is not an insuperable obstacle. Ross-on-Wye was one of the first courses to be built in Britain after World War II, and for all Cotton's skill and patience the work would have been impossible without the help of the small course committee, headed by the Welsh international, Albert Evans, whose loan of labour and machinery kept the cost, about £42,000 including a well-equipped clubhouse, within bearable limits. Work started in the autumn of 1961 on clearing thousands of trees and filling in marshland. By August 1964, the first 9 holes were open and the new clubhouse was completed by the following June. Although the official opening of the second 9 by Gerald Micklem, then president of the English Golf Union, did not take place until May 1967, the character of the golf was always apparent.

There are challenging tree-lined holes demanding control and accuracy, yet not at the expense of discouraging the attacking stroke; and from the higher points, to underline the sense of escape, there are wonderful views of rural England. In what is remote country in the golfing sense, Ross-on-Wye is a rare jewel, far removed in quality from some of the club's earlier homes. Before moving in 1925 to Rudhall, whose 9 holes were laid out by J. H. Taylor, the Ross club was at Alton Court, described by one president of the club as qualifying for the prize for the worst course in Europe. Players had to cross a railway line twice, climb to a reservoir 150 ft above them and avoid the perils of a local rifle range.

Rotan, George V. AMERICAN
b. Waco, Tex., 1886. Texas Amateur 1912-15, 1919, runner-up 1920; Walker Cup 1923

One of the nation's most prominent amateurs from 1910 and through the 1920s, and a member of the 1923 Walker Cup Team. Rotan, a Yale graduate, set a competitive record at Pine Valley with a 70 in 1922. He failed to qualify in the 1930 US Amateur at Merion when his tee shot at the 16th hit a spectator and bounded into the

on voluntary help, and by 1918 a full 18 was ready. Foremost in improving the course was C. H. Redhead, a golf architect, whose proposals for new bunkering were adopted after much discussion.

Rotorua is not long by modern standards but it demands plenty of control and Peter Thomson described it as 'very humbling'.

On a base of pumice, it drains freely and its situation is magnificent. Not surprisingly Rotorua is popular with visitors: the club caters for some 10,000 to 12,000 a year.

Rough

That part of the course which is neither tee, green, fairway nor hazard. Colloquial words

quarry. Rotan was a member of the US Golf Association executive committee in 1927 and 1928.

Rotorua GC NEW ZEALAND
Rotorua, N. Island. 18 holes; 6,012 yd (5,497 m)

Before golf reached Rotorua in 1906, thermal activity and Maori culture had made the area known. Rotorua was at the time a straggling town with something under a thousand inhabitants. In the early days, the game was played on areas of doubtful quality and tenure. Pukeroa Hill, the home of the first course, is now the site of the King George v hospital. In 1911 a new course was laid out on the perimeter of an active thermal area in a reserve that borders Whaka Village and covers nearly 300 acres. From the fairways, steam can be seen rising from Pohutu geyser in great white heads behind the clubhouse and the 17th tee is flanked by two fumeroles gently puffing out subterranean heat.

The acquisition of the area, administered by the Tourist Department, was largely the work of Sir Joseph Ward. On the terms that the grounds should be cleared of all noxious weeds and prepared as a golf course, a third of the reserve was leased on a 21-year basis for the peppercorn rental of one shilling a year, and in May 1911, 9 holes were open for play.

Although no alcoholic liquor was permitted for a time, the club thrived, largely

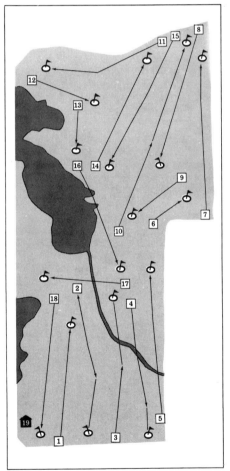

George V. Rotan

Rotorua GC, *top*, part of the course and, *above*, its course plan

Centre, and *above*, rough: Jim Simmons and Trevor Homer in trouble

for thicker areas of rough are cabbage, jungle, or tiger country.

Royal – For clubs other than the two below see under the next key-word.

Royal and Ancient GC SCOTLAND
St Andrews, Fife

The present name was given to a club which came into existence in 1754. In that year twenty-two gentlemen 'being admirers of the anticient and healthfull exercise of the Golf' formed themselves into the Society of St Andrews Golfers. They were made up of Fife noblemen and lairds, university professors and professional men. They adopted the code of rules laid down by the Honour-

others flowed, that club lost ground through having to change its site, and with St Andrews attracting by the quality of its turf and the pleasantness of its surroundings the elite of the game, clubs turned more and more to St Andrews for leadership and guidance. It had been one of the clubs invited by Prestwick to send a pair to compete in an Open championship, and one of the clubs which formed part of the committee in starting the British Open. After being approached by several leading clubs the Royal and Ancient club agreed in 1897 to become the governing authority on the rules of golf. That was the first authority invested in the club, and slowly its authority increased as other countries sought affiliation

approval. The R. and A. provides a selection committee for international teams, and co-operates with the USGA in the running of the international championships, such as the Eisenhower Trophy.

Other matters of an international scope dealt with by committees of the club are amateur status and the size of the ball. The need for a separate body to deal with the growing influence of commercialism and requests for reinstatement to amateur rank became gradually irresistible, and in 1964 a rules of amateur status committee was set up, with overseas connections similar to the rules of golf committee.

The other two levels on which the Royal and Ancient functions are national and club.

able Company of Edinburgh Golfers 11 years before. They met at the Golf House, the site of which is not known, and they frequently fed at Baillie Glass's. Later they met in the Union Parlour and it was not until 1854 that the present clubhouse was opened. Twenty years before that in 1834 the club had applied to the reigning monarch, King William IV, for permission to take the name of the Royal and Ancient Golf Club. This was granted and after some hesitation the king agreed to become the first captain of the newly named club. A full list of captains is given on p. 471.

Although the Honourable Company had preceded them as a club and had been responsible for a code of rules from which all

to the committee, until the number has now reached 52, not counting various bodies such as the Ladies' Golf Union, the European Golf Federation, the South American and Asian golf federations. The rules of golf committee reviews the rules from time to time and makes decisions of interpretation on the hundreds of queries put to it; the committee consists of 12 members with 10 co-opted members from abroad. As the only other governing authority for the rules is the United States Golf Association, the R. and A. works closely with that body when changes are proposed, and a joint meeting is held every four years for this purpose. There are subcommittees to deal with rules decisions and with implements submitted for

Royal and Ancient GC – a crowd around the 17th green of the Old Course

K. R. T. Mackenzie, who became secretary of the R. and A. in 1967

Before World War I a small group of clubs had been responsible for the running of the Open and Amateur championships, but in 1919 it was agreed that the Royal and Ancient should assume responsiblity for the two championships; for this purpose a championship committee was formed, and to its duties were subsequently added, in 1949,

RULES

FOR

THE GAME OF GOLF

AS IT IS PLAYED BY THE

Royal and Ancient

GOLF CLUB OF ST ANDREWS

Over their Links.

1842.

the Boys' Championship, in 1963 the Youths', and in 1970 the Seniors'. The committee to control these five events consists of 12 members. The work of these men has increased greatly in recent years, especially since they are also responsible for the running of such international events as the Walker Cup, the Eisenhower Trophy, the St Andrews Trophy and the Commonwealth Tournament when they are held in Britain. The selection committee for these teams consists of a chairman and one representative from each of the four home countries. They normally hold office for four years.

Finally the club is responsible to the 1,750 members, 700 of whom are overseas members from 45 different countries. This widely scattered membership allows for broad and effective representation on all the club committees with international and national functions. The club does not own the four courses at St Andrews, but through the medium of the joint links committee it exercised a powerful influence on their maintenance and was partly responsible with the

St Andrews town council for the finances of it. The 1974 reorganization of local government in the United Kingdom made necessary a new system of controlling the courses, hitherto owned by one local authority, and the formation of a new links trust was adopted in 1974.

For Golf at St Andrews see page 335.

Royal Burgess Golfing Society of Edinburgh SCOTLAND

Barnton, Edinburgh. 18 holes; 6,604 yd (6,039 m); par 72

The Royal Burgess was founded in 1735 and may thus claim to be the longest continuously established golfing society or club in the world (predating the Royal and Ancient, St Andrews, by 19 years and the Honourable Company of Edinburgh Golfers by nine years). Originally the Edinburgh Golfing Society, it became the Edinburgh Burgess in 1787 (although by no means confined to 'burgesses') and in 1929 the 'Royal' was added in recognition of the Duke of York (later King George VI) having played there several times. His brother, the Prince of Wales, accepted the captaincy of the club in 1936, the year in which he succeeded to the throne as King Edward VIII. The Burgess thus became the only club in Britain since 1834 with a reigning sovereign as its captain, and the customary ball which he presented to be attached to the captain's club is the only gold one among some hundred silver.

The original society shared Edinburgh's Bruntsfield Links (where golf is known to have been played before 1450), the round consisting of 5 or 6 holes. Over the years, by vigilance, persistence and occasional recourse to law, incursions were repelled of horsemen, troops, shinty players, the opening of quarries and new roads, but by 1874 congestion and encroachment of housing forced a move to Musselburgh with which club the Burgess amalgamated. But again the snowballing popularity of the game drove the Burgess to seek its own private course and in 1894 the Barnton estate, five miles west from Edinburgh's centre, was chosen, and the course was laid out by Tom Morris (later alterations were by James Braid). In 1814 and again in 1817 the society established a bizarre prerogative by granting Charters and Diplomas for the foundation of affiliated golfing societies in St Vincent and Barbados, in the West Indies. The fate of these clubs is unknown but St Vincent later expressed its gratitude by sending a gift of 54¼ gallons of rum to the society.

After the move to Barnton the world's senior society became in 1895 the first to

allow Sunday golf in Scotland. The Burgess has been host to several major professional events in postwar years.

Rub of the Green

Any chance deflection of the ball while in play.

Rubin, Mrs Claudine SEE CROS, CLAUDINE

Rudolph, Mason AMERICAN

b. Clarksville, Tenn., 1934. Walker Cup 1957; New Orleans Open 1964; Thunderbird Classic 1966; Green Island Open 1970; Ryder Cup 1971

Mason Rudolph, having turned professional in 1958, has made a steady rather

than spectacular income from the American tour. He was elected *Golf Digest's* 'Rookie of the Year' in 1959 and in the 1963 to 1965 seasons had a streak of 52 straight tournaments in which he won money.

He was long active in tour affairs and was a member of the USPGA tournament committee, 1965-7. Though his game fell into a slight decline in 1968 and 1969, particularly his putting, he had a good year in 1970 and won a place in the 1971 American team at St Louis, thus becoming one of the few who have played in both the Ryder and Walker Cup matches.

Rules of Golf

Golf is essentially a simple game, consisting (to quote Rule 1) 'in playing a ball from the teeing ground into the hole by successive strokes in accordance with the Rules', the fewer the strokes the better. At first sight, therefore, the need to have 40 other Rules, not to mention 35 Definitions, three Appendices and a section on Etiquette, is hard to understand: the game was at least three centuries old before any written rules ap-

Title page in one of the R. and A's scrapbooks

Mason Rudolph

peared, and between 1744, when the first 'Articles and Laws in Playing at Golf' were framed, and 1875, the number of written rules increased by only seven. In the past hundred years, however, there have been far-reaching changes in methods of play, in the implements used, in greenkeeping and, above all, in golfers' attitudes to the game itself. The length and apparent complexity of the present Rules reflect these changes.

Originally, each links had its own unwritten tradition of golf law and procedure. Matchplay (either singles or foursomes) was the only method used, and disputes, which were frequent, were settled by the parties themselves or by informal arbitration. The existence at this period of a traditional rule that the ball must be played as it lies or the hole conceded has been questioned, but it is clear that the 'rules' were simple and few.

In 1744 a Silver Club was offered for open competition over Leith Links, and the organizers (afterwards The Honourable

Company of Edinburgh Golfers), wishing to forestall controversy among the entrants, some of whom might be unfamiliar with local practice, drew up the first code of 13 rules. In 1754 the Leith code was adopted almost word for word for a similar competition by the society that later became the Royal and Ancient Golf Club of St Andrews. Both competitions were originally scored by holes, all playing all in notional matches, but this method was so complicated, even with a small field, that scoring by strokes was introduced at St Andrews in 1759. The sophistication of the modern Rules dates from these 15 years which saw the birth of open competitions and strokeplay.

Other golfing societies were formed, each of which framed its own rules of play. Although these naturally reflected differing traditions in different places, the lead of the Honourable Company in matters of golf law was fairly generally acknowledged, at least until the 1830s. Many of the basic principles

that underlie the present-day Rules were embodied in these early codes, but the act of codification clearly led to some traditional procedures being questioned, and there was no common or constant opinion about the most equitable way of dealing with certain situations. The penalty for a lost ball, for example, varied at different times and at different centres between stroke and distance, stroke only and, in matchplay, loss of hole. The right to play on an opponent's ball (i.e. to knock it further from the hole) and the right, in medal play, to have the opponent's (i.e. the fellow competitor's) ball lifted were also hotly disputed.

When the gutty superseded the feathery ball about 1848, the influence of the Royal and Ancient was already making itself felt, although individual clubs and societies continued to make their own rules. Golf's popularity and competitiveness during the latter half of the 19th century, however, produced a demand for a single code of rules which

Four cartoons illustrating some of the rules of golf by Charles Crombie

would be both comprehensive and universally applicable. In 1888, therefore, the R. and A. drew up a code which, for the first time, relegated to a separate section the rules peculiar to St Andrews. An even more comprehensive code was published in 1893 and, with the appointment of the first rules of golf committee in 1897, charged with responsibility for framing and interpreting the Rules, the R. and A.'s position as golf's legislative body was established.

Acceptance of a single legislative body was one thing: agreement with its rules and decisions was another. Golf had spread throughout the British Isles and had travelled overseas, notably to America where the United States Golf Association, formed in 1894, added its own rulings to the R. and A. code. Everywhere a new generation of golfers was springing up which had not been bred to the game's traditions, whose golf was played on terrain and in conditions quite unlike those of the old Scottish links, and which questioned many traditional attitudes: the preoccupation with matchplay, the acceptance, as part of the 'spirit of the game', of what it could only regard as inequities, and the reluctance to approve the use of more sophisticated equipment.

The 'traditionalists' were to lose many battles in the next 30 years: the ousting of the gutty by the rubber-cored ball, the recognition of four-ball matches and bogey competitions, the legalization of steel shafts, and a general tendency to reconcile the rules governing matchplay with those of strokeplay, in particular by allowing a match player whose ball was 'lost' or 'unplayable' to complete the hole under penalty instead of conceding. The occasions on which the ball could be 'handled' also increased.

Perhaps the fiercest battle raged over the stymie (the situation in matchplay in which the player on the green is forced to play over or round his opponent's ball to reach the hole). Always unpopular in the United States (although Bobby Jones was later to plead eloquently for its re-introduction), the rule was experimentally varied there in the 1930s after unnegotiable stymies had decided more than one important match. For the time being, however, the R. and A. stood firm on what many considered to be a vital ingredient of the matchplay ethos.

At the same time as it varied the stymie rule, the USGA reduced the penalty for 'out of bounds' to distance only, and after World War II there was a danger that the R. and A. and USGA might drift further apart. More than 20 years had passed since the Rules had last been comprehensively revised, and each body now published its own code, the

R. and A. experimenting with a system of reduced penalties. In 1951, however, at an international conference at which a joint committee of the R. and A. and the USGA was joined by representatives from the Commonwealth, a unified code was hammered out, to take effect in 1952. The old penalties were restored, but the R. and A. agreed to abolish the stymie and to approve the centre-shafted putter, which had been a bone of contention for half a century; agreement was not reached, however, on a standard size of ball. Further codes were published jointly in 1954 and 1956 when a procedure was established for the regular revision of the Rules at four-yearly intervals; this procedure now includes full consultation with golf unions and associations throughout the world. The uniformity achieved in 1952 was broken in 1964 on the issues of the flagstick rule and the penalty for an 'unplayable' ball; it was re-established and maintained in the 1968 and 1972 revisions.

How the Rules may evolve in the future is difficult to forecast; revisions are, to a large extent, based on the many queries answered by the rules of golf committees of the R. and A. and the USGA each year. Simplification and clarification of the existing code will, of course, continue, but a return to the Arcadian innocence of the 18th century would only be possible if a profound change were to take place in the climate of golfing opinion – if the game were again to be played according to the spirit rather than the letter of the law. The development of professional tournament golf over the past 20 years, with its rich prizes and fierce competition, has made such a revision most unlikely. As long as the Rules are expected to provide unequivocal and wholly equitable answers in every situation, they will continue to be long and complex, but if all golfers everywhere made up their minds to accept the 'rigour of the game', the legislators would be delighted to accommodate them.

Rumania

Before World War II, golf was reasonably popular in Rumania with courses at Bucharest, Sinaia and Ploesti but in the postwar years very little was heard about it. The first sign of revival came at the 1968 World Cup in Rome when Paul Tomita, professional at the Banessa Diplomatic Club in Bucharest, played in the event and was royally received by everyone. Not unnaturally, he said, 'I'm just so happy to be here. I have waited 31 years to see you all' but he only just made it as he encountered passport trouble and was a late arrival.

Even then, he was without his team mate,

Constantin Muntianu, who had broken his ankle in a last-minute accident, but the continued presence of a Rumanian team at subsequent events is proof that the game is growing again.

Run

The course of the ball after it has ceased to bounce and rolls along the ground. On soft ground there is little run; on hard ground the bounce and run of the ball have to be anticipated far more carefully.

Runfelt, Erik G. W. SWEDISH

b. 1893. Swedish Open Amateur 1911, 1913, 1917-18, 1920, 1922-3, 1927, 1929, 1938; Swedish Close Amateur 1912-13, 1918, 1934; Scandinavian Amateur 1913, 1919-21, 1924; Swedish Strokeplay 1947

Secretary of the Swedish Golf Union 1958-64, editor of its official magazine *Svensk Golf* 1946-66, and foremost Swedish expert on the rules of golf. Runfelt played 13 times for Sweden between 1914 and 1948, and was captain of the Swedish team for the Eisenhower Trophy in 1960 and 1964. Runfelt's career as a golfer is already a legend in his own country and throughout Scandinavia. As a writer on golf subjects, and in particular on the rules, he has educated several generations of Swedish golfers. He is still active within the Swedish Golf Union as a rules expert. He won the Swedish Seniors Championship 11 consecutive years from 1944 and again in 1957 and 1958.

Rungsted GC DENMARK

Rungsted. 18 holes; 6,040 yd (5,523 m)

A true parkland course situated 17 miles north of Copenhagen within a mile of the Sound which separates Denmark and Sweden. Although one of the best-known courses in Denmark and the scene of many Danish and Scandinavian championships, it

Rumania's Paul Tomita

is a relatively young club, dating from an opening in September 1937. The course was designed by Major C. A. Mackenzie. It is slightly undulating, protected from the prevailing westerly wind by picturesque beechwoods over almost its entire length.

Rungsted had the honour of housing the first Scandinavian International Amateur Championship in 1956, a tournament that is remembered for the fact that the then virtually unknown Michael Bonallack holed in one at the old 1st in one match; and a 19-year-old Swede, Stig Carlander, was 10 under par for the last 10 holes of his match with Henry Longhurst.

Run-up

An approach shot in which the ball travels close to or on the ground. It is usually played with a straight-faced club.

Runyan, Paul Scott AMERICAN

b. Hot Springs, Ark., 1908. Ryder Cup 1933, 1935; USPGA 1934, 1938; Argentine Open 1938; US Senior Professional 1961-2; World Senior Professional 1961-2

A trim stylist who maintained his game at a peak until well past the age of a senior. Runyan made his name as a player by winning the USPGA Championship in 1934 and 1938; in 1934 he beat Craig Wood at the 38th hole in one of the three longest finals, having saved himself at the 37th with a marvellous pitch; and in 1938 recorded the biggest margin in the history of the event, an 8 and 7 victory against Sam Snead. He won dozens of tournaments, including seven in 1934, when he was leading money winner. His victories for the World Seniors' title were against Sam King, the British champion.

In addition to his fame as a player, Runyan became known as one of the games outstanding teachers.

Ruspoli, Francesco, Duke of Morignano
ITALIAN

b. 1891; d. 1970.

Educated in England at Eton and Oxford, and of an illustrious family, Francesco Ruspoli was one of the pioneers of golf in Italy; in fact, he might safely be called the father of Italian golf. Although a keen sports-

man, he was only a moderate golfer, unlike his brothers who featured prominently in the early Italian chmpionships. He was president of the Italian Golf Federation from 1946 to 1968, president of the European GA in 1957 and also president of the Acquasanta and Olgiata Clubs in Rome.

Rut Iron

An obsolete club used for striking the ball out of narrow ruts on rough tracks. It had a narrow round head so that it could get into all but the smallest ruts.

Ruwa CC RHODESIA

Salisbury. 18 holes; 6,344 yd (5,801 m)

The club, 14 miles from the city of Salisbury on the Marandellas road, started as purely a tennis club but in 1944 the local farmers of Ruwa and Bromley decided to expand its activities.

Some 250 acres (100 ha) were bought three miles away and work began on new tennis courts, a cricket ground, gymkhana ground and a 9-hole golf course designed by Mr Waterfield in 1946. A second 9 was opened in 1948 and today Ruwa, with its fairways cut out among the natural trees, is one of the most attractive and demanding in Rhodesia. Large msasa trees line the course and provide a setting of great beauty. To begin with, the club faced great difficulty in obtaining adequate water supplies, and for the first few years the greens were watered by a bowser which was filled from boreholes. However, in 1968 a 60-million-gallon dam was constructed on the Ruwa with the result that water is now pumped $1\frac{1}{4}$ miles to a reservoir and from there boosted over fairways and greens. The clubhouse, consisting of two main wings with a large lounge in between, was built in the old Dutch style with white walls and thatched roof from materials provided by the local farmers.

Ryder Cup

The Ryder Cup series between the professionals of Great Britain and the United States would never have started under that name if a Manchester youth with ideas had been able to persuade his father to sell flower seeds in penny packets. He failed, left the family business, set up his own firm in St Albans, Hertfordshire, and flourished. In later life Samuel Ryder took up golf, engaged the great Abe Mitchell as his private coach, and presented a golf cup for the international series after Britain had won an unofficial contest at Wentworth by $13\frac{1}{2}$-$1\frac{1}{2}$. It was a different story a year later, in 1927, when the first British Ryder Cup team took the trophy to America and left it there,

Top, Rungsted GC

Centre, Paul S. Runyan

Above, rut iron of 1830

Walter Hagen's team winning 9½-2½.

Britain levelled the score in the second match at Moortown, Yorkshire, in 1929 when George Duncan led his men to victory and beat Hagen 10 and 8 in the singles. British resistance melted away in a heat wave at Columbus, Ohio, in 1931 but it was level pegging again two years later after an exciting match at Southport, with Syd Easterbrook beating Denny Shute on the home green in the decisive game. That contest was watched by the Duke of Windsor (then Prince of Wales) who presented the Cup to the non-playing captain, five times Open Champion J. H. Taylor. At that time there seemed to be no reason why the sequence of home wins should not continue – but 24 years were to pass before the trophy was again handed to a British captain.

There were great hopes of a British victory in 1937, particularly as Henry Cotton, who had been absent from the 1931, 1933 and 1935 matches because he was domiciled in Belgium, was once more available. But the Americans sent a very strong team to Southport and won 8-4, the only home winners in

the singles being Cotton and a 24-year-old Welshman named Dai Rees, the reigning British matchplay champion. No blooding of a tenderfoot was ever more auspicious for Rees, after partnering his captain, Charles Whitcombe, in a halved foursome, defeated Byron Nelson, then America's top golfer, by 3 and 1.

The 1939 match did not take place and after six years of war without serious competitive golf, British professionals who went to Portland, Ore., in 1947 to resume the series were in no condition to give of their best. That they went at all was remarkable, and made possible only by the generosity of Robert Hudson, a Portland business man who more or less financed the expedition and played host to the visitors. His benevolence was not emulated by his compatriots on the field of battle, for the Americans won all four foursomes and seven of the eight singles, Sam King escaping the whitewash brush by defeating Herman Keiser in the bottom match. The first postwar match on British soil, at Ganton, Yorkshire, in 1949, started well for the home team with a 3-1 foursomes lead. But the Americans counterattacked to win six of the eight singles, urged on to victory by the great Ben Hogan who, slowly recovering from an almost-fatal car accident, hobbled about as non-playing captain and was a constant inspiration to his side.

Two years later Hogan, miraculously

restored to playing fitness, won both his games as a contribution to another US victory by 9½-2½. In 1953 Britain came very close to winning, even after losing the foursomes 1-3, but home-green disappointments for the two youngest players, Peter Alliss and Bernard Hunt, turned the hoped-for victory into a 1-point win for the Americans. Nevertheless the portents suggested that success could not long be delayed, and this came in dramatic fashion at Lindrick, Yorkshire, in 1957, after a 1955 encounter in California which gave the British their best performance in America thus far. They lost by only 4 points and took six of their American conquerors to the 34th green or beyond.

And so to Lindrick where Dai Rees,

youthful hero of 20 years earlier, had the tremendous thrill of receiving the Ryder Cup from the hands of Sir Stuart Goodwin, whose £10,000 contribution to the Ryder Cup fund had set a new standard of promotion in this biennial event. Britain had lost the foursomes 3-1 but so dominated the singles that they won overall by 7½-4½. The home supporters were wild with delight but none wore a bigger smile than that displayed by Robert Hudson. 'A shot in the arm for British golf' he said, and so everyone thought, but the injection had no lasting effect.

Britain continued to lose away matches and in 1961 and 1965 suffered defeats at home by unpleasantly large margins. Changes in the format – matches over 18 holes instead of 36 were introduced in 1961 and fourball games on an extra day were added in 1963 – merely served to emphasize American superiority.

Nevertheless, British supporters anticipated the 1969 match at Birkdale with optimistic feelings based not only on Tony Jacklin's great victory in the Open Championship earlier that year, but also on the conviction that a new generation of golfers was about to make an impact. No doubt the whole team also felt stimulated, and the result was not victory, but a most honourable draw. There was nothing in it after the foursomes and fourball games, but in the first round of singles Jacklin scored a great victory over Jack Nicklaus, by 4 and 3, to give Britain a lead of two points. The Americans fought back during the intensely exciting final round and in the end everything depended on Huggett's game with Billy Casper and the return match between Nicklaus and Jacklin. Britain wanted 1½ points from these two games to win the Cup but actually it was only by means of two brave putts – Huggett on the home green and Jacklin at the 17th – that Britain halved both games and with them the contest.

After this it was not surprising that the next match at St Louis, Mo., in 1971 should produce the best-ever performance by a British team on American soil. The margin in favour of America was 5 points – 18½-13½ – and those 5 points were gained in the fourball games. So the British players returned home feeling they had done their duty and encouraged to hope that another 'Lindrick' would not be too long delayed, but at Muirfield in 1973, after leading at lunchtime on the second day, they fell to the increasing American pressure on the first occasion the match was held in Scotland.

Rye GC ENGLAND
Rye, Sussex. 18 holes

The Ryder Cup Trophy and, *right,* the cup being presented to Jackie Burke, captain of the American team in 1973 by Edward Heath (then Prime Minister of the United Kingdom)

the inland side of the road to Camber and used to extend beyond the row of coast-guard's cottages in which Leonard Crawley, who perhaps played Rye better than anyone, used to live.

A number of changes have taken place but the present course, shaped by the hand of Sir Guy Campbell, is post-1945 and most unlikely to be changed further. His last alteration – re-routing the 10th away from the busy road through a fiendish avenue of gorse – took place in the early 1960s and brought a feeling of near perfection to the course as a whole.

The par of something like 68 is alarmingly elusive even with 5 short holes which make as classic a batch as any, for if the player is not an accomplished strokemaker, he must be content to take 5s at the par 4s far more often than he likes. It is often said that the most important shots at Rye are the second shots at the short holes.

For years, Rye's clubhouse, almost de-capitated by a flying bomb during World War II, was a cluster of corrugated iron but with its conversion into a clubhouse full of character, the club took on a new identity. In 1970 Rye housed its first major cham-pionship when Dinah Oxley became English Ladies' Champion, beating Mrs Sally Barber in the final by 3 and 2.

It is not, however, in championship terms that the golfer thinks of Rye, although it has nearly all the suitable qualities, but as the place where so many societies like to hold their meetings, and where members always find enjoyment. In addition to the golf, the view of the harbour, the Brede Valley, the desolate marshlands and the old town stand-ing firm on its hill make an irresistible com-bination. In 1974 work was started on a third 9 holes.

There is nothing quite like Rye anywhere in the golfing world. It is a course of distinc-tive charm a mile or two from the ancient town that gives it its name. The course is joyously seaside by nature with the variety of stances changing as often as the wind and there is a deceptive fierceness about the golf which demands precision rather than power.

There is one major range of sandhills with the holes skilfully arranged on either side of it. The present version is the last of several course lay-outs. The first came into being in 1894 as the work of Harry Colt, at the time a solicitor in Hastings though later one of the greatest of all golf-course architects. Colt also had something to do with the founding of the club, with Parson Tindall, a school-

master in Hastings, and two others.

Rye's alliance with the Oxford and Cambridge Golfing Society in the early years of this century helped forge a link that has been a source of equal pride to both. It has been a frequent home for the university match and each January it opens its hospit-able doors to the President's Putter which, though more often than not threatened by the weather and accused of being an acute form of winter madness, is one of the great tournaments of the world. Certainly the Putter would not be the same played anywhere other than Rye. Nobody loved Rye or the Putter more than Bernard Darwin; his early accounts remind the present generation that the course began on

Rye GC, *top*, a view of the short 5th and, *above*, a view from the 7th tee – two of Rye's classic short holes

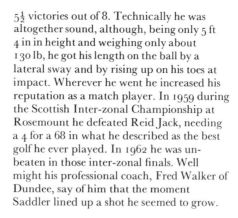

Saddler, Alexander BRITISH

b. Forfar, Angus, 1935. Tied 1st David Low Professional 1959; European Amateur Team Championship 1960, 1962, 1966; runner-up Scottish Amateur 1960; Berkshire Trophy 1962; Eisenhower Trophy 1962; Walker Cup 1963, 1965, 1967

Perhaps the most resolute player to come out of Scotland since the war, his courage and dourness amply making up for his lack of inches. Brought up in Forfar where his father ran a bakery, Sandy Saddler was the scourge of the county as a youth. At that time he had no thought of travel and his career might not have expanded, but he tied with John Panton in a Scottish professional tournament, playing four rounds over the

tough Carnoustie course in 283, and losing the 18-hole play-off by only 1 stroke. At that time players in all parts of the country were coming under detailed scrutiny for international teams, and in the Walker Cup trials he finished 2nd. But he had to wait another four years before joining the team. When he was picked he at once showed himself the bonniest of fighters, holding both Charles Coe and Deane Beman, two of America's strongest, to halves at his first appearance. He played in two more contests and of six singles he lost only one, a remarkable record by British standards.

Saddler was chosen for the Commonwealth Tournament in South Africa in 1959 and finished with the best British record of

Sandy Saddler

5½ victories out of 8. Technically he was altogether sound, although, being only 5 ft 4 in in height and weighing only about 130 lb, he got his length on the ball by a lateral sway and by rising up on his toes at impact. Wherever he went he increased his reputation as a match player. In 1959 during the Scottish Inter-zonal Championship at Rosemount he defeated Reid Jack, needing a 4 for a 68 in what he described as the best golf he ever played. In 1962 he was unbeaten in those inter-zonal finals. Well might his professional coach, Fred Walker of Dundee, say of him that the moment Saddler lined up a shot he seemed to grow.

St Andrews, Golf at

The origins of golf remain a matter for discussion and dispute but, even if St Andrews was not the first place where the game was played, it was undoubtedly one of the first and has always been accepted as the home of the game.

As a town situated on the eastern shores of Scotland in the Kingdom of Fife, it dates back into the mists of history. The first precise date concerning St Andrews is AD 747 but when the university, the oldest in Scotland, was founded in 1413, 289 years after the town was created a royal burgh, what is now the Old Course was primitively in existence. It is quite possible that some equally primitive form of golf was played on it in the next century and a half, but the

St Andrews, looking down on the 9th hole and green with the 10th running parallel to it

earliest documented evidence of golf at St Andrews takes the form of a licence dated 25 January 1552, granted by John Hamilton. It seems that this was merely confirmation of rights already established; but so closely are the links bound up with the life of the town that the charter included certain privileges allowing local residents to graze sheep as well as play golf. Indeed, until 1913 neither residents nor visitors were charged for a round on the Old Course. Even today the charge is absurdly low compared with many other great championship courses throughout the world. Restrictions were only introduced to provide some check on the immense traffic the course was being forced to bear, and it took a special Act of Parliament to legalize them.

However, apart from having to ballot for times in the summer and allowing members of the Royal and Ancient some concessions on the first tee during May, August and September, anyone in the world has the right to pay a green fee.

Golfers from overseas have often been heard to express surprise that the Old Course does not look like a course at all. Somehow they expect the most famous links in the world to have more appearance, more shape and more magnificence and, if they do not play their best, there are frequent accusations that it is too blind, too open or too fluky. Its merits are not always apparent at first sight and, in calm weather, it has become somewhat outdated as a test of the modern professional but, as Bobby Jones said so often, it improves on knowing. It was perhaps this factor that influenced Jones's comment that, if he had to pick one course on which he was obliged to play all his golf, it would be the Old Course. Certainly it has never been successfully copied, though there

reduced from 22 holes to 18. It was in this purely arbitrary way that a round of golf was adopted as 18 holes.

With the increase of those playing the course, St Andrews also discovered the advisability of having separate fairways and greens for the outward and homeward journeys, although the solution was still to

The Swilcan burn masks the distant innocence of the 1st hole, which has as wide a fairway as any in the world, and the danger of being foolish enough to stray down the right at holes named Dyke, Cartgate and Ginger Beer usually induces a tendency to over-compensate.

The famous 'loop' at the far end with the

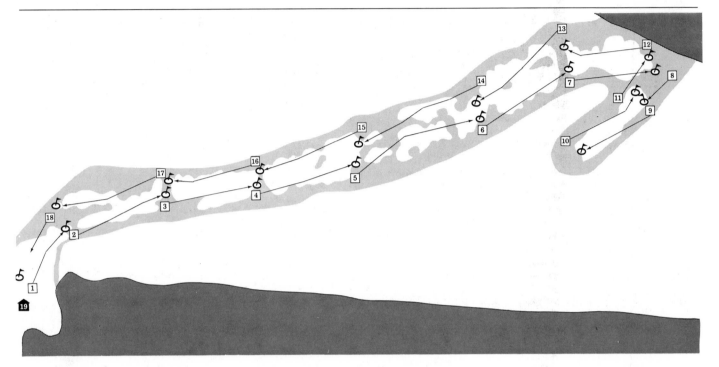

have been many attempts, but if there are those who do not like the golf at St Andrews and will deny any charm to the links, there must surely be none who will deny a charm to the place as a whole.

As a golf course, or a tract of land on which golf is played, it remains faithful to nature, occupying the narrowest of strips between the old railway and the dunes along St Andrews Bay. The strip, shaped like a shepherd's crook, was in fact so narrow that until about 1840 there was only room for single greens.

To begin with, there were 12 holes running out to the Eden. The golfers struck off from beside the home hole and played 11 holes out to the far end before turning and playing 11 holes home; the same holes as on the outward journey They finished off by holing out at the home hole from which they started and a round at St Andrews thus consisted of 22 holes.

In 1764, however, the Royal and Ancient suggested that the first 4 holes should become 2, thus converting the 4 holes on the way home into 2. The round was therefore

share. Two holes were cut on the huge double greens that are such a feature of St Andrews and the fairways were widened so that the course became, in effect, one long fairway. Only 4 holes have their own green and it is to the peculiar arrangement of St Andrews that we owe the familiar terms 'out' and 'home'.

Nowadays the course is a little more refined and with automatic watering of the greens and the help of modern equipment, very much easier. Years ago on ground that was hard and bare in summer, the line to each hole had to be strategically planned and adjusted with every little shift of the wind. The stranger had to follow the advice of one of the host of local caddies like some navigator in a dangerous channel.

St Andrews' main defence is its bunkers, most of them with their own names, some hidden and some only just big enough to accommodate an irate golfer and his niblick. It takes a long time to locate them all and even longer to remember the funereal ring of Hell, Coffin, Grave, and others such as the Principal's Nose, Strath, and Walkinshaw's.

course's only short holes, the 8th and 11th, offers the chance of redeeming a poor score, but the 11th is a terror and the long haul home is scattered with menace. If the Elysian Fields are safely reached between the out-of-bounds wall and the Beardies, the 14th still has Hell bunker up its sleeve, and if the 16th can be negotiated without an encounter with the track of the now sadly defunct railway, the Road Hole can always be relied upon to claim another victim.

The sliced drive over the old sheds, which used to end up in the stationmaster's garden, now reaches a more sophisticated resting place before the front door of the modern British Railways Hotel with the humiliating thought that the guests have been watching; and then there is one of the most feared shots in golf to be played on to a green angled between the Road and the Road bunker.

All this time the golfer may be wishing that he had chosen a round on the New Course, constructed in 1894 to the east of the Old; the Eden, laid out in 1912 on each side of the railway; or the Jubilee, which is the

The plan of the Old Course at St Andrews

least demanding of the four. All are maintained by the Links Management Committee of the town and the R. and A. and are in constant use in the summer. Yet, however much tantalized or frustrated a player has been by the Old Course, the march up the 18th to Tom Morris's green brings a special thrill that no other setting can arouse.

a long tradition of golf in St Andrews, it was not long before the fame of outstanding local golfers began to spread.

The first of the great professional players, Allan Robertson, was a St Andrean born on the 11 September 1815. His family had long since been established ballmakers but Allan, with an easy, graceful style, was the first

From the time that Tom Kidd won the first St Andrews Open in 1873, its champions have included J. H. Taylor, James Braid, Jock Hutchison and Bobby Jones. Jones remains the only amateur to have won at St Andrews, although in 1921 Roger Wethered tied with Hutchison. Despite suggestions that the Old Course is not the

It was on 12 May 1754 that, following the example of the Honourable Company of Edinburgh Golfers 10 years earlier, the Royal and Ancient GC, or as it was first known, the Society of St Andrews Golfers, was founded by a small and select number of devotees to the game. Members of the club were then largely local gentry, but with such

of the great players. He is given the distinction of being the first person to break 80 at St. Andrews. Other famous names are the Tom Morrises, Old and Young, Willie Fernie, Andrew Kirkaldy, Jamie Anderson, the Straths and the Auchterlonies.

Tales of these great men can be found elsewhere under separate headings, but the fame of St Andrews does not owe everything to its origins and its sons. Its history is as much wrapped up in the championships that have taken place there. They may have occupied only a small part of the time that the game has been played in the town but no course can claim to have held a greater number or a greater assortment of championships than St Andrews.

In the beginning, the Open Championship was run by the Prestwick Club and it was not until 1872, following Young Tom Morris's three consecutive victories which made the original Champion Belt his own property, that the present cup was subscribed by the Prestwick Club, the Royal and Ancient, and the Honourable Company of Edinburgh Golfers.

test it was, it continues to produce worthy winners.

Since World War II, Sam Snead, Peter Thomson, Bobby Locke, Kel Nagle, Tony Lema and Jack Nicklaus have all won and each championship deserves a chapter to itself. The Centenary Open in 1960 is particularly remembered for the first appearance of Arnold Palmer, who was 2nd to Nagle, and for the violent thunderstorm that caused the postponement of the last round on Friday afternoon.

Another equally violent storm stopped play 10 years later on the first afternoon with the defending champion, Tony Jacklin, in sight of breaking the course record after covering the first 9 holes in 29 strokes. He hit his second to the 14th into the whins, however, and the following morning could do no better than finish in 67.

After a dramatic finish in which Doug Sanders took three putts on the 18th green, Jack Nicklaus beat him in an equally dramatic play-off and spoke of his delight at winning at St Andrews. Not normally a man given to emotion, he said that a champion's

Above, The Royal and Ancient clubhouse at St Andrews from the 18th tee on the Old Course

Top, golfers at St Andrews in the 1850s

career was incomplete without a victory over the Old Course. Probably the most remarkable victory, however, was that of Tony Lema in 1964. In defiance of the view that St Andrews calls for a long apprenticeship he won without having seen the course before. His play was a revelation of adaptability in conditions entirely new to him. He conquered the high winds of the first two days and in the last two rounds scored 68 and 70 for a winning total of 279, five better than that of Jack Nicklaus.

Of the British Amateur Championships at St Andrews, none was more memorable than Bobby Jones's victory by 7 and 6 against Roger Wethered which formed part of the Grand Slam; the triumph of Joe Carr in 1958 against Alan Thirlwell; or the success in 1963 of Michael Lunt who was the first British player to win from a field which included most of a visiting American Walker Cup side.

Scottish Amateur, Scottish and British Ladies' championships have been held regularly at St Andrews as well as several other international meetings of great significance. In 1938 came the first British victory in the Walker Cup and then, after a gap of 33 years, Britain scored her only other victory in May 1971 with a tremendous rally on the last afternoon.

In 1954 a large Commonwealth meeting was held to celebrate the bi-centenary of the Royal and Ancient, and in 1958 the first Eisenhower Trophy tournament took place over the Old Course. Though the Australian side narrowly defeated the Americans, the American non-playing captain on that occasion was Bobby Jones who, at an unforgettable ceremony, was granted the Freedom of the City of St Andrews on the evening of Thursday 9 October.

As the list of six or eight persons who had been similarly honoured contained some of the great figures in literary and political circles, it was a unique honour. Before a packed hall with thousands waiting outside, the Provost welcomed the new Freeman in a touching address and a few minutes later Jones was faced with the task of replying. He spoke movingly for about ten minutes without reference to the notes he had prepared and left the hall in his electric golf cart as the entire company sang spontaneously, 'Will ye no come back again'. Jones perhaps summed up his sentiments best when he said near the end, 'I could take out of my life everything except my experiences at St Andrews and I'd still have a rich, full life.'

St Andrew's GC USA
Ardsley-on-Hudson, N.Y.

It is fitting that a club named after the most famous course in the world should be the oldest permanent golf club in the United States. Late in 1887 Robert Lockhart, of New York, returned from a trip to Scotland with several sets of golf clubs and some golf balls that his friend John Reid of Yonkers had asked him to purchase for him. Mr Reid and a few cronies played a little rudimentary golf the following year, and they enjoyed it so much that in November they decided to form a golf club and to call it St Andrew's. Their first course was three holes in John Reid's pasture. Their next consisted of 6 holes in Henry Tallmadge's larger pasture. In 1892 they moved to an apple orchard on Palisades Avenue, and it was here that they became known as the 'Apple Tree Gang'; this course again consisted of 6 holes. Two years later, the expanding club moved again, this time to Grey Oaks where they built a 9-hole course. Finally, in 1897, the club settled at Mount Hope in Ardsley-on-Hudson, where the present 18-hole course was established. It was very active in the early days of American golf, being one of the five charter members of the USGA.

The American St Andrew's, it might be pointed out, hardly resembles a Scottish course. Set in the hills of Westchester County a little way back from the Hudson River, it has the rolling terrain, the wooded passages, and the lush turf of the typical American inland layout. However, the club is very proud of its Scottish background and is well known in America for the salient role it has played in spreading the gospel of another old Scottish game – curling.

St Andrews Trophy
Trophy awarded for the match held every two years between the amateurs of Great Britain and Ireland and the Continent of Europe.

St Charles CC CANADA
Winnipeg, Man. South and North Nines 18 holes, 6,473 yd (5,919 m), par 72; West Nine 9 holes, 3,503 yd (3,203 m), par 36

It cannot be contended that these courses offer great difficulty to the expert golfer, but there is much to justify the claim that they are among the best conditioned and most pleasant courses to be found anywhere in Canada. Occupying some 325 acres (130 ha) of land on the banks of the lovely Assiniboine River, and lined with magnificent, spreading elms and other native trees, the courses are a never-ending delight to play. The club was organized in 1904 and opened its present clubhouse in 1916 after suffering the loss of two previous buildings by fire. The keen interest of the members in promoting the welfare of golf is shown by the national championships it has entertained. The club has been host to the Canadian Open of 1952, the Canadian Amateurs of 1936 and 1957, the Senior Championships of Canada of 1962 and 1970 and the Americas Golf Cup Team Matches of 1965. Two of these events stand out particularly. In 1952 John Palmer, of Badin, N. Car., set the all-time record for the Canadian Open, winning it with a score of 263, 25 strokes under par. It is, perhaps, almost as great a tribute to the fine greens of St Charles as it is to his phenomenal putting streak that Palmer was able to achieve his brilliant rounds of 66, 65, 66 and 66. In 1965 the Canadian team played inspired golf to earn Canada's only victory, and to inflict upon the United States their only loss, in the now-defunct Americas Cup Matches.

St-Cloud GC FRANCE
St-Cloud, Seine-et-Oise. Green Course 18 holes, 6,616 yd (6,050 m), par 72; Yellow Course 18 holes, 5,670 yd (5,185 m), par 68

Early golfing at America's oldest permanent golf club – St Andrew s GC

One of the most important courses in the Paris region, both from the quality of its golf and from its association with major national and international events. It is situated on high ground to the southwest of Paris, occupying the wooded park of what was formerly royal property, the Châtaignerie de Buzenval. In 1871 during the Franco-Prussian war the battle of Buzenval, marking the most westerly point of the German advance, was fought on these heights. The chestnut trees are still much in evidence. The idea of building a golf course in the park belonged to a group of Frenchmen in 1909, but it was 1913 before the course, which had been developed by British interests, was opened under its first president, an American lawyer, Henri Cachard. That course, now the Green, was designed by Harry Colt; after World War II a second course, the Yellow, was added in the direction of Vaucresson. It is much less undulating than the first course, except over the last few holes. The main championship course starts with four strong holes on the top plateau before plunging down at the short 6th to the lower part of the course. The 9th returns to the clubhouse. The second half contains some severe undulations, including two more short holes from plateau tees, before regaining the higher ground for a testing last two holes. One of the best holes is the 15th with its long subtle second shot to a green well guarded by trees and bunkers. The soil is clay with a consequent lush growth of fairway grass and greens containing plenty of nap.

The national championship was first held there in 1926 when it was won by Aubrey Boomer who with his brother, Percy, was professional at the course between the wars. Since 1946 the championship has returned to St-Cloud more often than to any other club. The international character of the club is reflected by the presence on the staff of St-Cloud of David Mills, a young British professional, and for some years Peter Butler divided his time between that club and his home course outside Birmingham. Several international matches have been held there – Continental teams playing against the American Ryder Cup team in 1953 and the American Curtis Cup team in 1968, and an amateur match between Great Britain and the Continent. It has become the home also of the French Girls' Championship.

St David's GC, Royal WALES

Harlech, Merioneth. 18 holes, 6,606 yd (6,040 m)

There is something inspiring about golf played against a background of mountains,

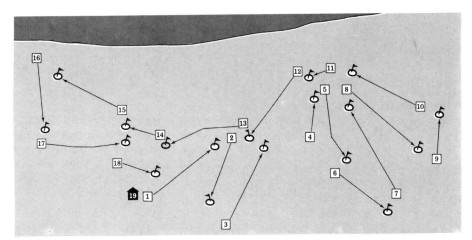

but Royal St David's, as well as mountains, has the old castle, built in the reign of King Edward I. The castle, standing at the top of a sheer precipice of rock looking down over the links and the sea, makes an incomparable setting.

The history of Harlech makes that of Royal St David's seem ridiculously modern, yet the club dates from 1894, a year after Harold Finch-Hatton had led a party of men out on to the 'Morfa', the sheep-grazing area below the castle, to try their luck at what they regarded as the Scottish game of golf. With W. H. More to guide them as Secretary, an office he held for 20 years, they obtained the rights of the Morfa in a matter of months and laid out 18 holes which were opened in the autumn of 1894. The occasion was marked by a special competition which John Ball won. In 1902 Charles Hutchings and Harold Hilton tied for the Harlech Town Bowl playing off plus 6.

The course underwent changes before staging its maiden championship in which Cecil Leitch won her fourth British Ladies' title in 1926.

Today, the course twists and turns naturally in all directions, so that the wind is never constantly in the player's face or on his back, and it is still a popular choice for championships and other events. Apart from innumerable Welsh championships, it has been a particular favourite for the British Ladies', Miss Leitch's victory being followed by Frances Stephens defeating Mrs Val Reddan in 1949, Barbara McIntire adding the British to her American title in 1960, and Elizabeth Chadwick successfully defending her title in a final against Mary Everard in 1967.

The club received the prefix 'Royal' about 15 years after its founding and in 1935 the Duke of Windsor, when Prince of Wales, became captain, travelling there specially to play himself in.

St Enodoc GC ENGLAND

Rock, Cornwall. 18 holes and 9 holes

St Enodoc is a holiday course of rare delight. It nestles above the tiny village of Rock opposite Padstow and is laid out on

The course plan of Royal St David's GC and a scene near the 13th hole

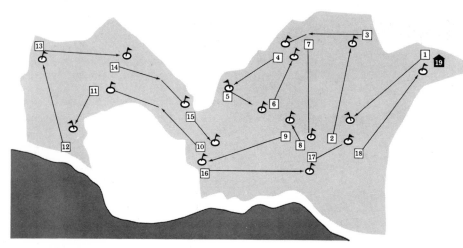

some of the most eminently natural golfing country in Britain with a view commanding the estuary of the River Camel. The ground is both varied and dramatic, with a section among the most glorious and tremendous sandhills; the Himalaya bunker at the 6th must surely be the highest in the world over which golf is played. The golf is fine, adventurous and fun; but it is demanding as well and it would be quite wrong to regard the course's reputation as confined to its own little corner of England. In 1937 the club housed the English Ladies' Championship won by Wanda Morgan; it is a popular and regular choice for women's and county events.

Yet a good part of its character lies in its remote beauty which has remained largely unchanged since the day in 1888 when a party of undergraduates first played on part of the present course. That was in the area around St Enodoc's ancient church and Daymer Bay with its golden sands. In 1889 a few holes were laid out in the sandhills at Rock and the present club was formed about 1891.

In 1907, James Braid laid out a full 18 holes, two years after Dr Theophilus Hoskin granted the club a lease of most of the land on which the course now stands. With the resiting of the clubhouse to coincide with the building of a motor road to the village, Braid paid a further visit to design the existing 17th and 18th holes. In 1950 the club became tenants to the Duchy of Cornwall, and shortly after King George VI and Queen Elizabeth, with Princess Margaret, took tea with the captain and committee.

St George's, Royal ENGLAND
Sandwich, Kent. 6,748 yd (6,170 m); par 70

One of a trio of great courses on the Kentish coast, sharing with Prince's a view over the waters of Pegwell Bay, a true links

course of tradition threading its way between and over formidable dunes. Throughout its long history it has been criticized for the number of blind shots it contains, most of them occurring in the first half, but for the average golfer its charm far outweighs any such considerations. Chief summer ingredients of this charm are the lark song and the bright sunshine, and the sense of solitude. But the golfer should not top his drives, for on this course more than on most, the fine raking carry off the tee is called for. The foundation of a low score must come in the outward half, which is some 400 yd (366 m) shorter than the remaining 9 and contains three of the four short holes. In contrast the finishing holes at Sandwich form one of the toughest challenges in the country. Starting with the 13th, the last 6 holes contain four challenging par 4s, and one of the remainder is a long par 5, along the boundary with the Prince's club, and called Suez Canal because of the water hazard running the width of the fairway. The 13th itself, turning away towards Prince's clubhouse, is a magnificent example of a links two-shotter, with a slightly offset drive and a singularly subtle second.

The St George's Club was founded in 1877 through the initiative of Dr Laidlaw Purves. The course quickly took shape, and in 1892 the first British Amateur Championship was held there. Eighty years later 10 more Amateur titles had been won over that course, and in the same period eight Open championships were held there. Great are the names of the champions at Sandwich, as the course was known for many years before Royal St George's became the official title: and there in 1894 J. H. Taylor won the first Open ever to be held in England; Vardon in 1899 and again in 1911; Jack White in 1904; Hagen for the first time in 1922, making good his vow after taking more than 80 in the final round at Deal two years before that

he would be back and win the championship, and again in 1928. Then came Henry Cotton's great 'turning of the tide' victory in 1934 and four years later the windswept one of Reg Whitcombe when tents were flattened and their contents tossed through the air by the gale. In Taylor's year the hopes of Sandy Herd were washed away by a thunderstorm which the winner missed, and Vardon in finishing seventh won £4. Taylor's winning score of 326 was 43 strokes more than Henry Cotton's 40 years later, bearing testimony to the changes made in the game by the rubber-cored ball and the steel shaft. The description of the final of the 1904 Amateur, in which Walter Travis became at Sandwich the first overseas winner of a British championship, contained reference to two splendid second shots with a spoon to the 2nd and 12th greens, a further indication of the shrinking of the course.

One last postwar Open was played there in 1949 before the course fell out of favour as the event moved into the big-money age, and the remoteness and solitude of the place which constitutes much of its appeal became a disadvantage. Its length also has been called in question as an Open championship test. If Sandwich does return to the championship roster it will be warmly received, for the South of England relied much on it in the past. In matters amateur the club has never been idle for long, and great men have won the championship there, John Ball, F. G. Tait, Harold Hilton, Walter Travis, and Cyril Tolley among them. The club was host to the first Walker Cup match to be held in England, in 1930 when the great Bobby Jones was at the height of his powers, and the first European Team Championship to be held in Britain in 1965 when champagne and fireworks galore heralded Ireland's first victory in the event. As though all this were not enough, the club has its own historic competition, the Champion Grand Challenge Cup, or St George's Cup, which boasts as proud a list of winners as any 36-hole tournament.

Sandwich has always been well supported by the chroniclers. Back in 1910 Horace Hutchinson wrote of it: 'On the whole Sandwich is a very good course. A good many say it is the best in the world, and some really think so.' 'Confound their politics!' wrote Bernard Darwin; 'Why do they want to alter this adorable place? I know that they are perfectly right and I have even agreed with them that this is a blind spot and that an indefensibly bad hole, but what does it matter? This is perfect bliss.' The last word, and the most recent, may be left to Sir Peter Allen in his *Famous Fairways*:

The course plan of St Enodoc GC

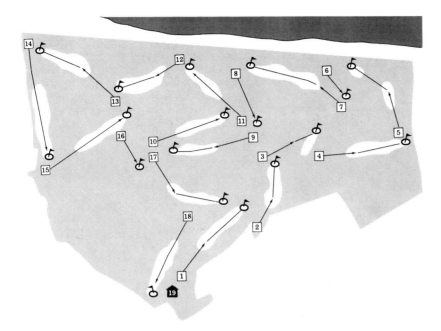

The course plan of Royal St George's

'There is a pleasant, conservative air about the place; the course has hardly been altered in the last 40 years, nor should it have been, and the club-house, save for the elimination of sand-boxes and earth closets, is equally unchanged. A relaxed peaceful leather-furnished smoking room persists and you can still get a tankard of ale from the wood.'

St Knuds GC DENMARK

Nyborg. 18 holes; 6,555 yd (5,994 m)

Sankt Knuds Golf Klub bears the name of a Danish saint who was the nephew and namesake of Cnut, King of England and Denmark. The club was founded in 1950 and opened in May 1954 on completion of the course which is situated on a peninsula just outside the old town of Nyborg. Designed by the British architect, C. K. Cotton, St Knuds is varied and picturesque with some of the holes cut out of the woods, some next to the shallow waters of Nyborg Fjord and some in more open land. Although the course has been in existence only a short time, it has quickly established a reputation and in August 1971 housed the Scandinavian International Amateur Championship.

St Louis CC USA

St Louis, Mo. 18 holes; 6,628 yd (6,061 m); par 71

Few Open championships have ended as dramatically as the 1947 tournament, played at the St Louis CC, and it was probably watched by more people than had ever seen an Open before. Sam Snead came to the home hole in the fourth round needing a putt for a birdie 3 to tie Lew Worsham, and he holed it from 18 ft. Next day he came to the 18th needing a putt of 30 inches to tie Worsham again, but this time he missed, and with that miss went his best chance ever of winning the Open. This was the first US Open, and quite possibly the first American golf tournament of any description, to be televised. It was done locally and the St Louis station showed only the 18th green. That seems quite primitive from this distance in time, but it was a major breakthrough in those early days of American sports telecasting.

The St Louis CC was organized in 1892, and since 1914 it has occupied its present site about 10 miles west of St Louis in the village of Ladue. It is a family-type club offering tennis, paddle tennis, and swimming in addition to golf.

The golf course was designed by Charles Blair Macdonald, and it has been the site of the United States Amateur championships of 1921 and 1960, the 1947 Open, and the Women's Amateur of 1925. At 6,628 yd from the back tees, the course is not particularly long, and so the big hitter does not have much of an advantage. There are a few exceptions. Two par-5 holes can be reached in two, the 537-yd (491-m) 9th by a very strong player, and the 500-yd (457-m) 15th by the moderately long hitter. The course is unusual in that it has five par-3 holes, two of them together.

St Pierre GCC WALES

Chepstow, Monmouthshire. 18 holes

For some years before 1960 golfers felt the need of a first-class course in the area around Ross-on-Wye and Chepstow. Golf had always been sparse in the hills of the Welsh Marches because there was little land that was not used for agriculture but within a year or two of each other C. K. Cotton had designed two courses which filled this gap admirably.

The one at Ross was a new home for an existing club but St Pierre was something entirely new for Britain, although some of its membership was from Chepstow's old 9-hole course down by the racecourse.

A golfing visionary, Bill Graham, who had spent the war as mess caterer to the Coldstream Guards, acquired the land for a course within the walls of the old deer park on the road between Chepstow and Newport. The grass was almost ready made for fairways and the profusion of stately trees was the answer to an architect's prayer. The site had another asset: in the middle of the park stood an ancient mansion. This was originally the seat of the St Pierre family who acquired the manor in Norman times. At the time of the Battle of Agincourt in 1415 the crown jewels were stored in the small tower which still commands the entrance to the inner courtyard. For 500 years a family named Lewis resided there. More recently it passed through several hands but none was destructive and Graham needed to do little to convert it for his purposes.

Within a year of work starting the house had become a club and within 10 years it had become a thriving golf and country club, offering accommodation, squash, billiards, tennis, swimming, badminton and bridge.

Golf remained Graham's trump card for 500 of the 1,400 members which the club had attracted within three years of opening were golfers. He was helped, too, by the opening of the Severn road bridge which brought Bristol, London and Birmingham within striking distance.

In 1968, the first 9 were altered by C. K. Cotton to include the escarpment – originally part of the St Pierre Estate – which looks down on the remainder of the course, although their construction on extremely rocky ground presented many problems.

At the time of its construction, which was remarkably straightforward, St Pierre was among the first new courses to be built in Britain in postwar years and quickly gained a reputation. The golf was thought of sufficient quality in 1971 to house a first-class field of professionals for the Dunlop Masters. It was held there again in 1973 and 1974 by which time work was well advanced on a second 18 holes.

Saint-Sauveur, Vicomtesse de see
SEGARD, LALLY

Salisbury GC, Royal RHODESIA
Salisbury. 18 holes; 7,115 yd (6,506 m)

A delightful parkland course with an abundance of trees, Royal Salisbury lies two miles from the centre of the city, its smooth fairways far removed from the weeds and tough veldt grass of 50 years ago. The club acts regularly as host to professional tournaments and has ample room. A comprehensive watering system is maintained by numerous boreholes. An average of more than 110 rounds a day played over it throughout the year makes it one of the busiest courses in the world.

In 1899, only nine years after colonial pioneers had occupied Mashonaland, eight enthusiasts met to form the Salisbury club. One of them, Ernest Montagu, was elected captain, honorary secretary and treasurer, and it was Sir Ernest, as he later became, who nursed the club through its infancy, holding the office of president from 1927 to 1949. In those early days no attempt was made to compete against the heavy rains, and the club simply closed from December to April. In 1901 a move had to be made. After an alternative site beyond the Makabusi River had been turned down because of warnings of the danger of malaria and blackwater fever, the club found its present site. In 1922 L. B. Waters, who has been called the father of golf in South Africa, became professional there, and was responsible for developing and improving the course before his retirement in 1939. The Prince of Wales played there while on a visit to the country in 1925 and four years later the title 'Royal' was conferred on the club. A facelift was given in 1968 by the British firm of Hawtree and Son to a course which has entertained such great names as Bobby Locke, Gary Player, Sam Snead, Arnold Palmer, and Billy Casper.

Sander, Mrs Anne (née Anne Quast; formerly Mrs J. D. Decker, Mrs D. Welts)
AMERICAN
b. Everett, Wash., 1937. Western Women's Amateur 1956, 1961; Curtis Cup 1958, 1960, 1962, 1966, 1968, 1974; US Women's Amateur 1958, 1961, 1963, runner-up 1965, 1968, 1974; semi-finalist British Ladies' 1960, 1974; World Women's Amateur Team Championship 1966, 1968

A highly intelligent, highly strung golfer who, like Polly Riley, has a long connection with the US Amateur. In 13 appearances in that event she finished in the last 8 or better 11 times, and her three victories in it have been surpassed only by the five-time winner, Mrs Carner (JoAnne Gunderson). She burst upon the scene in 1958 when as a senior at Stanford University she won the final of the US Women's Amateur by playing the last 7 holes in 4 under par to defeat Barbara Romack by 3 and 2. But she had been noted before that, for she had reached the quarter-finals in 1955 as a girl of 17, and had in the year she won the title finished leading amateur in the US Women's Open. On her way to the final she had beaten JoAnne Gunderson after being 3 down at the turn. Her greatest triumph was in winning the national amateur title in 1961; her victim in the final was Phyllis Preuss whom she defeated by 14 and 13, one hole more than the previous record set by Glenna Collett (Mrs Vare) in 1928. She played brilliantly throughout the championship, being 9 under par for the whole week and in that time losing only six holes.

Sanders, George Douglas AMERICAN
b. Cedartown, Ga., 1933. Canadian Open 1956; tied 2nd USPGA 1959; tied 2nd US Open 1961; Ryder Cup 1967; runner-up British Open 1970, tied 2nd 1966

A typically successful product of the American tour, on which he was victorious in 18 of the larger tournaments, without ever having won a major championship, Doug Sanders is remembered primarily for

Doug Sanders missing the putt on the 18th green at St Andrews which lost him the 1970 British Open

his love of gaily coloured clothes, for his good-natured approach to the game, and for a backswing which must be the shortest among any of the first-class professionals. He has a follow-through to match, and in between he makes the stroke from an exaggeratedly wide, stiff-legged stance and after endless waggles. He attributes his short swing with the clubhead stopping only just past the vertical on the backswing to the narrow fairways at Cedartown where he learned his golf and to a personal shortage of golf balls at that time.

Sanders turned professional after winning the 1956 Canadian Open as an amateur and quickly became one of the most consistent money winners on the tour. In the 1961 US Open at Oakland Hills, Sanders was leading the field with 9 holes to play but Gene Littler slipped in ahead of him by 1 stroke with a string of birdies. In 1959 he was second to Bob Rosburg in the PGA and finished equal 3rd and 3rd in 1960 and 1961. In the British Open he has twice been thwarted by Jack Nicklaus – the second time, in 1970, only after a play-off. Having pre-qualified for that event at Panmure, Sanders came to the 72nd hole needing a 4 to win, but he pitched his second too strong, putted short, and missed one of the most expensive and painful putts in history. His total of 283 equalled that of Jack Nicklaus who beat him by one shot in the play-off (72 to 73) after a most stirring recovery over the last few holes by Sanders. It was a cruel outcome but Sanders accepted it with dignity and commanded as much respect in defeat as if he had won.

The peak years in his career seem to have been 1966 and 1967, after which he went through a comparatively lean time. Unlike some professionals who make spectacular showings but never in the major events, Sanders thrives on difficult courses and on the big occasion. In his earlier days he may have had a reputation of being happy-go-lucky, but he has also shown a high regard for tradition.

Sand Iron
A lofted, broad-soled club used to extricate the ball from sand. Also used for pitching from heavy places or when the player wants to get the ball up quickly. The development of the sand iron has revolutionized bunker play.

Sandwich see ST GEORGE'S GC, ROYAL;
PRINCE'S GC

San Francisco GC USA
San Francisco, Cal. 18 holes; 6,307 yd (5,767 m); par 71

At the time of its opening in 1895, the club was the first in the San Francisco area and only the seventh west of the Allegheny Mountains. It is surprising that golf was played on the West Coast so early, considering that the first American club, St Andrew's (in Yonkers, N.Y.) was established in 1888.

The first known set of clubs to arrive on the Coast passed customs as 'miscellaneous agricultural instruments' in Tacoma, Wash., in 1893, and the game was on its way. Two years later a group of devotees organized an unincorporated association and laid out a 9-hole course on the Presidio Reservation near the Golden Gate. They played this rudimentary course until 1904 when the club

became incorporated, purchased enough land to build a clubhouse, and leased enough from the Spring Valley Water Company to build an 18-hole course. The site was somewhat removed from the city, and so the United Railways converted one of their funeral trolleys into a spacious club bar, and the members came out in style. Vardon and Ray played this old course in a match against Vincent Whitney, Robin Hayne, and Jack Neville, who later collaborated in designing Pebble Beach, and Walter Hagen won the Panama Pacific International Open there in 1915. The water company subsequently sold the land, but the club bought more further south. In 1918 a new course, designed by A. W. Tillinghast, was completed.

duel had ended differently, California and its wealth of gold and silver would have gone to the Confederacy and the outcome might have been different. The 1974 Curtis Cup was held at the club.

São Paulo GC BRAZIL

Santo Amaro, São Paulo. 18 holes; 6,475 yd (5,921 m)

The club, the oldest in Brazil, was founded at the turn of the century by English and Scottish engineers working for the São Paulo Railway Company.

Its first position was near the railway company's main station but later the course was moved to a part of the town which today bears the name 'Morro dos Inglêses' (Hill of the Englishmen). In 1915 the Club bought the land in Santo Amaro on which the present course is sited.

The course has undergone modifications, notably the redesigning and introduction of grass greens in 1935. It has housed the Brazilian Open more times than any other course and has seen such players as Sam Snead, Roberto de Vicenzo, Billy Casper, Kel Nagle and Peter Alliss.

Brazil's own Mário Gonzalez was brought up and acquired his fame at the São Paulo club where his father, José Maria Gonzalez, was head professional from 1924 until his death in 1971.

Sarazen, Eugene AMERICAN

b. Harrison, N.Y., 1902. US Open 1922,

This is the course in use today. It is comfortable for members with only three par-4 holes over 400 yd (366 m) and two of its three par 5s barely over 500 yd (457 m). The land itself is quite historic. Two granite obelisks stand 10 ft apart near the 7th tee to mark the spot where a duel was fought during the Civil War era. It is said that if the

1932, runner-up 1934, 1940, 3rd 1927, tied 3rd 1926, 1929; USPGA 1922-3, 1933; British Open 1932, runner-up 1928, tied 3rd 1931, 1933; US Masters 1935, 3rd 1936

Gene Sarazen competed in his first US Open in 1920 at Toledo and played in the British Open at Troon in 1973 where 50

Top, Sand iron: the Walter Hagen hollow-ground sand wedge

Above, a buried ball that requires the use of a sand iron

Top, a diagram to illustrate the use of the sand iron

Above, part of the course at San Francisco GC

years before he had failed to qualify for the same event while reigning American champion. His career thus spans more than half a century from Vardon to Jacklin and is the longest in the history of the game. It is also one of the most distinguished. He was the first of the quartet (Hogan, Nicklaus and Player are the other three) to win the four

major championships of the world. Only three others besides him have won the American and British Opens in the same year, 1932. His name – he was christened Eugene Saraceni but changed it because he thought it sounded too much like a violinist – is one of the legendary ones of golf, going back to that noble era of Hagen and Jones when the United States was wresting from Britain world dominance in the game. A cheerful, olive-complexioned little man full of muscle, his personality is lively and positive. A realist, he is not one to linger in the past, and this has been an important factor in the unique position he has achieved in the game. Bernard Darwin said that it was impossible to think of him without his smile because it was the outward and visible sign of a charming and at the same time very strong and resolute personality. In British eyes Sarazen is among the country's most loyal visitors, having begun with Hagen the trend of travelling in pursuit of the oldest of all major championships. Sarazen is credited with having put the idea of competing in the British Open into the mind of Ben Hogan,

whose victory in 1953 bridged the gap between Snead's victory in 1946 and the advent of Palmer. His interest in the British Open was crowned when in the second round of the 1973 championship, the last one in which he took part, he holed in one at Troon's 8th hole (the Postage Stamp), a punched 5 iron flying straight on the flag and

trickling into the hole. The shot, made in the presence of two other Open champions, Fred Daly and Max Faulkner, was caught by the television camera and will go down in history.

Sarazen's father was a carpenter who had studied to be a priest back in Italy. He was steadfastly against his son's career in golf, and it is possible that Gene might never have played at all if he had not contracted pleurisy while apprenticed to his father in Connecticut. The doctors ordered him to find less strenuous work and, while recuperating, he started to turn himself into a golfer at a nearby public course. In a matter of months he had landed an assistant's post, and it was not long before he announced himself to the world by winning the 1922 US Open at Skokie, thanks to a last round of 68. He was unknown at the time and had entered chiefly to gain experience. During the championship he slept, so the story goes, in a dormitory of fellow professionals and was usually the last one into bed. Sarazen soon gave evidence of a rare talent by winning the USPGA Championship the

same year, and, almost more important to him, beating Hagen in a set match over 72 holes. He beat Hagen again in the 1923 final of the USPGA, but in the British Open the same year, the last which a British player won for 11 years, he failed to qualify, having had the worst of the weather. This was the beginning of a setback to his game, as a result of which for perhaps the only time in his life, he dabbled in technique. Until then he had played largely by the light of nature, and will be remembered for his simple, sturdy, straightforward swing, utterly without frills. Bobby Jones said of him: 'Sarazen has ever been the impatient player who went for everything in the hope of feeling the timely touch of inspiration. When the wand touches him, he is likely to win in a great finish, as he did at Fresh Meadow and Skokie, or in a parade, as he did at Prince's, but if it touch him not throughout the four rounds, the boldness of his play leaves no middle ground. When he is in the right mood, he is probably the greatest scorer in the game, possibly, that the game has ever seen.'

Sarazen had to contend with Jones as well as Hagen during that period, but he emerged a sounder and better player, finishing 2nd to Hagen in the British Open at Sandwich in 1928. The championship of 1932 turned out to be his only victory in Britain. On a fast-running course he showed great confidence and scored a convincing victory, winning by 5 strokes from another American, Macdonald Smith. Suitably inspired he returned home to win the US Open at Fresh Meadow on Long Island with a last round of 66. For sheer consistency and brilliance nothing could match his playing of the last 28 holes in 100 strokes, a feat which Bobby Jones described as 'the finest competitive exhibition on record'. The following year he won the PGA Championship again, 10 years after his last one. In the British Open he finished only 1 stroke behind Densmore Shute and Craig Wood, in spite of taking 6 at the short 11th in the second round and on the last round seeing his second to the 14th fail to carry Hell bunker.

There remained one more major victory – the second US Masters tournament of 1935, which was in a way the most dramatic of them all. No single shot has won more fame than his 4-wood shot which he holed for a double eagle at the 15th in the last round of that event. It enabled him to catch Craig Wood, seemingly assured of victory in the clubhouse, and to beat him in the play-off. Many years later Sarazen confessed that the shot had earned him more money than any of his Open titles. It certainly enabled him

Gene Sarazen in the 1958 British Open Championship at Royal Lytham and St Annes

Opposite, An early map of the course at St Andrews

Overleaf, South Africa, the Metropolitan GC, Cape Town

Plan
of the
GOLFING COURSE
The Links of
S.t Andrews

to become the first person to win all four major titles. After World War II his chances of victory grew less as he approached and passed 50, but he continued to play in championships and remains a regular at the Masters. His interest and fitness also persuaded him to become an adviser in designing new courses and for several years he was associated with the Shell company in their film series 'Wonderful World of Golf'. His book, written in conjunction with Herbert Warren Wind, *Thirty Years of Championship Golf* was a best-seller. He was made an honorary member of the Royal and Ancient.

Sargent, George AMERICAN
b. Dorking, Surrey, 1882; d. 1962. US Open 1909, tied 3rd 1914; Canadian Open 1912, runner-up 1908

Sargent moved from England, where at 17 he had been assistant to Harry Vardon, to Canada before reaching the United States where he was successively professional at Scioto, Interlachen, Chevy Chase and East Lake, remaining at the last club until his retirement in 1947. He was a pioneer in the use of motion pictures to demonstrate the golf swing. Sargent had five sons and five daughters; three of the sons became golf professionals, the best known being Harold who succeeded his father at East Lake and became president of the USPGA, as his father had been in 1921-6. The 1909 US Open was the first in which he played; he overtook Tom McNamara with a final 71, winning by 4 strokes in 290, a tournament record. In 1916 he became a charter member of the PGA.

Saudi Arabia SEE DESERT COURSES

Saunders, Vivien Inez BRITISH
b. Sutton, Surrey, 1946. Runner-up British Ladies' 1966; Commonwealth Tournament 1967; Curtis Cup 1968

After a promising beginning in girl's golf, Vivien Saunders reached the final of the 1966 British Ladies' Championship where she lost to Elizabeth Chadwick at Ganton. She was one of the leading players in Britain for a short while until she turned professional in 1969.

Saunton GC ENGLAND
Saunton, Devon. 18 holes; 6,728 yd (6,152 m)

The course, which lies across the estuary from Westward Ho!, was formed in 1897. Its headquarters were in the local post office and its 9 holes spread over the flat open fields east of the present course. The first permanent clubhouse – now the tennis

club – was built in 1906 when the course was extended to 18 holes by making use of land nearer the sea. The course was redesigned after World War I by Herbert Fowler and the present clubhouse was opened in 1929. In 1935 Fowler designed a second course but this had hardly become established before the whole area was taken over as a battle

school during World War II. Much clearance had to be undertaken before reconstruction could be attempted, and the New Course was never replaced; but with the help of Ken Cotton the 'Old', with new holes for the first and last two, was reopened in 1950 – one of England's finest links and a paradise for botanists and birdwatchers. It is ideal golfing country, made up of sandhills and scrub, which would have played a larger part in championships if it had been more accessible. The start is severe with three of the first four holes being over 440 yd (400 m). The 8th sets a blind drive over undulating dunes, and the finish is suitably testing with the 16th and 17th among the dunes providing two of the course's best.

Enid Wilson won the second of her three consecutive victories at Saunton in the British Ladies' Championship in 1932, and Frank Pennink the first of his two English championships. The English county finals have been taken to Saunton on three occasions, and in 1967 Ronnie Shade won the Brabazon Trophy there. In April 1966, the Schweppes PGA Championship was won by Guy Wolstenholme.

Throughout its history the club has been closely associated with the Christie family, of Glyndebourne Opera House fame. They are the landlords, having leased the course to the members in 1960 after operating it themselves through a committee for the first 63 years. Work on a second 18 holes was completed in 1972.

Sayers, Bernard BRITISH
b. Leith, Midlothian, 1857; d. North Berwick, East Lothian, 1924

One of the well-known old Scottish professionals who just missed winning the Open championship although he was very successful in the tournaments and big matches of his day. Ben Sayers was joint 2nd in the Open of 1888, 3rd in 1889 and joint 5th in 1894. He won 24 tournaments; beat Andrew Kirkaldy in a £100 match over North Berwick and St Andrews by 2 holes; partnered D. Grant to victory over Andrew and Hugh Kirkaldy in 1891 by 12 and 11; and beat Willie Campbell over North Berwick and Prestwick for a £100 stake, winning by 6 and 5.

Like Andrew Kirkaldy, Sayers was essentially a 'character', though of a quieter and subtler nature. He was also excitable and enthusiastic and it was these characteristics combined with his alertness which made him such a good salesman. His personality should not obscure his skill as a player, for never did so small a man have such control of so big a club.

His name will be forever linked with North Berwick where he ran a small shop on the West Course opposite Point Garry before becoming club professional. By then he had a name as a clubmaker and invented an approaching club called the 'Benny' which came out just after the introduction of the Haskell ball. It was a great success and he followed by inventing another club, the 'Jigger', and still later a driver with a very big head called the 'Dreadnought'.

Ben Sayers had a son, Young Ben, who was professional for some years at Wimbledon Park but with the success of their new clubs, the Sayers family decided to form a clubmaking firm which is still flourishing. Their factory remains in North Berwick.

Scarboro GCC CANADA
Toronto, Ont. 18 holes; 6,772 yd (6,192 m); par 71

Possibly one of the best tournament sites in Canada. It is endowed with natural hazards in such abundance that artificial ones are almost superfluous. It has steep hills, towering trees and the winding Highland Creek which comes into play on no fewer than 15 shots throughout the 18 holes. The grass is Scarboro bent, a strain developed by the club and widely used throughout Canada and the northern United States. Tournaments played at Scarboro are almost always exciting because accurate placement of shots permits of good scoring. The penalties are severe for shots off line, and long hitting gives no great advantage. Started as a 9-hole course in 1912, it

Opposite, St Andrews, the Walker Cup of 1971 *above*; Spain, Real Club de Golf 'El Prat', Barcelona *below*

George Sargent

was lengthened to 18 holes two years later. Its present form is the product of two noted golf architects, A. W. Tillinghast of New York who carried out extensive remodelling from 1924 to 1926, and Stanley Thompson of Canada who later introduced some modifications.

An unusual feature of the course is an extra par-3 19th hole which members usually play after completing the regulation 18, and on which many wagers are settled. Sam Snead won the Canadian Open Championship at Scarboro in 1940 after a play-off with Harold McSpaden. In 1947 Bobby Locke had a remarkable score of 268 to win the same championship. Other champions which the course has produced are Dave Douglas in 1953 with a score of 273 and Doug Ford in 1963 with 280. One of the club's most brilliant players was Donald D. Carrick who won the Canadian Amateur Championship there in both 1925 and 1927. He is a co-holder of the course record of 63. Another well-known member is Phil Farley, six times winner of the Ontario Amateur Championship and twice winner of the Ontario Open. The Canadian Amateur Championship, in which he has been a finalist on three occasions, has eluded him by only the narrowest of margins. Scarboro has a requirement dating from 1921 that all new members must receive from the club professional a certificate stating that they have sufficient knowledge of the rules of golf to be allowed to play over the course.

Scioto CC USA

Columbus, Ohio. 18 holes

Scioto is thought of now as the course where a pudgy local boy named Jack Nicklaus first began to hit golf balls enormous distances. However, Scioto was well known before that momentous day when Charlie Nicklaus, a pharmacist, first took his 10-year-old son out to play a few holes. Nor should it be forgotten that it was at Scioto in 1926 that Bobby Jones became the first man to win both the British and the US Opens in the same year. And Walter Hagen's angry statement to his fellow professionals in the Scioto locker room afterward cannot be allowed to slip into limbo: 'All that damned amateur has to do is show up on the first tee, and the best pros in the world throw in the sponge. What are we going to do about it?' It should also be remembered that the Ryder Cup match of 1931 was played at Scioto as well as the 1950 PGA Championship in which the defending champion, Sam Snead, was beaten on the first day. The 1968 Amateur was also played there.

Scioto was built by Donald Ross in 1916

and revised in the 1960s by Dick Wilson. Although it has the look of a gentle course, it is long and tight and testing. But today the player does not have to worry about the impossibly high rough that was a feature of Scioto about the time that the Open was played there. In that championship, Bobby Cruickshank drove into a veritable wheatfield of rough on one round. His caddie put the bag down, the better to look for the ball, and then they could not find the bag.

Sclaff

Old Scottish expression for hitting the ground behind the ball. Often referred to as 'fat' or 'heavy', a sort of smother.

Scotch Foursomes see FOURSOMES

Scott, Lady Margaret (Lady Margaret Hamilton-Russell) BRITISH
b. 1875; d. 1938. British Ladies' 1893-5

At the close of the last century Lady Margaret Scott was in a class of her own. Besides having a style that was pleasing to the eye, she had an admirable temperament

and was never known to be ruffled. She played in the first three Ladies' Championships to be held, and the margin of her three victories indicates her supremacy. The first of these was at Royal Lytham and St Annes ladies' course (9 holes) with a scratch score of 90 for the two 9s. In her first match she was out in 40, in spite of a 6 at the 9th, and 8 up on her opponent; she went on to win by 9 and 7. Her remaining victories were by 8 and 7, 6 and 4, and in the final she defeated Isette Pearson by 7 and 5. Her speech on the presentation was made on her behalf by her father, Lord Eldon. Her other two victories, at Littlestone and Portrush, were equally convincing, her narrowest escape being in the 1895 semi-final which she won on the last green after being four down at the 9th. She held two course records, at Bath (70) and at Royal Lytham (80), the latter immediately after winning her first championship. The hat trick complete, she retired from golf and gave up membership of the three clubs to which she belonged – Cotswold Hills, Cheltenham and Westward Ho! She became Lady Margaret Hamilton-Russell on her marriage.

Scott, The Hon. Michael BRITISH
b. London 1873; d. 1959. Australian Open 1904, 1907; Australian Amateur 1907, 1909-10; French Open Amateur 1912, 1922; Walker Cup 1924, 1934; British Amateur 1933

Michael Scott was best known to golfers as the oldest winner of the Amateur Championship, being 55 and a grandfather at the time; but he was in fact a very fine player throughout his career. He was a modest, diffident man and with a stronger personality would no doubt have made a bigger impact in international golf. He belonged to a notable golfing family, for his brothers Osmund and Denys were scratch players, the former being runner-up for the Amateur title in 1905; and their sister Lady Margaret Scott won the first three British Ladies' championships. Michael Scott made only two appearances in Walker Cup matches, the first being almost sensational: he defeated Jess Sweetser 7 and 6, and in the foursomes, partnered by Robert Scott, he won against the formidable combination of R. T. Jones Jr and W. C. Fownes.

Scott, Robert Jr BRITISH
b. Glasgow 1883. Semi-finalist British Amateur 1922; leading amateur British Open 1924; Walker Cup 1924

Scott, Sydney Simeon BRITISH
b. Armathwaite, Cumberland, 1913. Tied

Top, Scioto CC, the 17th hole

Above, Sclaff—this one the result of Bobby Nichols attempting to emulate Larry Ziegler's ability to play left-handed, having borrowed Bob Charles's club

2nd British Open 1954; Ryder Cup 1955; British Seniors 1964

During the 1950s, Scott, despite not hitting the ball great distances, was one of the most reliable players on the British professional circuit. He came an honourable 2nd with Dai Rees in the 1954 British Open at Royal Birkdale and earned a place in the 1955 Ryder Cup team at Palm Springs. He did not play so much in the 1960s but won the British Seniors' title at Gosforth Park in 1964, losing the world title to Sam Snead at Wentworth. Possessor of a smooth stylish swing, he is a sought-after teacher.

Scratch Player

A player who needs no handicap.

Scrutton, Philip F. BRITISH

b. 1933; d. 1958. Berkshire Trophy 1950-2; Brabazon Trophy (English Amateur Open Strokeplay) 1952, 1954-5; Walker Cup 1955, 1957

Temperamentally better suited to strokeplay than matchplay as any perfectionist in the game tends to be, Scrutton won the Brabazon Trophy in 1952, 1954, and 1955, the first player to win it three times. He also won the Berkshire Trophy, one of the stepping stones to international recognition, in 1950, 1951 and 1952. Because of his distinguished record in the Brabazon and Berkshire, a commemorative trophy, the Scrutton Jug, has been awarded since 1959 to the player with the lowest aggregate in these two events. He played several times for England, and twice against the United States, in 1955 and 1957. He was killed in a car crash returning from a day's golf at Sunningdale.

Sea Island GC USA

Sea Island, Ga. 3 9-hole courses

Off the coast of South Carolina and

Philip F. Scrutton

Georgia, there lies an almost continuous stretch of islands, extending down nearly to Florida and forming an inland waterway of hundreds of miles. With their innumerable bays, bayous, coves, inlets, and lagoons, these islands once served as hideouts and refuges for buccaneers, and privateers. Now one after another of these lovely islets, ideal

for luxury exploitation, are being developed.

Sea Island is almost the southernmost of these delightful places. The golf here is tied to The Cloister, a charming and famous old resort hotel, and 18 of the 27 holes have been there since 1927 when they were designed by Colt and Alison, a firm of British architects. The newest 9 was laid out by Dick Wilson in 1959. These three 9s occupy land that was part of an old Colonial property called Retreat Plantation, and the golf clubhouse is made from a huge corn barn more than 150 years old. The ruins of the old mansion, along with the slave quarters and hospital, have been carefully preserved. The golfer, however, needs no quaint atmosphere to reward his visit to Sea Island. The three 9s are named Retreat, Plantation, and Seaside, and the latter two combine to form a course of distinctive quality. Seaside, which lies along St Simon Sound, has a little of the character of an English links, although the turf is different. On five of the holes, the water is a very real hazard. The inside 9s are more like the inland courses of the United States in general character. There is little rise and fall to the land, but, for all that, a pleasant variety of holes, largely because eight lakes come into play.

Seascale GC ENGLAND

Seascale, Cumberland. 18 holes; 6,307 yd (5,767 m)

Situated on the Cumberland coast west of the Lake District and only a short drive from

Top, Sea Island GC

the Scottish Border country, this is a traditional British links course. It was founded in 1892 by the Earl of Erroll and some 60 colleagues who chose their site wisely. They also engaged a famous Scot, Willie Campbell, to lay out the course and six years later called in George Low from Lytham and St Annes to extend Campbell's original work

from 9 to 18 holes. Over the years Seascale has remained a much respected course; its relative inaccessibility explains why it is not better known. It has been widely used for Cumberland and Westmorland championships and in 1971 housed the finals of the English County Championship.

Seattle GC USA

Seattle, Wash. 18 holes

Seattle is a real golfing community, one of the most ardent in the Pacific Northwest, and its climate seems ideally suited to the game. It has been called an English-type climate, possibly erroneously, but there nearly always is year-round play in this region. Consequently there are a score and

Above, Seattle GC's clubhouse

more of public and private courses in and around the city, and perhaps the best of them is the Seattle GC, up in what are called the Highlands, about 10 miles from the city centre. The fact that this course was chosen for both a US Amateur Championship and a Walker Cup match speaks for its worth. Here in 1952 Jack Westland, a native of Washington who has represented his state in Congress and his country in international golf matches, won the Amateur. Westland was 47 when he won the title and so he was a little too old to play against Britain again when the Cup match came to Seattle in 1961.

Seaver, Charles AMERICAN
b. 1912. Semi-finalist US Amateur 1930; Walker Cup 1932; California Amateur 1933; Northern California Amateur 1933; Southern California Amateur 1934, runner-up 1928

Stanford football player and golfer who reached the semi-finals of the US Amateur in 1930 and won both his matches in the 1932 Walker Cup. In the 1930 Amateur, Seaver met Gene Homans in the semi-finals to see who would try to stop Bobby Jones from completing the Grand Slam. Homans won, 1 up, and was routed by Jones the next day.

Seaview CC USA
Atlantic City, N.J. 36 holes; Bay Course 6,350 yd (5,806 m), par 71; Pines Course 6,900 yd (6,309 m), par 72

It is difficult to imagine two courses belonging to the same club so totally different as the Bay Course and the Pines Course at Seaview. The Bay, the older of the two, was a creation of Donald Ross, laid out about 1915 over flattish, somewhat marshy, almost barren land, wide open but with the usual subtleties of a Ross design. The other

course, the Pines, was hewn from a dense forest, the first 9 in 1932 when not many golf courses were being built, and the second 9 in 1957 by Bill and Dave Gordon. Before the second 9 was completed, the usual practice whenever a tournament was held at Seaview was to play 9 holes of the Pines and 9 more from the Bay. This is how it was set up in 1942 when Sam Snead won his first USPGA Championship. Contrary to its name, Seaview is not next to the water. It is about eight miles inland from Atlantic City – just over 50 miles from Philadelphia, an hour's drive on a modern expressway. The club can trace its origin to Clarence H. Geist, an improbably wealthy Philadelphia businessman who was a member of the Atlantic City CC. In about 1914 or thereabouts, Geist went to his club to play one day and found five groups ahead of him on the first tee. Geist vowed to build his own club where he would not have to wait. He moved inland to Absecon, New Jersey, invested $1.5 million, and wound up with a golf course and a huge clubhouse with 250 rooms (it has been expanded since then) and an indoor salt-water swimming pool. It is one of the few clubs in the United States where motorized carts are not permitted.

Seeding
Spreading the best entrants for a knock-out competition evenly throughout the draw so that they do not eliminate each other in the early rounds; 4, 8 or 16 is the usual number of seeds.

Segard, Mrs P. (née Lally Vagliano) FRENCH
b. Paris 1920. British Girls' 1937; French Ladies' Close 1939, 1946, 1949-51, runner-up 1952-3, 1964, 1967; French Ladies' Open 1948, 1950-2; Italian Ladies' Open 1949, 1951; Swiss Ladies' Open 1949, 1965; British

Ladies' 1950; Spanish Ladies' 1951; Kayser-Bondor Foursomes (with Brigitte Varangot) 1960; Worplesdon Foursomes (with David Frame) 1962

Lally Segard, who was the Vicomtesse de Saint-Sauveur before her remarriage in 1970, is one of the greatest woman golfers in Europe and her career lasted for more than 30 years. Ever since, as Lally Vagliano, she won the British Girls' Championship in 1937, she has taken an active part in British golf and in matches against the British Isles. In 1950 she won the British Championship, the third Frenchwoman to do so. In 1961 she won the Avia women's foursomes with her young protégée, Brigitte Varangot, who later went on to become a triple British champion; and in 1962 she won the Worplesdon Foursomes with David Frame.

Mrs Segard is petite and elegant, yet she hit the ball as far as almost anyone in her day. She had a faultless style with a wide arc and a perfect grip, and she swung at the ball with all the controlled force that her lissom figure could muster. It is significant that her victory in the British came at Royal County Down, one of the longest and toughest courses in the British Isles. She came of a golfing family – the Vagliano Trophy, competed for between teams representing the British Isles and the Continent, was presented by her father – and in addition to her sound technique she had an attacking spirit which seldom left her short of the hole. Thanks to her encouragement and enthusiasm there grew up around her a little group of players of the highest quality – Brigitte Varangot, Claudine Cros-Rubin, and most recently Catherine Lacoste-de Prado. Her record shows the enduring quality of her game. Most of her successes came in the postwar years, but she won her first French championship in 1939. She won five times after the war, and finished runner-up as late as 1964. Similarly she won the Swiss Ladies' Open in 1949 and again 16 years later. Her appearances for France in international matches against other Continental countries cover a span of 26 years from 1937 to 1965.

Selangor GC, Royal MALAYSIA
Kuala Lumpur. 36 holes; Championship Course 6,793 yd (6,212 m)

In 1893, a few years before the widespread planting of rubber began which has helped give Malaysia its 20th-century prosperity, the Selangor club was founded and a 9-hole course laid out and opened the same year in the Petaling Hills southeast of the capital, on the site of a disused Chinese graveyard. Needless to say, the British had a hand at

Charles Seaver

Mrs P. Segard

Selangor where the principal pioneers were the brothers Glassford, coffee planters on the Mount Estate who hailed from Grantown-on-Spey, Moray, and Kit and Robert Meikle.

The Petaling site was chosen in preference to one in Lake Gardens, where a course, but no club, had been started in 1889 by A. B. Venning, Treasurer of the State of Selangor. A clubhouse or pavilion was built at Selangor and improvements steadily maintained under the influence of the Glassfords, although for some time there was need of a local rule that read 'Graves, with their mounds and trenches, roads, paths and any other part of the course over which the turf has been removed must be treated as hazards . . . long grass is not a hazard.' The first club match, Scotland against the Rest, is recorded in the club history *Twelve under Fours*.

These were good days for the golfers at Petaling Hills. About 1918, however, the government wanted to turn the area into a park and a new home was found at Circular Road on ground occupied by the Department of Forestry. The area was swampy and favoured for snipe shooting. But in spite of many drainage and construction problems, this has proved a wise choice since the opening of the first 9 holes in 1921. In 1924 the old 'cow grass' on the greens was replaced by Bermuda grass, which in turn gave way in 1935 to Serangoon grass, already a success at Royal Singapore. The addition of a 'relief 9'

in 1924 to cope with increased demand alleviated matters only temporarily and by May 1931 the club's amenities, which included tennis and, later, swimming, were extended by the completion of a fourth 9 holes, the bunkering suggested by the British architect, H. S. Colt, to whom a plan had been sent.

The impact of World War II was little felt for a while, but the Japanese invasion in January 1942 brought organized golf to a halt. At first the Japanese, who did their best to destroy all trace of the British connection, allowed any civilian to join the club for a virtually nominal fee and subscription, but this did not last long. The Japanese Army eventually took over the club for use as a small-arms training school. The courses either became desolate, or were put to use for growing tapioca, bananas and vegetables.

The postwar task of restoring the full 36 holes was somehow completed by 1948 and today's flourishing club owes much to those responsible for the rehabilitation. By 1953, the diamond jubilee year, membership was 1,799. Since then Asians of the various communities have begun to take a much keener interest in the game.

The well-attended Malaysian Open held there each year has marked the beginning of an exciting new era. To maintain Selangor as a test for the modern professionals, Frank Pennink, the British golf architect, undertook extensive lengthening and tightening of the flat, tree-lined Championship Course,

chosen to house the 1974 World Amateur Team Championship which, alas, at the last moment was transferred to the Dominican Republic.

Selected Drive Foursome see GREENSOME

Seminole GC USA

Florida. 18 holes; 6,500 yd (5,944 m); par 72

There is an art to golf-course architecture that defies explanation: the great courses 'play' and the lesser courses do not, even if they have excellent natural features and the correct measurements. Seminole is a course that plays as well as any in the United States, and this is the reason why it is such a favourite with average golfers wintering in the south, top-level amateurs like Bob Sweeney (who is a member), and top professionals like Ben Hogan (also a member).

Seminole, which hugs the Atlantic 10 miles or so north of Palm Beach, Fla., is a Donald Ross course. It was opened for play in October 1929, and has not been greatly changed since that time. From the championship markers it measures just about 6,900 yd (6,310 m); from the middle markers, a little over 6,500 yd; and from the ladies' markers, about 5,900 yd (5,400 m). To be at its best, Seminole needs a touch of wind, which it has as often as not. It has just about everything else: a nice proportion of doglegs on which the bunkers are set perfectly; a wonderful variety of green sites, including those crown greens which Ross built better than anyone else; enough water and sand and stands of palms to keep the golfer on the *qui vive* throughout his round; and inspired routing that features constant changes of direction and pace. It is invariably in superb condition.

Seminole draws the bulk of its membership from the wealthy Palm Beach set. Its clubhouse, modest in size, has the feel of a Mediterranean villa. During the 1950s, the club conducted an annual 36-hole pro-am which was a high point on the winter tour, but the members are very keen on their golf and not disposed towards the idea of tournaments except among themselves and their friends. For many years, Claude Harmon was the club professional, a position now filled by Henry Picard.

Semi-rough

The lighter, graded rough nearest to the fairway.

Setterberg, Viktor H. SWEDISH

b. 1895; d. 1945. Runner-up Swedish Close Amateur 1904-7; runner-up Swedish Open Amateur 1911

Royal Selangor GC, the 18th tee

The 'Father of Swedish Golf', Setterberg's interest in the game was aroused by some Britons who used to play on a primitive course outside Gothenburg (Göteborg). He sent for literature and learned all he could theoretically. He started playing in 1894 with friends, and in 1901 laid out a new course almost singlehanded. In 1904, with Tor Törnsten, first president of the Gothenburg GC, he initiated the building of a third and more permanent course at Hovås, south of the city. Setterberg was founder and first honorary secretary/treasurer of the Gothenburg club and also, again with Törnsten, of the Swedish Golf Union and its first secretary (1903-14). He was a prolific writer on golf, the first in Sweden.

Sewell, Douglas BRITISH

b. Woking, Surrey, 1929. English Open Amateur Strokeplay 1957, 1959; Walker Cup 1957, 1959; English Amateur 1958, 1960; joint winner Martini Tournament 1970; Club Professionals' 1973

Doug Sewell, who worked on the railways and played as an artisan at Woking, was one

of the leading British amateurs in the late 1950s. He combined a steady though unspectacular swing with a deadliness round the greens. He had a wonderful record in medal events, particularly in the London area, and earned a place in the Walker Cup team through winning the English Open Amateur Strokeplay at Moortown in 1957. He won again in very fast conditions at Hollinwell in 1959. In 1960 he played the longest English final before defeating Martin Christmas at Hunstanton at the 41st hole.

It is possible that Sewell would have turned professional earlier if the PGA's qualification system had not been so severe, but he took advantage of the reduction in restrictions in 1960 and since then has had

some good performances in several tournaments, and notable success and popularity as a teacher both at Parkstone and Ferndown.

Shade, Ronnie David Bell Mitchell
BRITISH

b. Edinburgh 1938. English Open Amateur Strokeplay 1961, 1963, 1967; Walker Cup 1961, 1963, 1965, 1967; leading amateur British Open 1962; Eisenhower Trophy 1962, 1964, 1966, 1968; Scottish Amateur 1963-7, runner-up 1962; runner-up British Amateur 1966; Carroll's International Tournament 1969; Scottish Professional 1970

Intensively coached by his father, John Shade, the Duddingston club professional, Shade developed a swing of mechanical appearance and repetitiveness. Its principal characteristic is the unusual time he keeps his head down after the ball has gone. He very rarely missed a fairway and few amateurs of his generation have so consistently had first putts for birdies.

Shade's outstanding achievement as an amateur was to capture the Scottish title in

five successive years, twice more than Jack M'Lean did in the 1930s. In the process Shade won 40 matches, 35 of them over 18 holes. His game travelled well, too; in World Amateur Team Championships he broke a course record in Japan and in Mexico he had the lowest individual aggregate. Shade prepared meticulously, almost professionally, for an important event, and so when he actually turned – belatedly in 1968, as he readily admitted afterwards – he quickly found his feet and won a major tournament in each of his first two seasons. As an amateur he was awarded the MBE.

Shaft
The part of the club which is not the head.

Shank
The part of the club nearest to the hosel. Used as a verb it means to hit the ball on the shank, one of the most dreaded 'diseases' in golf. Also known as a socket.

Shannon GCC see LUCAYAN/SHANNON COMPLEX

Shaw, Andrew J. NEW ZEALANDER
b. Troon, Ayrshire, 1898. NZ Open 1926, 1929-32, 1934, 1936; NZ Professional 1928-9, 1931-4

Shaw was the finest player New Zealand produced before World War II. Born a Scot, he knew Vardon and Braid as a boy and played from an early age. In 1919, he decided to join his two brothers who were already in New Zealand.

Well built though not tall, Shaw based his game on his ability to hit the ball a long way but, while professional at Napier, he improved his control and his putting appreciably and in the next few years set new standards and scores for New Zealand golf. He more or less dominated the NZ Open and Professional championships from 1926 to 1936 and, when he went to Melbourne in 1934 for the Centenary tournament, greatly impressed leading American players there. Later, in a series with Gene Sarazen, he lost only once, and he also beat Walter Hagen. In 1930 he won the NZ Open by 18 strokes.

His successes, however, and his travel were largely limited to New Zealand and, to that extent, he belonged to the wrong generation. Today he would almost certainly have enjoyed a rich living from the tournaments.

Sheahan, Dr David B. IRISH
Irish Close Amateur 1961, 1966; Walker Cup 1963

In between his student days and early life as a doctor, David Sheahan was one of the best amateurs in Ireland, winning the Irish Amateur Close Championship in 1961 and 1970.

He followed his first victory with a quite remarkable triumph in the 1962 Jeyes Professional tournament at Royal Dublin while still at University College, and qualified for the 1963 Walker Cup team at Turnberry where he won singles victories over Labron Harris and Richard Davies, then British Amateur Champion. Sheahan played for Ireland seven times.

Shepperson, Alec BRITISH

b. 1936. British Boys' 1953, runner-up 1952; President's Putter 1957; Walker Cup 1957, 1959; runner-up English Open Amateur

Hollinwell, but faded from the scene thereafter.

Sheridan, James BRITISH
b. East Lothian 1885; d. Sunningdale, Berkshire, 1970

James Sheridan took up his appointment as caddiemaster of Sunningdale in 1911 on a trial basis and, though he used to delight in saying that it was never confirmed, retired after 56 years in office.

He was the last of the old race of caddiemasters and also the last of the old generation of Scots who have exerted a healthy influence on the game in many parts of the world. He was a man of strong will and high principle, never afraid to speak his mind.

But, for all his occasional gruffness, Sheridan was a scrupulously fair and kind master to the caddies, a respected and loyal friend to distinguished men in many corners of the world and, above all, a man with an abiding love of golf and golfers.

His decision to go south was a bold step for a young man of 26 but he had had a sound upbringing, caddying on the great links of Muirfield, North Berwick and Musselburgh, and knew far more about the game than most people of his age.

In 1955 Sheridan was made an honorary life member of Sunningdale, which touched him deeply, although in thanking the committee he is said to have commented, 'Ah well, I have been making my own rules around here for 45 years'. He also had the distinction of seeing his portrait hung in the clubhouse. There was one more honour to be bestowed upon him, the presentation by the captain, Gerald Micklem, of a silver salver to mark his 50 years' service in 1961; and then six more years before he retired to the little village of Sunningdale.

It ended a remarkable career in which he

Strokeplay 1962; semi-finalist English Amateur 1964

Alec Shepperson first came to prominence when he lost the 1952 final of the Boys' Championship to Michael Bonallack. He went one better the following year and graduated to international golf during a distinguished career at Oxford University where he studied law. He gained a place in the Walker Cup teams of 1957 and 1959, winning his single at Muirfield against Tommy Aaron by 2 and 1. But building a business career severely restricted his competitive appearances. Shepperson tied in the English Amateur Strokeplay at Woodhall Spa in 1962 and reached the semi-final of the English Championship in 1964 at

befriended princes and peers, but he was best loved by those who served him. He passed on the spirit of loyalty to his son, John, who has been professional at Denham for more than 25 years.

Sherlock, James G.
b. High Wycombe, Buckinghamshire, 1876;

Top, David B. Sheahan playing from the 6th tee at Turnberry during the 1963 Walker Cup

Above, Alec Shepperson

James G. Sherlock

d. 1966. British Professional Matchplay 1910

Sherlock learned to be a very fine golfer on one of the worst courses in Europe, at Hinksey outside Oxford. He could juggle with the ball on the mud there but could hardly learn to be a long driver. He was an original thinker befriended there by generations of young Oxford golfers. When he moved to Stoke Poges, Buckinghamshire, his long game gradually developed; he looked as though he had reduced the game to its elements, and he appeared always to be doing the easiest thing in the most straightforward manner. His putting was outstanding with the most natural of styles, and when he defeated Duncan in the final of the British Matchplay (*News of the World* Tournament) in 1910 he was probably for that year the best golfer in the country. He ended a long career as professional at Hunstanton.

Shillong GC INDIA

Shillong, Assam. 18 holes; 5,926 yd (5,419 m); par 70

In the northeast of India, among the Khasi and Jaintia Hills of Assam, is the beautiful golf course of Shillong at an altitude of 5,000 ft. A course was first laid out in 1898 on the present racecourse and polo ground, with a small thatch-roofed pavilion. It was mainly used by tea planters and visitors escaping from the steamy heat of Calcutta. One of the first major tournaments was for ladies, the Bachelor's Cup presented by R. A. Collie in 1903, and for men came the Kelner Cup in the same year. After World War I, as golf increased in popularity, it was decided to construct a good clubhouse, acquire more land and lay out a better and larger course. In 1923 the present clubhouse was built, and with its lovely surrounding countryside nostalgic Scottish tea planters soon called Shillong the 'Gleneagles of the East'. The grass is an indigenous hill species and there is a profusion of pine and rhododendron. The best season is in September and October after the heavy monsoons.

Shillong was a headquarters of Eastern Command during the Burma campaign of World War II, and during the fighting in Bangladesh in 1971, and the golf course is much patronized by the armed forces. Plans are in hand for major improvements as a tourist attraction, and India's golfing vice-president, Sri G. S. Pathak, has enthused over the beauty of the course.

The course record of 67 is shared by an amateur, L. S. Foster, and the professional Srikissen Ram Koiri, who is also the greenkeeper. Longer than any hole either at Calcutta or Delhi, the 594-yd (543-m) 6th would with an adverse wind require three

well-struck shots to reach the green. The local rules tell golfers that they may stop for shelter during rain, a reminder of the fact that only 36 miles by road, and a third of that distance as the vulture flies, is Cherrapunji, famous for having the highest average rainfall in the world.

Shinnecock Hills GC USA

Southampton, Long Island, N.Y. 18 holes

It often is difficult to get at the true beginnings of the earliest golf clubs in the United States, but about the fact that Shinnecock Hills was the first course built on Long Island and about its quality there can be no doubt. The most attractive story told of its beginnings relates that one day in the winter of 1889, William K. Vanderbilt, sojourning in Biarritz, saw Willie Dunn, the famous Scottish professional and golf architect, hit a few balls and, turning to his companions, made the understatement of the dying century, if not of the one yet unborn: 'Gentlemen,' he said, 'this beats rifle shooting. It is a game I think might go in our country.'

That is how Dunn came to be called to Southampton, the fashionable gathering place of the wealthy at the tip of the island, to design and build Shinnecock. The club went through its share of vicissitudes, but the course stands today, handsomely revised by Dick Wilson in the 1930s, as one of the very best in the country.

The terrain is ideal – as near to the linksland that Willie Dunn knew in Scotland as can be found in the United States. The course lies alongside, almost touching, the National Golf Links of America, built a little later by Charles Blair Macdonald, partly along Peconic Bay, and any visitor who gets out that far on the island, about 100 miles from the city, should try to play both.

Shinnecock was named after a tribe of

Indians that once occupied the far end of Long Island. Its brown shingled clubhouse, not much changed from the day it was designed by Stanford White, was the first golf clubhouse built in the States. The club itself, they say, was the first American club to be incorporated and the first to have a waiting list.

Short Game

The part of the game centred around the green when the need for control, finesse and accuracy replaces the need for power and distance. It includes pitching, chipping, greenside bunker play, and putting.

Short Set

British term for a set in which about half the normal complement of 14 clubs is carried. A typical example would be a wood, four irons, wedge and putter contained in a small bag. A short set is ideal for young beginners. Experienced players often score as well with such a set as with a full one.

Shute, Herman Densmore AMERICAN

b. Cleveland, Ohio, 1904; d. 1973. Ryder Cup 1931, 1933, 1937; British Open 1933; USPGA 1936-7; 3rd US Open 1939

Shute had the unusual experience in 1933 of going from nadir to apex of his fortunes in the space of two weeks. At Southport, Lancashire, playing Syd Easterbrook in the decisive single of the Ryder Cup match, he took three putts on the home green and lost. He then went to St Andrews, where he had four rounds each of 73 in the Open Championship, tied with Craig Wood, and beat his fellow American in the play-off with rounds of 74 and 76. Shute, of Devon stock, was a slightly-built, dark man with deep-set eyes, an engaging manner, and a great capacity for concentration. In addition to a successful tournament career he twice had

Shinnecock Hills GC

the satisfaction of beating a reigning US Open champion in 72-hole challenge matches – Johnny Goodman in 1933 and Ralph Guldahl in 1937. But in the latter year, following Henry Cotton's second victory in the Open at Carnoustie, Shute was beaten 6 and 5 by the British master over 72 holes at Walton Heath.

Sikes, Daniel D. AMERICAN

b. Jacksonville, Fla., 1930. US Amateur Public Links 1958; Doral Open 1963; Cleveland Open 1965; Jacksonville Open 1967; Philadelphia Classic 1967; Ryder Cup 1969

Dan Sikes turned professional later than most. He graduated from law school and is still a member of the Florida Bar Association. This training he put to good use as a member of the old USPGA tournament committee, especially in the stormy years of the late 1960s. He also became a consistent player on the circuit, a keen analyst of courses and of styles. His own was based on a study of Cary Middlecoff. He was a fine putter; his best years were 1967-70 and this earned him a place in the 1969 Ryder Cup

team. He partnered Nicklaus on the latter's first appearance in the foursomes and again in the fourball matches. In 1967, while engaged in steering the PGA tournament committee through its darkest days, he won two tournaments. He also finished 2nd at Westchester, a tournament from which he had withdrawn once and missed the cut once, but both rounds were washed out and Sikes was back in the tournament.

Sikes, Richard H. AMERICAN

b. Paris, Ark., 1940. US Amateur Public Links 1961-2; Eisenhower Trophy 1962; runner-up US Amateur 1963; Walker Cup 1963; Sahara Invitational 1964; Cleveland Open 1966

Sikes came to the front as a student at the University of Arkansas, and achieved the rare distinction of defending his title as Public Links Champion successfully. This earned him a place in the Walker Cup and Eisenhower teams. He won a tournament while still a recruit on the tour in 1964 and has made a steady income since.

Silk, Bryan Martell NEW ZEALANDER

b. 1910. NZ Amateur 1934, 1937, 1947; Bledisloe Cup (leading amateur NZ Open) 1934, 1936, 1948, 1963; North Island Amateur 1948-9, 1951, 1956, 1958

Bryan Silk entered Wanganui Collegiate School in 1925 along with J. P. Hornabrook, against whom he contested the final of the 1935 NZ Amateur and with whom he took the Amateur Foursomes in 1938.

In 1929, Silk finished 13th in his first NZ Open, an event he subsequently missed only once until the late 1960s. He represented his country from the age of 21 and later became one of the best known of all New Zealand golfers. He won the NZ Amateur three times. Although his work as an accountant did not leave him as much time for golf as he would

have liked, he maintained his game at a high pitch for a long time.

During World War II he was awarded the US Legion of Merit in the Pacific. Later he used borrowed clubs to win the Inter-Allied Army Golf Tournament in Italy by 20 strokes. In 1954 he took part in the Commonwealth Tournament at St Andrews to mark the bi-centenary of the R. and A., and while in Britain, investigated the merits of the newly formed Golf Foundation for fostering junior golf through the schools. He was sufficiently impressed to prepare a local scheme and, as chairman of the New Zealand Golf Foundation from the outset in 1955, has helped to guide its success and expansion.

Silloth on Solway GC ENGLAND

Silloth, Cumberland. 18 holes

Silloth on Solway, 20 miles west of Carlisle, is one of the delights of British golf. It is a traditional seaside links of subtlety, entertainment and distinction, not long by modern standards, but demanding enough to have housed a major championship if its situation had not been regarded as remote. Its setting by the shining Solway Firth, not far from the Lakeland fells and the Lowland peaks of Scotland, is not the least part of the charm that attracted the small band of Carlisle businessmen who founded the club in 1892, known until fairly recently as Carlisle and Silloth. Much of the club's fame and reputation was spread by the skills of Miss Cecil Leitch. She and her four sisters, all daughters of the local doctor, formed the basis of the club's team in the early days and legend has it that when they alighted from their coach one day for a match in the Borders, it was believed that they were caddies. Their male hosts had not considered them as players but the four sisters, though not quite as good as Cecil, were still un-usually talented and the resounding success they scored left a trail of embarrassment among the men.

Cecil Leitch went on to win the British Ladies' Championship four times, owing much to her formative years spent on the glorious Cumberland turf at Silloth.

Simons, Jim AMERICAN

b. Butler, Pa., 1950. 2nd Canadian Amateur 1970; runner-up British Amateur 1971; tied 5th US Open 1971; Walker Cup 1971

A relatively inexperienced player when he gained selection for the Walker Cup match at St Andrews in 1971, where he failed to win a point in two outings. He was paired in the leading foursome on the first day with Lanny Wadkins, a fellow student of Wake

Top. Densmore Shute

Above. Dan Sikes

R. H. Sikes

Forest University where he had won an Arnold Palmer scholarship. It came as a surprise, therefore, when he reached the final the following week of the British Amateur at Carnoustie losing to Steve Melnyk by 3 and 2, and an even greater surprise when he led after three rounds in the US Open at Merion shortly afterwards.

He finished with a 76 in a tie for 5th place, but was low amateur by a comfortable margin. He has since turned professional.

Simpson, Jack BRITISH
b. Earlsferry, Fife. British Open 1884

Simpson, Tom BRITISH
b. 1876

Tom Simpson is remembered not only for his design and construction of golf courses but also for his authoritative and lucid writings on golf-course architecture. His most active period was between the two world wars when he worked not only in Britain but also in continental Europe.

He took a degree in law at Trinity Hall, Cambridge, and was called to the bar although he never practised. He was a scratch golfer, a member of the Oxford and Cambridge Golfing Society and the Royal and Ancient GC. A man of considerable private means he devoted the greater part of his active life to golf-course architecture. Simpson always insisted that a proper understanding of the principles of course design could only be achieved by a detailed study of the Old Course at St Andrews. As regards construction work, his view was that it should appear as natural as possible and should also make for easy maintenance.

Probably his best work was done abroad, as at Morfontaine and Chiberta (France), and Royal Antwerp, Keerbergen and Spa (Belgium). In Britain some of the best

examples of the artistry of his work can be seen at Sunningdale New Course, Royal Porthcawl, Ashridge, Liphook and Muirfield. He also worked in the Irish Republic where Baltray is a good example.

Simpson's outstanding work as a writer on golf-course architecture was *The Architectural Side of Golf*, published in 1929 in collaboration with H. N. Wethered. This was illustrated profusely with his own inimitable drawings and plans, the former mainly in ink and wash. He was also an authority on etchings and wrote a book on the subject; and he did beautiful work in silk embroidery. He travelled in a chauffeur-driven Rolls Royce and was generally to be seen, shooting stick in hand, wearing a beret and cloak.

Singapore Island CC SINGAPORE
72 holes; Bukit Course 6,715 yd (6,140 m); Island Course 6,365 yd (5,820 m); New Course 6,874 yd (6,286 m); Sime Course 6,314 yd (5,774 m)

The Singapore Island CC is an amalgamation of the original Royal Singapore and Royal Island GCs. They were merged on 21 June 1963 and today form an international, inter-communal club without equal in Southeast Asia with a multiplicity of other interests besides golf and a membership, at the end of 1971, of 7,000. Such interest reflects the rising tide of enthusiasm in modern Singapore where the Prime Minister and many Government officials are keen golfers. But organized golf in Singapore

dates from 1891 when Mr Justice Goldney founded the Singapore GC on a 9-hole circuit at the old racecourse in Farrer Park and, wearing knickerbockers, stiff collar, white tie, red coat and bowler hat, drove the first ball, to much local curiosity.

At the start, the legal profession dominated Singapore golf at the racecourse which was its home for 33 years. Women were admitted in 1907 although they were barred from the clubhouse until a part of the veranda had been curtained off for their use. In 1924 a move was made to the Bukit site where some 275 acres (110 ha) of jungle, home of tiger and wild boar, had to be cleared.

Thanks to the energy and foresight of John Sime, Bukit was opened for play in 1924. In 1930, another 12 holes were constructed east of the clubhouse and these were later lengthened and combined to form the first 9 of the present course, later to be renamed the Sime Course. About 1938, the second 9 of the Sime Course were completed, and in 1966, the whole course was considerably improved. The Royal Singapore GC, as it had then become, thus had a delightful setting in surroundings similar to an English park.

By 1927 the Island GC, later the Royal Island, had also come to life not far away, in the same reservoir area, and this became the centre for the most cosmopolitan club on the island.

During World War II the Japanese used

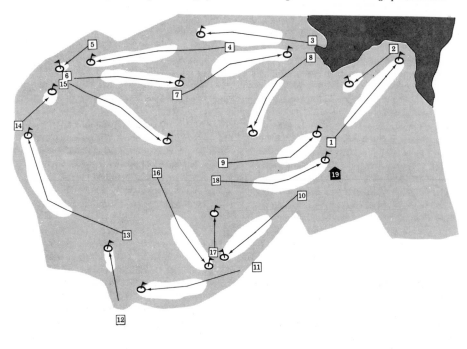

Jim Simons playing from a bunker during the semi-final of the 1971 British Amateur Championship

The course plan of Singapore Island GC

large areas of the course for growing tapioca and, at Bukit, laid an asphalt road to their shrine on top of the hill overlooking the reservoir.

All traces of these were removed after the war and the clubs slowly got back to normal. The Royal Island had a new clubhouse in 1951 but Singapore's two premier golf clubs only retained their separate identities for a little while longer. By 1963, important national developments had taken place on the Island and it was natural that these changes should affect golf which had become so popular. The merger of the two clubs was completed swiftly; the golf, to the Prime Minister's delight, has flourished. A new course, designed by Frank Pennink, was opened in August 1970, at the Island location where facilities include swimming and an air-conditioned eight-lane automatic bowling alley; and interest has been accentuated among the golf-minded people of Singapore by the staging of the Singapore Open which forms part of the Far East circuit, and of the World (formerly Canada) Cup in 1969.

Single

A match between two players. Often erroneously used of one player playing on his own.

Smith, Alex

b. Carnoustie, Angus, 1872; d. 1930. US Open 1906, 1910, 2nd 1901, 3rd 1908

One of the early Scottish professionals who made such a significant impact on early American golf. Alex, brother of Willie Smith from Carnoustie who won the US Open in 1899, captured the title in 1906. A congenial and fine-looking man who was professional at the Nassau CC, Glen Cove, N.Y., Smith scored 295 (73, 74, 73, 75), a remarkable total which beat 300 for the first time. He defeated his brother by 7 strokes. Alex, playing from the Wykagyl CC, New Rochell, N.Y., won again in 1910 at the St Martin's course of the Philadelphia Cricket Club after the first three-way tie. Smith's original score was 298 (73, 73, 79, 73) and in the play-off he had 71 against Johnny McDermott's 75 and the 77 of Macdonald, another of his four brothers.

Alex also gained fame as a teacher and is credited with having developed the games of Jerry Travers and Glenna Collett.

Smith, Charles B. AMERICAN

b. 1931. North and South Amateur 1960; Southern Amateur 1960; Eastern Amateur 1962; Walker Cup 1961, 1963

Smith, Eric Martin BRITISH

b. 1908; d. 1951. British Amateur 1931

Son of an international golfer, Smith was only recently down from Cambridge, where he had won a Blue, when he yielded reluctantly to the suggestions of his friends and entered for the British Amateur Championship. He was 22, comparatively inexperienced, and bound to be regarded as insignificant in a field containing several good Americans and all the leading British amateurs. One by one the best faded out, leaving him to contest the final with John de Forest. It was not a thrilling match except in the closeness of the finish, Martin Smith winning at the 36th. In the last year of his life he was MP for Grantham, Lincolnshire.

Smith, Mrs Frances (née Frances Stephens) BRITISH

b. 1924. English Ladies' 1948, 1954-5, runner-up 1959; British Ladies' 1949, 1954, runner-up 1951-2; Worplesdon Foursomes 1949-50, 1954, 1961; Curtis Cup 1950, 1952, 1954, 1956, 1958, 1960 (non-playing captain 1962, 1972)

For 10 years and more after World War II Frances Smith was the outstanding competitor in British women's golf and her tally of achievements would have been even greater had she been blessed with a stronger physique. As it was she won the British Ladies' in 1949 and 1954 and was runner-up twice; she was English champion three times and losing finalist once, and won a host of lesser events at stroke and matchplay. Her record in the Curtis Cup matches against the United States remains incomparable; from 1950 to 1958 she was undefeated in five singles, won three of five foursomes and, together with Elisabeth Price Fisher, was largely responsible for British victories in 1952 and 1956, and for halving the 1958

match in Boston. She was non-playing captain of Britain in 1962 and 1972.

In 1956 at Prince's, Sandwich, the destiny of the whole match rested upon the final hole of her single against Polly Riley. A flawless medium iron shot to the heart of the green won the day for Britain and, by extraordinary coincidence, two years later she

and Miss Riley again had to play for the trophy. Again Mrs Smith's perfect strokes on the closing holes prevailed, but these were the two most famous instances of her classic temperament in a crisis. No golfer of that period, man or woman, played more perfect shots under severe pressure.

Writing after the 1958 match Herbert Warren Wind paid tribute to her in these words: 'She holds on to her timing in the most nerve-racking situations because she has superb concentration. She holds on to her concentration because she has a purposefulness that never wavers and a wondrous heart.'

Thoughts of defeat had no place at all in the philosophy of Frances Smith; her determination to win, beneath a gentle, retiring manner, was almost beyond belief. In this she was helped by a phlegmatic, unexcitable nature not given to imagining the consequences of failure, and an outlook that was ever positive and, in the golfing sense, aggressive.

Perfectionism is a rare trait in women amateur golfers but Frances Smith forever sought perfection. Her father, Fred Stephens, was a gifted teacher and together they worked and worked for years to create a swing that would withstand all pressures. It was not beautiful; it lacked the fluency of a natural athletic movement, with its pronounced pause just before the top, but in every phase was perfectly positioned. Her vigilance over its mechanics never ceased; in

Charles B. Smith   Mrs Frances Smith

common with the greatest players she was never entirely satisfied, but the years of dedicated practice gave her a confidence in her method that rarely failed. No woman golfer ever was more consistently straight over a longer period, and had she been more powerful few, if any, of her time could have lived with her.

Smith, Horton AMERICAN

b. Springfield, Mo., 1908; d. 1963. Ryder Cup 1929, 1933, 1935; US Masters 1934, 1936

Horton Smith is remembered as the first winner of the US Masters at Augusta, a victory by 1 stroke from Craig Wood, but he took the tournament scene by storm in the

winter of 1928-9, winning eight tournaments and finishing leading money winner. Although he never matched that sort of brilliance again, he was throughout the 1930s a prominent figure of whose putting Bernard Darwin once wrote, 'a joy to watch, easy, elegant and of a horrid certainty. The United States have sent us a number of great putters from whom to choose models, but I am disposed to doubt if they have sent a better than Horton Smith.' In many ways, his career was similar to that of his namesake, Macdonald Smith, who won almost everything in his own country except The Open. Horton added a second Masters title in 1936 and was a regular and loyal member of the PGA tournament committee, joining in 1932 and becoming president in 1952. He was a member of several Ryder Cup teams and in 1929 was one of only two Americans to win a singles match.

He became seriously ill in 1957 and underwent a series of operations but he continued his job and in 1961 received the Ben Hogan Award for his fortitude in overcoming a physical handicap.

Smith, Macdonald AMERICAN

b. Carnoustie, Angus, 1890; d. 1949. 3rd US Open 1910, runner-up 1930; Western Open 1912, 1925, 1933; Canadian Open 1926; runner-up British Open 1930, 1932

Mac Smith has the somewhat depressing reputation of being probably the best player who never won the British or American Open championships. He had a fine, smooth, elegant swing and came from a Scots family of champions; his brothers Alex and Willie Smith won the US Open three times between them.

A quiet, pleasant man, Smith learned his golf at Carnoustie but, like so many citizens of that ancient town, he went to America and before he was 20 had tied for the Open

championship there and lost a play-off. He disappeared from the golfing scene and worked in a shipyard but, when he came back to golf in 1923, he won a whole host of tournaments including the Canadian Open in 1926.

Because of his Scottish origins, he was a frequent visitor to the British Open during the era of Jones, Hagen and Sarazen but never quite won despite always travelling over early to get acclimatized and to learn the course.

His record of near misses was remarkable. From the time he tied in 1910 until the time he was 4th in the US Open of 1936 at Baltusrol, he came within 3 strokes of the winner in the British or US Opens nine times –

the US Opens of 1913, 1930, 1934; and the British Opens of 1923-5, 1930-2.

In the long run, he must be said to have lacked that indefinable something which separates the champions from the good players. He had the knack of being able to play a great last round when the chance of winning had almost gone but not such a

great one when the chance was there for the taking.

The most bitter example of the latter was in the British Open of 1925 when he needed 78 to win at Prestwick and took 82, being beaten by Jim Barnes.

An enthusiastic Scottish crowd obviously upset him through wanting too much the Scotsman to win. The effects on Smith were deep and lasting but he became one of the most consistent professionals in the world, swinging unusually heavy clubs with an easy grace and becoming a most popular figure on both sides of the Atlantic.

Smith, Margaret C. AMERICAN

b. 1937. Mexican Women's 1953; quarter-finalist US Women's Amateur 1954-5; British Ladies' 1956; Curtis Cup 1956; French Ladies' 1956

For three weeks in the summer of 1956 Wiffi Smith could do no wrong. Her defeat of Mary Patten Janssen by 8 and 7 in the final of the British followed her French victory and 2 points scored in the Curtis Cup match. She was still only 19. An abundance of freckles and a sunny disposition endeared her to spectators, and her splendidly solid physique enabled her to hit the ball a long way without undue effort. She turned professional in 1956. Her best finishes in the US Women's Open were 7th in 1958 and 6th in 1960. Illness hindered her from reaching her full potential as a professional.

Horton Smith

Macdonald Smith

Margaret C. Smith

Smith, William Dickson BRITISH

b. Glasgow 1918. Indian Amateur 1945; Scottish Amateur 1958; Walker Cup 1959; Portuguese Open Amateur 1967, 1970

Dick Smith holds the distinction of having won the amateur championships of three countries. He came into the Walker Cup side at Muirfield in 1959, when Jimmy Walker withdrew because of injury, and was beaten 5 and 4 in the singles by Jack Nicklaus. In 1957, when he had established himself as a Scottish International, Smith was leading amateur, and took joint 5th place overall in the British Open.

Smith, Willie AMERICAN

b. Carnoustie, Angus; d. 1915. US Open 1899, runner-up 1906, 1908, 3rd 1901

Willie Smith, a member of the famous Carnoustie golfing family, went to the United States as professional at the Midlothian CC and in 1899 won the US Open championship at the Baltimore CC.

His total of 315 (77, 82, 79, 77) gave him a winning margin of 11 strokes which has never been equalled. In 1907 he became professional to the New Mexico City CC where he remained until his death in 1915, the direct result of the fighting in the 1914-15 revolution when the clubhouse was badly shelled. Smith, refusing to leave, hid in the cellar but was in poor condition when found.

Smooth

Said of an even, rhythmic swing with no suspicion of a 'hit'. Gene Littler provides a perfect example of a smooth swing.

Smye, Catherine (Mrs P. G. MacCann) IRISH

b. Clonmel, Co. Tipperary, 1922. Irish Ladies' 1949, 1961, runner-up 1947, 1952, 1957, 1960; British Ladies' 1951; Curtis Cup 1952

Like all her generation in Ireland Catherine Smye was prevented from winning more honours by Philomena Garvey who defeated her in three finals. In her only Curtis Cup appearance she did not take part in the match. She represented Ireland in Home International matches for 15 years and was non-playing captain in 1965. A strong, workmanlike striker of the ball, she played, in company with many of her countrywomen, an attacking game, in which her command of the irons was outstanding.

Snead, Samuel Jackson AMERICAN

b. Hot Springs, Va., 1912. Ryder Cup 1937, 1939, 1947, 1949, 1951, 1953, 1955, 1959, (captain 1951, 1959, 1969); runner-up US Open 1937, 1947, 1953, joint runner-up 1949; Canadian Open 1938, 1940-1; Vardon Trophy 1938, 1949-50, 1955; US Masters 1949, 1952, 1954, runner-up 1939; USPGA 1942, 1949, 1951; British Open 1946

In many respects Sam Snead was the equal of the great golfing names of his year – he was born in 1912, the same year as Hogan and Nelson. He won the British Open in 1946, and both the USPGA Championship and the Masters three times. He had a swing which for fluency, rhythm and classic proportions has probably never been equalled. Yet his failure to win the US Open, in spite of coming very close to doing so, has always set him slightly apart from the big all-time names. Had he won he would have joined the elite few who have won the Big Four events; he has not done that, but his reputation of possessing the best swing in the world is a powerful compensation.

Snead took little time to reach the top. He became professional in 1933 and four years later he won five major tournaments, came within 2 strokes of winning the US Open at his first appearance in it, and finished 3rd leading money winner. The following year he became leading money winner in spite of a poor performance in the US Open. That championship became a bugbear for him; the nearest he came to winning it was in 1947 at the old St Louis CC. He made a birdie on the 72nd hole to tie Lew Worsham, but in the play-off he missed from 30 inches to keep the contest alive on the 18th green. That was not the only time he came within sight of winning the US Open. In 1939 he came to the 72nd hole at Philadelphia, needing a par 5 to win and a 6 to tie with Byron Nelson. Putting his third into a greenside bunker, took 2 to get out and 3 putts for an 8 which relegated him to 5th place. His failure to hold Worsham in the 1947 play-off might have deterred

Willie Smith

The smooth swing of Gene Littler

some from continuing the fight, but Snead's swing was one to last him a lifetime and he challenged twice more for the one title that still eluded him. In 1949 he had a chance to catch Cary Middlecoff at Medinah, needing a 33 on the final 9 holes; he failed by 1 stroke and ended in a tie for 2nd with Clayton Heafner. His fourth finish

Sam Snead

in 2nd place, at Oakmont in 1953, was more decisive, for he finished 6 strokes behind Ben Hogan, then at the height of his powers after his car accident.

Snead's victory in the British Open, though genuine enough, lacked the lustre of some later victories by his fellow countrymen. British golf had not recovered from the war years in the sense that the leading players lacked competitive edge. Snead made up his mind to play only at the last moment and arrived two days before the championship started. Yet his preparation was enough for he drove magnificently in rough weather. Snead had played once before in the British Open, in 1937, the year of the American Ryder Cup visit, when he finished 11th.

The best chance the British public had of watching his classical swing – it was once described as being as graceful as the spring of a cat – was his visit with the Ryder Cup team. His record in this event is one of the strongest of all Americans. He was a member of eight teams, including 1939 when the match was not played. Of the six singles he played he won all except one, and that was his dramatic defeat by Weetman in 1953 at Wentworth, when after being 4 up with 6 to play in his 36-hole match he lost five of the remaining holes and brought the United States to the brink of defeat. He captained the 1951 and 1959 teams and 10 years later he was again nominated to lead the Americans when they came to Royal Birkdale for the memorable tied match.

When all the long list of Snead's achievements – in 1971 he was credited with 131 victories including team events – has been recorded, it is the memory of his style that will endure longest. It was based on a well-proportioned and supremely supple body, and this allied with perfect timing, which seemed to come naturally to him, gave him immense length in his driving without any apparent effort. He played by the light of nature. In all his many victories he did not need to bring to his game the depth of concentration and intelligence that players like Hogan, Cotton and Nicklaus devoted to it; some have attributed to this lack of the highest golfing intelligence his failure to win the Open championship of his country.

Snead's putting was the first part of his game to let him down, and until the rule was changed he used to putt for a time standing astride the ball and with one hand right down the shaft gripping the club almost at the neck. But his game had astonishing endurance. More than 30 years after he had turned professional he was still showing up well in the prize lists. Thus in 1966 he was in

a tie for 6th place in the USPGA Championship, in 1967 he was tied 10th in the Masters, and the following year he was 9th in the Open, all this while in his mid-fifties. That same year he tied 4th in the Canadian Open and finished 2nd on his own in the Greater Milwaukee event. In the Canada Cup (later the World Cup), a team event between pairs of professionals, he had three different partners – Ben Hogan in 1956, Arnold Palmer in 1960, and Jimmy Demaret in 1961; on that last occasion he won the individual title in his 50th year. His total prize earnings are more than half a million dollars, but even more impressive is his extraordinary longevity as a golfer. In 1971 he finished tied 4th in one of the biggest tournaments of the year, the Westchester, was in contention in the 1972 US Masters until well into the final round and was still playing as well as ever in 1974, finishing equal 3rd in the USPGA.

Snell, David BRITISH
b. Whitwell, Nottinghamshire, 1933. British Professional Matchplay 1959; tied Rediffusion Tournament 1963; World (Canada) Cup 1965

Snell played on the British professional circuit with steady rather than spectacular success, though he won the Matchplay Championship at Birkdale in 1959 when he beat Harry Weetman in the final. He had a fine, free swing.

Social Sporting Club EGYPT
Alexandria. 18 holes; 6,393 yd (5,846 m); par 72

All grass, including the greens, with luxuriant fairway turf which survives lack of maintenance. It was renamed from the old Smouha course, situated within the Smouha racecourse. It is flat but has numerous trees and other features.

David Snell

Society of St Andrews Golfers see ROYAL AND ANCIENT GC OF ST ANDREWS

Socket see SHANK

Sole
That part of the club which rests on the ground when the player addresses the ball.

Somerville, Charles Ross CANADIAN
b. London, Ont., 1903. Canadian Amateur 1926, 1928, 1930-1, 1935, 1937; US Amateur 1932; semi-finalist British Amateur 1938; Canadian Seniors' GA 1960-1, 1965-6

An athlete of renown in Canadian football, ice hockey and cricket, Sandy Somerville became Canada's finest amateur golfer of his time, playing partly during the Bob Jones era. His iron play was acknowledged to rank with the best in the world. A powerful figure on the golf course, he was accustomed to play with little conversation and intense concentration. Such was his aggressive style that he was seldom known to leave a putt short of the hole.

He became the second foreign winner in history of the United States Amateur Championship. To his six victories in the Canadian Amateur Championship must be added four occasions on which he was runner-up. Among his other triumphs were four in the Ontario Amateur and one in the Manitoba Amateur Championship. Bob Jones wrote that his fourth win in his Grand Slam year of 1930 was made possible by one break in his first-round match against Somerville in the United States Amateur Championship. Jones holed for a birdie from 8 ft on the 7th hole to go 1 up, and he felt that had he not managed to do so, Somerville would have made his 7-footer and won the hole and the tide of play might have gone the other way.

It was not only as a player that Somerville made a great contribution to golf in Canada. He served for many years as a governor of the Royal Canadian Golf Association and was its president in 1957. In 1969-70 he was president of the Canadian Seniors' Golf Association.

Sorenson, Carol AMERICAN
b. Janesville, Wis., 1942. Western Amateur 1962; semi-finalist US Women's Amateur 1963; British Ladies' 1964; Curtis Cup 1964, 1966; Trans-Mississippi Women's 1964

A bronzed blonde from Arizona State University, Carol Sorenson completed a most successful year in 1964 by defeating Bridget Jackson at the 37th in the final of the British Ladies' at Prince's. In 1962, on her way to gaining a place in the Curtis Cup

team, she became the Women's Collegiate Champion, and she is a four-time winner of the State championship of her native Wisconsin. Now Mrs Flenniken, she plays only an occasional tournament.

Sota, Ramón SPANISH

b. Santander, 1939. Spanish Open 1963; Dutch Open 1966, 1971; Portuguese Open 1963, 1969, 1970; French Open 1965; Algarve Open 1971; Italian Open 1971

Through sheer application Sota worked himself into the position of being the leading professional on the Continent. He enjoyed his most successful year in 1971. He learned golf the hard way as a caddie at the Santander course with little chance of sound coaching, so that when he first tried his chance in a wider competitive field his long game was not good enough, although endless practice had given him a strong short game. Sota's serious-minded approach to golf and the attention he gives to every detail of grip and stance reflects the modesty of his origins and the hardship endured by his family in his youth. He first made his mark in winning his native championship in 1963 at a time when the Miguel brothers reigned supreme in Spain. The same year he and Sebastián Miguel came within 3 strokes of winning the World (Canada) Cup in Paris but were beaten, largely by a wonderful last round from Nicklaus for the United States. Sota tried his luck in the United States, but found the going there too tough for a foreigner, even though the experience has since stood him in good stead. His best performance was to finish tied 6th in the 1965 US Masters, the best position ever reached by a Continental player. He played in 1966 on the Caribbean tour with marked success, but with the onset of bad rheumatism he returned to Europe and after two years recovering his health and his putting,

he appeared with renewed vigour on the European circuit. His victory in the 1965 French Open owed much to a third round of 62 which lowered the record of St-Nom-la-Bretèche by 6 strokes, and in the course of which he scored an albatross 2 at the 16th. In the World Cup he has a fine record, having finished 3rd in Madrid in 1965 and

twice 4th in the individual rating. In 1972 during the international matches of the Double Diamond tournament he made history by becoming the first professional to be penalized for slow play in Britain, a decision which caused much resentment among his fellow countrymen and which hastened his decision to leave the tour. He was Spanish Professional champion four times.

Sotogrande GC SPAIN

Sotogrande, Costa del Sol. 36 holes; par 74
Club de Golf Sotogrande, about 22 miles from Gibraltar with a view of two continents, was the first course in Spain to be built as the centre of a real-estate development. The club was founded in 1964 and the course designed by the American, Robert Trent Jones, from a sandy wilderness and a forest of cork trees. Several artificial lakes were added. Jones's course embodies the American concept of design probably to a greater extent than anywhere else in Europe and the result is a spectacular course of great merit

Carol Sorenson playing in the British Ladies' Championship, 1964

Top, Ramón Sota

Above, Sotogrande GC, with the Rock of Gibraltar in the background

which has become popular with visitors from all over the world. A second 18 holes were added after a few years. From the back tees, the course is on the grand scale though in the Spanish Open Championship which was held there in 1966, the winner, Roberto de Vicenzo, had a second round of 66 which included three putts from about 5 yd on the last green. Chalets in which golfers can stay adjoin the clubhouse and a short distance away the Sotogrande Tennis Club provides equally pleasant accommodation.

Souchak, Mike AMERICAN
b. Berwick, Pa., 1927. Ryder Cup 1959, 1961

Mike Souchak turned professional in 1952

after leaving the US Navy and looked as though he would win many major championships. He was a likeable bear of a man with massive strength and a fine rhythmic swing, who won several tournaments between 1955 and 1961. His consistently good showing earned him a place in the Ryder Cup teams of 1959 and 1961. Although he never won a major championship, he still holds the PGA record for the lowest individual 9-hole score in tournament play. He achieved both in the 1955 Texas Open on the Brackebridge Park course in San Antonio, putting together rounds of 60, 68, 64, 65 for a total of 257. It was in his first round of 60 that he played the last 9 holes in 27 (2,4,4,3,3,3,3,3,2).

South Africa
As in other countries the origin of the game is traceable to the Scots and the army. The first recorded golf was in 1882 when a 6-hole affair was started at Waterloo Green adjoining the British military camp at Wynberg, near Cape Town. The ground was rough and stony, the greens uneven, but it was golf,

and within a few years there were other equally rough courses at Port Elizabeth, Kimberley and Johannesburg. Within 20 years of that date there were at least 50 courses of sorts on the Rand alone. General Torrens, not content with a few holes on Waterloo Green, was also instrumental in forming the Cape GC – now the Royal Cape – and mother club of the country's golf. Golf balls, clubs and a hole cutter were obtained from North Berwick in Scotland; the first balls to arrive were the Eclipse 'gutties' together with some wooden niblicks, and in 1886 the first recorded monthly medal in the Union was won by the General with a score of 94. Lieutenant Gardiner of the Royal Scots was 2nd on 99, and such were the

rigours of the course that three competitors took 144 each to complete the round. Interest in the Cape club, which languished after the departure of the Royal Scots, was revived by the appearance of the East Yorkshire regiment, and by the interest in the game of such personalities as Sir David Gill, the Astronomer Royal. In those early days Rondebosch Common was open to the public and it was not unusual for children to play hopscotch on the greens, lovers to wander across the line of play, and for carts and wagons to use the ground indiscriminately until the Rondebosch club obtained a lease of the ground in 1911. To the Royal Durban club belongs the honour of having the oldest permanent home for the game, since 1902.

Mike Souchak

South Africa: Drakensberg Gardens course. Natal

In Port Elizabeth there were even earlier signs of golf, but in contrast Johannesburg made a troubled start, courses repeatedly being laid down too close to the centre of a quickly expanding mining and industrial area. The early established courses at Durban and Port Elizabeth were of the inland type; development of a links-type course was first seen at Port Alfred. These were followed by the construction of the Durban CC and Humewood which have since developed into links courses of the highest quality.

South Africa was slow to establish a controlling body for the game. Not until the South African championships were held at Potchefstroom in 1909 was it decided to form

growth of grass, and it was only in the second half of this century with the installation of watering systems that all-grass courses have been possible in parts of the Orange Free State. In 1913 the South African championships were held for the last time on sand greens.

With South Africans distinguishing themselves now in all corners of the world, it seems strange that some 25 years passed after the start of the game before a championship was won by a South African. For 30 years Scottish professionals dominated the South African Open, as they had done in the United States, while a group of Scottish-born amateurs that included such outstanding names as H. M. Ballingall, J. A. W. Prentice,

championships have been lost, but the first of them, sponsored by a committee of club captains, was believed to have been at Port Elizabeth in 1893. In those days the Amateur was the important event, and the professionals seem to have been invited to the championship and played in a series of matches. Such professionals as there were made their mark – prominent among them Laurie Waters, a young assistant to Tom Morris at St Andrews who emigrated for his health's sake. With his flat St Andrews swing and his little pigtail wave of the clubhead at the top he won four championships between 1903 and 1920, but his most important contribution was his construction work on a number of courses and introducing grass tees

the South African Golf Union. Up to that time only a minority of clubs could boast of grass greens, and sand greens were generally in use. The blue ground from the Kimberley diamond mines provided a specially suitable surface and was in demand by clubs throughout the country. Irregular rainfall in the central areas of the Union restricted the

and H. Gordon Stewart monopolized the Amateur. The first home-born professional to break through was Fred Jangle, an ex-caddie from Cape Town with a free, full swing; and only twice in the first 27 years of the Amateur did South African-born players win – J. R. Southey in 1904 and Dr E. L. Steyn in 1910. Early records of both these

and greens. Two other Scots, George and John Fotheringham, won the Open six times in seven years from 1908, before moving on to the United States.

They were followed by two other brothers, Jock and Sid Brews, sons of a professional at Minchinhampton, who between them won the Open on 12 occasions between 1921 and

South Africa: the Tzaneen golf course.
East Transvaal

1952. Sid won the title for the eighth time in the latter year at the age of 52 as evidence of his sustained capacity for the game.

Sid Brews was the first South African professional to make his mark abroad when he was runner-up to Henry Cotton in the British Open at Sandwich in 1934. A beautiful iron player, he won several Continental championships and one tournament in the United States.

It was the arrival first of Bobby Locke and then Gary Player that made South Africa prominent in the international scene. They were the first foreign players in the United States to break the monotonous supremacy that American professionals had established on their own courses.

Only with the advent of Gary Player was there a general rise in the standard of golf in the Republic, both in the amateur and professional ranks. Player was an inspiration to the game by personal example and his readiness to encourage and help others.

In the international sphere South Africa supported the World Cup and the Eisenhower Trophy from their inauguration and had the satisfaction of Player and Harold Henning winning the former event in Spain in 1965 and finishing runners-up to Nicklaus and Palmer at Tokyo the following year.

A number of South African professionals compete on the world circuits and two young players, Bobby Cole, who won the British Amateur before turning professional, and Dale Hayes are watched with close interest as possible successors to Locke and Player. Both are players of good potential.

The South African Indian golfer, 'Papwa' Sewgolum, competed in the British Open and won the Dutch Open Championship in 1959-60 and 1964. He is famous for his left-hand-below-right grip.

In recent years a successful professional circuit has been established in the Republic for some 10 weeks in December, January and February. It attracts wide support from Britain and America by players seizing the opportunity of playing in the sun while so many of their home courses are weather bound.

Altogether there were 325 golf courses in South Africa in 1972 of which about 90 have sand greens. There were 39,000 amateurs registered with the South African Golf Union and approximately 10,000 under the auspices of the South African Ladies' Golf Union.

Southerndown GC WALES
nr Bridgend (Pen-y-bont ar Ogwr), Glamorgan. 18 holes; 6,750 yd (6,172 m)

Southerndown, as its name suggests, is a classic example of downland golf. It is situ-

ated on Ogmore Down, a bold headland overlooking the Ogmore River, the Ewenny and the sea, and dates from 1905 when John Alexander, an auctioneer in Cardiff, was largely responsible for the formation of the club. The course was laid out under the direction of W. Fernie from Penarth and was later revised and improved by Herbert Fowler, Willie Park Jr and H. S. Colt. Its main defence on such an exposed perch is the wind but in summer the bracken lining the fairways is thick enough to make control essential.

Southerndown is a regular choice for Welsh championships and has also housed major professional events but its most important connection with Welsh golf has been

through the Duncan family. Tony Duncan, for many years the mainspring of the Welsh team, learned to play there as a small boy and has retained a great affection for the course. In 1959 he inaugurated the Duncan Putter, a 72-hole medal played at Southerndown every Easter as a means of encouraging young Welsh players and providing early-season competition for the more established.

Southern Hills CC USA
Tulsa, Okla.

Tulsa is a city typical of the American Southwest, founded at the turn of the century when oil was discovered on the opposite side of the Arkansas River at Red Fork. The

Top, Southerndown GC

Above, Southern Hills CC

city is probably the only one anywhere built on the site of a former Indian community, and took the name of that settlement which in the Creek tongue was called a *tulsa* or council. Like most oil towns, Tulsa became a boom town, but it went on to develop into a sound, rich city of 500,000 people, half of whom may be connected with the petroleum industry. A friendly city, though, like its favourite native son, Will Rogers.

In the midst of the Depression – in fact, right at the rock bottom of it, in 1933 – the civic leaders of Tulsa decided they wanted a place to play golf. That was all that was needed to produce Southern Hills with its handsome, extensive clubhouse and its course of championship calibre fashioned by Perry Maxwell. The tournament that brought the course to national attention was the US Open of 1958. Tommy Bolt, playing exquisite golf in all four rounds, won that Open with a total of 283. Only two other men broke 290 – Gary Player with 287 and Julius Boros with 289. As the scoring suggests, Southern Hills was a fearsome test that week. It took driving of the highest class to keep the ball on the narrow fairways set up by the USGA, and those fairways were bordered by Bermuda-grass rough that was much more punishing than the officials intended or perhaps appreciated. In the extreme heat, the greens came very close to burning out, and to prevent this the USGA allowed them to be syringed with water at certain periods while the Open was actually in progress. It can get almost intolerably hot in the Southwest, and during that championship the temperature rose close to 100°F, with strong hot winds blowing in off Oklahoma's open spaces. The course is at its best in late spring or early autumn, and that best is very good indeed. The course is over gently undulating parkland. The first 9 return to the clubhouse, and only at the opening and closing holes of the two halves are there gradients.

In more recent years, two other national championships have been staged at Southern Hills. In 1965, when Bob Murphy won the first strokeplay Amateur Championship there, his score was rather high, 291, although the course was hardly as severe as it had been for Bolt's Open. For the 1970 PGA Championship, it was set up on the lenient side, and this time the scoring was suitably low, Dave Stockton compiling a winning total of 279 which included a superb 66 in the third round.

Southport and Ainsdale GC ENGLAND
Southport, Lancashire. 18 holes; 6,452 yd (5,900 m)

The South Lancashire coast is renowned for its strip of duneland country on which many fine golf courses are built. A traveller by train from Liverpool to Southport could count half a dozen on either side of the line, Southport and Ainsdale among them. The club came into being in 1906 with a little 9-hole course later absorbed in a housing estate. A move to the site of the present course was soon made and in 1923 James Braid planned a new lay-out. Southport and Ainsdale quickly gained a reputation for itself and has housed many professional events – principally the old Dunlop-Southport Tournament. Its most famous link with golfing history lies in its staging of the 1933 and 1937 Ryder Cup matches. In 1933 the British won one of their rare victories, but before another enormous crowd, the Americans gained their revenge in 1937. More recently, Southport and Ainsdale has been used as one of the qualifying places when the British Open has been held at Royal Birkdale and the club has continued to produce its own fine players such as David Marsh, twice English champion, Dixie Rawlinson and Geoff Roberts, English champion in 1951.

Spade Mashie
An obsolete hickory-shafted iron a little stronger than a mashie niblick. It corresponds roughly to the modern 6 iron.

Spain
Golf began in Spanish territory in 1891 with the formation of the Las Palmas GC in the Canary Islands, but it was another 13 years before it invaded the mainland and the Madrid Polo GC became established on the site of the old Castellaña racecourse. In 1914 the Madrid Polo Club moved to Puerta de Hierro and became the Real Club de la Puerta de Hierro, the setting for a great

many of the early Spanish championships.

Things were also on the move by this time in the north where the Real Sociedad de Golf de Neguri was founded near Bilbao in 1911 and the Real Club de Golf de San Sebastián 'Jaizkibel' at Fuenterrabia in 1910 but generally the game developed slowly. For one reason it was practised only by a wealthy minority and for another it was interrupted in many places by the Spanish Civil War. By 1954, when El Prat was built in Barcelona, there were still only 14 clubs in existence. By 1970 the number had increased to 35 with the promise of at least a dozen more by 1975.

The country steadily became more golf minded, the Spanish professionals made their mark in European competition and two big international events were held in Madrid, the World (Canada) Cup at Hipica Española Club de Campo in 1965, and the World Amateur Team Championship (Eisenhower Trophy) at Puerta de Hierro in 1970. In addition, a small band of enthusiasts began the Madrid Open Championship which was officially recognized by

Spain, *above,* the course of Atalaya Park Hotel on the Costa del Sol: the opening exhibition is in progress with Peter Alliss putting on the 17th green

Top, a spade mashie, or lofting iron of 1700

the British PGA in 1972. In the same year Spain's supremacy in Europe was emphasized when their team finished third in the world amateur team championship in Buenos Aires. However, the chief reason for the increase in the number of courses was not so much a spread in the popularity of the game, which remains very largely a pursuit of the rich, but its effectiveness as a means of attracting tourists.

With a virtual guarantee of sunshine, the east coast of Spain from Sotogrande in the south to Pals (Gerona) in the north has seen many highly financed projects involving the building of courses, hotels, apartments and bungalows which are sold or let to overseas visitors. Some courses are among the best in Europe; one or two stand even sterner comparison.

Spearman, Mrs A. D. see HARRIS, MRS MARLEY

Square

Short for all square: position in a match when two players or two sides are level. Of a clubface: set or swung through the ball at right angles to the line of aim, or to the line of swing. Of a swing: having the clubface held through the backswing, downswing and at impact at the natural angle, in relation to hands, wrists and arms, in which it was held at the address. The clubface is not 'shut', 'opened' or 'rolled'.

Sri Lanka (Ceylon)

Golf began in Sri Lanka in 1882 when the British founded the Royal Colombo Club, which has remained the most revered name in Ceylonese golf. Also well-known are Nuwara Eliya, in the hills among tea plantations, which has shared the Ceylon Amateur and Ceylon Ladies' with Royal Colombo since these championships began in 1920; and the Kandy Club at Peredeniya. The most famous name among Sri Lanka's golfers is probably that of W. P. Fernando, winner of the Ceylon Amateur. His wife also won the Ceylon Ladies' Championship twice.

S.S.S. see STANDARD SCRATCH SCORE

Stableford

A popular system of scoring by points formulated by Dr Frank B. Stableford with the primary intention of securing a more accurate reflection of the standard of play in bogey competitions held over difficult courses.

The Stableford is a form of stroke competition in which play is against a fixed score

at each hole. The reckoning is made by points awarded at each hole in relation to the fixed score, which is usually par. Thus:

hole done in 1 over fixed score	1 point
hole done in fixed score	2 points
hole done in 1 under fixed score	3 points
hole done in 2 under fixed score	4 points
hole done in 3 under fixed score	5 points

The winner is the competitor who scores the highest number of points. In handicap singles events, seven-eighths of handicap is allowed, strokes being taken at the holes indicated and the points assessed on the net score.

As a relief from the more strenuous exercise of medal play, the system has been widely played since the first competition under Stableford rules took place on the Wallasey Links, Cheshire, England, on 16 May 1932.

Dr Stableford served with distinction in his younger days as a surgeon attached to the RAMC in the South African War. He was also a fine golfer and on returning to Britain in 1907 he acquired a handicap of plus 1 and was a semi-finalist in the Welsh Amateur Championship. He joined the Royal Liverpool and Wallasey clubs in 1914 and continued his membership at Wallasey until his death in 1959 at the age of 89.

Stacy, Hollis AMERICAN

b. Savannah, Ga., 1954. US Girls' Junior 1969-71; Curtis Cup 1972

Hollis Stacy's achievement was unique in twice successfully defending her title in the US Girls' Junior Championship, a highly competitive field which included the reigning US Champion, 16-year-old Laura Baugh. She has an upright swing, not perhaps seen at its best on the British windswept links in 1972.

Stance

The position of the player's feet when addressing the ball.

Hollis Stacy in the 1972 Curtis Cup

Standard Scratch Score (S.S.S.)

The Standard Scratch Score is the score in which a scratch player is expected to go round the course, playing from the medal tees, in summer conditions. The S.S.S. is not allocated among the individual holes. *See also* Course Rating and Par.

Stanton, Robert James AUSTRALIAN

b. Sydney, N.S.W., 1946. Australian Dunlop International 1966; German Open 1966

A young Australian professional who went to seek his fortune on the American circuit. He qualified for his USPGA player's card in Florida in 1966, the year in which he won the Dunlop International Tournament and the German Open. After winning three tournaments in Australia in 1967, he started a run of success in the United States during which he twice finished 2nd and twice 3rd in tournaments in 1968 and 1970. He had another good year in the United States in 1969, but 1971 was a lean year for him when he won only $4,691 in America.

Stanwich Club USA

Greenwich, Conn. 18 holes

The Stanwich Club, it will be noted, has neither the word golf nor county in its title, which is an indication of this comparatively new organization's character. Its prospectus, circulated in 1965, declared that the growing need for a new club in Greenwich, Conn., had led a group of prominent residents to create Stanwich. This document set forth minimum requirements that had to be and were met in the construction of course and clubhouse, and if it had not also stated minimum requirements for membership, they were implied.

The group of prominent residents, all rated in the tycoon class by the news magazines, bought an old estate with an attractive mansion surrounded by 184 acres of naturally beautiful land; from its highest point stretches of Long Island Sound may be seen. Many Stanwich members retain membership also in other attractive and exclusive clubs in the area.

The course was built by William Gordon, a man of long experience who made excellent use of streams, ponds, and the many fine trees, to lay out an interesting 18 holes which have the look of becoming a real test of golf as the course ages. The property is quite hilly, but the holes are so well arranged that there is only one real climb. The club sits in a secluded spot well back from Stanwich Road on the high ground to the west of the Merritt Parkway. Billy Farrell, son of Johnny Farrell, the former US Open Champion, is the professional.

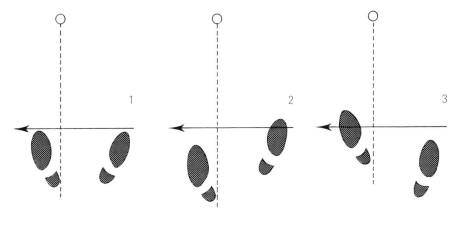

Stewards

Those people appointed by a tournament committee responsible for special duties, usually crowd control. They generally wear some kind of identifying uniform.

Stewart, J. E. Douglas see ROLLAND, DOUGLAS

Still, Kenneth A. AMERICAN
b. Tacoma, Wash., 1935. Ryder Cup 1969; Florida Citrus 1969; Greater Milwaukee Open 1969; Kaiser Open 1970; semi-finalist USPGA Matchplay 1971

Still had thoughts of becoming a baseball player but turned to golf as a professional in 1953. It was not until 1960 that he tried his

luck on the tour and it took him several years to make a name for himself. The third of his three tour victories came in the Kaiser Open after a sudden-death play-off with Lee Trevino and Bert Yancey.

Stirling, Alexa (Mrs W. G. Fraser) AMERICAN
US Women's Amateur 1916, 1919-20, runner-up 1921, 1923, 1925; Canadian Women's Open 1920, 1934, runner-up 1922, 1925

Three American National Amateur Championships in succession, but not consecutive years, owing to the break caused by World War I, measure the greatness of her golfing abilities. Of Scottish parentage, she was coached by Stewart Maiden, and played with a neighbour, Bobby Jones. This trio has immortalized Atlanta, Ga., in golfing annals. Like her mentor, and her great colleague, she was a stylist, and set new standards in the women's sphere. She could play the pitch shot in a truly professional manner, was an outstandingly fine putter, and was never known to be flustered.

Staying Down

Completing the shot fully after impact, and driving the clubhead through on the intended line. The opposite of lifting the head, quitting, or 'coming off' the ball.

Stephens, Frances see SMITH, MRS FRANCES

Stevenson, Charlotte (Mrs J. B. Watson; Mrs E. C. Beddows) BRITISH
b. Edinburgh 1887. Scottish Ladies' 1920, 1921-2, runner-up 1923, 1950; Curtis Cup 1932

Charlotte Stevenson played hockey for Scotland between 1905 and 1912, before representing her country at golf. She won her first medal, a bronze, in the Scottish Ladies' in 1905, and her 11th, a silver, 45 years later. She regularly represented Scotland in the Home Internationals over a period of 38 years (1913-51), during which she captained her country five times and played in 60 matches, winning 37 games in them. Her span of county golf extended from 1909 to 1966.

She was also four times winner of the

Veteran Women's Championship – 1947, 1949, 1950-1.

She lives at Gullane, on the edge of the course, and her unabated enthusiasm and zest for golf has enabled her to enjoy an exceptional innings as a first-class player. Even now, in her eighties, she plays most days and regularly takes lessons.

Top, a series of diagrams to illustrate the stance for various strokes: 1. square; 2. open; 3. closed, all for drives; 4. long irons; 5. medium irons; 6. short irons

Above, Robert Stanton

Kenneth A. Still

She visited Europe in 1921, when she was undisputed leader of women's golf in North America, as holder of both the US and the Canadian titles. Unluckily she drew Miss Cecil Leitch in the first round of the British Ladies' Championship at Turnberry, and in a match played in rough weather lost at the 16th. She went to Paris for the French Open at Fontainebleau, won the medal in the qualifying round, and continued to the semi-final where she was defeated by Joyce Wethered.

In 1917, with Elaine Rosenthal, Perry Adair, and Bobby Jones, she toured the Eastern United States giving charity exhibition matches which raised $150,000 for the Red Cross.

Stockton, Dave AMERICAN
b. San Bernardino, Cal., 1941
USPGA 1970; Ryder Cup 1971

Dave Stockton, a direct descendant of Richard Stockton who signed the Declaration of Independence for New Jersey, and the son of a golf professional, earned a golf scholarship to the University of California and graduated in 1964 with a degree in business management. That same year he joined the professional tour; he made a modest beginning but in 1967 won the Colonial, added two more victories (the Cleveland and Milwaukee Opens) in 1968 – and over $100,000 in prize money – and in 1970 captured his first major title. This was the USPGA Championship at Southern

Hills, Tulsa, with a total of 279, 2 strokes better than Arnold Palmer and Bob Murphy. Victory means a great deal in the PGA Championship – particularly in providing free exemption into PGA tournaments – and Stockton quickly became one of the steadiest players in America, winning the Massachusetts Golf Classic and qualifying for a

place in the American Ryder Cup team.

Storey, Edward Francis BRITISH
b. 1901. Runner-up British Amateur 1924; Walker Cup 1924, 1926, 1928; tied President's Putter 1926; leading amateur British Open 1938

Eustace Storey, as he was generally known, was only 23 when he reached the final of the British Amateur, being beaten 3 and 2 by E. W. E. (later Sir Ernest) Holderness, then at the height of his powers. This performance earned Storey a place in the Walker Cup team and later the same year he became an England international. He also captained the Cambridge University team. He was a strong painstaking player, full of progressive ideas and a great experimenter. In later years he adopted a curious and awkward-looking putting stance which he maintained solved his own problems, although he had no imitator.

Stout, James Alfred BRITISH
b. Whitehaven, Cumberland, 1896; d. 1973. English Amateur 1928; Walker Cup 1930, 1932

Stout was a dentist at Bridlington, in Yorkshire, a big and strong golfer who played only infrequently in important events. Apart from his English championship win his best performance was in 1932 when, at Brookline, Mass., he halved with Jess Sweetser in the Walker Cup match. Two years later at Sandwich, Kent, he was the

victim of a remarkable second-round recovery by Don K. Moe of America in the Walker Cup match.

Stowe, Charles BRITISH
b. Sedgley, Staffordshire, 1909. Walker Cup 1938, 1947; runner-up British Amateur 1948, semi-finalist 1937, 1939; English Open Amateur Strokeplay 1948, 1953

One of the victorious British Walker Cup team of 1938 who contributed his share in the singles by defeating Charles Kocsis by 2 and 1. He was a player of uncertain brilliance, immensely powerful and on his day an exceptional iron player. With the 1953 Walker Cup team away in the United States, Stowe entered the English Strokeplay Championship (Brabazon Trophy) and won it in the most convincing manner with a splendid display of approach shots from his quick, flashing swing. He was a rapid player who could not easily stand delays and let people know it with a sharp tongue, but there were many who thought he should have had more than two Walker Cup matches. At all events, the World War II came at a time to hinder a player of great promise.

Stranahan, Frank R. AMERICAN
b. Toledo, Ohio, 1922. US North and South Amateur 1946, 1949, 1952; US Western Amateur 1946, 1949, 1951, 1953; joint runner-up British Open 1947, 1953; Canadian Amateur 1947-8; Walker Cup 1947, 1949, 1951; British Amateur 1948, 1950; runner-up US Amateur 1950; Tam O'Shanter World's Amateur 1950-4

Son of a sparking-plug millionaire, Stranahan achieved fame in world amateur golf not by stylish methods but by almost obsessive devotion to detail, a passion for physical fitness, and through the will to win that has characterized so many American sportsmen. His swing was almost mechanical in its execution, but he had great strength of mind and body, and maintained fitness by daily exercises with weight-lifting equipment that even accompanied him on trips abroad. Stranahan was twice runner-up for the British Open title as an amateur. In 1947 at Hoylake he was within inches of holing an iron shot at the 72nd hole which would have given him a tie with Fred Daly; and at Carnoustie in 1953 he had a final round of 69, against Ben Hogan's 68, to share 2nd place with three professionals. Stranahan turned professional in 1954 at the age of 32, but surprisingly had comparatively little success in prize-money golf. But his amateur record, particularly his five-year monopoly of the Tam O'Shanter World Amateur

Alexa Stirling

Dave Stockton

title, is sufficient to give him an exalted place among amateur golfers.

Strath Brothers, The BRITISH

b. St Andrews, Fife: Andrew 1836-1868; David 1840-1879

Andrew and David Strath belonged to the early professional era begun by Allan Robertson. Andrew won the 1865 British Open at Prestwick. David, a great friend of Young Tom Morris, was considered to be the better player on account of his effortless style, although he never emulated his brother's feat. David was involved in 1876 in one of the strangest incidents in the championship's history. On a day when the course was unusually heavy, he appeared to have the championship won after 13 holes of the second round but at the 14th his drive hit and felled a player, an upholsterer named Hutton, who was going to the 5th. Though Hutton recovered almost immediately from the blow, the incident so upset David that he dropped a stroke both there and at the 15th.

Two 5s, par figures in those days at the 17th and 18th, would still have given him victory but the 18th cost him 6, and after he tied with Bob Martin on 176, some of Martin's supporters asked for Strath's disqualification, claiming that he had played his approach to the 17th before the couple in front had left the green. It was typical of the casual atmosphere of championships in those days that the committee could not decide

whether to sustain or overrule the objection. Strath, believing that the issue should be decided before a play-off, refused to turn up and the title was awarded to Martin. Soon after David moved to North Berwick, became ill and died on a voyage to Australia. His brother, Andrew, went to Prestwick as greenkeeper. He was also a good clubmaker

but he too died young. A third brother, George, became Troon's first professional and later one of the first to emigrate to the United States. The Strath bunker, strategically placed to guard the right-hand side of the 11th green on the Old Course, and the graveyard of many hopes, commemorates the name of one of St Andrews's most famous families.

Streit, Mrs Marlene Stewart CANADIAN

b. Cereal, Alta., 1934. Canadian Ladies' Close 1951-7, 1963, 1968; Canadian Ladies' Open 1951, 1954-6, 1958-9, 1963, 1968-9, 1972-3; British Ladies' 1953; US Women's National Intercollegiate 1956; US North and South 1956; US Women's Amateur 1956; low amateur US Women's Open 1961; Australian Ladies' 1963

Canada's pre-eminent woman golfer of all time and one of the great woman players of the world. Only slightly over 5 ft tall, she has always possessed a compact and beautiful swing that has produced golf of amazing consistency from tee to green. This engendered a confidence which, when coupled with her courage and fierce determination, resulted in greatness. It was from Fonthill, Ont., where she had grown up, that Marlene Stewart burst into prominence at the age of 17 by winning the Ontario Junior Championship, the Ontario Ladies', the Canadian Ladies' Close and the Canadian Ladies' Championships, all in the same year. Combining her education at Rawlins College in

Florida with year-round golf, she went on to win the national championship of her own country a record 10 times, and also to win the national championships of three other countries as well – Britain, the United States and Australia. Her golfing accomplishments are too numerous to list; they include four victories in each of the Ontario Ladies' Championship, the United States Mixed Foursome Championship and the Helen Lee Doherty Championship, and a win in the United States National Two Ball Championship. Twice she has been voted Canada's Outstanding Athlete of the Year, and five times Canadian Woman Athlete of the Year. She has been elected to both the Canadian Golf Hall of Fame and Sports Hall of Fame.

She married in 1957 and has two daughters.

Stringer, Mable E. BRITISH

b. 1869; d. Walmer, Kent, 1958

A pioneer during the early days of the Ladies' Golf Union, in which she worked as an assistant honorary secretary. Mabel Stringer helped in founding four golfing associations, the Parliamentary (1911), Legal (1912), United Services (1912), Veterans' (1921), and the Girls' Golfing Society (1923). While editor of the Sports Section of *The Gentlewoman*, she persuaded the publishers to sponsor a championship for girl golfers. The inaugural championship was arranged for 1914, but had to be deferred until 1919. It has subsequently evolved into the British Girls' Amateur Open Championship.

A scratch golfer for many years, her autobiography *Golfing Reminiscences* is a delightful record of the game from the 1880s to the early 1920s. The last golfing event of importance at which she was present was the Curtis Cup match at Prince's, Sandwich, in 1956, when she was 87.

Stroke

A forward movement of the club made with the intention of hitting the ball. A stroke does not necessarily move the ball.

Stroke Index

A chart showing at which holes players receive their handicap strokes. It is usually shown on the scorecard. It applies in matchplay when there is a difference of handicap and in Stableford competitions where a player receives seven-eighths of his handicap. A club committee decides the arrangement of stroke index and usually bases it on the relative difficulty of the holes, and on the desire to balance the stroke index between the two 9s.

Frank R. Stranahan

Mrs Marlene Streit

Strokeplay

A competition in which the player's total strokes for the round are recorded and compared with the scores of other players in the field. Usually reckoned a more testing form than matchplay and therefore as a better indication of ability. *See also* Medal play.

Strong

The opposite of short; a ball struck too powerfully; one that travels too far.

Stuffy

A slang term used of an excessively steady player who gives little away, who rarely hits a destructive stroke or does anything stupid. Probably a limited player who rarely gambles but a consistent one who makes a frustrating opponent and is difficult to beat.

Stuttgart see MONSHEIM GC

Stutt, John Hamilton BRITISH

b. Renfrewshire, 1924

Hamilton Stutt has been engaged in golf-course design and construction since about 1946, having graduated in botany at St Andrews where he played golf and tennis for the university. His initial concern was mainly with construction but this aroused his interest in design and, after studying under John Morrison and P. Mackenzie Ross, he became a leading architect and a founder of the British Association of Golf Course Architects.

Courses for which he has done work include Carlyon Bay GC, Cornwall; Fort William GC, Inverness-shire; Prestwick, Ayrshire; the Costa Brava GC, Spain.

Styles and Methods

In his classic work, *The Art of Golf*, 1887, Sir Walter Simpson wrote: 'Do I maintain, then, the reader may ask, that everyone ought to have the same style? By no means; on the contrary, for you or me to model ourselves on a champion is about as profitless as to copy out Hamlet in the hope of becoming Shakespeare. There is no more fruitful source of bad golf than to suppose that there is some best style for each individual which must be searched out by him if he is to get the best results out of himself. In a broad and general way, each player ought to have and has, a style which is the reflection of himself, his build, his mind, the age at which he began and his previous habits.'

Although hundreds of instructional books have claimed that their message is new, wiser or better, the simple answer is that little has changed. No matter what method Palmer, Sanders or Player may choose, the only purpose of the golf swing is to present

the club to, and move it through, the ball square to the target at maximum speed. The good swings are those that do it again and again. That is the creed on which John Jacobs bases his teachings, but there are one or two fundamentals of nearly all good swings, such as the grip and stance, (qq.v.), which offer a better chance of achieving elusive perfection. Method is a word used loosely to describe a player's manner of striking and swinging, whereas style is more than just that. It is a combination of several factors: mechanical efficiency, grace, balance, smoothness, rhythm and consistency. Everyone is envious of a classic style, and each generation has had its shining examples. Allan Robertson, Harry Vardon, Bobby Jones, Sam Snead, Gene Littler, Tom Weiskopf – all have come closer to what most people regard as technical perfection than their contemporaries, and have excelled as a result of it. They have maintained the beliefs of Willie Park who in the last century declared: 'In the majority of cases it is hardly possible to play a good game unless you have a good style'; but a good stylist may not necessarily be a successful golfer because style takes no account of temperament, dedication, or competitive flair.

In modern professional golf there are many who have made a rich living out of the game without an attractive method, but they are a product of their times and, if the technical differences that have taken place in the last century are studied, it is clear that

it is changes in equipment that have exercised the great influence on those methods. Most people would agree that modern equipment has made the game easier since the days when red-coated or Norfolk-jacketed golfers had to coax the feathery or gutty ball in playing conditions which now seem primitive. The game then was more of

an art than a science, but contrary to the widely held belief that the nature of their clothing was restrictive, photographs of the old masters generally reveal swings which were full, flowing and uninhibited. The full swing was the logical outcome of the equipment. Thick grips were needed on hickory-shafted clubs to absorb the shock of hard hitting which was demanded far more, for anyone seeking to achieve distance, in the case of the less responsive gutty ball than in the case of the rubber-cored one that succeeded it. In order both to generate power and to grip the club properly swings were generally full and loose. The first refinement of the grip came with the 'overlapping' method of Harry Vardon who, as the game developed, was regarded as the great model of style. His results were so impressive that it was obvious that his method was a significant factor; but another reason was that an improvement in the composition of the gutty ball reduced the amount of sweeping action hitherto necessary to overcome the ball's lack of resilience. Vardon's swing required less effort and control, and it had a profound influence on the game. Another step that had a bearing on technique was the advent of the Haskell, rubber-cored ball which arrived about the middle of Vardon's career. Players moulded their styles, of course, to match their strength, and no finer example can be quoted than the Triumvirate. Braid, tall and wiry, was flexible and variable. Vardon, an ideal build, was more uniform and J. H. Taylor, shorter and sturdier, was a golfer of strong forearms. But the hickory shaft with its torsion effect encouraged a bigger variety of strokes, and there was an almost artistic note about the inventiveness of some of the great players' shots.

Until May 1921, when the Royal and

Ancient insisted upon certain specifications, the type of ball used also entered into their calculations. Variations of size and weight brought about different flight characteristics, and the right choice of ball was an important factor. In contrast to modern times it produced an individuality of style. This individuality was swept away by the introduction

of a standard ball, by improvement in courses, and above all by the development of steel shafts and matched sets. Steel shafts caused the biggest upheaval since the arrival of the Haskell ball, although they had been known for some time before they were recognized in 1929, the year before Bobby Jones, always faithful to hickory, retired.

It was the prospect of greater length that made steel popular because golfers would do anything for a few extra yards; but the general impression was that the new clubs helped the weaker players to get perceptibly more length without giving the big hitters much advantage. This to many was a sad step. The rewards for skill were lessened

Style and method demonstrated by three golfers: *top*, Lanny Wadkins of the USA; *centre*, Lu Liang Huan of Taiwan; *above*, Roberto de Vicenzo of the Argentine

until the point was reached when players who thrived on the steel shaft might well have foundered with the hickory. The steel shaft was more forgiving and because it was easier to hit straight with the new clubs, they immediately became popular. Although a few, mostly in Scotland, remain faithful to the craft, it was the beginning of the end of the traditional clubmaker who could whittle a special club and fashion it with care. Mass production took over and clubs began to be turned out on the end of a conveyor belt. Their matched sets introduced a mechanical element to the game which had perhaps the biggest influence of all on the way it was played. Theoretically, a golfer bought a matched set, used one swing only, and employed a good caddie who gave him the right club. The hard thing was to find the right swing and, as clubmaking advanced, the right shaft. Clubs were soulless numbers rather than romantic names, their shafts freed from torsion, made stroke production easier. To many players it has become a purely functional exercise, a more predictable science without any frills. The

old-fashioned 'Scottish' swing began to disappear. For the first time the influence of the Americans began to be felt. They cared less about style, more about results, but they were emphatic about the importance of good teaching. Their adoption of the bigger ball (1.68 in) during the 1930s made them generally better and more reliable strikers. The marked lowering of scores showed how well they eliminated bad error, but this also owed as much to watered greens, less rough and the advent of the sand wedge which, more than any other single club, revolutionized the game. Inevitably there have been variations in the grip such as the interlocking and the two handed. New theories on technique have been tried out and sometimes rejected. There will never be a perfect swing or indeed two the same, but technical interpretation is one of the reasons why golf is such a fascinating and frustrating study, and why all new ideas are merely variations on the same, endless theme.

Stymie
An obsolete golfing term that has become a

word in everyday use. It meant a situation in matchplay golf in which an opponent's ball on the putting green blocked the line to the hole. The opponent was then said 'to have laid a stymie' and the victim 'to be stymied'. The answer was for the stymied player to play round his opponent's ball or, if skilled enough, to chip over it with a niblick. A stymie, however, did not apply if the balls were less than 6 in apart; or in strokeplay where there is no direct opponent.

The stymie was an accepted part of the game for many years and a legitimate tactic in matchplay. It also played a crucial part in many famous matches. Jack M'Lean was laid a cruel stymie by Johnny Fischer at the 34th hole of their final of the US Amateur Championship which M'Lean lost at the 37th; and in Bobby Jones's Grand Slam year, he beat Cyril Tolley in the 4th round of the British Amateur when Tolley laid himself an impossible stymie at the 19th. The English championship of 1951 was decided at the 39th hole when H. Bennett was laid a hopeless stymie by G. P. Roberts in the final.

There is no denying that the stymie was a source of great controversy from beginning to end. In 1833 the Royal and Ancient even adopted a 'no stymie' rule for about a year. Stymies were always unpopular in the United States. After a number of matches were decided by unintentional stymies, the R. and A. and the USGA abolished the stymie in 1951.

The derivation of the word itself is obscure.

Sucker
A plugged ball, usually in soft ground rather than in sand.

Sudden Death
A form of play-off in strokeplay competitions used when one or more players tie with the same score. The first person to win a hole outright is the winner. With more than two players, a process of elimination is involved.

Suggs, Louise AMERICAN
b. Atlanta, Ga., 1923. US Women's Amateur 1947; British Ladies' 1948; Curtis Cup 1948; US Women's Open 1949, 1952, runner-up 1951, 1955, 1958-9, 1963; LPGA 1957

The second American to win the British Ladies' Championship. She gained this title in 1948 at Royal Lytham and St Annes, on the 36th green, after a thrilling final with Jean Donald. The previous autumn she had won the US Women's National Amateur, and she had played in Britain with the US Curtis Cup team.

The classical style of Sam Snead

The achievement of the American-British 'double' was followed by tempting offers to turn professional, which she did with conspicuous success by capturing all the major honours in that field during the next decade. Besides setting standards as a player, she helped considerably to further the activities of the women professionals at a time when they were trying to establish a circuit of tournaments. Her reward for these efforts was election as president of the LPGA in 1956-7, and Member at Large, 1959, 1961.

Sugimoto, Hideyo JAPANESE
b. nr Ito, Shizuoka Prefecture, 1938. Japanese Open 1964, 1969, runner-up 1971: runner-up Thailand Open 1965; runner-up Hong Kong Open 1966; Kanto Open 1966; runner-up Singapore Open 1967; Taiwan Open 1969, runner-up 1967; Philippines Open 1972

One of the Japanese circuit's 'big boys', weighing more than 190 lb, Sugimoto became a full professional in 1959 after spending several years as a caddie at the two courses of the Kwana club near his home. He represented Japan in three Canada Cup matches, before it became the World Cup in 1968. His best performance was in the third of them in 1966 in Tokyo, when he led the field by 2 strokes with the 72nd hole – a short one – to play. He took 5 at the hole, dropping 2 strokes, and lost the play-off to George Knudson.

Sunningdale GC ENGLAND
Sunningdale, Berkshire. 36 holes; Old Course 6,506 yd (5,944 m); New Course 6,565 yd (6,003 m)

Sunningdale stands in the belt of sand, heather and pine that is the basis of all the best courses around London. It is one of the most famous names in British golf. Its two courses are as fine a pair as any in

Louise Suggs

Europe and afford for many an easy escape from the pressures of city life.

The founding of the club in 1900 was largely due to the influence of T. A. Roberts and his brother George, together with friends and a few members of nearby clubs. Roberts eventually became agent for St John's College, Cambridge, owners of the land.

When the Old Course opened in what proved to be the last days of the gutty ball, Sunningdale was a wilderness of heathery scrub. Old photographs show nothing of the enclosed look familiar today; it was the growing of trees and a general redesign of Willie Park's lay-out by H. S. Colt, the club secretary at the time, that gave character, beauty and identity to the golf.

If the Royal and Ancient ever broke with tradition and took the British Open away from the seaside, Sunningdale would surely be considered on purely golfing merit. In 1926 the southern qualifying stages of the championship were held there – in which Bobby Jones played some of his most illustrious golf. His first round of 66, which contained all 3s and 4s, broke the previous course record by 6 strokes and his second round of 68 was almost equally impressive. Afterwards he said 'I'm afraid I've reached my peak too early' – but he went on to win his first Open at Royal Lytham and St Annes.

Sunningdale became a highly fashionable club in the pre-World War II years. The Duke of York, later George VI, and the Prince of Wales, later Duke of Windsor, played there. Tournaments became part of the scene. The first unofficial Curtis Cup match between the women of the British Isles and the United States took place there in 1930. Since 1934 the club has run the annual Sunningdale Foursomes, a unique knock-out competition of assorted pairings.

Top, Hideyo Sugimoto

Above, Sunningdale GC's Old Course: the 4th green and, beyond, the 5th and 6th

And it was at Sunningdale in 1955 that Gary Player won his first major professional event. The Dunlop Masters was played there in 1948, 1953, 1960 and 1968. Sunningdale was also the home until recently of the *Golf Illustrated* Gold Vase tournament, one of the oldest amateur events, and was host to the 1956 British Boys' Championship and the 1970 Curtis Cup trials.

Both these took place over the Old Course, lengthened and tightened in recent years. But one of Sunningdale's great virtues is the presence of a second course of almost equal distinction. The New, laid out by H. S. Colt in 1922, is less confined but, despite five short holes, extremely demanding, particularly when the wind blows.

Largely because of the fine golf it offers, Sunningdale has always attracted a number of formidable players. Besides Jack White, who won the 1904 British Open, and other faithful professionals such as Ernest Sales, Michael Bingham, Percy Boomer and Arthur Lees, the most famous name connected with the club may well be that of James Sheridan. He moved south from his native Scotland on the recommendation of Jack White in 1910 to take up the post of caddiemaster on a trial basis, and went on to serve the club for 56 years.

Swartkop CC SOUTH AFRICA
Pretoria, Transvaal. 18 holes; 6,838 yd (6,253 m)

Situated by the Henops River beside the main Pretoria-Johannesburg road, the course came into being in 1933. The farmland on which the course was built was purchased by the South African Iron and Steel Corp. in 1938 and a new clubhouse added later. In 1948 Robert Grimsdell redesigned the course, using the hazard of the Henops River to such effect that it is featured either crossing the fairways or as a lateral hazard at 10 of the holes. A number of Transvaal championships have been held there, and in 1955 the club staged its first South African Open. In the Amateur Championship, held there the same year, a new course record of 65 was set by A. D. Jackson. The club had a membership of more than 1,500 by 1960. It is the home course of Dale Hayes.

Sway
A lateral movement of the head, shoulders or body, most often seen in the backswing. It is one of the most common faults in golf, involving the movement of weight onto the right foot on the backswing. The need to compensate for this by swaying back into the shot makes it difficult to achieve a consistent strike.

A sway can be used to add extra length and in the days of hickory-shafted clubs it used to be considered more orthodox with the freer and more flowing swings.

Sweden
Golf was introduced to Sweden by two brothers, Robert and Edvard Sager, who laid out a private 6-hole course on their estate at Ryfors, near Jönköping, in 1888. Although a further 3 holes were added later, no club as such was formed, and interest in the game did not spread at that point. At about the same time an Anglican clergyman in Gothenburg (Göteborg), the Rev. A. V. Despard, had started playing golf on fields at Sandviken on the northern side of the Göta estuary, near the city. He formed the Gothenburg Golf Club, which existed between 1891 and 1894. This club used English as its language and had among its members men with such names as Edward and James Carnegie, Robert and Osborne Dickson, John Millar, Arthur Seaton and James Keiller.

The vicar did not have enough time to lay out a proper course, and when Viktor H. Setterberg, a businessman, took up the idea of golf in 1894 he had to start from scratch, first at Arendal, later at Sandviken. In 1904 a more permanent course was laid out at Hovås, south of Gothenburg in an area already 'discovered' by Despard 15 years earlier. This is regarded as the start of the game in Sweden.

During the first 40 years the game developed slowly, although enthusiasm was great. Stockholms Golfklubb was formed in 1904, Falsterbo was added in 1909. Not until 1929, however, did the country get its first complete 18-hole course, at Lidingö, outside Stockholm. As late as 1945 there were still only 22 clubs in the country with a total membership of 3,000. Real growth did not in fact begin until the 1960s when most of the present 120 or so courses were constructed. The rate of growth has slackened lately, but among the recreational activities of the country golf enjoys a central position. Only ice hockey has grown faster as a popular sport, and more than 40,000 Swedes now regard themselves as golfers. In their own thoroughgoing way Swedes have taken to

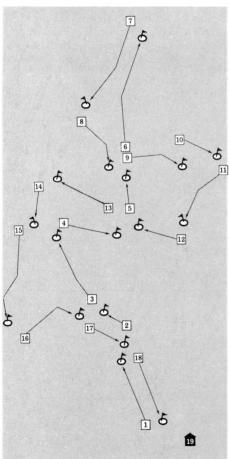

The plan of Sunningdale GC's New Course

A portrait of the Duke of Windsor, then the Prince of Wales, who was captain of Sunningdale in 1930

the game with the same serious determination they apply when paying their taxes. Courses are today to be found all over the country, and Sweden boasts the second most northerly course in the world – at Boden.

Internationally, Sweden's golfing contacts were initially conducted at club level. Falsterbo GC from the start played a match against Copenhagen GC (formed in 1898). There was a match with Germany as early as 1914, and this fixture became a regular feature during the inter-war years. Matches were also played against the Netherlands and from 1942 full international matches have been played against Denmark.

Since the war a regular four-country golf meeting has been held in the Scandinavian countries and Sweden has been the dominant power. It has developed into the Scandinavian Amateur Team Championship. Sweden took part from the outset in European amateur golf, winning the European Team Championship in 1959 and again in 1961 when England entered the competition for the first time. There was also for a time a popular match between Scandinavia and Scotland, and several individual Swedes, notably Claes Jöhncke, have scored successes in the biennial match between the British Isles and the Continent of Europe.

Sweden has always had a strong contingent of British professionals serving various clubs. Edward Roberts, born in 1893 at Hoylake, started at Stockholms Golfklubb in 1914 and is still active. Douglas Brasier, born in 1906 at Limpsfield, Surrey, arrived in 1929. He is well known also as a golf architect. James Dodd, born in 1890 and also from Hoylake, served the Djursholm club near Stockholm for more than 30 years and Alfred Perry, who was British Open Champion in 1935, worked for a period at Falsterbo as an assistant in 1928.

Sweeny, Robert, Jr AMERICAN

b. Pasadena, Cal., 1911. British Amateur 1937, runner-up 1946; *Golf Illustrated* Golf Vase 1937; Walker Cup (reserve) 1947; runner-up Metropolitan (N.Y.) 1948, 1957; runner-up US Amateur 1954.

A player of almost classical simplicity and elegance and a completely cosmopolitan figure, equally at home whether playing golf with leading American professionals, in the rough and tumble of earlier British championships, or in the more cloistered atmosphere of Continental resorts. Above all he has been a sincere Anglo-American, and it was ironical that circumstances prevented his taking part in that most Anglo-American of occasions, the Walker Cup match. Such was the rhythm and balance of

his swing that he has remained a regular and successful participant in British and European amateur events long past the age when others have given up.

Like his brother, Charles, he won a golf Blue at Oxford in 1932, having previously spent much of his holidays at Le Touquet playing the game. First signs of champion-

ship quality came in 1935 when he reached the semi-finals of the British Amateur, and two years later he joined the select band of American winners of the title, defeating Lionel Munn by 3 and 2 in the final. Munn knew Royal St George's backwards, but he was in his fiftieth year and yielded to the younger man in a match which was described by Bernard Darwin as 'the most entirely enjoyable final of its kind I ever saw'. When war broke out Sweeny joined the Eagle Squadron of the RAF and was later awarded the Distinguished Flying Cross. He reached the final again in the first championship after the war, but found James Bruen in irresistible form. He continued a loyal supporter of the event, and in 1954 was

prevented from winning the US Amateur only by Arnold Palmer who was making his last appearance as an amateur. On the death of another admirer of British golf, Bobby Jones, Sweeny had the idea which led to a memorial service in St Andrews, the town of which Jones had been made a freeman.

Sweetser, Jess W. AMERICAN

b. St Louis, Mo., 1902. US National Collegiate 1920; US Amateur 1922, runner-up 1923; Walker Cup 1922-4, 1926, 1928, 1932 (captain 1967, 1973); British Amateur 1926

One of the few double Amateur champions of Britain and the United States, Jess Sweetser belonged to the Jones era and was the second American to win the British Amateur Championship – the first was Walter Travis in 1904.

Sweetser had travelled over with the American Walker Cup team and won one of the most overwhelming victories in the championship's history, knocking out one fine player after another at Muirfield by commanding margins except in a 21-hole semi-final with Brownlow; eventually he

Robert Sweeny

Jess W. Sweetser

defeated A. F. Simpson, a good Edinburgh golfer, by 6 and 5 in the final.

He had impressed all those who saw him in previous Walker Cup matches and, as might be expected of a former Yale quarter-miler, was big and strong and had an impressively 'grooved' swing, but it was in winning the 1922 US Amateur that he perhaps played his finest golf. He accounted for the holder, Jesse Guilford, Bob Jones, Chick Evans and Willie Hunter. He beat Evans 3 and 2 in the final and the following year lost his title only at the 38th hole of the final against Max Marston. He lost to Jones in the semi-final of Jones's historic year of 1930 at Merion. An amateur golfer in the finest tradition, he was a constant figure in the early days of the Walker Cup and has the distinction of being the only player ever to have lost at extra holes. In 1922 he and C. V. L. Hooman, all square after 36 holes and not knowing what to do, were told to play on but thereafter it was decided that matches all square after 36 holes should remain halved.

Swing

The sweep or arc of the club employed with the purpose of hitting the ball. No two players have ever swung quite alike.

Swing Weight

The 'weight' of the club's head that the golfer senses when the club is swung. Although not the same as the total (or club) weight, it is a measurable factor and is an aid to the golfer in his choice of clubs.

Sydney GC, Royal AUSTRALIA

Sydney, N.S.W. 18 holes; 6,722 yd (6,147 m)

It is hard, looking at the urban growth which has sprouted on all sides of Royal Sydney's present course, to realize that the area between Rose Bay and the sea used to be virgin country. Those were the days when 'Nosey Bob the Hangman' was one of the few inhabitants of the ridge which ran from the site of the old Ostrich Farm at South Head to the fort at Ben Buckler; and when the green committee was authorized to spend not more than £2 per month on the upkeep of the links.

Nowadays, row upon row of houses obscure any sort of view but, rather like Royal Lytham in England, the course retains many of its seaside characteristics and, with a good deal of judicious planting which gives it more of a parkland appearance, it has built up a justifiable reputation as a championship course.

It has been a regular host to all the major

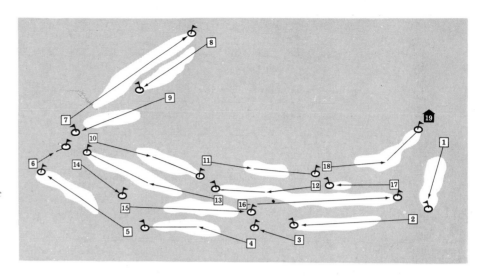

Australian events but, more important, the game in Australia has been much influenced by the club which has also maintained the best interests of its members and kept a friendly welcome for its hundreds of visitors.

Originally, permission to use land owned by Miss (later Dame) Eadith Walker as a golf course led to the formation of the Sydney GC in 1893. In October of that year the first competition was held, but, despite the hospitality of Miss Walker, the members were keen to secure a seaside course.

An area was found in the Bondi sandhills between Old South Head Road and the sea and a 9-hole course laid out. In later years, land was acquired for 18 holes on the western side of Old South Head Road. In 1897 it was reported that 'the new holes completing the full course of 18 are very picturesque, and make fine sporting holes. One drive is right over a Chinaman's garden, others are over pretty groves of trees.'

In August 1897, a new clubhouse was ready and at its official opening a month later the club was granted the title of 'Royal'.

In 1898 a 10-year lease was granted to the club and with some measure of security thus attained, the committee turned its attention to improving the amenities of the club. They arranged 'to have members' boots cleaned' and 'to procure some Gin and Brandy, also Cigars and Cigarettes, to see whether the Demand for these Goods would justify the Club in keeping a regular supply'. It is presumed that there was and that sales expanded as the membership grew.

Late in 1914 the list of full playing ordinary members was closed at 400 and in 1916 the freehold of most of the club's present area was secured. Although there was a decrease in membership during World War I, it rose steeply again afterwards and in

December 1919 it was decided to make substantial alterations and additions to the clubhouse. No sooner had work started, however, than the clubhouse was destroyed by fire but with the help of a temporary structure and an offer from the Australian GC, continuity was maintained until July 1922 when the new clubhouse, still in use today, was completed.

Syria

Syria has one golf course, consisting of 7 grass holes, built, owned and run by the Iraq Petroleum Co. at Banias, the Mediterranean terminus of the company's pipeline which carries crude oil from northern Iraq. The Banias course is primarily for resident staff and company visitors, but other visitors are made welcome.

The course plan of Royal Sydney GC

T

Tait, Frederick Guthrie BRITISH
b. Dalkeith, Midlothian 1870; d. 1900.
British Amateur 1896, 1898, runner-up
1899, tied 3rd; British Open 1896-7

Although only 30 when he was killed in
the South African War, Tait had already
made his mark very strongly in golf at a
time when the game abounded with distinguished amateurs. He achieved this as much
by his magnetic personality as by the excellence of his record. The third son of a professor at Edinburgh University, he spent
many childhood holidays at St Andrews
where he developed a love for the Old
Course. He was educated at Sedbergh and
commissioned into the Leinster Regiment
from where he was posted to the Black
Watch, and was serving with them when he
was killed leading his company into action
against the Boers. Tait was an all-rounder,
an expert rifle shot, and a first-class rugby
player and cricketer. He also took his duties
as a soldier most seriously, and yet he still
found time to build a high reputation in golf,
while all the time seeking an opportunity for
service abroad.

His career as a golfer covers the last
decade of the 19th century. He won the
British Amateur in 1896 and 1898, both
times on an English course, Sandwich and
Hoylake. Being stationed at Shorncliffe and
Hythe in Kent enabled him to compete in
the St George's Challenge Cup at Sandwich
which he won in 1896, 1898 and 1899. In
1899 he also reached the final of the
Amateur Championship where he was
beaten at the 37th by John Ball over the
Prestwick links. In the British Open he
missed only one year between 1891 and
1899; his best performances were in 1896
when he finished equal 3rd to Vardon and
Taylor, and the following year when he was
again equal 3rd behind Braid and Hilton.

Tait is looked on primarily as a match
player, a form of the game he himself preferred to medal play. He loved the challenge
of a match, and although he was normally a
very accurate driver as well as an exceptionally long one, he was capable of startling
recoveries from losing positions. Yet he
achieved many scoring feats. His love of St
Andrews brought him a rich harvest of 15
medals, including the George Glennie medal

three times, awarded to the lowest aggregate
scores at the spring and autumn meetings. In
the course of one of these rounds he lowered
the existing record for the Old Course to 78.
He once holed the Old Course in 72: this
was not allowed as a record because it was
not played over the strictly medal course.
He also held the course record at Carnoustie
with a 72 and at Luffness New, East
Lothian, a course which he helped to form.
Tait had immensely strong arms and hands
and was capable of prodigious length, although as his game matured he sacrificed it
for accuracy and seldom called upon the full
shot. One of his drives has gone down in
history, that made from the 13th tee on the
Old Course at St Andrews which on frozen
ground carried 250 yd and finished 340 yd
away. Much of the glamour that surrounds
his name is connected with his personality;
he was high-spirited and firm in his views,
but always courteous and kind, and observed
the best spirit of the game. Large crowds
followed him on the course in England as in
Scotland, and in the army he was adored by
his men.

Taiwan

Golf in Taiwan began at Tamsui about 50
years ago when the country was known as
Formosa and occupied by the Japanese. At
the end of World War II, the Nationalist
Chinese moved in and found the American
forces establishing a golf course on a battle
training area. A sympathetic golfing general

appointed a sergeant in charge of golf, an
activity that came under the heading of
special services. The Americans brought in
equipment and ran caddies' competitions,
allowing them to play at certain times, giving
prizes and grading them on their ability as
players. It was as a result of this training
that Chen Ching Po, who later became
known as the Ben Hogan of Asia, emerged,
followed by many others who were in effect
sponsored caddies. Chen Ching Po played in
the Canada Cup at Wentworth in 1956 with
Lu Liang Huan, the first time that Taiwan
had broken into world golf. The climax came
in 1972 at Melbourne when Lu and Hsieh
Min Nam won for Taiwan. A steady flow of
highly proficient players began to make their
mark on tournaments in the Far East and
elsewhere. Much of the credit for this must
go to the caddies' scheme and to the remarkable Old Man Chen, who taught
relations who included Chen Ching Po,
Hsieh Min Nam and Hsieh Yung Yo.

Old Man Chen was one of the original
Taiwanese professionals whose influence was
as great as that of Ernest Jones in America.
He taught his pupils simply to swing the
clubhead and it is no coincidence that most
of the Taiwanese professionals swing the
club the same way.

In the last few years, as the American
forces have been withdrawn and the Taiwanese have acquired greater influence, golf
has increasingly been organized by the local
people. There are now seven courses:

M. C. Ho of Taiwan playing in the 1973 Indian
Open at Delhi

Tamsui (now the Taiwan GCC) is naturally the most famous. Set on a hill overlooking the Formosa Straits, it was founded in 1919.

Takeaway

The act of taking the club away from the ball to start the swing. Although covering only a few inches, it is generally reckoned to be a movement of prime importance.

Target Golf

Expression used to describe golf that is analogous to darts or archery and played on well-watered courses with little run: the shots can be flighted so that they pitch and stop almost in their pitchmarks. It encourages high-flying shots with backspin. The term embraces competitions staged at driving ranges in which a target is laid out on the ground and points are scored for finishing nearest to the bull's eye.

Tasmania GC AUSTRALIA

nr Hobart, Tasmania. 18 holes; 6,748 yd (6,170 m)

The course, in its new home at Barilla Bay

close to Hobart Airport, occupies what must be the most beautiful setting of all Australian courses. The clubhouse overlooks the pleasantly undulating, tree-lined course which gives commanding views to seaward and inland. In January 1971 the new club was opened by the Governor of Tasmania, Sir Eric Bastyan, but its history goes back to 1902 when it began life as the Lindisfarne Club.

It owed its name to the suburb in which it was situated on the eastern shore of the Derwent River and until 1948 it was linked with Hobart only by ferry. A year later the club decided to expand to 18 holes but the growth of housing in Lindisfarne, caused by the building of Hobart's unique floating bridge giving easier access to the city, eventually enforced the club's move to its present site. The new course, designed by Al Howard of New South Wales, was opened in the autumn of 1970 and in 1971 housed the Tasmanian Open Championship.

Taylor, Frank M., Jr AMERICAN

b. 1926. California Amateur 1954-5; runner-up US Amateur 1957; Walker Cup 1957, 1959, 1961

A dentist by profession, Taylor was prominent in Southwestern golf for several years. He won every tournament in California at least once and reached the final of the 1957 US Amateur, losing to Hillman Robbins. In three Walker Cup appearances he won four matches out of four.

Taylor, John Henry BRITISH

b. Northam, Devon, 1871; d. 1963. British Open 1894-5, 1900, 1909, 1913; runner-up 1896, 1906, 1914, joint runner-up 1904-5; runner-up US Open 1900; British Professional Matchplay 1904, 1908; French Open 1908-9; German Open 1912

J. H. Taylor's death marked the passing of the last of the great golfers of the 19th century, who had dominated championship golf for almost 30 years. A member of the famous Triumvirate, he was the first outstanding English professional, winning the first of his five victories in the Open at Sandwich in 1894 on its first appearance outside Scotland.

In his early days professionals lived from hand to mouth and often ended where they began, as caddies. Taylor, throughout his career, worked hard for his brother professionals and together with his illustrious contemporaries, Braid and Vardon, raised their status considerably. As a natural leader of men, 'J.H.' played a major part in the formation of the British PGA and lent enthusiastic support to artisan golf.

After leaving school at 11, Taylor was variously engaged as a caddie at Westward Ho!, a bootboy in the home of Horace Hutchinson's father, a gardener's boy and a mason's labourer. At the age of 17 he became a member of the greenkeeping staff at Westward Ho!

The army and the navy turned him down on account of his eyesight but when he was 19, already a good player and by now professional and greenkeeper at Burnham in Somerset, he beat the famous Andrew Kirkaldy in a match; and, after Kirkaldy had spread good news about his conqueror, Taylor succeeded him at Winchester, later taking up posts at Wimbledon and finally at Royal Mid-Surrey, where he remained for over 40 years.

Taylor's strong, firm-footed stance and short, punched swing first began to be noticed when he nearly surprised the Scots in the Open at Prestwick in 1893. The following year at Sandwich he found that extra steadiness and so recorded the first of the 16 Open victories won by himself, Braid and Vardon.

He defended his title successfully the next year at St Andrews and in 1896 tied with Vardon at Muirfield before losing the play-off. Vardon won again in 1898 and 1899 and pipped Taylor once more in the US Open Championship at the Chicago GC in 1900. Taylor scored his second success at St Andrews that same year with some magnificent golf. The next few years brought the establishment of James Braid and it was 1909 before Taylor re-asserted his supremacy.

That was at Deal; his last and his finest victory came at Hoylake in 1913 where his compact swing showed a control which nobody could match in appalling conditions of wind and rain. After qualifying by holing a putt of 6 ft on the last green, he played heroically and long afterwards referred to this as some of the best golf in his life. When he pulled down his cap, stuck out his chin and embedded his large boots in the ground, he could hit straight through the wind as though it were not there.

He was a stern competitor, though a highly strung and emotional man, and he approached every championship as though it were a battle. Characteristically, he ceased to take part when he felt he could no longer win, but as late as 1924, at the age of 53, his score for six rounds, which included the two qualifying rounds, was the lowest of the entire field. He finished 5th.

In 1933, as non-playing captain, he led the British team to victory in the Ryder Cup at Southport and Ainsdale. Although he had left school so young, he took great pains to

Takeaway, *top,* Jessie Valentine starts her swing

Above, Frank M. Taylor

educate himself, was a frequent reader of Dickens and Boswell and the book he wrote, *Golf, My Life's Work* was produced entirely by his own efforts.

He wrote regularly, was a warm-hearted, affectionate man and was always good company. In 1950, he was elected an honorary member of the Royal and Ancient GC of St Andrews together with James Braid and Willie Auchterlonie, a singular honour. Later, on the occasion of his 90th birthday, the captain and past captains of the club presented him with a silver salver bearing their signatures.

His long career ended in retirement in his home on the hill above Westward Ho! where he described the view as 'the finest in Christendom'. It was there that his love and respect for the game he served so faithfully was born.

In 1957 the Royal North Devon Club paid him the highest honour of his life by electing him president. Taylor lost his wife in 1956 shortly after their diamond wedding.

Taylor, Reginald Carden SOUTH AFRICAN
South African Open 1954; South African Amateur 1956; Eisenhower Trophy 1960, 1962, 1964; Canadian Amateur 1962; German Open Amateur 1958; French Open Amateur 1970

Reg Taylor is probably the best South African amateur who has remained an amateur throughout a career in which he has been at the top for over twenty years. He has certainly been the most successful overseas, having won championships in three continents. His victories in the German and his capture of the French twelve years later coincided with two of his many private visits to Europe. He is a popular figure in many countries. The peak of his career came in 1954, when he won the South African Open in the heyday of Bobby Locke, a rare feat.

Tee
A wooden or, more commonly, plastic peg on which the ball is placed for the initial shot to each hole. Almost always used for a driver, it is sometimes waived by good players for irons or a spoon. In earlier days golfers or their caddies made tees with sand. 'Tee' also refers to the teeing ground, usually raised and suitably marked, from which the player begins each hole. *See also* Equipment.

Teeing Ground SEE TEE

Texas Wedge
American term for a putter when used from off the green. When the ground short of the green is dry and hard, and the use of a

broad-soled club difficult, a putter is often the most effective club.

Thailand
The origins of golf in Thailand go back to 1890 when the Royal Bangkok club was founded. The King of Siam, having played the game a good deal in Europe, helped things along and British influence also played a large part. A team of engineers, building the railway from Malaya to Siam, formed the Hua Hin club at a seaside resort more than 100 miles from Bangkok, but the real development in the game has come recently, long after Siam changed its name to Thailand in June 1939.

The Thai Tourist Association has now

become interested and several new courses have helped to swell the total to over 20. Of these, Rose Garden, designed by a Japanese architect, and the Siam CC, built in 18 months and designed by Robert Trent Jones, are the most notable. Two long established clubs are the Royal Dusit and the Royal Thai Air Force GC, both in Bangkok. The latter is situated between the civilian and military runways of the airport and is flat, the only feature being some small trees and the *klongs* (drains).

Today golf in Thailand falls more under American influence and this has helped its development. Although the game is expensive, the country can boast something like 30,000 golfers, of whom about 40 are professionals; the most famous of these is the diminutive Sukree Onsham. The most senior is Chalaw Chalakua, a jockey at the end of World War II, who took to golf and became professional at the Royal Bangkok Sports Club. He has never been an outstanding player but has done much for his fellow professionals in securing contracts for caddies in order to allow them to develop their golf. Without this help, many could never have afforded to play.

The growth of the Far East circuit, with the Thailand Open as one of its main events, has helped foster interest in the game.

Thin
A ball hit off the bottom of the club that does not attain normal height or flight and tends to finish beyond its target.

Thirlwell, Alan BRITISH
b. 1928. English Amateur 1954-5; runner-up 1963; semi-finalist Canadian Amateur 1957; Walker Cup 1957; runner-up British Amateur 1958, 1972

Alan Thirlwell has played more championship golf since World War II than almost any other British player; a majestic swinger whose great power made him an effortless striker. For a time after he won the first of his English championships he was one of the best amateurs in Britain and was unlucky not to have been picked for the Walker Cup more than once.

In his first English final, he beat Harry Bentley at Royal St George's by 2 and 1 and the following year at Ganton joined the small band of players who have successfully defended their titles by beating Michael Burgess 7 and 6. This established him in a succession of appearances for England exceeded only by Crawley, Foster, Bonallack and Marsh. In the final of the British Amateur at St Andrews in 1958 he lost to Joe Carr by 3 and 2. Carr, 1 up after the

Above, teeing ground: Peter Alliss on the 7th at Parkstone

Texas Wedge – Michael Attenborough in action at Rye

11th in the afternoon, made two cruel thrusts driving the 12th green and reaching the 13th green with a huge shot from a bunker into which he had driven.

Thirlwell had to swallow another hard defeat in the final of the English Championship at Burnham and Berrow in 1963 when Bonallack's short game was deadly even for him and blunted Thirlwell's superiority through the green. He remained a good player for a long time, helping Northumberland many times in the county championship, and showing up well in championships such as the 1969 English at Sandwich, when he became the first man for three years to beat Michael Bonallack in that event. However, an even more remarkable performance was in reaching the final of the Amateur Championship on the same course in 1972, testimony to an enduring swing.

Thom, Kenneth Gordon BRITISH
b. 1922. Runner-up British Boys' 1939; runner-up English Amateur 1946; Walker Cup 1949

Ken Thom played all his early golf at Southend-on-Sea, Essex, and was one of many players to have a promising career affected by war. He was 24 when championships were resumed and quickly made his mark. Later in life he took over a London golf school and taught as a professional.

Thomas, David C. BRITISH
b. 1934. Runner-up British Open 1958; joint runner-up 1966; Ryder Cup 1959, 1963, 1965, 1967; British Professional Matchplay 1963; French Open 1959

Ever since David Thomas emerged as a young assistant of 16, the golfing world was impressed by his potential. His massive frame allied to a sound simple swing made him probably the best driver in professional golf of his day and on courses where long

driving was called for, he had a tremendous advantage. Yet for more than 15 years, Thomas remained something of an enigma.

He took a little while to break through and did not win anything like as much as his majestic driving suggested he might, mainly because he developed a sort of paralysis over his short pitching, rare in first-class golfers, and partly because he later had eyesight and back troubles.

His pitching affliction was a source of great anguish to him and he worked hard to overcome it. He still fashioned a fine career in which he came nearer to winning the Open than any British player for 18 years. His performance at Lytham and St Annes in 1958 was confirmation of his talent. Making up 2 strokes on Thomson at the 15th in the 4th round, he went 1 stroke ahead with a 3 at the 16th but understandably tightened up on his second to the 17th. Although he finished bravely, unlike so many of the leading contenders, at the 18th and tied with Thomson on 278, Thomson won the play-off with 139 to 143. Another fine performance came in the 1966 Open at Muirfield when his driving stood up on one of the narrowest championship courses in history. He put in a rousing finish and had the lowest score for the last two rounds, but he and Doug Sanders were edged out by Jack Nicklaus.

Though real success escaped him in the United States, where he spent a good deal of time, he won on the Continent (victories in

the Belgian, Dutch and French Opens), established a place in the Ryder Cup team, and had frequent victories at home including the 1963 Professional Matchplay when he beat J. A. Macdonald by 3 and 2 at Turnberry. He also represented Wales 11 times in the World (formerly Canada) Cup.

Now retired as a tournament player, he is

well known as a golf-course architect in partnership with Peter Alliss.

Thomson, Hector BRITISH
b. Machrihanish, Argyll, 1913. British Boys' 1931; Irish Open Amateur 1934-5; Scottish Amateur 1935; British Amateur 1936; Walker Cup 1936, 1938

A member of one of the best-known Scottish golfing families, Thomson was one of the most complete players of his generation, which he overshadowed along with his great friend and keenest rival, the late Jack M'Lean. Thomson's swing was so consistent that it was said of him that from a distance it was impossible to tell whether he was taking a practice swing or actually hitting the ball.

Having achieved all there was for him to do as an amateur, Thomson turned professional in 1940. But his tournament career, interrupted by World War II, never approached its amateur eminence. He became attached to a number of overseas clubs in Egypt, Switzerland, Italy, and Greece.

Thomson, Peter William AUSTRALIAN
b. Melbourne, Victoria, 1929. New Zealand Open 1950-1, 1953, 1955, 1959-61, 1965, 1971; Australian Open 1951, 1967, 1972; British Professional Matchplay 1954, 1961, 1966-7; British Open 1954-6, 1958, 1965

Only Harry Vardon, with six victories, won the British Open more often and only J. H. Taylor and James Braid as often. In modern times nobody has enjoyed such success and from the time that Peter Thomson travelled to Britain as a young man in 1951, he has been something of a scourge to British professionals. For many years he could justly claim to be the absolute master with the small ball on fast courses. He was excluded from the highest rank because of a comparative failure in the United States, although he was more successful there than some of his critics care to acknowledge.

Thomson's first steps in golf were taken during the war years in Melbourne when, living near a course, he began to play on his own. There was nobody to instruct him but, by the end of World War II, he had built himself the basis of one of the most orthodox and rhythmic swings, and was able to hold his own with the good players on their return from the services. He turned professional at the age of 19 in 1949 and, because of the lack of tournament golf in Australia, had to focus his ambitions upon Britain where he made an immediate impact. He was 6th equal in his first Open Championship at Royal Portrush in 1951, 2nd in 1952 at Royal Lytham,

Alan Thirlwell

David C. Thomas

2nd equal in 1953 at Carnoustie and winner of Royal Birkdale's first Open in 1954.

This was the first of three successive victories, the first such since Bob Ferguson in 1880-2, and part of a prolonged domination by him and Bobby Locke. From 1952 to 1958 Thomson never finished worse than equal 2nd; from 1949 to 1957 Locke won four times,

and was equal 2nd, 4th, tied 6th and 8th.

With such a disarmingly simple method and a pleasant poise and self-assurance, it was obvious that Thomson was destined for more success after Birkdale. The following year he began a happy association with the Old Course by winning at St Andrews, and in 1956 at Hoylake made the most of some

Peter Thomson, *top*, with the British Open trophy in 1956 having won it for the third consecutive time; *above*, about to hit his tee shot in the 1961 Dunlop Masters

good fortune with the weather.

He completed his sequence with another victory in 1958, this time after a play-off with David Thomas at Royal Lytham. During the 1950s there was no great invasion of Britain from overseas although Van Donck, Cerda, de Vicenzo, Locke and Stranahan were regular visitors. From 1960, however, the pattern changed and Thomson's fifth victory at Birkdale in 1965 was achieved from the strongest Open field yet.

During the mid and late 1950s Thomson spent a large part of the year in the United States, winning the Texas Open in Dallas in 1956, finishing equal 4th in the US Open after leading for two rounds, and 5th in the Masters in 1957. But it was elsewhere in the world that he really made his name.

Thomson and Kel Nagle won the Canada Cup for Australia in 1954 and 1959; his supremacy in Britain was maintained throughout the 1960s in ordinary professional events; and he was largely responsible for the rich development of the Far East tour. For his services to the game, he was made an MBE.

He also became well known for writing his own newspaper articles, for frequent commentaries on television, as an administrator of the Australian PGA, a wise counsellor, co-author of 'This Wonderful World of Golf' and as a golf-course architect; a natural outlet for his imagination and intellect.

Threeball

A match in which three players compete against each other, each player playing his own ball.

Threesome

A match in which two players combine as a pair, hitting alternate shots with the same ball, against a third player who hits his own.

Through the Green

'Through the green' is the whole area of the course except: (1) the teeing ground and the green of the hole being played; (2) all hazards on the course.

Tie

This occurs when two or more players or pairs return the same score in a strokeplay competition. Sometimes the result is left as a tie but more often is decided by a play-off.

Tight

Of a course – one that is narrow with well-guarded greens; of a shot – one with a great challenge and the smallest margin for error; of a lie – one in which the ball does not sit too well, but hugs the ground.

Tin

The metal casing inside the hole.

Titirangi GC NEW ZEALAND

Titirangi, Auckland, N. Island. 18 holes

When the Auckland GC gave up One Tree Hill in 1909 to move to Middlemore, a band of enthusiasts took over the playing rights to form the Maungakiekie club. Congestion was a problem as the club became popular and a new site was acquired near New Lynn. Much of the site was cleared by 1915 when the course was given the Maori name of Titirangi.

World War I halted plans but the course was kept open and in 1921 the Maungakiekie Club brought Titirangi to real life. The course, laid out by F. G. Hood and Gilbert Martin, was officially opened on 23 April of that year.

In 1926 Dr Alister Mackenzie, creator of Cypress Point and Augusta who was visiting Australia, submitted a new design for the course. It was a wise move and Titirangi undoubtedly benefited from the only work the architect undertook in New Zealand. In Mackenzie's opinion, the ground was 'exceptionally well adapted for golf, undulating without being hilly'. The tight course had long rough and open ditches amply supplemented by trees and shrubs. Though amendments were later made, Titirangi, one of New Zealand's best courses, preserved Mackenzie's ideas.

In 1933, it housed the New Zealand Amateur and Open championships and has remained a regular choice for both. It may be a little short by modern standards and the threat of urban development casts doubt on its future. In 1971, a special committee was facing the problem. Those who have enjoyed the combination of its setting and playing merits hope that Titirangi, 'the fringe of heaven', will continue to hold its respected place in New Zealand golf.

Tobago GC TOBAGO

18 holes; 6,687 yd (6,115 m)

Tobago GC, on the shores of Mount Irvine Bay looking over to the famous Bucco Reef, is by common consent the best course in the West Indies. It was opened in 1968 and designed by the British architect, John Harris, on land that was an old coconut estate. The whole project was the brainchild of Patrick Coghlan, an Englishman who had a house beside what is now the 15th green and thought the area ideal for golf. He formed a small private syndicate to buy the estate and build the course, which took three years to complete. The course is not steep but undulates nicely; Harris made

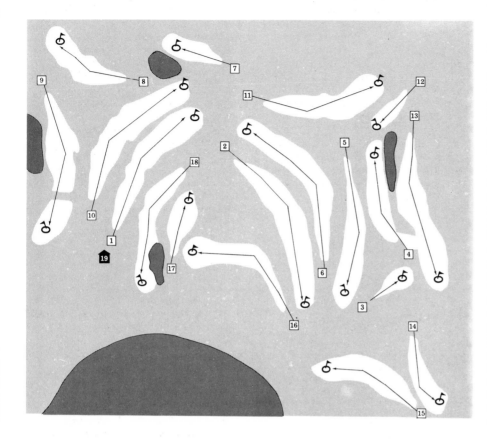

admirable use of the rises and falls in building tees which offer inviting drives. Bermuda grass was flown in from Tifton in Georgia to provide tees, greens and fairways which are watered by underground pipes.

The Tobago club with its delightful clubhouse has made a notable addition to golf in Trinidad and Tobago, an area which

hitherto had little to offer, and was soon considered to have enough scenic attraction and golfing merit to house a match in the Shell film series, 'Wonderful World of Golf'.

Toe
The part of the clubhead furthest from the shaft.

The course plan of the Tobago GC and a view from the 9th tee

Tolley, Cyril James Hastings BRITISH
b. London, 1895. British Amateur 1920, 1929; Walker Cup 1922, 1923, 1924, 1926, 1930, 1934; French Open 1924, 1928; President's Putter 1938

One of the dominant figures in British amateur golf after World War I from which he emerged, having been a prisoner of war, with the MC. He was extremely powerful, long and relatively straight driving being a feature of his game. He drove the 18th green at St Andrews (370 yd; 338 m) and the 1st at Troon (350 yd; 320 m). Wearing plus-fours and smoking a pipe he cut an imposing figure which frequently earned him the adjective 'majestic', but though he usually rose to an occasion he was not free from nerves. Bernard Darwin has left a picture of him as he defeated a former US Open champion, Chick Evans, in the unofficial match against the United States which preceded the first Walker Cup match in 1922. 'Menacing and Napoleonic, he looked every inch a champion. To see him filling his pipe while studying the line of his putt and then tap the ball in, walking away to the next tee before the ball dropped, was a truly inspiring spectacle.' His first victory in the British Amateur came in 1920 when he was an undergraduate at Oxford, and consisted of a dramatic win at the 36th against Bob Gardner, an American and one of the first to compete in this country.

In the next 15 years Tolley won most of the leading amateur tournaments, including the Worsplesdon Foursomes with Joyce Wethered, but it was not until 1938 that he captured the President's Putter in which he had competed for years. In 1929 Tolley won again at Sandwich and a year later at St Andrews came the titanic battle with Bobby Jones in the year of the American's grand slam. The whole of St Andrews seemed to turn out to watch, and the match in the 4th round, changed six times from 1 up to all square with each in turn holding the lead. When all square at the 17th, Jones's second with a 4 iron struck spectators at the back of the green, but since there was no telling where his ball would have finished, it is impossible to say whether it affected the result, which was victory for Jones at the 19th where Tolley stymied himself. Tolley won two out of six Walker Cup singles, his biggest defeat coming at the hands of Jones, by 12 and 11, in 1926 the year when Jones had his 'perfect' round at Sunningdale in pre-qualifying for the Open.

In 1938 Tolley was chairman of the selectors in Britain's only pre-war victory and in 1948 was nominated captain of the Royal and Ancient. Two of Tolley's most striking successes came in Paris where against a strong professional field he carried off the French Open, thereby establishing himself in medal play against the best professionals.

Top

To strike the ball above the centre line, so that it cannot leave the ground properly. The commonest cause of it is failure to keep the head still.

Topspin

Forward rotation of the ball in flight. It is caused by striking the ball an upward blow. Its effect is to add run to the ball.

Toronto GC CANADA

Toronto, Ont. 18 holes, 6,441 yd (5,890 m), par 70; 9 holes, 2,495 yd (2,281 m), par 33

Only Royal Montreal GC (founded 1873) and Royal Quebec GC (1875) take North American precedence over Toronto GC, which was formed in 1876.

Early headquarters were in a room in the Woodbine Hotel and Tavern which was used for lunches and as a locker room. In 1914 a deserted mansion was rebuilt as a permanent clubhouse and a grocery store was converted into the professional's house. The latter was occupied for several years by George Cumming, who died in 1950 after 50 years of service with the club. The club was instrumental in establishing a legal precedent in 1915 which has since remained a landmark of golfing jurisprudence. Three of its members were convicted by the magistrate at Little York of playing golf on a Sunday contrary to the provisions of the Lord's Day Act. However, they were successful in their appeal against the conviction, the judge holding that 'golf is not a game of ball similar in any sense to the games enumerated in, or intended to be prohibited by, the statute, and also it is not a noisy game'. That decision has never been successfully challenged.

It was in 1911 that the club purchased its present ground of 270 acres (110 ha) on the Dixie Road on the banks of the Etobicoke River. H. S. Colt was brought from England to lay out the new course, which was completed in 1912. Colt's finished work is ranked among his masterpieces, with something reminiscent of Sunningdale about the holes. The architect was particularly proud of the 187-yd (171-m) 4th hole, which was named after him. Excellent turf covers the sandy soil throughout the whole of the beautifully-conditioned course. Although not particularly difficult, it resists low scoring in surprising fashion. The professional course record of 68 held by Tommy Armour

and Leo Diegel attests to this. Five of the early Canadian Open championships were contested at Toronto GC. It was here also that Canada's immortal amateurs, George S. Lyon in 1898 and C. Ross Somerville in 1926, each scored the first of the 14 Canadian Amateur Championship victories they were to account for between them. One of the club's remarkable players was Archie Kerr, who won the same championship in 1897, only three years after he had first taken up golf, and who repeated his victory in 1901.

Torrance, T. A. BRITISH

b. Edinburgh 1891. Worplesdon Foursomes 1921, 1934; Walker Cup 1924, 1928, 1930, 1934 (captain 1932); Irish Open Amateur 1925; German Amateur 1927, 1929; semi-finalist British Amateur 1935

Tony Torrance had a notable international career both for Scotland and Britain in the 1920s and early 1930s. He played in five of the first eight Walker Cup matches and although he lost all four foursome games in which he took part, Torrance lost only one of five singles, winning three and halving the other. As captain of the team in 1932 Torrance halved with Francis Ouimet, the US Champion of that year, whom he had beaten two years previously for Britain's only singles point.

Torrance, W. B. BRITISH

b. Edinburgh. Walker Cup 1922

Willie Torrance preceded his brother Tony in playing for Britain against the United States when he was a member of the first Walker Cup team in 1922. He also played for Scotland for several years and was twice captain of the side. Torrance tied for the place of first British amateur in the 1927 Open Championship, in which the leading amateur was also the winner, Bobby Jones.

Torrey Pines Men's GC USA

San Diego, Cal. 36 holes; North Course 6,667 yd (6,096 m), par 72; South Course 7,050 yd (6,447 m)

The Torrey Pines municipal golf complex near San Diego is composed of the North and the South Courses. It has been said that the South is the finest municipal golf course in the United States, a rather broad claim perhaps, but it is good enough to have been the site of the Andy Williams-San Diego Open for a number of years. The South measures slightly over 7,000 yd and is in the tradition of modern architecture with long par-4 holes, three of them 450 yd (411 m), and two par-3 holes over 200 yd (183 m). The North is slightly less ambitious, measuring 6,667 yd from the back tees.

Both are set on headlands 300 ft above the waters of the Pacific – so high that the sea does not come into play as at Pebble Beach.

Construction began in 1956, and both courses were opened for play in 1957. Since then, over 2,000,000 rounds have been played. William Bell Sr was the original architect, but he died before the project was completed, and it was taken over by his son, William Bell Jr. At one time the land where Torrey Pines now stands seemed destined to be an automobile racecourse. During World War II it was an army base. The Government declared it surplus, and the city of San Diego was under pressure to convert the paved streets into a racecourse. Leo Calland, the city's Parks and Recreation Director, helped persuade the city council to turn the tract into a golf complex.

Torsion

Golf clubs are capable of having torsion applied to them in two ways. Laterally, when the shaft 'springs', as seen in high-speed photographs of a club at impact, and in the sense of the shaft twisting against the clubhead. The hickory shaft was far more susceptible to torsion than the steel. The new graphite-shafted clubs are liable to torsion.

Townsend, Peter Michael Paul BRITISH

b. Cambridge 1946. British Boys' 1962, 1964; Walker Cup 1965; English Open Amateur Strokeplay 1966; Dutch Open 1967; British PGA 1968; runner-up Alcan

Golfer of the Year 1968; Ryder Cup 1969, 1971; Swiss Open 1971

Townsend provides a good example of the indirect benefit that a golfer can derive from subjecting his game to the toughening process of the American circuit, and at the same time of the frustrations that it may provide. He spent at least two long stretches on the

Peter Townsend recovering from the rough

US tour and endured the hardships of having to try to pre-qualify. Finishing 2nd in the 1969 Milwaukee tournament and 4th in another later that season marked his best performances in the United States, but there was little doubt that the chastening experience improved his performance back in Britain and on the Continent.

Townsend came on the golf scene as a small boy. He first played in the Boys' Championship in 1960 at the age of 13; the first of his two victories in the event came two years later when he was 15, and he won again in 1964 at Formby. It was obvious that he had an unusual talent for the game and he quickly graduated to play for England and for Britain in the 1965 Walker

Cup team which tied the United States in Baltimore, Townsend winning three out of his four matches. He did not give himself time to win either the English or the British championships, but he carried off the English Amateur Strokeplay Championship in fine style in 1966. During that season he proved himself as a medal player, for his scoring in more than a dozen consecutive rounds of tournament play averaged below 70. After playing in the Eisenhower Trophy team that autumn he turned professional.

This coincided with a loss of form so complete, especially during his first winter in South Africa, that he lost confidence, all the more serious in a golfer whose nature is to attack. He recovered to win the Dutch Open in 1967 and the following summer found his best form again, winning the British PGA at Royal Mid-Surrey, scene of victory in his first Boys' Championship, and finishing runner-up a fortnight later to Gay Brewer in the Alcan. He won a place in the Ryder Cup team four years after playing in the Walker Cup; both then and two years later in St Louis he played with distinction.

Peter Townsend

Track Iron
A club with a small head used in the old days to play the ball from cart tracks. Similar to the rut iron.

Tradesman's Entrance
British slang for the back of the hole; applied to putts that run round the rim of the hole before dropping in at the back. In America the equivalent term is back door.

Trap
American term for bunker.

Travers, Jerome Dunstan AMERICAN
b. New York 1887. Nassau Invitation 1904; Metropolitan Amateur 1906-7, 1911-13;

US Amateur 1907-8, 1912-13; runner-up 1914; US Open 1915
Born of a wealthy New York family, Travers was one of the most brilliant amateurs of his age. His habit of playing only when he felt inclined to was carried to the point where he omitted one year to enter for the Amateur championship of which he was the title holder. His game resembled in certain aspects that of Walter Travis, an older champion than he and one with whom he frequently clashed. His strength lay in his putting – he switched to Travis's kind of putter, the Schenectady, when he won his first big event, the National Nassau Invitation, and met Travis in the final. Travers was an indifferent driver and

Jerome D. Travers

frequently took a cleek off the tee, but he recovered well and had a first-class temperament. Alex Smith, who taught him to play, said that unlike most players it was impossible to tell of Travers whether he was winning or losing. In the *World of Golf* Charles Price has a story of him topping his tee shot at a short hole which left him an awkward shot from the muddy bank of a stream. Travers hit his niblick shot in mid-air as he was jumping across the stream; the ball overshot the green into a wheatfield, from where he just made the green and holed the putt; his opponent took three and Travers walked off the green without saying a word, as though it had been a fair and ordinary half. In spite of his four national amateur titles, Travers's victory in the 1915 US Open came as only less of a surprise than Ouimet's at the Country Club three years before. He finished the last 6 holes at Baltusrol in 1 under par. He declined to defend his title the following year and his golfing career came to an abrupt end at that point.

Travis, Walter J. AUSTRALIAN
b. Maldon, Victoria, 1862; d. 1927. US Amateur 1900-1, 1903; tied 2nd US Open 1902; British Amateur 1904
Somewhat lightly regarded at first, Walter Travis became one of the famous early names in amateur golf. His achievement in winning the US Amateur Championship three times in four years has only been approached by Bobby Jones who won five years out of seven. In 1904 Travis became the first overseas player to win the British Amateur. When he travelled from America to Britain, a small man with a black cigar, he was already over 40. Partly because he had not taken up the game when he was young, he was essentially a made player without much power but he was an accurate striker, had an aggressive, competitive temperament and, above all, was a marvellously gifted putter. He used a famous centre-shafted Schenectady putter which for a long time after his victory at Sandwich was made illegal in Britain. He had to play a great many second shots with wooden clubs at Sandwich, but his control enabled him to beat James Robb, Harold Hilton, Horace Hutchinson and in the final Edward Blackwell.

Blackwell, markedly longer off the tee, was outputted, and Travis, four up at lunch, won on the 15th green in the afternoon. Travis clearly did not enjoy himself in Britain and on his return home said uncomplimentary things about Sandwich and its members. No doubt there were faults on both sides, but it cannot have seemed a gracious acceptance of Travis's victory when his Schenectady putter was barred in Britain, though not in America.

Travis continued to win championships until he was well in his fifties. His last notable triumph was the 1915 Metropolitan Amateur. He was a gifted person in other respects. An excellent writer and 'idea man', he founded and edited the famous magazine, *The American Golfer*. He was a capable golf-course architect and was one of the builders of the Garden City Golf Club's demanding course over which the 1924 Walker Cup and the 1936 US Amateur were played. He is credited with having helped Bobby Jones develop into a fine putter.

Trevino, Lee AMERICAN

b. Dallas, Tex., 1939. US Open 1968, 1971; Ryder Cup 1969, 1971, 1973; Vardon Trophy 1970-71; leading money winner US 1970; British Open 1971-2; Canadian Open 1971.

When Lee Trevino finished 5th in the 1967 US Open at Baltusrol, having had his entry money paid by his wife, it was widely felt that, though he might make a pleasant and prosperous living on the professional golf tour, he would not make a champion. When he won the following year at Rochester, therefore, his victory was hailed as the biggest surprise since Jack Fleck beat Ben Hogan in a play-off in 1955; and most of the critics found it hard to retract their opinions despite the fact that Trevino became the first man to return four rounds under par in the event.

They maintained that the natural swing that had been moulded on a public par-3 course was not reliable enough and that Trevino himself liked to make money fast and spend it faster. People failed to take him seriously but though he continued after Rochester to project himself as an enlivening, generous character who always had something to say, his golf subsequently began to make everyone take notice. Within three years he silenced the doubters by becoming perhaps one of the most consistent players in the world, the main threat to Nicklaus's championship supremacy, and the most gifted shotmaker on the tour.

For someone brought up in an old maintenance shack in Dallas, this graduation inevitably brought a remarkable change of life but, as so often happens, Trevino came at exactly the right moment and has had an invigorating influence on the game. His victory in the Open in 1968 was decidedly comfortable on paper. His final total of 275 (69, 68, 69, 69) was four shots better than Jack Nicklaus – but it followed a disastrous finish in the Champions' Tournament at

Houston and, considering that he had never previously won any big event, let alone an Open, his triumph over the pressures that built up was remarkable. He tied the Open record of Nicklaus; in doing so he topped his second to the 17th, pitched and holed from 12 ft, and at the 18th, hit his first two shots into the rough, wedged to within 4 ft, and again holed for his par.

Not surprisingly, Trevino was good copy for the writers and he was soon reported in all parts of the world. He finished 1968 in 6th place on the money winners' list, a rise of 39 places, and won the Hawaiian Open, giving $10,000 of his winnings to the family of his former roommate and fellow professional, Ted Makalena, who was killed in a

surfing accident. This was the first of several examples of the charitableness of Trevino who knows better than most what hard times are like.

In 1970 he won the Harry Vardon Trophy and rose from 7th the year before to leading money winner; he had a strokeplay average of 70.642 for 109 rounds, and won two tournaments. He also led the British Open after three rounds, letting slip on St Andrews' huge greens a good chance of victory. As important as his improvement in shotmaking had been his growing belief in himself; and in 1971 he gave spectacular evidence of this.

Within the space of 23 days, he won the US, Canadian and British Opens, an unparalleled performance; but it was not just a sudden, haphazard streak. His record for six weeks before that had been two victories, once 2nd and three times tied 3rd. Even without the momentous weeks which followed, this was a proud sequence. At Merion, he and Nicklaus, the two best players in the world, contested a play-off after both had tied with totals of 280. In Montreal, he won another play-off, this time with the veteran, Art Wall; and at Birkdale, he equalled the feats of Bobby Jones (1930), Gene Sarazen (1932) and Ben Hogan (1953) by winning the British and American Opens the same summer.

Here his total was 278 (69, 70, 69, 70) but after establishing a commanding position by going out in 31 on the final afternoon, threatening to lower Arnold Palmer's record aggregate, and also equal Palmer's feat of returning three rounds under 70 in the British Open, he almost came to grief. A skirmish with the left-hand sandhill at the 17th cost him 7, and it needed a brave 4 at the 18th to withstand the challenge of his playing partner, Lu Huan Liang.

Only a player of Trevino's buoyancy and spirit could have endured such prolonged physical and mental pressures. And soon he was everywhere – on news stands, radio and television; wisecracking, smiling and bubbling over. It was easy, in fact, to forget just how far the likeable little Mexican-American had come in four years. It was possible only to one completely absorbed in playing, completely dedicated to competing. Nobody ever expended more nervous energy while playing; yet his ability to concentrate on the shot in hand within seconds of an unquenchable flow of chatter was absolute. His swing is distinctly individual but his arc is true and solid and extends through the ball longer than any of his contemporaries. Throughout that golden month, he was rarely off line and he showed himself an exceptional putter

Lee Trevino: in the lower picture he is registering displeasure during the 1973 British Open

with a stroke in which the putter always remained close to the ground.

He was the player of 1971 and his confidence stood by him despite an appendix operation which almost prevented him from playing in the Ryder Cup in September; but though he at one time established a good lead in the race for leading money winner, Jack Nicklaus, not to be outdone, produced a tremendous finish to the year and beat him, winning the last tournament of the tour. He and Nicklaus won a big victory in the World Cup, thereby capping a memorable season which the two of them dominated throughout.

Trevino could not expect to maintain that pace through 1972 but, despite playing at Pebble Beach when barely recovered from pneumonitis, he made a brave defence of his US Open title, finishing equal 4th with a 78 in the last round; and, then, just as all eyes were on Nicklaus to complete the third leg of the Grand Slam, Trevino won an extraordinary victory in the British Open at Muirfield. In the last 21 holes, he holed a freak bunker shot and two chips, the final thrust coming at the 17th in the final round. This gave him an unlikely 5 at a time when he had virtually surrendered to his partner, Tony Jacklin, who followed by taking 3 putts and a 5 at the last. Trevino's total was 278, 1 better than Nicklaus; but it may be a hundred years before anyone else enjoys such a streak in the Open with a wedge.

Trevose GCC ENGLAND

Constantine Bay, Cornwall. 18 holes and short par 3

Trevose is on the Atlantic coast not far from Padstow, near the ruins of the church that gave its name to the bay which forms the western boundary of the course. It is a fine stretch of coast and the main features of the course, designed by H. S. Colt, are those of a seaside links. The course comes closest to the sea at the 4th green with its sight of surf and sand. Trevose, now run as a successful country club, was opened in 1926 and has been a regular home for Cornish championships. It is well known to legions of holiday golfers.

Troon Golf Course SCOTLAND

Troon, Ayrshire. 18 holes; 6,735 yd (6,159 m); par 73

A proud, rigorous links on the Ayrshire coast, it contains the longest and shortest holes in British championship golf. Its opening and closing holes lie along the Clyde shore, yet to some the old links lack charm. Certain outside factors may have contributed to this: one is that airliners shatter the

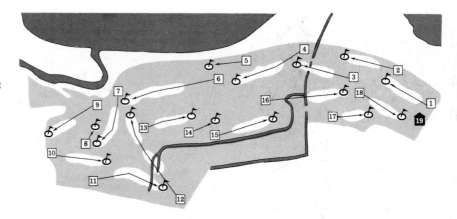

silence as they take off from nearby Prestwick and soar over the course; another is the unfortunate memory of the 1962 Open when crowd control round the 18th green broke down as Arnold Palmer completed the successful defence of his title. One difficulty affecting championships is enclosing the links so that everybody pays. Yet Troon is seaside golf at its best and has justifiably remained on the championship roster. The club was founded in 1878 and was first included on the Open Championship list in 1923, the year when Arthur Havers withstood the American challenge headed by Walter Hagen. In 1950 Bobby Locke won the second Open to be held there; in spite of taking a five at the 5th, an excellent links

short hole somewhat overshadowed by the more notorious 'Postage Stamp' 8th. Then in 1962 Arnold Palmer, playing some of the finest golf of his career in alien, dried-up conditions, won his second Open with 276, 6 strokes ahead of Kel Nagle, and a record for the championship. The third British Amateur to be held there gave Michael Bonallack his third title. Although for some years the club earned itself a reputation for not making the ladies welcome, the Scottish and British Ladies' championships were held there in the first decade of the century and have returned since. Troon has in fact been the home of every possible championship, the first-class hotel standing hard by the 18th green easing problems of accom-

Troon Golf Course, the plan and a view of the 8th green – known as the Postage Stamp

Opposite. Switzerland, the golf course at Lenzerheide

modation. Although not especially old by Scottish standards, the club is the home of some notable antiques, including a set of eight clubs dating back to the Stuart kings.

The start is somewhat flat and guileless with the waters of the open Clyde seeming almost to lap the side of the fairways. Notable holes are the redesigned 6th, which is the longest championship hole in the British Isles, measuring 580 yd (530 m), the 8th which is the shortest at 127 yd (116 m), and the redesigned 11th with its green against the railway fence, where Nicklaus once took 10, and where in the same championship Palmer played it in 1 under par and virtually won the championship there. The real name for the 8th is the Ailsa, for from the pulpit tee a fine view across the water to the island can be had, but the meagreness of the target at short range has caused it to be called the Postage Stamp. Hagen took a 5 at the hole in the 1923 Open final round, and finished 2nd. Roberto de Vicenzo deemed his tee shot unplayable in a bunker, returned to the tee (playing two according to the rules at the time) and nearly holed his second shot. On the other hand Gene Sarazen crowned a sentimental return to the course by holing in one there when the Open Championship revisited it in 1973 and Tom Weiskopf equalled Palmer's record aggregate of 276.

This return after 12 years was in the nature of a trial to see whether the course was still suitable for an Open from the point of view of access, aircraft noise interference, and the space needed to house the modern championship. Its claims at this time were being challenged by the resurgence of Turnberry further down the Ayrshire coast. With gloriously springy turf and fairly uncomplicated greens, Troon has thus much to offer the visitor.

Tucson National GC USA Tucson, Ariz. From a flat plain the Santa Catalina Mountains rise over 9,000 ft near Tucson, and at their base sits the Tucson National. Mount Lemmon, the dominant peak of the range, becomes covered with snow during the winter and turns into a skier's paradise, but the golf course is always open, except for a brief period in August, an uncomfortable month in the Southwest, when employees take a brief vacation.

Tucson sits 2,400 ft above sea level, and at that altitude and in that dry climate a golf ball travels great distances. For this reason, the course's 7,305-yd (6,680-m) maximum length is not really as overpowering as it may seem. From the more modest regular tees, it measures 6,670 yd (6,099 m). In addition to its great length, Tucson National

is spread over a vast area, 198 acres (80 ha). Because the course was built on barren wasteland, more than 5,000 trees have been planted to add beauty and course definition. There is something romantic about playing a shot from beneath a mysterious Joshua tree, so symbolic of the American West.

The club has a membership of about 530, among them Fred Waring, Gene Sarazen, Barry Goldwater, Mrs Westbrook Pegler, and Dr Ed Updegraff.

Tufts, Richard S. AMERICAN b. 1896 For knowledge of the game of golf, Tufts has had few if any peers in the United States. To some degree, this is understandable. As the grandson of James W. Tufts, who founded Pinehurst in the late 1890s, he practically grew up on the four 18-hole courses at the famous golf colony in North Carolina. After his graduation from Harvard University he returned to Pinehurst, and from the mid-1920s until late in 1970 when the Tufts family sold the resort to the Diamondhead Corporation, he directed the golf there. A man of great personal charm and intellectual honesty, he has been a traditionalist in all things, and it was fitting that his office on the village green in Pinehurst conjured up perfectly the flavour of a small Massachusetts town in the era of Rutherford B. Hayes.

There is hardly a facet of golf that Tufts does not know well. He was a very good player who scored in the low 70s. Although he was too modest by nature to let it be generally known, he was an authority on technique and a remarkably good judge of a golfer's true abilities. He was in the administrative side of the game for half a century, starting with the Carolinas Golf Association. He was a member of the USGA for three decades, heading nearly all the important committees at one time or another before serving as president in 1956-7. During that

time, he was one of the moving spirits in the formation of the World Amateur Golf Council. A close friend and admirer of Donald Ross, he took over after Ross's death as the resident architect at Pinehurst. In revising the No. 4 course and building No. 5, he showed a nice command of the orthodox principles and a flair for design.

Tufts has written a number of excellent treatises on golf and his book *The Principles Behind the Rules of Golf*, published in 1960, sheds more light on that subject than any other.

There has been no one single climax to Tufts' career, but he has confided to friends that serving as captain of the 1963 US Walker Cup team was 'far and away the greatest thrill I've had in golf'. That team was trailing the British 6 points to 3 after the first day's play, but Tufts succeeded in rallying his men and they pulled away on the second day to win 12 to 8.

Tunisia
Tunisia, tucked into the Mediterranean coast between Libya and Algeria, with a marvellous golfing climate, beautiful beaches, and a variety of tourist attractions, has great potential for golf. At present, however, the country has only one course, in Tunis.

There are indications that the government is interested in developing the game along the pattern established by Spain and followed by Morocco. Habib Bourguiba Jr, son of the president of Tunisia, has looked closely at golf development in these countries, and has said that Tunisia should follow suit. Coming from him, a leading figure in investment banking and tourist promotion in his country, and a keen golfer, that statement holds promise.

Tupling, L. Peter BRITISH
b. Sheffield, Yorkshire, 1950. British Boys'

Richard S. Tufts

Peter L. Tupling

Opposite. Tasmania GC *above* and Tobago GC *below*

1967; Yorkshire Amateur 1968; Walker Cup 1969; 2nd Wills Open 1971

Tupling reached the last 8 of the British Amateur at Hoylake in 1969, later finished leading amateur in the British Open at Lytham and was picked for the 1969 England and Walker Cup teams.

He turned professional and has made steady progress. He tied for 4th place in the Daks tournament, finished 2nd in the Wills of 1971 and led the 1972 British Open at Muirfield after one round.

Turkey

Golf in Turkey is scarce. Istanbul, the country's largest and most colourful city, has one 18-hole course. Ankara, the nation's capital in Central Anatolia, has one; and so has Izmir, formerly Smyrna, on the Aegean Sea in the southwest.

These three courses are open to tourists; but, generally speaking, they are not sufficiently developed to be classed as tourist attractions. Basically, they are grass, with sand greens, but poorly designed and maintained. They are mostly used by foreign residents as few Turks have taken to golf, and the Ministry of Tourism has, until recently at least, done little to develop courses. The US Air Force has limited golf facilities at some of the American bases, including a small course at Incirli near Adana. These, however, are normally restricted to American military and civilian personnel and their dependants, and thus generally excluded from tourist consideration.

Turnberry Hotel GC SCOTLAND
Turnberry, Ayrshire. 36 holes; 2 courses

Turnberry is an unforgettable place in an incomparable setting by the sea, with Ailsa Craig and the peaks of the isle of Arran across the water. British golf has nothing better to offer. Yet the history of Turnberry is full of upheaval and costly endeavour and, but for continued faith and financial backing, it would have ceased to exist long ago. In World War II, its future was threatened by conversion into an airfield, but, even before 1939, its well-being was uncertain.

It was due to the Marquis of Ailsa, who had a private course in his Culzean Estate, that golf got under way at Turnberry. Later he agreed to the takeover and development of the golfing facilities by the Glasgow and South Western Railway. By 1907 Turnberry had become a golf centre with a first-class hotel. A branch line from Ayr through Turnberry to Girvan was opened providing a frequent train service from Glasgow, and a direct sleeper service from London and the Midlands.

A plan dated April 1909 shows two 18-hole golf courses. It is assumed that Willie Fernie, the professional/greenkeeper at Old Troon, advised on their construction; a view supported by the fact that his son, Tom Fernie, became Turnberry's first professional.

Despite the criticism of Sunday golf by the Kirk, its introduction helped to bring Turnberry to the forefront of Scottish golf and the courses progressed favourably until the outbreak of war in 1914 when an airfield was established. The links became a training station for pilots of the Royal Flying Corps and other Empire flying units; a memorial to their dead still stands beside the 12th green of the Ailsa course.

Although Turnberry was under military control for five years, the damage to the courses was not so great as 30 years later and, soon after the land was reclaimed, a new No. 2 course was built which proved so popular that it became the principal course, used for many championship events.

Until the 1926 regrouping of the railways, Turnberry had been developed by David Cooper, General Manager of the Glasgow and South Western Railway. After the reorganization Turnberry, as part of the LMS Hotels group, came under the enthusiastic direction of Arthur Tawle, a keen golfer who was responsible for the appointment of James Macdonald as professional and for christening the courses 'Ailsa' and 'Arran'.

In order that the Ailsa course should regain some of its lost popularity, Major C. K. Hutchison, who played a part in the construction of Gleneagles, was commissioned to revise the layout. His main directives were to reduce the number of blind shots and to increase its length, alterations that were completed by 1938. They never became established as, within a year, war had broken out again and the land requisitioned as an airfield by RAF Coastal Command.

Runways were relaid and golf forgotten, as some thought forever, but not only was Turnberry miraculously reborn, its rapid reestablishment brought it new acclaim. Within a few years it housed its first Amateur Championship, its first Walker Cup match, its first Home Internationals and its first Professional Matchplay Championship.

Turnberry owed its resuscitation to the skill of Mackenzie Ross, the Scottish architect who achieved his finest work in turning bulldozers, grabs and scoops into instruments of creation; and to James Alexander, Superintendent of British Transport Hotels, who was responsible for organizing the reconstruction.

A Glasgow firm was engaged to demolish the concrete runways and airfield buildings but it needed a good deal of hard work and persuasion by Frank Hole, Tawle's successor, to make this possible and to coax the government into giving proper financial compensation. In convincing the hotel directors

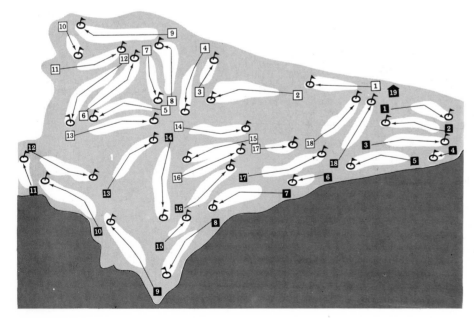

The course plan of Turnberry Hotel GC; the tees of the Ailsa course are in black and those of the Arran course in open squares

that Turnberry had a great future, Frank Hole deserved the gratitude of the golfing world.

All traces of Turnberry's belligerent past were quickly removed and by June 1951, the Ailsa Course was reopened, having first been turfed rather than seeded on tee, fairway and green, a most unusual undertaking. The natural features were preserved and Mackenzie Ross made good use of the line of dunes skirting the shore. By taking holes such as the 4th, 9th and 10th alarmingly close to the beach he gave Turnberry a spectacular new identity. The drive at the 9th from an isolated island tee above the rocks has been much photographed and is a symbol of true linksland golf. In addition to preserving the beauty, Mackenzie Ross introduced a sternness fit for an Open championship. With the opening up of approach roads to the course, Turnberry was scheduled for its first Open Championship in 1977.

After the Home Internationals had been

staged there in 1960, the Royal and Ancient chose it for the British Amateur of 1961 in which Michael Bonallack won his first major title, beating the Ayrshire golfer, Jimmy Walker, in the final by 6 and 4. In 1963 the Walker Cup produced a wonderful match in which Britain's first-day lead was offset by America's recovery in the second.

The *News of the World* British Professional Matchplay Championship had become a fairly regular visitor, producing champions in Christy O'Connor (1957), Eric Brown (1960) and David Thomas (1963). It also staged the novel Braemar tournament played with seven clubs in 1964 and in 1972 and 1973 it housed the John Player Classic in which many of the world's leading professionals competed there for the first time, although Turnberry had naturally been the scene of many filmed matches.

To James Alexander goes the credit for replanning the Arran course, reopened in 1954. The idea was to have two courses of differing character. In fact the Arran, a little flatter and more sheltered although more gorse-fringed, is a fine test in itself.

Turnberry Hotel GC; *top*, the 9th tee and, *above*, the 16th green

Turnesa, Jim AMERICAN
b. New York 1909. USPGA 1952; Ryder Cup 1953

Sixth son of Vitale Turnesa, father of one of golf's most famous golfing families, Turnesa became the first and only Turnesa to win the USPGA championship, although all the others tried. He was 3 down to Chick Harbert after 18 holes, and led for the first time when he won on the 36th green. He was 39 and the following year in the Ryder Cup match he was left out of the foursomes; in the singles he was Peter Alliss's opponent in the dramatic match in which Turnesa just got home on the last green.

Turnesa, Joe AMERICAN
b. New York 1901. Runner-up US Open 1926; Ryder Cup 1927, 1929; runner-up USPGA 1927

Third son of Vitale Turnesa, greenkeeper at the Fairview club (*see* William Turnesa), Joe was the tallest and possibly the most easy going of the family. He came within sight of winning the US Open and the USPGA in successive years; in the 1926 Open he had a 4-stroke lead at one time over Bobby Jones in the final round, but slipped to a 77, and Jones grimly sticking to par got home by 1 stroke. In the final of the PGA championship against Hagen the following year, Turnesa was leading until 5 holes from the end but could not prevent Hagen from recording his fourth consecutive victory in the event. His Ryder Cup record was 1½ points out of 4.

Turnesa, William AMERICAN
b. New York 1914. US Amateur 1938, 1948; semi-finalist 1949; British Amateur 1947; runner-up 1949; Walker Cup 1947, 1949, 1951 (captain)

One of the great wedge players of all time and a magnificent match player. From an early age Willie Turnesa lived golf: he was the seventh and youngest son of an Italian immigrant, who was greenkeeper at the Fairview CC in suburban Westchester, and whose other six sons all became golf professionals. Willie ('the Wedge' as he was known) was the only one to remain amateur, the family fortunes by then being sound enough to stand it. There was nothing exceptional about his long game, indeed by championship standards it was below average in consistency, but he was a phenomenal player round the greens. Two examples out of many can be taken from matches directly involved in his championship record. In the final of his first US Amateur victory in 1938 at Oakmont, where the greens are notoriously tricky and bunkers abundant, he was in traps at 13 of the 29 holes he needed to

beat Pat Abbott, and every single time he got down in 2 strokes from them. In the semi-final of the British Amateur in 1949 Turnesa missed the prepared surface 15 times out of 18 from the tee, yet he was round in 71 and beat Ernest Millward on the last green.

Willie went to Holy Cross University on the savings of his brothers, and learned the game at the 'Turnesa Country Club', a rough-hewn course laid out by his elder brothers. He scored several victories in the New York area, winning the Metropolitan, the Westchester (amateur), the North and South and the New York State, before breaking through with his 1938 victory in the Amateur. He scored three victories in six matches in the Walker Cup series, but failed to score a point in 1949, coming up against Ronnie White at his greatest both times. Turnesa helped to found and run the Westchester Caddie Fund which has sent more than one hundred caddies to college.

Tuthill, Jack AMERICAN
A native of Cutchogue, Long Island, N.Y., Tuthill became a professional baseball player after he had graduated from high school. He played for Hartford in the Eastern League in 1947, and was with Eau Claire, Wis., and Watertown, N.Y., in the Border League the following season.

He matriculated at Cortland, N.Y., State Teachers College in 1948 and earned a physical education degree. He continued his education at Ithaca College and received a master's degree in education.

Tuthill was associated with the New York State Labor Department, the Federal Bureau of Investigation, and Republic Aviation, Inc., before joining the tournament staff of the PGA of America in December 1960. Since 1964 he has been head of the team which presides over the day-to-day operation of the USPGA tour. Presently his title is Tournament Director.

Tutwiler, Edgar M. AMERICAN b. 1920.
Runner-up US Amateur 1964; Eisenhower Trophy 1964; Walker Cup 1965, 1967; Indiana Amateur 1966

Tutwiler was beaten in the final of the 1964 Amateur by a fellow Virginian, Bill Campbell, who achieved a lifelong ambition in winning the title. Like Dr Updegraff his international career did not begin until he was in the forties. His victory in the final series of singles against Ronnie Shade in the 1965 Walker Cup, at the age of 45, led a remarkable recovery by the United States who were 5 points behind with the final eight singles to come. His own recovery was

no less remarkable for he was 3 down with 5 holes played.

Tweddell, William BRITISH
b. Whickham, Co. Durham, 1897. British Amateur 1927; runner-up 1935; Midland Amateur 1927; Walker Cup 1928, 1936 (captain); captain Royal and Ancient 1961

Dr William Tweddell, who brought to golf the precision and infinite capacity for taking pains that could be expected from a surgeon, was one of three Worcestershire amateurs who dominated Midland competitions in the 1920s, the others being Eric Fiddian and Stanley Lunt. All three won national titles, and Tweddell had the best record although his practice gave him little time in which to prepare for big events. His 1927 win in the Amateur Championship was gained easily – he beat D. E. Landale 7 and 6 in the final – but a more striking performance in that event was in 1935 when, in his 39th year, and not in the best of health, he again reached the final and took the young American Lawson Little, holder of the title, to the 36th hole.

Twitch
An uncontrollable nervous 'disease' of putting. A convulsive movement of the hands particularly during short putts which leads to great anguish and frustration. It is largely incurable, and liable to attack even the best players.

Ed Tutwiler

UAR see EGYPT; SYRIA

Uganda

On 29 August 1969, the Uganda GC in Kampala celebrated its 50th anniversary and though it is possible that golf was played in other centres before 1919, no records exist to prove it. Nearly all the country's 15 courses were started by Provincial or District Commissioners of the old Colonial Service, the notable exception being the Kilembe Mines GC which came into play in 1956 largely through the efforts of Alf Pugsley, general manager of the mine at the time. Kilembe Mines was extended from 9 to 18 in 1969. Kilembe and Uganda GC are the country's only 18-hole courses, but some of the smaller clubs have very good lay-outs, particularly Jinja, Entebbe, and the Toro club at Fort Portal.

Jinja and Entebbe lie close to the shores of Lake Victoria and from the 2nd hole at Jinja the obelisk marking the source of the Nile can be seen. Hippo no longer worry the golfers at Jinja although a unique local rule still exists allowing players a free drop if the ball lies in a hippo's footprint. Golf at Fort Portal is played against the background of the famous Mountains of the Moon and is another good test.

A number of open fixtures attract entries from all over Uganda. The premier event is the Uganda Amateur Championship, usually played in Kampala but staged at Kilembe in 1970. The possibility of an Open championship linking up with the professional circuit of other parts of Africa is being studied.

Until about 1970 golf in Uganda was played mostly by expatriate residents but nowadays more and more Ugandans are taking an interest. Many of them show a natural aptitude for the game and it might not be long before one of them emerges as Ugandan champion. Another indication of golf's spread was that on 8 August 1971 the Uganda Golfing Society invited the former President of Uganda, General Idi Amin Dada, to become an honorary member.

Caddie fees are low and in June 1971 the government abolished import duty on sports equipment, thereby making it cheaper to buy clubs there than in the United States.

Uganda GC UGANDA

Kampala. 18 holes; 6,684 yd (6,112 m)

The club, the oldest in Uganda, is situated in the heart of Kampala barely five minutes' walk from the Kampala International Hotel. It has been at its present site since about 1940 when it was moved out from even nearer the city centre when Kampala expanded.

Before 1948, only 13 holes were in play because of lack of money and a small membership – about 70; in 1948, however, the extra 5 holes were revived and the full course covered 6,495 yd (5,939 m). Playing membership is now nearly 500. The course contains many natural features, not the least of which is a water furrow, known locally as the 'Kitante', which comes into play on at least 9 holes.

Ugolino GCC ITALY

nr Florence (Firenze). 18 holes; 6,105 yd (5,582 m); par 71

This course is situated some seven miles from the city on a picturesque hillside. Some of the holes, notably the 4th and the short 8th, running like narrow funnels through the trees, are first class. But the course is perhaps most memorable for the silver-grey of the olive trees, the distinctive green of the umbrella pines, and the slender cypresses. The Ugolino club will also be remembered for its unusually friendly atmosphere, and its cuisine. It has produced one of the best amateurs from that side of the Alps, Baldovino Dassu, the 1970 British Youths' Champion.

United Services Club INDIA

Colaba Point, Bombay Island. 18 holes; 5,836 yd (5,336 m); par 70

This club has what is perhaps India's only true seaside links. As the name suggests, members are mostly from the Indian armed forces. Water is scarce, the course is dry and the greens shrivel as the hot weather advances. But even if the golf is not of championship calibre, the sight of the sun dipping clear into the Arabian Sea behind silhouetted casuarinas more than compensates.

United States of America

There are more golfers and courses in the United States than in all the rest of the world. Some 10 million people play at least 15 rounds a year, and 2¼ million others play fewer. They use over 11,250 courses, of which 9,750 are conventional and 1,500 are composed mostly of par-3 holes. Still the game grows, with an annual net increase of at least 250 courses.

Golf in the United States is not only vast but widely varied in its physical elements of turf, courses and climate, even without tropical conditions. The player at the northern summer course is restricted to four months of golf a year, whereas his brother in the deep South has '13 months of sunshine'. Links courses are comparatively few, but there is otherwise great diversity – golfers trudge meadow and mountain, seaside and savannah, forest and desert.

What first was a pastime mainly for a privileged few has become a national game available to almost everyone. It is a game of economic extremes. A plush new club may have a membership initiation fee of $5,000 and annual dues of $2,000; yet it is possible to play the same game on a public course in a small town for $1 or less a round. Metropolitan public courses are more costly, and crowded: players sometimes register as early as 4 a.m., then sleep nearby in their automobiles until dawn signals their starting times.

All this started less than a century ago. There is reason to believe that golf was played in 1779 near New York, in 1786 at Charleston, S. Car., and in 1795 at Savannah, Ga., but there was no continuity. A tiny club formed in 1884 at Oakhurst near White Sulphur Springs, W. Va., also did not endure. The real beginnings came soon after. Three clubs claim to be the oldest with continuous existence. It is said that golf was played in 1885 at Foxburg, Pa., and that the Foxburg CC was organized in 1887; there is no documentation. The Dorset Field Club, in Dorset, Vt., is said to have had golf since 1886, and at its present site; again there is no documentation. Golf was played in Yonkers, New York, on 22 February 1888, and the St Andrew's GC was founded there on 14 November 1888; its organization is well authenticated. The Middlesboro GC, in Middlesboro, Ky., is reputed to have started in 1889.

Once well rooted, the game caught American fancy and enthusiasm. By the turn of the century there were over 1,000 courses. Although golf was then primarily a club game for people of means, New York City opened the first public course in July 1895 in Van Cortlandt Park; its 9th hole was 700 yd (640 m) long, but the entire 9 measured only 2,561 yd (2,342 m).

In the lavish 1920s golf had a boom – only to be followed by a bust in the next decade. A long downward slide in the number of golf facilities reached a low point of 4,808 in 1945. Since then, in a quarter-century, there has been an increase of about 135% to the present 11,250 courses. It is notable that there are now more courses open to the public (6,200) than private courses (5,050).

Before 1962 there were always more private than public courses. California has more facilities than any other State, nearly 700, closely followed by New York. Every State except Alaska has at least 20. Among the regions the Midwest is the most abundant in courses.

Statisticians have a glorious time with golf figures; to wit the following estimates in 1972:

Acres devoted to golf facilities 1,127,012

Rounds played annually 215,000,000

Capital investment $3,273,400,000

Annual maintenance costs $423,000,000

There are pronounced extremes in quality of courses and upkeep. On the whole, standards are high, with growing appreciation of the aid which science and engineering can give in maintenance. It is not uncommon for a club to spend $100,000 a year for the upkeep of 18 holes. Course superintendents at many clubs are college graduates with degrees in agronomy; the top salaries of a few go to $25,000 a year; unskilled unionized workers in some areas earn $3.50 an hour.

Notable advances in course conditions have been made in the South, where golf can be played the year round, but cool-season grasses cannot be used generally. Since World War II the South has had a revolution in its turf cover. Science has developed hybrid Bermuda grasses which produce fine-bladed putting green turf comparable with the best bent grasses.

Clubhouses tend to be family and social centres, rather than pure temples of golf. One consequence is an elaboration of services, especially for women's weekday patronage. Since club restaurants are notorious for not paying their way, the clubhouse tail often wags the golfing dog. The cost of clubhouse services is one of the increasing financial difficulties facing private clubs. Real-estate taxes and labour costs continually rise. There are Federal limits on the amount of non-member income which a club may receive without forfeiting income-tax exemption. Clubs are widely used by members in entertaining business customers, but stringent rules govern allocation of costs as an individual's business expenses, thus tending to dampen club income.

A most significant aspect of the game in America finds expression in programmes to assist school-age caddies, in training, recreation, and with college scholarship funds. Twenty-six regional golf associations help 1,788 former caddies with college expenses.

The bellwethers are the Chick Evans Scholars Foundation of the Western Golf Association and the Francis Ouimet Scholarship Fund of the Massachusetts Golf Association. Caddies are carefully chosen for scholarship aid on the bases of need and ability. But, on the whole, caddies are vanishing. They are available in metropolitan areas where rates are high (e.g. $14 for two bags over 18 holes), but many first-class courses literally have no caddies.

In the place of the caddie have come trolleys and a fleet of motorized carts, some 200,000 of them, powered by electric batteries or gasoline, suitable for carrying at least two players and their bags. Purists dislike the motor carts because they curtail exercise in a game meant to be played for exercise. They minimize sociability, especially in a land where sociable four-ball games are the custom. On the other hand, they extend the golfing life of older men. A cartoon typifies an attitude which carts foster. A golfer has just dismounted from his motorized vehicle, and, club in hand, is standing over the ball, about to hit it, and is saying: 'This is the part of the game I don't like.'

Even so, with one person in 20 charged with being a golfer, it is suspected that golf is in America to stay.

United States Golf Association (USGA)
The governing body of golf in the United States is more than a governing body. It is at once a service organization, with agronomists who give scientific advice on course upkeep; it is a public information medium which publishes a general-interest golf magazine and produces motion pictures; it is a custodian of physical memorabilia and the intangible traditions of the game, as well as a maker of rules and a sponsor of national and international championships.

The United States Golf Association is distinguished not only for the scope of its work but for the motive force behind it. It started as an amateur organization with the aim of serving the best interests of golf. It has remained true to that purpose, even as the game has grown and commercial influences have swirled around it. The USGA's sense of mission to golf and sportsmanship is kept clear by the fact that its hundreds of committeemen serve for love of the game, without compensation, and pay their own expenses to meetings and championships.

The USGA consists of nearly 4,000 golf clubs and courses. There were five members when it was founded on 22 December 1894, as the Amateur Golf Association of the United States, with subsequent name changes to American Golf Association and United States Golf Association. It came into being because there were no uniform standards for the fledgling game. Earlier in 1894 two clubs had independently held 'Amateur Golf Championships of the United States' – the Newport GC at Newport, R.I., and the St Andrew's GC at Yonkers, N.Y. The

United States of America: members of the victorious 1970 team raise the Espirito Santo Trophy with the help of P. H. Strubing, President of the USGA; from left to right: Mrs H. Prunaret (captain), Martha Wilkinson, Cynthia Hill, Jane Booth

catalyst was Henry O. Tallmadge, honorary secretary of St Andrew's, who brought the charter member clubs together at a dinner in New York.

Although the first Amateur Championship in 1895 was a focal point, the new organization appended an Open and a Women's Amateur Championship. A year later the Open had a significant racial test when a number of professionals threatened not to play if the entry of a 16-year-old coloured caddie, John Shippen, was accepted. The USGA president, Theodore A. Havemeyer – the 'Sugar King' – is said to have assured the hesitant ones that the tournament would go on with or without them. It went on with them. A crisis was weathered. John Shippen tied for 5th place.

Today the USGA's work is in three principal areas: regulations, competitions and general services.

Regulations In formulating and interpreting codes for the game, the USGA touches every golfer. The Rules of Golf are framed jointly by the USGA and the Royal and Ancient GC of St Andrews in quadrennial conferences. The first modern negotiations took place in 1951, when the respective chairmen were Isaac B. Grainger for the USGA and Dr Harold Gardiner-Hill for the R. and A. A national handicap system has been in effect for many years, formulated by the USGA and applied by clubs and several hundred regional, State and district golf associations, which have a cooperative relationship with the USGA although organizationally independent. Electronic computers are widely used in revising handicaps every few weeks in the season.

The USGA long ago anticipated the need for limiting the distance qualities of the golf ball and established in January 1942, a test of impact velocity in addition to specifications for size and weight. This has prevented the obsolescence of many courses. To emphasize skill, the USGA at the same time introduced specifications for markings on iron clubs. It had limited the number of clubs carried to 14 beginning in January 1938.

The growth of commercial forces in golf has threatened the amateur code but the USGA has staunchly upheld it, even though amateur competition has declined in public estimation as the professional player's star has ascended.

Competitions The three original championships – Amateur, Open and Women's Amateur – had no additions until the Amateur Public Links Championshop was started in 1922. Subsequently there were added the Junior Amateur, Girls' Junior,

Women's Open, Senior Amateur and Women's Senior. The nine USGA Championships constitute a vast programme, with 13,431 entrants in 1971; several Championships require a network of sectional qualifying rounds to produce the final fields. The extent of player interest is shown in the following numbers of entrants in 1971: Open – 4,279; Public Links – 4,174; Amateur – 2,327. The USGA participates in five international competitions – the Walker Cup and Curtis Cup with British amateurs and women amateurs, respectively, and three World Amateur Team Championships for amateurs, women amateurs and seniors. The USGA took the initiative in organization of the World Amateur Golf Council in 1958.

General Services Since the early 1920s the USGA has had a Green Section whose scientists first researched, and now give extension service, in problems of golf-course maintenance. There are 13 agronomists in five regional offices.

USGA headquarters is an information centre for virtually all aspects of golf. Publications, brochures and films are available to the golfing public. A Golf Museum and Library was started in 1936 at the instance of George W. Blossom Jr. Its growth resulted in the purchase of a New York town house in 1950 which, as 'Golf House', served as USGA headquarters until 1972, when a brick mansion on 62 acres became 'Golf House', in Far Hills, N.J., not far from Manhattan. It houses a treasure trove of historic golf clubs and other memorabilia and one of the great golf libraries of the world, as well as the USGA's executive staff of 27.

The USGA has 21 standing subcommittees comprising more than 500 members. The governing Executive consists of 15 business and professional gentlemen who are elected annually. The Executive Director and his staff handle an income of $1½ millions a year. The Association's surplus exceeds $1 million. Its Presidents are listed on p. 473.

Up

A player is said to be up when in a match he has won more holes than his opponent. 'Never up, never in' is a saying applied to putts that do not reach the hole.

Updegraff, Edgar R. AMERICAN

b. 1922. Western Amateur 1957, 1959; semi-finalist British Amateur 1963; Walker Cup 1963, 1965, 1969

A US Army captain in World War II, Edgar Updegraff graduated in 1945 from

the University of Iowa College of Medicine. He began a career as urologist and it was not until he was over 40 that he made his first Walker Cup appearance. In 1963 he made a notable contribution to the US victory by winning both his matches on the last day when the United States were trailing, including a single against Joe Carr. In the ensuing British Amateur at St Andrews he was beaten in the semi-finals by the eventual winner, Michael Lunt. Updegraff won the Arizona Amateur three times and the Southwestern Amateur seven times.

Upright

Opposite of flat; a swing which is nearer the vertical than the horizontal plane.

Top, Edgar R. Updegraff

Above, the upright swing of Gay Brewer

Uruguay GC URUGUAY
Montevideo

Club de Golf del Uruguay is the leading club in a relatively small golfing country – although the Uruguayan team of Juan Sereda and José Esmori finished 6th with Brazil in the 1962 World Cup in Buenos Aires. Sereda is probably the best of all Uruguyan players, dominating professional golf in the country throughout the 1960s. In 1964 he achieved one of the rare holes in 1 in the World Cup, at the 16th of Royal Kaanapali in Hawaii. The Uruguayan amateur team ventured into the Eisenhower Trophy event in 1964, an example of the competitive spirit fostered by the Uruguyan Open and other championships.

Urzetta, Sam AMERICAN
b. Rochester, N.Y., 1926. US Amateur 1950; Walker Cup 1951, 1953

Sam Urzetta won the 1950 US Amateur after the longest final in history. His match with Frank Stranahan lasted 39 holes. Urzetta, a former caddie, won four matches out of four in the 1951 and 1953 Walker Cups. Since the middle 1950s, this sound technician and excellent teacher has been the professional at Rochester CC.

USGA Men's National Championship
see p. 452.

US Masters Tournament
The United States Masters Tournament is now firmly entrenched as one of the four world events which have become known as the 'Big Four'. The other three are the US and British Opens and the USPGA. The Masters is the most recent of them and the only one to be held at the same course every year. It has never been claimed for the tournament that it is held on the greatest championship course in the world, nor that the entry is absolutely the strongest that could be found, nor that victory in it is necessarily the most treasured prize of all. The Augusta National course, as is explained elsewhere, is essentially a course of opportunity. At 5 of the last 9 holes water plays a spectacular part; scores may be ruined, but a player who takes his courage in his hands and who has the skill may string the birdies together. This, as much as anything, has given the tournament its impetus and its panache. The entry each year contains all the very great names, but as Bobby Jones's wish was that the tournament should retain its invitational character, and that overseas players as well as amateurs should be represented, the main body of American players do not muster in full strength.

What has been achieved is the creation of a classic – a tournament which has become the most colourful and spectacular in the world, and which has still retained its basic qualities of enjoyment and high golfing principles. If in prestige the US or British Opens stand as first in the world, there are material benefits to be obtained from the chance that the Masters comes at the beginning of the golfing season. Because of this the winner can make season-long contracts, plan exhibition matches and accept invitations to other events which victory in the later tournaments cannot offer to the same extent.

First among the factors that have brought the Masters to the front must be counted the personality of its founder, and the only president in perpetuity of the Augusta National GC, Bobby Jones. He set the tone, not only by the quality of the friends he invited to play in those early days, but by his insistence on the highest standards of sportsmanship. The Masters has remained an invitation tournament, and anyone falling below the high level of behaviour that has been set is in danger of not being asked again.

The first Masters was in 1934. Bobby Jones, although he had officially retired four years before, took part because the club was short of money and needed someone to draw the local public. Jones had invited those with whom he had done battle in the past, which meant the best in the land, but also invited were former champions and anyone with a distinguished record. There were none of the trappings of modern tournament play, and the informal spirit is typified by the story told of Bobby Jones's father, a notable character affectionately known as the Colonel. Having a fair grasp of the rules of golf he was given official status and took up his station on the course. In the final round a fine old champion, struggling to put on a good show in this the great man's own tournament, pitched short of the water-ringed 12th green and was in doubt whether he might get a free drop because of casual water. He approached the Colonel who countered with the question: 'How do you stand at present, old timer?' On being told that the former champion was 17 over par, the Colonel replied: 'As far as I am concerned, sir, you can do what the hell you like!'

Jones finished tied 13th, but a start had been made, and when in the following year Gene Sarazen overtook Craig Wood by holing his second to the 15th (485 yd; 443 m) with a 4-wood, the tournament made front-page news and has stayed there ever since. Two years later Byron Nelson picked up 6 strokes in two holes and overtook the probable winner, Ralph Guldahl, and the pattern of challenge and disaster over the last 9 holes of the course was beginning to form. For example, in 1939 Guldahl had his triumph by coming home in a final 33 and overtaking Sam Snead. The belief that the last 9 formed the area of opportunity was confirmed in 1940 when Jimmy Demaret, who later became the first player to win the Masters three times, came home in 30 to win by 4 strokes.

After 1942 when Byron Nelson recorded his second victory the course was closed for the duration of the war. For a time cattle were allowed to graze on it to help the war effort, but they became too destructive of what had been the greens and of the rare bushes and trees. A solution was reached when it was found that the head greenkeeper had had experience breeding turkeys, and from then on the Augusta National became a turkey farm.

Augusta is essentially a course for the specialist. It takes time to appreciate the problems set by pin placements on the spacious greens. Some of the finest golfers have only won there after repeated efforts. Craig Wood, after two near misses, finally had his reward in 1941; it was 10 years after first playing that Ben Hogan won the Masters title in 1951. Then, and again in 1953 in winning, he played some of the finest golf ever seen there. For his second victory, in 1953, he returned a total of 274, the lowest up to that point; the weather was favourable, but the golf he turned on has been reckoned to be as good as has ever been played.

No amateur has ever won the Masters but three have finished in 2nd place, on their own or in a tie – Frank Stranahan in 1947, Ken Venturi in 1956, and Charlie Coe in 1961. Venturi appeared to be in a winning position in 1956 when he led the field by 4 strokes with one round to go, but in rough weather he took a final 80 and Jack Burke slipped ahead of him with a 71. Coe holds the most consistent record of any amateur in the Masters. He has been low amateur six times and has nine times finished in the first

the next nine titles, Palmer taking four of them in every alternate year from 1958. In 1960 he led the field all the way, the first player to have done so since Craig Wood in 1941. Nicklaus became the youngest ever to win the event at the age of 23 in 1963; his score in rough weather was the third highest recorded, but two years later his 271 was the lowest winning total. In the course of it he scored 64, equalling the record for the course set by Lloyd Mangrum in 1940. The only player to break the Big Three's grip on the Masters in that period was Art Wall in 1959 who, with an electrifying run of birdies finished with 66, gaining 8 strokes on Palmer and 9 on Stan Leonard of Canada.

In 1966 Nicklaus scored his third victory,

respect it differed from the US Masters: it is switched from courses in one part of the country to another and seldom revisits a course, whereas the Masters is fixed at Augusta, Ga., which tends to breed course specialists. Also the USGA, which is responsible for the championship, has more and more followed a policy of making special preparations to increase the difficulties. Its practice has been to move in over a year in advance, so that by the time the championship comes round the rough has been allowed to grow and encroach on the fairways, holes have been lengthened and bunkers trimmed. At times the professionals have complained, as they did at Brookline, Mass., in 1963, that the course had been

24, which secures an invitation for the following year. He owed his 2nd place in 1961 to closing rounds of 69 and 69 which gained him 6 strokes on Palmer, with whom he tied, and 5 on the winner, Player. The victory of the South African was the first time an American had not won and emphasized in a different direction the all-round character of the event. The best finishes by other players from outside the American continent have been Ramón Sota's tied 6th in 1965, Peter Thomson's 5th in 1957, and Peter Oosterhuis's tied 3rd in 1973.

More than any other major championship the Masters felt the impact of the Big Three. Starting in 1958 Arnold Palmer, followed by Gary Player and Jack Nicklaus, won eight of

but after that the Big Three did not score again until 1972 when Nicklaus equalled Palmer's record of four victories. Of the intervening winners the most sensational was Bob Goalby who appeared to have tied with Roberto de Vicenzo until it came to light that the Argentinian had signed for a 4 at the 17th instead of the 3 he had taken.

US Open Championship

One of the Big Four championships, the US Open became, until the British Open began again to challenge its supremacy, the most important of them, and the title which Americans and non-Americans coveted most both for its prestige and for the indirect financial benefits it offered. In one important

'tricked up' so much that it produced a freak winner. But the USGA, while relenting a little, has adhered strictly to its opinion that the Open is a supreme test of skill and as such must be made as difficult as possible.

In 1973 Oakmont became the first course to be used for a fifth championship; Baltusrol with four is the next most frequented. The USGA has a difficult task to find courses of the required quality in the different areas under its control. There has been criticism that it has never taken the Open to Florida, for example, or to Southern states such as Georgia; the latter is a strange omission as Georgia was the home state of Bob Jones. In the four years beginning in 1970 the USGA found such extremes of the continent as

Houston in Texas, Hazeltine in Michigan, Merion on the Atlantic side and Pebble Beach on the Pacific.

The championship originated in much the same haphazard way as the British Open had done. In both cases the event started as an appendage of the Amateur championship. The US Open was first held over a 9-hole course at Newport, R.I., at the beginning of October 1895. For the first 16 years the championship was dominated by Britons who had emigrated to the United States, and in 1900 the Americans suffered the final indignity of finding Harry Vardon, who had spent most of the summer in that country, victorious with J. H. Taylor 2nd. Vardon's final round of 80 included a fresh-air shot on the last green when he stabbed carelessly at a putt. The first American-born winner was J. J. McDermott in 1911; he proved it to have been no fluke by winning again in 1912. He has been described as a 'self-assured, determined alumnus of the Philadelphia caddie sheds'. His second winning score of 294 was described as the first below par, the term being first employed then in official national usage.

Five amateurs have won the US Open. The first of them was Jerome D. Travers in 1915; the last was Johnny Goodman in 1933. Like Charles Evans (1916), Francis Ouimet (1913) and Bobby Jones (1923, 1926, 1929, and 1930), Goodman won the Open before he was successful in the Amateur. The last British victory in the Open until Jacklin's in 1970 (if that of Tommy Armour, the Scottish-born naturalized American is not included) took place in 1920 when Ted Ray won at Inverness, beating Vardon, who was 50 years old, into a tie for 2nd place.

In 1924 the growing popularity of the game made necessary the holding of Eastern and Western qualifying rounds; and for the first time the use of steel clubs was permitted. That year there were 319 entries; 40 years later there were more than 4,000 and regional qualifying rounds to reduce the field to 150 were held all round the country. Prize money has increased in much the same way as the British. Starting in 1895 with a 1st prize of $150, it had risen to $500 in 1919 when play was resumed after a two-year war break. By 1946, after a similar break of four years, prize money stood at $8,000 with a 1st prize of $1,500. Today it is around the $200,000 mark, one of the biggest prize totals.

Two years stand out in the history of the US Open. The first was the improbable defeat of Vardon and Ray in 1913 after a play-off with Francis Ouimet. It was not until several years later that the historic

significance of this, as the point when the tide turned in favour of the Americans, became clear. At the time it was simply a sensational victory comparable to, say a local Scottish amateur, persuaded into competing at the last hour, forcing a play-off with Nicklaus and Trevino and defeating them. The other year was 1930 – which in golf means only one thing, Bobby Jones's Grand Slam. That year at Interlachen he won his fourth National Open, defeating the luckless Macdonald Smith. Before Jones only Willie Anderson had won four times, and after Jones only Hogan achieved it. That year also marked the end of the Jones era. The championship has had its emotional victories: that of Ken Venturi in 1964, a comeback that cost him so much he could hardly drag himself up the last fairway; that of Lloyd Mangrum, a recently demobilized and bemedalled war veteran winning the first Open after World War II in 1946; and Hogan's return after his nearly fatal car accident to win the 1950 Open with bandaged legs at Merion.

In spite of the efforts of the USGA to make the Open a supreme test of skill, the list of winners includes several outsiders. Sam Parks, who in 1935 won the Open at Oakmont with the only score under 300, was an outstanding surprise; and when after World War II such players as Ed Furgol, Jack Fleck, Dick Mayer and Orville Moody were successful, there were rumblings that this was the result of courses that had been made too difficult.

Table of results on p. 452.

Utrecht GC NETHERLANDS

nr Utrecht. 18 holes; 6,272 yd (5,735 m)

The club was started in 1894 as the Doornsche Golf Club on the initiative of E. Cremers, Dutch Amateur Champion in 1905 and 1906, and a committee of six. The course, situated 15 miles southeast of Utrecht near the village of Doorn (where the Kaiser went into exile after World War I), was opened on 18 July 1894. It had sand greens and the first professional was a Scotsman named Dunn. The Doornsche, however, did not survive long because the owner of the land did not like golf being played on his property. An alternative site had to be found at Huis ter Heide, six miles east of Utrecht. The course, one of the most beautiful inland courses in continental Europe, was designed under the direction of Messrs Morrison and Colt and was officially opened under its new name in April 1929.

The Utrechtse Golf Club 'De Pan' now has a membership of 650 with 150 junior members, and has housed several Dutch

Amateur and Open championships. An indication of its fine wooded setting was its selection for one of Shell's colour films in the series 'Wonderful World of Golf' in which Peter Thomson played Dave Marr. The club has produced two figures notable in Dutch golf: Jonkheer Calkoen van Limmen, a good player and former president of the Netherlands Golf Committee, and Joyce de Witt Puyt who at a young age became one of the leading women golfers in continental Europe.

V

The pattern created by the thumb and fore-finger of both left and right hand during the grip. It is the angle of the V of the left hand that decrees how many knuckles are shown and also determines the angle of the V of the right hand. *See also* GRIP

Vagliano, Lally see SEGARD, LALLY

Vale do Lobo GC PORTUGAL
Almansil, Algarve. 18 holes

Vale do Lobo was the brainchild of Sir Richard Costain who planned to retire to the Algarve and keep an eye on the whole programme there of a golf course, hotel and building development. He died before his dream could be realized and the course, a dozen miles west of Faro, was opened in 1967.

As the architect Henry Cotton faced a different set of problems from the flat, swampland conditions at Penina, also in the Algarve. Vale do Lobo was cut out of trees on sandy, rolling country which in places runs down to the sea. Thus Cotton was able

to remain true to his principle of never making two courses alike: Vale do Lobo has a few elevated tee shots into tree-lined valleys and rather more tricky greens than Penina.

As is usual in a popular holiday centre, the course receives a great deal of traffic and further development has been carried out with a few alterations to some of the holes. In 1971 the Algarve Open was played there and won by Ramón Sota.

Valentine, Mrs George (née Jessie Anderson) BRITISH
b. Perth, 1915. New Zealand Open Match-play, 1935; French Open 1936; British Ladies' 1937, 1955, 1958, runner-up 1950, 1957, semi-finalist 1935, 1947; Curtis Cup 1936, 1938, 1950, 1952, 1954, 1956, 1958; Scottish Ladies' 1938-9, 1951, 1953, 1955-6, runner-up 1934, 1954, semi-finalist 1933, 1936, 1950, 1957; Commonwealth Tournament 1953, Worplesdon Foursomes (with John Behrend) 1963-5

Known universally as 'Wee Jessie', a sobriquet she does not particularly enjoy, but which has stayed with her since she made her debut as a teenager.

The first of her three British Ladies' Championships was gained before World War II, and so were two of her six Scottish Championships. She arrived in big golf by reaching the semi-final of the Scottish, and winning the British Girls' Championship in 1933. The following season she played in the Home Internationals, and was runner-up in the Scottish. After reaching the semi-final of the British in 1935 she was chosen for the British team that toured Australia and New Zealand, and during that trip won her first national title, the New Zealand Open Matchplay Championship. Her second, the French Open, in 1936, was followed by the British in 1937, and the Scottish in 1938 and 1939.

When play was resumed after the war, she soon began adding to her collection of titles, and in 1955 became the first Scottish player to win the British Ladies' Championship and the Scottish title in the same season. In 1956 she set another record for her country-women by taking the Scottish title for the sixth time. She was the first woman golfer to be decorated for her services to the game, being awarded the MBE in 1959.

She relinquished her amateur status by taking over her father's sports business and designing equipment for women.

Like the majority of outstanding women players, she has always been good with all her woods. The control and variety of her strokes with the irons is where she has always

excelled, and in this department of the game, particularly on seaside courses, with unequal lies and stances, she has a mastery few women have equalled.

Valentine, Joseph AMERICAN
b. 1887; d. 1966

The most publicized grass in America in the 1950s – and still used in more than 50 per cent of sod grown for sale in that country – is Merion Blue. Its name derives from the Philadelphia suburban course where it was discovered by an Italian immigrant who became one of the most respected golf-course superintendents in the United States. Joe Valentine, who had landed in America at the age of 19, was a construction foreman for Merion's famous East Course and was hired as its greenkeeper shortly before it was opened in 1912. Over a stretch of 52 years, Valentine groomed the East Course for many major tournaments, including two US Open Championships, three US Amateur Championships, and a World Amateur team event. On his retirement in 1963, Joe was succeeded by his son Richie, but continued as a consultant until his death in 1966.

Largely through Joe Valentine's efforts, the first greenkeepers' short instruction course was held at Penn State University in 1919. Penn State is now one of America's best-known turf research centres. A fund devoted to research and scholarship has been established there as a 'living memorial' to him.

Valley GC PHILIPPINES
Antipolo, Rizal. 18 holes; 7,097 yd (6,489 m)

The club was founded in 1958 by 200 *aficionados* who wanted a course which would be neither too hard for them nor too easy for the modern professional. The gently rolling terrain in a small valley in the Rizal hills was shown to two course architects, Fred

Mrs G. Valentine

Joseph Valentine

Smith, an Englishman, and James Scott, an Australian. From their respective plans, which did not differ materially, a fine test of golf emerged. The course can be reduced from its full 7,097 yd to a more manageable 6,475 yd (5,921 m). When construction started, samples of Tifton 328 grass were brought from Texas and propagated in a nursery. The strain, used on all greens, is quick to recover after rain and makes Valley one of the outstanding courses of the Philippines.

The latest underground watering system keeps the fairways in prime condition and the outstanding clubhouse is unique in design. Situated on high ground looking out over the course, it has the appearance from the air of a golf ball on a tee; and near Valley's 10th tee stands a 25,000-gal water tank also in the form of a golf ball 22 ft in diameter on a 20-ft high tee.

The course, which took three years to build, was opened for play in November 1962 and in 1972, when membership had risen to over 730, a third 9 holes was under construction.

Van Cortlandt Park USA

New York. 18 holes; 5,702 yd (5,214 m); par 68

Van Cortlandt Park, in the heavily populated borough of the Bronx in New York City, was the first municipal golf course in the United States. It dates back to 1895, and it is still in use today, although its condition is far from ideal. When the golf course was first proposed to Park Commissioner James Roosevelt in 1895, Van Cortlandt Park was a quiet area remote from the frenetic and gaseous atmosphere of the city. Today it is sliced by two major expressways – the Major Deegan and Mosholu Parkway – and besides the normal problems facing the golfer, he must also contend with blaring car horns, the screech of brakes, and the blue fog of exhaust fumes.

The golf course is not the test it once was. It measures just 5,702 yd after being altered to make room for the expressways, but while the holes themselves are fairly short, another 1,800 yd (1,650 m) of walking must be added in covering the course. The walk from the clubhouse to the first tee, for example, is 750 yd (685 m), to which a similar distance should be added for the return from the 18th green. The course weaves under Mosholu Parkway and back and forth for 14 holes across railroad tracks and over relatively level country. It then crosses over to the far side of the Major Deegan where 4 holes range up and down steep hills forming the toughest part of the course.

When the layout was changed in the late 1930s to make room for the roads, the old 9th and 10th holes were combined into a 602-yd (550-m) par 5 which is now the 12th. It is one of two par 5s on the course. The other is the 2nd which measures 590 yd (540 m) and parallels the 12th. Six of the holes are par 3s.

One reason for the poor condition of the course is its heavy use. Nearly 60,000 rounds are played at Van Cortlandt annually for comparatively low green fees.

Vancouver GC CANADA

Coquitlam, B.C. 18 holes; 6,661 yd (6,091 m); par 72

One of the older clubs of the Vancouver area, it now enjoys a beautiful course which is a tribute to the pioneering spirit of the group of hardy Scots who dared to choose its first and only location. It is also a reward for the perseverance and loyalty of its later members who fought to hold on to their land and to bring their club to a high standard of prosperity. The course is one of the finest in the vicinity of British Columbia's mainland coast. It is hilly and wooded, and so lush that it plays somewhat longer than its adequate yardage would suggest. The first 9 is a pleasant one, with one hole of over 600 yd (550 m) in length. The second 9 is better and more difficult. With a total length of more than 3,500 yd (3,200 m) and a par of 37, it features narrow fairways which wind through the seclusion of tall stands of thick timber. Were it not for the hum of urban traffic which may be heard beyond the trees, the golfer might believe himself here to be in some remote part of British Columbia's forested wilds.

For the golfer capable of combining accuracy with length, the inward 9 is a good test of ability; and for the rest it offers respite from the tensions of modern metropolitan living.

The enthusiasm of the founders of the club in 1911 evokes admiration. For when they selected their site it was well beyond the limits of civilized development. In the early days the members had to travel from the city by railway, climb a rugged embankment from the nearest station and hike a considerable distance to the course. Later they went by tram and horse-drawn vehicle. Because of this the first members stayed in tents set up in a clearing in the woods, and the earliest clubhouse included men's and ladies' dormitories.

The club was constantly in straitened circumstances until the approach of urban development enabled it to triumph over earlier financial adversities.

Van Wie, Virginia AMERICAN

Curtis Cup 1932, 1934; US Women's Amateur 1932-4, runner-up 1928, 1930, semi-finalist 1931

A shy, unobtrusive triple champion of the early 1930s in the United States. Bernard Darwin wrote later of her that he thought she had the most beautiful swing he ever saw. No one is likely to question that authority, and even 40 years after her appearance in Britain as a Curtis Cup player, those who had seen her were still asking after 'the girl with the glorious swing'. Before winning the first of her titles at Salem, Virginia Van Wie had been frustrated twice in the final and once in the semi-finals by her principal rival, Glenna Collett (Mrs E. H. Vare). The first of Miss Van Wie's defeats at the hands of the great player was by the margin of 13 and 12 at Hot Springs, Va., and it must have given her particular satisfaction that the opponent she defeated in the final on the way to her first title was the same Mrs Vare, and that the margin was 10 and 8. Miss Van Wie scored three and a half points out of four in her two Curtis Cup matches, but after her third national title she slipped quietly out of the limelight. She was last heard of teaching in the Chicago area.

Varangot, Brigitte FRENCH

b. Biarritz, Basses-Pyrénées, 1940. French Ladies' Close 1959, 1962-3, 1966, 1970; French Ladies' Open 1961-2, 1964-6, 1973; British Ladies' 1963, 1965, 1968

Virginia Van Wie

tégée she was. Brigitte Varangot became a regular visitor to British championships. Her solid build and firm, three-quarter swing which seemed to punch the ball, far more in the manner of a man than a woman, was well suited to seaside golf; but equally important to her success was a wonderfully competitive spirit. This was well illustrated in the third of her British victories, over her friend and compatriot, Claudine Cros-Rubin, in the 1968 final at Walton Heath. She played badly all the week, scraping through round after round, until the final; here too she seemed to be beaten but she holed from 10 feet on the last green for a birdie to keep the match alive and won at the 20th.

With her two compatriots, Claudine Cros-Rubin and Catherine Lacoste, she played in the first five World Women's Amateur Team Championships (Espirito Santo Trophy), which her team won when it was first held in Paris in 1964 and was subsequently always in the first three. She was not the first champion to find that it could be easier to win an individual title than to contribute supremely well to a team cause, especially when one's involvement in the match is deep. She registered four victories in the beginning of the season foursomes competition in England which has been staged under a series of sponsors, but at present is called the Avia. One of these victories, with Mrs Marley Spearman (Mrs Harris) in 1965, was by a huge margin over 72 holes.

Vardon, Harry BRITISH

b. Grouville, Jersey, 1870; d. London, 1937. British Open 1896, 1898-9, 1903, 1911, 1914, runner-up 1900-2, 1912, 3rd 1906, tied 3rd 1913; US Open 1900, runner-up 1913, tied 2nd 1920; German Open 1911; runner-up French Open 1912, 1914, 3rd 1909-10

In his time Vardon's genius for the game was unsurpassed and his influence upon it great. His six victories in the British Open are a record; Braid and Taylor, the other two members of the Great Triumvirate as they were called, each won it five times, a feat equalled later only by Peter Thomson. Although Vardon won the last of his Opens in 1914, 18 years after his first, it was at the turn of the century that he was in his prime. At that time he went up and down the country winning tournaments and breaking records. He did what only a very great player can do: he raised the general conception of what was possible in his game and forced his nearest rivals to attempt a higher standard than they would have thought possible. He had a great influence, too, on

methods of playing. When he first appeared his notably upright swing, though rhythmic and graceful, surprised the majority who at the time favoured a sweeping stroke with a wide arc. He made popular the overlapping grip, which is generally known by his name, though J. E. Laidlay had used it before him.

He adopted an open stance when a somewhat closed stance was the fashion of the day, and he allowed his left arm to bend, straightening it again as he began the downswing, though the effect was smooth and graceful and the rhythm superb. Horace Hutchinson, the writing golfer of those times, described him as playing with considerably shorter and lighter clubs than those used by the majority of golfers, and he drove a very long ball. If he was away from home and wished to borrow a set, it was often ladies' clubs that he chose. All accounts agree on his length and on his ability, although a modest 5 ft 9 in tall, to call on greater length with no apparent extra effort.

In his own book, *The Complete Golfer*, he listed his own clubs as 10 in number, but two of those were accounted for by a spare driver and brassie: the tendency for shafts to break and heads to fly off was much greater in those days. A driving cleek, a light cleek which he preferred to the driving mashie, an iron mashie, niblick and putter made up the complement. During his finest years he was so accurate that he seldom made use of the niblick. He was of a singularly serene disposition, playing, in the words of Horace Hutchinson 'with a certain gay and gallant courage'. Well might Bernard Darwin, who was not given to extreme opinions, say of him: 'I do not think anyone who saw him in his prime, will disagree as to this, that a greater golfing genius is inconceivable.'

Three of Vardon's six championships were won after the introduction of the rubber-cored ball in 1902, but it was with the gutty before his serious illness that he was supreme. After that his putting began to betray him, but he was never a bad putter. He was at least a fine approach putter and a competent holer-out. Otherwise he could not have accomplished half of what he did. He learned to play as a caddie at Grouville, near St Helier, in the Channel Islands where he was born, and it was on the advice of his younger brother, Tom, who had gone as assistant professional to St Annes, that he took up a post at Ripon, Yorkshire, in 1890.

A year later he moved to Bury, and thence in 1896 to Ganton. Here J. H. Taylor, who was reigning Open champion, came to play him and went home defeated by 8 and 6 but full of Vardon's praise. In the Open

After the decline of the Vicomtesse de Saint-Sauveur and before the rise of Catherine Lacoste, Brigitte Varangot reigned supreme as a golfer in France and throughout the Continent; for a time her dominion extended over almost the whole of the British Isles. A measure of her ability was that although her French victories were won almost exclusively on inland, park courses where she had learned the game, her three British titles were achieved on courses of a very different kind, and which varied also from each other: Royal County Down, St. Andrews and Walton Heath. She had the great advantage of being introduced to the game by the Vicomtesse de Saint-Sauveur (Mrs Segard), herself a champion of both countries, whose pro-

Brigitte Varangot, top, during the 1971 European Ladies' Team Championship and, above, in the final of the foursomes at Sunningdale GC

that year they tied for 1st place and Vardon won the play-off. There followed his best years. He beat Willie Park by 1 stroke in the 1898 Open and won easily at Sandwich in 1899. The same year he beat Taylor who was playing well by 11 and 10 in the final of a tournament at Newcastle, Co. Down, and also beat Willie Park in a challenge match

over North Berwick and Ganton. In 1905 he played another great match in which he and Taylor beat Braid and Herd by 11 and 10 over four greens. Their play at Troon where they won 14 holes was astonishingly fine, though Vardon had a haemorrhage the night before and was hardly fit.

In January 1900 Vardon started a year's tour of the United States, playing a great many matches and arousing much enthusiasm in a country where the game was still young. He hardly lost a match and won the US Open, Taylor finishing 2nd. He returned to defend his title in the British Open and the positions were reversed. But the work of the tour took its toll and it is doubtful if he was ever so brilliant again. After being twice runner-up in the British Open he won at Prestwick in 1903 with a total of 300, and this he regarded as the best of his achievements for he was so unwell that he nearly fainted several times during the last round. Soon afterwards he went to a sanatorium but made an almost complete recovery.

In 1911 he won the Open yet again, beat-

ing Arnaud Massy so convincingly in a play-off that the Frenchman gave up at the 35th hole. Two years later on the other side of the Atlantic he was involved in yet another tie, losing this time to Francis Ouimet, a victory that was significant in the history of American golf because it marked the end of a dominant British phase.

It was a blow for Vardon but he had one more championship in his bag, the Open at Prestwick in 1914 when he was 44 years old, beating Taylor by 3 strokes. In 1920, by which time he was 50, Vardon returned to the United States and tied for 2nd, one place behind Ray. With 7 holes to play he was 6 strokes ahead, but a vicious half-gale swept down as he stood on the 12th tee. He was still hitting the ball beautifully but it took him 4 strokes to reach the green, and, tiring, he dropped more strokes allowing Ray to slip in ahead of him. 'Fate,' wrote O. B. Keeler, the American chronicler, 'and nothing else, beat Harry Vardon that day.' From 1903 to the end of his life he was professional to the South Herts club in North London.

Vare, Mrs E. H. see COLLET, GLENNA

Venice GC ITALY
Lido di Venezia. 18 holes; 6,385 yd (5,838 m); par 72
The Lido di Venezia club began with a course designed in 1928. This was increased

to 18 in the late 1950s by the addition of a second 9 for which C. K. Cotton was responsible. It contains a number of par 4s in the best tradition and three exceptional par 5s, the 6th, 8th and 11th, where the temptation to 'go for it' often ends in disaster, for the rough is stern and comparable to that of Muirfield at its best. The Italian Open was held there in 1974.

Venturi, Ken AMERICAN
b. San Francisco, Cal., 1931. Walker Cup 1953; runner-up US Masters 1956, 1960; US Open 1964; Ryder Cup 1965
Venturi's victory in the 1964 US Open Championship, with all the human sentiments involved, is one of the most remark-

able in the whole history of championship golf. Venturi, one of the very few to represent his country as an amateur and as professional, emerges from it as an heroic figure, the more so since his background was one of frustration and poor health, after showing early promise as one of the best iron players American golf has ever seen. He was for a time a protégé of Byron Nelson.

Venturi, son of the manager of the Harding Park professionals shop, graduated from San Jose State University in 1953 and played in the Walker Cup match the same year. His early promise bore fruit when he outplayed the entire field for three rounds in the US Masters while still an amateur in 1956. Four strokes ahead with one round to go, he finished with an 80 which was not as bad as it sounds but left him in 2nd place behind Jack Burke Jr. He turned professional later that year after a tour of duty in the army.

In 1958, paired with Arnold Palmer in the last round, he finished only 2 strokes behind the winner in a tie for 4th place, then in 1960 he was foiled again. While Venturi was back in the clubhouse after a total of 283, and

Harry Vardon, shown here on the right of the photograph with, from left to right of the driver James Braid, Ted Ray and J. H. Taylor

Ken Venturi

being prematurely congratulated as the probable winner, Palmer slipped in 1 stroke ahead of him with birdies at the last two holes. Not surprisingly some of the sting went out of Venturi's game and he lost his power as a handsome shotmaker. The slump continued through 1961, 1962, when he hardly ever finished higher than 18th, and 1963, when he failed to qualify for the US Open and won less than $4,000. But he kept plugging away at his practice, as far as his back trouble would allow. His uncomplaining behaviour won the admiration of his fellow professionals, and in 1964 the tide turned dramatically. That spring his game had revived sufficiently for him to tie 3rd in the Thunderbird Tournament and tie 6th in

the Buick Open. However, his putting remained uncertain and a victory for him in the US Open seemed unlikely until, after rounds of 72 and 70, he took the lead for a time in the third round with six birdies in the first 12 holes. Venturi significantly ended that third round by missing short putts on the 17th and 18th, and at lunchtime was nearly in a state of collapse from the severe heat. Some thought it was physically impossible for him to last another round – it was the last year in which two rounds were played on the last day – let alone make a score, but somehow he made it. Looking pale and drawn, and accompanied throughout by a doctor, he caught Tommy Jacobs and took the lead with a

beautifully played par 4 at the 9th. He widened it to 4 strokes, forcing his nearest rivals, Jacobs and Palmer, to take risks. With the sun still beating down mercilessly, he came up to the last fairway to a hero's welcome. He was champion at last, and although, after playing in the Ryder Cup match at Royal Birkdale in 1965, he never again played quite like one, he had had his just hour.

Vicenzo, Roberto de ARGENTINIAN
b. Buenos Aires 1923. British Open 1967, runner-up 1950, 3rd 1949, 1956, 1964, tied 3rd 1948, 1960, 1969; runner-up US Masters 1968; World Seniors' 1974

A most popular international figure, both

for his disposition and for his classical style. In his long career he has won more than 140 professional tournaments and over 20 national championships in 14 countries. Never a regular competitor on the American circuit, he has nevertheless won eight of its tournaments. Like many large, magnificently proportioned men, he has a kindly, gentle nature; he also has immense self-restraint and calmness.

Vicenzo was born of humble parents who had no connection with golf, his interest being formed by living close to a Buenos Aires course where he and his brothers used to caddie. He turned professional at the age of 18 – four of his brothers are also professionals. Golf was not popular in Argentina at the time, and he had to wait before becoming a world-class professional.

In 1947 he first played in North America and in 1948 made his first appearance in the British Open, an event which drew from him much of his best golf. In his first three championships he finished equal 3rd, 3rd and 2nd, thus beginning one of the best and most consistent records in its history. After

some 10 appearances it did, however, begin to look as though he was not destined to win; he himself said he had just come over to see his friends. But just when people were beginning to give up hope, his moment came. After three rounds at Hoylake in 1967 he led the field and, throughout the final round on which depended his whole destiny as a golfer, he maintained it gallantly despite a tremendous challenge by Jack Nicklaus, the reigning US Open champion. The final stages, with all their richly human undertones, were moving. Following a superb spoon across the corner of the out-of-bounds at the 16th, he completed a round of 70 (his other rounds were 70, 71, 67) and was assured of a place in golfing history. Victory for a man of 44 was a triumph of faith and perseverance. The effect on his confidence was also marked and the following spring he tied with Bob Goalby for the US Masters title but was deprived by a now famous technicality of the chance of a play-off.

He failed to notice that his partner, Tommy Aaron, had credited his birdie three at the 17th, which millions had watched on television, as a four on the scorecard. Vicenzo signed for this as the correct figure and, under the rules, it had to stand.

Although Vicenzo was the first to acknowledge the correctness of the decision and accepted the disappointment with dignity and grace, (and in 1970 received the Bob Jones award for 'distinguished sportsmanship') it left its mark upon him. For a while, his great appetite and enthusiasm for practice waned but nothing could break his spirit. In the 1970 World Cup in Buenos Aires he won the individual championship and so extended a list of successes that only Sam Snead could match in number. Among the national titles he has captured are the French, the Spanish, the Dutch, the Argentine, the Chilean and the Colombian Opens. He cut down his appearances after that but was still good enough to win the Brazilian Open at the end of 1973, and in 1974 the World Seniors' Championship and the Panama Open.

Victoria GC AUSTRALIA
Melbourne, Victoria. 18 holes; 6,830 yd (6,245 m)

A parkland-type course on the famous Melbourne 'sand belt' at Cheltenham, the new club cost $A 53,000 and was opened in 1927 by the Prime Minister, Mr S. M. Bruce. Designed by Dr Alister Mackenzie, it is of championship calibre and has staged the 1961 Australian Open won by Frank Phillips, the 1968 World Women's Amateur Team Championship won by the United

Roberto de Vicenzo, *above,* and *right*

States, and several professional tournaments. The course was founded in 1903 at Fishermen's Bend, a stretch of natural country swept by cold winds which earned it the nickname of 'Siberia'. In 1954, the year that Lord Bruce, as he had become, was made captain of the Royal and Ancient, two members of Victoria brought the club distinction. Peter Thomson by winning the British Open; Doug Bachli by becoming the first Australian to win the British Amateur.

Victoria GC CANADA

Oak Bay, Victoria, B.C. 18 holes; 5,948 yd (5,439 m); par 70

The Victoria course is a golfing gem in a beautiful setting at Oak Bay, only three

are three successive par-3 holes, respectively of 215, 120 and 198 yd (197, 110 and 181 m), which call for particular skill and accuracy. Just to play them once is to remember them always.

From many of the holes there are spectacular views of the Olympic Mountains and snow-capped Mt Baker in the State of Washington across the United States border. And on a clear day even the peak of Mt Ranier, over 14,000 ft high and 170 miles away, may be seen. Closer at hand, several of the beautiful Gulf Islands which dot the strait attract attention. The 1967 Commonwealth matches were played over the course, resulting in a tie between the teams of Great Britain and New Zealand.

Vilamoura GC PORTUGAL

Boliqueime, Algarve. 18 holes

Vilamoura, about 15 miles west of Faro and the third of the Algarve courses to be built, came into being as part of a development financed by a consortium of banks. The designer was the British architect Frank Pennink, who was given a choice of three sites on 4,000 acres of land close to the sea. The soil was light and ideal for golf. Vilamoura was carved out of a miniature forest of smaller umbrella pines and calls to mind the sand-and-heather courses south of London. Splendid variety has been achieved on pleasantly undulating land although, as scoring in the 1970 Algarve Open proved, the golf is far from straightforward.

miles from the centre of the city of Victoria on Vancouver Island. But it contains a flaw that is due to its age and cannot be repaired. Although adequately long when it was established in 1893 in the era of the gutty ball and wooden shaft, it is incapable of being extended to the length of a modern championship course, The course, which is playable all year round, still provides exciting golf, particularly when the normal, strong winds blow. Overlooking the Strait of Georgia, an extension of the Pacific Ocean separating Vancouver Island from the mainland, the portion of the course from the 3rd hole to the 10th furnishes true linksland golf reminiscent of some of the best to be found in the British Isles. Among the holes which play out onto a promontory jutting into the sea

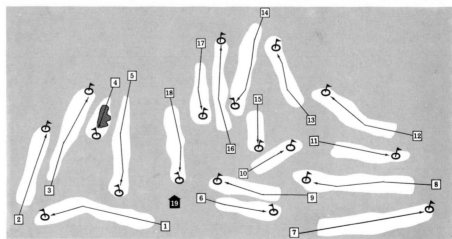

Top, a view of the Victoria GC   *Above,* the course plan of Vilamoura GC   *Opposite,* Siam GC, Thailand

The course opened before the rest of the development in April 1969 and is kept busy. The Portuguese Open of 1973 played one round there. Plans exist for two more courses.

Villa d'Este GC ITALY
nr Como. 18 holes; 6,070 yd (5,550 m); par 71

The course belongs to the owners of the luxury hotel of the same name situated on Lake Como. It winds its way through a thick forest of pine and chestnut on sandy soil of the highest quality. Though on the short side, it has been the traditional venue of countless Italian championships. Some holes have been lengthened, and it has always, with its narrow fairways bordered by fern and heather, offered a tough challenge to inaccurate hitters.

Virginia CC USA
Richmond, Va. 36 holes

The Country Club of Virginia has two courses. The Westhampton Course lies at the heart of club activity at the western end of Richmond; the James River Course is six miles away on heavily wooded land that tumbles down to the historic river. It is of the James River Course that the golfer thinks when the CC of Virginia is mentioned, and for good reason. It is an extremely interesting 18 designed by Bill Flynn, started in 1926 and completed two years later. Harvie Ward won the 1955 US Amateur there, defeating Bill Hyndman in the final.

The James River Course begins with a par 4 of 425 yd (390 m) that carries the player down a gentle slope. From there it turns left to another open par 4, then it ducks into pine and oak forests and really does not come out again until the 17th. Both the 6th and the 18th are par-5 holes for the members, but there is a tendency to play them as par 4s from the women's tees during major competitions.

The club was established in 1910, and its red-brick clubhouse with tall white columns sits on one of the highest points in Richmond, overlooking the James River Valley. It is quite a big building, and well it might be, for the membership – over 5,000 – is among the largest in the United States.

Virginia Hot Springs Golf and Tennis Club USA
Hot Springs, Va. 54 holes

Hot Springs, in the heart of the Appalachian Mountains, is one of America's most scenic resorts and includes the Homestead, the name of the oldest of the three courses there. It is a fairly short layout that

meanders around in the general vicinity of the hotel's tall main building. The Cascades, the best of the courses, lies about three miles or so down the road, and it takes its name from the appealing little water chute in that area. The Curtis Cup match of 1966 was played on the Cascades, and the next summer it was the scene of the dazzling victory in the US Women's Open by Catherine Lacoste. Miss Lacoste compiled a total of 294 – very fine scoring – in becoming the first amateur to win that event.

The third and newest of the courses in Hot Springs is the Lower Cascades, a Robert Trent Jones course. It has the strong points of that architect's style but it does not have the charm and diversity of the older Cas-

cades – few courses do. Some of its fans believe that it is nothing less than the finest 'mountain course' in the world. A main reason for this is that it presents only a few holes of definite upland character and, for the rest, is simply an aggregation of solid golf holes, some of which stress a defined tightness, others a variety of routes to the green. In this town Sam Snead was born and grew up.

Voigt, George AMERICAN
Semi-finalist British Amateur 1930; Walker Cup 1930, 1932

Once described as an amateur of almost professional quality, Voigt played in two Walker Cup matches. In the first, he defeated Sir Ernest Holderness by 10 and 8 and in the other lost to Leonard Crawley. But he is best remembered as the man who almost altered the course of history by preventing Bobby Jones from winning the 'impregnable quadrilateral'.

The place was St Andrews, the year 1930 and the championship the British Amateur, the one which Jones had never won. Their

meeting came in the semi-final and Jones, with so much at stake and with a long time to wait between matches, became unsettled, missed a number of putts and even fluffed a short pitch at the 13th. Voigt was 2 up with 5 to play and as Jones wrote later: 'I did not think that Voigt was the kind of player who would toss away this sort of lead, and I was quite certain that I was not capable of the golf needed to wrest it away from him. All I could do was what I did, namely, resolve to swallow the medicine, whatever it might be, and to keep on trying as best I could.'

Voigt drove out of bounds over the stone wall at the 14th and the rot set in. His tee shot caught the Principal's Nose at the 16th and though the 17th was halved in a valiant 4, Voigt's second at the 18th fell back into the Valley of Sin and he failed, as so many have done, to get down in 2.

Von Elm, George AMERICAN
b. Salt Lake City, Utah, 1901. Tied 3rd British Open 1926; US Amateur 1926, runner-up 1924; Walker Cup 1926, 1928,

Opposite, Peter Thomson

Above, part of the Cascades course of Virginia Hot Springs Golf and Tennis Club

Top, George Voigt

1930; French Amateur 1930; runner-up US Open 1931, tied 4th 1928

In the vintage years of American amateur golf after World War 1, Von Elm was among the finest, overshadowed only by Bobby Jones during his years of glory. But for Jones, Von Elm might have won other championships; when Jones won his first Amateur in 1924 Von Elm opposed him in the final and suffered a humiliating defeat by 9 and 8. The following year Jones won again, this time beating Von Elm in the semi-finals. But in 1926 Von Elm, having struggled to qualify for the championship, improved with every round and kept his best for the final. Jones had been through hard matches against Ouimet and Evans and had reached his peak too soon; in a 36-hole final, in which Jones needed a par to finish in one over fours and in which he never holed a putt all day, Von Elm won at the 35th – a contest marked by a high spirit of sportsmanship on both sides.

At the British Open that same year, following his first appearance in a Walker Cup match, Von Elm without ever threatening

to pass Jones, finished strongly to tie Hagen in 3rd place. Von Elm was of German descent and O. B. Keeler wrote of him 'when the handsome Uhlan went swaggering down the fairway, you could hear the sabres clink'. The outstanding feature of his swing was the violence of his pivot, causing a positive wrench of the shoulders. In the first Open

after Jones's retirement Von Elm birdied the last hole to tie Billy Burke, birdied the last hole again to draw level in the first 36 holes of the play-off and lost the second 36-hole play-off by 1 stroke. It was the longest Open ever recorded. In his three Walker Cup appearances Von Elm played six matches; his only defeat was in the 1930 foursomes with George Voigt against Tolley and Wethered. In the 1925 US Amateur he was involved in a remarkable match in the first round against a youngster of 17, Roland McKenzie. Von Elm, who by then already had a reputation as a formidable match player, was 8 up with 15 to play against the unknown. However, partly from his own lapses and partly from his opponent's birdies he was brought back to all square and only won at the 37th.

Von Hagge, Robert AMERICAN

One of the most talented golf architects in the United States, he grew up in Texas in a golfing environment. A capable player, he entered golf architecture about 1960 when he joined Dick Wilson's staff at Delray Beech, Fla. He worked with Wilson on his designs for most of his important courses, such as Doral. Upon Wilson's death, Von Hagge, a handsome and articulate man, went into business for himself. Working mainly in Florida and the Caribbean, he soon made a name as a builder of interesting, imaginative courses, such as Boca Rio and Conquistador. In the late 1960s, he and Bruce Devlin, the well-known Australian professional, formed the firm of Von Hagge and Devlin (with headquarters in Coral Gables, Fla., and Mascot, N.S.W.), and they have done some excellent work on both continents.

Von Nida, Norman AUSTRALIAN

b. Sydney, N.S.W., 1914
Vardon Trophy 1947; Dunlop Masters 1948; Australian Open 1950, 1952-3; Australian Professional 1946, 1948, 1950-1

Von Nida's achievements in tournaments far exceeded his record in championships, although he won his native title three times. But his reputation is based on far more than the ability to win tournaments. In a sense he was the father of Australian golf; not only did he blaze the trail abroad after World War II, but he guided and helped numerous young golfers of promise, notably Peter Thomson, five times British Open champion, who recognizes a debt to him for his early encouragement. In the years immediately after the war Von Nida enjoyed a success in Britain which was all the more remarkable for the not always favourable publicity that accompanied him.

He won two tournaments in 1946, his first appearance in Britain, and then in a seven-month spell in 1947, during which he captured four of the first six tournaments he played in, he earned a record £3,250 in prize money and won the Vardon Trophy with a score average of 71.25 over 52 rounds.

Brought up near the poverty line in Brisbane whither his family moved, he was first employed in an abattoir and attributes the abnormal strength of his wrists and hands to the heavy work he did there. In his spare time he caddied at the Royal Queensland Club and his first success came at the age of 15 in winning the Queensland Amateur. Short of stature, and weighing about 126 lb he could not rely on outstanding length, although using a full swing he hit a good average length. The strength of his game lay in his accuracy and in his short game, which he had practised with fierce intensity as a young man. He was as hard as flint and fearless in saying what he thought in a voice that was crisp even by Australian standards, but in his actions he has been genuine and generous. His best finish in the

British Open was tied 3rd in 1948. His best chance of winning had come the year before when he had tied in the lead after three rounds with two others; but Fred Daly got in his final blow before the wind got up and Von Nida could only finish tied 6th. A prolonged visit to the United States in 1948 was not a great success, largely owing to a much-publicized incident when after a dispute with an American professional over the marking of a card, they came to blows in front of the clubhouse and had to be separated. In Australia, where horse racing was his second love, he built a reputation as a coach in his later years.

George Von Elm

Norman Von Nida

W

Wack Wack GCC PHILIPPINES

Mandaluyong, Rizal. 36 holes; East Course 7,078 yd (6,472 m), West Course 5,798 yd (5,302 m)

In April 1930 the work of building the first 18 holes was started at Wack Wack and in a speech delivered the following year, Bill Shaw, the club's founder and first president, said: 'Where before there stood nothing but impenetrable thickets of thorny, unsightly bushes, favourite habitation for reptiles and loathsome vermin, the hand of man has replaced it with a veritable garden of beauty, converting it into pleasurable strolling grounds for tired bodies and minds.' In April 1931 the work was completed and shortly afterwards Shaw purchased more land for another 18. In 1935 the first Philippines Open was held at Wack Wack, Guillermo Navajo winning a play-off with Sixto Andrales. The courses were designed by Jim Black.

The club's unusual name derives from the cry of crows disturbed in their nests by the wayward shots of a foursome who played an important part in the eventual establishment of a club on the site of the old municipal links. Wack Wack soon became a meeting place of international repute and has served as a powerful force in boosting golf in the Philippines. It has been the scene of every Philippines Open since 1935, except for 1968 when it was held at the Holiday Hills GCC.

Wadkins, Jerry L. AMERICAN

b. Richmond, Va., 1949. Walker Cup 1969, 1971; US Amateur 1970; Eisenhower Trophy 1970

Lanny Wadkins gave a number of impressive performances both in amateur and professional events after leaving Wake Forest, Arnold Palmer's old university. He was only 17 when he won the Southern Amateur Championship, and at 18 was the youngest member of the Walker Cup team at Milwaukee in 1969. Less than 5 ft 9 in tall, he has a fast swing and compact style, and he won his single on the final afternoon of the 1971 Walker Cup at St Andrews against Michael Bonallack. He had already scored well in two professional tournaments at the end of 1970, and led the field in the Greensboro tournament in the first round.

He turned professional in the autumn of 1971. It took him no time to adapt and he finished in a tie for 3rd place in the last tournament of the year, the Walt Disney. The following year he was runner-up in the Bob Hope Desert tournament and again the following week, after a play-off with Homero Blancas in the Phoenix Open. Perhaps no young player since Jack Nicklaus has been rated so highly in his prospects during his first year on the circuit, at least until the appearance of Ben Crenshaw in 1973. Wadkins's earnings in 1972, his first full year as a professional, exceeded $100,000. In 1973 he won the USI Classic and had another wonderful year.

Wagga Wagga CC AUSTRALIA

Wagga Wagga, N.S.W. 18 holes; 6,557 yd (5,995 m); par 70

This club was formed in 1928 when a group of businessmen bought land adjoining the foreshore of Lake Albert, a few miles from the provincial city of Wagga Wagga. The course is well sprinkled with trees and flowering shrubs. A winding creek provides a natural hazard on several of the holes. The greens are basically of New Zealand Brown Top bent grass. It is one of the best Australian non-championship courses.

Waggle

The movement of the club once the stance has been taken up before the club is taken away at the beginning of the backswing. Generally used to lessen tension.

Waialae CC HAWAII

Maunalua Bay. 7,029 yd (6,427 m)

The land beside Maunalua Bay behind Diamond Head, that majestic rock on the island of Oahu that symbolizes Hawaii, is monotonously flat, ideal land for a dairy farm, utterly boring for a golf course – or so it would seem. Until 1927 it really was a dairy farm, and since then it has been a golf course, providing far from boring golf. Waialae is among the older courses in Hawaii. It was designed by Seth Raynor and Charles Banks, who recognized the problems of this level terrain and compensated for it by building a number of doglegs into the design and adding deep bunkers and huge greens. Several holes approach the waters of the bay, pale green in the shallows. Hawaii lies in the path of the trade winds, and any hole that plays into them can be terribly long. Raynor and Banks worked concepts of some well-known holes into their par 3s. The 210-yd (192-m) 8th is patterned on the Redan at North Berwick; the 210-yd 13th, on the Biarritz, at Biarritz; and the 190-yd

(174-m) 16th, on the 6th at the National Golf Links at Southampton, N.Y. The 12th hole is a 418-yd (382-m) par 4. Francis H. I. Brown, the most famous name in Hawaiian golf, once drove this green and, naturally enough, the hole is named after him.

Wairakei Hotel International Golf Course NEW ZEALAND

Wairakei, N. Island. 18 holes; 6,903 yd (6,312 m)

Wairakei, about midway between Wellington and Auckland, and served by Taupo airport about six miles distant, is a fairly recent creation. It is rated by Peter Thomson the best course in New Zealand and it is certainly one of the principal attractions at this resort which includes a first-class hotel with conference facilities. In a magnificent setting, somewhat reminiscent of Gleneagles in Scotland, the site for the course was something of an architect's dream. It lies on the high central plateau of North Island, with no possibility of intrusion from industry or housing, and meanders through rolling green acres fringed with trees. The pumice turf and the free-draining volcanic cinder make an excellent foundation. Its architect, John Harris, did fine work in blending the course into its surroundings and producing a fair but demanding test for everyone.

It was the first course in New Zealand to have an underground, automatic watering system. One of the features of the course is

Lanny Wadkins

the subtle variety in the shaping of the greens. Wairakei has no club membership and is open to all comers the year round. It is immensely popular. Another feature is that each hole has three sets of tees, providing, in effect, three courses of varying difficulty, the White, the Red and the Blue.

Waiting for it

Not rushing a shot. Making a full, controlled shoulder turn and giving time for the hands to work the clubhead to its fullest extent.

Wakonda GC USA

Des Moines, Iowa. 18 holes; 6,896 yd (6,306 m)

Wakonda is a hilly course that demands at least two qualities of its members: the ability to play shots from uphill, downhill or side-hill lies, and reasonably good physical condition. The usual impression of the American Midwest is of flat terrain broken by some scrub growth, or unending fields of grain. The ground where Wakonda wanders is far from level, and its fairways are bordered by several varieties of oak, elm and locust trees.

It is a well-tended course with smooth, undulating greens that putt very true. A couple of creeks wander through the course without affecting play very much. Many approach shots are blind. The heart of the course is the first 6 holes, made up of four par 4s over 420 yd (384 m), a 190-yd (174-m) par 3, and a 530-yd (485-m) par 5. The opening three are particularly testing. Wakonda dates back to the early 1920s when a number of the older Des Moines families joined in the venture to build the club. It was completed in 1922 at a cost of $650,000, and former Senator Clyde L. Herring served as its first president. Wakonda is an Indian word meaning a holy spirit, or the god of movement or light. He is sometimes of immense help in negotiating the golf course.

Walker, Carol Michelle BRITISH

b. Leeds, Yorkshire, 1952. British Ladies' 1971-2, runner-up 1973; Commonwealth Tournament 1971; French Girls' 1971; Curtis Cup 1972; English Ladies' 1972; Women's Trans-Mississippi Amateur 1972; World Women's Amateur Team Championship 1972

Although she now lives in Kent, Mickey Walker learned her golf in her native Yorkshire. She returns regularly to the professional at Ilkley, Bill Ferguson, who has been her principal teacher. Within two years of being runner-up in the British Girls' Championship she reached the top, becoming the youngest British champion this century when she won in 1971 at the age of 18. She successfully defended her title the following year at Hunstanton. She had made a notable first appearance in the Curtis Cup match against the United States a few weeks before, winning 3½ points out of 4; in doing so she halved with the young American champion, Laura Baugh, and won a classic encounter on the final day against Jane Booth, one of America's outstanding players.

A classic swing and sound method soon marked her out for international honours; and a quiet and modest charm conceals a strongly competitive spirit. This enabled her to overcome strong opposition from Beverly Huke in her first final, but her finest triumph was in defeating the American challenge in the 1972 British Ladies', and beating Claudine Cros-Rubin of France in her most determined mood. In the course of a very busy year, during which she did not neglect her county and international loyalties, she found time to visit the United States and to win the important Trans-Mississippi Amateur at her first appearance in that country. In the final she defeated Mrs Booth for the third time that season. Her place in the British side for the World Women's Amateur Team event (for the Espirito Santo Trophy) that autumn in Buenos Aires was assured, but she gave further evidence of her all-round ability by finishing runner-up to Belle Robertson in the British Strokeplay Championship in September.

Mickey Walker turned professional in 1973, joining the Mark McCormack organization when women's golf in such countries as Japan and Australia was showing signs of becoming increasingly worthwhile.

Walker, Cyril BRITISH

US Open 1924

The diminutive professional from England who defeated Bobby Jones for the 1924 US Open Championship at Oakland Hills. In a strong wind Jones, the defending champion, finished with a birdie 4 for a total of 300, but Walker later beat him by 3 strokes with a total of 297 (74, 74, 74, 75). It was the first championship in which steel-shafted putters were permitted.

Walker, George Herbert AMERICAN

b. St Louis, Mo., 1874; d. 1953

Donor of the Walker Cup and president of the United States Golf Association, 1920. George Herbert Walker, though not an international golfer, was a low handicap player at the National Golf Links of America and also a keen advocate of the game who took a great interest in its administration. He was part of the USGA's representation at a meeting with the R. and A. on the Rules of Golf in the spring of 1920, the year of his presidency, and on their return was so taken with the idea of a plan for an international golf championship, that he offered to give a trophy.

The original idea was that the competition might include other countries, but it was appropriate that the Walker Cup should

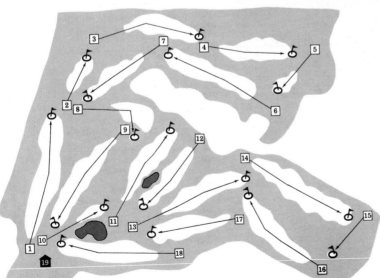

Left, the course plan of Wairakei International Golf Course

Above, Michelle Walker

become exclusively a meeting between the United States and Britain because Walker was partly educated in England (he went to school at Stonyhurst before going on to the Washington University, St Louis) and had many sentimental attachments with the country.

He believed in and loved sports of all

kinds and had a great will to win. Walker had also an acute sense of fair play and fittingly the Walker Cup has preserved all that is good in golf.

Walker, James BRITISH

b. Bartonholm, Irvine, Ayrshire, 1921. Semi-finalist British Amateur 1960; runner-

up 1961; Scottish Amateur 1961; Walker Cup 1961

A policeman in his early playing days – he won the British and Scottish Police championships for four consecutive years from 1949 – Jimmy Walker steadily established himself during the 1950s. Like many prominent Ayrshire golfers before and since, he gained several of his most important successes on courses in the county. He was chosen for the Walker Cup match in 1959, only to lose his place when he was injured in a car accident. He was, however, selected again two years later and played at Seattle. A straddling stance, a quick three-quarter swing, and a decisive putting stroke from a squatting, wrap-around stance were the characteristics of Walker's style. When he became Scottish champion he was the second of three players from the same club, Irvine Bogside, to win the title, following Hamilton McInally (1937, 1939, 1947) and preceding Jack Cannon (1969).

Walker Cup see INTERNATIONAL MATCH FOR THE WALKER CUP

Wall, Art AMERICAN

b. Honesdale, Pa., 1923. Ryder Cup 1957, 1959, 1961; leading money winner US 1959; US Masters 1959; Vardon Trophy 1959

Wall graduated from Duke University in 1949, turned professional and became a regular on the US circuit. He was in the American Ryder Cup Team in 1957 but it

was his victory in the 1959 Masters that changed his life in a day. At the start of the last round, Wall was 6 shots behind Stan Leonard and Arnold Palmer but a last round of 66, which included eight birdies, five of them on the last six holes, gave him victory by 1 stroke. His total was 284 (73, 74, 71, 66) with Cary Middlecoff 2nd and

Palmer 3rd. This climaxed a notable season in which he was named Player of the Year and finished leading money winner. Through the 1960s his golf weathered well and he so preserved his skill that in 1971 he tied for the Canadian Open with Lee Trevino. He has won 12 events on the American tour.

Wall was a member of the USPGA committee in 1959-60 and 1970.

Walton Heath GC ENGLAND

Walton on the Hill, Surrey. 36 holes; Old Course 6,735 yd (6,159 m), par 72; New Course 6,516 yd (5,958 m)

At the turn of the century a new generation of courses arose round London. Previously courses had been generally confined to public commons or to fields interspersed by trees and artificial ramparts. Most of them were on clay, like glue in winter and concrete in summer; but within a few years of each other a chain of courses began to appear on stretches of sand and heather south of the Thames. Woking and Sunningdale were among the first and they were quickly followed in 1904 by Walton Heath. Both courses, apart from the opening hole on the Old, lie across the Dorking road from the clubhouse, and stretch far out over the vast expanse of heath. It is out and back on mature, springy turf drained by the chalk of the North Downs. This makes for plenty of run on fairways that are generous but imprisoned by unyielding heather, bracken and gorse. The wind is also nearly always in attendance for the courses lie close to where the Downs plunge towards Reigate and Dorking. A man is alone with his golf at Walton Heath, apart from an occasional horseman or a bird startled out of a blackberry bush. He is closer to nature than on perhaps any other great course. This comfort the golfer needs, for Walton Heath can be a stern master, merciless to the crooked shot, and even though the prevailing wind tends to help, the holes from the 13th in, with three long holes of which the greatest is the 16th, provide one of the toughest finishes in the game.

Herbert Fowler, on horseback, first saw the possibilities of Walton Heath. A daring and original architect, he laid out both courses in the grand manner, specially to suit the rubber-cored ball which two years before, in 1902, had won its first British Open. James Braid's long, happy professional association with the club began in 1904 and lasted till his death in 1950, and the formidable test the courses offer was of great benefit to his game. The course was opened by the Triumvirate of Vardon,

Top, George H. Walker

Above, James Walker

Art Wall

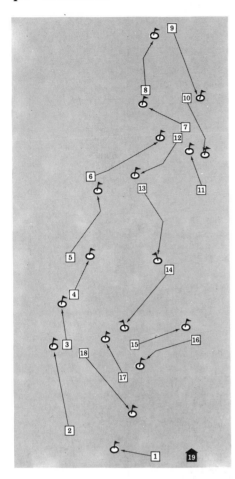

Braid and Taylor, and within three years its merit was recognized when the third British Matchplay Championship was held there. Not surprisingly, Braid was the winner. Until 1969, when the *News of the World* gave up sponsorship of the event, it was a regular venue for the championship and latterly, thanks to the continuing influence of the Carr family, its permanent home. Because gate money cannot be charged on common land, other championship events have been confined to the English, won by Doug Sewell in 1958, the Brabazon Trophy won by Michael Bonallack in 1968, and the British Ladies' which gave Brigitte Varangot her third victory.

The club eventually became the property of the members. When a piece of ground at the far end of the course had to be given up for a motorway, there was no difficulty in readjusting the course, such is the amount of ground to spare.

Wanganui GC NEW ZEALAND
Wanganui, N. Island. 18 holes
    The club owes its present home in the

sand-dune country at Belmont largely to the influence of Jock Harold, a local schoolmaster, and Dr George Saunders who were fired with the idea of building a links in the best Scottish tradition and whose sons became stalwarts of the club. Nine holes were laid out in 1894 at Encampment Flats and given the name Balgownie Links, possibly after the course of that name in faraway Aberdeen. Conditions became too cramped and a move was made to Belmont, members undertaking a good deal of the work of clearing scrub from a pure wilderness. The speed with which the course became established is reflected in the fact that in 1911 the New Zealand Open and Amateur championships were held there. The course recovered quickly from the neglect of the World War I years and trees were planted. In June 1922, a 12-year-old, Bryan Silk, was admitted as a junior; in 1934 he won at Belmont the first of three national amateur titles, and his skill both in the game and as an administrator have been highly valued by the club. Another Wanganui member, Jack Goss, also won the NZ Amateur at Belmont, in 1923. Throughout, the club has been a regular venue for national championships and has preserved the best traditions of the game.

Ward, Angela SEE BONALLACK, MRS ANGELA

Ward, Charles BRITISH
b. Birmingham 1911. Ryder Cup 1947, 1949, 1951; Vardon Trophy 1948-9; Dunlop Masters 1949, runner-up 1950; British PGA Close 1956

    It was not until he was over 30 that Charlie Ward made his mark in British professional golf. World War II was partly responsible for this, but it also gave him the opportunity to perfect his short game. At Torquay, Devon, where he had been em-

ployed before the war, he worked in an RAF rehabilitation centre and he was able to polish his short game on the short course. When the war was over he at once began to show his worth, winning 12 tournaments in five years from 1946. His best year was 1948 when he won four tournaments and the Vardon Trophy for the best stroke average, and he followed this up with three victories in 1949. Wiry and short of figure, Ward had a lightning swing and used a high tee and a straight-faced driver, but he was bound to suffer in length by comparison with the power golfers beginning to come into prominence, and he had to rely mainly on his short game, in which he developed great accuracy with the short chip. He also missed fewer putts than most from six feet in. In the winter of 1946-7 he visited the United States with Dai Rees and this gave him added reason to believe in the importance of what he called the 'third shot'. His best performance in the British Open was 3rd in 1951.

Ward, E. Harvie AMERICAN
b. 1926. British Amateur 1952, runner-up 1953; Walker Cup 1953, 1955, 1959; US Amateur 1955-6
    During the early 1950s Harvie Ward was one of the most accomplished golfers in the world, and supreme as an amateur. He won the British Amateur at Prestwick in 1952, was runner-up the following year and in 1955-6 was US Amateur Champion. Before he could attempt a second successful defence of his title he was suspended for a year by the USGA. It was alleged that he had been paid expenses by his employer for playing in amateur events; the irony of it was that had he received a larger salary and paid his own there would have been no debate. As it was the USGA clearly decided to make an example of their amateur champion. The effect upon Ward was immediate; his golf

The plan of the Old course at Walton Heath GC   Charles Ward   E. Harvie Ward *(right)* with Joe Carr

lost its tremendous flair, and although he finished 4th in the Masters at Augusta in 1957, and competed with distinction in his last Walker Cup match in 1959, he was never quite the same player again.

At his finest Ward had a classic style, simple, perfectly balanced and beautifully rhythmic; and he was a great competitor. The depth of his quality as a golfer became obvious at Prestwick where conditions were extremely fast and fortuitous, but his touch around the greens, often with a putter from far away, was wonderfully delicate and after beating Joe Carr in the semi-final he overwhelmed Frank Stranahan in the final. It was generally expected that he would retain his title the following year at Hoylake. His passage to the final was far more impressive than that of Carr, who survived several desperate matches, but beautiful though Ward's swing remained his golf on the last day was not his best, and in the end Carr's great holing out was the decisive factor in his victory on the last green.

Two years later Ward played a great part in the American victory in the Walker Cup

cation of this occurred in winning the first of his two US Amateur championships in 1939, when he had single putts at 29 holes in his semi-final and final matches, covering 48 holes. In the 1947 Walker Cup match at St Andrews he beat Leonard Crawley, to whom he was 3 down at lunch, by 5 and 3 having seven consecutive 3s from the 7th hole. On his return to the United States he finished 5th in the US Open and later turned professional.

Ward-Thomas, Pat Ainsworth BRITISH
b. Marple, Cheshire, 1913

Pat Ward-Thomas has become one of the world's leading golf writers, combining deep knowledge of the game and enthusiasm for it with a rare descriptive ability. As a boy he had a love of games, particularly cricket, and it was not surprising that he developed an urge to write about them. He first wrote about golf in unusual circumstances. He joined the Royal Air Force early in World War II and was shot down over Holland in 1940. He spent the war in a German prison camp where he was largely responsible for

An enthusiastic and devoted watcher, he soon established himself as a responsible and highly respected judge of the game, and succeeded Bernard Darwin as the main contributor on golf for *Country Life*. He has broadcast regularly for the BBC for more than 20 years, and is the author of *Masters of Golf* and *The Long Green Fairway*.

Waterloo GC, Royal BELGIUM
Ohain. 18 holes, 6,850 yd (6,264 m), par 74; 18 holes, 5,150 yd (4,709 m), par 69

Founded in 1923, the club moved to its present site, off the Brussels–Charleroi road in partly wooded country near Ohain, in 1961. A large clubhouse overlooks both courses. The course has always taken trouble in its choice of professional. One of the first to occupy the post was Henry Cotton who moved there from England in 1932. It was from Royal Waterloo club that he won his first British Open in 1934. He left in 1936 to go to Ashridge. During World War II the club was turned over to pasture for army horses, and when peace returned it was some time before the course picked up again. Now

match at St Andrews, and again four years later at Muirfield. By then his golf through the green was not the flawless expression that it had been, but his putting was devastating as his opponents have good reason to recall. Thereafter the great occasions of golf saw little of Ward, although he was still a young man, but he will be remembered as one of the most attractive golfers of his age.

Ward, Marvin H. AMERICAN
b. Washington 1913; d. San Mateo, Cal., 1967. Walker Cup 1938, 1947; US Amateur 1939, 1941, semi-finalist 1937

Bud Ward was a hard competitor with the reputation of being one of the greatest players in the United States. Some indi-

the introduction of golf and the construction of the Sagan course round the compound which helped prisoners to retain their sanity.

With the help of the Red Cross and the Royal and Ancient GC, the P.O.W.s obtained clubs, and manufactured balls out of rubber cushions and shoes. The idea of writing about golf prompted him to send a 10,000-word manuscript on golf to Henry Longhurst. Ward-Thomas continued in the RAF in the early postwar years. Then on leaving the service in 1950, a spell of writing about several sports ended with his appointment as golf correspondent for the *Manchester Guardian*, (now the *Guardian*), a post he has held ever since.

it has a membership of more than one thousand; the senior course is restricted to handicaps of better than 24. The rough is not severe, but the course represents a good test of handicap. The present professional is Donald Swaelens who followed the Channel Islander, Aubrey Boomer.

Watrous, Andrew Albert AMERICAN
b. Yonkers, N.Y., 1899. Canadian Open 1922; runner-up British Open 1926; Ryder Cup 1927, 1929; US Seniors' 1950-1, 1957

Watrous turned professional in 1920 having served in the US Navy, and quickly became one of America's leading players although he understandably never ranked with such formidable contemporaries as

Marvin H. Ward

Pat Ward-Thomas

Al Watrous

Hagen, Sarazen and Jones. Bernard Darwin once wrote of him, 'He had no tremendous power, but he had all the American virtues of smoothness and rhythm and he was a very fine putter'; and in the 1926 British Open he came as near as any man could to beating Bobby Jones.

On the last day at Lytham and St Annes, Jones and Watrous were drawn together and, with Jones unhappy over his putting, Watrous was 2 strokes ahead with 5 holes to play; but the pair were level on the 17th tee and then came Jones's historic shot from the sandy wilderness; Watrous, on in 2, took 3 putts, as anyone has a right to after that, and Jones went on to the first of his three Open victories.

Watrous, winner of the Michigan Open six times and the Michigan PGA title nine times, played in more National Opens and PGA events than anyone except Gene Sarazen. He was also a fine teacher and was engaged as professional for 37 years by the Oakland Hills Club, Birmingham, Mich.

Altogether he won 34 tournaments, and in addition to two Ryder Cup appearances, played in the unofficial match of 1926.

Watson, Mrs J. B. see STEVENSON, CHARLOTTE

Wee Burn CC USA
Darien, Conn.

There is an interesting pattern repeated many times in the beginnings of the earliest golf clubs in the United States. In a particu-

meetings came any number of the country's oldest and best clubs. So it was with Wee Burn, a pleasant club with a splendid course in the hills of Darien, back from Long Island Sound. This particular meeting was held in 1896, a few holes were dug and, as one account has it, 'the original members played with great seriousness and no little pomp, for it was the custom to play wearing red coats'. George Strath built the first course. The club prospered but had no name until one of the founders asked his friend Andrew Carnegie for a suggestion. When that great old Scot heard that a small brook ran through the property, there was no possibility of calling the club by any other name.

Interest in the game and the club grew rapidly as the holes increased, but the present course was not built until the early 1920s. It was designed by Devereux Emmett, a leading architect of the day, and the result is described as outstanding. Few golfers, comparatively speaking, know what a joy Wee Burn is to play, for it has not been advertised much by word of mouth. But the women know. Three times their national amateur championship has been played over the course – in 1939, 1958, and 1970 – and it also has been host to many Metropolitan District tournaments.

Weetman, Harry BRITISH
b. Oswestry, Shropshire, 1920; d. 1972. British Professional Matchplay 1951, 1958, runner-up 1956, 1959-60; Ryder Cup 1951,

ball. Broad of shoulder and of thigh, he hit the ball violently with an air of truculence. He would almost swagger up to the ball and appear to take no trouble in addressing it. He frequently drove off line, but he scorned to reduce his power, and more often than not his huge hands would contrive a recovery that would surprise his opponent. It was not surprising that he should have such a good matchplay record; in the Ryder Cup he scored a notable victory against Sam Snead at Wentworth in 1953, after being 4 down with 6 to play. As often happens he combined great strength with an almost velvet touch on the greens and this contributed to numerous victories in medal play. He was a delightful player to watch. Bold and uncomplicated he made putting look delightfully simple. A certain fierceness of expression added to the general impression of violence on the course, but off the course he had an engaging humour and a ready smile. There was much of the countryside about his personality; he was a son of the land having been born in a small country town. He was professional at Hartsbourne, before moving to Selsdon Park, Surrey. He was killed in a car accident.

Weiskopf, Tom AMERICAN
b. Massillon, Ohio, 1942. British Open 1973; Canadian Open 1973; tied 2nd US Masters 1969, 1972

From the time that Weiskopf turned professional in 1964 and started to play the

lar community some resident who had encountered the game in Scotland would ask a few neighbours for dinner to talk over the possibility of setting up some kind of ground on which they could play. Nearly always, someone present owned suitable pasture land where a few holes could be managed and a start made. Out of such informal

1953, 1955, 1957, 1959, 1961, 1963, non-playing captain 1965; Dunlop Masters 1952, 1958; Vardon Trophy 1952, 1956; World (Canada) Cup 1953-4, 1956, 1960; runner-up French Open 1955; German Open 1957

One of the leading English professional golfers after World War II and a favourite with the crowds for the distance he hit the

Part of the course at the Wee Burn CC

Harry Weetman

Opposite, Lee Trevino

Overleaf, Waialae GC

tour in 1965, everyone talked about his tremendous potential. Jack Nicklaus, a senior at Ohio State for one year when Weiskopf was a sophomore, more than once hinted that if Weiskopf ever realized how good he was, nobody would ever catch him. But Weiskopf also had a temper which could unsteady a swing that might have come straight out of an instruction book. It was not until the summer of 1973 at Troon that he showed that he could hang on and not beat himself in a major championship.

He had come close at the US Masters twice, 1969 and 1972, and was 3rd in the US Open at Oakmont in 1973 a month or so before Troon, but it was there that he finally became a real champion, doing things in the grand manner – he led after all four rounds, something not achieved since Henry Cotton in 1934. Only fleetingly in the third round did he lose his lead to Johnny Miller, his partner for the last two rounds who was striving to become a double champion in the same year. However, despite not really liking the course and not knowing how to play it, Weiskopf eventually won by 3 strokes

and equalled Palmer's record aggregate for the British Open – also at Troon – of 276.

It was in 1968 that Weiskopf began to give evidence of his class, a year in which he finished 3rd in the money list with victories in the Andy Williams San Diego Open and the Buick. In 1971 he won two more tour

Tom Weiskopf giving a victory wave at the end of the 1973 British Open Championship

Opposite, Vilamoura GC *above* and Wentworth GC, Gary Player in the Piccadilly World Matchplay of 1963 *below*

events. Then victory in the Jackie Gleason Inverary Classic early in 1973 with a record 1st prize of $52,000, and another in the Piccadilly Matchplay Championship at Wentworth, really made him believe in himself, the more so as in the latter event he beat Lee Trevino in the 36-hole final by 4 and 3. But an influence of a very different kind was responsible for the quite astonishing form he showed throughout 1973. The death of his father made Tom realize that it was time he revealed the champion's qualities which his father always believed he possessed.

By June Tom Weiskopf had won the Colonial, the Kemper and the Philadelphia Classic, finished 2nd three times and been 3rd in the US Open. It was a sequence that Hogan or Nelson might have envied. Within days of returning from Troon he had won the Canadian Open with all the cool self-assurance of a man who, with the blessings of a big, strong physique (6 ft 3 in and 185 lb), was for a few months at least, one of the two best in the world.

Wellington GC NEW ZEALAND

Heretaunga, N. Island. 27 holes; Main Course 6,930 yd (6,337 m)

One of the oldest clubs in New Zealand, Wellington was founded in 1895 with a course at Miramar, a suburb of Wellington, but at the beginning of the century it moved to Heretaunga, 14 miles out of Wellington on Highway 2, where the course, designed by Mr Marshall, the club's professional at Miramar, enjoys a most attractive setting bordered on all sides by green hills, with two tributaries of the Hutt River, which flows along the northern boundary, winding through the course.

The clubhouse, built in 1908, is a fine all-timber building which blends with the surroundings and looks out onto a true parkland course, notable for the variety of trees lining its fairways. Although the old course was not long at 6,217 yd (5,685 m) with a par of 69, a swirling wind through the valley could make life difficult; in winning the 1954 NZ Open Championship, Bob Charles's winning total was as high as 280.

This was one of three NZ Opens the club has held (the other two were in 1912 and 1932), but recent changes make it a regular championship venue. The construction of 7 new holes under the direction of J. S. Watson of Melbourne added some 700 yd (640 m) to the course. An additional 9 holes of 2,350 yd (2,149 m) were built inside the main 18 and an electronically controlled watering system installed. Extensions were also made to the clubhouse to accommodate

the 1,500 members, care being taken to preserve the features of the original building.

Welts, Mrs D. see MRS ANNE SANDER

Wentworth GC ENGLAND

Virginia Water, Surrey. 45 holes; West Course 6,997 yd (6,398 m); East Course 6,202 yd (5,671 m); Short Course (9 holes) 1,731 yd (1,583 m)

Wentworth, which snakes its way through a large, private residential estate on the edge of the road between London and Southamp-

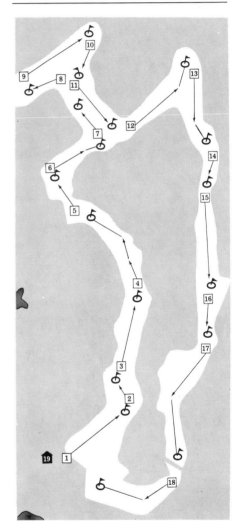

The plan of the West course at Wentworth

ton, reached its present eminence only in fairly recent times. The club was founded in 1924 with the opening of the East Course designed by H. S. Colt. It was laid out in heather, fir and silver birch country similar to that of its near neighbour, Sunningdale, and it was on the East Course that the first of Wentworth's international events took

place. On 4 and 5 June 1926 the forerunner to the Ryder Cup was held, followed by the 1929 British Professional Matchplay Championship, won by Abe Mitchell, and the first Curtis Cup match.

It is somewhat surprising that the East is the senior of the two courses and that, when the West was opened a few years later, it was found to be not unduly difficult. In the Dunlop Metropolitan tournament of 1938, Alf Perry won with four rounds under 70. After World War II, during which Wentworth became the emergency headquarters from which the Imperial General Staff would have conducted the war had London been put out of action, the course was lengthened and its reputation grew.

The Ryder Cup of 1953, which Britain came near to winning, really put Wentworth on the map, but the crowds were even larger for the Canada Cup of 1956 which Ben Hogan and Sam Snead won for the United States of America. After that Wentworth was in constant demand for major tournaments. It was the regular home of the Daks Tournament from 1952 until 1970; the club ran the popular Wentworth Foursomes each spring for the same period, eventually giving up the event because the growth of the Continental tournaments affected the professional entry; and in 1961 it was the scene of the English Amateur in which Ian Caldwell defeated Gordon Clark at the 37th hole in the final.

Although the enclosed and meandering nature of the West Course makes it difficult for the crowds, it is widely regarded as one of the finest tests of inland golf in Britain and it is an obvious choice for society bookings and green fees. Visitors are as much perhaps attracted by the club's facilities, which are more in the style of the American country club than almost any in Britain. The latest link between Wentworth and the professionals, who are generous in their praise of its challenge, was the inauguration there in 1964 of the Piccadilly World Matchplay Championship. With a cast of eight of the world's leading players engaged in matches over 36 holes, the event has captured public imagination in Britain to a degree only surpassed by the Open Championship.

Werden, Lincoln A. AMERICAN
b. New York

Linc Werden has been on the sports staff of the *New York Times* since 1928 and has been its golf writer since 1947, when he succeeded Bill Richardson. Werden graduated from Columbia University in 1925. He has garnered many honours through the years. He was instrumental in setting up the Golf Writers' Association of America, and has served as chairman of the board for well over a decade. A gifted organizer, he has made the annual dinner of the Metropolitan Golf Writers' Association the most prestigious affair of its kind in America. He is the first American newspaperman who has covered the full professional tour as his

'beat'. He departs periodically from the circuit to attend the other top golf events. Werden, who writes a crisp, direct prose, has been the trusted friend of four decades of champions.

Werkell, Arne SWEDISH
b. 1919

Professional at the Stockholm GC and brother of Elis, Arne Werkell dominated the professional game in Scandinavia between 1945 and 1955.

Werkell, Elis SWEDISH
b. 1918. Swedish Open Amateur 1946, 1950, 1952; Swedish Close Amateur 1947, 1949-50, 1952, 1955

Wentworth GC, the 12th hole of the West Course

Lincoln A. Werden

Elis Werkell was the dominant Swedish amateur golfer of his generation. He played 20 times for his country, and for Scandinavia v. Scotland in 1956 and 1958, for Europe v. British Isles in 1956 and 1960. He was a member of the winning Swedish team in the European Amateur Team Championship in 1959.

Weslock, Nick CANADIAN
b. Winnipeg, Man., 1917. Ontario Open 1946, 1949, 1959, 1962, 1964-5, 1969; Canadian Amateur 1957, 1963-4, 1966

Though born in Manitoba, Nick Weslock lived in Ontario throughout his golfing career. He represented that province in the Willingdon Cup Interprovincial Team matches a record 21 times. Internationally he has played for Canada in many teams, including the World Amateur matches three times, the Americas Cup matches seven times, and the Commonwealth matches three times. In no fewer than 11 years he has been low amateur in the Canadian Open.

Weslock has always been at his best in strokeplay rather than matchplay. His prowess with the shorter irons has earned for him the pseudonym of 'Nick-the-wedge', and he has long been a leading exponent and student of putting. Gay Brewer, the American professional, attributes his victory in the 1972 Canadian Open in large measure to advice on putting which Weslock gave him.

Westchester CC USA
Rye, N.Y.

In America, the Westchester CC is one of the nearest things to Gleneagles in the way of golf and living facilities. Although it now is a private membership club and a huge one, it began back in the fabulous 1920s as a great luxury complex: a 350-room hotel, two golf courses, polo fields, bathing beaches, half a dozen restaurants and night clubs, and many tennis courts, all surrounded by the magnificent homes of the wealthy. Then called the Westchester-Biltmore, it became a victim of the Depression and changed gradually, and painfully, to more modest though still luxurious standards.

The club now is the site of one of the world's richest golf tournaments, the annual Westchester Classic, whose winner pockets $50,000. The course on which the tournament is played is short at 6,500 yd (5,944 m), and though not really difficult for the top professionals (Jack Nicklaus won the tournament with 270 one year), it is a beautiful and rewarding course for lesser golfers. The fairways are not at all narrow but just a little

looseness off the tees can provide sidehill lies in many places. It is considered a hilly course but there are not too many arduous climbs.

West Hill GC ENGLAND
Brookwood, Surrey. 18 holes

With Woking and Worplesdon, West Hill forms a famous trio of courses within a stone's throw of each other in the sand and heather country of Surrey. It is not very different from its distinguished neighbours but, perhaps because it was the last to be built, it has never quite been given the attention it deserves. The holes have a better balance than the other two, it poses a fine test of driving down avenues skirted with heather, pine and silver birch, and it can make the rare boast for a club of being founded by a woman, Mrs Geoffrey Lubbock who, tired of being unable to play anywhere on a Sunday, decided to take steps of her own.

She saw the possibilities of the ground in an area which was then only beginning to be developed. The design was the handiwork of Willie Park, architect of the Old Course at Sunningdale a few years earlier, and Jack White, Sunningdale's first professional who won the British Open in 1904. It is a tribute to their skill that few alterations have since been found necessary. The club has housed many Surrey championships and also the widely supported and well-established Fathers and Sons tournament.

West Norfolk GC, Royal ENGLAND
Brancaster, Norfolk. 18 holes

The links of the Royal West Norfolk at Brancaster is a classic example of the traditional British seaside course. It lies on a narrow strip, at times less than 200 yds (183 m) across, between a great sweep of sea marsh on the one hand and the dunes of the north Norfolk coast on the other, which reaches down to the beautiful estuary running into Brancaster Staithe. The land undulates gently, owing nothing to the bulldozer. As Horace Hutchinson, first of an illustrious company of captains, wrote a few years after the course was opened in 1892, 'its distinguishing features are the absence of all artificiality and the great variety to be found in the holes'.

Every hole has its own individual character, emphasized by the marsh that borders most of the outward holes and then cuts across the 8th, making islands of its tee, fairway and approaches to the green. When the tides are high the marsh fills and the hole becomes a perilously beautiful examination of a golfer's nerve, but normally the marsh

and the seashore are in play and therein lies a rare charm of Brancaster. It must be one of the few courses in the world where it is impossible to go out of bounds, except for an insanely overclubbed shot to the 18th.

Other features of the course are the huge black-sleepered bunkers which have to be carried at short holes like the 4th, and the

superb 15th; the 3rd, one of the great short par 4s in England; the 9th on its distant plateau; and the last, where the green sits within a horseshoe of sand. This may sound formidable but the golf, except when the wind is hard, is not too severe for the man hitting reasonably good shots, but the bad ones are less likely to escape punishment than on most other courses.

Distinctive, appealing and challenging though the golf may be, and the course rarely plays the same from one day to the next, the enduring attraction of Brancaster is its unchanging nature, the purity of its strong, bracing air and the unspoiled beauty of the setting against the varying colours of sea and marsh. There a golfer may find solitude and quiet, and be at one with golf of an older kind.

Wethered, Joyce (Lady Heathcoat Amory)
BRITISH
b. 1901. English Ladies' 1920-4; runner-up French Ladies' Open 1921; British Ladies' 1922, 1924-5, 1929, runner-up 1921, semi-finalist 1923; Worplesdon Foursomes 1922-3; 1927-8, 1931-3, 1936

The supreme woman golfer of her age, perhaps of all time, and crowned by the remark of Bobby Jones after he had played with her that he thought she was the best golfer – man or woman – he had ever seen. In the British Championships for which she entered she would have needed to have won 43 matches to have won all six titles; she

Joyce Wethered (Lady Heathcoat Amory)

won 38 of them, and was defeated by Cecil Leitch in the 1921 final and by Mrs Allan Macbeth in the 1923 semi-finals. The English Championship she made her absolute property by winning it five years in succession, involving 33 matches without a defeat. Besides the challenge of the game, she was fascinated by its artistry and the perfection of style. Though most pictures of her striking the ball show her on her toes, she was perfectly balanced and as poised as a ballerina. The rhythm of her swing, full-pivoted yet giving the impression of economy of movement, was effortless, but it was productive of a clubhead speed and a crispness of stroke that enabled her to outdistance her contemporaries by many yards. She also had a flawless temperament – strung up to the right degree, a touch of humour, the power of pegging away, and above all a legendary power of concentration, focused on swinging the club and playing each hole as it came.

Her entry into and departure from championship golf – over a span of nine years – were equally remarkable. As a 19-year-old unknown, she entered for the 1920 English Ladies' at Sheringham, Norfolk, and to everyone's amazement, including her own, defeated the dominant figure in women's golf, Cecil Leitch, in the final. This marked the beginning of an epic series of contests between these two great golfers and their future encounters were avidly followed. In 1921 they met again twice; in the final of the British at Turnberry and of the French Open at Fontainebleau where Miss Leitch had her revenge. The next met in 1922 in the final of the British at Prince's when Miss Wethered levelled the score with a convincing victory. Their paths did not cross again until 1924, in the fifth round of the British. This was their only meeting over 18 holes in a championship, and like boxers sparring for an opening, they halved the first seven holes before Joyce Wethered drew away to win.

In 1925 a third great player entered the arena, Glenna Collett (Mrs Vare), champion of the United States; she was beaten by Joyce Wethered in the third round with golf that was better than par, then Miss Wethered went on to win her most difficult and memorable final – against Miss Leitch at the 37th. Having achieved supremacy, she withdrew from competition for three seasons but was tempted back once more when the 1929 British Ladies' was held on the Old Course at St Andrews. This produced yet another fabulous final in which she prevailed over Glenna Collett by 3 and 1. The American, 5 up after 11 holes, and 4 under 4s, relaxed her bombardment and

lunched only 2 up, having gone round in 75. A counter-attack by Miss Wethered made her 4 up after reaching the turn in 35, but her opponent won back the next two holes in 3s, and the huge crowd was kept in suspense until the end came on the 35th.

In only one other field did she continue to compete thereafter – the mixed foursomes at Worplesdon, a most delightful fixture which attracted some of the best amateur golfers of both sexes and which she made famous. Altogether she won the event eight times with seven different partners, who were successively amazed by the accuracy of her play and appalled by the number of times she had to play from positions into which she would never have got herself. In 1935 she toured the United States, played a foursome over the Augusta course against Bobby Jones, and taking part in exhibition matches, two of which allow a comparison with another great golfer of that time, Babe Zaharias. At Oak Ridge, Chicago, in a fourball, the scores were Miss Wethered 78, Horton Smith 71 against Miss Zaharias 88 and Gene Sarazen 71. Later at Meadowbrook in another match the scores were Joyce Wethered 77, George Nagell 73, Babe Zaharias 81, Sarazen 72.

Wethered, Roger Henry BRITISH
b. 1899. Runner-up British Open 1921; Walker Cup 1922-3, 1926, 1930, 1934; British Amateur 1923, runner-up 1928, 1930, semi-finalist 1924, 1927; *Golf Illustrated* Gold Vase 1927; captain Royal and Ancient GC 1946

One of the most famous of all British amateur golfers, even if he had not been the brother of Joyce Wethered. With Cyril Tolley he dominated the British scene from the moment he went up to Oxford immediately after World War I. While still an undergraduate he achieved the greatest performance of his career, tying for 1st place in the British Open at St Andrews, and losing the play-off.

On the golf course his manner was reserved, as became his upbringing which included grounding in the game on the remote, elite links of Dornoch. He was above all a magnificent iron player with exceptional powers of recovery and of stopping the ball. He was a long driver but, except at his best, not a reliable one.

In the President's Putter, which in the years between the wars commanded about as strong an entry as the English Championship, he was four times successful and on a fifth occasion tied when a halt was called in semi-darkness at the 24th hole with Eustace Storey. In his five Walker Cup matches, not

counting the match in 1921 that preceded them, he scored a total of 5½ points out of 8; apart from his final foursome with his old partner, Tolley, when he was beaten by Goodman and Lawson Little, he lost only to Bobby Jones throughout his career in them.

In the Open of 1921 he lost the play-off to Jock Hutchison who had returned a 70 in the last round to tie. Wethered had begun with a 78, but followed this with 75, and on the last day 72 and 71. The controversial penalty stroke for walking back onto his ball came in the third round, but it would not be justified to assume that it necessarily affected the result of the championship. More clearly to be regretted was his taking 5 at the 72nd hole. He had wanted to go south that night to play in a cricket match, but was persuaded to stay on and give himself the chance of being the first amateur to win the title this century. He failed with a score of 159 to 150. He was to have been captain of the Royal and Ancient in 1939 but had to wait until 1946 to take up office. When a memorial service was held in St Andrews to Bobby Jones after his death in 1972, Wethered as the senior of 11 past captains present gave the address.

Whigham, H. J. AMERICAN
US Amateur 1896-7
H. J. Whigham from Onwentsia Club, Lake Forest, Ill., was a graduate of Oxford and an English-trained golfer. In the 1896 US Amateur, Whigham, son-in-law of

H. J. Whigham

C. B. Macdonald, led the qualifying before going on to defeat J. G. Thorp in the final; in 1897 he repeated the whole performance, this time defeating W. R. Betts in the final.

Whipping

The thread or twine used in wrapping or binding the space where the head and the shaft of the club are joined together. Nowadays used only on wooden clubs.

Whitcombe, Charles Albert BRITISH

b. Burnham, Somerset, 1895. West of England Open 1921, 1924, 1929; Ryder Cup 1927, 1929, 1931, 1933, 1935, 1937 (non-playing captain 1949); British Professional Matchplay 1928, 1930, runner-up 1934; 3rd British Open 1935; Irish Open 1930

Prominent with his two brothers, Ernest and Reggie, in professional golf in the 1930s. He never quite fulfilled his promise in the British Open, taking a final 76, when his best chance seemed to offer, in 1935 and finishing 3rd to Perry. However, he beat Henry Cotton twice in the final of the Matchplay Championship and played in six Ryder Cup matches.

Whitcombe, Ernest R. BRITISH

b. Burnham, Somerset, 1890; d. 1971. Runner-up British Open 1924; British Professional Matchplay 1924; Dutch Open 1928; Irish Open 1928, 1935; Ryder Cup 1929, 1931, 1935; French Open 1930

Ernest Whitcombe, eldest of the three sons of a Burnham gamekeeper who learned their golf on the windswept Somerset sandhills, never won the Open Championship but only the irrepressible Hagen prevented him from doing so in 1924. Whitcombe led by 3 strokes at one time but took 43 for the first 9 holes at Hoylake in the final round. He came back in 35 for what looked like a winning total, but Hagen, with a series of remarkable recovery shots from bad drives, edged him out by a stroke. During the next 15 years Whitcombe achieved many fine performances in national events and tournaments, although he had to bow to youth when Dai Rees beat him in the British Matchplay Championship final of 1936. Whitcombe's son Eddie carried on the family tradition and is professional at Chigwell, Essex.

Whitcombe, Reginald A. BRITISH

b. Burnham, Somerset, 1898. West of England Open 1922, 1931, 1933, 1934, 1938, 1948, 1950; Ryder Cup 1935; British Open 1938, runner-up 1937; British Open 1936

Reg Whitcombe was not only the youngest of the brothers but also matured rather later,

and to compare his record with that of Charles, for instance, is to revive wonder that he alone of the three won the British Open. Until he finished 2nd to Henry Cotton on the rain-soaked Carnoustie links in 1937 he had never been in the first 8. Twelve months later, on one of the windiest days in the history of the championship, he achieved at Sandwich what had so often eluded his brothers.

White, Jack BRITISH

b. East Lothian 1873; d. 1949. British Open 1904, runner-up 1899, 3rd 1903

He became in 1904 the first man to win the Open with a score under 300, namely 296, at Sandwich. He had no great physique, nor was his long game consistent, yet this Scotsman was one of the few to interrupt the reign of the Great Triumvirate (Vardon, Taylor and Braid) over the British Open Championship. Like Willie Park he was an outstandingly fine putter, using a thin-bladed cleek and a crouching stance with his head sunk low between his shoulders. In an age when little attention was paid generally to the theory of putting, White was an exception. His view, expressed in his book *Easier Golf*, was that if the blade of the putter were to be kept at right angles to the line of the putt throughout the backswing, it could be done only by crooking the right elbow outwards on the backswing and the left elbow on the forward swing. Although such theory would not be accepted today, White had a talent for finding out what was wrong and putting it right. He had also an intense earnestness combined with a lovable optimism: if he was off his game he was very soon going to be on it again. His Open total of 296 was a brilliant score for those days, but even so he was chased home by Braid and Taylor, each of whom had tremendous last rounds and needed a 3 to tie at the last hole at Sandwich. White was a nephew of Ben Sayers and had much of his uncle's mixture of shrewdness and enthusiasm. He served as professional at York, Workington, Mitcham and Seaford before settling at Sunningdale where he worked for 25 years.

White, Ronald James BRITISH

b. Wallasey, Cheshire, 1921. Walker Cup 1947, 1949, 1951, 1953, 1955; English Amateur 1949, runner-up 1953; *Golf Illustrated* Gold Vase 1949; English Open Amateur Strokeplay 1950-1

Few golfers, amateur or professional have been as gifted in the art of striking a ball through the green as Ronnie White. His talent came to light immediately before World War II, and for several years after-

wards he had no peer in British amateur golf. He won the English Championship in 1949 but his fame largely rests upon a remarkable record in the Walker Cup matches. In the first four postwar contests he won all his singles, and lost only one of four foursomes. His match with Charles Coe at Birkdale in 1951 was a classic of unshakeable courage; all day he was behind but finally beat Coe with a series of masterful strokes.

His swing was compact, simple and true; he stood very solid and still, well over the ball, and struck it with an authority, power and accuracy that in those days recalled Henry Cotton at his best. The flight of his shots, even in strong winds on seaside courses, had an implacable, piercing quality that only superb timing and control can achieve.

And yet, for all his tremendous gifts, White rarely played in national championships. After 1949 he made only one appearance when at the peak of his powers, and his defeat in the English final in 1953 was the triumph of a lifetime for Gerald Micklem. Eventually lack of first-class competition told on his performance and his last Walker Cup match in 1955 was a sad anti-climax to his career, but the quality of his striking remained a legend in the North West for some years afterwards.

White was criticized for not appearing more often in major events but he had little spare time from his profession as a solicitor. Had he turned professional after the war he would have reached the game's highest places. A talent such as his is rarely seen in a generation.

Whitton, Ivo Harrington AUSTRALIAN

b. Melbourne, Victoria, 1893; d. 1967. Australian Open 1912-13, 1926, 1929, 1931; Victoria Amateur 1919-20, 1922-4; Australian Amateur 1922-3, runner-up 1913, 1926; Queensland Amateur 1922, 1931, 1933; New South Wales Amateur 1929

One of the most famous names in Australian golf and one of the finest amateur players. Ivo Whitton's record of winning the Australian Open five times over a period of 19 years is remarkable and only Gary Player has more victories to his credit. He was also a notable figure in the administration of the game in Australia once his serious playing days were over. He was the Australian representative on the Rules committee of the Royal and Ancient GC, 1948-53; represented Australia on the negotiating committee of Rules of Golf at St Andrews in 1951; and was captain of Royal Melbourne GC 1947-50.

Whitworth, Kathrynne Ann AMERICAN
b. Monahans, Tex., 1939

Kathy Whitworth turned professional in 1959, but it was four years before she made a name for herself. In 1962 she won her first two events and finished 2nd in eight others; this won her the award for the most improved professional of the year. The following year she won eight tournaments. She developed into the most consistent player on the tour, and its most dominant figure after Mickey Wright had reached her peak. By 1974 she had won more than 70 victories, including two LPGA titles, and earned more than $500,000. Surprisingly, however, she has never won the U S Women's Open.

Wilkinson, Martha SEE KIROUAC, MRS MARTHA

Will, George BRITISH
b. Ladybank, Fife, 1937. British Youths' 1957; Ryder Cup 1963, 1965, 1967; Esso Golden Tournament 1965

After a promising beginning in boys' and youths' golf, George Will became a good tournament player with a fine swing. He made three appearances in the Ryder Cup, earning his selection by good, general consistency.

Wilson, Dick AMERICAN
Many knowledgeable golf men consider Dick Wilson to be the best architect the

United States has produced. Wilson started in with the well-known Philadelphia firm of Toomey & Flynn in the middle 1920s when he was hardly more than a boy. By 1931 he had become a key figure in the firm and deserved perhaps the bulk of the credit for rebuilding Shinnecock Hills into one of the finest courses in the United States.

A friendly, earthy, and warm-hearted man, Wilson, after years of good solid work had given him a national reputation and enabled him to go into business for himself, suddenly burst into prominence in the middle 1950s. By this time he had moved to Florida, and in the Delray Beach area he put together an organization of extremely talented people, among them his right-hand

man Joe Lee, Bob Von Hagge, a very creative designer, and, over a number of winters, Shelley Mayfield, a top-rank professional golfer. Wilson was sought out by clubs all over the country to remodel their layouts or to build new ones for them. Among his best remodelling works are Bel-Air, in Los Angeles, and Inverness, in Toledo. Among the northern courses Wilson designed during this period were the new Meadow Brook and Deepdale, on Long Island, Laurel Valley, east of Pittsburgh, Pa., and the National Cash Register Company's courses, in Akron, Ohio. He came to do an increasing proportion of his work in Florida where his credits include Doral, Bay Hill, the P.G.A. National, and Pine Tree. Many of Wilson's admirers believe that Pine Tree, which is in Delray Beach and was the architect's home course, is probably his masterpiece.

From the back tees, Wilson's courses demand both power and accuracy. The approach cannot be half-missed and still work out all right, for it was Wilson's practice, particularly in the latter years of his life, to place his greens above the level of the fairway and to protect them with a large frontal bunker. Since he was also disposed to building rather shallow greens, the approach shot had to be nicely gauged. He gave his greens interesting and subtle contours, and they demand careful reading and an excellent touch. Dick Wilson was a good player himself, and this developed his feeling for shot values.

Wilson, Enid BRITISH
b. Stonebroom, Derbyshire, 1910. British Girls' 1925; Midland Women's 1926, 1928-30; English Ladies' 1928, 1930; British Ladies' 1931, 1932-3; semi-finalist American Women's 1931-3; Curtis Cup 1932

Widely regarded as the finest British woman golfer between the wars after Joyce Wethered, Enid Wilson has played and been connected with golf all her life. She was a devoted and model pupil willing to apply herself wholeheartedly to practice, although she never allowed herself to become enslaved by the game and maintained an admirable sense of proportion. She had a sound rather than graceful swing but she was a resolute competitor capable of her best when it mattered most, and had a remarkable record in championships, despite giving up playing seriously at a comparatively young age.

She won her two finals in the English championship by commanding margins but her outstanding performance was in equalling Cecil Leitch's record of three victories in three successive years in the

Kathrynne Ann Whitworth

Top, George Will

Above, Enid Wilson

British Ladies' Championship, again winning the finals with comfort. In 1931 she beat Wanda Morgan at Portmarnock by 7 and 6; in 1932 Clementine Montgomery at Saunton by 7 and 6; and in 1933, Diana Plumpton (Mrs N. Sabine) at Gleneagles by 5 and 4.

Her early retirement was a great loss to the Curtis Cup sides of the 1930s although she played as champion in the first one, winning in 1932 at Wentworth her single against Helen Hicks; she maintained her interest in the game and, after World War II, turned to golf writing, contributing to the *Daily Telegraph* for many years.

To generations of young golfers who never saw her play, Enid Wilson became known as a highly respected figure whose knowledge and authority were second to none and who was always ready with kindly and helpful advice. She wrote *A Gallery of Women Golfers* (1961), one of the best books on women's golf ever published.

Wilson, Hugh AMERICAN
b. 1879; d. 1925

When the rubber-cored ball made obsolete the original course of the Merion Cricket Club in suburban Philadelphia, it was decided to scrap that course and build anew at another site. The planning was turned over to a six-man committee, which took an unusual step. Rather than hire a professional golf architect, in 1910 it sent its junior member, Hugh Wilson, to study the great courses of Scotland and England. Wilson, a young insurance man only a few years out of Princeton University, was an enthusiastic but not particularly skilled golfer. He was chosen mainly because he was able to leave his business for an extended period and because it was felt that the trip might be good for his none-too-robust health. Wilson stayed abroad seven months and returned with hundreds of drawings of what he had seen. Better still, he brought back a 'remarkable concept of golf architecture', which was reflected in great measure in what became the East Course of the Merion GC (now long since divorced from the parent Cricket Club). Built on 127 acres (51 ha), the East Course was opened for play in 1912. Four of its holes crossed a country road, and when this became a busy highway, some revisions were necessary. Otherwise, the course – especially its five breath-taking finishing holes – is essentially the same as Wilson designed it. Eleven championships and other major competitions have been played there, most recently the 1971 US Open.

In 1918 Hugh Wilson and his brother

Allan supervised the completion of the last four holes (the present 12th, 13th, 14th, and 15th) at Pine Valley, another world-renowned course in the Philadelphia area. Wilson did not live long enough to gain the full acclaim due him for his talents in the still-young field of architecture.

Wilson, James C. BRITISH
Walker Cup 1947, 1953; runner-up Scottish Amateur 1951-2

James Wilson represented Scotland from 1948 to 1954, and toured South Africa with the British team in 1951-2. In the 1953 Walker Cup match he lost his single in 1953 to Ken Venturi and played in the famous foursome when one of the American couple was found to be carrying 15 clubs. Wilson also won the Antlers of Royal Mid-Surrey three times with Leonard Crawley.

Wilson, John BRITISH
b. Girvan, Ayrshire, Scotland, 1892. Scottish Amateur 1922, 1931; Walker Cup 1923

John Wilson beat Ted Blackwell at the 19th hole of the final at St Andrews to become the first winner of the Scottish Amateur Championship in 1922. He played for Scotland from 1922 to 1926, and again in 1932. He won both his matches in the 1923 Walker Cup.

Wimbledon GC, Royal ENGLAND
Wimbledon, Surrey. 18 holes; 6,335 yd (5,793 m); par 72

Wimbledon Common in the southwestern suburbs of London was one of the early landmarks of golf in England, a near contemporary of Westward Ho! and Hoylake. In 1865 the London Scottish GC was formed, an organization under control of the military that allowed civilians also to be members. This uneasy situation gradually grew more stormy as the civilian membership came to represent a larger proportion of the club, but military influence, sustained by the unyielding personality of Lord Elcho, stood its ground. There were men of character on both sides, and after a number of unpleasant scenes the inevitable split came. The iron buildings that housed the club had become too small; the civilians withdrew to their own clubhouse on the town side of the Common, and about 1881 called themselves Wimbledon, later Royal Wimbledon, GC.

In spite of this acrimonious start, Wimbledon soon gained a reputation for being a friendly club with strong golfing traditions. Partly because of its length, but partly also because it lies close to London, it has not encouraged outside events but has been content to go its own busy way. It is claimed

for it that no other golf course can be reached so quickly from the centre of London, and for this reason it is sought after by the growing number of overseas diplomats resident in London. While heated debates were going on in committee between the spirited leaders of opinion – Lord Elcho on the one side, Dr Laidlaw Purves and Mr Bob Grant on the other – the course had become the home of the earliest of inter-club encounters, that annual meeting between Oxford and Cambridge University. They first met in 1878 and apart from 1881 when there was no match they remained there until 1893. It was not until 1908 that the separated club acquired a new course at Caesar's Camp alongside the common course. It is on this higher ground that the heather and gorse character of the old course is retained; elsewhere the holes are more parkland in character with trees exercising considerable influence. After the first hole with its violent dogleg, the course divides into three loops so that the remainder of it can be played in a variety of sequences. In the middle of the round, looking across to the neighbouring club of Coombe Hill on the other side of the valley, it is still difficult to believe that London's West End may be only 15 minutes distant if the traffic is kind. For the golfer playing the holes in the rear of the Camp in their heather and silver birch setting, the atmosphere is indistinguishable from pure countryside. There are holes like the 6th and 9th where the handicap player may look to improve his score, but whatever the length of the course there are a good number of stiff par 4s that will, specially in the autumn, provide a more than adequate test. The reputation of Royal Wimbledon as a friendly club is still maintained. A special welcome can be found by overseas players and trying to see that no player is without a game is a deep-rooted tradition. A high-class practice putting green bordered by spring flowers has long been the scene of an inter-club putting competition held in the evenings, in which the seriousness of the competitive spirit takes second place to the conviviality of the occasion. Julius Boros, a distinguished visitor to the course, is of the opinion that the long dogleg 12th hole, with its change from 'moorland' to park, is one of the course's best.

Winged Foot GC USA
Mamaroneck, N.Y.

Few clubs and few courses are so well known throughout the American world of golf as Winged Foot and its West Course, a few miles north of New York City in Westchester County. This is because of the

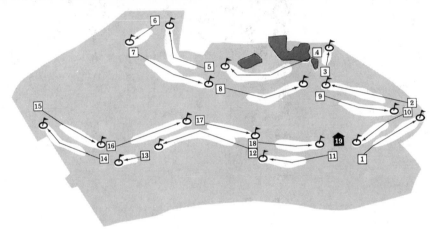

significant things that have happened there and the prominent personalities associated with club and course.

Bobby Jones won the third of his four US Open titles on the West in 1929; Billy Casper won his first Open there in 1959; Dick Chapman won the US Amateur there in 1940; and the Walker Cup matches were held there in 1949. Craig Wood was head professional at Winged Foot when he won the Masters and the US Open in 1941. Claude Harmon, his successor, won the Masters in 1948. Dick Mayer, the US Open champion of 1957, played his amateur golf as a Winged Foot member. From Harmon's pro shop has come a seemingly unending stream of young assistants to win fame after perfecting their games on the West – Jackie Burke, Jay Hebert, Dave Marr, Shelley Mayfield, Al Mengert, Mike Souchak. Finally, Tommy Armour, that colourful old Scot, was long a member and held court at a table in the grill room daily until he died. In addition to all this, there probably have been more scratch and plus golfers attached, with great affection, to the club than to any other in America. All this makes Winged Foot – it takes its name from the emblem of the New York Athletic Club, some of whose members founded the club in the early 1920s – not only a famous golf place but a fabulous and delightful club.

The West Course, though now perhaps a bit cramped for space in places, is still a fine course after half a century, although it is not,

in truth, a great course in the classic meaning of the term. It was designed by A. W. Tillinghast, a careful architect whose trademark was the pear-shaped green, tightly bunkered. As for the East Course, many members maintain that it is better than the West, though mostly they whisper it around the club. Playing the East is a different sort of experience because it is a different sort of playground – not so long, not so muscular. It has plenty of challenging holes of the kind known as sporting, and nobody comes off it with a low score without playing good solid golf all the way round. The US Women's Open was played on it in 1957 and 1972, and the girls loved it. In 1974 the US Open was held there and won by Hale Irwin.

Wit, Gerard de DUTCH
b. Wassenaar 1918

Gerry de Wit has won the Dutch National Close Championship 14 times and the Dutch Professional 14 times. As this record indicates, Gerry de Wit is the best known of all Dutch golfers. His victories in the close and professional championships are un-approached but curiously he never managed to win the Dutch Open title, although he was runner-up five times and 3rd five times. He also lost three play-offs by 1 stroke to Sewgolum, Angelini and Grappasonni.

Woking GC ENGLAND
Woking, Surrey. 18 holes
Until 1893 when the Woking course was

Winged Foot GC, the clubhouse and course plan

carved out of boggy ground thickly covered with gorse and heather by 'a few mad barristers', as Bernard Darwin once called them, golf around London was mainly confined to public commons such as Wimbledon and Blackheath, and to open parkland inclined to muddiness in the winter. Woking opened up a whole new area of pine, heather and silver birch country in Surrey and Berkshire which was quickly acknowledged as an ideal form of inland golf. The responsibility for Woking brightening the Londoner's horizon belonged largely to Stuart Paton, educated at Loretto alongside the old championship course at Musselburgh, and one of the very few men who is said to have declined the captaincy of the Royal and Ancient GC.

with the universities of Oxford and Cambridge, the Seniors and the Bar golfing societies. It was the course on which Douglas Sewell, a member of the Hook Heath Artisans' Club, first became known, winning the Woking club's annual Alba Trophy many times.

Wollin, Mrs L. see FORSELL, LIV

Wolstenholme, Guy B. BRITISH
b. Leicester 1931. English Amateur 1956, 1959; Walker Cup 1957, 1959; English Open Amateur Strokeplay 1960; British PGA Close 1966

A leading British amateur in the latter half of the 1950s with a flair for attack and an

tage and began new lives as professionals. Although they started a trend that quickly became fashionable, both were in their thirties at the time and Wolstenholme found progress hard in tournament golf. But gradually, after adjustments to his swing which became shorter and less powerful, he made his mark. He won the British PGA in 1966 at Saunton with a score of 278, made a steady, if unspectacular, income from tournaments all over the world and later settled in Australia where his successes continued.

Women's World Amateur Team Championship for the Espirito Santo Trophy see table on p. 470

Paton was regarded as an autocrat, but he was the most benevolent of autocrats with only the good of the club in mind. Although he only allowed one medal competition a year, Woking has always been a delightful place to play. The bunker in the middle of the 4th fairway remains as a conspicuous memorial to his influence.

Woking may lack the grandeur of Sunningdale or Wentworth but it possesses a distinct quality, which does not prevent it being recognized as essentially a members' club where the tradition of foursomes play is strongly preserved. Little attempt has been made to extend the course beyond comfortable limits.

The club has always had close connections

inspired putting touch. He won two English Amateur Championships and remains to this day the only man who has beaten Michael Bonallack in a national final. That was in 1959 after a wonderful match at Formby when, 1 down and 2 to play, he won the 17th in 4 and the 18th in 3. Wolstenholme also won by 1 hole in 1956 against H. Bennett at Royal Lytham, added the English Open Amateur Strokeplay at Ganton in 1960 after a play-off with Martin Christmas and finished 6th in the Centenary Open Championship at St Andrews the same year.

A few months later the British PGA relaxed their qualification period for membership from five years to six months and Wolstenholme and Doug Sewell took advan-

Wood, Craig Ralph AMERICAN
b. Lake Placid, N.Y., 1901; d. 1968. Ryder Cup 1931, 1933, 1935; runner-up British Open 1933; runner-up USPGA 1934; US Masters 1941, runner-up 1934-5; US Open 1941, runner-up 1939, 3rd 1933, 4th 1940; Canadian Open 1942

Craig Wood seemed destined to succeed Macdonald Smith as the great runner-up, for on several occasions when he seemed about to raise the cup of victory to his lips it was dashed from him. At the first US Masters tournament ever played Horton Smith holed from 20 ft on the 17th and finished 1 shot ahead of him, and in the following year he was already being congratulated in the clubhouse for his winning final round, in which he had played the last 8 holes 4 under par, when Sarazen holed his second for a double-eagle at the 485-yd (443-m) 15th, forced a play-off, and won by 5 strokes. Another case of bad luck for Wood was in the play-off with Byron Nelson for the 1939 US Open. They had shaken off Densmore Shute in the first round of the play-off but in the second Nelson won by 70-73. In

Gerard de Wit

Guy Wolstenholme

Craig R. Wood

the course of it Nelson holed a no. 1-iron second shot which put him into a lead he never relinquished. On his first visit to Britain in 1933 Craig Wood tied 1st with Densmore Shute, the first of three encounters with him in deciding a championship, but lost the play-off. Since he also finished runner-up to Paul Runyan in the 1934 USPGA championship, he could eventually claim to have been runner-up in all the Big Four events, and in some others besides. But he had his reward at last, and his revenge: he won the 1941 US Open, beating Shute into 2nd place. After his retirement, he went to live in the Bahamas and became professional at the Lucayan Club; both there and in the United States he enjoyed great popularity.

For a number of years in the 1940s, Wood was professional at Winged Foot, and later was succeeded by his assistant, Claude Harmon.

Woodbridge GC ENGLAND

Woodbridge, Suffolk. 27 holes; 18-hole course 6,282 yd (5,744 m)

Woodbridge is one of those British courses which, though not of major championship status, combine a charm and quality that make them delightful places to play. It lies a mile or so out of the town of Woodbridge among gorse and heather, and is one of the oldest and best in East Anglia.

The club was founded in 1893 and began life as a 9-hole course. In 1895 it was extended to 18 'clear of the rifle range where firing interfered with the play'. It graduated naturally to the list of Suffolk championship courses and has been a regular choice for the East Anglian Open, an example of inland golf at its best. In the period before the great golfing boom of the early 1960s, its membership, like those of many similar clubs, dwindled. It now thrives and boasts an extra 9-hole course, designed by Fred Hawtree, and a fine modern clubhouse near the tee of the old short 2nd hole.

Woodhall Spa GC ENGLAND

Woodhall Spa, Lincolnshire. 18 holes; 6,823 yd (6,239 m)

About 1810, long before golf invaded the quiet reaches of Lincolnshire, man's quest in the area of Woodhall was for coal. It was in vain, but water that accumulated in the derelict holes sunk by the prospectors was found to contain a health-giving constituent. Woodhall became a spa town that more recently has earned at least equal distinction from its golf course, which is as fine an inland test as any in Britain. Reminiscent of the heather, broom, and silver birch country in

Surrey or Berkshire, it contrasts with the rich agricultural Fenland soil, but it makes an immediate and lasting appeal and its remote peacefulness is much sought after. After four severe opening holes and a short 5th surrounded by gaping bunkers, a single-track, disused railway is crossed and the course runs out to a distant turn, but so beguiling is the mixture of woodland and heath and so easy the turf underfoot, that neither its length nor the strikingly severe bunkering gives offence. The short 12th is also policed by bunkers that swallow man and club as well as ball, and the remaining holes in the more wooded part offer little let-up.

The present course is Woodhall's third.

Woodhall Spa GC, *top*, looking towards the 3rd green and, *above*, down the 18th fairway

The first was close to the river, and the second in the grounds of what is now the Petwood Hotel and Jubilee Park. In 1903 Harry Vardon surveyed a stretch of heathland, owned by Colonel S. V. Hotchkin, which was covered with thick heather, devoid of grass, and too rocky to come under the plough. The wet summer of 1903 washed away all the seed that had been sown, and in 1904 the reseeded fairways had to be protected from an unparalleled drought by being covered by bracken. It was not until 1905 that the course was opened. The course, with its huge bunkers shaped so naturally from the sandy soil, was reconstructed in 1911 by H. S. Colt, and after World War I was completely redesigned by Hotchkin, who was also responsible for work at Ashridge and West Sussex, in addition to several courses in South Africa. The family name has been continued at Woodhall by his son, Neil, president of the English Golf Union in 1972, who has helped to raise the course to championship status. It has already housed two English, two English Strokeplay Championships, and four English Ladies' championships. It is also the home of the Central England Foursomes. But it is part of Woodhall's charm that it appeals no less to those many visitors who are not in the championship class.

Woodlands GC AUSTRALIA

Mordialloc, Victoria. 18 holes; 6,615 yd (6,049 m)

Originally the Mordialloc GC, a 9-hole course laid out in 1913, and extended to 18 in 1919. It changed its name in 1925 to Woodlands, appropriately enough in view of the club's delightful setting on the fringes of Melbourne's famous sand-belt area. The course has retained much of the original atmosphere and charm, and at the same time

voted officers of the club, W. E. P. Prendergast, and J. Lovett, have both been presidents of the Australian Golf Union and of the Victorian Golf Association.

The club's most notable golfer was Margaret Masters who before successfully entering the women's professional circuit in the United States, won the Ladies' championships of Australia and South Africa.

Woods

The wooden-headed clubs, with the exception nowadays of wooden-headed putters. Originally most of the game was played with woods, but by about 1920 a uniform set generally consisted of three woods and the rest irons. There were, and still are, variations but the absence of woods from a player's bag is often an indication that he cannot get on with them.

Woods are the clubs usually played when distance is required. In the early days the club used to drive off the tee was known as the 'play club', the club used to get the ball 'in play', but gradually it acquired the name of driver.

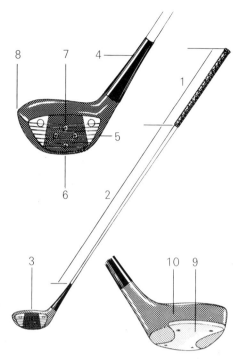

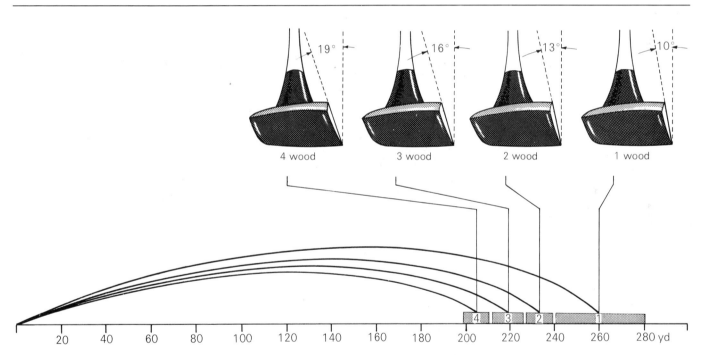

4 wood   3 wood   2 wood   1 wood

provides a first-class modern test of golf.

During 1964, abundant underground water was discovered and a semi-automatic system installed, enabling championship conditions to be enjoyed throughout the year.

The present clubhouse was built in 1927 and has a fine view of the course. Two de-

Drivers have varying degrees of loft and varying depths to the face; the amounts are personal matters. Then there came the brassie, for hitting the ball as far as possible from a lie on the ground; the spoon, a club with a little more loft than the brassie; and the baffy, a short wood used more for recovery work.

Modern terminology, and more is the pity, seems to scorn names for clubs and replaces them with numbers as though, Bernard Darwin once wrote, they were convicts. The driver retains its title over the no. 1 wood but increasingly the brassie has become the no. 2 wood, the spoon the 3 wood and so on. The modern no. 4 wood

Above, woods: normal distances achieved by average golfers

Top, the parts of a wooden club: 1. grip, surmounted by plug; 2. shaft; 3. head; 4. socket and hozel; 5. heel; 6. sole; 7. face; 8. toe; 9. sole plate; 10. back

corresponds more perhaps to the baffy but things have not been allowed to rest there. Many professionals, including Lee Trevino, carry a no. 5 wood and there are some amateurs who carry as many as eight, the 8 wood corresponding roughly in terms of loft to the 7 iron.

In recent times, some manufacturers have marketed heads made of nylon and other compositions but these are still known as woods.

Work, Bertram AMERICAN

b. Staten Island, N.Y. 1868; d. St Moritz, Switzerland, 1927

The man who collaborated with Coburn Haskell in perfecting the rubber-wound golf ball. Together they submitted their specifications to the US Patent Office in 1898 before the Goodrich Rubber Company started production of the new balls. In 1907 Bertram Work became President of the Goodrich Rubber Company.

World Amateur Team Championship

see table on p. 470.

World Cup: *top,* George Knudson and Al Balding pose beside the World Cup after the 1968 presentation ceremony: *above,* the presentation to Gary Player after winning the individual title in 1965

World Cup (formerly Canada Cup)

The Canada Cup was founded by John Jay Hopkins, an American industrialist, for 'the furtherance of good fellowship and better understanding among the nations of the world through the medium of international golf competition'. It was Hopkins's belief that because more countries were playing golf, and the Ryder Cup was limited to Britain and the United States, there was a need for a truly international tournament.

Hopkins was not only the father of the idea, he was the man who backed it and nurtured it from 1953, when seven nations responded to his invitation to take part in the first tournament in Montreal, until his death in 1957. The project has been continued by his successors as president of the International Golf Association, which he founded in 1952, and by the enthusiasm of its tournament director, Fred Corcoran, who has been its guiding light for many years.

Argentina was the first winner of the two-man event and the following year Australia captured the title, also in Montreal, from a field of 25. To promote interest the tournament began to move around, setting up its annual camp in places as far removed as Tokyo, Hawaii, Puerto Rico, Buenos Aires and Mexico. The number of participant countries has increased significantly and by 1964 32 nations took part. In 1965 in Madrid, Czechoslovakia became the first East European country to file an entry and in 1969 the field reached 45. In 1967 the tournament changed its name to the World Cup.

It has lacked the excitement of other international occasions, has traded largely on goodwill, modest prize money and a somewhat wearisome form of play.

The winner is the two-man team with the lowest combined medal score for four rounds, during which time play is by four-balls. It demands a good deal of teamwork. The event, largely dominated by the Americans, has produced some memorable moments, notably when Ben Hogan and Sam Snead scored America's second victory and, almost on their own, drew enormous crowds to Wentworth in 1956.

The list of results is given on p. 450.

Worlington and Newmarket GC, Royal
ENGLAND

Worlington, Suffolk. 9 holes

No 9-hole course in the world has greater distinction, tradition or romantic appeal than Royal Worlington and Newmarket, which has the geological luck to form a sandy oasis a few miles north of the famous racing town of Newmarket. It has been the home of

generations of Cambridge undergraduate golfers and, if not wholly responsible, is certainly a significant reason for their supremacy over Oxford through the years.

It is a classical course of humble origin situated close to the hamlet of Worlington, a mile or so from the ancient market town of Mildenhall. Although the piece of warren land was planned as 18 holes, some of the marshy ground was found to be unsuitable and, on the advice of Captain A. M. Ross (himself a fine golfer judging by his club handicap of plus 6), only 9 holes were made. The course was constructed three years before the club was formed in 1893, and six years before it was granted the title 'Royal' by Queen Victoria.

Whereas so many courses are attributable to the hand of man, Worlington is the design of nature where the golfer learns, if he ever does, the subtleties of finesse, control and artistry. Power is no substitute for craft and thought; and, above all, Worlington teaches the joys of fast, true greens which have no equals among British inland courses in the winter. Worlington, in fact, is the golfer's ideal. Yet at first sight it looks dull, flat and featureless; and, when you have been round once, you have to go round again; maybe four times in a single day. What could be easier than that?

The truth is, however, rather the opposite. Nobody ever grows tired of its pleasures and variations, or of respecting its many qualities. It is ideal for foursomes, which are much favoured there, with its nine different tee shots for each player.

Its triangular shape demands that the holes are always changing direction, each one offering something different. Bernard Darwin himself called them 'the sacred nine'. Each therefore has its special admirers but, if Worlington owes its fame to a few in particular, the 3rd, 5th, 6th and 9th are the most often named. The short 5th, played at right angles over a corner of the 4th green, is a gem of devilish intrigue in which the architect had no need for bunkers, its green, shaped like a vaulting horse, proving no easier to hold with a scuttling pitch from its sides than a 5 iron from the tee.

In 1907 J. F. Ireland, a member of the Cambridge side that year, holed in one at the 5th and 7th in the same 9 holes. But Worlington has the power to get its own back, if not with the pitch to the 4th, then at the 6th along the row of majestic pines, the 8th with its good old-fashioned cross bunker or at the 9th, a superb short par 4.

Since the time of its inauguration, successive generations of Cambridge golfers have built up an undying affection for Worlington or Mildenhall, as so many, including Henry Longhurst, prefer to call it. Its attractions are many. There is the feeling of escape that a 21-mile journey inevitably brings, a knowledge that no better training ground exists for young golfers, and for many there has been the benefit of a lesson

A course made famous by the mixed foursomes competition held there since 1921, but an attractive course in its own right, on a heather and woodland strip in the heart of Surrey. Though too short for most national events the course responded perfectly to the needs of the mixed foursome, providing a number of holes ideally fitted in length to this

drew attention to the competition by winning it eight times with six different partners. It came to be regarded as an event in which victory depended largely on a class woman player, and subsequent history has certainly borne this out. Female winners of the event include several Curtis Cup players, among them Molly Gourlay, Wanda

with Jack Beverley, the club's faithful professional for many years, or perhaps a round with Leonard Crawley who lives a brassie shot from the 9th tee.

Few who play at Worlington fail to benefit in some way but undoubtedly its greatest blessing is that nothing seems to change. The quiet, rural beauty of its setting, the little farmhouse clubhouse, the glass hatch behind which the drinks are dispensed, the friendly welcome of the members and, for the hungry undergraduate, quite the best chocolate cake in the land.

Worplesdon GC ENGLAND
Woking, Surrey. 18 holes; 6,304 yd
(5,764 m); par 70

unusual form of competition. Worplesdon lies about a mile from Brookwood station, and was founded in 1908. It has suffered only slight alteration since. Its first professional, Johnnie Heron, made a reputation as a teacher over 36 years, and was succeeded by Alan Waters.

Tucked away in the wooded Surrey lanes it is one of those courses where the golfer seems to enjoy complete solitude, yet four of the holes lie across the Guildford-Bagshot road which needs careful negotiating, and there are numerous short cuts. For years the mixed foursomes attracted the highest class of entry and made a cheerful and enjoyable end to the amateur season. Joyce Wethered Morgan, Mrs Bunty Smith, Mrs Angela

Bonallack, who with her husband became in 1958 the first married couple to win, and Mrs G. Valentine (Jessie Anderson).

An unusual feature of the course is that it comes early back to the clubhouse, at the 4th a long one-shotter for the women. Thereafter the course is a mixture of heather and pine, and there are several holes to test the combination. This is specially true of the finish, for the one-shot 16th usually requires wood from the women, the 17th pitch needs most careful judging if the ball is not to run on or run back, and the 18th behaves as the best finishing holes should, clearly offering the choice between playing safe for a 5 or attempting glory with a spoon-shot

Worplesdon GC – Peter Benka chipping onto the 10th green

second. Another hole of note is the 10th, the Pond, straightforward enough but one at which even the best have at times lifted their heads and seen the water splash.

In 1971 the Vagliano Trophy match was held at Worplesdon.

Worsham, Lewis Elmer AMERICAN

b. Alta., Va., 1917. Atlanta Open 1946; Ryder Cup 1947; US Open 1947; Phoenix Open 1951; Tam O'Shanter World Championship 1953

Two of the peaks in Worsham's golfing career occurred under the television camera. In 1947, when he defeated Sam Snead in a play-off for the Open at St Louis, television was used for the first time in a national championship. Snead had tied him by holing from 18 ft for a birdie at the 18th in the fourth round, but coming to the last green with the same score in the play-off, both second putts were just less than a yard from the hole. After measurement Snead putted first and missed, and Worsham became the winner by 69 to 70. An even more publicized occasion was his winning of the World

Championship in George S. May's tournament at the Tam O'Shanter club. Needing a birdie 3 to tie Chandler Harper for the title, Worsham, left with an approach of about 110 yd, chose a wedge and in front of a large crowd and television audience holed the shot for an eagle, which won him $25,000 dollars outright.

A Virginian by birth, Worsham came up through the caddie ranks and turned professional at 18. He has been professional at Fort Lauderdale and Oakmont, dividing his time between the two. In his only appearance in a Ryder Cup match in 1947 he and Ed Oliver had a spectacular victory by 10 and 9 in the top foursome against Henry Cotton and Arthur Lees.

Lew Worsham

Wright, Mrs Innes see ROBERTSON, JANETTE

Wright, Mary Kathryn AMERICAN

b. San Diego, Cal., 1935. US Junior Girls' 1952, runner-up 1950; runner-up US Women's Amateur 1954; US Women's Open 1958-9, 1961, 1964

Four times winner of the US Women's Open, Mickey Wright ranks among the few really great players of women's golf. She was considered to have greater length than her famous compatriot, Babe Zaharias, and her record in professional tournaments in the United States during the early 1960s set a completely new standard in women's golf. In the 10 years after turning professional in 1956, she lowered the best women's scoring average from the 75-76 mark to 72-73.

She was the daughter of an attorney who had already decided the baby would be a boy and had chosen the name Michael, which gave rise to the name by which Mary Kathryn Wright became known. She won the US Junior in 1952, the year she entered Stanford University to study psychology.

She had been runner-up two years before at the age of 15, when she won a long-driving contest by driving three balls a total of 680 yd (622 m). Before turning professional in 1954 she was runner-up to Barbara Romack in the US Women's Amateur. She made history by becoming the first player to be fined by the LPGA, because she spoke out

Mickey Wright

plainly at the end of a round-robin tournament in which she had scored generally better than her opponents but, because of the scoring system, had failed to win.

One of Mickey Wright's best years was 1961 when she won an unprecedented 10 tournaments, four of them in a row. Her victory by 6 strokes in the Open the same year, over a specially severe course at Baltusrol, included a 69 which, considering the length of the course – 6,400 yd (5,850 m) – must rank as one of the greatest played by a woman. Her retiring nature may have been an obstacle to her achieving the fame of other golfers, but her record and her game leave no doubt that she is among them. She once hit a drive in normal conditions more than 270 yd (247 m), and her usual length has been reckoned as 230 yd (210 m). Yet her driving was not her only strong point, and it was in her long iron play that she was considered supreme.

She was leading money winner in 1961-4, won the LPGA Vare Trophy 1960-4 and in 1966 won seven victories and over $40,000. Altogether she has had 82 wins. Not surprisingly she is a member of the LPGA Hall of Fame.

Wry Neck

Similar to the goose neck, but applied more often to iron clubs. A wry-necked putter is designed so that the shaft turns back at the angle of the blade's loft for an inch or two, and then goes forward until it reaches the line of the heel, whence it turns upwards to take the shaft.

Wry necks used to be thought proof against shanking. *See also* Goose neck.

Yale GC USA

New Haven, Conn.

People have been known to come a long way just for the pleasure of playing the Yale University course, which winds through hilly woodland on the outskirts of New Haven, just west of the famous football arena, Yale Bowl. Certainly, this is one of the best college courses in America.

It was built out of resistant wilderness in the mid-1920s by Charles Blair Macdonald from land made available by the widow of Ray Tompkins, who also underwrote the cost of construction – the official name of the lay-out is the Ray Tompkins Memorial Course. It plays long from the back tees and is on the tough side even from the shortest. Greist Pond and a second unnamed pond are right in the middle and come into play on a number of holes. The greens are large, some enormous. On the very first hole a second shot could be hooked so badly as to appear out of bounds, but the ball might be found on the green, although a long way from the pin.

The fact that many of its holes have been called 'best' by someone indicates only that Yale stirs a golfer's imagination. Tommy Armour designated the 440-yd (402-m) 4th, which has water on the right and runs to an elevated green, a great golf hole, but there are more votes for the 9th than any other. It is, in truth, a spectacular hole – a par 3 that measures from 190 yd (174 m) to 225 yd (206 m), according to the tee, and presents a long carry over water from all of them. What people remember most vividly about the 9th is a deep, V-shaped dip that cuts right across the green at a right angle to the line of the tee shot. Much of the terrain has this Brobdingnagian quality about it.

Yarra Yarra GC AUSTRALIA

nr Melbourne, Victoria. 18 holes; 6,657 yd (6,087 m)

This club came into existence in 1911 as the successor of the old Eaglemont club. It thrived until in the mid-1920s members began to be drawn to the newly established courses in the famous sand-belt area. In order to survive the club decided to move to a site in the same region, not far from the courses at Commonwealth and Metro-politan. Under the direction of Alex Russell, who joined forces with Dr Alister Mac-kenzie, swift progress was made. The pleasant tree-lined course was opened in 1929, together with the distinctive new club-house embodying features of Spanish, Moorish and Italian architecture. No sooner had the club settled in than the Depression overtook it. By 1934, however, Yarra Yarra was moving towards its present healthy state.

It has produced its own share of good players, in particular Kevin Hartley, winner of the Australian Amateur in 1958. It was a proud moment for the club when the 1969 Dunlop International tournament was staged there, attracting such players as Tony Jacklin, Bruce Devlin, Lee Trevino and Gary Player.

Yasuda, Haruo JAPANESE

b. Tokyo 1943. Runner-up Malaysia Open 1967; runner-up Thailand Open 1968; Philippines Open 1969, runner-up 1971; runner-up Hong Kong Open 1970; runner-up Singapore Open 1970; Yomiuri Open

1971; Taiwan Open 1972

Yasuda, who turned professional in 1961, attracts a large following because of his aggressive play. He is full of determination and not one to play safe. Taking his pro-fession seriously, he maintains a strict train-ing programme which is said to include the practice of Zen meditation.

Haruo Yasuda

Yates, Charles Richard AMERICAN

b. Atlanta, Ga., 1913. Georgia Amateur 1931-2; US National Collegiate 1934; Western Amateur 1935; Walker Cup 1936, 1938; British Amateur 1938

Not an elegant golfer but a forceful one, Yates employed almost a wrench of the shoulders in his swing. He won the British Amateur at Troon in 1938 as a member of the US Walker Cup team, defeating Cecil Ewing by 3 and 2 in the final. Of a cheerful and lovable disposition with a rich, deep Southern accent, he was easily persuaded to break into song, which he did at the ceremony after Britain had won the Walker Cup match at St Andrews. His rendering of 'A wee deochan doruis' won over the crowd. If not the greatest golfer ever to win the British championship he was certainly a most popular one, and on his game he was one of the finest putters. In 1971 his voice was heard again proposing a toast at the jubilee dinner of the Walker Cup match at St Andrews. A devoted member of the Augusta National, he has been for many years one of its lieutenants with special responsibility for running the press section with its scores of writers attending the Masters.

Yost, Richard L. AMERICAN

Oregon State Medal Play 1952; Pacific Northwest 1953; Walker Cup 1955

Yost won both his matches in the 1955 Walker Cup competition.

Yugoslavia

Before World War II and the virtual ex-tinction of golf in Yugoslavia, there were courses at Belgrade and Zagreb. Yugoslav Open Amateur and Ladies' championships were held for one year only, in 1938.

Among the East European countries Yugoslavia has, however, shown the most signs of encouraging the game again, al-though largely, as in Spain and Portugal, to attract tourists. Donald Harradine designed a new course at Bled in 1972 and there have been reports of several other developments.

Z

Zaharias, Mrs G. (née Mildred Didrikson)
AMERICAN

b. Port Arthur, Tex., 1914; d. 1956. US
Women's Amateur 1946; British Ladies'
1947; US Women's Open 1948, 1950, 1954

A great athlete, not only in golf but in a
variety of other sports. Babe Zaharias won
two gold medals in the 1932 Olympics at
Los Angeles and it was not until later that
she became taken with golf, eventually to
the exclusion of all other sports. Her overwhelming success in golf did not come
instantly, although it is said that the first
time she swung a golf club she struck the ball
more than 200 yd. Her success came from
her prodigious length and from the long
hours of practice she cheerfully undertook.
Her exceptional agility gave her great
powers of acceleration, but it was some years
before she gained the control necessary to
win championships. She once said that
round Muirfield she had not wanted anything more than an 8 iron for her second
shots. Enid Wilson saw her finish over the
back of a hole 540 yd (494 m) long at
Gullane with a 4-iron second. The fairways

Mrs G. Zaharias

were soft and the last 140 yd (128 m) of the
hole was uphill.

Enid Wilson in her *Gallery of Women
Golfers* (1961) has left this picture of her:
'Above average height but not abnormally
tall and of slender build, the "Babe" moved
like a ballerina, as though she did not have a
bone in her body. Her hair and fingernails
were worn long and she used cosmetics just
like any other smart woman of her time. She
smoked in moderation but had no use for
alcohol. She played in two exhibition
matches with Joyce Wethered with whom
comparisons have often been drawn, but
none was possible at that time, because
whereas the Briton was at her peak Mrs
Zaharias did not reach hers for another 10
years.' Charles Price, an American sports
writer, put it neatly when he said 'the Babe
had convinced many that she was the best
woman player since Miss Wethered, and
many more who had never seen her play
that she was even better.'

Two years after graduating from high
school she became an American basketball
player. She then entered for seven events in
the National Track and Field Championships that preceded the Olympics of 1932.
She was placed 1st in six of them. Limited to
three events in the Olympics she finished 1st
in all three, setting three world records in
the low hurdles, the javelin, and the high
jump. Her medal in the last event was dis-
allowed because of a then unorthodox
method. After winning the Texas Open in
1935 she was banned from playing in amateur golf events, but after her marriage in
1938 to an all-in wrestler, she applied for reinstatement, which was granted in 1943.

In 1946 Babe Zaharias won the US
Amateur, not going beyond the 15th hole in
any of her matches and winning the 36-hole
final by 11 and 9. The following year, she
travelled to Britain and became the first
American to win that championship. Her
extrovert manner was somewhat coolly received by the crowds at Gullane, and she
was asked to go back and change out of her
red and white check shorts on the final day,
but she won as convincingly over Jacqueline
Gordon as she had done over all others. She
at once reverted to her professional status on
returning to the United States, and the
following year won the first of her three US
Opens. She had a strong sense of publicity
and attracted crowds wherever she went, so
that she was largely instrumental in giving
impetus to the women's professional circuit,
which was just coming into being. She made
one more trip to Britain, in 1951, as part of a
sponsored show. The team of women made a
triumphal progress which culminated in

winning all their singles against a team of
first-class males playing on level terms.

Most appealing of all to the American
public was the fight Babe Zaharias put up
against cancer. After undergoing surgery for
it in 1953 she proceeded to win her third US
Open in the following year by a record 12
strokes. She won four other events that year
and two more in 1955 before she had to give
up. Altogether she won more than 50 events.

Zahrani CC LEBANON
nr Sidon. 9 holes; 5,384 yd (4,923 m); par 68
(for 18 holes)

This club lies 30 miles south of Beirut,
near Sidon and a mile inland from the
Mediterranean. Zahrani is run by the Trans
Arabian Pipeline Co. as a private course for
its staff and invited guests.

Zoute GC, Royal BELGIUM
Knokke-Het Zoute (Knocke-Le-Zoute).
3 courses

At the end of the 19th or the beginning of
the 20th century, a few retired Englishmen
began to play golf on the dunes belonging to
the Compagnie Immobilière du Zoute.
Count Maurice Lippens was chairman of
the company and it was he who started to
build a proper course and clubhouse, which
came into operation in 1908. A few years
later a second course was added, and about
1930 a third. All three courses were destroyed by the Germans during World War
II. At the end of the war Yvan Feyerick, a
former president of the club and of the
Fédération Royale Belge de Golf, got in
touch with British and Canadian military
officers to see if it would be possible to have
the bulldozer and mine school occupying the
dunes moved. His efforts were successful
enough to restore 9 holes by the end of 1945,
although it was necessary for golfers to play
their shots from small movable mats or
carpets because time was still needed for the
fairways either to recover or to be resown.

By 1947 two courses were playable and
the club became a regular host to Belgian
championships. The main course has many
of the characteristics of British seaside golf
and is one of the best in Belgium. In August
1970 it was the scene of the biennial match
between the amateurs of Great Britain and
Ireland and the Continent of Europe.

The town itself, about 30 miles along the
coast from Ostend, is a popular holiday
resort.

Zürich GC SWITZERLAND
Zumikon, nr Zürich. 18 holes; 6,300 yd
(5,760 m); par 72

Zürich's course, some 1,450 ft above sea

level, has replaced the almost miniature one at Dolder which was only just outside the centre of the city. In recent years new courses have been started on the outskirts of Zürich; in 1972 the course at Zumikon was, at the time at least, the greenest, the most picturesque and in the best order. It is laid out in the verdant and wooded country round this largest city in Switzerland. Through it runs a river which here and there makes the golf more pleasurable without imposing many difficulties.

Royal Zoute GC

Tables of Results

1922 NATIONAL GOLF LINKS OF AMERICA, N.Y.	Great Britain and Ireland		United States	
Great Britain and Ireland 4 *Captain: R. Harris*	*Foursomes*	*1*	*Foursomes*	*3*
	C. J. H. Tolley & B. Darwin	0	J. P. Guilford & F. D. Ouimet (8 & 7)	1
	R. H. Wethered & C. C. Aylmer (5 & 4)	1	C. Evans Jr & R. A. Gardner	0
United States 8 *Captain: W. C. Fownes Jr*	W. B. Torrance & C. V. L. Hooman	0	R. T. Jones Jr & J. W. Sweetser (3 & 2)	1
	J. Caven & W. W. Mackenzie	0	M. R. Marston & W. C. Fownes Jr (2 & 1)	1
	Singles	*3*	*Singles*	*5*
	C. J. H. Tolley	0	J. P. Guilford (2 & 1)	1
	R. H. Wethered	0	R. T. Jones Jr (3 & 2)	1
	J. Caven	0	C. Evans Jr (5 & 4)	1
	C. C. Aylmer	0	F. D. Ouimet (8 & 7)	1
	W. B. Torrance	0	R. A. Gardner (7 & 5)	1
	W. W. Mackenzie (6 & 5)	1	M. R. Marston	0
	B. Darwin (3 & 1)	1	W. C. Fownes Jr	0
	C. V. L. Hooman (37th)	1	J. W. Sweetser	0

1923 ST ANDREWS, SCOTLAND	Great Britain and Ireland		United States	
Great Britain and Ireland 5 *Captain: R. Harris*	*Foursomes*	*3*	*Foursomes*	*1*
	C. J. H. Tolley & R. H. Wethered (6 & 5)	1	F. D. Ouimet & J. W. Sweetser	0
	R. Harris & C. V. L. Hooman	1	R. A. Gardner & M. R. Marston (7 & 6)	1
United States 6 *Captain: R. A. Gardner*	E. W. E. Holderness & W. L. Hope (1 up)	1	G. V. Rotan & S. D. Herron	0
	J. Wilson & W. A. Murray (4 & 3)	1	H. R. Johnston & J. F. Neville	0
	Singles	*2*	*Singles*	*5*
	R. H. Wethered (halved)	0	F. D. Ouimet (halved)	0
	C. J. H. Tolley (4 & 3)	1	J. W. Sweetser	0
	R. Harris	0	R. A. Gardner (1 up)	1
	W. W. Mackenzie	0	G. V. Rotan (5 & 4)	1
	W. L. Hope	0	M. R. Marston (6 & 5)	1
	E. W. E. Holderness	0	F. J. Wright Jr (1 up)	1
	J. Wilson (1 up)	1	S. D. Herron	0
	W. A. Murray	0	O. F. Willing (2 & 1)	1

1924 GARDEN CITY GC, N.Y.	Great Britain and Ireland		United States	
Great Britain and Ireland 3 *Captain: C. J. H. Tolley*	*Foursomes*	*1*	*Foursomes*	*3*
	E. F. Storey & W. A. Murray	0	M. R. Marston & R. A. Gardner (3 & 1)	1
	C. J. H. Tolley & C. O. Hezlet	0	J. P. Guilford & F. D. Ouimet (2 & 1)	1
United States 9 *Captain: R. A. Gardner*	Hon. M. Scott & R. Scott Jr (1 up)	1	R. T. Jones Jr & W. C. Fownes Jr	0
	T. A. Torrance & O. C. Bristowe	0	J. W. Sweetser & H. R. Johnston (4 & 3)	1
	Singles	*2*	*Singles*	*6*
	C. J. H. Tolley (1 up)	1	M. R. Marston	0
	C. O. Hezlet	0	R. T. Jones Jr (4 & 3)	1
	W. A. Murray	0	C. Evans Jr (2 & 1)	1
	E. F. Storey	0	F. D. Ouimet (1 up)	1
	Hon. M. Scott (7 & 6)	1	J. W. Sweetser	0
	W. L. Hope	0	R. A. Gardner (3 & 2)	1
	T. A. Torrance	0	J. P. Guilford (2 & 1)	1
	D. H. Kyle	0	O. F. Willing (3 & 2)	1

1926 ST ANDREWS, SCOTLAND	Great Britain and Ireland		United States	
Great Britain and Ireland 5 *Captain: R. Harris*	*Foursomes*	*1*	*Foursomes*	*3*
	R. H. Wethered & E. W. E. Holderness (5 & 4)	1	F. D. Ouimet & J. P. Guilford	0
	C. J. H. Tolley & A. Jamieson Jr	0	R. T. Jones Jr & W. Gunn (4 & 3)	1
United States 6 *Captain: R. A. Gardner*	R. Harris & C. O. Hezlet	0	G. Von Elm & J. W. Sweetser (8 & 7)	1
	E. F. Storey & Hon. W. G. E. Brownlow	0	R. A. Gardner & R. R. MacKenzie (1 up)	1
	Singles	*4*	*Singles*	*3*
	C. J. H. Tolley	0	R. T. Jones Jr (12 & 11)	1
	E. W. E. Holderness	0	J. W. Sweetser (4 & 3)	1
	R. H. Wethered (5 & 4)	1	F. D. Ouimet	0
	C. O. Hezlet (halved)	0	G. Von Elm (halved)	0
	R. Harris (2 & 1)	1	J. P. Guilford	0
	W. G. E. Brownlow	0	W. Gunn (9 & 8)	1
	E. F. Storey (2 & 1)	1	R. R. MacKenzie	0
	A. Jamieson Jr (5 & 4)	1	R. A. Gardner	0

	Great Britain and Ireland		United States	
1928 CHICAGO GC, ILL.				
	Foursomes	0	*Foursomes*	4
Great Britain and Ireland 1	T. P. Perkins & W. Tweddell	0	J. W. Sweetser & G. Von Elm (7 & 6)	1
Captain: W. Tweddell	C. O. Hezlet & W. L. Hope	0	R. T. Jones Jr & C. Evans Jr (5 & 3)	1
	T. A. Torrance & E. F. Storey	0	F. D. Ouimet & H. R. Johnston (4 & 2)	1
United States 11	J. B. Beck & A. R. MacCallum	0	W. Gunn & R. R. MacKenzie (7 & 5)	1
Captain: R. T. Jones Jr				
	Singles	1	*Singles*	7
	T. P. Perkins	0	R. T. Jones Jr (13 & 12)	1
	W. Tweddell	0	G. Von Elm (3 & 2)	1
	C. O. Hezlet	0	F. D. Ouimet (8 & 7)	1
	W. L. Hope	0	J. W. Sweetser (5 & 4)	1
	E. F. Storey	0	H. R. Johnston (4 & 2)	1
	T. A. Torrance (1 up)	1	C. Evans Jr	0
	R. H. Hardman	0	W. Gunn (11 & 10)	1
	G. N. C. Martin	0	R. R. MacKenzie (2 & 1)	1

	Great Britain and Ireland		United States	
1930 ROYAL ST GEORGE'S GC, ENGLAND				
	Foursomes	1	*Foursomes*	3
Great Britain and Ireland 2	C. J. H. Tolley & R. H. Wethered (2 up)	1	G. Von Elm & G. J. Voigt	0
Captain: R. H. Wethered	R. W. Hartley & T. A. Torrance	0	R. T. Jones Jr & O. F. Willing (8 & 7)	1
	E. W. E. Holderness & J. A. Stout	0	R. R. MacKenzie & D. K. Moe (2 & 1)	1
United States 10	W. Campbell & J. N. Smith	0	H. R. Johnston & F. D. Ouimet (2 & 1)	1
Captain: R. T. Jones Jr				
	Singles	1	*Singles*	7
	C. J. H. Tolley	0	H. R. Johnston (5 & 4)	1
	R. H. Wethered	0	R. T. Jones Jr (9 & 8)	1
	R. W. Hartley	0	G. Von Elm (3 & 2)	1
	E. W. E. Holderness	0	G. J. Voigt (10 & 8)	1
	J. N. Smith	0	O. F. Willing (2 & 1)	1
	T. A. Torrance (7 & 6)	1	F. D. Ouimet	0
	J. A. Stout	0	D. K. Moe (1 up)	1
	W. Campbell	0	R. R. MacKenzie (6 & 5)	1

	Great Britain and Ireland		United States	
1932 THE COUNTRY CLUB, BROOKLINE, MASS.				
	Foursomes	0	*Foursomes*	4
Great Britain and Ireland 1	R. W. Hartley & W. L. Hartley	0	J. W. Sweetser & G. J. Voigt (7 & 6)	1
Captain: T. A. Torrance	T. A. Torrance & J. G. de Forest	0	C. H. Seaver & G. T. Moreland (6 & 5)	1
	J. A. Stout & J. Burke	0	F. D. Ouimet & G. T. Dunlap Jr (7 & 6)	1
United States 8	E. W. Fiddian & E. A. McRuvie	0	D. K. Moe & W. Howell (5 & 4)	1
Captain: F. D. Ouimet				
	Singles	1	*Singles*	4
	T. A. Torrance (halved)	0	F. D. Ouimet (halved)	0
	J. A. Stout (halved)	0	J. W. Sweetser (halved)	0
	R. W. Hartley	0	G. T. Moreland (2 & 1)	1
	J. Burke (halved)	0	J. Westland (halved)	0
	L. G. Crawley (1 up)	1	G. J. Voigt	0
	W. L. Hartley	0	M. J. McCarthy Jr (3 & 2)	1
	E. W. Fiddian	0	C. H. Seaver (7 & 6)	1
	E. A. McRuvie	0	G. T. Dunlap Jr (10 & 9)	1

	Great Britain and Ireland		United States	
1934 ST ANDREWS, SCOTLAND				
	Foursomes	1	*Foursomes*	3
Great Britain and Ireland 2	R. H. Wethered & C. J. H. Tolley	0	J. G. Goodman & W. L. Little Jr (8 & 6)	1
Captain: Hon. M. Scott	H. G. Bentley & E. W. Fiddian	0	G. T. Moreland & J. Westland (6 & 5)	1
	Hon. M. Scott & S. L. McKinlay	0	H. C. Egan & M. R. Marston (3 & 2)	1
United States 9	E. A. McRuvie & J. McLean (4 & 2)	1	F. D. Ouimet & G. T. Dunlap Jr	0
Captain: F. D. Ouimet				
	Singles	1	*Singles*	6
	Hon. M. Scott	0	J. G. Goodman (7 & 6)	1
	C. J. H. Tolley	0	W. L. Little Jr (6 & 5)	1
	L. G. Crawley	0	F. D. Ouimet (5 & 4)	1
	J. McLean	0	G. T. Dunlap Jr (4 & 3)	1
	E. W. Fiddian	0	J. W. Fischer (5 & 4)	1
	S. L. McKinlay	0	G. T. Moreland (3 & 1)	1
	E. A. McRuvie (halved)	0	J. Westland (halved)	0
	T. A. Torrance (4 & 3)	1	M. R. Marston	0

1936 PINE VALLEY GC, N.J.

Great Britain and Ireland 0
Captain: W. Tweddell

United States 9
Captain: F. D. Ouimet

Great Britain and Ireland		United States	
Foursomes	0	*Foursomes*	2
H. Thomson & H. G. Bentley	0	J. G. Goodman & A. E. Campbell (7 & 5)	1
J. McLean & J. D. A. Langley	0	R. Smith & E. White (8 & 7)	1
G. B. Peters & J. M. Dykes (halved)	0	C. R. Yates & W. Emery (halved)	0
G. A. Hill & R. C. Ewing (halved)	0	H. L. Givan & G. J. Voigt (halved)	0
Singles	0	*Singles*	7
H. Thomson	0	J. G. Goodman (3 & 2)	1
J. McLean	0	A. E. Campbell (5 & 4)	1
R. C. Ewing	0	J. W. Fischer (8 & 7)	1
G. A. Hill	0	R. Smith (11 & 9)	1
G. B. Peters	0	W. Emery (1 up)	1
J. M. Dykes	0	C. R. Yates (8 & 7)	1
H. G. Bentley (halved)	0	G. T. Dunlap Jr (halved)	0
J. D. A. Langley	0	E. White (6 & 5)	1

1938 ST ANDREWS, SCOTLAND

Great Britain and Ireland 7
Captain: J. B. Beck

United States 4
Captain: F. D. Ouimet

Great Britain and Ireland		United States	
Foursomes	2	*Foursomes*	1
H. G. Bentley & J. Bruen Jr (halved)	0	J. W. Fischer & C. R. Kocsis (halved)	0
G. B. Peters & H. Thomson (4 & 2)	1	J. G. Goodman & M. H. Ward	0
A. T. Kyle & C. Stowe	0	C. R. Yates & R. E. Billows (3 & 2)	1
J. J. F. Pennink & L. G. Crawley (3 & 1)	1	R. Smith & F. Haas Jr	0
Singles	5	*Singles*	3
J. Bruen Jr	0	C. R. Yates (2 & 1)	1
H. Thomson (6 & 4)	1	J. G. Goodman	0
L. G. Crawley	0	J. W. Fischer (3 & 2)	1
C. Stowe (2 & 1)	1	C. R. Kocsis	0
J. J. F. Pennink	0	M. H. Ward (12 & 11)	1
R. C. Ewing (1 up)	1	R. E. Billows	0
G. B. Peters (9 & 8)	1	R. Smith	0
A. T. Kyle (5 & 4)	1	F. Haas Jr	0

1947 ST ANDREWS, SCOTLAND

Great Britain and Ireland 4
Captain: J. B. Beck

United States 8
Captain: F. D. Ouimet

Great Britain and Ireland		United States	
Foursomes	2	*Foursomes*	2
J. B. Carr & R. C. Ewing	0	S. E. Bishop & R. H. (Skee) Riegel (3 & 2)	1
L. G. Crawley & P. B. Lucas (5 & 4)	1	M. H. Ward & S. L. Quick	0
A. T. Kyle & J. C. Wilson	0	W. P. Turnesa & A. F. Kammer Jr (5 & 4)	1
R. J. White & C. Stowe (4 & 3)	1	F. R. Stranahan & R. D. Chapman	0
Singles	2	*Singles*	6
L. G. Crawley	0	M. H. Ward (5 & 3)	1
J. B. Carr (5 & 3)	1	S. E. Bishop	0
G. H. Micklem	0	R. H. (Skee) Riegel (6 & 5)	1
R. C. Ewing	0	W. P. Turnesa (6 & 5)	1
C. Stowe	0	F. R. Stranahan (2 & 1)	1
R. J. White (4 & 3)	1	A. F. Kammer Jr	0
J. C. Wilson	0	S. L. Quick (8 & 6)	1
P. B. Lucas	0	R. D. Chapman (4 & 3)	1

1949 WINGED FOOT GC, N.Y.

Great Britain and Ireland 2
Captain: P. B. Lucas

United States 10
Captain: F. D. Ouimet

Great Britain and Ireland		United States	
Foursomes	1	*Foursomes*	3
J. B. Carr & R. J. White (3 & 2)	1	R. E. Billows & W. P. Turnesa	0
J. Bruen Jr & S. M. McCready	0	C. R. Kocsis & F. R. Stranahan (2 & 1)	1
R. C. Ewing & G. H. Micklem	0	S. E. Bishop & R. H. (Skee) Riegel (9 & 7)	1
K. G. Thom & A. H. Perowne	0	J. W. Dawson & B. N. McCormick (8 & 7)	1
Singles	1	*Singles*	7
R. J. White (4 & 3)	1	W. P. Turnesa	0
S. M. McCready	0	F. R. Stranahan (6 & 5)	1
J. Bruen Jr	0	R. H. (Skee) Riegel (5 & 4)	1
J. B. Carr	0	J. W. Dawson (5 & 3)	1
R. C. Ewing	0	C. R. Coe (1 up)	1
K. G. Thom	0	R. E. Billows (2 & 1)	1
A. H. Perowne	0	C. R. Kocsis (4 & 2)	1
G. H. Micklem	0	J. B. McHale Jr (5 & 4)	1

1951 ROYAL BIRKDALE GC, ENGLAND

Great Britain and Ireland 3
Captain: R. Oppenheimer

United States 6
Captain: W. P. Turnesa

Great Britain and Ireland		United States	
Foursomes	0	*Foursomes*	2
R. J. White & J. B. Carr (halved)	0	F. R. Stranahan & W. C. Campbell (halved)	0
R. C. Ewing & J. D. A. Langley (halved)	0	C. R. Coe & J. B. McHale Jr (halved)	0
A. T. Kyle & I. Caldwell	0	R. D. Chapman & R. W. Knowles Jr (1 up)	1
J. Bruen Jr & J. L. Morgan	0	W. P. Turnesa & S. Urzetta (5 & 4)	1
Singles	3	*Singles*	4
S. M. McCready	0	S. Urzetta (4 & 3)	1
J. B. Carr (2 & 1)	1	F. R. Stranahan	0
R. J. White (2 & 1)	1	C. R. Coe	0
J. D. A. Langley	0	J. B. McHale Jr (2 up)	1
R. C. Ewing	0	W. C. Campbell (5 & 4)	1
A. T. Kyle (2 up)	1	W. P. Turnesa	0
I. Caldwell (halved)	0	H. D. Paddock Jr (halved)	0
J. L. Morgan	0	R. D. Chapman (7 & 6)	1

1953 KITTANSETT CLUB, MASS.

Great Britain and Ireland 3
Captain: A. A. Duncan

United States 9
Captain: C. R. Yates

Great Britain and Ireland		United States	
Foursomes	1	*Foursomes*	3
J. B. Carr & R. J. White	0	S. Urzetta & K. Venturi (6 & 4)	1
J. D. A. Langley & A. H. Perowne	0	E. H. Ward Jr & J. Westland (9 & 8)	1
J. C. Wilson & R. C. MacGregor	0	J. G. Jackson & G. A. Littler (3 & 2)	1
G. H. Micklem & J. L. Morgan (4 & 3)	1	W. C. Campbell & C. R. Coe	0
Singles	2	*Singles*	6
J. B. Carr	0	E. H. Ward Jr (4 & 3)	1
R. J. White (1 up)	1	R. D. Chapman	0
G. H. Micklem	0	G. A. Littler (5 & 3)	1
R. C. MacGregor	0	J. Westland (7 & 5)	1
N. V. Drew	0	D. R. Cherry (9 & 7)	1
J. C. Wilson	0	K. Venturi (9 & 8)	1
J. L. Morgan (3 & 2)	1	C. R. Coe	0
J. D. A. Langley	0	S. Urzetta (3 & 2)	1

1955 ST. ANDREWS, SCOTLAND

Great Britain and Ireland 2
Captain: G. A. Hill

United States 10
Captain: W. C. Campbell

Great Britain and Ireland		United States	
Foursomes	0	*Foursomes*	4
J. B. Carr & R. J. White	0	E. H. Ward Jr & D. R. Cherry (1 up)	1
G. H. Micklem & J. L. Morgan	0	W. J. Patton & R. L. Yost (2 & 1)	1
I. Caldwell & E. B. Millward	0	J. W. Conrad & D. Morey (3 & 2)	1
D. A. Blair & J. R. Cater	0	B. H. Cudd & J. G. Jackson (5 & 4)	1
Singles	2	*Singles*	6
R. J. White	0	E. H. Ward Jr (6 & 5)	1
P. F. Scrutton	0	W. J. Patton (2 & 1)	1
I. Caldwell (1 up)	1	D. Morey	0
J. B. Carr	0	D. R. Cherry (5 & 4)	1
D. A. Blair (1 up)	1	J. W. Conrad	0
E. B. Millward	0	B. H. Cudd (2 up)	1
R. C. Ewing	0	J. G. Jackson (6 & 4)	1
J. L. Morgan	0	R. L. Yost (8 & 7)	1

1957 MINIKAHDA CLUB, MINN.

Great Britain and Ireland 3
Captain: G. H. Micklem

United States 8
Captain: C. R. Coe

Great Britain and Ireland		United States	
Foursomes	1	*Foursomes*	2
J. B. Carr & F. W. G. Deighton	0	R. Baxter Jr & W. J. Patton (2 & 1)	1
A. F. Bussell & P. F. Scrutton	0	W. C. Campbell & F. M. Taylor Jr (4 & 3)	1
R. R. Jack & D. Sewell (1 up)	1	A. S. Blum & C. R. Kocsis	0
A. E. Shepperson & G. B. Wolstenholme (halved)	0	H. Robbins Jr & E. M. Rudolph (halved)	0
Singles	2	*Singles*	6
R. R. Jack	0	W. J. Patton (1 up)	1
J. B. Carr	0	W. C. Campbell (3 & 2)	1
A. Thirlwell	0	R. Baxter Jr (4 & 3)	1
F. W. G. Deighton	0	W. Hyndman III (7 & 6)	1
A. F. Bussell (2 & 1)	1	J. E. Campbell	0
D. Sewell	0	F. M. Taylor Jr (1 up)	1
P. F. Scrutton	0	E. M. Rudolph (3 & 2)	1
G. B. Wolstenholme (2 & 1)	1	H. Robbins Jr	0

1959 LINKS OF THE HONOURABLE COMPANY OF
EDINBURGH GOLFERS, SCOTLAND

Great Britain and Ireland 3
Captain: G. H. Micklem

United States 9
Captain: C. R. Coe

Great Britain and Ireland		United States	
Foursomes	0	*Foursomes*	4
R. R. Jack & D. N. Sewell	0	E. H. Ward Jr & F. M. Taylor Jr (1 up)	1
J. B. Carr & G. B. Wolstenholme	0	W. Hyndman III & T. D. Aaron (1 up)	1
M. F. Bonallack & A. H. Perowne	0	W. J. Patton & C. R. Coe (9 & 8)	1
M. S. R. Lunt & A. E. Shepperson	0	H. W. Wettlaufer & J. W. Nicklaus (2 & 1)	1
Singles	3	*Singles*	5
J. B. Carr (2 & 1)	1	C. R. Coe	0
G. B. Wolstenholme	0	E. H. Ward Jr (9 & 8)	1
R. R. Jack (5 & 3)	1	W. J. Patton	0
D. N. Sewell	0	W. Hyndman III (4 & 3)	1
A. E. Shepperson (2 & 1)	1	T. D. Aaron	0
M. F. Bonallack	0	D. R. Beman (2 up)	1
M. S. R. Lunt	0	H. W. Wettlaufer (6 & 5)	1
W. D. Smith	0	J. W. Nicklaus (5 & 4)	1

1961 SEATTLE GC, WASHINGTON

Great Britain and Ireland 1
Captain: C. D. Lawrie

United States 11
Captain: J. Westland

Great Britain and Ireland		United States	
Foursomes	0	*Foursomes*	4
J. Walker & B. H. G. Chapman	0	D. R. Beman & J. W. Nicklaus (6 & 5)	1
D. A. Blair & M. J. Christmas	0	C. R. Coe & D. R. Cherry (1 up)	1
J. B. Carr & G. Huddy	0	W. Hyndman III & R. W. Gardner (4 & 3)	1
M. F. Bonallack & R. D. B. M. Shade	0	R. E. Cochran & E. S. Andrews (4 & 3)	1
Singles	1	*Singles*	7
M. F. Bonallack	0	D. R. Beman (3 & 2)	1
M. S. R. Lunt	0	C. R. Coe (5 & 4)	1
J. Walker	0	F. M. Taylor Jr (3 & 2)	1
D. W. Frame	0	W. Hyndman III (7 & 6)	1
J. B. Carr	0	J. W. Nicklaus (6 & 4)	1
M. J. Christmas (3 & 2)	1	C. B. Smith	0
R. D. B. M. Shade	0	R. W. Gardner (1 up)	1
D. A. Blair	0	D. R. Cherry (5 & 4)	1

1963 AILSA COURSE, TURNBERRY, SCOTLAND

Great Britain and Ireland 8
Captain: C. D. Lawrie

United States 12
Captain: R. S. Tufts

Great Britain and Ireland		United States	
Foursomes	1	*Foursomes*	2
M. F. Bonallack & S. W. T. Murray (4 & 3)	1	W. J. Patton & R. H. Sikes	0
J. B. Carr & C. W. Green	0	A. D. Gray Jr & L. E. Harris Jr (2 up)	1
M. S. R. Lunt & D. B. Sheahan	0	D. R. Beman & C. R. Coe (5 & 3)	1
J. F. D. Madeley & R. D. B. M. Shade (halved)	0	R. W. Gardner & E. R. Updegraff (halved)	0
Singles	5	*Singles*	1
S. W. T. Murray (3 & 1)	1	D. R. Beman	0
M. J. Christmas	0	W. J. Patton (3 & 2)	1
J. B. Carr (7 & 5)	1	R. H. Sikes	0
D. B. Sheahan (1 up)	1	L. E. Harris Jr	0
M. F. Bonallack (1 up)	1	R. E. Davies	0
S. Saddler (halved)	0	C. R. Coe (halved)	0
R. D. B. M. Shade (4 & 3)	1	A. D. Gray Jr	0
M. S. R. Lunt (halved)	0	C. B. Smith (halved)	0
Foursomes	0	*Foursomes*	4
M. F. Bonallack & S. W. T. Murray	0	W. J. Patton & R. H. Sikes (1 up)	1
M. S. R. Lunt & D. B. Sheahan	0	A. D. Gray Jr & L. E. Harris Jr (3 & 2)	1
C. W. Green & S. Saddler	0	R. W. Gardner & E. R. Updegraff (3 & 1)	1
J. F. D. Madeley & R. D. B. M. Shade	0	D. R. Beman & C. R. Coe (3 & 2)	1
Singles	2	*Singles*	5
S. W. T. Murray	0	W. J. Patton (3 & 2)	1
D. B. Sheahan (1 up)	1	R. D. Davies	0
J. B. Carr	0	E. R. Updegraff (4 & 3)	1
M. F. Bonallack	0	L. E. Harris Jr (3 & 2)	1
M. S. R. Lunt	0	R. W. Gardner (3 & 2)	1
S. Saddler (halved)	0	D. R. Beman (halved)	0
R. D. B. M. Shade (2 & 1)	1	A. D. Gray Jr	0
C. W. Green	0	C. R. Coe (4 & 3)	1

1965 BALTIMORE CC FIVE FARMS OLD COURSE, MD.

Great Britain and Ireland 11
Captain: J. B. Carr

United States 11
Captain: J. W. Fischer

Great Britain and Ireland		United States	
Foursomes	2	*Foursomes*	1
M. Lunt & G. Cosh (1 up)	1	W. C. Campbell & A. D. Gray Jr	0
M. Bonallack & C. Clark (halved)	0	D. R. Beman & D. C. Allen (halved)	0
R. Foster & G. Clark	0	W. J. Patton & E. M. Tutwiler (5 & 4)	1
P. Townsend & R. D. B. M. Shade (2 & 1)	1	J. M. Hopkins & D. Eichelberger	0
Singles	6	*Singles*	2
M. Bonallack	0	W. C. Campbell (6 & 5)	1
R. Foster	0	D. R. Beman (2 up)	1
R. D. B. M. Shade (3 & 1)	1	A. D. Gray Jr	0
C. Clark (5 & 3)	1	J. M. Hopkins	0
P. Townsend (3 & 2)	1	W. J. Patton	0
A. C. Saddler (2 & 1)	1	D. Morey	0
G. Cosh (2 up)	1	D. C. Allen	0
M. Lunt (2 & 1)	1	E. R. Updegraff	0
Foursomes	2	*Foursomes*	2
A. C. Saddler & R. Foster	0	W. C. Campbell & A. D. Gray Jr (4 & 3)	1
R. D. B. M. Shade & P. Townsend (2 & 1)	1	D. R. Beman & D. Eichelberger	0
G. Cosh & M. Lunt	0	E. M. Tutwiler & W. J. Patton (2 & 1)	1
C. Clark & M. Bonallack (2 & 1)	1	D. C. Allen & D. Morey	0
Singles	1	*Singles*	6
R. Foster	0	W. C. Campbell (3 & 2)	1
A. C. Saddler	0	D. R. Beman (1 up)	1
R. D. B. M. Shade	0	E. M. Tutwiler (5 & 3)	1
G. Cosh (4 & 3)	1	D. C. Allen	0
P. Townsend	0	A. D. Gray Jr (1 up)	1
C. Clark (halved)	0	J. M. Hopkins (halved)	0
M. Bonallack	0	D. Eichelberger (5 & 3)	1
M. Lunt	0	W. J. Patton (4 & 2)	1

1967 ROYAL ST GEORGE'S GC, ENGLAND

Great Britain and Ireland 7
Captain: J. B. Carr

United States 13
Captain: J. W. Sweetser

Great Britain and Ireland		United States	
Foursomes	0	*Foursomes*	3
R. D. B. M. Shade & P. A. Oosterhuis (halved)	0	R. J. Murphy Jr & R. J. Cerrudo (halved)	0
R. Foster & A. C. Saddler	0	W. C. Campbell & J. W. Lewis Jr (1 up)	1
M. Bonallack & M. F. Attenborough	0	A. D. Gray Jr & E. M. Tutwiler (4 & 2)	1
J. B. Carr & T. Craddock	0	R. B. Dickson & J. A. Grant (3 & 1)	1
Singles	1	*Singles*	5
R. D. B. M. Shade	0	W. C. Campbell (2 & 1)	1
R. Foster	0	R. J. Murphy Jr (2 & 1)	1
M. Bonallack (halved)	0	A. D. Gray Jr (halved)	0
M. F. Attenborough	0	R. J. Cerrudo (4 & 3)	1
P. A. Oosterhuis	0	R. B. Dickson (6 & 4)	1
T. Craddock	0	J. W. Lewis Jr (2 & 1)	1
A. K. Pirie (halved)	0	D. C. Allen (halved)	0
A. C. Saddler (3 & 2)	1	M. A. Fleckman	0
Foursomes	3	*Foursomes*	1
M. Bonallack & T. Craddock (2 up)	1	R. J. Murphy Jr & R. J. Cerrudo	0
A. C. Saddler & A. K. Pirie	0	W. C. Campbell & J. W. Lewis Jr (1 up)	1
R. D. B. M. Shade & P. A. Oosterhuis (3 & 1)	1	A. D. Gray Jr & E. M. Tutwiler	0
R. Foster & D. J. Millensted (2 & 1)	1	D. C. Allen & M. A. Fleckman	0
Singles	3	*Singles*	4
R. D. B. M. Shade	0	W. C. Campbell (3 & 2)	1
M. Bonallack (4 & 2)	1	R. J. Murphy Jr	0
A. C. Saddler (3 & 2)	1	A. D. Gray	0
R. Foster (halved)	0	R. J. Cerrudo (halved)	0
A. K. Pirie	0	R. B. Dickson (4 & 3)	1
T. Craddock (5 & 4)	1	J. W. Lewis Jr	0
P. A. Oosterhuis	0	J. A. Grant (1 up)	1
D. J. Millensted	0	E. M. Tutwiler (3 & 1)	1

1969 MILWAUKEE CC, WIS.

Great Britain and Ireland 8
Captain: M. Bonallack

United States 10
Captain: W. J. Patton

Great Britain and Ireland		United States	
Foursomes	*1*	*Foursomes*	*2*
M. Bonallack & T. Craddock	0	M. Giles III & S. Melnyk (3 & 2)	1
P. Benka & B. Critchley (halved)	0	B. Fleisher & A. Miller (halved)	0
C. Green & A. Brooks (3 & 2)	1	L. Wadkins & R. L. Siderowf	0
R. Foster & G. Marks	0	W. Hyndman III & J. Inman Jr (2 & 1)	1
Singles	*2*	*Singles*	*5*
M. Bonallack (halved)	0	B. Fleisher (halved)	0
C. Green	0	M. Giles III (1 up)	1
B. Critchley	0	A. Miller III (1 up)	1
L. Tupling	0	R. L. Siderowf (6 & 5)	1
P. Benka (3 & 1)	1	S. Melnyk	0
G. Marks (1 up)	1	L. Wadkins	0
M. King	0	J. Bohmann (2 & 1)	1
R. Foster	0	E. R. Updegraff (6 & 5)	1
Foursomes	*2*	*Foursomes*	*1*
C. Green & A. Brooks (halved)	0	M. Giles III & S. Melnyk (halved)	0
P. Benka & B. Critchley (2 & 1)	1	B. Fleisher & A. Miller III	0
R. Foster & M. King	0	R. L. Siderowf & L. Wadkins (6 & 5)	1
M. Bonallack & P. Tupling (4 & 3)	1	E. R. Updegraff & J. Bohmann	0
Singles	*3*	*Singles*	*2*
M. Bonallack (5 & 4)	1	B. Fleisher	0
B. Critchley (halved)	0	R. L. Siderowf (halved)	0
M. G. King	0	A. Miller III (1 up)	1
T. Craddock (halved)	0	M. Giles III (halved)	0
P. Benka	0	J. Inman Jr (2 & 1)	1
A. Brooks (4 & 3)	1	J. Bohmann	0
C. W. Green (halved)	0	W. Hyndman III (halved)	0
G. Marks (3 & 2)	1	E. R. Updegraff	0

1971 ST ANDREWS, SCOTLAND

Great Britain and Ireland 13
Captain: M. F. Bonallack

United States 11
Captain: J. M. Winters Jr

Great Britain and Ireland		United States	
Foursomes	*4*	*Foursomes*	*0*
M. Bonallack & W. Humphreys (1 up)	1	L. Wadkins & J. B. Simons	0
C. W. Green & R. J. Carr (1 up)	1	S. Melnyk & M. Giles III	0
D. M. Marsh & G. Macgregor (2 & 1)	1	A. L. Miller III & J. Farquhar	0
J. S. Macdonald & R. Foster (2 & 1)	1	W. C. Campbell & T. O. Kite Jr	0
Singles	*1½*	*Singles*	*6½*
C. W. Green	0	L. Wadkins (1 up)	1
M. Bonallack	0	M. Giles III (1 up)	1
G. C. Marks	0	A. L. Miller III (1 up)	1
J. S. Macdonald	0	S. Melnyk (3 & 2)	1
R. J. Carr (halved)	½	W. Hyndman III (halved)	½
W. Humphreys	0	J. R. Gabrielsen (1 up)	1
H. B. Stuart (3 & 2)	1	J. Farquhar	0
R. Foster	0	T. O. Kite Jr (3 & 2)	1
Foursomes	*1½*	*Foursomes*	*2½*
G. C. Marks & C. W. Green	0	S. Melnyk & M. Giles III (1 up)	1
H. B. Stuart & R. J. Carr (1 up)	1	W. Wadkins & J. R. Gabrielsen	0
D. M. Marsh & M. Bonallack	0	A. L. Miller III & J. Farquhar (5 & 4)	1
J. S. Macdonald & R. Foster (halved)	½	W. C. Campbell & T. O. Kite Jr (halved)	½
Singles	*6*	*Singles*	*2*
M. Bonallack	0	L. Wadkins (3 & 1)	1
H. B. Stuart (2 & 1)	1	M. Giles III	0
W. Humphreys (2 & 1)	1	S. Melnyk	0
C. W. Green (1 up)	1	A. L. Miller III	0
R. J. Carr (2 up)	1	J. B. Simons	0
G. Macgregor (1 up)	1	J. R. Gabrielsen	0
D. M. Marsh (1 up)	1	W. Hyndman III	0
G. C. Marks	0	T. O. Kite Jr (3 & 2)	1

1973 THE COUNTRY CLUB, BROOKLINE, MASS.

Great Britain and Ireland		United States	
Foursomes	*0*	*Foursomes*	*3*
M. G. King & P. Hedges (halved)	0	M. Giles & G. Koch (halved)	0
H. B. Stuart & J. Davies	0	R. Siderowf & M. Pfeil (5 & 4)	1
C. W. Green & W. T. Milne	0	D. Edwards & J. Ellis (2 & 1)	1
R. Foster & T. W. B. Homer	0	M. West & D. Ballenger (2 & 1)	1
Singles	*5*	*Singles*	*3*
H. B. Stuart	0	M. Giles (5 & 4)	1
M. F. Bonallack	0	R. Siderowf (4 & 2)	1
J. Davies (1 hole)	1	G. Koch	0
H. K. Clark (2 & 1)	1	M. West	0
R. Foster	0	D. Edwards (2 holes)	1
M. G. King (1 hole)	1	M. Killian	0
C. W. Green (1 hole)	1	W. Rodgers	0
W. T. Milne (4 & 3)	1	M. Pfeil	0
Foursomes	*0*	*Foursomes*	*3*
T. W. B. Homer & R. Foster	0	M. Giles & G. Koch (7 & 5)	1
H. K. Clark & J. Davies (halved)	0	R. Siderowf & M. Pfeil (halved)	0
P. Hedges & M. G. King	0	D. Edwards & J. Ellis (2 & 1)	1
H. B. Stuart & W. T. Milne	0	W. Rodgers & M. Killian (1 hole)	1
Singles	*3*	*Singles*	*3*
H. B. Stuart (5 & 4)	1	J. Ellis	0
J. Davies (3 & 2)	1	R. Siderowf	0
T. W. B. Homer	0	D. Edwards (2 & 1)	1
C. W. Green (halved)	0	M. Giles (halved)	0
M. G. King	0	M. West (1 hole)	1
W. T. Milne (2 & 1)	1	M. Killian	0
P. Hedges (halved)	0	G. Koch (halved)	0
H. K. Clark	0	M. Pfeil (1 hole)	1

Great Britain and Ireland 8
Captain: D. M. Marsh

United States 12
Captain: J. Sweetser

1932 WENTWORTH GC, ENGLAND

Great Britain and Ireland 3½
Captain: Joyce Wethered

United States 5½
Captain: Marion Hollins

Great Britain and Ireland		United States	
Foursomes	*0*	*Foursomes*	*3*
Joyce Wethered & Wanda Morgan	0	Glenna Collett Vare & Mrs O. S. Hill (1 up)	1
Enid Wilson & J. B. Watson	0	Virginia Van Wie & Helen Hicks (2 & 1)	1
Molly Gourlay & Doris Park	0	Maureen Orcutt & Mrs L. D. Cheney (1 up)	1
Singles	*3½*	*Singles*	*2½*
Joyce Wethered (6 & 4)	1	Glenna Collett Vare	0
Enid Wilson (2 & 1)	1	Helen Hicks	0
Wanda Morgan	0	Virginia Van Wie (2 & 1)	1
Diana Fishwick (4 & 3)	1	Maureen Orcutt	0
Molly Gourlay (halved)	½	Mrs O. S. Hill (halved)	½
Elsie Corlett	0	Mrs L. D. Cheney (4 & 3)	1

1934 CHEVY CHASE CLUB, MD.

Great Britain and Ireland 2½
Captain: Doris Chambers

United States 6½
Captain: Glenna Collett Vare

Great Britain and Ireland		United States	
Foursomes	*1½*	*Foursomes*	*1½*
Molly Gourlay & Pamela Barton (halved)	½	Virginia Van Wie & Charlotte Glutting (halved)	½
Diana Fishwick & Wanda Morgan	0	Maureen Orcutt & Mrs L. D. Cheney (2 up)	1
Diana Plumpton & Mrs J. B. Walker (2 & 1)	1	Mrs O. S. Hill & Lucile Robinson	0
Singles	*1*	*Singles*	*5*
Diana Fishwick	0	Virginia Van Wie (2 & 1)	1
Molly Gourlay	0	Maureen Orcutt (4 & 2)	1
Pamela Barton	0	Mrs L. D. Cheney (7 & 5)	1
Wanda Morgan	0	Charlotte Glutting (3 & 2)	1
Diana Plumpton	0	Mrs O. S. Hill (3 & 2)	1
Mrs J. B. Walker (3 & 2)	1	Mrs Frank Goldthwaite	0

1936 KING'S COURSE, GLENEAGLES, SCOTLAND

Great Britain and Ireland 4½
Captain: Doris Chambers

United States 4½
Captain: Glenna Collett Vare

Great Britain and Ireland		United States	
Foursomes	*1½*	*Foursomes*	*1½*
Wanda Morgan & Marjorie Ross Garon (halved)	½	Glenna Collett Vare & Patty Berg (halved)	½
Pamela Barton & Mrs J. B. Walker	0	Maureen Orcutt & Mrs L. D. Cheney (2 & 1)	1
Jessie Anderson & Mrs Andrew M. Holm (3 & 2)	1	Mrs O. S. Hill & Charlotte Glutting	0
Singles	*3*	*Singles*	*3*
Wanda Morgan	0	Glenna Collett Vare (3 & 2)	1
Mrs Andrew M. Holm (4 & 3)	1	Patty Berg	0
Pamela Barton	0	Charlotte Glutting (1 up)	1
J. B. Walker	0	Maureen Orcutt (1 up)	1
Jessie Anderson (1 up)	1	Mrs L. D. Cheney	0
Marjorie Ross Garon (7 & 5)	1	Mrs O. S. Hill	0

1938 ESSEX COUNTY CLUB, MASS.

Great Britain and Ireland 3½
Captain: Mrs. R. H. Wallace-Williamson

United States 5½
Captain: Frances E. Stebbins

Great Britain and Ireland		United States	
Foursomes	*2½*	*Foursomes*	*½*
Mrs Andrew M. Holm & Clarrie Tiernan (2 up)	1	Mrs Julius A. Page Jr & Maureen Orcutt	0
Jessie Anderson & Elsie Corlett (1 up)	1	Glenna Collett Vare & Patty Berg	0
Mrs J. B. Walker & Phyllis Wade (halved)	½	Marion Miley & Kathryn Hemphill (halved)	½
Singles	*1*	*Singles*	*5*
Mrs Andrew M. Holm	0	Mrs Julius A. Page Jr (6 & 5)	1
Jessie Anderson	0	Patty Berg (1 up)	1
Elsie Corlett	0	Marion Miley (2 & 1)	1
Mrs J. B. Walker	0	Glenna Collett Vare (2 & 1)	1
Clarrie Tiernan (2 & 1)	1	Maureen Orcutt	0
Nan Baird	0	Charlotte Glutting (1 up)	1

1948 ROYAL BIRKDALE GC, ENGLAND

Great Britain and Ireland 2½
Captain: Doris E. Chambers

United States 6½
Captain: Glenna Collett Vare

Great Britain and Ireland		United States	
Foursomes	*1*	*Foursomes*	*2*
Jacqueline Gordon & Jean Donald (3 & 2)	1	Louise Suggs & Grace Lenczyk	0
Philomena Garvey & Zara Bolton	0	Glenna Collett Vare & Dorothy Kirby (4 & 3)	1
Maureen Ruttle & Mrs Val Reddan	0	Dorothy Kielty & Mrs Julius A. Page Jr (5 & 4)	1
Singles	*1½*	*Singles*	*4½*
Philomena Garvey (halved)	½	Louise Suggs (halved)	½
Jean Donald (2 up)	1	Dorothy Kirby	0
Jacqueline Gordon	0	Grace Lenczyk (5 & 3)	1
Mrs Andrew M. Holm	0	Mrs Julius A. Page Jr (3 & 2)	1
Maureen Ruttle	0	Polly Riley (3 & 2)	1
Zara Bolton	0	Dorothy Kielty (2 & 1)	1

1950 COUNTRY CLUB OF BUFFALO, N.Y.

Great Britain and Ireland 1½
Captain: Mrs. A. C. Critchley

United States 7½
Captain: Mrs Glenna Collett Vare

Great Britain and Ireland		United States	
Foursomes	*1*	*Foursomes*	*2*
Jean Donald & Mrs George Valentine	0	Dorothy Germain Porter & Beverly Hanson (3 & 2)	1
Frances Stephens & Elizabeth Price (1 up)	1	Helen Sigel & Peggy Kirk	0
Philomena Garvey & Jeanne Bisgood	0	Dorothy Kielty & Dorothy Kirby (6 & 5)	1
Singles	*½*	*Singles*	*5½*
Frances Stephens (halved)	½	Dorothy Germain Porter (halved)	½
Mrs George Valentine	0	Polly Riley (7 & 6)	1
Jean Donald	0	Beverly Hanson (6 & 5)	1
Philomena Garvey	0	Dorothy Kielty (3 & 1)	1
Jeanne Bisgood	0	Peggy Kirk (1 up)	1
Elizabeth Price	0	Grace Lenczyk (5 & 4)	1

1952 LINKS OF THE HONOURABLE COMPANY OF EDINBURGH GOLFERS, SCOTLAND

Great Britain and Ireland 5
Captain: Lady Katharine Cairns

United States 4
Captain: Mrs Frank Goldthwaite

Great Britain and Ireland		United States	
Foursomes	*2*	*Foursomes*	*1*
Jean Donald & Elizabeth Price (3 & 2)	1	Dorothy Kirby & Grace DeMoss	0
Frances Stephens & Mrs George Valentine	0	Claire Doran & Marjorie Lindsay (6 & 4)	1
Moira Paterson & Philomena Garvey (2 & 1)	1	Polly Riley & Patricia O'Sullivan	0
Singles	*3*	*Singles*	*3*
Jean Donald	0	Dorothy Kirby (1 up)	1
Frances Stephens (2 & 1)	1	Marjorie Lindsay	0
Moira Paterson	0	Polly Riley (6 & 4)	1
Jeanne Bisgood (6 & 5)	1	Mae Murray	0
Philomena Garvey	0	Claire Doran (3 & 2)	1
Elizabeth Price (3 & 2)	1	Grace DeMoss	0

1954 MERION GC (EAST COURSE), PA.

Great Britain and Ireland 3
Captain: Mrs John B. Beck

United States 6
Captain: Mrs Harrison F. Flippin

Great Britain and Ireland		United States	
Foursomes	*0*	*Foursomes*	*3*
Frances Stephens & Elizabeth Price	0	Mary Lena Faulk & Polly Riley (6 & 4)	1
Mrs George Valentine & Philomena Garvey	0	Claire Doran & Patricia Lesser (6 & 5)	1
Mrs R. T. Peel & Janette Robertson	0	Dorothy Kirby & Barbara Romack (6 & 5)	1
Singles	*3*	*Singles*	*3*
Frances Stephens (1 up)	1	Mary Lena Faulk	0
Jeanne Bisgood	0	Claire Doran (4 & 3)	1
Elizabeth Price	0	Polly Riley (9 & 8)	1
Philomena Garvey (3 & 1)	1	Dorothy Kirby	0
Mrs George Valentine	0	Grace DeMoss Smith (4 & 3)	1
Janette Robertson (3 & 1)	1	Joyce Ziske	0

1956 PRINCE'S GC, ENGLAND

Great Britain and Ireland 5
Captain: Mrs Sloan Bolton

United States 4
Captain: Mrs Harrison F. Flippin

Great Britain and Ireland		United States	
Foursomes	*1*	*Foursomes*	*2*
Mrs George Valentine & Philomena Garvey	0	Patricia Lesser & Margaret Smith (2 & 1)	1
Mrs Roy Smith & Elizabeth Price (5 & 3)	1	Polly Riley & Barbara Romack	0
Janette Robertson & Veronica Anstey	0	Mary Ann Downey & Philip J. Cudone (6 & 4)	1
Singles	*4*	*Singles*	*2*
Mrs George Valentine (6 & 4)	1	Patricia Lesser	0
Philomena Garvey	0	Margaret Smith (9 & 8)	1
Mrs Roy Smith (1 up)	1	Polly Riley	0
Janette Robertson	0	Barbara Romack (6 & 4)	1
Angela Ward (4 & 3)	1	Mary Ann Downey	0
Elizabeth Price (7 & 6)	1	Jane Nelson	0

1958 BRAE BURN GC, MASS.

Great Britain and Ireland 4½
Captain: Daisy Ferguson

United States 4½
Captain: Mrs Charles Dennehy

Great Britain and Ireland		United States	
Foursomes	*2*	*Foursomes*	*1*
Angela Ward Bonallack & Elizabeth Price (2 & 1)	1	Barbara Romack & Polly Riley	0
Janette Robertson & Frances Smith (3 & 2)	1	JoAnne Gunderson & Anne Quast	0
Bridget Jackson & Mrs George Valentine	0	Barbara McIntire & Ann Casey Johnstone (6 & 5)	1
Singles	*2½*	*Singles*	*3½*
Mrs George Valentine	0	JoAnne Gunderson (2 up)	1
Angela Ward Bonallack (halved)	½	Barbara McIntire (halved)	½
Elizabeth Price	0	Anne Quast (4 & 2)	1
Janette Robertson (3 & 2)	1	Ann Casey Johnstone	0
Bridget Jackson	0	Barbara Romack (4 & 2)	1
Frances Smith (2 up)	1	Polly Riley	0

1960 LINDRICK GC, ENGLAND

Great Britain and Ireland 2½
Captain: Mrs Maureen Garrett

United States 6½
Captain: Mrs Henri Prunaret

Great Britain and Ireland		United States	
Foursomes	1	*Foursomes*	2
Angela Ward Bonallack & Elizabeth Price (1 up)	1	JoAnne Gunderson & Barbara McIntire	0
Belle McCorkindale & Janette Robertson	0	Judy Eller & Anne Quast (4 & 2)	1
Ruth Porter & Frances Smith	0	Joanne Goodwin & Ann Casey Johnstone (3 & 2)	1
Singles	1½	*Singles*	4½
Elizabeth Price (halved)	½	Barbara McIntire (halved)	½
Angela Ward Bonallack	0	JoAnne Gunderson (2 & 1)	1
Janette Robertson	0	Anne Quast (2 up)	1
Philomena Garvey	0	Judy Eller (4 & 3)	1
Belle McCorkindale	0	Judy Bell (8 & 7)	1
Ruth Porter (1 up)	1	Joanne Goodwin	0

1962 BROADMOOR GC, COLO.

Great Britain and Ireland 1
Captain: Frances Smith

United States 8
Captain: Polly Riley

Great Britain and Ireland		United States	
Foursomes	0	*Foursomes*	3
Angela Ward Bonallack & Mrs Marley Spearman	0	Anne Quast Decker & Barbara McIntire (7 & 5)	1
Ann Irvin & Sheila Vaughan	0	Clifford Ann Creed & JoAnne Gunderson (4 & 3)	1
Mrs Alastair Frearson & Ruth Porter	0	Jean Ashley & Ann Casey Johnstone (8 & 7)	1
Singles	1	*Singles*	5
Mrs Marley Spearman	0	Anne Quast Decker (5 & 4)	1
Angela Ward Bonallack	0	JoAnne Gunderson (2 & 1)	1
Mrs Alastair Frearson (8 & 7)	1	Judy Bell	0
Jean Roberts	0	Phyllis Preuss (1 up)	1
Sally Bonallack	0	Clifford Ann Creed (6 & 5)	1
Sheila Vaughan	0	Barbara McIntire (5 & 4)	1

1964 ROYAL PORTHCAWL GC, WALES

Great Britain and Ireland 7½
Captain: Elsie Corlett

United States 10½
Captain: Mrs T. W. Hawes

Great Britain and Ireland		United States	
Foursomes	2	*Foursomes*	1
Mrs Marley Spearman & Angela Ward Bonallack (2 & 1)	1	Barbara McIntire & Phyllis Preuss	0
Bridget Jackson & Susan Armitage	0	Carol Sorenson & Barbara Fay White (8 & 6)	1
Sheila Vaughan & Ruth Porter (3 & 2)	1	JoAnne Gunderson & Nancy Roth	0
Singles	2½	*Singles*	3½
Mrs Marley Spearman (halved)	½	Barbara McIntire (halved)	½
Angela Ward Bonallack	0	JoAnne Gunderson (6 & 5)	1
Joan Lawrence	0	Peggy Conley (1 up)	1
Julia Greenhalgh	0	Barbara Fay White (3 & 2)	1
Bridget Jackson (4 & 3)	1	Carol Sorenson	0
Ruth Porter (1 up)	1	Nancy Roth	0
Foursomes	1½	*Foursomes*	1½
Mrs Marley Spearman & Angela Ward Bonallack (6 & 5)	1	Barbara McIntire & Phyllis Preuss	0
Susan Armitage & Bridget Jackson	0	JoAnne Gunderson & Nancy Roth (2 up)	1
Ruth Porter & Sheila Vaughan (halved)	½	Carol Sorenson & Barbara Fay White (halved)	½
Singles	1½	*Singles*	4½
Mrs Marley Spearman (halved)	½	JoAnne Gunderson (halved)	½
Joan Lawrence	0	Barbara McIntire (4 & 2)	1
Julia Greenhalgh (5 & 3)	1	Phyllis Preuss	0
Bridget Jackson	0	Peggy Conley (1 up)	1
Angela Ward Bonallack	0	Barbara Fay White (3 & 2)	1
Ruth Porter	0	Carol Sorenson (3 & 2)	1

1966 CASCADES COURSE, HOT SPRINGS, VA.

Great Britain and Ireland 5
Captain: Mrs S. M. Bolton

United States 13
Captain: Dorothy Germain Porter

Great Britain and Ireland		United States	
Foursomes	½	*Foursomes*	2½
Angela Ward Bonallack &		Jean Ashley &	
Susan Armitage	0	Phyllis Preuss (1 up)	1
Mrs I. C. Robertson &		Anne Quast Welts &	
Joan Hastings (halved)	½	Barbara McIntire (halved)	½
Elizabeth Chadwick &		Barbara White Boddie &	
Pamela Tredinnick	0	Carol Sorenson Flenniken (1 up)	1
Singles	1½	*Singles*	4½
Mrs I. C. Robertson	0	Jean Ashley (1 up)	1
Susan Armitage (halved)	½	Anne Quast Welts (halved)	½
Angela Ward Bonallack	0	Barbara White Boddie (3 & 2)	1
Elizabeth Chadwick	0	Nancy Roth Syms (2 up)	1
Ita Burke (3 & 1)	1	Helen Sigel Wilson	0
Marjory Fowler	0	Carol Sorenson Flenniken (3 & 1)	1
Foursomes	1	*Foursomes*	2
Angela Ward Bonallack &		Jean Ashley &	
Susan Armitage	0	Phyllis Preuss (3 & 1)	1
Elizabeth Chadwick &		Anne Quast Welts &	
Ita Burke (1 up)	1	Barbara McIntire	0
Mrs I. C. Robertson &		Barbara White Boddie &	
Joan Hastings	0	Carol Sorenson Flenniken (2 & 1)	1
Singles	2	*Singles*	4
Angela Ward Bonallack (2 & 1)	1	Jean Ashley	0
Mrs I. C. Robertson (halved)	½	Anne Quast Welts (halved)	½
Susan Armitage	0	Barbara White Boddie (3 & 2)	1
Pamela Tredinnick (halved)	½	Nancy Roth Syms (halved)	½
Elizabeth Chadwick	0	Phyllis Preuss (3 & 2)	1
Ita Burke	0	Carol Sorenson Flenniken (2 & 1)	1

1968 ROYAL COUNTY DOWN GC, NORTHERN IRELAND

Great Britain and Ireland 7½
Captain: Mrs S. M. Bolton

United States 10½
Captain: Mrs Robert M. Monsted

Great Britain and Ireland		United States	
Foursomes	2	*Foursomes*	1
Mrs. I. C. Robertson & Ann Irvin (6 & 5)	1	Shelley Hamlin & Anne Quast Welts	0
Margaret Pickard & Vivien Saunders (3 & 2)	1	Mary Lou Dill & Peggy Conley	0
Ann Howard & Pamela Tredinnick	0	Phyllis Preuss & Jean Ashley (1 up)	1
Singles	3	*Singles*	3
Ann Irvin (3 & 2)	1	Anne Quast Welts	0
Vivien Saunders	0	Shelley Hamlin (1 up)	1
Mrs I. C. Robertson	0	Roberta Albers (1 up)	1
Bridget Jackson (halved)	½	Peggy Conley (halved)	½
Dinah Oxley (halved)	½	Phyllis Preuss (halved)	½
Margaret Pickard (2 up)	1	Jean Ashley	0
Foursomes	½	*Foursomes*	2½
Mrs. I. C. Robertson & Ann Irvin (halved)	½	Mary Lou Dill & Peggy Conley (halved)	½
Margaret Pickard & Vivien Saunders	0	Shelley Hamlin & Anne Quast Welts (2 & 1)	1
Dinah Oxley & Pamela Tredinnick	0	Phyllis Preuss & Jean Ashley (5 & 4)	1
Singles	2	*Singles*	4
Ann Irvin (3 & 2)	1	Shelley Hamlin	0
Mrs I. C. Robertson (halved)	½	Anne Quast Welts (halved)	½
Vivien Saunders (halved)	½	Roberta Albers (halved)	½
Margaret Pickard	0	Peggy Conley (1 up)	1
Ann Howard	0	Mary Lou Dill (4 & 2)	1
Bridget Jackson	0	Phyllis Preuss (2 & 1)	1

1970 BRAE BURN CC, MASS.

Great Britain and Ireland 6½
Captain: Jeanne Bisgood

United States 11½
Captain: Mrs Philip Cudone

Great Britain and Ireland		United States	
Foursomes	2	*Foursomes*	1
Dinah Oxley & Mary McKenna (4 & 3)	1	Shelley Hamlin & Jane Bastanchury	0
Mrs I. C. Robertson & Ann Irvin	0	Phyllis Preuss & Martha Wilkinson (4 & 3)	1
Mary Everard & Julia Greenhalgh (5 & 3)	1	Cynthia Hill & Jane Fassinger	0
Singles	1½	*Singles*	4½
Dinah Oxley	0	Jane Bastanchury (5 & 3)	1
Ann Irvin	0	Martha Wilkinson (1 up)	1
Mrs I. C. Robertson (even)	½	Shelley Hamlin (even)	½
Mary McKenna (4 & 2)	1	Phyllis Preuss	0
Margaret Pickard	0	Nancy Hager (5 & 4)	1
Julia Greenhalgh	0	Mrs Paul Dye Jr (1 up)	1
Foursomes	½	*Foursomes*	2½
Dinah Oxley & Mary McKenna	0	Phyllis Preuss & Martha Wilkinson (6 & 4)	1
Mrs I. C. Robertson & Ann Irvin	0	Shelley Hamlin & Jane Bastanchury (1 up)	1
Mary Everard & Julia Greenhalgh (even)	½	Cynthia Hill & Mrs Paul Dye Jr (even)	½
Singles	2½	*Singles*	3½
Dinah Oxley (even)	½	Shelley Hamlin (even)	½
Ann Irvin	0	Jane Bastanchury (4 & 3)	1
Mrs I. C. Robertson	0	Phyllis Preuss (1 up)	1
Julia Greenhalgh (6 & 4)	1	Martha Wilkinson	0
Mary Everard (4 & 3)	1	Nancy Hager	0
Mary McKenna	0	Cynthia Hill (2 & 1)	1

1972 WESTERN GAILES, SCOTLAND

Great Britain and Ireland 8
Captain: Mrs F. Smith

United States 10
Captain: Mrs J. Crawford

Great Britain and Ireland		United States	
Foursomes	2	*Foursomes*	1
Mary Everard & Beverly Huke	0	Laura Baugh & Mrs M. Kirouac (2 & 1)	1
Mrs I. C. Robertson & Mrs D. Frearson (2 & 1)	1	Jane Booth & Barbara McIntire	0
Michelle Walker & Mary McKenna (1 hole)	1	Beth Barry & Hollis Stacy	0
Singles	1½	*Singles*	4½
Michelle Walker	½	Laura Baugh	½
Mrs I. C. Robertson	0	Jane Booth (3 & 1)	1
Mary Everard	0	Mrs M. Kirouac (4 & 3)	1
Diana Oxley	0	Barbara McIntire (4 & 3)	1
Kathryn Phillips (2 holes)	1	Lancy Smith	0
Mary McKenna	0	Beth Barry (2 & 1)	1
Foursomes	1½	*Foursomes*	1½
Michelle Walker & Mary McKenna (3 & 2)	1	Laura Baugh & Mrs M. Kirouac	0
Mary Everard & Beverly Huke	0	Jane Booth & Barbara McIntire (5 & 4)	1
Mrs I. C. Robertson & Mrs D. Frearson	½	Beth Barry & Hollis Stacy	½
Singles	3	*Singles*	3
Mrs I. C. Robertson	0	Laura Baugh (6 & 5)	1
Mary Everard (6 & 5)	1	Barbara McIntire	0
Michelle Walker (1 hole)	1	Jane Booth	0
Mary McKenna (3 & 1)	1	Mrs M. Kirouac	0
Mrs D. Frearson	0	Lancy Smith (3 & 1)	1
Kathryn Phillips	0	Beth Barry (3 & 1)	1

1974 SAN FRANCISCO GC, CALIF.

Great Britain and Ireland 5
Captain: Mrs Belle Robertson

United States 13
Captain: Mrs Allison Choate

Great Britain and Ireland		United States	
Foursomes	1½	*Foursomes*	1½
Mary McKenna & Julia Greenhalgh	½	Carol Semple & Cynthia Hill	½
Jennifer Lee-Smith & Carol Le Feuvre	0	Anne Sander & Jane Booth (6 & 5)	1
Maureen Walker & Mary Everard (5 & 4)	1	Mary Budke & Bonnie Lauer	0
Singles	1½	*Singles*	4½
Maureen Walker (2 & 1)	1	Carol Semple	0
Mary McKenna	0	Jane Booth (5 & 3)	1
Mary Everard	0	Debbie Massey	1
Jennifer Lee-Smith	0	Bonnie Lauer	1
Julia Greenhalgh	0	Beth Barry	1
Tegwen Perkins	½	Cynthia Hill	½
Foursomes	1	*Foursomes*	2
Mary McKenna & Maureen Walker	0	Anne Sander & Jane Booth (5 & 4)	1
Mary Everard & Carol Le Feuvre	0	Mary Budke & Bonnie Lauer (5 & 3)	1
Julia Greenhalgh & Tegwen Perkins (3 & 2)	1	Carol Semple & Cynthia Hill	0
Singles	1	*Singles*	5
Mary Everard	0	Anne Sander (4 & 3)	1
Julia Greenhalgh	0	Jane Booth (7 & 5)	1
Carol Le Feuvre	0	Debbie Massey (6 & 5)	1
Maureen Walker	0	Carol Semple (2 & 1)	1
Tegwen Perkins	0	Mary Budke (5 & 4)	1
Mary McKenna (2 & 1)	1	Bonnie Lauer	0

1927 WORCESTER, MASS.

Great Britain and Ireland 2
Captain: E. Ray

United States 9
Captain: W. Hagen

Great Britain and Ireland		United States	
Foursomes	*1*	*Foursomes*	*3*
E. Ray & F. Robson	0	W. Hagen & J. Golden (2 & 1)	1
G. Duncan & A. Compston	0	J. Farrell & J. Turnesa (8 & 6)	1
A. Havers & H. Jolly	0	E. Sarazen & A. Watrous (3 & 2)	1
A. Boomer & C. A. Whitcombe (7 & 5)	1	L. Diegel & W. Mehlhorn	0
Singles	*1*	*Singles*	*6*
A. Compston	0	W. Mehlhorn (1 hole)	1
A. Boomer	0	J. Farrell (5 & 4)	1
H. C. Jolly	0	J. Golden (8 & 7)	1
E. Ray	0	L. Diegel (7 & 5)	1
C. A. Whitcombe (halved)	0	E. Sarazen (halved)	0
A. G. Havers	0	W. Hagen (2 & 1)	1
F. Robson	0	A. Watrous (3 & 2)	1
G. Duncan (1 hole)	1	J. Turnesa	0

1929 MOORTOWN, ENGLAND

Great Britain and Ireland 6
Captain: G. Duncan

United States 4
Captain: W. Hagen

Great Britain and Ireland		United States	
Foursomes	*1*	*Foursomes*	*2*
C. A. Whitcombe & A. Compston (halved)	0	J. Farrell & J. Turnesa (halved)	0
A. Boomer & G. Duncan	0	L. Diegel & A. Espinosa (7 & 5)	1
A. Mitchell & F. Robson (2 & 1)	1	E. Sarazen & E. Dudley	0
E. R. Whitcombe & T. H. Cotton	0	J. Golden & W. Hagen (2 up)	1
Singles	*5*	*Singles*	*2*
C. A. Whitcombe (8 & 6)	1	J. Farrell	0
G. Duncan (10 & 8)	1	W. Hagen	0
A. Mitchell	0	L. Diegel (9 & 8)	1
A. Compston (6 & 4)	1	E. Sarazen	0
A. Boomer (4 & 3)	1	J. Turnesa	0
F. Robson	0	H. Smith (4 & 2)	1
T. H. Cotton (4 & 3)	1	A. Watrous	0
E. R. Whitcombe (halved)	0	A. Espinosa (halved)	0

1931 SCIOTO, OHIO

Great Britain and Ireland 3
Captain: C. A. Whitcombe

United States 9
Captain: W. Hagen

Great Britain and Ireland		United States	
Foursomes	*1*	*Foursomes*	*3*
A. Compston & W. H. Davies	0	E. Sarazen & J. Farrell (8 & 7)	1
G. Duncan & A. Havers	0	W. Hagen & D. Shute (10 & 9)	1
A. Mitchell & F. Robson (3 & 1)	1	L. Diegel & A. Espinosa	0
S. Easterbrook & E. Whitcombe	0	W. Burke & W. Cox (3 & 2)	1
Singles	*2*	*Singles*	*6*
A. Compston	0	W. Burke (7 & 6)	1
F. Robson	0	E. Sarazen (7 & 6)	1
W. H. Davies (4 & 3)	1	J. Farrell	0
A. Mitchell	0	W. Cox (3 & 1)	1
C. A. Whitcombe	0	W. Hagen (4 & 3)	1
B. Hodson	0	D. Shute (8 & 6)	1
E. Whitcombe	0	A. Espinosa (2 & 1)	1
A. Havers (4 & 3)	1	C. Wood	0

1933 SOUTHPORT AND AINSDALE COURSES, ENGLAND

Great Britain and Ireland 6
Captain: J. H. Taylor

United States 5
Captain: W. Hagen

Great Britain and Ireland		United States	
Foursomes	*2*	*Foursomes*	*1*
P. Alliss & C. A. Whitcombe (halved)	0	E. Sarazen & W. Hagen (halved)	0
A. Mitchell & A. Havers (3 & 2)	1	O. Dutra & D. Shute	0
W. H. Davies & S. Easterbrook (1 up)	1	C. Wood & P. Runyan	0
A. H. Padgham & A. Perry	0	E. Dudley & W. Burke (1 up)	1
Singles	*4*	*Singles*	*4*
A. H. Padgham	0	E. Sarazen (6 & 4)	1
A. Mitchell (9 & 8)	1	O. Dutra	0
A. J. Lacey	0	W. Hagen (2 & 1)	1
W. H. Davies	0	C. Wood (4 & 3)	1
P. Alliss (2 & 1)	1	P. Runyan	0
A. Havers (4 & 3)	1	L. Diegel	0
S. Easterbrook (1 hole)	1	D. Shute	0
C. A. Whitcombe	0	H. Smith (2 & 1)	1

1935 RIDGEWOOD, N.J.

Great Britain and Ireland 2
Captain: C. A. Whitcombe

United States 8
Captain: W. Hagen

Great Britain and Ireland		United States	
Foursomes	*1*	*Foursomes*	*3*
A. Perry & J. J. Busson	0	E. Sarazen & W. Hagen (7 & 6)	1
A. H. Padgham & P. Alliss	0	H. Picard & J. Revolta (6 & 5)	1
W. J. Cox & E. W. Jarman	0	P. Runyan & H. Smith (9 & 8)	1
C. A. Whitcombe & E. R. Whitcombe (1 hole)	1	O. Dutra & K. Laffoon	0
Singles	*1*	*Singles*	*5*
J. J. Busson	0	E. Sarazen (3 & 2)	1
R. Burton	0	P. L. Runyan (5 & 3)	1
R. A. Whitcombe	0	J. L. Revolta (2 & 1)	1
A. H. Padgham	0	O. Dutra (4 & 2)	1
P. Alliss (1 hole)	1	C. Wood	0
W. J. Cox (halved)	0	H. Smith (halved)	0
E. R. Whitcombe	0	H. Pickard (3 & 2)	1
A. Perry (halved)	0	S. Parks (halved)	0

1937 SOUTHPORT AND AINSDALE COURSES, ENGLAND

Great Britain and Ireland 3
Captain: C. A. Whitcombe

United States 7
Captain: W. Hagen

Great Britain and Ireland		United States	
Foursomes	*1*	*Foursomes*	*2*
A. H. Padgham & T. H. Cotton	0	E. Dudley & B. Nelson (4 & 2)	1
A. J. Lacey & W. J. Cox	0	R. Guldahl & T. Manero (2 & 1)	1
C. A. Whitcombe & D. J. Rees (halved)	0	E. Sarazen & D. Shute (halved)	0
P. Alliss & R. Burton (2 & 1)	1	H. Picard & J. Revolta	0
Singles	*2*	*Singles*	*5*
A. H. Padgham	0	R. Guldahl (8 & 7)	1
S. L. King (halved)	0	D. Shute (halved)	0
D. J. Rees (3 & 1)	1	B. Nelson	0
T. H. Cotton (5 & 3)	1	T. Manero	0
· P. Alliss	0	E. Sarazen (1 hole)	1
R. Burton	0	S. Snead (5 & 4)	1
A. Perry	0	E. Dudley (2 & 1)	1
A. J. Lacey	0	H. Picard (2 & 1)	1

1947 PORTLAND, OREG.

Great Britain and Ireland 1
Captain: T. H. Cotton

United States 11
Captain: B. Hogan

Great Britain and Ireland		United States	
Foursomes	*0*	*Foursomes*	*4*
T. H. Cotton & A. Lees	0	E. Oliver & L. Worsham (10 & 9)	1
F. Daly & C. H. Ward	0	S. Snead & L. Mangrum (6 & 5)	1
J. Adams & M. Faulkner	0	B. Hogan & J. Demaret (2 holes)	1
D. J. Rees & S. King	0	B. Nelson & H. Barron (2 & 1)	1
Singles	*1*	*Singles*	*7*
F. Daly	0	E. J. Harrison (5 & 4)	1
J. Adams	0	L. Worsham (3 & 2)	1
M. Faulkner	0	L. Mangrum (6 & 5)	1
C. H. Ward	0	E. Oliver (4 & 3)	1
A. Lees	0	B. Nelson (2 & 1)	1
T. H. Cotton	0	S. Snead (5 & 4)	1
D. J. Rees	0	J. Demaret (3 & 2)	1
S. King (4 & 3)	1	H. Keiser	0

1949 GANTON, SCARBOROUGH, ENGLAND

Great Britain and Ireland 5
Captain: C. A. Whitcombe

United States 7
Captain: B. Hogan

Great Britain and Ireland		United States	
Foursomes	*3*	*Foursomes*	*1*
M. Faulkner & J. Adams (2 & 1)	1	E. J. Harrison & J. Palmer	0
F. Daly & K. Bousfield (4 & 2)	1	R. Hamilton & S. Alexander	0
C. Ward & S. L. King	0	J. Demaret & C. Heafner (4 & 3)	1
R. Burton & A. Lees (1 hole)	1	S. Snead & L. Mangrum	0
Singles	*2*	*Singles*	*6*
M. Faulkner	0	E. J. Harrison (8 & 7)	1
J. Adams (2 & 1)	1	J. Palmer	0
C. Ward	0	S. Snead (6 & 5)	1
D. J. Rees (6 & 4)	1	R. Hamilton	0
R. Burton	0	C. Heafner (3 & 2)	1
S. King	0	C. Harbert (4 & 3)	1
A. Lees	0	J. Demaret (7 & 6)	1
F. Daly	0	L. Mangrum (1 hole)	1

1951 PINEHURST, N.C.

Great Britain and Ireland 2
Captain: A. J. Lacey

United States 9
Captain: S. Snead

Great Britain and Ireland		United States	
Foursomes	*1*	*Foursomes*	*3*
M. Faulkner & D. J. Rees	0	C. Heafner & J. Burke (5 & 3)	1
C. H. Ward & A. Lees (2 & 1)	1	E. Oliver & H. Ransom	0
J. Adams & J. Panton	0	L. Mangrum & S. Snead (5 & 4)	1
F. Daly & K. Bousfield	0	B. Hogan & J. Demaret (5 & 4)	1
Singles	*1*	*Singles*	*6*
J. Adams	0	J. Burke (4 & 3)	1
D. J. Rees	0	J. Demaret (2 holes)	1
F. Daly (halved)	0	C. Heafner (halved)	0
H. Weetman	0	L. Mangrum (6 & 5)	1
A. Lees (2 & 1)	1	E. Oliver	0
C. H. Ward	0	B. Hogan (3 & 2)	1
J. Panton	0	S. Alexander (8 & 7)	1
M. Faulkner	0	S. Snead (4 & 3)	1

1953 WENTWORTH, ENGLAND

Great Britain and Ireland 5
Captain: T. H. Cotton

United States 6
Captain: L. Mangrum

Great Britain and Ireland		United States	
Foursomes	*1*	*Foursomes*	*3*
H. Weetman & P. Alliss	0	D. Douglas & E. Oliver (2 & 1)	1
E. C. Brown & J. Panton	0	L. Mangrum & S. Snead (8 & 7)	1
J. Adams & B. J. Hunt	0	T. Kroll & J. Burke (7 & 5)	1
F. Daly & H. Bradshaw (1 hole)	1	W. Burkemo & C. Middlecoff	0
Singles	*4*	*Singles*	*3*
D. J. Rees	0	J. Burke (2 & 1)	1
F. Daly (9 & 7)	1	T. Kroll	0
E. C. Brown (2 up)	1	L. Mangrum	0
H. Weetman (1 up)	1	S. Snead	0
M. Faulkner	0	C. Middlecoff (3 & 2)	1
P. Alliss	0	J. Turnesa (1 up)	1
B. J. Hunt (halved)	0	D. Douglas (halved)	0
H. Bradshaw (3 & 2)	1	F. Haas	0

1955 PALM SPRINGS, CALIF.

Great Britain and Ireland 4
Captain: D. J. Rees

United States 8
Captain: C. Harbert

Great Britain and Ireland		United States	
Foursomes	*1*	*Foursomes*	*3*
J. Fallon & J. R. M. Jacobs (1 hole)	1	C. Harbert & J. Barber	0
E. C. Brown & S. S. Scott	0	D. Ford & T. Kroll (5 & 4)	1
A. Lees & H. Weetman	0	J. Burke & T. Bolt (1 hole)	1
D. J. Rees & H. Bradshaw	0	S. Snead & C. Middlecoff (3 & 2)	1
Singles	*3*	*Singles*	*5*
C. O'Connor	0	T. Bolt (4 & 2)	1
S. S. Scott	0	C. Harbert (3 & 2)	1
J. Jacobs (1 hole)	1	C. Middlecoff	0
D. J. Rees	0	S. Snead (3 & 1)	1
A. Lees (3 & 1)	1	M. Furgol	0
E. C. Brown (3 & 2)	1	J. Barber	0
H. Bradshaw	0	J. Burke (3 & 2)	1
H. Weetman	0	D. Ford (3 & 2)	1

1957 LINDRICK, ENGLAND

Great Britain and Ireland 7
Captain: D. J. Rees

United States 4
Captain: J. Burke

Great Britain and Ireland		United States	
Foursomes	*1*	*Foursomes*	*3*
P. Alliss & B. J. Hunt	0	D. Ford & D. Finsterwald (2 & 1)	1
K. Bousfield & D. J. Rees (3 & 2)	1	A. Wall & F. Hawkins	0
M. Faulkner & H. Weetman	0	T. Kroll & J. Burke (4 & 3)	1
C. O'Connor & E. C. Brown	0	R. Mayer & T. Bolt (7 & 5)	1
Singles	*6*	*Singles*	*1*
E. C. Brown (4 & 3)	1	T. Bolt	0
R. P. Mills (5 & 3)	1	J. Burke	0
P. Alliss	0	F. Hawkins (2 & 1)	1
K. Bousfield (4 & 3)	1	L. Hebert	0
D. J. Rees (7 & 6)	1	E. Furgol	0
B. J. Hunt (6 & 5)	1	D. Ford	0
C. O'Connor (7 & 6)	1	D. Finsterwald	0
H. Bradshaw (halved)	0	R. Mayer (halved)	0

1959 PALM DESERT, CALIF.

Great Britain and Ireland 2
Captain: D. J. Rees

United States 7
Captain: S. Snead

Great Britain and Ireland		United States	
Foursomes	*1*	*Foursomes*	*2*
B. J. Hunt & E. C. Brown	0	R. Rosburg & M. Souchak (5 & 4)	1
C. O'Connor & P. Alliss (3 & 2)	1	D. Ford & A. Wall	0
D. J. Rees & K. Bousfield	0	J. Boros & D. Finsterwald (2 holes)	1
H. Weetman & D. C. Thomas (halved)	0	S. Snead & C. Middlecoff (halved)	0
Singles	*1*	*Singles*	*5*
N. V. Drew (halved)	0	D. Ford (halved)	0
K. Bousfield	0	M. Souchak (3 & 2)	1
H. Weetman	0	R. Rosburg (6 & 5)	1
D. C. Thomas	0	S. Snead (6 & 5)	1
D. J. Rees	0	D. Finsterwald (1 hole)	1
P. Alliss (halved)	0	J. Hebert (halved)	0
C. O'Connor	0	A. Wall (7 & 6)	1
E. C. Brown (4 & 3)	1	C. Middlecoff	0

1961 ROYAL LYTHAM AND ST ANNES, ENGLAND

Great Britain and Ireland 8
Captain: D. J. Rees

United States 13
Captain: J. Barber

Great Britain and Ireland		United States	
Foursomes	*2*	*Foursomes*	*6*
C. O'Connor & P. Alliss (4 & 3)	1	G. Littler & D. Ford	0
J. Panton & B. J. Hunt	0	A. Wall & J. Hebert (4 & 3)	1
D. J. Rees & K. Bousfield	0	W. Casper & A. Palmer (2 & 1)	1
T. B. Haliburton & N. C. Coles	0	M. Souchak & W. Collins (1 hole)	1
C. O'Connor & P. Alliss	0	A. Wall & J. Hebert (1 hole)	1
J. Panton & B. J. Hunt	0	W. Casper & A. Palmer (5 & 4)	1
D. J. Rees & K. Bousfield (4 & 2)	1	M. Souchak & W. Collins	0
T. B. Haliburton & N. C. Coles	0	J. Barber & D. Finsterwald (1 hole)	1
Singles	*6*	*Singles*	*7*
H. Weetman	0	D. Ford (1 hole)	1
R. L. Moffitt	0	M. Souchak (5 & 4)	1
P. Alliss (halved)	0	A. Palmer (halved)	0
K. Bousfield	0	W. Casper (5 & 3)	1
D. J. Rees (2 & 1)	1	J. Hebert	0
N. C. Coles (halved)	0	G. Littler (halved)	0
B. J. Hunt (5 & 4)	1	J. Barber	0
C. O'Connor	0	D. Finsterwald (2 & 1)	1
H. Weetman	0	A. Wall (1 hole)	1
P. Alliss (3 & 2)	1	W. Collins	0
B. J. Hunt	0	M. Souchak (2 & 1)	1
T. B. Haliburton	0	A. Palmer (2 & 1)	1
D. J. Rees (4 & 3)	1	D. Ford	0
K. Bousfield (1 hole)	1	J. Barber	0
N. C. Coles (1 hole)	1	D. Finsterwald	0
C. O'Connor (halved)	0	G. Littler (halved)	0

1963 ATLANTA, GA.	Great Britain and Ireland		United States	
Great Britain and Ireland 6 *Captain: J. Fallon* **United States 20** *Captain: A. Palmer*	*Foursomes*	1	*Foursomes*	5
	B. G. C. Huggett & G. Will (3 & 2)	1	A. Palmer & J. Pott	0
	P. Alliss & C. O'Connor	0	W. Casper & D. Ragan (1 hole)	1
	N. C. Coles & B. J. Hunt (halved)	0	J. Boros & A. Lema (halved)	0
	D. C. Thomas & H. Weetman (halved)	0	G. Littler & D. Finsterwald (halved)	0
	D. C. Thomas & H. Weetman	0	W. Maxwell & R. Goalby (4 & 3)	1
	B. G. C. Huggett & G. Will	0	A. Palmer & W. Casper (5 & 4)	1
	N. C. Coles & G. M. Hunt	0	G. Littler & D. Finsterwald (2 & 1)	1
	T. B. Haliburton & B. J. Hunt	0	J. Boros & A. Lema (1 hole)	1
	Four-ball	1	*Four-ball*	5
	B. G. C. Huggett & D. C. Thomas	0	A. Palmer & D. Finsterwald (5 & 4)	1
	P. Alliss & B. J. Hunt (halved)	0	G. Littler & J. Boros (halved)	0
	H. Weetman & G. Will	0	W. Casper & W. Maxwell (3 & 2)	1
	N. C. Coles & C. O'Connor (1 hole)	1	R. Goalby & D. Ragan	0
	N. C. Coles & C. O'Connor	0	A. Palmer & D. Finsterwald (3 & 2)	1
	P. Alliss & B. J. Hunt	0	A. Lema & J. Pott (1 hole)	1
	T. B. Haliburton & G. M. Hunt	0	W. Casper & W. Maxwell (2 & 1)	1
	B. G. C. Huggett & D. C. Thomas (halved)	0	R. Goalby & D. Ragan (halved)	0
	Singles	4	*Singles*	10
	G. M. Hunt	0	A. Lema (5 & 3)	1
	B. G. C. Huggett (3 & 1)	1	J. Pott	0
	P. Alliss (1 hole)	1	A. Palmer	0
	N. C. Coles (halved)	0	W. Casper (halved)	0
	D. C. Thomas	0	R. Goalby (3 & 2)	1
	C. O'Connor	0	G. Littler (1 hole)	1
	H. Weetman (1 hole)	1	J. Boros	0
	B. J. Hunt (2 holes)	1	D. Finsterwald	0
	G. Will	0	A. Palmer (3 & 2)	1
	N. C. Coles	0	D. Ragan (2 & 1)	1
	P. Alliss (halved)	0	A. Lema (halved)	0
	T. B. Haliburton	0	G. Littler (6 & 5)	1
	H. Weetman	0	J. Boros (2 & 1)	1
	C. O'Connor	0	W. Maxwell (2 & 1)	1
	D. C. Thomas	0	D. Finsterwald (4 & 3)	1
	B. J. Hunt	0	R. Goalby (2 & 1)	1

1965 ROYAL BIRKDALE, ENGLAND	Great Britain and Ireland		United States	
Great Britain and Ireland 11 *Captain: H. Weetman* **United States 18** *Captain: B. Nelson*	*Foursomes*	4	*Foursomes*	4
	D. C. Thomas & G. Will (6 & 5)	1	D. Marr & A. Palmer	0
	C. O'Connor & P. Alliss (5 & 4)	1	K. Venturi & D. January	0
	L. Platts & P. J. Butler	0	J. Boros & A. Lema (1 hole)	1
	B. J. Hunt & N. C. Coles	0	W. Casper & G. Littler (2 & 1)	1
	D. C. Thomas & G. Will	0	D. Marr & A. Palmer (6 & 5)	1
	J. Martin & J. Hitchcock	0	J. Boros & A. Lema (5 & 4)	1
	C. O'Connor & P. Alliss (2 & 1)	1	W. Casper & G. Littler	0
	B. J. Hunt & N. C. Coles (3 & 2)	1	K. Venturi & D. January	0
	Four-ball	2	*Four-ball*	4
	D. C. Thomas & G. Will	0	D. January & T. Jacobs (1 hole)	1
	L. Platts & P. J. Butler (halved)	0	W. Casper & G. Littler (halved)	0
	P. Alliss & C. O'Connor	0	D. Marr & A. Palmer (5 & 4)	1
	N. C. Coles & B. J. Hunt (1 hole)	1	J. Boros & A. Lema	0
	P. Alliss & C. O'Connor (1 hole)	1	D. Marr & A. Palmer	0
	D. C. Thomas & G. Will	0	D. January & T. Jacobs (1 hole)	1
	L. Platts & P. J. Butler (halved)	0	W. Casper & G. Littler (halved)	0
	N. C. Coles & B. J. Hunt	0	A. Lema & K. Venturi (1 hole)	1
	Singles	5	*Singles*	10
	J. Hitchcock	0	A. Palmer (3 & 2)	1
	L. Platts	0	J. Boros (4 & 2)	1
	P. J. Butler	0	A. Lema (1 hole)	1
	N. C. Coles	0	D. Marr (2 holes)	1
	B. J. Hunt (2 holes)	1	G. Littler	0
	P. Alliss (1 hole)	1	W. Casper	0
	D. C. Thomas	0	T. Jacobs (2 & 1)	1
	G. Will (halved)	0	D. January (halved)	0
	P. J. Butler	0	A. Palmer (2 holes)	1
	J. Hitchcock	0	J. Boros (2 & 1)	1
	C. O'Connor	0	A. Lema (6 & 4)	1
	P. Alliss (3 & 1)	1	K. Venturi	0
	B. J. Hunt	0	D. Marr (1 hole)	1
	N. C. Coles (3 & 2)	1	W. Casper	0
	G. Will	0	G. Littler (2 & 1)	1
	L. Platts (1 hole)	1	T. Jacobs	0

1967 HOUSTON, TEX.

Great Britain and Ireland 6
Captain: D. J. Rees

United States 21
Captain: B. Hogan

Great Britain and Ireland		United States	
Foursomes	2	*Foursomes*	5
B. G. C. Huggett & G. Will (halved)	0	W. Casper & J. Boros (halved)	0
P. Alliss & C. O'Connor	0	A. Palmer & G. Dickinson (2 & 1)	1
A. Jacklin & D. C. Thomas (4 & 3)	1	D. Sanders & G. Brewer	0
B. J. Hunt & N. C. Coles	0	B. Nichols & J. Pott (6 & 5)	1
B. G. C. Huggett & G. Will	0	J. Boros & W. Casper (1 hole)	1
M. Gregson & H. F. Boyle	0	G. Dickinson & A. Palmer (5 & 4)	1
A. Jacklin & D. C. Thomas (3 & 2)	1	G. Littler & A. Geiberger	0
P. Alliss & C. O'Connor	0	B. Nichols & J. Pott (2 & 1)	1
Four-ball	0	*Four-ball*	7
P. Alliss & C. O'Connor	0	W. Casper & G. Brewer (3 & 2)	1
B. J. Hunt & N. C. Coles	0	B. Nichols & J. Pott (1 hole)	1
A. Jacklin & D. C. Thomas	0	G. Littler & A. Geiberger (1 hole)	1
B. G. C. Huggett & G. Will	0	G. Dickinson & D. Sanders (3 & 2)	1
B. J. Hunt & N. C. Coles	0	W. Casper & G. Brewer (5 & 3)	1
P. Alliss & M. Gregson	0	G. Dickinson & D. Sanders (3 & 2)	1
G. Will & H. F. Boyle	0	A. Palmer & J. Boros (1 hole)	1
A. Jacklin & D. C. Thomas (halved)	0	G. Littler & A. Geiberger (halved)	0
Singles	4	*Singles*	9
H. F. Boyle	0	G. Brewer (4 & 3)	1
P. Alliss	0	W. Casper (2 & 1)	1
A. Jacklin	0	A. Palmer (3 & 2)	1
B. G. C. Huggett (1 hole)	1	J. Boros	0
N. C. Coles (2 & 1)	1	D. Sanders	0
M. Gregson	0	A. Geiberger (4 & 2)	1
D. C. Thomas (halved)	0	G. Littler (halved)	0
B. J. Hunt (halved)	0	B. Nichols (halved)	0
B. G. C. Huggett	0	A. Palmer (5 & 3)	1
P. Alliss (2 & 1)	1	G. Brewer	0
A. Jacklin	0	G. Dickinson (3 & 2)	1
C. O'Connor	0	B. Nichols (3 & 2)	1
G. Will	0	J. Pott (3 & 1)	1
M. Gregson	0	A. Geiberger (2 & 1)	1
B. J. Hunt (halved)	0	J. Boros (halved)	0
N. C. Coles (2 & 1)	1	D. Sanders	0

1969 ROYAL BIRKDALE, ENGLAND

Great Britain and Ireland 13
Captain: E. C. Brown

United States 13
Captain: S. Snead

Great Britain and Ireland		United States	
Foursomes	4	*Foursomes*	3
N. C. Coles, B. G. C. Huggett (3 & 2)	1	M. Barber & R. Floyd	0
B. Gallacher, M. Bembridge (2 & 1)	1	L. Trevino & K. Still	0
T. Jacklin & P. Townsend (3 & 1)	1	D. Hill & T. Aaron	0
C. O'Connor & P. Alliss (halved)	0	W. Casper & F. Beard (halved)	0
N. C. Coles, B. G. C. Huggett	0	D. Hill & T. Aaron (1 hole)	1
B. Gallacher & M. Bembridge	0	L. Trevino & G. Littler (2 holes)	1
A. Jacklin & P. Townsend (1 hole)	1	W. Casper & F. Beard	0
B. J. Hunt & P. J. Butler	0	J. Nicklaus & D. Sikes (1 hole)	1
Four-ball	2	*Four-ball*	3
C. O'Connor & P. Townsend (1 hole)	1	D. Hill & D. Douglass	0
B. G. C. Huggett & G. A. Caygill (halved)	0	R. Floyd & M. Barber (halved)	0
B. Barnes & P. Alliss	0	L. Trevino & G. Littler (1 hole)	1
A. Jacklin & N. C. Coles (1 hole)	1	J. Nicklaus & D. Sikes	0
P. Townsend & P. J. Butler	0	W. Casper & F. Beard (2 holes)	1
B. G. C. Huggett, B. Gallacher	0	D. Hill & K. Still (2 & 1)	1
M. Bembridge & B. J. Hunt (halved)	0	T. Aaron & R. Floyd (halved)	0
A. Jacklin & N. C. Coles (halved)	0	L. Trevino & M. Barber (halved)	0
Singles	7	*Singles*	7
P. Alliss	0	L. Trevino (2 & 1)	1
P. Townsend	0	D. Hill (5 & 4)	1
N. C. Coles (1 hole)	1	T. Aaron	0
B. Barnes	0	W. Casper (1 hole)	1
C. O'Connor (5 & 4)	1	F. Beard	0
M. Bembridge (1 hole)	1	K. Still	0
P. J. Butler (1 hole)	1	R. Floyd	0
A. Jacklin (4 & 3)	1	J. Nicklaus	0
B. Barnes	0	D. Hill (4 & 2)	1
B. Gallacher (4 & 3)	1	L. Trevino	0
M. Bembridge	0	M. Barber (7 & 6)	1
P. J. Butler (3 & 2)	1	D. Douglass	0
C. O'Connor	0	G. Littler (2 & 1)	1
B. G. C. Huggett (halved)	0	W. Casper (halved)	0
N. C. Coles	0	D. Sikes (4 & 3)	1
A. Jacklin (halved)	0	J. Nicklaus (halved)	0

1971 LOUIS, MO.

Great Britain and Ireland 11
Captain: E. C. Brown

United States 16
Captain: J. Hebert

Great Britain and Ireland		United States	
Foursomes	4	*Foursomes*	3
N. C. Coles & C. O'Connor (2 & 1)	1	W. J. Casper & M. Barber	0
P. M. P. Townsend & P. A. Oosterhuis	0	A. Palmer & G. Dickinson (2 holes)	1
B. G. C. Huggett & A. Jacklin (3 & 2)	1	J. W. Nicklaus & D. Stockton	0
M. E. Bembridge & P. J. Butler (1 hole)	1	C. Coody & F. Beard	0
H. Bannerman & B. J. Gallacher (2 & 1)	1	W. J. Casper & M. Barber	0
P. M. P. Townsend & P. A. Oosterhuis	0	A. Palmer & G. Dickinson (1 hole)	1
B. G. C. Huggett & A. Jacklin (halved)	0	L. Trevino & M. Rudolph (halved)	0
M. E. Bembridge & P. J. Butler	0	J. W. Nicklaus & J. C. Snead (5 & 3)	1
Four-ball	1	*Four-ball*	6
C. O'Connor & B. W. Barnes	0	L. Trevino & M. Rudolph (2 & 1)	1
N. C. Coles & J. Garner	0	F. Beard & J. C. Snead (2 & 1)	1
P. A. Oosterhuis & B. J. Gallacher	0	A. Palmer & G. Dickinson (5 & 4)	1
P. M. P. Townsend & H. Bannerman	0	J. W. Nicklaus & G. Littler (2 & 1)	1
B. J. Gallacher & P. A. Oosterhuis (1 hole)	1	L. Trevino & W. J. Casper	0
A. Jacklin & B. G. C. Huggett	0	G. Littler & J. C. Snead (2 & 1)	1
P. M. P. Townsend & H. Bannerman	0	A. Palmer & J. W. Nicklaus (1 hole)	1
N. C. Coles & C. O'Connor (halved)	0	C. Coody & F. Beard (halved)	0
Singles	6	*Singles*	7
A. Jacklin	0	L. Trevino (1 hole)	1
B. J. Gallacher (halved)	0	D. Stockton (halved)	0
B. W. Barnes (1 hole)	1	M. Rudolph	0
P. A. Oosterhuis (4 & 3)	1	G. Littler	0
P. M. P. Townsend	0	J. W. Nicklaus (3 & 2)	1
C. O'Connor	0	G. Dickinson (5 & 4)	1
H. Bannerman (halved)	0	A. Palmer (halved)	0
N. C. Coles (halved)	0	F. Beard (halved)	0
B. G. C. Huggett	0	L. Trevino (7 & 6)	1
A. Jacklin	0	J. C. Snead (1 hole)	1
B. W. Barnes (2 & 1)	1	M. Barber	0
P. M. P. Townsend	0	D. Stockton (1 hole)	1
B. J. Gallacher (2 & 1)	1	C. Coody	0
N. C. Coles	0	J. W. Nicklaus (5 & 3)	1
P. A. Oosterhuis (3 & 2)	1	A. Palmer	0
H. Bannerman (2 & 1)	1	G. Dickinson	0

1973 MUIRFIELD, SCOTLAND

Great Britain and Ireland 13
Captain: B. J. Hunt

United States 19
Captain: J. Burke

Great Britain and Ireland		United States	
Foursomes	4½	*Foursomes*	3½
B. Barnes & B. Gallacher (1 hole)	1	L. Trevino & W. Casper	0
M. Bembridge & E. Polland	0	J. Nicklaus & A. Palmer (6 & 5)	1
C. O'Connor & N. Coles (3 & 2)	1	T. Weiskopf & J. C. Snead	0
A. Jacklin & P. Oosterhuis (halved)	½	L. Graham & J. Rodriguez (halved)	½
B. Barnes & P. Butler	0	J. Nicklaus & T. Weiskopf (1 hole)	1
P. Oosterhuis & A. Jacklin (2 holes)	1	A. Palmer & D. Hill	0
B. Huggett & M. Bembridge (5 & 4)	1	L. Graham & J. Rodriguez	0
C. O'Connor & N. Coles	0	L. Trevino & W. Casper (2 & 1)	1
Four-ball	3½	*Four-ball*	4½
B. Barnes & B. Gallacher (5 & 4)	1	T. Aaron & G. Brewer	0
M. Bembridge & B. Huggett (3 & 1)	1	J. Nicklaus & A. Palmer	0
C. O'Connor & N. Coles	0	L. Trevino & H. Blancas (2 & 1)	1
A. Jacklin & P. Oosterhuis (3 & 1)	1	T. Weiskopf & W. Casper	0
B. Barnes & P. Butler	0	J. C. Snead & A. Palmer (2 holes)	1
A. Jacklin & P. Oosterhuis	0	G. Brewer & W. Casper (3 & 2)	1
E. Polland & C. Clark	0	T. Weiskopf & J. Nicklaus (3 & 2)	1
M. Bembridge & B. Huggett (halved)	½	L. Trevino & H. Blancas (halved)	½
Singles	5	*Singles*	11
B. Barnes	0	W. Casper (2 & 1)	1
B. Gallacher	0	T. Weiskopf (3 & 1)	1
P. Butler	0	H. Blancas (5 & 4)	1
A. Jacklin (3 & 1)	1	T. Aaron	0
N. Coles (halved)	½	G. Brewer (halved)	½
C. O'Connor	0	J. C. Snead (1 hole)	1
M. Bembridge (halved)	½	J. Nicklaus (halved)	½
P. Oosterhuis (halved)	½	L. Trevino (halved)	½
B. Huggett (3 & 2)	1	H. Blancas	0
B. Barnes	0	J. C. Snead (3 & 1)	1
B. Gallacher	0	G. Brewer (6 & 5)	1
N. Coles	0	L. Trevino (6 & 5)	1
A. Jacklin	0	W. Casper (2 & 1)	1
M. Bembridge	0	J. Nicklaus (2 holes)	1
C. O'Connor (halved)	½	T. Weiskopf (halved)	½
P. Oosterhuis (4 & 2)	1	A. Palmer	0

1953 MONTREAL *7 entries*

1. Argentina 287
R. de Vicenzo 147; A. Cerda 140

2. Canada 297
S. Leonard 144; B. Kerr 153

3. Australia 298
O. Pickworth 147; P. Thomson 151

4. England and South Africa 298
H. Weetman 148; A. D. Locke 150

5. United States 304
J. Boros 150; J. Turnesa 154

6. Germany 312
G. Bessner 151; Goermert 161

Individual title: A. Cerda 140

1954 MONTREAL *25 entries*

1. Australia 556
K. Nagle 279; P. Thomson 277

2. Argentina 560
A. Cerda 277; R. de Vicenzo 283

3. United States 565
J. Demaret 278; S. Snead 287

4. Canada 570
Hout 295; S. Leonard 275

5. Scotland 571
E. C. Brown 287; T. Haliburton 284

6. France 573
J. Garaialde 284; V. Saubaber 289

Individual title: S. Leonard 275

1955 WASHINGTON *25 entries*

1. United States 560
C. Harbert 281; E. Furgol 279

2. Australia 569
P. Thomson 279; K. Nagle 290

3. Scotland 571
E. Brown 285; J. Panton 286

4. Argentina 573
R. de Vicenzo 287; A. Cerda 286

4. Belgium 573
F. van Donck 279; A. de Vulder 294

6. Germany 575
G. Bessner 288; F. Schmaderer 287

6. England 575
N. Sutton 287; P. Alliss 288

Individual Title: E. Furgol, F. van Donck and
P. Thomson 279. Furgol won play-off

1956 WENTWORTH (ENGLAND) *29 entries*

1. United States 567
B. Hogan 277; S. Snead 290

2. South Africa 581
A. D. Locke 285; G. Player 296

3. Canada 583
A. Balding 297; S. Leonard 286

4. England 586
K. Bousfield 291; H. Weetman 295

4. Japan 586
Y. Hayashi 297; M. Ishii 289

6. Wales 587
D. J. Rees 284; D. Smalldon 303

Individual Title: Ben Hogan 277

1957 TOKYO *30 entries*

1. Japan 557
T. Nakamura 274; K. Ono 283

2. United States 566
S. Snead 281; J. Demaret 285

3. South Africa 569
G. Player 281; H. Henning 288

4. Australia 572
B. Crampton 285; P. Thomson 287

5. Wales 573
D. Thomas 281; D. Rees 292

6. Canada 576
S. Leonard 283; A. Balding 293

Individual Title: T. Nakamura 274

1958 MEXICO CITY *29 entries*

1. Ireland 579
H. Bradshaw 286; C. O'Connor 293

2. Spain 582
A. Miguel 286; S. Miguel 296

3. South Africa 584
H. Henning 293; G. Player 291

4. Scotland 588
E. Brown 289; J. Panton 299

4. Australia 588
K. Nagle 299; F. Phillips 289

6. England 593
P. Alliss 296; B. Hunt 297

Individual Title: A. Miguel and H. Bradshaw 286
Miguel won play-off

1959 MELBOURNE *30 entries*

1. Australia 563
P. Thomson 275; K. Nagle 288

2. United States 573
S. Snead 281; C. Middlecoff 292

3. Canada 574
S. Leonard 275; A. Balding 299

4. South Africa 580
G. Player 284; H. Henning 296

5. England 588
B. Hunt 295; P. Alliss 293

6. Wales 590
D. J. Rees 296; D. Thomas 294

Individual Title: S. Leonard and P. Thomson 275

1960 PORTMARNOCK DUBLIN *30 entries*

1. United States 565
A. Palmer 284; S. Snead 281

2. England 573
B. Hunt 289; H. Weetman 284

3. Australia 574
K. Nagle 288; P. Thomson 286

4. Ireland 575
N. Drew 289; C. O'Connor 286

5. South Africa 578
A. Locke 289; G. Player 289

6. Scotland 580
E. Brown 286; J. Panton 294

Individual Title: F. van Donck 279

1961 DORADO BEACH (PUERTO RICO) *33 entries*

1. United States 560
S. Snead 272; J. Demaret 288

2. Australia 572
P. Thomson 280; K. Nagle 292

3. Canada 579
A. Balding 283; A. Johnston 296

4. Ireland 582
N. Drew 300; C. O'Connor 282

5. Philippines 585
B. Arda 286; C. Tugot 299

6. Wales 587
D. Rees 295; D. Thomas 292

Individual Title: S. Snead 272

1962 BUENOS AIRES *34 entries*

1. United States 557
A. Palmer 278; S. Snead 279

2. Argentina 559
R. de Vicenzo 276; F. de Luca 283

3. Australia 569
K. Nagle 283; P. Thomson 286

4. England 572
P. Alliss 278; B. Hunt 294

5. France 585
J. Garaialde 287; R. Cotton 298

6. Brazil 586
M. Gonzalez 284; J. Gonzalez 302

6. Uruguay 586
J. Sereda 292; J. Esmori 294

Individual Title: R. de Vicenzo 276

1963 PARIS *33 entries*. Limited to 54 holes by fog

1. United States 482
J. Nicklaus 237; A. Palmer 245

2. Spain 485
R. Sota 243; S. Miguel 242

3. South Africa 492
G. Player 242; R. Waltman 250

4. Canada 495
A. Balding 245; S. Leonard 250

5. Australia 497
B. Crampton 245; B. Devlin 252

6. Belgium 508
F. van Donck 251; D. Swaelens 257

Individual Title: J. Nicklaus 237

1964 HAWAII *34 entries*

1. United States 554
J. Nicklaus 276; A. Palmer 278

2. Argentina 565
R. de Vicenzo 281; L. Ruiz 284

3. South Africa 568
G. Player 279; D. Hutchinson 289

4. Spain 572
A. Miguel 285; R. Sota 287

5. England 578
P. Alliss 289; B. Hunt 289

6. Hawaii 579
T. Makalena 279; P. Scodeller 300

Individual Title: J. Nicklaus 276

1965 MADRID *37 entries*

1. South Africa 571
G. Player 281; H. Henning 290

2. Spain 579
R. Sota 285; A. Miguel 294

3. United States 582
J. Nicklaus 284; A. Lema 298

4. Canada 585
G. Knudson 291; W. Homenui 294

4. England 585
G. Wolstenholme 292; D. Snell 293

6. Colombia 590
M. Sala 286; A. Bohorquez 304

Individual Title: G. Player 281

1966 TOKYO *35 entries*

1. United States 548
J. Nicklaus 273; A. Palmer 275

2. South Africa 553
H. Henning 276; G. Player 277

3. Taiwan 554
Lu Liang Huan 273; C. Chen 281

4. Australia 556
B. Devlin 277; K. Nagle 279

5. Japan 561
H. Sugimoto 272; M. Kono 289

6. Canada 565
G. Knudson 272; F. Fowler 293

6. Argentina 565
R. de Vicenzo 278; L. Ruiz 287

Individual Title: G. Knudson and H. Sugimoto 272
Knudson won play-off

1967 MEXICO CITY *40 entries*

1. United States 557
A. Palmer 276; J. Nicklaus 281

2. New Zealand 570
R. Charles 281; W. Godfrey 289

3. Mexico 574
A. Cerda 284; R. Cazares 290

4. South Africa 579
G. Player 289; H. Henning 290

5. Argentina 581
F. de Luca 287; F. Molina 294

5. Hawaii 581
T. Makalena 285; J. Ukauka 296

Individual Title: A. Palmer 276

1968 ROME *42 entries*

1. Canada 569
A. Balding 274; G. Knudson 295

2. United States 571
L. Trevino 283; J. Boros 288

3. Italy 573
R. Bernardini 279; A. Angelini 294

4. Taiwan 576
Lu Liang Huan 286; H. Yung-Yo 290

5. Spain 580
R. Sota 287; S. Miguel 293

6. South Africa 584
G. Player 285; C. Legrange 299

Individual Title: A. Balding 274

1969 SINGAPORE *45 entries*

1. United States 552
L. Trevino 275; O. Moody 277

2. Japan 560
T. Kono 279; H. Yasuda 281

3. Argentina 561
R. de Vicenzo 276; L. Ruiz 285

4. Thailand 562
S. Onchum 277; S. Suwanapomg 285

4. Taiwan 562
H. Yung-Yo 277; H. Chi-San 285

6. Philippines 564
B. Arda 278; E. Nival 286

Individual Title: L. Trevino 275

1970 BUENOS AIRES *43 entries*

1. Australia 544
D. Graham 270; B. Devlin 274

2. Argentina 554
R. de Vicenzo 269; V. Fernandez 285

3. South Africa 563
A. Henning 279; H. Henning 284

4. United States 565
D. Stockton 279; L. Trevino 286

5. Wales 572
B. Huggett 286; D. Thomas 286

5. Italy 572
E. Della Torre 283; E. Canessa 289

Individual Title: R. de Vicenzo 269

1971 PALM BEACH GARDENS, FLORIDA *46 entries*

1. United States 555
J. Nicklaus 271; L. Trevino 284

2. South Africa·567
G. Player 278; H. Henning 289

3. New Zealand 569
R. Charles 287; J. Lister 282

4. Argentina 575
R. de Vicenzo 281; F. Molina 294

5. Korea 581
H. C. Sang 290; K. S. Hack 291

6. England 582
A. Jacklin 290; P. Oosterhuis 292

Individual Title: J. Nicklaus 271

1972 ROYAL MELBOURNE (*limited to 54 holes*)

1. Taiwan 438
Hsieh Min Nam 217; Lu Liang Huan 221

2. Japan 440
T. Kono 219; T. Murakami 221

3. South Africa 444
G. Player 224; T. Britz 220

4. United States 445
T. Weiskopf 223; J. Jamieson 222

4. Australia 445
B. Crampton 221; W. Dunk 224

6. England 449
T. Jacklin 226; G. Hunt 223

Individual Title: H. Min Nam 217

1973 NUEVA ANDALUCIA, MARBELLA, SPAIN

1. United States 558
J. Miller 277; J. Nicklaus 281

2. South Africa 564
G. Player 280; H. Baiocchi 284

3. Taiwan 568
Lu Liang Huan 281; Hsieh Min Nam 287

4. Spain 582
V. Barrios 287; A. Gallardo 295

5. Argentina 582
R. de Vicenzo 288; F. de Luca 294

6. Japan 583
I. Aoki 287; T. Nakamura 296

Individual Title: J. Miller 277

1895 NEWPORT GC, R.I.

H. Rawlins *Newport*	45	46	41	41	173
W. Dunn *Shinnecock Hills*	43	46	44	42	175
J. Foulis *Chicago*	46	43	44	43	176
*A. W. Smith *Toronto*	47	43	44	42	176
W. F. Davis *Newport*	45	49	42	42	178
W. Campbell *Brookline*	41	48	42	48	179

1896 SHINNECOCK HILLS GC, N.Y.

J. Foulis *Chicago*	78	74	152
H. Rawlins *Sadequada*	79	76	155
G. Douglas *Brookline*	79	79	158
*A. W. Smith *Toronto*	78	80	158
J. Shippen *Shinnecock Hills*	78	81	159
*H. J. Whigham *Onwentsia*	82	77	159

1897 CHICAGO GC, ILL.

J. Lloyd *Essex*	83	79	162
W. Anderson *Watch Hill*	79	84	163
J. Foulis *Chicago*	80	88	168
W. Dunn *New York*	87	81	168
W. T. Hoare *Pittsburgh*	82	87	169
A. Ricketts *Albany*	91	81	172
B. Nicholls *Lenox*	87	85	172

1898 MYOPIA HUNT CLUB, MASS.

F. Herd *Washington Park*	84	85	75	84	328
A. Smith *Washington Park*	78	86	86	85	335
W. Anderson *Baltusrol*	81	82	87	86	336
J. Lloyd *Essex County*	87	80	86	86	339
W. Smith *Shinnecock*	82	91	85	82	340
W. V. Hoare *Dayton*	84	84	87	87	342

1899 BALTIMORE CC, MD.

W. Smith *Midlothian*	77	82	79	77	315
G. Low *Dyker Meadow*	82	79	89	76	326
V. Fitzjohn *Otsego*	85	80	79	82	326
W. H. Way *Detroit*	80	85	80	81	326
W. Anderson *New York*	77	81	85	84	327
J. Park *Essex County*	88	80	75	85	328

1900 CHICAGO GC, ILL.

H. Vardon *Ganton (England)*	79	78	76	80	313
J. H. Taylor *Richmond (England)*	76	82	79	78	315
D. Bell *Midlothian*	78	83	83	78	322
L. Auchterlonie *Glen View*	84	82	80	81	327
W. Smith *Midlothian*	82	83	79	84	328
G. Low *Dyker Meadow*	84	80	85	82	331

1901 MYOPIA HUNT CLUB, MASS.

W. Anderson *Pittsfield* (won play-off 85 to 86)	84	83	83	81	331
A. Smith *Washington Park*	82	82	87	80	331
W. Smith *Midlothian*	84	86	82	81	333
S. Gardner *Garden City*	86	82	81	85	334
L. Auchterlonie *Glen View*	81	85	86	83	335
B. Nicholls *Boston*	84	85	83	83	335

1902 GARDEN CITY GC, N.Y.

L. Auchterlonie *Chicago*	78	78	74	77	307
S. Gardner *Garden City*	82	76	77	78	313
*W. J. Travis *Garden City*	82	82	75	74	313
W. Smith *Chicago*	82	79	80	75	316
J. Shippen *New York*	83	81	75	79	318
W. Anderson *Montclair*	79	82	76	81	318

* Amateur

1903 BALTUSROL GC, N.J.

W. Anderson *Apawamis* (won play-off 82 to 84)	149	76 82	307
D. Brown *Wollaston*	156	75 76	307
S. Gardner *Garden City*	154	82 79	315
A. Smith *Nassau*	154	81 81	316
D. J. Ross *Oakley*	158	78 82	318
J. Campbell *Brookline*	159	83 77	319

1904 GLEN VIEW CLUB, ILL.

W. Anderson *Apawamis*	75	78	78	72	303
G. Nicholls *St Louis*	80	76	79	73	308
F. Mackenzie *Onwentsia*	76	79	74	80	309
L. Auchterlonie *Glen View*	80	81	75	78	314
B. Nicholls *Elyria, Ohio*	80	77	79	78	314
R. Simpson *Riverside, Ill.*	82	82	76	76	316
P. F. Barrett *Lambton, Ont.*	78	79	79	80	316
S. Gardner *Garden City*	75	76	80	85	316

1905 MYOPIA HUNT CLUB, MASS.

W. Anderson *Apawamis*	81	80	76	77	314
A. Smith *Nassau*	81	80	76	79	316
P. Robertson *Oakmont*	79	80	81	77	317
P. F. Barrett *Canada*	81	80	77	79	317
S. Gardner *Garden City*	78	78	85	77	318
A. Campbell *The Country Club*	82	76	80	81	319

1906 ONWENTSIA CLUB, ILL.

A. Smith *Nassau*	73	74	73	75	295
W. Smith *Mexico*	73	81	74	74	302
L. Auchterlonie *Glen View*	76	78	75	76	305
J. Maiden *Toledo*	80	73	77	75	305
W. Anderson *Onwentsia*	73	76	74	84	307
A. Ross *Brae Burn*	76	79	75	80	310

1907 PHILADELPHIA CRICKET CLUB, PA.

A. Ross *Brae Burn*	76	74	76	76	302
G. Nicholls *Woodland*	80	73	72	79	304
A. Campbell *The Country Club*	78	74	78	75	305
J. Hobens *Englewood*	76	75	73	85	309
P. Robertson *Oakmont*	81	77	78	74	310
G. Low *Baltusrol*	78	76	79	77	310
F. McLeod *Midlothian*	79	77	79	75	310

1908 MYOPIA HUNT CLUB, MASS.

F. McLeod *Midlothian* (won play-off 77 to 83)	82	82	81	77	322
W. Smith *Mexico*	77	82	85	78	322
A. Smith *Nassau*	80	83	83	81	327
W. Anderson *Onwentsia*	85	86	80	79	330
J. Jones *Myopia*	81	81	87	82	331
J. Hobens *Englewood*	86	81	85	81	333
P. Robertson *Oakmont*	89	84	77	83	333

1909 ENGLEWOOD GC, N.J.

G. Sargent *Hyde Manor*	75	72	72	71	290
T. McNamara *Wollaston*	73	69	75	77	294
A. Smith *Wykagyl*	76	73	74	72	295
I. Mackie *Fox Hills*	77	75	74	73	299
W. Anderson *St Louis*	79	74	76	70	299
J. Hobens *Englewood*	75	78	72	74	299

1910 PHILADELPHIA CRICKET CLUB, PA.

A. Smith *Wykagyl* (won play-off)	73	73	79	73	298	71
J.J. McDermott *Merchantville*	74	74	75	75	298	75
M. Smith *Claremont*	74	78	75	71	298	77
F. McLeod *St Louis*	78	70	78	73	299
T. McNamara *Boston*	73	78	73	76	300
G. Nicholls *Wilmington*	73	75	77	75	300

1911 CHICAGO GC, ILL.

J. J. McDermott *Atlantic City*	81	72	75	79	307
M. J. Brady *Wollaston*	76	77	79	75	307
G. O. Simpson *Wheaton*	76	77	79	75	307

Play-off: McDermott 80; Brady 82; Simpson 85

F. McLeod *St Louis*	77	72	76	83	308
G. Nicholls *Wilmington*	76	78	74	81	309
J. Hutchison *Allegheny*	80	77	73	79	309

1912 BUFFALO CC, N.Y.

J. J. McDermott *Atlantic City*	74	75	74	71	294
T. McNamara *Boston*	74	80	73	69	296
A. Smith *Wykagyl*	77	70	77	75	299
M. J. Brady *Wollaston*	72	75	73	79	299
A. Campbell *Brookline*	74	77	80	71	302
G. Sargent *Chevy Chase*	72	78	76	77	303

1913 BROOKLINE CC, MASS.

*F. Ouimet *Woodland*	77	74	74	79	304
H. Vardon *England*	75	72	78	79	304
E. Ray *England*	79	70	76	79	304

Play-off: Ouimet 72; Vardon 77; Ray 78

W. Hagen *Rochester*	73	78	76	80	307
J. M. Barnes *Tacoma*	74	76	78	79	307
M. Smith *Wykagyl*	71	79	80	77	307
L. Tellier *France*	76	76	79	76	307

1914 MIDLOTHIAN COUNTRY CLUB, ILL.

W. C. Hagen *Rochester*	68	74	75	73	290
*C. Evans Jr *Edgewater*	76	74	71	70	291
G. Sargent *Chevy Chase*	74	77	74	72	297
F. McLeod *Columbia*	78	73	71	77	297
*F. Ouimet *Woodland*	69	76	75	78	298
M. J. Brady *Wollaston*	78	72	74	74	298
J. A. Donaldson *Glen View*	72	79	74	73	298

1915 BALTUSROL GC, N.J.

*J. D. Travers *Upper Montclair*	148	73	76	297
T. McNamara *Boston*	149	74	75	298
R. G. MacDonald *Buffalo*	149	73	78	300
J. M. Barnes *Whitemarsh Valley*	146	76	79	301
L. Tellier *Canoe Brook*	146	76	79	301
M. J. Brady *Wollaston*	147	75	80	302

1916 MINIKAHDA CLUB, MINN.

*C. Evans Jr *Edgewater*	70	69	74	73	286
J. Hutchison *Allegheny*	73	75	72	68	288
J. M. Barnes *Whitemarsh Valley*	71	74	71	74	290
W. Reid *Wilmington*	70	72	79	72	293
G. Nicholls *Great Neck*	73	76	71	73	293
G. Sargent *Interlachen*	75	71	72	75	293

1919 BRAE BURN CC, MASS.

W. Hagen *Oakland Hills*	78	73	75	75	301
M. J. Brady *Oakley*	74	74	73	80	301

Play-off: Hagen 77; Brady 78

J. Hutchison *Glen View*	78	76	76	76	306
T. McNamara *New York*	80	73	79	74	306
G. McLean *Great Neck*	81	75	76	76	308
L. Tellier *Brae Burn*	73	78	82	75	308

1920 INVERNESS CLUB, OHIO

E. Ray *England*	74	73	73	75	295
H. Vardon *England*	74	73	71	78	296
J. Burke *Town and Country*	75	77	72	72	296
L. Diegel *Lake Shore*	72	74	73	77	296
J. Hutchison *Glen View*	69	76	74	77	296
*C. Evans Jr *Edgewater*	74	76	73	75	298
J. M. Barnes *Sunset Hills*	76	70	76	76	298

1921 COLUMBIA CC, MD.

J. M. Barnes *Pelham*	69	75	73	72	289
W. Hagen *New York*	79	73	72	74	298
F. McLeod *Columbia*	74	74	76	74	298
*C. Evans Jr *Edgewater*	73	78	76	75	302
*R. T. Jones Jr *Atlanta*	78	71	77	77	303
E. French *Youngstown*	75	77	74	77	303
A. Smith *Shennecossett*	75	75	79	74	303

1922 SKOKIE CC, ILL.

G. Sarazen *Highland, Pittsburgh*	72	73	75	68	288
J. L. Black *Oakland, Calif.*	71	71	75	72	289
*R. T. Jones Jr *Atlanta*	74	72	70	73	289
W. E. Mehlhorn *Shreveport*	73	71	72	74	290
W. Hagen *New York*	68	77	74	72	291
G. Duncan *England*	76	73	75	72	296

1923 INWOOD CC, N.Y.

*R. T. Jones Jr *Atlanta*	71	73	76	76	296
R. A. Cruickshank *Shackamaxon*	73	72	78	73	296

Play-off: Jones 76; Cruickshank 78

J. Hutchison *Glen View*	70	72	82	78	302
J. Forrester *Hollywood, N.J.*	75	73	77	78	303
J. J. Farrell *Quaker Ridge*	76	77	75	76	304
F. Gallett *Port Washington*	76	72	77	79	304
*W. M. Reekie *Upper Montclair*	80	74	75	75	304

1924 OAKLAND HILLS CC, MICH.

C. Walker *Englewood*	74	74	74	75	297
*R. T. Jones Jr *Atlanta*	74	73	75	78	300
W. E. Mehlhorn *Normandy, Mo.*	72	75	76	78	301
R. A. Cruickshank *Shackamaxon*	77	72	76	78	303
W. Hagen *New York*	75	75	76	77	303
M. Smith *San Francisco*	78	72	77	76	303

1925 WORCESTER CC, MASS.

W. Macfarlane *Oak Ridge*	74	67	72	78	291
*R. T. Jones Jr *Atlanta*	77	70	70	74	291

Play-off: Macfarlane 75, 72 (147);
Jones 75, 73 (148)

J. Farrell *Quaker Ridge*	71	74	69	78	292
*F. Ouimet *Woodland*	70	73	73	76	292
G. Sarazen *Fresh Meadow*	72	72	75	74	293
W. Hagen *Pasadena, Fla.*	72	76	71	74	293

1926 SCIOTO CC, OHIO

*R. T. Jones Jr *Atlanta*	70	79	71	73	293
J. Turnesa *Fairview*	71	74	72	77	294
W. E. Mehlhorn *Chicago*	68	75	76	78	297
G. Sarazen *Fresh Meadow*	78	77	72	70	297
L. Diegel *Mountain View Farm*	72	76	75	74	297
J. Farrell *Quaker Ridge*	76	79	69	73	297

1927 OAKMONT CC, PA.

T. Armour *Congressional*	78	71	76	76	301
H. Cooper *El Serreno*	74	76	74	77	301

Play-off: Armour 76; Cooper 79

G. Sarazen *Fresh Meadow*	74	74	80	74	302
E. French *Southern Pines*	75	79	77	73	304
W. E. Mehlhorn *New York*	75	77	80	73	305
W. Hagen *Pasadena, Fla.*	77	73	76	81	307

1928 OLYMPIA FIELDS CC, ILL.

J. Farrell *Quaker Ridge*	77	74	71	72	294
*R. T. Jones Jr *Atlanta*	73	71	73	77	294

Play-off: Farrell 70, 73 (143); Jones 73, 71 (144)

R. Hancock *Wilmington, N.C.*	74	77	72	72	295
W. Hagen *New York City*	75	72	73	76	296
*G. Von Elm *Tam O'Shanter*	74	72	76	74	296
J. Turnesa *Elmsford*	74	77	74	74	299
G. Sarazen *Fresh Meadow*	78	76	73	72	299
H. Ciuci *Mill River, Conn.*	70	77	72	80	299
W. W. Crowder *Cleveland*	74	74	76	75	299
W. Leach *Overbrook*	72	74	73	80	299
M. Smith *Lakeville*	75	77	75	72	299
D. Shute *Worthington, Ohio*	75	73	79	72	299
E. Dudley *Unattached*	77	79	68	75	299

1929 WINGED FOOT GC, N.Y.

*R. T. Jones *Atlanta*	69	75	71	79	294
A. Espinosa *Glencoe, Ill.*	70	72	77	75	294

Play-off: Jones 72, 69 (141); Espinosa 84, 80 (164)

G. Sarazen *Fresh Meadow*	71	71	76	78	296
D. Shute *Worthington, Ohio*	73	71	76	76	296
T. Armour *Tam O'Shanter*	74	71	76	76	297
*G. Von Elm *Tam O'Shanter*	79	70	74	74	297

1930 INTERLACHEN CC, MINN.

*R. T. Jones Jr *Atlanta*	71	73	68	75	287
M. Smith *Lakeville*	70	75	74	70	289
H. Smith *Cragston*	72	70	76	74	292
H. Cooper *Glen Elyn, Ill.*	72	72	73	76	293
J. Golden *Wee Burn*	74	73	71	76	294
T. Armour *Tam O'Shanter*	70	76	75	76	297

1931 INVERNESS CLUB, OHIO

B. Burke *Round Hill*	73	72	74	73	292
*G. Von Elm *Unattached*	75	69	73	75	292

Play-offs: Burke 73, 76 (149); Von Elm 75, 74 (149)
Burke 77, 71 (148); Von Elm 76, 73 (149)

L. Diegel *Mexico*	75	73	74	72	294
W. Cox *Brooklyn*	75	74	74	73	296
W. E. Mehlhorn *Pinewald, N.J.*	77	73	75	71	296
G. Sarazen *Lakeville*	74	78	74	70	296

1932 FRESH MEADOW CC, N.Y.

G. Sarazen *Lakeville*	74	76	70	66	286
R. A. Cruickshank *Willowbrook, N.Y.*					
	78	74	69	68	289
T. P. Perkins *Unattached*	76	69	74	70	289
L. Diegel *Mexico*	73	74	73	74	294
W. Cox *Brooklyn*	80	73	70	72	295
J. Jurado *Argentina*	74	71	75	76	296

1933 NORTH SHORE GC, ILL.

*J. Goodman *Omaha*	75	66	70	76	287
R. Guldahl *St Louis*	76	71	70	71	288
C. Wood *Hollywood*	73	74	71	72	290
W. Hagen *Unattached*	73	76	77	66	292
T. Armour *Medinah*	68	75	76	73	292
M. Dutra *Red Run*	75	73	72	74	294

1934 MERION CRICKET CLUB, PA.

O. Dutra *Brentwood, Calif.*	76	74	71	72	293
G. Sarazen *New York City*	73	72	73	76	294
W. Cox *Dyker Beach, N.Y.*	71	75	74	75	295
R. Cruickshank *Virginia CC*	71	71	77	76	295
H. Cooper *Glen Oak, Ill.*	76	74	74	71	295
B. Burke *Cleveland*	76	71	77	72	296
M. Smith *Nashville*	75	73	78	70	296

1935 OAKMONT CC, PA.

S. Parks Jr *South Hills, Pa.*	77	73	73	76	299
J. Thomson *Lakewood, Calif.*	73	73	77	78	301
W. Hagen *Detroit*	77	76	73	76	302
D. Shute *Chicago*	78	73	76	76	303
R. Mangrum *Los Angeles*	76	76	72	79	303
H. Picard *Hershey*	79	78	70	79	306
G. Sarazen *Brookfield, Conn.*	75	74	78	79	306
A. Krueger *Beloit, Wis.*	71	77	78	80	306
H. Smith *Oak Park, Ill.*	73	79	79	75	306

1936 BALTUSROL GC, N.J.

T. Manero *Sedgefield, N.C.*	73	69	73	67	282
H. E. Cooper *Glen Oak, Ill.*	71	70	70	73	284
C. Clark *Forest Hill Field, N.J.*	69	75	71	72	287
M. Smith *Glendale, Calif.*	73	73	72	70	288
H. Picard *Hershey, Pa.*	70	71	74	74	289
W. Cox *Kenwood, Md.*	74	74	69	72	289
K. Laffoon *Northmoor, Ill.*	71	74	70	74	289

1937 OAKLAND HILLS CC, MICH.

R. Guldahl *Chicago*	71	69	72	69	281
S. Snead *Greenbrier*	69	73	70	71	283
R. Cruickshank *Virginia CC*	73	73	67	72	285
H. E. Cooper *Chicago*	72	70	73	71	286
E. Dudley *Philadelphia*	70	70	71	76	287
A. Brosch *Bethpage State Park, N.Y.*					
	74	73	68	73	288

1938 CHERRY HILLS CLUB, COLO.

R. Guldahl *Braidburn, N.J.*	74	70	71	69	284
D. Metz *Mill Road Farm, Ill.*	73	68	70	79	290
H. Cooper *Chicopee*	76	69	76	71	292
T. Penna *Dayton, Ohio*	78	72	74	68	292
B. Nelson *Reading, Pa.*	77	71	74	72	294
E. Zimmerman *Columbia-Edgewater, Oreg.*					
	72	71	73	78	294

1939 PHILADELPHIA CC, PA.

B. Nelson *Reading, Pa.*	72	73	71	68	284
C. Wood *Winged Foot, N.Y.*	70	71	71	72	284
D. Shute *Huntington, W. Va.*	70	72	70	72	284

Play-off: Nelson 68, 70 (138); Wood 68, 73 (141);
Shute 76 (eliminated)

M. (Bud) Ward *Spokane, Wash.*	69	73	71	72	285
S. Snead *Greenbrier*	68	71	73	74	286
J. Bulla *Chicago*	72	71	68	76	287

1940 CANTERBURY GC, OHIO

L. Little *Bretton Woods, N.H.*	72	69	73	73	287
G. Sarazen *Brookfield Center, Conn.*					
	71	74	70	72	287

Play-off: Little 70; Sarazen 73

H. Smith *Oak Park*	69	72	78	69	288
C. Wood *Winged Foot, N.Y.*	72	73	72	72	289
B. Hogan *Century, N.Y.*	70	73	74	73	290
R. Guldahl *Chicago*	73	71	76	70	290
L. Mangrum *Oak Park*	75	70	71	74	290
B. Nelson *Inverness, Ohio*	72	74	70	74	290

1941 COLONIAL CLUB, TEX.

C. Wood *Winged Foot, N.Y.*	73	71	70	70	284
D. Shute *Chicago*	69	75	72	71	287
J. Bulla *Chicago*	75	71	72	71	289
B. Hogan *Hershey*	74	77	68	70	289
H. Barron *Fenway, N.Y.*	75	71	74	71	291
P. Runyan *Metropolis, N.Y.*	73	72	71	75	291

1946 CANTERBURY GC, OHIO

L. Mangrum *Los Angeles*	74	70	68	72	284
B. Nelson *Toledo, Ohio*	71	71	69	73	284
V. Ghezzi *Knoxville, Tenn.*	71	69	72	72	284

Play-offs: Mangrum 72; Nelson 72; Ghezzi 72
Mangrum 72; Nelson 73; Ghezzi 73

H. Barron *Fenway, N.Y.*	72	72	72	69	285
B. Hogan *Hershey*	72	68	73	72	285
J. Demaret *Houston*	71	74	73	68	286
E. S. Oliver Jr *Wilmington, Del.*	71	71	74	70	286

1947 ST LOUIS CC, MO.

L. Worsham *Oakmont*	70	70	71	71	282
S. Snead *Cascades, Va.*	72	70	70	70	282

Play-off: Worsham 69; Snead 70

A. D. (Bobby) Locke *Vereeniging (South Africa)*					
	68	74	70	73	285
E. S. Oliver Jr *Wilmington, Del.*	73	70	71	71	285
*M. (Bud) Ward *Spokane, Wash.*	69	72	73	73	287
J. Ferrier *Chicago*	71	70	74	74	289
V. J. Ghezzi *Victory Hills, Kans.*	74	73	73	69	289
L. Gibson *Blue Hills, Mo.*	69	76	73	71	289
B. Hogan *Hershey*	70	75	70	74	289
J. Palmer *Badin*	72	70	75	72	289
P. Runyan *Annandale, Calif.*	71	74	72	72	289

1948 RIVIERA CC, CALIF.

B. Hogan *Hershey*	67	72	68	69	276
J. Demaret *Houston*	71	70	68	69	278
J. Turnesa *Elmsford*	71	69	70	70	280
A. D. (Bobby) Locke *Vereeniging (South Africa)*					
	70	69	73	70	282
S. Snead *Greenbrier*	69	69	73	72	283
L. Worsham *Oakmont*	67	74	71	73	285

1949 MEDINAH CC, ILL.

C. Middlecoff *Colonial, Tenn.*	75	67	69	75	286
C. Heafner *Eastwood, N.C.*	72	71	71	73	287
S. Snead *Greenbrier*	73	73	71	70	287
J. Turnesa *Briar Hall, N.Y.*	78	69	70	72	289
A. D. (Bobby) Locke *Vereeniging (South Africa)*					
	74	71	73	71	289
B. White *Greenwood, Miss.*	74	68	70	78	290
D. Douglas *Newark, Del.*	74	73	70	73	290

1950 MERION GC, PA.

B. Hogan *Hershey*	72	69	72	74	287
L. Mangrum *Tam O'Shanter*	72	70	69	76	287
G. Fazio *Woodmont, Md.*	73	72	72	70	287

Play-off: Hogan 69; Mangrum 73; Fazio 75

E. J. (Dutch) Harrison *St Andrews, Ill.*					
	72	67	73	76	288
J. Kirkwood Jr *Kirkwood, Calif.*	71	74	74	70	289
J. Ferrier *Chicago*	71	69	74	75	289
H. Ransom *St Andrews, Ill.*	72	71	73	73	289

1951 OAKLAND HILLS CC, MICH.

B. Hogan *Hershey*	76	73	71	67	287
C. Heafner *Eastwood, N.C.*	72	75	73	69	289
A. D. (Bobby) Locke *Ohenimuri (South Africa)*					
	73	71	74	73	291
L. Mangrum *Tam O'Shanter*	75	74	74	70	293
J. Boros *Mid Pines, N.C.*	74	74	71	74	293
A. C. Besselink *Hillcrest, Mich.*	72	77	72	73	294
P. Runyan *Annandale, Calif.*	73	74	72	75	294
F. E. Hawkins *El Paso, Tex.*	76	72	75	71	294
D. Douglas *Newark, Del.*	75	70	75	74	294

1952 NORTHWOOD CLUB, TEX.

J. Boros *Mid Pines, N.C.*	71	71	68	71	281
E. S. Oliver Jr *Cog Hill, Ill.*	71	72	70	72	285
B. Hogan *Tamarisk, Calif.*	69	69	74	74	286
J. Bulla *Westmoreland, Pa.*	73	68	73	73	287
G. Fazio *Pine Valley, N.J.*	71	69	75	75	290
D. Metz *Maple City, Kans.*	70	74	76	71	291

1953 OAKMONT CC, PA.

B. Hogan *Tamarisk, Calif.*	67	72	73	71	283
S. Snead *Greenbrier, W. Va.*	72	69	72	76	289
L. Mangrum *Tam O'Shanter*	73	70	74	75	292
P. Cooper *Century, N.Y.*	78	75	71	70	294
G. Fazio *Pine Valley, N.J.*	70	71	77	76	294
J. Demaret *Concord, N.Y.*	71	76	71	76	294
T. Kroll *New Hartford*	76	71	74	74	295
D. Metz *Maple City, Kans.*	75	70	74	76	295

1954 BALTUSROL GC, N.J.

E. Furgol *Westwood, Mo.*	71	70	71	72	284
G. Littler *Thunderbird, Calif.*	70	69	76	70	285
R. Mayer *St Petersburg, Fla.*	72	71	70	73	286
L. Mangrum *Tam O'Shanter*	72	71	72	71	286
A. D. (Bobby) Locke *Ohenimuri CC (South Africa)*					
	74	70	74	70	288
T. Bolt *Memorial Park, Tex.*	72	72	73	72	289
B. Hogan *Fort Worth, Tex.*	71	70	76	72	289
S. Mayfield *Sequin, Tex.*	73	75	72	69	289
F. Haas *New Orleans*	73	73	71	72	289
*W. J. Patton *Mimosa, N.C.*	69	76	71	73	289

1955 OLYMPIC CC, CALIF.

J. Fleck *Davenport Municipal, Iowa*					
	76	69	75	67	287
B. Hogan *Fort Worth, Tex.*	72	73	72	70	287

Play-off: Fleck 69; Hogan 72

S. Snead *Greenbrier, W. Va.*	79	69	70	74	292
T. Bolt *Chattanooga*	67	77	75	73	292
J. Boros *Mid Pines, N.C.*	76	69	73	77	295
R. R. Rosburg *Palo Alto, Calif.*	78	74	67	76	295

1956 OAK HILL COUNTRY CLUB, N.Y.

C. Middlecoff *Riverlake, Tex.*	71	70	70	70	281
J. Boros *Mid Pines, N.C.*	71	71	71	69	282
B. Hogan *Fort Worth, Tex.*	72	68	72	70	282
E. Furgol *Westwood, Mo.*	71	70	73	71	285
P. Thomson *Victoria (Australia)*	70	69	75	71	285
T. Kroll *Fort Lauderdale*	72	70	70	73	285

1957 INVERNESS CLUB, OHIO

R. Mayer *St Petersburg, Fla*	70	68	74	70	282
C. Middlecoff *Riverlake, Tex.*	71	75	68	68	282

Play-off: Mayer 72; Middlecoff 79

J. Demaret *Concord International, N.Y.*					
	68	73	70	72	283
J. Boros *Mid Pines, N.C.*	69	75	70	70	284
W. Burkemo *Franklin Hills, Mich.*					
	74	73	72	65	284
K. Venturi *California*	69	71	75	71	286
F. E. Hawkins *El Paso, Tex.*	72	72	71	71	286

1958 SOUTHERN HILLS CC, OKLA.

T. Bolt *Paradise, Fla.*	71	71	69	72	283
G. Player *Killarney (South Africa)*					
	75	68	73	71	287
J. Boros *Mid Pines, N.C.*	71	75	72	71	289
G. Littler *Singing Hills, Calif.*	74	73	67	76	290
W. Burkemo *Franklin Hills, Mich.*					
	75	74	70	72	291
R. R. Rosburg *Silverado, Calif.*	75	74	72	70	291

1959 WINGED FOOT GC, N.Y.

W. Casper Jr *Apple Valley*	71	68	69	74	282
R. R. Rosburg *Palo Alto, Calif.*	75	70	67	71	283
C. Harmon *Winged Foot, N.Y.*	72	71	70	71	284
M. Souchak *Grossinger, N.Y.*	71	70	72	71	284
D. Ford *Paradise, Fla.*	72	69	72	73	286
E. Vossier *Midland, Tex.*	72	70	72	72	286
A. Palmer *Laurel Valley, Pa.*	71	69	72	74	286

1960 CHERRY HILLS CC, COLO.

A. Palmer *Laurel Valley, Pa.*	72	71	72	65	280
*J. Nicklaus *Scioto, Ohio*	71	71	69	71	282
E. J. (Dutch) Harrison *Old Warson, Mo.*					
	74	70	70	69	283
J. Boros *Mid Pines, N.C.*	73	69	68	73	283
M. Souchak *Grossinger, N.Y.*	68	67	73	75	283
E. Kroll *DeSoto Lakes, Fla.*	72	69	75	67	283
J. Fleck *El Caballero, Calif.*	70	70	72	71	283
D. Finsterwald *Tequesta, Fla.*	71	69	70	73	283

1961 OAKLAND HILLS CC, MICH.

G. Littler *Singing Hills, Calif.*	73	68	72	68	281
B. Goalby *Paradise, Fla.*	70	72	69	71	282
D. Sanders *Ojai, Calif.*	72	67	71	72	282
M. Souchak *Grossinger, N.Y.*	73	70	68	73	284
*J. Nicklaus *Scioto, Ohio*	75	69	70	70	284
D. Finsterwald *Tequesta, Fla.*	72	71	71	72	286
E. Monti *Hillcrest, Calif.*	74	67	72	73	286
D. Ford *Tuckahoe, N.Y.*	72	69	71	74	286

1962 OAKMONT CC, PA.

J. Nicklaus *Tucson National, Ariz.*					
	72	70	72	69	283
A. D. Palmer *Miami*	71	68	73	71	283

Play-off: Nicklaus 71; Palmer 74

P. Rodgers *La Jolla, Calif.*	74	70	69	72	285
B. Nichols *Midland, Tex.*	70	72	70	73	285
G. Brewer Jr *Paradise, Fla.*	73	72	73	69	287
T. Jacobs *Bermuda Dunes, Calif.*	74	71	73	70	288
G. Player *Ponte Vedra, Fla.*	71	71	72	74	288

USGA Men's Open Championship

1963 THE COUNTRY CLUB, BROOKLINE, MASS.

J. Boros *Mid Pines, N.C.*	71 74 76 72	293
J. D. Cupit *Mountain View, Calif.*		
	70 72 76 75	293
A. Palmer *Laurel Valley, Pa.*	73 69 77 74	293

Play-off: Boros 70; Cupit 73; Palmer 76

P. Harney *Sunset Oaks, Calif.*	78 70 73 73	294
B. Maxwell *Tropicana, Nev.*	73 73 75 74	295
B. Crampton *Sydney (Australia)*	74 72 75 74	295
T. Lema *San Leandro, Calif.*	71 74 74 76	295

1964 CONGRESSIONAL CC, WASHINGTON D.C.

K. Venturi *Paradise, Fla.*	72 70 66 70	278
T. Jacobs *Bermuda Dunes, Calif.*	72 64 70 76	282
R. J. Charles *De Soto Lakes, Fla.*	72 72 71 68	283
B. Casper *Mountain View, Calif.*	71 74 69 71	285
G. Brewer Jr *Dallas*	76 69 73 68	286
A. Palmer *Laurel Valley, Pa.*	68 69 75 74	286

1965 BELLERIVE CC, MO.

G. Player *Johannesburg (South Africa)*		
	70 70 71 71	282
K. Nagle *Pymble (Australia)*	68 73 72 69	282

Play-off: Player 71; Nagle 74

F. Beard *Seneca, Ky.*	74 69 70 71	284
J. Boros *Mid Pines, N.C.*	72 75 70 70	287
A. Geiberger *Carlton Oaks, Calif.*	70 76 70 71	287
R. L. Floyd *St Andrews, Ill.*	72 72 76 68	288
B. Devlin *Sydney (Australia)*	72 73 72 71	288

1966 OLYMPIC CC, CALIF.

W. Casper Jr *Peacock Gap, Calif.*	69 68 73 68	278
A. Palmer *Laurel Valley, Pa.*	71 66 70 71	278

Play-off: Casper 69; Palmer 73

J. Nicklaus *Scioto, Ohio*	71 71 69 74	285
T. Lema *Marco Island, Fla.*	71 74 70 71	286
D. Marr *Goodyear, Ariz.*	71 74 68 73	286
P. Rodgers *La Jolla, Calif.*	70 70 73 74	287

1967 BALTUSROL GC, N.J.

J. Nicklaus *Scioto, Ohio*	71 67 72 65	275
A. Palmer *Laurel Valley, Pa.*	69 68 73 69	279
D. January *Dallas*	69 72 70 70	281
W. Casper Jr *Bonita, Calif.*	69 70 71 72	282
L. Trevino *Horizon Hills, Tex.*	72 70 71 70	283
B. Goalby *Tamarisk, Calif.*	72 71 70 71	284
D. R. Beman *Bethesda, Md.*	69 71 71 73	284
G. Dickinson Jr *Lost Tree, Fla.*	70 73 68 73	284

1968 OAK HILL CC, N.Y.

L. Trevino *Horizon Hills, Tex.*	69 68 69 69	275
J. Nicklaus *Scioto, Ohio*	72 70 70 67	279
B. Yancey *Killearn, Fla.*	67 68 70 76	281
B. Nichols *Louisville, Ky.*	74 71 68 69	282
D. Bies *Seattle*	70 70 75 69	284
J. S. Spray *Cedar Rapids, Iowa*	73 75 71 65	284

1969 CHAMPIONS GC, TEX.

O. J. Moody *Yukon, Okla.*	71 70 68 72	281
D. R. Beman *Bethesda, Md.*	68 69 73 72	282
A. Geiberger *Santa Barbara, Calif.*		
	68 72 72 70	282
R. R. Rosburg *Westwood, Mo.*	70 69 72 71	282
B. Murphy Jr *Bartow, Fla.*	66 72 74 71	283
M. Barber *Woodlawn, Tex.*	67 71 68 78	284
B. Crampton *Bahama Reef*	73 72 68 71	284
A. Palmer *Laurel Valley, Pa.*	70 73 69 72	284

1970 HAZELTINE GC, MINN.

T. Jacklin *The Cloisters, Ga.*	71 70 70 70	281
D. Hill *Evergreen, Colo.*	75 69 71 73	288
R. J. Lunn *Haggin Oaks, Calif.*	77 72 70 70	289
R. J. Charles *Christchurch (New Zealand)*		
	76 71 75 67	289
K. Still *Fircrest, Wash.*	78 71 71 71	291
M. Barber *Woodlawn, Tex.*	75 75 72 70	292

1971 MERION GC, PA.

L. Trevino *El Paso, Tex.*	70 72 69 69	280
J. Nicklaus *Scioto, Ohio*	69 72 68 71	280

Play-off: Trevino 68; Nicklaus 71

R. R. Rosburg *French Lick, Ind.*	71 72 70 69	282
J. J. Colbert Jr *Prairie Creek, Ark.*	69 69 73 71	282
*J. Simons *Butler, Pa.*	71 71 65 76	283
J. L. Miller *San Francisco, GC*	70 73 70 70	283
G. Archer *Gilroy, Calif.*	71 70 70 72	283

1972 PEBBLE BEACH, CALIF.

J. Nicklaus *Scioto, Ohio*	71 73 72 74	290
B. Crampton *Australia*	74 70 73 76	293
A. Palmer *Laurel Valley, Pa.*	77 68 73 76	294
L. Trevino *El Paso, Tex.*	74 72 71 78	295
H. Blancas *Houston, Tex.*	74 70 76 75	295
K. Zarley *Houston, Tex.*	71 73 73 79	296

1973 OAKMONT CC, PA.

J. Miller *San Francisco, GC*	71 69 76 63	279
J. Schlee *Preston Trails, Tex.*	73 70 67 70	280
T. Weiskopf *Columbus, Ohio*	73 69 69 70	281
A. Palmer *Laurel Valley, Pa.*	71 71 68 72	282
L. Trevino *El Paso, Tex.*	70 72 70 70	282
J. Nicklaus *Scioto, Ohio*	71 69 74 68	282

1974 WINGED FOOT GC, N.Y.

H. Irwin *Boulder CC, Calif.*	73 70 71 73	287
F. Fezler *Indian Wells CG, Calif.*	75 70 74 70	289
L. Graham *Richland CC, Tenn.*	71 75 74 70	290
B. Yancey *Palm Aire CC, Fla.*	76 69 73 72	290
A. Palmer *Laurel Valley, Pa.*	73 70 73 76	292
J. Colbert *Overland Pk, Kan.*	72 77 69 74	292
T. Watson *Kansas City CC*	73 71 69 79	292

(Three rounds of 12 holes)

1860 PRESTWICK

W. Park *Musselburgh*	174
T. Morris Sr *Prestwick*	176
A. Strath *St Andrews*	180
R. Andrew *Perth*	191
G. D. Brown	192
C. Hunter *Prestwick*	195

1861 PRESTWICK

T. Morris Sr *Prestwick*	163
W. Park *Musselburgh*	167
W. Dow *Musselburgh*	171
D. Park *Musselburgh*	172
R. Andrew *Perth*	175
P. McEwen	178

1862 PRESTWICK

T. Morris Sr *Prestwick*	163
W. Park *Musselburgh*	176
C. Hunter *Prestwick, St Nicholas*	178
W. Dow *Musselburgh*	181
J. Knight	186
J. J. Johnstone	208

1863 PRESTWICK

W. Park *Musselburgh*	168
T. Morris Sr *Prestwick*	170
D. Park *Musselburgh*	172
A. Strath *St Andrews*	174
G. D. Brown	176
R. Andrew *Perth*	178

1864 PRESTWICK

T. Morris Sr *Prestwick*	167
A. Strath *St Andrews*	169
R. Andrew *Perth*	175
W. Park *Musselburgh*	177

1865 PRESTWICK

A. Strath *St Andrews*	162
W. Park *Musselburgh*	164
R. Kirk *St Andrews*	173
T. Morris Sr *Prestwick*	174
W. Doleman *Glasgow*	178
R. Andrew *Perth*	179

1866 PRESTWICK

W. Park *Musselburgh*	169
D. Park *Musselburgh*	171
R. Andrew *Perth*	176
T. Morris Sr *St Andrews*	178
R. Kirk *St Andrews*	180
A. Strath *St Andrews*	182

1867 PRESTWICK

T. Morris Sr *St Andrews*	170
W. Park *Musselburgh*	172
A. Strath *St Andrews*	174

1868 PRESTWICK

T. Morris Jr *St Andrews*	157
R. Andrew *Perth*	159
W. Park *Musselburgh*	162
R. Kirk *St Andrews*	171
J. Allen	172
C. Hunter *Prestwick*	172

1869 PRESTWICK

T. Morris Jr *St Andrews*		154
T. Morris Sr *St Andrews*		157
Mr Ferguson *Prestwick*		165
T. Dunn		167
R. Kirk *St Andrews*		168
D. Strath *St Andrews*		169

1870 PRESTWICK

T. Morris Jr *St Andrews*		149
R. Kirk *St Andrews*		161
D. Strath *St Andrews*		161
T. Morris Sr *St Andrews*		162
W. Doleman *Glasgow*		169
J. Anderson		174

1871 NO CHAMPIONSHIP

1872 PRESTWICK

T. Morris Jr *St Andrews*		166
D. Strath *St Andrews*		169
W. Doleman *Musselburgh*		177
D. Park *Musselburgh*		179
T. Morris Sr *St Andrews*		179
C. Hunter *Prestwick*		189

1873 ST ANDREWS

T. Kidd *St Andrews*		179
J. Anderson *St Andrews*		

1874 MUSSELBURGH

M. Park *Musselburgh*		159
T. Morris Jr *St Andrews*		161
G. Paxton *Musselburgh*		162

1875 PRESTWICK

W. Park *Musselburgh*		166
R. Martin *St Andrews*		168
M. Park *Musselburgh*		171
R. Ferguson *Musselburgh*		172
J. Rennie		177
D. Strath *St Andrews*		178

1876 ST ANDREWS

B. Martin *St Andrews*		176
D. Strath *St Andrews*		176

Martin was awarded the title when Strath refused to play-off

W. Park *Musselburgh*		183
J. O. F. Morris Sr *St Andrews*		185
W. Thomson *Elie*		185
M. Park *Musselburgh*		185

1877 MUSSELBURGH

J. Anderson *St Andrews*		160
B. Pringle *Musselburgh*		162
B. Ferguson *Musselburgh*		164
W. Cosgrove *Musselburgh*		164

1878 PRESTWICK

J. Anderson *St Andrews*		157
R. Kirk *St Andrews*		159
J. O. F. Morris *St Andrews*		161
J. Ball *Royal Liverpool*		165
B. Martin *St Andrews*		165
W. Park *Musselburgh*		166

1879 ST ANDREWS

J. Anderson *St Andrews*		170
A. Kirkaldy *St Andrews*		170

Anderson won play-off

1880 MUSSELBURGH

B. Ferguson *Musselburgh*		162
P. Paxton *Musselburgh*		167
N. Cosgrove *Musselburgh*		168

1881 PRESTWICK

B. Ferguson *Musselburgh*		170
J. Anderson *St Andrews*		173
N. Cosgrove *Musselburgh*		177
B. Martin *St Andrews*		178
T. Morris Sr *St Andrews*		181
W. Campbell *Prestwick*		
W. Park Jr *Musselburgh*		

1882 ST ANDREWS

B. Ferguson *Musselburgh*		171
W. Fernie *Dumfries*		

1883 MUSSELBURGH

W. Fernie *Dumfries* (won play-off)		159
B. Ferguson *Musselburgh*		159
F. Boothby		163

1884 PRESTWICK

J. Simpson *Carnoustie*		160
W. Fernie *Troon*		164
D. Rolland		164
W. Park Jr *Musselburgh*		169
W. Campbell *Prestwick*		169
B. Sayers *North Berwick*		171
T. Dunn		171
G. Fernie		171

1885 ST ANDREWS

B. Martin *St Andrews*		171
A. Simpson *Carnoustie*		172
D. Ayton *St Andrews*		172

1886 MUSSELBURGH

D. Brown *Musselburgh*		157
W. Campbell *Musselburgh*		159
B. Campbell *Musselburgh*		160

1887 PRESTWICK

W. Park Jr *Musselburgh*		161
B. Martin *St Andrews*		162
W. Campbell *Prestwick*		164
J. E. Laidlay *Honourable Company*		166
B. Sayers *North Berwick*		168
A. Simpson		168

1888 ST ANDREWS

J. Burns *Warwick*	86	85	171
D. Anderson Jr *St Andrews*	87	85	172
B. Sayers *North Berwick*	85	87	172
W. Campbell *Prestwick*	84	90	174
L. Balfour *Edinburgh*	86	89	175
A. Kirkaldy *St Andrews*	87	89	176
D. Grant *North Berwick*	88	88	176

1889 MUSSELBURGH

W. Park Jr *Musselburgh*	78	77	155
A. Kirkaldy *St Andrews*	77	78	155

Play-off: Park beat Kirkaldy 158 to 163

B. Sayers *North Berwick*	79	80	159
J. E. Laidlay *Honourable Company*	81	81	162
D. Brown *Musselburgh*	82	80	162
W. Fernie *Troon*	84	80	164

1890 PRESTWICK

J. Ball *Royal Liverpool*	82	82	164
W. Fernie *Troon*	85	82	167
A. Simpson *Carnoustie*	85	82	167
W. Park Jr *Musselburgh*	90	80	170
A. Kirkaldy *St Andrews*	81	89	170
H. Hutchinson *Royal North Devon*	87	85	172

1891 ST ANDREWS

H. Kirkaldy *St Andrews*	83	83	166
W. Fernie *Troon*	84	84	168
A. Kirkaldy *St Andrews*	84	84	168
S. M. Fergusson *Royal and Ancient*	86	84	170
W. D. More *Chester*	84	87	171
W. Park Jr *Musselburgh*	88	85	173

(From 1892 the competition was extended to 72 holes)

1892 MUIRFIELD

H. Hilton *Royal Liverpool*	78	81	72	74	305
J. Ball Jr *Royal Liverpool*	75	80	74	79	308
J. Kirkaldy *St Andrews*	77	83	73	75	308
A. Herd *Huddersfield*	77	78	77	76	308
J. Kay *Seaton Carew*					312
B. Sayers *North Berwick*					

1893 PRESTWICK

W. Auchterlonie *St Andrews*	78	81	81	82	322
J. E. Laidlay *Honourable Company*	80	83	80	81	324
A. Herd *Huddersfield*	82	81	78	84	325
H. Kirkaldy *St Andrews*	83	79	82	82	326
A. Kirkaldy *St Andrews*	85	82	82	77	326
J. Kay *Seaton Carew*	81	81	80	85	327
R. Simpson *Carnoustie*	81	81	80	85	327

1894 SANDWICH

J. H. Taylor *Winchester*	84	80	81	81	326
D. Rolland *Limpsfield*	86	79	84	82	331
A. Kirkaldy *St Andrews*	86	79	83	84	332
A. Toogood *Eltham*	84	85	82	82	333
W. Fernie *Troon*	84	84	86	80	334
H. Vardon *Bury St Edmunds*	86	86	82	80	334
B. Sayers *North Berwick*	85	81	84	84	334

1895 ST ANDREWS

J. H. Taylor *Winchester*	86	78	80	78	322
A. Herd *Huddersfield*	82	77	82	85	326
A. Kirkaldy *St Andrews*	81	83	84	84	332
G. Pulford *Royal Liverpool*	84	81	83	87	335
A. Simpson *Aberdeen*	88	85	78	85	336
W. Fernie *Troon*	86	79	86	86	337
D. Brown *Malvern*	81	89	83	84	337
D. Anderson *Panmure*	86	83	84	84	337

1896 MUIRFIELD

H. Vardon *Ganton*	83	78	78	77	316
J. H. Taylor *Winchester*	77	78	81	80	316

Play-off: Vardon beat Taylor 157 to 161

F. G. Tait *Black Watch*	83	75	84	77	319
W. Fernie *Troon*	78	79	82	80	319
A. Herd *Huddersfield*	72	84	79	85	320
J. Braid *Romford*	83	81	79	80	323

1897 HOYLAKE

H. H. Hilton *Royal Liverpool*	80	75	84	75	314
J. Braid *Romford*	80	74	82	79	315
F. G. Tait *Black Watch*	79	79	80	79	317
G. Pulford *Royal Liverpool*	80	79	79	79	317
A. Herd *Huddersfield*	78	81	79	80	318
H. Vardon *Ganton*	84	80	80	76	320

1898 PRESTWICK

H. Vardon *Ganton*	79	75	77	76	307
W. Park *Musselburgh*	76	75	78	79	308
H. H. Hilton *Royal Liverpool*	76	81	77	75	309
J. H. Taylor *Winchester*	78	78	77	79	312
F. G. Tait *Black Watch*	81	77	75	72	315
D. Kinnell *Leven*	80	77	79	80	316

1899 SANDWICH

H. Vardon *Ganton*	76	76	81	77	310
J. White *Seaford*	79	79	82	75	315
A. Kirkaldy *St Andrews*	81	79	82	77	319
J. H. Taylor *Mid-Surrey*	77	76	83	84	320
J. Braid *Romford*	78	78	83	84	322
W. Fernie *Troon*	79	73	82	78	322

1900 ST ANDREWS

J. H. Taylor *Mid-Surrey*	79	77	78	75	309
H. Vardon *Ganton*	79	81	80	78	317
J. Braid *Romford*	82	81	80	79	322
J. White *Seaford*	80	81	82	80	323
W. Auchterlonie *St Andrews*	81	85	80	80	326
W. Park Jr *Musselburgh*	80	83	81	84	328

1901 MUIRFIELD

J. Braid *Romford*	79	76	74	80	309
H. Vardon *Ganton*	77	78	79	78	312
J. H. Taylor *Royal Mid-Surrey*	79	83	74	77	313
H. H. Hilton *Royal Liverpool*	89	80	75	76	320
A. Herd *Huddersfield*	87	81	81	76	325
J. White *Seaford*	82	82	80	82	326

1902 HOYLAKE

A. Herd *Huddersfield*	77	76	73	81	307
H. Vardon *South Herts*	72	77	80	79	308
J. Braid *Walton Heath*	78	76	80	74	308
R. Maxwell *Honourable Company*	79	77	79	74	309
T. Vardon *Ilkley*	80	76	78	79	313
J. H. Taylor *Mid-Surrey*	81	76	77	80	314
D. Kinnell *Leven*	78	80	79	77	314
H. Hilton *Royal Liverpool*	79	76	81	78	314

1903 PRESTWICK

H. Vardon *South Herts*	73	77	72	78	300
T. Vardon *Ilkley*	76	81	75	74	306
J. White *Sunningdale*	77	78	74	79	308
A. Herd *Huddersfield*	73	83	76	77	309
J. Braid *Walton Heath*	77	79	79	75	310
R. Thomson	83	78	77	76	314
A. H. Scott	77	77	83	77	314

1904 SANDWICH

J. White *Sunningdale*	80	75	72	69	296
J. Braid *Walton Heath*	77	80	69	71	297
J. H. Taylor *Mid-Surrey*	77	78	74	68	297
T. Vardon *Ilkley*	77	77	75	72	301
H. Vardon *South Herts*	76	73	79	74	302
J. Sherlock *Stoke Poges*	83	71	78	77	309

1905 ST ANDREWS

J. Braid *Walton Heath*	81	78	78	81	318
J. H. Taylor *Mid-Surrey*	80	85	78	80	323
R. Jones *Wimbledon*	81	77	87	78	323
J. Kinnell *Purley Downs*	82	79	82	81	324
A. Massy *La Boulie*	81	80	82	82	325
E. Gray *Littlehampton*	82	81	84	78	325

1906 MUIRFIELD

J. Braid *Walton Heath*	77	76	74	73	300
J. H. Taylor *Mid-Surrey*	77	72	75	80	304
H. Vardon *South Herts*	77	73	77	78	305
J. Graham Jr *Royal Liverpool*	71	79	78	78	306
R. Jones *Wimbledon Park*	74	78	73	83	308
A. Massy *La Boulie*	76	80	76	78	310

1907 HOYLAKE

A. Massy *La Boulie*	76	81	78	77	312
J. H. Taylor *Mid-Surrey*	79	79	76	80	314
T. Vardon *Sandwich*	81	81	80	75	317
G. Pulford *Royal Liverpool*	81	78	80	78	317
E. Ray *Ganton*	83	80	79	76	318
J. Braid *Walton Heath*	82	85	75	76	318

1908 PRESTWICK

J. Braid *Walton Heath*	70	72	77	72	291
T. Ball *West Lancashire*	76	73	76	74	299
E. Ray *Ganton*	79	71	75	76	301
A. Herd *Huddersfield*	74	74	79	75	302
H. Vardon *South Herts*	79	78	74	75	306
D. Kinnell *Prestwick St Nicholas*	75	73	80	78	306

1909 DEAL

J. H. Taylor *Mid-Surrey*	74	73	74	74	295
J. Braid *Walton Heath*	79	73	73	74	299
T. Ball *West Lancashire*	74	75	76	76	301
C. Johns *Southdown*	72	76	79	75	302
T. G. Renouf *Manchester*	76	78	76	73	303
E. Ray *Ganton*	77	76	76	75	304

1910 ST ANDREWS

J. Braid *Walton Heath*	76	73	74	76	299
A. Herd *Huddersfield*	78	74	75	76	303
G. Duncan *Hanger Hill*	73	77	71	83	304
L. Ayton *Bishops Stortford*	78	76	75	77	306
E. Ray *Ganton*	76	77	74	81	308
W. Smith *Mexico*	77	71	80	80	308
J. Robson *West Surrey*	75	80	77	76	308

1911 SANDWICH

H. Vardon *South Herts*	74	74	75	80	303
A. Massy *St Jean de Lux*	75	78	74	76	303

Play-off: Vardon won; Massy conceded at the 35th hole

H. Hilton *Royal Liverpool*	76	74	78	76	304
A. Herd *Coombe Hill*	77	73	76	78	304
E. Ray *Ganton*	76	72	79	78	305
J. Braid *Walton Heath*	78	75	74	78	305
J. H. Taylor *Mid-Surrey*	72	76	78	79	305

1912 MUIRFIELD

E. Ray *Oxhey*	71	73	76	75	295
H. Vardon *South Herts*	75	72	81	71	299
J. Braid *Walton Heath*	77	71	77	78	303
G. Duncan *Hanger Hill*	72	77	78	78	305
L. Ayton *Bishops Stortford*	74	80	75	79	308
A. Herd *Coombe Hill*	76	81	76	76	309

1913 HOYLAKE

J. H. Taylor *Mid-Surrey*	73	75	77	79	304
E. Ray *Oxhey*	73	74	81	84	312
H. Vardon *South Herts*	79	75	79	80	313
M. Moran *Dollymount*	76	74	89	74	313
J. J. McDermott *USA*	75	80	77	83	315
T. G. Renouf *Manchester*	75	78	84	78	315

1914 PRESTWICK

H. Vardon *South Herts*	73	77	78	78	306
J. H. Taylor *Mid-Surrey*	74	78	74	83	309
H. B. Simpson *St Annes Old*	77	80	78	75	310
A. Mitchell *Sonning*	76	78	79	79	312
T. Williamson *Notts*	75	79	79	79	312
R. G. Wilson *Croham Hurst*	76	77	80	80	313

1920 DEAL

G. Duncan *Hanger Hill*	80	80	71	72	303
A. Herd *Coombe Hill*	72	81	77	75	305
E. Ray *Oxhey*	72	83	78	73	306
A. Mitchell *North Foreland*	74	73	84	76	307
L. Holland *Northampton*	80	78	71	79	308
J. Barnes *USA*	79	74	77	79	309

1921 ST ANDREWS

J. Hutchison *USA*	72	75	79	70	296
R. H. Wethered *R and A*	78	75	72	71	296
T. Kerrigan *USA*	74	80	72	72	298
A. G. Havers *West Lancs*	76	74	77	72	299
G. Duncan *Hanger Hill*	74	75	78	74	301

Play-off: Hutchison 150 74 76; Wethered 159 77 82

1922 SANDWICH

W. Hagen *USA*	76	73	79	72	300
G. Duncan *Hanger Hill*	76	75	81	69	301
J. Barnes *USA*	75	76	77	73	301
J. Hutchison *USA*	79	74	73	76	302
C. A. Whitcombe *Dorchester*	77	79	72	75	303
J. H. Taylor *Mid-Surrey*	73	78	76	77	304

1923 TROON

A. G. Havers *Coombe Hill*	73	73	73	76	295
W. Hagen *USA*	76	71	74	75	296
M. Smith *USA*	80	73	69	75	297
J. Kirkwood *Australia*	72	79	69	78	298
T. R. Fernie *Turnberry*	73	78	74	75	300
G. Duncan *Hanger Hill*	79	75	74	74	302
C. A. Whitcombe *Lansdowne*	70	76	74	82	302

1924 HOYLAKE

W. Hagen *USA*	77	73	74	77	301
E. R. Whitcombe *Came Down*	77	70	77	78	302
M. Smith *USA*	76	74	77	77	304
F. Ball *Langley Park*	78	75	74	77	304
J. H. Taylor *Mid-Surrey*	75	74	79	79	307
G. Duncan *Hanger Hill*	74	79	74	81	308
A. Boomer *St Cloud, Paris*	75	78	76	79	308

1925 PRESTWICK

J. Barnes *USA*	70	77	79	74	300
A. Compston *North Manchester*	76	75	75	75	301
E. Ray *Oxhey*	77	76	75	73	301
M. Smith *USA*	76	69	76	82	303
A. Mitchell *Unattached*	77	76	75	77	305

1926 ROYAL LYTHAM

R. T. Jones Jr *USA*	72	72	73	74	291
A. Watrous *USA*	71	75	69	78	293
W. Hagen *USA*	68	77	74	76	295
G. Von Elm *USA*	75	72	76	72	295
A. Mitchell *Unattached*	78	78	72	71	299
T. Barber *Cavendish*	77	73	78	71	299

1927 ST ANDREWS

R. T. Jones Jr *USA*	68	72	73	72	285
A. Boomer *St Cloud*	76	70	73	72	291
F. Robson *Cooden Beach*	76	72	69	74	291
J. Kirkwood *Australia*	72	72	75	74	293
E. R. Whitcombe *Bournemouth*	74	73	73	73	293
C. A. Whitcombe *Crews Hill*	74	76	71	75	296

1928 SANDWICH

W. Hagen *USA*	75	73	72	72	292
G. Sarazen *USA*	72	76	73	73	294
A. Compston *Unattached*	75	74	73	73	295
P. Alliss *Berlin*	75	76	75	72	298
F. Robson *Cooden Beach*	79	73	73	73	298
J. Jurado *Argentina*	74	71	76	80	301
A. Boomer *St Cloud*	79	73	77	72	301
J. Barnes *USA*	81	73	76	71	301

1929 MUIRFIELD

W. Hagen *USA*	75	67	75	75	292
J. Farrell *USA*	72	75	76	75	298
L. Diegel *USA*	71	69	82	77	299
A. Mitchell *St Albans*	72	72	78	78	300
P. Alliss *Berlin*	69	76	76	79	300
R. Cruickshank *USA*	73	74	78	76	301

1930 HOYLAKE

R. T. Jones Jr *USA*	70	72	74	75	291
L. Diegel *USA*	74	73	71	75	293
M. Smith *USA*	70	77	75	71	293
F. Robson *Cooden Beach*	71	72	78	75	296
H. Smith *USA*	72	73	78	73	296
A. Compston *Coombe Hill*	74	73	68	82	297
J. Barnes *USA*	71	77	72	77	297

1931 CARNOUSTIE

T. D. Armour *USA*	73	75	77	71	296
J. Jurado *Argentina*	76	71	73	77	297
P. Alliss *Berlin*	74	78	73	73	298
G. Sarazen *USA*	74	76	75	73	298
M. Smith *USA*	75	77	71	76	299
J. Farrell *USA*	72	77	75	75	299

1932 PRINCE'S

G. Sarazen *USA*	70	69	70	74	283
M. Smith *USA*	71	76	71	70	288
A. G. Havers *Sandy Lodge*	74	71	68	76	289
C. A. Whitcombe *Crews Hill*	71	73	73	75	292
P. Alliss *Beaconsfield*	71	71	78	72	292
A. H. Padgham *Royal Ashdown Forest*	76	72	74	70	292

1933 ST ANDREWS

D. Shute *USA*	73	73	73	73	292
C. Wood *USA*	77	72	68	75	292
S. Easterbrook *Knowle*	73	72	71	77	293
G. Sarazen *USA*	72	73	73	75	293
L. Diegel *USA*	75	70	71	77	293
O. Dutra *USA*	76	76	70	72	294

1934 SANDWICH

T. H. Cotton *Waterloo (Brussels)*	67	65	72	79	283
S. F. Brews *Durban (South Africa)*	76	71	70	71	288
A. H. Padgham *Sundridge Park*	71	70	75	74	290
M. Smith *USA*	77	71	72	72	292
J. Kirkwood *USA*	74	69	71	78	292
M. Dallemagne *St Germain (France)*	71	73	71	77	292

1935 MUIRFIELD

A. Perry *Leatherhead*	69	75	67	72	283
A. Padgham *Sundridge Park*	70	72	74	71	287
C. Whitcombe *Crews Hill*	71	68	73	76	288
B. Gadd *Brand Hall*	72	75	71	71	289
W. L. Little *Presido (USA)*	75	71	74	69	289
H. Picard *Hershey (USA)*	72	73	72	75	292

1936 HOYLAKE

A. H. Padgham *Sundridge Park*	73	72	71	71	287
J. Adams *Romford*	71	73	71	73	288
T. H. Cotton *Waterloo (Belgium)*	73	72	70	74	289
M. Dallemagne *St Germain (France)*	73	72	75	69	289
P. Alliss *Leeds Municipal*	74	72	74	71	291
T. Green *Burnham Beeches*	74	72	70	75	291
G. Sarazen *USA*	73	75	70	73	291

1937 CARNOUSTIE

T. H. Cotton *Ashridge*	74	72	73	71	290
R. A. Whitcombe *Parkstone*	72	70	74	76	292
C. Lacey *USA*	76	75	70	72	293
C. A. Whitcombe *Crews Hill*	73	71	74	76	294
B. Nelson *USA*	75	76	71	74	296
E. Dudley *USA*	70	74	78	75	297

1938 SANDWICH

R. A. Whitcombe *Parkstone*	71	71	75	78	295
J. Adams *Royal Liverpool*	70	71	78	78	297
T. H. Cotton *Ashridge*	74	73	77	74	298
A. H. Padgham *Sundridge Park*	74	72	75	82	303
J. J. Busson *Pannal*	71	69	83	80	303
R. Burton *Sale*	71	69	78	85	303
A. Dailey *Wanstead*	73	72	80	78	303

1939 ST ANDREWS

R. Burton *Sale*	70	72	77	71	290
J. Bulla *Chicago*	77	71	71	73	292
J. Fallon *Huddersfield*	71	73	71	79	294
W. Shankland *Templenewsam*	72	73	72	77	294
A. Perry *Leatherhead*	71	74	73	76	294
R. A. Whitcombe *Parkstone*	71	75	74	74	294
S. L. King *Knole Park*	74	72	75	73	294

1946 ST ANDREWS

S. Snead *USA*	71	70	74	75	290
A. D. Locke *South Africa*	69	74	75	76	294
J. Bulla *USA*	71	72	72	79	294
C. H. Ward *Little Aston*	73	73	73	76	295
T. H. Cotton *Royal Mid-Surrey*	70	70	76	79	295
D. J. Rees *Hindhead*	75	67	73	80	295
N. Von Nida *Australia*	70	76	74	75	295

1947 HOYLAKE

F. Daly *Balmoral (Belfast)*	73	70	78	72	293
R. W. Horne *Hendon*	77	74	72	71	294
F. R. Stranahan *USA*	71	79	72	72	294
W. Shankland *Templenewsam*	76	74	75	70	295
R. Burton *Coombe Hill*	77	71	77	71	296
C. H. Ward *Little Aston*	76	73	76	72	297
S. L. King *Wildernesse*	75	72	77	73	297
A. Lees *Dore and Totley*	75	74	72	76	297
J. Bulla *USA*	80	72	74	71	297
T. H. Cotton *Royal Mid-Surrey*	69	78	74	76	297
N. Von Nida *Australia*	74	76	71	76	297

1948 MUIRFIELD

T. H. Cotton *Royal Mid-Surrey*	71	66	75	72	284
F. Daly *Balmoral*	72	71	73	73	289
N. G. Von Nida *Australia*	71	72	76	71	290
R. de Vicenzo *Argentina*	70	73	72	75	290
J. Hargreaves *Sutton Coldfield*	76	68	73	73	290
C. H. Ward *Little Aston*	69	72	75	74	290

1949 SANDWICH

A. D. Locke *South Africa*	69	76	68	70	283
H. Bradshaw *Kilcroney (Eire)*	68	77	68	70	283
R. de Vicenzo *Argentina*	68	75	73	69	285
S. L. King *Knole Park*	71	69	74	72	286
C. H. Ward *Little Aston*	73	71	70	72	286
A. Lees *Dore and Totley*	74	70	72	71	287
M. Faulkner *Royal Mid-Surrey*	71	71	71	74	287

Play-off: Locke 135, Bradshaw 147

1950 TROON

A. D. Locke *South Africa*	69	72	70	68	279
R. de Vicenzo *Argentina*	72	71	68	70	281
F. Daly *Balmoral, Belfast*	75	72	69	66	282
D. J. Rees *South Herts*	71	68	72	71	282
E. Moore *South Africa*	74	68	73	68	283
M. Faulkner *Royal Mid-Surrey*	72	70	70	71	283

1951 ROYAL PORTRUSH

M. Faulkner *Unattached*	71	70	70	74	285
A. Cerda *Argentina*	74	72	71	70	287
C. H. Ward *Little Aston*	75	73	74	68	290
F. Daly *Balmoral*	74	70	75	73	292
J. Adams *Wentworth*	68	77	75	72	292
A. D. Locke *South Africa*	71	74	74	73	293
W. Shankland *Templenewsam*	73	76	72	72	293
N. Sutton *Leigh*	73	70	74	76	293
H. Weetman *Croham Hurst*	73	71	75	74	293
P. W. Thomson *Australia*	70	75	73	75	293

1952 ROYAL LYTHAM

A. D. Locke *South Africa*	69	71	74	73	287
P. W. Thomson *Australia*	68	73	77	70	288
F. Daly *Balmoral*	67	69	77	76	289
T. H. Cotton *Royal Mid-Surrey*	75	74	74	71	294
A. Cerda *Argentina*	73	73	76	73	295
S. L. King *Knole Park*	71	74	74	76	295

1953 CARNOUSTIE

B. Hogan *USA*	73 71 70 68	282
F. R. Stranahan *USA*	70 74 73 69	286
D. J. Rees *South Herts*	72 70 73 71	286
P. W. Thomson *Australia*	72 72 71 71	286
A. Cerda *Argentina*	75 71 69 71	286
R. de Vicenzo *Argentina*	72 71 71 73	287

1954 ROYAL BIRKDALE

P. W. Thomson *Australia*	72 71 69 71	283
S. S. Scott *Carlisle City*	76 67 69 72	284
D. J. Rees *South Herts*	72 71 69 72	284
A. D. Locke *South Africa*	74 71 69 70	284
J. Adams *Royal Mid-Surrey*	73 75 69 69	286
A. Cerda *Argentina*	71 71 73 71	286
J. Turnesa *USA*	72 72 71 71	286

1955 ST ANDREWS

P. W. Thomson *Australia*	71 68 70 72	281
J. Fallon *Huddersfield*	73 67 73 70	283
F. Jowle *Edgbaston*	70 71 69 74	284
A. D. Locke *South Africa*	74 69 70 72	285
A. Cerda *Argentina*	73 71 71 71	286
K. Bousfield *Coombe Hill*	71 75 70 70	286
H. Weetman *Croham Hurst*	71 71 70 74	286
B. J. Hunt *Hartsbourne*	70 71 74 71	286
F. van Donck *Belgium*	71 72 71 72	286

1956 HOYLAKE

P. W. Thomson *Australia*	70 70 72 74	286
F. van Donck *Belgium*	71 74 70 74	289
R. de Vicenzo *Mexico*	71 70 79 70	290
G. Player *South Africa*	71 76 73 71	291
J. Panton *Glenbervie*	74 76 72 70	292
T. H. Cotton *Temple*	72 76 71 74	293
E. Bertolino *Argentina*	69 72 76 76	293

1957 ST ANDREWS

A. D. Locke *South Africa*	69 72 68 70	279
P. W. Thomson *Australia*	73 69 70 70	282
E. C. Brown *Buchanan Castle*	67 72 73 71	283
A. Miguel *Spain*	72 72 69 72	285
D. C. Thomas *Sudbury*	72 74 70 70	286
T. B. Haliburton *Wentworth*	72 73 68 73	286
W. D. Smith *Prestwick*	71 72 72 71	286
F. van Donck *Belgium*	72 68 74 72	286

1958 ROYAL LYTHAM

P. W. Thomson *Australia*	66 72 67 73	278
D. C. Thomas *Sudbury*	70 68 69 71	278

Play-off: Thomson (68, 71) 139; Thomas (69, 74) 143

E. C. Brown *Buchanan Castle*	73 70 65 71	279
C. O'Connor *Killarney*	67 68 73 71	279
F. van Donck *Belgium*	70 70 67 74	281
L. Ruiz *Argentina*	71 65 72 73	281

1959 MUIRFIELD

G. Player *South Africa*	75 71 70 68	284
F. van Donck *Belgium*	70 70 73 73	286
F. Bullock *Prestwick St Ninians*	68 70 74 74	286
S. S. Scott *Roehampton*	73 70 73 71	287
C. O'Connor *Royal Dublin*	73 74 72 69	288
R. R. Jack *Dullatur*	71 75 68 74	288
S. L. King *Knole Park*	70 74 68 76	288
J. Panton *Glenbervie*	72 72 71 73	288

1960 ST ANDREWS

K. D. G. Nagle *Australia*	69 67 71 71	278
A. Palmer *USA*	70 71 70 68	279
B. J. Hunt *Hartsbourne*	72 73 71 66	282
H. R. Henning *South Africa*	72 72 69 69	282
R. de Vicenzo *Argentina*	67 67 75 73	282
G. B. Wolstenholme *Sunningdale*	74 70 71 68	283

1961 ROYAL BIRKDALE

A. Palmer *USA*	70 73 69 72	284
D. J. Rees *South Herts*	68 74 71 72	285
C. O'Connor *Royal Dublin*	71 77 67 73	288
N. C. Coles *Coombe Hill*	70 77 69 72	288
E. C. Brown *Unattached*	73 76 70 70	289
K. D. G. Nagle *Australia*	68 75 75 71	289

1962 TROON

A. Palmer *USA*	71 69 67 69	276
K. D. G. Nagle *Australia*	71 71 70 70	282
B. Huggett *Romford*	75 71 74 69	289
P. Rodgers *USA*	75 70 72 72	289
R. Charles *NZ*	75 70 70 75	290
S. Snead *USA*	76 73 72 71	292
P. W. Thomson *Australia*	70 77 75 70	292

1963 ROYAL LYTHAM

R. J. Charles *NZ*	68 72 66 71	277
P. Rodgers *USA*	67 68 73 69	277

Play-off: Charles 69 71 140; Rodgers 72 76 148

J. Nicklaus *USA*	71 67 70 70	278
K. D. G. Nagle *Australia*	69 70 73 71	283
P. W. Thomson *Australia*	67 69 71 78	285
C. O'Connor *Royal Dublin*	74 68 76 68	286

1964 ST ANDREWS

A. Lema *USA*	73 68 68 70	279
J. Nicklaus *USA*	76 74 66 68	284
R. de Vicenzo *Argentina*	76 72 70 67	285
B. J. Hunt *Hartsbourne*	73 74 70 70	287
B. Devlin *Australia*	72 72 73 73	290
C. O'Connor *Royal Dublin*	71 73 74 73	291
H. Weetman *Selsdon Park*	72 71 75 73	291

1965 ROYAL BIRKDALE

P. W. Thomson *Australia*	74 68 72 71	285
C. O'Connor *Royal Dublin*	69 73 74 71	287
B. Huggett *Romford*	73 68 76 70	287
R. de Vicenzo *Argentina*	74 69 73 72	288
K. D. G. Nagle *Australia*	74 70 73 72	289
A. Lema *USA*	68 72 75 74	289
B. J. Hunt *Hartsbourne*	74 74 70 71	289

1966 MUIRFIELD

J. Nicklaus *USA*	70 67 75 70	282
D. C. Thomas *Dunham Forest*	72 73 69 69	283
D. Sanders *USA*	71 70 72 70	283
G. Player *South Africa*	72 74 71 69	286
B. Devlin *Australia*	73 69 74 70	286
K. D. G. Nagle *Australia*	72 68 76 70	286
P. Rodgers *USA*	74 66 70 76	286

1967 HOYLAKE

R. de Vicenzo *Argentina*	70 71 67 70	278
J. Nicklaus *USA*	71 69 71 69	280
C. A. Clark *Sunningdale*	70 73 69 72	284
G. Player *South Africa*	72 71 67 74	284
A. Jacklin *Potters Bar*	73 69 73 70	285
S. Miguel *Spain*	72 74 68 72	286
H. Henning *South Africa*	74 70 71 71	286

1968 CARNOUSTIE

G. Player *South Africa*	74 71 71 73	289
J. Nicklaus *USA*	76 69 73 73	291
R. J. Charles *NZ*	72 72 71 76	291
W. Casper *USA*	72 68 74 78	292
M. Bembridge *Little Aston*	71 75 73 74	293
B. Barnes *Burnham & Berrow*	70 74 80 71	295
N. C. Coles *Coombe Hill*	75 76 71 73	295
G. Brewer *USA*	74 73 72 76	295

1969 ROYAL LYTHAM

A. Jacklin *Potters Bar*	68 70 70 72	280
R. J. Charles *NZ*	66 69 75 72	282
P. W. Thomson *Australia*	71 70 70 72	283
R. de Vicenzo *Argentina*	72 73 66 72	283
C. O'Connor *Royal Dublin*	71 65 74 74	284
J. Nicklaus *USA*	75 70 68 72	285
D. M. Love Jr *USA*	70 73 71 71	285

1970 ST ANDREWS

J. Nicklaus *USA*	68 69 73 73	283
D. Sanders *USA*	68 71 71 73	283

Play-off: Nicklaus 72; Sanders 73

H. Henning *South Africa*	67 72 73 73	285
L. Trevino *USA*	68 68 72 77	285
A. Jacklin *Potters Bar*	67 70 73 76	286
N. C. Coles *Coombe Hill*	65 74 72 76	287
P. A. Oosterhuis *Dulwich*	73 69 69 76	287

1971 ROYAL BIRKDALE

L. Trevino *USA*	69 70 69 70	278
Lu Liang Huan *Taiwan*	70 70 69 70	279
A. Jacklin *Potters Bar*	69 70 70 71	280
C. De Foy *Coombe Hill*	72 72 68 69	281
J. Nicklaus *USA*	71 71 72 69	283
C. Coody *USA*	74 71 70 68	283

1972 MUIRFIELD

L. Trevino *USA*	71 70 66 71	278
J. Nicklaus *USA*	70 72 71 66	279
A. Jacklin *Potters Bar*	69 72 67 72	280
D. Sanders *USA*	71 71 69 70	281
B. W. Barnes *Fairway DR*	71 72 69 71	283
G. Player *South Africa*	71 71 76 67	285

1973 TROON

T. Weiskopf *USA*	68 67 71 70	276
N. C. Coles *Holiday Inns*	71 72 70 66	279
J. Miller *USA*	70 68 69 72	279
J. Nicklaus *USA*	69 70 76 65	280
B. Yancey *USA*	69 69 73 70	281
P. J. Butler *Golf Domes*	71 72 74 69	286

1974 ROYAL LYTHAM

G. Player *South Africa*	69 68 75 70	282
P. Oosterhuis *Pacific Harbour*	71 71 73 71	286
J. Nicklaus *USA*	74 72 70 71	287
H. M. Green *USA*	71 74 72 71	288
D. Edwards *USA*	70 73 76 73	292
Lu Liang Huan *Taiwan*	72 72 75 73	292

1895 NEWPORT, R.I.
C. B. Macdonald *Chicago*

Semi-finals:
Macdonald beat C. Claxton 8 and 7
C. E. Sands beat F. I. Amory 3 and 2
Final:
Macdonald beat Sands 12 and 11

1896 SHINNECOCK HILLS, N.Y.
J. Whigham *Onwentsia*

Semi-finals
Whigham beat A. M. Coats 8 and 6
J. G. Thorp beat H. P. Toler 4 and 3
Final:
Whigham beat Thorp 8 and 7

1897 CHICAGO, ILL.
H. J. Whigham *Onwentsia*

Semi-finals:
Whigham beat F. S. Douglas 6 and 5
W. R. Betts beat C. B. Macdonald 1 up
Final:
Whigham beat Betts 8 and 6

1898 MORRIS COUNTY, N.J.
F. S. Douglas *Fairfield*

Semi-finals:
Douglas beat W. J. Travis 8 and 6
W. B. Smith beat C. B. Macdonald 2 and 1
Final:
Douglas beat Smith 5 and 3

1899 ONWENTSIA, ILL.
H. M. Harriman *Meadow Brook*

Semi-finals:
F. S. Douglas beat W. J. Travis 2 and 1
Harriman beat C. B. Macdonald 6 and 5
Final:
Harriman beat Douglas 3 and 2

1900 GARDEN CITY, N.Y.
W. J. Travis *Garden City*

Semi-finals:
Travis beat A. G. Lockwood 11 and 10
F. S. Douglas beat H. M. Harriman 4 and 3
Final:
Travis beat Douglas 2 up

1901 ATLANTIC CITY, N.J.
W. J. Travis *Garden City*

Semi-finals:
W. E. Egan beat C. H. Seeley 11 and 10
Travis beat F. S. Douglas at 38th
Final:
Travis beat Egan 5 and 4

1902 GLEN VIEW, ILL.
L. N. James *Glen View*

Semi-finals:
E. M. Byers beat D. P. Fredericks 4 and 3
James beat F. O. Reinhart 2 and 1
Final:
James beat Byers 4 and 2

1903 NASSAU, N.Y.
W. J. Travis *Garden City*

Semi-finals:
Travis beat F. O. Reinhart 5 and 4
E. M. Byers beat B. Smith 5 and 4
Final:
Travis beat Byers 5 and 4

1904 BALTUSROL, N.J.
H. C. Egan *Exmoor*

Semi-finals:
F. Herreshoff beat W. T. West 6 and 5
Egan beat D. P. Fredericks 2 and 1
Final:
Egan beat Herreshoff 8 and 6

1905 CHICAGO, ILL.
H. C. Egan *Exmoor*

Semi-finals:
D. E. Sawyer beat H. C. Fownes 2 up
Egan beat H. Weber 7 and 5
Final:
Egan beat Sawyer 6 and 5

1906 ENGLEWOOD, N.J.
E. M. Byers *Allegheny*

Semi-finals:
G. S. Lyon beat E. Knowles 5 and 4
Byers beat W. J. Travis 4 and 3
Final:
Byers beat Lyon 2 up

1907 EUCLID, OHIO
J. D. Travers *Montclair*

Semi-finals:
Travers beat E. M. Byers 6 and 5
A. Graham beat H. C. Fownes 4 and 3
Final:
Travers beat Graham 6 and 5

1908 GARDEN CITY, N.Y.
J. D. Travers *Montclair*

Semi-finals:
Travers beat W. J. Travis 2 up
M. Behr beat F. Herreshoff 37th
Final:
Travers beat Behr 8 and 7

1909 CHICAGO, ILL.
R. A. Gardner *Hinsdale*

Semi-finals:
H. C. Egan beat C. Evans 1 up
Gardner beat M. E. Phelps 2 up
Final:
Gardner beat Egan 4 and 3

1910 THE COUNTRY CLUB, BROOKLINE, MASS.
W. C. Fownes Jr *Oakmont*

Semi-finals:
Fownes beat C. Evans 1 up
W. K. Wood beat W. R. Tukerman 2 up
Final:
Fownes beat Wood 4 and 3

1911 APAWAMIS, N.Y.
H. H. Hilton *Royal Liverpool*

Semi-finals:
Hilton beat C. W. Inslee 8 and 6
F. Herreshoff beat C. Evans 3 and 2
Final:
Hilton beat Herreshoff 37th

1912 CHICAGO, ILL.
J. D. Travers *Upper Montclair*

Semi-finals:
Travers beat H. K. Kerr 7 and 5
C. Evans beat W. K. Wood 4 and 3
Final:
Travers beat Evans 7 and 6

1913 GARDEN CITY, N.Y.
J. D. Travers *Upper Montclair*

Semi-finals:
J. G. Anderson beat C. Evans 2 and 1
Travers beat F. Herreshoff 5 and 4
Final:
Travers beat Anderson 5 and 4

1914 EKWANOK, VT.
F. D. Ouimet *Woodland*

Semi-finals:
J. D. Travers beat W. J. Travis 5 and 3
Ouimet beat W. C. Fownes 1 up
Final:
Ouimet beat Travers 6 and 5

1915 DETROIT CC, MICH.
R. A. Gardner *Hinsdale*

Semi-finals:
Gardner beat M. Marston 37th
J. G. Anderson beat S. Sherman 2 and 1
Final:
Gardner beat Anderson 5 and 4

1916 MERION, PA.
C. Evans *Edgewater*

Semi-finals:
R. A. Gardner beat J. P. Guilford 4 and 3
Evans beat D. C. Corkran 3 and 2
Final:
Evans beat Gardner 4 and 3

1919 OAKMONT, PA.
S. D. Herron *Oakmont*

Semi-finals:
R. T. Jones Jr beat W. C. Fownes 5 and 3
Herron beat J. W. Platt 7 and 6
Final:
Herron beat Jones 5 and 4

1920 ENGINEERS, N.Y.
C. Evans Jr *Edgewater*

Semi-finals:
Evans beat E. P. Allis 10 and 8
F. Ouimet beat R. T. Jones Jr 6 and 5
Final:
Evans beat Ouimet 7 and 6

1921 ST LOUIS CC, MO.
J. P. Guilford *Woodland*

Semi-finals:
Guilford beat C. Evans Jr 5 and 4
R. A. Gardner beat W. I. Hunter 6 and 5
Final:
Guilford beat Gardner 7 and 6

1922 THE COUNTRY CLUB, BROOKLINE, MASS.
J. W. Sweetser *Siwanoy*

Semi-finals:
Sweetser beat R. T. Jones Jr 8 and 7
C. Evans Jr beat R. E. Knepper 11 and 9
Final:
Sweetser beat Evans 3 and 2

1923 FLOSSMOOR, ILL.
M. R. Marston *Pine Valley*

Semi-finals:
J. W. Sweetser beat R. A. Gardner 8 and 7
Marston beat F. Ouimet 3 and 2
Final:
Marston beat Sweetser at 38th

1924 MERION, PA
R. T. Jones Jr *Atlanta*

Semi-finals:
Jones beat F. Ouimet 11 and 10
G. Von Elm beat M. R. Marston 7 and 6
Final:
Jones beat Von Elm 9 and 8

1925 OAKMONT, PA.
R. T. Jones Jr *Atlanta*

Semi-finals:
W. Gunn beat R. A. Jones 5 and 3
Jones beat G. Von Elm 7 and 6
Final:
Jones beat Gunn 8 and 7

1926 BALTUSROL, N.J.
G. Von Elm *Rancho*

Semi-finals:
Von Elm beat G. Dawson 11 and 10
R. T. Jones beat F. Ouimet 5 and 4
Final:
Von Elm beat Jones 2 and 1

1927 MINIKAHDA CLUB, MINN.
R. T. Jones Jr *Atlanta*

Semi-finals:
C. Evans Jr beat R. Mackenzie at 37th
Jones beat F. Ouimet 11 and 10
Final:
Jones beat Evans 8 and 7

1928 BRAE BURN CC, MASS.
R. T. Jones Jr *Atlanta*

Semi-finals:
T. P. Perkins beat G. J. Voigt 6 and 4
Jones beat P. Finlay 13 and 12
Final:
Jones beat Perkins 10 and 9

1929 DEL MONTE CC, CALIF.
H. R. Johnston *White Bear*

Semi-finals:
O. F. Willing beat H. C. Egan 4 and 3
Johnston beat F. Ouimet 6 and 5
Final:
Johnston beat Willing 4 and 3

1930 MERION, PA.
R. T. Jones Jr *Atlanta*

Semi-finals:
E. V. Homans beat C. H. Seaver 1 hole
Jones beat J. W. Sweetser 9 and 8
Final:
Jones beat Homans 8 and 7

1931 BEVERLY CC, ILL.
F. Ouimet *Woodland*

Semi-finals:
Ouimet beat B. Howell 2 and 1
J. Westland beat M. J. McCarthy Jr 3 and 2
Final:
Ouimet beat Westland 6 and 5

1932 BALTIMORE CC, MD.
C. Ross Sommerville *London (Canada)*

Semi-finals:
Sommerville beat J. P. Guilford 7 and 6
J. Goodman beat F. Ouimet 4 and 2
Final:
Sommerville beat Goodman 2 and 1

1933 KENWOOD CC, OHIO
G. T. Dunlap *Pomonok*

Semi-finals:
M. R. Marston beat J. Munger 6 and 5
Dunlap beat W. Lawson Little 4 and 3
Final:
Dunlap beat Marston 6 and 5

1934 THE COUNTRY CLUB, BROOKLINE, MASS.
W. Lawson Little Jr *Presidio*

Semi-finals:
D. Goldman beat Reynolds Smith 4 and 2
Lawson Little beat D. Armstrong 4 and 3
Final:
Lawson Little beat Goldman 8 and 7

1935 THE COUNTRY CLUB, CLEVELAND, OHIO
W. Lawson Little Jr *Presidio*

Semi-finals:
Lawson Little beat J. Goodman 4 and 3
W. Emery beat J. P. Lynch 4 and 3
Final:
Lawson Little beat Emery 4 and 2

1936 GARDEN CITY GC, N.Y.
J. W. Fischer *Highland*

Semi-finals:
Fischer beat J. Goodman 2 and 1
J. M'Lean beat G. J. Voigt 8 and 7
Final:
Fischer beat M'Lean at 37th

1937 ALDERWOOD CC, ORE.
J. W. Goodman *Omaha*

Semi-finals:
R. Billows beat J. W. Fischer 6 and 5
Goodman beat M. Ward 1 hole
Final:
Goodman beat Billows 2 holes

1938 OAKMONT CC, PA.
N. Turnesa *Briar Hills*

Semi-finals:
B. P. Abbott beat R. D. Chapman 5 and 4
Turnesa beat E. C. Kingsley 4 and 3
Final:
Turnesa beat Abbott 8 and 7

1939 NORTH SHORE CC, ILL.
M. Ward *Spokane*

Semi-finals:
R. Billows beat D. Schumacher 6 and 5
Ward beat A. L. Doering 2 and 1
Final:
Ward beat Billows 7 and 5

1940 WINGED FOOT GC, N.Y.
R. D. Chapman *Winged Foot*

Semi-finals:
Chapman beat W. Wehrle 3 and 2
W. McCullogh beat R. Billows 5 and 3
Final:
Chapman beat McCullogh 11 and 9

1941 OMAHA FIELD, NEB.
M. Ward *Spokane*

Semi-finals:
Ward beat R. F. Riegel 9 and 8
B. P. Abbott beat T. Bishop 1 hole
Final:
Ward beat Abbott 4 and 3

1946 BALTUSROL GC
S. E. Bishop *Norfolk*

Semi-finals:
S. L. Quick beat A. F. Kammer Jr 3 and 1
Bishop beat R. W. Willits 10 and 9
Final:
Bishop beat Quick at 37th

1947 PEBBLE BEACH GL, CALIF.
R. H. Riegel *California*

Semi-finals:
J. W. Dawson beat J. H. Selby 5 and 4
Riegel beat F. Torza 2 and 1
Final:
Riegel beat Dawson 2 and 1

1948 MEMPHIS CC, TENN.
W. P. Turnesa *Knollwood*

Semi-finals:
R. E. Billows beat C. R. Coe 6 and 5
Turnesa beat E. Dahlbender 8 and 6
Final:
Turnesa beat Billows 2 and 1

1949 OAK HILL CC, N.Y.
C. R. Coe *Oklahoma City*

Semi-finals:
R. King beat W. P. Turnesa 2 and 1
Coe beat W. C. Campbell 8 and 7
Final:
Coe beat King 11 and 10

1950 MINNEAPOLIS GC, MINN.
S. Urzetta *Irondequoit*

Semi-finals:
Urzetta beat R. W. Knowles Jr 6 and 5
F. R. Stranahan beat J. P. Ward 1 hole
Final:
Urzetta beat Stranahan at the 39th

1951 SAUCON VALLEY CC, PA.
B. Maxwell *Odessa*

Semi-finals:
J. F. Gagliardi beat K. T. Jacobs Jr 6 and 5
Maxwell beat J. C. Benson 10 and 9
Final:
Maxwell beat Gagliardi 4 and 3

1952 SEATTLE GC, WASH.
J. Westland *Everett*

Semi-finals:
A. Mengert beat D. Cherry 3 and 2
Westland beat W. C. Mawhinney 5 and 4
Final:
Westland beat Mengert 3 and 2

1953 OKLAHOMA CITY CC, OKLA.
G. Littler *La Jolla*

Semi-finals:
D. Morey beat D. Albert 5 and 4
Littler beat B. Cudd 10 and 8
Final:
Littler beat Morey 1 hole

1954 DETROIT CC, MICH.
A. D. Palmer *Pine Ridge*

Semi-finals:
Palmer beat E. L. Meister at the 39th
R. Sweeny beat T. N. Lenczyk 5 and 4
Final:
Palmer beat Sweeny 1 hole

1955 VIRGINIA CC, VA.
E. H. Ward *San Francisco*

Semi-finals:
W. Hyndman III beat H. Robbins 4 and 3
Ward beat W. A. Booe 4 and 2
Final:
Ward beat Hyndman 9 and 8

1956 KNOLLWOOD C, ILL.
E. H. Ward *San Francisco*

Semi-finals:
C. Kocsis beat G. J. Magee 4 and 2
Ward beat J. Campbell 2 and 1
Final:
Ward beat Kocsis 5 and 4

1957 THE COUNTRY CLUB, BROOKLINE, MASS.
H. Robbins *Colonial*

Semi-finals:
F. M. Taylor beat E. M. Rudolph 5 and 4
Robbins beat R. Baxter Jr 2 holes
Final:
Robbins beat Taylor 5 and 4

1958 OLYMPIC CC, CALIF.
C. R. Coe *Oklahoma City*

Semi-finals:
Coe beat R. T. McManus 3 and 2
T. D. Aaron beat D. Foote 10 and 9
Final:
Coe beat Aaron 5 and 4

1959 BROADMOOR GC, COLO.
J. W. Nicklaus *Scioto*

Semi-finals:
C. R. Coe beat D. Wysong 6 and 4
Nicklaus beat G. Andrews 1 hole
Final:
Nicklaus beat Coe 1 hole

1960 ST LOUIS CC, MO.
D. R. Beman *Bethesda*

Semi-finals:
R. W. Gardner beat C. F. Lewis 2 and 1
Beman beat J. Farquhar 5 and 4
Final:
Beman beat Gardner 6 and 4

1961 PEBBLE BEACH GL, CALIF.
J. W. Nicklaus *Scioto*

Semi-finals:
H. D. Wysong beat J. B. Carr 2 holes
Nicklaus beat M. C. Methvin 9 and 8
Final:
Nicklaus beat Wysong 8 and 6

1962 PINEHURST CC, N.C.
L. E. Harris Jr *Oakwood*

Semi-finals:
Harris beat W. J. Patton 3 and 1
Downing Gray beat C. Coody 3 and 2
Final:
Harris beat Gray 1 hole

1963 WAKONDA, IOWA
D. R. Beman *Bethesda*

Semi-finals:
Beman beat G. W. Archer 5 and 4
R. H. Sikes beat C. R. Coe 2 and 1
Final:
Beman beat Sikes 2 and 1

1964 CANTERBURY GC, OHIO
W. C. Campbell *Guyan*

Semi-finals:
Campbell beat J. M. Hopkins 3 and 1
E. Tutwiler beat D. Eichelberger 3 and 2
Final:
Campbell beat Tutwiler 1 hole

Strokeplay introduced

1965 SOUTHERN HILLS CC, OKLA.

R. J. Murphy Jr *Long Palm*	73	69	76	73	291
R. B. Dickson *Muskogee*	71	75	72	74	292
D. C. Allen *Rochester CC*	70	74	76	73	293
C. Sanudo *Carlton Oaks*	71	76	72	74	293

1966 MERION GC, PA.

G. Cowan *Westmount (Canada)*	74	72	72	67	285
D. R. Beman *Bethesda*	71	67	76	71	285

Play-off: Cowan 75; Beman 76

J. W. Lewis *Florence CC*	73	69	75	69	286
R. Cerrudo *California GC*	70	75	70	71	286
A. Downing Gray *Pensacola*	74	72	68	72	286

1967 BROADMOOR GC (WEST), COLO.

R. B. Dickson *McAlester*	71	71	74	69	285
M. M. Giles III *Boonsboro*	76	69	72	69	286
R. Cerrudo *California GC*	75	73	73	68	289
A. D. Gray *Pensacola*	75	72	70	73	290

1968 SCIOTO CC, OHIO

B. Fleisher *Miami CC*	73	70	71	70	284
M. M. Giles III *Boonsboro*	75	72	73	65	285
J. Bohmann *Chaparral*	74	73	74	67	288
H. M. Green *Birmingham CC*	72	71	73	73	289

1969 OAKMONT CC, PA.

S. N. Melnyk *Brunswick*	70	73	73	70	286
M. M. Giles III *Boonsboro*	72	75	72	72	291
A. L. Miller *Pensacola*	77	69	73	74	293
R. I. Zender *Evanston*	75	78	72	70	295

1970 WAVERLEY CC, OREG.

L. Wadkins *Meadowbrook*	67	73	69	70	279
T. Kite Jr *Austin CC*	69	67	72	73	280
G. Cowan *West Mount*	69	70	73	72	284
J. R. Gabrielsen *Peachtree*	75	67	69	73	284
J. B. Simons *Butler*	69	72	69	74	284

1971 WILMINGTON CC, DEL.

G. Cowan *West Mount (Canada)*	70	71	69	70	280
E. Pearce *Temple Terrace*	70	69	73	71	283
M. M. Giles III *Virginia CC*	74	73	68	69	284
J. C. McLean *Rainier*	72	67	73	73	285

1972 CHARLOTTE CC, N.C.

M. M. Giles III *Virginia CC*	73	68	72	72	285
M. S. Hayes *Twin Hills*	73	72	69	74	288
B. Crenshaw *Austin*	71	75	71	71	288
M. R. West III *Columbia*	73	71	73	72	289

Reverted to Matchplay

1973 INVERNESS, ILL.
C. Stadler *La Jolla*

Semi-finals:
D. Strawn beat W. C. Campbell 6 and 5
C. Stadler beat M. M. Giles III 3 and 1
Final:
Stadler beat Strawn 6 and 5

**USGA Men's National Amateur
Championship**

1974 RIDGEWOOD CC, N.J.
J. Pate *Pensacola CC*

Semi-finals:
J. P. Grace beat G. Koch 2 and 1
Pate beat C. Strange 3 and 1
Final:
Pate beat Grace 2 and 1

1885 HOYLAKE
A. F. MacFie *Royal Liverpool*

Semi-finals:
H. G. Hutchinson beat W. J. Ball 2 holes
MacFie a bye
Final:
MacFie beat Hutchinson 7 and 6

1886 ST ANDREWS
H. G. Hutchinson *Royal and Ancient*

Semi-finals:
Hutchinson beat C. Chambers 5 and 3
H. A. Lamb beat J. Ball Sr 7 and 6
Final:
Hutchinson beat Lamb 7 and 6

1887 HOYLAKE
H. G. Hutchinson *Royal and Ancient*

Semi-finals:
J. Ball Jr beat J. G. Tait 3 and 1
Hutchinson beat Ball Sr 1 hole
Final:
Hutchinson beat Ball 1 hole

1888 PRESTWICK
J. Ball Jr *Royal Liverpool*

Semi-finals:
J. E. Laidlay beat L. M. Balfour Melville 6 and 5
Ball beat A. Stuart 4 and 3
Final:
Ball beat Laidlay 5 and 4

1889 ST ANDREWS
J. E. Laidlay *Hon Company*

Semi-finals:
Laidlay beat J. Ball Jr at 20th
L. M. Balfour beat W. S. Wilson 5 and 4
Final:
Laidlay beat Balfour 2 and 1

1890 HOYLAKE
J. Ball Jr *Royal Liverpool*

Semi-finals:
Ball beat L. M. Balfour Melville 6 and 4
J. E. Laidlay beat D. Leitch 1 hole
Final:
Ball beat Laidlay 4 and 3

1891 ST ANDREWS
J. E. Laidlay *Hon Company*

Semi-finals:
H. H. Hilton beat W. Ballingall 6 and 4
Laidlay beat T. Gilroy 5 and 4
Final:
Laidlay beat Hilton at 20th

1892 ROYAL ST GEORGE'S
J. Ball Jr *Royal Liverpool*

Semi-finals:
H. H. Hilton beat J. E. Laidlay 5 and 4
Ball beat L. M. Balfour Melville 1 hole
Final:
Ball beat Hilton 3 and 1

1893 PRESTWICK
P. C. Anderson *St Andrews Univ*

Semi-finals:
J. E. Laidlay beat F. G. Tait at 19th
Anderson beat S. Mure Fergusson 2 holes
Final:
Anderson beat Laidlay 1 hole

1894 HOYLAKE
J. Ball Jr *Royal Liverpool*

Semi-finals:
Ball beat J. E. Laidlay 5 and 3
S. Mure Fergusson beat F. G. Tait 4 and 3
Final:
Ball beat Mure Fergusson 1 hole

1895 ST ANDREWS
L. M. Balfour Melville *Royal and Ancient*

Semi-finals:
J. Ball Jr beat F. G. Tait 5 and 3
Balfour Melville beat L. Auchterlonie at 19th
Final:
Balfour Melville beat Ball at 19th

1896 ROYAL ST GEORGE'S
F. G. Tait *Black Watch GC*

Semi-finals:
Tait beat H. G. Hutchinson 3 and 2
H. H. Hilton beat J. H. Graham 4 and 3
Final:
Tait beat Hilton 8 and 7

1897 MUIRFIELD (36-hole final introduced)
A. J. T. Allan *Edinburgh Univ*

Semi-finals:
J. Robb beat J. L. Low at 21st
Allan beat L. M. Balfour-Melville 3 and 1
Final:
Allan beat Robb 4 and 2

1898 HOYLAKE
F. G. Tait *Black Watch GC*

Semi-finals:
Tait beat J. L. Low at 22nd
S. Mure Fergusson beat J. Robb 1 hole
Final:
Tait beat Mure Fergusson 7 and 5

1899 PRESTWICK
J. Ball Jr *Royal Liverpool*

Semi-finals:
Ball beat G. C. Whigham 8 and 7
F. G. Tait beat J. M. Williamson 3 and 1
Final:
Ball beat Tait at 37th

1900 ROYAL ST GEORGE'S
H. H. Hilton *Royal Liverpool*

Semi-finals:
J. Robb beat J. A. T. Bramston 3 and 1
Hilton beat J. Graham Jr 7 and 5
Final:
Hilton beat Robb 8 and 7

1901 ST ANDREWS
H. H. Hilton *Royal Liverpool*

Semi-finals:
Hilton beat H. G. Hutchinson 2 and 1
J. L. Low beat J. Graham Jr 1 hole
Final:
Hilton beat Low 1 hole

1902 HOYLAKE
C. Hutchings *Royal Liverpool*

Semi-finals:
Hutchings beat J. Robb 2 and 1
S. H. Fry beat R. Maxwell 1 hole
Final:
Hutchings beat Fry 1 hole

1903 MUIRFIELD
R. Maxwell *Tantallon*

Semi-finals:
Maxwell beat H. W. de Zoete at 19th
H. G. Hutchinson beat A. M'Donald 4 and 2
Final:
Maxwell beat Hutchinson 7 and 5

1904 ROYAL ST GEORGE'S
W. J. Travis *USA*

Semi-finals:
E. Blackwell beat J. E. Laidlay 2 and 1
Travis beat H. G. Hutchinson 4 and 2
Final:
Travis beat Blackwell 4 and 3

1905 PRESTWICK
A. G. Barry *St Andrews Univ*

Semi-finals:
Barry beat J. Graham Jr 1 hole
Hon O. Scott beat A. R. Aitken 2 and 1
Final:
Barry beat Scott 3 and 2

1906 HOYLAKE
J. Robb *Prestwick St Nicholas*

Semi-finals:
Robb beat H. S. Colt 3 and 2
C. C. Lingen beat E. A. Smirke 1 hole
Final:
Robb beat Lingen 4 and 3

1907 ST ANDREWS
J. Ball Jr *Royal Liverpool*

Semi-finals:
C. A. Palmer beat R. Harris 2 and 1
Ball beat G. Campbell 2 and 1
Final:
Ball beat Palmer 6 and 4

1908 ROYAL ST GEORGE'S
E. A. Lassen *Royal Lytham and St Annes*

Semi-finals:
H. E. Taylor beat J. Graham Jr 4 and 3
Lassen beat C. E. Dick 2 and 1
Final:
Lassen beat Taylor 7 and 6

1909 MUIRFIELD
R. Maxwell *Tantallon*

Semi-finals:
C. K. Hutchison beat R. Andrew 3 and 2
Maxwell beat B. Darwin 3 and 2
Final:
Maxwell beat Hutchison 1 hole

1910 HOYLAKE
J. Ball, Jr *Royal Liverpool*

Semi-finals:
C. C. Aylmer beat H. H. Hilton 4 and 3
Ball beat A. Mitchell 5 and 4
Final:
Ball beat Aylmer 10 and 9

1911 PRESTWICK
H. H. Hilton *Royal Liverpool*

Semi-finals:
Hilton beat G. Lockhart 4 and 3
E. A. Lassen beat L. B. Stevens 2 holes
Final:
Hilton beat Lassen 4 and 3

1912 WESTWARD HO!
J. Ball Jr *Royal Liverpool*

Semi-finals:
A. Mitchell beat C. B. Macfarlane 4 and 3
Ball beat A. V. Hambro 3 and 2
Final:
Ball beat Mitchell at 38th

1913 ST ANDREWS
H. H. Hilton *Royal Liverpool*

Semi-finals:
R. Harris beat E. P. Kyle 3 and 2
Hilton beat C. C. Aylmer 1 hole
Final:
Hilton beat Harris 6 and 5

1914 ROYAL ST GEORGE'S
J. L. C. Jenkins *Troon*

Semi-finals:
C. O. Hezlet beat R. P. Humphries 1 hole
Jenkins beat E. M. Smith 2 and 1
Final:
Jenkins beat Hezlet 3 and 2

1915–19 No Championship

1920 MUIRFIELD
C. J. H. Tolley *Rye*

Semi-finals:
R. A. Gardner beat Hon M. Scott 2 holes
Tolley beat G. T. Mellin 5 and 4
Final:
Tolley beat Gardner at 37th

1921 HOYLAKE
W. I. Hunter *Walmer and Kingsdown*

Semi-finals:
A. J. Graham beat H. S. B. Tubbs
Hunter beat B. Darwin 3 and 2
Final:
Hunter beat Graham 12 and 11

1922 PRESTWICK
E. W. E. Holderness *Walton Heath*

Semi-finals:
Holderness beat W. I. Hunter 2 and 1
J. Caven beat R. Scott Jr 1 hole
Final:
Holderness beat Caven 1 hole

1923 DEAL
R. H. Wethered *Worplesdon*

Semi-finals:
Wethered beat F. Ouimet 2 and 1
R. Harris beat D. Grant 5 and 4
Final:
Wethered beat Harris 7 and 6

1924 ST ANDREWS
E. W. E. Holderness *Walton Heath*

Semi-finals:
E. F. Storey beat R. H. Wethered 2 holes
Holderness beat W. A. Murray 3 and 2
Final:
Holderness beat Storey 3 and 2

1925 WESTWARD HO!
R. Harris *Royal and Ancient*

Semi-finals:
Harris beat E. N. Layton 1 hole
K. F. Fradgley beat R. H. Hardman 2 holes
Final:
Harris beat Fradgley 13 and 12

1926 MUIRFIELD
J. Sweetser *USA*

Semi-finals:
Sweetser beat Hon W. Brownlow at 21st
A. F. Simpson beat A. Jamieson Jr 2 and 1
Final:
Sweetser beat Simpson 6 and 5

1927 HOYLAKE
W. Tweddell *Stourbridge*

Semi-finals:
Tweddell beat R. H. Wethered 4 and 3
D. E. Landale beat R. H. Jobson 1 hole
Final:
Tweddell beat Landale 7 and 6

1928 PRESTWICK
T. P. Perkins *Castle Bromwich*

Semi-finals:
Perkins beat W. Tulloch 6 and 5
R. H. Wethered beat E. B. Tipping 4 and 3
Final:
Perkins beat Wethered 6 and 4

1929 ROYAL ST GEORGE'S
C. J. H. Tolley *Rye*

Semi-finals:
Tolley beat R. Hartley 1 hole
J. N. Smith beat J. Dawson at 19th
Final:
Tolley beat Smith 4 and 3

1930 ST ANDREWS
R. T. Jones Jr *USA*

Semi-finals:
Jones beat G. J. Voigt 1 hole
R. H. Wethered beat L. Hartley 2 and 1
Final:
Jones beat Wethered 7 and 6

1931 WESTWARD HO!
E. Martin Smith *Royal St George's*

Semi-finals:
J. de Forest beat W. Tulloch 1 hole
Martin Smith beat J. D. MacCormack 1 hole
Final:
Martin Smith beat de Forest 1 hole

1932 MUIRFIELD
J. de Forest *Addington*

Semi-finals:
de Forest beat L. O. M. Munn at 21st
E. W. Fiddian beat E. A. McRuvie 2 holes
Final:
de Forest beat Fiddian 3 and 1

1933 HOYLAKE
Hon M. Scott *Royal St George's*

Semi-finals:
Scott beat G. T. Dunlap Jr 4 and 3
T. A. Bourn beat C. J. H. Tolley at 20th
Final:
Scott beat Bourn 4 and 3

1934 PRESTWICK
W. Lawson Little *USA*

Semi-finals:
J. Wallace beat G. T. Dunlap Jr 2 and 1
Lawson Little beat L. G. Garnett at 19th
Final:
Lawson Little beat Wallace 14 and 13

1935 ROYAL LYTHAM AND ST ANNES
W. Lawson Little *USA*

Semi-finals:
W. Tweddell beat T. A. Torrance 2 and 1
Lawson Little beat R. Sweeny Jr 3 and 1
Final:
Lawson Little beat Tweddell 1 hole

1936 ST ANDREWS
H. Thomson *Williamwood*

Semi-finals:
Thomson beat C. Ewing 4 and 3
J. Ferrier beat G. A. Hill 1 hole
Final:
Thomson beat Ferrier 2 holes

1937 ROYAL ST GEORGE'S
R. Sweeny Jr *Royal and Ancient*

Semi-finals:
L. O. M. Munn beat J. de Forest 4 and 3
Sweeny beat C. Stowe 6 and 5
Final:
Sweeny beat Munn 3 and 2

1938 TROON
C. R. Yates *USA*

Semi-finals:
C. Ewing beat C. Ross Somerville 2 holes
Yates beat H. Thomson at 19th
Final:
Yates beat Ewing 3 and 2

1939 HOYLAKE
A. T. Kyle *Sand Moor*

Semi-finals:
Kyle beat W. E. Holt Jr 2 and 1
A. A. Duncan beat C. Stowe 3 and 2
Final:
Kyle beat Duncan 2 and 1

1940–45 No Championship

1946 ROYAL BIRKDALE
J. Bruen *Cork*

Semi-finals:
Bruen beat H. E. Walker 3 and 2
R. Sweeny Jr beat G. H. Micklem 5 and 3
Final:
Bruen beat Sweeny 4 and 3

1947 CARNOUSTIE
W. P. Turnesa *USA*

Semi-finals:
Turnesa beat J. G. Campbell 4 and 3
R. D. Chapman beat S. L. McKinlay 2 holes
Final:
Turnesa beat Chapman 3 and 2

1948 ROYAL ST GEORGE'S
F. R. Stranahan *USA*

Semi-finals:
Stranahan beat D. H. R. Martin 3 and 1
C. Stowe beat W. P. Turnesa 1 hole
Final:
Stranahan beat Stowe 5 and 4

1949 PORTMARNOCK
S. M. McCready *Sunningdale*

Semi-finals:
W. P. Turnesa beat E. P. Millward 1 hole
McCready beat K. G. Thom at 20th
Final:
McCready beat Turnesa 2 and 1

1950 ST ANDREWS
F. R. Stranahan *USA*

Semi-finals:
R. D. Chapman beat J. B. McHale 1 hole
Stranahan beat C. J. H. Tolley 4 and 3
Final:
Stranahan beat Chapman 8 and 6

1951 ROYAL PORTHCAWL
R. D. Chapman *USA*

Semi-finals:
C. R. Coe beat A. D. Evans 4 and 2
Chapman beat J. B. Carr 4 and 3
Final:
Chapman beat Coe 5 and 4

1952 PRESTWICK
E. Harvie Ward *USA*

Semi-finals:
Harvie Ward beat J. B. Carr 2 and 1
F. R. Stranahan beat J. R. Cater 2 holes
Final:
Harvie Ward beat Stranahan 7 and 5

1953 HOYLAKE
J. B. Carr *Sutton*

Semi-finals:
Carr beat C. H. Beamish at 19th
E. Harvie Ward beat A. H. Perowne 6 and 5
Final:
Carr beat Harvie Ward 2 holes

1954 MUIRFIELD
D. W. Bachli *Australia*

Semi-finals:
W. C. Campbell beat J. B. Carr 3 and 2
Bachli beat W. A. Slark 3 and 2
Final:
Bachli beat Campbell 2 and 1

1955 ROYAL LYTHAM AND ST ANNES
J. W. Conrad *USA*

Semi-finals:
A. Slater beat A. H. Perowne 3 and 2
Conrad beat P. F. Scrutton 5 and 4
Final:
Conrad beat Slater 3 and 2

1956 TROON (Quarter finals, semi-finals and final
played over 36 holes in 1956–57)
J. C. Beharrell *Little Aston*

Semi-finals:
Beharrell beat R. Reid Jack 2 and 1
L. G. Taylor beat G. G. Henderson 6 and 5
Final:
Beharrell beat Taylor 5 and 4

1957 FORMBY
R. Reid Jack *Dullatur*

Semi-finals:
Reid Jack beat A. F. Bussell 3 and 2
H. B. Ridgley beat A. Walker 13 and 12
Final:
Reid Jack beat Ridgley 2 and 1

1958 ST ANDREWS (Semi-finals and final only
played over 36 holes)
J. B. Carr *Sutton*

Semi-finals:
Carr beat M. F. Bonallack 4 and 3
A. Thirlwell beat T. Holland 4 and 3
Final:
Carr beat Thirlwell 3 and 2

1959 ROYAL ST GEORGE'S (Semi-finals and final
played over 36 holes)
D. Beman *USA*

Semi-finals:
W. Hyndman III beat B. Magee at 38th
Beman beat G. B. Wolstenholme 5 and 4
Final:
Beman beat Hyndman 3 and 2

1960 ROYAL PORTRUSH
J. B. Carr *Sutton*

Semi-finals:
Carr beat J. Walker 2 holes
B. Cochran beat G. Huddy 3 and 2
Final:
Carr beat Cochran 8 and 7

1961 TURNBERRY
M. F. Bonallack *Thorpe Hall*

Semi-finals:
J. Walker beat R. L. Morrow 1 hole
Bonallack beat M. J. Christmas 3 and 2
Final:
Bonallack beat Walker 6 and 4

1962 HOYLAKE
R. D. Davies *USA*

Semi-finals:
J. D. Povall beat B. H. G. Chapman 1 hole
Davies beat R. Foster 3 and 2
Final:
Davies beat Povall 1 hole

1963 ST ANDREWS
M. S. R. Lunt *Moseley*

Semi-finals:
Lunt beat E. Updegraff 1 hole
J. G. Blackwell beat R. Luceti 3 and 2
Final:
Lunt beat Blackwell 2 and 1

1964 GANTON
G. J. Clark *Whitley Bay*

Semi-finals:
M. S. R. Lunt beat J. Hall 4 and 3
Clark beat M. J. Christmas 2 holes
Final:
Clark beat Lunt at 39th

1965 ROYAL PORTHCAWL
M. F. Bonallack *Thorpe Hall*

Semi-finals:
Bonallack beat R. Foster 1 hole
C. A. Clark beat M. J. Christmas 1 hole
Final:
Bonallack beat Clark 2 and 1

1966 CARNOUSTIE
R. Cole *South Africa*

Semi-finals:
R. D. B. M. Shade beat G. B. Cosh 2 and 1
Cole beat H. de Lamaze 2 and 1
Final:
Cole beat Shade 3 and 2 (Final played over 18 holes)

1967 FORMBY
R. B. Dickson *USA*

Semi-finals:
Dickson beat G. J. Clark 4 and 3
R. Cerrudo beat M. Fleckman at 19th
Final:
Dickson beat Cerrudo 2 and 1

1968 TROON
M. F. Bonallack *Thorpe Hall*

Semi-finals:
J. B. Carr beat R. L. Glading 3 and 1
Bonallack beat G. C. Marks 3 and 2
Final:
Bonallack beat Carr 7 and 6

1969 HOYLAKE
M. F. Bonallack *Thorpe Hall*

Semi-finals:
Bonallack beat W. C. Davidson 4 and 3
W. Hyndman III beat D. Hayes 3 and 2
Final:
Bonallack beat Hyndman 3 and 2

1970 ROYAL COUNTY DOWN
M. F. Bonallack *Thorpe Hall*

Semi-finals:
Bonallack beat B. Critchley 2 and 1
W. Hyndman III beat T. B. C. Hoey 2 holes
Final:
Bonallack beat Hyndman 8 and 7

1971 CARNOUSTIE
S. Melnyk *USA*

Semi-finals:
J. Simons beat T. Kite 1 hole
Melnyk beat P. H. Moody 4 and 3
Final:
Melnyk beat Simons 3 and 2

1972 ROYAL ST GEORGE'S
T. W. B. Homer *Walsall*

Semi-finals:
A. Thirlwell beat M. F. Bonallack 2 and 1
Homer beat R. Revell 4 and 3
Final:
Homer beat Thirlwell 4 and 3

1973 ROYAL PORTHCAWL
R. Siderowf *USA*

Semi-finals:
Siderowf beat H. Ashby 6 and 5
P. H. Moody beat H. K. Clark 3 and 2
Final:
Siderowf beat Moody 5 and 3

1974 MUIRFIELD
T. W. B. Homer *Walsall*

Semi-finals:
J. Gabrielsen beat M. A. Poxon 5 and 4
Homer beat H. B. Stuart 1 hole
Final:
Homer beat Gabrielsen 2 holes

9. USPGA Championship

1916 SIWANOY CC, N.Y.
J. M. Barnes beat J. Hutchison 1 up

1919 ENGINEERS CC, N.Y.
J. M. Barnes beat F. McLeod 6 and 5

1920 FLOSSMOOR CC, ILL.
J. Hutchison beat J. D. Edgar 1 up

1921 INWOOD CC, N.Y.
W. Hagen beat J. M. Barnes 3 and 2

1922 OAKMONT CC, PA.
G. Sarazen beat E. French 4 and 3

1923 PELHAM CC, N.Y.
G. Sarazen beat W. Hagen at 38th

1924 FRENCH LICK CC, IND.
W. Hagen beat J. M. Barnes 2 up

1925 OLYMPIA FIELDS CC, ILL.
W. Hagen beat W. Mehlhorn 6 and 5

1926 SALISBURY GC, N.Y.
W. Hagen beat L. Diegel 5 and 3

1927 CEDAR CREST CC, TEX.
W. Hagen beat J. Turnesa 1 up

1928 BALTIMORE CC FIVE FARMS, MD.
L. Diegel beat A. Espinosa 6 and 5

1929 HILLCREST CC, CALIF.
L. Diegel beat J. Farrell 6 and 4

1930 FRESH MEADOW, N.Y.
T. Armour beat G. Sarazen 1 up

1931 WANNAMOISETT CC, R.I.
T. Creavy beat D. Shute 2 and 1

1932 KELLER GC, MINN.
O. Dutra beat F. Walsh 4 and 3

1933 BLUE MOUND CC, WIS.
G. Sarazen beat W. Goggin 5 and 4

1934 PARK CC, N.Y.
P. Runyan beat C. Wood at 38th

1935 TWIN HILLS CC, OKLA.
J. Revolta beat T. Armour 5 and 4

1936 PINEHURST CC, N.C.
D. Shute beat J. Thomson 3 and 2

1937 PITTSBURGH CC, PA.
D. Shute beat H. McSpaden at 37th

1938 SHAWNEE CC, PA.
P. Runyan beat S. Snead 8 and 7

1939 POMONOK CC, N.Y.
H. Picard beat B. Nelson at 37th

1940 HERSHEY CC, PA.
B. Nelson beat S. Snead 1 up

1941 CHERRY HILLS CC, COLO.
V. Ghezzi beat B. Nelson at 38th

1942 SEAVIEW CC, N.J.
S. Snead beat J. Turnesa 2 and 1

1944 MANITO G & CC, WASH.
B. Hamilton beat B. Nelson 1 up

1945 MORRAINE CC, OHIO
B. Nelson beat S. Byrd 4 and 3

1946 PORTLAND GC, ORE.
B. Hogan beat E. Oliver 6 and 4

1947 PLUM HOLLOW CC, MICH.
J. Ferrier beat C. Harbert 2 and 1

1948 NORWOOD HILLS CC, MO.
B. Hogan beat M. Turnesa 7 and 6

1949 HERMITAGE CC, VA.
S. Snead beat J. Palmer 3 and 2

1950 SCIOTO CC, OHIO
C. Harper beat H. Williams Jr 4 and 3

1951 OAKMONT CC, PA.
S. Snead beat W. Burkemo 7 and 6

1952 BIG SPRING CC, KY.
J. Turnesa beat C. Harbert 1 up

1953 BIRMINGHAM CC, MICH.
W. Burkemo beat F. Torza 2 and 1

1954 KELLER GC, MINN.
C. Harbert beat W. Burkemo 4 and 3

1955 MEADOWBROOK CC, MICH.
D. Ford beat C. Middlecoff 4 and 3

1956 BLUE HILL CC, MASS.
J. Burke beat T. Kroll 3 and 2

1957 MIAMI VALLEY GC, OHIO
L. Hebert beat D. Finsterwald 2 and 1

1958 LLANERCH CC, PA.
(Decided by strokeplay hereafter)

D. Finsterwald	67 72 70 67 276
B. Casper	73 67 68 70 278
S. Snead	73 67 67 73 280
J. Burke	70 72 69 70 281
J. Boros	72 68 73 72 285
T. Bolt	72 70 73 70 285

1959 MINNEAPOLIS GC, MINN.

B. Rosburg	71 72 68 66 277
J. Barber	69 65 71 73 278
D. Sanders	72 66 68 72 278
D. Finsterwald	71 68 71 70 280
M. Souchak	69 67 71 74 281
B. Goalby	72 69 62 68 281
K. Venturi	70 72 70 69 281

1960 FIRESTONE CC, OHIO

J. Hebert	72 67 72 70 281
J. Ferrier	71 74 66 71 282
S. Snead	68 73 70 72 283
D. Sanders	70 71 69 73 283
D. January	70 70 72 72 284
W. Ellis	72 72 72 69 285
A. Palmer	67 74 75 70 286

1961 OLYMPIA FIELDS CC, ILL.

| J. Barber | 69 67 71 70 277 |
| D. January | 72 66 67 72 277 |

Play-off: Barber 67; January 68

D. Sanders	70 68 74 68 280
T. Kroll	72 68 70 71 281
A. Palmer	73 72 69 68 282
W. Ellis	71 71 68 72 282
J. Pott	71 73 67 71 282
D. Ford	282
G. Littler	282
A. Wall	282

1962 ARONIMINK GC, PA.

G. Player	72 67 69 70 278
B. Goalby	69 72 71 67 279
J. Nicklaus	71 74 69 67 281
G. Bayer	69 70 71 71 281
D. Ford	69 69 73 71 282
B. Nichols	72 70 71 70 283

1963 DALLAS ATHLETIC CC, TEX.

J. Nicklaus	69 73 69 68 279
D. Ragan	75 70 67 69 281
D. Finsterwald	72 72 66 62 282
B. Crampton	70 73 65 74 282
A. Geiberger	72 73 69 70 284
B. Maxwell	73 71 69 71 284

1964 COLUMBUS CC, OHIO

B. Nichols	64 71 69 67 271
A. Palmer	68 68 69 69 274
J. Nicklaus	67 73 70 64 274
M. Rudolph	73 66 68 69 276
K. Venturi	72 65 73 69 279
T. Nieporte	68 71 68 72 279

1965 LAUREL VALLEY GC, PA.

D. Marr	70 69 70 71 280
B. Casper	70 70 71 71 282
J. Nicklaus	69 70 72 71 282
B. Winninger	73 72 72 66 283
G. Dickinson	67 74 69 74 284
B. Devlin	68 75 72 70 285

1966 FIRESTONE CC, OHIO

A. Geiberger	68 72 68 72 280
D. Wysong	74 72 66 72 284
W. Casper	73 73 70 70 286
G. Littler	75 71 71 70 286
G. Player	73 70 70 73 286

1967 COLUMBINE CC, COLO.

| D. January | 71 72 70 68 281 |
| D. Massengale | 70 75 70 66 281 |

Play-off: January 69; Massengale 71

J. Nicklaus	67 75 69 71 282
D. Sikes	69 70 70 73 282
J. Boros	69 76 70 68 283
A. Geiberger	73 71 69 70 283

1968 PECAN VALLEY CC, TEX.

J. Boros	71 71 70 69 281
B. Charles	72 70 70 70 282
A. Palmer	71 69 72 70 282
G. Archer	71 69 74 69 283
M. Fleckman	66 72 72 73 283
F. Beard	68 70 72 74 284
W. Casper	74 74 70 70 284

1969 NCR GC, DAYTON, OHIO

R. Floyd	69 66 67 74 276
G. Player	71 65 71 70 277
B. Greene	71 68 68 71 278
J. Wright	71 68 69 71 279
L. Ziegler	69 71 70 70 280
M. Barber	73 75 64 68 280

1970 SOUTHERN HILLS CC, OKLA.

D. Stockton	70 70 66 73 279
B. Murphy	71 73 71 66 281
A. Palmer	70 72 69 70 281
L. Hinson	69 71 74 68 282
G. Littler	72 71 69 70 282
J. Nicklaus	68 76 73 66 283
B. Crampton	73 75 68 67 283

1971 PGA NATIONAL GC, FLA.

J. Nicklaus	69 69 70 73 281
W. Casper	71 73 71 68 283
T. Bolt	72 74 69 69 284
M. Barber	72 68 75 70 285
G. Player	71 73 68 73 285
D. Hill	74 71 71 70 286
J. Jamieson	72 72 72 70 286
G. Gilbert	74 67 72 73 286

1972 OAKLAND HILLS GC, MICH.

G. Player	71 71 67 72 281
T. Aaron	71 71 70 71 283
J. Jamieson	69 72 72 70 283
W. Casper	73 70 67 74 284
R. Floyd	69 71 74 70 284
S. J. Snead	70 74 71 69 284

1973 CANTERBURY CLUB, OHIO

J. Nicklaus	72 68 68 69 277
B. Crampton	71 73 67 70 281
M. Rudolph	69 70 70 73 282
L. Wadkins	73 69 71 69 282
J. C. Snead	71 74 68 69 282
D. Sikes	72 68 72 71 283
T. Weiskopf	70 71 71 71 283
D. Iverson	67 72 70 74 283

1974 TANGLEWOOD GC, N.CAR.

L. Trevino	73 66 68 69 276
J. Nicklaus	69 69 70 69 277
R. Cole	69 68 71 71 279
H. Green	68 68 73 70 279
D. Hill	74 69 67 69 279
S. J. Snead	69 71 71 68 279

Play-off scores are in *italics*

1934

1. H. Smith	70 72 70 72	284
2. C. Wood	71 74 69 71	285
3. B. Burke	72 71 70 73	286
3. P. Runyan	74 71 70 71	286
5. E. Dudley	74 69 71 74	288
6. W. MacFarlane	74 73 70 74	291

1935

1. G. Sarazen	68 71 73 70	282 *144*
2. C. Wood	69 72 68 73	282 *149*
3. O. Dutra	70 70 70 74	284
4. H. Picard	67 68 76 75	286
5. D. Shute	73 71 70 73	287
6. L. Little Jr	74 72 70 72	288

1936

1. H. Smith	74 71 68 72	285
2. H. Cooper	70 69 71 76	286
3. G. Sarazen	78 67 72 70	287
4. B. Cruickshank	75 69 74 72	290
4. P. Runyan	76 69 70 75	290
6. R. Mangrum	76 73 68 76	293
6. E. Dudley	75 75 70 73	293
6. K. Laffoon	75 70 75 73	293

1937

1. B. Nelson	66 72 75 70	283
2. R. Guldahl	69 72 68 76	285
3. E. Dudley	70 71 71 74	286
4. H. Cooper	73 69 71 74	287
5. K. Laffoon	73 70 74 73	290
6. J. Thomson	71 73 74 73	291

1938

1. H. Picard	71 72 72 70	285
2. R. Guldahl	73 70 73 71	287
2. H. Cooper	68 77 71 71	287
4. P. Runyan	71 73 74 70	288
5. B. Nelson	73 74 70 73	290
6. E. Dudley	70 69 77 75	291
6. F. Serafin	72 71 78 70	291

1939

1. R. Guldahl	72 68 70 69	279
2. S. Snead	70 70 72 68	280
3. B. Burke	69 72 71 70	282
3. L. Little Jr	72 72 68 70	282
5. G. Sarazen	73 66 72 72	283
6. C. Wood	72 73 71 68	284

1940

1. J. Demaret	67 72 70 71	280
2. L. Mangrum	64 75 71 74	284
3. B. Nelson	69 72 74 70	285
4. E. Dudley	73 72 71 71	287
4. H. Cooper	69 75 73 70	287
4. W. Goggin	71 72 73 71	287

1941

1. C. Wood	66 71 71 72	280
2. B. Nelson	71 69 73 70	283
3. S. Byrd	73 70 68 74	285
4. B. Hogan	71 72 75 68	286
5. E. Dudley	73 72 75 68	288
6. S. Snead	73 75 72 69	289
6. V. Ghezzi	77 71 71 70	289

1942

1. B. Nelson	68 67 72 73	280 *69*
2. B. Hogan	73 70 67 70	280 *70*
3. P. Runyan	67 73 72 71	283
4. S. Byrd	68 68 75 74	285
5. H. Smith	67 73 74 73	287
6. J. Demaret	70 70 75 75	290

1946

1. H. Keiser	69 68 71 74	282
2. B. Hogan	74 70 69 70	283
3. B. Hamilton	75 69 71 72	287
4. K. Laffoon	74 73 70 72	289
4. J. Demaret	75 70 71 73	289
4. J. Ferrier	74 72 68 75	289

1947

1. J. Demaret	69 71 70 71	281
2. B. Nelson	69 72 72 70	283
2. F. Stranahan	73 72 70 68	283
4. B. Hogan	75 68 71 70	284
4. H. McSpaden	74 69 70 71	284
6. H. Picard	73 70 72 71	286
6. J. Ferrier	70 71 73 72	286

1948

1. C. Harmon	70 70 69 70	279
2. C. Middlecoff	74 71 69 70	284
3. C. Harbert	71 70 70 76	287
4. J. Ferrier	71 71 75 71	288
4. L. Mangrum	69 73 75 71	288
6. E. Furgol	70 72 73 74	289
6. B. Hogan	70 71 77 71	289

1949

1. S. Snead	73 75 67 67	282
2. J. Bulla	74 73 69 69	285
2. L. Mangrum	69 74 72 70	285
4. J. Palmer	73 71 70 72	286
4. J. Turnesa	73 72 71 70	286
6. L. Worsham Jr	76 75 70 68	289

1950

1. J. Demaret	70 72 72 69	283
2. J. Ferrier	70 67 73 75	285
3. S. Snead	71 74 70 72	287
4. B. Hogan	73 68 71 76	288
4. B. Nelson	75 70 69 74	288
6. L. Mangrum	76 74 73 68	291

1951

1. B. Hogan	70 72 70 68	280
2. S. Riegel	73 68 70 71	282
3. L. Mangrum	69 74 70 73	286
3. L. Worsham Jr	71 71 72 72	286
5. D. Douglas	74 69 72 73	288
6. L. Little Jr	72 73 72 72	289

1952

1. S. Snead	70 67 77 72	286
2. J. Burke Jr	76 67 78 69	290
3. A. Besselink	70 76 71 74	291
3. T. Bolt	71 71 75 74	291
3. J. Ferrier	72 70 77 72	291
6. L. Mangrum	71 74 75 72	292

1953

1. B. Hogan	70 69 66 69	274
2. E. Oliver Jr	69 73 67 70	279
3. L. Mangrum	74 68 71 69	282
4. B. Hamilton	71 69 70 73	283
5. T. Bolt	71 75 68 71	285
5. C. Harbert	68 73 70 74	285

1954

1. S. Snead	74 73 70 72	289 *70*
2. B. Hogan	72 73 69 75	289 *71*
3. W. J. Patton	70 74 75 71	290
4. E. J. Harrison	70 79 74 68	291
4. L. Mangrum	71 75 76 69	291
6. J. Barber	74 76 71 71	292
6. J. Burke Jr	71 77 73 71	292
6. B. Rosburg	73 73 76 70	292

1955

1. C. Middlecoff	72 65 72 70	279
2. B. Hogan	73 68 72 73	286
3. S. Snead	72 71 74 70	287
4. B. Rosburg	72 72 72 73	289
4. M. Souchak	71 74 72 72	289
4. J. Boros	71 75 72 71	289

1956

1. J. Burke Jr	72 71 75 71	289
2. K. Venturi	66 69 75 80	290
3. C. Middlecoff	67 72 75 77	291
4. L. Mangrum	72 74 72 74	292
4. S. Snead	73 76 72 71	292
6. J. Barber	71 72 76 75	294
6. D. Ford	70 72 75 77	294

1957

1. D. Ford	72 73 72 66	283
2. S. Snead	72 68 74 72	286
3. J. Demaret	72 70 75 70	287
4. E. H. Ward Jr	73 71 71 73	288
5. P. Thomson	72 73 73 71	289
6. E. Furgol	73 71 72 74	290

1958

1. A. Palmer	70 73 68 73	284
2. D. Ford	74 71 70 70	285
2. F. Hawkins	71 75 68 71	285
4. S. Leonard	72 70 73 71	286
4. K. Venturi	68 72 74 72	286
6. C. Middlecoff	70 73 69 75	287
6. A. Wall Jr	71 72 70 74	287

1959

1. A. Wall Jr	73 74 71 66	284
2. C. Middlecoff	74 71 68 72	285
3. A. Palmer	71 70 71 74	286
4. D. Mayer	73 75 71 68	287
4. S. Leonard	69 74 69 75	287
6. C. R. Coe	74 74 67 73	288

1960

1. A. Palmer	67 73 72 70	282
2. K. Venturi	73 69 71 70	283
3. D. Finsterwald	71 70 72 71	284
4. W. Casper Jr	71 71 71 74	287
5. J. Boros	72 71 70 75	288
6. W. Burkemo	72 69 75 73	289
6. B. Hogan	73 68 72 76	289
6. G. Player	72 71 72 74	289

1961

1. G. Player	69 68 69 74	280
2. A. Palmer	68 69 73 71	281
2. C. R. Coe	72 71 69 69	281
4. T. Bolt	72 71 74 68	285
4. D. January	74 68 72 71	285
6. P. Harney	71 73 68 74	286

1962

1. A. Palmer	70 66 69 75	280	68
2. G. Player	67 71 71 71	280	71
3. D. Finsterwald	74 68 65 73	280	77
4. G. Littler	71 68 71 72	282	
5. M. Souchak	70 72 74 71	287	
5. J. Demaret	73 73 71 70	287	
5. J. Barber	72 72 69 74	287	
5. B. Maxwell	71 73 72 71	287	

1963

1. J. Nicklaus	74 66 74 72	286
2. A. Lema	74 69 74 70	287
3. J. Boros	76 69 71 72	288
3. S. Snead	70 73 74 71	288
5. D. Finsterwald	74 73 73 69	289
5. E. Furgol	70 71 74 74	289
5. G. Player	71 74 74 70	289

1964

1. A. Palmer	69 68 69 70	276
2. D. Marr	70 73 69 70	282
2. J. Nicklaus	71 73 71 67	282
4. B. Devlin	72 72 67 73	284
5. W. Casper Jr	76 72 69 69	286
5. J. Ferrier	71 73 69 73	286
5. P. Harney	73 72 71 70	286
5. G. Player	69 72 72 73	286

1965

1. J. Nicklaus	67 71 64 69	271
2. A. Palmer	70 68 72 70	280
2. G. Player	65 73 69 73	280
4. M. Rudolph	70 75 66 72	283
5. D. Sikes	67 72 71 75	285
6. G. Littler	71 74 67 74	286
6. R. Sota	71 73 70 72	286

1966

1. J. Nicklaus	68 76 72 72	288	70
2. T. Jacobs	75 71 70 72	288	72
3. G. Brewer	74 72 72 70	288	78
4. A. Palmer	74 70 74 72	290	
4. D. Sanders	74 70 75 71	290	
6. D. January	71 73 73 75	292	
6. G. Knudson	73 76 72 71	292	

1967

1. G. Brewer	73 68 72 67	280
2. B. Nichols	72 69 70 70	281
3. B. Yancey	67 73 71 73	284
4. A. Palmer	73 73 70 69	285
5. J. Boros	71 70 70 75	286
6. P. Harney	73 71 74 69	287
6. G. Player	75 69 72 71	287

1968

1. R. Goalby	70 70 71 66	277
2. R. de Vicenzo	69 73 70 66	278
3. B. Yancey	71 71 72 65	279
4. B. Devlin	69 73 69 69	280
5. F. Beard	75 65 71 70	281
5. J. Nicklaus	69 71 74 67	281

1969

1. G. Archer	67 73 69 72	281
2. T. Weiskopf	71 71 69 71	282
2. G. Knudson	70 73 69 70	282
2. W. Casper	66 71 71 74	282
5. C. Coody	74 68 69 72	283
5. D. January	74 73 70 66	283

1970

1. W. Casper	72 68 68 71	279	69
2. G. Littler	69 70 70 70	279	74
3. G. Player	74 68 68 70	280	
4. B. Yancey	69 70 72 70	281	
5. T. Aaron	68 74 69 72	283	
5. D. Hill	73 70 70 70	283	
5. D. Stockton	72 72 69 70	283	

1971

1. C. Coody	66 73 70 70	279
2. J. Miller	72 73 68 68	281
2. J. Nicklaus	70 71 68 72	281
4. D. January	69 69 73 72	283
4. G. Littler	72 69 73 69	283
6. G. Player	72 72 71 69	284
6. T. Weiskopf	71 69 72 72	284
6. K. Still	72 71 72 69	284

1972

1. J. Nicklaus	68 71 73 74	286
2. T. Weiskopf	74 71 70 74	289
2. B. Crampton	72 75 69 73	289
2. R. Mitchell	73 72 71 73	289
5. B. Devlin	74 75 70 71	290
5. J. McGee	73 74 71 72	290
5. H. Blancas	76 71 69 74	290
5. J. Heard	73 71 72 74	290
5. J. Jamieson	72 70 71 77	290

1973

1. T. Aaron	68 73 74 68	283
2. J. C. Snead	70 71 73 70	284
3. P. Oosterhuis	73 70 68 74	285
3. J. Jamieson	73 71 70 71	285
3. J. Nicklaus	69 77 73 66	285
6. J. Miller	75 69 71 73	288
6. R. Goalby	73 70 71 74	288

1974

1. G. Player	71 71 66 70	278
2. D. Stockton	71 66 70 73	280
2. T. Weiskopf	71 69 70 70	280
4. J. Nicklaus	69 71 72 69	281
4. H. Irwin	68 70 72 71	281
4. J. Colbert	67 72 69 73	281

1958 ST ANDREWS, SCOTLAND

1. Australia 918
D. W. Bachli, P. A. Toogood, B. W. Devlin,
R. F. Stevens
2. United States 918
C. R. Coe, W. Hyndman III, W. J. Patton,
F. M. Taylor Jr
Play-off: USA 224; Australia 222
3. Great Britain and Ireland 919
J. B. Carr, R. Reid Jack, A. H. Perowne,
G. B. Wolstenholme

1960 MERION, PA.

1. United States 834
D. R. Beman, R. W. Gardner, W. Hyndman III,
J. W. Nicklaus
2. Australia 876
E. Ball, J. Doogan, B. W. Devlin, E. G. Routley
3. Great Britain and Ireland 881
M. F. Bonallack, J. B. Carr, D. N. Sewell,
G. B. Wolstenholme

1962 FUJI GC, KAWANA, JAPAN

1. United States 854
D. R. Beman, L. Harris Jr, W. J. Patton, R. H. Sikes
2. Canada 862
G. Cowan, W. Wakeham, N. Weslock, R. Wylie
3. Great Britain and Ireland 874
M. F. Bonallack, M. J. Christmas, A. C. Saddler,
R. D. B. M. Shade

1964 OLGIATA, ITALY

1. Great Britain and Ireland 895
M. F. Bonallack, R. Foster, M. S. R. Lunt,
R. D. B. M. Shade
2. Canada 897
R. K. Alexander, G. Cowan, D. H. Silverberg,
N. Weslock
3. New Zealand 900
J. D. Durry, S. G. Jones, E. J. McDougall,
R. C. Murray

1966 CLUB DE GOLF MEXICO, MEXICO CITY, MEXICO

1. Australia 877
H. W. Berwick, P. K. Billings, K. L. Donohoe,
K. W. Hartley
2. United States 879
D. R. Beman, R. J. Cerrudo, A. Downing Gray,
R. J. Murphy Jr
3. Great Britain and Ireland 883
M. F. Bonallack, G. B. Cosh, R. D. B. M. Shade,
P. M. Townsend

1968 ROYAL MELBOURNE, AUSTRALIA

1. United States 868
B. Fleisher, M. Giles III, J. W. Lewis Jr,
R. L. Siderowf
2. Great Britain and Ireland 869
M. F. Bonallack, G. B. Cosh, P. A. Oosterhuis,
R. D. B. M. Shade
3. Canada 885
G. Cowan, J. Doyle, J. Johnston, R. L. Wylie

1970 PUERTO DE HIERRO, MADRID, SPAIN

1. United States 854
M. Giles III, T. Kite Jr, A. L. Miller III, L. Wadkins
2. New Zealand 869
G. E. Clarke, S. G. Jones, E. J. McDougall,
R. C. Murray
3. South Africa 870
H. J. Baiocchi, J. A. Fourie, D. Hayes, D. H. Symons

1972 OLIVOS GC, BUENOS AIRES, ARGENTINA

1. United States 865
B. Crenshaw, V. Giles, M. Hayes, M. West
2. Australia 870
M. Cahill, T. Gale, T. Gresham, N. Ratcliffe
3. South Africa 878
C. Dreyer, Y. Murray, K. Suddards, N. Sundelson

1974 LA ROMANA, DOMINICAN REPUBLIC

1. United States 888
G. Burns, G. Koch, J. Pate, C. Strange
2. Japan 898
G. Nakake, T. Irie, T. Sakata, S. Yamazaki
3. Brazil 901
J. Gonzalez, J. Diniz, R. Rossi, R. Navarro

12. Women's World Amateur Team Championship for the Espirito Santo Trophy

1964 ST GERMAIN, FRANCE

1. France 588
Claudine Cros, Catherine Lacoste, Brigitte Varangot
2. United States 589
Barbara McIntire, Carol Sorenson, Barbara F. White
3. England 597
Bridget Jackson, Ruth Porter, Marley Spearman

1966 MEXICO CITY CC, MEXICO

1. United States 580
Barbara White Boddie, Shelley Hamlin, Anne Quast Welts
2. Canada 589
Gayle Hitchens, Gail Harvey Moore,
Marlene Stewart Streit
3. France 597
Claudine Cros, Catherine Lacoste, Brigitte Varangot

1968 VICTORIA GC, AUSTRALIA

1. United States 616
Jane Bastanchury, Shelley Hamlin, Anne Quast Welts
2. Australia 621
Elizabeth Blackmore, Marea Hickey, Ray Thomas
3. France 622
Claudine Cros-Rubin, Catherine Lacoste,
Brigitte Varangot

1970 MADRID, SPAIN

1. United States 598
Jane Bastanchury, Cynthia Hill, Martha Wilkinson
2. France 599
Catherine Lacoste De Prado, Claudine Cros-Rubin,
Brigitte Varangot
3. South Africa 606
Judy Angel, Jeanette Joan Burd, Sally Knight Little

1972 HINDU GC, BUENOS AIRES, ARGENTINA

1. United States 583
Laura Baugh, Jane Booth, Mary Budke
2. France 587
Anne-Marie Palli, Claudine Cros-Rubin,
Brigitte Varangot
3. Sweden 594
Birgit Forssman, Christina Westerberg, Liv Wollin

1974 LA ROMANA, DOMINICAN REPUBLIC

1. United States 620
Cynthia Hill, Debbie Massey, Carol Semple
2. Great Britain and Ireland 636
Mary McKenna, Julia Greenhalgh, Tegwen Perkins
2. South Africa 636
Lisle Nel, Alison Sheard, Jenny Bruce

1754 William Landale,
St Andrews

1755 Thomas Boswall,
Edinburgh

1756 Alexander Duncan,
Craigton, Edinburgh

1757

1758 Hugh Fraser,
Lovat

1759 Sir James Carnegie, Bt, MP

1760

1761 Alexander Duncan,
Cragton

1762 Hugh Fraser,
Lovat

1763 Sir Harry Seton, Bt

1764 William St Clair,
Roslin

1765 The Hon Francis Charteris,
Aimsfield

1766 William St Clair
Roslin

1767 James Durham,
Largo

1768 William St Clair,
Roslin

1769 Dr George Forrest,
St Andrews

1770 Henry Bethune,
Nydie

1771 Ninian Imrie,
Denmuir

1772 James Morrison,
Naughton

1773 Patrick Rigg,
Downfield

1774 John Hay,
Leys

1775 The Earl of Balcarres

1776 Roger Ayton,
Inchdairnie

1777 John Balfour,
Fernie

1778 Walter Boswell

1779 James Morrison,
Naughton

1780 James Durham,
Largo

1781 Alexander Duncan

1782 The Earl of Balcarres

1783 Major William Morrison

1784 Robert Low,
Clatto

1785 Captain John Cheape,
Rossie

1786 Colonel John Thomson,
Charlton

1787 James Cheape,
Strathtyrum

1788 Captain James Dalrymple

1789 Captain William Nairne

1790 Patrick Rigg,
Downfield

1791 Alexander Duncan

1792 The Earl of Crawford

1793 John Pattullo,
Balhouffie

1794 Captain Alexander Aytone,
Kippo

1795 Alexander Anderson,
Newbigging

1796 James Morrison,
Naughton

1797 Thomas Erskine,
Cambo

1798 Methven Erskine,
Airdrie

1799 John Dalyell,
Lingo

1800 Robert Patullo

1801 George Cheape

1802 Hugh Cleghorn,
Stravithy

1803 George Paterson,
Cunnoquhie

1804 John Anstruther Thomson,
Charlton

1805 Colonel David Dewar,
Gilston

1806 William Dalgleish,
Scotscraig

1807 General George Moncrieff

1808 Alexander Guthrie,
Craigie

1809 James Home Rigg,
Morton

1810 John Maitland,
Kilmaron

1811 Thomas Bruce,
Grangemuir

1812 R. Gillespie Smyth,
Gibleston

1813 General James Durham,
Largo

1814 George Cheape,
Pusk

1815 John Makgill,
Kemback

1816 Sir John Anstruther Bt,
Anstruther

1817 David Moncreiffe, younger,
Moncreiffe

1818 John Murray,
Lintrose

1819 Robert Bruce,
Kennet

1820 David, Earl of Leven and Melville

1821 Colonel Alexander Bethune,
Blebo

1822 Alexander Binny,
St Andrews

1823 John Whyte Melville,
Strathkinness

1824 Colonel James Lindsay,
Balcarres

1825 Sir Ralph Anstruther Bt,
Balcaskie

1826 Charles M. Christie,
Durie

1827 James Cheape, of Balgove, Captain RN

1828 John Dalyell,
Lingo

1829 Sir David Erskine Bt,
Cambo

1830 Francis Balfour,
Fernie

1831 James Stuart Oliphant,
Rossie

1832 C. Halket Craigie,
Dumbarnie

1833 Major Robert Anstruther,
Third Part

1834 General Sir John Oswald GCB
Dunnikier

1835/1836 Colonel J. Murray Belshes,
Buttergask

1837 Captain George Moncrieff

1838 O. T. Bruce,
Falkland

1839 John Grant,
Kilgraston

1840 Henry Stewart,
St Fort

1841 David Gillespie,
Mountquhanie

1842 John Balfour,
Balbirnie

1843 Sir David Baird Bt,
Newbyth

1844 Sir Thomas Moncreiffe Bt,
Moncreiffe

1845 George Makgill,
Kemback

1846 Robert Lindsay,
Straiton

1847 F. L. S. Wedderburn,
Wedderburn

1848 James Wolfe Murray,
Cringletie

1849 James Townsend Oswald,
Dunnikier

1850 James O. Fairlie,
Coodham

1851 George Whyte-Melville younger,
Mount Melville

1852 E. J. Jackson

1853 The Earl of Eglinton and Winton KT

1854 Hay Erskine Wemyss,
Wemyss and Torrie

1855 Lord Loughborough

1856 Sir Hugh Lyon Playfair

1857 Robert Cathcart younger,
Pitcairlie

1858 John Anstruther Thomson,
Charleton

1859 Sir David Baird Bt,
Newbyth

1860 Sir Thomas Erskine Bt,
Cambo

1861 George Dempster,
Skibo

1862 The Earl of Dalhousie KT

1863 HRH the Prince of Wales

1864 Viscount Dupplin

1865 Lt-General Sir John Low,
Clatto

1866 Sir Robert Anstruther Bt,
Balcaskie

1867 Sir John T. Bethune Bt,
Kilconquhar

1868 Sir Coutts Lindsay Bt,
Balcarres

1869 Alexander Bethune,
Blebo

1870 Sir Robert Hay Bt,
Hayston and Kingsmeadows

1871 John Blackwood

1872 Alexander Kinloch yr,
Gilmerton

1873 William Baillie Skene,
Pitlour

1874 William Patrick Adam MP,
Blairadam

1875 The Hon Charles Carnegie

1876 HRH Prince Leopold

1877 John Inglis,
Glencorse

1878 The Hon George Waldegrave Leslie

1879 The Earl of Elgin and Kincardine

1880 The Earl of Glasgow

1881 Captain Randle Jackson

1882 The Hon Robert Preston Bruce

1883 Vacant*

1884 George Glennie

1885 The Earl of Aberdeen

1886 Captain Daniel Shaw Stewart

1887 J. H. A. Macdonald MP

1888 Captain G. C. Cheape,
Wellfield

1889 Sir Robert Anstruther Dalyell KCIE, CSI,
Lingo

1890 John Henry Baxter,
Gilston

1891 Sir Ralph W. Anstruther Bt,
Balcaskie

1892 Andrew Graham Murray QC, MP

1893 J. Ogilvy R. Fairlie,
Myres

1894 Sir A. J. Balfour, MP, Bt,
Whittingehame

1895 John Oswald,
Dunnikier

1896 James G. Baird Hay,
Belton

1897 Henry S. Wedderburn,
Birkhill

1898 William John Mure CB

1899 The Hon Thomas Cochrane

*John Whyte Melville of Bennochy and
Strathkinness was elected but died before entering
office. He had previously held office in 1823.

1900 John Blair Balfour, Lord Justice General

1901 Walter T. J. S. Steuart Fothringham,
Pourie and Grandtully

1902 Sir John Gilmour Bt,
Lundin and Montrave

1903 Sir Robert B. Finlay KC, MP

1904 Ralph Dalyell, of Lingo CB

1905 Colonel David Alexander Kinloch,
Younger of Gilmerton CB, MVO

1906 Leslie Balfour-Melville

1907 The Earl of Stair

1908 Horace G. Hutchinson

1909 Lord Kinross

1910 Samuel Mure Fergusson

1911 Sir Ludovic James Grant Bt

1912 Walter Edwin Fairlie

1913 Henry William Forster MP

1914/1918 World War I

1919 Lt-Colonel Henry Alexander Bethune
Mountquhanie

1920 Field-Marshal Earl Haig KT

1921 Robert Tuite Boothby

1922 HRH the Prince of Wales KG, KT

1923 Colonel Sir Alexander Sprot CMG, Bt,
Stravithie

1924 James Younger,
Mount Melville

1925 Edward Baird Hay Blackwell

1926 Lt-Colonel Sir John Gilmour DSO, MP, Bt,
Lundin and Montrave

1927 James Tennent Inglis

1928 Angus Valdemar Hambro

1929 Colonel Philip George Moncrieff Skene
OBE, DL,
Halliards and Pitlour

1930 HRH the Duke of York KG, KT

1931 John William Beaumont Pease

1932 The Earl of Lindsay

1933 Sir Ernley Robertson Hay Blackwell KCB

1934 Bernard Darwin

1935 William Norman Boase CBE

1936 Sir John Simon PC, GCSI, KCVO, KC, MP

1937 HRH the Duke of Kent KG, KT

1938 Colonel Henry Holmes Sutherland DSO, DL

1939/1945 World War II

1946 Roger Henry Wethered

1947 Lord Teviot of Burghclere DSO, MC

1948 Cyril James Hastings Tolley MC

1949 Lord Balfour of Burleigh

1950 Sir George Cunningham GCIE, KCSI, OBE, LL D

1951 Francis De Sales Ouimet

1952 Lord Brabazon of Tara PC, GBE, MC

1953 Lt-Colonel John Inglis CMG, DSO

1954 Viscount Bruce of Melbourne PC, CH, MC, FRS

1955 Lord MacAndrew PC, TD, DL

1956 Dr Harold Gardiner-Hill

1957 John Beaumont Beck MC

1958 Lord Morton of Henryton PC, MC

1959 Henry Hutchison Turcan

1960 Lord Cohen PC

1961 William Tweddell MC, MB, CH B

1962 Sir William Giles Newsom Walker

1963 Thomas Francis Blackwell MBE

1964 George Alec Hill DSO

1965 James Lockhart Mitchell

1966 John Geoffrey Blackwell

1967 Major Thomas Steuart Fothringham MC, TD

1968 Gerald Hugh Micklem CBE

1969 Rt Hon William Stephen Ian Whitelaw MC, MP

1970 George William Mackie JP

1971 Alan Darlington Cave

1972 Sir Iain Stewart

1973 Donald Neil Vaughan Smith

1974 Sir John Carmichael KBE

1894/95/96 T. A. Havemeyer
Newport GC, R.I.

1879/98 L. Curtis
The Country Club, Mass.

1899/1900 W. B. Thomas
The Country Club, Mass.

1901/1902 R. H. Robertson
Shinnecock Hills GC, N.Y.

1903/1904 G. H. Windeler
The Country Club, Mass.

1905/1906 R. H. Thomas
Morris County GC, N.J.

1907/1908 D. Chauncey
Garden City GC, N.Y.

1909/1910 H. Jaques
The Country Club, Mass.

1911/12 S. H. Strawn
Glen View C, Ill.

1913/14 R. C. Watson
National Golf Links of America, N.Y.

1915/16 F. L. Woodward
Denver CC, Colo.

1917 H. W. Perrin
Merion Cricket C, Pa.

1918/19 F. S. Wheeler
Apawamis C, N.Y.

1920 G. H. Walker
National Golf Links of America, N.Y.

1921 H. F. Whitney
Nassau CC, N.Y.

1922/23 J. F. Byers
Allegheny CC, Pa.

1924/25 W. D. Vanderpool
Morris County GC, N.J.

1926/27 W. C. Fownes Jr
Oakmont CC, Pa.

1928 M. A. Traylor
Glen View C, Ill.

1929/30 F. S. Douglas
Apawamis C, N.Y.

1931/32 H. H. Ramsay
National Golf Links of America, N.Y.

1933/34 H. Jaques
The Country Club, Mass.

1935 P. S. Bush
Round Hill C, Conn.

1936/37 J. G. Jackson
Deepdale GC, N.Y.

1938/39 A. M. Reid
St Andrew's GC, N.Y.

1940/41 H. W. Pierce
The Country Club, Mass.

1942/43 G. W. Blossom Jr
Onwentsia C, Ill.

1944/45 M. G. Bogue
Deepdale GC, N.Y.

1946/47 C. W. Littlefield
Montclair GC, N.J.

1948/49 F. Wallace
Augusta National GC, Ga.

1950/51 J. D. Standish Jr
CC of Detroit, Mich.

1952/53 T. P. Heffelfinger
Minikahda C, Minn.

1954/55 I. B. Grainger
Montclair GC, N.J.

1956/57 R. S. Tufts
Pinehurst CC, N.C.

1958/59 J. D. Ames
Onwentsia C, Ill.

1960/61 J. G. Clock
Virginia CC, Calif.

1962/63 J. M. Winters Jr
Southern Hills CC, Okla.

1964/65 C. W. Benedict
Winged Foot GC, N.Y.

1966/67 W. W. Foshay
Round Hill C, Conn.

1968/69 H. H. Hardin
Bellerive CC, Mo.

1970/71 P. H. Strubing
Sunnybrook GC, Pa.

1972/73 L. Lardner Jr
Milwaukee GC, Wis.

1974/75 H. S. Semple
Sewickley Heights GC, Pa.

Index of Golf Courses

The golf clubs listed below, in the countries in which they occur, have entries in this encyclopedia. Information on a number of other clubs may be found under the entry of the country concerned, e.g. Afghanistan. Many clubs have more than one course, the most important of which are described in the text.

Picture Credits

106 centre, USGA; right, Danish Tourist Board
107 top, Golf Promotion Services; below, USGA
109 left, FG; centre, USGA; right (top), FG; right (below), FG
110 left, USGA; centre, USGA; right, FG
111 top, FG
114 left (top), USGA; left (below), HWN; right, Tom Scott by courtesy of the R. and A.
115 right, USGA
116 HWN
117 left, USGA; centre, USGA; right, Tom Scott by courtesy of the Scottish National Portrait Gallery
118 centre, USGA
119 centre (top), USGA; centre (below), USGA
120 left, Golf Promotion Services; right, USGA
121 left (top), USGA; left (below), HWN; centre, USGA
122 USGA
123 Slazengers Ltd
124 FG
125 USGA
126 FG
127 HWN
128 centre, Belgian National Tourist Office; right, USGA
129 left, FG; right, USGA
130 USGA
131 USGA
132 left, USGA; centre, HWN
133 left (top), FG; left (below), USGA; centre (top), FG; centre, FG; centre (below), FG; right, FG
134 left, FG; right, HWN
135 left, FG; centre, HWN; right, FG
136 left, USGA; centre (top), HWN; centre (below), HWN
137 top, French Government Tourist Office; below, French Government Tourist Office
138 left, HWN; centre (top), FG; centre (below), USGA
139 left, FG; centre (top), FG; centre (below), FG; right, HWN
140 HWN
141 left (top), USGA; left (below), USGA; right, HWN
142 centre, EDL; right, USGA
143 USGA
144 left (top), FG; left (below), USGA
145 British Tourist Authority
146 left, EDL
147 left and centre, Tom Scott by courtesy of the R. and A.
148 Tom Scott by courtesy of the R. and A.

149 Tom Scott by courtesy of the R. and A.
151 The National Galleries of Scotland
152 Slazengers Ltd
155 top, FG; below, FG
156 top, FG; right, USGA
157 top, FG; below, HWN
158 left, Fred Kuehn Studios; right; USGA
159 top, USGA; below, Topix
160 centre, HWN; right, FG
161 left, FG; centre, EDL; right (centre), FG; right (below), HWN
162 centre, FG
163 left (top), USGA; left (below), EDL; centre, FG
164 USGA
165 left, HWN; right, USGA
166 top, Netherlands National Tourist Office; right, HWN
167 left, FG; right, USGA
168 left, HWN; right, USGA
169 left, USGA; centre, USGA; right, USGA
170 centre (top), USGA; centre (below), HWN; right (top), HWN; right (below), HWN
171 Australian News and Information Bureau
172 left, Golf Promotion Services; centre, USGA; right, HWN
173 left (centre), FG; left (below), Source Perrier; right, USGA
174 left (top), USGA; left (below), USGA; centre, FG
175 centre (top), USGA; centre (below), USGA; right, FG
176 top, FG; centre, FG
178 top, FG
179 centre (top), HWN; centre (below), HWN
180 centre, FG; right, FG
181 left (top), FG; left (below), HWN; centre, Eyre Methuen
182 centre, HWN
183 HWN
184 centre, HWN; centre (below), Topix; right, USGA
185 centre (top), EDL; centre (below), EDL; right (top), HWN; right (below), Topix
187 left, FG; centre, FG
189 left (top), USGA; left (below), FG
190 top, Keshub Mahindra; right (centre), Keshub Mahindra; right (below), Keshub Mahindra
191 USGA
193 top, Eyre Methuen; left, HWN
194 top, USGA; centre, USGA
195 right (centre), Tom Scott by courtesy of the R. and A.
197 top, FG; below, HWN
198 HWN

199 left (top), FG; left (below), HWN; centre (top), EDL; centre (below), Topix
200 left (top), FG; centre, USGA; right (top), EDL; right (below), HWN
201 left (top), USGA; left (below), USGA; right, HWN
202 left, HWN; centre (top), HWN; centre (below), HWN
203 Eyre Methuen
204 left, USGA; right, Richard Elm/Robert Trent Jones
206 top, USGA; below, USGA
208 USGA
210 centre, USGA; right, EDL
211 Kennemer GCC
212 centre, FG; right, FG
213 centre, FG; centre (below), USGA
214 left, USGA; right (top), USGA; right (below), FG
215 below, HWN
216 left, USGA; right, Japan Uni Agency
217 USGA
218 top, EDL; centre, EDL
219 USGA
220 HWN
221 centre, FG
222 left, HWN; right, USGA
223 left, HWN; right, EDL
224 left, FG; right, FG
225 USGA
226 top, FG; bottom, HWN
227 top, HWN; below, FG
228 top, HWN; below, HWN
229 left, USGA; centre, FG; centre (below), FG
231 centre, HWN; centre (below), HWN; right, HWN
233 left, USGA; right, HWN
234 FG
235 left, FG; right, HWN
236 right, HWN
237 HWN
238 left, USGA; centre, USGA; right, HWN
239 left, FG; right, Topix
240 left (top), USGA; left (below), USGA
241 top, USGA; below, USGA
242 Visual Communications (Malta) Ltd
243 top, USGA; centre, USGA; centre (below), HWN
244 top, British Tourist Authority; below, British Tourist Authority
245 centre, FG; centre (below), FG; right, HWN
246 left, Keshub Mahindra; centre, USGA; right, FG
247 left, Tom Scott by courtesy of the R. and A.; right, USGA
248 USGA
249 top, USGA; below, USGA
250 below, Melbourne Age

251 top, Melbourne Age; below, USGA
252 USGA
253 centre (top), HWN; centre (below), HWN; right, EDL
254 FG
255 left (top), EDL; left (below), EDL; centre, EDL; centre (below), FG; right, EDL
256 centre (top), FG; centre, HWN; right, USGA
258 centre, USGA; right, FG
259 FG
260 top, HWN; below, HWN
261 left, HWN; right, USGA
263 left, Tom Scott by courtesy of the R. and A.; centre, Tom Scott by courtesy of the R. and A.
264 top, J. Pugh; below, USGA
265 top, FG; below, EDL
267 top, FG; below, HWN
269 Eyre Methuen
270 left, FG; right (top), HWN; right (below), USGA
272 left, High Commissioner for New Zealand; right (top), Tom Scott by courtesy of the R. and A.; right (below), FG
273 HWN
274 centre, FG; right (top), FG; right (below), FG
275 HWN
276 USGA
277 HWN
279 top, USGA; below, USGA
280 J. W. Newsome
281 centre (top), EDL; centre, FG
282 left, USGA; top, USGA
283 centre, Eyre Methuen
284 centre, HWN; right, FG
285 EDL
286 left, FG; right, USGA
288 left, USGA; right, HWN
289 HWN
291 left, HWN; centre, FG; right, EDL
292 USGA
293 left, FG; right, High Commissioner for New Zealand
294 Tom Scott by courtesy of the R. and A.
295 left, USGA; right, FG
296 left, USGA
297 Eyre Methuen
299 left, HWN; right, FG
300 left, HWN; centre, EDL
301 below, Eyre Methuen
303 left (top), EDL; left (below), FG; centre (top), USGA; centre (below), FG; right, Tom Scott by courtesy of the R. and A.
304 centre, FG; right (top), HWN; right (below), Topix
305 Australian News and Information Bureau
306 FG

307 centre, Northern Ireland
     Tourist Board
308 top, HWN; below, HWN
309 right, FG
310 centre (top), USGA; centre,
     USGA; right, FG
314 centre, FG; right, FG
315 left (top), EDL; left (below)
     HWN; right, Tom Scott by
     courtesy of the R. and A.
316 USGA
317 left, HWN; centre, USGA;
     right, USGA
318 left, USGA; centre, USGA
319 top, HWN; below, FG
320 left, FG; centre, USGA;
     right, USGA
321 centre, USGA; right, USGA
322 USGA
323 left, J. Pugh; centre, FG;
     right, HWN
324 top, USGA; below, USGA
325 left, USGA; centre, HWN
327 left, USGA; centre (top),
     High Commissioner for New
     Zealand; right (centre),
     HWN; right (below), FG
328 centre, HWN; right, HWN
329 left, Tom Scott by courtesy of
     the R. and A.; right, USGA
330 Source Perrier
331 HWN
332 top, Danish Tourist Board;
     centre, HWN; centre
     (below), Tom Scott by
     courtesy of the R. and A.
333 left, HWN; centre, FG
334 top, FG; below, HWN
335 left, FG; right, HWN
337 top, Tom Scott by courtesy
     of the R. and A.; left (below),
     FG
338 USGA
339 centre, FG
342 FG
343 left (centre), Tom Scott by
     courtesy of the R. and A.;
     left (below), HWN; right,
     USGA
344 left, HWN; centre, HWN
345 USGA
346 centre, USGA; centre
     (below), FG
347 left, HWN; right (top),
     USGA; right (below), USGA
348 left, USGA; centre, HWN
349 Straits Times Press
350 left, FG; centre, FG; right, FG
351 centre, HWN; centre
     (below), HWN; right HWN
352 USGA
353 left (top), USGA; left
     (below), EDL; centre, EDL
354 FG
355 centre, USGA; right, HWN
356 left, USGA; centre, USGA;
     right, USGA
357 left, USGA; centre, FG;
     right, FG

358 FG
359 left, EDL; centre (top),
     HWN; right, Ward Wallace
360 left, HWN; right, South
     African Tourist Corporation
361 South African Tourist
     Corporation
362 top, HWN; below, USGA
363 right, Tom Scott by courtesy
     of the R. and A.; right
     (below), HWN
364 FG
365 centre, Australian News and
     Information Bureau;
     right, USGA
366 left, USGA; centre, Topix
367 left, USGA; centre, HWN
368–70 all sequences, FG
371 left, USGA; centre, Japan
     Uni Agency; centre (below),
     The Field
372 centre, Tom Scott by courtesy
     of the R. and A.
373 centre, USGA; right, USGA
375 Keshub Mahindra
376 left (top), FG; left (below),
     USGA
377 left, FG; centre, FG
378 left, EDL; centre, Topix
379 left (top), HWN; left
     (below), HWN
380 Cogllan's Corporation
381 EDL
382 left, FG; centre, USGA
383 centre (top), FG; centre, FG
384 HWN
385 centre, USGA; right, EDL
387 top, British Tourist Authority;
     below, HWN
388 EDL
390 HWN
391 right (top), USGA; right
     (below), FG
392 USGA
393 USGA
395 left, HWN; right, HWN
396 USGA
397 left (top), HWN; left (below),
     FG
398 left, Harry Braid; right, FG
399 left, EDL; centre, FG
400 The National Film Board of
     Canada
401 right, USGA; centre,
     USGA
402 left, USGA; right, FG
403 USGA
404 HWN
405 left (top), USGA; left
     (below), HWN; centre,
     USGA
406 centre, FG; right, HWN
407 left, USGA; centre, FG;
     right, USGA
408 left, USGA; right, FG
409 FG
410 top, FG; right, USGA
411 Central Press
412 USGA

414 left, USGA; centre (top),
     FG; centre, Sport and
     General
416 Eyre Methuen
417 left, HWN; centre, FG;
     right, USGA
418 top, HWN; below, HWN
420 left (top), HWN; left
     (below), FG
421 FG
422 left, USGA; centre, USGA
423 EDL
424 HWN
425 Belgian National Tourist
     Office